U0856247

图书在版编目(CIP)数据

新疆统计年鉴. 2016：汉英对照 / 新疆维吾尔自治区统计局编. -- 北京 : 中国统计出版社, 2016.9
ISBN 978-7-5037-7902-2

Ⅰ. ①新… Ⅱ. ①新… Ⅲ. ①统计资料－新疆－2016－年鉴-汉、英 Ⅳ. ①C832.45-54

中国版本图书馆CIP数据核字(2016)第192235号

新疆统计年鉴—2016

作　　者/新疆维吾尔自治区统计局
责任编辑/佘竞雄　熊　威
装帧设计/王红刚
出版发行/中国统计出版社
地　　址/北京市丰台区西三环南路甲6号　邮政编码/100073
电　　话/邮购（010）63376909　书店（010）68783171
网　　址/http://www.zgtjcbs.com
印　　刷/新疆统计印刷厂
经　　销/新华书店
开　　本/890mm×1240mm　1/16
字　　数/1370千字
印　　张/46.5
版　　别/2016年9月第1版
版　　次/2016年9月第1次印刷
定　　价/460.00元

本书附同版本CD-ROM一张，光盘内容以书面文字为准。
如有印装差错，由本社发行部调换。

《新疆统计年鉴——2016》编辑委员会

XINJIANG STATISTICAL YEARBOOK-2016
NAME LIST OF EDITORIAL BOARD

生产总值（GDP）
Gross Domestic Product

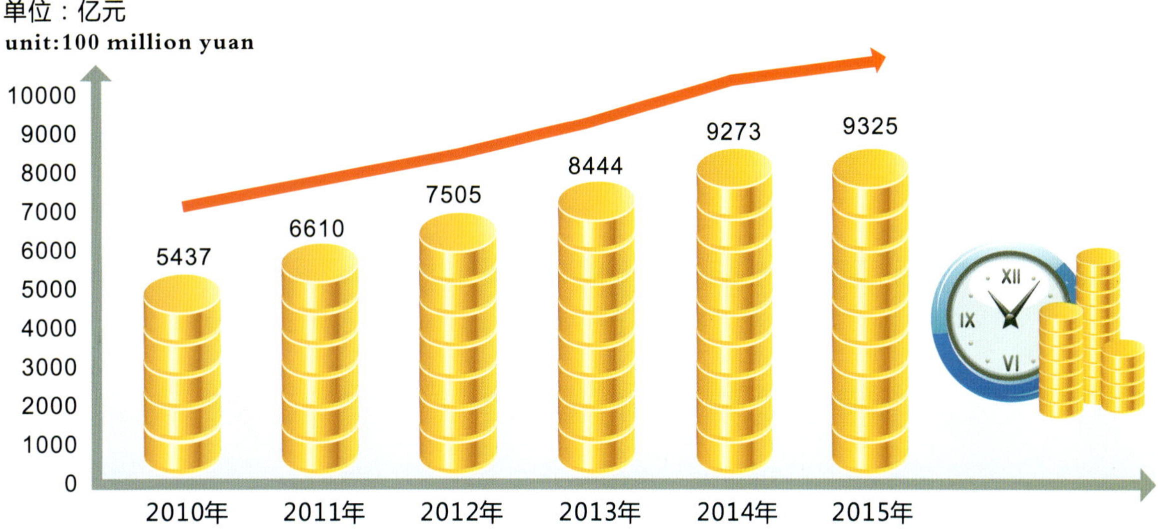

人均生产总值
Per Capita Gross Domestic Product

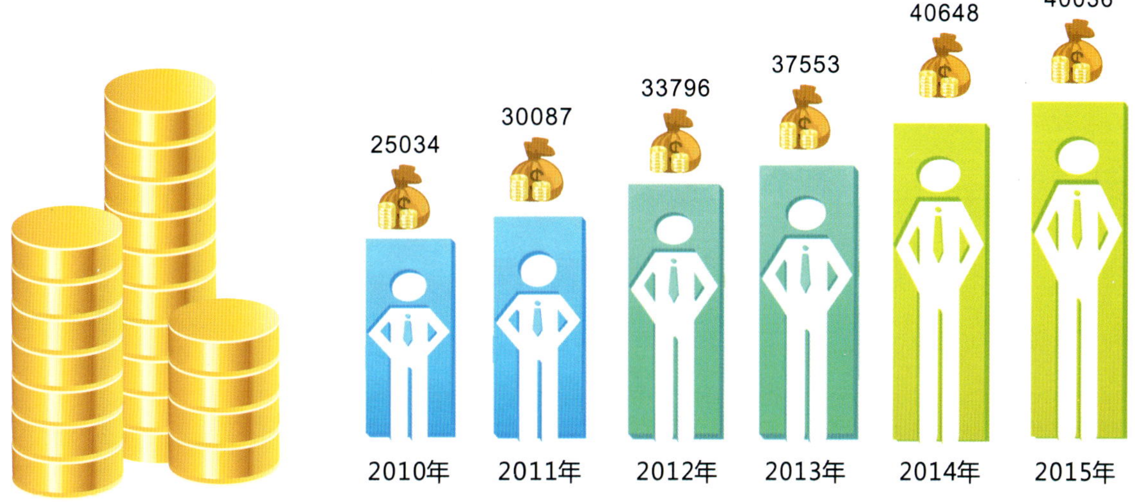

三次产业增加值占地区生产总值比重
Three Industry Composition of Gross Domestic Product

单位：%
unit:%

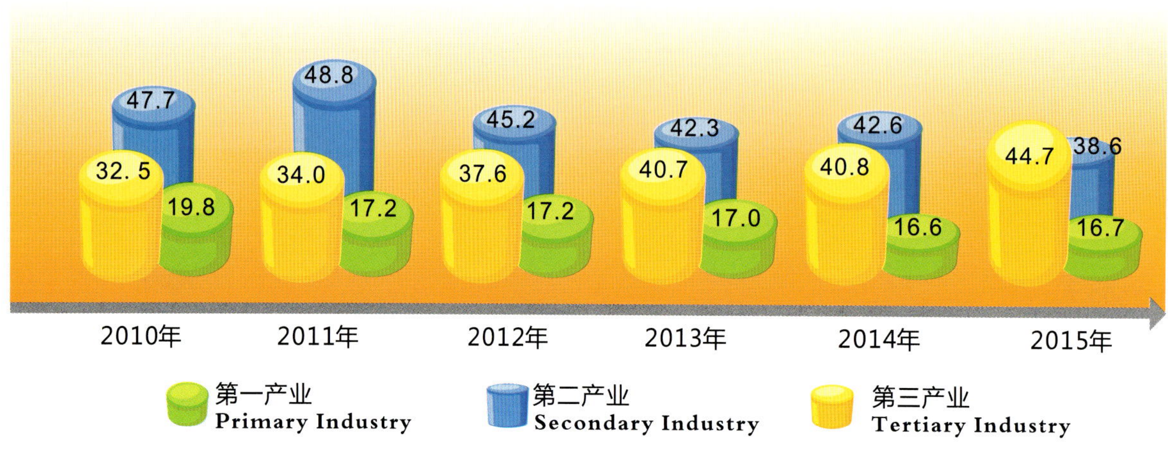

年末人口数
Population at Year-end

单位：万人
unit: 10000 persons

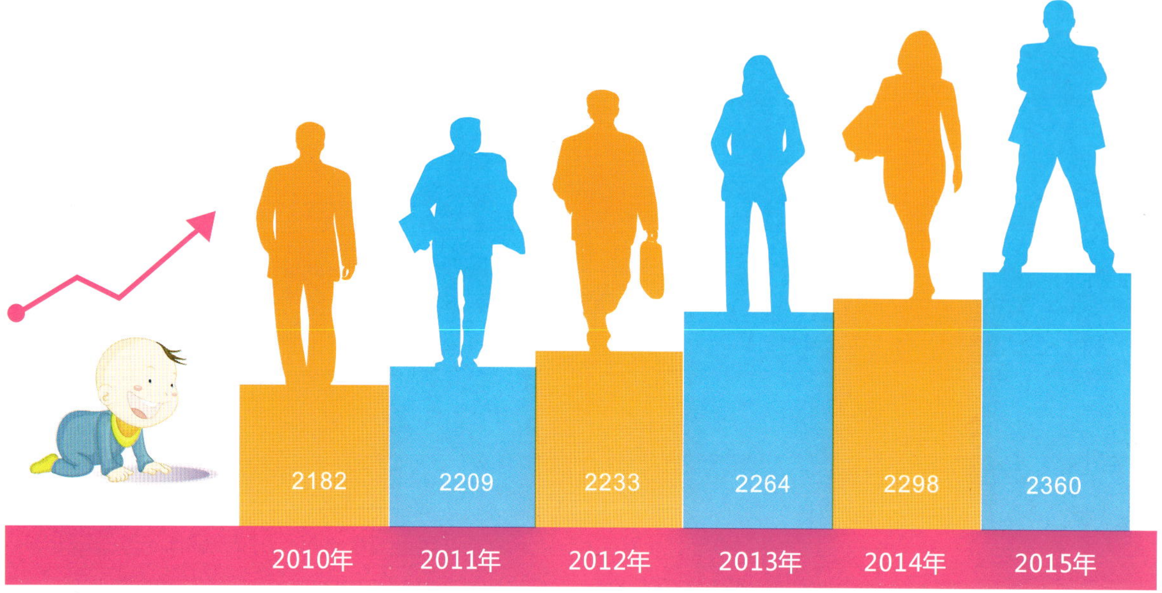

全社会分三次产业从业人员
Three Industry of Total Employed Persons

单位：万人
unit:10000 persons

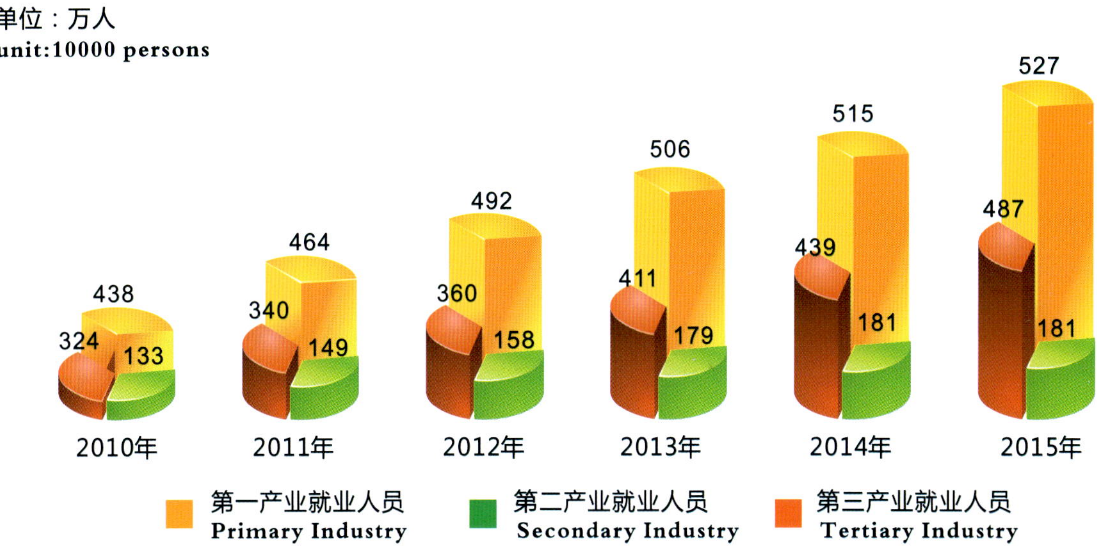

非私营单位在岗职工工资总额
Total Wage Bill of Employed Persons in Non-Private Units

单位：亿元
unit: 100 million yuan

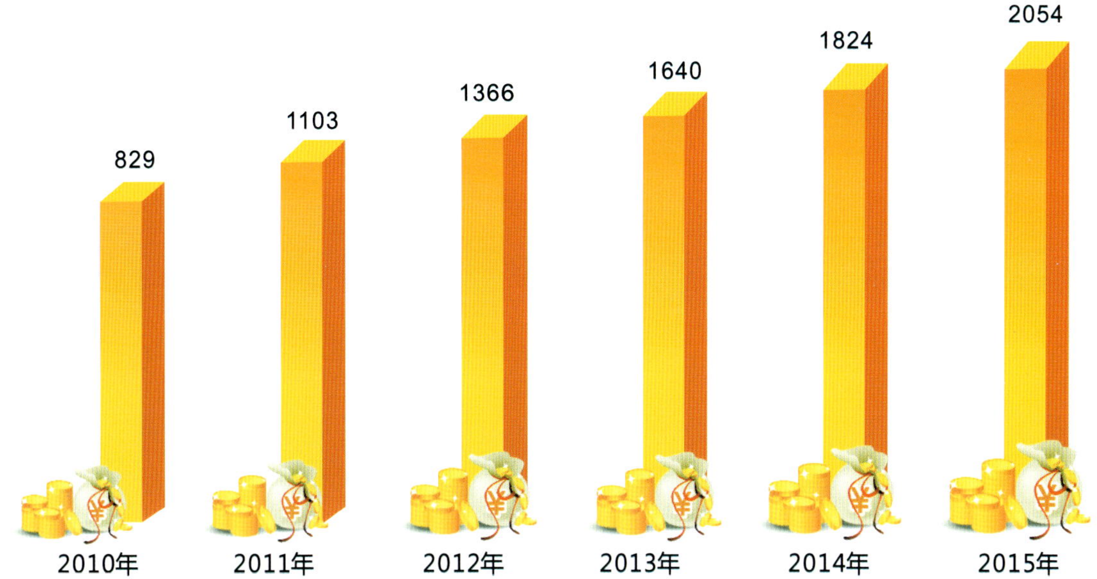

城镇非私营单位在岗职工平均工资
Average Wage of Employed Persons in Urban Non-Private Units

单位：元
unit:yuan

固定资产投资（不含农户）总额
Total Investment in Fixed Assets (Excluding Rural Households)

单位：亿元
unit: 100 million yuan

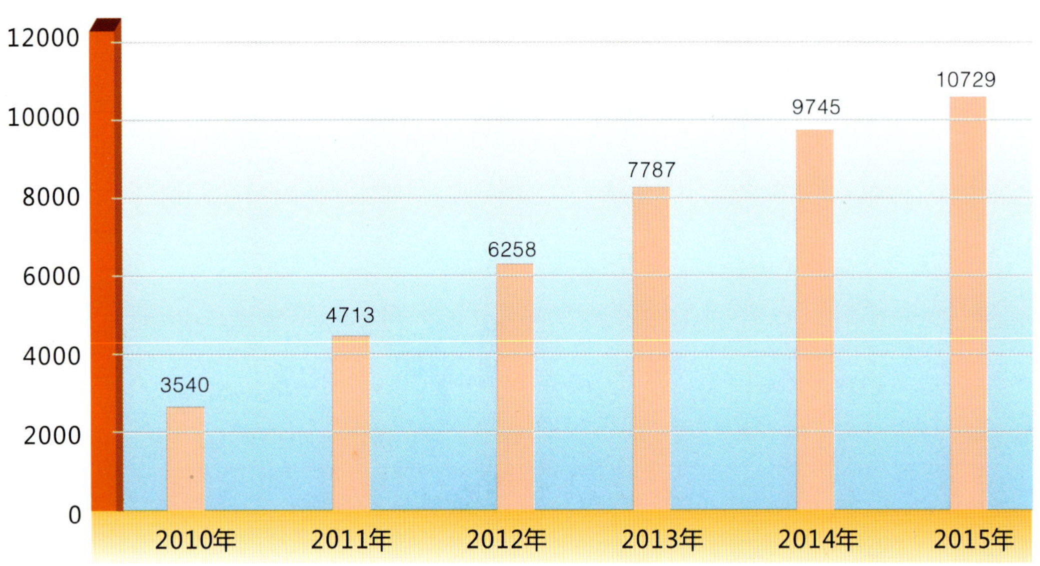

2015年按领域分固定资产投资构成

Investment in Fixed Assets by Setor in 2015

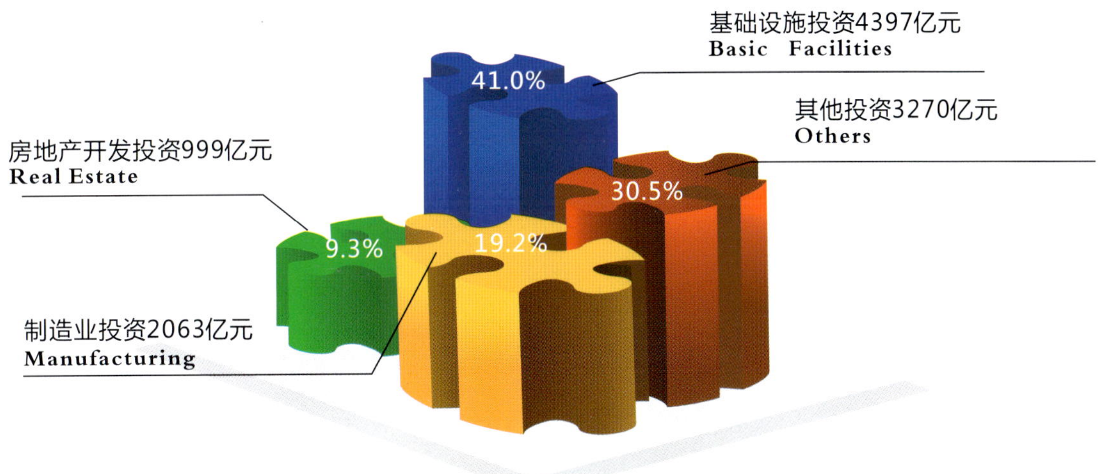

房地产投资

Investment in Real Estate

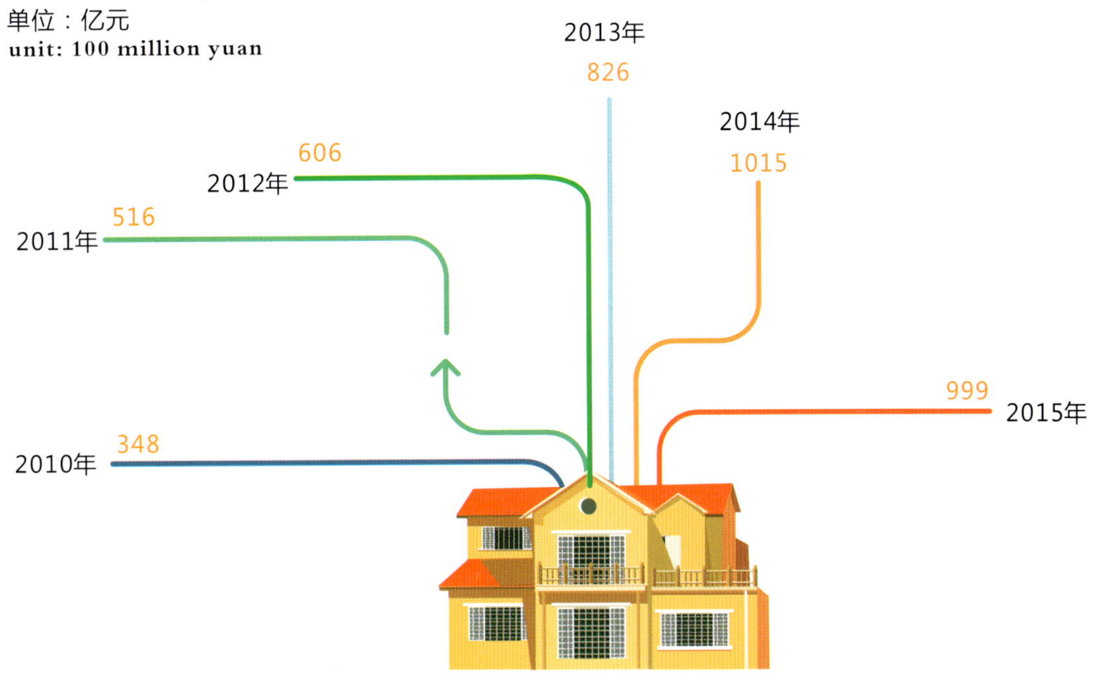

货物进出口总额
Total Value of Imports and Exports

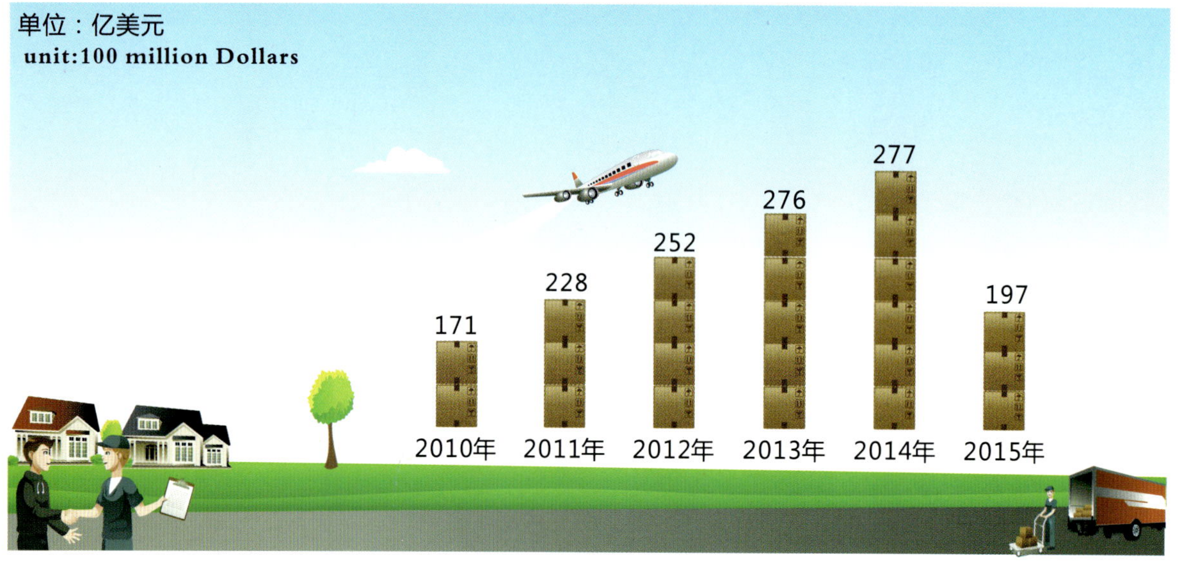

能源消费总量
Total Eneygy Consumption

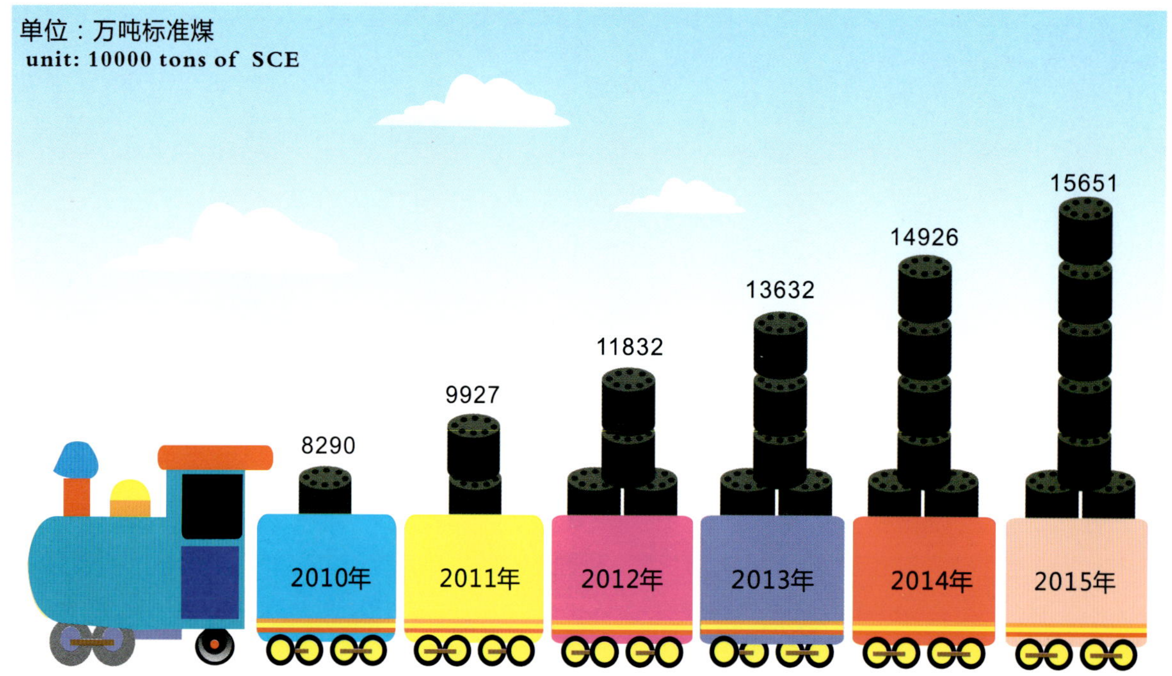

一般公共预算收支
Local Public Budgetary Financial Revenue and Expenditure

单位：亿元
unit: 100 million yuan

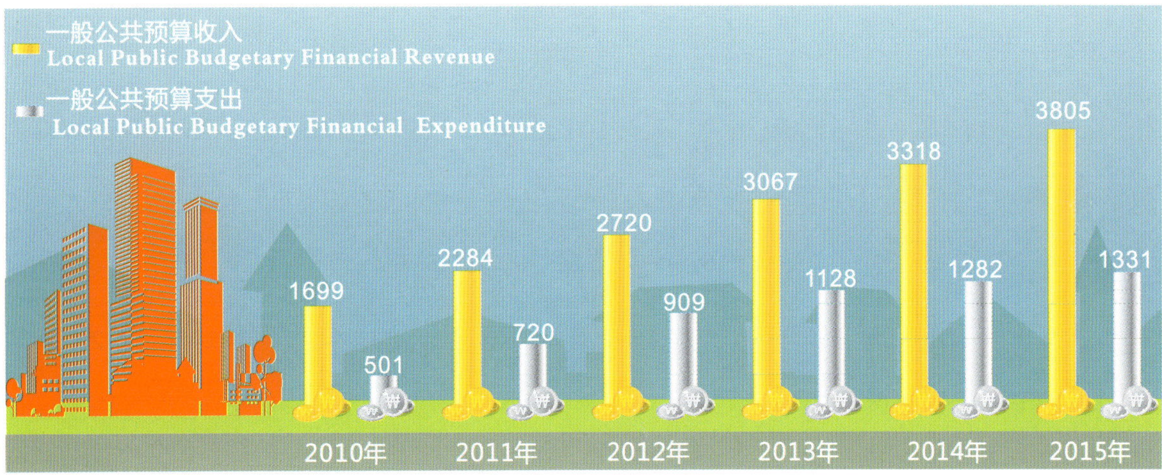

城乡居民人民币储蓄存款余额
Savings Desposit of Households by Urban and Rural

单位：亿元
unit: 100 million yuan

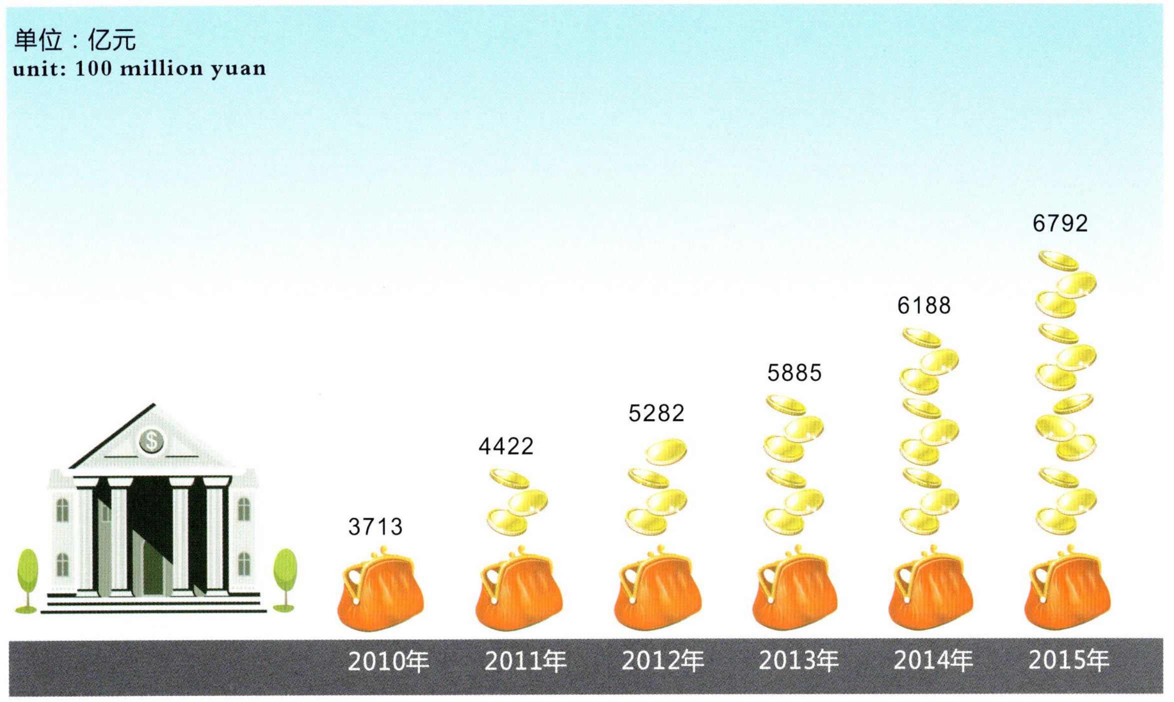

城镇居民人均可支配收入
Per Capita Disposable Income of Urban Residents

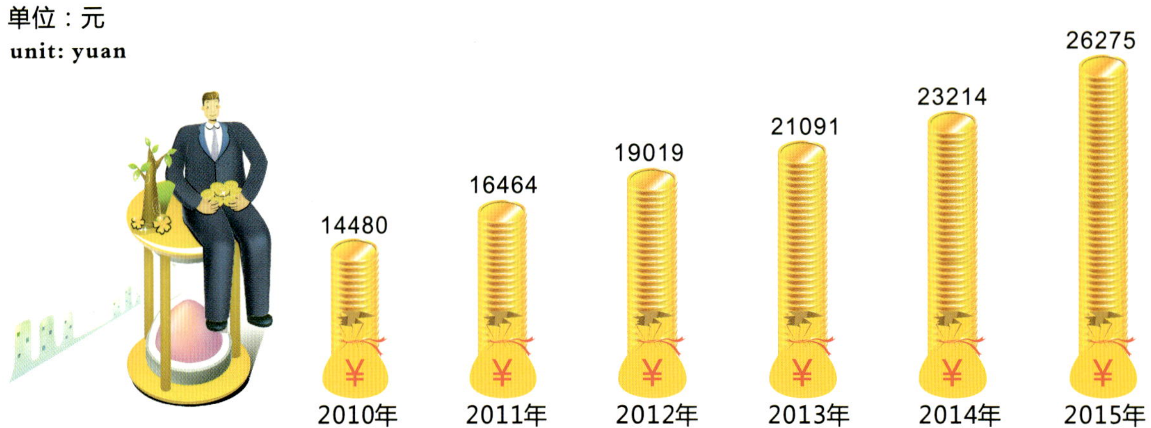

注：图中数据按城乡一体化新口径计算。

note:The data of the chart were caculated according to the new caliber of urban and Rural in intergration

农村居民人均可支配收入
Per Capita Disposable Income of Rural Residents

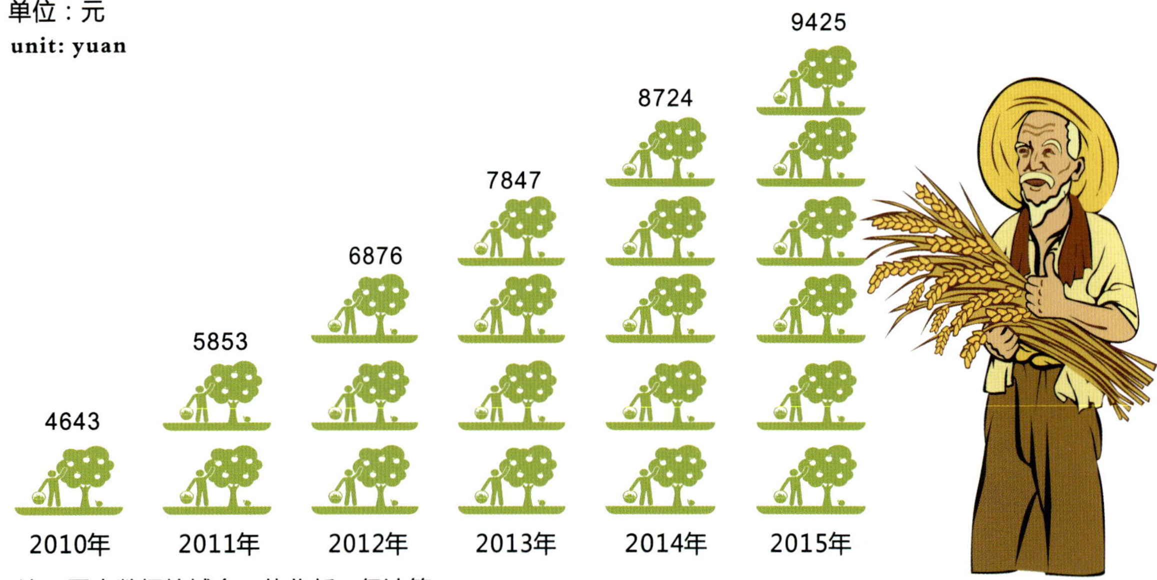

注：图中数据按城乡一体化新口径计算。

note:The data of the chart were caculated according to the new caliber of urban and Rural in intergration

2015年农林牧渔业总产值

Gross Output Value of Agriculture Forestry Animal Husbandry and Fishery

单位：亿元
unit: 100 million yuan

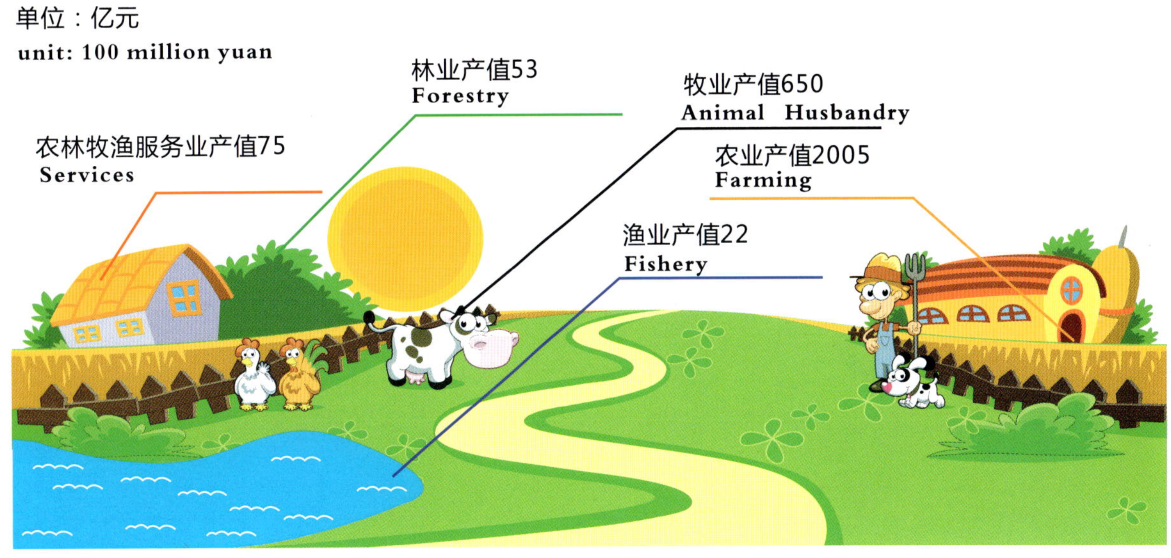

粮食产量

Output of Grain

单位：万吨
unit: 10000 tons

各级各类学校在校学生数
Enrolled Students in Various Schools

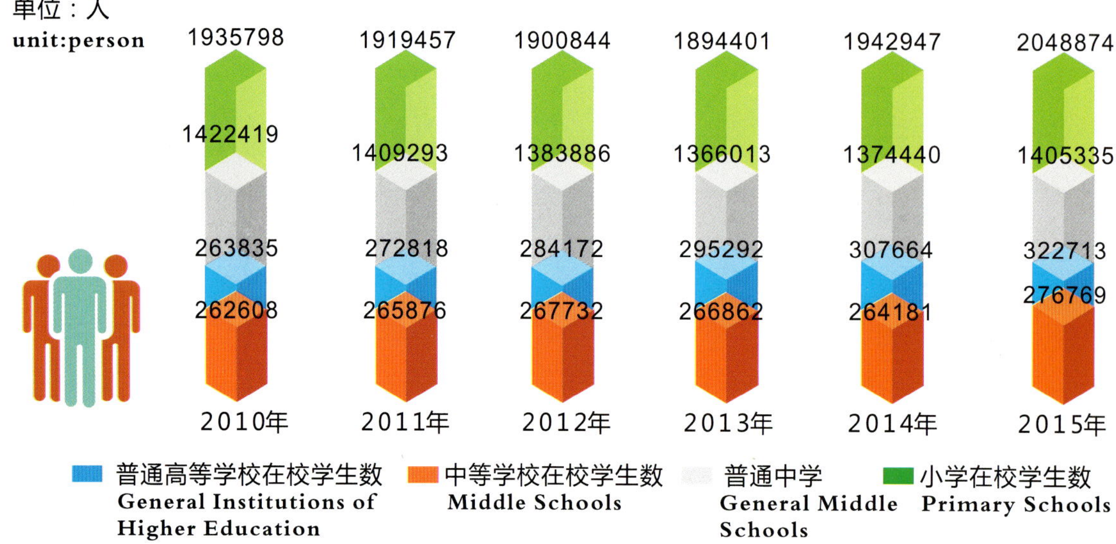

卫生技术人员
Medical Technical Personnel

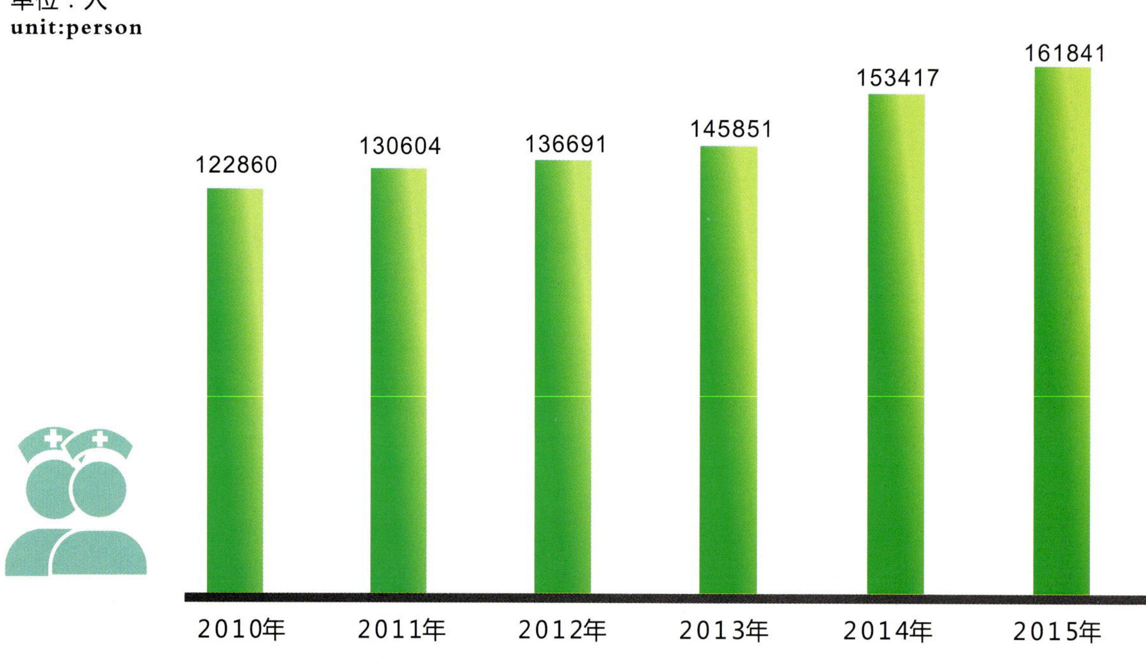

编者说明

一、《新疆统计年鉴—2016》系统收录了全区和各地、县（市）2015 年经济和社会各方面的统计数据，以及重要历史年份和近年全区主要统计数据，并收录了全国及各省市区 2015 年的主要统计数据，是一部全面反映新疆维吾尔自治区经济和社会发展情况的资料性年刊。

二、全书内容分为：特载（新疆维吾尔自治区 2015 年国民经济和社会发展统计公报）；综合；国民经济核算；人口与就业；固定资产投资；对外经济贸易和旅游；资源与环境；能源生产和消费；财政；物价；人民生活；城市概况；农业；工业；建筑业；运输和邮电；批发和零售、住宿和餐饮业；金融业；教育、科技和文化；卫生及其他；各地、州、市主要经济指标排序；附录（各省、市、区主要经济指标排序）。各篇前有简要说明，篇末附有《主要统计指标解释》。

三、本《年鉴》的资料来源，大部分来自年度报表，部分来自抽样调查资料。

四、资料中所使用的度量衡单位均采用国家法定计量单位。

五、本《年鉴》总量指标计算所采用的价格均为现行价格。

六、本《年鉴》伊犁哈萨克自治州的数据包括伊犁州直属县（市）、塔城地区和阿勒泰地区。

七、本《年鉴》使用符号说明："#"表示其中项；"..."表示不足小数位的数据；"空"表示没有或未掌握该指标数据。

八、本《年鉴》在编辑过程中得到自治区内外许多单位和同志们的大力支持，在此深表谢意。限于我们的水平，加之时间仓促，不足之处，敬请各级领导、各界人士和统计战线的同仁批评指正。

Editor's Explanatory Notes

Ⅰ.Xinjiang statistical yearbook 2016 systemly included the economic and social aspects of statistical data by region and throughout the county (city) in 2015,and the main statistical data in historically important years and recent years, and included the major statistical data of provinces and regions in 2015.The book is an annual statistic publication of fully reflect the developmen of economic and social in Xinjiang Uygur Autonomous Region.

Ⅱ.The yearbook comprises such sections as: Special Article (Statistical Communique on National Economy and Social Development of Xinjiang Uygur Autonomous Region in the year 2015); general survey; national accounts; population and employment; investment in fixed assets; foreign trade & economic cooperation and tourism; resources and environment; production and consumption of energy; government finance; price; people' s livelihood; general survey of cities; agriculture; industry; construction; transport and telecommunication services; wholesale & retail trades, hotels and catering services; financial;education, science & technology and culture; public health and others; ranking of main economic indicators by region of Xinjiang; appendix (ranking of main economic indicators by region),etc. Each section is equipped with Explanatory Notes on Main Statistical Indicators at the end.

Ⅲ. The Yearbook of sources are mostly from the annual statements, in part from the sample survey data.

Ⅳ.The units of measurement used in this yearbook are internationally standard measurement units.

Ⅴ.The computation of all the gross indicators in the yearbook is equipped with current prices.

Ⅵ.The data about Yili Kazak Autonomous Prefecture in the present Xinjiang Statistical Yearbook covers counties (cities) direct under Yili Prefecture, Tacheng Prefecture and Altay Prefecture.

Ⅶ.Description of signs or symbols in the yearbook "#" stands for interim item; "..." for data with insufficient decimal place ; "blank" for absence of data indicators or ignorance of them.

Ⅷ.In the course of complication, the yearbook has received great support from many units and comrades in and out of Autonomous Region, we acknowledge their help to the book. Mistakes and faults are inevitable to take place for inadequate proficiency and limited time. Leaders, personnel from all walks of life and colleagues from statistical sector are welcome to make their critical comments and suggestions.

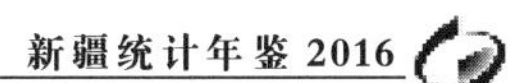

目 录 CONTENTS

第一篇 综 合

CHAPTER 1 GENERAL SURVEY

第 二 篇 国民经济核算

CHAPTER 2 NATIONAL ACCOUNTS

第 三 篇 人口与就业

CHAPTER 3 POPULATION AND EMPLOYMENT

第 四 篇　固定资产投资

CHAPTER 4 INVESTMENT IN FIXED ASSETS

第 五 篇 对外经济贸易和旅游

CHAPTER 5 FOREIGN TRADE AND ECONOMIC COOPERATION & TOURISM

第 十一 篇 城市概况

CHAPTER 11 GENERAL SURVEY OF CITIES

第十二篇 农 业

CHAPTER 12 AGRICULTURE

第十三篇 工 业

CHAPTER 13 INDUSTRY

第十四篇 建筑业

CHAPTER 14 CONSTRUCTION

第 十五 篇　运输和邮电

CHAPTER 15　TRANSPORT, POSTAL AND TELECOMMUNICATION SERVICES

第十六篇 批发和零售业、住宿和餐饮业

CHAPTER 16 WHOLESALE & RETAIL TRADES, HOTELS AND CATERING SERVICES

第 十七 篇 金融业

CHAPTER 17 FINANCIAL INTERMEDIATION

第十八篇 教育、科技和文化

CHAPTER 18 EDUCATION SCIENCE & TECHNOLOGY AND CULTURE

第 十九 篇　卫生及其他

CHAPTER 19 PUBLIC HEALTH AND OTHERS

第二十篇 各地州市主要经济指标排序

CHAPTER 20 RANKING OF MAIN ECONOMIC INDICATORS BY PREFECTURE, AUTONOMOUS PREFECTURE, CITY AND COUNTY OF XINJIANG

附录：各省市区主要经济指标排序

APPENDIX: RANKING OF MAIN ECONOMIC INDICATORS BY REGION

特 载

SPECIAL ARTICLE

新疆统计年鉴2016
XINJIANG STATISTICAL YEARBOOK

2015

2015年，面对复杂多变的国际环境和"三期叠加"的国内形势，自治区党委、人民政府团结带领全区各族人民，坚定不移地贯彻落实中央决策部署，牢牢把握国内外发展大势，坚持"稳中求进、改革创新"工作总基调，主动引领经济发展新常态，着力创新宏观调控，奋力激发市场活力，努力培育创新动力，国民经济在新常态下平稳运行，结构调整出现积极变化，民生事业持续改善，经济社会持续稳定发展，实现了"十二五"圆满收官，为"十三五"经济社会发展和全面建成小康社会奠定了坚实的基础。

一、综　合

初步核算，全年实现地区生产总值（GDP）9324.80 亿元，按可比价计算，比上年增长 8.8%。其中，第一产业增加值 1559.08 亿元，增长 5.9%；第二产业增加值 3596.40 亿元，增长 7.3%；第三产业增加值 4169.32 亿元，增长 12.2 %。三次产业结构为 16.7:38.6:44.7。按常住人口计算，全年人均地区生产总值 40036 元，增长 6.6%；按 2015 年全年平均汇率折算为 6428 美元，增长 5.1%。

全年居民消费价格比上年上涨0.6%，其中，食品价格下降0.8%。工业生产者出厂价格下降17.6%，其中，轻工业下降1.3%，重工业下降20.3%。工业生产者购进价格下降15.7%。截至2015年12月，工业生产者出厂价格连续43个月下降，工业生产者购进价格连续42个月下降。固定资产投资价格下降1.7%。农业生产资料价格下降1.4%。

表1　　**2015年居民消费价格变动情况**

指　　标	涨跌幅度（%）
居民消费价格	0.6
城　市	0.5
农　村	0.6
食　品	-0.8
#粮　食	1.7
肉禽及其制品	-6.5
油脂类	-2.3
蛋　类	-7.2
水产品	-1.7
菜　类	1.3
烟　酒	2.0
衣　着	3.4
家庭设备用品及维修服务	0.6
医疗保健和个人用品	1.5
交通和通信	-0.7
娱乐教育文化用品及服务	0.9
居　住	2.0

二、农　业

全年实现农林牧渔业总产值2804.42亿元，按可比价计算，比上年增长6.3%，其中，农业产值2005.38亿元，增长6.9%；林业产值53.15亿元，增长7.9%；畜牧业产值649.51亿元，增长4.1%；渔业产值21.77亿元，增长9.5%；农林牧渔服务业产值74.61亿元，增长7.4%。

全年农作物播种面积9189.09万亩，增长2.2%。其中，粮食（含薯类）3592.53万亩，增长6.2%；棉花3409.67万亩，同口径对比下降6.1%；油料327.50万亩，下降1.0%；甜菜91.85万亩，下降2.6%；蔬菜485.51万亩，增长4.4%（工业番茄104.12万亩，下降0.9%；工业辣椒73.35万亩，增长19.7%）。特色林果2396.11万亩，增长3.6%，其中，园林水果1457.68万亩，增长2.2%。

全年粮食产量(含薯类)1521.26万吨，增长7.5%。棉花429.8万吨，同口径对比下降4.7%。油料62.88万吨，增长6.0%。甜菜448.32万吨，下降5.0%。蔬菜1933.92万吨，增长6.3%（工业番茄761.30万吨，增长3.6%；工业辣椒198万吨，增长29.6%）。特色林果产量1708.14万吨，增长11.8%，其中，园林水果961.44万吨，增长12.0%。

表2　　2015年特色林果产量及变动情况

指　　标	产量（万吨）	比上年增长（%）
特色林果	1708.14	11.8
水果（含果用瓜）	1635.02	11.5
#园林水果	961.44	12.0
#红枣	305.43	18.6
香梨	113.98	9.1
葡萄	275.60	19.0
果用瓜	673.58	10.7
坚果	73.12	18.9

年末猪牛羊存栏4687.04万头（只），比上年增长2.5%。全年猪牛羊出栏4154.49万头（只），增长2.8%。猪牛羊肉总产量128.96万吨，增长1.8%，其中，牛肉产量40.45万吨，增长3.3%；羊肉产量55.43万吨，增长3.4%；猪肉产量33.08万吨，下降2.3%。禽肉产量14.29万吨，增长10.0%。禽蛋产量32.64万吨，增长6.9%。生牛奶产量155.77万吨，增长5.6%。水产品产量15.14万吨，增长5.1%。

年末农业机械总动力2483.49万千瓦，增长6.2%。拥有大中型拖拉机47.06万台，增长6.4%；小型拖拉机28.09万台，下降6.1%。化肥施用量（折纯）248.09万吨，增长4.7%。农村用电量104.07亿千瓦时，增长7.8%。

拥有农业产业化经营组织11862家，比上年增加855家。自治区级以上农业产业化重点龙头企业507家，增加113家。农产品加工（流通）企业13758家，增加1678家；实现农产品加工（流通）业总产值1729亿元，增长9.2%。

三、工业和建筑业

全年实现全部工业增加值2740.71亿元，按可比价计算，比上年增长5.8%。规模以上工业企业2707家，增长9.3%；实现规模以上工业增加值2662.70亿元，按可比价计算，增长5.2%。在规模以上工业中，按轻重工业划分，轻工业增加值329.00亿元，增长6.1%；重工业2333.70亿元，增长4.9%。按石油非石油工业划分，石油工业增加值1090.95亿元，增长0.8%；非石油工业1571.75亿元，增长9.0%。按经济类型划分，公有制经济工业增加值1857.76亿元，增长4.0%；非公有制经济804.94亿元，增长8.9%。按隶属关系划分，中央企业工业增加值1527.29亿元，增长1.0%；地方企业1135.41亿元，增长11.8%。按企业规模划分，大型企业工业增加值1691.97亿元，增长4.8%；中型企业355.98亿元，增长2.8%；小型企业566.81亿元，增长8.1%；微型企业47.94亿元，增长3.7%。

园区工业实现工业增加值729.04亿元，增长4.1%。建成工业园区94家，其中，国家级23家，自治区级71家。

在自治区重点监测的十大产业中，石油工业增加值1090.95亿元，增长0.8%；有色工业204.08亿元，增长25.7%；电力工业328.25亿元，增长10.9%；化学工业203.13亿元，下降4.4%；钢铁工业14.31亿元，下降38.5%；煤炭工业131.55亿元，增长5.3%；纺织工业52.38亿元，增长5.7%；农副食品加工工业95.68亿元，增长6.3%；装备制造工业110.03亿元，增长32.4%；建材工业111.66亿元，下降9.2%。

表3　2015年工业企业主要产品产量及变动情况

产品名称	单　位	产　量	比上年增长（%）
原　油	万吨	2795.09	-2.8
天然气	亿立方米	293.02	-1.2
原油加工量	万吨	2424.55	-8.3
发电量	亿千瓦时	2478.51	18.5
成品糖	万吨	44.02	-1.1
卷　烟	亿支	201.50	6.1
罐　头	万吨	87.65	5.4
#番茄酱	万吨	82.52	5.2
纱	万吨	60.23	37.0
布	万米	6859.22	4.9
服装	万件	4110.55	91.3
轻革	万平方米	626.93	-22.2
机制纸及纸板	万吨	37.62	-23.0
化肥(折纯)	万吨	322.40	3.2
十种有色金属	万吨	601.46	35.1
电解铝	万吨	586.45	37.4
粗　钢	万吨	785.78	-38.1
钢　材	万吨	1124.01	-28.3
生　铁	万吨	759.52	-43.3
水　泥	万吨	4278.53	-15.8
变压器	万千伏安	7311.22	3.5
化学纤维	万吨	49.45	-10.8
塑料制品	万吨	228.07	7.5

全年规模以上工业企业产品销售率97.7%，比上年提高0.4个百分点。完成工业品出口交货值62.97亿元，

增长21.1%。实现利润总额340.97亿元，下降50.1%。

全年实现建筑业增加值959.03亿元，增长10.3%。具有资质等级的总承包和专业承包建筑企业总产值2255.73亿元，下降2.2%。

四、固定资产投资

全年完成固定资产投资（不含农户）10729.32亿元，比上年增长10.1%，扣除价格因素，实际增长12.0%。其中，第一产业投资366.33亿元，增长21.8%；第二产业投资5179.17亿元，增长6.7%；第三产业投资5183.82亿元，增长13.0%。在第二产业投资中，工业投资5060.53亿元，增长6.3%。

在固定资产投资（不含农户）中，国有及国有控股投资6289.39亿元，增长13.3%，占固定资产投资（不含农户）的比重为58.6%；民间投资4358.89亿元，增长7.2%，占固定资产投资（不含农户）的比重为40.6%；基础设施投资4396.72亿元，增长25.4%，占固定资产投资（不含农户）的比重为41.0%。

房地产开发投资998.88亿元，下降1.6%，其中，住宅投资603.66亿元，下降2.1%。房屋施工面积11465.44万平方米，增长1.6%；房屋竣工面积1608.58万平方米，下降22.9%。商品房销售面积1825.18万平方米，增长0.5%；销售额849.18亿元，增长1.0%。

五、国内贸易

全年实现社会消费品零售总额2605.96亿元，比上年增长7.0%，扣除价格因素，实际增长7.4%。

按经营地划分，城镇消费品零售额2373.80亿元，增长6.9%；乡村消费品零售额232.16亿元，增长7.6%。

按消费形态划分，餐饮收入329.84亿元，增长11.2%；商品零售2276.12亿元，增长6.4%。

按规模划分，限额以上单位消费品零售额1079.88亿元，增长1.4%；限额以下单位消费品零售额1526.08亿元，增长11.3%。

按商品类别划分，限额以上单位粮油、食品类零售额增长6.0%，服装、鞋帽、针纺织品类增长6.0%，烟酒类增长5.7%，饮料类增长3.2%，家用电器和音像制品类增长2.6%，汽车类增长1.4%，金银珠宝类下降2.2%，石油及制品类下降9.4%。

全年疆内企业通过国内第三方电子商务交易平台实现网上零售额44.40亿元，比上年增长20.3%；新疆本地消费者通过国内第三方电子商务交易平台实现网上零售额319.50亿元，增长26.7%，占同期新疆社会消费品零售总额12.3%。

六、对外经济

全年货物进出口总额196.78亿美元，比上年下降28.9%。其中，出口175.06亿美元，下降25.5%；进口21.72亿美元，下降48.1%。

全年拥有172个贸易伙伴国家和地区，其中，对美国进出口额20.72亿美元，增长1.7倍；哈萨克斯坦57.48亿美元，下降43.3%；吉尔吉斯斯坦32.37亿美元，下降21.0%；塔吉克斯坦13.93亿美元，下降30.7%；俄罗斯9.38亿美元，下降56.4%。

表4　　2015年货物进出口总额及变动情况

指　　标	绝对数（亿美元）	比上年增长（%）
货物进出口总额	196.78	-28.9
货物出口额	175.06	-25.4
其中：一般贸易	68.21	-19.7
加工贸易	1.48	-50.6
边境小额贸易	93.50	-27.2
其中：机电产品	50.17	-11.4
高新技术产品	3.22	-29.3
货物进口额	21.72	-48.2
其中：一般贸易	15.55	-37.9
加工贸易	1.15	-24.2
边境小额贸易	2.69	-80.5
其中：机电产品	7.38	37.8
高新技术产品	1.63	36.2
原油	0.79	-96.1

按登记注册类型划分，国有企业进出口 28.93 亿美元，下降47.6%；集体企业1.01亿美元，下降50.6%；外商投资企业 2.51 亿美元，增长 18.5%；私营企业164.17 亿美元，下降 24.5%。

新批准设立外商直接投资企业 50 个，增长2.0%；外商直接投资合同金额 8.57 亿美元，增长62.8%；实际利用外商直接投资 4.53 亿美元，增长8.5%。

七、交通、邮电和旅游

全年完成货运量80190.60万吨，比上年下降11.1%。其中，铁路货运量6234万吨，下降17.2%；

公路货运量64505万吨，下降13.3%；民航货运量6.6万吨，下降7.8%。

全年完成客运量35824万人，比上年下降35.9%。其中，铁路客运量2751万人，增长16.8%；公路客运量32310万人，下降38.8%；民航客运量763万人，增长5.0%。

年末铁路营业里程6165公里，增长7.0%；民航通航里程20.93万公里，下降1.2%；公路线路年末里程17.83万公里，增长1.6%，其中，高速公路4316公里。

年末民用汽车保有量298.26万辆（包括三轮车和低速货车），增长7.6%。其中，年末私人汽车保有量234.52万辆，增长12.4%。年末私人轿车保有量129.97万辆，增长12.3%。

全年完成邮电业务总量402.03亿元，比上年增长8.7%，其中，邮政业务总量22.25亿元，增长10.0%；电信业务总量379.78亿元，增长15.1%。年末固定电话用户523.60万户，下降2.2%。固定电话普及率每百人22.8部。年末移动电话用户2067.20万户，下降0.5%，其中，3G移动电话用户1213.70万户，增长36.2%。移动电话普及率每百人89.9部。互联网宽带接入用户322.60万户，增长5.5%。

全年接待旅游总人数6097.36万人次，增长23.1%。其中，接待入境旅游168.36万人次，增长12.1%；国内旅游5929万人次，增长23.5%。实现旅游总消费1022亿元，其中，国内旅游消费985亿元，入境旅游消费6.08亿美元。

八、财政和金融

全年全口径财政收入2441亿元，比上年下降0.7%。地方财政收入1666亿元，下降2.6%。其中，一般公共预算收入1331亿元，增长3.8%。

全年地方财政支出4169亿元，增长10.4%。其中，一般公共预算支出3805亿元，增长14.7%。全年民生财政支出2812亿元，增长21.7%，占公共预算财政支出73.9%。

年末金融机构（含外资）人民币各项存款余额17123.95亿元，比上年增长10.9%。其中，非金融企业及机关团体存款余额9342.59亿元，增长14.5%；储蓄存款余额6791.62亿元，增长9.8%。

年末金融机构（含外资）人民币各项贷款余额13041亿元，比上年增长11.7%。其中，短期贷款4063.04亿元，增长5.5%；中长期贷款7557.13亿元，增长10.9%。个人消费贷款1559.46亿元，增长14.3%。

年末拥有境内上市公司43家，其中，H股上市公司4家。A股总股本526.76亿股，增长44.0%；股票市价总值6141.01亿元，增长36.0%；全年通过发行、配售股票共筹集资金226.11亿元，增长99.0%；证券交易额32635.27亿元，增长1.8倍；期货交易额19213.78亿元，增长1.1倍。

全年保险公司各项保费收入367.43亿元，比上年增长15.8%。其中，人寿险169.43亿元，增长20.0%；财产险142.96亿元，增长8.6%；健康险41.86亿元，增长29.5%；意外伤害险13.18亿元，增长7.7%。

全年各类保险赔款及给付支出136.85亿元，增长12.9%。其中，财产险赔款76.91亿元，增长0.4%；健康险赔付15.46亿元，增长18.7%；意外伤害险赔付3.79亿元，增长18.8%。

九、教育和科学技术

年末共有普通高等学校39所；全年研究生教育招生0.65万人，增长6.3%；在校研究生1.80万人，增长4.6%；毕业研究生0.55万人，增长11.3%。本专科招生9.02万人，增长5.8%；在校生30.47万人，增长4.9%；毕业生6.97万人，增长3.2%。

中等职业教育学校172所；全年招生8.95万人，增长4.1%；在校生22.17万人，增长1.0%；毕业生6.52万人，下降7.9%。

普通高中357所；全年招生18.77万人，增长7.9%；在校生49.79万人，增长7.6%；毕业生13.91万人，下降1.6%。

初中1069所；全年招生29.93万人，下降2.1%；在校生90.74万人，下降0.4%；毕业生29.75万人，下降0.8%。

小学3501所；全年招生39.77万人，增长7.9%；在校生204.89万人，增长5.5%；毕业生30.04万人，下降2.8%。

特殊教育学校28所；全年招生0.14万人，增长5.8%；在校生0.65万人，增长9.2%；毕业生706人，下降11.4%。

幼儿园4247所；全年招生38.98万人，增长4.4%；在园幼儿81.03万人，增长7.7%；毕业幼儿33.90万人，增长3.8%。

小学学龄儿童净入学率99.85%；小学毕业生升入初中升学率99.62%；初中毕业升入普通高中升学

率68.03%。

全年安排自治区级科技计划项目1433项，其中，科技支撑计划87项，高技术研究发展计划55项，科技兴新项目68项，科技成果转化专项资金项目51项，科技中小企业技术创新基金项目88项。共获得省部级以上科技成果220项。

年末拥有县以上部门属研究与技术开发机构119个。其中，自然科学研究与技术开发机构95个，科技信息与文献机构7个，社会与人文科学领域研究与技术开发机构6个，转制科学研究与技术开发机构11个。重点实验室53个，其中，国家重点实验室1个。工程技术研究中心20个，其中，国家级5个，已挂牌的自治区级工程技术中心15个。高新技术企业424个。高新技术工业园区17个，其中，国家级2个，自治区级15个。农业科技园区21个，其中，国家级7个。生产力促进中心82个，其中，国家级示范中心9个，国家级创新型企业5个，国家级创新型试点企业7个。

全年受理专利申请12250项，其中，受理发明专利申请3024项，占24.7%；获得专利授权8761项，其中，获得发明专利授权950项，占10.8%。签订技术合同656项，技术合同成交金额3.53亿元，其中，技术交易额3.47亿元。

十、文化、卫生和体育

年末共有文化馆118个，公共图书馆107个，博物馆86个。国家综合档案馆110个，开放档案63.49万卷。全区广播综合人口覆盖率96.60%。电视综合人口覆盖率97.04%。有线电视用户217.73万户，其中，有线数字电视用户207.95万户。

年末共有医疗卫生机构18798个，其中，医院、卫生院1841个，妇幼保健院（所、站）92个，专科疾病防治院（所、站）4个。医院、卫生院拥有床位14.36万张，增长9.7%。卫生技术人员12.85万人，增长12.3%，其中，执业医师和执业助理医师4.13万人，注册护士5.39万人。疾病预防控制中心223个。卫生监督检验机构1个。乡镇卫生院927个，拥有床位2.56万张，乡镇卫生院卫生技术人员2.35万人。89个县（市）开展了新型农村合作医疗试点工作，覆盖农村人口1141.06万人。实际参加农村合作医疗农民1138.19万人，参合率为99.75%。

全年建成5个县级全民健身活动中心，14个乡镇农民体育健身工程，3158个行政村农牧民体育健身工程。全区运动健儿在国际比赛中荣获金牌5枚，银牌2枚，铜牌8枚。在全国比赛中荣获金牌63枚，银牌51枚，铜牌78枚。

十一、人口与人民生活

年末常住总人口2359.73万人，其中，城镇人口1114.50万人，乡村人口1245.23万人。城镇人口占总人口比重（常住人口城镇化率）为47.23%。全年人口出生率15.60‰，死亡率4.54‰，自然增长率11.06‰。

全年全体居民人均可支配收入16859.11元，比上年增长11.7%，扣除价格因素，实际增长11.0%。按常住地分，城镇居民人均可支配收入26274.66元，比上年增长13.2%，扣除价格因素，实际增长12.6%。其中，工资性收入17943.27元，增长16.5%；经营净收入2693.15元，增长8.1%；财产净收入1267.84元，增长2.2%；转移净收入4370.39元，增长7.2%。农村居民人均可支配收入9425.08元，增长8.0%，扣除价格因素，实际增长7.4%。其中，工资性收入2131.37元，增长15.3%；经营净收入5397.48元，增长4.2%；财产净收入209.49元，下降8.4%；转移净收入1686.74元，增长14.9%。

十二、劳动就业和社会保障

年末就业人员1195.06万人，增长5.3%。全年通过各种途径实现城镇就业再就业46万人，其中，就业困难人员实现就业5.79万人。全年消除“零就业”家庭654户，帮助实现就业674人。城镇登记失业率3.52%。

年末参加职工基本养老保险345.35万人，其中，在职人员250.20万人，离退休人员95.15万人。参加城乡居民基本养老保险530.83万人。参加城镇基本医疗保险656.89万人，其中，城镇职工376.48万人，城镇居民280.41万人。参加失业保险229.45万人。参加工伤保险253.55万人，其中，参加工伤保险农民工45.20万人。参加生育保险241.10万人。

年末城镇居民最低生活保障人数77.86万人，农村居民最低生活保障人数131.76万人。年末各类收养性社会服务机构及设施4004个；拥有床位数7.15万张；收养人数2.47万人。全区共有各类社区服务设施2136个，其中，一百平米以上的社区服务站1766个。全年销售福利彩票39.81亿元，增长7.5%；筹集公益金11.58亿元，增长9.5%。直接接受社会捐赠16850万元。

十三、资源、环境和安全生产

全区已发现矿种142种。查明资源储量的矿种99种，其中，能源矿产6种，金属矿产33种，非金属矿产60种。新增查明资源储量中，石油储量1.67亿吨，天然气1846.06亿立方米，煤炭储量176亿吨。

全年完成造林面积18.67万公顷，退耕还林面积3.33万公顷。森林覆盖率4.7%。

初步核算，全年能源消费总量1.57亿吨标准煤，比上年增长4.9%。万元地区生产总值能耗比上年下降3.63%。

全年在监测的19个城市中，有4个城市空气质量达到国家Ⅱ级以上标准；城市空气质量优良天数占70.2%。首府乌鲁木齐市空气质量好于Ⅱ级的优良天数占65.2%，与上年相比，年度优良天数比例增加7.9个百分点。在监测的78条河流169个断面中，Ⅰ～Ⅲ类优良水质断面比例为95.9%，比上年提高1.3个百分点；Ⅳ～Ⅴ类轻中度污染水质断面比例为2.9%，降低0.7个百分点；劣Ⅴ类重度污染水质断面比例为1.2%，降低1.2个百分点。在监测的20座湖库中，Ⅰ～Ⅲ类优良水质的湖库比例为63.3%，Ⅳ～Ⅴ类轻中度污染水质湖库比例为13.4%，劣Ⅴ类重度污染水质的湖库比例为23.3%。

自治区级以上自然保护区29个，其中，国家级自然保护区11个，自治区级自然保护区18个，保护区总面积2136万公顷，占新疆国土总面积的12.9%。

全年共发生各类生产经营性安全事故1513起，死亡953人。亿元GDP安全生产事故死亡人数0.233人，工矿商贸十万从业人员生产安全事故死亡人数3.187人，道路交通万车死亡人数4.417人，煤矿百万吨死亡人数0.093人。

注释：

[1]地区生产总值（GDP）、总产值及各产业增加值绝对数按现价计算，增长速度按可比价格计算。

[2]科技、文化、劳动就业、社会保障及环境数据不含兵团。

资料来源：

本公报中主要经济指标数据来源于自治区统计局和国家统计局新疆调查总队，其他数据来源于相关部门。其中，农业机械动力来源于自治区农机局；农业产业化数据来源于自治区农业产业化发展局；林业数据来源于自治区林业厅；利用外资数据来源于自治区商务厅；货物进出口数据来源于乌鲁木齐海关；铁路客货运量及年末营业里程数据来源于乌鲁木齐铁路局；公路客货运量及公路线路年末营业里程数据来源于自治区交通运输厅；民航客货运量来源于中国南方航空股份有限公司新疆分公司；民用汽车数据来源于自治区公安厅；邮政业务数据来源于新疆邮政管理局；电信业务数据来源于自治区通信管理局；旅游数据来源于自治区旅游局；财政数据来源于自治区财政厅；金融信贷数据来源于中国人民银行乌鲁木齐中心支行；上市公司数据来源于中国证券监督管理委员会新疆监管局；保险业数据来源于中国保监会新疆监管局；教育数据来源于自治区教育厅；艺术表演团体、博物馆、公共图书馆、文化馆数据来源于自治区文化厅；科技数据来源于自治区科技厅；广播、电视、电影数据来源于自治区广播电视总局；档案数据来源于自治区档案局；卫生数据来源于自治区卫生计生委；体育数据来源于自治区体育局；就业与社会保障数据来源于自治区人力资源和社会保障厅；销售福利彩票及筹集公益金数据来源于自治区福利彩票发行中心；矿产资源数据来源于自治区国土资源厅；环境监测及自然保护区数据来源于自治区环境保护厅；安全生产数据来源于自治区安全生产监督管理局。

Statistical Communique on the 2015 National Economic & Social Development of the Xinjiang Uygur Autonomous Region

2015, in the face of complex and volatile international environment and the three phase of the superposition of the domestic situation.Autonomous Region Party committee, the people's government to unite and lead the people of all ethnic groups in the region, firmly implement the central decision-making arrangements, firmly grasp the general trend of development at home and abroad,Insist on maintaining stability, reform and innovation, the overall tone of "initiative to lead the new normal economic development, focus on innovation, macro-control struggling to stimulate the vitality of the market, efforts to foster innovation power, national economy under the new normal stable operation, adjust the structure appeared positive changes, continuous improvement of people's livelihood, sustained and stable economic and social development, the realization of the "the 12th Five-year Plan successful ending, "the 13th Five-year Plan economic and social will development and completion of a comprehensive well-off society has laid a solid foundation.

I General Outlook

The gross domestic product (GDP) of Xinjiang was 932.480 billion yuan,up by 8.8% over the previous year, of which, the added value of the primary industry was 155.908 billion yuan,up by 5.9%; that of the secondary industry was 359.640 billion yuan,up by 7.3%; And that of the tertiary industry was 416.932 billion yuan,up by 12.2% over the previous year. The permanent-population-based per-capita GDP reached 40036 yuan, up by 6.6% over the previous year.

The total consumer price index of the year was up by 0.6% over the previous year, of which,the price of food was down by 0.8%.

The ex-factory price index of industrial product was down by 17.6%, of which, light industry was down by 1.3%, heavy industry was down by 20.3%. The purchasing price of industrial product was down by15.7%. The production price of agriculture products down by1.4%. The price of fixed asset investment was up by1.7%.

Table 1 Span of rise and decrease on the consumer price indices

unit: %

Item	Span of rise and decrease
Consumer price index	0.6
Rural	0.6
Uban	0.5
Food	-0.8
#Grain	1.7
Meal poultry and processed products	-6.5
Oil and Fat	-2.3
Eggs	-7.2
Aquatic products	-1.7
Greengrocery	1.3
Tobacco,Liquor and Articles	2.0
Clothing	3.4
Household Facilities, Articles and Services	0.6
Health Care and Personal Articles	1.5
Transportation and Communication	-0.7
Recreation, Education and Culture Articles	0.9
Residence	2.0

II. Agriculture

The gross output value of agriculture,forestry,animal husbandry and fishery was 280.442 billion yuan,up by 6.9%,of which,gross output of agriculture was 200.538 billion yuan ,up by 6.9%, gross output of frostry was 5.315 billion yuan ,up by 7.9%, gross output of animal husbandry was 64.951 billion yuan ,up by 4.1%, gross output of fishery was2.177billion yuan,up by9.5%,gross output of services of agriculture,forestry,animal husbandry and fishery was 7.461 billion yuan,up by 7.4%.

The total sown areas of farm crops was 91.8909 million mus,up by 2.2% over the previous year. Of which, The sown area of grain crops was 35.9253 million mus, up by 6.2% The sown area of cotton crops was 34.0967 million mus; The sown area of oil bearing-crops was 3.2750 million mus,down by 1.0% The sown area of sugar crops was 0.9185 million mus,down by 2.6%

over the previous year. The sown area of vegetable crops was 4.8551 million mus,up by 4.4% over the previous year. The sown area of fruit crops was 23.9611 million mus,up by 3.6%,of which,garden fruit was 14.5768 million mus,up by 2.2%.

The total output of grain was 1521.26 ten thousand tons,up by 7.5% over the previous year The output of cotton was 429.8 ten thousand tons.The output of oil-bearing was 62.88 ten thousand tons, up by 6.0% The output of sugar was 448.32 ten thousand tons,down by 5.0%. The output of vegetable was 1933.92 ten thousand tons, up by 6.3%(tomato in industry was 761.30 ten thousand tons,up by 3.6%;Pepper in industry was 198.00 ten thousand tons,up by 29.6%). The output of fruit was 1708.14 ten thousand tons, up by 11.8%,of which,garden fruit was 961.44 ten thousand tons,up by 12.0%.

Table 2 The output and changes of Characteristics fruit in 2015

Item	Output (10 000 tons)	Increase by previons year
Characteristics of fruit	1708.14	11.8
Fruit	1635.02	11.5
#Garden fruit	961.44	12.0
#Red dates	305.43	18.6
Pear	113.98	9.1
Grape	275.60	19.0
Melon	673.58	10.7
Muslcmelon	234.95	-1.9
Nut	73.12	18.9
Walnut	50.14	24.5
Almond	5.08	42.0

At the end of the year, livestock (only)were 46.8704million heads,up by 2.5%.The annual livestock slaughter were 41.5449 million heads, up by 2.8%. Total meat output were 1.2896 million tons, up by 1.8%, of which, the mutton output were 554.3 thousand tons, up by 3.4%; The beef output were 404.5 thousan tons, up by 3.3%; The pork output were 3.30.8 thousand tons,down by 2.3%. The poultry output was 142.9 thousand tons,up by 10.0%;The production of egg were 326.4 thousand tons, up by 6.9%.The output of Milk were 1557..thousand tons, up by 5.6%. Aquatic products output were 151.4 thousand tons,up by 5.1%.

The year-end total agricultural machinery power was 24.8349 million kilowatt,up by 6.2% over the previous year. There were 47.06 ten thousand large and medium-size tractors,up by 6.4%;And 28.09 ten thousand small-size tractors,down by 6.1%. The consumption of chemical fertilizer was 248.09ten thousand tons(100% equivalent),up by 4.7%. Electricity consumed in rural areas was 10.407 billion kwh, up by 7.8%.

There were 11862 agricultural industrialization management organizations an increase of 855 over the previous year. Above the regional level agricultural industrialization leading enterprises were 507, increased 113. Agricultural products processing (circulation) enterprises were 13758, an increase of 1678. agricultural product processing (Liu Tong) industry output value achieved 172.9 billion yuan, an increase of 9.2%.

III. Industry and Construction

The total value-added of the industrial sector was 274.071 billion yuan,up by 5.8% over the previous year. In the scale of the industry, according to the severityquan of industrial division, light industry added value were 32.900 billion yuan, an increase of 6.1%; Heavy industry added value were 233.370 billion yuan, up by 4.9%.According to the petroleum industry, the oil industry added value were 109.095 billion yuan, up by 0.8%; The non oil industry added value were 157.175 billion yuan ,up by 9.0%. According to the economic classification, the public ownership of economic and industrial added value were 185.776 billion yuan, up by4.0%; Non-public economic added value were 80.494billion yuan, up by8.9%. According to the affiliation of the division, the central enterprise industrial added value were 152.729 billion yuan, up by 1.0%; Local enterprises added value were 113.541 billion yuan, up by 11.8%. Grouped by size of enterprises, large industrial enterprises added value were169.197 billion yuan ,up by 4.8%, and medium-sized enterprises were 35.598 billion yuan, up by 2.8%; small-sized enterprises were 56.681 billion yuan, up by 8.1%; Micro enterprises were 4.794 billion yuan, up by 3.7%.

Table3: Output of Major Industrial Products 2015

Item	Unit	Output	Increase over 2014(%)
Crude oil	10 000 tons	2795.09	-2.8
Natural gas	100 million cubic meters	293.02	1.2
Processed oil	10 000 tons	2424.55	-8.3
Electricity	100 million kilowatt-hours	2478.51	18.5
Refind sugar	10 000 tons	44.02	-1.1
Cigarettes	100 million pieces	201.50	6.1
Can	10 000 tons	87.65	5.4
#Tomato	10 000 tons	82.52	5.2
Yarn	10 000 tons	60.23	37.0
Cloth	10 000meters	6859.22	4.9
Clothing	10 000 sets	4110.55	91.3
Light leather	square meters	626.93	-22.2
Machine-made paper and paperbord	10 000 tons	37.62	-23.0
Chemical fertilizers	10 000 tons	322.40	3.2
Plastics	10 000 tons	228.07	7.5
Ten kinds of nonferrous metals	10 000 tons	601.46	35.1
Aluminum solutio	10 000 tons	586.45	37.4
Crude steel	10 000 tons	785.78	-38.1
Rolled steel	10 000 tons	1124.01	-28.3
Pig Iron	10 000 tons	759.52	-43.3
Cement	10 000 tons	4278.53	-15.8
Transformer	kilovolt-ampere	7311.22	3.5
Chemical fiber	10 000 tons	49.45	-10.8

Among the ten proportion of industrial enterprises above designated, oil industry was 109.095 billion yuan,up by 0.8%. Non-ferrous of industry was 20.408 billion yuan ,up by 25.7%. Production of electric power was 32.825 billion yuan,up by 10.9%. Manufacture of chemical products was 20.313billion yuan,down by 4.4%. Iron and steel industry was 1.431 billion yuan,down by 38.5%. Minging of coal was 13.155 billion yuan,up by 5.3%. Manufacture of textile was 5.238 billion yuan,up by 5.7%. Processing of food from agriculture products was 9.568billion yuan,up by 6.3%.Equipment manufactory industry was 11.003billion yuan,up by 32.4%.

Annual product sales rate of Industrial enterprises above designated size was97.7%,up by0.4%.Completion of export delivery value of industrial goods was 6.297 billion yuan,up by 21.1%.Total profit was 34.162 billion yuan,down by 50.1%.

Added value of construction industry was 95.903billion yuan,up by 10.3%.General contracting and special contracting construction enterprises with qualification grade reaped profits of 225.573 billion yuan, down by 2.2%.

IV. Investment in Fixed Asset

The completed investment in fixed assets(excluding rural households) was 1072.932 billion yuan,up by 10.1%.After deducting price factors, the actual growth12.0%. over the previous year. In terms of three industries, the investment in the primary industry was 36.633 billion yuan,up by 21.8% The investment in the secondary industry was 517.917 billion yuan,up by 6.7%,The tertiary industry investment was 518.382billion yuan, up by 13.0%. Among the investment in the secondary industry, the investment in industry was506.053billion yuan,up by 6.3%.

In the investment in fixed assets (excluding rural households), the state-owned and state-controlled investment was 628.939 billion yuan, up by 13.3%; The proportion of investment in fixed assets was 58.6%. Private investment was 435.889 billion yuan,up by 7.2%,the proportion of investment in fixed assets was 40.6%; Investment in the people's livelihood was 439.672 9 billion yuan, up by 25.4%, The proportion of investment in fixed assets was 41.0%.

The investment in real estate development was 99.888 billion yuan, down by 1.6% over the previous year. The investment of residential was 60.366 billion yuan,down by 2.1%.The floor space of buildings under construction was 114.6544 million square meters, up by 1.6%. The floor space of building completed was 16.0858million square meters, down by 22.9%. The total sales area of commercial buildings for the whole year reached 18.2518million square meters,up by 0.5%. The total sales of commercial building was 84.918 billion yuan,up by 1.0%.

V. Domestic Trades

The total retail sales of consumer goods reached 260.596 billion yuan,up by 7.0% over the previous year. Really up by 7.4%.

In terms of urban and rural areas,the retail sales of consumer goods in urban areas reached 237.380 billion yuan,up by 6.9% And the retail sales of consumer goods in rural areas reached 23.216 billion yuan,up by 7.6%.

According to consumption patterns, Food and beverage revenue was 32.984 billion yuan,up by 11.2%.Retail sales of goods was 227.612 billion yuan,up by 6.4%.

In terms of different sectors,the sales of the wholesale and retail trade reached 107.988 billion yuan, up by 1.4% The sales of the accommodation and catering service was 152.608billion yuan,up by 11.3%.

In the enterprises of wholesale retailsale trade, the volume of food retail sales increased up by 6.0%, the volume of clothing,shoses & hat and textiles, up by 6.0%, household appliance and audiovisual products up by 2.6%, petroleum product down by 9.4%, gold silver and jewelry down by 2.2%,automobiles down by1.4%. Tobacco and Liquor up by 5.7%,beverage category up by 3.2%.

The annual Xinjiang enterprises through third party e-commerce trading platform for retail sales was 4.440 billion yuan,up by 20.3%; Xinjiang local consumers through the online third party e-commerce trading platform to achieve online retail sales was 31.950 billion yuan,up by 26.7%. Accounted for one percent of total retail sales of social consumer goods in the same 12.3% in Xinjiang.

VI Foreign Economic

The total value of import and export reached US$ 19.678 billion,down by 28.9% over the previous year. Of which,the value of export was US$ 17.506 billion, down by 25.5%; And the value of import was US$ 2.172 billion,down by48.1%.

With 172 trade partner countries and regions, including the total import and export value of Russia was$0.938 billion, down by 56.4%.Tajikistan $1.393 billion, down by 30.7%; Kazakhstan $5.748 billion, down by 43.3%; Kyrgyzstan $3.237,down by 21.0%; America $2.072 billion, up by 1.7 times.

Grouped by registration status, state-owned enterprises import and export were $2.893 billion, down by 47.6%; Collective enterprises were $0.101 billion,down by 50.6%; Enterprises with foreign investment of $251 million, up by 18.5%; Private enterprises were $16.417 billion, down by 24.5%.

Newly approved foreign direct investment enterprises 50,

up by 2.0%. Foreign direct investment in the contract amount of $0.857 billion, up by 62.8%; The actual utilization of foreign direct investment of $0.453 billion, up by 8.5%.

Table4 Total Value of Imports and Exports and Growth Rates

unit: US$ 100 million

Item	2015	Increase over 2014(%)
Total value of imports and exports	196.78	-28.9
Total exports	175.06	-25.4
#Ordinary trade	68.21	-19.7
Processing trade	1.48	-50.6
Frontier small trade	93.50	-27.2
Total imports	21.72	-48.2
#Ordinary trade	15.55	-37.9
Processing trade	1.15	-24.2
Frontier small trade	2.69	-80.5

VII Transportation, Postal & Telecommunication and Tourism

Annual freight volume was 801.906 million tons, down by 11.1%. The freight turnover by railways was 62.34 million tons,down by 17.2% That by highways 645.05 million tons,down by 13.3%;That by civil aviation 0.66 ten thousands tons,down by 7.8%.

The annual volume of passenger traffic was 358.24 million passengers, down by 35.9%. Passenger traffic by railways was 27.51 million passengers,up by 16.8%;That by highways 323.10million passengers,down by 38.8% That by civil aviation 7.63 million passengers,up by 5.0%.

At the end of the year, railway in operation reached 6.615 thousand kilometers,up by 7.0%.Total road routes reached 17.83 ten thousand kilometers,dpwn by1.6%.Of which ,highway routes reached 4.316 thousand kilometers.

At the end of the year, there were 298.26 ten thousand civilian automobiles, up by 7.6%, of which, there were 234.52 ten thousand private automobiles, up by 12.4%.

The total volume of telecommunication was 40.203 billion yuan,up by 8.7% over the previous year. The total volume of post stood at 2.225 billion yuan,up by 10.0%. Number of fixed phone users 52360 ten thousang,down by 2.2%. The popularization rate of fixed telephone was 22.8 sets/100 persons.Number of mobile phone users 20.6720 million,down by 0.5%.of which,the number of 3G mobile phone uses was 12.1370 million,up by 36.2%.The popularization rate of mobile telephone was 89.9sets/100 persons. Year-end Internet customer 3.2260 million,up by5.5%.

Tourists through customs to Xinjiang numbered 60.97 million, up by 23.1%,of which, foreign tourists numbered 1.6836 million, up by 12.1%.Domesic tourists numbered 5929 ten thousand, up by 23.5%. Income from tourism amounted to 102.2 billion yuan .Of which, income from foreign tourists amounted 0.608 billion US$.

VIII Finance and Intermediation

The overall-caliber financial revenue stood at 244.1 billion yuan,down by 0.7%. Local government revenue was 166.6 billion yuan,down by 2.6%,of which,the public financial budget revenue was 133.31 billion yuan, up by 3.8%.

The local government expenditure stood at 416.69 billion yuan,up by 10.4%,of which,the general budgetary expenditure was 380.5 billion yuan,up by 14.7%.Annual expenditure on people's livelihood was 281.2 billion yuan,up by 21.7%.

By the end of 2015,savings deposits of all kinds in financial institutions reached 1712.395 billion yuan,up by10.9% over the previous year. Of which,units savings deposits were 934.259 billion yuan, up by 14.5%; Savings deposits were 679.162 billion yuan, up by 9.8%.

Loans of all kinds in financial institutions were 1304.1 billion yuan, of which, Loans of short-term were 406.304 billion yuan, up by 5.5%; Loan of medium-and long-term were 755.713 billion yuan,up by 10.9%. Individual consumption loans were 155.946 0billion yuan, up by 14.3%.

At the end of 2015, there were 43 listed companies, Total market capitalization were 614.101 billion yuan, up by 36.0%. In the year of 2015, the refinancing totaled 22.611 billion yuan,up by 99.0%. Total futures trading volume were 3263.527 billion yuan, up by 1.8 times.

The total premium of insurance companies reached 36.743 billion yuan,up by 15.8% over the previous year. of the total,life insurance premium was 16.943 billion yuan,up by 20.0%; Property insurance premium 14.296 billion yuan, up by 8.6%; Health and casualty insurance premium were 4.186 billion yuan,up by29.5%; That against health and accidental injury were 1.318 billion yuan, up by 7.7%.

Insurance companies paid an indemnity of 13.685 billion yuan as reparation for various property and life insurance programs, up by 12.9%. Of which, and that against property was 7.690 billion yuan, up by 0.4%; The indemnity against life insurance was1.546 billion yuan, down by 18.7%; The health insurance was 0.379 billion yuan,up by 18.8%.

IX Education and Scientific Technology

By the end of 2015,there were totally 39 general colleges .The enrollment of postgraduate students were 6500 new entrants,up by 6.3%; The enrollment of post- graduate students was 18000,up by 4.6%, graduates students were 5500, up by 11.3%. The enrollment of regular under-graduates and college student were 9.02 ten thousand, up by 5.8%; The enrollment of students was 30.47 ten thousand,up by 4.9%, graduates students were 6.97 ten thousand, down by3.2%.

There were 172 secondary schools,the recruit students were 8.95 ten thousand,up by 4.1%. Enrollment of students were 22.17ten thousand,up by 1.0%;Graduates students were 6.52 ten thousand, down by 7.9%.

There were 357 ordinary high school, the annual enrollment of 18.77 ten thousand people, an increase of 7.9%; 47.79 ten thousand students, an increase of 7.6%; 13.91ten thousand graduates, an increase of 1.6%.

There were 1069 regular secondary schools,the recruit students were 29.93 ten thousand,down by2.1%. Enrollment of students were 90.74 ten thousand,down by 0.4%;Graduates students were29.75ten thousand,down by 0.8%.

There were 3501 primary schools,the recruit students were 39.77 ten thousand,up by 7.9%;Enrollment of student were 204.89 ten thousand,up by 5.5%;Graduates students were 30.04 ten thousand,down by 2.8%.

There were 28 special schools,the recruit students were 1400, up by 5.8%;Enrollment of student were 6500,up by 9.2%;Graduates students were 706,down by 11.4%.

There were 4247 kindergartens, the recruit students were 38.98 ten thousand,up by 4.4%;Enrollment of student were 81.03 ten thousand,up by 7.7%; Graduated children in kindergartens were 33.90 ten thousand,up by 3.8%.

The enrollment rate of school-age children reached 99.85%. Enrollment rate of junior secondary school-age youth was 99.62%.Promotion rate from junior sendary school to senior secondary school was 68.03%.

In 2015, the autonomous region formulated 1433 sci-tech project plans, of which, science and technology support program 87, high technology research and development program 55, science and technology of new projects 68, scientific and technological achievements into a special fund project 51, tech SME Technology Innovation Fund Project 88. Has won provincial and ministerial level scientific and technological achievements 220.

At the end of the year, there were 119 above the county department of research and technological development institutions, the natural scientific research and technological development institutions were 95, science and technology information and literature were 7, social sciences and Humanities Research and technological development institutions were 6. There were 53 key laboratories, of which,national key laboratores were 1. Engineering and technological research centers were 20, of which, national level 5, autonomous Level15. By the end of 2015 we had 424 high and new tech enterprises, There are17 new and high tech zones, of which, 2 national level ,15 autonomous level. There were 21 agricultural science and technology park , of which ,7 national level. There were 82 productivity Promotion center, of which 9 national innovation centers5, national innovation enterprises, 7 national innovation pilot enterprise.

There are totally 12250 patent applications, of which, there are 3024 for a patent for invention taking up 24.7%, and 8761 patent licenses, including 950 invention patent licenses accounting for 10.8%. 656 technology contracts were signed, and the turnover reached 353 million yuan, of which, the volume of technology trade was 347 million yuan.

X Culture and Sports

At the end of 2015,there were 118 cutural centers, 107 public library, 86 museums;110 national comprehensive archives. Open the record rooms were 63.49 ten thousand units. telivision stations. radio broadcasting coverage rate was 97.04%; television coverage rate was 96.94%. Number of users of cable television was 217.73 ten thousand, number of Users of digital TV was 207.95ten thousand.

At the end of the year, there were 18798 medical institutions, including 1841 hospitals, maternal and child health hospital (the station) 92, specialized disease prevention (the station) 4. The hospital has 143.6 thousand beds, up by 9.7%. health and technical personnel were 128.5 thousand, up by 12.3%, among them, practice doctors and practicing assistant doctors were 41.3 thousand, registered nurses were.53.9 thousand The Centers for Disease Control and prevention were 223. Health supervision and inspection agencies was 1. There were 927 township hospitals, with 25.6 thousand beds, township hospitals and health workers were 23.5 thousand.89 County (city) carried out the pilot work of new rural cooperative medical care coverage in rural areas the population of 11.4106 million people. The rural participated cooperative medical farmers were 11.3819 million people, the participation rate was 99.75%.

Built 5 county level nationwide fitness activities center. There were 14 the rural fitnes centers,the farm fitness projects were 3158 administrative village farmer sports fitness project. In the international competition Athletes from the Autonomous Region won 5 gold medal, 2 silver medal, 8 bronze medal. In the national competition Athletes from the Autonomous Region in matches home and abroad won 63 gold medals, 51 silver medals,

78 bronze medals..

XI Populatin and People's Life

By the end of 2015,the population of autonomous region was 23.5973 million, of which, the population in urban areas was 11.1450 million, rural areas 12.4523 million; The urbanization rate was 47.23%.The birthrate was 15.60‰; The deathrate was 4.54‰. The natural growth rate of population was 11.06‰.

The per capital family income reached 16859.11 yuan,up by 11.7%,of which,the per capital disposable income of urban residents reached 26274.66 yuan,up by 13.2% over the previous year. Of which, income of salary and wage was 17943.27 yuan, up by 16.5%, Net operating income were 2693.15yuan, down by 8.1%, income of property were 1267.84 yuan, up by 2.2%, metastatic income were 4370.39 yuan, up by 7.2%. The per capital auunal net income of rural households was 9425.08yuan, up by 8.0%, of which, income of salaries and wages was 2131.37 yuan, up by 15.3%; income from household operations was 5397.48 yuan, up by 4.2%; Income from properties was 209.49 yuan, down by 8.4%. Income from transfers was 1686.74 yuan, up by 14.9%.

XII.Employment and Social Security

Number of employed person was 11.9506 million at year-end, up by 5.3%. Number of urban employed persons were 46 ten thousand, of which,the reemployment of zero-employment workers was 5.79 ten thousand. The elimination of zero employment family 654 households, helping to realize the employment of 674 people.Registered unemployment rate in urban areas was 3.52%.

A total of 3.4535 million people participated in basic social endowment insurance programs, Among them, 250.20 ten thousands were in-service staff. 95.15 ten thousand were retirees.

530.83 ten thousands people participated in urban and rural basic endowment insurance. 656.89 ten thousands people participate urban basic medical insurance, among them ,376.48 ten thousands urban staff, 280.41 ten thousands urban residents. 229.45ten thousands people participated in unemployment insurance. 253.55 ten thousands people participated in work-related injury insurance, among them,45.20 ten thousands were peasant-worker, 241.10 ten thousands people participated in maternity insurance.

There were 77.86ten thousand people recevied the basic welfare for urban residents. 131.76 ten tgousand people received the basic welfare for rural residents.Number of all lcinds of adoption of sacial services and facilities were 4004;Number of beds were 7.15 ten thousand in social welfare institutions at the end of year; Number of inmates were 2.47 ten thousand. The number of community service equipment were 2136. Of which, the number of more than one hunclred squar meters of community services stations wcre 1766. Revenue from social welfare lottery tickets were 3.981 billion yuan, up by 7.5%; Social welfare fund were 1158 million yuan, up by 9.5%. 168.50 million yuan of donatioas were received from the general public.

XIII Rsources Environment and Safe production

142 mineral products were found, of which, 99 mineral products have resources. Of which, there were 6 energy minerals, 33 metal minerals, 60 non-metal minerals. An increase of mineral products have resources,of which,coal resources were 17.6 billion tons. petroleum reserves were 0.167 billion tons,atural gas were 184606 million cubic meters.

The annual afforestation area of 186.7 thousand hectares, returning farmland to forest area of 33 thousand and 300 hectares. The forest coverage rate is 4.7%.

Preliminary accounting, the annual total energy consumption of 1.57 tons of standard coal, up by 4.9%.Yuan GDP energy consumption down by 3.63%.

In the 19 monitored cities, 4 cities had their air quality reach national standard Grade II. In the Autonomous Region about 70.2% of the year the air quality was better than Grade II. And 65.2% of the year in Urmqi the air quality was better than Grade II, up by 7.9% over the previous year. Monitoring of water quality on 169 sections of the 78rivers showed that good quality water of standard Grade I ~III accounted for 95.9%, up by 1.3%. Quality water of standard Grade IV~V accounted for 2.9%, down by 0.7%, Quality water of standard Grade V accounted for 1.2%, down by 1.2%. Monitoring of water quality of 20 lakes and reservoirs showed that good quality water of standard Grade I III accounted for 63.3%, Quality water of standard Grade V accounted for 23.3%.

There were 29 national and regional nature reserves.of which,national nature reserves were 11. Area of nature reserves were 2136 ten thousand sqkm, proportion of nature reserves in total area of territory was 12.9%.

There were 1513 safety accidents occurred, with 953 person died. The 100-million- GDP-based death rate in production safety accidents was 0.233. Among every 100 000 employees in trade sectors 3.187 persons died, for every 10 000 vehicles 4.417 persons died, for every one million tons output of coal mines 0.093persons died.

综 合
COMPREHENSIVE
STATISTICS
1

第一篇 综合

本篇主要内容和资料来源

综合资料主要包括新疆行政区划、国民经济和社会发展综合资料以及基本单位资料三部分。

行政区划资料由新疆维吾尔自治区民政厅根据国务院批准的、截止到2015年末新疆行政区划变更情况汇总整理并提供；国民经济和社会发展综合资料由新疆维吾尔自治区统计局国民经济综合统计处根据各篇主要指标加工整理而成；基本单位统计资料由新疆维吾尔自治区统计局普查中心依据基本单位年报整理提供。

Comprehensive Statistics

Main Content and Source of Data

This chapter mainly covers three parts: the data of division of administrative areas, summary data on the national economy and grass-roots unit.

Data on division of administrative areas are provided by the Bureau of Civil Affairs of Xinjiang Uygur Autonomous Region on the basis of the changes in the divisions of administrative areas as approred by the state council at the end of 2015.Data on the national economy and social development are compiled and processed by the Department of Comprehensive Statistics of the Xinjiang Bureau of Statistics using relevant. Data on grass-roots units are compiled and processed by the Census Center.

1-1 行 政 区 划
Divisions of Administrative Areas in Xinjiang Uygur Autonomous Region

单位：个　　(2015 年)　　(unit)

区划名称	Region	地级区划数 Number of Regions at Prefecture Level	县级区划数 Number of Regions at County level	#地州辖市 Cities under the Prefectures	#市辖区 Districts under the Jurisdiction of Cities	#县 Counties	#自治县 Autonomous Counties
总　计	**Total**	**14**	**103**	**16**	**12**	**62**	**6**
乌鲁木齐市	Urumqi City	1	8		7	1	
克拉玛依市	Karamay City	1	4		4		
吐鲁番市	Turpan City	1	3		1	2	
哈密地区	Hami [Kumul] Administrative Offices	1	3	1		1	1
昌吉回族自治州	Changji Hui Autonomous Prefecture	1	7	2		4	1
伊犁哈萨克自治州	Ili Kazak Autonomous Prefecture	3	25	6		17	2
伊犁州直属县(市)	Counties (Cities) Direct Under Ili Prefecture	1	11	3		7	1
塔城地区	Tacheng [Tarbagatai] Administrative Offices	1	7	2		4	1
阿勒泰地区	Altay Administrative Offices	1	7	1		6	
博尔塔拉自治州	Bortala Mongol Autonomous Prefecture	1	4	2		2	
巴音郭楞自治州	Bayangol Mongol Autonomous Prefecture	1	9	1		7	1
阿克苏地区	Aksu Administrative Offices	1	9	1		8	
克孜勒苏自治州	Kizilsu Kirgiz Autonomous Prefecture	1	4	1		3	
喀什地区	Kashgar [Kaxgar] Administrative Offices	1	12	1		10	1
和田地区	Hotan Administrative Offices	1	8	1		7	
自治区直辖市	Cities under the Autonomous Region		7				
石河子市	Shihezi City		1				
阿拉尔市	Aral City		1				
图木舒克市	Tumxuk City		1				
五家渠市	Wujiaqu City		1				
北屯市	Beitun City		1				
铁门关市	Tiemenguan City		1				
双河市	Shuanghe City		1				

1-1 续表 Continued

单位：个 (unit)

区划名称	Region	乡镇级区划数 Number of Regions at Town-ships Level	#镇 Towns	#乡 Townships	#民族乡 National Townships	#街道办事处 Street Communities
总　计	**Total**	**1046**	**320**	**506**	**42**	**178**
乌鲁木齐市	Urumqi City	95	8	13	1	73
克拉玛依市	Karamay City	14	1	1		12
吐鲁番市	Turpan City	30	14	12	1	3
哈密地区	Hami [Kumul] Administrative Offices	42	14	20	3	5
昌吉回族自治州	Changji Hui Autonomous Prefecture	79	43	16	11	9
伊犁哈萨克自治州	Ili Kazak Autonomous Prefecture	247	93	109	17	28
伊犁州直属县(市)	Counties (Cities) Direct Under Ili Prefecture	114	35	52	10	17
塔城地区	Tacheng [Tarbagatai] Administrative Offices	75	34	28	5	8
阿勒泰地区	Altay Administrative Offices	58	24	29	2	3
博尔塔拉自治州	Bortala Mongol Autonomous Prefecture	21	9	8		4
巴音郭楞自治州	Bayangol Mongol Autonomous Prefecture	90	32	52	1	5
阿克苏地区	Aksu Administrative Offices	96	36	47	2	11
克孜勒苏自治州	Kizilsu Kirgiz Autonomous Prefecture	39	6	30	1	2
喀什地区	Kashgar [Kaxgar] Administrative Offices	176	38	128	3	7
和田地区	Hotan Administrative Offices	95	20	69	2	4
自治区直辖市	Cities under the Autonomous Region	22	6	1		15
石河子市	Shihezi City	7	2			5
阿拉尔市	Aral City	6	1	1		4
图木舒克市	Tumxuk City	4	1			3
五家渠市	Wujiaqu City	5	2			3
北屯市	Beitun City					
铁门关市	Tiemenguan City					
双河市	Shuanghe City					

1-2 县级以上行政区划
Divisions of Administrative Areas at and above the County Level

(2015 年)

<table>
<tr><th colspan="2">地、州、市名称
Name of Administrative Offices, Autonomous Prefectures, Cities</th><th>市、县(市辖区)名称
Name of Cities and Counties (Districts under Cities)</th></tr>
<tr><td colspan="2">乌鲁木齐市
Urumqi City</td><td>天山区、沙依巴克区、高新区(新市区)、水磨沟区、经济技术开发区(头屯河区)、达坂城区、米东区、乌鲁木齐县
Tianshan District, Shayibak District, Gaoxin District(Xinshi District), Shui Mogou District, Economic and Technological Development Zone(Tou Tunhe District), Da Bancheng District, Midong District, Urumqi County</td></tr>
<tr><td colspan="2">克拉玛依市
Karamay City</td><td>克拉玛依区、独山子区、白碱滩区、乌尔禾区
Karamay District, Dushanzi District, Bai Jiantan District, Urhe District</td></tr>
<tr><td colspan="2">吐鲁番市
Turpan City</td><td>高昌区、鄯善县、托克逊县
Gaochang District, Shanshan [Piqan] County, Toksun County</td></tr>
<tr><td colspan="2">哈密地区
Hami [Kumul] Administrative Offices</td><td>哈密市、巴里坤哈萨克自治县、伊吾县
Hami [Kumul] City, Barkol Kazak Autonomous County, Yiwu[Araturuk] County</td></tr>
<tr><td colspan="2">昌吉回族自治州
Changji Hui Autonomous Prefecture</td><td>昌吉市、阜康市、呼图壁县、玛纳斯县、奇台县、吉木萨尔县、木垒哈萨克自治县
Changji City, Fukang City, Hutubi County, Manas County, Qitai County, Jimsar County, Mori Kazak Autonomous County</td></tr>
<tr><td rowspan="3">伊犁哈萨克自治州
Ili Kazak Autonomous Prefecture</td><td>伊犁州直属县(市)
Counties (Cities) Direct Under Ili Prefecture</td><td>伊宁市、奎屯市、伊宁县、察布查尔锡伯自治县、霍城县、巩留县、新源县、昭苏县、特克斯县、尼勒克县、霍尔果斯市
Yining [Gulja] City, Kuytun City , Yining [Gulja] County, Qapqal Xibe AutonomousCounty, Huocheng [Korgas] County, Gongliu [Tokkuzlara] County, Xinyuan [Kunes] County, Zhaosu [Mongolkure] County, Tekes County, Nilka County Huoerguosi City</td></tr>
<tr><td>塔城地区
Tacheng [Tarbagatai] Administrative Offices</td><td>塔城市、乌苏市、额敏县、沙湾县、托里县、裕民县、和布克赛尔蒙古自治县
Tacheng [Qoqek] City, Usu City, Emin [Dorbiljin] County, Shawan County, Toli County, Yumin [Qagantokay] County, Hoboksar Mongol Autonomous County</td></tr>
<tr><td>阿勒泰地区
Altay Administrative Offices</td><td>阿勒泰市、布尔津县、富蕴县、福海县、哈巴河县、青河县、吉木乃县
Altay City, Burqin County, Fuyun [Koktokay] County, Fuhai [Burultokay] County, Habahe [Kaba] County, Qinghe [Qinggil] County, Jeminay county</td></tr>
<tr><td colspan="2">博尔塔拉蒙古自治州
Bortala Mongol Autonomous Prefecture</td><td>博乐市、精河县、温泉县、阿拉山口市
Bole [Bortala] City, Jinghe [Jing] County, Wenquan [Arxang] County， Alashankou City</td></tr>
<tr><td colspan="2">巴音郭楞蒙古自治州
Bayangol Mongol Autonomous Prefecture</td><td>库尔勒市、轮台县、尉犁县、若羌县、且末县、焉耆回族自治县、和静县、和硕县、博湖县
Korla City, Luntai [Bugur] County, Yuli [Lopnur] County, Ruoqiang [Qarkilik] County, Qiemo [Qarqan] County, Yanqi Hui Autonomous County, Hejing County, Bohu [Bagrax] County</td></tr>
<tr><td colspan="2">阿克苏地区
Aksu Administrative Offices</td><td>阿克苏市、温宿县、库车县、沙雅县、新和县、拜城县、乌什县、阿瓦提县、柯坪县
Aksu City, Wensu [Onsu] County, Kuqa County, Xayar County, Xinhe [Toksu] County, Baicheng [Bay] County, Wushi [Uqturpan] County, Awat County, Kalpin County</td></tr>
<tr><td colspan="2">克孜勒苏柯尔克孜自治州
Kizilsu Kirgiz Autonomous Prefecture</td><td>阿图什市、阿克陶县、阿合奇县、乌恰县
Artux City, Akto County, Akqi County, Wuqia [Ulugqat] County</td></tr>
<tr><td colspan="2">喀什地区
Kashgar [Kaxgar] Administrative Offices</td><td>喀什市、疏附县、疏勒县、英吉沙县、泽普县、莎车县、叶城县、麦盖提县、岳普湖县、伽师县、巴楚县、塔什库尔干塔吉克自治县
Kashgar [Kaxgar] City, Shufu County, Shule County, Yengisar County, Zepu [Poskam] County, Shache [Yarkant] County, Yecheng [Kagilik] County, Makit County, Yopurga County, Jiashi [Payzawat] County, Bachu [Maralbexi] County, Taxkorgan Tajik Aotonomous County</td></tr>
<tr><td colspan="2">和田地区
Hotan Administrative Offices</td><td>和田市、和田县、墨玉县、皮山县、洛浦县、策勒县、于田县、民丰县
Hotan City, Hotan County, Moyu [Karakax] County, Pishan [Guma] County, Lop County, Qira County, Yutian [Keriya] County, Minfeng [niya] County</td></tr>
<tr><td colspan="2">自治区直辖县级市
County level City directly under the Autonomous Region</td><td>石河子市、 阿拉尔市、图木舒克市、五家渠市、北屯市、铁门关市、双河市
Shihezi City,Aral City,Tumxuk City,Wujiaqu City,Beitun City,Tiemenguan City Shuanghe City</td></tr>
</table>

1-3 主要年份国民经济和社会发展总量与速度指标

指 标	Item	1978
人口与就业	**Population and Employment**	
人口(万人)	**Population (10 000 persons)**	
年末总人口	Population at the Year-end	1233.01
男 性	Male	630.18
女 性	Female	602.83
就业(万人)	**Employment (10 000 persons)**	
就业人员数	Employment	491.25
#在岗职工人数	Staff and Workers	226.69
城镇登记失业人数	Urban Registeration Unemployment	
宏观经济	**Macro Economy**	
国民经济核算(亿元)	**National Accounting (100 million yuan)**	
新疆生产总值	Gross Domestic Product	39.07
第一产业	Primary Industry	13.97
第二产业	Secondary Industry	18.35
第三产业	Tertiary Industry	6.75
支出法新疆生产总值	Gross Domestic Product by Expenditure Approach	
#最终消费	Final Consumption Expenditure	27.64
居民消费	Houshold Consumption Expenditure	22.61
政府消费	Government Consumption Expenditure	5.03
资本形成总额	Gross Capital Formation	18.43
固定资本形成	Gross Fixed Capital Formation	13.25
存货增加	Changes in Inventories	5.18
货物和服务净出口	Net Export of Goods and Services	-7.00
固定资产投资	**Investment in Fixed Assets**	
全社会固定资产投资总额(亿元)	Total Investment in Fixed Assets (100 million yuan)	13.00
#房地产	Real Estate Development	
全社会施工房屋建筑面积(万平方米)	Floor Space of Buildings under Construction (10 000 sq.m)	
全社会竣工房屋建筑面积(万平方米)	Floor Space of Building Completed (10 000 sq.m)	
消 费	**Consumption**	
社会消费品零售总额(亿元)	Total Retail Sales of Consumer Goods (100 million yuan)	21.89
对外贸易	**Foreign Trade**	
进出口总额(亿美元)	Total Value of Imports and Exports (USD 100 million)	0.23
出口额	Exports	0.09
进口额	Imports	0.14
利用外资(万美元)	**Utilization of Foreign Capital (USD 10 000)**	
签订利用外资协议额	Amount of Foreign Capital for Utilization through Signed Contracts or Agreements	
实际利用外资额	Amount of Foreign Capital Actually Utilized	
财政(亿元)	**Public Finance (100 million yuan)**	
一般公共预算收入	General Budgetary Revenue	7.14
#税收收入	Various Taxes	4.34

Principal Aggregate Indicators on National Economic and Social Development and Growth Rates in Main Years

总量指标 Aggregate Data				速度指标(%) Indices and Growth Rates(%)						
				指数(2015 年比以下各年) Index (2015 as percentuage of the following years)				平均增长速度 Average Annual Growth Rate		
2000	2010	2014	2015	1978	2000	2010	2014	1979-2015	2001-2015	2011-2015
1849.41	2181.58	2298.47	2359.73	191.4	127.6	108.2	102.7	1.8	1.6	1.6
957.07	1127.01	1164.38	1199.47	190.3	125.3	106.4	103.0	1.8	1.5	1.3
892.34	1054.57	1134.09	1160.26	192.5	130.0	110.0	102.3	1.8	1.8	1.9
672.50	894.65	1135.24	1195.06	243.3	177.7	133.6	105.3	2.4	3.9	6.0
255.75	245.48	305.60	307.77	135.8	120.3	125.4	100.7	0.8	1.2	4.6
11.00	10.99	11.21	13.42		122.0	122.1	119.7		1.3	4.1
1363.56	5437.47	9273.46	9324.80	3905.3	444.6	166.6	108.8	10.4	10.5	10.8
288.18	1078.63	1538.60	1559.08	1355.5	236.2	136.6	105.9	7.3	5.9	6.4
537.58	2592.15	3948.96	3596.40	3692.7	505.4	170.9	107.3	10.2	11.4	11.3
537.80	1766.69	3785.90	4169.32	10703.9	516.9	177.7	112.2	13.5	11.6	12.2
760.20	2865.56	5024.50	5639.84							
492.32	1578.93	2837.02	3187.11							
267.88	1286.63	2187.48	2452.73							
618.12	3371.22	8282.49	8785.27							
648.12	3233.00	8301.43	8755.72							
-30.00	138.22	-18.94	29.55							
-14.76	-799.31	-4033.53	-5100.31							
610.38	3539.69	9744.79	10729.32	82533.2	1757.8	303.1	110.1	19.9	21.1	24.8
57.43	347.72	1014.81	998.88		1739.3	287.3	98.4		21.0	23.5
4485.77	11361.96	25797.54	22689.17		505.8	199.7	88.0		11.4	14.8
2633.23	4649.89	7072.93	5935.82		225.4	127.7	83.9		5.6	5.0
374.50	1386.06	2436.50	2605.96	11904.8	695.8	188.0	107.0	13.8	13.8	13.5
22.64	171.28	276.69	196.78	85556.5	869.2	114.9	71.1	20.0	15.5	2.8
12.04	129.70	234.82	175.06	194511.1	1454.0	135.0	74.6	22.7	19.5	6.2
10.60	41.58	41.87	21.72	15514.3	204.9	52.2	51.9	14.6	4.9	-12.2
9212.00	30091.00	52604.00	85651.00		929.8	284.6	162.8		16.0	23.3
1923.00	23742.00	41700.00	45250.00		2353.1	190.6	108.5		23.4	13.8
79.07	500.58	1282.34	1330.85	18639.4	1683.1	265.9	103.8	15.2	20.7	21.6
64.53	416.23	887.79	861.73	19855.5	1335.4	207.0	97.1	15.4	18.9	15.7

1-3 续表 1

指　标	Item	1978
一般公共预算支出	General Budgetary Expenditures	17.02
#一般公共服务	General Common Service	
教育与科学技术	Operating Expenses for Education and Operating Expenses for Science and Technology	
社会保障和就业	Operating Expenses for Social Safety and Employ ment Effort	
节能环保	Energy Saving and Environmental Protection	
城乡社区事务	Expenses of Community	
农林水事务	Expenses of Agriculture, Forest and Irrigation	
物价总指数(上年=100)	**Price Indices (preceding year=100)**	
居民消费价格总指数	Consumer Price Indices	101.2
商品零售价格总指数	Retail Price Indices	101.4
工业生产者出厂价格指数	Producer Price Indices for Industrial Products	
工业生产者购进价格指数	Purchasing Price Indices for Industrial Products	
固定资产投资价格指数	Investment in Fixed Assets Price Indices	
能源生产与消费(万吨标准煤)	**Production and Consumption of Energy (10 000 tons of SCE)**	
能源生产总量	Total Energy Production	1410.75
能源消费总量	Total Energy Consumption	979.27
产　业	**Industry**	
农　业	**Agriculture**	
农林牧渔业总产值(亿元)	Gross Output Value of Agriculture Forestry, Animal Husbandry and Fishery (100 million yuan)	19.12
主要农产品产量(万吨)	Output of Major Farm Products (10 000 tons)	
粮　食	Grain	370.01
棉　花	Cotton	5.50
油　料	Oil-bearing Crops	10.33
甜　菜	Beet Roots	16.37
水　果	Fruits	13.98
肉　类	Meat	9.65
奶　类	Milk	5.25
水产品	Aquatic Products	0.57
工　业	**Industry**	
主要工业产品产量	Output of Major Industrial Products	
纱(万吨)	Yarn (10 000 tons)	2.80
布(亿米)	Cloth (100 million meter)	1.56
绒线(吨)	Woolen Knitting (ton)	1239
呢绒(万米)	Woolen Goods (10 000 meter)	189
原盐(万吨)	Crude Salt (10 000 tons)	51.71
机制纸及纸板(万吨)	Machine-Made Paper and Paperboards (10 000 tons)	1.99
成品糖(万吨)	Refined Sugar (10 000 tons)	2.08
原煤(万吨)	Coal(10 000 tons)	1079.01
原油(万吨)	Crude Oil (10 000 tons)	353.05
天然气(亿立方米)	Natural Gas (100 million cu.m)	2.51
发电量(亿千瓦小时)	Electricity (100 million kwh)	21.17

Continued

总量指标 Aggregate Data				速度指标(%) Indices and Growth Rates						
				指数(2015 年比以下各年) Index (2015as percentuage of the following years)				平均增长速度 Average Annual Growth Rate		
2000	2010	2014	2015	1978	2000	2010	2014	1979-2015	2001-2015	2011-2015
190.95	1698.91	3317.79	3804.87	22355.3	1992.6	224.0	114.7	15.7	22.1	17.5
	195.57	324.88	366.41			187.4	112.8			13.4
	334.02	607.54	689.57			206.4	113.5			15.6
	166.40	300.85	371.90			223.5	123.6			17.5
	51.02	70.86	71.51			140.2	100.9			7.0
	95.28	286.76	323.04			339.0	112.7			27.7
	220.50	477.27	605.34			274.5	126.8			22.4
99.4	104.3	102.1	100.6							
98.3	104.6	101.7	99.6							
129.4	125.3	96.2	82.4							
115.2	123.9	97.5	84.3							
103.6	104.6	100.3	98.3							
5419.77	14696.76	19473.20	19779.97	1402.1	365.0	134.6	101.6	7.4	9.0	6.1
3316.03	8290.20	14926.08	15651.20	1598.3	472.0	188.8	104.9	7.8	10.9	13.6
487.20	1846.18	2744.01	2804.42	1497.8	255.5	139.8	106.3	7.6	6.5	6.9
808.60	1150.20	1390.81	1501.30	405.7	185.7	130.5	107.9	3.9	4.2	5.5
150.00	247.90	451.00	429.80	7814.5	286.5	173.4	95.3	12.5	7.3	11.6
60.14	66.62	59.33	62.88	608.7	104.6	94.4	106.0	5.0	0.3	-1.1
292.65	486.97	471.94	448.32	2738.7	153.2	92.1	95.0	9.4	2.9	-1.6
151.87	593.85	858.61	961.45	6877.3	633.1	161.9	112.0	12.1	13.1	10.1
90.00	121.74	149.10	155.84	1614.9	173.2	128.0	104.5	7.8	3.7	5.1
78.23	132.82	150.70	158.56	3020.2	202.7	119.4	105.2	9.6	4.8	3.6
6.01	10.11	14.40	15.14	2656.1	251.9	149.8	105.1	9.3	6.4	8.4
33.43	41.58	43.99	60.23	2151.1	180.2	144.9	136.9	8.6	4.0	7.7
2.81	1.51	0.65	0.69	44.2	24.6	45.7	106.2	-2.2	-8.9	-14.5
1184	741	230	225	18.2	19.0	30.4	98.0	-4.5	-10.5	-21.2
754	326	272	391	206.9	51.9	119.9	143.8	2.0	-4.3	3.7
31.78	174.67	383.05	415.74	804.0	1308.2	238.0	108.5	5.8	18.7	18.9
17.65	37.10	48.81	37.62	1890.5	213.1	101.4	77.1	8.3	5.2	0.3
30.76	45.10	44.53	44.02	2116.3	143.1	97.6	98.9	8.6	2.4	-0.5
2798.90	9926.72	14519.53	15221.48	1410.7	543.8	153.3	104.8	7.4	12.0	8.9
1848.43	2558.16	2875.28	2795.09	791.7	151.2	109.3	97.2	5.8	2.8	1.8
35.39	249.91	296.70	293.02	11674.1	828.0	117.3	98.8	13.7	15.1	3.2
182.98	679.33	2090.94	2478.51	11707.7	1354.5	364.8	118.5	13.7	19.0	29.5

1-3 续表 2

指　标	Item	1978
粗钢(万吨)	Crude Steel (10 000 tons)	8.46
钢材(万吨)	Steel Products (10 000 tons)	6.83
水泥(万吨)	Cement (10 000 tons)	78.15
全部工业总产值(亿元)	Gross industrial Output Value (100 million yuan)	33.91
规模以上工业企业主要经济指标	Main Economic Indicators of Industrial Enterprises Above Designated Size	
工业总产值(亿元)	Gross Industrial Output Value (100 million yuan)	28.43
资产总计(亿元)	Total Assets (100 million yuan)	
主营业务收入(亿元)	Revenue from Principal Business (100 million yuan)	
利润总额(亿元)	Profits (100 million yuan)	4.28
建筑业	**Construction**	
建筑业企业从业人员(万人)	Number of Employed Persons (10 000 persons)	
建筑业企业总产值(亿元)	Gross Output Value (100 million yuan)	
施工房屋面积(万平方米)	Floor Space of Buildings under Construction (10 000 sq.m)	
竣工房屋面积(万平方米)	Floor Space of Buildings Completed (10 000 sq.m)	
交通运输	**Transportation**	
货运量(万吨)	Freight TrafficVolume (10 000 tons)	6064
铁　路	Railways	923
公　路	Highways	4843
管　道	Pipelines	298
航　空	Civil Aviation	0.12
客运量(万人)	Passenger Traffic Volume (10 000 persons)	941
铁　路	Railways	148
公　路	Highways	786
航　空	Civil Aviation	7
邮电通信业	**Postal and Telecommunication Services**	
邮政业务总量(亿元)	Business Volume of Postal Services (100 million yuan)	
电信业务总量(亿元)	Business Volume of Telecommunication Services (100 million yuan)	
函　件(万件)	Number of Letters Delivered (10 000 pieces)	4843
报刊期发数(万份)	Number of Newspapers and Magazines Distributed (10 000 copies)	224
局用交换机容量(万门)	Capacity of Office Telephone Exchanges (10 000 lines)	
固定电话年末用户(万部)	Local Telephone Subscribers at Year-end (10 000 subscribers)	2.90
移动电话用户(万户)	Number of Mobile Telephone Subscribers (10 000 subscribers)	
旅　游	**Tourism**	
入境旅游过夜者人数(万人)	Number of Oversea Visitor Arrivals (10 000 person-times)	0.01
入境旅游消费(万美元)	Foreign Exchange Eearnings from International Tourism (USD 10 000)	5
金　融	**Banking**	
金融机构各项存款(亿元)	Deposits of Finacial Institution (100 million yuan)	32.07
金融机构各项贷款(亿元)	Loans of Finacial Institution (100 million yuan)	18.26
教育、科技、文化	**Education, Science & Technology and Culture**	
教　育	**Education**	
专任教师数(人)	Full-time Teachers (person)	
普通高等学校	Regular Institutions of Higher Education	2458

Continued

总量指标 Aggregate Data				速度指标(%) Indices and Growth Rates						
				指数(2015 年比以下各年) Index (2015as percentuage of the following years)				平均增长速度 Average Annual Growth Rate		
2000	2010	2014	2015	1978	2000	2010	2014	1979-2015	2001-2015	2011-2015
109.70	825.54	1270.32	785.78	9288.2	716.3	95.2	61.9	13.0	14.0	-1.0
131.26	891.70	1566.95	1124.01	16457.0	856.3	126.1	71.7	14.8	15.4	4.7
895.67	2400.96	5081.66	4279.00	5475.4	477.7	178.2	84.2	11.4	11.0	12.3
1061.29	5766.51	9877.27	8668.64	6183.9	618.1	185.6	106.6	11.8	12.9	13.2
852.01	5341.90	9431.76	8132.55							
1708.81	7911.97	16770.08	18164.16		1063.0	229.6	108.3		17.1	18.1
821.26	5492.61	9320.05	8203.73		998.9	149.4	88.0		16.6	8.4
90.49	852.43	732.06	340.97	7966.6	376.8	40.0	46.6	12.6	9.2	-16.7
26.16	56.48	75.84	72.19		276.0	127.8	95.2		7.0	5.0
234.95	969.47	2332.12	2304.07		980.7	237.7	98.8		16.4	18.9
2241.48	6620.14	14340.27	12233.29		545.8	184.8	85.3		12.0	13.1
1261.42	2891.45	6115.37	5247.30		416.0	181.5	85.8		10.0	12.7
33091	64597	90249	80191	1322.4	242.3	124.1	88.9	7.2	6.1	4.4
4199	6853	7529	6234	675.4	148.5	91.0	82.8	5.3	2.7	-1.9
27048	50448	74432	64505	1331.9	238.5	127.9	86.7	7.2	6.0	5.0
1840	7292	8281	9445	3169.5	513.3	129.5	114.1	9.8	11.5	5.3
3.50	3.70	7.16	6.60	5500.0	188.6	178.4	92.2	11.4	4.3	12.3
23191	46346	55880	35824	3807.0	154.5	77.3	64.1	10.3	2.9	-5.0
1147	1523	2355	2751	1858.8	239.8	180.6	116.8	8.2	6.0	12.6
21877	44333	52798	32310	4110.7	147.7	72.9	61.2	10.6	2.6	-6.1
167	490	727	763	10900.0	456.9	155.7	105.0	13.5	10.7	9.3
5.94	16.58	20.23	22.25		374.6	134.2	110.0		9.2	6.1
41.36	565.47	329.03	379.78		918.2	67.2	115.4		15.9	-7.7
7148	2926	1908	2049	42.3	28.7	70.0	107.4	-2.3	-8.0	-6.9
535	307	358	350	156.3	65.4	114.0	97.8	1.2	-2.8	2.7
241.67	928.20	669.30	453.90		187.8	48.9	67.8		4.3	-13.3
191.03	547.50	535.40	523.60	18055.2	274.1	95.6	97.8	15.1	7.0	-0.9
78.00	1359.80	2077.70	2067.20		2650.3	152.0	99.5		24.4	8.7
25.61	106.53	150.17	168.36	1683600.0	657.4	158.0	112.1	30.1	13.4	9.6
			60775							
1863.48	8870.72	15055.39	17123.95	53395.5	918.9	193.0	113.7	18.5	15.9	14.1
1403.13	4973.16	11671.39	13041.00	69635.3	929.4	262.2	111.7	19.4	16.0	21.3
7924	16506	19081	19374	788.2	244.5	117.4	101.5	5.7	6.1	3.3

1-3 续表 3

指　标	Item	1978
中等学校	Regular Secondary Schools	44417
小　学	Regular Primary Schools	82616
在校学生数(万人)	Students Enrollment (10 000 persons)	
普通高等学校	Regular Institutions of Higher Education	1.02
中等学校	Regular Secondary Schools	83.86
小　学	Regular Primary Schools	202.88
科　技	**Science and Technology**	
研究与发展经费支出(万元)	Expenditures on Research and Development (10 000 yuan)	
技术市场交易额(万元)	Volume of Transaction in Technical Markets (10 000 yuan)	
文　化	**Culture**	
电视节目制作时间(小时)	Time for TV Programs Production (hour)	
家庭、生活、环境	**Family, People's Livelihood and Environment**	
家　庭	**Family**	
家庭总户数(万户)	Total Number of Households (10 000 households)	
婚　姻	**Marriages and Divorces**	
结婚数(万对)	Number of Marriages (10 000 couples)	
离婚数(万对)	Number of Divorces (10 000 couples)	
生　活	**People's Livelihood**	
城镇居民人均可支配收入(元)	Per Capita Disposable Income of Urban Households (yuan)	319
农村居民人均可支配收入(元)	Per Capita Disposable Incom of Rural Households (yuan)	119
城乡居民储蓄存款余额(亿元)	Outstanding Amount of Saving Deposits in Urban and Rural Areas (100 million yuan)	6.42
卫　生	**Health Care**	
医院、卫生院(个)	Number of Hospitals and Health centers (unit)	806
医生(人)	Number of Doctors (person)	16898
医院、卫生院床位数(张)	Number of Hospital and Health centers Beds (unit)	39179
市政建设	**Municipal Works**	
自来水供应量(亿立方米)	Volume of Tapping Water Supply(100 million cu.m)	
下水道长度(公里)	Length of Sewer Pipelines (km)	
铺装道路长度(公里)	Length of Paved Roads (km)	
环境、灾害	**Environment and Disaster**	
化学需氧量排放量(万吨)	COD Discharge (10 000 tons)	
二氧化硫排放量(万吨)	Sulphur Dioxide Emission (10 000 tons)	
火灾发生数(起)	Number of Fire Disasters (times)	
火灾损失(万元)	Fire Loss (10 000 yuan)	
交通事故发生数(起)	Number of Traffic Accidents (times)	
交通事故损失(万元)	Loss of Traffic Accidents (10 000 yuan)	

注：2014 年以前农村居民人均可支配收入为农牧民人均纯收入，2014 年以后城乡居民人均可支配收入为城乡一体化新口径，指数和平均增速按可比口径计算。

Continued

总量指标 Aggregate Data				速度指标(%) Indices and Growth Rates						
				指数(2015 年比以下各年) Index (2015 as percentuage of the following years)				平均增长速度 Average Annual Growth Rate		
2000	2010	2014	2015	1978	2000	2010	2014	1979-2015	2001-2015	2011-2015
89211	128306	141295	141627	318.9	158.8	110.4	100.2	3.2	3.1	2.0
131259	133963	145067	144767	175.2	110.3	108.1	99.8	1.5	0.7	1.6
7.41	26.38	30.77	32.27	3163.7	435.5	122.3	104.9	9.8	10.3	4.1
131.18	168.40	163.86	168.21	200.6	128.2	99.9	102.7	1.9	1.7	0.0
247.74	193.58	194.29	204.89	101.0	82.7	105.8	105.5	0.0	-1.3	1.1
32381	266545	491587	520010		1605.9	195.1	105.8		20.3	14.3
66168	43146	29835	34748		52.5	80.5	116.5		-4.2	-4.2
29261	76467	93188	93441		319.3	122.2	100.3		8.0	4.1
481.91	639.86	692.06	689.94		143.2	107.8	99.7		2.4	1.5
16.25	26.40	27.92	29.26		180.1	110.8	104.8		4.0	2.1
5.90	9.78	10.80	10.63		180.2	108.7	98.4		4.0	1.7
5645	13644	23214	26275	77641	488.5	188.4	113.2	12.5	11.2	13.5
1618	4646	8724	9425	7365.9	541.5	188.8	108.0	12.3	11.9	13.6
908.55	3713.47	6187.67	6791.62	105788.5	747.5	182.9	109.8	20.7	14.4	12.8
1352	1712	1807	1841	228.4	136.2	107.5	101.9	2.3	2.1	1.5
45402	48166	53789	56272	333.0	123.9	116.8	104.6	3.3	1.4	3.2
65916	109851	136722	143575	366.5	217.8	130.7	105.0	3.6	5.3	5.5
5.00	7.73	8.00	7.91		160.0	103.5	98.9		3.2	0.7
2008	4372	5140	5655		281.6	129.3	110.0		7.1	5.3
2809	5178	5686	6139		218.5	118.6	108.0		5.4	3.5
	29.60	67.02	66.02			230.0	98.5			17.4
31.10	58.85	85.30	77.82		250.2	132.0	91.2		6.3	5.7
3050	5209	13496	11969		392.4	229.8	88.7		9.5	18.1
2329	3041	8984	11775		505.6	387.2	131.1		11.4	31.1
10048	4949	4919	4992		49.7	100.9	101.5		-4.6	0.2
4443	864	1228	1263		28.4	146.1	102.8		-8.0	7.9

Note:Before 2014,the per capita disaposable income of rural honseholds refer to the per capita net income of farmers and herdsmen.After 2014,the per capita disposable income of urban and rural residents is adjusted to the nen caliber of urban and rural integration. The average growth rate 's calculated by the comparable caliber

1-4 主要年份国民经济和社会发展结构指标
Composition Indicators on National Economic and Social Development in Main Years

单位：% (%)

指标	Item	1978	2000	2010	2014	2015
人口与就业	**Population and Employment**					
人口	**Population**					
性别结构	Sexual Composition					
男	Male	51.1	51.8	51.7	50.7	50.8
女	Female	48.9	48.2	48.3	49.3	49.2
就业	**Employment**					
产业结构	Industrial Composition					
第一产业	Primary Industry	72.1	57.7	49.0	45.4	44.1
第二产业	Secondary Industry	14.3	13.8	14.8	16.0	15.2
第三产业	Tertiary Industry	13.6	28.5	36.2	38.6	40.7
宏观经济	**Macro Economy**					
国民经济核算	**National Accounting**					
新疆生产总值产业结构	Industrial Composition					
第一产业	Primary Industry	35.8	21.1	19.8	16.6	16.7
第二产业	Secondary Industry	47.0	39.4	47.7	42.6	38.6
第三产业	Tertiary Industry	17.2	39.5	32.5	40.8	44.7
固定资产投资	**Investment in Fixed Assets**					
全社会固定资产投资产业结构	Industrial Composition of Total Investment in Fixed Assets					
第一产业	Primary Industry		8.9	6.0	3.1	3.4
第二产业	Secondary Industry		41.7	47.1	50.4	48.3
第三产业	Tertiary Industry		49.4	46.9	46.5	48.3
资金来源结构	Composition of Funded Sources					
国家预算内资金	State Budgetary Appropriation	79.0	8.3	16.8	13.5	14.7
国内贷款	Domestic Loans		22.1	15.2	14.0	14.8
利用外资	Foreign Investment		1.6	0.3		
自筹和其他投资	Fundraising and Other Investment	21.0	68.0	67.7	70.5	70.5
对外经济贸易	**Foreign Economic Trade**					
进出口总额结构	Composition of total Value of Exports and Imports					
出口额	Exports	39.9	53.2	75.7	84.9	89.0
进口额	Imports	60.1	46.8	24.3	15.1	11.0
财政	**Finance**					
一般公共预算收入结构	Composition of General Budgetary Revenue					
税收收入	Various Taxes	60.8	81.6	83.2	69.2	64.8
非税收入	Nontax Revenues	39.2	18.4	16.8	30.8	35.2
一般公共预算支出结构	Composition of General Budgetary Expenses					
一般公共服务	Expenses of General Common Service			11.5	9.8	9.6
教育与科学技术	Expenses for Education, Science and Technology			19.7	18.3	18.1
社会保障和就业	Expenses for Social Safety Net and Employment Effort			9.8	9.1	9.8
节能环保	Expenses of Energy Saving and Environmental Protection			3.0	2.1	1.9
城乡社区事务	Expenses of Community			5.6	8.6	8.5
农林水事务	Expenses of Agriculture, Forest and Irrigation			13.0	14.4	15.9
其他各项支出	Other Expense			37.4	37.7	36.2
能源生产与消费	**Energy Production and Consumption**					
能源生产总量结构	Composition of Total Energy Production					
原煤	Coal	60.0	40.6	49.2	53.0	53.3
原油	Petroleum Crude Oil	35.8	48.7	24.9	21.1	20.2
天然气	Natural Gas	2.4	7.9	22.6	20.3	19.7
水风电	Hydro and Wind Power	1.8	2.8	3.3	5.6	6.8

1-4 续表 1 Continued

单位: % (%)

指　标	Item	1978	2000	2010	2014	2015
能源消费总量结构	Composition of Total Energy Consumption					
煤　炭	Coal	72.5	63.6	66.3	65.1	65.8
石　油	Petroleum Oil	21.5	23.3	15.8	12.4	13.2
天然气	Natural Gas	3.4	8.6	12.4	15.2	12.4
水电、风电	Hydro-power, Wind Power	2.6	4.5	5.5	7.3	8.6
产　业	**Industrial**					
农　业	**Agriculture**					
农林牧渔业产值结构	Composition of Gross Output Value of Agriculture, Forestry, Animal Husbandry, Fishery					
农　业	Farming	74.5	74.0	74.6	71.1	71.5
林　业	Forestry	1.8	1.7	1.9	1.9	1.9
牧　业	Animal Husbandry	23.5	23.5	20.4	23.8	23.1
渔　业	Fishery	0.2	0.8	0.7	0.7	0.8
农林牧渔服务业	Services for Agriculturel, Forestry, Animal Husbandry and Fishery			2.4	2.5	2.7
工　业	**Industry**					
工业总产值规模结构	Composition of Gross Output Value of Industry					
大型企业	Large Enterprises		53.7	55.2	63.0	53.0
中型企业	Medium-sized Enterprises		10.1	24.4	15.2	13.3
小微企业	Small Enterprises		36.2	20.4	21.8	33.7
建筑业	**Construction**					
建筑业总产值结构	Composition of Gross Output Value of Construction Industry					
建筑工程	Construction Projects		88.3	87.2	90.0	90.6
安装工程	Installation Projects		9.1	11.4	8.1	7.8
其　他	Others		2.6	1.4	1.9	1.6
交通运输业	**Transportation**					
货运量结构按运输方式分	Composition of Freight Traffic by Means of Transportation					
铁　路	Railways	15.2	12.7	10.6	8.8	7.8
公　路	Highways	79.9	81.7	78.1	81.9	80.4
民用航空	Civil Aviation					
输油(气)管道	Petroleum and Gas Pipelines	4.9	5.6	11.3	9.3	11.8
国际旅游业	**International Tourism**					
入境旅游人数结构	Composition of Overseas Tourists					
外国人	Foreigners	100.0	81.4	94.8	94.4	95.7
港澳台同胞	Compatriots form Hong Kong, Macao and Taiwan		18.6	5.2	5.6	4.3
金　融	**Banking**					
金融机构资金来源结构	Composition of Sources of Funds in Financial Institution					
各项存款	Various Deposits		122.8	110.1	99.9	98.9
应付及暂收款	Payable and Temporary Collection		…	1.5	1.9	2.1
所有者权益	Owner's Right and Interest		0.1	3.6	4.9	5.4
其　他	Others		-22.9	-15.3	-6.7	-6.4
金融机构资金运用结构	Composition of Fund Uses in Financial Institution					
各项贷款	Loans		92.5	61.8	69.8	75.2
股权及其他投资	Securities and Investment		4.4	5.6	5.6	5.1
联行往来（净）	Inter-branch Accounts		1.6	29.1	16.6	12.6
固定资产	Cash in Stock					1.2
其　他	Others		1.5	3.5	8.0	5.9
教育、科技	**Education Science and Technology**					
教　育	**Education**					
在校学生结构	Composition of Student Enrollment					
大学生	College and University Students	0.4	2.0	6.8	7.7	8.0
中学生	Secondary School Students	29.1	30.8	43.4	42.7	41.5

1-4 续表 2 Continued

单位: % (%)

指 标	Item	1978	2000	2010	2014	2015
小学生	Primary School Students	70.5	67.2	49.8	49.6	50.5
专任教师结构	Full-time Teachers by Type					
大 学	Colleges and Universities	1.9	3.5	5.9	6.2	6.3
中 学	Secondary Schools	34.3	39.1	46.0	46.5	46.3
小 学	Primary Schools	63.8	57.4	48.1	47.3	47.4
科 技	**Science and Technology**					
科学研究与试验发展经费支出结构	Composition of Expenditure on Research and Development					
基础研究	Basic Research		4.7	5.4	6.8	6.9
应用研究	Supplied Research		27.4	23.6	15.3	20.5
试验发展	Experimental Development		67.9	71.0	77.9	72.6
卫 生	**Health Care**					
卫生技术人员结构	Medical Technical Personnel by Types					
执业医师(西医师)	Licensed Doctors (Western Medicine)	14.4	76.9	32.0	29.3	29.2
执业助理医师(西医士)	Licensed Assistant Doctors (Western Medicine)	18.7	23.1	7.2	6.4	6.2
注册护士	Registered Nurses	21.1		36.0	38.9	39.5
药剂人员	Pharmacists			5.2	4.7	4.7
技师(士)	Laboratory Technicians			6.3	5.8	5.8
其他	Others			13.3	14.7	14.6
人民生活	**People's Livelihood**					
城镇居民消费结构	**Consumption Composition of Urban Residents**					
食品类	Food				32.4	31.8
衣着类	Clothing				10.1	9.9
家庭设备、用品及服务	Articles for Daily Use and Others				18.7	17.3
医疗保健	Health Care and Medical Services				5.6	6.1
交通通讯	Transport and Communication				13.6	14.3
教育文化娱乐服务	Education,Cultral and Recreation Services				9.3	10.0
居 住	Residence				8.2	8.4
杂项商品和服务	Miscellaneous Goods and Services				2.0	2.2
农村居民消费结构	**Consumption Composition of Rural Residents**					
食品类	Food				34.5	34.1
衣着类	Clothing				8.8	9.0
家庭设备、用品及服务	Articles for Daily Use and Others				19.2	19.3
医疗保健	Health Care and Medical Services				4.6	5.1
交通和通讯	Transport and Communication				13.7	13.4
文教娱乐用品及服务	Education,Cultural and Recreation Services				8.2	8.2
居 住	Residence				9.7	9.5
其他商品和服务	Other Goods and Services				1.3	1.4
环境、灾害	**Environment and Disasters**					
工业污染治理投资结构	**Composition of Investment in the Treatment of Industrial Pollution**					
治理废水	Waste Water Treatment		38.2	29.5	17.3	19.0
治理废气	Waste Gas Treatment		40.9	69.3	74.8	79.3
治理固体废物	Solid Wastes Treatment		1.6	1.2	3.6	0.2
治理噪声	Noise Abatement		18.4		...	
其 他	Others		0.9	...	4.3	1.5
火灾事故损失额结构	**Composition of Fire Losses Converted into Cash**					
特 大	Extraordinarily Serious Fires		15.7			
重 大	Serious Fires		14.3	...		
较 大	Big Fires			0.1		1.6
一 般	Ordinary Fires		70.0	99.9	100.0	98.4

1-5 主要年份国民经济和社会发展比例和效益指标
Indicators on Proportions and Efficiency in National Economic and Social Development in Main Years

指　标	Item	1978	2000	2010	2014	2015
人口与就业	**Population and Employment**					
出生率(‰)	Birth Rate(‰)	22.55	17.57	14.85	16.44	15.60
死亡率(‰)	Death Rate(‰)	7.69	5.40	4.14	4.97	4.54
自然增长率(‰)	Natural Growth Rate(‰)	14.86	12.17	10.71	11.47	11.06
城镇登记失业率(%)	Registered Unemployment Rate in Urban Areas (%)		3.8	3.2	3.2	3.5
国民经济核算	**National Accounting**					
人均生产总值(元/人)	Per Capita GDP (yuan/person)	313	7372	25034	40648	40036
固定资产投资	**Investment in Fixed Assets**					
全社会固定资产投资相当于新疆生产总值比例(%)	Proportion of Investment in Fixed Assets to GDP of Xinjiang (%)	33.3	44.8	65.1	105.1	115.1
全社会房屋建筑面积竣工率(%)	Rate of Total Floor Space of Buildings Completed in Construction (%)		58.7	40.9	27.4	26.2
消　费	**Consumption**					
人均社会消费品零售额(元)	Per Capita Retail Sales of Consumer Goods(yuan)	179	2066	6388	10680	11188
对外贸易	**Foreign Trade**					
进出口总额相当于新疆生产总值比例(%)	Proportion of Total Value of Imports & Exports to GDP (%)	1.01	13.74	21.32	18.32	13.10
财　政	**Finance**					
一般公共预算收入相当于新疆生产总值比例(%)	Proportion of General Budgetary Revenue to GDP of Xinjiang (%)	18.3	5.8	9.2	13.8	14.3
一般公共预算支出相当于新疆生产总值比例(%)	Proportion of General Budgetary Expenditure to GDP of Xinjiang (%)	43.6	14.0	31.2	35.8	40.8
利用外资	**Utilization of Foreign Capital**					
实际利用外资额相当于签订利用外资额比例(%)	Proportion of Actually Foreign Direct Investment for Foreign Direct Investment (%)		20.87	78.90	79.27	52.83
能　源	**Energy**					
能源生产弹性系数	Elasticity Ratio of Energy Production	1.20	0.40	0.80	0.28	0.18
电力生产弹性系数	Elasticity Ratio of Electricety Production		0.99	2.02	2.54	2.10
能源消费弹性系数	Elasticity Ratio of Energy Consumption	0.74	0.38	0.92	0.95	0.56
电力消费弹性系数	Elasticity Ratio of Electricity Consumption		0.99	2.20	1.96	1.81

1-5 续表 1 Continued

指　标	Item	1978	2000	2010	2014	2015
农　业	**Agriculture**					
每公顷播种面积农产品产量(公斤)	Output of Farm Crops per Hectare of Sown Area (kg)					
粮　食	Grain	1650	5595	5771	6264	6347
棉　花	Cotton	375	1485	1697	1863	1891
油　料	Oil-bearing Crops	510	1935	2437	2690	2880
工　业(规模以上)	**Industry(Above Designated Size)**					
总资产贡献率(%)	Rate of Total Assets to Industrial Output Value (%)		11.2	18.2	11.1	7.4
资产负债率(%)	Assets-Liability Ratio (%)		62.7	50.8	63.0	64.1
成本费用利润率(%)	Rate of Profits to Industrial Cost (%)		12.8	19.3	8.9	4.5
流动资产周转次数(次/年)	Number of Times of Annual Turnover Working Capitals (times/year)		1.6	2.2	1.9	1.5
建筑业	**Construction**					
全员劳动生产率(按总产值计算) (元/人)	Overall Labor Productivity (yuan/person) (in terms of gross output value per employee)		74994	176404	285958	290120
交通运输业	**Transportation**					
铁路网密度(公里/万平方公里)	Railway Density (km/10 000 sq.km)	6.19	18.08	26.39	34.60	37.03
公路网密度(公里/万平方公里)	Highway Density (km/10 000 sq.km)	143	208	918	1054	1071
邮电通信业	**Post and Communications**					
固定电话普及率(部/百人)	Popularization Rate of Telephones (set/100 persons)		15.0	25.4	23.4	22.8
移动电话普及率(部/百人)	Popularization Rate of Mobile Telephones (set/100 persons)			63.0	90.8	89.9
旅游业	**Tourism**					
每一入境游客花费(美元)	Expenditure per Overseas Tourist(USD)		371	346	331	361
国内旅游人均花费(元)	Expenditure per Domestic Tourism(yuan)		827	925	1290	1661

1-5 续表 2 Continued

指　标	Item	1978	2000	2010	2014	2015
金融业	**Banking**					
金融机构存款相当于新疆生产总值比例(%)	Bank Deposits as Percentage of GDP in Xinjiang (%)	82.08	136.62	163.13	162.35	183.63
金融机构贷款相当于新疆生产总值比例(%)	Bank Loans as Percentage of GDP in Xinjiang (%)	46.74	102.87	91.46	125.86	139.85
教　育	**Education**					
学龄儿童入学率(%)	Rate of School-age Children Enrollment (%)	96.00	97.03	99.78	99.81	99.85
小学升学率(%)	Rate of Graduates of Primary Schools Entering Junior Secondary Schools (%)	88.67	92.01	100.53	98.90	99.62
初中升学率(%)	Rate of Graduates of Junior Secondary Schools Entering Senior Secondary Schools (%)	48.22	30.30	45.40	57.97	63.08
学校教师负担系数(%)	Student-teacher Ratio (in percentage) (%)					
高等学校	Colleges and Universities	4.16	9.34	15.22	15.22	15.73
普通中学	Secondary Schools	19.36	14.92	12.48	11.01	11.28
小学	Primary Schools	24.56	18.87	14.45	13.39	14.15
科　技	**Science and Technology**					
研究与开发经费支出相当于新疆生产总值比例(%)	R&D Expenditures as Percentage of GDP (%)		0.38	0.49	0.53	0.56
文　化	**Culture**					
每百万人有艺术表演团体(个)	Number of Troupes per Million Persons(unit)	5.24	4.76	6.08	4.74	4.83
每百万人有公共图书馆(个)	Number of Public Libraries per Million Persons(unit)	0.41	4.33	4.75	4.66	4.74
每百万人有博物馆(个)	Number of Museums per Million Persons(unit)	0.08	1.24	3.27	3.57	3.81
卫　生	**Health Care**					
每万人医院、卫生院数(个)	Number of Hospitals and Health Centers per 10 000 Persons (unit)	0.66	0.73	0.79	0.79	0.78
每万人医生数(人)	Number of Doctors per 10 000 Persons (person)	13.70	24.55	22.25	23.40	23.85
每万人医院、卫生院床位数(张)	Number of Hospital and Health Centers Beds per 10 000 Persons (unit)	31.78	35. 64	50.36	59.48	60.84
医院病床使用率(%)	Utilization Rate of Hospital Beds (%)		66.31	89.19	86.80	86.93
市政建设	**City Construction**					
城市自来水普及率(%)	Percentage of Households with Access to Tap Water (%)	59.0	98.8	99.2	98.2	99.1
城市燃气普及率(%)	Percentage of Households with Access to Tap Gas (%)	11.0	92.8	95.8	97.3	98.0
建成区绿化覆盖率(%)	Green Covrage Rate in Completed Area(%)		29.1	36.4	37.5	37.9
灾　害	**Disasters**					
平均每起火灾损失(元)	Average Loss of per Fire Disaster (yuan)		7635	5422	6657	9838
平均每起交通事故损失(元)	Average Loss of per Traffic Accident (yuan)		4775	1746	2496	2530

1-6 主要年份人均主要工农业产品产量
Per Capita Output of Major Industrial and Agricultural Products in Main Years

年份 Year	粮食(公斤) Grain (kg)	棉花(公斤) Cotton (kg)	油料(公斤) Oil-bearing Crops (kg)	甜菜(公斤) Sugar Crops (kg)	水果(公斤) Fruits (kg)	猪牛羊肉(公斤) Pork, Beef and Mutton (kg)	水产品(公斤) Aquatic Products (kg)
1978	303.0	4.5	8.5	13.4	11.4	7.9	0.5
1980	304.1	6.2	13.9	30.3	12.3	9.4	0.5
1985	367.2	13.9	25.3	30.1	36.4	12.8	0.7
1990	453.8	31.4	26.1	150.4	53.6	18.6	1.6
1995	443.3	56.8	30.0	174.9	69.4	27.9	2.7
2000	446.2	82.8	33.2	161.5	83.8	42.4	3.3
2001	427.3	84.3	22.9	244.3	82.8	44.5	3.3
2002	463.3	79.3	23.5	246.9	104.8	46.9	3.4
2003	417.6	83.4	26.1	198.8	113.7	50.4	3.5
2004	425.2	89.9	22.9	176.7	135.6	55.2	3.8
2005	441.5	98.5	19.6	211.0	146.6	60.5	4.0
2006	441.0	131.8	16.2	273.6	169.0	66.5	4.1
2007	418.3	139.9	19.4	283.2	214.7	67.1	4.3
2008	430.2	142.7	26.9	207.7	213.4	47.4	4.4
2009	537.1	117.7	29.8	195.1	263.5	46.5	4.5
2010	530.1	114.2	30.7	224.4	275.1	48.6	4.7
2011	547.0	132.0	30.4	236.4	274.1	50.1	5.3
2012	567.3	159.4	26.6	259.9	331.8	51.5	5.6
2013	605.2	156.5	27.0	211.9	348.1	52.9	5.9
2014	609.6	197.7	26.0	206.9	376.4	55.5	6.3
2015	644.5	184.5	27.0	192.5	412.8	55.4	6.5

年份 Year	布(米) Cloth (m)	机制纸及纸板(公斤) Machine-made Paper and Paperboard (kg)	纱(公斤) Yarn (kg)	原油(公斤) Crude Oil (kg)	发电量(千瓦小时) Electricity (kwh)	粗钢(公斤) Steel (kg)	水泥(公斤) Cement (kg)
1978	13.0	1.6	2.3	289	173	7	64
1980	13.0	1.9	2.5	308	186	8	72
1985	16.0	3.1	2.9	369	282	15	149
1990	20.0	6.1	6.8	466	468	23	191
1995	18.0	11.0	14.9	770	731	43	297
2000	15.0	9.7	18.5	1021	1011	61	495
2001	14.0	10.4	16.3	1045	1061	72	527
2002	11.0	12.0	16.7	1077	1123	93	545
2003	8.0	12.2	15.3	1116	1222	106	588
2004	7.0	13.5	15.0	1156	1367	128	623
2005	7.0	14.6	17.2	1212	1545	154	625
2006	8.0	14.5	17.6	1219	1759	194	657
2007	8.0	12.2	19.7	1257	2011	216	742
2008	7.2	14.3	18.8	1285	2315	254	792
2009	7.1	16.6	18.0	1171	2664	305	956
2010	7.0	17.1	19.2	1179	3131	380	1106
2011	2.0	19.3	18.2	1146	3987	407	1445
2012	3.0	18.5	18.1	1203	5351	513	1943
2013	3.0	20.3	19.3	1242	7417	568	2406
2014	2.8	21.4	19.3	1260	9165	557	2227
2015	3.0	16.2	25.9	1200	10642	337	1837

1-7 主要年份人均国民经济主要指标
Per Capita Main Indicators on National Economy in Main Years

指　　标	Item	1978	2000	2010	2014	2015
新疆生产总值(元)	Gross Domestic Product of Xinjiang (yuan)	313	7372	25034	40648	40036
工农业总产值(元)	Gross Output Value of Industry and Agriculture (yuan)	450	8544	35082	55323	49260
工业总产值	Gross Output Value of Industriy	278	5856	26574	43295	37219
农林牧渔业总产值	Gross Output Value of Agriculture, Forestry, Animal Husbandry and Fishery	172	2688	8508	12028	12041
固定资产投资总额(元)	Total Investment in Fixed Assets (yuan)	106	3368	16312	42714	46064
一般公共预算收入(元)	General Budgetary Revenue in Local Finance (yuan)	58	436	2307	5621	5714
一般公共预算支出(元)	General Budgetary Expenditure in Local Finance (yuan)	139	1054	7829	14543	16335
主要工农业产品产量	Output of Major Industrial and Agricultural Products					
粮食(公斤)	Grain Yield (kg)	303.0	446.2	530.1	609.6	644.5
棉花(公斤)	Cotton Yield (kg)	4.5	82.8	114.2	197.7	184.5
油料(公斤)	Oil-bearing Crops Yield (kg)	8.5	33.2	30.7	26.0	27.0
甜菜(公斤)	Beet Roots Yield (kg)	13.4	161.5	224.4	206.9	192.5
猪牛羊肉(公斤)	Pork, Beef and Mutton Yield (kg)	7.9	42.4	48.6	55.5	55.4
水产品(公斤)	Aquatic Products Yield (kg)	0.5	3.3	4.7	6.3	6.5
水果(公斤)	Fruits Yield (kg)	11.4	83.8	275.1	376.4	412.8
果用瓜(公斤)	Fruit Melon Yield (kg)	36.1	83.3	200.5	266.6	289.2
布(米)	Cloth (m)	13	15	7	3	3
机制纸和纸板(公斤)	Machine-made Paper and Paperboard (kg)	1.6	9.7	17.1	21.4	16.2
纱(公斤)	Yarn (kg)	2.3	18.5	19.2	19.3	25.9
原油(公斤)	Crude Oil (kg)	289	1021	1179	1260	1200
发电量(千瓦小时)	Electric Power (kwh)	173	1011	3131	9165	10642
水泥(公斤)	Cement (kg)	64	495	1106	2227	1837
社会消费品零售总额(元)	Total Retail Sales of Consumer Goods (yuan)	179	2066	6104	10680	11189
海关出口总额(美元)	Value of Exports (USD)	0.8	66.5	789.3	1212.8	844.9
高等学校在校学生数(人/万人)	Students Enrollment in Institions of Higher Education (person/10 000 persons)	8.3	41.1	115.1	135.0	138.5
中等专业学校在校学生数(人/万人)	Students Enrollment in Specialized Secondary Schools (person/10 000 persons)	19.2	56.9	69.8	96.2	65.2
普通中学在校学生数(人/万人)	Students Enrollment in Regular Secondary Schools (person/10 000 persons)	654.0	638.0	652.1	602.5	603.3
医院、卫生院床位数(张/万人)	Beds of Medical and Health Centers (unit/10 000 persons)	31.8	35.6	50.4	59.5	60.8
卫生技术人员数(人/万人)	Medical Technical Personnel (person/10 000 persons)	41.4	53.0	56.3	66.7	68.0
#医　生	Doctors	13.7	24.6	22.3	23.4	23.9
城乡居民储蓄存款余额(元)	Urban and Rural Savings Deposits (yuan)	57	4913	17113	27122	29158

1-8 新疆建区以来主要年份国民经济主要指标

年 份 Year	年末总人口(万人) Year-end Population (10 000 persons)	就业人员(万人) Employed Persons (10 000 persons)	新疆生产总值(亿元) Gross Domestic Product of Xinjiang (100 million yuan)	第一产业 Primary Industry	第二产业 Secondary Industry	第三产业 Tertiary Industry	#工 业 Industry	人均新疆生产总值(元) Per Capita GDP (yuan)
1955	511.78	254.58	12.31	6.69	3.22	2.40	2.10	241
1960	686.33	338.32	25.20	9.27	11.06	4.87	8.12	374
1965	789.10	350.25	24.20	12.48	7.32	4.40	5.03	312
1970	976.58	410.33	23.08	10.35	8.67	4.06	6.19	236
1975	1154.53	466.43	28.12	11.21	12.20	4.71	8.86	240
1978	1233.01	491.25	39.07	13.97	18.35	6.75	14.48	313
1980	1283.24	506.35	53.24	21.53	21.44	10.27	17.48	410
1985	1361.14	565.81	112.24	42.89	40.50	28.85	32.14	820
1990	1529.16	617.70	261.44	104.09	83.18	74.17	71.50	1713
1991	1554.57	638.49	335.91	111.86	107.99	116.06	84.07	2101
1992	1580.63	646.94	402.31	114.50	147.64	140.17	106.29	2477
1993	1605.26	655.98	495.25	126.85	205.07	163.33	155.92	2964
1994	1632.70	657.54	662.32	187.69	249.11	225.52	190.00	3888
1995	1661.35	676.00	814.85	240.71	283.97	290.17	219.01	4701
1996	1689.29	684.00	900.93	249.31	313.70	337.92	239.07	5102
1997	1718.08	715.40	1039.85	279.73	385.37	374.75	302.50	5848
1998	1747.35	680.92	1106.95	291.05	395.75	420.15	298.53	6174
1999	1775.00	694.34	1163.17	268.51	420.48	474.18	315.86	6443
2000	1849.41	672.50	1363.56	288.18	537.58	537.80	418.63	7372
2001	1876.19	685.38	1491.60	288.12	573.91	629.57	445.60	7945
2002	1905.19	701.49	1612.65	305.00	603.15	704.50	463.59	8457
2003	1933.95	721.27	1886.35	412.90	719.54	753.91	563.57	9828
2004	1963.11	744.49	2209.09	446.13	914.47	848.49	734.10	11337
2005	2010.35	791.62	2604.14	510.00	1164.80	929.34	961.62	13108
2006	2050.00	811.75	3045.26	527.80	1459.30	1058.16	1241.33	15000
2007	2095.19	830.42	3523.16	628.72	1647.55	1246.89	1405.11	16999
2008	2130.81	847.58	4183.21	691.07	2070.76	1421.38	1755.35	19797
2009	2158.63	866.15	4277.05	759.74	1929.59	1587.72	1555.84	19942
2010	2181.58	894.65	5437.47	1078.63	2592.15	1766.69	2161.39	25034
2011	2208.71	953.34	6610.05	1139.03	3225.90	2245.12	2700.20	30087
2012	2232.78	1010.44	7505.31	1290.42	3294.50	2820.39	2841.57	33796
2013	2264.30	1096.60	8443.84	1434.83	3574.88	3434.13	2925.74	37553
2014	2298.47	1135.24	9273.46	1538.60	3948.96	3785.90	3179.60	40648
2015	2359.33	1195.06	9324.80	1559.08	3596.40	4169.32	2740.71	40036
			平均增长速度(%)					
1956-2015	2.6	2.6	8.4	5.0	9.4	9.9	9.6	5.5
1979-2015	1.8	2.4	10.4	7.3	10.2	13.5	10.0	10.6
2001-2015	1.6	3.9	10.5	5.9	11.4	11.6	11.3	8.3

注：1.农村居民人均可支配收入 1980-2013 年为农村居民纯收入。 2.全社会固定资产投资从 2014 年起为不含农户数。

Main Indicators of National Economic since Xinjing Established in Main Years

全社会固定资产投资总额(亿元) Total Investment in Fixed Assets (100 million yuan)	社会消费品零售总额(亿元) Total Retail Sales of Consumer Goods (100 million yuan)	公共财政预算收入(亿元) General Budgetary Revenue in Local Finance (100 million yuan)	公共财政预算支出(亿元) General Budgetary Expenditure in Local Finance (100 million yuan)	金融机构存款余额(亿元) Deposits of National Banking System (100 million yuan)	金融机构贷款余额(亿元) Loans of National Banking System (100 million yuan)	进出口总额(亿美元) Total Imports And Exports (USD 100 million)	#出口额 Exports	农村居民人均可支配收入(元) Annual Per capita Net Income of Rural Residents (yuan)	城镇居民人均可支配收入(元) Annual Per capita Disposable Income of Urban Residents (yuan)
2.62	6.14	1.73	1.83	2.72	3.41	0.51	0.20		
10.59	11.91	6.36	9.58	6.89	15.50	0.73	0.48		
4.03	11.30	4.53	4.89	11.52	9.70	0.14	0.13		
4.50	13.23	3.57	6.05	17.25	14.35	0.02	...		
6.11	16.85	1.01	8.85	26.88	14.71	0.09	0.04		
13.00	21.89	7.14	17.02	32.07	18.26	0.23	0.09	119	319
20.47	29.36	4.03	16.22	38.56	24.74	0.32	0.17	201	427
44.48	57.38	8.47	28.60	82.96	72.68	2.92	1.80	394	735
88.78	104.30	21.78	47.62	221.80	233.72	4.10	3.35	684	1314
124.93	121.52	26.47	50.34	282.21	299.59	4.59	3.63	703	1476
170.03	138.25	26.07	56.09	336.58	380.26	7.50	4.54	740	1952
248.44	168.37	35.13	64.71	397.39	467.81	9.22	4.95	778	2423
285.48	197.11	28.70	71.10	634.44	632.32	10.41	5.76	936	3170
333.34	253.65	38.28	96.40	838.42	843.38	14.28	7.69	1137	4163
387.85	295.36	48.31	114.88	1012.47	1016.20	14.04	5.50	1290	4650
446.81	310.42	54.52	123.35	1180.78	1215.39	14.47	6.65	1500	4845
519.77	327.52	65.39	145.99	1336.58	1318.41	15.32	8.08	1600	5001
534.65	347.40	71.31	166.28	1548.72	1386.78	17.65	10.27	1473	5320
610.38	374.50	79.07	190.95	1863.48	1403.13	22.64	12.04	1618	5645
706.00	406.35	95.09	263.32	1972.55	1584.73	17.71	6.68	1710	6215
813.02	442.88	116.47	361.17	2225.31	1801.15	26.92	13.08	1863	6554
1002.13	421.16	128.22	368.47	2661.65	2099.09	47.72	25.42	2106	7006
1161.52	563.41	155.70	421.04	2959.78	2214.66	56.36	30.47	2245	7503
1352.27	640.20	180.32	519.02	3427.48	2272.08	79.42	50.40	2482	7990
1567.05	733.20	219.46	678.47	4040.78	2412.69	91.03	71.39	2737	8871
1850.84	857.50	285.86	795.15	4614.62	2685.00	137.16	115.03	3183	10313
2259.97	1041.50	361.06	1059.36	5399.34	2826.53	222.17	192.99	3503	11432
2827.24	1180.06	388.78	1346.91	6845.07	3782.92	138.28	108.23	3883	12258
3539.69	1386.06	500.58	1698.91	8870.02	4973.16	171.28	129.70	4643	13644
4712.77	1662.35	720.43	2284.49	10387.00	6270.21	228.22	168.29	5442	15514
6258.38	1916.06	908.97	2720.27	12330.89	7914.00	251.71	193.47	6394	17921
8148.41	2179.45	1128.49	3067.12	14088.83	9840.46	275.62	222.70	7296	19874
9744.79	2436.50	1282.34	3317.79	15055.39	11671.39	276.69	234.83	8724	23214
10729.32	2605.96	1330.85	3804.87	17123.95	13041.00	196.78	175.06	9425	26275
Average Annual Growth Rate (%)									
14.9	10.6	11.7	13.6	15.7	14.7	10.4	12.0		
19.9	13.8	15.2	15.7	18.5	19.4	20.0	22.7	12.5	12.5
21.1	13.8	20.7	22.1	15.9	16.0	15.5	19.5	11.9	11.2

Note: 1.Annual per capita disposabie income of rural residents of 1980-2013refer to net income of rural residents. 2.Since 2014 data on total investment in fixed assets do not include rural individual investment.

1-8 续表

年 份 Year	主要农产品产量(万吨) Output of Major Farm(10 000 tons)					年末牲畜存栏数(万头(只)) The Year-end Domesticated Animals in Stock (10 000 heads)	
	粮食 Grain	棉花 Cotton	油料 Oil-bearing Crops	甜菜 Beet	水果 Fruit		#羊 Sheep and Goats
1955	147.02	2.51	6.84	0.10	12.33	1640.07	1224.33
1960	197.98	3.19	5.88	7.09	16.10	1911.59	1529.89
1965	261.74	7.59	6.97	15.97	22.35	2697.53	2192.31
1970	303.21	6.46	6.84	21.06	13.70	2431.32	1949.67
1975	310.96	4.67	9.04	15.12	14.25	2436.08	1916.15
1978	370.01	5.50	10.33	16.37	13.98	2476.98	1927.54
1980	386.13	7.92	17.59	38.52	15.62	2672.60	2105.43
1985	496.65	18.78	34.25	40.69	49.25	3016.04	2431.91
1990	676.89	46.88	38.96	224.37	79.88	3496.40	2830.81
1991	672.52	63.95	40.49	256.85	81.10	3494.00	2830.65
1992	706.27	66.76	35.62	329.07	91.89	3495.41	2830.36
1993	720.37	68.00	37.02	236.91	99.82	3514.72	2842.83
1994	666.17	88.21	50.76	299.24	107.52	3599.01	2905.80
1995	730.16	93.50	49.41	288.14	114.43	3724.32	3009.02
1996	818.20	94.04	30.95	354.52	115.99	3863.80	3136.21
1997	825.34	115.00	29.95	388.71	123.67	4007.66	3261.81
1998	830.00	140.00	37.52	513.12	121.48	4223.99	3447.38
1999	838.78	140.75	60.46	354.24	136.42	4396.54	3592.29
2000	808.60	150.00	60.14	292.65	151.87	4524.67	3690.21
2001	796.00	157.00	42.64	455.12	154.25	4603.78	3764.88
2002	875.87	150.00	44.37	466.81	198.20	4781.77	3908.23
2003	801.64	160.00	50.13	381.65	218.34	5026.54	4104.30
2004	828.53	175.25	44.54	344.21	264.22	5206.37	4266.73
2005	877.21	195.70	38.94	419.12	291.26	5333.60	4355.50
2006	895.22	267.53	32.82	555.53	343.14	5339.71	4359.50
2007	867.04	290.00	40.30	586.93	411.98	5023.37	4083.44
2008	909.00	301.55	56.85	438.88	450.87	3746.11	3025.70
2009	1152.00	252.40	63.91	418.41	565.15	3844.75	3127.50
2010	1150.20	247.90	66.62	486.97	593.85	3722.15	3013.37
2011	1200.75	289.77	66.76	518.95	601.65	3697.60	3016.40
2012	1259.83	353.95	59.04	577.19	736.74	4333.25	3502.05
2013	1360.83	351.80	60.63	476.47	782.69	4502.86	3663.22
2014	1390.81	451.00	59.33	471.94	858.61	4763.46	3883.98
2015	1501.30	429.80	62.88	448.32	961.45	4875.05	3995.65
			平均增长速度(%)				
1956-2015	3.9	8.9	3.8	15.0	7.5	1.8	2.0
1979-2015	3.9	12.5	5.0	9.4	12.1	1.8	2.0
2001-2015	4.2	7.3	0.3	2.9	13.1	0.5	0.5

Continued

主要畜产品产量(万吨) Output of Major Livestock Products(10 000 tons)			水产品产量(万吨) Output of Aquatic Products (10 000 tons)	主要工业产品产量 Output of Major Industrial Products			
肉类 Meat	羊毛 Wool	奶类 Milk		原油(万吨) Crude Oil (10 000 tons)	天然气(亿立方米) Natural Gas (100 million cu.m)	发电量(亿千瓦时) Volume of Electric Generation (100 million kwh)	钢材(万吨) Steel Rolled (10 000 tons)
6.69			0.07	3.29	0.01	0.55	0.66
6.08			0.57	166.23	0.06	3.44	3.63
9.17			0.46	97.31	0.01	4.46	3.94
8.84		8.53	0.65	153.60	0.66	7.95	4.21
9.16	3.16	6.35	0.50	300.19	3.76	13.23	2.20
9.65	3.08	5.25	0.57	353.05	2.51	21.17	6.83
12.70	3.31	7.28	0.66	390.58	3.53	23.58	8.59
18.37	7.07	19.70	0.90	499.00	5.46	38.11	16.73
30.46	5.09	35.64	2.32	695.00	5.02	69.79	28.48
32.94	5.19	37.49	2.52	762.00	5.54	78.04	33.80
36.02	5.20	39.79	2.66	831.66	6.75	86.80	40.30
38.30	5.28	40.85	2.88	1065.50	8.43	95.78	45.98
42.81	5.46	44.83	3.53	1156.62	9.06	106.17	57.71
52.38	5.66	49.81	4.44	1267.83	11.48	120.43	66.55
60.31	5.99	54.22	4.79	1457.10	14.06	136.03	86.70
64.40	6.25	58.78	5.24	1629.25	21.30	150.58	99.89
75.19	6.48	65.02	5.34	1628.38	23.78	157.76	116.19
81.36	6.76	70.43	5.58	1739.65	31.06	169.30	117.30
90.00	6.98	78.23	6.01	1848.43	35.39	182.98	131.25
97.00	7.30	87.85	6.09	1946.95	41.74	197.62	134.42
105.44	7.78	100.71	6.39	2036.19	48.52	212.24	173.07
115.00	8.21	119.21	6.73	2141.40	50.29	234.62	203.10
128.13	8.91	139.73	7.33	2253.02	57.48	266.30	238.52
141.46	9.38	157.84	7.93	2408.32	106.64	306.92	326.96
158.21	9.62	185.41	8.45	2474.74	164.21	357.15	411.45
160.58	9.34	201.77	8.89	2604.31	210.33	416.87	470.94
114.74	9.03	137.40	9.26	2715.13	235.89	489.17	576.62
115.31	7.60	125.15	9.70	2512.86	245.39	571.31	690.81
121.74	8.69	132.82	10.11	2558.16	249.91	679.32	891.70
127.28	9.01	133.91	11.69	2615.63	235.38	875.19	985.14
134.23	9.20	136.32	12.53	2670.68	253.01	1187.48	1289.84
139.26	9.68	139.19	13.17	2792.47	283.98	1667.82	1512.90
149.10	9.68	150.70	14.40	2875.28	296.70	2090.94	1566.95
155.84	10.11	158.56	15.14	2795.09	293.02	2478.51	1124.01
Average Annual Growth Rate (%)							
5.4			9.4	11.9	18.7	15.1	13.2
7.8	3.3	9.6	9.3	5.8	13.7	13.7	14.8
3.7	2.5	4.8	6.4	2.8	15.1	19.0	15.4

1-9 各时期经济发展主要指标

Major Economic Development Indicators of Each Period

时　期	Period	新疆生产总值（亿元） Gross Domestic Product of Xinjiang (100 million yuan)	第一产业 Primary Industry	第二产业 Secondary Industry	第三产业 Tertiary Industry	#工 业 Industry	全社会固定资产投资总额（亿元） Total Investment in Fixed Assets (100 million yuan)
"一五"时期	"First Five-year Plan" Period	60.35	33.86	15.54	10.95	8.82	
"二五"时期	"Second Five-year Plan" Period	102.65	43.27	39.48	19.90	28.37	31.42
	1963—1965	64.76	33.56	19.27	11.93	13.64	10.43
"三五"时期	"Third Five-year Plan" Period	111.94	53.53	38.02	20.39	27.84	18.82
"四五"时期	"Fourth Five-year Plan" Period	128.37	54.38	50.55	23.44	36.84	24.72
"五五"时期	"Fifth Five-year Plan" Period	205.39	77.27	91.75	36.37	72.34	69.12
"六五"时期	"Sixth Five-year Plan" Period	405.19	165.70	146.99	92.50	117.51	149.13
"七五"时期	"Seventh Five-year Plan" Period	948.99	356.55	318.96	273.48	263.20	331.97
"八五"时期	"Eighth Five-year Plan" Period	2710.64	781.61	993.78	935.25	755.30	1162.22
"九五"时期	"Ninth Five-year Plan" Period	5574.46	1376.78	2052.88	2144.80	1574.58	2499.46
"十五"时期	"Tenth Five-year Plan" Period	9803.83	1962.15	3975.87	3865.81	3168.48	5034.95
"十一五"时期	"Eleventh Five-year Plan " Period	20466.15	3685.96	9699.35	7080.84	8119.02	12044.80
"十二五"时期	"Twelfth Five-year Plan " Period	41157.46	6961.96	17740.64	16454.86	14387.82	39593.67
	2011	6610.05	1139.03	3225.90	2245.12	2700.20	4712.77
	2012	7505.31	1290.42	3394.50	2820.39	2841.57	6258.38
	2013	8443.84	1434.83	3574.88	3434.13	2925.74	8148.41
	2014	9273.46	1538.60	3948.96	3785.90	3179.60	9744.79
	2015	9324.80	1559.08	3596.40	4169.32	2740.71	10729.32

时　期	Period	住宅竣工建筑面积（万平方米） Floor Space of Building Completed (10 000 sq.m)	一般公共预算收入（亿元） General Budgetary Revenue in Local Finance (100 million yuan)	一般公共预算支出（亿元） General Budgetary Expenditure in Local Finance (100 million yuan)	进出口总　额（万美元） Total Imports And Exports (USD 10 000)	#出口额 Exports	社会消费品零售总额（亿元） Total Retail Sales of Consumer Goods (100 million yuan)
"一五"时期	"First Five-year Plan" Period		8.65	9.50	20819	10945	31.38
"二五"时期	"Second Five-year Plan" Period		21.39	27.16	26197	17976	53.43
	1963—1965		12.20	11.61	4806	4632	31.92
"三五"时期	"Third Five-year Plan" Period		15.38	21.78	1243	633	63.75
"四五"时期	"Fourth Five-year Plan" Period		11.11	39.78	2922	1217	76.26
"五五"时期	"Fifth Five-year Plan" Period		18.24	54.80	10255	4310	113.51
"六五"时期	"Sixth Five-year Plan" Period	3279.57	27.35	100.30	81536	57445	215.35
"七五"时期	"Seventh Five-year Plan" Period	4175.39	75.48	197.04	190173	142124	323.14
"八五"时期	"Eighth Five-year Plan" Period	4928.74	155.63	338.64	460033	265704	878.89
"九五"时期	"Ninth Five-year Plan" Period	8341.78	318.60	741.45	841181	425462	1655.20
"十五"时期	"Tenth Five-year Plan" Period	12466.98	675.80	1933.02	2281284	1260601	2474.00
"十一五"时期	"Eleventh Five-year Plan " Period	19074.22	1755.75	5578.82	7599235	6173465	5198.32
"十二五"时期	"Twelfth Five-year Plan " Period	22330.72	5371.08	15194.34	12290210	9943407	10800.32
	2011	4504.94	720.43	2284.49	2282225	1682886	1662.35
	2012	6152.03	908.97	2720.07	2517075	1934686	1916.06
	2013	4228.72	1128.49	3067.12	2756191	2226980	2179.45
	2014	4052.72	1282.34	3317.79	2766930	2348255	2436.50
	2015	3392.31	1330.85	3804.87	1967789	1750600	2605.96

1-10 各时期经济发展主要指标平均增长率
Average Growth Rate of Major Economic Development Indicators of Each Period

单位：% (%)

时　期	Period	新疆生产总值 Gross Domestic Product of Xinjiang	第一产业 Primary Industry	第二产业 Secondary Industry	第三产业 Tertiary Industry	#工 业 Industry	全社会固定资产投资总额 Total Investment in Fixed Assets
"一五"时期	"First Five-year Plan" Period	9.0	5.1	12.6	18.8	8.8	
"二五"时期	"Second Five-year Plan" Period	4.5	2.8	11.0	-1.3	24.5	-14.8
	1963—1965	12.9	17.9	8.4	5.4	3.3	28.4
"三五"时期	"Third Five-year Plan" Period	0.3	-3.1	3.8	4.8	4.3	2.2
"四五"时期	"Fourth Five-year Plan" Period	2.9	…	7.2	-0.5	7.3	6.3
"五五"时期	"Fifth Five-year Plan" Period	10.5	7.4	11.6	14.5	14.3	34.1
"六五"时期	"Sixth Five-year Plan" Period	12.5	13.0	9.2	17.6	9.3	10.9
"七五"时期	"Seventh Five-year Plan" Period	9.8	7.9	8.2	14.7	9.2	14.8
"八五"时期	"Eighth Five-year Plan" Period	11.8	6.7	14.2	15.0	13.5	30.3
"九五"时期	"Ninth Five-year Plan" Period	7.7	5.8	6.8	10.3	5.9	12.9
"十五"时期	"Tenth Five-year Plan" Period	10.0	5.6	10.6	11.2	11.3	17.2
"十一五"时期	"Eleventh Five-year Plan " Period	10.6	5.6	11.8	11.4	12.1	21.2
"十二五"时期	"Twelfth Five-year Plan " Period	10.8	6.4	11.2	12.3	10.4	26.4
	2011	12.0	6.5	12.0	15.2	11.4	33.1
	2012	12.0	7.0	13.1	13.1	12.7	35.1
	2013	11.0	6.9	12.5	10.9	12.0	30.2
	2014	10.0	5.9	11.2	10.4	10.0	25.2
	2015	8.8	5.9	7.3	12.2	5.8	10.1

时　期	Period	住宅竣工建筑面积 Floor Space of Building Completed	一般公共预算收入 General Budgetary Revenue in Local Finance	一般公共预算支出 General Budgetary Expenditure in Local Finance	进出口总　额 Total Imports And Exports	#出口额 Exports	社会消费品零售总额 Total Retail Sales of Consumer Goods
"一五"时期	"First Five-year Plan" Period		25.0	30.7	17.8	17.8	18.5
"二五"时期	"Second Five-year Plan" Period		4.7	-0.4	-12.5	-9.6	4.3
	1963—1965		16.8	30.5	-20.4	-13.8	2.3
"三五"时期	"Third Five-year Plan" Period		-4.7	4.3	-34.4	-50.3	3.2
"四五"时期	"Fourth Five-year Plan" Period		-22.3	7.9	40.6	58.0	5.0
"五五"时期	"Fifth Five-year Plan" Period		31.9	12.9	28.4	35.5	11.7
"六五"时期	"Sixth Five-year Plan" Period		16.0	12.0	56.0	60.2	14.3
"七五"时期	"Seventh Five-year Plan" Period	2.3	20.8	10.7	7.0	13.2	12.7
"八五"时期	"Eighth Five-year Plan" Period	3.1	11.9	15.1	28.3	18.1	19.4
"九五"时期	"Ninth Five-year Plan" Period	12.1	15.6	14.6	9.7	9.4	8.1
"十五"时期	"Tenth Five-year Plan" Period	14.0	17.9	22.1	28.5	33.2	11.3
"十一五"时期	"Eleventh Five-year Plan " Period	-1.9	22.7	26.8	16.6	20.8	16.7
"十二五"时期	"Twelfth Five-year Plan " Period	0.7	21.6	17.5	2.8	6.2	13.5
	2011	36.8	43.9	34.5	33.2	29.8	19.9
	2012	36.6	26.2	19.1	10.3	15.0	15.3
	2013	-31.2	24.2	12.8	9.5	15.1	13.7
	2014	-4.2	13.6	8.2	0.4	5.4	11.8
	2015	-16.1	3.8	14.7	-28.9	-25.4	7.0

1-11 天山北坡经济带主要经济指标

(2015 年)

指　　标	Item	全区合计 Total of the whole region	北坡经济带合计 Total of the economic belt	北坡经济带占全区比重(%) Percentage of Belt on the Northern Scope to total(%)	乌鲁木齐市 Urumqi City
人　口(万人)	**Population (10 000 persons)**				
年末总人口	Total Population at Year-end	2359.73	891.95	37.8	266.83
城镇人口	Urban Population	1114.50	545.88	56.4	206.35
乡村人口	Rural Population	1245.23	346.07	24.9	60.48
综　合	**General**				
新疆生产总值(亿元)	Gross Domestic Produc in Xinjiang (100 million yuan)	9324.80	6462.48	69.3	2631.64
第一产业	First Industry	1559.08	671.07	43.0	31.65
第二产业	Second Industry	3596.40	2553.51	71.0	787.37
第三产业	Tertiary Industry	4169.32	3237.9	77.7	1812.62
#工　业	Industry	2740.71	2100.32	76.6	632.14
新疆生产总值构成(%)	Composition of Gross Domestic Produc in Xinjiang (%)				
第一产业	First Industry	16.7	10.4		1.2
第二产业	Second Industry	38.6	39.5		29.9
第三产业	Tertiary Industry	44.7	50.1		68.9
#工　业	Industry	29.4	32.5		24.0
一般公共预算收入相当于新疆生产总值比重(%)	Ratio of GDP covered by financial Expenditure (%)	14.3	11.4		14.0
一般公共预算支出相当于新疆生产总值比重(%)	Ratio of GDP covered by financial Expenditure (%)	40.8	17.1		17.0
固定资产投资(亿元)	**Fixed Asset Investment (100 million yuan)**	9730.45	5325.22	54.7	1226.06
财政、金融(亿元)	**Finance and Public Money(100 million yuan)**				
公共财政预算收入	General Budgetary Revenue	1330.58	738.8	55.5	368.67
#各项税收	Various Tax Incomes	861.73	453.24	52.6	181.80
公共财政预算支出	Expenditure of Local Expenses	3804.87	93.56	25.3	446.67
#一般公共服务	General Common Service	366.41	204.29	31.5	30.75
教　育	Operating Expenses for Education	647.93	89.31	24.0	70.42
社保和就业	Operating Expenses for Medical Treatment and Sanitation	371.90	85.48	23.0	40.88
金融机构年末存款余额	Year-end Deposit Balance of Finance	17123.95	11778.07	68.8	6984.60
金融机构年末贷款余额	Year-end Loan Balance of Finance	13041.00	8233.33	63.1	4957.43
物价(上年=100)	**Commodity Price (Preceding year=100)**				
商品零售价格指数	Indices of Commodity Retail Price	99.6			99.4
居民消费价格指数	Indices of Price for Residents' Consumption	100.6			100.7
人民生活	**People's life**				
在岗职工平均货币工资(元)	Average Staff's Money Wage (yuan)	60914			68603
农村居民家庭人均纯收入(元)	Per capita Net Income of Rural Residents (yuan)	9425			15007
城乡居民储蓄存款余额(亿元)	Balance of Both Urban and Rural Deposit(100 million yuan)	6791.62	4210.24	62.0	2157.31
建成区绿化覆盖率(%)	Ratio of Green Coverage in Completed Areas(%)	37.86			40.30

Main Economic Indicators for Economic Belt on the Northern Scope of the Tianshan Mountains

克拉玛依 市 Karamay City	石河子市 Shihezi City	五家渠市 Wujiaqu City	哈密市 Hami [Kumul] City	高昌区 Gaochang District	鄯善县 Shanshan [Piqan] County	托克逊县 Toksun County	伊宁市 Yining [Gulja] City	奎屯市 Kuytun City	伊宁县 Yining [Gulja] County	察布查尔锡伯自治县 Qapqal Xibe Autonomous county	霍城县 Huocheng [Korgas] County	乌苏市 Usu City	沙湾县 Shawan County
29.97	63.26	9.31	48.90	29.72	23.06	12.40	58.75	28.94	43.92	19.67	43.38	22.47	20.63
29.68	42.69	7.29	29.68	11.31	7.64	4.64	41.17	19.69	6.17	4.92	15.98	8.06	10.56
0.29	20.57	2.02	19.22	18.41	15.42	7.76	17.58	9.25	37.75	14.75	27.40	14.41	10.07
629.43	315.78	123.03	330.74	76.04	89.93	42.94	205.32	120.36	75.99	47.64	119.58	167.79	185.83
5.14	10.75	6.65	24.36	19.74	16.16	9.89	6.89	7.11	30.94	23.00	33.61	63.81	86.99
410.53	185.40	85.11	172.56	17.06	40.19	21.29	44.02	47.94	20.03	9.70	35.79	58.92	34.83
213.76	119.63	31.27	133.81	39.24	33.57	11.77	154.41	65.31	25.01	14.95	50.19	45.06	64.01
465.89	134.56	68.62	116.05	10.81	34.96	13.57	17.44	32.04	15.69	6.42	30.90	44.42	24.50
0.8	3.4	5.4	7.4	26.0	18.0	23.0	3.4	5.9	40.7	48.3	28.1	38.0	46.8
65.2	58.7	69.2	52.2	22.4	44.7	49.6	21.4	39.8	26.4	20.4	29.9	35.1	18.7
34.0	37.9	25.4	40.5	51.6	37.3	27.4	75.2	54.3	32.9	31.4	42.0	26.9	34.4
74.0	42.6	55.8	35.1	14.2	38.9	31.6	8.5	26.6	20.6	13.5	25.8	26.5	13.2
11.9	11.7	9.5	12.7	9.8	12.2	19.2	32.5	9.4	6.1	5.6	3.6	8.0	4.5
14.2	14.1	11.3	15.8	30.5	24.6	37.9	59.9	17.5	32.3	37.3	19.5	17.3	12.9
396.54	210.83	65.46	626.09	204.39	116.34	119.57	98.64	119.81	59.47	55.60	120.81	97.78	117.54
74.99	36.83	11.71	41.87	7.48	11.00	8.27	24.69	11.37	4.64	2.67	4.31	13.34	8.28
61.82	29.11	10.90	28.32	5.20	6.03	4.95	22.00	9.46	3.72	2.01	3.64	9.07	3.14
89.66	44.59	13.94	52.32	23.19	21.62	16.28	45.49	21.04	24.58	17.77	23.27	29.01	24.06
10.40	2.44	0.75	5.29	2.54	3.39	1.90	5.19	1.75	1.56	1.38	1.66	2.78	2.20
21.93	5.33	1.11	8.27	5.22	5.12	4.04	11.00	3.94	7.65	4.32	5.97	5.49	5.10
6.91	1.77	0.77	4.41	1.40	1.39	1.04	4.84	1.18	3.47	1.98	2.46	2.60	2.45
1286.78	538.85	111.65	472.49	100.10	90.98	37.52	423.45	246.49	45.86	39.06	79.97	118.33	95.44
509.73	374.50	111.77	434.33	87.75	57.68	27.37	312.81	196.01	77.65	33.23	35.07	78.45	61.66
99.7	100.2	100.5	99.6	100.3			99.6	100.3					99.4
100.4	100.5	100.6	100.9	101.4			101.2	101.1					100.0
83194	60819	59776	60414	63189	78381	56987	58640	54271	48444	49743	46776	43326	49421
		15033	13810	10348	10367	10220	13639	14456	11876	12012	12408	15035	15714
290.00	345.47	57.81	230.85	53.03	51.67	19.98	186.93	151.72	27.26	20.89	48.34	66.10	63.21
43.05	37.30	31.08	36.26	37.72	38.20	38.30	35.85	39.37	29.29	35.24	40.26	32.09	30.96

1-11 续表 1

指标	Item	全区合计 Total of the whole region	北坡经济带合计 Total of the economic belt	北坡经济带占全区比重(%) Percentage of Belt on the Northern Scope to total(%)	乌鲁木齐市 Urumqi City
农　业	**Agriculture**				
农林牧渔业总产值(亿元)	Value of Farm, Forestry, Animal Husbandry and Fishery (100 million yuan)	2804.42	1405.61	50.1	40.23
农　业	Farming	2005.38	875.22	43.6	17.01
林　业	Forestry	53.15	22.11	41.6	1.10
牧　业	Animal Husbandry	649.51	437.49	67.4	20.77
渔　业	Fishery	21.77	9.46	43.5	0.72
农林牧渔服务业	Services for Farming, Forestry, Animal Husbandary and Fishery	74.61	61.10	81.9	0.63
主要农产品产量(万吨)	Main Rural Products Output (10 000 tons)				
粮　食	Grain	1501.30	696.87	46.4	10.29
棉　花	Cotton	429.80	130.17	30.3	0.12
油　料	Oil-bearing Crops	62.88	34.13	54.3	0.80
甜　菜	Beet Roots	448.32	219.07	48.9	0.05
水　果	Fruits	961.45	118.89	12.4	0.71
肉　类	Meat	155.84	118.54	76.1	6.53
工　业	**Industry**				
工业总产值(规模以上)(亿元)	Total Value of Industrial Products (100 million yuan)	8132.55	6009.62	73.9	2063.25
轻工业	Light Industry	1311.84	713.02	54.4	252.98
重工业	Heavy Industry	6820.71	5072.32	74.4	1801.78
主要工业产品产量	Output of Main Industrial Products				
纱(万吨)	Cotton Yarn (10 000 tons)	60.23	23.32	38.7	1.11
布(万米)	Cloth (10 000 m)	6859.00	2285.00	33.3	70.00
绒线(吨)	Woolen knitting wool (ton)	225.00	98.00	43.6	98.00
呢绒(万米)	Woolen Goods (10 000 m)	391.00			
原盐(万吨)	Crude Salt (10 000 tons)	415.74	283.09	68.2	9.00
成品糖(万吨)	Sugar (10 000 tons)	44.02	19.17	43.5	
原油(万吨)	Crude Oil (10 000 tons)	2795.09	2294.06	82.1	703.00
发电量(亿千瓦小时)	Volume of Electric Generation (100 million kwh)	2478.51	1992.50	80.4	320.12
粗钢(万吨)	Grude steel (10 000 tons)	785.78	469.91	59.8	417.17
钢材(万吨)	Steel Rolled (10 000 tons)	1124.01	697.15	62.0	585.91
水泥(万吨)	Cement (10 000 tons)	4279.00	1718.95	40.2	226.60
国内商业	**Domestic Trades**				
社会消费品零售总额(亿元)	Retail sales of Consumer Goods (100 million yuan)	2605.96	2053.47	78.8	940.51
教育、卫生	**Education and Health**				
在校学生数(人)	Number of Students Enrollment(person)				
高等学校	Institutions of Higher Education	322713	240722	74.6	179829
中等职业学校	Specialized Secondary School	276789	216419	78.2	52121
普通中学	Ordinary Middle School	1405335	584337	41.6	154614
小　学	Elementary School	2048874	588661	28.7	198982
毕业生数(人)	Number of Graduates (person)				
高等学校	Institutions of Higher Education	75113	52383	69.7	39633
中等职业学校	Specialized Secondary School	69481	39133	56.3	19132
普通中学	Ordinary Middle School	436574	183062	41.9	50432
小　学	Elementary School	300407	104635	34.8	28387
医院、卫生院床位数(张)	Number of Hospital and Health centers Beds (unit)	143575	79485	55.4	28052
卫生技术人员数(人)	Number of Medical Technical Personnel (person)	161841	94160	58.2	35516

Continued

克拉玛依市 Karamay City	石河子市 Shihezi City	五家渠市 Wujiaqu City	哈密市 Hami [Kumul] City	高昌区 Gaochang District	鄯善县 Shanshan [Piqan] County	托克逊县 Toksun County	伊宁市 Yining [Gulja] City	奎屯市 Kuytun City	伊宁县 Yining [Gulja] County	察布查尔锡伯自治县 Qapqal Xibe Autonomous county	霍城县 Huocheng [Korgas] County	乌苏市 Usu City	沙湾县 Shawan County
12.58	28.44	15.78	26.70	33.67	27.57	16.73	12.83	4.17	52.47	30.58	30.89	71.99	85.24
4.56	16.87	10.36	18.93	28.37	23.58	12.61	6.89	2.85	23.33	18.88	16.73	55.12	59.05
2.95	0.40	0.09	0.35	0.31	0.14	0.19	0.04	0.01	0.26	1.08	0.43	0.54	0.30
4.16	7.46	3.74	6.95	4.41	3.67	3.66	5.34	1.16	26.91	10.01	13.01	15.47	24.16
0.10	0.37	0.22	0.20	0.06	0.01		0.23		0.98	0.15	0.11	0.11	0.28
0.80	3.34	1.37	0.28	0.52	0.17	0.27	0.33	0.16	0.98	0.45	0.63	0.75	1.47
3.52	3.65	2.67	4.16			1.27	10.24	2.66	78.42	50.75	27.26	46.72	38.38
	2.44	0.44	5.18	0.69	0.72	1.83		1.06		0.06	0.21	18.63	21.81
0.48	0.04	1.38	0.11			0.17	0.08		0.83	1.10	1.03	0.08	0.08
2.64	0.01	0.20					0.82		3.05	13.60	31.79	2.42	6.82
0.05	6.32	1.58											
1.14	1.96	1.53	2.21	1.22	0.90	3.28	1.48	0.51	6.26	1.83	4.61	3.96	5.84
1062.01	479.79	299.70	265.70	33.96	114.82	60.64	34.95	90.22	55.68	13.87	48.33	72.38	49.47
13.03	120.28	65.60	4.80	6.24	0.64	0.72	5.97	0.65	0.86	0.21	0.99	8.31	25.59
1048.97	359.51	227.80	260.90	27.71	114.18	59.92	5.45	9.69	8.00	1.21	0.56	64.07	23.88
	11.13	1.90	0.70	0.35				1.06				0.87	0.08
1.00	2214.00												
	391.00												
				163.05	-	102.00							
									3.86		4.41		
1180.01					210.00							191.00	
63.44	378.44	187.70	238.70	7.72	6.08	43.01	32.30	1.35	9.36	0.32	5.34		2.12
								32.80					1.37
		21.40						43.60					1.25
	262.92		121.40	59.81		104.31	43.49			172.55	16.57	42.87	39.75
58.82	92.37	33.96	75.62	25.88	13.5	4.97	76.09	24.85	14.97	3.29	17.41	15.72	17.65
5228	7428	4375	4929	2433			28638						566
829	1788	1749	6727	14803	13817	6498	11290	234	913	354	347	12605	13119
25546	18602	6925	27278	25040	22025	9746	38063	14099	21368	8147	15568	16361	13831
23773	12450	6529	27066	8849	6926	3496	51631	10336	39197	14272	26366	6990	5411
1323	2111	686	1006			-	6495						
142	846	691	2307	723	86	137	2618	65	226	285	85		1
8092	6053	2466	9234	4773	3881	1809	11402	4881	7137	2767	4774	4298	13
3673	1868	1108	4263	3353	2959	1550	7920	1682	5847	1953	3723	2692	18
1564	4016	1705	2496	1518	790	620	5893	2408	1961	725	1117	1463	886
3199	6616	1070	3421	1806	874	787	2307	2497	1009	1014	906	1412	1358

1-11 续表 2

指　　标	Item	昌吉市 Changji City	阜康市 Fukang City	呼图壁县 Hu Tubi County	玛纳斯县 Manas County	奇台县 Qitai County	吉木萨尔县 Jimsar County
人　口（万人）	**Population (10 000 persons)**						
年末总人口	Total Population at Year-end	37.14	16.70	21.50	17.42	23.86	13.85
城镇人口	Urban Population	22.94	8.58	7.95	6.58	6.55	3.26
乡村人口	Rural Population	14.20	8.12	13.55	10.84	17.31	10.59
综　合	**General**						
新疆生产总值(亿元)	Gross Domestic Produc in Xinjiang (100 million yuan)	390.96	140.50	137.90	170.31	130.41	115.19
第一产业	First Industry	39.91	27.45	43.27	61.49	46.49	20.06
第二产业	Second Industry	200.24	76.54	51.35	64.08	49.67	75.25
第三产业	Tertiary Industry	150.81	36.51	43.28	44.74	34.26	19.88
#工　业	Industry	160.56	60.69	34.75	53.69	33.15	68.91
新疆生产总值构成(%)	Composition of Gross Domestic Produc in Xinjiang (%)						
第一产业	First Industry	10.2	19.5	31.4	36.1	35.6	17.4
第二产业	Second Industry	51.2	54.5	37.2	37.6	38.1	65.3
第三产业	Tertiary Industry	38.6	26.0	31.4	26.3	26.3	17.3
#工　业	Industry	41.1	43.2	25.2	31.5	25.4	59.8
财政收入相当于新疆生产总值比重(%)	Ratio of GDP covered by financial Expenditure (%)	9.0	14.2	7.1	5.8	6.9	10.7
财政支出相当于新疆生产总值比重(%)	Ratio of GDP covered by financial Expenditure (%)	12.7	19.2	17.5	12.6	19.2	17.9
固定资产投资(亿元)	**Fixed Asset Investment (100 million yuan)**	278.56	227.38	147.07	129.6	316.31	347.26
财政、金融(亿元)	**Finance and Public Money(100 million yuan)**						
公共财政预算收入	Local Financial Income	35.30	19.92	9.78	9.90	9.04	12.35
#各项税收	Various Tax Incomes	22.53	11.72	6.18	5.91	6.48	9.54
公共财政预算支出	Expenditure of Local Finance	49.52	26.93	24.07	21.38	25.10	20.67
#一般公共服务	General Common Service	4.77	2.39	1.98	2.01	1.78	1.59
教　育	Operating Expenses for Education	6.19	4.85	4.55	4.34	5.93	4.13
社保和就业	Operating Expenses for Medical Treatment and Sanitation	1.92	1.26	1.60	1.20	1.45	1.50
金融机构年末存款余额	Year-end Loan Balance of Finance	473.56	88.23	90.56	84.10	93.07	64.46
金融机构年末贷款余额	Year-end Deposit Balance of Finance	435.66	81.28	75.19	60.67	80.41	29.81
物价(上年=100)	**Commodity Price (Preceding year=100)**						
商品零售价格指数	Index of Commodity Retail Price	100.5					
居民消费价格指数	Index of Price for Residents' Consumption	101.4					
人民生活	**People's life**						
在岗职工平均货币工资(元)	Average Staff"s Money Wage (yuan)	63574	62277	55301	57604	62582	75425
农村居民家庭人均纯收入(元)	Annual Per capita Net Income of Rural Residents (yuan)	16889	16132	17576	18816	15097	15010
城乡居民储蓄存款余额(亿元)	Balance of Both Urban and Rural Deposit(100 million yuan)	208.53	58.53	58.88	48.81	57.09	32.68
建成区绿化覆盖率(%)	Ratio of Green Coverage in Completed Areas(%)	35.50	33.00	35.62	38.96	24.42	34.98

Continued

博乐市 Bole [Bortala] City	精河县 Jinghe [Jing] County	农四师 XJPCC No.4 Division	农五师 XJPCC No.5 Division	农六师 XJPCC No.6 Division	农七师 XJPCC No.7 Division	农八师 XJPCC No.8 Division	农十一师 XJPCC No.11 Division	农十二师 XJPCC No.12 Division	农十三师 XJPCC No.13 Division	兵团直属 Directly under XPCG
25.80	14.47									
14.36	6.66									
11.44	7.81									
144.87	70.30									
30.20	25.51									
45.83	19.81									
68.83	24.98									
28.87	11.69									
20.8	36.3									
31.6	28.2									
47.5	35.5									
19.9	16.6									
32.5	4.8									
95.9	21.4									
180.83	63.28									
9.06	3.34									
6.91	2.79									
26.74	15.03									
2.94	1.12									
5.02	4.37									
1.80	1.03									
160.16	52.33									
84.68	31.64									
100.3										
100.5										
50823	49131									
13451	13294									
69.26	30.6									
35.65	33.99									

1-11 续表 3

指 标	Item	昌吉市 Changji City	阜康市 Fukang City	呼图壁县 Hu Tubi County	玛纳斯县 Manas County	奇台县 Qitai County	吉木萨尔县 Jimsar County
农 业	**Agriculture**						
农林牧渔业总产值(亿元)	Value of Farm, Forestry, Animal Husbandry and Fishery (100 million yuan)	51.19	44.41	57.87	66.51	75.49	30.76
农 业	Farming	17.97	19.88	21.21	35.89	28.45	14.30
林 业	Forestry	0.44	0.24	0.46	0.31	0.39	0.62
牧 业	Animal Husbandry	31.30	24.04	34.30	28.92	46.62	15.50
渔 业	Fishery	1.07	0.05	0.47	0.28	0.00	0.21
农林牧渔服务业	Services for Farming, Forestry, Animal Husbandary and Fishery	0.42	0.20	1.43	1.11	0.03	0.13
主要农产品产量(万吨)	Main Rural Products Output (10 000 tons)						
粮 食	Grain	26.16	14.41	35.35	22.69	74.46	28.18
棉 花	Cotton	2.99	0.19	4.27	7.54		
油 料	Oil-bearing Crops	5.57	3.44	1.81	0.45	0.81	0.68
甜 菜	Beet	10.40	13.29	9.75	0.83	8.91	1.01
水 果	Fruit						
肉 类	Meat	10.86	5.77	7.93	5.57	13.00	4.53
工 业	**Industry**						
工业总产值(规模以上)(亿元)	Total Value of Industrial Products (100 million yuan)	351.70	220.40	81.73	180.76	63.47	325.08
轻工业	Light Industry	108.79	2.34	23.48	31.98	14.50	8.83
重工业	Heavy Industry	242.91	218.06	58.25	148.77	48.97	316.25
主要工业产品产量	Output of Main Industrial Products						
纱(万吨)	Cotton Yarn (10 000 tons)	0.27	0.00	2.39	0.26		
布(万米)	Cloth (10 000 m)						
绒线(吨)	Woolen knitting wool (ton)						
呢绒(万米)	Woolen Goods (10 000 m)						
原盐(万吨)	Crude Salt (10 000 tons)						
成品糖(万吨)	Sugar (10 000 tons)	3.39				3.85	
原油(万吨)	Crude Oil (10 000 tons)						10.05
发电量(亿千瓦小时)	Volume of Electric Generation (100 million kwh)	38.48	107.36	31.14	103.20	0.11	409.22
粗钢(万吨)	Grude steel (10 000 tons)		18.56				
钢材(万吨)	Steel Rolled (10 000 tons)		27.32	17.67			
水泥(万吨)	Cement (10 000 tons)	62.23	158.28			186.44	133.83
国内商业	**Domestic Trades**						
社会消费品零售总额(亿元)	Retail Volume of Social Commodities (100 million yuan)	99.57	32.24	27.41	30.2	26.63	12.67
教育、卫生	**Education and Health**						
在校学生数(人)	Number of Registered Students (person)						
高等学校	Institutions of Higher Education						
中等职业学校	Specialized Secondary School						
普通中学	Ordinary Middle School	13667	8189	6709	8406	5712	11416
小 学	Elementary School	25321	8497	8189	11130	6859	11762
毕业生数(人)	Number of Graduates (person)						
高等学校	Institutions of Higher Education						
中等职业学校	Specialized Secondary School						
普通中学	Ordinary Middle School	4557	2670	2445	2919	1998	4252
小 学	Elementary School	3955	1345	1377	1742	1172	1950
医院床位数(张)	Number of Sick Beds (unit)						
卫生技术人员数(人)	Number of Medical Technical personnel (person)						

Continued

博尔市 Bole [Bortala] City	精河县 Jinghe [Jing] County	农四师 XJPCC No.4 Division	农五师 XJPCC No.5 Division	农六师 XJPCC No.6 Division	农七师 XJPCC No.7 Division	农八师 XJPCC No.8 Division	农十一师 XJPCC No.11 Division	农十二师 XJPCC No.12 Division	农十三师 XJPCC No.13 Division	兵团直属 Directly under XPCG
32.04	41.15	81.35	38.35	102.34	82.48	160.71	0.14	20.92	30.02	
23.61	35.29	54.04	28.64	69.56	63.48	112.75	0.14	13.89	20.98	
0.10	0.23	0.98	0.48	0.94	0.98	6.46		1.18	0.12	
6.61	3.09	21.70	5.59	21.66	13.24	24.05		3.79	6.22	
0.29	0.07	1.35	0.14	0.48	0.41	0.80		0.30	0.02	
1.43	2.48	3.38	3.20	9.69	4.37	16.64		1.77	2.68	
41.36	8.91	70.50	12.41	46.85	13.71	15.87	0.05	2.34	3.63	
5.77	10.71	1.68	10.49	11.34	17.86	45.19	0.03	0.03	3.63	
0.01	0.35	6.28	0.67	6.59	0.37	0.56	0.03	0.29	0.04	
2.03	4.50	63.26	5.27	4.97	27.69	5.76				
		37.15	12.20	5.83	9.25	22.14	0.01	9.11	14.54	
1.16	0.64	5.10	1.72	6.81	2.77	6.82		0.84	1.76	
24.87	16.84									
7.82	8.41									
17.05	8.43									
0.13	3.08									
	9.04									
3.66										
1.94	5.05									
45.56	42.33									
29.31	6.79	23.46	17.87	84.73	43.41	100.09	1.44	54.18	12.54	35.33
2499										
1559		478	92	1749	585	3813	835	239	958	14818
6649	5514	12955	8206	15066	8082	18636	3888	5112	5170	6088
14651	9553	15255	8701	17732	8060	20824	3943	6898	6960	1563
1129										
193		1035	118	691	181	1074	395	130	37	5882
2047	2042	4661	2930	5494	3114	6230	1603	1926	1526	8424
2225	1434	2740	1553	2921	1728	4093	610	1144	1135	234
1427	508	1499	786	2073	2093	5055	89	314	1122	912
2016	668	1857	1050	2884	2122	6605	133	376	1327	1121

1-12 法人单位数和产业活动单位数
Number of Legal Entities and Establishment Entities

单位：个 (unit)

年份 Year	地区 Region	法人单位数 Number of Legal Entities	单产业法人 Single Sector	多产业法人 Multi-sector	产业活动单位数 Number of Establishments Entities	#多产业法人的活动单位 Establishments Entities of Multi-sector
	2000	53982	47574	6408		
	2001	66477	60857	5620	114912	54055
	2002	66186	60736	5450	114141	53405
	2003	68203	62895	5308	115782	52887
	2004	63429	58196	5233	112499	54303
	2005	69756	64157	5599	122055	57898
	2006	75447	69724	5723	128165	58441
	2007	79767	73984	5783	132750	58766
	2008	88115	82100	6015	139686	57586
	2009	93673	87408	6265	148845	61437
	2010	96727	90456	6271	151303	60847
	2011	101926	95614	6312	155890	60276
	2012	110109	103664	6445	164313	60649
	2013	135357	127219	8138	192348	65129
	2014	177084	167351	9733	244093	76742
	2015	196439	186520	9919	263239	76719
乌鲁木齐市	Urumqi City	60996	58950	2046	67377	8427
克拉玛依市	Karamay City	4901	4613	288	6079	1466
吐鲁番市	Turpan City	6129	5884	245	7445	1561
哈密地区	Hami [Kumul] Administrative Offices	6900	6454	446	9179	2725
昌吉回族自治州	Changji Hui Autonomous Prefecture	14168	13528	640	17988	4460
伊犁哈萨克自治州	Ili Kazak Autonomous Prefecture	29844	28264	1580	39521	11257
伊犁州直属县(市)	Counties (Cities) Direct Under Ili Prefecture	14685	14031	654	18946	4915
塔城地区	Tacheng [Tarbagatai] Administrative Offices	8162	7755	407	11256	3501
阿勒泰地区	Altay Administrative Offices	6997	6478	519	9319	2841
博尔塔拉蒙古自治州	Bortala Mongol Autonomous Prefecture	4534	4175	359	6217	2042
巴音郭楞蒙古自治州	Bayangol Mongol Autonomous Prefecture	17635	16594	1041	22399	5805
阿克苏地区	Aksu Administrative Offices	12889	11771	1118	23334	11563
克孜勒苏柯尔克孜自治州	Kizilsu Kirgiz Autonomous Prefecture	3089	2921	168	5314	2393
喀什地区	Kashgar [Kaxgar] Administrative Offices	14767	13667	1100	32801	19134
和田地区	Hotan Administrative Offices	13452	12945	507	16251	3306
自治区直辖县级市	County level City directly under the Autonomous Region	7135	6754	381	9334	2580
石河子市	Shihezi City	4157	3906	251	5013	1107
阿拉尔市	Aral City	1555	1491	64	2303	812
图木舒克市	Tumxuk City	484	464	20	890	426
五家渠市	Wujiaqu City	939	893	46	1128	235

注：2004 年数据不包括农、林、牧、渔业。
Note: Data in 2004 does not include statistics of agriculture,forestry,animal husbandry and fishery.

1-13 按三次产业分的法人单位数及构成
Number of Legal Entities by Three Strata of Industry and Its Composition

单位：个 (unit)

年 份 Year	地 区 Region	法人单位数 Number of Legal Entities	第一产业 Primary Industry 绝对数 Value	 构成 (%) Composition (%)
	2000	53982		
	2001	66477	3439	5.17
	2002	66186	3421	5.17
	2003	68203	3195	4.68
	2004	63429		
	2005	69756	1449	2.08
	2006	75447	1524	2.02
	2007	79767	1715	2.15
	2008	88115	203	0.23
	2009	93673	2439	2.60
	2010	96727	2842	2.94
	2011	101926	3650	3.58
	2012	110109	4773	4.34
	2013	135357	4692	3.47
	2014	177084	15907	8.98
	2015	196439	12622	6.43
乌鲁木齐市	Urumqi City	60996	899	1.47
克拉玛依市	Karamay City	4901	140	2.86
吐鲁番市	Turpan City	6129	553	9.02
哈密地区	Hami [Kumul] Administrative Offices	6900	810	11.74
昌吉回族自治州	Changji Hui Autonomous Prefecture	14168	2168	15.30
伊犁哈萨克自治州	Ili Kazak Autonomous Prefecture	29844	2405	8.06
伊犁州直属县(市)	Counties (Cities) Direct Under Ili Prefecture	14685	353	2.41
塔城地区	Tacheng [Tarbagatai] Administrative Offices	8162	1078	13.20
阿勒泰地区	Altay Administrative Offices	6997	974	13.92
博尔塔拉蒙古自治州	Bortala Mongol Autonomous Prefecture	4534	449	9.90
巴音郭楞蒙古自治州	Bayangol Mongol Autonomous Prefecture	17635	1836	10.41
阿克苏地区	Aksu Administrative Offices	12889	751	5.83
克孜勒苏柯尔克孜自治州	Kizilsu Kirgiz Autonomous Prefecture	3089	344	11.14
喀什地区	Kashgar [Kaxgar] Administrative Offices	14767	611	4.14
和田地区	Hotan Administrative Offices	13452	1295	9.63
自治区直辖县级市	County level City directly under the Autonomous Region	7135	361	5.06
石河子市	Shihezi City	4157	73	1.75
阿拉尔市	Aral City	1555	142	9.13
图木舒克市	Tumxuk City	484	52	10.74
五家渠市	Wujiaqu City	939	94	10.01

注：2004 年数据不包括农、林、牧、渔业。
Note: Data in 2004 does not include statistics of agriculture,forestry,animal husbandry and fishery.

1-13 续表 Continued

年 份 Year	地 区 Region	第二产业 Secondary Industry 绝对数 Value	构成(%) Composition	第三产业 Tertiary Industry 绝对数 Value	构成 (%) Composition (%)
	2000				
	2001	8446	12.71	54592	82.12
	2002	8360	12.63	54405	82.20
	2003	8529	12.51	56479	82.81
	2004	7824	12.34	55605	87.66
	2005	8713	12.49	59594	85.43
	2006	9425	12.49	64498	85.49
	2007	10226	12.82	67826	85.03
	2008	11276	12.80	76636	86.97
	2009	12034	12.85	79200	84.55
	2010	13005	13.45	80880	83.62
	2011	14595	14.32	83681	82.10
	2012	16510	14.99	88826	80.67
	2013	18707	13.82	111958	87.71
	2014	23858	13.47	137319	77.54
	2015	26222	13.35	157595	80.22
乌鲁木齐市	Urumqi City	5684	9.32	54413	89.21
克拉玛依市	Karamay City	696	14.20	4065	82.94
吐鲁番市	Turpan City	1289	21.03	4287	69.95
哈密地区	Hami [Kumul] Administrative Offices	1345	19.49	4745	68.77
昌吉回族自治州	Changji Hui Autonomous Prefecture	2727	19.25	9273	65.45
伊犁哈萨克自治州	Ili Kazak Autonomous Prefecture	3903	13.08	23536	78.86
伊犁州直属县(市)	Counties (Cities) Direct Under Ili Prefecture	2033	13.84	12299	83.75
塔城地区	Tacheng [Tarbagatai] Administrative Offices	1024	12.55	6060	74.25
阿勒泰地区	Altay Administrative Offices	846	12.09	5177	73.99
博尔塔拉蒙古自治州	Bortala Mongol Autonomous Prefecture	642	14.16	3443	75.94
巴音郭楞蒙古自治州	Bayangol Mongol Autonomous Prefecture	2460	13.95	13339	75.64
阿克苏地区	Aksu Administrative Offices	2029	15.74	10109	78.43
克孜勒苏柯尔克孜自治州	Kizilsu Kirgiz Autonomous Prefecture	462	14.95	2283	73.91
喀什地区	Kashgar [Kaxgar] Administrative Offices	2354	15.94	11802	79.92
和田地区	Hotan Administrative Offices	1101	8.18	11056	82.19
自治区直辖县级市	County level City directly under the Autonomous Region	1530	21.44	5244	73.50
石河子市	Shihezi City	835	20.09	3249	78.16
阿拉尔市	Aral City	397	25.53	1016	65.34
图木舒克市	Tumxuk City	110	22.73	322	66.53
五家渠市	Wujiaqu City	188	20.02	657	69.97

1-14 按登记注册、机构类型分的法人单位数和产业活动单位数
Number of Legal Entities and Establishment Entities by Status of Registration and Institutions

单位：个 (2015 年) (unit)

类　型		法人单位数 Number of Legal Entities	单产业法人 Single Sector	多产业法人 Multi-sector	产业活动单位数 Number of Establishments Entities	#多产业法人的活动单位 Establishments Entities of Multi-sector
总　计	**Total**	**196439**	**186520**	**9919**	**263239**	**76719**
按登记注册类型分组	**By Status of Registration**					
内　资	**Domestic Funded**	**195986**	**186115**	**9871**	**262406**	**76291**
国　有	State-owned Enterprises	30927	26163	4764	60523	34360
集　体	Collective-owned Enterprises	1271	1128	143	2894	1766
股份合作	Cooperative Enterprises	427	331	96	661	330
联　营	Joint Ownership Enterprises	330	320	10	733	413
国有联营	State Joint Ownership Enterprises	68	65	3	170	105
集体联营	Collective Joint Ownership Enterprises	121	116	5	259	143
国有与集体联营	Joint State-collective Enterprises	24	23	1	61	38
其他联营	Other Joint Ownership Enterprises	117	116	1	243	127
有限责任公司	Limited Liability Corporations	25661	24169	1492	31244	7075
国有独资公司	State Sole Funded Corporations	888	744	144	1163	419
其他有限责任公司	Other Limited Liability Corporations	24773	23425	1348	30081	6656
股份有限公司	Share-holding Corporations Ltd	1565	1234	331	4026	2792
私　营	Private Enterprises	89097	86309	2788	96426	10117
私营独资	Private-funded Enterprises	14299	14058	241	15454	1396
私营合伙	Private Partnership Enterprises	2320	2289	31	2449	160
私营有限责任公司	Private Limited Liability Corporations	71156	68696	2460	77018	8322
私营股份有限公司	Private Share-holding Corporations Ltd.	1322	1266	56	1505	239
其他内资	Other Enterprises	46708	46461	247	65899	19438
港澳台商投资	**Enterprises with Funds from Hong Kong, Macao and Taiwan**	**157**	**136**	**21**	**278**	**142**
与港澳台商合资经营	Joint-venture Enterprises	73	64	9	97	33
与港澳台商合作经营	Cooperative Enterprises	4	4		7	3
港澳台商独资	Enterprises with Sole Investment	60	54	6	102	48
港澳台商投资股份有限公司	Enterprises with Sole Investment Share-holding Corporations Ltd.	15	12	3	65	53
其他港、澳、台商投资	Other	5	2	3	7	5
外商投资	**Foreign Funded Enterprises**	**296**	**269**	**27**	**555**	**286**
中外合资经营	Joint-venture Enterprises	115	103	12	147	44
中外合作经营	Cooperation Enterprises	17	13	4	19	6
外资企业	Enterprises with Sole Funds	118	114	4	280	166
外商投资股份有限公司	Share-holding Corporations Ltd.	14	12	2	49	37
其他外商投资	Other	32	27	5	60	33
按机构类型分组	**by Status of Organization**					
企　业	Enterprise	129581	123989	5592	155412	31423
事业单位	Institution	17287	15869	1418	33833	17964
机　关	Organ	8700	6030	2670	12999	6969
社会团体	Social Organization	6306	6202	104	6881	679
民办非企业单位	Private Non-enterprises Units	2650	2634	16	2634	
基金会	Foundation	32	32		36	4
居委会	Neighborhood Committee	2362	2335	27	2457	122
村委会	Village Committee	9219	9212	7	9316	104
其他组织机构	Other Units	20302	20217	85	39671	19454

1-15 按行业分的法人单位数和产业活动单位数
Number of Legal Entities and Establishment Entities by Sector

单位：个　　(2015 年)　　(unit)

类型		法人单位数 Number of Legal Entities	单产业法人 Single Sector	多产业法人 Multi-sector	产业活动单位数 Number of Establishments Entities	#多产业法人的活动单位 Establishments Entities of Multi-sector
总　计	**Total Farming**	**196439**	**186520**	**9919**	**263239**	**76719**
农、林、牧、渔业	**AgricultureForestry, Animal Husbandry and Fishery**	**17640**	**17333**	**307**	**21407**	**4074**
农　业	Farming	4542	4359	183	6664	2305
林　业	Forestry	647	635	12	724	89
畜牧业	Animal Husbandry	7192	7156	36	7347	191
渔　业	Fishery	241	237	4	253	16
农、林、牧、渔服务业	Services for Agriculture Forestry, Animal Husbandry and Fishery	5018	4946	72	6419	1473
采矿业	**Mining Ores**	**3029**	**2945**	**84**	**3284**	**339**
煤炭开采和洗选业	Mining and Washing of Coal	519	492	27	568	76
石油和天然气开采业	Extraction of Petroleum and Natural Gas	33	30	3	55	25
黑色金属矿采选业	Mining and Processing of Ferrous Metal Ores	583	571	12	612	41
有色金属矿采选业	Mining and Processing of Non-Ferrous Metal Ores	481	472	9	492	20
非金属矿采选业	Mining and Processing of Non-metal Ores	996	979	17	1077	98
开采辅助活动	Support Activities for Mining	280	265	15	340	75
其他采矿业	Mining of Other Ores	137	136	1	140	4
制造业	**Manufacture**	**17083**	**16702**	**381**	**17937**	**1235**
农副食品加工业	Processing of Food from Agricultural Products	1910	1849	61	2072	223
食品制造业	Manufacture of Foods	669	642	27	693	51
酒、饮料和精制茶制造业	Manufacture of Liguor, Beverage and Refined Tea	574	551	23	600	49
烟草制品业	Manufacture of Tobacco	1	1		2	1
纺织业	Manufacture of Textile	595	578	17	611	33
纺织服装、服饰业	Manufacture of Textile, Wearing Apparel and Accessories	423	421	2	434	13
皮革、毛皮、羽毛(绒)及其制品业	Manufacture of Leather, Fur, Feather and Related Products	90	89	1	95	6
木材加工及木、竹、藤、棕、草制品业	Processing of Timber, Manufacture of Wood, Bamboo,Rattan,Palm,and Straw Products	322	319	3	339	20
家具制造业	Manufacture of Furniture	200	198	2	207	9
造纸及纸制品业	Manufacture of Paper and Paper Products	314	308	6	323	15
印刷业和记录媒介的复制	Printing,Reproduction of Recording Media	401	396	5	426	30
文教、工美、体育和娱乐用品制造业	Manufacture of Cultural, Educational,Sports and Entertainment Articles	495	492	3	503	11
石油加工、炼焦及核燃料加工业	Processing of Petroleum, Coking, Processing of Nuclear Fuel	316	303	13	325	22
化学原料及化学制品制造业	Manufacture of Raw Chemical Materials and Chemical Products	1264	1208	56	1339	131
医药制造业	Manufacture of Medicines	167	158	9	173	15
化学纤维制造业	Manufacture of Chemical Fibers	43	41	2	44	3
橡胶和塑料制品业	Manu facture of Rubber and Plastic Products	1554	1533	21	1596	63
非金属矿物制品业	Manufacture of Non-metallic Mineral Products	3838	3771	67	4059	288
黑色金属冶炼及压延加工业	Smelting and Pressing of Ferrous Metals	335	330	5	341	11
有色金属冶炼及压延加工业	Smelting and Pressing of Non-ferrous Metals	175	169	6	183	14
金属制品业	Manufacture of Metal Products	1304	1293	11	1356	63
通用设备制造业	Manufacture of General Purpose Machinery	492	483	9	508	25

1-15 续表 1 Continued

单位：个 (unit)

类型		法人单位数 Number of Legal Entities	单产业法人 Single Sector	多产业法人 Multi-sector	产业活动单位数 Number of Establishments Entities	#多产业法人的活动单位 Establishments Entities of Multi-sector
专用设备制造业	Manufacture of Special Purpose Machinery	642	632	10	680	48
汽车制造业	Manufacture of Automobile	83	81	2	85	4
铁路、船舶、航空航天和其他运输设备制造业	Manufacture of Railway ,Ship,Aeronautics and Other	24	22	2	24	2
电气机械及器材制造业	Manufacture of Electrical Machinery and Equipment	473	461	12	489	28
计算机、通信和其他电子设备制造业	Manufacture of Computers Communication, and Other Electronic Equipment	31	30	1	36	6
仪器仪表制造业	Manufacture of Mesuring Instruments and Maehtnrey	40	39	1	45	6
其他制造业	Other Manufactures	75	75		81	6
废弃资源综合利用业	Comprehensive Utilization of Waste Resources	85	84	1	94	10
金属制品、机械和设备修理业	Repair Serrice Manufacture of Metal Products, Machinery and Equipment	148	145	3	174	29
电力、燃气及水的生产和供应业	**Production and Supply of Electric Power,Gas and Water**	**1776**	**1656**	**120**	**2280**	**624**
电力、热力的生产和供应业	Production and Supply of Electric Power and Heat Power	1390	1335	55	1722	387
燃气生产和供应业	Production and Supply of Gas	165	128	37	257	129
水的生产和供应业	Production and Supply of Water	221	193	28	301	108
建筑业	**Construction**	**4762**	**4346**	**416**	**6373**	**2027**
房屋建筑业	Construction Decoration	1199	982	217	2067	1085
土木工程建筑业	Building and Civil Engineering	968	879	89	1250	371
建筑安装业	Construction Installation	865	802	63	1121	319
建筑装饰和其他建筑业	Other Construction	1730	1683	47	1935	252
批发和零售业	**Wholesale and Retail Trades**	**50652**	**48717**	**1935**	**61143**	**12426**
批发业	Wholesalel Trade	34610	33357	1253	40710	7353
零售业	Retail Trade	16042	15360	682	20433	5073
交通运输、仓储和邮政业	**Transport,Storage and Postal**	**6146**	**5722**	**424**	**8556**	**2834**
铁路运输业	Railway Transport	88	82	6	180	98
道路运输业	Road Transport	3401	3168	233	4057	889
水上运输业	Water Transport	3	3		6	3
航空运输业	Air Transport	72	68	4	99	31
管道运输业	Pipeline Transport	23	17	6	35	18
装卸搬运和运输代理业	Loading,Unloading and Other	1690	1597	93	1883	286
仓储业	Storage	545	530	15	682	152
邮政业	Posts	324	257	67	1614	1357
住宿和餐饮业	**Hotels and Catering Services**	**1746**	**1638**	**108**	**2365**	**727**
住宿业	Hotels	1044	973	71	1402	429
餐饮业	Catering Services	702	665	37	963	298
信息传输、软件和信息技术服务业	**Information Transmission, Software and Information Technology**	**2896**	**2772**	**124**	**4300**	**1528**
电信、广播电视和卫星传输服务	Telecommunications and Other Information Services	386	305	81	1596	1291
互联网和相关服务	Internet and Related Services	396	389	7	477	88
软件和信息技术服务业	Software and Information Techology	2114	2078	36	2227	149
金融业	**Financial Intermediation**	**2315**	**1905**	**410**	**6323**	**4418**
货币金融服务	Bank	874	628	246	3854	3226

1-15 续表 2 Continued

单位：个 (unit)

类型		法人单位数 Number of Legal Entities	单产业法人 Single Sector	多产业法人 Multi-sector	产业活动单位数 Number of Establishments Entities	#多产业法人的活动单位 Establishments Entities of Multi-sector
资本市场服务	Securities	620	608	12	696	88
保险业	Insurance	286	142	144	1174	1032
其他金融活动	Other Services	535	527	8	599	72
房地产业	**Real Estate**	**7024**	**6427**	**597**	**8040**	**1613**
房地产业	Real Estate	7024	6427	597	8040	1613
租赁和商务服务业	**Leasing and Business Services**	**14494**	**14060**	**434**	**16238**	**2178**
租赁业	Leasing	1129	1113	16	1204	91
商务服务业	Business Services	13365	12947	418	15034	2087
科学研究和技术服务业	**Scientific Research, and Technical Services**	**7035**	**6690**	**345**	**9455**	**2765**
研究与试验发展	Research and Experimental Development	416	402	14	446	44
专业技术服务业	Technical Services	4777	4515	262	6199	1684
科技交流和推广服务业	Services of Science and Technology Exchange and Promtion	1842	1773	69	2810	1037
水利、环境和公共设施管理业	**Management of Water Conservancy,Enviroment and Public Facilities**	**1530**	**1401**	**129**	**2790**	**1389**
水利管理业	Management of Water Conservancy	520	427	93	1512	1085
生态保护和环境治理业	Ecological Protection and Enviromental Governance	236	227	9	327	100
公共设施管理业	Management of and Public Facilities	774	747	27	951	204
居民服务和其他服务业	**Services to Households and other services**	**3165**	**3073**	**92**	**3605**	**532**
居民服务业	Services to Households	950	921	29	1169	248
机动车、电子产品和日用产品修理业	Motor Vehicle,Electronic Products and Baily Products repair	1452	1411	41	1614	203
其他服务业	Other services	763	741	22	822	81
教 育	**Education**	**7114**	**6585**	**529**	**10883**	**4298**
教 育	Education	7114	6585	529	10883	4298
卫生和社会工作	**Health and,Social Service**	**3529**	**3320**	**209**	**5328**	**2008**
卫 生	Public Health	3005	2804	201	4623	1819
社会工作	Social Service	524	516	8	705	189
文化、体育和娱乐业	**Culture,Sports and Entertainment**	**3900**	**3828**	**72**	**5012**	**1184**
新闻出版业	Journalism and Publishing Activities	164	160	4	182	22
广播、电视、电影和音像业	Broadcasting,Movies,Television and Audiovisual Activies	507	480	27	989	509
文化艺术业	Culture and Art Activities	799	782	17	1331	549
体 育	Sports Activities	179	175	4	224	49
娱乐业	Entertainment	2251	2231	20	2286	55
公共管理、社会保障和社会组织	**Public Management,Social Security and Social Organization**	**40603**	**37400**	**3203**	**67920**	**30520**
中国共产党机关	Communist Party of China	1117	922	195	1338	416
国家机构	Government Agencies	12146	9301	2845	22195	12894
人民政协和民主党派	People's Political Consultative Conference and Democratic Parties	133	128	5	137	9
社会保障	Social Security	251	234	17	598	364
群众团体、社会团体和宗教组织	Non-Government Organizations,Social Organizations and Religion Organizations	15375	15268	107	31879	16611
基层群众自治组织	Grass Roots Self-governing Organizations	11581	11547	34	11773	226

1-16 各地区按机构类型分法人单位数

Number of Legal Entities by Type of Institutions and Region

单位：个 (2015 年) (unit)

地　区	Region	法人单位数 Number of Legal Entities	企业法人 Business Entity	事业法人 Institution Entity	机关法人 Governmint Entity	社会团体 Social Organization	其 他 Others
总　计	**Total**	**196439**	**129581**	**17287**	**8700**	**6306**	**34565**
乌鲁木齐市	Urumqi City	60996	53956	2067	949	1023	3001
克拉玛依市	Karamay City	4901	3855	199	282	203	362
吐鲁番市	Turpan City	6129	3645	553	255	221	1455
哈密地区	Hami [Kumul] Administrative Offices	6900	4162	757	352	218	1411
昌吉回族自治州	Changji Hui Autonomous Prefecture	14168	8078	1327	617	553	3593
伊犁哈萨克自治州	Ili Kazak Autonomous Prefecture	29844	13916	4893	2127	1213	7695
伊犁州直属县(市)	Counties (Cities) DirectUnderIliPrefecture	14685	7537	2296	915	378	3559
塔城地区	Tacheng[Tarbagatai]AdministrativeOffices	8162	3467	1347	622	373	2353
阿勒泰地区	Altay Administrative Offices	6997	2912	1250	590	462	1783
博尔塔拉蒙古自治州	Bortala Mongol Autonomous Prefecture	4534	2780	524	315	188	727
巴音郭楞蒙古自治州	BayangolMongolAutonomous Prefecture	17635	12288	1339	718	482	2808
阿克苏地区	Aksu Administrative Offices	12889	8039	1429	790	551	2080
克孜勒苏柯尔克孜自治州	Kizilsu Kirgiz Autonomous Prefecture	3089	1519	339	376	69	786
喀什地区	Kashgar [Kaxgar] Administrative Offices	14767	7692	1751	1008	1034	3282
和田地区	Hotan Administrative Offices	13452	4236	1430	633	360	6793
自治区直辖县级市	County level City directly under the Autonomous Region	7135	5415	679	278	191	572
石河子市	Shihezi City	4157	3341	222	94	126	374
阿拉尔市	Aral City	1555	1166	203	46	16	124
图木舒克市	Tumxuk City	484	300	110	58	10	6
五家渠市	Wujiaqu City	939	608	144	80	39	68

1-17 按地区和营业状态分企业法人单位数
Number of Business Entities by Region and Operation Status

单位：个　　(2015 年)　　(unit)

地　区	Region	企业法人单位数 Number of Business Entities	营业 In Business or Operating	停业（歇业） Closed	筹建 In Preparation	当年关闭 Closed in the Year	当年破产 Bankrupted in the Year	其他 Others
总　计	**Total**	**129581**	**100706**	**10469**	**15619**	**1294**	**223**	**1270**
乌鲁木齐市	Urumqi City	53956	43864	4551	4764	426	39	312
克拉玛依市	Karamay City	3855	3153	180	386	122	1	13
吐鲁番市	Turpan City	3645	2820	376	413	15	3	18
哈密地区	Hami [Kumul] Administrative Offices	4162	2666	652	774	19	1	50
昌吉回族自治州	Changji Hui Autonomous Prefecture	8078	6126	560	1218	79	23	72
伊犁哈萨克自治州	Ili Kazak Autonomous Prefecture	13916	10932	1242	1405	110	26	201
伊犁州直属县(市)	Counties (Cities) Direct Under Ili Prefecture	7537	5988	593	748	83	7	118
塔城地区	Tacheng [Tarbagatai] Administrative Offices	3467	2842	398	179	14	8	26
阿勒泰地区	Altay Administrative Offices	2912	2102	251	478	13	11	57
博尔塔拉蒙古自治州	Bortala Mongol Autonomous Prefecture	2780	2306	161	247	12	1	53
巴音郭楞蒙古自治州	Bayangol Mongol Autonomous Prefecture	12288	8863	602	2537	75	15	196
阿克苏地区	Aksu Administrative Offices	8039	6127	597	1088	115	27	85
克孜勒苏柯尔克孜自治州	Kizilsu Kirgiz Autonomous Prefecture	1519	1091	192	194	19	6	17
喀什地区	Kashgar [Kaxgar] Administrative Offices	7692	5874	464	1039	163	32	120
和田地区	Hotan Administrative Offices	4236	2360	490	1149	92	47	98
自治区直辖县级市	County level City directly under the Autonomous Region	5415	4524	402	405	47	2	35
石河子市	Shihezi City	3341	2853	302	141	12		33
阿拉尔市	Aral City	1166	926	60	153	26	1	
图木舒克市	Tumxuk City	300	246	15	35	4		
五家渠市	Wujiaqu City	608	499	25	76	5	1	2

1-18 各地区非公有制企业法人单位数
Number of Non-public Enterprise Legal Entities by Region

单位：个　　　　(2015 年)　　　　(unit)

地　区	Region	全部企业法人单位数 Number of Total Enterprises	非公有制企业法人单位数 Number of Non-public Enterprises	非公有制占全部比例(%) As Percentage of Total Enterprises
总　计	**Total**	**129581**	**124495**	**96.08**
乌鲁木齐市	Urumqi City	53956	52588	97.46
克拉玛依市	Karamay City	3855	3778	98.00
吐鲁番市	Turpan City	3645	3466	95.09
哈密地区	Hami [Kumul] Administrative Offices	4162	3975	95.51
昌吉回族自治州	Changji Hui Autonomous Prefecture	8078	7794	96.48
伊犁哈萨克自治州	Ili Kazak Autonomous Prefecture	13916	12961	93.14
伊犁州直属县(市)	Counties (Cities) Direct Under Ili Prefecture	7537	7025	93.21
塔城地区	Tacheng [Tarbagatai] Administrative Offices	3467	3206	92.47
阿勒泰地区	Altay Administrative Offices	2912	2730	93.75
博尔塔拉蒙古自治州	Bortala Mongol Autonomous Prefecture	2780	2576	92.66
巴音郭楞蒙古自治州	Bayangol Mongol Autonomous Prefecture	12288	11808	96.09
阿克苏地区	Aksu Administrative Offices	8039	7681	95.55
克孜勒苏柯尔克孜自治州	Kizilsu Kirgiz Autonomous Prefecture	1519	1414	93.09
喀什地区	Kashgar [Kaxgar] Administrative Offices	7692	7262	94.41
和田地区	Hotan Administrative Offices	4236	4036	95.28
自治区直辖县级市	County level City directly under the Autonomous Region	5415	5156	95.22
石河子市	Shihezi City	3341	3185	95.33
阿拉尔市	Aral City	1166	1138	97.60
图木舒克市	Tumxuk City	300	277	92.33
五家渠市	Wujiaqu City	608	556	91.45

1-19 服务业法人单位数和从业人员数

Number of Services to Legal Entities and Employed Persons

年份 Year	合计 Total	企业 Enterprises	行政事业 Administrative	社会团体及其他 Social Organizations and Others
单位数(个) Number of Enterprises(unit)				
2009	79200	36738	20616	21846
2010	80880	38226	20636	22018
2011	83681	40854	20729	22098
2012	88826	45569	21021	22236
2013	111958	58758	23520	29457
2014	137319	80760	25149	31410
2015	152150	95693	25262	31195
从业人数(万人) Number of Employed Persons(10000 persons)				
2009	173.31	64.48	93.70	15.12
2010	178.72	68.24	95.05	15.43
2011	184.51	73.15	95.76	15.60
2012	194.80	82.11	96.65	16.04
2013	250.13	103.01	113.25	33.87
2014	271.76	118.53	117.05	36.18
2015	280.64	125.45	118.06	37.13

1-20 服务业分行业法人单位数及从业人员数

Number of Services to Legal Entities and Employed Persons by Industry

(2015年)

行业	Sector	法人单位数(个) Number of Legal Entities (unit)	从业人数(万人) Employed Persons (10000 persons)
总计	**Total**	**152150**	**280.64**
交通运输、仓储和邮政业	Transport,Storage and Post	6146	17.68
信息传输、计算机服务和软件业	Information Transmission,Comupter Services and Software	2896	4.93
批发和零售业	Wholesale and Retail Trades	50653	39.14
住宿和餐饮业	Hotels and Catering Services	1746	6.09
金融业	Financil Intermediation	2315	9.52
房地产业	Real Estate	7024	14.02
租赁和商务服务业	Leasing and Business Services	14494	23.69
科学研究、技术服务和地质勘查业	Scientific Research,Technical Services and Geological Prospecting	7035	11.81
水利、环境和公共设施管理业	Mangement of Water Conservancy,Environment and Public Facilities	1530	5.86
居民服务和其他服务业	Services to Households and other Services	3165	3.66
教育	Education	7114	39.45
卫生、社会保障和社会福利业	Health,Social Securities and Social Welfare	3529	18.54
文化、体育和娱乐业	Culture,Sports and Entertainment	3900	4.43
公共管理和社会组织	Public Mangement and Social Organization	40603	81.81

1-21 各地区服务业法人单位数
Number of Services to Legal Entities by Region

单位：个 (2015 年) (unit)

地区	Region	合计 Total	交通运输仓储及邮政业 Traffic, Transport, Storage and Post	信息传输计算机服务和软件业 Information Transmission, Computer, Services and Software	批发和零售业 Wholesale and Retail Trade	住宿和餐饮业 Accommodation and Restaurants
总计	**Total**	**152150**	**6146**	**2896**	**50653**	**1746**
乌鲁木齐市	Urumqi City	54229	2020	1968	26884	595
克拉玛依市	Karamay City	3901	214	141	1329	49
吐鲁番市	Turpan City	4181	200	16	762	74
哈密地区	Hami [Kumul] Administrative Offices	4643	281	28	1292	59
昌吉回族自治州	Changji Hui Autonomous Prefecture	8626	635	97	1630	84
伊犁哈萨克自治州	Ili Kazak Autonomous Prefecture	21174	802	139	3682	312
伊犁州直属县(市)	Counties (Cities) Direct Under Ili Prefecture	11115	491	72	2293	180
塔城地区	Tacheng [Tarbagatai] Administrative Offices	5220	144	27	654	43
阿勒泰地区	Altay Administrative Offices	4839	167	40	735	89
博尔塔拉蒙古自治州	Bortala Mongol Autonomous Prefecture	3357	190	32	1003	31
巴音郭楞蒙古自治州	Bayangol Mongol Autonomous Prefecture	12825	585	126	5119	173
阿克苏地区	Aksu Administrative Offices	9638	385	101	2771	86
克孜勒苏柯尔克孜自治州	Kizilsu Kirgiz Autonomous Prefecture	2249	100	28	465	24
喀什地区	Kashgar [Kaxgar] Administrative Offices	11519	355	125	2586	134
和田地区	Hotan Administrative Offices	10697	153	43	1465	56
自治区直辖县级市	County level City Directly under the Autonomous Region	5111	226	52	1665	69
石河子市	Shihezi City	3207	138	34	1184	44
阿拉尔市	Aral City	956	38	13	352	10
图木舒克市	Tumxuk City	304	12	1	38	7
五家渠市	Wujiaqu City	644	38	4	91	8

1-21 续表 1 Continued

单位：个 (unit)

地　区	Region	金融业 Finance	房地产业 Real Estate	租赁和商务服务业 Leasing and Business Services	科学研究技术服务和地质勘察业 ScientificResearch, TechnicalService andGeologic Perambulation	水利、环境和公共设施管理业 Managementof WaterConservancy, Environmentand PublicEstablishment
总　计	**Total**	**2315**	**7024**	**14494**	**7035**	**1530**
乌鲁木齐市	Urumqi City	1160	2367	7566	2992	406
克拉玛依市	Karamay City	59	188	495	247	48
吐鲁番市	Turpan City	49	148	291	164	42
哈密地区	Hami [Kumul] Administrative Offices	56	290	368	215	45
昌吉回族自治州	Changji Hui Autonomous Prefecture	121	521	809	427	124
伊犁哈萨克自治州	Ili Kazak Autonomous Prefecture	226	1068	1445	976	342
伊犁州直属县(市)	Counties (Cities) Direct Under Ili Prefecture	111	689	917	492	157
塔城地区	Tacheng [Tarbagatai] Administrative Offices	55	176	199	223	86
阿勒泰地区	Altay Administrative Offices	60	203	329	261	99
博尔塔拉蒙古自治州	Bortala Mongol Autonomous Prefecture	59	160	200	139	40
巴音郭楞蒙古自治州	Bayangol Mongol Autonomous Prefecture	154	624	1075	620	122
阿克苏地区	Aksu Administrative Offices	111	575	617	365	96
克孜勒苏柯尔克孜自治州	Kizilsu Kirgiz Autonomous Prefecture	26	61	115	94	28
喀什地区	Kashgar [Kaxgar] Administrative Offices	105	516	674	254	94
和田地区	Hotan Administrative Offices	46	151	283	282	67
自治区直辖县级市	County level City directly under the Autonomous Region	143	355	556	260	76
石河子市	Shihezi City	115	192	390	152	21
阿拉尔市	Aral City	4	67	89	58	29
图木舒克市	Tumxuk City	2	19	19	15	9
五家渠市	Wujiaqu City	22	77	58	35	17

1-21 续表 2 Continued

单位：个 (unit)

地区	Region	居民服务和其他服务业 Resident Services and other Services	教育 Education	卫生、社会保障和社会福利业 Sanitation, Social Security and Social Welfare	文化、体育和娱乐业 Culture, Sports and Entertainment	公共管理和社会组织 Public Management and Social Organization
总计	**Total**	**3165**	**7114**	**3529**	**3900**	**40603**
乌鲁木齐市	Urumqi City	1446	1205	516	1036	4068
克拉玛依市	Karamay City	154	188	52	83	654
吐鲁番市	Turpan City	85	281	81	138	1850
哈密地区	Hami [Kumul] Administrative Offices	65	250	120	133	1441
昌吉回族自治州	Changji Hui Autonomous Prefecture	134	569	468	328	2679
伊犁哈萨克自治州	Ili Kazak Autonomous Prefecture	254	1654	822	842	8610
伊犁州直属县(市)	Counties (Cities) Direct Under Ili Prefecture	136	967	392	417	3801
塔城地区	Tacheng [Tarbagatai] Administrative Offices	61	433	247	233	2639
阿勒泰地区	Altay Administrative Offices	57	254	183	192	2170
博尔塔拉蒙古自治州	Bortala Mongol Autonomous Prefecture	39	177	101	124	1062
巴音郭楞蒙古自治州	Bayangol Mongol Autonomous Prefecture	338	514	306	180	2889
阿克苏地区	Aksu Administrative Offices	195	663	243	372	3058
克孜勒苏柯尔克孜自治州	Kizilsu Kirgiz Autonomous Prefecture	26	91	50	46	1095
喀什地区	Kashgar [Kaxgar] Administrative Offices	166	815	392	237	5066
和田地区	Hotan Administrative Offices	111	395	267	76	7302
自治区直辖县级市	County level City directly under the Autonomous Region	152	312	111	305	829
石河子市	Shihezi City	112	220	50	149	406
阿拉尔市	Aral City	20	41	22	98	115
图木舒克市	Tumxuk City	5	20	18	28	111
五家渠市	Wujiaqu City	15	31	21	30	197

主要统计指标解释

行政区划 指国家对行政区域的划分。根据有关法规规定，我国的行政区域划分如下：(1)全国分为省、自治区、直辖市；(2)省、自治区分为自治州、县、自治县、市；(3)自治州分为县、自治县、市；(4)县、自治县分为乡、民族乡、镇；(5)直辖市和较大的市分为区、县；(6)国家在必要时设立的特别行政区。

平均增长速度 平均增长速度表明社会经济现象在一个较长的时期内逐期平均增长变化的程度，它不能根据各个环比增长速度直接求得，但与平均发展速度之间存在着一定的数量关系：平均增长速度 = 平均发展速度 – 1

平均发展速度是一种根据环比发展速度计算的序时平均数，由于各时期对比的基础不同，所以计算平均发展速度不能采用一般的序时平均数的计算方法，计算方法分为水平法和累计法。水平法，又称几何平均法，即将环比发展速度按连乘法用几何平均数公式计算。累计法，也称方程法，根据一段时期内各年发展水平总和与基期水平的关系，列出方程式计算平均发展速度。水平法着重考虑最后一年所达到的发展水平；累计法着重考虑整个时期累计发展水平的总量。

本《年鉴》内所列的平均增长速度，均用“水平法”计算。从某年到某年平均增长速度的年份，均不包括基期年在内。如2011-2015年的平均增长速度是以2010年为基期计算的，则写为2011-2015年平均增长速度，其余类推。

国民经济行业分类 自 2012 年定期报表开始使用新的《国民经济行业分类》(GB/T4754-2011)，该分类是由国家统计局组织修订，国家质量监督检验检疫总局和中国国家标准化管理委员会于 2011 年 4 月 29 日发布。这次修订是在 2002 年分类标准的基础上，参照联合国《全部经济活动的国际标准产业分类》(ISIC/Rev.4) 进行的。修订后的《国民经济行业分类》(GB/T4754-2011)共有门类 20 个，大类 96 个，中类 432 个，小类 1094 个。

企业(单位)登记注册类型 是以在工商行政管理机关登记注册的各类企业为划分对象，以工商行政管理部门对企业登记注册的类型为依据，将企业登记注册类型分为内资企业、港澳台商投资企业和外商投资企业三大类。内资企业包括国有企业、集体企业、股份合作企业、联营企业、有限责任公司、股份有限公司、私营公司和其他企业；港澳台商投资企业和外商投资企业分别包括合资经营企业、合作经营企业、独资经营企业和股份有限公司等。对不在工商行政管理部门进行登记注册的行政机关、事业单位和社会团体，主要按其经费来源和管理方式进行划分。

国有企业 指企业全部资产归国家所有，并按《中华人民共和国企业法人登记管理条例》规定登记注册的非公司制的经济组织。不包括有限责任公司中的国有独资公司。

集体企业 指企业资产归集体所有，并按《中华人民共和国企业法人登记管理条例》规定登记注册的经济组织。

股份合作企业 指以合作制为基础，由企业职工共同出资入股，吸收一定比例的社会资产投资组建，实行自主经营，自负盈亏，共同劳动，民主管理，按劳分配与按股分红相结合的一种集体经济组织。

联营企业 指两个及两个以上相同或不同所有制性质的企业法人或事业单位法人，按自愿、平等、互利的原则，共同投资组成的经济组织。联营企业包括国有联营企业、集体联营企业、国有与集体联营企业和其他联营企业。

有限责任公司 指根据《中华人民共和国公司登记管理条例》规定登记注册，由两个以上、五十个以下的股东共同出资，每个股东以其所认缴的出资额对公司承担有限责任，公司以其全部资产对其债务承担责任的经济组织。有限责任公司包括国有独资公司以及其他有限责任公司。

股份有限公司 指根据《中华人民共和国公司登记管理条例》规定登记注册，其全部注册资本由等额股份构成并通过发行股票筹集资本，股东以其认购的股份对公司承担有限责任，公司以其全部资产对其债务承担责任的经济组织。

私营企业 指由自然人投资设立或由自然人控股，以雇佣劳动为基础的营利性经济组织。包括按照《公司法》、《合伙企业法》、《私营企业暂行条例》规定登记注册的私营有限责任公司、私营股份有限公司、私营合伙企业和私营独资企业。

其他企业 指上述企业之外的其他内资经济组织。

合资经营企业 (港或澳、台商) 指港澳台地区投资者与内地的企业依照《中华人民共和国中外合资经营企业法》及有关法律的规定，按合同规定的比例投资设立、分享利润和分担风险的企业。

合作经营企业 (港或澳、台资) 指港澳台地区投资者与内地企业依照《中华人民共和国中外合作经营企业法》及有关法律的规定，依照合作合同的约定进行投资或提供条件设立、分配利润和分担风险的企业。

港澳台商独资经营企业 指依照《中华人民共和国外资企业法》及有关法律的规定，在内地由港澳台地区投资者全额投资设立的企业。

港澳台商投资股份有限公司 指根据国家有关规定，经原外经贸部依法批准设立，其中港、澳、台商的股本占公司注册资本的比例达 25% 以上的股份有限公司。凡其中港、澳、台商的股本占公司注册资本的比例小于 25%的，属于内资企业中的股份有限公司。

其他港澳台商投资企业 指在中国境内参照《外国企业或个人在中国境内设立合伙企业管理办法》和《外商投资合伙企业登记管理规定》，依法设立的港、澳、台商投资合伙企业等。

中外合资经营企业 指外国企业或外国人与中国内地企业依照《中华人民共和国中外合资经营企业法》及有关法律的规定，按合同规定的比例投资设立、分享利润和分担风险的企业。

中外合作经营企业 指外国企业或外国人与中国内地企业依照《中华人民共和国中外合作经营企业法》及有关法律的规定，依照合作合同的约定进行投资或提供条件设立、分配利润和分担风险的企业。

外资企业 指依照《中华人民共和国外资企业法》及有关法律的规定，在中国内地由外国投资者全额投资设立的企业。

外商投资股份有限公司 指根据国家有关规定，经商务部依法批准设立，并且其中外资的股本占公司注册资本的比例达 25% 以上的股份有限公司。凡其中外资股本占公司注册资本的比例小于 25%的，属于内资中的股份有限公司。

其他外商投资企业 指在中国境内依照《外国企业或个人在中国境内设立合伙企业管理办法》和《外商投资合伙企业登记管理规定》，依法设立的外商投资合伙企业等。

行政机关、事业单位和社会团体 参照企业登记注册类型，主要按其经费来源和管理方式划分。具体规定如下：

(1)行政机关：包括国家机关和政党机关，原则上均列为“国有”。但有特殊规定的，如供销社等，则列为“集体”。

(2)事业单位：包括经国家机构编制部门和有关业务主管部门批准成立的各类事业单位，不包括实行企业化管理的事业单位。事业单位的划分办法如下：

①由国家财政预算拨款或列入财政预算外资金管理以及经费主要来源于国有主管部门或国有上级单位的事业单位，列为“国有”。

②经费主要来源于集体单位的事业单位，列为“集体”。

③公民个人(或个人合伙)开办的事业单位，列为“私营”。

④上述以外的其他事业单位，如果其经费来源不明确，按管理方式进行归类。

(3)社会团体：包括经民政部门批准成立以及未纳入社会团体管理条例范围的工会、妇联等各类社会团体。社会团体的划分办法如下：

①未纳入民政部社会团体管理条例范围的工会、妇联、共青团、青联、工商联、科协、侨联等社会团体，国家拨款设立的基金会或基金管理组织以及经费主要来源于国有业务主管部门或国有上级单位的社会团体，列为“国有”。

②经费主要来源于集体单位的社会团体，列为“集体”。

③公民个人(或个人合伙)开办的社会团体，划为“私营”。

④上述以外的其他社会团体，如果其经费来源不明确，改按管理方式进行归类。

各个计划时期 表内所用各个“时期”代表的年份如下：恢复时期为 1950 到 1952 年；第一个五年计划时期(简称“一五”时期)为 1953 到 1957 年；第二个五年计划时期(简称“二五”时期)为 1958 到 1962 年；第三个五年计划时期(简称“三五”时期)为 1966 到 1970 年；第四个五年计划时期(简称“四五”时期)为 1971 到 1975 年；第五个五年计划时期(简称“五五”时期)为 1976 到 1980 年；第六个五年计划时期(简称“六五”时期)为 1981 到 1985 年；第七个五年计划时期(简称“七五”时期)为 1986 到 1990 年；第八个五年计划时期(简称“八五”时期)为 1991 到 1995 年；第九个五年计划时期(简称“九五”时期)为 1996 到 2000 年；第十个五年计划时期(简称“十五”时期)为 2001 到 2005 年；第十一个五年计划时期(简称“十一五”时期)为 2006 到 2010 年；第十二个五年计划时期（简称“十二五”时期）为 2011 到 2015 年；第十三个五年计划时期（简称“十三五”时期）为 2016 到 2020 年。

法人单位 指具备：

(1)依法成立、有自己的名称、组织机构和场所、能够独立承担民事责任；

(2)独立拥有和使用（或授权使用）资产、承担负债、有权与其它单位签订合同；

(3)会计上独立核算、能够编制资产负债表。法人单位包括企业法人、事业单位法人、机关法人、社会团体法人和其他法人。

单产业法人 指只在一个地点，主要从事一种生产经营活动的法人单位。

多产业法人 指坐落于两个及两个以上地点、或主要从事两种及两种以上生产经营活动的，按照单位划分规定可以划分为两个或两个以上产业活动单位的法人单位。

产业活动单位 是法人单位的附属单位。产业活动单位应具备下列条件：

(1)在一个场所从事一种或主要从事一种社会经济活动；

(2)相对独立组织生产经营和业务活动；

(3)能够掌握收入和支出等业务核算资料。

服务业 指生产和销售产品的生产部门和企业的集合。在国民经济核算中，将服务业视同为第三产业，即除农业、工业、建筑业以外的其它所有产业部门。

Explanatory Notes on Main Statistical Indicators

Divisions of Administrative Areas refer to the division of administrative areas by the State. The relative laws stipulate that 1) the whole country is divided into provinces, autonomous regions and municipalities directly under the Central Government; 2) provinces and autonomous regions are further divided into autonomous prefectures, counties, autonomous counties and cities; 3) autonomous prefectures are further divided into counties, autonomous counties and cities; 4) counties and autonomous counties are further divided into townships, ethnic townships and towns; 5) municipalities directly under the Central Government and large cities are divided into districts and counties, 6) the State shall, when necessary, establish special administrative regions.

Average Annual Growth Rate shows the average growth rate of social and economic development during a longer period. It can not be directly calculated by chain based growth rate. The relation is:

Average Annual Growth Rate = Average Speed of Development – 1

Average speed of development is the time series average of speed which calculated by chain based. Because the reference bases during the different periods are not same, average speed of development can not be calculated by the general method. Level approach and accumulative approach for calculating average speed of development rate are applied. The "level approach", or the method of calculating the geometric average, is derived by the formula of geometric average of the chain-based speeds of development, or comparing the level of the last year of the interval with that of the beginning year; the other is called the "accumulative approach" or the "algebraic average", "equation" method, which is derived by the summation of the actual figure of each year in the interval divided by the figure in the base year. The level approach focuses on the level of the last year, while the accumulative approach emphasizes the aggregate development in the duration.

The average annual growth rates listed in this statistical yearbook are calculated by level approach. The base years are not listed when the years are listed for average annual growth rates. For instance,the average annual growth rate of 2011-2015 is listed as average annual growth rate of 2011-2015 without listing the base year 2010.

Industrial Classification of the National Economy The new Industrial Classification of the National Economy (GB/T 4754-2011) is introduced starting from the compilation of 2012 annual statistics. The revision, based on the 2002 classification, was organized by the National Bureau of Statistics taking into consideration of the International Standards of the Industrial Classification of All Economic Activities (ISIC/Rev.4) of the United Nations. The new Classification was promulgated by the National Administration of Quality Supervision, Inspection and Quarantine and the Standardization Administration of the People's Republic of China on April 29, 2011. The revised version of the Industrial Classification of the National Economy (GB/T 4754-2012) is composed of 20 sections, 96 divisions, 432 groups and 1094 classes.

Registration Status of Enterprises (Units) Enterprises are classified into 3 categories, namely domestic-funded enterprises, enterprises with investment from Hong Kong, Macao and Taiwan, and enterprises with foreign investment, according to the registration status of an enterprise in industrial and commercial administration agencies. Domestic-funded enterprises include State-owned enterprises, collective-owned enterprises, cooperative enterprises, joint ownership enterprises, limited liability corporations, share-holding corporations Ltd., private enterprises and other enterprises. Included in the enterprises with investment from Hong Kong, Macao and Taiwan and enterprises with foreign investment are joint-venture enterprises, cooperative enterprises, sole investment enterprises and share-holding corporations Ltd. For government agencies, institutions and social organizations which are not registered in industrial and commercial administration agencies, they are classified mainly by their sources of funding and manner of management.

State-owned Enterprises refer to non-corporation economic units where the entire assets are owned by the state and which have been registered in accordance with the Regulation of the People's Republic of China on the Management of Registration of Corporate Enterprises. Not included from this category are solely state-funded corporations in the limited liability corporations.

Collective-owned Enterprises refer to economic units where the assets are owned collectively and which have been registered in accordance with the Regulation of the People's Republic of China on the Management of Registration of Corporate Enterprises.

Cooperative Enterprises refer to a form of collective economic units (enterprises) where capitals come mainly from employees as their shares, with certain proportion of capital from the outside, where production is organized on the basis of independent operation, independent accounting for profits and losses, joint work, democratic management, and a distribution

system that integrates remuneration according to work with dividend according to capital share.

Joint Ownership Enterprises refer to economic units established by two or more corporate enterprises or corporate institutions of the same or different ownership, through joint investment on the basis of voluntary participation , equality, and mutual benefits. They include State joint ownership enterprises; collective joint ownership enterprises; joint State-collective enterprises; and other joint ownership enterprises.

Limited Liability Corporations refer to economic units established with investment from 2-50 investors and registered in accordance with the Regulation of the People's Republic of China on the Management of Registration of Corporations, each investor bearing limited liability to the corporation depending on its share of investment, and the corporation bearing liability to its debt to the maximum of its total assets. Limited liability corporations include exclusive state-funded limited liability corporations and other limited liability corporations.

Share-holding Corporations Ltd. refer to economic units registered in accordance with the Regulation of the People's Republic of China on the Management of Registration of Corporations, with total registered capitals divided into equal shares and raised through issuing stocks. Each investor bears limited liability to the corporation depending on the holding of shares, and the corporation bears liability to its debt to the maximum of its total assets.

Private Enterprises refer to profit-making economic units invested and established by natural persons, or controlled by natural persons using employed labour. Included in this category are private limited liability corporations, private share-holding corporations Ltd., private partnership enterprises and private-funded enterprises registered in accordance with the Company Law, the Law on Partnership Business and Interim Regulations on Private Enterprises.

Other Domestic-funded Enterprises refer to domestic-funded economic units other than those mentioned above.

Joint Venture Enterprises(Funds are from Hong Kong, Macao or Taiwan .) are enterprises established by investors from Hong Kong, Macao and Taiwan with enterprises in the mainland of China in accordance with the Law of the People's Republic of China on Sino-foreign Equity Joint Ventures and other relevant laws, where the establishment of the investment and the sharing of profits and risks are stipulated under joint venture contracts.

Cooperative Enterprises(Funds are from Hong Kong ,Macao orTaiwan .) established by investors from Hong Kong, Macao and Taiwan with enterprises in the mainland of China in accordance with the Law of the People's Republic of China on Sino-foreign Contractual Joint Venture and other relevant laws, where the investment or provision of facilities and the sharing of profits and risks are stipulated under cooperative contracts.

Enterprises with Sole (exclusive) Investment from Hong Kong, Macao and Taiwan refer to enterprises established in the mainland of China with exclusive investment from investors from Hong Kong, Macao and Taiwan in accordance with the Law of the People's Republic of China on *Wholly Foreign-owned Enterprises* and other relevant laws.

Share-holding Corporations Ltd. with Investment from Hong Kong, Macao and Taiwan refer to share-holding corporations Ltd. established with the approval from the former Ministry of Foreign Trade and Economic Relations in line with relevant State regulations, where the share of investment from Hong Kong, Macao or Taiwan businessmen exceeds 25% of the total registered capital of the corporation. In case the share of investment from Hong Kong, Macao or Taiwan is less than 25% of the total registered capital, the enterprise is to be classified as domestic-funded share-holding corporation Ltd.

Other Enterprises with Funds are from Hong Kong ,Macao and Taiwan refer to partnership enterprises with investment from Hong Kong, Macao and Taiwan established within the territory of China in accordance with Administrative Measures on the Establishment of Partnership Enterprises in China by Foreign Enterprises or Foreign Individuals and Regulations for the Administration of the Registration of Foreign-invested Partnership Enterprises.

Joint Venture Enterprises with Foreign Investment refer to enterprises jointly established by foreign enterprises or foreigners with enterprises in the mainland of China in accordance with the Law of the People's Republic of China on Sino-foreign Equity Joint Ventures and other relevant laws, where the sharing of investment, profits and risks is stipulated under contract.

Cooperative Enterprises with Foreign Investment refer to enterprises jointly established by foreign enterprises or foreigners with enterprises in the mainland of China in accordance with the Law of the People's Republic of China on Sino-foreign *Contractual Joint Venture* and other relevant laws, where the investment or provision of facilities and the sharing of profits and risks are stipulated under cooperative contracts.

Enterprises with Sole (exclusive) Foreign Investment refer to enterprises established in the mainland of China with exclusive investment from foreign investors in accordance with the Law of the People's Republic of China on Wholly Foreign-owned Enterprises and other relevant laws.

Share-holding Corporations Ltd. with Foreign Investment refer to share-holding corporations Ltd. established with the approval from the former Ministry of Foreign Trade and Economic Relations in line with relevant State regulations, where the share of investment from foreign investors exceeds 25% of the total registered capital of the corporation. In case the share of foreign investment is less than 25% of the total registered capital, the enterprise is to be classified as domestic-funded share-holding corporation Ltd.

Other Enterprises with Foreign Funds refer to partnership enterprises established within the territory of China in accordance with Administrative Measures on the Establishment of Partnership Enterprises in China by Foreign Enterprises or Foreign Individuals and Regulations for the Administration of the Registration of Foreign-invested Partnership Enterprises.

Government Agencies, Institutions and Social Organizations are classified into the following categories by source of funds and manner of management taking reference of the registration status of enterprises:

(1) Government agencies: include State and party agencies, classified in principle as State-owned. There are exceptions, such as supply and marketing cooperatives which are classified as collective-owned.

(2) Institutions: include institutions of various types established with the approval by organization and staffing departments of the government, but exclude institutions where enterprise management system is introduced. Institutions are further classified as follows:

(a) Institutions for which their main budgets are from government budget appropriations or extra-budget funds, or allocated from the budget of their competent government agencies. Such institutions are classified as state-owned.

(b) Institutions for which their budget mainly come from collective units. Such institutions are classified as collective-owned.

(c) Social institutions established by individual or a group of citizens, which are classified as private.

(d) Institutions other than those mentioned above for which their sources of budget are not clear. Such institutions are classified by the manner of management.

(3) Social organizations: include social organizations established with the approval from the Ministry of Civil Affairs, and organizations that are not covered by social organization management regulations such as trades unions, women's federations etc.. Social organizations are further classified as follows:

(a) Social organizations that are not covered by social organization management regulations of the Ministry of Civil Affairs such as trades unions, women federations, communist youth leagues, youth associations, industrial and commerce associations, scicntists associations, overseas Chinese associations, etc.foundations and fund management organizations established with funds from the state, and social organizations whose funds mainly come from the budget of their competent government agencies. Such institutions are classified as state-owned.

(b) Social organizations for which their budget mainly come from collective units. Such institutions are classified as collective-owned.

(c) Social organizations established by individual or a group of citizens, which are classified as private.

(d) Social organizations other than those mentioned above for whose their source of budget is not clear. Such organizations are classified by the manner of management.

Each Plan Period recovery period refer to 1950-1952;the first five-year plan refer to 1953-1957;the second five-year plan refer to 1958-1962;the third five-year plan refer to 1966-1970;the fourth five-year plan refer to 1971-1975; the fifth five-yaer plan refer to 1976-1980;the sixth five-year plan refer to 1981-1985;the seventh five-yaer plan refer to 1986-1990;the eighth five-yaer plan refer to 1991-1995;the ninth five-year plan refer to 1996-2000;the tenth five-year plan refer to 2001-2005;the eleventh five-year plan refer to 2006-2010; the twelvth five-yaer plan refer to 2011-2015; the thirteenth five-yaer plan refer to 2010-2020.

Legal person units refer to unit that have following conditions:

(1) legally Estabilished,have own name,organization,location and can undertake a civil case responsibility independently by law.

(2) independently own and use (or authorizable usage)a property,undertake liabilities and can make a bargain with other units.

(3) can independently account and workout balance sheet.artificial person unit Includes business artificial person,artifial person organization,artifial person,meeting group artificial person and other.

Single sector legal person refer to the unit that have only one location and be engaged in one kind of production mangement activity.

Multi-sector legal person refer to the unit that have 2 or above 2 locations,or mainly be engaged in 2 kinds or above 2 kinds of production management activity,and who can be diviede 2 or above 2 establishment units.

Industrial activity unit refer to the subsidiary unit of legal person unit.It should have following conditions:

(1) Be engaged in only one kind of social economic activities in excusive conditon.

(2) Opposite independtly organize management and business activity.

(3) Predominate data of business,such as income and expenditure ect.

Service refer to the enterprises and prodution department for production and selling the products.In the national economy accounting,service is regarded as the third industry,other said that refers to all sectors except agriculture,industry and construction.

2 国民经济核算

NATIONAL ACCOUNTS

第二篇 国民经济核算

本篇主要内容和资料来源

国民经济核算篇资料主要包括新疆维吾尔自治区主要年份生产总值的绝对值、构成和指数，居民消费水平，各地、州、市、县生产总值、构成和指数等资料。本篇资料由新疆维吾尔自治区统计局国民经济核算处根据不同产业部门、不同支出构成的特点和资料来源，严格按照国家国民经济核算制度计算。

根据自治区第三次全国经济普查结果,对2013年新疆生产总值数据进行了调整。

本篇所列分地、州（市）、县的数据来自各地、州（市）、县统计局的国民经济核算资料，由于采用分级核算，各地区数据相加不等于全疆总计，地区所辖县、市数据相加不等于地区合计。

本篇中人均地区生产总值按年平均常住人口计算。

National Accounts

Main Content and Source of Data

Statistics on national accounts include mainly gross domestic product of Xinjiang Bureau of Statistics, it' s composition and indices of gross domestic product, household consumption level, composition and indices of gross domestic product by prefecture, autonomous prefecture, city and county. Data on GDP are calculated by the Department of National Accounts Statistics of the Xinjiang Bureau of Statistics with various approaches in the light of the features of various sectors, various expenditure structures and the data sources and National Accounts system.

According to the results of the Third National Economy Census in the autonomous region, the total production value of Xinjiang in 2013 was adjusted.

Data on the table come from national accounts statistics by prefecture, autonomous prefecture, city and county. Due to the adoption of hierarchical accounting, regional data do not add up to a total area of Xinjiang, under the jurisdiction of county, city is not equal to the sum of the data region total.

Per-capita Gross Domestic Product are calculated at annual permanent population.

2-1 1978-2015 年历年新疆生产总值
Gross Domestic Product in Xinjiang(1978-2015)

单位：亿元 (100 million yuan)

年 份 Year	新疆生产总值 Gross Domestic Product	第一产业 Primary Industry	第二产业 Secondary Industry	第三产业 Tertiary Industry	#工 业 Industry	#建筑业 Construction	#交通运输仓储和邮政业 Transport, Storage and Post	#批发和零售业 Wholesale and Retail Trades	人均新疆生产总值(元) Per Capita GDP (yuan)
1978	39.07	13.97	18.35	6.75	14.48	3.87	1.19	2.07	313
1979	45.63	16.32	21.43	7.88	17.16	4.27	1.52	2.34	359
1980	53.24	21.53	21.44	10.27	17.48	3.96	1.91	2.91	410
1981	59.41	25.18	22.39	11.84	17.93	4.46	2.25	3.41	450
1982	65.24	28.11	23.35	13.78	18.66	4.69	2.53	3.84	488
1983	78.55	32.84	29.10	16.61	23.33	5.77	3.01	4.75	583
1984	89.75	36.68	31.65	21.42	25.45	6.20	4.01	6.29	661
1985	112.24	42.89	40.50	28.85	32.14	8.36	4.59	8.97	820
1986	129.04	46.00	45.63	37.41	36.79	8.84	5.98	10.48	924
1987	148.50	56.18	50.30	42.02	41.16	9.14	7.73	12.45	1053
1988	192.72	72.27	66.02	54.43	53.53	12.49	11.60	16.11	1347
1989	217.29	78.01	73.83	65.45	60.21	13.62	12.90	17.59	1493
1990	274.01	94.62	83.50	95.89	68.09	15.41	19.73	27.70	1799
1991	335.91	111.86	107.99	116.06	84.07	23.92	22.63	36.88	2101
1992	402.31	114.50	147.64	140.17	106.29	41.35	28.32	39.85	2477
1993	495.25	126.85	205.07	163.33	155.92	49.15	32.58	43.46	2964
1994	662.32	187.69	249.11	225.52	190.00	59.11	44.40	57.67	3888
1995	814.85	240.71	283.97	290.17	219.01	64.96	59.63	73.78	4701
1996	900.93	249.31	313.70	337.92	239.07	74.63	73.74	87.25	5102
1997	1039.85	279.73	385.37	374.75	302.50	82.87	85.70	94.23	5848
1998	1106.95	291.05	395.75	420.15	298.53	97.22	106.87	98.06	6174
1999	1163.17	268.51	420.48	474.18	315.86	104.62	129.60	102.26	6443
2000	1363.56	288.18	537.58	537.80	418.63	118.95	148.63	110.10	7372
2001	1491.60	288.12	573.91	629.57	445.60	128.31	148.38	118.45	7945
2002	1612.65	305.00	603.15	704.50	463.59	139.56	168.58	123.88	8457
2003	1886.35	412.90	719.54	753.91	563.57	155.97	159.43	141.32	9828
2004	2209.09	446.13	914.47	848.49	734.10	180.37	186.70	160.30	11337
2005	2604.14	510.00	1164.80	929.34	961.62	203.18	149.61	145.10	13108
2006	3045.26	527.80	1459.30	1058.16	1241.33	217.97	165.60	163.15	15000
2007	3523.16	628.72	1647.55	1246.89	1405.11	242.44	177.28	187.10	16999
2008	4183.21	691.07	2070.76	1421.38	1755.35	315.41	191.84	222.74	19797
2009	4277.05	759.74	1929.59	1587.72	1555.84	373.75	209.10	253.60	19942
2010	5437.47	1078.63	2592.15	1766.69	2161.39	430.76	222.47	276.28	25034
2011	6610.05	1139.03	3225.90	2245.12	2700.20	525.70	256.72	371.90	30087
2012	7505.31	1290.42	3394.50	2820.39	2841.57	631.50	357.90	426.65	33796
2013	8443.84	1434.83	3574.88	3434.13	2925.74	750.33	386.97	559.01	37553
2014	9273.46	1538.60	3948.96	3785.90	3179.60	867.54	480.44	550.67	40648
2015	9324.80	1559.08	3596.40	4169.32	2740.71	959.03	536.06	523.58	40036

注：1.根据自治区第六次全国人口普查结果,对 2010 年人均新疆生产总值数据进行了调整。2.2012 年及以后年份的新疆生产总值行业分类执行《国民经济行业分类》(GB/T 4754-2011)，产业分类执行《三次产业划分规定》(国统字 (2012) 108 号)。(下表同)

Note: a)According to the results of the sixth national population census of 2010,per capita GDP of Xinjiang data were adjusted. b)Since 2012,the data of gross domestic product classified by the Classification of National Economy of Sector (GB/T4754-2011),industry classification adopted by the Regulation of the Three Industrial Division [National Statistics (2012)108]. (the following table)

2-2 1978-2015 年历年新疆生产总值构成
Composition of Gross Domestic Product in Xinjiang(1978-2015)

单位：% (%)

年 份 Year	新疆生产总值构成 Composition of Gross Domestic Product	第一产业 Primary Industry	第二产业 Secondary Industry	第三产业 Tertiary Industry	#工 业 Industry	#建筑业 Construction	#交通运输仓储和邮政业 Transport, Storage and Post	#批发和零售业 Wholesale and Retail Trades
1978	100	35.8	47.0	17.2	37.1	9.9	3.0	5.3
1979	100	35.7	47.0	17.3	37.6	9.4	3.3	5.1
1980	100	40.4	40.3	19.3	32.9	7.4	3.6	5.5
1981	100	42.4	37.7	19.9	30.2	7.5	3.8	5.7
1982	100	43.1	35.8	21.1	28.6	7.2	3.9	5.9
1983	100	41.8	37.1	21.1	29.8	7.3	3.8	6.0
1984	100	40.9	35.2	23.9	28.3	6.9	4.5	7.0
1985	100	38.2	36.1	25.7	28.7	7.4	4.1	8.0
1986	100	35.6	35.4	29.0	28.5	6.9	4.6	8.1
1987	100	37.8	33.9	28.3	27.7	6.2	5.2	8.4
1988	100	37.5	34.3	28.2	27.8	6.5	6.0	8.4
1989	100	35.9	34.0	30.1	27.7	6.3	5.9	8.1
1990	100	34.5	30.5	35.0	24.8	5.6	7.2	10.1
1991	100	33.3	32.1	34.6	25.0	7.1	6.7	11.0
1992	100	28.5	36.7	34.8	26.4	10.3	7.0	9.9
1993	100	25.6	41.4	33.0	31.5	9.9	6.6	8.8
1994	100	28.3	37.6	34.1	28.7	8.9	6.7	8.7
1995	100	29.5	34.9	35.6	26.9	8.0	7.3	9.1
1996	100	27.7	34.8	37.5	26.5	8.3	8.2	9.7
1997	100	26.9	37.1	36.0	29.1	8.0	8.2	9.1
1998	100	26.3	35.7	38.0	27.0	8.7	9.7	8.9
1999	100	23.1	36.1	40.8	27.1	9.0	11.1	8.8
2000	100	21.1	39.4	39.5	30.7	8.7	10.9	8.1
2001	100	19.3	38.5	42.2	29.9	8.6	9.9	7.9
2002	100	18.9	37.4	43.7	28.7	8.7	10.5	7.7
2003	100	21.9	38.1	40.0	29.8	8.3	8.5	7.5
2004	100	20.2	41.4	38.4	33.2	8.2	8.5	7.3
2005	100	19.6	44.7	35.7	36.9	7.8	5.7	5.6
2006	100	17.3	47.9	34.8	40.7	7.2	5.4	5.4
2007	100	17.8	46.8	35.4	39.9	6.9	5.0	5.3
2008	100	16.5	49.5	34.0	42.0	7.5	4.6	5.3
2009	100	17.8	45.1	37.1	36.4	8.7	4.9	5.9
2010	100	19.8	47.7	32.5	39.8	7.9	4.1	5.1
2011	100	17.2	48.8	34.0	40.8	8.0	3.9	5.6
2012	100	17.2	45.2	37.6	37.9	8.4	4.8	5.7
2013	100	17.0	42.3	40.7	34.6	8.9	4.6	6.6
2014	100	16.6	42.6	40.8	34.3	9.4	5.2	5.9
2015	100	16.7	38.6	44.7	29.4	10.3	5.7	5.6

注：本表按当年价格计算。
Note: Data in value terms in this table are calculated at current prices.

2-3 1978-2015 年历年新疆生产总值指数

Indices of Gross Domestic Product in Xinjiang(1978-2015)

(上年=100) (preceding year=100)

年份 Year	新疆生产总值 Gross Domestic Product	第一产业 Primary Industry	第二产业 Secondary Industry	第三产业 Tertiary Industry	#工业 Industry	#建筑业 Construction	#交通运输仓储和邮政业 Transport, Storage and Post	#批发和零售业 Wholesale and Retail Trades	人均新疆生产总值 Per Capita GDP
1978	109.8	110.2	110.3	107.2	112.8	101.8	102.1	109.3	106.9
1979	112.4	109.8	111.5	120.8	111.2	112.6	121.6	117.5	110.2
1980	107.3	106.0	105.2	116.6	108.5	93.1	115.6	125.5	105.0
1981	108.5	115.2	99.3	113.4	99.1	100.3	119.4	117.9	106.6
1982	109.9	111.2	104.3	117.1	104.6	102.8	118.9	119.8	108.5
1983	113.5	112.1	111.9	118.7	112.4	109.8	113.3	108.8	112.5
1984	114.1	113.6	114.7	114.0	115.1	112.9	100.0	109.2	113.2
1985	116.9	112.9	116.6	125.0	116.1	119.0	100.3	126.6	115.9
1986	111.7	108.3	109.5	120.7	111.0	102.5	124.7	110.0	109.2
1987	110.0	110.7	105.6	114.7	108.5	91.4	119.3	111.0	108.7
1988	109.6	103.3	114.6	112.9	113.6	120.2	118.8	114.7	108.0
1989	106.1	101.8	105.0	113.5	106.9	94.5	112.7	107.5	104.1
1990	111.7	116.0	106.7	112.0	106.4	108.6	106.7	104.5	106.8
1991	114.4	111.2	117.0	115.7	113.1	140.6	128.8	101.6	109.0
1992	113.1	105.5	119.4	115.7	112.6	152.8	124.6	112.6	111.3
1993	110.2	101.1	113.3	117.7	111.4	120.3	118.3	121.3	106.9
1994	112.1	111.2	110.2	115.3	111.3	106.3	109.7	105.6	110.2
1995	109.1	104.9	111.5	110.9	113.3	105.0	119.5	108.9	107.4
1996	106.5	103.5	107.8	108.0	107.4	109.5	113.0	109.6	104.5
1997	108.4	110.8	105.2	109.7	103.4	112.0	119.6	105.8	107.6
1998	107.5	107.2	105.7	109.6	103.0	115.0	117.5	104.9	106.6
1999	107.4	102.7	106.8	112.3	106.5	107.7	114.7	107.9	106.6
2000	108.7	104.8	108.6	112.1	109.1	107.3	114.4	109.6	106.2
2001	108.6	102.8	108.1	112.1	107.8	109.0	109.5	105.0	107.0
2002	108.2	105.0	107.4	110.4	107.7	106.3	114.3	110.3	106.5
2003	111.2	108.2	111.6	112.3	111.2	112.8	115.1	110.9	110.5
2004	111.4	105.7	114.0	111.5	114.5	112.2	115.1	112.6	109.7
2005	110.9	106.5	114.4	109.4	115.7	109.7	109.0	111.9	108.8
2006	111.0	105.7	111.2	113.6	112.5	105.0	107.2	110.5	108.7
2007	112.2	107.1	112.7	114.3	114.1	105.4	106.1	109.1	109.9
2008	111.0	106.4	114.3	109.2	114.3	114.1	108.7	110.3	108.9
2009	108.1	104.5	108.5	109.2	106.2	120.9	107.0	113.4	106.5
2010	110.6	104.5	112.6	110.8	113.5	108.3	107.9	108.3	109.3
2011	112.0	106.5	112.0	115.2	111.4	115.0	117.3	116.6	110.7
2012	112.0	107.0	113.1	113.1	112.7	118.2	124.1	107.8	110.8
2013	111.0	106.9	112.5	110.9	112.0	117.2	111.8	108.8	109.6
2014	110.0	105.9	111.2	110.4	110.0	115.3	116.1	97.1	108.4
2015	108.8	105.9	107.3	112.2	105.8	113.1	114.1	103.2	106.6

注：本表按可比价计算。

Note: Data in this table are calculated at constant prices.

2-4 1978-2015 年历年新疆生产总值指数
Indices of Gross Domestic Product in Xinjiang(1978-2015)

(1978 年=100)

年 份 Year	新疆生产总值 Gross Domestic Product	第一产业 Primary Industry	第二产业 Secondary Industry	第三产业 Tertiary Industry	#工 业 Industry	#建筑业 Construction	#交通运输仓储和邮政业 Transport, Storage and Post	#批发和零售业 Wholesale and Retail Trades	人均新疆生产总值 Per Capita GDP
1978	100	100	100	100	100	100	100	100	100
1979	112.4	109.8	111.5	120.8	111.2	112.6	121.6	117.5	110.2
1980	120.6	116.4	117.3	140.9	120.7	104.8	140.6	147.5	115.7
1981	130.9	134.1	116.5	159.8	119.6	105.1	167.9	173.9	123.3
1982	143.9	149.1	121.5	187.1	125.1	108.0	199.6	208.3	133.8
1983	163.3	167.1	136.0	222.1	140.6	118.6	226.1	226.6	150.6
1984	186.3	189.8	156.0	253.2	161.8	133.9	226.1	247.4	170.4
1985	217.8	214.3	181.9	316.5	187.8	159.3	226.8	313.2	197.5
1986	243.3	232.1	199.2	382.0	208.5	163.3	282.8	344.5	215.7
1987	267.6	256.9	210.4	438.2	226.2	149.3	337.4	382.4	234.5
1988	293.3	265.4	241.1	494.7	257.0	179.5	400.8	438.6	253.2
1989	311.2	270.2	253.2	561.5	274.7	169.6	451.7	471.5	263.6
1990	347.6	313.4	270.2	628.9	292.3	184.2	482.0	492.7	281.5
1991	397.7	348.5	316.1	727.6	330.6	259.0	620.8	500.6	306.9
1992	449.8	367.7	377.4	841.8	372.3	395.8	773.5	563.7	341.6
1993	495.7	371.7	427.6	990.8	414.7	476.1	915.1	683.8	365.1
1994	555.7	413.3	471.2	1142.4	461.6	506.1	1003.9	722.1	402.4
1995	606.3	433.6	525.4	1266.9	523.0	531.4	1199.7	786.4	432.1
1996	645.7	448.8	566.4	1368.3	561.7	581.9	1355.7	861.9	451.6
1997	699.9	497.3	595.9	1501.0	580.8	651.7	1621.4	911.9	485.9
1998	752.4	533.1	629.9	1645.1	598.2	749.5	1905.1	956.6	518.0
1999	808.1	547.5	672.7	1847.4	637.1	807.2	2185.1	1032.2	552.2
2000	878.4	573.8	730.6	2070.9	695.1	866.1	2499.8	1131.3	586.4
2001	953.9	589.9	789.8	2321.5	749.3	944.0	2737.3	1187.9	627.4
2002	1032.1	619.4	848.2	2562.9	807.0	1003.5	3128.7	1310.3	668.2
2003	1147.7	670.2	946.6	2878.1	897.4	1131.9	3601.1	1453.1	738.4
2004	1278.5	708.4	1079.1	3209.1	1027.5	1270.0	4144.9	1636.2	810.0
2005	1417.9	754.4	1234.5	3510.8	1188.8	1393.2	4517.9	1830.9	881.3
2006	1573.9	797.4	1372.8	3988.3	1337.4	1462.9	4843.2	2023.1	958.0
2007	1765.9	854.0	1547.1	4558.6	1526.0	1541.9	5138.6	2207.2	1052.8
2008	1960.1	908.7	1768.3	4978.0	1744.2	1759.3	5585.7	2434.5	1146.5
2009	2118.9	949.5	1918.6	5436.0	1852.4	2127.0	5976.7	2760.8	1221.0
2010	2343.5	992.2	2160.3	6023.1	2102.5	2303.5	6448.9	2989.9	1334.6
2011	2624.7	1056.7	2419.5	6938.6	2342.2	2649.0	7564.6	3486.2	1477.4
2012	2939.7	1130.7	2751.0	7792.0	2639.7	3131.1	9387.7	3758.1	1637.0
2013	3263.1	1208.7	3094.9	8641.3	2956.5	3669.6	10495.4	4088.8	1794.2
2014	3589.4	1280.0	3441.5	9540.0	3252.2	4231.0	12185.2	3970.2	1944.9
2015	3905.3	1355.5	3692.7	10703.9	3440.8	4785.3	13903.3	4097.2	2073.3

注：本表按可比价计算。
Note: Data in this table are calculated at constant prices.

2-5 分行业新疆生产总值
Gross Domestic Product by Sector in Xinjiang

指　标	Item	增加值(亿元) Added Value (100 million yuan)		构　成(%) Composition (%)		指数(上年=100) Indices (preceding year=100)	
		2014	2015	2014	2015	2014	2015
新疆生产总值	**Gross Domestic Product**	**9273.46**	**9324.80**	**100**	**100**	**110.0**	**108.8**
按产业分	**By Industry**						
第一产业	Primary Industry	1538.60	1559.08	16.6	16.7	105.9	105.9
第二产业	Secondary Industry	3948.96	3596.40	42.6	38.6	111.2	107.3
第三产业	Tertiary Industry	3785.90	4169.32	40.8	44.7	110.4	112.2
按行业分	**By Sector**						
工　业	Industry	3179.60	2740.71	34.3	29.4	110.0	105.8
建筑业	Construction	867.54	959.03	9.4	10.3	115.3	113.1
交通运输、仓储和邮政业	Transport, storage and Post	480.44	536.06	5.2	5.7	116.1	114.1
批发和零售业	Wholesale and Retail Trades	550.67	523.58	5.9	5.6	97.1	103.2
住宿和餐饮业	Hotels and Catering Services	142.85	155.62	1.5	1.7	104.5	107.3
金融业	Financial Intermediation	536.94	563.80	5.8	6.0	112.6	112.4
房地产业	Real Estate	281.56	285.38	3.0	3.1	95.0	100.6
其他服务业	Others	1793.44	2104.88	19.3	22.6	114.5	115.5

注：本表按当年价格计算，指数按不变价格计算，采用 GB/T4754-2011 国民经济行业分类标准。

Note: Data in value terms in this table are calculated at current prices, indices in this table are caculated at constant prices, adopted the new Industrial Classification of National Economy (GB/T4754-2011).

2-6 新疆生产总值收入法构成项目
Income Approach Components of Gross Domestic Product in Xinjiang

(2015 年)

指 标	Item	生产总值 Gross Domestic Product	劳动者报酬 Compensation of Employees	生产税净额 Net Taxes on Production	固定资产折旧 Depreciation of Fixed Assets	营业盈余 Operating Surplus
新疆生产总值(亿元)	**Gross Domestic Product (100 million yuan)**	**9324.80**	**5499.12**	**1250.87**	**1565.01**	**1009.80**
按产业分	**By Industry**					
第一产业	Primary Industry	1559.08	1501.08		58.00	
第二产业	Secondary Industry	3596.40	1425.88	868.91	878.39	423.22
第三产业	Tertiary Industry	4169.32	2572.16	381.96	628.62	586.58
按行业分	**By Sector**					
工 业	Industry	2740.71	827.90	744.58	849.39	318.84
建筑业	Construction	959.03	663.74	141.92	46.98	106.39
交通运输、仓储和邮政业	Transport, storage and Post	536.06	229.88	31.16	124.36	150.66
信息传输、软件和信息技术服务业	Information Transmission, Software and Information Technology	126.24	46.87	4.36	68.34	6.67
批发和零售业	Wholesale and Retail Trades	523.58	251.10	157.35	40.24	74.89
住宿和餐饮业	Hotels and Catering Services	155.62	144.23	9.39	9.07	-7.07
金融业	Financial Intermediation	563.80	178.36	60.63	22.79	302.02
房地产业	Real Estate	285.38	49.28	67.82	148.69	19.59
租赁和商务服务业	Leasing and Business Services	93.03	46.60	9.25	9.14	28.04
科学研究和技术服务业	Scientific Research, and Technical Service	76.13	50.32	6.48	4.26	15.07
水利、环境和公共设施管理业	Management of Water Conservancy, Environment and Public Facility	107.77	31.20	3.77	71.97	0.83
居民服务、修理和其他服务业	Servicer to Househld, Repair and Other Services	156.88	140.47	9.66	11.42	-4.67
教 育	Education	409.35	378.93	1.34	31.17	-2.09
卫生和社会工作	Health, Social Service	212.25	197.00	1.40	13.57	0.28
文化、体育和娱乐业	Culture, Sports and Entertainment	45.13	36.26	1.34	6.44	1.09
公共管理、社会保障和社会组织	Public Management , Social Security and Social Organization	735.18	687.79	0.42	47.71	-0.74

注：本表按当年价格计算。
Note: Data in value terms in this table are calculated at current prices.

2-7 主要年份支出法新疆生产总值

Gross Domestic Product by Expenditure Approach in Xinjiang in Main Years

单位：亿元 (100 million yuan)

年 份 Year	支出法新疆生产总值 Gross Domestic Product by Expenditure	最终消费 Final Consumption Expenditures	资本形成总额 Gross Capital Formation	货物和服务净出口 Net Export of Goods and Services	最终消费率(消费率)(%) Final Consumption Rate (%)	资本形成率(投资率)(%) Capital Formation Rate (%)
1978	39.07	27.64	18.43	-7.00	70.7	47.2
1980	53.24	39.82	23.15	-9.73	74.8	43.5
1985	112.24	78.04	58.43	-24.23	69.5	52.1
1986	129.04	92.38	60.26	-23.60	71.6	46.7
1987	148.51	103.77	69.94	-25.20	69.9	47.1
1988	192.72	126.09	98.31	-31.67	65.4	51.0
1989	217.29	137.50	117.84	-38.05	63.3	54.2
1990	261.44	166.77	141.17	-46.50	63.8	54.0
1991	335.91	196.58	169.15	-29.81	58.5	50.4
1992	402.31	221.57	249.26	-68.52	55.1	61.9
1993	495.25	269.92	356.16	-130.83	54.5	71.9
1994	662.32	336.94	487.55	-162.17	50.9	73.6
1995	814.85	444.62	473.71	-103.48	54.6	58.1
1996	900.93	553.90	456.96	-109.93	61.5	50.7
1997	1039.85	611.81	564.92	-136.89	58.8	54.3
1998	1106.95	642.48	685.85	-221.37	58.0	62.0
1999	1163.17	690.57	581.59	-108.99	59.4	50.0
2000	1363.56	760.20	618.12	-14.76	55.8	45.3
2001	1491.60	859.00	771.42	-138.82	57.6	51.7
2002	1612.65	963.71	864.27	-215.33	59.8	53.6
2003	1886.35	1027.22	1119.21	-260.08	54.5	59.3
2004	2209.09	1125.11	1350.47	-266.50	50.9	61.1
2005	2604.14	1266.52	1505.97	-168.35	48.6	57.8
2006	3045.26	1464.53	1654.70	-73.97	48.1	54.3
2007	3513.16	1740.56	1970.06	-197.46	49.5	56.1
2008	4183.21	2073.05	2301.50	-191.34	49.6	55.0
2009	4277.05	2266.20	2549.75	-538.90	53.0	59.6
2010	5437.47	2865.56	3371.22	-799.31	52.7	62.0
2011	6610.05	3518.82	4162.32	-1071.09	53.2	63.0
2012	7505.31	4262.51	5792.16	-2549.36	56.8	77.2
2013	8443.84	4599.24	7192.45	-3347.85	54.5	85.2
2014	9273.46	5024.50	8282.49	-4033.53	54.2	89.3
2015	9324.80	5639.84	8785.27	-5100.31	60.5	94.2

注：2005 年以后数据依据 2008 年经济普查资料已修订。

Note: Since 2005 the data has adjusted according to the economic census in 2008.

2-8 主要年份资本形成总额及其构成
Gross Capital Formation and Its Composition in Main Years

年　份	Year	资本形成总额 (亿元) Gross Capital Formation (100 million yuan)	固定资本形成 Gross Fixed Capital Formation	存货增加 Change in Inventories	以资本形成总额为 100 Gross Capital Formation=100 固定资本形成 (%) Gross Fixed Capital Formation	存货增加 (%) Change in Inventories
	1978	18.43	13.25	5.18	71.9	28.1
	1980	23.15	18.14	5.01	78.3	21.7
	1985	58.43	46.78	11.65	80.1	19.9
	1990	141.17	91.50	49.67	64.8	35.2
	1991	169.15	124.77	44.38	73.8	26.2
	1992	249.26	181.17	68.09	72.7	27.3
	1993	356.16	264.90	91.26	74.4	25.6
	1994	487.55	376.95	110.60	77.3	22.7
	1995	473.71	377.91	95.80	79.8	20.2
	1996	456.96	422.87	34.09	92.5	7.5
	1997	564.92	461.41	103.51	81.7	18.3
	1998	685.85	543.78	142.06	79.3	20.7
	1999	581.59	551.72	29.87	94.9	5.1
	2000	618.12	648.12	-30.00	104.9	-4.9
	2001	771.42	720.12	51.30	93.3	6.7
	2002	864.27	856.70	7.57	99.1	0.9
	2003	1119.21	1079.24	39.98	96.4	3.6
	2004	1350.47	1239.50	110.97	91.8	8.2
	2005	1505.97	1384.33	121.63	91.9	8.1
	2006	1654.70	1596.16	58.54	96.5	3.5
	2007	1970.06	1885.24	84.83	95.7	4.3
	2008	2301.50	2285.60	15.90	99.3	0.7
	2009	2549.75	2473.24	76.51	97.0	3.0
	2010	3371.22	3233.00	138.22	95.9	4.1
	2011	4162.32	3948.87	213.45	94.9	5.1
	2012	5792.16	5477.61	314.55	94.6	5.4
	2013	7192.45	6943.72	248.73	96.5	3.5
	2014	8282.49	8301.43	-18.94	100.2	-0.2
	2015	8785.27	8755.72	29.55	99.7	0.3
"一五"时期	"First Five-year Plan" Period	16.26	14.33	1.94	88.1	11.9
"二五"时期	"Second Five-year Plan" Period	36.39	26.69	9.70	73.3	26.7
	1963—1965	19.40	14.34	5.06	73.9	26.1
"三五"时期	"Third Five-year Plan" Period	30.65	20.96	9.68	68.4	31.6
"四五"时期	"Fourth Five-year Plan" Period	51.70	32.13	19.57	62.1	37.9
"五五"时期	"Fifth Five-year Plan" Period	87.76	62.50	25.26	71.2	28.8
"六五"时期	"Sixth Five-year Plan" Period	191.38	158.48	32.91	82.8	17.2
"七五"时期	"Seventh Five-year Plan" Period	487.52	361.64	125.88	74.2	25.8
"八五"时期	"Eighth Five-year Plan" Period	1735.83	1325.70	410.12	76.4	23.6
"九五"时期	"Ninth Five-year Plan" Period	2907.43	2627.90	279.53	90.4	9.6
"十五"时期	"Tenth Five-year Plan" Period	5611.34	5279.89	331.45	94.1	5.9
"十一五"时期	"Eleventh Five-year Plan " Period	11847.23	11473.23	374.00	96.8	3.2
"十二五"时期	"Twelfth Five-year Plan " Period	34214.69	33427.35	787.34	97.7	2.3

注：本表按当年价格计算。
Note: Data in value terms in this table are calculated at current prices.

2-9 主要年份最终消费及其构成

Final Consumption Expenditure and Its Composition in Main Years

年 份	Year	最终消费（亿元） Final Consumption Expenditures (100 million yuan)	居民消费 Household Consumption	农村居民 Rural Household	城镇居民 Urban Household	政府消费 Government Consumption	最终消费=100 Final Consumption Expenditure=100 居民消费 Household Consumption	政府消费 Government Consumption	居民消费=100 Houshold Consumption=100 农村居民 Rural Household	城镇居民 Urban Household
	1978	27.64	22.61	12.08	10.53	5.03	81.8	18.2	53.4	46.6
	1980	39.82	32.78	16.20	16.58	7.04	82.3	17.7	49.4	50.6
	1985	78.04	58.51	26.41	32.10	19.53	75.0	25.0	45.1	54.9
	1990	166.77	121.12	45.67	75.46	45.65	72.6	27.4	37.7	62.3
	1991	196.58	145.55	52.30	93.26	51.02	74.0	26.0	35.9	64.1
	1992	221.57	159.20	55.18	104.02	62.37	71.9	28.1	34.7	65.3
	1993	269.92	197.78	63.96	133.82	72.14	73.3	26.7	32.3	67.7
	1994	336.94	242.79	83.04	159.75	94.15	72.1	27.9	34.2	65.8
	1995	444.62	320.70	108.43	212.27	123.93	72.1	27.9	33.8	66.2
	1996	553.90	397.61	156.07	241.54	156.29	71.8	28.2	39.3	60.7
	1997	611.81	436.67	164.84	271.84	175.14	71.4	28.6	37.7	62.3
	1998	642.48	457.38	175.72	281.66	185.10	71.2	28.8	38.4	61.6
	1999	690.57	475.74	158.98	316.76	214.83	68.9	31.1	33.4	66.6
	2000	760.20	492.32	159.97	332.34	267.88	64.8	35.2	32.5	67.5
	2001	859.00	545.49	176.00	369.49	313.51	63.5	36.5	32.3	67.7
	2002	963.71	615.47	190.85	424.62	348.25	63.9	36.1	31.0	69.0
	2003	1027.22	623.61	202.67	420.94	403.61	60.7	39.3	32.5	67.5
	2004	1125.11	671.28	209.99	461.29	453.84	59.7	40.3	31.3	68.7
	2005	1266.52	764.26	238.98	525.28	502.26	60.3	39.7	31.3	68.7
	2006	1464.53	853.88	253.58	600.31	610.65	58.3	41.7	29.7	70.3
	2007	1740.56	1013.48	295.52	717.96	727.09	58.2	41.8	29.2	70.8
	2008	2073.05	1171.05	340.69	830.36	902.00	56.5	43.5	29.1	70.9
	2009	2266.20	1284.66	385.66	898.99	981.54	56.7	43.3	30.0	70.0
	2010	2865.56	1578.93	456.31	1122.62	1286.63	55.1	44.9	28.9	71.1
	2011	3518.82	1954.33	560.30	1394.03	1564.49	55.5	44.5	28.7	71.3
	2012	4262.51	2370.67	675.64	1695.03	1891.84	55.6	44.4	28.5	71.5
	2013	4599.24	2563.54	745.18	1818.36	2035.70	55.7	44.3	29.1	70.9
	2014	5024.50	2837.02	856.28	1980.74	2187.48	56.5	43.5	30.2	69.8
	2015	5639.84	3187.11	955.88	2231.23	2452.73	56.5	43.5	30.0	70.0
“一五”时期	"First Five-year Plan" Period	42.97	38.62	23.89	14.73	4.35	89.9	10.1	61.9	38.1
“二五”时期	"Second Five-year Plan" Period	71.40	64.02	39.30	24.72	7.38	89.7	10.3	61.4	38.6
	1963—1965	47.00	42.42	30.93	11.49	4.58	90.3	9.7	72.9	27.1
“三五”时期	"Third Five-year Plan" Period	80.09	72.97	49.13	23.84	7.12	91.1	8.9	67.3	32.7
“四五”时期	"Forth Five-year Plan" Period	97.46	83.75	51.78	31.97	13.71	85.9	14.1	61.8	38.2
“五五”时期	"Fifth Five-year Plan" Period	149.77	123.11	65.02	58.09	26.66	82.2	17.8	52.8	47.2
“六五”时期	"Sixth Five-year Plan" Period	289.27	227.00	107.93	119.06	62.28	78.5	21.5	47.5	52.5
“七五”时期	"Seventh Five-year Plan" Period	626.51	464.17	186.47	277.70	162.34	74.1	25.9	40.2	59.8
“八五”时期	"Eighth Five-year Plan" Period	1469.63	1066.03	362.91	703.12	403.60	72.5	27.5	34.0	66.0
“九五”时期	"Ninth Five-year Plan" Period	3258.96	2259.72	815.58	1444.14	999.24	69.3	30.7	36.1	63.9
“十五”时期	"Tenth Five-year Plan" Period	5241.57	3220.11	1018.50	2201.61	2021.46	61.4	38.6	31.6	68.4
“十一五”时期	"Eleventh Five-year Plan " Period	10409.90	5902.00	1731.76	4170.24	4507.90	56.7	43.3	29.3	70.7
“十二五”时期	"Twelfth Five-year Plan " Period	23044.91	12912.67	3793.28	9119.39	10132.24	56.0	44.0	29.4	70.6

注：本表按当年价格计算。
Note: Data in value terms in this table are calculated at current prices.

2-10 各地、州、市、县(市)地区生产总值

单位：万元 (2015 年)

地 区	Region	地区生产总值 Gross Regional Product	第一产业 Primary Industry
乌鲁木齐市	**Urumqi City**	**26316398**	**316439**
#乌鲁木齐县	Urumqi County	215201	74403
克拉玛依市	**Karamay City**	**6294299**	**51436**
石河子市	**Shihezi City**	**3157843**	**107540**
吐鲁番市	**Turpan City**	**2085846**	**457903**
高昌区	Gaochang District	760387	197376
鄯善县	Shanshan [Piqan] County	899289	161631
托克逊县	Toksun County	429444	98896
哈密地区	**Hami [Kumul] Administrative Offices**	**4235687**	**394773**
哈密市	Hami [Kumul] City	3307375	243603
巴里坤哈萨克自治县	Barkol Kazak Autonomous County	485752	101320
伊吾县	Yiwu [Araturuk] County	443308	49849
昌吉回族自治州	**Changji Hui Autonomous Prefecture**	**11400132**	**2491462**
昌吉市	Changji City	3909619	399071
阜康市	Fukang City	1404974	274511
呼图壁县	Hutubi County	1378957	432722
玛纳斯县	Manas County	1703140	614902
奇台县	Qitai County	1304109	464851
吉木萨尔县	Jimsar County	1151885	200575
木垒哈萨克自治县	Mori Kazak Autonomous County	278682	121167
伊犁哈萨克自治州	**Ili Kazak Autonomous Prefecture**	**16243371**	**4486234**
伊犁州直属县(市)	**Counties (Cities) Direct Under Ili Prefecture**	**8090572**	**1879565**
伊宁市	Yining [Gulja] City	2053177	68879
奎屯市	Kuytun City	1203643	71148
伊宁县	Yining [Gulja] County	759896	309449
察布查尔锡伯自治县	Qapqal Xibe Autonomous County	476440	229955
霍城县	Huocheng [Korgas] County	1195828	336085
巩留县	Gongliu [Tokkuztara] County	433761	141729
新源县	Xinyuan [Kunes] County	802914	277296
昭苏县	Zhaosu [Mongolkure] County	441027	180559
特克斯县	Tekes County	265352	108282
尼勒克县	Nilka County	460799	156181

Gross Regional Product by Prefecture, Autonomous Prefecture, City and County

(10 000 yuan)

第二产业 Secondary Industry	第三产业 Tertiary Industry	#工　业 Industry	#建筑业 Construction	#交通运输、仓储和邮政业 Transport,storage And Post	#批发和零售业 Wholesale and Retail Trades	人均地区生产总值（元） Per Capita GDP (yuan)
7873749	**18126210**	**6321387**	**1566916**	**3359386**	**2452890**	**74340**
44662	96136	36000	8662	8060	9860	34213
4105309	**2137554**	**4658887**	**244851**	**126526**	**115213**	**131014**
1854032	**1196271**	**1345620**	**508413**	**137506**	**151224**	**83701**
785413	**842530**	**593394**	**286200**	**142022**	**61478**	**32415**
170613	392398	108114	62500	74290	33210	26741
401919	335739	349599	146500	67879	12953	38415
212882	117666	135682	77200	10781	7547	35698
2282926	**1557988**	**1516057**	**767000**	**388797**	**229144**	**68669**
1725646	1338126	1160491	565286	351864	200803	68252
236524	147908	144705	91819	23377	22790	46262
321746	71713	211852	109894	13609	5555	189679
5399622	**3509048**	**4278685**	**1122965**	**452081**	**616856**	**71251**
2002446	1508102	1605633	396813	264679	148517	78982
765410	365053	606880	158530	46076	72055	84030
513460	432775	347470	165990	52682	99836	63139
640828	447410	536863	103965	48510	79053	66924
496673	342585	331497	165176	43192	73475	54474
752521	198789	689061	63460	18225	43189	88949
53436	104079	21839	31597	9615	18411	31313
4827709	**6929428**	**3146938**	**1685695**	**557238**	**1157902**	**34277**
2342445	**3868562**	**1542071**	**805000**	**320295**	**723059**	**28755**
440159	1544139	174421	266425	86688	340527	37957
479365	653130	320395	159814	83110	116219	77256
200303	250144	156855	43447	26216	30518	17407
96978	149507	64229	33373	8502	11550	24130
357858	501885	309007	49733	68305	148090	28767
166534	125498	118652	48089	8730	6852	21457
263916	261702	162893	101516	25906	26161	24943
106855	153613	83780	23075	12477	24837	23200
43075	113995	27439	15636	5821	6721	16595
188866	115752	125464	63891	3197	14896	24394

2-10 续表 1

单位：万元

地　　区	Region	地区生产总值 Gross Regional Product	第一产业 Primary Industry
塔城地区	**Tacheng [Tarbagatai] Administrative Offices**	**5931633**	**2140806**
塔城市	Tacheng [Qoqek] City	825951	216086
乌苏市	Usu City	1677908	638062
额敏县	Emin [Dorbiljin] County	740010	236347
沙湾县	Shawan County	1858326	869903
托里县	Toli County	389524	65958
裕民县	Yumin [Qagantokay] County	155604	57499
和布克赛尔蒙古自治县	Hoboksar Mongol Autonomous County	346245	68535
阿勒泰地区	**Altay Administrative Offices**	**2221166**	**465863**
阿勒泰市	Altay City	607916	88424
布尔津县	Burqin County	210363	34809
富蕴县	Fuyun [Koktokay] County	426546	62429
福海县	Fuhai [Burultokay] County	406810	138602
哈巴河县	Habahe [Kaba] County	340762	75612
青河县	Qinghe [Qinggil] County	143357	37287
吉木乃县	Jeminay County	112441	13096
博尔塔拉蒙古自治州	**Bortala Mongolian Autonomous Prefecture**	**2872055**	**636151**
博乐市	Bole [Bortala] City	1448654	302012
精河县	Jinghe [Jing] County	702981	255080
温泉县	Wenquan [Araxang] County	230044	79060
阿拉山口市	Alashankou City	490377	
巴音郭楞蒙古自治州	**Bayangol Mongol ian Autonomous Prefecture**	**10390002**	**1814339**
库尔勒市	Korla City	6637443	400500
轮台县	Luntai [Bugur] County	480255	161982
尉犁县	Yuli [Lopnur] County	511704	294122
若羌县	Ruoqiang [Qarkilik] County	669203	202900
且末县	Qiemo [Qarqan] County	237878	118302
焉耆回族自治县	Yanqi Hui Autonomous County	600020	140584
和静县	Hejing County	701463	206819
和硕县	Hoxud County	327543	195861
博湖县	Bohu [Bagrax] County	246667	96323
阿克苏地区	**Aksu Administrative Offices**	**8101842**	**2362121**
阿克苏市	Aksu City	1672126	208866
温宿县	Wensu [Onsu] County	537783	204069
库车县	Kuqa County	1619915	220892

Continued

(10 000 yuan)

第二产业 Secondary Industry	第三产业 Tertiary Industry	#工业 Industry	#建筑业 Construction	#交通运输、仓储和邮政业 Transport,storage And Post	#批发和零售业 Wholesale and Retail Trades	人均地区生产总值(元) Per Capita GDP (yuan)
1682422	**2108407**	**1073902**	**608520**	**129260**	**350308**	**45964**
146278	463587	44108	102170	49796	87506	49491
589235	450611	444235	145000	50503	107399	54635
220369	283294	114426	105943	27190	56633	34419
348296	640127	244997	103299	65135	150087	51461
217280	106286	157157	60123	21790	9742	43807
25004	73101	6950	18054	2653	10309	26032
173640	104070	93890	79750	12843	14286	53219
802842	**952461**	**530965**	**272175**	**107683**	**84535**	**34996**
110053	409439	41253	69100	34494	42360	31255
89911	85643	49411	40500	5157	8764	30095
261650	102467	209750	51900	24783	7862	44852
136614	131594	98969	37700	13200	16591	50661
174161	90989	140589	33600	15140	6490	39027
49106	56964	29306	19800	2766	4627	20867
68600	30745	52200	16400	2033	2183	28905
817767	**1418137**	**521642**	**296125**	**215339**	**317214**	**59641**
458342	688300	288678	169664	51997	92003	55841
198103	249798	116900	81203	39726	45409	48523
50275	100709	24515	25760	7327	10059	30448
111047	379330	91549	19498	116290	169744	206259
5846537	**2729126**	**5157800**	**810000**	**379118**	**309129**	**73649**
4939658	1297285	4410784	592554	127572	180914	112222
49814	268459	45970	17144	49830	21883	40619
82623	134959	43692	38931	13078	14813	48349
372443	93860	350788	21655	9965	6271	152284
31697	87879	18229	13468	5178	1280	34204
132433	327003	66023	66410	67788	44159	44135
210249	284395	184012	26237	89776	15151	36668
35912	95770	19973	15939	9766	6040	45737
41730	108614	24069	17661	7985	13486	40852
2561723	**3177998**	**1835723**	**726000**	**254466**	**458172**	**28477**
367146	1096114	180729	186417	101692	199630	32514
117710	216004	63476	54234	13489	15729	20660
825270	573753	674135	151135	146718	28297	32844

2-10 续表 2

单位：万元

地　　区	Region	地区生产总值 Gross Regional Product	第一产业 Primary Industry
沙雅县	Xayar County	515265	149767
新和县	Xinhe [Toksu] County	354306	127316
拜城县	Baicheng [Bay] County	560386	124811
乌什县	Wushi [Uxturpan] County	258904	88330
阿瓦提县	Awat County	457581	178976
柯坪县	Kalpin County	95839	21629
克孜勒苏柯尔克孜自治州	**Kizilsu Kirgiz Autonomous Prefecture**	**1000297**	**141662**
阿图什市	Artux City	451236	64303
阿克陶县	Akto County	260931	57926
阿合奇县	Akqi County	88121	9427
乌恰县	Wuqia [Ulugqat] County	200765	10008
喀什地区	**Kashgar [Kaxgar] Administrative Offices**	**7801202**	**2267496**
喀什市	Kashgar [Kaxgar] City	2161929	78307
疏附县	Shufu County	410064	155420
疏勒县	Shule County	700980	223649
英吉沙县	Yengisar County	401001	122056
泽普县	Zepu [Poskam] County	494771	153605
莎车县	Shache [Yarkant] County	889048	440602
叶城县	Yecheng [Kagilik] County	830274	341030
麦盖提县	Makit County	433072	215301
岳普湖县	Yopurga County	380071	98071
伽师县	Jiashi [Payzawat] County	646137	245006
巴楚县	Bachu [Maralbexi] County	651404	221691
塔什库尔干塔吉克自治县	Taxkorgan Tajik Autonomous County	110639	14807
和田地区	**Hotan Administrative Offices**	**2340523**	**626682**
和田市	Hotan City	655113	38760
和田县	Hotan County	298868	96152
墨玉县	Moyu [Karakax] County	410844	204381
皮山县	Pishan [Guma] County	230790	90138
洛浦县	Lop County	247828	64549
策勒县	Qira County	170197	54218
于田县	Yutian [Keriya] County	236660	71867
民丰县	Minfeng [Niya] County	90223	15396

Continued

(10 000 yuan)

第二产业 Secondary Industry	第三产业 Tertiary Industry	#工　业 Industry	#建筑业 Construction	#交通运输、仓储和邮政业 Transport,storage And Post	#批发和零售业 Wholesale and Retail Trades	人均地区生产总值(元) Per Capita GDP (yuan)
102317	263181	60017	42300	18077	21474	18670
72740	154250	53179	19561	13418	11304	18355
223426	212149	178382	45044	26817	16469	23038
33880	136694	15800	18080	2621	880	11156
73803	204802	30805	42997	9139	7259	17399
19109	55101	9168	9941	3382	110	17303
300533	**558102**	**169533**	**131000**	**31064**	**28378**	**16777**
114904	272029	71981	42923	24830	15701	16732
77329	125676	38472	38857	2350	4042	11833
23717	54977	14617	9100	2144	2130	19996
84583	106174	44463	40120	5126	6489	32983
2407990	**3125716**	**1331400**	**1076590**	**213290**	**764454**	**17431**
674499	1409123	503999	170500	127050	539069	32316
80910	173734	28932	51978	5576	14002	14809
328316	149015	205325	122991	4719	11562	18798
120005	158940	35936	84069	7091	16682	13333
114405	226761	53005	61400	8366	58660	22131
130571	317875	67001	63570	9580	28100	10473
221612	267632	134547	87065	14464	36391	16005
83368	134403	37375	45993	6271	22489	17891
152635	129365	59876	92759	6829	14488	21977
220351	180780	134113	86238	18300	30815	14776
134736	294977	55821	78915	7264	134634	17139
56564	39268	8168	48396	1344	3224	27403
347220	**1366621**	**105193**	**242027**	**30469**	**140422**	**10215**
123223	493130	6389	116834	28736	61553	18718
68059	134657	34247	33812	1616	1103	9500
30821	175642	9316	21505	9509	16240	7169
24121	116531	10321	13800	1817	2844	7797
44675	138604	17667	27008	2607	3612	8886
24168	91811	4475	19693	1141	6236	10250
32942	131851	8094	24848	4646	5512	8458
13949	60878	6942	7007	1680	2300	23269

2-11 各地、州、市、县(市)地区生产总值构成

单位：%　　(2015 年)

地　　区	Region	地区生产总值 Gross Regional Product	第一产业 Primary Industry
乌鲁木齐市	**Urumqi City**	**100.0**	**1.2**
#乌鲁木齐县	Urumqi County	100.0	34.6
克拉玛依市	**Karamay City**	**100.0**	**0.8**
石河子市	**Shihezi City**	**100.0**	**3.4**
吐鲁番市	**Turpan City**	**100.0**	**22.0**
高昌区	Gaochang District	100.0	26.0
鄯善县	Shanshan [Piqan] County	100.0	18.0
托克逊县	Toksun County	100.0	23.0
哈密地区	**Hami [Kumul] Administrative Offices**	**100.0**	**9.3**
哈密市	Hami [Kumul] City	100.0	7.4
巴里坤哈萨克自治县	Barkol Kazak Autonomous County	100.0	20.9
伊吾县	Yiwu [Araturuk] County	100.0	11.2
昌吉回族自治州	**Changji Hui Autonomous Prefecture**	**100.0**	**21.9**
昌吉市	Changji City	100.0	10.2
阜康市	Fukang City	100.0	19.5
呼图壁县	Hutubi County	100.0	31.4
玛纳斯县	Manas County	100.0	36.1
奇台县	Qitai County	100.0	35.6
吉木萨尔县	Jimsar County	100.0	17.4
木垒哈萨克自治县	Mori Kazak Autonomous County	100.0	43.5
伊犁哈萨克自治州	**Ili Kazak Autonomous Prefecture**	**100.0**	**27.6**
伊犁州直属县(市)	**Counties (Cities) Direct Under Ili Prefecture**	**100.0**	**23.2**
伊宁市	Yining [Gulja] City	100.0	3.4
奎屯市	Kuytun City	100.0	5.9
伊宁县	Yining [Gulja] County	100.0	40.7
察布查尔锡伯自治县	Qapqal Xibe Autonomous County	100.0	48.3
霍城县	Huocheng [Korgas] County	100.0	28.1
巩留县	Gongliu [Tokkuztara] County	100.0	32.7
新源县	Xinyuan [Kunes] County	100.0	34.5
昭苏县	Zhaosu [Mongolkure] County	100.0	40.9
特克斯县	Tekes County	100.0	40.8
尼勒克县	Nilka County	100.0	33.9

Composition of Gross Regional Product by Prefecture, Autonomous Prefecture, City and County

(%)

第二产业 Secondary Industry	第三产业 Tertiary Industry	#工业 Industry	#建筑业 Construction	#交通运输、仓储和邮政业 Transport,storage And Post	#批发和零售业 Wholesale and Retail Trades
29.9	**68.9**	**24.0**	**6.0**	**12.8**	**9.3**
20.8	44.6	16.8	4.0	3.7	4.6
65.2	**34.0**	**74.0**	**3.9**	**2.0**	**1.8**
58.7	**37.9**	**42.6**	**16.1**	**4.4**	**4.8**
37.7	**40.3**	**28.4**	**13.7**	**6.8**	**2.9**
22.4	51.6	14.2	8.2	9.8	4.4
44.7	37.3	38.9	16.3	7.5	1.4
49.6	27.4	31.6	18.0	2.5	1.8
53.9	**36.8**	**35.8**	**18.1**	**9.2**	**5.4**
52.2	40.4	35.1	17.1	10.6	6.1
48.7	30.4	29.8	18.9	4.8	4.7
72.6	16.2	47.8	24.8	3.1	1.3
47.4	**30.7**	**37.5**	**9.9**	**4.0**	**5.4**
51.2	38.6	41.1	10.1	6.8	3.8
54.5	26.0	43.2	11.3	3.3	5.1
37.2	31.4	25.2	12.0	3.8	7.2
37.6	26.3	31.5	6.1	2.8	4.6
38.1	26.3	25.4	12.7	3.3	5.6
65.3	17.3	59.8	5.5	1.6	3.7
19.2	37.3	7.9	11.3	3.5	6.6
29.7	**42.7**	**19.3**	**10.4**	**3.4**	**7.1**
29.0	**47.8**	**19.1**	**9.9**	**4.0**	**8.9**
21.4	75.2	8.4	13.0	4.2	16.6
39.8	54.3	26.6	13.3	6.9	9.7
26.4	32.9	20.7	5.7	3.4	4.0
20.4	31.3	13.5	7.0	1.8	2.4
29.9	42.0	25.8	4.2	5.7	12.4
38.4	28.9	27.3	11.1	2.0	1.6
32.9	32.6	20.3	12.6	3.2	3.3
24.2	34.9	19.0	5.2	2.8	5.6
16.2	43.0	10.3	5.9	2.2	2.5
41.0	25.1	27.2	13.9	0.7	3.2

2-11 续表 1

单位：%

地　　区	Region	地区生产总值 Gross Regional Product	第一产业 Primary Industry
塔城地区	**Tacheng [Tarbagatai] Administrative Offices**	**100.0**	**36.1**
塔城市	Tacheng [Qoqek] City	100.0	26.2
乌苏市	Usu City	100.0	38.0
额敏县	Emin [Dorbiljin] County	100.0	31.9
沙湾县	Shawan County	100.0	46.8
托里县	Toli County	100.0	16.9
裕民县	Yumin [Qagantokay] County	100.0	37.0
和布克赛尔蒙古自治县	Hoboksar Mongol Autonomous County	100.0	19.8
阿勒泰地区	**Altay Administrative Offices**	**100.0**	**21.0**
阿勒泰市	Altay City	100.0	14.5
布尔津县	Burqin County	100.0	16.5
富蕴县	Fuyun [Koktokay] County	100.0	14.6
福海县	Fuhai [Burultokay] County	100.0	34.1
哈巴河县	Habahe [Kaba] County	100.0	22.2
青河县	Qinghe [Qinggil] County	100.0	26.0
吉木乃县	Jeminay County	100.0	11.6
博尔塔拉蒙古自治州	**Bortala Mongolian Autonomous Prefecture**	**100.0**	**22.1**
博乐市	Bole [Bortala] City	100.0	20.8
精河县	Jinghe [Jing] County	100.0	36.3
温泉县	Wenquan [Araxang] County	100.0	34.4
阿拉山口市	Alashankou City	100.0	
巴音郭楞蒙古自治州	**Bayangol Mongol ian Autonomous Prefecture**	**100.0**	**17.5**
库尔勒市	Korla City	100.0	6.0
轮台县	Luntai [Bugur] County	100.0	33.7
尉犁县	Yuli [Lopnur] County	100.0	57.5
若羌县	Ruoqiang [Qarkilik] County	100.0	30.3
且末县	Qiemo [Qarqan] County	100.0	49.7
焉耆回族自治县	Yanqi Hui Autonomous County	100.0	23.4
和静县	Hejing County	100.0	29.5
和硕县	Hoxud County	100.0	59.8
博湖县	Bohu [Bagrax] County	100.0	39.0
阿克苏地区	**Aksu Administrative Offices**	**100.0**	**29.2**
阿克苏市	Aksu City	100.0	12.5
温宿县	Wensu [Onsu] County	100.0	37.9
库车县	Kuqa County	100.0	13.6

Continued

(%)

第二产业 Secondary Industry	第三产业 Tertiary Industry	#工 业 Industry	#建筑业 Construction	#交通运输、仓储和邮政业 Transport,storage And Post	#批发和零售业 Wholesale and Retail Trades
28.4	**35.5**	**18.1**	**10.3**	**2.2**	**5.9**
17.7	56.1	5.3	12.4	6.0	10.6
35.1	26.9	26.5	8.6	3.0	6.4
29.8	38.3	15.5	14.3	3.7	7.7
18.7	34.5	13.1	5.6	3.5	8.1
55.8	27.3	40.4	15.4	5.6	2.5
16.1	46.9	4.5	11.6	1.7	6.6
50.1	30.1	27.1	23.0	3.7	4.1
36.1	**42.9**	**23.8**	**12.3**	**4.8**	**3.8**
18.1	67.4	6.7	11.4	5.7	7.0
42.7	40.8	23.4	19.3	2.5	4.2
61.3	24.1	49.1	12.2	5.8	1.8
33.6	32.3	24.3	9.3	3.2	4.1
51.1	26.7	41.2	9.9	4.4	1.9
34.3	39.7	20.5	13.8	1.9	3.2
61.0	27.4	46.4	14.6	1.8	1.9
28.5	**49.4**	**18.2**	**10.3**	**7.5**	**11.0**
31.6	47.6	19.9	11.7	3.6	6.4
28.2	35.5	16.6	11.6	5.7	6.5
21.9	43.7	10.7	11.2	3.2	4.4
22.6	77.4	18.6	4.0	23.7	34.6
56.3	**26.2**	**49.6**	**7.8**	**3.6**	**3.0**
74.4	19.6	66.5	8.9	1.9	2.7
10.4	55.9	9.6	3.6	10.4	4.6
16.1	26.4	8.5	7.6	2.6	2.9
55.7	14.0	52.5	3.2	1.5	0.9
13.3	37.0	7.6	5.7	2.2	0.5
22.1	54.5	11.0	11.1	11.3	7.4
30.0	40.5	26.3	3.7	12.8	2.2
11.0	29.2	6.1	4.9	3.0	1.8
16.9	44.1	9.7	7.2	3.2	5.5
31.6	**39.2**	**22.6**	**9.0**	**3.1**	**5.7**
22.0	65.5	10.9	11.1	6.1	11.9
21.9	40.2	11.8	10.1	2.5	2.9
50.9	35.5	41.6	9.3	9.1	1.7

2-11 续表 2

单位：%

地　　区	Region	地区生产总值 Gross Regional Product	第一产业 Primary Industry
沙雅县	Xayar County	100.0	29.1
新和县	Xinhe [Toksu] County	100.0	35.9
拜城县	Baicheng [Bay] County	100.0	22.3
乌什县	Wushi [Uxturpan] County	100.0	34.1
阿瓦提县	Awat County	100.0	39.1
柯坪县	Kalpin County	100.0	22.6
克孜勒苏柯尔克孜自治州	**Kizilsu Kirgiz Autonomous Prefecture**	**100.0**	**14.2**
阿图什市	Artux City	100.0	14.3
阿克陶县	Akto County	100.0	22.2
阿合奇县	Akqi County	100.0	10.7
乌恰县	Wuqia [Ulugqat] County	100.0	5.0
喀什地区	**Kashgar [Kaxgar] Administrative Offices**	**100.0**	**29.1**
喀什市	Kashgar [Kaxgar] City	100.0	3.6
疏附县	Shufu County	100.0	37.9
疏勒县	Shule County	100.0	31.9
英吉沙县	Yengisar County	100.0	30.4
泽普县	Zepu [Poskam] County	100.0	31.0
莎车县	Shache [Yarkant] County	100.0	49.6
叶城县	Yecheng [Kagilik] County	100.0	41.1
麦盖提县	Makit County	100.0	49.7
岳普湖县	Yopurga County	100.0	25.8
伽师县	Jiashi [Payzawat] County	100.0	37.9
巴楚县	Bachu [Maralbexi] County	100.0	34.0
塔什库尔干县	Taxkorgan Tajik Autonomous County	100.0	13.4
和田地区	**Hotan Administrative Offices**	**100.0**	**26.8**
和田市	Hotan City	100.0	5.9
和田县	Hotan County	100.0	32.2
墨玉县	Moyu [Karakax] County	100.0	49.7
皮山县	Pishan [Guma] County	100.0	39.1
洛浦县	Lop County	100.0	26.0
策勒县	Qira County	100.0	31.9
于田县	Yutian [Keriya] County	100.0	30.4
民丰县	Minfeng [Niya] County	100.0	17.1

Continued

(%)

第二产业 Secondary Industry	第三产业 Tertiary Industry	#工 业 Industry	#建筑业 Construction	#交通运输、仓储和邮政业 Transport,storage And Post	#批发和零售业 Wholesale and Retail Trades
19.9	51.0	11.7	8.2	3.5	4.2
20.5	43.6	15.0	5.5	3.8	3.2
39.9	37.8	31.9	8.0	4.8	2.9
13.1	52.8	6.1	7.0	1.0	0.3
16.1	44.8	6.7	9.4	2.0	1.6
19.9	57.5	9.5	10.4	3.5	0.1
30.0	**55.8**	**16.9**	**13.1**	**3.1**	**2.8**
25.5	60.2	16.0	9.5	5.5	3.5
29.6	48.2	14.7	14.9	0.9	1.5
26.9	62.4	16.6	10.3	2.4	2.4
42.1	52.9	22.1	20.0	2.6	3.2
30.9	**40.0**	**17.1**	**13.8**	**2.7**	**9.8**
31.2	65.2	23.3	7.9	5.9	24.9
19.7	42.4	7.0	12.7	1.4	3.4
46.8	21.3	29.3	17.5	0.7	1.6
29.9	39.7	8.9	21.0	1.8	4.2
23.1	45.9	10.7	12.4	1.7	11.9
14.7	35.7	7.5	7.2	1.1	3.2
26.7	32.2	16.2	10.5	1.7	4.4
19.3	31.0	8.7	10.6	1.4	5.2
40.2	34.0	15.8	24.4	1.8	3.8
34.1	28.0	20.8	13.3	2.8	4.8
20.7	45.3	8.6	12.1	1.1	20.7
51.1	35.5	7.4	43.7	1.2	2.9
14.8	**58.4**	**4.5**	**10.3**	**1.3**	**6.0**
18.8	75.3	1.0	17.8	4.4	9.4
22.8	45.0	11.5	11.3	0.5	0.4
7.5	42.8	2.3	5.2	2.3	4.0
10.5	50.4	4.5	6.0	0.8	1.2
18.0	56.0	7.1	10.9	1.1	1.5
14.2	53.9	2.6	11.6	0.7	3.7
13.9	55.7	3.4	10.5	2.0	2.3
15.5	67.4	7.7	7.8	1.9	2.5

2-12 各地、州、市、县(市)地区生产总值指数

(上年=100) (2015年)

地区	Region	地区生产总值 Gross Regional Product	第一产业 Primary Industry
乌鲁木齐市	**Urumqi City**	**110.5**	**106.1**
#乌鲁木齐县	Urumqi County	108.8	104.0
克拉玛依市	**Karamay City**	**100.5**	**102.5**
石河子市	**Shihezi City**	**111.8**	**105.0**
吐鲁番市	**Turpan City**	**105.5**	**105.7**
高昌区	Turpan City	107.6	105.8
鄯善县	Shanshan [Piqan] County	108.5	105.7
托克逊县	Toksun County	93.6	105.2
哈密地区	**Hami [Kumul] Administrative Offices**	**110.4**	**106.0**
哈密市	Hami [Kumul] City	111.2	107.6
巴里坤哈萨克自治县	Barkol Kazak Autonomous County	110.6	103.4
伊吾县	Yiwu [Araturuk] County	102.5	105.3
昌吉回族自治州	**Changji Hui Autonomous Prefecture**	**112.0**	**104.9**
昌吉市	Changji City	111.0	105.1
阜康市	Fukang City	110.5	103.7
呼图壁县	Hutubi County	111.2	104.5
玛纳斯县	Manas County	103.6	104.4
奇台县	Qitai County	114.6	104.8
吉木萨尔县	Jimsar County	127.0	104.5
木垒哈萨克自治县	Mori Kazak Autonomous County	108.3	104.9
伊犁哈萨克自治州	**Ili Kazak Autonomous Prefecture**	**109.3**	**106.9**
伊犁州直属县(市)	**Counties (Cities) Direct Under Ili Prefecture**	**107.5**	**105.1**
伊宁市	Yining [Gulja] City	107.6	103.1
奎屯市	Kuytun City	107.5	109.8
伊宁县	Yining [Gulja] County	109.1	104.4
察布查尔锡伯自治县	Qapqal Xibe Autonomous County	104.1	107.8
霍城县	Huocheng [Korgas] County	109.2	102.7
巩留县	Gongliu [Tokkuztara] County	108.0	98.5
新源县	Xinyuan [Kunes] County	106.1	105.2
昭苏县	Zhaosu [Mongolkure] County	108.0	110.8
特克斯县	Tekes County	107.8	105.6
尼勒克县	Nilka County	105.1	105.4

Indices of Gross Regional Product by Prefecture, Autonomous Prefecture, City and County

(preceding year=100)

第二产业 Secondary Industry	第三产业 Tertiary Industry	#工业 Industry	#建筑业 Construction	#交通运输、仓储和邮政业 Transport,storage And Post	#批发和零售业 Wholesale and Retail Trades
105.1	**114.3**	**103.9**	**114.2**	**114.7**	**97.3**
100.5	117.4	97.5	124.1	120.2	104.6
98.6	**107.0**	**99.0**	**103.7**	**82.6**	**103.9**
113.5	**109.7**	**108.4**	**131.8**	**116.6**	**110.7**
106.1	**104.4**	**103.6**	**109.1**	**96.6**	**118.7**
109.6	106.9	105.7	124.3	95.5	107.2
112.8	98.3	112.6	98.3	97.0	98.0
86.8	111.4	79.9	122.6	104.7	111.8
113.5	**105.5**	**114.6**	**110.7**	**95.7**	**103.6**
116.1	104.1	123.4	99.6	95.0	103.9
113.7	109.2	101.7	152.1	95.7	100.8
100.3	115.7	86.8	164.6	111.5	109.6
115.5	**111.2**	**115.5**	**115.1**	**110.9**	**112.4**
111.8	111.5	108.7	126.0	107.9	104.5
111.9	110.7	110.6	117.8	104.1	115.9
117.8	110.4	121.2	108.8	106.0	109.1
99.2	110.9	99.0	100.0	114.1	107.6
123.1	114.2	128.2	112.5	115.1	116.1
134.2	112.5	138.1	91.6	102.7	112.6
114.1	108.6	92.4	139.4	102.5	111.3
107.8	**106.7**	**110.8**	**112.6**	**107.1**	**110.9**
104.6	**110.7**	**103.0**	**108.5**	**107.5**	**111.3**
97.6	111.6	86.9	107.7	103.0	120.5
106.5	107.9	106.3	106.8	109.2	100.8
110.0	113.5	111.1	103.8	109.1	111.8
91.6	112.4	86.1	109.8	106.8	138.6
113.3	110.2	113.6	110.1	106.2	109.1
114.1	110.6	115.5	111.2	87.2	115.7
104.0	111.7	102.7	109.3	112.0	120.3
106.5	106.7	105.5	109.0	125.4	115.6
104.4	111.6	101.6	112.1	114.6	109.3
101.6	112.3	97.0	114.1	107.2	110.4

2-12 续表 1

(上年=100)

地　　区	Region	地区生产总值 Gross Regional Product	第一产业 Primary Industry
塔城地区	**Tacheng [Tarbagatai] Administrative Offices**	**112.3**	**108.4**
塔城市	Tacheng [Qoqek] City	112.8	105.6
乌苏市	Usu City	113.8	105.7
额敏县	Emin [Dorbiljin] County	107.2	106.0
沙湾县	Shawan County	113.3	107.6
托里县	Toli County	105.9	105.4
裕民县	Yumin [Qagantokay] County	107.5	101.7
和布克赛尔蒙古自治县	Hoboksar Mongol Autonomous County	103.5	102.9
阿勒泰地区	**Altay Administrative Offices**	**107.2**	**106.2**
阿勒泰市	Altay City	106.9	104.2
布尔津县	Burqin County	110.8	101.7
富蕴县	Fuyun [Koktokay] County	95.6	107.0
福海县	Fuhai [Burultokay] County	108.3	107.4
哈巴河县	Habahe [Kaba] County	106.2	104.4
青河县	Qinghe [Qinggil] County	105.0	102.3
吉木乃县	Jeminay County	109.8	102.1
博尔塔拉蒙古自治州	**Bortala Mongolian Autonomous Prefecture**	**112.0**	**105.8**
博乐市	Bole [Bortala] City	112.4	106.3
精河县	Jinghe [Jing] County	111.9	105.4
温泉县	Wenquan [Araxang] County	108.9	105.1
阿拉山口市	Alashankou City	111.4	
巴音郭楞蒙古自治州	**Bayangol Mongol ian Autonomous Prefecture**	**104.3**	**105.2**
库尔勒市	Korla City	103.8	106.7
轮台县	Luntai [Bugur] County	88.5	80.6
尉犁县	Yuli [Lopnur] County	113.2	115.7
若羌县	Ruoqiang [Qarkilik] County	108.0	106.1
且末县	Qiemo [Qarqan] County	103.6	115.6
焉耆回族自治县	Yanqi Hui Autonomous County	108.0	103.2
和静县	Hejing County	97.6	100.5
和硕县	Hoxud County	104.2	104.5
博湖县	Bohu [Bagrax] County	106.5	109.4
阿克苏地区	**Aksu Administrative Offices**	**110.9**	**108.0**
阿克苏市	Aksu City	109.6	107.9
温宿县	Wensu [Onsu] County	110.3	107.8
库车县	Kuqa County	111.7	107.8

Continued

(preceding year=100)

第二产业 Secondary Industry	第三产业 Tertiary Industry	#工　业 Industry	#建筑业 Construction	#交通运输、仓储和邮政业 Transport,storage And Post	#批发和零售业 Wholesale and Retail Trades
113.9	**114.7**	**113.5**	**115.0**	**106.0**	**112.5**
115.3	114.0	110.3	118.8	109.4	108.4
116.9	116.1	119.8	102.1	116.7	117.3
106.8	108.6	105.1	109.9	110.6	110.2
115.9	119.5	115.6	117.0	119.7	116.8
104.7	110.9	104.5	105.6	111.1	113.1
97.3	117.2	101.0	96.0	114.2	130.4
100.7	110.4	106.3	94.2	107.7	107.1
101.5	**115.6**	**99.4**	**108.6**	**107.6**	**100.5**
101.5	109.3	100.6	102.1	102.2	97.3
115.8	110.1	108.0	123.5	101.6	113.9
90.2	111.0	87.3	108.5	121.4	106.1
103.8	114.6	102.3	107.9	101.5	125.5
105.4	110.5	105.1	107.7	107.4	110.5
104.4	107.1	105.1	104.0	99.2	101.8
117.0	105.2	105.2	134.4	104.8	114.7
121.5	**109.7**	**124.2**	**116.3**	**94.5**	**113.5**
121.2	109.5	124.7	114.5	106.5	115.6
122.5	112.5	126.5	116.8	94.3	145.7
108.5	112.0	108.7	108.3	104.5	152.2
123.5	107.6	123.9	120.9	89.5	106.0
102.3	**108.8**	**102.2**	**101.7**	**102.7**	**110.0**
102.9	106.5	101.9	107.5	104.8	108.9
82.2	94.6	81.0	86.1	96.8	102.9
117.5	104.6	126.2	109.0	103.0	115.1
104.9	126.3	104.5	113.6	129.9	195.2
69.5	107.4	66.5	74.5	110.2	130.9
105.4	112.2	113.3	95.8	110.7	110.8
85.4	110.2	83.9	98.3	102.1	131.2
92.3	112.8	86.0	109.6	103.3	98.0
87.3	114.9	96.4	77.7	107.9	117.2
113.2	**110.8**	**110.8**	**119.0**	**102.1**	**116.0**
111.7	108.8	110.7	113.7	104.5	135.1
107.4	116.3	105.5	110.0	119.2	61.7
110.2	116.4	109.7	111.6	115.4	116.2

2-12 续表 2

(上年=100)

地 区	Region	地区生产总值 Gross Regional Product	第一产业 Primary Industry
沙雅县	Xayar County	107.0	104.8
新和县	Xinhe [Toksu] County	109.7	108.5
拜城县	Baicheng [Bay] County	109.1	107.3
乌什县	Wushi [Uxturpan] County	109.0	107.5
阿瓦提县	Awat County	109.8	108.6
柯坪县	Kalpin County	109.4	107.9
克孜勒苏柯尔克孜自治州	**Kizilsu Kirgiz Autonomous Prefecture**	**112.3**	**105.4**
阿图什市	Artux City	110.6	107.2
阿克陶县	Akto County	111.2	105.2
阿合奇县	Akqi County	112.4	113.2
乌恰县	Wuqia [Ulugqat] County	112.0	100.2
喀什地区	**Kashgar [Kaxgar] Administrative Offices**	**112.2**	**106.2**
喀什市	Kashgar [Kaxgar] City	111.5	100.3
疏附县	Shufu County	115.4	107.9
疏勒县	Shule County	107.9	108.0
英吉沙县	Yengisar County	117.0	106.3
泽普县	Zepu [Poskam] County	114.8	114.3
莎车县	Shache [Yarkant] County	116.5	111.7
叶城县	Yecheng [Kagilik] County	115.0	109.2
麦盖提县	Makit County	112.3	108.7
岳普湖县	Yopurga County	115.0	106.0
伽师县	Jiashi [Payzawat] County	119.4	112.1
巴楚县	Bachu [Maralbexi] County	110.8	108.3
塔什库尔干县	Taxkorgan Tajik Autonomous County	104.8	112.8
和田地区	**Hotan Administrative Offices**	**111.6**	**105.4**
和田市	Hotan City	113.7	126.1
和田县	Hotan County	110.6	105.5
墨玉县	Moyu [Karakax] County	111.2	105.2
皮山县	Pishan [Guma] County	111.6	103.6
洛浦县	Lop County	112.1	106.2
策勒县	Qira County	110.9	101.2
于田县	Yutian [Keriya] County	110.7	104.4
民丰县	Minfeng [Niya] County	111.0	104.3

Continued

(preceding year=100)

第二产业 Secondary Industry	第三产业 Tertiary Industry	#工　业 Industry	#建筑业 Construction	#交通运输、仓储和邮政业 Transport,storage And Post	#批发和零售业 Wholesale and Retail Trades
106.6	108.6	103.2	113.8	109.2	82.2
114.4	108.0	113.2	118.6	108.0	94.7
105.0	117.1	102.3	122.7	104.7	116.1
119.2	107.8	118.2	120.0	80.2	109.9
112.8	109.9	106.2	116.7	103.1	113.5
110.3	109.7	110.8	109.4	105.4	112.0
111.6	**114.3**	**107.4**	**115.7**	**101.1**	**115.3**
94.3	118.2	73.4	121.1	105.6	118.0
111.7	113.8	108.5	115.0	98.3	112.1
112.2	112.4	110.6	114.5	102.1	115.0
108.1	118.4	105.7	112.2	106.6	121.4
114.4	**115.0**	**111.5**	**118.1**	**101.5**	**102.0**
112.0	111.9	112.7	109.9	101.4	107.8
123.3	118.8	122.7	123.6	101.7	127.4
101.5	115.0	101.4	101.6	102.7	101.4
123.4	123.2	124.5	122.9	114.0	115.2
118.1	113.4	114.2	122.0	99.3	128.7
121.8	121.7	130.0	115.0	113.2	114.8
122.9	117.8	128.6	114.8	115.2	117.8
109.2	118.3	114.1	105.1	99.0	120.2
118.6	117.8	125.0	115.2	94.8	122.2
131.9	117.5	125.0	147.4	72.3	111.0
116.5	110.4	124.9	107.0	110.5	107.8
100.8	107.3	43.3	169.3	106.3	102.9
104.2	**117.5**	**97.7**	**108.4**	**104.3**	**105.1**
113.5	112.7	97.5	114.5	122.3	149.4
125.3	106.4	147.3	110.4	102.9	144.1
118.0	116.0	114.3	119.7	113.0	109.7
106.9	120.8	117.8	102.0	108.4	115.4
106.9	116.2	102.1	108.1	104.2	105.4
117.3	115.1	136.3	114.0	111.1	113.1
110.7	114.4	83.6	122.1	125.5	130.1
109.8	113.6	111.3	108.7	105.4	112.1

2-13 三次产业贡献率

Share of the Contributions of Three Strata of Industry to the Increase of the GDP

单位：%　　(%)

年 份 Year	新疆生产总值 Gross Domestic Product	第一产业 Primary Industry	第二产业 Secondary Industry	第三产业 Tertiary Industry	#工 业 Industry	#建筑业 Construction
2001	100	12.9	44.0	43.1	34.3	9.7
2002	100	12.0	38.2	49.8	28.2	10.0
2003	100	13.8	42.7	43.5	29.5	13.2
2004	100	9.2	50.5	40.3	37.7	12.8
2005	100	11.1	52.9	36.0	45.1	7.8
2006	100	10.1	45.8	44.1	41.9	3.9
2007	100	10.9	46.2	42.9	43.2	2.9
2008	100	10.3	58.5	31.2	49.6	8.9
2009	100	9.5	48.6	41.8	30.2	18.5
2010	100	7.0	55.4	37.6	49.2	6.3
2011	100	10.8	47.8	41.4	37.9	9.9
2012	100	10.8	51.0	38.2	41.9	12.4
2013	100	11.1	53.9	35.0	43.4	13.4
2014	100	10.0	53.5	36.5	40.1	13.8
2015	100	10.9	39.9	49.2	26.5	14.2

注：三次产业贡献率指可比价各产业增加值增量与 GDP 增量之比。

Note: Share of the contributions of the three strata of industry to increase of GDp refers to the proportion of the increment of the value-added of each industry to the increment of GDP

2-14 三次产业对地区生产总值增长的拉动

Contribution of the Three Strata of Industry to GDP Growth

单位：百分点　　(percentage points)

年 份 Year	新疆生产总值 Gross Domestic Product	第一产业 Primary Industry	第二产业 Secondary Industry	第三产业 Tertiary Industry	#工 业 Industry	#建筑业 Construction
2001	8.6	1.1	3.8	3.7	2.9	0.8
2002	8.2	1.0	3.1	4.1	2.3	0.8
2003	11.2	1.5	4.8	4.9	3.3	1.5
2004	11.4	1.1	5.8	4.6	4.3	1.5
2005	10.9	1.2	5.8	3.9	4.9	0.9
2006	11.0	1.1	5.0	4.9	4.6	0.4
2007	12.2	1.3	5.7	5.2	5.3	0.4
2008	11.0	1.1	6.5	3.4	5.5	1.0
2009	8.1	0.8	3.9	3.4	2.4	1.5
2010	10.6	0.7	5.9	4.0	5.2	0.7
2011	12.0	1.3	5.7	5.0	4.5	1.2
2012	12.0	1.3	6.1	4.6	5.0	1.5
2013	11.0	1.2	5.9	3.9	4.8	1.5
2014	10.0	1.0	5.4	3.6	4.0	1.4
2015	8.8	1.0	3.5	4.3	2.3	1.2

注：三次产业对地区生产总值增长的拉动指各产业贡献率与 GDP 增速之乘积。

Note: Contributions of the three strata of industry to GDP growth refers to the growth rate of GDP multiplied by the contribution share of every industry.

2-15 主要年份居民消费水平及指数
Household Consumption Expenditure and Its Indices in Main Years

年份 Year	居民消费水平(元) Household Consumption (yuan)	农村居民 Rural Households	城镇居民 Urban Households	居民消费水平指数(1952年=100) Index of Residents' Consumption Level (1952=100)	农村居民 Rural Households
1978	181	131	323	140.5	144.5
1980	252	180	417	182.4	184.4
1990	796	447	1508	299.5	236.3
1995	1852	977	3414	344.1	246.5
1996	2266	1387	3836	377.1	312.6
1997	2455	1445	4261	384.6	313.9
1998	2539	1520	4364	396.1	339.3
1999	2606	1358	4841	413.1	319.3
2000	2662	1308	5131	415.2	299.2
2001	2905	1427	5743	434.3	307.6
2002	3228	1525	6483	484.7	325.4
2003	3249	1603	6427	488.6	338.1
2004	3445	1652	6808	502.3	339.8
2005	3814	1884	7221	556.0	385.7
2006	4151	2000	7728	596.2	400.6
2007	4831	2320	8833	661.4	432.7
2008	5521	2686	9882	700.1	452.7
2009	5945	3029	10366	753.6	503.9
2010	7400	3674	12665	894.8	587.6
2011	8895	4495	14663	991.5	644.6
2012	10675	5410	17442	1149.1	749.0
2013	11401	5942	18285	1191.6	794.7
2014	12436	6859	19176	1275.0	902.0
2015	13684	7694	20532	1382.1	981.4

年份 Year	城镇居民 Urban Households	居民消费水平指数(上年=100) Index of Residents' Consumption Level (preceding year=100)	农村居民 Rural Households	城镇居民 Urban Households
1978	99.0	104.7	102.3	102.8
1980	119.3	111.9	107.6	113.1
1990	226.4	103.8	98.8	105.0
1995	257.4	109.0	102.3	112.3
1996	260.7	109.6	126.8	101.3
1997	268.5	102.0	100.4	103.0
1998	268.5	103.0	108.1	100.0
1999	297.8	104.3	94.1	110.9
2000	315.7	100.5	93.7	106.0
2001	338.7	104.6	102.8	107.3
2002	386.8	111.6	105.8	114.2
2003	386.8	100.8	103.9	100.0
2004	396.1	102.8	100.5	102.4
2005	421.1	110.7	113.5	106.3
2006	445.3	107.2	103.9	105.7
2007	489.7	110.9	108.0	110.0
2008	512.3	105.9	104.6	104.6
2009	540.7	107.6	111.3	105.5
2010	627.2	118.7	116.6	116.0
2011	676.7	110.8	109.7	107.9
2012	776.9	115.9	116.2	114.8
2013	793.2	103.7	106.1	102.1
2014	815.4	107.0	113.5	102.8
2015	866.0	108.4	108.8	106.2

2-16 居民消费支出
Household Consumption Expenditure

单位：亿元 (100 million yuan)

项　　目	Item	2014	2015
居民消费支出	**Household Consumption Expenditure**	**2837.02**	**3187.11**
食品烟酒	Food, Tobacco, Liquor	802.14	877.94
衣着	Clothing	266.27	294.65
居住（含自有住房服务）	Residence	464.68	533.60
生活用品及服务	Household Facilities, Articles and Services	154.89	178.99
交通和通信	Transport and Communications	350.98	421.99
教育文化娱乐	Education , Cultural and Recreation	223.53	277.32
医疗保健	Health Care and Medical Services	265.62	295.28
银行中介服务	Bank Intermediary Services	200.04	197.93
保险服务	Insurance Service	47.72	41.72
其他商品和服务	Miscellaneous Goods and Services	61.15	67.69
按城乡分支出	**By Residence**		
农村居民	Rural Household Expenditure	856.28	955.88
食品烟酒	Food, Tobacco, Liquor	230.97	245.82
衣着	Clothing	68.74	75.88
居住（含自有住房服务）	Residence	179.39	224.24
生活用品及服务	Household Facilities, Articles and Services	42.55	49.20
交通和通信	Transport and Communications	102.39	120.17
教育文化娱乐	Education , Cultural and Recreation	43.70	58.52
医疗保健	Health Care and Medical Services	110.17	130.41
银行中介服务	Insurance Service	62.06	34.29
保险服务	Miscellaneous Goods and Services	4.77	4.17
其他商品和服务	Food, Tobacco, Liquor	11.54	13.18
城镇居民支出	Urban Households Expenditure	1980.74	2231.23
食品烟油	Food, Tobacco, Liquor	571.17	632.12
衣着	Clothing	197.53	218.77
居住（含自有住房服务）	Residence	285.29	309.36
生活用品及服务	Household Facilities, Articles and Services	112.34	129.79
交通和通信	Transport and Communications	248.59	301.82
教育文化娱乐	Education , Cultural and Recreation	179.83	218.80
医疗保健	Health Care and Medical Services	155.45	164.87
银行中介服务	Bank Intermediary Services	137.98	163.64
保险服务	Insurance Service	42.95	37.55
其他商品和服务	Miscellaneous Goods and Services	49.61	54.51

主要统计指标解释

国内生产总值(GDP) 指按市场价格计算的一个国家(或地区)所有常住单位在一定时期内生产活动的最终成果。国内生产总值有三种表现形态，即价值形态、收入形态和产品形态。从价值形态看，它是所有常住单位在一定时期内生产的全部货物和服务价值与同期投入的全部非固定资产货物和服务价值的差额，即所有常住单位的增加值之和；从收入形态看，它是所有常住单位在一定时期内创造并分配给常住单位和非常住单位的初次收入之和；从产品形态看，它是所有常住单位在一定时期内最终使用的货物和服务价值与货物和服务净出口价值之和。在实际核算中，国内生产总值有三种计算方法，即生产法、收入法和支出法。三种方法分别从不同的方面反映国内生产总值及其构成。

对于一个地区来说，称为地区生产总值或地区GDP.

三次产业 三次产业的划分是世界上较为常用的产业结构分类，但各国的划分不尽一致。根据《国民经济行业划分》（GT/T 4754—2011），我国的三次产业划分是：

第一产业是指农、林、牧、渔业（不含农、林、牧、渔服务业）。

第二产业是指采矿业（不含开采辅助活动），制造业（不含金属制品、机械和设备修理业），电力、热力、燃气及水的生产和供应业，建筑业。

第三产业是指除第一、二产业以外的其他行业。

劳动者报酬 指劳动者因从事生产活动所获得的全部报酬。包括劳动者获得的各种形式的工资、奖金和津贴，既包括货币形式的，也包括实物形式的，还包括劳动者所享受的公费医疗和医药卫生费、上下班交通补贴、单位支付的社会保险费、住房公积金等。

生产税净额 指生产税减生产补贴后的余额。生产税指政府对生产单位从事生产、销售和经营活动以及因从事生产活动使用某些生产要素(如固定资产、土地、劳动力)所征收的各种税、附加费和规费。生产补贴与生产税相反，指政府对生产单位的单方面转移支出，因此视为负生产税，包括政策亏损补贴、价格补贴等。

固定资产折旧 指一定时期内为弥补固定资产损耗按照规定的固定资产折旧率提取的固定资产折旧，或按国民经济核算统一规定的折旧率虚拟计算的固定资产折旧。它反映了固定资产在当期生产中的转移价值。各类企业和企业化管理的事业单位的固定资产折旧是指实际计提的折旧费；不计提折旧的政府机关、非企业化管理的事业单位和居民住房的固定资产折旧是按照统一规定的折旧率和固定资产原值计算的虚拟折旧。原则上，固定资产折旧应按固定资产的重置价值计算，但是目前我国尚不具备对全社会固定资产进行重估价的基础，所以暂时只能采用上述办法。

营业盈余 指常住单位创造的增加值扣除劳动者报酬、生产税净额和固定资产折旧后的余额。它相当于企业的营业利润加上生产补贴，但要扣除从利润中开支的工资和福利等。

支出法国内生产总值 是从最终使用的角度反映一个国家(或地区)一定时期内生产活动最终成果的一种方法，包括最终消费支出、资本形成总额及货物和服务净出口三部分。计算公式为：

支出法国内生产总值=最终消费支出+资本形成总额+货物和服务净出口

最终消费支出 指常住单位为满足物质、文化和精神生活的需要，从本国经济领土和国外购买的货物和服务的支出。它不包括非常住单位在本国经济领土内的消费支出。最终消费支出分为居民消费支出和政府消费支出。

居民消费支出 指常住住户在一定时期内对于货物和服务的全部最终消费支出。居民消费支出除了直接以货币形式购买的货物和服务的消费支出外，还包括以其他方式获得的货物和服务的消费支出，即所谓的虚拟消费支出。居民虚拟消费支出包括如下几种类型：单位以实物报酬及实物转移的形式提供给劳动者的货物和服务；住户生产并由本住户消费了的货物和服务，其中的服务仅指住户的自有住房服务和付酬的家庭雇员提供的家庭和个人服务；金融机构提供的金融媒介服务。

政府消费支出 指政府部门为全社会提供的公共服务的消费支出和免费或以较低的价格向居民住户提供的货物和服务的净支出，前者等于政府服务的产出价值减去政府单位所获得的经营收入的价值，后者等于政府部门免费或以较低价格向居民住户提供的货物和服务的市场价值减去向住户收取的价值。

资本形成总额 指常住单位在一定时期内获得减去处置的固定资产和存货的净额，包括固定资本形成总额和存货变动两部分。

固定资本形成总额 指常住单位在一定时期内获得的固定资产减处置的固定资产的价值总额。固定资产是通过生产活动生产出来的，且其使用年限在一年以上、单位价值在规定标准以上的资产，不包括自然资产。可分为有形固定资本形成总额和无形固定资本形成总额。有形固定资本形成总额包括一定时期内完成的建筑工程、安装工程和设备工器具购置(减处置)价值，以及土地改良、新增役、种、奶、毛、娱乐用牲畜和新增经济林木价值。无形固定资本形成总额包括矿藏的勘探、计算机软件等获得减处置。

存货变动 指常住单位在一定时期内存货实物量变动的市场价值，即期末价值减期初价值的差额，再扣除当期由于价格变动而产生的持有收益。存货变动可以是正值，也可以是负值，正值表示存货上升，负值表示存货下降。存货包括生产单位购进的原材料、燃料和储备物资等存货，以及生产单位生产的产成品、在制品和半成品等存货。

货物和服务净出口 指货物和服务出口减货物和服务进口的差额。出口包括常住单位向非常住单位出售或无偿转让的各种货物和服务的价值；进口包括常住单位从非常住单位购买或无偿得到的各种货物和服务的价值。由于服务活动的提供与使用同时发生，一般把常住单位从非常住单位得到的服务作为进口，非常住单位从常住单位得到的服务作为出口。货物的出口和进口都按离岸价格计算。

Explanatory Notes on Main Statistical Indicators

Gross Domestic Product (GDP) refers to the final products at market prices produced by all resident units in a country during a certain period of time. Gross domestic product is expressed in three different perspectives, namely value, income, and products respectively. GDP in its value perspective refers to the balance of total value of all goods and services produced by all resident units during a certain period of time, minus the total value of input of goods and services of the nature of non-fixed assets; in other words, it is the sum of the value-added of all resident units. GDP from the perspective of income includes the primary income created by all resident units and distributed to resident and non-resident units. GDP from the perspective of products refers to the value of all goods and services for final demand by all resident units plus the net exports of goods and services during a given period of time. In the practice of national accounting, gross domestic product is calculated from three approaches, namely production approach, income approach and expenditure approach, which reflect gross domestic product and its composition from different angles.

For a region, it is called as Gross Regional Product(GRP) or regional GDP.

Three Strata of Industry Classification of economic activities into three strata of industry is a common practice in the world, although the grouping varies to some extent from country to country. In China, according to Industrial classification for National Economic Activities (GB/T 4754—2011), economic activities are categorized into the following three strata of industry:

Primary industry refers to agriculture, forestry, animal husbandry and fishery industries (not including services in support of agriculture, forestry, animal husbandry and fishery industries).

Secondary industry refers to mining and quarrying(not including support activities for mining), manufacturing(not including repair service of metal products, machinery and equipment), production and supply of electricity, heat, gas and water, and construction.

Tertiary industry refers to all other economic activities not included in the primary or secondary industries.

Compensation of Employees refers to the total payment of various forms to employees for the productive activities they are engaged in. It includes wages, bonuses and allowances, which the employees earn in cash or in kind. It also includes the free medical services provided to the employees and the medicine expenses, transport subsidies and social insurance, and housing fund paid by the employers.

Net Taxes on Production refers to taxes on production less subsidies on production. The taxes on production refers to the various taxes, extra charges and fees levied on the production units on their production, sale and business activities as well as on the use of some factors of production, such as fixed assets, land and labour in the production activities they are engaged in. In contrast to taxes on production, subsidies on production refer to the unilateral government transfer to the production units and are therefore regarded as negative taxes on production. They include subsidies on the loss due to implementation of government policies, price subsidies, etc.

Depreciation of Fixed Assets refers to the depreciation of fixed assets in a given period, drawn in accordance with the stipulated depreciation rate for the purpose of compensating the wear-and-tear loss of the fixed assets or the depreciation of fixed assets imputed in accordance with the stipulated unified depreciation rate in the national economic accounting system. It reflects the value of transfer of the fixed assets in the production of the current period. The depreciation of fixed assets in various enterprises and institutions managed as enterprises refers to the depreciation expenses actually drawn. In government agencies and institutions not managed as enterprises which do not draw the depreciation expenses, as well as for the houses of residents, the depreciation of fixed assets is the imputed depreciation, which is calculated in accordance with the stipulated unified depreciation rate. In principle, the depreciation of fixed assets should be calculated on the basis of the re-purchased value of the fixed assets. However, currently the conditions in China do not facilitate the revaluation of all the fixed assets. Therefore, only the above-mentioned methods can be adopted at present.

Operating Surplus refers to the balance of the value added created by the resident units after deducting the labourers remuneration, net taxes on production and the depreciation of fixed assets. It is equivalent to the business profit of the enterprises plus subsidies to production, but the wages and welfare expenses paid from the profits should be deducted.

GDP by Expenditure Approach refers to the method of measuring the final results of production activities of a country (region) during a given period from the perspective of final uses. It includes final consumption expenditure, gross capital formation and net export of goods and services. The formula for computation is.:

GDP by expenditure approach = final consumption expenditure + gross capital formation + net export of goods and services

Final Consumption Expenditure refers to the total expenditure of resident units for purchases of goods and services from both the domestic economic territory and abroad to meet the needs of material, cultural and spiritual life. It does not include the expenditure of non-resident units on consumption in the economic territory of the country. The final consumption expenditure is broken down into household consumption expenditure and government consumption expenditure.

Households Consumption Expenditure refers to the total expenditure of resident households on the final consumption of goods and services. In addition to the consumption of goods and services bought by the households directly with money, the households consumption expenditure also includes expenditure on goods and services obtained by the households in other ways, i.e. the so-called imputed consumption expenditure, which includes the following: (a) the goods and services provided to households by employer in the form of payment in kind and transfer in kind; (b) goods and services produced and consumed by the households themselves, in which the services refer to the owner-occupied housing and services offered by paid family employees; (c) financial intermediate services provided by financial institutions.

Government Consumption Expenditure refers to the consumption expenditure spent for the provision of public services provided by the government to the whole country and the net expenditure on the goods and services provided by the government to households free of charge or at reduced prices. The former equals to the output value of the government services minus the value of operating income obtained by the government departments. The latter equals to the market value of the goods and services provided by the government free of charge or at reduced prices to the households minus the value received by the government from the households.

Gross Capital Formation refers to the fixed assets acquired less disposals and the net value of inventory, thus including gross fixed capital formation and changes in inventories.

Gross Fixed Capital Formation refers to the value of acquisitions less those disposals of fixed assets during a given period. Fixed assets are the assets produced through production activities with unit value above a specified amount and which could be used for over one year. Natural assets are not included. Gross fixed capital formation can be categorized into total tangible fixed capital formation and total intangible fixed capital formation. Total tangible fixed capital formation includes the value of the construction projects and installation projects completed and the equipment, apparatus and instruments purchased (less those disposed) as well as the value of land improved, the value of draught animals, breeding stock and animals for milk, for wool and for recreational purposes and the newly increased forest with economic value. Total intangible fixed capital formation includes the prospecting of minerals and the acquisition of computer software minus the disposal of them.

Changes in Inventories refers to the market value of the change in the physical volume of inventory of resident units during a given period, i.e. the difference between the values at the beginning and at the end of the period minus the gains due to the change in prices. The changes in inventories can have a positive or a negative value. A positive value indicates an increase in inventory while a negative value indicates a decrease in inventory. The inventory includes raw materials, fuels and reserve materials purchased by the production units as well as the inventory of finished products, semi-finished products and work-in-progress.

Net Export of Goods and Services refers to the exports of goods and services subtracting the imports of goods and services. Exports include the value of various goods and services sold or gratuitously transferred by resident units to non-resident units. Imports include the value of various goods and services purchased or gratuitously acquired resident units from non-resident units. Because the provision of services and the use of them happen simultaneously, the acquisition of services by resident units from abroad is usually treated as import while the acquisition of services by non-resident units in this country is usually treated as export. The exports and imports of goods are calculated at FOB.

3 人口与就业

POPULATION AND EMPLOYMENT

第三篇　人口与就业

本篇主要内容和资料来源

本篇内容主要包括人口、婚姻登记、计划生育、就业、工资等资料。人口资料包括全区、各地、州、市、县及兵团人口情况、人口普查的主要数据等。

本篇人口及相关分组数据，除3-1、3-2表是由新疆维吾尔自治区统计局人口与就业统计处根据人口变动调查数据推算外，其他表中数据均取自新疆维吾尔自治区公安厅户籍处所提供的公安户籍年报；计划生育资料由新疆维吾尔自治区卫生和计划生育委员会提供；失业资料由新疆维吾尔自治区人力资源和社会保障厅提供；人口普查资料、就业和劳动报酬资料由新疆维吾尔自治区统计局人口与就业统计处提供。

Population and Employment

Main Content and Source of Data

Data in this chapter show the basic condition of population, marriage registry, employment, wages of staff and workers, family planning. Data of population mainly include the condition of population by whole region, prefecture, autonomous prefecture, city, country and Xinjiang Production and Construction Group, and the data of 5 national population censuses.

The data on household registered population are provided by Municipal Bureau of Public Security of Xinjiang Uygur Autonomous Region,except the data of 3-1,3-2 are estimated from the national sample survey on population changes by the Department of Population and Social.Science and Technology Statistic.of the Xinjiang Bureau of Statistics. Data on marriang registry are provided by Department of Civil Affairs.Data on family planning come from Municipal Family Planning Commission. Data on unemployment are provided by Bureau of Labor and Social Security.The data of population census, employment and wages are provided by the Department of Population and Social Science and Technology Statistic of the Xinjiang Bureau of Statistics.

3-1 主要年份人口数及构成
Population and Its Composition in Main Years

单位：万人、% (10 000 persons,%)

年份 Year	年末总人口 Total Population (Year-end)	按性别分 By Sex				按城乡分 By Residence			
		男 Male		女 Female		城镇人口 Urban		乡村人口 Rural	
		人口数 Population	比重 Proportion	人口数 Population	比重 Proportion	人口数 Population	比重 Proportion	人口数 Population	比重 Proportion
1978	1233.01	630.18	51.11	602.83	48.89	321.40	26.07	911.61	73.93
1980	1283.24	654.90	51.03	628.34	48.97	372.74	29.05	910.50	70.95
1985	1361.14	696.81	51.19	664.33	48.81	582.24	42.78	778.90	57.22
1990	1529.16	785.06	51.34	744.10	48.66	685.96	44.86	843.20	55.14
1995	1661.35	848.12	51.05	813.23	48.95	822.53	49.51	838.82	50.49
1996	1689.29	869.59	51.48	819.70	48.52	846.17	50.09	843.12	49.91
1997	1718.08	883.03	51.40	835.05	48.60	860.76	50.10	857.32	49.90
1998	1747.35	897.90	51.39	849.45	48.61	875.42	50.10	871.93	49.90
1999	1775.00	910.98	51.32	864.02	48.68	929.00	52.34	846.00	47.66
2000	1849.41	957.07	51.75	892.34	48.25	624.18	33.75	1225.23	66.25
2001	1876.19	954.23	50.86	921.96	49.14	633.21	33.75	1242.98	66.25
2002	1905.19	975.46	51.20	929.73	48.80	644.72	33.84	1260.47	66.16
2003	1933.95	994.24	51.41	939.71	48.59	665.11	34.39	1268.84	65.61
2004	1963.11	1008.02	51.30	955.09	48.70	690.11	35.15	1273.00	64.85
2005	2010.35	1029.70	51.22	980.65	48.78	746.85	37.15	1263.50	62.85
2006	2050.00	1050.01	51.22	999.99	48.78	777.77	37.94	1272.23	62.06
2007	2095.19	1072.53	51.19	1022.66	48.81	820.27	39.15	1274.92	60.85
2008	2130.81	1083.94	50.87	1046.87	49.13	844.65	39.64	1286.16	60.36
2009	2158.63	1098.31	50.88	1060.32	49.12	860.21	39.85	1298.42	60.15
2010	2181.58	1127.01	51.66	1054.57	48.34	933.58	42.79	1248.01	57.21
2011	2208.71	1128.75	51.10	1079.96	48.90	961.67	43.54	1247.04	56.46
2012	2232.78	1145.21	51.29	1087.57	48.71	981.98	44.00	1250.80	56.00
2013	2264.30	1151.77	50.87	1112.53	49.13	1006.93	44.47	1257.37	55.53
2014	2298.47	1164.38	50.66	1134.09	49.34	1058.91	46.07	1239.56	53.93
2015	2359.73	1199.47	50.83	1160.26	49.17	1114.50	47.23	1245.23	52.77

3-2 主要年份人口出生率、死亡率、自然增长率
Birth Rate,Death Rate and Natural Growth Rate of Population in Main Years

单位：‰ (‰)

年份 Year	出生率 Birth Rate	死亡率 Death Rate	自然增长率 Natural Growth Rate	年份 Year	出生率 Birth Rate	死亡率 Death Rate	自然增长率 Natural Growth Rate
1978	22.55	7.69	14.86	2000	17.57	5.40	12.17
1980	21.28	7.62	13.66	2001	16.82	5.69	11.13
1985	19.80	6.39	13.41	2002	16.30	5.43	10.87
1986	20.54	6.13	14.41	2003	16.01	5.23	10.78
1987	21.03	5.96	15.07	2004	16.00	5.09	10.91
1988	19.72	5.99	13.73	2005	16.42	5.04	11.38
1989	21.15	5.77	15.38	2006	15.97	5.03	10.94
1990	26.41	7.81	18.60	2007	16.79	5.01	11.78
1991	24.45	7.86	16.59	2008	16.05	4.88	11.17
1992	22.80	7.84	14.96	2009	15.99	5.43	10.56
1993	21.53	7.68	13.85	2010	14.85	4.14	10.71
1994	20.82	7.43	13.39	2011	14.99	4.42	10.57
1995	18.90	6.45	12.45	2012	15.32	4.48	10.84
1996	19.45	6.60	12.85	2013	15.84	4.92	10.92
1997	19.66	6.55	13.11	2014	16.44	4.97	11.47
1998	19.74	6.93	12.81	2015	15.60	4.54	11.06
1999	18.76	6.96	11.80				

3-3 新疆人口普查基本情况

Basic Statistics on National Population Census in Xinjiang

单位：万人 (10 000 persons)

指 标	Items	第二次普查 (1964 年) 1964 Census	第三次普查 (1982 年) 1982 Census	第四次普查 (1990 年) 1990 Census	第五次普查 (2000 年) 2000 Census	第六次普查 (2010 年) 2010 Census
总人口	**Total Population**	**727.01**	**1308.15**	**1515.69**	**1845.95**	**2181.58**
男	Male	389.47	673.22	782.32	955.22	1127.01
女	Female	337.54	634.93	733.37	890.73	1054.57
总户数(万户)	**Total Household (10 000 household)**	**178.00**	**293.79**	**337.41**	**491.66**	**690.29**
家 庭 户	Family Households		292.70	334.89	479.38	670.56
集 体 户	Collective Households		1.09	2.52	12.28	19.73
各年龄组人口	**Population by Age Group**					
0-5 岁	Age 0-5	121.86	186.70	218.85	165.12	185.03
6-14 岁	Age 6-14	146.77	330.85	282.12	338.18	261.15
15-64 岁	Age 15-64	428.73	742.42	955.49	1256.40	1593.99
65 岁及以上	Aged 65 and Over	29.65	48.18	59.23	86.25	141.41
民族人口	**Nationality Population**					
汉 族	Han Nationality	232.12	528.40	569.54	748.99	882.99
少数民族	Minority Nationalities	494.89	779.75	946.15	1096.96	1298.59
各种文化程度人口	**Population by Educational Level**					
大专及以上	College and Above	4.10	8.37	27.98	94.65	231.53
高中和中专	Senior Secondary School and Specialized Secondary School	15.51	84.28	157.42	224.79	254.56
初 中	Junior Secondary School	50.37	228.63	313.51	508.59	790.62
小 学	Primary School	197.34	442.57	552.55	699.78	656.32
不识字或识字很少	Illiterate and Semi-iliterate	249.03	265.39	198.11	103.68	63.52

注：不识字或识字很少除 1964 年包含 12-14 岁人口外，其他均为 15 岁及以上人口。
Note: Illiterate or semi-illiterate population refers to the population aged above 15 except for the population aged between 12 and 14 in 1964.

3-4 主要年份婚姻登记情况

Statistics on Marriage Registration in Main Years

指 标	Item	2010	2014	2015
登记结婚(对)	**Registered Marriages (couple)**	**264013**	**279188**	**292598**
初婚(人)	First Marriage (person)	389342	525027	390188
再婚(人)	Remarriage (person)	138684	33349	195008
#男	Male	73863	16858	94752
#再婚中恢复结婚(对)	Resumed Marriages (couple)	11108	10260	24670
登记离婚(对)	**Registered Divorces (couple)**	**97817**	**108009**	**106316**
民政部门批准	Approved by the Civil Administration	69137	76733	74979
法院调判	Mediated by the court	28680	31276	31337
涉外及华侨港澳台居民婚姻	**Marital status of OverseasChinese ,Foreigner and Hong Kong, Macao and Taiwan Compatriots**			
登记结婚(对)	Registered Marriages (couple)	235	296	247
国内公民(人)	Citizen (person)	235	296	247
港澳台居民(人)	Compatriots of Hong Kong, Macao and Taiwan (person)	31	14	49
华 侨(人)	Overseas Chinese (person)	13	1	
外国人(人)	Foreigner (person)	191	281	198
登记离婚(对)	Registered Divorces (couple)	26	45	53

3-5 各地、州、市、县(市)户数、人口数、土地面积

Household, Population, Land Area by Prefecture, Autonomous Prefecture,City and County

(2015 年)

地　区	Region	户 数 (万户) Number of Households (10 000 households)	年末人口 (万人) Population at Year-end (10 000 persons)	#男 Male	平均每户人口 (人) Average Persons Per Household (person)	土地面积 (平方公里) Land Area (sq.km)
总　计	**Total**	**689.94**	**2321.72**	**1178.36**	**3.37**	**1664897.17**
乌鲁木齐市	**Urumqi City**	**80.72**	**266.83**	**136.85**	**3.31**	**14875.50**
天山区	Tianshan District	16.50	57.26	28.84	3.47	47.31
沙依巴克区	Shayibak District	17.69	55.15	27.91	3.12	38.60
新市区	Xinshi District	18.17	64.12	33.58	3.53	57.07
水磨沟区	Shui Mogou Distric	7.68	29.22	14.99	3.80	10.76
头屯河区	Tou Tunhe District	6.51	21.94	11.45	3.37	20.11
达坂城区	Da Bancheng District	1.23	4.13	2.22	3.36	1111.85
米东区	Midong District	10.46	28.72	14.76	2.74	3789.22
乌鲁木齐县	Urumqi County	2.47	6.29	3.09	2.55	9800.58
克拉玛依市	**Karamay City**	**11.25**	**29.97**	**15.10**	**2.67**	**8654.08**
独山子区	Dushanzi District	2.28	5.79	2.92	2.54	379.11
克拉玛依区	Karamay District	7.44	20.01	10.04	2.69	4231.56
白碱滩区	Bai Jiantan District	1.45	3.96	2.04	2.73	2618.76
乌尔河区	Urhe District	0.07	0.22	0.11	2.92	1424.65
吐鲁番市	**Turpan City**	**20.34**	**65.19**	**32.84**	**3.21**	**67562.91**
高昌区	Gaochang District	8.44	29.72	14.94	3.52	13589.22
鄯善县	Shanshan [Piqan] County	7.76	23.06	11.55	2.97	38281.46
托克逊县	Toksun County	4.14	12.40	6.35	2.99	15692.23
哈密地区	**Hami [Kumul] Administrative Offices**	**21.69**	**61.67**	**31.73**	**2.84**	**142094.88**
哈密市	Hami [Kumul] City	17.01	48.90	25.25	2.87	85587.23
巴里坤哈萨克自治县	Barkol Kazak Autonomous County	3.86	10.45	5.30	2.71	36988.55
伊吾县	Yiwu [Araturuk] County	0.82	2.33	1.18	2.85	19519.10

注：1.全区年末人口数、各地、州、市、县、区人口数据为 2015 年公安年报数据。
2.本表全疆及各地州市土地面积为国土资源厅 2008 年数据。

Note: a) The data in this table of population by prefecture,antonomous prefecture,city and county come from the annual data of public security of 2015
b) The land area of different prefectures and cities come from the Department of land resources of 2008.

3-5 续表 1 Continued

地区	Region	户数(万户) Number of Households (10 000 households)	年末人口(万人) Population at Year-end (10 000 persons)	#男 Male	平均每户人口(人) Average Persons Per Household (person)	土地面积(平方公里) Land Area (sq.km)
昌吉回族自治州	**Changji Hui Autonomous Prefecture**	**48.49**	**139.28**	**70.50**	**2.87**	**73139.75**
昌吉市	Changji City	12.94	37.14	18.58	2.87	7505.12
阜康市	Fukang City	5.78	16.70	8.44	2.89	8534.97
呼图壁县	Hutubi County	7.74	21.50	10.88	2.78	9421.03
玛纳斯县	Manas County	6.47	17.42	8.79	2.69	9597.27
奇台县	Qitai County	7.73	23.86	12.15	3.08	16635.92
吉木萨尔县	Jimsar County	4.87	13.85	7.10	2.84	8144.58
木垒哈萨克自治县	Mori Kazak Autonomous County	2.95	8.82	4.55	2.99	13300.86
伊犁哈萨克自治州	**Ili Kazak Autonomous Prefecture**	**154.84**	**469.63**	**237.40**	**3.03**	**268778.72**
伊犁州直属县(市)	**Counties (Cities) Direct Under Ili Prefecture**	**95.88**	**300.42**	**152.11**	**3.13**	**56381.53**
伊宁市	Yining [Gulja] City	19.51	58.75	29.04	3.01	524.94
奎屯市	Kuytun City	10.83	28.94	14.44	2.67	1109.89
伊宁县	Yining [Gulja] County	11.07	43.92	22.59	3.97	4681.90
察布查尔锡伯自治县	Qapqal Xibe Autonomous County	6.61	19.67	10.05	2.98	4471.95
霍城县	Huocheng [Korgas] County	13.93	41.38	21.09	2.97	5429.83
巩留县	Gongliu [Tokkuztara] County	6.31	20.35	10.34	3.22	4326.90
新源县	Xinyuan [Kunes] County	10.23	32.17	16.42	3.14	6813.74
昭苏县	Zhaosu [Mongolkure] County	6.69	18.77	9.48	2.80	11127.91
特克斯县	Tekes County	5.43	17.49	8.95	3.22	7764.10
尼勒克县	Nilka County	5.26	18.98	9.70	3.61	10130.37
塔城地区	**Tacheng [Tarbagatai] Administrative Offices**	**36.09**	**102.42**	**51.65**	**2.84**	**94698.18**
塔城市	Tacheng [Qoqek] City	5.88	16.87	8.47	2.87	3991.25
乌苏市	Usu City	7.28	22.47	11.41	3.09	14299.86
额敏县	Emin [Dorbiljin] County	8.21	21.29	10.77	2.59	9448.37
沙湾县	Shawan County	7.47	20.63	10.39	2.76	12676.58
托里县	Toli County	3.02	9.69	4.85	3.21	28192.65
裕民县	Yumin [Qagantokay] County	2.17	5.96	3.00	2.74	6112.13
和布克赛尔蒙古自治县	Hoboksar Mongol Autonomous County	2.06	5.50	2.76	2.67	19977.34

3-5 续表 2 Continued

地　区	Region	户 数 (万户) Number of Households (10 000 households)	年末人口 (万人) Population at Year-end (10 000 persons)	#男 Male	平均每户人口 (人) Average Persons Per Household (person)	土地面积 (平方公里) Land Area (sq.km)
阿勒泰地区	**Altay Administrative Offices**	**22.87**	**66.80**	**33.64**	**2.92**	**117699.01**
阿勒泰市	Altay City	7.59	23.15	11.65	3.05	10829.06
布尔津县	Burqin County	3.69	7.24	3.65	1.96	10357.35
富蕴县	Fuyun [Koktokay] County	2.88	9.71	4.89	3.37	32186.11
福海县	Fuhai [Burultokay] County	2.47	7.55	3.83	3.06	33250.74
哈巴河县	Habahe [Kaba] County	2.75	8.74	4.42	3.18	8166.58
青河县	Qinghe [Qinggil] County	1.96	6.53	3.28	3.33	15756.87
吉木乃县	Jemnay County	1.53	3.89	1.93	2.54	7152.30
博尔塔拉蒙古自治州	**Bortala Mongol Autonomous Prefecture**	**17.24**	**47.97**	**24.28**	**2.78**	**24934.33**
博乐市	Bole [Bortala] City	9.16	25.80	12.99	2.82	7877.34
阿拉山口市	Alashankou City	0.08	0.17	0.09	2.16	
精河县	Jinghe [Jing] County	5.00	14.47	7.37	2.90	11175.25
温泉县	Wenquan [Araxang] County	3.00	7.53	3.84	2.51	5881.74
巴音郭楞蒙古自治州	**Bayangol Mongol Autonomous Prefecture**	**47.37**	**139.38**	**70.16**	**2.94**	**470954.25**
库尔勒市	Korla City	19.15	55.90	27.83	2.92	7215.90
轮台县	Luntai [Bugur] County	4.68	14.62	7.40	3.12	14156.61
尉犁县	Yuli [Lopnur] County	3.59	10.31	5.21	2.87	59234.48
若羌县	Ruoqiang [Qarkilik] County	1.16	3.40	1.73	2.93	198793.52
且末县	Qiemo [Qarqan] County	2.05	6.95	3.53	3.38	137831.05
焉耆回族自治县	Yanji Hui Autonomous County	5.82	17.29	8.74	2.97	2440.73
和静县	Hejing County	6.64	18.35	9.36	2.77	34886.74
和硕县	Hoxud County	2.35	6.57	3.31	2.80	12816.49
博湖县	Bohu [Bagrax] County	1.93	5.99	3.07	3.10	3578.73
阿克苏地区	**Aksu Administrative Offices**	**63.30**	**253.05**	**128.57**	**4.00**	**127144.91**
阿克苏市	Aksu City	13.98	51.37	25.88	3.67	13987.61
温宿县	Wensu [Onsu] County	6.70	25.93	13.23	3.87	14202.46
库车县	Kuqa County	11.45	49.25	24.97	4.30	14602.95
沙雅县	Xayar County	7.10	27.44	13.98	3.87	31955.15
新和县	Xinhe [Toksu] County	4.85	19.59	9.88	4.04	5817.82
拜城县	Baicheng [Bay] County	6.85	24.11	12.37	3.52	15553.70
乌什县	Wushi [Uxturpan] County	5.59	23.53	12.03	4.21	9082.00
阿瓦提县	Awat County	5.51	26.28	13.39	4.77	13233.57
柯坪县	Kalpin County	1.28	5.54	2.84	4.34	8709.65

3-5 续表 3 Continued

地　区	Region	户 数 (万户) Number of Households (10 000 households)	年末人口 (万人) Population at Year-end (10 000 persons)	#男 Male	平均每户人口 (人) Average Persons Per Household (person)	土地面积 (平方公里) Land Area (sq.km)
克孜勒苏柯尔克孜自治州	**Kizilsu Kirgiz Autonomous Prefecture**	**15.25**	**59.61**	**30.28**	**3.91**	**72468.08**
阿图什市	Artux City	6.23	26.93	13.67	4.32	16151.17
阿克陶县	Akto County	5.83	22.15	11.30	3.80	24539.86
阿合奇县	Akqi County	1.23	4.47	2.24	3.65	12737.09
乌恰县	Wuqia [Ulugqat] County	1.96	6.06	3.07	3.08	19039.96
喀什地区	**Kashgar [Kaxgar] Administrative Offices**	**111.12**	**449.92**	**227.02**	**4.05**	**137578.51**
喀什市	Kashgar [Kaxgar] City	16.35	62.83	31.33	3.84	199.38
疏附县	Shufu County	6.50	27.79	14.15	4.28	3323.12
疏勒县	Shule County	9.09	37.70	19.13	4.15	2485.31
英吉沙县	Yengisar County	6.83	30.25	15.45	4.43	3223.87
泽普县	Zepu [Poskam] County	6.63	22.37	11.21	3.38	826.90
莎车县	Shache [Yarkant] County	19.31	85.14	43.18	4.41	9066.86
叶城县	Yecheng [Kagilik] County	12.49	52.00	26.20	4.16	29359.29
麦盖提县	Makit County	7.16	27.20	13.62	3.80	10276.57
岳普湖县	Yopurga County	4.77	17.80	8.95	3.73	2700.48
伽师县	Jiashi [Payzawat] County	10.90	44.58	22.65	4.09	6668.59
巴楚县	Bachu [Maralbexi] County	9.92	38.22	19.11	3.85	18903.70
塔什库尔干塔吉克自治县	Taxkorgan Tajik Autonomous County	1.18	4.04	2.03	3.41	50544.44
和田地区	**Hotan Administrative Offices**	**59.64**	**232.43**	**118.65**	**3.90**	**249146.59**
和田市	Hotan City	8.55	34.83	17.54	4.08	495.84
和田县	Hotan County	7.17	32.75	16.82	4.57	40876.80
墨玉县	Moyu [Karakax] County	14.52	57.74	29.66	3.98	25624.02
皮山县	Pishan [Guma] County	7.75	29.61	15.09	3.82	39819.75
洛浦县	Lop County	6.90	28.76	14.67	4.17	14286.97
策勒县	Qira County	5.21	16.67	8.51	3.20	31342.58
于田县	Yutian [Keriya] County	8.20	28.22	14.41	3.44	39126.14
民丰县	Minfeng [Niya] County	1.36	3.85	1.95	2.83	57574.49
自治区直辖县级市	**County level City directly under the Autonomous Region**	**38.70**	**106.80**	**54.98**	**2.76**	**7267.04**
石河子市	Shihezi City	23.80	63.26	31.70	2.66	459.94
阿拉尔市	Aral City	6.69	17.92	9.58	2.68	4196.00
图木舒克市	Tumxuk City	4.47	16.31	9.04	3.65	1901.10
五家渠市	Wujiaqu City	3.75	9.31	4.65	2.48	710.00

3-6 各地、州、市、县(市)城乡人口及自然变动情况
Population Natural Changes by Prefecture, Autonomous Prefecture, City and County

单位：人、‰ (2015 年) (person ‰)

地区	Region	总人口按城乡划分 城镇人口 Urban Population	乡村人口 Rural Population	出生率 Birth Rate	死亡率 Death Rate	自然增长率 Natural Growth Rate
乌鲁木齐市	**Urumqi City**	**2063494**	**604821**	**9.51**	**3.43**	**6.08**
天山区	Tianshan District	489644	82912	9.37	2.70	6.67
沙依巴克区	Shayibak District	478795	72703	8.78	3.70	5.08
新市区	Xinshi District	488877	152371	9.50	3.72	5.78
水磨沟区	Shui Mogou Distric	219551	72621	8.20	2.67	5.53
头屯河区	Tou Tunhe District	177700	41719	8.33	3.98	4.35
达坂城区	Da Bancheng District	14806	26523	9.92	4.57	5.35
米东区	Midong District	189007	98195	11.94	3.52	8.42
乌鲁木齐县	Urumqi County	5114	57777	16.14	5.20	10.94
克拉玛依市	**Karamay City**	**296799**	**2921**	**11.78**	**3.98**	**7.80**
独山子区	Dushanzi District	57852		12.81	4.08	8.73
克拉玛依区	Karamay District	198461	1617	12.27	3.91	8.36
白碱滩区	Bai Jiantan District	39613		7.95	4.24	3.71
乌尔河区	Urhe District	873	1304	8.73	2.76	5.97
吐鲁番市	**Turpan City**	**235840**	**416013**	**18.44**	**15.30**	**3.14**
高昌区	Gaochang District	113076	184139	19.76	23.12	-3.36
鄯善县	Shanshan [Piqan] County	76363	154235	18.22	9.03	9.19
托克逊县	Toksun County	46401	77639	15.66	8.22	7.44
哈密地区	**Hami [Kumul] Administrative Offices**	**337146**	**279565**	**10.18**	**6.70**	**3.48**
哈密市	Hami [Kumul] City	296750	192214	9.64	6.06	3.58
巴里坤哈萨克自治县	Barkol Kazak Autonomous County	33612	70847	11.69	9.39	2.30
伊吾县	Yiwu [Araturuk] County	6784	16504	14.81	8.20	6.61
昌吉回族自治州	**Changji Hui Autonomous Prefecture**	**576085**	**816677**	**11.03**	**7.40**	**3.63**
昌吉市	Changji City	229428	141931	11.35	6.24	5.11
阜康市	Fukang City	85829	81126	11.22	6.82	4.40
呼图壁县	Hutubi County	79470	135563	11.45	6.39	5.06
玛纳斯县	Manas County	65823	108383	9.70	8.91	0.79
奇台县	Qitai County	65491	173093	11.02	9.90	1.12
吉木萨尔县	Jimsar County	32586	105880	10.62	5.71	4.91
木垒哈萨克自治县	Mori Kazak Autonomous County	17458	70701	11.65	8.73	2.92

3-6 续表 1 Continued

单位：人、‰ (person ‰)

地 区	Region	总人口按城乡划分 城镇人口 Urban Population	乡村人口 Rural Population	出生率 Birth Rate	死亡率 Death Rate	自然增长率 Natural Growth Rate
伊犁哈萨克自治州	**Ili Kazak Autonomous Prefecture**	**2035781**	**2660541**	**16.05**	**6.95**	**9.10**
伊犁州直属县(市)	**Counties (Cities) Direct Under Ili Prefecture**	**1310776**	**1693394**	**17.53**	**7.12**	**10.41**
伊宁市	Yining [Gulja] City	411711	175796	18.53	5.22	13.31
奎屯市	Kuytun City	196914	92483	6.83	5.34	1.49
伊宁县	Yining [Gulja] County	61733	377446	22.39	4.97	17.42
察布查尔锡伯自治县	Qapqal Xibe Autonomous County	49234	147508	16.87	13.21	3.66
霍城县	Huocheng [Korgas] County	159761	253997	15.49	10.86	4.63
巩留县	Gongliu [Tokkuztara] County	71387	132105	19.57	8.93	10.64
新源县	Xinyuan [Kunes] County	193790	127949	17.97	7.38	10.59
昭苏县	Zhaosu [Mongolkure] County	56865	130845	16.94	6.33	10.61
特克斯县	Tekes County	55716	119167	21.51	5.03	16.48
尼勒克县	Nilka County	53665	136098	18.65	6.50	12.15
塔城地区	**Tacheng [Tarbagatai] Administrative Offices**	**455476**	**568688**	**12.65**	**6.90**	**5.75**
塔城市	Tacheng [Qoqek] City	91003	77739	10.59	4.94	5.65
乌苏市	Usu City	80561	144146	12.95	7.29	5.66
额敏县	Emin [Dorbiljin] County	92986	119940	13.11	6.44	6.67
沙湾县	Shawan County	105606	100712	11.22	8.39	2.83
托里县	Toli County	34024	62849	16.14	8.36	7.78
裕民县	Yumin [Qagantokay] County	24661	34891	12.69	5.99	6.70
和布克赛尔蒙古自治县	Hoboksar Mongol Autonomous County	26635	28411	15.17	5.89	9.28
阿勒泰地区	**Altay Administrative Offices**	**269529**	**398459**	**14.58**	**6.26**	**8.32**
阿勒泰市	Altay City	123827	107639	11.03	5.90	5.13
布尔津县	Burqin County	22218	50160	16.03	7.17	8.86
富蕴县	Fuyun [Koktokay] County	34158	62955	19.01	6.00	13.01
福海县	Fuhai [Burultokay] County	27727	47759	13.29	6.09	7.20
哈巴河县	Habahe [Kaba] County	20904	66452	16.30	7.10	9.20
青河县	Qinghe [Qinggil] County	23699	41591	18.59	5.59	13.00
吉木乃县	Jemnay County	16996	21903	13.91	6.99	6.92
博尔塔拉蒙古自治州	**Bortala Mongol Autonomous Prefecture**	**231423**	**248314**	**12.21**	**6.15**	**6.06**
博乐市	Bole [Bortala] City	143551	114451	11.75	5.57	6.18
阿拉山口市	Alashankou City	1716		11.07	1.17	9.90
精河县	Jinghe [Jing] County	66551	78138	13.28	7.03	6.25
温泉县	Wenquan [Araxang] County	19605	55725	11.76	6.56	5.20
巴音郭楞蒙古自治州	**Bayangol Mongol Autonomous Prefecture**	**637553**	**756259**	**15.20**	**6.87**	**8.33**
库尔勒市	Korla City	363728	195240	14.17	5.13	9.04
轮台县	Luntai [Bugur] County	39642	106577	18.54	7.32	11.22
尉犁县	Yuli [Lopnur] County	41942	61201	14.83	8.27	6.56
若羌县	Ruoqiang [Qarkilik] County	13158	20862	15.29	7.47	7.82
且末县	Qiemo [Qarqan] County	21157	48307	21.65	7.23	14.42
焉耆回族自治县	Yanji Hui Autonomous County	43139	129722	13.30	6.92	6.38
和静县	Hejing County	74879	108654	16.21	10.25	5.96
和硕县	Hoxud County	25116	40588	12.39	8.33	4.06
博湖县	Bohu [Bagrax] County	14792	45108	15.28	6.83	8.45

3-6 续表 2 Continued

单位：人、‰ (person.‰)

地　　区	Region	总人口按城乡划分 城镇人口 Urban Population	乡村人口 Rural Population	出生率 Birth Rate	死亡率 Death Rate	自　然 增长率 Natural Growth Rate
阿克苏地区	**Aksu Administrative Offices**	**830433**	**1700073**	**28.40**	**9.99**	**18.41**
阿克苏市	Aksu City	307727	205955	23.74	7.96	15.78
温宿县	Wensu [Onsu] County	59812	199493	23.16	10.39	12.77
库车县	Kuqa County	172403	320132	23.71	14.23	9.48
沙雅县	Xayar County	68240	206142	30.59	15.06	15.53
新和县	Xinhe [Toksu] County	71451	124469	51.86	9.30	42.56
拜城县	Baicheng [Bay] County	48581	192498	14.43	8.64	5.79
乌什县	Wushi [Uxturpan] County	38721	196615	24.92	6.26	18.66
阿瓦提县	Awat County	48162	214680	49.76	6.22	43.54
柯坪县	Kalpin County	15336	40089	18.37	6.06	12.31
克孜勒苏柯尔克孜自治州	**Kizilsu Kirgiz Autonomous Prefecture**	**127315**	**468749**	**22.91**	**6.51**	**16.40**
阿图什市	Artux City	92044	177273	22.84	6.69	16.15
阿克陶县	Akto County	9065	212461	22.53	5.88	16.65
阿合奇县	Akqi County	9790	34866	24.18	6.92	17.26
乌恰县	Wuqia [Ulugqat] County	16416	44149	23.63	7.73	15.90
喀什地区	**Kashgar [Kaxgar] Administrative Offices**	**1090095**	**3409063**	**36.31**	**10.25**	**26.06**
喀什市	Kashgar [Kaxgar] City	310134	318168	30.03	5.29	24.74
疏附县	Shufu County	45701	232176	18.73	6.23	12.50
疏勒县	Shule County	60612	316417	26.22	10.24	15.98
英吉沙县	Yengisar County	42361	260181	39.26	17.37	21.89
泽普县	Zepu [Poskam] County	54433	169261	31.16	13.89	17.27
莎车县	Shache [Yarkant] County	220986	630388	61.32	11.14	50.18
叶城县	Yecheng [Kagilik] County	112459	407503	29.93	12.62	17.31
麦盖提县	Makit County	48192	223818	29.97	13.30	16.67
岳普湖县	Yopurga County	34765	143190	34.81	7.31	27.50
伽师县	Jiashi [Payzawat] County	85924	359922	35.06	12.48	22.58
巴楚县	Bachu [Maralbexi] County	63542	318734	31.40	5.06	26.34
塔什库尔干塔吉克自治县	Taxkorgan Tajik Autonomous County	11076	29305	19.61	9.58	10.03
和田地区	**Hotan Administrative Offices**	**618404**	**1705883**	**22.79**	**5.52**	**17.27**
和田市	Hotan City	297307	50982	19.42	5.10	14.32
和田县	Hotan County	14135	313398	21.35	4.99	16.36
墨玉县	Moyu [Karakax] County	96220	481171	20.80	4.75	16.05
皮山县	Pishan [Guma] County	38097	257978	21.45	4.33	17.12
洛浦县	Lop County	35779	251811	25.97	6.38	19.59
策勒县	Qira County	33230	133505	25.32	7.07	18.25
于田县	Yutian [Keriya] County	90096	192086	29.56	7.69	21.87
民丰县	Minfeng [Niya] County	13540	24952	21.10	5.64	15.46
自治区直辖县级市	**County level City directly under the Autonomous Region**	**603536**	**464443**	**7.28**	**4.74**	**2.54**
石河子市	Shihezi City	426885	205721	5.83	4.82	1.01
阿拉尔市	Aral City	56112	123102	9.84	4.15	5.69
图木舒克市	Tumxuk City	47668	115433	10.02	4.05	5.97
五家渠市	Wujiaqu City	72871	20187	7.32	6.59	0.73

3-7 各地、州、市、县(市)分民族人口数

单位：人 (2015 年)

地　区	Region	合　计 Total	#少数民族 Minority Nationalities	维吾尔族 Uygur	汉　族 Han	哈萨克族 Kazak
乌鲁木齐市	**Urumqi City**	**2668315**	**694666**	**339951**	**1973649**	**63780**
天山区	Tianshan District	572556	240619	176527	331937	11978
沙依巴克区	Shayibak District	551498	110270	57698	441228	7448
新市区	Xinshi District	641248	95137	40348	546111	3887
水磨沟区	Shui Mogou Distric	292172	48339	30344	243833	3015
头屯河区	Tou Tunhe District	219419	43905	21427	175514	1635
达坂城区	Da Bancheng District	41329	23019	2387	18310	6839
米东区	Midong District	287202	93154	10278	194048	4708
乌鲁木齐县	Urumqi County	62891	40223	942	22668	24270
克拉玛依市	**Karamay City**	**299720**	**75800**	**46575**	**223920**	**12281**
独山子区	Dushanzi District	57852	15414	9415	42438	2658
克拉玛依区	Karamay District	200078	48284	29259	151794	7912
白碱滩区	Bai Jiantan District	39613	11054	7535	28559	1659
乌尔河区	Urhe District	2177	1048	366	1129	52
吐鲁番市	**Turpan City**	**651853**	**530284**	**489135**	**121569**	**355**
高昌区	Gaochang District	297215	248010	227610	49205	28
鄯善县	Shanshan [Piqan] County	230598	176834	165086	53764	39
托克逊县	Toksun County	124040	105440	96439	18600	288
哈密地区	**Hami [Kumul] Administrative Offices**	**616711**	**189054**	**109072**	**427657**	**55550**
哈密市	Hami [Kumul] City	488964	133082	99036	355882	12804
巴里坤哈萨克自治县	Barkol Kazak Autonomous County	104459	40563	142	63896	38189
伊吾县	Yiwu [Araturuk] County	23288	15409	9894	7879	4557
昌吉回族自治州	**Changji Hui Autonomous Prefecture**	**1392762**	**386116**	**68144**	**1006646**	**146831**
昌吉市	Changji City	371359	102668	11172	268691	20160
阜康市	Fukang City	166955	50551	10835	116404	15331
呼图壁县	Hutubi County	215033	53360	6508	161673	26914
玛纳斯县	Manas County	174206	34782	6224	139424	19306
奇台县	Qitai County	238584	66611	20439	171973	27616
吉木萨尔县	Jimsar County	138466	45230	7801	93236	12129
木垒哈萨克自治县	Mori Kazak Autonomous County	88159	32914	5165	55245	25375

Population of Major Nationalities by Prefecture, Autonomous Prefecture, City and County

(person)

回 族 Hui	柯尔克孜族 Kirgiz	蒙古族 Mongolian	锡伯族 Xibo	俄罗斯族 Russion	塔吉克族 Tajik	乌孜别克族 Uzbek	塔塔尔族 Tatar	满 族 Manchu	达斡尔族 Daur	其 它 Others
244210	**1900**	**10343**	**5686**	**3836**	**215**	**2129**	**1042**	**11215**	**638**	**9721**
39272	870	2790	1626	1162	107	1287	568	2498	188	1746
33809	457	2658	1409	1014	50	387	198	2733	153	2256
39757	317	2397	1477	919	29	242	119	3176	169	2300
10733	106	1075	549	354	13	112	35	1106	49	848
17662	61	591	450	154	10	40	19	941	36	879
13583	11	23	4	6	2	2	5	63	2	92
74833	40	670	163	224	4	9	27	684	36	1478
14561	38	139	8	3		50	71	14	5	122
7388	**150**	**2888**	**986**	**646**	**34**	**346**	**101**	**1365**	**161**	**2879**
1620	8	515	148	152	5	85	7	306	25	470
4975	106	1509	729	440	25	223	65	908	120	2013
770	36	265	104	54	4	38	28	151	16	394
23		599	5				1			2
39079	**3**	**225**	**26**	**54**		**28**	**6**	**275**	**6**	**1092**
19399		113	19	36		9	2	135	6	653
11141	1	87	3	15		19	4	107		332
8539	2	25	4	3				33		107
17588	**15**	**2716**	**158**	**100**		**12**	**27**	**1794**	**14**	**2008**
16378	13	1078	149	82		10	5	1727	14	1786
327	2	1628	9	18			22	62		164
883		10				2		5		58
146885	**181**	**6900**	**651**	**753**	**6**	**2378**	**909**	**3295**	**61**	**9122**
64412	101	1628	400	330	6	155	91	1371	34	2808
21810	17	416	69	110		46	58	238	10	1611
17296	5	319	42	95		3	29	170	1	1978
7763	35	123	31	108		19	9	170	8	986
13548	9	1765	76	77		658	459	1183	4	777
21105	8	2619	23	20		502	169	121	3	730
951	6	30	10	13		995	94	42	1	232

3-7 续表 1

单位：人

地　区	Region	合　计 Total	#少数民族 Minority Nationalities	维吾尔族 Uygur	汉　族 Han	哈萨克族 Kazak
伊犁哈萨克自治州	**Ili Kazak Autonomous Prefecture**	**4696322**	**2761751**	**819701**	**1934571**	**1257003**
伊犁州直属县(市)	**Counties (Cities) Direct Under Ili Prefecture**	**3004170**	**1906405**	**768113**	**1097765**	**637147**
伊宁市	Yining [Gulja] City	587507	351940	264534	235567	26863
奎屯市	Kuytun City	289397	15768	1018	273629	5222
伊宁县	Yining [Gulja] County	439179	373633	207446	65546	54533
察布查尔锡伯自治县	Qapqal Xibe Autonomous County	196742	131660	56700	65082	40181
霍城县	Huocheng [Korgas] County	413758	248956	94946	164802	37878
巩留县	Gongliu [Tokkuztara] County	203492	148602	47571	54890	63108
新源县	Xinyuan [Kunes] County	321739	211594	34001	110145	150145
昭苏县	Zhaosu [Mongolkure] County	187710	139542	18938	48168	94120
特克斯县	Tekes County	174883	140985	20010	33898	76904
尼勒克县	Nilka County	189763	143725	22949	46038	88193
塔城地区	**Tacheng [Tarbagatai] Administrative Offices**	**1024164**	**454846**	**42154**	**569318**	**267695**
塔城市	Tacheng [Qoqek] City	168742	64426	5081	104316	27731
乌苏市	Usu City	224707	84945	17118	139762	22766
额敏县	Emin [Dorbiljin] County	212926	101609	8080	111317	76084
沙湾县	Shawan County	206318	72049	9406	134269	37824
托里县	Toli County	96873	72040	1220	24833	68958
裕民县	Yumin [Qagantokay] County	59552	24576	170	34976	18799
和布克赛尔蒙古自治县	Hoboksar Mongol Autonomous County	55046	35201	1079	19845	15533
阿勒泰地区	**Altay Administrative Offices**	**667988**	**400500**	**9434**	**267488**	**352161**
阿勒泰市	Altay City	231466	96849	4890	134617	79626
布尔津县	Burqin County	72378	50905	1008	21473	41583
富蕴县	Fuyun [Koktokay] County	97113	76325	1929	20788	71384
福海县	Fuhai [Burultokay] County	75486	35333	509	40153	31191
哈巴河县	Habahe [Kaba] County	87356	61713	346	25643	53437
青河县	Qinghe [Qinggil] County	65290	53398	558	11892	50091
吉木乃县	Jemnay County	38899	25977	194	12922	24849
博尔塔拉蒙古自治州	**Bortala Mongol Autonomous Prefecture**	**479737**	**172749**	**68514**	**306988**	**49792**
博乐市	Bole [Bortala] City	258002	91736	44749	166266	21022
阿拉山口市	Alashankou City	1716	207	40	1509	24
精河县	Jinghe [Jing] County	144689	47997	20090	96692	14047
温泉县	Wenquan [Araxang] County	75330	32809	3635	42521	14699
巴音郭楞蒙古自治州	**Bayangol Mongol Autonomous Prefecture**	**1393812**	**567749**	**440283**	**826063**	**1289**
库尔勒市	Korla City	558968	150815	129411	408153	102
轮台县	Luntai [Bugur] County	146219	95681	95078	50538	8
尉犁县	Yuli [Lopnur] County	103143	34862	33752	68281	15
若羌县	Ruoqiang [Qarkilik] County	34020	15037	13328	18983	5
且末县	Qiemo [Qarqan] County	69464	51099	50754	18365	3
焉耆回族自治县	Yanji Hui Autonomous County	172861	81636	45786	91225	39
和静县	Hejing County	183533	92371	51069	91162	1061
和硕县	Hoxud County	65704	23978	10641	41726	37
博湖县	Bohu [Bagrax] County	59900	22270	10464	37630	19

Continued

(person)

回　族 Hui	柯尔克孜族 Kirgiz	蒙古族 Mongolian	锡伯族 Xibo	俄罗斯族 Russion	塔吉克族 Tajik	乌孜别克族 Uzbek	塔塔尔族 Tatar	满　族 Manchu	达斡尔族 Daur	其　它 Others
433045	**22428**	**75597**	**34457**	**5394**	**153**	**8298**	**2852**	**5199**	**5875**	**91749**
323318	**20154**	**34603**	**32384**	**1566**	**145**	**7702**	**1292**	**4018**	**535**	**75428**
39844	727	2209	5318	815	91	4666	543	2177	73	4080
6364	29	1059	267	90	3	13	5	424	38	1236
74136	382	258	230	31	8	759	61	349	5	35435
11035	300	167	20426	100		140	10	103	19	2479
89093	297	788	3252	237	4	241	113	342	338	21427
29226	466	2283	1550	95	1	184	117	278	6	3717
23117	483	179	410	102	6	742	145	157	7	2100
5353	5539	14025	69	37	5	397	271	38	1	749
25000	11202	4549	202	5	20	291	20	75	2	2705
20150	729	9086	660	54	7	269	7	75	46	1500
84845	**2207**	**34454**	**1990**	**3407**	**7**	**419**	**506**	**812**	**5324**	**11026**
13954	1791	1764	1553	2333	2	160	245	232	5128	4452
35167	7	7921	139	139	1	60	33	124	32	1438
7743	354	6074	91	537		126	70	155	67	2228
22386	13	496	43	119	4	24	19	186	24	1505
1074	19	445	56	16		24	41	50	6	131
4017	5	145	54	233			9	26	44	1074
504	18	17609	54	30		25	89	39	23	198
24882	**67**	**6540**	**83**	**421**	**1**	**177**	**1054**	**369**	**16**	**5295**
6972	30	2864	37	191	1	121	318	196	5	1598
4758	6	1763	11	141		4	338	48	2	1243
2027	18	304	9	37		13	91	41	4	468
2713	1	222	9	37			53	40	3	555
6356	5	440	8			11	51	8		1051
1330	2	914	7	11		28	192	11		254
726	5	33	2	4			11	25	2	126
20995	**95**	**28388**	**432**	**196**	**3**	**168**	**16**	**378**	**31**	**3741**
10678	35	13050	309	152	3	99	12	275	14	1338
62		47	1					6		27
7001	32	4990	67	41		42	3	71		1613
3254	28	10301	55	3		27	1	26	17	763
64979	**213**	**50091**	**233**	**265**	**4**	**149**	**3**	**1375**	**28**	**8837**
10997	15	5481	199	234	2	81	1	1059	19	3214
351	1	54	8	3		6	1	24		147
522		34	2	9		16		39	5	468
1184	1	26	2					7		484
182		16	3		1	12		4		124
31052	89	3621	2	1	1	26		74	1	944
7140	92	30816	12	10		8		99	3	2061
6746	3	5740	2	8			1	30		770
6805	12	4303	3					39		625

3-7 续表 2

单位：人

地　　区	Region	合　计 Total	#少数民族 Minority Nationalities	维吾尔族 Uygur	汉　族 Han	哈萨克族 Kazak
阿克苏地区	**Aksu Administrative Offices**	**2530506**	**2064523**	**2030600**	**465983**	**162**
阿克苏市	Aksu City	513682	286901	278210	226781	38
温宿县	Wensu [Onsu] County	259305	203970	197360	55335	11
库车县	Kuqa County	492535	443514	440125	49021	58
沙雅县	Xayar County	274382	232919	230129	41463	2
新和县	Xinhe [Toksu] County	195920	185019	184399	10901	11
拜城县	Baicheng [Bay] County	241079	214520	212272	26559	22
乌什县	Wushi [Uxturpan] County	235336	223874	216579	11462	12
阿瓦提县	Awat County	262842	219882	217722	42960	6
柯坪县	Kalpin County	55425	53924	53804	1501	2
克孜勒苏柯尔克孜自治州	**Kizilsu Kirgiz Autonomous Prefecture**	**596064**	**554626**	**389437**	**41438**	**172**
阿图什市	Artux City	269317	247563	216651	21754	60
阿克陶县	Akto County	221526	213179	161687	8347	29
阿合奇县	Akqi County	44656	40121	1193	4535	39
乌恰县	Wuqia [Ulugqat] County	60565	53763	9906	6802	44
喀什地区	**Kashgar [Kaxgar] Administrative Offices**	**4499158**	**4206186**	**4140255**	**292972**	**211**
喀什市	Kashgar [Kaxgar] City	628302	539719	534848	88583	98
疏附县	Shufu County	277877	272471	271556	5406	7
疏勒县	Shule County	377029	351320	350301	25709	4
英吉沙县	Yengisar County	302542	298141	297290	4401	14
泽普县	Zepu [Poskam] County	223694	187744	181256	35950	7
莎车县	Shache [Yarkant] County	851374	825970	818379	25404	10
叶城县	Yecheng [Kagilik] County	519962	496554	490417	23408	31
麦盖提县	Makit County	272010	226769	225608	45241	2
岳普湖县	Yopurga County	177955	168154	167860	9801	2
伽师县	Jiashi [Payzawat] County	445846	437504	437073	8342	13
巴楚县	Bachu [Maralbexi] County	382186	364370	363488	17816	8
塔什库尔干塔吉克自治县	Taxkorgan Tajik Autonomous County	40381	37470	2179	2911	15
和田地区	**Hotan Administrative Offices**	**2324287**	**2253054**	**2248113**	**71233**	**113**
和田市	Hotan City	348289	312392	311050	35897	23
和田县	Hotan County	327533	325510	325117	2023	3
墨玉县	Moyu [Karakax] County	577391	563869	563606	13522	4
皮山县	Pishan [Guma] County	296075	292287	290016	3788	
洛浦县	Lop County	287590	282695	282513	4895	31
策勒县	Qira County	166735	163814	163705	2921	1
于田县	Yutian [Keriya] County	282182	277504	277206	4678	18
民丰县	Minfeng [Niya] County	38492	34983	34900	3509	33
自治区直辖县级市	**County level City directly under the Autonomous Region**	**1067979**	**149705**	**113519**	**918274**	**3710**
石河子市	Shihezi City	632606	32638	6380	599968	3583
阿拉尔市	Aral City	179214	11517	6036	167697	28
图木舒克市	Tumxuk City	163101	102187	101042	60914	1
五家渠市	Wujiaqu City	93058	3363	61	89695	98

Continued

(person)

回 族 Hui	柯尔克孜族 Kirgiz	蒙古族 Mongolian	锡伯族 Xibo	俄罗斯族 Russion	塔吉克族 Tajik	乌孜别克族 Uzbek	塔塔尔族 Tatar	满 族 Manchu	达斡尔族 Daur	其 它 Others
14056	**11386**	**835**	**161**	**126**	**9**	**208**	**14**	**582**	**2**	**6382**
4825	231	552	79	62		43		351		2510
821	4175	42	6	3	4	6		18		1524
2482	153	80	34	22	2	47	1	107	1	402
2178	8	27	14	20		3	1	33		504
340	9	16	6	12	2			39		185
852	1148	32	9			12	1	19	1	152
1338	5613	19	11			78	10	6		208
1193	20	59	2	7	1	19	1	9		843
27	29	8								54
661	**157717**	**81**	**28**	**6**	**5829**	**175**	**34**	**87**	**2**	**397**
279	30174	43	13	6	24	17	2	69		225
191	45279	18	6		5759	106	32	3	1	68
80	38765	4	2		3			5		30
111	43499	16	7		43	52		10	1	74
6395	**7036**	**740**	**150**	**100**	**42746**	**4767**	**74**	**603**	**13**	**3096**
1603	350	168	57	68	172	1372	23	293	5	662
74	669	5	3		6	9	5	1	1	135
346	379	98	8	2	1	21	2	30	1	127
67	599	9	4	4	21	27	3	21	2	80
1076	144	128	11	9	4452	152	1	65		443
974	1238	101	32	7	2932	1856	33	41	1	366
862	1324	53	11	6	2288	1170	1	45		346
612	2	43	1	1	4	46	1	32		417
103		51	4		2	1	1	3		127
55	7	41	6	1		73	3	36		196
593	4	34	6	1	1	40	1	27	3	164
30	2320	9	7	1	32867			9		33
1585	**1017**	**156**	**55**	**12**	**1095**	**41**	**16**	**107**	**2**	**742**
760	15	84	31	12	9	26	7	68	2	305
346	1						9	2		32
125	1	13	8			4		8		100
94	991	15	4		1081	7				79
53		15	2					6		75
55	1	5	4		1			1		41
142	5	24	6		1			22		80
10	3				3	4				30
18891	**57**	**1600**	**188**	**305**	**18**	**47**	**1**	**1238**	**23**	**10108**
15618	38	820	153	235	17	9	1	923	19	4842
846	18	245	11	15	1			78		4239
501	1	58	5	4		38		39	1	497
1926		477	19	51				198	3	530

3-8 主要年份分民族人口数
Population by Nationality in Main Years

单位：万人 (10 000 persons)

年份 Year	维吾尔族 Uygur	汉族 Han	哈萨克族 Kazak	回族 Hui	柯尔克孜族 Kirgiz	蒙古族 Mongolian	锡伯族 Xibo
1978	555.53	512.90	82.10	53.12	10.40	10.74	2.55
1980	576.46	531.03	87.68	56.56	10.89	11.32	2.59
1985	629.44	534.92	98.72	59.96	12.35	12.33	2.93
1990	724.95	574.66	113.92	68.89	14.44	14.28	3.42
1995	780.00	631.81	123.77	74.76	15.78	15.28	3.82
1996	791.60	643.28	125.70	76.02	16.05	15.54	3.89
1997	802.00	660.13	127.08	77.06	16.27	15.75	3.90
1998	813.95	674.11	128.70	78.20	16.41	15.91	3.95
1999	825.03	687.15	130.45	79.26	16.64	16.13	4.00
2000	852.33	725.08	131.87	83.93	16.47	16.20	4.05
2001	860.56	742.20	131.92	84.42	17.01	16.19	4.13
2002	869.23	759.57	133.35	85.46	17.13	16.38	4.10
2003	882.35	771.10	135.21	86.67	17.37	16.69	4.03
2004	897.67	780.25	138.16	87.63	17.12	16.96	4.08
2005	923.50	795.66	141.39	89.35	17.15	17.17	4.15
2006	941.38	812.16	143.50	90.96	17.59	17.46	4.19
2007	965.06	823.93	148.39	94.30	18.19	17.71	4.24
2008	983.18	836.33	151.05	95.30	18.64	18.10	4.32
2009	1001.98	841.69	151.48	98.04	18.93	17.96	4.28
2010	1017.15	832.29	151.16	98.40	18.92	17.74	4.23
2011	1037.04	844.42	154.26	100.34	19.40	17.89	4.27
2012	1052.86	847.29	155.75	102.31	19.44	18.08	4.29
2013	1074.41	860.06	158.54	104.57	19.85	18.43	4.35
2014	1127.19	859.51	159.87	105.85	20.24	18.53	4.35
2015	1130.33	861.10	159.12	101.58	20.22	18.06	4.32

年份 Year	俄罗斯族 Russian	塔吉克族 Tajik	乌孜别克族 Uzbek	塔塔尔族 Tatar	满族 Manchu	达斡尔族 Daur	其他民族 Others
1978	0.06	2.28	0.77	0.31	0.42	0.41	1.42
1980	0.06	2.41	0.79	0.31	0.50	0.40	2.24
1985	0.43	2.89	0.93	0.33	0.95	0.48	4.49
1990	0.75	3.44	1.14	0.40	1.66	0.56	6.65
1995	0.90	3.82	1.33	0.47	1.99	0.62	7.00
1996	0.92	3.89	1.35	0.47	2.05	0.63	7.90
1997	0.92	3.90	1.35	0.46	2.06	0.63	6.56
1998	0.93	3.96	1.37	0.47	2.09	0.64	6.66
1999	0.94	4.01	1.39	0.48	2.12	0.65	6.75
2000	1.09	4.09	1.36	0.48	2.31	0.66	9.48
2001	1.08	4.12	1.37	0.47	2.30	0.67	9.75
2002	1.12	4.07	1.39	0.48	2.35	0.67	9.89
2003	1.11	4.09	1.46	0.49	2.39	0.67	10.32
2004	1.13	4.35	1.42	0.47	2.41	0.67	10.79
2005	1.12	4.40	1.51	0.47	2.46	0.65	11.37
2006	1.14	4.47	1.60	0.47	2.52	0.66	11.91
2007	1.16	4.48	1.61	0.47	2.56	0.67	12.42
2008	1.16	4.54	1.69	0.49	2.59	0.68	12.74
2009	1.17	4.72	1.67	0.49	2.62	0.69	12.91
2010	1.16	4.69	1.70	0.49	2.61	0.67	13.23
2011	1.16	4.73	1.74	0.49	2.64	0.69	13.59
2012	1.17	4.86	1.77	0.50	2.66	0.68	14.39
2013	1.18	4.90	1.82	0.51	2.71	0.68	14.61
2014	1.20	5.01	1.85	0.51	2.81	0.69	14.94
2015	1.18	5.01	1.87	0.51	2.75	0.69	14.99

3-9 各地、州、市采取各种避孕措施情况

Condition of Adopting Various Contraceptives by Prefecture, Autonomous Prefecture, City and County

单位：人　　(2015 年)　　(person)

地　区	Region	合　计 Total	男性绝育 Masculine Sterilization	女性绝育 Female Sterilization	宫内节育器 IUD Intrauterine Device	皮下埋植 Subdermal Implant
总　计	**Total**	**3543577**	**3476**	**123752**	**2879629**	**5605**
城　镇	Urban	1221581	987	21014	935051	1312
农　村	Rural	2321996	2489	102738	1944578	4293
乌鲁木齐市	Urumqi City	466918	408	8923	234157	788
克拉玛依市	Karamay City	73741	119	1596	45561	118
吐鲁番市	Turpan City	110301	24	1413	97880	235
哈密地区	Hami [Kumul] Administrative Offices	84417	58	2886	66038	240
昌吉回族自治州	Changji Hui Autonomous Prefecture	231825	325	8789	186767	451
伊犁州直属县(市)	Counties (Cities) Direct Under Ili Prefecture	429519	337	10224	347648	420
塔城地区	Tacheng [Tarbagatai] Administrative Offices	165930	248	8065	135392	1199
阿勒泰地区	Altay Administrative Offices	105216	76	1998	81756	284
博尔塔拉蒙古自治州	Bortala Mongol Autonomous Prefecture	66483	190	3370	48023	183
巴音郭楞蒙古自治州	Bayangol Mongol Autonomous Prefecture	283185	1093	13508	239684	127
阿克苏地区	Aksu Administrative Offices	437744	380	20281	387130	1206
克孜勒苏柯尔克孜自治州	Kizilsu Kirgiz Autonomous Prefecture	96011	2	1501	88445	25
喀什地区	Kashgar [Kaxgar] Administrative Offices	652692	128	19168	613600	306
和田地区	Hotan Administrative Offices	339595	88	22030	307548	23

地　区	Region	口服药及注射针 Medicine and Entry Needle	避孕套 Contraceptives	外用药 Drug for Exterior Use	其他 Other
总　计	**Total**	**14284**	**489661**	**17356**	**9814**
城　镇	Urban	7444	248429	2623	4721
农　村	Rural	6840	241232	14733	5093
乌鲁木齐市	Urumqi City	7353	207464	638	7187
克拉玛依市	Karamay City	618	25407	173	149
吐鲁番市	Turpan City	449	9604	495	201
哈密地区	Hami [Kumul] Administrative Offices	154	14950	15	76
昌吉回族自治州	Changji Hui Autonomous Prefecture	763	34355	267	108
伊犁州直属县(市)	Counties (Cities) Direct Under Ili Prefecture	1132	68158	404	1196
塔城地区	Tacheng [Tarbagatai] Administrative Offices	265	20688	59	14
阿勒泰地区	Altay Administrative Offices	162	20861	55	24
博尔塔拉蒙古自治州	Bortala Mongol Autonomous Prefecture	246	14420	51	0
巴音郭楞蒙古自治州	Bayangol Mongol Autonomous Prefecture	202	28376	147	48
阿克苏地区	Aksu Administrative Offices	1059	23234	3893	561
克孜勒苏柯尔克孜自治州	Kizilsu Kirgiz Autonomous Prefecture	800	4007	1101	130
喀什地区	Kashgar [Kaxgar] Administrative Offices	961	8906	9514	109
和田地区	Hotan Administrative Offices	120	9231	544	11

3-10 主要年份新疆生产建设兵团人口情况
Population of Xinjiang Production and Construction Group in Main Years

单位：人 (person)

年份 Year	总人口 Total Population	按性别分 by sex 男 Male	女 Female	按农业非农业分 by Agricultural and Non-agricultural 农业人口 Agricultural Population	非农业人口 Non-Agricultural Population	出生人口 Birth Population	死亡人口 Death Population	出生率(‰) Birth Rate (‰)	死亡率(‰) Death Rate (‰)	自然增长率(‰) Natural Growth Rate (‰)
1978	2119835	1090674	1029161			32749	6203	16.56	3.14	13.42
1980	2200755	1127050	1073705			26972	7162	12.27	3.26	9.01
1990	2143528	1110475	1033053	1132435	1044093	24589	9305	11.48	4.35	7.13
1995	2287896	1194166	1093730	1230151	1057745	22519	10044	9.98	4.45	5.53
2000	2427920	1272719	1155201	1379913	1048007	22674	12525	9.40	5.20	4.20
2001	2453575	1289954	1163621	1325998	1127577	19061	9014	7.80	3.70	4.10
2002	2501189	1311750	1189439	1355526	1145663	18179	9842	7.37	3.99	3.38
2003	2542170	1330666	1211504	1377224	1164946	17218	9914	6.84	3.94	2.90
2004	2563837	1341213	1222624	1413197	1150640	15860	9864	6.21	3.86	2.35
2005	2569756	1346901	1222855	1332458	1237298	16381	11934	6.38	4.65	1.73
2006	2579435	1352541	1226894	1312908	1266527	14687	11858	5.71	4.61	1.10
2007	2584732	1353053	1231679	1316590	1268142	13289	10131	5.15	3.92	1.23
2008	2573077	1344445	1228632	1289450	1283627	14612	11183	5.67	4.34	1.33
2009	2573145	1346229	1226918	1296755	1276390	14447	11285	5.61	4.39	1.22
2010	2607184	1376580	1230604	1252049	1321154	19205	10572	6.30	4.08	2.22
2011	2613724	1372606	1241118	1244796	1368928	13838	12198	5.33	4.70	0.63
2012	2648636	1390548	1258088	1192468	1456168	14916	14794	5.67	5.62	0.05
2013	2701427	1423075	1278352	1075898	1625529	15305	13203	5.72	4.94	0.78
2014	2732868	1434671	1298197	1072998	1659870	17126	12666	6.30	4.66	1.64
2015	2765608	1447041	1318567	1035634	1729974	16619	13303	6.04	4.84	1.20

3-11 按县、市分列的团场户数、人口数
Household and Population of Regiment Farms by City and County

(2015 年)

团 场	Regiment Farm	户数(户) Number of Households (household)	人口数(人) Population (person)
总 计	**Total**	**633125**	**1789627**
乌鲁木齐市	**Urumqi City**	**23871**	**62020**
沙依巴克区	Shayibake District	10247	27578
104 团	No.104 Regiment Farm	7974	21306
西山农场	Xishan Farm	2273	6272
头屯河区	Tou Tunhe District	13624	34442
三平农场	Sanping Farm	3802	11403
五一农场	MayIst Farm	4239	11588
头屯河农场	Tou Tunhe Farm	5583	11451
克拉玛依市	**Karamay City**	**13581**	**35884**
129 团	No.129 Regiment Farm	6731	17209
136 团	No.136 Regiment Farm	3584	10031
137 团	No.137 Regiment Farm	3266	8644
石河子市	**Shihezi City**	**17594**	**52403**
152 团	No.152 Regiment Farm	2135	6026
石河子总场	General Shihezi Farm	15459	46377
吐鲁番市	**Turpan City**	**1886**	**5185**
高昌区	Gaochang District	1886	5185
221 团	No.221 Regiment Farm	1886	5185
哈密地区	**Hami [Kumul] Administrative Offices**	**27165**	**80441**
哈密市	Hami [Kumul] City	21906	65674
红星一场	Red Star No.1 Farm	3413	8726
红星二场	Red Star No.2 Farm	3012	7543
红星四场	Red Star No.4 Farm	2510	7916
黄田农场	Huangtian Farm	3267	11079
火箭农场	Huojian Farm	6281	19495
柳树泉农场	Liu Shuquan Farm	3423	10915
巴里坤哈萨克自治县	Barkol Kazak Autonomous County	4275	12184
红山农场	Hongshan Farm	4275	12184
伊吾县	Yiwu [Araturuk] County	984	2583
淖毛湖农场	Nao Maohu Farm	984	2583
昌吉回族自治州	**Changji Hui Autonomous Prefecture**	**121625**	**317763**
五家渠市	Wujiaqu City	16777	43472
101 团	No.101 Regiment Farm	3198	9029
102 团	No.102 Regiment Farm	6756	18648
103 团	No.103 Regiment Farm	6823	15795
昌吉市	Changji City	9219	25066
共青团农场	Communist League Farm	3593	10520
军户农场	Junhu Farm	5626	14546
呼图壁县	Hutubi County	29768	77239
105 团	No.105 Regiment Farm	4894	13412
106 团	No.106 Regiment Farm	1652	5428
芳草湖农场	Fang Caohu Farm	23222	58399
玛纳斯县	Manas County	40390	105980
147 团	No.147 Regiment Farm	5389	14152
148 团	No.148 Regiment Farm	9321	24500
149 团	No.149 Regiment Farm	6521	16331
150 团	No.150 Regiment Farm	5321	13644
新湖农场	Xinhu Farm	13838	37353
奇台县	Qitai County	11566	31378
奇台农场	Qitai Farm	10639	27662
北塔山牧场	Bei Tashan Ranch	927	3716
阜康市	Fukang City	8888	21555
222 团	No.222 Regiment Farm	4052	10322
土墩子农场	Tu Dunzi Farm	2096	5395
六运湖农场	Liu Yunhu Farm	2740	5838
吉木萨尔县	Jimsar County	5017	13073
红旗农场	Red Flag Farm	5017	13073
伊犁哈萨克自治州	**Ili Kazak Autonomous Prefecture**	**213170**	**565437**
伊犁州直属县(市)	**Counties (Cities) Direct Under Ili Prefecture**	**72075**	**193693**
奎屯市	Kuytun City	8035	18023
131 团	No.131 Regiment Farm	8035	18023
伊宁县	Yining [Gulja] County	3646	9618
70 团	No.70 Regiment Farm	3646	9618
察布查尔锡伯自治县	Qapqal Xibe Autonomous County	9241	26640
67 团	No.67 Regiment Farm	3761	12204
68 团	No.68 Regiment Farm	3341	8306
69 团	No.69 Regiment Farm	2139	6130
霍城县	Huocheng [Korgas] County	29407	81654
61 团	No.61 Regiment Farm	3997	11551
62 团	No.62 Regiment Farm	5335	15490
63 团	No.63 Regiment Farm	3283	8222

注：总计中包括农一师的阿拉尔农场和幸福城农场，两个农场共计 5044 户、13574 人。
Note: Total in this table includes Alaer and Xinfu farms of division 1,there are 5044 households and 13574 persons in this two farms.

3-11 续表 1 Continued

团　场	Regiment Farm	户数(户) Number of House-Holds (house-hold)	人口数(人) Popula-tion (person)	团　场	Regiment Farm	户数(户) Number of House-holds (house-hold)	人口数(人) Popula-tion (person)
64 团	No.64 Regiment Farm	7949	21657	134 团	No.134 Regiment Farm	8522	18838
66 团	No.66 Regiment Farm	8843	24734	141 团	No.141 Regiment Farm	3647	9197
巩留县	Gongliu [Tokkuztara] County	2752	7441	142 团	No.142 Regiment Farm	8776	23496
73 团	No.73 Regiment Farm	2752	7441	143 团	No.143 Regiment Farm	12871	31143
新源县	Xinyuan [Kunes] County	8020	19468	144 团	No.144 Regiment Farm	4853	11497
71 团	No.71 Regiment Farm	4172	9736	托里县	Toli County	1152	3098
72 团	No.72 Regiment Farm	3848	9732	170 团	No.170 Regiment Farm	1152	3098
昭苏县	Zhaosu [Mongolkure] County	7771	21884	裕民县	Yumin [Qagantokay] County	1954	5127
74 团	No.74 Regiment Farm	1192	3167	161 团	No.161 Regiment Farm	1954	5127
75 团	No.75 Regiment Farm	1025	2678	和布克赛尔蒙古自治县	Hoboksar Mongol Autonomous County	2388	6801
76 团	No.76 Regiment Farm	3365	9388	184 团	No.184 Regiment Farm	2388	6801
77 团	No.77 Regiment Farm	2189	6651	**阿勒泰地区**	**Altay Administrative Offices**	**16603**	**44527**
特克斯县	Tekes County	1660	4485	阿勒泰市	Altay City	3416	9865
78 团	No.78 Regiment Farm	1660	4485	181 团	No.181 Regiment Farm	3416	9865
尼勒克县	Nilka County	1543	4480	福海县	Fuhai [Burultokay] County	1769	4943
79 团	No.79 Regiment Farm	1543	4480	182 团	No.182 Regiment Farm	1769	4943
塔城地区	**Tacheng [Tarbagatai] Administrative Offices**	**124492**	**327217**	北屯市	Beitun City	9335	24063
塔城市	Tacheng City	5564	15160	183 团	No.183 Regiment Farm	3130	8068
163 团	No.163 Regiment Farm	3266	9480	187 团	No.187 Regiment Farm	2310	6110
164 团	No.164 Regiment Farm	2298	5680	188 团	No.188 Regiment Farm	3895	9885
额敏县	Emin [Dorbiljin] County	11258	30463	哈巴河县	Habahe [Kaba] County	1129	3126
165 团	No.165 Regiment Farm	1636	5131	185 团	No.185 Regiment Farm	1129	3126
166 团	No.166 Regiment Farm	2394	7607	吉木乃县	Jeminay County	954	2530
167 团	No.167 Regiment Farm	1960	5446	186 团	No.186 Regiment Farm	954	2530
168 团	No.168 Regiment Farm	3976	8958	**博尔塔拉蒙古自治州**	**Bortala Mongol Autonomous Prefecture**	**30344**	**91742**
团结农场	Tuanjie Farm	1292	3321	博乐市	Bole [Bortala] City	18823	58092
乌苏市	Usu City	41124	114488	81 团	No.81 Regiment Farm	3495	10577
123 团	No.123 Regiment Farm	8051	22178	84 团	No.84 Regiment Farm	2458	7335
124 团	No.124 Regiment Farm	5487	16348	86 团	No.86 Regiment Farm	4869	15187
125 团	No.125 Regiment Farm	6739	17899	89 团	No.89 Regiment Farm	5037	15563
126 团	No.126 Regiment Farm	3723	10876	90 团	No.90 Regiment Farm	2964	9430
127 团	No.127 Regiment Farm	4978	13955	精河县	Jinghe [Jing] County	8423	25161
128 团	No.128 Regiment Farm	5014	13634	83 团	No.83 Regiment Farm	7058	21275
130 团	No.130 Regiment Farm	7132	19598	91 团	No.91 Regiment Farm	1365	3886
沙湾县	Shawan County	61052	152080	温泉县	Wenquan [Araxang] County	3098	8489
121 团	No.121 Regiment Farm	14525	37011	87 团	No.87 Regiment Farm	1599	4300
133 团	No.133 Regiment Farm	7858	20898	88 团	No.88 Regiment Farm	1499	4189

3-11 续表 2 Continued

团　场	Regiment Farm	户数(户) Number of Households (household)	人口数(人) Population (person)	团　场	Regiment Farm	户数(户) Number of Households (household)	人口数(人) Population (person)
巴音郭楞蒙古自治州	**Bayangol Mongol Autonomous Prefecture**	**51559**	**141369**	乌什县	Wushi [Uxturpan] County	2786	7924
铁门关市	Tiemenguan city	12747	35213	4 团	No.4 Regiment Farm	2786	7924
29 团	No.29 Regiment Farm	9667	26327	阿瓦提县	Awat County	5124	14648
30 团	No.30 Regiment Farm	3080	8886	3 团	No.3 Regiment Farm	5124	14648
尉犁县	Yuli [Lopnur] County	10472	30624	**克孜勒苏柯尔克孜自治州**	**Kizilsu Kirgiz Autonomous Prefecture**	**1242**	**4619**
31 团	No.31 Regiment Farm	3155	8515	阿图什市	Artux City	956	3720
33 团	No.33 Regiment Farm	4076	12058	红旗农场	Red Flag Farm	956	3720
34 团	No.34 Regiment Farm	3241	10051	乌恰县	Wuqia [Ulugqat] County	286	899
若羌县	Ruoqiang [Qarkilik] County	2987	7045	托云牧场	Tuoyun Ranch	286	899
36 团	No.36 Regiment Farm	2987	7045	**喀什地区**	**Kashgar [Kaxgar] Administrative Offices**	**50672**	**182914**
焉耆回族自治县	Yanji Hui Autonomous County	1613	6217	疏勒县	Shule County	3058	7646
27 团	No.27 Regiment Farm	668	2264	41 团	No.41 Regiment Farm	3058	7646
和静县	Hejing County	945	3953	英吉莎县	Yengisar County	435	1510
21 团	No.21 Regiment Farm	4220	10256	东风农场	Dong Feng Farm	435	1510
22 团	No.22 Regiment Farm	4220	10256	叶城县	Yecheng [Kagilik] County	353	1275
223 团	No.223 Regiment Farm	13499	35513	叶城牧场	Yechen Ranch	353	1275
和硕县	Hoxud County	3641	10003	麦盖提县	Makit County	8320	26319
24 团	No.24 Regiment Farm	6866	17516	45 团	No.45 Regiment Farm	7069	22713
博湖县	Bohu [Bagrax] County	2992	7994	46 团	No.46 Regiment Farm	1251	3606
25 团	No.25 Regiment Farm	4304	11519	岳普湖县	Yopurga County	1265	3264
且末县	Qiemo County	4304	11519	42 团	No.42 Regiment Farm	1265	3264
37 团	No.37 Regiment Farm	1717	4982	伽师县	Jiashi [Payzawat] County	3705	11716
38 团	No.38 Regiment Farm	1717	4982	伽师总场	General Jiashi Farm	3705	11716
阿克苏地区	**Aksu Administrative Offices**	**61817**	**190389**	巴楚县	Bachu [Maralbexi] County	2056	6559
阿克苏市	Aksu City	9927	32162	48 团	No.48 Regiment Farm	2056	6559
1 团	No.1 Regiment Farm	6352	20956	图木舒克市	Tumxuk City	31480	124625
2 团	No.2 Regiment Farm	3575	11206	44 团	No.44 Regiment Farm	6681	25186
阿拉尔市	Alar City	34489	107003	49 团	No.49 Regiment Farm	4172	14918
7 团	No.7 Regiment Farm	3849	11152	50 团	No.50 Regiment Farm	5588	18591
8 团	No.8 Regiment Farm	3353	10031	51 团	No.51 Regiment Farm	9912	44982
10 团	No.10 Regiment Farm	5060	15600	53 团	No.53 Regiment Farm	5127	20948
11 团	No.11 Regiment Farm	3340	10020	**和田地区**	**Hotan Administrative Offices**	**13555**	**45887**
12 团	No.12 Regiment Farm	6287	19086	墨玉县	Moyu [Karakax] County	5458	17223
13 团	No.13 Regiment Farm	5103	18191	47 团	No.47 Regiment Farm	1905	5142
14 团	No.14 Regiment Farm	2663	7882	224 团	No.224 Regiment Farm	3553	12081
16 团	No.16 Regiment Farm	4834	15041	皮山县	Pishan [Guma] County	7107	25949
温宿县	Wensu [Onsu] County	9491	28652	皮山农场	Pishan Farm	7107	25949
5 团	No.5 Regiment Farm	6032	18696	策勒县	Qira County	990	2715
6 团	No.6 Regiment Farm	3459	9956	一牧场	No.1Ranch	990	2715

3-12 主要年份按三次产业分的就业人员
Number of Employed Persons by Three Strata of Industry in Main Years

单位：万人 (10 000 persons)

年份 Year	经济活动人口 Economically Active Population	就业人员合计 Total Number of Employed persons	第一产业 Primary Industry	第二产业 Secondary Industry
1978		491.25	353.99	70.42
1980		506.35	354.49	75.12
1985		565.81	363.24	89.64
1990		617.70	378.47	107.42
1995		676.00	388.16	124.21
1996		684.00	390.98	119.39
1997		715.40	421.30	105.40
1998		680.92	387.80	106.22
1999		694.34	385.57	104.51
2000		672.50	387.90	92.70
2001	697.45	685.38	388.19	92.19
2002	714.17	701.49	391.84	95.82
2003	734.02	721.27	397.20	95.69
2004	755.36	744.49	403.31	98.49
2005	802.75	791.62	408.00	122.81
2006	823.73	811.75	414.45	111.28
2007	842.12	830.42	417.73	118.34
2008	859.35	847.58	421.32	120.05
2009	878.01	866.15	427.48	127.28
2010	905.64	894.65	438.13	132.75
2011	964.46	953.34	463.91	149.04
2012	1022.29	1010.44	492.36	157.71
2013	1108.50	1096.59	506.35	178.79
2014	1146.45	1135.24	515.21	181.30
2015	1208.48	1195.06	526.82	181.12

年份 Year		构成(合计=100) (%) Composition in Percentage (total=100)(%)		
	第三产业 Tertiary Industry	第一产业 Primary Industry	第二产业 Secondary Industry	第三产业 Tertiary Industry
1978	66.84	72.06	14.33	13.61
1980	76.74	70.01	14.84	15.15
1985	112.93	64.20	15.84	19.96
1990	131.81	61.27	17.39	21.34
1995	163.63	57.42	18.37	24.21
1996	173.63	57.16	17.45	25.39
1997	188.70	58.89	14.73	26.38
1998	186.90	56.95	15.60	27.45
1999	204.26	55.53	15.05	29.42
2000	191.90	57.68	13.78	28.54
2001	205.00	56.64	13.45	29.91
2002	213.83	55.86	13.66	30.48
2003	228.38	55.07	13.27	31.66
2004	242.69	54.17	13.23	32.60
2005	260.81	51.54	15.51	32.95
2006	286.02	51.06	13.71	35.23
2007	294.35	50.30	14.25	35.45
2008	306.21	49.71	14.16	36.13
2009	311.39	49.35	14.70	35.95
2010	323.77	48.97	14.84	36.19
2011	340.39	48.66	15.63	35.71
2012	360.37	48.73	15.61	35.66
2013	411.46	46.17	16.31	37.52
2014	438.73	45.38	15.97	38.65
2015	487.12	44.08	15.16	40.76

3-13 主要年份城镇登记失业人数及失业率

Number of Registered Unemployed Persons and Unemployment Rate in Urban Areas in Main Years

单位：万人 (10 000 persons)

年 份 Year	城镇登记失业人数 Number of Registered Unemployment Persons in Urban Area	城镇登记失业率(%) Registered Unemployment Rate in Urban Areas (%)	年 份 Year	城镇登记失业人数 Number of Registered Unemployment Persons in Urban Area	城镇登记失业率(%) Registered Unemployment Rate in Urban Areas (%)
1980	13.55	7.5	2002	12.68	3.6
1985	4.04	1.9	2003	12.75	3.8
1990	9.60	3.8	2004	10.87	3.8
1991	9.95	3.8	2005	11.13	3.9
1992	9.81	3.7	2006	11.98	3.9
1993	9.50	3.6	2007	11.70	3.9
1994	10.00	3.8	2008	11.77	3.7
1995	10.24	3.9	2009	11.86	3.8
1996	9.81	3.8	2010	10.99	3.2
1997	10.20	3.8	2011	11.12	3.2
1998	11.06	3.9	2012	11.85	3.4
1999	10.30	3.7	2013	11.90	3.4
2000	11.00	3.8	2014	11.21	3.2
2001	12.07	3.7	2015	13.42	3.5

3-14 各地、州、市城镇登记失业率

Registered Unemployment Rate in Urban Area by Prefecture, Autonomous Prefecture and City

单位：% (%)

地 区	Region	2014	2015
总 计	**Total**	**3.17**	**3.52**
乌鲁木齐市	Urumqi City	3.62	3.46
克拉玛依市	Karamay City	0.48	2.00
吐鲁番市	Turpan City	2.68	2.98
哈密地区	Hami [Kumul] Administrative Offices	2.73	2.74
昌吉回族自治州	Changji Hui Autonomous Prefecture	2.53	2.13
伊犁州直属县(市)	Counties (Cities) Direct Under Ili Prefecture	3.60	3.77
塔城地区	Tacheng [Tarbagatai] Administrative Offices	1.22	1.40
阿勒泰地区	Altay Administrative Offices	2.78	2.70
博尔塔拉蒙古自治州	Bortala Mongol Autonomous Prefecture	3.65	2.27
巴音郭楞蒙古自治州	Bayangol Mongol Autonomous Prefecture	2.57	2.20
阿克苏地区	Aksu Administrative Offices	2.23	2.08
克孜勒苏柯尔克孜自治州	Kizilsu Kirgiz Autonomous Prefecture	1.14	1.56
喀什地区	Kashgar [Kaxgar] Administrative Offices	3.92	3.31
和田地区	Hotan Administrative Offices	2.90	2.61

3-15 分行业分地区城镇非私营单位年末就业人员

Number of Employed Persons in Urban Non-Private Units at Year-end by Sectors and Region

单位：人 (2015 年) (person)

项目	Item	合计 Total	国有单位 State-owned Units	集体单位 Urban Collective-Owned Units	其他单位 Units of Other Types Of Ownership
总计	**Total**	**3172483**	**2052250**	**27993**	**1092240**
按国民经济行业分组	**Grouped by Sectors**				
农林牧渔业	Agriculture Forestry, Animal Husbandry and Fishery	517464	503923	80	13461
采矿业	Mining	178515	12859	184	165472
制造业	Manufacturing	348394	8882	2345	337167
电力、热力、燃气及水生产和供应业	Production and Supply of Electricity, Heat Gas and Water	89279	41166	323	47790
建筑业	Construction	247312	33769	2065	211478
批发和零售业	Wholesale and Retail Trades	82386	11920	2872	67594
交通运输、仓储和邮政业	Traffic Transport, Storage and Post	167098	130937	643	35518
住宿和餐饮业	Hotels and Catering Services	24060	11104	499	12457
信息传输、软件和信息技术服务业	Information Transmission, Software and Information fechnology	28662	6948	20	21694
金融业	Financial Intermediation	90236	29170	10119	50947
房地产业	Real Estate	50588	4301	530	45757
租赁和商务服务业	Leasing and Business Services	85118	27643	5838	51637
科学研究和技术服务业	Scientific Research and Technical Services	64250	48185	460	15605
水利、环境和公共设施管理业	Management of Water Conservancy, Environment and Public Facilitys	58597	52884		5713
居民服务、修理和其他服务业	Services to households,Repair and Other Services	7125	4370	255	2500
教育	Education	383961	380927	114	2920
卫生和社会工作	Health and Social Service	180220	175713	1631	2876
文化、体育和娱乐业	Culture, Sports and Entertainment	29783	28144	4	1635
公共管理、社会保障和社会组织	Public Management, Social Security and Social Organization	539435	539405	11	19
按地区分	**By Region**				
乌鲁木齐市	Urumqi City	742958	437105	6521	299332
克拉玛依市	Karamay City	182812	35191	1472	146149
吐鲁番市	Turpan City	85660	54629	687	30344
哈密地区	Hami [Kumul] Administrative Offices	102910	62450	1717	38743
昌吉回族自治州	Changji Hui Autonomous Prefecture	249587	135161	3042	111384
伊犁哈萨克自治州	Ili Kazak Autonomous Prefecture	636921	496012	4862	136047
伊犁州直属县(市)	Counties (Cities) Direct Under Ili Prefecture	293875	209210	2300	82365
塔城地区	Tacheng [Tarbagatai] Administrative Offices	227542	188718	1613	37211
阿勒泰地区	Altay Administrative Offices	115504	98084	949	16471
博尔塔拉蒙古自治州	Bortala Mongol Autonomous Prefecture	89569	73563	738	15268
巴音郭楞蒙古自治州	Bayangol Mongol Autonomous Prefecture	211514	147561	2090	61863
阿克苏地区	Aksu Administrative Offices	213376	151181	2185	60010
克孜勒苏柯尔克孜自治州	Kizilsu Kirgiz Autonomous Prefecture	57786	46097	310	11379
喀什地区	Kashgar [Kaxgar] Administrative Offices	249242	187477	3250	58515
和田地区	Hotan Administrative Offices	129104	113925	1119	14060
石河子市	Shihezi City	110651	44038		66613
阿拉尔市	Aral City	48835	35687		13148
图木舒克市	Tumxuk City	21657	14189		7468
五家渠市	Wujiaqu City	39901	17984		21917

3-16 各地区城镇非私营单位年末在岗职工（含劳务派遣工）人数

Number of Employed Persons (including the dispatched employees) in Urban Non-Private Units at Year-end by Region

单位：万人 (10 000 persons)

年份 Year	地区 Region	合计 Total	国有单位 State-owned Units	集体单位 Urban Collective-owned Units	其他单位 Units of Other Types of Ownership
	2002	242.26	189.26	9.31	43.69
	2003	237.94	184.02	7.55	46.37
	2004	235.97	182.80	6.43	46.74
	2005	237.84	181.92	5.96	49.96
	2006	238.95	182.91	5.19	50.85
	2007	239.45	181.46	4.58	53.41
	2008	239.16	180.29	3.64	55.23
	2009	239.54	175.90	3.54	60.10
	2010	245.48	178.40	3.00	64.08
	2011	270.77	187.78	3.00	79.99
	2012	280.33	195.47	3.26	81.60
	2013	298.93	196.42	2.79	99.72
	2014	305.60	199.47	2.89	103.24
	2015	307.77	200.67	2.74	104.36
乌鲁木齐市	Urumqi City	73.11	43.22	0.63	29.26
克拉玛依市	Karamay City	17.39	3.38	0.15	13.86
吐鲁番市	Turpan City	7.78	4.92	0.07	2.79
哈密地区	Hami [Kumul] Administrative Offices	9.85	6.12	0.17	3.56
昌吉回族自治州	Changji Hui Autonomous Prefecture	24.63	13.41	0.30	10.92
伊犁哈萨克自治州	Ili Kazak Autonomous Prefecture	62.00	48.80	0.48	12.72
伊犁州直属县(市)	Counties (Cities) Direct Under Ili Prefecture	28.70	20.67	0.23	7.80
塔城地区	Tacheng [Tarbagatai] Administrative Offices	22.09	18.60	0.16	3.33
阿勒泰地区	Altay Administrative Offices	11.21	9.53	0.09	1.59
博尔塔拉蒙古自治州	Bortala Mongol Autonomous Prefecture	8.85	7.30	0.07	1.48
巴音郭楞蒙古自治州	Bayangol Mongol Autonomous Prefecture	19.83	13.86	0.21	5.76
阿克苏地区	Aksu Administrative Offices	21.26	15.09	0.22	5.95
克孜勒苏柯尔克孜自治州	Kizilsu Kirgiz Autonomous Prefecture	5.30	4.44	0.03	0.83
喀什地区	Kashgar [Kaxgar] Administrative Offices	23.93	18.39	0.30	5.24
和田地区	Hotan Administrative Offices	12.07	10.71	0.11	1.25
石河子市	Shihezi City	10.89	4.32		6.57
阿拉尔市	Aral City	4.87	3.56		1.31
图木舒克市	Tumxuk City	2.16	1.42		0.74
五家渠市	Wujiaqu City	3.85	1.73		2.12

3-17 分行业城镇非私营单位年末在岗职工(含劳务派遣工)人数
Number of Employed Persons (including the dispatched employees) in Urban Non-Private Units at Year-end by Sectors

单位：人 (2015 年) (person)

项目	Item	合计 Total	国有单位 State-owned Units	集体单位 Urban Collective-owned Units	其他单位 Units of Other Types of Ownership
总计	**Total**	**3077670**	**2006681**	**27400**	**1043589**
农林牧渔业	**Agriculture , Forestry, Animal Husbandry and Fishery**	**507432**	**494011**	**80**	**13341**
农业	Agriculture	415388	407423	53	7912
林业	Forestry	6979	5106		1873
畜牧业	Animal Husbandry	63972	61739	19	2214
渔业	Fishery	134	58		76
农林牧渔服务业	Services in Support of Agriculture, Forestry, Animal Husbandry and Fishery	20959	19685	8	1266
采矿业	**Mining**	**175671**	**12804**	**184**	**162683**
煤炭开采和洗选业	Mining and Washing of Coal	52511	1401	153	50957
石油和天然气开采业	Extraction of Petroleum and Natural Gas	68474			68474
黑色金属矿采选业	Mining and Processing of Ferrous Metal Ores	5620	10		5610
有色金属矿采选业	Mining and Processing of Non-Ferrous Metal Ores	7251	20		7231
非金属矿采选业	Mining and Processing of Non-metal Ores	2255	467	28	1760
开采辅助活动	Activities for Mining	39519	10887	3	28629
其他采矿业	Mining of Other Ores	41	19		22
制造业	**Manufacturing**	**343316**	**8741**	**2301**	**332274**
农副食品加工业	Processing of Food from Agriculture Products	29758	631	11	29116
食品制造业	Manufacture of Foods	19947	156	88	19703
酒、饮料和精制茶制造业	Manufacture of liguor, Beverage and Refined Tea	10192	181	7	10004
烟草制品业	Manufacture of Tobacco	764			764
纺织业	Manufacture of Textile	25952	500	92	25360
纺织服装、服饰业	Manufacture of Textile ,Wearing Apparel, and Accessories	7460	83	38	7339
皮革、毛皮、羽毛及其制品和制鞋业	Manufacture of Leather, Fur, Feather and Related Products	264		4	260
木材加工和木、竹、藤、棕、草制品业	Processing of Timber, Manufacture of Wood, Bamboo, Rattan, Palm and Straw Products	843	4	5	834
家具制造业	Manufacture of Furniture	220	36	23	161
造纸及纸制品业	Manufacture of Paper and Paper Products	2481		83	2398
印刷业和记录媒介的复制业	Printing and Reproduction of Recording Media	2923	1663	69	1191
文教、工美、体育和娱乐用品制造业	Manufacture of Articles For Culture, Education ,Arts and Crafts, Sport and Entertain ment Activities	836		65	771
石油加工、炼焦及核燃料加工业	Processing of Petroleum, cokingc Refining and Nuclear-fuel	38052		2	38050
化学原料及化学制品制造业	Manufacture of Raw Chemical Materials and Chemical Products	65213	1292	477	63444
医药制造业	Manufacture of Medicines	5687	31		5656
化学纤维制造业	Manufacture of Chemical Fibers	5108			5108
橡胶和塑料制品业	Manufacture of Rubber and Plastic Products	8898	611	69	8218
非金属矿物制品业	Manufacture of Non-metal Mineral Products	38488	756	529	37203
黑色金属冶炼及压延加工业	Smelting and Pressing of Ferrous Metals	29838	590	389	28859
有色金属冶炼及压延加工业	Smelting and Pressing of Non-ferrous Metals	25570	91	24	25455
金属制品业	Manufavture of Metal Products	6197	172	19	6006
通用设备制造业	Manufacturie of General Purpose Machinery	1987	133		1854
专用设备制造业	Manufacture of Special Purpose Machinery	3415	879	47	2489

3-17 续表 1 Continued

单位：人 (person)

项目	Item	合计 Total	国有单位 State-owned Units	集体单位 Urban Collective-owned Units	其他单位 Units of Other Types of Ownership
汽车制造业	Manufacture of Automobiles	2503		15	2488
铁路、船舶、航空航天和其他运输设备制造业	Manufacture of Transport Equipment	881	722		159
电气机械和器材制造业	Manufacture of Electrical Machinery and Apparatus	8122	88	22	8012
计算机、通信和其他电子设备制造业	Manufacture of Computers Communication and Other Electronic Equipment	122			122
仪器仪表制造业	Manufacture of Measuring Instruments and Machinery	175			175
废弃资源综合利用业	Utiligation of Waste	239	50		189
金属制品、机械和设备修理业	Repair Service of Metal Products,Machinery and Equipment	1181	72	223	886
电力、热力、燃气及水的生产和供应业	**Production and Supply of Electric,Power, Heat, Gas and Water**	**88421**	**40897**	**311**	**47213**
电力、热力的生产和供应业	Production and Supply of Electric Power, Heat Power	71512	36454	40	35018
燃气生产和供应业	Production and Supply of Gas	7892	56		7836
水的生产和供应业	Production and Supply of Water	9017	4387	271	4359
建筑业	**Construction**	**231400**	**33663**	**2058**	**195679**
房屋建筑业	Construction of Buildings	151022	22383	413	128226
土木工程建筑业	Construction of Civil Engineering	60638	6502	1274	52862
建筑安装业	Building Installation	11888	797	361	10730
建筑装饰和其他建筑业	Other Construction	7852	3981	10	3861
批发和零售业	**Wholesale and Retail Trades**	**80411**	**11654**	**2618**	**66139**
批发业	Wholesale Trades	49694	8737	2288	38669
零售业	Retail Trades	30717	2917	330	27470
交通运输、仓储和邮政业	**Transport, Storage and Post**	**165967**	**130482**	**633**	**34852**
铁路运输业	Railway Transport	53321	52816		505
道路运输业	Road Transport	80030	59211	38	20781
航空运输业	Air Transport	12744	6886		5858
管道运输业	Pipeline Transport	3675			3675
装卸搬运和运输代理业	Loading ,unloading and Forwandrding Agency	2123	657	504	962
仓储业	Storage	2572	1324	91	1157
邮政业	Post	11502	9588		1914
住宿和餐饮业	**Hotels and Catering Services**	**23051**	**10584**	**473**	**11994**
住宿业	Hotels	18295	8276	472	9547
餐饮业	Catering Services	4756	2308	1	2447
信息传输、软件和信息技术服务业	**Information Transmission, Software and Information technology**	**28277**	**6923**	**20**	**21334**
电信、广播电视和卫星传输服务	Telecommunication and Other I.T Transmission Service	24935	6486	6	18443
互联网和相关服务	Internet Service	356	112		244
软件和信息技术服务业	Software and Information technology	2986	325	14	2647
金融业	**Financial Intermediation**	**76335**	**28133**	**10025**	**38177**
货币金融服务业	Banking	53015	25178	9963	17874
资本市场服务业	Security Activities	579	125		454
保险业	Insurance	22352	2753	62	19537

3-17 续表 2 Continued

单位：人 (person)

项目	Item	合计 Total	国有单位 State-owned Units	集体单位 Urban Collective-owned Units	其他单位 Units of Other Types of Ownership
其他金融活动	Other Finance Activities	389	77		312
房地产业	**Real Estate**	**47467**	**4044**	**456**	**42967**
#房地产开发经营	Development and Management of Real Estate	21220	612	49	20559
物业管理	Real Estate Management	23493	2176	214	21103
房地产中介服务	Agency Service for Real Estate	465	161	6	298
租赁和商务服务业	**Leasing and Business Service**	**79790**	**26964**	**5825**	**47001**
租赁业	Leasing	1972	175	876	921
商务服务业	Business Service	77818	26789	4949	46080
科学研究、技术服务和地质勘查业	**Scientific Research, Technology Service and Geological Prospecting**	**61790**	**46736**	**433**	**14621**
研究与试验发展	Research and Experiment Development	6392	6121		271
专业技术服务业	Professional Technique Service	46129	31460	416	14253
科技推广和应用服务业	Science and Technology Popularization and Application Services	9269	9155	17	97
水利、环境和公共设施管理业	**Management of Water Conservancy, Environment and Public Facility**	**57007**	**51342**		**5665**
水利管理业	Management of Water Conservance	19704	19452		252
生态保护和环境治理业	Environmental Management	2408	2228		180
公共设施管理业	Management of Public Facilities	34895	29662		5233
居民服务、修理和其他服务业	**Service to Households and Other Services**	**6997**	**4267**	**255**	**2475**
居民服务业	Services to Households	2640	1679	89	872
机动车、电子产品和日用产品修理业	Repair of motor car,electruical products	633	371	4	258
其他服务业	Other Services	3724	2217	162	1345
教　育	**Education**	**381570**	**378646**	**114**	**2810**
#初等教育	Junior Education	142670	141979		691
中等教育	Secondary Education	183851	183578	15	258
高等教育	Senior Education	31664	31573		91
卫生和社会工作	**Health and Social Service**	**174390**	**170022**	**1606**	**2762**
卫　生	Health	171302	167004	1606	2692
社会工作	Social Service	3088	3018		70
文化、体育和娱乐业	**Culture, Sports and Entertainment**	**29168**	**27578**	**4**	**1586**
新闻和出版业	Journalism and Publishing Activities	6117	5612		505
广播、电视、电影和影视录音制作业	Broadcasting, Movies, Televisions and Audiovisual Activities	9957	9858		99
文化艺术业	Culture and Art Activities	11389	10881	4	504
体　育	Sports	906	804		102
娱乐业	Entertainment	799	423		376
公共管理、社会保障和社会组织	**Public Management Social Security and Social Organization**	**519210**	**519190**	**4**	**16**
中国共产党机关	Organs of Communist Party of China	22895	22895		
国家机关	Government Agencies	481212	481202		10
人民政协和民主党派	People's Political Consultative Conference and Democratic Parties	2536	2536		
社会保障	Social Security	7528	7528		
群众社团、社会团体和其他成员组织	Non-Governmental Organizations, Social Organizations and Religion Organizations	5039	5029	4	6

3-18 各地、州、市分行业城镇非私营单位年末在岗职工(含劳务派遣工)人数

Number of Employed Persons in Urban Non-Private Units at Year-end by Sector and Prefecture, Autonomous Prefecture and City(including the dispatched employees)

单位：人　　(2015 年)　　(person)

地　区	Region	合 计 Total	农林牧渔业 Agriculture, Forestry, Animal Husbandry and Fishery	采 矿 业 Mining	制 造 业 Manufacturing	电力、热力、燃气及水的生产和供应业 Production and Supply of Electic Power, Heat Power Gas and Water
总　计	**Total**	**3077670**	**507432**	**175671**	**343316**	**88421**
乌鲁木齐市	Urumqi City	731110	11054	20026	79561	35474
克拉玛依市	Karamay City	173854	7664	71523	28231	700
吐鲁番市	Turpan City	77762	2857	18953	11094	2671
哈密地区	Hami [Kumul] Administrative Offices	98533	18027	14244	8044	4628
昌吉回族自治州	Changji Hui Autonomous Prefecture	246321	55785	8880	58831	7185
伊犁哈萨克自治州	Ili Kazak Autonomous Prefecture	620010	219593	15785	44807	15039
伊犁州直属县(市)	Counties (Cities) Direct Under Ili Prefecture	287033	56703	4214	30011	9528
塔城地区	Tacheng [Tarbagatai] Administrative Offices	220867	116817	6900	12526	2801
阿勒泰地区	Altay Administrative Offices	112110	46073	4671	2270	2710
博尔塔拉蒙古自治州	Bortala Mongol Autonomous Prefecture	88451	27235	86	3974	1939
巴音郭楞蒙古自治州	Bayangol Mongol Autonomous Prefecture	198346	43792	17438	16669	3287
阿克苏地区	Aksu Administrative Offices	212609	30615	7247	17446	4140
克孜勒苏柯尔克孜自治州	Kizilsu Kirgiz Autonomous Prefecture	53025	2197	812	2290	801
喀什地区	Kashgar [Kaxgar] Administrative Offices	239348	16338	480	13180	3009
和田地区	Hotan Administrative Offices	120681	16529	197	4347	1079
石河子市	Shihezi City	108891	10120		27435	6275
阿拉尔市	Aral City	48694	29018		9617	90
图木舒克市	Tumxuk City	21609	8427		3797	702
五家渠市	Wujiaqu City	38426	8181		13993	1402

地　区	Region	建 筑 业 Construction	批发和零售业 Wholesale and Retail Trades	交通运输、仓储和邮政业 Transport, Storage and Post	住宿和餐饮业 Hotels and Catering Services	信息传输、软件和信息技术服务业 Information Transmission, Software and Information technology
总　计	**Total**	**231400**	**80411**	**165967**	**23051**	**28277**
乌鲁木齐市	Urumqi City	107119	31038	124779	11134	9458
克拉玛依市	Karamay City	10659	1666	2547	568	1271
吐鲁番市	Turpan City	2390	1495	1449	296	580
哈密地区	Hami [Kumul] Administrative Offices	2003	2142	1439	883	1061
昌吉回族自治州	Changji Hui Autonomous Prefecture	13398	4207	4287	569	1799
伊犁哈萨克自治州	Ili Kazak Autonomous Prefecture	18726	12159	11572	4262	5828
伊犁州直属县(市)	Counties (Cities) Direct Under Ili Prefecture	10654	7689	6867	2432	2831
塔城地区	Tacheng [Tarbagatai] Administrative Offices	6565	2951	2199	577	1338
阿勒泰地区	Altay Administrative Offices	1507	1519	2506	1253	1659
博尔塔拉蒙古自治州	Bortala Mongol Autonomous Prefecture	5646	2185	1838	467	793
巴音郭楞蒙古自治州	Bayangol Mongol Autonomous Prefecture	7396	6070	4168	1148	1487
阿克苏地区	Aksu Administrative Offices	8487	7513	3148	715	1895
克孜勒苏柯尔克孜自治州	Kizilsu Kirgiz Autonomous Prefecture	3350	673	1348	256	501
喀什地区	Kashgar [Kaxgar] Administrative Offices	14367	6964	5610	1966	1551
和田地区	Hotan Administrative Offices	2323	1347	1972	402	932
石河子市	Shihezi City	28541	1628	1167	178	1076
阿拉尔市	Aral City	2266	504	7		
图木舒克市	Tumxuk City	2999	62	74	28	
五家渠市	Wujiaqu City	1730	758	562	179	45

3-18 续表 Continued

单位：人 (person)

地区	Region	金融业 Financial Intermedia-tion	房地产业 Real Estate	租赁和商务服务业 Leasing and Business Services	科学研究、技术服务业 Scientific Research, Technical Service	水利、环境和公共设施管理业 Management of Water Conservancy, Environment and Public Facility
总计	**Total**	**76335**	**47467**	**79790**	**61790**	**57007**
乌鲁木齐市	Urumqi City	19595	16482	25073	25164	6756
克拉玛依市	Karamay City	3061	6359	11726	1998	1094
吐鲁番市	Turpan City	1835	694	999	1337	793
哈密地区	Hami [Kumul] Administrative Offices	3213	463	2197	3013	4116
昌吉回族自治州	Changji Hui Autonomous Prefecture	7938	5429	3425	4789	6059
伊犁哈萨克自治州	Ili Kazak Autonomous Prefecture	12886	6593	4265	9769	12186
伊犁州直属县(市)	Counties (Cities) Direct Under Ili Prefecture	7029	4909	2970	4611	6189
塔城地区	Tacheng [Tarbagatai] Administrative Offices	3593	1131	587	2513	3745
阿勒泰地区	Altay Administrative Offices	2264	553	708	2645	2252
博尔塔拉蒙古自治州	Bortala Mongol Autonomous Prefecture	1897	711	6492	1277	2354
巴音郭楞蒙古自治州	Bayangol Mongol Autonomous Prefecture	4472	1915	3824	3258	5872
阿克苏地区	Aksu Administrative Offices	5428	2502	3740	3119	7808
克孜勒苏柯尔克孜自治州	Kizilsu Kirgiz Autonomous Prefecture	885	273	2721	1996	603
喀什地区	Kashgar [Kaxgar] Administrative Offices	6335	2991	9984	3160	3685
和田地区	Hotan Administrative Offices	2240	809	995	1237	2082
石河子市	Shihezi City	5350	349	3723	915	1803
阿拉尔市	Aral City		256	201	158	634
图木舒克市	Tumxuk City			116	148	286
五家渠市	Wujiaqu City	1200	1641	309	452	876

地区	Region	居民服务、修理和其他服务业 Service to Households, Repcuir and Other Services	教育 Education	卫生和社会工作 Health, and Social Service	文化、体育和娱乐业 Culture, Sports and Entertainment	公共管理、社会保障和社会组织 Public Management, Social and Social Organizations Security
总计	**Total**	**6997**	**381570**	**174390**	**29168**	**519210**
乌鲁木齐市	Urumqi City	1343	52218	36309	12285	106242
克拉玛依市	Karamay City	1792	7391	3187	594	11823
吐鲁番市	Turpan City		9713	3558	520	16528
哈密地区	Hami [Kumul] Administrative Offices	254	10957	5657	1080	15112
昌吉回族自治州	Changji Hui Autonomous Prefecture	205	21313	12853	1345	28024
伊犁哈萨克自治州	Ili Kazak Autonomous Prefecture	639	81557	36340	4281	103723
伊犁州直属县(市)	Counties (Cities) Direct Under Ili Prefecture	527	48089	21834	2456	57490
塔城地区	Tacheng [Tarbagatai] Administrative Offices	35	20970	9121	909	25589
阿勒泰地区	Altay Administrative Offices	77	12498	5385	916	20644
博尔塔拉蒙古自治州	Bortala Mongol Autonomous Prefecture	16	10076	4711	880	15874
巴音郭楞蒙古自治州	Bayangol Mongol Autonomous Prefecture	128	23769	13021	888	39744
阿克苏地区	Aksu Administrative Offices	78	37762	15132	1961	53873
克孜勒苏柯尔克孜自治州	Kizilsu Kirgiz Autonomous Prefecture	2048	13685	3939	945	13702
喀什地区	Kashgar [Kaxgar] Administrative Offices	191	68978	20330	2459	57770
和田地区	Hotan Administrative Offices	166	28640	10945	1139	43300
石河子市	Shihezi City	79	7978	5099	505	6670
阿拉尔市	Aral City		3169	1224	125	1425
图木舒克市	Tumxuk City		2141	750		2079
五家渠市	Wujiaqu City	58	2223	1335	161	3321

3-19 分行业城镇非私营单位年末女性就业人员

Number of Female Employed Persons in Urban Non-Private Units at Year-end by Sectors

单位：人 (2015 年) (person)

项目	Item	合计 Total	国有单位 State-owned Units	集体单位 Collective-owned Units	其他单位 Units of Other Types of Ownership
总计	**Total**	**1267840**	**922536**	**11452**	**333852**
农林牧渔业	Agriculture, Forestry, Animal Husbandry and Fishery	224558	219602	16	4940
采矿业	Mining	44785	3927	13	40845
制造业	Manufacturing	110027	3015	1055	105957
电力、热力、燃气及水生产和供应业	Production and Supply of Electric,Power, Heat, Gas and Water	24385	11157	67	13161
建筑业	Construction	37197	3699	358	33140
批发和零售业	Wholesale and Retail Trades	34488	4545	983	28960
交通运输、仓储和邮政业	Transport, Storage and Post	41336	31271	339	9726
住宿和餐饮业	Hotels and Catering Services	13304	5951	261	7092
信息传输、软件和信息技术服务业	Information Transmission, Software and Information technology	13254	3295	10	9949
金融业	Financial Intermediation	51953	15294	4842	31817
房地产业	Real Estate	22325	2134	269	19922
租赁和商务服务业	Leasing and Business Services	27415	10026	1656	15733
科学研究、技术服务业	Scientific Research, Technology Services	21150	16631	167	4352
水利、环境和公共设施管理业	Management of Water Conservancy, Environment and Public Facilitys	25101	22437		2664
居民服务、修理和其他服务业	Services to households and Other Services	3916	2320	208	1388
教育	Education	240260	238650	73	1537
卫生和社会工作	Health, and Social Service	122834	119750	1128	1956
文化、体育和娱乐业	Culture, Sports and Entertainment	14179	13479	1	699
公共管理、社会保障和社会组织	Public Management Social Security and Social Organization	195373	195353	6	14

3-20 城镇非私营单位在岗职工（含劳务派遣工）工资总额
Total Wages of Employed Persons (including the dispatched employees) and Its Composition in Urban Non-Private Units

单位：万元 (10 000 yuan)

年份 Year	地区 Region	工资总额 Total wages Bill	国有单位 State-owned Units	集体单位 Collective-owned Units	其他单位 Units of Other Types of Ownership
	1978	159409	148278	11131	
	1980	212446	196711	15735	
	1985	339110	304999	33789	322
	1990	668808	601300	65858	1650
	1995	1677257	1521670	135990	19597
	2000	2344694	2007823	125510	211361
	2001	2677431	2092155	105861	479415
	2002	2915398	2211411	93605	610382
	2003	3315399	2497369	77460	740570
	2004	3563312	2691462	78224	793626
	2005	3874068	2871542	75971	926555
	2006	4429959	3318694	77978	1033287
	2007	5332395	3951882	82215	1298298
	2008	6198976	4428784	84187	1686005
	2009	6912058	4796811	91488	2023759
	2010	8286857	5669760	105413	2511684
	2011	11034557	7021538	140410	3872609
	2012	13662181	8543738	174136	4944307
	2013	16395372	9173367	167510	7054495
	2014	18237746	10085377	176204	7976165
	2015	20540556	11986753	179301	8374502
乌鲁木齐市	Urumqi City	5662789	3074650	38124	2550015
克拉玛依市	Karamay City	1442757	277278	7322	1158157
吐鲁番市	Turpan City	528650	327675	2819	198156
哈密地区	Hami [Kumul] Administrative Offices	588571	339439	7761	241371
昌吉回族自治州	Changji Hui Autonomous Prefecture	1666109	854313	24586	787210
伊犁哈萨克自治州	Ili Kazak Autonomous Prefecture	3369645	2382146	32619	954880
伊犁州直属县(市)	Counties (Cities) Direct Under Ili Prefecture	1735115	1121401	15840	597874
塔城地区	Tacheng [Tarbagatai] Administrative Offices	1119406	865407	7922	246077
阿勒泰地区	Altay Administrative Offices	515124	395338	8857	110929
博尔塔拉蒙古自治州	Bortala Mongol Autonomous Prefecture	465993	388243	8299	69451
巴音郭楞蒙古自治州	Bayangol Mongol Autonomous Prefecture	1395886	739621	17873	638392
阿克苏地区	Aksu Administrative Offices	1218043	827816	14331	375896
克孜勒苏柯尔克孜自治州	Kizilsu Kirgiz Autonomous Prefecture	296340	253282	1327	41731
喀什地区	Kashgar [Kaxgar] Administrative Offices	1588689	1235476	18720	334493
和田地区	Hotan Administrative Offices	697898	611548	5520	80830
石河子市	Shihezi City	960628	386160		574468
阿拉尔市	Aral City	281092	108987		172105
图木舒克市	Tumxuk City	140386	84740		55646
五家渠市	Wujiaqu City	237080	95379		141701

3-21 主要年份城镇非私营单位在岗职工（含劳务派遣工）工资总额指数

Indices of Total Wages of Employed Persons (including the dispatched employees) in Urban Non-Private Units in Main Years

年份 Year	指数(上年=100) Indices (preceding year=100)				指数(1978年=100) Indices (1978=100)			
	合计 Total	国有单位 State-owned Units	集体单位 Urban Collective-owned Units	其他单位 Units of Other Types of Ownership	合计 Total	国有单位 State-owned Units	集体单位 Urban Collective-owned Units	其他单位 Units of Other Types of Ownership
1978	114.2	114.5	109.6		100.0	100.0	100.0	
1980	120.5	120.1	125.2		133.3	132.7	141.4	
1985	117.4	117.5	116.0	167.5	212.7	205.7	303.6	100.0
1990	116.6	116.3	126.9	132.6	419.6	405.5	591.7	513.4
1995	126.3	126.8	119.3	146.6	1052.2	1026.2	1221.7	6097.7
2000	110.7	108.1	91.4	171.0	1470.9	1354.1	1127.6	65762.7
2001	114.2	104.2	84.3	226.8	1679.6	1411.0	951.0	149164.7
2002	108.9	105.7	88.4	127.3	1828.9	1491.4	840.9	189913.4
2003	113.7	112.9	82.8	121.3	2079.8	1684.2	695.9	230420.0
2004	107.5	107.8	101.0	107.2	2235.3	1815.1	702.8	246927.8
2005	108.7	106.7	97.1	116.7	2430.3	1936.6	682.5	288287.3
2006	114.3	115.6	102.6	111.5	2779.0	2238.2	700.5	321896.3
2007	120.4	119.1	105.4	125.6	3345.1	2665.2	738.6	403198.1
2008	116.3	112.1	102.4	129.9	3888.7	2986.8	756.3	523604.0
2009	111.5	108.3	108.7	120.0	4336.1	3235.0	821.9	628496.6
2010	119.9	118.2	115.2	124.1	5198.5	3823.7	947.0	780026.1
2011	133.2	123.8	133.2	154.2	6922.2	4735.4	1261.4	1202673.7
2012	123.8	121.7	124.0	127.7	8570.5	5762.0	1564.4	1535499.1
2013	120.0	107.4	96.2	142.7	10285.1	6186.6	1504.9	2190837.0
2014	111.2	109.9	105.2	113.1	11440.9	6801.7	1583.0	2477069.9
2015	112.6	118.9	101.8	105.0	12885.4	8084.0	1610.8	2600777.0

注：2000年起职工工资总额指数由在岗职工工资总额计算而得。
Note: Since 2000,total wages of staff and worders were caculated by indices of total wages of stuff and workers.

3-22 主要年份城镇非私营单位在岗职工（含劳务派遣工）工资情况

Wages of Employed Persons (including the dispatched employees) in Urban Non-Private Units in Main Years

年份 Year	在岗职工工资总额(亿元) Total Wages of staff and workers (100 million yuan)	国有单位 State-owned Units	集体单位 Urban Collective-owned Units	其他单位 Units of Other Types of Ownership	在岗职工平均工资(元) Average Wage of Staff and Workers (yuan)	国有单位 State-owned Units	集体单位 Urban Collective-owned Units	其他单位 Units of Other Types of Ownership
1999	211.86	185.77	13.73	12.36	7611	7614	6815	8681
2000	234.47	200.78	12.55	21.14	8717	8731	7489	9498
2001	267.74	209.22	10.59	47.94	10278	10145	8197	11594
2002	291.54	221.14	9.36	61.04	11605	11435	9353	12767
2003	331.54	249.74	7.75	74.06	13255	13199	9966	13937
2004	356.33	269.15	7.82	79.36	14484	14477	11594	14870
2005	387.41	287.15	7.60	92.66	15558	15364	12738	16503
2006	443.00	331.87	7.80	103.33	17819	17704	14209	18566
2007	533.24	395.19	8.22	129.83	21434	21369	17780	21921
2008	619.90	442.88	8.42	168.60	24687	24016	22060	26815
2009	691.21	479.68	9.15	202.38	27753	26872	22862	30409
2010	828.69	566.98	10.54	251.17	32361	31390	31997	34807
2011	1103.46	702.15	14.04	387.26	38820	36752	40102	43177
2012	1366.22	854.37	17.41	494.43	45243	43115	47248	49380
2013	1639.54	917.34	16.75	705.45	49843	46523	57518	54749
2014	1823.77	1008.54	17.62	797.61	54407	50582	60394	60014
2015	2054.06	1198.68	17.93	837.45	60914	59518	63811	62967

3-23 分行业分地区城镇非私营单位就业人员平均工资

Average Wage of Employed Persons in Urban Non-Private Units by Sector and Region

单位：元 (yuan)

项 目	Item	2014	2015
总 计	**Total**	**53471**	**60117**
按行业分	**Grouped by Industrial Sector**		
农、林、牧、渔业	Agriculture Forestry, Animal Husbandry and Fishery	33872	38070
采 矿 业	Mining	85241	86253
制 造 业	Manufacturing	57397	58752
电力、热力、燃气及水生产和供应业	Production and Supply of Electricity, Heat Gas and Water	69737	70708
建筑业	Construction	51299	56238
批发和零售业	Wholesale and Retail Trades	53353	56573
交通运输、仓储和邮政业	Traffic Transport, Storage and Post	71957	78215
住宿和餐饮业	Hotels and Catering Services	41040	43885
信息传输、软件和信息技术服务业	Information Transmission, Software and Information fechnology	70757	78238
金融业	Financial Intermediation	79653	88212
房地产业	Real Estate	45377	47160
租赁和商务服务业	Leasing and Business Services	44272	44595
科学研究、技术服务业	Scientific Research and Technical Services	65981	75478
水利、环境和公共设施管理业	Management of Water Conservancy, Environment and Public Facilitys	38981	46068
居民服务、修理和其他服务业	Services to households,Repair and Other Services	35928	40614
教育	Education	53792	69813
卫生和社会工作	Health and Social Service	53203	65463
文化、体育和娱乐业	Culture, Sports and Entertainment	52299	64906
公共管理、社会保障和社会组织	Public Management, Social Security and Social Organization	48680	59598
按地区分	**By Region**		
乌鲁木齐市	Urumqi City	61689	68181
克拉玛依市	Karamay City	79144	80519
吐鲁番地区	Turpan Administrative Offices	57272	64971
哈密地区	Hami [Kumul] Administrative Offices	52595	58462
昌吉回族自治州	Changji Hui Autonomous Prefecture	54791	62034
伊犁哈萨克自治州	Ili Kazak Autonomous Prefecture	42354	49493
伊犁州直属县(市)	Counties (Cities) Direct Under Ili Prefecture	45975	53369
塔城地区	Tacheng [Tarbagatai] Administrative Offices	40300	45810
阿勒泰地区	Altay Administrative Offices	36684	43772
博尔塔拉蒙古自治州	Bortala Mongol Autonomous Prefecture	42270	50070
巴音郭楞蒙古自治州	Bayangol Mongol Autonomous Prefecture	53126	58183
阿克苏地区	Aksu Administrative Offices	46430	54460
克孜勒苏柯尔克孜自治州	Kizilsu Kirgiz Autonomous Prefecture	44605	53320
喀什地区	Kashgar [Kaxgar] Administrative Offices	49412	62561
和田地区	Hotan Administrative Offices	49238	54046
石河子市	Shihezi City	56536	60603
阿拉尔市	Aral City	49392	55823
图木舒克市	Tumxuk City	52516	57707
五家渠市	Wujiaqu City	54701	58417

3-24 分行业分地区城镇私营单位就业人员平均工资

Average Wage of Employed Persons in Urban Private Unites by Sector and Region

单位：元 (yuan)

项　目	Item	2014	2015
总　计	**Total**	**36199**	**37598**
按行业分	**Grouped by Industrial Sector**		
农、林、牧、渔业	Agriculture Forestry, Animal Husbandry and Fishery	28853	30352
采矿业	Mining	45958	50312
制造业	Manufacturing	37519	39527
电力、煤气及水的生产和供应	Production and Supply of Electricity, HeatGas and Water	40183	43090
建筑业	Construction	44311	45672
批发和零售业	Wholesale and Retail Trades	29320	29650
交通运输、仓储和邮政业	Traffic Transport, Storage and Post	40413	40532
住宿和餐饮业	Hotels and Catering Services	24777	32798
信息传输、计算机服务和软件	Information Transmission, Software andInformation fechnology	34976	37964
金融业	Financial Intermediation	41620	44239
房地产业	Real Estate	35320	38798
租赁和商务服务业	Leasing and Business Services	30620	28449
科学研究、技术服务和地质勘查业	Scientific Research and Technical Services	38642	43162
水利、环境和公共设施管理	Management of Water Conservancy, Environment and Public Facilitys	31363	36161
居民服务和其他服务业	Services to households,Repair and Other Services	29672	29206
教　育	Education	34559	31574
卫生、社会保障和社会福利	Health and Social Service	41638	43449
文化、体育和娱乐业	Culture, Sports and Entertainment	34479	35444
公共管理和社会组织	Public Management, Social Security and Social Organization		
按地区分	**By Region**		
乌鲁木齐市	Urumqi City	30390	31617
克拉玛依市	Karamay City	49467	48808
吐鲁番市	Turpan City	32478	34952
哈密地区	Hami [Kumul] Administrative Offices	40940	39730
昌吉回族自治州	Changji Hui Autonomous Prefecture	39957	41531
伊犁州直属县(市)	Counties (Cities) Direct Under Ili Prefecture	40150	38196
塔城地区	Tacheng [Tarbagatai] Administrative Offices	29248	30695
阿勒泰地区	Altay Administrative Offices	32973	37198
博尔塔拉蒙古自治州	Bortala Mongol Autonomous Prefecture	37029	38508
巴音郭楞蒙古自治州	Bayangol Mongol Autonomous Prefecture	30319	36065
阿克苏地区	Aksu Administrative Offices	37722	38942
克孜勒苏柯尔克孜自治州	Kizilsu Kirgiz Autonomous Prefecture	33560	34439
喀什地区	Kashgar [Kaxgar] Administrative Offices	25373	32928
和田地区	Hotan Administrative Offices	32327	33336
生产建设兵团	Xinjiang Production and Construction Group	47439	50081

3-25 主要年份城镇非私营单位在岗职工（含劳务派遣工）平均工资

Average Wage of Employed Persons in (including the dispatched employees) Urban Non-Private Units in Main Years

单位：元 (yuan)

年 份 Year	全部职工 Full Staff and Workers	国有单位 State-owned Units	城镇集体单位 Urban Collective-owned Units	其他单位 Units of Other Types of Ownership
1978	717	726	614	
1980	882	904	676	
1985	1277	1310	1038	1707
1990	2272	2345	1765	2498
1995	5348	5431	4509	5973
2000	8717	8731	7489	9498
2001	10278	10145	8197	11594
2002	11605	11435	9353	12767
2003	13255	13199	9966	13937
2004	14484	14477	11594	14870
2005	15558	15364	12738	16503
2006	17819	17704	14209	18566
2007	21434	21369	17780	21921
2008	24687	24016	22060	26815
2009	27753	26872	22862	30409
2010	32361	31390	31997	34807
2011	38820	36752	40102	43177
2012	45243	43115	47248	49380
2013	49843	46523	57518	54749
2014	54407	50582	60394	60014
2015	60914	59518	63811	62967

3-26 主要年份城镇非私营单位在岗职工（含劳务派遣工）平均工资指数

Indices of Average Wage of Employed Persons in (including the dispatched employees)Urban Non-Private Units in Main Years

(上年=100) (preceding year=100)

年 份 Year	货币工资 Money Wage				实际工资 Real Wage			
	合 计 Total	国有单位 State-owned Units	城镇集体单位 Urban Collective-owned Units	其他单位 Units of Other Types of Ownership	合 计 Total	国有单位 State-owned Units	城镇集体单位 Urban Collective-owned Units	其他单位 Units of Other Types of Ownership
1978		105.2				103.9		
1980	114.5	115.3	108.3		109.3	110.0	103.4	
1985	115.7	116.0	112.5	124.6	105.9	106.0	102.7	113.7
1990	113.2	113.3	113.6	96.5	108.3	108.4	108.7	92.3
1995	125.8	125.7	125.8	120.9	105.7	105.6	105.7	101.6
2000	114.5	114.7	109.9	109.4	115.2	115.4	110.6	110.1
2001	117.9	116.2	109.5	122.1	113.4	111.7	105.3	117.4
2002	112.9	112.7	114.1	110.1	113.6	113.4	114.8	110.8
2003	114.2	115.4	106.6	109.2	113.6	114.8	106.1	108.7
2004	109.3	109.7	116.3	106.7	107.0	107.4	113.9	104.5
2005	107.4	106.1	109.9	111.0	106.7	105.4	109.1	110.2
2006	114.5	115.2	111.5	112.5	113.7	114.4	110.7	111.7
2007	120.3	120.7	125.1	118.1	114.0	114.4	118.6	111.9
2008	115.2	112.4	124.1	122.3	106.6	104.0	114.8	113.1
2009	112.4	111.9	103.6	113.4	111.6	111.1	102.9	112.6
2010	116.6	116.8	140.0	114.5	111.8	112.0	134.2	109.7
2011	120.0	117.1	125.3	124.0	113.3	110.6	118.3	117.1
2012	116.5	117.3	117.8	114.4	112.2	113.0	113.5	110.2
2013	110.2	107.9	121.7	110.9	106.0	103.8	117.2	106.7
2014	109.2	108.7	105.0	109.6	107.0	106.5	102.8	107.3
2015	112.0	117.7	105.7	104.9	110.7	116.4	104.4	103.7

3-27 各地、州、市分行业城镇非私营单位在岗职工(含劳务派遣工)平均工资

Average Wage of Employed Persons in Urban Non-Private Unites (including the dispatched employees) by Sector and Prefecture, Autonomous Prefecture and City

单位：元　　(2015 年)　　(yuan)

地　区	Region	合 计 Total	农林牧渔业 Agriaulfure Forestry, Animal Husbandry and Fishery	采 矿 业 Mining	制 造 业 Manufacturing	电力、热力、燃气及水的生产和供应业 Production and Supply of Electric,Power, Heat,Gas and Water
总　　计	**Total**	**60914**	**38377**	**87007**	**58996**	**70996**
乌鲁木齐市	Urumqi City	68603	45551	87050	63998	67672
克拉玛依市	Karamay City	83194	54221	95344	85011	90109
吐鲁番市	Turpan City	67829	41540	85112	54304	92900
哈密地区	Hami [Kumul] Administrative Offices	59601	37097	65300	57618	99052
昌吉回族自治州	Changji Hui Autonomous Prefecture	62231	47775	70838	63024	83443
伊犁哈萨克自治州	Ili Kazak Autonomous Prefecture	49493	32640	60660	49195	68287
伊犁州直属县(市)	Counties (Cities) Direct Under Ili Prefecture	53780	36907	66220	50894	70402
塔城地区	Tacheng [Tarbagatai] Administrative Offices	46288	36477	57976	45980	59285
阿勒泰地区	Altay Administrative Offices	44266	17281	59544	45515	69808
博尔塔拉蒙古自治州	Bortala Mongol Autonomous Prefecture	50431	45830	47758	37901	44254
巴音郭楞蒙古自治州	Bayangol Mongol Autonomous Prefecture	60118	37297	114495	58923	74855
阿克苏地区	Aksu Administrative Offices	54544	28293	70878	49070	61210
克孜勒苏柯尔克孜自治州	Kizilsu Kirgiz Autonomous Prefecture	55551	50821	82841	49384	65979
喀什地区	Kashgar [Kaxgar] Administrative Offices	63804	50034	48441	41795	50858
和田地区	Hotan Administrative Offices	55829	45481	44041	39017	52080
石河子市	Shihezi City	60819	59074		53610	80669
阿拉尔市	Aral City	55941	36858		44934	56209
图木舒克市	Tumxuk City	57739	48610		52720	79103
五家渠市	Wujiaqu City	59000	39832		60615	69307

地　区	Region	建 筑 业 Construction	批发和零售业 Wholesale and Retail Trades	交通运输、仓储和邮政业 Transport, Storage and Post	住宿和餐饮业 Hotels and Catering Services	信息传输、软件和信息技术服务业 Information Transmission, Software and Information fechnology
总　　计	**Total**	**56960**	**57184**	**78640**	**44280**	**78529**
乌鲁木齐市	Urumqi City	60049	61993	85465	51960	86604
克拉玛依市	Karamay City	71242	74545	60846	46816	90672
吐鲁番市	Turpan City	65529	70488	43857	32103	83606
哈密地区	Hami [Kumul] Administrative Offices	55974	73418	54044	37605	78757
昌吉回族自治州	Changji Hui Autonomous Prefecture	54105	59470	53908	36760	72765
伊犁哈萨克自治州	Ili Kazak Autonomous Prefecture	48039	50509	55850	35684	64898
伊犁州直属县(市)	Counties (Cities) Direct Under Ili Prefecture	52094	51103	54112	33476	71261
塔城地区	Tacheng [Tarbagatai] Administrative Offices	41763	39615	57278	37305	57429
阿勒泰地区	Altay Administrative Offices	43809	68433	59322	39438	59942
博尔塔拉蒙古自治州	Bortala Mongol Autonomous Prefecture	37624	50037	60096	39147	67716
巴音郭楞蒙古自治州	Bayangol Mongol Autonomous Prefecture	59301	56568	56237	34734	83653
阿克苏地区	Aksu Administrative Offices	54277	44390	55361	40932	70858
克孜勒苏柯尔克孜自治州	Kizilsu Kirgiz Autonomous Prefecture	40421	37091	56634	39327	58548
喀什地区	Kashgar [Kaxgar] Administrative Offices	60600	48601	65798	35781	91989
和田地区	Hotan Administrative Offices	48798	56401	54673	36726	65191
石河子市	Shihezi City	54046	71456	71492	46481	91461
阿拉尔市	Aral City	80999	53530	81429		
图木舒克市	Tumxuk City	56647	77688	61824	42000	
五家渠市	Wujiaqu City	50349	57396	58796	44071	67889

3-27 续表 Continued

单位：元 (yuan)

地　区	Region	金融业 Financial Intermedition	房地产业 Real Estate	租赁和商务服务业 Leasing and Business Services	科学研究、技术服务 Scientific Research and Technical Services	水利、环境和公共设施管理业 Management of Water Conservancy, Environment and Public Facility
总　计	**Total**	**97489**	**48201**	**44887**	**77018**	**46972**
乌鲁木齐市	Urumqi City	139237	59188	61047	91093	53033
克拉玛依市	Karamay City	111802	35186	44947	87944	54646
吐鲁番市	Turpan City	83185	55655	39933	61681	60693
哈密地区	Hami [Kumul] Administrative Offices	97471	51860	42297	65928	35339
昌吉回族自治州	Changji Hui Autonomous Prefecture	81379	42480	39138	68642	56102
伊犁哈萨克自治州	Ili Kazak Autonomous Prefecture	83510	42667	41240	64455	44343
伊犁州直属县(市)	Counties (Cities) Direct Under Ili Prefecture	88241	43176	36792	64884	38102
塔城地区	Tacheng [Tarbagatai] Administrative Offices	73005	44354	41047	67524	51460
阿勒泰地区	Altay Administrative Offices	85483	34678	54613	60793	48971
博尔塔拉蒙古自治州	Bortala Mongol Autonomous Prefecture	102273	35566	18891	80246	39970
巴音郭楞蒙古自治州	Bayangol Mongol Autonomous Prefecture	95432	37244	42252	66599	38094
阿克苏地区	Aksu Administrative Offices	77118	39999	31604	61900	36756
克孜勒苏柯尔克孜自治州	Kizilsu Kirgiz Autonomous Prefecture	55293	42535	19487	57999	61502
喀什地区	Kashgar [Kaxgar] Administrative Offices	70059	34557	36386	68172	61714
和田地区	Hotan Administrative Offices	63728	56686	37608	61688	44078
石河子市	Shihezi City	74213	118628	47844	73791	59089
阿拉尔市	Aral City		53050	31396	58579	53553
图木舒克市	Tumxuk City			53450	57859	64086
五家渠市	Wujiaqu City	86614	63942	57056	84721	74888

地　区	Region	居民服务、修理和其他服务业 Services to households,Repair and Other Services	教　育 Education	卫生和社会事业 Health and Social Service	文化、体育和娱乐业 Culture, Sports and Entertainment	公共管理、社会保障和社会组织 Public Management, Social Security and Social Organization
总　计	**Total**	**40670**	**70050**	**66459**	**65645**	**60797**
乌鲁木齐市	Urumqi City	57351	64009	79396	69323	52759
克拉玛依市	Karamay City	33744	97894	114994	85372	79614
吐鲁番市	Turpan City		69932	66014	59674	59962
哈密地区	Hami [Kumul] Administrative Offices	52745	70199	69952	56702	59400
昌吉回族自治州	Changji Hui Autonomous Prefecture	45756	82682	69040	74650	75144
伊犁哈萨克自治州	Ili Kazak Autonomous Prefecture	34029	65693	58753	58914	60891
伊犁州直属县(市)	Counties (Cities) Direct Under Ili Prefecture	31155	64536	55589	58039	59144
塔城地区	Tacheng [Tarbagatai] Administrative Offices	61314	66840	60548	57377	62458
阿勒泰地区	Altay Administrative Offices	41558	68223	68716	62758	63739
博尔塔拉蒙古自治州	Bortala Mongol Autonomous Prefecture	42529	67853	63482	62558	58989
巴音郭楞蒙古自治州	Bayangol Mongol Autonomous Prefecture	41040	68112	59544	61898	59313
阿克苏地区	Aksu Administrative Offices	35872	66204	54745	61746	59828
克孜勒苏柯尔克孜自治州	Kizilsu Kirgiz Autonomous Prefecture	31670	58762	62961	58222	65238
喀什地区	Kashgar [Kaxgar] Administrative Offices	58652	78430	59042	62491	66636
和田地区	Hotan Administrative Offices	48577	66702	56848	65285	55541
石河子市	Shihezi City	66392	84946	97132	72065	82586
阿拉尔市	Aral City		59322	61121	46412	67082
图木舒克市	Tumxuk City		65675	69792		86465
五家渠市	Wujiaqu City	58069	76794	74667	72200	66292

3-28 各地、州、市、县(市)城镇非私营单位在岗职工(含劳务派遣工)平均工资

Average Wages of Fully Employed Persons in Urban Non-Private Units (including the dispatched employees)by Prefecture, Autonomous Prefecture, City and County

单位：元 (2015 年) (yuan)

地 区	Region	合 计 Total	国有单位 State-owned Units	城镇集体单 位 Urban Collective-owned Units	其他单位 Units of Other Types of Ownership
总 计	**Total**	**60914**	**59518**	**63811**	**62967**
乌鲁木齐市	**Urumqi City**	**68603**	**69791**	**57746**	**67410**
天山区	Tianshan District	70407	72021	51373	68697
沙依巴克区	Shayibak District	62669	64470	68986	60578
新市区	Xinshi District	71808	68261	81075	77140
水磨沟区	Shui Mogou Distric	60691	58196	37549	66240
头屯河区	Tou Tunhe District	56774	51941	52811	60054
达坂城区	Da Bancheng District	58871	51672	34692	63280
米东区	Midong District	67971	60010	39561	73733
经济技术开发区（头屯河区）	Economic and Technological DeveloPment Zone（Tou Tunhe District）	62081	48715		62680
高新技术开发区	New and High-tech Industrial DeveloPment Zone	65366	58827		65544
乌鲁木齐县	Urumqi County	61254	59278	128311	53370
克拉玛依市	**Karamay City**	**83194**	**81689**	**48423**	**83946**
独山子区	Dushanzi District	87059	87332	42775	89471
克拉玛依区	Karamay District	84539	83281	65496	84881
白碱滩区	Bai Jiantan District	63096	85978	34000	55071
乌尔河区	Urhe District	52293	49226		67459
吐鲁番市	**Turpan City**	**67829**	**68943**	**41161**	**66661**
高昌区	Gaochang District	63189	65175	40062	59136
鄯善县	Shanshan [Piqan] County	78381	77713	93225	79513
托克逊县	Toksun County	56987	54566	30960	58785
哈密地区	**Hami [Kumul] Administrative Offices**	**59601**	**55562**	**47529**	**66997**
哈密市	Hami [Kumul] City	60414	56510	43901	67121
巴里坤哈萨克自治县	Barkol Kazak Autonomous County	54587	51576	81363	71528
伊吾县	Yiwu [Araturuk] County	60046	56019	38167	63779
昌吉回族自治州	**Changji Hui Autonomous Prefecture**	**62231**	**63469**	**82754**	**60483**
昌吉市	Changji City	63574	73220	97994	55358
阜康市	Fukang City	62277	62127	110567	61848
呼图壁县	Hutubi County	55301	51529	140734	60441
玛纳斯县	Manas County	57604	55538	51624	61396
奇台县	Qitai County	62582	68452	51400	51192
吉木萨尔县	Jimsar County	75425	69661	140687	77273
木垒哈萨克自治县	Mori Kazak Autonomous County	76059	82370	138857	52662
伊犁哈萨克自治州	**Ili Kazak Autonomous Prefecture**	**49493**	**48511**	**69165**	**51597**
伊犁州直属县(市)	**Counties (Cities) Direct Under Ili Prefecture**	**53780**	**53681**	**68188**	**53665**
伊宁市	Yining [Gulja] City	58640	60040	76740	56581
奎屯市	Kuytun City	54271	59381	28757	51340
霍尔果斯市	Huoerguosi City	59813	63481		52366
伊宁县	Yining [Gulja] County	48444	44262	36267	57191
察布查尔锡伯自治县	Qapqal Xibe Autonomous County	49743	50068	86800	44574
霍城县	Huocheng [Korgas] County	46776	46585	71657	46669
巩留县	Gongliu [Tokkuztara] County	56817	58896	78398	43097

3-28 续表 1 Continued

单位：元 (yuan)

地　区	Region	合 计 Total	国有单位 State-owned Units	城镇集体单位 Urban Collective-owned Units	其他单位 Units of Other Types of Ownership
新源县	Xinyuan [Kunes] County	53499	52484	65634	54917
昭苏县	Zhaosu [Mongolkure] County	52577	52487	129871	30720
特克斯县	Tekes County	55700	56381	86104	44688
尼勒克县	Nilka County	51894	50201	96914	53945
塔城地区	**Tacheng [Tarbagatai] Administrative Offices**	**46288**	**46196**	**53563**	**46411**
塔城市	Tacheng [Qoqek] City	51801	51873	54338	51225
乌苏市	Usu City	43326	41361	43824	52557
额敏县	Emin [Dorbiljin] County	39454	39054	96103	40796
沙湾县	Shawan County	49421	53431	42164	40802
托里县	Toli County	58070	57309	29711	59955
裕民县	Yumin [Qagantokay] County	41913	42062	49909	27287
和布克赛尔蒙古自治县	Hoboksar Mongol Autonomous County	41908	35971	86708	59589
阿勒泰地区	**Altay Administrative Offices**	**44266**	**41694**	**96899**	**53758**
阿勒泰市	Altay City	48323	45899	122301	56127
布尔津县	Burqin County	48153	46302	132807	51950
富蕴县	Fuyun [Koktokay] County	34273	26739	101851	60161
福海县	Fuhai [Burultokay] County	42851	41168	45844	54288
哈巴河县	Habahe [Kaba] County	43450	43426	41955	43584
青河县	Qinghe [Qinggil] County	48281	48798	121220	38348
吉木乃县	Jemnay County	44185	42782	55091	60322
博尔塔拉蒙古自治州	**Bortala Mongol Autonomous Prefecture**	**50431**	**52066**	**62396**	**42081**
博乐市	Bole [Bortala] City	50823	52052	81654	43659
阿拉山口市	Alashankou City	60250	53240		76376
精河县	Jinghe [Jing] County	49131	53341	53533	32725
温泉县	Wenquan [Araxang] County	49603	49415	112205	47855
巴音郭楞蒙古自治州	**Bayangol Mongol Autonomous Prefecture**	**60118**	**53130**	**89276**	**70167**
库尔勒市	Korla City	66035	55740	86635	74651
轮台县	Luntai [Bugur] County	54291	47089	118584	76195
尉犁县	Yuli [Lopnur] County	47221	51703	98329	24789
若羌县	Ruoqiang [Qarkilik] County	79741	65090	99173	98061
且末县	Qiemo [Qarqan] County	53031	52119	50086	63114
焉耆回族自治县	Yanji Hui Autonomous County	57808	57542	102667	52609
和静县	Hejing County	47002	48035	48336	44492
和硕县	Hoxud County	46504	45701	120106	45136
博湖县	Bohu [Bagrax] County	52429	52066	52600	56461
阿克苏地区	**Aksu Administrative Offices**	**54544**	**56669**	**66346**	**50070**
阿克苏市	Aksu City	58292	63466	80152	51329
温宿县	Wensu [Onsu] County	40952	44415	58733	32235
库车县	Kuqa County	54767	52149	57271	58651
沙雅县	Xayar County	56612	58252	85502	49521

3-28 续表 2 Continued

单位：元 (yuan)

地　区	Region	合计 Total	国有单位 State-owned Units	城镇集体单位 Urban Collective-owned Units	其他单位 Units of Other Types of Ownership
新和县	Xinhe [Toksu] County	53000	56176	103497	37932
拜城县	Baicheng [Bay] County	61244	61317	98594	60385
乌什县	Wushi [Uxturpan] County	59431	60298	58063	46211
阿瓦提县	Awat County	48387	52393	44909	35943
柯坪县	Kalpin County	60231	59635	23800	112835
克孜勒苏柯尔克孜自治州	**Kizilsu Kirgiz Autonomous Prefecture**	**55551**	**57061**	**43792**	**48216**
阿图什市	Artux City	54740	56503	34400	46211
阿克陶县	Akto County	57455	62678	51574	40343
阿合奇县	Akqi County	46350	46207	48929	55806
乌恰县	Wuqia [Ulugqat] County	60286	57514	43447	78046
喀什地区	**Kashgar [Kaxgar] Administrative Offices**	**63804**	**68372**	**60781**	**51290**
喀什市	Kashgar [Kaxgar] City	55204	53620	65361	56544
疏附县	Shufu County	73698	76856	39458	36805
疏勒县	Shule County	66885	68524	75777	56690
英吉沙县	Yengisar County	66004	68087	27529	53699
泽普县	Zepu [Poskam] County	59851	60114	46980	59753
莎车县	Shache [Yarkant] County	69673	84532	61686	30040
叶城县	Yecheng [Kagilik] County	74607	81705	64797	40866
麦盖提县	Makit County	62181	62801	45981	54308
岳普湖县	Yopurga County	52682	53073	55333	51103
伽师县	Jiashi [Payzawat] County	73345	76807		36125
巴楚县	Bachu [Maralbexi] County	72629	75291	82130	40412
塔什库尔干塔吉克自治县	Taxkorgan Tajik Autonomous County	86581	89473		53990
和田地区	**Hotan Administrative Offices**	**55829**	**57315**	**49957**	**46986**
和田市	Hotan City	55707	57112	34514	52391
和田县	Hotan County	64584	66598	66008	52851
墨玉县	Moyu [Karakax] County	60194	63315	27000	38037
皮山县	Pishan [Guma] County	42646	43650	66846	27674
洛浦县	Lop County	58967	60772	52543	41243
策勒县	Qira County	53098	52303	98529	55405
于田县	Yutian [Keriya] County	60284	61653		39084
民丰县	Minfeng [Niya] County	58756	58913	53189	37600
自治区直辖县级市	**County level City directly under the Autonomous Region**	**59377**	**59456**		**59321**
石河子市	Shihezi City	60819	67156		57191
阿拉尔市	Aral City	55941	44030		67506
图木舒克市	Tumxuk City	57739	59172		55685
五家渠市	Wujiaqu City	59000	56112		61117

主要统计指标解释

人口数 指一定时点、一定地区范围内的有生命的个人的总和。

年度统计的年末人口数指每年12月31日24时的人口数。

户籍人口 指公民依照《中华人民共和国户口登记条例》已在其经常居住地的公安户籍管理机关登记了常住户口的人。

常住人口 指在某地区实际居住半年以上的人口。

城镇人口和乡村人口 城镇人口是指居住在城镇范围内的全部常住人口；乡村人口是除上述人口以外的全部人口。

出生率(又称粗出生率) 指在一定时期内(通常为一年)一定地区的出生人数与同期内平均人数(或期中人数)之比，用千分率表示。本资料中的出生率指年出生率，其计算公式为：

出生率＝年出生人数／年平均人数×1000‰

式中：出生人数指活产婴儿，即胎儿脱离母体时(不管怀孕月数)，有过呼吸或其他生命现象。年平均人数指年初、年底人口数的平均数，也可用年中人口数代替。

死亡率(又称粗死亡率) 指在一定时期内(通常为一年)一定地区的死亡人数与同期内平均人数(或期中人数)之比，用千分率表示。本资料中的死亡率指年死亡率，其计算公式为：

死亡率＝年死亡人数／年平均人数×1000‰

人口自然增长率 指在一定时期内(通常为一年)人口自然增加数(出生人数减死亡人数)与该时期内平均人数(或期中人数)之比，用千分率表示。计算公式为：

人口自然增长率＝(本年出生人数－本年死亡人数)／年平均人数×1000‰＝人口出生率－人口死亡率

经济活动人口 指在16周岁及以上，有劳动能力，参加或要求参加社会经济活动的人口；包括就业人员和失业人员。

就业人员 指一定年龄及以上，有劳动能力，为取得劳动报酬或经营收入而从事一定社会劳动的人员。具体指年满16周岁，为取得劳动报酬或经营利润，在调查周内从事1小时（含1小时）以上劳动或由于学习、休假等原因在调查周内暂时处于未工作状态，但有工作单位或场所的人口。

单位就业人员 指报告期末最后一日24时在本单位中工作，并取得工资或其他形式劳动报酬的人员数。该指标为时点指标，不包括最后一日当天及以前已经与单位解除劳动合同关系的人员，是在岗职工、劳务派遣人员及其他就业人员之和。就业人员不包括：

(1)离开本单位仍保留劳动关系，并定期领取生活费的人员；

(2)利用课余时间打工的学生及在本单位实习的各类在校学生；

(3)本单位因劳务外包而使用的人员。

国有单位 指资产归国家所有的经济组织。包括按《中华人民共和国企业法人登记管理条例》规定登记注册的非公司制的经济组织，以及中央、地方各级国家机关、事业单位和社会团体。

集体单位 指生产资料归集体所有，并按《中华人民共和国企业法人登记管理条例》规定登记注册的经济组织。

其他单位 包括股份合作单位、联营单位、有限责任公司、股份有限公司、港澳台商投资单位以及外商投资单位等其他登记注册类型单位。

城镇私营和个体就业人员 城镇私营就业人员指在工商管理部门注册登记，其经营地址设在县城关镇(含县城关镇)以上的私营企业就业人员，包括私营企业投资者和雇工。城镇个体就业人员指在工商管理部门注册登记，并持有城镇户口或在城镇长期居住，经批准从事个体工商经营的就业人员，包括个体经营者和在个体工商户劳动的家庭帮工和雇工。

在岗职工 指在本单位工作且与本单位签订劳动合同，并由单位支付各项工资和社会保险、住房公积金的人员，以及上述人员中由于学习、病伤、产假等原因暂未工作仍由单位支付工资的人员。在岗职工还包括：

(1)应订立劳动合同而未订立劳动合同人员(如使用的农村户籍人员)；

(2)处于试用期人员；

(3)编制外招用的人员；

(4)派往外单位工作，但工资仍由本单位发放的人员(如挂职锻炼、外派工作等情况)。

工资总额 指根据《关于工资总额组成的规定》(1990年1月1日国家统计局发布的一号令)进行修订，在报告期内(季度或年度)直接支付给本单位全部就业人员的劳动报酬总额。包括计时工资、计件工资、奖金、津贴和补贴、加班加点工资、特殊情况下支付的工资，是在岗职工工资总额、劳务派遣人员工资总额和其他就业人员工资总额之和。

工资总额是税前工资，包括单位从个人工资中直接为其代扣或代缴的房费、水费、电费、住房公积金和社会保险基金个人缴纳部分等。

工资总额不论是计入成本的还是不计入成本的，不论是以货币形式支付的还是以实物形式支付的，均应列入工资总额的计算范围。

平均工资　指单位就业人员在一定时期内平均每人所得的工资额。它表明一定时期职工工资收入的高低程度，是反映就业人员工资水平的主要指标。计算公式为:

平均工资 = 报告期就业人员工资总额 / 报告期就业人员平均人数

平均工资指数　指报告期就业人员平均工资与基期就业人员平均工资的比率，是反映不同时期就业人员货币工资水平变动情况的相对数。计算公式为:

平均工资指数 = 报告期就业人员平均工资 / 基期就业人员平均工资

平均实际工资指数　就业人员平均实际工资指扣除物价变动因素后的就业人员平均工资。就业人员平均实际工资指数是反映实际工资变动情况的相对数，表明就业人员实际工资水平提高或降低的程度。计算公式为：

平均实际工资指数 = 报告期就业人员平均工资指数 / 报告期城镇居民消费价格指数×100%

城镇登记失业人员　指有非农业户口，在一定的劳动年龄内（16 周岁至退休年龄），有劳动能力，无业而要求就业，并在当地劳动保障部门进行失业登记的人员。

城镇登记失业率　城镇登记失业人员与城镇单位就业人员（扣除使用的农村劳动力、聘用的离退休人员、港澳台及外方人员）、城镇单位中不在岗职工、城镇私营业主、个体户主、城镇私营企业和个体就业人员、城镇登记失业人数之和的比。

Explanatory Notes on Main Statistical Indicators

Total Population refers to the total number of people alive at a certain point of time within a given area.

The annual statistics on total population is taken at midnight, the 31st of December.

The household register population refers to citizens in accordance with the "people's Republic of Household Registration Ordinance" has been registered permanent residence.

The resident population refers to the practical living more than half year of the population.

Urban Population and Rural Population Urban population refers to all people residing in cities and towns, while rural population refers to population other than urban population.

Birth Rate(or Crude Birth Rate) refers to the ratio of the number of births to the average population (or mid-period population) during a certain period of time (usually a year), expressed in ‰. Birth rate in the chapter refers to annual birth rate. The following formula is used:

Brith Rate= Number of Births/Annual Average Number of Population*1000‰

Number of births in the formula refers to live births, i.e. when a baby has breathed or showed any vital phenomena regardless of the length of pregnancy.

Annual average population is the average of the number of population at the beginning of the year and that at the end of the year. Sometimes it is substituted by the mid-year population.

Death Rate(or Crude Death Rate) refers to the ratio of the number of deaths to the average population (or mid- period population) during a certain period of time (usually a year), expressed in‰. Death rate in the chapter refers to annual death rate. The following formula is used:

Death Rate =Number of Deaths/ Annual Average Number of Population*1000‰

Natural Growth Rate of Population refers to the ratio of natural increase in population(number of births minus number of deaths)in a certain period of time(usually a year)to the average population(or mid-period population)of the same period , expressed in‰. The following formula is applied:

Natural Growth Rate of Population= Number of Births-Number of Deaths / Annual Average Number of Population *1000‰

Natural Growth Rate of Population=Birth Rate-Death Rate

Economically Active Population refers to the population aged 16 and over who are capable of working, are participating in or willing to participate in economic activities, including employed persons and unemployed persons.

Employed Persons refers to persons above a specified age who had labour capacity and performed some social work for compensation or business gains.Specifically,it refers to all persons,aged 16 and over,who performed some work for compensation or business gains for one hour or more during the reference period;or who had work units or sites but were temporarily not at work during the reference period.

Persons Employed in Various Units refer to the total number of employees who work at his unit and obtain wages or other forms of payment at the end of the reporting period. This indicator is a kind of time point index and it equals to the sum of the number of employed staff and workers, labor dispatch personnel and other employed persons. Employed persons do not include:

1)persons who have left their working units while keeping their labour contract (employment relation) unchanged and receiving regular alimony;

2)students who do part-time jobs in spare time and all kinds of enrolled students who do internship in various units;

3)persons employed due to labor outsourcing;

4)persons who dissolve labor contracts with their units on the last day of reporting period or before.

State-owned Units refer to economic units whose assets are owned by the state.Included are non-corporation units registered according to Regulation of the People's Republic of China on the Registration of Enterprises and Corporation ,state argans,institutions and social organizations at the central and local levels.

Collective-owned Units refer to economic units registered according to Regulation of the People's Republic of China on the Registration of Enterprises and Corporations where the means of production are collectively owned.

Units of Other Types of Ownership refer to units registered with other types of ownership,including cooperative units,joint ownership units,limited companies,share holding corporation,units invested by entrepreneurs from Hong Kong, Macao,and Taiwan,and foreign-invested units.

Persons Employed in Private Enterprises and Self-Employed Individuals in Urban Areas Persons employed in private enterprises refer to the persons employed in the private enterprises which have been registered at the departments of industrial and commercial administration for which the business operation are situated at a county town (i.e. a town where the county government is located), or at urban areas with administrative hierarchy higher than a county town. The self-employed individuals in urban areas refer to persons who hold the certificates of residence in urban areas or have resided in the urban areas for a long time and have been registered at the departments of industrial and commercial administration and approved to be engaged in individual industrial or commercial business, including self-employed persons as well as helpers and hired laborers who work in individual households.

Employed Staff and Workers refer to persons who signed labor contracts with working units and working units would pay wages, social insurance and housing funds for them. Persons who have their work posts but are temporarily absent from work for reasons of study or on sick, injury or maternal leave and still receive wages from their working units are also included. Employed staff and workers also include:

1)Persons who should have signed the labor contracts but not (like people with rural household registration);

2)Employees on probation;

3)Employees beyond the staffing quota;

4)Employees who are sent to other working units but still obtain wages from their original units (situations like on-the-job placement, expatriated assignment, etc.)

1)Employed Staff and Workers do not include: Dispatched personnel who work and are paid directly by the working units; they shall be counted into "labour dispatch personnel" of the working units;

2)Personnel through labor outsourcing, they shall be counted into "employed staff and workers" of the units which contracted them.

Total Wage Bill It is revised according to the "Provision of Composition of Total Wages" (Order No.1 by National Bureau of Statistics on January, 1st, 1990), total wage bill refers to the total remuneration payment to all employed persons in various units during the reporting period (by quarter or by year), including hourly-paid wages, piece-rate wages, bonuses, allowance and subsidies, overtime wages and wages paid under special circumstances. It equals to the sum of total wages of employed staff and workers, dispatch labors and other employed persons.

Total wage bill is pre-tax wages, including the room charges, utility bills, housing funds and social insurance paid or withheld by employee's units.

Total wage bill, whether or not included in cost, whether or not paid in money or in kind, shall be included in the calculation of total wage.

Average Wage refers to the average per capita wage in money terms during a certain period of time for employed persons. It shows the general level of wage income of staff and worker during a certain period of time, one major indicator to reflect the wage level. It is calculated as follows:

Average Wage =Total Wage Bill of Empioyed Perons at Reference Time / Average Number of Persons Employed at Reference Time

Average Wage Indices refers to the ratio of average wage of employed persons the reporting period to that at the base period, which reflects the change of wage of employed persons at the different period. It is calculated as follows:

Average Wage Indices = Average Wage of Employed Persons at Reference Time / Average Wage of Persons Employeds at Base Period *100%

Average Real Wage Indices average real wage of employed persons refers to the average wage of employed persons after removing the effects of the price changes and average real wage indices of employed persons refers to the change of real wage, which reflects the relative increasing or decreasing level of real wage of employed persons ,which is calculated as follows:

Average Real Wage Indices =Average Wage Indices of Employed Persons at the Reference Time / Urban Consumer Price Indices at Reference Time *100%

Registered Unemployed Persons in Urban Areas refer to the persons with non-agricultural household registration at certain working ages (16 years old to retirement age), who are capable of working, unemployed and willing to work, and have been registered at the local employment service agencies to apply for a job.

Registered Unemployment Rate in Urban Areas refers to the ratio of the number of the registered unemployed persons to the sum of the number of persons employed in various units (minus the employed rural labour force, re-employed retirees, and Hong Kong, Macao, Taiwan or foreign employees), laid-off staff and workers in urban units, owners of private enterprises in urban areas, owners of self-employed individuals in urban areas, employees of private enterprises in urban areas, employee of self-employed individuals in urban areas, and the registered unemployed persons in urban areas.

固定资产投资

INVESTMENT IN FIXED ASSETS

第四篇 固定资产投资

本篇主要内容和资料来源

本篇资料包括主要年份全社会固定资产投资及其主要分组；2015年及同期的全区固定资产投资及其细化分组；2015年新增主要产品生产能力(或效益)；房地产开发企业基本情况；农村非农户固定资产投资情况。

本篇资料来自新疆维吾尔自治区统计局固定资产投资统计处。

本篇资料的统计范围，2011年及以前年份，固定资产投资统计起点为50及50万元以上；2012年开始，按照国家统计局相关规定，固定资产投资统计起点调整为500万元及以上。自2014年起固定资产投资中不包括农村个人投资。

Investment in Fixed Assets

Main Content and Source of Data

Statistics in this chapter cover the total investment in fixed assets of the whole society and its composition, total investment in fixed assets and its refining grouping by region in 2013.Newly increased production capacity of major production in 2015.Basic condition of enterprises for real estate development, basic condition of individual investment in fixed assets of farm households and non-farm households.

The data of investment in fixed assets in rural areas come from the Division of Investment in Fixed Assets, Xinjiang Bureau of Statistics.

Scope of statistics: Before and in 2011,the starting point of fixed assets is changed from RMB 500,000 and above; From 2012,the stating point of fixed assets is changed to RMB 5 million according to relevant regulations of National Bureau of Statistics.Since 2014 data of investment in fixed assets include individial investment in rural.

4-1 全社会固定资产投资
Total Investment in Fixed Assets in the Whole Country

单位：万元 (2015 年) (10 000 yuan)

项 目	Item	合 计 Total	#房地产 Real Estate Development
投资总额	**Total Investment**	**107293206**	**9988751**
#住 宅	Residential Buildings	10325134	6036606
#国有经济控股	State-holding	62893850	1235213
按构成分	**Grouped by Use of Funds**		
建筑工程	Construction	68622738	7437445
安装工程	Installation	8694195	1092660
设备工器具购置	Purchase of Equipment and Instruments	22562789	173309
其他费用	Other Expenses	7413484	1285337
按三次产业分	**Grouped by Three Strata of Industry**		
第一产业	Primary Industry	3663277	
第二产业	Secondary Industry	51791738	
第三产业	Tertiary Industry	51838191	9988751
按登记注册类型分	**Grouped by Types of Registration**		
内资企业	Domestic Fund Enterprises	106286909	9876409
国 有	State-owned	50991563	118751
集 体	Collective-owned	308076	2450
股份合作	Share-holding Cooperative	432148	1000
联营企业	Joint Ownership Enterprises	310463	
国有联营企业	State Joint Ownership Enterprises	243175	
集体联营企业	Collective-owned Joint Ownership Enterprises	6494	
国有与集体联营企业	State and Collective-owned Joint Ownership Enterprises	5442	
其他联营企业	Others	55352	
有限责任公司	Limited Liability Corporations	25997086	4719234
国有独资公司	State-funded Corporations	2502140	446532
其他有限责任公司	Other Limited Liability Corporations	23494946	4272702
股份有限公司	Share-holding Corporations Ltd	6494282	173797
私营企业	Private Enterprises	20394986	4860397
其他企业	Others	1358305	780
港澳台商投资企业	Funds from Hongkong,Macao and Taiwan	315804	112342

注：本表不包括农村个人投资。
Note: Total investment in this table do not include rural individual investment.

4-1 续表 Continued

单位：万元 (10 000 yuan)

项　目	Item	合 计 Total	#房地产 Real Estate Development
合资经营企业(港或澳、台资)	Joint-venture Enterprises (Hongkong,Macao and Taiwan)	147067	108341
合作经营企业(港或澳、台资)	Cooperation Enterprises (Hongkong,Macao and Taiwan)	98784	
港、澳、台商独资经营企业	Enterprises With Sole Investment from Hongkong,Macao and Taiwan	48001	4001
港、澳、台商投资股份有限公司	Share-holding Corporation Ltd from Hongkong,Macao and Taiwan	5390	
其他港、澳、台商投资企业	Others	16562	
外商投资企业	Foreign Funded Enterprises	518083	
中外合资经营企业(港或澳、台资)	Joint-venture Enterprises (Hongkong,Macao and Taiwan)	22584	
中外合作经营企业(港或澳、台资)	Cooperation Enterprises (Hongkong,Macao and Taiwan)		
外资企业	Enterprises With Sole Funds	351769	
外商投资股份有限公司	Share-holding Corporations Ltd.	96505	
其他外商投资企业	Others	47225	
个体经营	Individual Operate	172410	
#个 体 户	Self-employed Personel	113107	
个人合伙	Individual Partnership	59303	
按隶属关系分	**By Administrative Relationship**		
中 央	Central Government	19374771	483948
地 方	Local	87918435	9504803
资金来源小计	**All Sources**	**106565250**	**11347246**
国家预算内资金	State Budget Funds	15615189	
国内贷款	Domestic Loans	15739471	1244560
债 券	Bonds	86635	
利用外资	Foreign Investment	41409	
自筹资金	Self-raising Funds	64836103	4922646
其他资金来源	Others	10246443	5180040
本年新增固定资产	**Newly Increased Fixed Assets**	**72039763**	**4226009**
房屋施工面积(万平方米)	**Floor Space of Buildings (10 000 sq.m)**	**22689.17**	**11465.44**
#住 宅	Residential Buildings	11917.86	7370.42
房屋竣工面积(万平方米)	**Floor Space of Buildings Completed (10 000 sq.m)**	**5935.82**	**1608.58**
#住 宅	Residential Buildings	3392.31	1206.44

4-2 按构成分全社会固定资产投资
Total Investment in Fixed Asset by structure

单位：万元 (10 000 yuan)

年 份 Year	地 区 Region	合计 Total	建筑工程 Construction Works	安装工程 Installation Works	设备工具器具购置 Purchase of Equipment and Instruments	其他费用 Others
	1978	129999	86667		35686	7646
	1985	444758	323395		93254	28109
	1990	887775	571461		274647	41667
	1995	3333404	2145762		810995	376647
	1996	3878472	2245924	278445	929463	424640
	1997	4468148	2725428	310687	988070	443963
	1998	5197673	3435120	278895	920992	562666
	1999	5346468	3245779	344130	1039617	716942
	2000	6103843	3833328	416759	1254077	599679
	2001	7059970	4232768	454765	1616907	755530
	2002	8130223	4815707	593242	1787899	933375
	2003	10021256	6075091	690459	2030335	1225371
	2004	11615245	7133323	806705	2304931	1370286
	2005	13522757	8499303	993311	2637777	1392366
	2006	15670521	9776613	1014851	3166617	1712440
	2007	18508415	10667717	1517359	4312525	2010814
	2008	22599746	13071829	1773200	5488261	2266456
	2009	28272359	17511739	1938944	5855684	2965992
	2010	35396941	22224487	1943535	7960420	3268499
	2011	47127699	29541315	3362813	10626129	3597442
	2012	62583830	39278692	4507946	14260205	4536987
	2013	77874141	50280291	6153338	16516828	4923684
	2014	97447919	63506160	8235754	19956552	5749453
	2015	107293206	68622738	8694195	22562789	7413484
乌鲁木齐市	Urumqi City	16074304	9099166	1662126	2825212	2487800
克拉玛依市	Karamay City	4199548	3231076	407043	420037	141392
吐鲁番市	Turpan City	4587089	2818815	429955	1218662	119657
哈密地区	Hami [Kumul] Administrative Offices	9159381	3004080	1035062	4387535	732704
昌吉回族自治州	Changji Hui Autonomous Prefecture	16026331	8985146	1414412	5292653	334120
伊犁哈萨克自治州	Ili Kazak Autonomous Prefecture	14483694	10491600	894850	2371118	726126
伊犁州直属县(市)	Counties (Cities) Direct Under Ili Prefecture	7017654	4703188	527875	1271254	515337
塔城地区	Tacheng [Tarbagatai] Administrative Offices	4875188	3653019	256399	807637	158133
阿勒泰地区	Altay Administrative Offices	2590852	2135393	110576	292227	52656
博尔塔拉蒙古自治州	Bortala Mongol Autonomous Prefecture	3010301	2080453	128509	694027	107312
巴音郭楞蒙古自治州	Bayangol Mongol Autonomous Prefecture	7198562	4754290	318967	1610048	515257
阿克苏地区	Aksu Administrative Offices	6264621	4580829	836677	776763	70352
克孜勒苏柯尔克孜自治州	Kizilsu Kirgiz Autonomous Prefecture	1354750	1116053	44405	189023	5269
喀什地区	Kashgar [Kaxgar] Administrative Offices	9081682	7162484	593615	968380	357203
和田地区	Hotan Administrative Offices	3284914	2849295	229174	121605	84840
石河子市	Shihezi City	2347728	1001379	356194	839736	150419
阿拉尔市	Aral City	1260219	840607	59607	306642	53363
图木舒克市	Tumxuk City	651989	410297	23007	184182	34503
五家渠市	Wujiaqu City	1371841	932340	211878	189172	38451
跨地区投资	Trans-regional Investment	6936252	5264828	48714	167994	1454716

注：本表自 2013 年起不包括农村个人投资。
Note: Since 2013,total investment in this table do not include rural individual investment.

4-3 全社会固定资产投资资金来源情况
Sources of Funds of Total Investment in Fixed Assets in the Whole Country

单位：万元 (10 000 yuan)

年份 Year	地区 Region	合计 Total	国家预算内资金 State Budget	国内贷款 Domestic Loans	债券 Bonds	利用外资 Foreign Investment	自筹及其他资金 Self-raising Fund And Others
	1978	129999	102693				27306
	1985	444758	117439	72227		7708	247384
	1990	887775	105423	294985		40927	446440
	1995	3333404	98004	818914		307619	2108867
	1996	3878472	128725	756412		324532	2668803
	1997	4468148	269106	749345		109629	3340068
	1998	5197673	384195	1116497		133936	3563045
	1999	5346468	512364	1097949	12376	93895	3629884
	2000	6103843	506867	1346175	19429	99942	4131430
	2001	7059970	545176	1321317	8340	64834	5120303
	2002	8130223	1323660	1607535	30504	62992	5105532
	2003	10021256	1626261	1896104	21586	95287	6382018
	2004	11490824	1799593	1555105	46095	87388	8002643
	2005	13543432	2093022	1677020	15428	109968	9647994
	2006	15773966	2119253	1854512	8193	88675	11703333
	2007	19070184	2258779	2480410	5526	110034	14215435
	2008	22725814	3388141	3020001	3410	90233	16224029
	2009	30345365	5813486	5246186	54636	94000	19137057
	2010	37844438	6347565	5750361	11544	120367	25614601
	2011	51265602	6266348	6679368	22559	137967	38159360
	2012	66725427	8684685	8897975	59736	91197	48991834
	2013	82681763	11177239	10013972	211314	37902	61241336
	2014	97939630	13267770	13706202	277371	32550	70655737
	2015	106565250	15615189	15739471	86635	41409	75082546
乌鲁木齐市	Urumqi City	16526280	708844	3741588	4001		12071847
克拉玛依市	Karamay City	4198207	168602	288833			3740772
吐鲁番市	Turpan City	5294834	306066	1153831			3834937
哈密地区	Hami [Kumul] Administrative Offices	8206621	1858260	3410906			2937455
昌吉回族自治州	Changji Hui Autonomous Prefecture	15865486	1253527	596293			14015666
伊犁哈萨克自治州	Ili Kazak Autonomous Prefecture	14702239	2707250	964338	39858	4854	10985939
伊犁州直属县(市)	Counties (Cities) Direct Under Ili Prefecture	6540392	947502	404993		3354	5184543
塔城地区	Tacheng [Tarbagatai] Administrative Offices	5984180	1001654	414874			4567652
阿勒泰地区	Altay Administrative Offices	2177667	758094	144471	39858	1500	1233744
博尔塔拉蒙古自治州	Bortala Mongol Autonomous Prefecture	3001900	476011	131490			2394399
巴音郭楞蒙古自治州	Bayangol Mongol Autonomous Prefecture	6551807	939505	611947	12776	2663	4984916
阿克苏地区	Aksu Administrative Offices	6811923	1388440	279166		33892	5110425
克孜勒苏柯尔克孜自治州	Kizilsu Kirgiz Autonomous Prefecture	1161642	530535	157856			473251
喀什地区	Kashgar [Kaxgar] Administrative Offices	8763791	2473422	199327			6091042
和田地区	Hotan Administrative Offices	3739206	2030938	169631			1538637
石河子市	Shihezi City	1935039	112668	409928			1412443
阿拉尔市	Aral City	1158058	333354	209977			614727
图木舒克市	Tumxuk City	260957	149766	300			110891
五家渠市	Wujiaqu City	1374292	31698	36480			1306114
跨地区投资	Trans-regional Investment	7012968	146303	3377580	30000		3459085

注：1.自 2004 年起资金来源为本年实际到位资金。2.该表资金来源不包括农村个人资金。

Note: a) Sources of capital caculated on actual arrived investment from 2004. b) Sources of Capital in this table do not include rural individual fund.

4-4 按行业分全社会固定资产投资
Total Investment in Fixed Assets in the Whole Country by Sector

单位：万元 (10 000 yuan)

行　业	Sector	2014	2015
总　计	**Total**	**97447919**	**107293206**
农、林、牧、渔业	**Farming, Forestry, Animal Husbandry and Fishery**	**2996668**	**3663277**
农　业	Farming	546079	647822
林　业	Forestry	173893	307129
畜牧业	Animal Husbandry	1036800	912559
渔　业	Fishery	15027	16971
农、林、牧、渔服务业	Services in Support of Farming, Forestry, Animal Husbandry and Fishery	1224869	1778796
采矿业	**Mining**	**10360408**	**8887233**
#煤炭开采和洗选业	Mining and Washing of Coal	2658721	2433880
石油和天然气开采业	Extraction of Petroleum and Natural Gas	6056438	5430955
黑色金属矿采选业	Mining and Processing of Ferrous Metals Ores	594255	355839
#铁矿采选	Mining and Processing of Iron Ore	557021	313328
有色金属矿采选业	Mining and Processing of Non-ferrous Metals Ores	458056	300473
#常用有色金属矿采选	Mining and Processing of Common Non-ferrous Metal	321720	172580
非金属矿采选业	Mining and Processing of Non-metal Ores	168808	154982
#土砂石开采	Mining of Earth and Gravel	56589	102875
化学矿采选	Extracting of Chemical Ore	10826	5789
制造业	**Manufacturing**	**21296335**	**20629865**
#农副食品加工业	Processing of Food from Agricultural Products	1036179	920061
食品制造业	Manufacture of Food	910693	494928
烟草制品业	Manufacture of Tobacco	3081	33188
纺织业	Manufacture of Textile	732130	2681102
皮革、毛皮、羽绒及其制品业	Manufacture of Leather, Fur, Feather and Related Products	9086	17800
木材加工和木、竹、藤、棕、草制品业	Processing of Timber, Wood, Bamboo, Cane, Grass Products	108404	128836
家具制造业	Manufacture of Furniture	22942	26577
造纸及纸制品业	Manufacture of Paper and Paper Products	141594	82740
印刷和记录媒介复制业	Printing and Reproduction of Recording Media	44527	33068
石油加工及炼焦业	Processing of Petroleum, Coking and Nuclear Fuel	3657578	2740979
#精炼石油产品制造	Manufacture of Oil Products	2243883	1755659
炼　焦	Coking	1413695	985320
化学原料及化学制品制造业	Manufacture of Raw Chemical Material and Chemical Products	4226151	5402302
#基础化学原料制造	Manufacture of Basic Chemical Material	1910868	3265173
肥料制造	Manufacture of Fertilizer Making	438381	753495
医药制造业	Manufacture of Medicine	361874	242077
#中药饮片加工	Processing of Chinese Herbs and Tablet	58300	40495
中成药制造	Manufacture of Chinese Herbs and Patent Medicine	50494	34411
化学纤维制造业	Manufacture of Chemical Fiber	77321	131998
橡胶和塑料制品业	Manufacture of Rubber and Plastics	879570	509599
橡胶制品业	Manufacture of Rubber	28133	23804
塑料制品业	Manufacture of Plastic	851437	485795

注：分行业不包括农村个人投资。
Note: The major category in this table do not include rural individual investment.

4-4 续表 1 Continued

单位：万元 (10 000 yuan)

行　业	Sector	2014	2015
非金属矿物制品业	Manufacture of Non-metallic Mineral Products	2201499	1562732
#水泥、石灰和石膏的制造	Cement Manufacturing	485524	263139
黑色金属冶炼及压延加工业	Smelting and Pressing of Non-Ferrous Metals	926093	438808
#钢压延加工	Steel Rolling	131667	132629
有色金属冶炼及压延加工业	Smelting and Pressing of Nonferrous Metals	2597681	1710438
#常用有色金属冶炼	Smeltering of Common Non-ferrous Metal	1913741	848560
金属制品业	Manufacture of Metal Products	574757	476722
通用设备制造业	Manufacture of General Purpose Machinery	268144	414280
专用设备制造业	Manufacture of Special Purpose Machinery	432028	366802
汽车制造	Manufacture of Aufomobiles	166633	115230
电气机械及器材制造业	Manufacture of Electricial Machinery and Apparatus	322370	291641
电力、热力、燃气及水的生产和供应业	**Production and Supply of Electricity,Heat,Gas and Water**	**16520454**	**21088179**
电力、热力的生产和供应业	Production and Supply of Electric Power and Heat Power	14020212	18731748
电力生产	Production of Electric Power	10802455	15793899
电力供应	Supply of Electric Power	2415448	2232604
热力生产和供应	Production and Supply of Heat Power	802309	705245
燃气生产和供应业	Production and Supply of Gas	1610740	1547006
水的生产和供应业	Production and Supply of Water	889502	809425
#自来水的生产和供应	Production and Supply of Running Water	553364	484241
污水处理及其再生利用	Treatment and Recycle of Waste Water	265938	283364
建筑业	**Construction**	**961695**	**1186461**
#房屋和土木工程建筑业	Construction of Buildings and Civil Engineering	924032	1035362
建筑安装业	Building Installation	18445	36224
交通运输、仓储和邮政业	**Transport, Storage and Post**	**8278762**	**10613588**
铁路运输业	Railway Transport	1325100	1514534
道路运输业	Road Transport	5581853	7424890
#城市公共交通业	Urban Public Transport	181315	613621
航空运输业	Air Transport	153280	246243
管道运输业	Via Pipeline Transport	294154	157930
装卸搬运和其他运输服务业	Loading, Unloading and Other Transport Services	40264	68089
仓储业	Storage	876488	1194919
邮政业	Post	7223	5983
信息传输、软件和信息技术服务业	**Information Transmission, Software and Information Technology**	**1079247**	**1325991**
#电信、广播电视和卫星传输服务	Telecommunication and Other Information Transmission Services	925513	1170783
#电　信	Telecommunication	901710	1143370
批发和零售业	**Wholesal and Retail Trades**	**2042237**	**1820998**
批发业	Wholesale Trade	830799	934318
零售业	Retail Trade	1211438	886680
住宿和餐饮业	**Hotels and Catering Services**	**910974**	**837862**
住宿业	Hotels	686071	556206
#旅游饭店	Tourist Restaurant	505258	435001
餐饮业	Catering Service	224903	281656
金融业	**Financial Intermediation**	**48650**	**119420**

4-4 续表 2 Continued

单位：万元 (10 000 yuan)

行　业	Sector	2014	2015
#银行业	Banks	44488	103523
保险业	Insurance	1200	1498
其他金融活动	Other Financial Activities	2962	12797
房地产业	**Real Estate**	**19255327**	**19323079**
#房地产开发与经营业	Real Estate Development and Operation	10431815	307918
物业管理	Real Estate Management	6918	10660
租赁和商务服务业	**Leasing and Business Services**	**426179**	**1047293**
租赁业	Leasing	11672	142309
商务服务业	Business Services	414507	904984
科学研究和技术服务业	**Scientific Research, and Technical Service**	**179871**	**300913**
研究与试验发展	Research and Experimental Development	38158	30716
专业技术服务业	Professional Technical Service	77248	116835
科技推广和应用服务业	Services of Science and Technology Popularization and Application	64465	153362
水利、环境和公共设施管理业	**Management of Water Conservancy, Environment and Public Facilities**	**8655455**	**10939460**
水利管理业	Management of Water Conservancy	1496342	1564180
生态保护和环境治理业	Ecological protection and Environmental Treatment	160202	317756
公共设施管理业	Management of Public Facilities	6998911	9057524
#市政设施管理	Management of Public Facilities	5846749	6799834
绿化管理	Urban Greening Management	278898	313365
公园和游览景区管理	Scenic-Spot Management	516334	1551032
居民服务、修理和其他服务业	**Services to Households ,Repair and Other Services**	**159739**	**224709**
教　育	**Education**	**1361111**	**1612067**
#初等教育	Junion Education	195550	299107
中等教育	Secondary Education	665362	772430
高等教育	Senior Education	259863	281301
卫生和社会工作	**Health, Social Service**	**568022**	**874934**
卫　生	Health	450760	668719
#医　院	Hospital	373430	493538
社会工作	Social Service	117262	206215
文化、体育和娱乐业	**Culture, Sports and Entertainment**	**820738**	**803012**
新闻和出版业	Journalism and Publishing Activities	1800	453
广播、电视、电影和影视录音制作	Broadcasting,Movies,Televisions and Audiovisual Activites	17299	30767
文化艺术业	Culture and Art Activities	401470	414861
体　育	Sports Activities	330270	229089
娱乐业	Entertainment	69899	127842
公共管理、社会保障和社会组织	**Public Management,Social Security and Social Organization**	**1526047**	**1994865**
中国共产党机关	Orgars of Communist Party of China	42124	57674
国家机构	Govemment Agencies	1241654	1744535
人民政协、民主党派	People's Political Consultative Conference and Democratic Parties		
社会保障	Social Security	110875	34310
群众团体、社会团体和其他成员组织	Non-Govemmental Organizations,Social Organizations and Membership Organizations	33222	26998
基层群众自治组织	Grass Roots Self-governing Organizations	98172	131348

4-5 按构成及建设性质分固定资产投资

Investment in Fixed Assets in Area by Composition of Funds and Type of Construction

单位：万元 (10 000 yuan)

年份 Year	地区 Region	合计 Total	按构成分 By Composition of Funds 建筑安装工程 Construction and Installation	设备工具器具购置 Purchase of Equipment and Instruments	#用于更新的设备 Update Equipment	其他费用 Others
	1978	129999	86667	35686		7646
	1985	408435	314651	67295	5499	26489
	1990	782099	516443	224673	25153	40983
	1995	2864148	1817364	754369	64612	292415
	1996	3339710	2167304	825067	66119	347339
	1997	3817221	2600884	858958	61094	357379
	1998	4561217	3333948	792449	71986	434820
	1999	4613116	3294346	831951	82363	486819
	2000	4994145	3531280	1103399	104850	359466
	2001	5490569	3638754	1392920	186605	458895
	2002	6596964	4379556	1558818	181920	658590
	2003	8188381	5599787	1718853	105728	869741
	2004	9482471	6451184	2047000	232343	984287
	2005	11215637	7926905	2230165	145514	1058567
	2006	12971324	8943879	2686125	188170	1341320
	2007	14908734	9646247	3746476	177062	1516011
	2008	17970126	11542024	4772937	311014	1655165
	2009	22999843	15632380	5026513	552733	2340950
	2010	28338644	18973774	6938417	346525	2426453
	2011	36881064	25313983	9102251	726850	2464830
	2012	49877126	34176800	12344316	1048785	3356010
	2013	65587266	46037812	15830049	2022503	3719405
	2014	77266659	56629747	16880754	673690	3756158
	2015	97304455	68786828	22389480	1319062	6128147
乌鲁木齐市	Urumqi City	12260603	7686997	2790650	130545	1782956
克拉玛依市	Karamay City	3965392	3437431	415054	40311	112907
吐鲁番市	Turpan City	4402973	3100824	1210883	21536	91266
哈密地区	Hami [Kumul] Administrative Offices	8830537	3749727	4385414	5329	695396
昌吉回族自治州	Changji Hui Autonomous Prefecture	15302294	9739905	5282729	162018	279660
伊犁哈萨克自治州	Ili Kazak Autonomous Prefecture	12549623	9671183	2337112	430567	541328
伊犁州直属县(市)	Counties (Cities) Direct Under Ili Prefecture	5812843	4178281	1242112	117659	392450
塔城地区	Tacheng [Tarbagatai] Administrative Offices	4237180	3334084	803093	292105	100003
阿勒泰地区	Altay Administrative Offices	2499600	2158818	291907	20803	48875
博尔塔拉蒙古自治州	Bortala Mongol Autonomous Prefecture	2649368	1888755	691375	30400	69238
巴音郭楞蒙古自治州	Bayangol Mongol Autonomous Prefecture	6671759	4624591	1596408	86502	450760
阿克苏地区	Aksu Administrative Offices	5671254	4886061	770407	65459	14786
克孜勒苏柯尔克孜自治州	Kizilsu Kirgiz Autonomous Prefecture	1263787	1079228	183815	28983	744
喀什地区	Kashgar [Kaxgar] Administrative Offices	8908018	7614459	957807	163967	335752
和田地区	Hotan Administrative Offices	3283853	3077408	121605	11631	84840
石河子市	Shihezi City	2108337	1145196	838190	48474	124951
阿拉尔市	Aral City	1211213	855308	305942	1840	49963
图木舒克市	Tumxuk City	634630	415945	184182		34503
五家渠市	Wujiaqu City	654562	500268	149913		4381
跨地区投资	Trans-regional Investment	6936252	5313542	167994	91500	1454716

注：表4-5，4-6，4-7，4-8，4-9 投资额未含房地产投资。
Note: in table 4-5，4-6，4-7，4-8，4-9 urban investment exclude real estate.

4-5 续表 Continued

单位：万元 (10 000 yuan)

年 份 Year	地 区 Region	按建设性质分 By Type of Construction 新 建 New Construction	扩 建 Expansion	改 建 Reconstruction	其 他 Others
	1978	93462	34399		2138
	1985	110236	160639	116006	21554
	1990	299356	148222	277007	57514
	1995	1067281	886882	646081	263904
	1996	1240585	820966	967022	311137
	1997	1405259	911902	1155121	344939
	1998	1648622	1017786	1338994	555815
	1999	1381764	1226797	1326775	677780
	2000	1410065	1424339	1558514	601227
	2001	891146	2373927	1614961	610535
	2002	1429874	2687996	1984657	494437
	2003	2207269	3128374	2237752	614986
	2004	2358662	3595847	2781101	746861
	2005	3397472	3657464	3063457	1097244
	2006	3633284	5436397	2430373	1471270
	2007	3759028	7439715	2386806	1323185
	2008	5350574	8078708	2759536	1781308
	2009	9465044	7634515	4113649	1786635
	2010	13612835	8408038	4177527	2140244
	2011	19799225	9910989	4216233	2954617
	2012	29842768	12229771	4387038	3417549
	2013	43552033	13405908	5259439	3369886
	2014	51293596	15748578	6534071	3690414
	2015	72815388	12306278	9101065	3081724
乌鲁木齐市	Urumqi City	7949619	3356218	327124	627642
克拉玛依市	Karamay City	3886775	31862	25288	21467
吐鲁番市	Turpan City	3718691	551645	121234	11403
哈密地区	Hami [Kumul] Administrative Offices	8361169	249160	16397	203811
昌吉回族自治州	Changji Hui Autonomous Prefecture	13512534	889326	793933	106501
伊犁哈萨克自治州	Ili Kazak Autonomous Prefecture	7751750	2944095	1104567	749211
伊犁州直属县(市)	Counties (Cities) Direct Under Ili Prefecture	4163832	1004943	358007	286061
塔城地区	Tacheng [Tarbagatai] Administrative Offices	2821092	488284	650723	277081
阿勒泰地区	Altay Administrative Offices	766826	1450868	95837	186069
博尔塔拉蒙古自治州	Bortala Mongol Autonomous Prefecture	1862474	671353	82312	33229
巴音郭楞蒙古自治州	Bayangol Mongol Autonomous Prefecture	5054040	1315318	147558	154843
阿克苏地区	Aksu Administrative Offices	5072132	307930	248412	42780
克孜勒苏柯尔克孜自治州	Kizilsu Kirgiz Autonomous Prefecture	1205651	29541	10450	18145
喀什地区	Kashgar [Kaxgar] Administrative Offices	7210147	866485	724457	106929
和田地区	Hotan Administrative Offices	2046083	583422	46557	607791
石河子市	Shihezi City	1548204	57093	317845	185195
阿拉尔市	Aral City	666332	155288	351407	38186
图木舒克市	Tumxuk City	410389	21742	129517	72982
五家渠市	Wujiaqu City	456733	107187	80533	10109
跨地区投资	Trans-regional Investment	2102665	168613	4573474	91500

4-6 分行业固定资产投资主要指标

Main Indicators of Investment in Fixed Assets in Area by Sector

(2015 年)

行业	Sector	投资额（万元）Total Investment (10 000 yuan)	#地方 Local	施工项目个数（个）Number of Projects under Construction (unit)	竣工项目个数（个）Number of Projects Completed (unit)	本年新增固定资产（万元）Newly Increased Fixed Assets (10 000 yuan)
总 计	**Total**	**97304455**	**78413632**	**16352**	**11670**	**67813754**
农、林、牧、渔业	**Farming, Forestry, Animal Husbandry and Fishery**	**3663277**	**2450135**	**2067**	**1683**	**3440337**
农 业	Farming	647822	412870	344	275	582310
林 业	Forestry	307129	255143	155	144	321499
畜牧业	Animal Husbandry	912559	637974	477	390	873451
渔 业	Fishery	16971	9411	9	7	14291
农、林、牧、渔服务业	Services in Support of Farming, Forestry, Animal Husbandry and Fishery	1778796	1134737	1082	867	1648786
采矿业	**Mining**	**8887233**	**3415304**	**461**	**302**	**4174966**
#煤炭开采和洗选业	Mining and Washing of Coal	2433880	2065616	152	91	1594008
石油和天然气开采业	Extraction of Petroleum and Natural Gas	5430955	406212	89	46	1565450
黑色金属矿采选业	Mining and Processing of Ferrous Metals Ores	355839	355839	69	51	342717
#铁矿采选	Mining and Processing of Iron Ore	313328	313328	61	45	300482
有色金属矿采选业	Mining and Processing of Non-ferrous Metals Ores	300473	300473	69	58	458309
#常用有色金属矿采选	Mining and Processing of Common Non-ferrous Metal	172580	172580	40	33	255996
非金属矿采选业	Mining and Processing of Non-metal Ores	154982	154982	49	41	141613
#土砂石开采	Mining of Earth and Gravel	102875	102875	27	22	70195
制造业	**Manufacturing**	**20629865**	**19496841**	**2423**	**1648**	**12779263**
#农副食品加工业	Processing of Food from Agricultural Products	920061	873273	337	258	1047198
食品制造业	Manufacture of Foods	494928	365749	140	97	408528
酒、饮料和精制茶制造业	Manufacture of Tobacco,Wine and Tea	405937	392682	109	75	374678
烟草制品业	Manufacture of Tobacco	33188	33188	2		
纺织业	Manufacture of Textile	2681102	2518186	166	86	1282786
纺织服装、服饰业	Manufacture of Textile Wearing Apparel, Footware and Caps	366299	366299	88	62	270471
皮革、毛皮、羽毛及其制品和制鞋业	Manufacture of Leather,Fur,Feather and Related Products	17800	17800	7	5	9501
木材加工和木、竹、藤、棕、草制品业	Processing of Timber, Wood, Bamboo, Cane, Grass Products	128836	128836	29	24	129142
造纸和纸制品业	Manufacture of Paper and Paper Products	82740	82740	31	23	64175
印刷和记录媒介复制业	Printing,Reproduction,of Recording Media	33068	30568	16	11	30703
石油加工、炼焦和核燃料加工业	Processing of Petroleum,Coking and Nuclera Fuel	2740979	2585800	113	68	1714314
#精炼石油产品制造	Manufacture of Oil Products	1755659	1630210	74	49	1291751
炼 焦	Coking	985320	955590	39	19	422563
化学原料和化学制品制造业	Manufacture of Raw Chemical Material and Chemical Products	5402302	4994703	257	168	3438236

4-6 续表 1 Continued

行　业	Sector	投资额 (万元) Total Investment (10 000 yuan)	#地 方 Local	施工项目个数 (个) Number of Projects under Construction (unit)	竣工项目个数 (个) Number of Projects Completed (unit)	本年新增固定资产 (万元) Newly Increased Fixed Assets (10 000 yuan)
医药制造业	Manufacture of Medicine	242077	206960	36	25	143799
化学纤维制造业	Manufacture of Chemical Fibers	131998	128498	15	14	155064
橡胶和塑料制品业	Manufacture of Rubber and Plastic Products	509599	504409	152	112	444852
非金属矿物制品业	Manufacture of Non-metallic Mineral Products	1562732	1479944	376	283	1432113
#水泥、石灰和石膏制造	Cement Manufacturing	263139	241590	44	36	515554
玻璃制造	Manufacture of Glasses	26770	26770	4	3	21320
黑色金属冶炼和压延加工业	Smelting and Pressing of Ferrous Metals	438808	429792	51	37	268921
#炼　铁	Iron Making	67880	58864	8	5	18653
炼　钢	Steel Making	172318	172318	11	6	49293
有色金属冶炼和压延加工业	Smelting and Pressing of Nonferrous Metals	1710438	1708738	39	20	248482
金属制品业	Manufacture of Metal Products	476722	467389	108	69	356571
通用设备制造业	Manufacture of General Purpose Machinery	414280	413480	69	50	335178
专用设备制造业	Manufacture of Special Purpose Machinery	366802	340206	88	49	191127
汽车制造业	Manufacture of Automobiles	115230	100685	17	9	71350
计算机、通信和其他电子设备制造业	Manufacture of Communication Equipment, Comuputer and othe Elctronic Equipment	56731	56618	15	7	66094
电力、热力、燃气及水生产和供应业	**Production and Supply of Electricity,Heaf,Gas and Water**	**21088179**	**17403448**	**1670**	**1102**	**13263554**
电力、热力生产和供应业	Production and Supply of Electricity Power and Heat Power	18731748	15513527	1156	765	11779675
电力生产	Production of Electric Power	15793899	13395925	535	324	10006751
电力供应	Supply of Electric Power	2232604	1607232	383	267	1053010
热力生产和供应	Production and Supply of Heat Power	705245	510370	238	174	719914
燃气生产和供应业	Production and Supply of Gas	1547006	1258321	213	126	593034
水的生产和供应业	Production and Supply of Water	809425	631600	301	211	890845
#自来水生产和供应	Production and Supply of Running Water	484241	340105	207	150	580211
污水处理及其再生利用	Treatment and Recycle of Waste Water	283364	254375	78	50	243054
建筑业	**Construction**	**1186461**	**1062043**	**421**	**317**	**915947**
#房屋建筑业	Construction of Buildings	317481	293089	127	91	303693
土木工程建筑业	Buildings and Civil Engineering Construction	717881	624616	245	191	514914
建筑安装业	Building Installation	36224	31135	10	7	44669
批发和零售业	**Wholesale&Retail Trades**	**1820998**	**1612405**	**454**	**320**	**1498573**
批发业	Wholesale Trades	934318	852252	186	123	670401

4-6 续表 2 Continued

行　业	Sector	投资额 (万元) Total Investment (10 000 yuan)	#地 方 Local	施工项目个数 (个) Number of Projects under Construction (unit)	竣工项目个数 (个) Number of Projects Completed (unit)	本年新增固定资产 (万元) Newly Increased Fixed Assets (10 000 yuan)
零售业	Retail Trades	886680	760153	268	197	828172
交通运输、仓储和邮政业	**Transport, Storage and Post**	**10613588**	**8242451**	**1036**	**711**	**6593303**
#铁路运输业	Railway Transport	1514534	426427	34	11	336263
道路运输业	Road Transport	7424890	6422949	732	540	5246121
航空运输业	Air Transport	246243	212534	24	8	191260
管道运输业	Via Pipelines Transport	157930	67244	14	6	78694
仓储业	Storage	1194919	1038225	213	135	685631
邮政业	Post	5983	5983	8	3	4600
住宿和餐饮业	**Hotels and Catering Services**	**837862**	**817392**	**211**	**130**	**644419**
住宿业	Hotels	556206	540126	137	98	466362
#旅游饭店	Tourist Restaurant	435001	421031	92	65	360553
餐饮业	Catering Services	281656	277266	74	32	178057
信息传输、软件和信息技术服务业	**Information Transmission, and Information Technology Software**	**1325991**	**1018012**	**106**	**81**	**953781**
#电信、广播电视和卫星传输服务	Telecommunication and Other Information Transmission Services	1170783	870748	88	71	797480
电 信	Telecommunication	1143370	843997	68	57	773258
金融业	**Financial Intermediation**	**119420**	**107198**	**57**	**46**	**108105**
#货币金融服务	Monetary and Financial Service	103523	92853	50	39	98207
资本市场服务	Capital Market Service	1602	50	2	2	1602
保险业	**Insurance**	**1498**	**1498**	**1**	**1**	**1498**
房地产业	**Real Estate**	**9334328**	**7981728**	**1849**	**1347**	**9090111**
#房地产开发经营	Real Estate Development and Operation	307918	295325	46	28	310451
物业管理	Management of Real Estate	10660	8400	3	2	10260
其他房地产业	Other Real Estate	8953619	7615872	1781	1305	8735499
租赁和商务服务业	**Leasing and Business Services**	**1047293**	**1003588**	**146**	**75**	**409110**
租赁业	Leasing	142309	130309	17	7	20710
商务服务业	Business Services	904984	873279	129	68	388400
科学研究和技术服务业	**Scientific Research, and Technical Service**	**300913**	**273594**	**119**	**85**	**203538**
研究和试验发展	Research and Experiment Development	30716	29348	9	6	32195
专业技术服务业	Professional Technical Service	116835	107425	66	46	77662
科技推广和应用服务业	Services of Science and Technology Popularigation and Appliction	153362	136821	44	33	93681

4-6 续表 3 Continued

行 业	Sector	投资额 (万元) Total Investment (10 000 yuan)	#地 方 Local	施工项目个数 (个) Number of Projects under Construction (unit)	竣工项目个数 (个) Number of Projects Completed (unit)	本年新增固定资产 (万元) Newly Increased Fixed Assets (10 000 yuan)
水利、环境和公共设施管理业	**Management of Water Conservancy, Environment and Public Facilities**	**10939460**	**8704756**	**2754**	**2029**	**9214981**
水利管理业	Management of Water Conservancy	1564180	1220016	524	404	1233364
生态保护和环境治理业	Environmental Management	317756	304873	98	84	275053
公共设施管理业	Management of Public Facilities	9057524	7179867	2132	1541	7706564
市政设施管理	Management of Public Facilities	6799834	5153714	1647	1176	5567300
环境卫生管理	Ecological Protection and Enviroment Treatment	117043	93741	59	46	108514
城乡市容管理	Management of Apperance City	276250	262008	120	106	257500
绿化管理	Management of Urban Greening	313365	188504	110	73	240333
公园和游览景区管理	Scenic-Spot Management	1551032	1481900	196	140	1532917
居民服务、修理和其他服务业	**Resident Service and ,Repair Other Services**	**224709**	**204835**	**98**	**75**	**169390**
教 育	**Education**	**1612067**	**1344470**	**851**	**589**	**1227356**
#初等教育	Elementary Education	299107	272169	234	164	241238
中等教育	Secondary Education	772430	648172	389	282	605577
高等教育	Higher Education	281301	194233	62	24	134516
卫生和社会工作	**Health, Social Service**	**874934**	**765229**	**349**	**213**	**736499**
卫 生	Health	668719	586945	252	141	546255
#医 院	Hospital	493538	428528	124	69	419720
社会工作	Social Service	206215	178284	97	72	190244
文化、体育和娱乐业	**Culture, Sports and Entertainment**	**803012**	**694293**	**328**	**219**	**701381**
新闻和出版业	Journalism and Publishing Activities	453		1	1	5053
广播、电视、电影和影视录音制作业	Broadcasting,Movies,Televisions and Audiovisual Activites	30767	29132	19	13	29722
文化艺术业	Cultural and Art Activities	414861	333540	201	128	362731
体 育	Sports Activities	229089	205129	75	55	207339
娱乐业	Entertainment	127842	126492	32	22	96536
公共管理、社会保障和社会组织	**Public Management ,Social Security and Social Organization**	**1994865**	**1815910**	**952**	**698**	**1689140**
中国共产党机关	Organ of Communist Party of China	57674	57674	30	24	55688
国家机构	Government Agencies	1744535	1574754	797	571	1460912
人民政协、民主党派	People's Political Consultative Conference and Democratic Parties					
社会保障	Social Security	34310	31983	19	17	29586
群众团体、社会团体和其他成员组织	Non-Governmental Organigations,Social Organizations and Membership Organizations	26998	26998	16	11	19168
基层群众自治组织	Grass Roots Self-governing Organizations	131348	124501	90	75	123786

4-7 分行业固定资产投资资金来源情况

单位：万元 (2015 年)

行　业	Sector	本年资金来源小计 Sub-total Funds This Year
总　计	**Total**	**95218004**
农、林、牧、渔业	**Farming, Forestry, Animal Husbandry and Fishery**	**3652740**
农　业	Farming	707687
林　业	Forestry	290817
畜牧业	Animal Husbandry	915631
渔　业	Fishery	16891
农、林、牧、渔服务业	Services in Support of Farming, Forestry, Animal Husbandry and Fishery	1721714
采矿业	**Mining**	**8694659**
#煤炭开采和洗选业	Mining and Washing of Coal	2263066
石油和天然气开采业	Extraction of Petroleum and Natural Gas	5428625
黑色金属矿采选业	Mining and Processing of Ferrous Metals Ores	331702
#铁矿采选	Mining and Processing of Iron Ore	290175
有色金属矿采选业	Mining and Processing of Non-ferrous Metals Ores	287782
#常用有色金属矿采选	Mining and Processing of Common Non-ferrous Metal	159410
非金属矿采选业	Mining and Processing of Non-metal Ores	179412
#土砂石开采	Mining of Earth and Gravel	113919
制造业	**Manufacturing**	**20920673**
#农副食品加工业	Processing of Food from Agricultural Products	908617
食品制造业	Manufacture of Foods	544846
酒、饮料和精制茶制造业	Manufacture of Tobacco,Wine and Tea	399117
烟草制品业	Manufacture of Tobacco	33190
纺织业	Manufacture of Textile	2440255
纺织服装、服饰业	Manufacture of Textile Wearing Apparel,Footware and Caps	447401
皮革、毛皮、羽毛及其制品和制鞋业	Manufacture of Leather,Fur,Feather and Related Products	15800
木材加工和木、竹、藤、棕、草制品业	Processing of Timber, Wood, Bamboo, Cane, Grass Products	132964
造纸和纸制品业	Manufacture of Paper and Paper Products	92598
印刷和记录媒介复制业	Printing,Reproduction,of Recording Media	29194
石油加工、炼焦和核燃料加工业	Processing of Petroleum,Coking and Nuclera Fuel	2938912
#精炼石油产品制造	Manufacture of Oil Products	1863727
炼　焦	Coking	1075185

Sources of Funds of Investment in Fixed Assets in Area by Sector

(10 000 yuan)

国家预算内资金 State Budget	国内贷款 Domestic Loans	债　券 Bonds	利用外资 Foreign Investment	自筹资金 Self-raising Funds	其他资金来　源 Others
15615189	**14494911**	**86635**	**41409**	**59913457**	**5066403**
1130464	**33021**		**2663**	**2275989**	**210603**
215367	14500			439416	38404
76350				205564	8903
100181	3656			728197	83597
				16891	
738566	14865		2663	885921	79699
262989	**1352374**			**6833874**	**245422**
17436	116289			2034180	95161
170673	1196900			3996573	64479
53500	6700			207575	63927
53500	6700			196275	33700
19000	26485			234957	7340
19000	10000			126770	3640
1200	6000			170312	1900
	3000			109019	1900
905223	**1665903**		**3000**	**17591918**	**754629**
25891	9490			824342	48894
17068	5150			509634	12994
5612	11400			370876	11229
				33190	
121723	453736			1844096	20700
7750				421541	18110
				15800	
				130464	2500
				84598	8000
249				20245	8700
13413	89150			2570575	265774
13413	4000			1663040	183274
	85150			907535	82500

4-7 续表 1

单位：万元

行　业	Sector	本年资金来源小计 Sub-total Funds This Year
化学原料和化学制品制造业	Manufacture of Raw Chemical Material and Chemical Products	4946220
医药制造业	Manufacture of Medicine	250798
化学纤维制造业	Manufacture of Chemical Fibers	90562
橡胶和塑料制品业	Manufacture of Rubber and Plastic Products	524840
非金属矿物制品业	Manufacture of Non-metallic Mineral Products	1615661
#水泥、石灰和石膏制造	Cement Manufacturing	347372
玻璃制造	Manufacture of Glasses	27675
黑色金属冶炼和压延加工业	Smelting and Pressing of Ferrous Metals	531937
#炼 铁	Iron Making	233181
炼 钢	Steel Making	157598
有色金属冶炼和压延加工业	Smelting and Pressing of Nonferrous Metals	1836633
金属制品业	Manufacture of Metal Products	395480
通用设备制造业	Manufacture of General Purpose Machinery	413873
专用设备制造业	Manufacture of Special Purpose Machinery	367763
汽车制造业	Manufacture of Automobiles	323937
电气机械和器材制造业	Manufacture of Electric Equipment and Machinery	463536
计算机、通信和其他电子设备制造业	Manufacture of Communication Equipment,Comuputer and othe Elctronic	57406
电力、热力、燃气及水生产和供应业	**Production and Supply of Electricity,Heat,Gas and Water**	**20143328**
电力、热力生产和供应业	Production and Supply of Electricity Power and Heat Power	17444331
电力生产	Production of Electric Power	14541517
电力供应	Supply of Electric Power	2230927
热力生产和供应	Production and Supply of Heat Power	671887
燃气生产和供应业	Production and Supply of Gas	1949515
水的生产和供应业	Production and Supply of Water	749482
#自来水生产和供应	Production and Supply of Running Water	445265
污水处理及其再生利用	Treatment and Recycle of Waste Water	262378
建筑业	**Construction**	**1171050**
#房屋建筑业	Consturction of Buildings	299926
土木工程建筑业	Buildings and Civil Engineering Construction	717882
建筑安装业	Building Installation	37541
批发和零售业	**Wholesale&Retail Trades**	**1801288**
批发业	Wholesale Trades	911600

Continued

(10 000 yuan)

国家预算内资金 State Budget	国内贷款 Domestic Loans	债券 Bonds	利用外资 Foreign Investment	自筹资金 Self-raising Funds	其他资金来源 Others
688520	381001		3000	3819789	53910
1596				244202	5000
	21408			69154	
2184	13660			495509	13487
2505	121405			1298834	192917
	4500			174872	168000
				27675	
	82916			425085	23936
				233181	
	80000			75898	1700
	139063			1696870	700
550	1290			372900	20740
	158487			244106	11280
1200	8907			357156	500
				323937	
2037	110350			329999	21150
				57406	
2641831	**6611857**	**11600**		**10450522**	**427518**
2322884	6591354			8163916	366177
1902793	5686935			6751856	199933
281290	872591			1032721	44325
138801	31828			379339	121919
31455	13006			1873852	31202
287492	7497	11600		412754	30139
193318	1000	11600		225760	13587
71333	6497			174151	10397
481368	**14279**	**4001**		**586277**	**85125**
88002	2800	4001		181393	23730
317380	11479			344928	44095
26612				10929	
43470	**29144**			**1582134**	**146540**
32929	23144			827023	28504

4-7 续表 2

单位：万元

行　业	Sector	本年资金来源小计 Sub-total Funds This Year
零售业	Retail Trades	889688
交通运输、仓储和邮政业	**Transport Storage and Post**	**10591772**
#铁路运输业	Railway Transport	1609957
道路运输业	Road Transport	7453865
航空运输业	Air Transport	274079
管道运输业	Pipelines Transport	157525
仓储业	Storage	1048904
邮政业	Post	6084
住宿和餐饮业	**Hotels and Catering Services**	**903989**
住宿业	Hotels	515921
#旅游饭店	Tourist Restaurant	403151
餐饮业	Catering Services	388068
信息传输、软件和信息技术服务业	**Information Transmission, Software and Information Technology**	**1370414**
#电信、广播电视和卫星传输服务	Telecommunication and Other Information Transmission Services	1211153
#电　信	Telecommunication	1185178
金融业	**Financial Intermediation**	**119776**
#货币金融服务	Monetary and Financial Service	103776
资本市场服务	Capital Market Service	1602
保险业	**Insurance**	**1498**
房地产业	**Real Estate**	**9064525**
#房地产开发经营	Real Estate Development and Operation	303237
物业管理	Management of Real Estate	7660
其他房地产业	Other Real Estate	8694019
租赁和商务服务业	**Leasing and Business Services**	**1022824**
租赁业	Leasing	79560
商务服务业	Business Service	943264
科学研究和技术服务业	**Scientific Research and Technical Service**	**370447**
研究和试验发展	Research and Experiment Development	34514
专业技术服务业	Professional Technical Service	184871
科技推广和应用服务业	Services of Science and Technology Popularigaion and Application	151062

Continued

(10 000 yuan)

国家预算内资金 State Budget	国内贷款 Domestic Loans	债　券 Bonds	利用外资 Foreign Investment	自筹资金 Self-raising Funds	其他资金来　源 Others
10541	6000			755111	118036
1431948	**2803899**	**44659**		**5991340**	**319926**
159229	489569	40000		870802	50357
1138099	2280077	4659		3851303	179727
104504				143335	26240
5700	15073			136702	50
22792	19180			943380	63552
500				5584	
44874	**17616**			**814139**	**27360**
15045	16855			462491	21530
9461	7200			380435	6055
29829	761			351648	5830
9380	**113488**			**1195373**	**52173**
2912	96500			1060773	50968
1300	96500			1040632	46746
4209				**108769**	**6798**
3709				94767	5300
				1602	
					1498
3164646	**147592**	**12776**		**4367431**	**1372080**
2620	11301			284856	4460
1750	3200			2710	
3148653	133091	12776		4033170	1366329
48293	**128749**			**815655**	**30127**
2950				76610	
45343	128749			739045	30127
43943	**10010**		**2892**	**299766**	**13836**
300				34214	
20042	9010			155189	630
23601	1000		2892	110363	13206

4-7 续表 3

单位：万元

行　业	Sector	本年资金来源小计 Sub-total Funds This Year
水利、环境和公共设施管理业	**Management of Water Conservancy, Environment and Public Facilities**	**10207426**
水利管理业	Management of Water Conservancy	1501432
生态保护和环境治理业	Ecological Protection and Environmental Treatment	300918
公共设施管理业	Management of Public Facilities	8405076
市政设施管理	Management of Public Facilities	6324538
环境卫生管理	Management of Enviroment	90624
城乡市容管理	Management of Apperance City	221964
绿化管理	Management of Urban Greening	216525
公园和游览景区管理	Scenic-Spot Management	1551425
居民服务、修理和其他服务业	**Services to Households,Repair and other Services**	**228564**
教　育	**Education**	**1544135**
#初等教育	Elementary Education	293135
中等教育	Secondary Education	696073
高等教育	Higher Education	287859
卫生和社会工作	**Health, Social Service**	**842968**
卫　生	Health Care	632321
#医　院	Hospital	465709
社会工作	Social Service	210647
文化、体育和娱乐业	**Culture, Sports and Entertainment**	**688317**
新闻和出版业	Journalism and Publishing Activities	1020
广播、电视、电影和影视录音制作业	Broadcasting,Movies,Televisions and Audiovisual Activites	33052
文化艺术业	Cultural and Art Activities	313529
体　育	Sports Activities	208095
娱乐业	Entertainment	132621
公共管理、社会保障和社会组织	**Public Management ,Social Security and Social Organization**	**1879109**
中国共产党机关	Organ of Communist Party of China	56791
国家机构	Government Agencies	1629278
人民政协、民主党派	People's Political Consultative Conference and Democratic Parties	
社会保障	Social Security	31892
群众团体、社会团体和其他成员组织	Non-Governmental Organigations,Social Organizations and Membership Organizations	28513
基层群众自治组织	Grass Roots Self-governing Organizations	132635

Continued

(10 000 yuan)

国家预算内资金 State Budget	国内贷款 Domestic Loans	债券 Bonds	利用外资 Foreign Investment	自筹资金 Self-raising Funds	其他资金来源 Others
2835744	**1418674**	**13599**	**32854**	**4906954**	**999601**
896086	69600			414273	121473
107929	5289		1500	183550	2650
1831729	1343785	13599	31354	4309131	875478
1454244	1307776	13599	31354	2761909	755656
37277	310			42704	10333
91597				85579	44788
74157	550			135307	6511
174454	35149			1283632	58190
58942	**2485**			**131336**	**35801**
878945	**61445**			**505906**	**97839**
246506				38150	8479
465047	5593			156938	68495
51667	45852			190340	
286610	**16031**			**469061**	**71266**
207673	16031			345509	63108
141587	16031			260552	47539
78937				123552	8158
238243	**30881**			**379512**	**39681**
1020					
7692	1000			16955	7405
147379	21232			133622	11296
54600	8649			127661	17185
27552				101274	3795
1104067	**37463**			**607501**	**130078**
38469				6240	12082
943632	37463			558228	89955
23955				7937	
12501				12636	3376
85510				22460	24665

4-8 各地、州、市、县(市)固定资产投资和新增固定资产
Total Investment and Newly Increased Fixed Assets in Area by Prefecture, Autonomous Prefecture, City and County

单位：万元　　　　(2015 年)　　　　(10 000 yuan)

地　区 Region	投资总额 Total Investment	第一产业 Primary Industry	第二产业 Secondary Industry	第三产业 Tertiary Industry	新增固定资产 Newly Increased Fixed Assets	房屋建筑面积(万平方米) Floor Space of Buildings (10 000 sq.m) 施工面积 Floor Space Under Construction	竣工面积 Floor Space Completed
总　计 Total	**97304455**	**3663277**	**51791738**	**41849440**	**67813754**	**11223.73**	**4327.23**
按隶属关系分 Grouped By Administrative Relationship							
中　央 Central Government	18890823	1213142	10414102	7263579	13324805	3033.03	1966.01
地　方 Local	78413632	2450135	41377636	34585861	54488949	8190.70	2361.22
按区域分 Grouped by Region							
乌鲁木齐市 Urumqi City	**12260603**	**54027**	**4227439**	**7979137**	**6229896**	**1490.82**	**394.26**
#乌鲁木齐县 Urumqi County	220798		116621	104177	129510	1.36	1.36
克拉玛依市 Karamay City	**3965392**	**47232**	**3325810**	**592350**	**2233399**	**269.20**	**57.51**
吐鲁番市 Turpan City	**4402973**	**46047**	**2668008**	**1688918**	**3407093**	**153.14**	**15.60**
高昌区 Gaochang District	2043884	10810	629261	1403813	1966106	131.19	4.76
鄯善县 Shanshan [Piqan] County	1163387	18083	1036012	109292	856200	10.33	5.50
托克逊县 Toksun County	1195702	17154	1002735	175813	584787	11.62	5.34
哈密地区 Hami [Kumul] Administrative Offices	**8830537**	**92547**	**8013621**	**724369**	**5614662**	**329.83**	**126.31**
哈密市 Hami [Kumul] City	6260865	55024	5661401	544440	4104129	290.12	123.42
巴里坤哈萨克自治县 Barkol Kazak Autonomous County	1782902	16922	1685736	80244	1056179	29.11	1.50
伊吾县 Yiwu [Araturuk] County	786770	20601	666484	99685	454354	10.60	1.38
昌吉回族自治州 Changji Hui Autonomous Prefecture	**15302294**	**394421**	**10930239**	**3977634**	**7788305**	**434.05**	**165.36**
昌吉市 Changji City	2785588	87673	924112	1773803	983447	105.56	4.03
阜康市 Fukang City	2273813	46112	1656881	570820	1533031	29.70	20.92
呼图壁县 Hutubi County	1470712	18267	949795	502650	1714139	35.54	27.17
玛纳斯县 Manas County	1296022	177672	697648	420702	492882	148.06	97.00
奇台县 Qitai County	3163078	45848	2618571	498659	1449628	61.38	15.51
吉木萨尔县 Jimsar County	3472637	17125	3309828	145684	1312783	8.97	0.72
木垒哈萨克自治县 Mori Kazak Autonomous County	840444	1724	773404	65316	302395	44.85	
伊犁哈萨克自治州 Ili Kazak Autonomous Prefecture	**12549623**	**1237734**	**5649613**	**5662276**	**10602829**	**2208.28**	**1000.33**
伊犁州直属县(市) Counties (Cities) Direct Under Ili Prefecture	**5812843**	**276365**	**3002206**	**2534272**	**4252448**	**1029.34**	**373.81**
伊宁市 Yining [Gulja] City	986405	16733	436980	532692	495628	204.87	61.75

4-8 续表 1 Continued

单位：万元 (10 000 yuan)

地 区 Region	投资总额 Total Investment	第一产业 Primary Industry	第二产业 Secondary Industry	第三产业 Tertiary Industry	新增固定资产 Newly Increased Fixed Assets	房屋建筑面积(万平方米) Floor Space of Buildings (10 000 sq.m) 施工面积 Floor Space Under Construction	竣工面积 Floor Space Completed
奎屯市 Kuytun City	1198133	15333	796130	386670	664014	300.30	115.50
伊宁县 Yining [Gulja] County	594665	26979	421750	145936	835490	107.83	69.04
察布查尔锡伯自治县 Qapqal Xibe Autonomous County	555970	60123	186871	308976	297269	44.20	18.86
霍城县 Huocheng [Korgas] County	1208117	50289	563150	594678	901622	162.54	41.16
巩留县 Gongliu [Tokkuztara] County	280790	11220	155271	114299	285645	54.77	35.04
新源县 Xinyuan [Kunes] County	298516	8149	185445	104922	254252	30.73	15.86
昭苏县 Zhaosu [Mongolkure] County	264175	57213	61575	145387	250483	85.22	12.22
特克斯县 Tekes County	100698	8800	63502	28396	36322	1.01	0.79
尼勒克县 Nilka County	325374	21526	131532	172316	231723	37.86	3.59
塔城地区 Tacheng [Tarbagatai] Administrative Offices	**4237180**	**713931**	**1747097**	**1776152**	**4018103**	**782.33**	**375.63**
塔城市 Tacheng [Qoqek] City	553152	196610	85060	271482	483337	122.10	46.37
乌苏市 Usu City	977815	66520	606347	304948	895730	166.28	65.06
额敏县 Emin Ciunty	598779	101086	177444	320249	613468	83.05	16.84
沙湾县 Shawan County	1175442	304313	289991	581138	1260890	343.04	220.30
托里县 Toli County	456210	21426	239701	195083	329993	25.06	11.23
裕民县 Yumin [Qagantokay] County	89218	8904	28034	52280	73877	20.47	1.04
和布克赛尔蒙古自治县 Hoboksar Mongol Autonomous County	386564	15072	320520	50972	360808	22.33	14.78
阿勒泰地区 Altay Administrative Offices	**2499600**	**247438**	**900310**	**1351852**	**2332278**	**396.61**	**250.89**
阿勒泰市 Altay City	791658	32179	209966	549513	703113	201.53	119.70
布尔津县 Burqin County	461842	61779	116150	283913	462146	37.43	35.51
富蕴县 Fuyun [Koktokay] County	390241	6330	194446	189465	359696	47.30	24.54
福海县 Fuhai [Burultokay] County	267865	87472	94433	85960	213615	41.81	18.56
哈巴河县 Habahe [Kaba] County	232783	36848	67093	128842	346283	28.09	27.68
青河县 Qinghe [Qinggil] County	150974	13964	75256	61754	151304	22.60	13.16
吉木乃县 Jeminay County	204237	8866	142966	52405	96121	17.85	11.73
博尔塔拉蒙古自治州 Bortala Mongol Autonomous Prefecture	**2649368**	**181948**	**1178415**	**1289005**	**3037009**	**841.99**	**243.90**
博乐市 Bole [Bortala] City	1808258	117617	675325	1015316	2245500	637.01	215.37

4-8 续表 2 Continued

单位：万元 (10 000 yuan)

地区 Region	投资总额 Total Investment	第一产业 Primary Industry	第二产业 Secondary Industry	第三产业 Tertiary Industry	新增固定资产 Newly Increased Fixed Assets	房屋建筑面积(万平方米) Floor Space of Buildings (10 000 sq.m) 施工面积 Floor Space Under Construction	竣工面积 Floor Space Completed
精河县 Jinghe [Jing] County	632757	48823	432066	151868	561512	199.95	23.50
温泉县 Wenquan [Araxang] County	208353	15508	71024	121821	229997	5.04	5.04
巴音郭楞蒙古自治州 Bayangol Mongol Autonomous Prefecture	**6671759**	**280796**	**4552402**	**1838561**	**3401705**	**1415.73**	**808.63**
库尔勒市 Korla City	4378999	31532	3389753	957714	1692541	345.56	125.22
轮台县 Luntai [Bugur] County	159794		122208	37586	57837	67.78	34.86
尉犁县 Yuli [Lopnur] County	348859	48501	163251	137107	301604	80.70	61.73
若羌县 Ruoqiang [Qarkilik] County	385008	27254	231284	126470	255942	26.54	19.30
且末县 Qiemo [Qarqan] County	321898	67300	105056	149542	241024	133.29	29.63
焉耆回族自治县 Yanqi Hui Autonomous County	316147	41144	137894	137109	286498	73.33	43.63
和静县 Hejing County	515184	25817	349272	140095	338231	561.69	464.61
和硕县 Hoxud County	160348	25821	28740	105787	168853	84.85	15.99
博湖县 Bohu [Bagrax] County	85522	13427	24944	47151	59175	42.00	13.66
阿克苏地区 Aksu Administrative Offices	**5671254**	**233002**	**3213420**	**2224832**	**4327891**	**456.68**	**83.44**
阿克苏市 Aksu City	1122874	60452	457083	605339	893455	145.98	27.68
温宿县 Wensu [Onsu] County	783768	18594	423695	341479	614418	65.43	40.77
库车县 Kuqa County	1533331	5250	897073	631008	1166912	7.34	
沙雅县 Xayar County	512030	50000	368633	93397	162192	2.38	
新和县 Xinhe [Toksu] County	219367	15446	110145	93776	201579	3.88	
拜城县 Baicheng [Bay] County	735757		508933	226824	596373	76.53	
乌什县 Wushi [Uxturpan] County	313452	62593	96072	154787	235671	84.59	5.38
阿瓦提县 Awat County	308924	17116	233311	58497	330687	60.74	9.62
柯坪县 Kalpin County	141751	3551	118475	19725	126604	9.81	
克孜勒苏柯尔克孜自治州 Kizilsu Kirgiz Autonomous Prefecture	**1263787**	**73331**	**745706**	**444750**	**1214113**	**348.75**	**223.29**
阿图什市 Artux City	400561	18333	135840	246388	519982	195.51	124.90
阿克陶县 Akto County	466557	36113	350071	80373	266591	62.70	55.28
阿合奇县 Akqi County	69317	3164	45808	20345	84239	34.25	
乌恰县 Wuqia [Ulugqat] County	327352	15721	213987	97644	343301	56.29	43.10

4-8 续表 3 Continued

单位：万元 (10 000 yuan)

地区 Region	投资总额 Total Investment	第一产业 Primary Industry	第二产业 Secondary Industry	第三产业 Tertiary Industry	新增固定资产 Newly Increased Fixed Assets	房屋建筑面积(万平方米) Floor Space of Buildings (10 000 sq.m) 施工面积 Floor Space Under Construction	竣工面积 Floor Space Completed
喀什地区 Kashgar [Kaxgar] Administrative Offices	**8908018**	**451022**	**2628099**	**5828897**	**7396997**	**967.66**	**193.38**
喀什市 Kashgar [Kaxgar] City	2088595	26302	298672	1763621	773746	39.84	19.72
疏附县 Shufu County	544545		15017	529528	782642	91.73	66.40
疏勒县 Shule County	895040	34509	428596	431935	884523	168.92	60.44
英吉沙县 Yengisar County	641575	83977	248141	309457	634783	67.03	2.30
泽普县 Zepu [Poskam] County	429013	6201	90899	331913	380488	165.65	
莎车县 Shache [Yarkant] County	610102	15350	193851	400901	435311	210.72	10.76
叶城县 Yecheng [Kagilik] County	778406	34199	209902	534305	942742	77.18	5.88
麦盖提县 Makit County	552852	65936	203448	283468	458030	28.20	3.98
岳普湖县 Yopurga County	650717	91370	345236	214111	649450	33.35	7.91
伽师县 Jiashi [Payzawat] County	715236	69944	266626	378666	482297	14.26	2.47
巴楚县 Bachu [Maralbexi] County	692520	23234	162333	506953	675552	62.72	13.52
塔什库尔干塔吉克自治县 Taxkorgan Tajik Autonomous County	309417		165378	144039	297433	8.05	
和田地区 Hotan Administrative Offices	**3283853**	**359078**	**675856**	**2248919**	**3209617**	**1126.87**	**510.04**
和田市 Hotan City	811471	26628	57459	727384	1003170	34.88	
和田县 Hotan County	730439	110072	92119	528248	735639	175.45	127.56
墨玉县 Moyu [Karakax] County	549778	64616	191771	293391	364054	329.05	239.53
皮山县 Pishan [Guma] County	360429	25985	150182	184262	316196	282.35	88.82
洛浦县 Lop County	276202	66670	40676	168856	276577	110.14	45.93
策勒县 Qira County	214872	36890	51745	126237	184705	62.49	4.27
于田县 Yutian [Keriya] County	245993	27167	60181	158645	248993	111.51	3.94
民丰县 Minfeng [Niya] County	94669	1050	31723	61896	80283	21.01	
自治区直辖县级市 County level City directly under the Autonomous Region	**4608742**	**212092**	**2713810**	**1682840**	**4316052**	**1173.70**	**503.21**
石河子市 Shihezi City	2108337	52448	1560937	494952	2467117	428.28	119.35
阿拉尔市 Aral City	1211213	105898	528834	576481	1178366	345.45	236.39
图木舒克市 Tumxuk City	634630	31190	170769	432671	389163	248.71	122.67
五家渠市 Wujiaqu City	654562	22556	453270	178736	281406	151.26	24.80
跨地区投资 Trans-regional Investment	**6936252**		**1269300**	**5666952**	**5034186**	**7.02**	**1.97**

4-9 各地、州、市分行业固定资产投资

单位：万元 (2015 年)

行业 Sector	合计 Total	乌鲁木齐市 Urumqi City	克拉玛依市 Karamay City	吐鲁番市 Turpan City	哈密地区 Hami [Kumul] Administrative Offices	昌吉回族自治州 Changji Hui Autonomous Prefecture	伊犁哈萨克自治州 Ili Kazak Autonomous Prefecture	伊犁州直属县(市) Counties (Cities) Direct Under Ili Prefecture
总计 Total	**97304455**	**12260603**	**3965392**	**4402973**	**8830537**	**15302294**	**12549623**	**5812843**
农、林、牧、渔业 Farming, Forestry, Animal Husbandry and Fishery	3663277	54027	47232	46047	92547	394421	1237734	276365
采矿业 Mining	8887233	40980	1815340	757390	275243	1468440	586158	304158
制造业 Manufacturing	20629865	2270481	1233073	894144	409103	6318208	2068850	1295295
电力、热力、燃气及水生产和供应业 Production and Supply of Electricity, Heat,Gas and Water	21088179	1768706	211602	1014960	7329275	3098498	2749476	1204099
建筑业 Construction	1186461	147272	65795	1514		45093	245129	198654
交通运输、仓储及邮政业 Transport, Storage, Postal and Telecommunications Services	10613588	1675845	114581	144558	134587	905374	1043416	493562
信息传输、软件和信息技术服务业 Information Transmission, Software and Information Technology	1325991	900406	65597	2099	10062	30000	142267	27119
批发和零售业 Wholesale&Retail Trades	1820998	310486	45700	22460	103180	252498	282479	119151
住宿和餐饮业 Hotels and Catering Services	837862	98952	14706	5800	10849	378736	74367	19216
金融业 Financial Intermediation	119420	43365		6297	1852	19270	14059	4035
房地产业 Real Estate	9334328	1060285	48528	91347	170281	550948	1059981	405147
租赁和商务服务业 Leasing and Business Services	1047293	204322	29511	1300	21857	334641	224856	214386
科学研究和技术服务业 Scientific Research and Technical Service	300913	39606	10150	22112	9532	47626	40198	14421
水利、环境和公共设施管理业 Management of Water Conservancy, Environment and Public Facilities	10939460	3122877	90025	1194270	175764	910826	1817941	725387
居民服务、修理和其他服务业 Service to Households ,Repair and Others Services	224709	2100	285	19250	147	58263	50041	23242
教育 Education	1612067	211103	55716	43010	21961	140346	332467	194993
卫生和社会工作 Health, Social Service	874934	160194	45474	53779	37812	59813	154627	90297
文化、体育和娱乐业 Culture, Sports and Entertainment	803012	42482	55505	5415	8855	160508	167561	71466
公共管理、社会保障和社会组织 Public Management ,Social Security and Social Organization	1994865	107114	16572	77221	17630	128785	258016	131850

Investment in Fixed Assets in Area by Sectors in Prefecture, Autonomous Prefecture and City

(10 000 yuan)

塔城地区 Tacheng [Tarbagatai] Administra-tive Offices	阿勒泰地区 Altay Administra-tive Offices	博尔塔拉蒙古自治州 Bortala Mongol Autono-mous Prefecture	巴音郭楞蒙古自治州 Bayangol Mongol Autono-mous Prefecture	阿克苏地区 Aksu Administra-tive Offices	克孜勒苏柯尔克孜自治州 Kizilsu Kirgiz Autono-mous Prefecture	喀什地区 Kashgar [Kaxgar] Administra-tive Offices	和田地区 Hotan Administra-tive Offices	石河子市 Shihezi City	阿拉尔市 Aral City	图木舒克市 Tumxuk City	五家渠市 Wujiaqu City	跨地区投资 Trans-regional Investment
4237180	**2499600**	**2649368**	**6671759**	**5671254**	**1263787**	**8908018**	**3283853**	**2108337**	**1211213**	**634630**	**654562**	**6936252**
713931	247438	181948	280796	233002	73331	451022	359078	52448	105898	31190	22556	
182527	99473	61450	1888000	576459	67803	150810	21360					1177800
588777	184778	491622	1900888	1348071	85681	1559084	211969	825923	459774	53864	407630	91500
939323	606054	581978	749083	757163	516541	903465	440813	735014	69060	116905	45640	
36470	10005	43365	14431	531727	75681	14740	1714					
272993	276861	170334	288584	281473	50231	365223	107251	97132	174540	19490	16317	5024652
110003	5145	9708	2183	48121		27693	4132	4703	3700	5320		70000
90436	72892	43446	87722	123481	23560	394681	65905	33033	22097	6670	3600	
44473	10678	4902	25358	24758	2000	182573	9121		5500	240		
5202	4822	6902	6913	2000	6191	3465		8376	730			
470592	184242	374285	388220	972561	155243	2810564	1320548	137585	48911	135181	9860	
8770	1700	6290	60341	20994	447	106935	24466		3000		8333	
16135	9642	8200	41286	21352	1098	28930	1673	20797	1593		6760	
486980	605574	357485	720707	374798	67174	667438	181877	112168	248779	221017	104014	572300
23850	2949	18578	1420	19122	4361	42723	900	1500		1154	4865	
47584	89890	32036	109903	165016	40459	296782	107352	18982	21255	13732	1947	
40369	23961	45186	29988	41800	11376	135559	52774	24364	7235	7443	7510	
69344	26751	77692	30358	54067	9822	138135	5879	12738	13755	14710	5530	
89421	36745	133961	45578	75289	72788	628196	367041	23574	25386	7714	10000	

4-10 全社会房屋施工面积、竣工面积

Floor Space of Buildings under Construction and Completed in Whole Country

单位：万平方米 (10 000 sq.m)

年份 Year	地区 Region	施工面积 Floor Space of Buildings under Construction	#住宅 Residential Buildings	竣工面积 Floor Space of Buildings Completed	#住宅 Residential Buildings	房屋建筑面积竣工率(%) Rate of Floor Space of Building Completed (%)	#住宅 Residential Buildings
	1985	1670.30	945.76	1327.69	816.26	79.5	86.3
	1990	1740.94	1074.98	1337.06	912.57	76.8	84.9
	1995	2420.38	1368.84	1634.33	1064.14	67.5	77.7
	1996	2952.02	1901.01	2095.58	1441.22	71.0	75.8
	1997	2574.79	1732.19	1903.96	1393.11	73.9	80.4
	1998	2946.76	2057.08	2148.75	1604.68	72.9	78.0
	1999	3439.11	2470.41	2618.98	2020.89	76.2	81.8
	2000	4485.77	2509.17	2633.23	1881.88	58.7	75.0
	2001	4940.70	3282.51	3386.60	2411.78	68.5	73.5
	2002	3986.81	2358.04	2706.44	1790.82	67.9	75.9
	2003	5004.13	2863.92	3599.74	2347.04	71.9	82.0
	2004	5290.77	2999.85	4273.02	2298.56	80.8	76.6
	2005	6677.06	4522.20	4705.07	3618.78	70.5	80.0
	2006	7854.43	5694.75	4773.93	3785.46	60.8	66.5
	2007	8028.32	5915.83	5441.23	4458.77	67.8	75.4
	2008	8317.15	5938.78	5184.01	4125.67	62.3	69.5
	2009	9511.02	6344.39	4598.79	3412.43	48.4	53.8
	2010	11361.96	7640.58	4649.89	3291.89	40.9	43.1
	2011	16804.88	11357.36	5899.06	4504.94	35.1	39.7
	2012	21626.33	14159.68	7821.44	6152.03	36.2	43.4
	2013	25595.40	13455.29	6085.61	4228.72	23.8	31.4
	2014	25797.54	13289.42	7072.93	4052.72	27.4	30.5
	2015	22689.17	11917.86	5935.82	3392.31	26.2	28.5
乌鲁木齐市	Urumqi City	5435.24	3351.73	828.21	627.16	15.2	18.7
克拉玛依市	Karamay City	666.08	323.72	137.24	82.36	20.6	25.4
吐鲁番市	Turpan City	336.52	83.36	33.31	14.87	9.9	17.8
哈密地区	Hami [Kumul] Administrative Offices	801.91	433.95	245.14	121.78	30.6	28.1
昌吉回族自治州	Changji Hui Autonomous Prefecture	1361.71	803.90	294.59	173.08	21.6	21.5
伊犁哈萨克自治州	Ili Kazak Autonomous Prefecture	4560.83	2214.54	1376.40	689.40	30.2	31.1
伊犁州直属县(市)	Counties (Cities) Direct Under Ili Prefecture	2638.36	1312.61	597.30	327.05	22.6	24.9
塔城地区	Tacheng [Tarbagatai] Administrative Offices	1366.92	665.32	497.75	218.58	36.4	32.9
阿勒泰地区	Altay Administrative Offices	555.55	236.61	281.35	143.77	50.6	60.8
博尔塔拉蒙古自治州	Bortala Mongol Autonomous Prefecture	1174.52	386.78	279.58	186.50	23.8	48.2
巴音郭楞蒙古自治州	Bayangol Mongol Autonomous Prefecture	2278.09	1021.83	981.42	365.28	43.1	35.7
阿克苏地区	Aksu Administrative Offices	1102.96	576.46	174.47	92.58	15.8	16.1
克孜勒苏柯尔克孜自治州	Kizilsu Kirgiz Autonomous Prefecture	444.37	285.93	273.75	200.15	61.6	70.0
喀什地区	Kashgar [Kaxgar] Administrative Offices	1270.21	652.35	213.06	167.24	16.8	25.6
和田地区	Hotan Administrative Offices	1129.10	859.31	510.04	440.88	45.2	51.3
石河子市	Shihezi City	838.61	391.20	145.63	61.94	17.4	15.8
阿拉尔市	Aral City	409.87	68.14	251.92	33.06	61.5	48.5
图木舒克市	Tumxuk City	282.15	198.39	139.36	106.51	49.4	53.7
五家渠市	Wujiaqu City	589.96	266.27	49.71	29.52	8.4	11.1
跨地区投资	Trans-regional Investment	7.04		1.99		28.1	

注：该表房屋施工面积、竣工面积未包括农村个人。
Note: Floor space under construction and completed floor space in this table do not include rural individual.

4-11 固定资产投资效果指标
Result of Investment in Fixed Assets in Area

指　标	Item	2014	2015
建设周期(年)	Construction Cycle (year)	3	3
计划总投资(亿元)	Total Planned Investment (100 million yuan)	21549.97	25751.00
本年完成投资(亿元)	Completed Invetsment for the Current Year (100 million yuan)	7726.67	9730.45
本年新增固定资产(亿元)	Newly Increased Fixed Assets for the Current Year (100 million yuan)	5119.79	6781.38
固定资产交付使用率(%)	Rate of Projects of Fixed Assets Completed and Put into Operation (%)	66.3	69.7
施工项目个数(个)	Number of Projects under Construction (unit)	12751	16352
竣工项目个数(个)	Number of Projects Completed (unit)	8258	11670
建设项目投产率(%)	Rate of Projects Completed&Put into Use (%)	64.8	71.4

4-12 全社会基础设施投资
Investment of Basic Facilities in the Whole County

单位：亿元 (100 million yuan

指　标	Item	2014	2015
总　计	**Total**	**3453.40**	**4396.73**
电力、燃气及水的生产和供应业	Production and Supply of Electricity, Gas and Water	1652.05	2108.82
交通运输、仓储和邮政业	Transport, Storage, Postal and Telecommunications Services	827.88	1061.36
信息传输、计算机服务和软件业	Information Transmission, Software and Information Technology	107.92	132.60
水利、环境和公共设施管理业	Management of Water Conservancy, Environment and Public Facilities	865.55	1093.95

4-13 主要年份房地产开发企业基本情况

Basic Condition of Enterprises for Real Estate Development in Main Years

指　　标	Item	2005	2010	2015
企业单位数(个)	**Number of Enterprises (unit)**	**756**	**1233**	**1855**
#亏损企业	Loss- Suffering Enterprises	410	606	1249
主要财务指标（万元)	**Main Financial Indices (10 000 yuan)**			
年末资产负债情况	Situation of Year-end Liabilities			
资产总计	Total Assets	4861415	12591584	42944251
固定资产累计折旧	Accumulated Depreciation of Fixed Assets	81096	156739	420571
#本年折旧	Depreciation This Year	17981	34814	81769
负债总计	Total Liabilities	2932694	9422446	35862691
所有者权益合计	Total of Owner’s Right and Interest	1928721	3169138	7081560
实收资本	Total of Actual Capital	970103	2109245	4703767
损益情况	Situation of Profit and Loss			
经营收入总计	Total Income of Business	1084796	4119413	6784087
#土地转让收入	Income of Land Transfer	11295	19029	8405
商品房销售收入	Sales Income of Commercial Flat	1047965	4022490	6533598
房屋出租收入	Income of Renting House	15773	39343	136227
其他收入	Others	9763	38550	105857
经营成本	Operating Cost	871320	3040741	5089329
经营税金及附加	Operating Tax and Extra Charges	63562	295011	546802
销售费用	Expenses of Sales	27319	100896	369397
其他业务利润	Other Business Profits	9161	28592	14691
管理费用及财务费用	Expenses of Both Management and Finance	80949	257405	736008
投资收益及营业外收入	Income of Investment Earnings and Extra-business	7829	14881	281777
营业外支出	Expenditure of Extra-business	3456	14909	44145
利润总额	Total Profits	34320	454814	433052

4-14 主要年份房地产开发投资主要指标
Main Indicators of Real Estate Investment in Main Years

指 标	Item	2005	2010	2015
本年购置土地面积(万平方米)	**Land Space Purchased This Year (10 000 sq. m)**	**447.30**	**557.69**	**754.07**
房地产开发投资额(万元)	**Total Investment of Real-Estate Development (10 000 yuan)**	**1016618**	**3477185**	**9988751**
按中央和地方分	Grouped by Central and Local			
中央企业	Central Enterprises	54128	175564	483948
地方企业	Local Enterprises	962490	3301621	9504803
按投资构成分	Grouped by Use of Funds			
建筑工程	Construction	810003	2742491	7437445
安装工程	Installation	49559	161703	1092660
设备工器具购置	Purchase of Equipment and Instruments	14135	51777	173309
其他费用	Other Expenses	142921	521214	1285337
#土地购置费	Expenses of Land Purchase	94230	313568	882083
按工程用途分	Grouped by Purpose of Projects			
住 宅	Residential buildings	679521	2815620	6036606
办公楼	Office Building	40977	102895	586586
商业营业用房	Houses for Commercial and Business Purpose	247033	380275	2669691
其 他	Others	49087	178395	695868
本年资金来源小计 (万元)	**Sub-total of Capital Sources This Year (10 000 yuan)**	**1137693**	**5380739**	**11347246**
国内贷款	Domestic Loans	113887	684191	1244560
利用外资	Foreign Investment	160		
自筹资金	Self-raising Funds	479948	1397982	4922646
其它资金	Others	543698	3298566	5180040

4-15 按用途分房地产开发企业（单位）投资完成额

Investment Actually Completed by Enterprises for Real Estate Development by Use

单位：万元 (10 000 yuan)

年份 Year	地区 Region	企业个数（个） Number of Enterprises (unit)	本年完成投资 Investment Completed This Year	住宅 Residential Buildings	#别墅、高档公寓 Villas, High-grade Apartments
	1996	139	156232	80728	
	1997		169906	81886	1668
	1998		148577	95225	1000
	1999	165	234481	174446	2994
	2000	209	574347	500381	2390
	2001	293	979184	757490	3126
	2002	335	877060	570643	11001
	2003	492	1024908	547770	20212
	2004	709	1125577	599276	29585
	2005	756	1016618	679521	26634
	2006	824	1208786	899482	48542
	2007	909	1683160	1390360	57776
	2008	1130	2286267	1937460	94256
	2009	1159	2358805	1882530	148916
	2010	1233	3477185	2815620	194136
	2011	1421	5163895	4163926	258846
	2012	1509	6060939	4442667	368122
	2013	1634	8256855	5556183	475062
	2014	1808	10148108	6163046	556746
	2015	1855	9988751	6036606	427515
乌鲁木齐市	Urumqi City	399	3813701	2535623	113243
克拉玛依市	Karamay City	46	234156	164241	41583
吐鲁番市	Turpan City	47	184116	63047	
哈密地区	Hami [Kumul] Administrative Offices	92	328844	164625	3650
昌吉回族自治州	Changji Hui Autonomous Prefecture	166	724037	461358	40940
伊犁哈萨克自治州	Ili Kazak Autonomous Prefecture	451	1934071	1149097	82893
伊犁州直属县(市)	Counties (Cities) Direct Under Ili Prefecture	278	1204811	700571	15654
塔城地区	Tacheng [Tarbagatai] Administrative Offices	89	638008	423762	66019
阿勒泰地区	Altay Administrative Offices	84	91252	24764	1220
博尔塔拉蒙古自治州	Bortala Mongol Autonomous Prefecture	68	360933	175259	42979
巴音郭楞蒙古自治州	Bayangol Mongol Autonomous Prefecture	176	526803	249747	17464
阿克苏地区	Aksu Administrative Offices	148	593367	344197	1000
克孜勒苏柯尔克孜自治州	Kizilsu Kirgiz Autonomous Prefecture	25	90963	58637	
喀什地区	Kashgar [Kaxgar] Administrative Offices	85	173664	93037	665
和田地区	Hotan Administrative Offices	4	1061	1061	
石河子市	Shihezi City	71	239391	136082	2800
阿拉尔市	Aral City	21	49006	33373	1260
图木舒克市	Tumxuk City	13	17359	3763	
五家渠市	Wujiaqu City	43	717279	403459	79038

4-15 续表 Continued

单位：万元 (10 000 yuan)

年 份 Year	地 区 Region	办公楼 Office buildings	商业营业用房 Houses for Business Use	其 他 Others
	1996	18108	42562	14834
	1997	25347	41935	20738
	1998	17394	22027	13931
	1999	9133	27068	23834
	2000	13171	42601	18194
	2001	41911	111028	68755
	2002	81119	153498	71800
	2003	81497	286896	108745
	2004	77843	390566	57892
	2005	40977	247033	49087
	2006	28233	236945	44126
	2007	27629	205590	59581
	2008	56358	221418	71031
	2009	81926	281946	112403
	2010	102895	380275	178395
	2011	155400	572602	271967
	2012	120840	976135	521297
	2013	249894	1628450	822328
	2014	613946	2672112	699004
	2015	586586	2669691	695868
乌鲁木齐市	Urumqi City	352179	555729	370170
克拉玛依市	Karamay City	10382	47447	12086
吐鲁番市	Turpan City	1600	113017	6452
哈密地区	Hami [Kumul] Administrative Offices	10075	138270	15874
昌吉回族自治州	Changji Hui Autonomous Prefecture	32541	186644	43494
伊犁哈萨克自治州	Ili Kazak Autonomous Prefecture	65444	626371	93159
伊犁州直属县(市)	Counties (Cities) Direct Under Ili Prefecture	60828	392588	50824
塔城地区	Tacheng [Tarbagatai] Administrative Offices	2749	171027	40470
阿勒泰地区	Altay Administrative Offices	1867	62756	1865
博尔塔拉蒙古自治州	Bortala Mongol Autonomous Prefecture	385	180912	4377
巴音郭楞蒙古自治州	Bayangol Mongol Autonomous Prefecture	50963	195122	30971
阿克苏地区	Aksu Administrative Offices	23985	192115	33070
克孜勒苏柯尔克孜自治州	Kizilsu Kirgiz Autonomous Prefecture	910	29695	1721
喀什地区	Kashgar [Kaxgar] Administrative Offices	24000	54777	1850
和田地区	Hotan Administrative Offices			
石河子市	Shihezi City	7678	66403	29228
阿拉尔市	Aral City		14008	1625
图木舒克市	Tumxuk City		13516	80
五家渠市	Wujiaqu City	6444	255665	51711

4-16 房地产开发企业（单位）施工、销售和待售情况

单位：万平方米

年 份 Year	地 区 Region	本年施工房屋面积 Floor Space of Building under Construction This Year	#住宅 Residential Buildings	#商业营业用房 Houses for Business Use	本年新开工房屋面积 Floor Space Started This Year	#住宅 Residential Buildings	#商业营业用房 Houses for Business Use
	1996	224.90	150.80	41.67	103.87	69.84	19.52
	1997	222.20	144.50	47.68	90.24	70.08	12.81
	1998	252.61	188.38	40.72	133.26	120.95	6.35
	1999	343.38	295.62	34.33	212.73	194.77	12.48
	2000	771.86	665.30	74.20	453.63	397.77	43.00
	2001	1433.54	1207.89	150.63	912.06	778.55	97.24
	2002	1246.89	946.11	204.52	577.04	433.57	98.13
	2003	1382.14	962.89	298.51	782.78	557.28	175.73
	2004	1333.03	863.19	357.53	771.47	550.66	178.43
	2005	1371.15	941.58	340.63	793.55	639.98	130.90
	2006	1567.70	1188.61	307.19	1035.59	875.99	131.90
	2007	2053.76	1715.00	271.52	1347.11	1216.39	101.82
	2008	2639.06	2247.80	259.78	1703.86	1500.75	129.11
	2009	3064.41	2560.67	305.81	1718.17	1482.86	158.07
	2010	3980.80	3317.68	410.96	2177.24	1852.88	214.50
	2011	5481.44	4574.72	543.12	2974.51	2510.68	304.46
	2012	6896.54	5482.59	841.24	2823.64	2149.35	421.32
	2013	9459.55	6982.71	1545.44	3729.88	2499.16	838.51
	2014	11288.65	7632.93	2203.59	3561.09	2170.53	842.10
	2015	11465.44	7370.42	2516.62	2994.75	1877.08	722.41
乌鲁木齐市	Urumqi City	3944.41	2621.38	495.62	916.80	614.94	107.80
克拉玛依市	Karamay City	396.88	309.19	56.91	70.70	51.81	13.25
吐鲁番市	Turpan City	183.39	75.89	93.54	68.51	11.13	53.90
哈密地区	Hami [Kumul] Administrative Offices	472.08	285.05	146.17	138.00	52.66	78.64
昌吉回族自治州	Changji Hui Autonomous Prefecture	927.66	657.61	128.75	278.89	183.18	37.67
伊犁哈萨克自治州	Ili Kazak Autonomous Prefecture	2352.56	1421.12	722.40	836.54	554.03	227.92
伊犁州直属县(市)	Counties (Cities) Direct Under Ili Prefecture	1609.02	985.65	464.84	429.29	293.31	115.40
塔城地区	Tacheng [Tarbagatai] Administrative Offices	584.60	361.56	181.56	372.36	245.24	96.78
阿勒泰地区	Altay Administrative Offices	158.94	73.91	76.00	34.88	15.48	15.74
博尔塔拉蒙古自治州	Bortala Mongol Autonomous Prefecture	332.53	189.53	119.28	114.29	66.63	42.89
巴音郭楞蒙古自治州	Bayangol Mongol Autonomous Prefecture	862.36	553.80	196.45	178.34	114.25	45.88
阿克苏地区	Aksu Administrative Offices	642.36	419.26	176.17	188.48	112.14	53.82
克孜勒苏柯尔克孜自治州	Kizilsu Kirgiz Autonomous Prefecture	95.62	62.05	31.04	21.62	15.85	5.77
喀什地区	Kashgar [Kaxgar] Administrative Offices	302.54	196.95	65.44	37.92	25.48	12.20
和田地区	Hotan Administrative Offices	2.23	2.23				
石河子市	Shihezi City	410.33	268.62	82.55	58.09	30.75	15.20
阿拉尔市	Aral City	68.35	33.03	33.67	16.11	10.51	4.77
图木舒克市	Tumxuk City	33.44	15.53	17.44	7.59	4.41	3.18
五家渠市	Wujiaqu City	438.70	259.18	151.19	62.88	29.31	19.52

Condition of Under Construction, Sale and Idle of Enterprises for Real Estate Development

(10 000 sq.m)

本年竣工房屋面积 Floor Space of Buindings Completed This Year	#住宅 Residential Buildings	#商业营业用房 Houses for Business Use	本年房屋销售面积 Floor Space of Building Sold This Year	#住宅 Residential Buildings	#商业营业用房 Houses for Business Use	房屋销售额(万元) Sales Value of Buildings (10 000 yuan)	#住宅 Residential Buildings	#商业营业用房 Houses for Business Use
81.19	64.51	8.14	45.60	41.29	2.91	67514	57024	5883
93.56	73.32	6.93	55.43	52.48	0.98	75110	67585	1569
94.28	79.92	6.23	83.29	75.97	3.46	118386	98803	8544
159.99	143.93	13.52	127.48	120.44	4.67	177683	158304	12599
330.11	298.79	23.07	262.52	250.95	9.82	373801	333166	35153
633.25	559.91	57.01	419.87	381.67	31.77	643814	537818	90441
727.21	616.12	85.03	506.66	455.68	46.34	879287	658157	208821
791.14	626.50	126.42	587.02	516.48	53.44	1066640	768012	224579
704.25	511.61	156.54	635.53	538.33	81.27	1106143	784408	281856
717.43	553.48	121.37	687.20	606.48	68.16	1235410	915191	288747
679.06	551.63	104.13	892.41	806.46	73.96	1658176	1358136	265450
890.55	798.12	72.07	1144.34	1078.28	51.57	2381520	2113425	211508
1049.29	943.40	67.30	954.35	886.35	51.22	2137859	1861169	212861
1032.72	900.87	76.28	1406.55	1326.67	65.81	3662638	3271682	317310
1012.90	859.92	98.40	1564.90	1450.02	94.42	4830392	4164140	523153
1270.48	1108.02	109.66	1728.23	1570.56	123.12	6133128	5162366	779898
1736.19	1438.43	177.43	1430.30	1274.79	116.33	5604508	4581386	759812
1722.16	1394.08	220.40	2017.03	1799.94	172.46	8609530	7107384	1231744
2086.08	1594.27	314.32	1815.88	1541.25	210.38	8404657	6253483	1691206
1608.58	1206.44	271.86	1825.18	1536.49	206.10	8491847	6416249	1536999
433.96	354.25	27.22	578.47	511.72	26.24	3676977	2997248	352663
79.73	67.83	5.85	96.18	84.33	3.88	362987	302704	40260
17.72	13.11	4.00	13.94	11.15	2.77	46473	33908	12325
118.83	83.65	27.10	57.10	49.47	7.02	220060	166426	51822
129.23	102.36	19.96	172.24	149.11	14.05	707211	542663	108848
376.07	263.68	80.12	437.07	355.81	67.53	1663997	1158862	447339
223.49	157.71	37.38	301.19	247.83	43.61	1151129	823228	286582
122.12	86.46	32.53	107.18	91.13	15.66	406562	295573	109628
30.46	19.51	10.20	28.69	16.84	8.25	106306	40061	51129
35.68	26.18	9.45	58.30	42.94	14.36	176657	119635	54543
172.79	126.53	31.07	104.24	94.92	5.42	357031	275108	58809
91.03	64.27	20.43	70.40	58.31	10.83	248330	184206	57579
50.46	41.68	8.79	42.66	39.57	3.09	120884	92592	28292
19.68	13.53	6.15	18.67	10.88	7.42	64770	30160	32271
			0.76	0.76		1525	1525	
26.29	15.57	9.19	54.78	39.60	11.30	312819	187563	84733
15.53	2.63	12.91	15.60	10.07	5.29	55795	29495	25338
16.68	8.45	7.92	3.45	2.35	1.10	10297	4687	5610
24.90	22.72	1.71	101.33	75.51	25.81	466034	289467	176567

4-16 续表 Continued

单位：万平方米 (10 000 sq.m)

年份 Year	地区 Region	房屋待售面积 Floor Space At Idle	#住宅 Residential Buildings	#商业营业用房 Houses for Business Use
	1996	33.20	27.41	4.44
	1997	36.33	25.58	3.76
	1998	27.20	20.33	2.78
	1999	63.01	49.00	8.91
	2000	69.75	58.92	6.35
	2001	200.46	169.78	20.26
	2002	353.23	285.87	51.33
	2003	422.11	313.93	84.81
	2004	400.40	248.38	125.31
	2005	460.99	269.07	151.02
	2006	406.25	208.02	157.83
	2007	289.22	115.39	150.68
	2008	389.70	245.81	119.10
	2009	419.83	254.36	121.41
	2010	348.98	195.47	106.55
	2011	367.02	220.45	92.77
	2012	459.21	277.72	93.42
	2013	731.88	472.59	155.43
	2014	988.81	643.98	221.16
	2015	1136.62	701.45	299.58
乌鲁木齐市	Urumqi City	248.87	132.62	40.17
克拉玛依市	Karamay City	15.13	7.85	4.70
吐鲁番市	Turpan City	20.60	10.19	9.81
哈密地区	Hami [Kumul] Administrative Offices	75.18	43.08	26.39
昌吉回族自治州	Changji Hui Autonomous Prefecture	60.15	42.18	14.14
伊犁哈萨克自治州	Ili Kazak Autonomous Prefecture	181.35	114.75	46.45
伊犁州直属县(市)	Counties (Cities) Direct Under Ili Prefecture	106.49	59.69	29.12
塔城地区	Tacheng [Tarbagatai] Administrative Offices	46.03	37.77	6.40
阿勒泰地区	Altay Administrative Offices	28.83	17.29	10.93
博尔塔拉蒙古自治州	Bortala Mongol Autonomous Prefecture	22.95	13.87	8.95
巴音郭楞蒙古自治州	Bayangol Mongol Autonomous Prefecture	226.26	176.75	33.46
阿克苏地区	Aksu Administrative Offices	119.89	83.09	34.38
克孜勒苏柯尔克孜自治州	Kizilsu Kirgiz Autonomous Prefecture	10.43	6.47	3.95
喀什地区	Kashgar [Kaxgar] Administrative Offices	55.39	28.43	23.98
和田地区	Hotan Administrative Offices	0.87		0.87
石河子市	Shihezi City	32.95	7.28	22.93
阿拉尔市	Aral City	12.82	2.48	10.33
图木舒克市	Tumxuk City	6.29	1.54	4.75
五家渠市	Wujiaqu City	47.49	30.87	14.32

4-17 房地产开发企业（单位）资金来源
Sources of Funds of Enterprises for Real Estate Development

单位：万元 (10 000 yuan)

年份 Year	地区 Region	合计 Total	国内贷款 Domestic Loans	利用外资 Foreign Investment	自筹资金 Self-raising Funds	其他资金来源 Others
	1996	154995	51048	742	45104	58101
	1997	161399	51443	500	60573	48883
	1998	151094	22419	500	49427	78748
	1999	244252	29665	5770	73899	134918
	2000	701332	113823	600	232768	354141
	2001	890102	106794	1278	303975	478055
	2002	1064031	158511		455707	449813
	2003	1117659	208348		448441	460870
	2004	1215850	125553		546282	544015
	2005	1137693	113887	160	479948	543698
	2006	1446593	145340		478871	822382
	2007	2243755	217380		766344	1260031
	2008	2427323	253427		961343	1212553
	2009	3683795	453692	50	915219	2314834
	2010	5380739	684191		1397982	3298566
	2011	6843313	731550	1666	2314233	3795864
	2012	7979461	908749		2976896	4093816
	2013	11131481	1066046		4121799	5943636
	2014	11364803	1045811		4882973	5436019
	2015	11347246	1244560		4922646	5180040
乌鲁木齐市	Urumqi City	4487304	808036		1303429	2375839
克拉玛依市	Karamay City	311422	15197		63205	233020
吐鲁番市	Turpan City	208932	4060		152231	52641
哈密地区	Hami [Kumul] Administrative Offices	387537	8000		131517	248020
昌吉回族自治州	Changji Hui Autonomous Prefecture	871242	123226		218050	529966
伊犁哈萨克自治州	Ili Kazak Autonomous Prefecture	2135428	129443		1244370	761615
伊犁州直属县(市)	Counties (Cities) Direct Under Ili Prefecture	1283142	101323		522283	659536
塔城地区	Tacheng [Tarbagatai] Administrative Offices	777389	26350		660298	90741
阿勒泰地区	Altay Administrative Offices	74897	1770		61789	11338
博尔塔拉蒙古自治州	Bortala Mongol Autonomous Prefecture	380520	2200		294138	84182
巴音郭楞蒙古自治州	Bayangol Mongol Autonomous Prefecture	570793	34453		311571	224769
阿克苏地区	Aksu Administrative Offices	676169	30130		468851	177188
克孜勒苏柯尔克孜自治州	Kizilsu Kirgiz Autonomous Prefecture	84004	1426		76352	6226
喀什地区	Kashgar [Kaxgar] Administrative Offices	197318	42109		88094	67115
和田地区	Hotan Administrative Offices	1709			1709	
石河子市	Shihezi City	229121	9500		44655	174966
阿拉尔市	Aral City	59678	300		39824	19554
图木舒克市	Tumxuk City	19825			16675	3150
五家渠市	Wujiaqu City	726244	36480		467975	221789

4-18 新增主要产品生产能力
Newly Increased Production Capacity of Major Products

项　目	Item	2014	2015
原煤开采(万吨/年)	Coal Mining (10 000 tons/year)	2514.28	4567.58
焦炭(万吨/年)	Coke (10 000 tons/year)	1733.00	1583.00
天然原油开采(万吨/年)	Petroleum Extractin (10 000 tons/year)	313.93	831.80
天然气开采(亿立方米/年)	Natural Gas Extraction (100 million cu.m/year)	61.21	261.35
裂化设备能力(处理万吨/年)	Cracking Equipment Capabillity(handle 10 000 tons/year)	51.15	276.85
铁矿石开采(原矿) (万吨/年)	Iron-Ore Mining (10 000 tons/year)	1423.00	518.00
铁矿选矿处理原矿量(万吨/年)	Iron-ore Dressing (10 000 tons/year)	319.10	70.00
生铁(万吨/年)	Pig Iron(10 000 tons/year)	547.18	220.00
粗钢(万吨/年)	Crude Steel(10 000 tons/year)	445.00	410.00
铜采矿(原矿)(万吨/年)	Copper Ore Mining (10 000 tons/year)	523.25	746.20
处理原矿(万吨/年)	Crude Ore Dressing (10 000 tons/year)	395.25	300.00
铅锌采矿(原矿) (万吨/年)	Plumbum/Zinc Ore Mining (10 000 tons/year)	30.10	231.00
铝加工(吨/年)	Aluminium Processing (ton/year)	207425.00	878265.00
发电机组容量(万千瓦)	Capacity of Generating Setes (10 000 kw/year)		
水力发电	Hydraulic Power	471.69	12125.96
火力发电	Fire Power	1012.75	1885.50
其他发电	Others	2.00	98.37
输电线路长度(11 万伏及以上)(公里)	Transmission Line (110 000V)(km)	5887.87	7502.75
水泥(万吨/年)	Cement (10 000 tons/year)	3341.50	2030.71

4-18 Continued

项　目	Item	2014	2015
农用氮、磷、钾化学肥料(吨/年)	Farm-use Nitrogen, Phosphorus and Potassium Fertilizer (ton/year)		
氮肥	Nitrogen Fertilizer	1693324	323016
磷肥	Phoshate Fertilizer	81825	32313
钾肥	Potash Fertilizer	33750	233206
塑料树脂及共聚物(吨/年)	Plastic Colophony and Polymer (ton/year)	634150	26070
棉纺锭(锭)	Cotton Spindle (spindle)	228000	2033400
酒(万吨/年)	Liquors (10 000 tons/year)	3.05	0.33
其他酒	Others	23.98	4.64
新建公路(公里)	Length of New Highways (km)	2293.05	5521.40
二级公路	Second Class highways	261.77	475.95
改建公路(公里)	Length of Reconstructed Highways(km)	5910.92	6354.26
二级公路	Second Class highways	1892.87	1560.80
新建独立公路桥梁(延长米)	New-Built Separate Highway and Bridge (Extended Length m)	4533	7255.54
(座)	(unit)	10	42
新(扩)建客、货运站(个)	Number of Newly-Built or Expanded Passenger and Freight Stations (unit)	12	22
(平方米)	(sq.m)	41317	75046
城市自来水供水能力(万吨/日)	Capacity of City Tap Water Supply (10 000 tons/day)	14.13	51.09
城市污水处理能力(万吨/日)	Disposal Capacity of Sewer (10 000 tons/day)	32.26	87.32

主要统计指标解释

全社会固定资产投资 以货币形式表现的在一定时期内全社会建造和购置固定资产的工作量以及与此有关的费用的总称。该指标是反映固定资产投资规模、结构和发展速度的综合性指标,又是观察工程进度和考核投资效果的重要依据。全社会固定资产投资按登记注册类型可分为国有、集体、联营、股份制、私营和个体、港澳台商、外商、其他等。

固定资产投资（不含农户）指城镇和农村各种登记注册类型的企业、事业、行政单位及城镇个体户进行的计划总投资500万元及500万元以上的建设项目投资和房地产开发投资，包含原口径的城镇固定资产投资加上农村企事业组织项目投资，该口径自2011年起开始使用。

房地产开发投资 指各种登记注册类型的房地产开发法人单位统一开发的包括统代建、拆迁还建的住宅、厂房、仓库、饭店、宾馆、度假村、写字楼、办公楼等房屋建筑物，配套的服务设施，土地开发工程（如道路、给水、排水、供电、供热、通讯、平整场地等基础设施工程）和土地购置的投资；不包括单纯的土地开发和交易活动。

固定资产投资的实际到位资金 根据固定资产投资的资金来源不同，分为国家预算资金、国内贷款、利用外资、自筹资金和其他资金。

(1)国家预算资金: 国家预算包括一般预算、政府性基金预算、国有资本经营预算和社保基金预算。各类预算中用于固定资产投资的资金全部作为国家预算资金填报，其中一般预算中用于固定资产投资的部分包括基建投资、车购税、灾后恢复重建基金和其他财政投资。各级政府债券也应归入国家预算资金。

(2)国内贷款: 指报告期固定资产项目投资单位向银行及非银行金融机构借入的用于固定资产投资各种国内借款，包括银行利用自有资金及吸收存款发放的贷款、上级主管部门拨入的国内贷款、国家专项贷款（包括煤代油贷款、劳改煤矿专项贷款等），地方财政专项资金安排的贷款、国内储备贷款、周转贷款等。

(3)利用外资: 指报告期收到的境外（包括外国及港澳台地区）资金(包括设备、材料、技术在内)。包括对外借款(外国政府贷款、国际金融组织贷款、出口信贷、外国银行商业贷款、对外发行债券和股票)、外商直接投资、外商其他投资(包括利用外商投资收益在国内进行固定资产再投资活动的资金)。不包括我国自有外汇资金(国家外汇、地方外汇、留成外汇、调剂外汇和国内银行自有资金发放的外汇贷款等)。各类外资按报告期末的外汇牌价（中间价）折成人民币计算。

(4)自筹资金: 指固定资产投资单位在报告期收到的，由各企、事业单位筹集用于固定资产投资的资金，包括各类企事业单位的自有资金和从其他单位筹集的用于固定资产投资的资金，但不包括各类财政性资金、从各类金融机构借入资金和国外资金。

(5)其他资金: 指在报告期收到的除以上各种资金之外的用于固定资产投资的资金，包括社会集资、个人资金、无偿捐赠的资金及其他单位拨入的资金等。

固定资产投资按国民经济行业分 指根据其从事的社会经济活动性质对各类单位进行的分类。应根据建设项目建成投产后的主要产品种类或主要用途及社会经济活动种类来划分，不能根据项目单位本身的行业类别来划分。如果项目投产后有几种产品，应根据主要产品来确定行业类别。一般情况下，一个建设项目只能属于一种国民经济行业。

固定资产投资按隶属关系分 是按建设单位或企业、事业、行政单位的主管上级机关确定的。

(1)中央 是指中共中央、人大常委会和国务院各部、委、局、总公司以及直属机构直接领导的建设项目和企业、事业、行政单位。这些单位的固定资产投资计划由国务院各部门直接编制和下达，统一组织或委托下级实施。包括有中央垂直管理的部门（如国家统计局各级调查队）和中央直属企业、事业单位（如工商银行、中国电信、中国石油）等。

(2)地方 是由省（自治区、直辖市）、地（区、市、州、盟）、县（区、市、旗）三级政府及业务主管部门直接领导和管理的建设项目、企业、事业、行政单位。地方项目还包括不隶属以上各级政府及主管部门的建设项目和企业、事业单位，如外商投资企业和无主管部门的企业等。

固定资产投资按建设性质分 按整个建设项目情况来确定。建设项目的性质一般分为新建、扩建、改建和技术改造、单纯建造生活设施、迁建、恢复、单纯购置。房地产开发单位、农户投资不划分建设性质。

(1)新建 指从无到有“平地起家”开始建设的项目。现有企业、事业、行政单位投资的项目一般不属于新建。但如有的单位原有基础很小，经过建设后新增的固定资产价值超过该企业、事业、行政单位原有固定资产价值（原值）三倍以上的，也应作为新建。

(2)扩建 指在厂内或其他地点，为扩大原有产品的生产能力(或效益)或增加新的产品生产能力，而增建的生产车间(或主要工程)、分厂、独立的生产线的企业、事业单位。行政、事业单位在原单位增建业务性用房(如学校增建教学用房、医院增建门诊部、病房等)也作为扩建。

现有企、事业单位为扩大原有主要产品生产能力或增加新的产品生产能力，增建一个或几个主要生产车间(或主要工程)、分厂，同时进行一些更新改造工程的，也应作为扩建。

(3)改建和技术改造　指现有企业、事业单位对原有设施进行技术改造或更新(包括相应配套的辅助性生产、生活福利设施) 的建设项目。改建项目包括现有企业、事业单位为适应市场变化的需要，而改变企业的主要产品种类(如军工企业转民产品等) 的建设项目，原有产品生产作业线由于各工序(车间)之间能力不平衡，为填平补齐充分发挥原有生产能力而增建不增加本企业主要产品设计能力的车间的建设项目。技术改造是指企业、事业单位在现有基础上，用先进的技术代替落后的技术，用先进的工艺和装备代替落后的工艺和装备，以改变企业落后的技术经济面貌，实现以内涵为主的扩大再生产，达到提高产品质量、促进产品更新换代、节约能源、降低消耗、扩大生产规模、全面提高社会经济效益的目的。技术改造具体包括以下内容：机器设备和工具的更新改造；生产工艺改革、节约能源和原材料的改造；厂房建筑和公共设施的改造；保护环境进行的“三废”治理改造；劳动条件和生产环境的改造等。

固定资产投资按构成分

(1)建筑工程　指各种房屋、建筑物的建造工程，又称建筑工作量。这部分投资额必须兴工动料，通过施工活动才能实现，是固定资产投资额的重要组成部分。

(2)安装工程　指各种设备、装置的安装工程，又称安装工作量。

在安装工程中，不包括被安装设备本身价值。

(3)设备工具器具购置　指报告期内购置或自制的，达到固定资产标准的设备、工具、器具的价值。新建单位及扩建单位的新建车间，按照设计或计划要求购置或自制的全部设备、工具、器具，不论是否达到固定资产标准均计入“设备工具器具购置”中。

(4)其他费用　指在固定资产建造和购置过程中发生的，除建筑安装工程和设备、工器具购置投资完成额以外的应当分摊计入固定资产投资的费用，不指经营中财务上的其他费用。

施工项目个数　是指本年正式进行过建筑或安装施工活动的建设项目个数。包括本年新开工项目，以前年度开工跨入本年继续施工项目，本年全部建成投产项目、以前年度全部停缓建在本年恢复施工的项目，本年进行过施工又在本年内全部停缓建的项目。施工项目个数可以反映一定时期固定资产投资的实际规模，与同期全部建成投产项目个数相比，可以从建设速度的角度反映固定资产投资的效果。

本年投产项目个数　指报告期内按设计文件规定建成主体工程和相应配套的辅助设施，形成生产能力或工程效益，经过验收合格，并且已正式投入生产或交付使用的建设项目。

新增生产能力(或工程效益)　指通过固定资产投资活动而增加的设计能力(或工程效益)，主要指标包括建设规模、本年施工规模、自开始建设累计新增生产能力（或工程效益）、本年新增生产能力（或工程效益）等。

房屋施工面积　指报告期内施工的全部房屋建筑面积。包括本期新开工的面积、上期跨入本期继续施工的房屋建筑面积、上期停缓建在本期恢复施工的房屋建筑面积、本期竣工的房屋建筑面积以及本期施工后又停缓建的房屋建筑面积。多层建筑应填各层建筑面积之和。

房屋竣工面积　指在报告期内房屋建筑按照设计要求已经全部完工，达到住人和使用条件，经验收鉴定合格或达到竣工验收标准，可正式移交使用的各栋房屋建筑面积的总和。

新增固定资产　是指已经完成建造和购置过程，并已交付生产或使用单位的固定资产的价值，包括已经建成投入生产或交付使用的工程投资和达到固定资产标准的设备、工具、器具的投资及有关应摊入的费用。该指标是表示固定资产投资成果的价值指标，也是反映建设进度，计算固定资产投资效果的重要指标。

项目建成投产率　指一定时期内全部建成投产项目个数与同期施工项目个数的比率。该指标从建设单位建设速度的角度反映投资效果。

固定资产交付使用率　指一定时期新增固定资产与同期完成投资额的比率。该指标是反映固定资产动用速度，衡量建设过程中宏观投资效果的综合指标。由于新增固定资产是较长时期内形成的结果，而投资额则是当年完成的，因此，该指标一般适宜于反映较长时期内固定资产的动用情况。

商品房销售面积　指报告期内出售商品房屋的合同总面积（即双方签署的正式买卖合同中所确定的建筑面积）。由现房销售面积和期房销售面积两部分组成。

商品房销售额　指报告期内出售商品房屋的合同总价款（即双方签署的正式买卖合同中所确定的合同总价）。该指标与商品房销售面积同口径，由现房销售额和期房销售额两部分组成。

Explanatory Notes on Main Statistical Indicators

Total Investment in Fixed Assets in the Whole Country refers to the volume of activities in construction and purchases of fixed assets of the whole country and related fees, expressed in monetary terms during the reference period. It is a comprehensive indicator which shows the size, structure and growth of the investment in fixed assets, providing a basis for observing the progress of construction projects and evaluating results of investment. Total investment in fixed assets in the whole country includes, by type of ownership, the investment by State-owned units, collective-owned units, joint ownership units, share-holding units, private units, individuals as well as investments by entrepreneurs from Hong Kong, Macao and Taiwan, foreign investors and others.

Investment in Fixed Assets (Excluding Rural Households) refers to the investment in construction projects with a total planned investment of 5 million yuan and over by enterprises of various ownerships, institutions, administrative units and urban self-employed individuals, and the investment in real estate development in both urban and rural areas. Since 2011, it covers the urban investment in fixed assets under the previous statistical coverage plus project investments by rural enterprises and institutions.

Investment in Real Estate Development refers to investment by real estate development companies, commercialized buildings construction companies and other real estate development units of various types of ownership in the construction of buildings, such as residential buildings, factory buildings, warehouses, hotels, guesthouses, holiday villages, office buildings, the complementary service facilities and land development projects, such as roads, water supply, water drainage, power supply, heating supply, telecommunications, land leveling and other infrastructural projects. It does not include activities in pure land transactions.

Actual Funds in Place for Investment in Fixed Assets are categorized as funds from the State budget, domestic loans, foreign investment, self-raised funds, and others, depending on the sources of investment.

(1) Fund from the State budget: State budget consists of general budget, government fund budget, operation budget of state-owned assets and social security fund budget. Funds for investment in fixed assets from various budgets are reported as fund from the state budget, of which, the general budget utilized on fixed assets investment includes investment on infrastructure construction, vehicle purchase tax, post-disaster restoration and reconstruction funds and other financial investment. Government bonds at all levels should also be included.

(2) Domestic loans refer to loans of various forms borrowed by investing units from banks and non-bank financial institutions during the reference period for the purpose of investment in fixed assets, including loans issued by banks from their self-owned funds and deposit, loans appropriated by higher responsible authorities, special loans by government (including loan for substituting petroleum with coal, special loans for reform-through-labour coal mines), loans arranged by local government from special funds, domestic reserve loan, and revolving loan, etc.

(3) Foreign investment refers to overseas (including foreign countries, Hongkong, Macao and Taiwan) funds received during the reference period (covering equipment, materials and technology), including foreign borrowings (loans from foreign governments and international financial institutions, export credit, commercial loans from foreign banks, issue of bonds and stocks overseas), foreign direct investment and other foreign investments (including funds from foreign direct investment income that are reinvested in fixed assets domestically). Excluded from this category is capital in foreign exchanges owned by China (foreign exchanges owned by the central and local governments, foreign exchanges retained by enterprises, foreign exchanges by enterprises through the regulating mechanism, loans in foreign exchanges issued by the Bank of China with its own fund, etc.). In calculating the utilization of foreign capital, foreign currencies are converted into Chinese Renminbi applying the exchange rate (central parity rate) at the end of the reference period.

(4) Self-raised funds refer to funds for investment in fixed assets received during the reference period by investing units, including investment in fixed assets using own funds of various enterprises and institutions or funds raised from other units other than financial funds, funds borrowed from financial institutions and overseas funds.

(5) Others refer to funds for investment in fixed assets received from sources other than those listed above, including funds raised from individuals and through donations, and funds transferred from other units.

Investment in Fixed Assets by Sector refers to the classification of investment by the nature of social economic activities the investing units are engaged in. The classification of construction projects by sector is determined by the major products or the purpose of the projects when they are put into production or use, and by the nature of their social economic activities, instead of being determined by industrial classification of the project enterprises. The project will be classified according to major product if there are several kinds of products yielded. In general, one project can only be classified into one sector.

Investment in Fixed Assets by Jurisdiction of Management refers to the classification of investment by the competent authorities under which investment is made by construction units, enterprises, institutions or administrative units.

(1) Central investment refers to the investment in projects or by enterprises, institutions or administrative units which are under the direct leadership and management of the State Council and of the national commissions, ministries, agencies and State-owned large corporations. Various ministries and departments of the State Council prepare and implement plans through unified organization or lower-level commissions, which include departments direct under central government (i.e. survey offices at all level of the National Bureau of Statistics) and enterprises and institutions directly under central government (like the Industrial and Commercial Bank of China, China Telecom and China National Petroleum Corporation)..

(2) Local investment refers to the investment in projects or by enterprises, institutions or administrative units which are under the direct leadership and management of competent departments and governments at the level of province (autonomous regions and municipalities directly under the Central Government), prefecture (prefectures, cities and leagues) and county (districts, cities and banners). Also included are projects by foreign-invested enterprises and enterprises without competent managing authorities.

Investment in Fixed Assets by Type of Construction Construction projects in general can be classified, by the type of construction, into new construction, expansion, reconstruction and technical transformation, purely construction of living facilities, moving, restoration and purely purchasing. However, investment by type of construction is not applied to investment by real-estate development units and investment by rural households.

(1) New construction in general refers to construction projects, which start from scratch. The existing projects invested by enterprises, institutions and administrative agencies cannot be classified as new construction. In case the size of the existing unit is quite small, and the value of newly added fixed assets is more than three times of the original value, the expansion will be considered as new construction.

(2) Expansion refers to construction of new production workshop, branch factory or independent production line within a factory or in other locations, for the purpose of increasing the production capacity (or improving efficiency) or adding new production capacity by enterprises and institutions. Newly constructed accommodation for the operation of institutions and administrative organizations (such as newly constructed buildings for teaching in schools, buildings for clinics or wards in hospitals, etc.) are also classified as expansion.

Also included in expansion are investments by existing enterprises or institutions in building major production line(s) or branch factory (ies) along with some work on innovation, for the purpose of expanding the production capacity of original products or producing new products.

(3) Reconstruction and technical transformation refers to construction projects by existing enterprises or institutions in innovation or technical transformation of the old facilities (including auxiliary production equipment and welfare facilities). Also considered as reconstruction is the construction of new workshops by the existing enterprises or institutions to change the variety of products to meet the market demand (such as the production of civil products by defence industries), or to bring the designed production capacity into full play through a more balanced production process on production lines. Technical transformation refers to replacement of old technology or equipment by new technology or equipment, in order to expand the reproduction through improvement of technology contents in production, to improve product quality, to promote new products, to save energy, to reduce consumption, to expand the production scale and to improve overall social-economic efficiency. Contents of technical transformation include: updating of machinery, equipment and tools; reforming production process by using energy or materials saving technology; construction of factory workshops and transformation of public facilities; treatment transformation of “three wastes” (waste gas, waste water and industrial residue) aiming at environmental protection; improvement of working conditions and environment, etc.

Investment in Fixed Assets by Structure

(1) Construction refers to the construction of houses and buildings, also known as work volume of construction. This part of investment can only be achieved through construction activities, it is the major component of the total investment in fixed assets.

(2) Installation refers to the installation of various kinds of equipment and instruments, also known as work volume of installation.

The value of equipment installed itself is not included in the value of installation projects.

(3) Purchase of equipment and instruments refers to the total value of equipment, tools, and instruments purchased or self-produced which come up to the cut-off point for fixed assets during the reference period. Equipment, tools and

instruments purchased or self-produced for new workshops by newly established or expanded units are categorized as "purchase of equipment and instruments" no matter whether they come up to the cut-off point for fixed assets.

(4) Other expenses refer to expenses arising during the construction or purchase of fixed assets other than those expenses on construction, installation and purchase of equipment and instruments. Other financial expenses arising in operation are not included.

Number of Projects under Construction refers to number of all projects with actual construction or installation activities in current year, including newly started projects, projects started previously and extended into the current year, projects completed and put into operation in current year, projects suspended previously and resumed in current year, and projects started this year but suspended or postponed in current year. The number of projects under construction can reflect the actual size of investment in fixed assets during a given period, and when compared with the number of projects completed and put into use during the same period, it demonstrates the results of investment in fixed assets from the angle of the speed of the construction.

Number of Projects Put into Use This Year refer to projects have completed the main construction and correspondent auxiliary facilities in accordance with the design documents, resulting in forming production capacity (efficiency) and have been checked and accepted after relevant tests, and have been formally delivered for use.

Newly Increased Production Capacity (or Project Efficiency) refers to the increase in design capacity (or project efficiency) through investment in fixed assets. The main indicators include: construction scale, scale of projects under construction in current year, the accumulated newly increased production capacity (project efficiency) since the start of the projects and the newly increased production capacity (project efficiency) of current year.

Floor Space of Buildings under Construction refers to total floor space of the horizontal section of outer walls above the plinth of the building, including the effective area and the area occupied by the structure. This indicator is one of the important indicators in physical terms to reflect the scale and accomplishment of the construction industry, and important basis for monitoring the pr ogress, calculating the cost, analyzing the efficiency and studying the sup ply of building materials in relation with the construction projects.

Floor Space of Residential Buildings refers to the floor space of the residential buildings among the total space of buildings under construction or completed.

Newly Increased Fixed Assets refer to the value of fixed assets that has completed the construction and purchase, and has been delivered to the production or owner units, including investment in projects that have been completed and put into operation in current year and the investment in equipment, tools and appliance that meet the standard of fixed assets and fees that should be apportioned. This is an indicator that demonstrates the results of investment in fixed assets in monetary terms, and an important indicator to reflect the speed of construction and to calculate the efficiency of investment.

Rate of Construction Projects Completed and Put into Use refers to the ratio of the number of construction projects completed and put into use in a certain period of time to the number of projects under construction in the same period. This reflects the investment efficiency from the perspective of the speed of projects construction.

Rate of Projects of Fixed Assets Completed and Put into Operation refers to the ratio of the newly increased fixed assets to the total investment made in the same period. This is a comprehensive indicator reflecting the speed of the employment of fixed assets and the investment efficiency at the macro-level. As the newly increase fixed assets is the result of a long period while the investment is completed in the current year, this indicator is expected to be used to reflect the employment of fixed assets over a long period of time.

Area of Commercialized Housing Sold refers to total contracted area of commercialized housing (i.e. area of floor space as designated in the formal contracts signed by both sides) during the reference time. It constitutes floor space of completed housing and floor space of future housing.

Value of Commercialized Housing Sold refers to the total contracted value (i.e. value of sales/purchase for selling/purchase of commercialized housing as designated in the contract signed by both sides) during the reference time. This indicator has the same coverage as the area of commercialized housing sold, which constitutes floor space of completed housing and floor space of housing yet to be completed.

对外经济贸易和旅游

FOREIGN TRADE AND ECONOMIC COOPERATION & TOURISM

第五篇 对外经济贸易和旅游

本篇主要内容和资料来源

本篇内容包括海关进出口额、主要进出口商品数量及金额、对外承包工程和劳务合作、利用外资、外国和港澳台地区在新疆直接投资情况、新疆在国外和港澳台地区直接投资、经济技术开发（合作）主要情况、旅游情况等。

海关进出口额、利用外资、旅游资料由新疆维吾尔自治区统计局贸易外经统计处分别根据乌鲁木齐海关、新疆维吾尔自治区商务厅、新疆维吾尔自治区工商管理局和新疆维吾尔自治区旅游局的有关资料加工整理。

Foreign Trade and Economic Cooperation & Tourism

Main Content and Source of Data

Data in this chapter cover mainly total imports and exports at customs, main imports and exports in volume and value, contracted projects and labor services cooperation, utilization of foreign capital, basic condition of direct investment in Xinjiang by foreign countries and compatriots from Hong Kong, Macao and Taiwan, main condition of economic and technological development and cooperation zones, condition of tourism.

Data on imports and exports, utilization of foreign capitals, tourism are collected and processed by the Department of Trade Statistics, the Xinjiang Bureau of Statistics in accordance with the data from custom of Urumqi, Foreign Economic and Trade Commission of Xinjiang, Xinjiang Administration for Industry and Commerce, Tourist Bureau of Xinjiang.

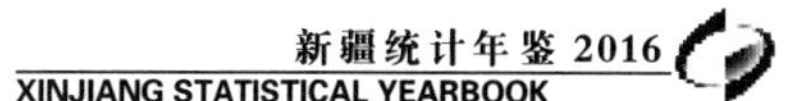

5-1 进出口贸易总额
Total Value of Imports and Exports

单位：万美元 (USD 10 000)

年份 Year	地区 Region	进出口总额 Total Imports and Exports	出口额 Exports	#一般贸易 Ordinary Trade	#边境贸易 Border Trade	进口额 Imports	#一般贸易 Ordinary Trade	#边境贸易 Border Trade
	1978	2346	937			1409		
	1985	29197	18020			11177		
	1990	41025	33530		3506	7495		3416
	1995	142798	76880	44550	27562	65918	17640	41888
	1996	140367	54975	30281	18647	85392	25982	54484
	1997	144667	66547	36061	22962	78120	24061	52031
	1998	153214	80789	32268	37599	72425	20972	49354
	1999	176534	102743	37120	57329	73791	25723	44976
	2000	226399	120408	55060	58020	105991	28020	73950
	2001	177148	66849	29523	18418	110299	24895	79661
	2002	269186	130849	54404	47218	138337	26028	107152
	2003	477198	254221	71115	160411	222977	72510	143504
	2004	563563	304658	50194	223782	258905	101540	147058
	2005	794189	504024	88036	386237	290165	108894	167648
	2006	910327	713923	158842	522038	196404	61915	126429
	2007	1371623	1150311	294000	806885	221312	75418	134778
	2008	2221680	1929925	290237	1576911	291755	92279	187279
	2009	1382771	1082325	168078	754206	300446	128702	157390
	2010	1712834	1296981	208909	767478	415853	154567	236745
	2011	2282225	1682886	476788	881882	599339	170863	401754
	2012	2517075	1934686	700915	891987	582389	144347	408382
	2013	2756191	2226980	850994	1063308	529211	100235	372450
	2014	2766930	2348255	849589	1284704	418675	250380	137849
	2015	1967789	1750600	682147	935045	217189	155459	26901
乌鲁木齐市	Urumqi City	584311	481117			103194		
克拉玛依市	Karamay City	9522	5915			3607		
石河子市	Shihezi City	120093	115835			4258		
吐鲁番市	Turpan City	4200	1919			2281		
哈密地区	Hami [Kumul] Administrative Offices	43345	40129			3216		
昌吉回族自治州	Changji Hui Autonomous Prefecture	142422	124522			17900		
伊犁哈萨克自治州	Ili Kazak Autonomous Prefecture	594712	571322			23390		
伊犁州直属县(市)	Counties (Cities) Direct Under Ili Prefecture	469564	456656			12908		
塔城地区	Tacheng [Tarbagatai] Administrative Offices	38506	35400			3106		
阿勒泰地区	Altay Administrative Offices	86642	79266			7376		
博尔塔拉蒙古自治州	Bortala Mongol Autonomous Prefecture	217505	188683			28822		
巴音郭楞蒙古自治州	Bayangol Mongol Autonomous Prefecture	36930	13523			23407		
阿克苏地区	Aksu Administrative Offices	28094	27836			258		
克孜勒苏柯尔克孜自治州	Kizilsu Kirgiz Autonomous Prefecture	28196	25258			2938		
喀什地区	Kashgar [Kaxgar] Administrative Offices	157480	153793			3687		
和田地区	Hotan Administrative Offices	979	748			231		

注：1998 年以前的资料由商务厅提供，1998 年以后资料由乌鲁木齐海关提供(5-2、5-3、5-4 表相同)。
Note: The data prior to 1998 is offered by the Bureau of Foreign Economic and Trades , data after 1998 is offered by Urumqi Customs (The same in the 5-2, 5-3, 5-4 tables).

5-2 主要进出口商品数量和金额
Main Imports and Exports Commodities in Volume and Value

项　目	Item	2014		2015	
		数　量 Volume	金　额 (万美元) Value (USD 10 000)	数　量 Volume	金　额 (万美元) Value (USD 10 000)
主要出口商品	**Main Export Commodities**				
棉纱(吨)	Cotton Yarn (ton)	4700	2740	3344	1966
棉机织物(万米)	Cotton cloth(10 000 m)	5590	9918	5802	9978
肠衣(吨)	Casings (ton)	293	1508	355	1554
番茄酱(万吨)	Tomato Jam (10 000 tons)	39	42357	45	40695
电视机(万台)	TV Sets (10 000 sets)	28	4576	8	1015
地毯(吨)	Carpets (ton)	2189	1599	1749	1253
药材(吨)	Medical Materials (ton)	662	367	108	35
鞋　类	Shoes		341794		246313
主要进口商品	**Main Import Commodities**				
羊毛及条(吨)	Wool and Wool Tops (ton)	6073	805	10869	1582
钢材(万吨)	Rolled Steel (10 000 tons)	3	1861	4	4245
纸及纸板(未切成型的)(吨)	Paper and Paperboard in Rolls (ton)	23	35	853	318
原木(吨)	Logs (ton)	7196	164	9772	289
医疗仪器及器械	Medical Instruments and Appliances		5379		5080
肥料(万吨)	Fertilizers (10 000 tons)	3	758	0.01	4
原油(万吨)	Crude Oil (10 000 tons)	309	200346	14	7862
成品油(万吨)	Petroleum Products Refined (10 000 tons)	19	10407	2	884
牛皮革及马皮革(吨)	Cattle and Horse Leather (ton)	41789	4091	49198	5321

5-3 新疆同各国(地区)海关进出口总额
Value of Xinjiang's Imports and Exports by Countries(Region) of Destination

单位：万美元 (USD 10 000)

国别(地区)	Country (Region)	2014			2015		
		进出口总额 Total Value of Imports and Exports	出口额 Exports	进口额 Imports	进出口总额 Total Value of Imports and Exports	出口额 Exports	进口额 Imports
合　计	**Total**	**2766930**	**2348255**	**418675**	**1967789**	**1750600**	**217189**
亚　洲	**Asia**	**2191244**	**1995487**	**195757**	**1375576**	**1268808**	**106768**
阿富汗	Afghanistan	7532	7419	113	6540	6384	156
巴　林	Bahrain	3360	3360		232	232	
孟加拉国	Bangladesh	3333	3326	7	2001	1946	55
文　莱	Brunei Darussalam	2418	2418		511	511	
缅　甸	Myanmar	3049	3049		913	911	2
柬埔寨	Cambodia	441	441		185	185	
塞浦路斯	Cyprus	211	211		19	19	
朝　鲜	Korea DPR	4041	2995	1046	462	462	
香　港	Hong Kong, China	7097	7092	5	2460	2453	7
印　度	India	44518	41316	3202	22023	19795	2228
印度尼西亚	Indonesia	17921	17503	418	6934	5914	1020
伊　朗	Iran	79647	79503	144	59121	57101	2020
伊拉克	Iraq	1289	1236	53	704	692	12
以色列	Israel	2431	1893	538	2326	2110	216
日　本	Japan	14863	8704	6159	13565	7558	6007
约　旦	Jordan	2740	2740		398	396	2
科威特	Kuwait	854	854		315	315	
老　挝	Laos	12	12		65	65	
黎巴嫩	Lebanon	1786	1786		1202	1202	
澳　门	Macao	8	8		930	930	
马来西亚	Malaysia	38399	37082	1317	16370	14646	1724
马尔代夫	Maldives	16	16		48	48	
蒙　古	Mongolia	41837	37681	4156	9981	4125	5856
尼泊尔联邦民主共和国	Nepal	61	61		60	15	45
阿　曼	Aman	2809	2809		788	788	
巴基斯坦	Pakistan	31853	29051	2802	31255	26221	5034
巴勒斯坦	Palestine	100	100		22	22	
菲律宾	Philppines	6390	6358	32	5913	5636	277
卡塔尔	Qatar	2089	2073	16	128	128	
沙特阿拉伯	Saudi Arabia	15787	15564	223	9921	9517	404
新加坡	Singapore	27403	26477	926	20551	19643	908
韩　国	Korea Rep.	30700	27972	2728	11480	8521	2959
斯里兰卡	Sri Lanka	1519	1459	60	1267	1213	54
叙利亚	Syria	247	247		76	76	
泰　国	Thailand	12199	12053	146	13442	13130	312
土耳其	Turkey	12993	9540	3453	8823	5554	3269
阿联酋	United Arab Emirates	25307	25151	156	11565	11479	86
也　门	Yemen	2251	2251		1164	1164	
越　南	Vietnam	22774	21958	816	7510	7261	249
中华人民共和国	P.R.China	245		245	1672	21	1651
台湾省	Taiwan,China	5057	3907	1150	2912	2833	79
东帝汶	Timor Leste	15	15		9	9	
哈萨克斯坦	Kazakhstan	1012954	878754	134200	574789	526152	48637
吉尔吉斯斯坦	Kirghizia	409776	405974	3802	323737	319972	3765
塔吉克斯坦	Tadzhikistan	201164	200119	1045	139308	137797	1511
土库曼斯坦	Turkmenistan	13291	13013	278	9153	8466	687
乌兹别克斯坦	Uzbekistan	76457	49936	26521	52726	35190	17536
非　洲	**Africa**	**86300**	**85116**	**1184**	**55228**	**54478**	**750**
阿尔及利亚	Algeria	6490	6490		5353	5353	
安哥拉	Angola	10629	10560	69	23662	23428	234

5-3 续表 1 Continued

单位：万美元 (USD 10 000)

国 别 (地 区)	Country (Region)	2014			2015		
		进出口总额 Total Value of Imports and Exports	出口额 Exports	进口额 Imports	进出口总额 Total Value of Imports and Exports	出口额 Exports	进口额 Imports
贝 宁	Benin	1905	1905		491	491	
博茨瓦纳	Botswana	61	61		31	31	
喀麦隆	Cameroon	2137	2137		1598	1598	
佛得角	Cape Verde	23	23				
乍 得	Chad	2	2				
科摩罗	Comoros	39	39				
刚果(布)	Congo	1129	1129		133	133	
吉布提	Djibouti	923	923		851	851	
埃及	Egypt	3175	2715	460	1735	1465	270
赤道几内亚	Eq. Guinea	10	10				
埃塞俄比亚	Ethiopia	766	766		649	649	
加 纳	Ghana	3320	3320		3740	3740	
冈比亚	Gambia	201	201		37	37	
加 蓬	Gabon	313	313		104	104	
几内亚	Guinea	2056	2056		454	454	
几内亚比绍	Guinea Bissau	15	15				
科特迪瓦	Cote d'lvoire	1375	1375		907	907	
肯尼亚	Kenya	4921	4921		3002	3002	
利比里亚	Liberia	202	202		95	95	
利比亚	Libya	1719	1719		230	230	
马达加斯加	Madagascar	510	509	1	183	183	
马拉维	Malawi	67	67		133	133	
毛里塔尼亚	Mauritania	246	246		65	65	
毛里求斯	Mauritius	828	828		99	99	
摩洛哥	Morocco	1071	1071		501	500	1
莫桑比克	Mozambique	2255	2255		159	159	
纳米比亚	Namibia	581	577	4	222	222	
尼日尔	Niger	100	100		27	27	
尼日利亚	Nigeria	14279	14210	69	3436	3423	13
留尼汪	Reunion	27	27		18	18	
卢旺达	Rwanda	2	2		13	13	
塞内加尔	Senegal	3308	3308		1470	1470	
塞拉利昂	Sierra Leone	35	35		23	23	
塞舌尔	Seychelles	20	20				
索马里	Somalia	114	114		4	4	
南 非	South Africa	6942	6367	575	2569	2346	223
苏 丹	Sudan	1986	1986		1365	1364	1
坦桑尼亚	Tanzania	2665	2665		571	571	
多 哥	Togo	3091	3091		320	320	
突尼斯	Tunisia	447	441	6	81	73	8
乌干达	Uganda	249	249		335	335	
布基纳法索	Burkina Faso	4	4				
刚果(金)	Congo DR	599	599		199	199	
赞比亚	Zambia	5165	5165		315	315	
莱索托	Lesotho	49	49				
津巴布韦	Zimbabwe	198	198		7	7	
南苏丹共和国	Republic of South Sudan				41	41	
斯威士兰	Swaziland	10	10				
厄立特里亚	Eritrea	41	41				

5-3 续表 2 Continued

单位：万美元 (USD 10 000)

国 别 (地 区)	Country (Region)	2014			2015		
		进出口总额 Total Value of Imports and Exports	出口额 Exports	进口额 Imports	进出口总额 Total Value of Imports and Exports	出口额 Exports	进口额 Imports
欧 洲	**Europe**	**357980**	**169966**	**188014**	**269939**	**216389**	**53550**
比利时	Belgium	3567	3425	142	5425	5205	220
丹 麦	Denmark	734	387	347	305	132	173
英 国	United Kingdom	15202	13988	1214	23416	22719	697
德 国	Germany	32728	15678	17050	44182	20712	23470
法 国	France	6417	5082	1335	6482	5329	1153
爱尔兰	Ireland	495	239	256	320	43	277
意大利	Italy	9458	6345	3113	14030	9224	4806
卢森堡	Luxembourg	88		88			
荷 兰	Netherlands	11655	11547	108	29653	28886	767
希 腊	Greece	1634	1619	15	1848	1845	3
葡萄牙	Portugal	589	584	5	1442	726	716
西班牙	Spain	6254	6186	68	9772	9718	54
阿尔巴尼亚	Albania	137	137		73	73	
奥地利	Austria	865	386	479	1012	458	554
保加利亚	Bulgaria	267	267		392	264	128
芬 兰	Finland	1661	494	1167	2623	250	2373
匈牙利	Hungary	113	76	37	123	93	30
冰岛	Iceland				2	2	
马耳他	Malta	1085	1085		796	796	
摩纳哥	Monaco	8	8				
挪 威	Norway	905	725	180	530	346	184
波 兰	Poland	3830	3519	311	4999	4992	7
罗马尼亚	Romania	2084	1817	267	2121	1593	528
瑞 典	Sweden	2543	296	2247	2580	1075	1505
瑞 士	Switzerland	2542	547	1995	1709	331	1378
爱沙尼亚	Estonia	43	41	2	17	13	4
拉脱维亚	Latvia	57	57		125	125	
立陶宛	Lithuania	421	414	7	364	303	61
格鲁吉亚	Georgia	3226	3143	83	1570	1423	147
亚美尼亚	Armenia	25	25		7	7	
阿塞拜疆	Azerbaijan	14001	12495	1506	10488	9053	1435
白俄罗斯	Byelorussia	332	70	262	608	73	535
摩尔多瓦	Moldavia	18	18		14	14	
俄罗斯联邦	Russia	215089	59468	155621	93809	81657	12152
乌克兰	Ukraine	17754	17684	70	7905	7849	56
斯洛文尼亚	Slovenia	442	430	12	509	509	
克罗地亚	Croatia	182	182		106	106	
捷 克	Czech	844	817	27	514	379	135
斯洛伐克	Slovak	573	573		9	9	
前南马其顿	Macedonia	6	6		2		2
波 黑	Bosnia & Herzegovina	1	1				
塞尔维亚	Serbia	56	56		55	55	
黑 山	Montenegro	49	49		2	2	
拉丁美洲	**Latin America**	**30604**	**28628**	**1976**	**31683**	**28362**	**3321**
阿根廷	Argentina	1546	687	859	1482	1028	454
阿鲁巴	Aruba	23	23		25	25	
巴哈马	Bahamas	68	68				
巴巴多斯	Barbados	6	6				

5-3 续表 3 Continued

单位：万美元 (USD 10 000)

国别 (地区)	Country (Region)	2014			2015		
		进出口总额 Total Value of Imports and Exports	出口额 Exports	进口额 Imports	进出口总额 Total Value of Imports and Exports	出口额 Exports	进口额 Imports
伯利兹	Belize				2	2	
多民族玻利维亚国	Bolivia	15	15		4	4	
巴　西	Brazil	6736	6580	156	5294	3979	1315
智　利	Chile	3118	2374	744	4259	3884	375
哥伦比亚	Colombia	1406	1406		1365	1365	
多米尼克	Dominica	19	19				
哥斯达黎加	Costa Rica	91	91		123	123	
古　巴	Cuba	37	37		59	59	
多米尼加共和国	Dominica Rep	73	73		151	151	
厄瓜多尔	Ecuador	335	335		201	175	26
格林纳达	Granada	20	20				
危地马拉	Guatemala	100	100		355	355	
圭亚那	Guyana	8	8				
海　地	Haiti	111	111		220	220	
洪都拉斯	Honduras	55	41	14	86	20	66
牙买加	Jamaica	520	520		457	457	
墨西哥	Mexico	4794	4713	81	9710	9160	550
尼加拉瓜	Nicaragua	5	5		8	8	
巴拿马	Panama	8751	8751		3813	3813	
巴拉圭	Paraguay	54	54		25	25	
秘　鲁	Peru	1063	1003	60	1987	1730	257
波多黎各	Puerto Rico	41	41		136	136	
圣卢西亚	Saint Lucia	73	73		3	3	
萨尔瓦多	EL Salvador	75	75		11	11	
苏里南	Surinam	71	71		372	372	
特立尼达和多巴哥	Trinidad and Tobago	21	21		19	19	
乌拉圭	Uruguay	339	277	62	724	446	278
委内瑞拉	Venezuela	970	970		790	790	
荷属安的列斯群岛	Andreas Islands (N)	60	60		2	2	
北美洲	**North America**	**84986**	**61151**	**23835**	**220803**	**173611**	**47192**
加拿大	Canada	8247	6312	1935	13618	10131	3487
美　国	United States	76739	54839	21900	207185	163480	43705
大洋洲	**Oceanic**	**15816**	**7907**	**7909**	**14560**	**8952**	**5608**
澳大利亚	Australia	14351	6476	7875	13163	7571	5592
斐　济	Fiji	112	112		103	103	
新喀里多尼亚	New Caledonia (Fr)	12	12		4	4	
瓦努阿图	Vanuatu	8	8		1	1	
新西兰	New Zealand	1194	1166	28	1160	1144	16
巴布亚新几内亚	Papua New Guinea	81	81		46	46	
所罗门群岛	Solomon Islands	37	37		78	78	
汤　加	Tonga	10	10				
萨摩亚	Samoa	2	2		5	5	
法属波利尼西亚	Polynesia (F)	1	1				
大洋洲其他国家（地区）	Other Counties (Regions)	2	2				
其　他	**Others**	**6**		**6**			

5-4 按贸易方式和登记注册类型分的海关进出口额
Total Value of Imports and Exports by Customs Type and Registration

单位：万美元 (USD 10 000)

项目	Item	2014			2015		
		进出口总额 Total Imports and Exports	出口额 Exports	进口额 Imports	进出口总额 Total Imports and Exports	出口额 Exports	进口额 Imports
总　计	**Total**	**2766930**	**2348255**	**418675**	**1967789**	**1750600**	**217189**
按贸易方式分	**By Customs Regime**						
一般贸易	Ordinary Trades	1099969	849589	250380	837606	682147	155459
加工贸易	Processing Trades	45138	29927	15211	26307	14779	11528
边境小额贸易	Petty-volume Border Trades	1422553	1284704	137849	961946	935045	26901
其它贸易	Other Trades	199270	184035	15235	141930	118629	23301
按登记注册类型分	**By Registration Status**						
国有经济	State-owned Units	552224	242683	309541	289282	202702	86580
集体经济	Collective-owned Units	20390	17373	3017	10063	8826	1237
私营经济	Private-owned Units	2173090	2079336	93754	1641693	1531399	110294
三资企业	Three Kinds of Ventures	21219	8863	12356	25143	7426	17717
其它经济	Other Types of Ownership	7		7	1608	247	1361

5-5 主要年份人民币对主要外币年平均汇价(中间价)
Average Exchange Rate of RMB Yuan Against Main Foreign Currency in Main Years (Medium Rate)

单位：人民币元 (RMB yuan)

年份 Year	100美元 100 US Dollars	100日元 100 JapaneseYen	100港元 100 Hong Kong Dollars	100欧元 100 Euros
1985	293.66	1.25	37.57	
1990	478.32	3.32	61.39	
1995	835.10	8.92	107.96	
1996	831.42	7.64	107.51	
1997	828.98	6.86	107.09	
1998	827.91	6.35	106.88	
1999	827.83	7.29	106.66	
2000	827.84	7.69	106.18	
2001	827.70	6.81	106.08	
2002	827.70	6.62	106.07	800.58
2003	827.70	7.15	106.24	936.13
2004	827.68	7.66	106.23	1029.00
2005	819.17	7.45	105.30	1019.53
2006	797.18	6.86	102.62	1001.90
2007	760.40	6.46	97.46	1041.75
2008	694.51	6.74	89.19	1022.27
2009	683.10	7.29	88.12	952.70
2010	676.95	7.73	87.13	897.25
2011	645.88	8.11	82.97	900.11
2012	631.25	7.90	81.38	810.67
2013	619.32	6.30	79.80	822.19
2014	614.28	5.80	79.20	816.51
2015	622.84	5.15	80.34	691.41

5-6 对外承包工程和劳务合作
Contracted Projects and Labour Services with Foreign Countries or Territories

单位：万美元 (USD 10 000)

项　目	Item	2014	2015
新签合同金额	Newly Signed Contracted Value	206491	204640
实际营业额	Actual Business Volume	217309	218479

5-7 外商直接投资
Foreign Direct Investment

单位：个、万美元 (unit, USD 10 000)

指　标	Item	2014			2015		
		项　目 Number of Projects	合同金额 Contract Value	实际使用金额 Used Value	项　目 Number of Projects	合同金额 Contract Value	实际使用金额 Used Value
总　计	**Total**	**49**	**52604**	**41700**	**50**	**85651**	**45250**
独资经营企业	Foreign Investment Enterprises	32	21683	15600	35	32318	12150
合资经营企业	Joint Ventures Enterprises	15	25849	11470	13	20225	12973
合作经营企业	Cooperative Operation Enterprises	2	5000	117	1	680	4
股份制企业	Share-holding Corporations Ltd.		72	14513	1	32428	20123

5-8 外国和港澳台地区在新疆直接投资情况

Basic Conditions of Direct Investment in China by Foreign Countries and Compatriots from Hongkong, Macao and Taiwan

单位：个、万美元　　(2015 年)　　(unit, USD 10 000)

项　目	Item	签订协议情况 Signed Agreements		实际使用外资金额 Used Amount of Foreign Investment	年末实有企业个数 Number of Enterprises at Year-end
		企业(项目)个数 Number of Contracts	合同外资金额 Actually Used Amount of Region Investment		
总　计	**Total**	**50**	**85651**	**45250**	**554**
按企业类型分	**Grouped by Status of Enterprises**				
独资经营企业	Foreign Investment Enterprises	35	32318	12150	311
合资经营企业	Joint Ventures Enterprises	13	20225	12973	209
合作经营企业	Cooperative Operation Enterprises	1	680	4	24
外商投资股份制企业	Foreign Investment Share Enterprises	1	32428	20123	10
按国民经济行业分	**Grouped by Economic Sector**				
农、林、牧、渔业	Agriculture Forestry, Animal Husbandry and Fishery	6	9948	1311	39
采矿业	Mining		161	2577	29
制造业	Manufacturing	7	19937	27015	200
电力、煤气及水的生产和供应业	Production and Supply of Electricity, Gas and Water	2	7131	3466	32
建筑业	Construction				19
交通运输、仓储及邮电通讯业	Transport, Storage, Post and Telecommunications	2	17842	5360	56
信息传输、计算机服务和软件业	Information Transmission, Computer Servics and Software	1	78		306
批发和零售业	Wholesale and Retail Trades	17	3331	3327	367
住宿和餐饮业	Accommodation and Catering Service	3	13	6	79
金融业	Financial Intermediation	4	26010		42
房地产业	Real Estate			273	20
租赁和商务服务业	Leasing and Business Services	5	771	209	113
科学研究、技术服务和地质勘察业	Scientific Research, Technical Service and Geological Prospecting	2	328	1651	39
水利、环境和公共设施管理业	Water Conservancy, Environment and Public Facility Management				8
居民服务和其他服务业	Services to Households and Other Services	1	100	55	24
教　育	Education		1		10
文化、体育和娱乐业	Culture,Sports and Entertainment				1
按国别、地区分	**By Country or Territory**				
中国香港	Hong Kong,China	23	53263	16634	197
中国台湾	Taiwan,China	2	388	3	23
日　本	Japan			80	10
美　国	United States		25	5	28
加拿大	Canada	3	96	65	13
德　国	Federal Republic of Germany	1	1000	1144	8
土耳其	Turkey	1	8	13	
英　国	United Kingdom	1	3	18	6
荷　兰	Netherlands	1	7	1359	
新加坡	Singapore			810	
澳大利亚	Australia	1	82	661	15
哈萨克斯坦	Kazarhstan	5	-227	1184	
俄罗斯联邦	Russia	1		24	7
马来西亚	Malaysia			500	
韩　国	Republic of Korea	4	-483	8	26

注：年末实有企业个数，按企业类型分 554 个；按国民经济行业分 1384 个（其中包括了 828 个外商投资企业分支机构和 2 个外商投资合伙企业）；按国别地区分 554 个。

Note:There are number of enterprises at the end of year auordhing to the type of entewprise 554,auording to the national economy 1384.(of which in cluding 828 branches of foreign invesed enterprises and 2 foreign invested enterprises) auording to the counery 554.

5-9 各地、州、市利用外商直接投资情况

Conditions of Foreign Direct Investment Used by Prefecture, Autonomous Prefecture and City

单位：个、万美元 (unit, USD 10 000)

地区	Region	2014			2015		
		签订合同数 Number of Contracts	合同金额 Contract Value	实际使用投资 Amount of Foreingn Capital Actually Used	签订合同数 Number of Contracts	合同金额 Contract Value	实际使用投资 Amount of Foreign Capital Actually Used
总　计	**Total**	**49**	**52604**	**41700**	**50**	**85651**	**45250**
乌鲁木齐市	Urumqi City	30	15363	18309	26	41791	24079
克拉玛依市	Karamay City				1	2	
石河子市	Shihezi City	2	12813	5282	5	1384	2820
吐鲁番市	Turpan City			8	2	684	518
哈密地区	Hami [Kumul] Administrative Offices			1406	1	8333	3365
昌吉回族自治州	Changji Hui Autonomous Prefecture	4	4346	6096	3	3748	3597
伊犁哈萨克自治州	Ili Kazak Autonomous Prefecture	4	4685	3091	5	26310	3755
伊犁州直属县(市)	Counties (Cities) Direct Under Ili Prefecture	2	2952	819	4	24610	2335
塔城地区	Tacheng [Tarbagatai] Administrative Offices	1	668	664	1	500	2
阿勒泰地区	Altay Administrative Offices	1	1065	1608		1200	1418
博尔塔拉蒙古自治州	Bortala Mongol Autonomous Prefecture			22	1	472	
巴音郭楞蒙古自治州	BayangolMongol Autonomous Prefecture	6	12599	2941	2	536	2737
阿克苏地区	Aksu Administrative Offices			3315		126	572
克孜勒苏柯尔克孜自治州	Kizilsu Kirgiz Autonomous Prefecture	1	-852	917			570
喀什地区	Kashgar [Kaxgar] Administrative Offices	2	3649	313	3	35	1008
和田地区	Hotan Administrative Offices		1		1	2230	2229

5-10 新疆在外国和港澳台地区直接投资

Direct Investment in Foreign Countries and Hong Kong，Macao and Taiwan Made by Xinjiang Partner

单位：万美元 (USD 10 000)

年份 Year	投资额 Investment	年份 Year	投资额 Investment
2005	5280	2012	25920
2008	6863	2013	39968
2009	28619	2014	58884
2010	47809	2015	90823
2011	41803		

5-11 主要年份旅游事业发展情况
Development of Tourism in Main Years

项　目	Item	2000	2010	2015
旅行社总数(个)	**Total Number of Travel Agencies (unit)**	**130**	**462**	**339**
入境旅游人数(人)	**Total Number of Overseas Vistor Arrivals (person)**	**256082**	**1065261**	**1683550**
外国人	Foreigners	208374	1010294	1611535
#日　本	Japan	51974	32629	6252
新加坡	Singapore	5137	6269	5365
美　国	United States	10231	27603	8045
英　国	United Kingdom	3702	18289	6254
法　国	France	5218	10818	8643
德　国	Federal Republic of Germany	6310	10540	8346
独联体	Commonwealth of Independent States	76966	689063	1375807
香港同胞	Compatriots from Hong Kong	12710	17111	17248
澳门同胞	Compatriots from Macao	1387	5395	7859
台湾同胞	Compatriots from Taiwan	33611	32461	46908
按地区分	**By Regions**			
乌鲁木齐市	Urumqi City	144830	581624	287182
克拉玛依市	Karamay City	505	1325	6942
石河子市	Shihezi City	532	510	129
吐鲁番市	Turpan City	43641	71210	23945
哈密地区	Hami [Kumul]Administrative Offices	624	20145	14007
昌吉回族自治州	Changji Hui Autonomous Prefecture	213	1120	16091
伊犁哈萨克自治州	Ili Kazak Autonomous Prefecture	18204	266934	1235225
伊犁州直属县(市)	Counties (Cities) Direct Under Ili Prefecture	15356	217613	1046272
塔城地区	Tacheng [Tarbagatai] Administrative Offices	298	13693	38027
阿勒泰地区	Altay Administrative Offices	2550	35628	150926
博尔塔拉蒙古自治州	Bortala Mongol Autonomous Prefecture	672	27105	50918
巴音郭楞蒙古自治州	BayangolMongol Autonomous Prefecture	7313	6012	18034
阿克苏地区	Aksu Administrative Offices	6028	3001	3891
克孜勒苏柯尔克孜自治州	Kizilsu Kirgiz Autonomous Prefecture	2100	20861	10267
喀什地区	Kashgar [Kaxgar] Administrative Offices	27510	43665	14026
和田地区	Hotan Administrative Offices	3910	21749	2893
国内旅游人数(万人)	**Number of Domestic Visitors (10 000 persons)**	**758**	**3038**	**5929**
疆内居民出境游(人)	**Number of Domestic Resident Outbound Visitors (person)**	**4535**	**12499**	**63972**
旅游消费	**Consumption Tourism**			
入境旅游消费(万美元)	Inbound Tourism Consumption (USD 10 000)			60775
国内旅游消费(亿元)	Domestic Tourism Consumption (100 million yuan)			985

注：1. 从2015年开始,旅游部门对旅游主要经济指标进行了调整，将"旅游收入"调整为"旅游消费"。 2. 旅游消费是指人们在旅行游览过程中，为了满足其自身发展和享受的需要所消费的旅游产品和服务的价值总和。通俗是指游客以旅游为目的在准备旅游阶段及进行旅游阶段所产生的消费，如：在交通、住宿、餐饮、购物、娱乐、参观等等环节所产生的消费。

Note:Since 2015,the Sector of Tourism has adjusted the main economic indicators of tourisn ,the tourism revenue was adjusted to tourism consumotion.Tourism consumption is the sum of the value of tourism products and services that are consumed in order to meet the needs of their own development and enjoyment.Popular refers to the tourism to travel for the purpose of tourism in the preparation stage and the stage of consumption,such as in transportation, accommodation ,catering, shopping, entertainment ,tourism and other aspects of the production or consumption.

5-12 各地、州、市旅行社及旅游宾馆(酒店)基本情况
Accommodation of Travel Agencies and Tourist Hotels by Prefecture, Autonomous Prefecture and City

(2015 年)

地区	Region	旅行社(个) Number of Travel Agencies (unit)	星级宾馆(个) Number of Star-rated Hotels (unit)	客房(间) Number of Rooms (unit)	床位(张) Number of Beds (unit)
总计	**Total**	**339**	**404**	**46715**	**85109**
乌鲁木齐市	Urumqi City	159	60	10805	19015
克拉玛依市	Karamay City	14	16	1424	2468
吐鲁番市	Turpan City	11	30	2505	4888
哈密地区	Hami [Kumul] Administrative Offices	6	14	1671	2950
昌吉回族自治州	Changji Hui Autonomous Prefecture	13	32	2820	5140
伊犁哈萨克自治州	Ili Kazak Autonomous Prefecture	69	113	11308	21332
伊犁州直属县(市)	Counties (Cities) Direct Under Ili Prefecture	39	56	5030	9567
塔城地区	Tacheng [Tarbagatai] Administrative Offices	6	15	1303	2410
阿勒泰地区	Altay Administrative Offices	24	42	4975	9355
博尔塔拉蒙古自治州	Bortala Mongol Autonomous Prefecture	4	9	660	1244
巴音郭楞蒙古自治州	Bayangol Mongol Autonomous Prefecture	18	37	4309	7895
阿克苏地区	Aksu Administrative Offices	6	38	4198	7749
克孜勒苏柯尔克孜自治州	Kizilsu Kirgiz Autonomous Prefecture	3	3	454	804
喀什地区	Kashgar [Kaxgar] Administrative Offices	30	37	5323	9443
和田地区	Hotan Administrative Offices	6	15	1238	2181

注：本表数据不含兵团数据。
Note:The date of this table don't cover the date of XJPCC.

5-13 各地、州、市旅游消费情况
Tourism Consumption by Prefecture, Autonomous Prefecture and City

(2015 年)

地　区	Region	入境旅游消费 (万美元) Inbond Tourism Consumption (USD 10 000)	国内旅游消费 (万元) Domestic Tourism Consumption (10 000 yuan)
总　计	**Total**	**60775**	**9850000**
乌鲁木齐市	Urumqi City	17771	3827131
克拉玛依市	Karamay City	336	402176
石河子市	Shihezi City	6	381759
吐鲁番市	Turpan City	1204	702109
哈密地区	Hami [Kumul] Administrative Offices	746	157076
昌吉回族自治州	Changji Hui Autonomous Prefecture	756	1030871
伊犁哈萨克自治州	Ili Kazak Autonomous Prefecture	35659	1874620
伊犁州直属县(市)	Counties (Cities) Direct Under Ili Prefecture	29839	974180
塔城地区	Tacheng [Tarbagatai] Administrative Offices	1211	289345
阿勒泰地区	Altay Administrative Offices	4609	611095
博尔塔拉蒙古自治州	Bortala Mongol Autonomous Prefecture	1523	174910
巴音郭楞蒙古自治州	BayangolMongol Autonomous Prefecture	951	726501
阿克苏地区	Aksu Administrative Offices	169	245910
克孜勒苏柯尔克孜自治州	Kizilsu Kirgiz Autonomous Prefecture	761	39806
喀什地区	Kashgar [Kaxgar] Administrative Offices	762	228631
和田地区	Hotan Administrative Offices	131	58500

5-14 入境旅游消费及构成
Inbound Tourism Consumption and Composition

单位：万美元、% (USD 10 000,%)

指　　标	Item	2014 金额 Value	2014 比重 Percentage	2015 金额 Value	2015 比重 Percentage
总　计	**Total**	**49704**	**100**	**60775**	**100**
长途交通费	Long Distance Transportation	19583	39.4	25921	42.65
民　航	Air	13967	28.1	18682	30.74
铁　路	Railway	3678	7.4	5646	9.29
汽　车	Highway	1398	3.9	1593	2.62
游　览	Sightseeing	3479	7	1349	2.22
住　宿	Accommodation	5915	11.9	5585	9.19
餐　饮	Food anf Beverage	3628	7.3	4163	6.85
商品销售	Shopping	7804	15.7	11292	18.58
娱　乐	Entertainment	3181	6.4	1513	2.49
邮电通信	Postul and Communication Services	1292	2.6	3823	6.29
市内交通	Local Transportation	1243	2.5	650	1.07
其他服务	Other Service	3579	7.2	6479	10.66

5-15 接待外国旅游人数(按国别分)
Number of Foreign Tourists Received by Country

单位：人 (person)

国　别	Country	2014	2015	国　别	Country	2014	2015
总　计	**Total**	**1438259**	**1611535**	德　国	Federal Republic of Germany	7045	8346
亚　洲	**Asia**	**1218641**	**1432496**	法　国	France	6836	8643
印　度	India	803	1161	意大利	Italy	1650	3795
印度尼西亚	Indonesia	771	921	西班牙	Spain	773	2088
日　本	Japan	7013	6252	瑞　典	Sweden	1136	1747
马来西亚	Malaysia	8527	6167	瑞　士	Switzerland	2645	2510
蒙　古	Mongolia	80353	110360	独联体(欧洲部分)	Commonwealth of Independent States (Europe)	167172	105502
菲律宾	The Philppines	966	891	其　他	Others	4530	4345
新加坡	Singapore	5083	5365	**北美洲**	**North America**	**12711**	**18472**
韩　国	Republic of Korea	9072	7591	加拿大	Canada	3809	6856
泰　国	Thailand	1438	2574	美　国	United States	6861	8045
巴基斯坦	Pakistan	5133	10297	其　他	Others	2041	3571
哈萨克斯坦	Haskistan	1090080	1270305	**大洋洲**	**Oceania**	**8381**	**11838**
其　他	Others	9402	10612	澳大利亚	Australia	5542	2822
非　洲	**Africa**	**625**	**1983**	新西兰	New Zealand	1879	2167
欧　洲	**Europe**	**197172**	**143230**	其　他	Others	960	6849
英　国	United Kingdom	5385	6254	**其他小计**	**Other sub-total**	**729**	**3516**

注：表中独联体仅指独联体在欧洲部分的国家。
Note: Commonwealth of Independent State in the table only refer to the part of the countries in Europe.

主要统计指标解释

货物进出口总额 指实际进出我国国境的货物总金额。包括对外贸易实际进出口货物，来料加工装配进出口货物，国家间、联合国及国际组织无偿援助物资和赠送品，华侨、港澳台同胞和外籍华人捐赠品，租赁期满归承租人所有的租赁货物，进料加工进出口货物，边境地方贸易及边境地区小额贸易进出口货物(边民互市贸易除外)，中外合资企业、中外合作经营企业、外商独资经营企业进出口货物和公用物品，到、离岸价格在规定限额以上的进出口货样和广告品(无商业价值、无使用价值和免费提供出口的除外)，从保税仓库提取在中国境内销售的进口货物，以及其他进出口货物。该指标可以观察一个国家在对外贸易方面的总规模。我国规定出口货物按离岸价格统计，进口货物按到岸价格统计。

外商直接投资 是指外国投资者在我国境内通过设立外商投资企业、合伙企业、与中方投资者共同进行石油资源的合作勘探开发以及设立外国公司分支机构等方式进行投资。外国投资者可以用现金、实物、无形资产、股权等投资，还可以用从外商投资企业获得的利润进行再投资。

对外承包工程 根据《对外承包工程管理条例》，对外承包工程是指中国的企业或者其他单位承包境外建设工程项目的活动。

对外劳务合作 指组织劳务人员赴其他国家或地区为国外的企业或机构工作的经营性活动。

入境游客 指报告期内来中国（大陆）观光、度假、探亲访友、就医疗养、购物、参加会议或从事经济、文化、体育、宗教活动的外国人、港澳台同胞等游客（即入境旅游人数）。统计时，入境游客按每入境一次统计1人次。入境旅游人数包括入境过夜游客和入境一日游游客。

出境人数(出境游客） 指中国（大陆）居民因公或因私出境前往其他国家、中国香港特别行政区、澳门特别行政区和台湾省观光、度假、探亲访友、就医疗养、购物、参加会议或从事经济、文化、体育、宗教活动的人数 即出境游客 。统计时，出境游客按每出境一次统计1人次。

国内游客 指在报告期内在中国（大陆）观光游览、度假、探亲访友、就医疗养、购物、参加会议或从事经济、文化、体育、宗教活动的中国（大陆）居民人数，其出游的目的不是通过所从事的活动谋取报酬。统计时，国内游客按每出游一次统计1人次。

国际旅游(外汇)收入 指入境游客在中国（大陆）境内旅行、游览过程中用于交通、参观游览、住宿、餐饮、购物、娱乐等全部花费。

国内旅游收入(旅游总花费) 指国内游客在国内旅行、游览过程中用于交通、参观游览、住宿、餐饮、购物、娱乐等全部花费。

星级饭店 指设备、设施、服务符合《旅游饭店星级的划分与评定》（GB/T14308-2003），通过相关旅游管理部门评定，并取得星级饭店称号的饭店（含预备星级饭店）。

Explanatory Notes on Main Statistical Indicators

Total Import and Export of Goods refer to the real value of commodities imported and exported across the border of China. They include the actual imports and exports through foreign trade, imported and exported goods under the processing and assembling trades and materials, supplies and gifts as aid given gratis between governments and by the United Nations and other international organizations, and contributions donated by overseas Chinese, compatriots in Hong Kong and Macao and Chinese with foreign citizenship, leasing commodities owned by tenant at the expiration of leasing period, the imported and exported commodities processed with imported materials, commodities trading in border areas (excluding mutual exchange goods), the imported and exported commodities and articles for public use of the Sino-foreign joint ventures, cooperative enterprises and ventures with sole foreign investment. Also included is import or export of samples and advertising goods for which CIF or FOB value are beyond the permitted ceiling (excluding goods of no trading or use value and free commodities for export), imported goods sold in China from bonded warehouses and other imported or exported goods. The indicator of the total imports and exports at customs can be used to observe the total size of external trade in a country. In accordance with the stipulation of the Chinese government, imports are calculated at CIF, while exports are calculated at FOB.

Foreign Direct Investment refers to foreign investment in China through the establishment of foreign invested enterprises, cooperative exploration and development of petroleum resources with domestic investors and the establishment of branch organizations of foreign enterprises. Foreign investment can be made in forms of cash, physical investment, intangible assets and equity, in addition with reinvestment of the foreign enterprises with the profits gained from the investment.

Overseas Contracted Projects refer to activities of contracting overseas construction projects by Chinese enterprises or any other units, which are stipulated in the *Regulations on Administration of Foreign Contracted Project*.

Overseas Labour Services refer to operational activities of organizing labour force to go abroad providing services to foreign enterprises or agencies.

Overseas Visitor Arrivals refer to the number of tourists of foreigners, Chinese compatriots from Hong Kong, Macao and Taiwan who come to China (mainland) within the reference period for sight-seeing, vacation, visiting relatives, medical treatment, shopping, attending conference, or to engage in economic, cultural, sports and religious activities (namely the number of overseas visitor arrivals). In compiling statistics, each arrival is counted as one person-time. The number of overseas visitor arrivals includes inbound overnight tourists and one-day tourists.

Number of Chinese Residents Going Abroad (Chinese Outbound Visitors) refers to the number of Chinese (mainland) residents going to other countries, Hong Kong Special Administrative region, Macao Special Administrative region and Taiwan for on official or private purposes, for sight-seeing, vacation, visiting relatives, medical treatment, shopping, attending conference, or to engage in economic, cultural, sports and religious activities (namely the Chinese outbound visitors). In compiling statistics, each time of leaving is counted as one person-time.

Number of Domestic Tourists refers to the number of Chinese (mainland) residents who travel within China (mainland) for sight-seeing, vacation, visiting relatives, medical treatment, shopping, attending conference, or to engage in economic, cultural, sports and religious activities. In compiling statistics, each time of travelling is counted as one person-time.

Foreign Exchange Earnings from International Tourism refer to the total expenditure of foreigners, overseas Chinese, Chinese compatriots from Hong Kong, Macao and Taiwan during their stay in the mainland of China on transportation, sighting, accommodation, food, shopping and entertainment.

Income from Domestic Tourism refer to expenditure of domestic tourists on transportation, sighting, accommodation, food, shopping and entertainment while they travel.

Star-rated Hotels refer to hotels rated with stars as assessed by the relevant tourism authorities according to GB/T14308-2003 standard with reference to their infrastructure, facilities and service levels.

6 资源与环境

NATURAL RESOURCES AND ENVIRONMENT PROTECTION

第六篇 资源与环境

本篇主要内容和资料来源

本篇主要反映新疆维吾尔自治区自然资源、自然状况及环境保护事业发展等情况。主要包括自然资源储量和自然状况及水环境、大气环境、固体废物、声环境、生态环境、环境污染治理投资等内容。

水资源、城市生活垃圾清运及处理、地质灾害、矿产资源资料、土地资源情况、林木资源等资料分别由新疆维吾尔自治区水利厅、住建厅、地震局、国土资源厅、林业厅提供；气象资料由新疆维吾尔自治区气象局提供。环境污染与治理、声环境、工业污染治理投资等情况由新疆维吾尔自治区环境保护厅依据年报资料整理提供。

土地资源仍沿用2008年数据。

Natural Resources and Environment Protection

Main Content and Source of Data

This chapter contain information that reflect the natural conditions and natural resources and data on development of environment protection in Xinjiang Uygur Autonomous Region, including natural resources and natural condition, total water resources, atmosphere environment, solid wastes, environmental noise, eco-environment protection, natural disaster and investments in the treatment of environmental pollution etc.

Data on water resource, collection and disposal of urban consumption wastes, geological disasters, land use, forest resource, etc. are provided respectively by Bureau of Water Conservancy, Bureau of Construction, Seismological Bureau, Bureau of Land and Resources, Forestry Bureau in Xinjiang Uygur Autonomous Region.Meteorological data are provided by the Xinjiang Uygur Autonomous Region Meteorological Bureau. Data on environment pollution and treatment, noise monitoring and on investment in the treatment of industrial pollution are provided by the Xinjiang Environmental Protection Bureau.

Data of land resources still followed 2008 annual data.

6-1 自然资源
Natural Resources

指　　标	Item	2015
自然状况	**State of the Nature**	
经纬度	Longitude and Latitude	
东　经	East Longitude	73　40　96　23
北　纬	North Latitude	34　25　49　10
气　候	Climate	
年平均气温(摄氏度)	Annual Average Temperature (℃)	11.0
北　疆	North Xinjiang	9.0
南　疆	South Xinjiang	13.6
东　疆	East Xinjiang	13.7
年平均降水量(毫米)	Annual Average Precipitation (mm)	195.3
北　疆	North Xinjiang	295.9
南　疆	South Xinjiang	71.3
东　疆	East Xinjiang	52.6
平均日照时数(小时)	Average Sunshine Hours (hour)	2680.3
北　疆	North Xinjiang	2588.6
南　疆	South Xinjiang	2770.8
东　疆	East Xinjiang	2866.5
自然资源	**Natural Resources**	
土地资源(万公顷)	Land Resources (10 000 hectares)	
土地总面积	Total Land Area	16648.97
农用地	Land for Farm Use	6308.48
耕地面积	Cultivated Land	412.46
园地面积	Garden Land	36.42
林地面积	Forest Land	676.48
牧草地面积	Grass Land	5111.38
其他农用地	Other Land for Agriculture use	71.75
建设用地	Land for Construction	123.98
未利用地	Land yet to be Used	10216.51
土地利用率(%)	Land Utilization Rate (%)	38.64
林木资源	Forest Resources	
活立木总蓄积量(万立方米)	Total Standing Forest Stock Volume (10 000 cu.m)	38679
森林蓄积量(万立方米)	Forest Stock Volume (10 000 cu.m)	33654

6-1 续表 Continued

指　标	Item	2015
有林地面积(万公顷)	Woodland Area (10 000 hectares)	236
灌木林地面积(万公顷)	Bush Woodland Area (10 000 hectares)	466
四旁树(万株)	Surrounding Woods (10 000 trees)	25095
森林覆盖率(%)	Forest Coverage Rate (%)	4.24
水资源(亿立方米)	Water Resources (100 million cu.m)	
水资源总量	Total Water Resources Volume	930.40
地表水水资源量	Surface Water Volume	880.10
地下水水资源量	Underground Water Volume	545.00
重复计算量	Volume of Repeated Computation	494.70
主要矿产资源保有储量	**Reserve of Mafor Mineral Resources**	
铁矿(亿吨)	Iron Ore (100 million tons)	26.30
铬铁矿(万吨)	Chromium Ore (10 000 tons)	160.40
铜矿(金属)(万吨)	Copper Ore (10 000 tons)	907.22
铅矿(金属)(万吨)	Lead Ore (10 000 tons)	450.62
锌矿(金属)(万吨)	Zinc Ore (10 000 tons)	1150.77
铝土矿(万吨)	Bauxite(10 000 tons)	55.26
镍矿(金属)(万吨)	Nickel Ore (10 000 tons)	153.23
煤(亿吨)	Coal (100 million tons)	3773.13
耐火粘土(万吨)	Fire-proof Clay (10 000 tons)	539.37
钠硝石(万吨)	Nitratite (10 000 tons)	50394.99
芒硝(Na2SO4) (亿吨)	Mirabilite(Na2SO4) (100 million tons)	915.75
盐矿(NaCl) (亿吨)	Solidum Salt(NaCI) (100 million tons)	132.95
钾盐(KCl) (万吨)	Potassium(KCI) (10 000 tons)	19677.04
石棉(万吨)	Asbest (10 000 tons)	844.14
云母(工业原料) (吨)	Mica(Industrial raw materials) (ton)	54253.04
蛭石(万吨)	Roseite (10 000 tons)	1646.26
水泥用灰岩(亿吨)	Limestone Used for Cement (100 million tons)	41.89
膨润土(万吨)	Bentonite (10 000 tons)	45715.78
饰面用花岗岩(万立方米)	Granite as Veneer (10 000 cu.m)	53645.46

注：1.林木资源为2011年第八次全国森林资源清查、自治区森林资源第六次复查数据（2012年公布）。2.因2009年第二次全国土地调查数据国家尚未反馈，土地资源仍沿用2008年度数据。

Note: a) Figures of 2011 forest resources were form the sixth Autonomous Region Forest Survey(2012 announced).b) Data of land resources followed in 2008.

6-2 主要城市平均气温

Monthly Average Temperature of Major Cities

单位：摄氏度 (2015 年) (℃)

城 市	City	一月 Jan.	二月 Feb.	三月 Mar.	四月 Apr.	五月 May	六月 June	七月 July
乌鲁木齐市	Urumqi City	-8.7	-6.6	1.6	12.0	19.1	21.7	26.6
克拉玛依市	Karamay City	-11.5	-8.5	2.9	14.0	22.6	26.1	29.7
石河子市	Shihezi City	-11.0	-8.7	2.7	14.0	21.7	24.2	27.3
阜康市	Fukang City	-12.2	-8.8	2.7	13.6	21.1	23.6	27.8
米东区	Midong Distrct	-9.7	-7.0	3.0	13.6	21.0	24.4	29.1
伊宁市	Yining [Gulja] City	-4.0	0.1	5.4	14.3	20.0	22.1	26.3
塔城市	Tacheng [Qoqek] City	-7.3	-4.5	0.7	12.2	18.1	22.6	25.2
阿勒泰市	Altay City	-13.3	-10.9	-3.9	9.3	16.8	21.6	23.4
博乐市	Bole [Bor tala] City	-12.1	-8.6	1.6	12.5	20.5	23.0	26.2
库尔勒市	Korla City	-5.1	0.9	9.8	17.2	23.0	24.8	30.7
阿克苏市	Aksu City	-5.2	-0.3	9.4	16.8	21.1	22.6	27.9
阿图什市	Artux City	-2.1	2.1	11.6	17.6	23.0	24.5	30.0
喀什市	Kashgar [Kaxgar] City	-3.1	0.9	10.1	16.4	21.6	23.5	28.3
和田市	Hotan City	-1.0	3.6	12.3	18.3	22.8	24.1	29.6
高昌区	Gaocang Distrct	-3.9	2.6	11.5	20.8	27.6	29.6	33.7
哈密市	Hami [Kumul] City	-7.1	-2.0	6.6	15.2	21.8	24.0	28.2

城 市	City	八月 Aug.	九月 Sept.	十月 Oct.	十一月 Nov.	十二月 Dec.	全年平均 Annual Average
乌鲁木齐市	Urumqi City	23.0	14.5	8.8	0.0	-6.6	8.8
克拉玛依市	Karamay City	26.0	16.4	10.2	1.9	-9.6	10.0
石河子市	Shi Hezi City	23.6	16.1	9.4	1.7	-9.4	9.3
阜康市	Fukang City	23.6	15.1	8.5	0.2	-10.9	8.7
米东区	Midong Distrct	25.1	16.6	9.9	1.1	-8.6	9.9
伊宁市	Yining [Gulja] City	22.2	15.8	11.0	2.3	-2.7	11.1
塔城市	Tacheng [Qoqek] City	22.3	13.4	8.5	0.9	-3.0	9.1
阿勒泰市	Altay City	21.1	11.3	6.7	-1.8	-9.1	5.9
博乐市	Bole [Bor tala] City	22.7	14.4	8.2	1.2	-9.6	8.3
库尔勒市	Korla City	28.1	18.9	13.2	4.8	-4.8	13.5
阿克苏市	Aksu City	24.2	18.0	12.4	4.2	-5.0	12.2
阿图什市	Artux City	26.2	20.5	14.4	6.3	-2.2	14.3
喀什市	Kashgar [Kaxgar] City	24.6	19.2	13.6	5.5	-3.1	13.1
和田市	Hotan City	25.9	20.5	15.5	7.1	-1.2	14.8
高昌区	Gaocang Distrct	29.9	22.0	13.8	6.0	-1.6	16.0
哈密市	Hami [Kumul] City	26.8	17.1	10.1	2.4	-6.5	11.4

6-3 主要城市降水量
Monthly Precipitation of Major Cities

单位：毫米 (2015 年) (millimeter)

城　　市	City	一月 Jan.	二月 Feb.	三月 Mar.	四月 Apr.	五月 May	六月 June	七月 July
乌鲁木齐市	Urumqi City	15.0	15.0	14.5	55.0	23.7	74.3	3.8
克拉玛依市	Karamay City	3.3	0.9	7.0	9.3	4.2	2.2	26.5
石河子市	Shi Hezi City	5.2	15.3	10.5	21.4	16.1	20.9	9.9
阜康市	Fukang City	5.1	4.3	3.7	29.0	17.2	52.4	8.3
米东区	Midong Distrct	7.5	12.4	6.6	39.9	15.7	44.1	3.2
伊宁市	Yining [Gulja] City	20.3	13.2	36.6	27.0	11.9	56.1	34.7
塔城市	Tacheng [Qoqek] City	28.6	23.1	23.1	15.4	31.8	14.2	17.0
阿勒泰市	Altay City	25.4	20.3	15.9	6.8	8.0	5.1	26.9
博乐市	Bole [Bortala] City	2.5	1.2	26.0	14.2	29.4	21.4	21.4
库尔勒市	Korla City	0.5	0.3		7.3	27.4	10.4	2.7
阿克苏市	Aksu City	4.2	3.5		2.2	9.7	11.6	4.9
阿图什市	Artux City	2.6	4.5		2.8	4.5	33.5	2.8
喀什市	Kashgar [Kaxgar] City	1.1	6.6		5.4	1.6	24.2	8.2
和田市	Hotan City	0.8	0.8			9.6	10.5	1.3
高昌区	Gaocang Distrct	0.7				4.0	6.3	0.1
哈密市	Hami [Kumul] City	1.2			10.3	3.5	32.5	13.5

城　　市	City	八月 Aug.	九月 Sept.	十月 Oct.	十一月 Nov.	十二月 Dec.	全年合计 Annual Total
乌鲁木齐市	Urumqi City	53.9	36.5	33.4	32.7	51.1	408.9
克拉玛依市	Karamay City	3.5	24.0	8.6	15.7	6.7	111.9
石河子市	Shihezi City	31.7	15.4	10.5	48.9	21.7	227.5
阜康市	Fukang City	46.5	35.5	12.7	34.7	21.4	270.8
米东区	Midong Distrct	43.7	33.0	23.6	39.4	33.3	302.4
伊宁市	Yining [Gulja] City	20.1	14.5	35.5	105.9	31.8	407.6
塔城市	Tacheng [Qoqek] City	10.6	108.6	24.5	56.2	47.6	400.7
阿勒泰市	Altay City	6.5	46.8	14.7	34.6	56.5	267.5
博乐市	Bole [Bortala] City	29.3	16.9	25.1	55.1	23.0	265.5
库尔勒市	Korla City	12.3	21.1	2.0	1.8	11.9	97.7
阿克苏市	Aksu City	9.4	33.8	0.6	0.3	18.3	98.5
阿图什市	Artux City	11.5	2.4				64.6
喀什市	Kashgar [Kaxgar] City	9.1	2.5	0.4		0.3	59.4
和田市	Hotan City	2.7	9.0			1.8	36.5
高昌区	Gaocang Distrct	2.1	12.4		0.8		26.4
哈密市	Hami [Kumul] City	6.0	3.7	6.0	2.1		78.8

6-4 主要城市日照时数
Monthly Sunshine Hours of Major Cities

单位：小时　　(2015 年)　　(hour)

城　市	City	一月 Jan.	二月 Feb.	三月 Mar.	四月 Apr.	五月 May	六月 June	七月 July
乌鲁木齐市	Urumqi City	127.9	172.2	228.7	282.7	298.8	300.6	353.8
克拉玛依市	Karamay City	128.3	172.9	203.5	242.5	285.1	273.8	321.6
石河子市	Shi Hezi City	68.8	106.9	208.5	271.6	309.7	307.6	371.7
阜康市	Fukang City	57.1	127.4	220.3	279.7	293.7	289.3	332.8
米东区	Midong Distrct	33.0	96.4	203.8	266.0	268.2	268.1	300.3
伊宁市	Yining [Gulja] City	147.1	181.8	228.0	286.9	331.8	297.9	359.8
塔城市	Tacheng [Qoqek] City	136.5	168.3	215.9	278.7	304.2	330.7	349.5
阿勒泰市	Altay City	140.2	183.2	242.9	305.6	315.4	302.1	353.6
博乐市	Bole [Bortala] City	126.6	142.2	186.9	250.5	300.9	284.7	342.3
库尔勒市	Korla City	154.9	166.7	231.4	269.4	301.9	288.4	333.2
阿克苏市	Aksu City	182.5	188.9	266.7	285.2	306.5	321.7	340.5
阿图什市	Artux City	137.1	116.0	203.3	205.6	259.9	291.7	251.3
喀什市	Kashgar [Kaxgar] City	163.0	141.0	225.5	251.7	298.6	340.9	289.9
和田市	Hotan City	181.9	146.7	201.4	217.5	272.2	263.3	282.3
高昌区	Gaocang Distrct	60.5	124.9	187.2	269.2	330.5	282.6	316.2
哈密市	Hami [Kumul] City	209.5	239.3	306.6	293.7	351.3	309.1	359.5

城　市	City	八月 Aug.	九月 Sept.	十月 Oct.	十一月 Nov.	十二月 Dec.	全年合计 Annual Total
乌鲁木齐市	Urumqi City	310.0	263.0	236.7	103.4	121.0	2798.8
克拉玛依市	Karamay City	308.1	216.0	198.6	89.4	35.3	2475.1
石河子市	Shi Hezi City	312.6	263.2	230.7	78.6	19.4	2549.3
阜康市	Fukang City	299.2	256.5	217.4	78.3	34.2	2485.9
米东区	Midong Distrct	283.5	237.1	187.9	36.2	7.2	2187.7
伊宁市	Yining [Gulja] City	299.8	273.1	201.6	115.0	150.1	2872.9
塔城市	Tacheng [Qoqek] City	298.0	236.0	186.9	95.2	103.6	2703.5
阿勒泰市	Altay City	336.5	229.6	203.8	88.5	92.6	2794.0
博乐市	Bole [Bortala] City	301.6	229.2	148.1	55.5	61.6	2430.1
库尔勒市	Korla City	284.8	265.2	264.7	167.6	97.8	2826.0
阿克苏市	Aksu City	276.7	290.1	273.9	212.4	148.8	3093.9
阿图什市	Artux City	232.8	252.3	178.1	143.7	110.8	2382.6
喀什市	Kashgar [Kaxgar] City	275.6	292.1	261.4	205.1	154.6	2899.4
和田市	Hotan City	180.2	254.8	264.2	225.4	162.6	2652.5
高昌区	Gaocang Distrct	277.1	211.9	177.7	81.3	46.3	2365.4
哈密市	Hami [Kumul] City	359.5	289.4	260.9	176.8	211.9	3367.5

6-5 环境保护基本情况
Basic Statistics on Environmental Protection

项　　目	Item	2014	2015
水环境	**Water Environment**		
废水排放总量(亿吨)	Waste Water Discharged (100 million tons)	10.27	9.99
#工业废水排放量	Industrial Waste Water Discharged	3.28	2.84
城镇生活废水排放量	Urban Living Waste Water Discharged	6.99	7.14
集中式治理设施废水排放量	Centralized Treatment for Waste Water Facilities		0.01
化学需氧量排放量(万吨)	COD Emission (10 000 tons)	67.02	66.02
#工业化学需氧量排放量	Industryial COD Emission	18.70	18.34
城镇生活化学需氧量排放量	Urban Living COD Emission	11.74	12.93
农业化学需氧量排放量	Agricutral COD Emission	36.16	34.52
集中式治理设施化学需氧量排放量	Amount of Centralized Treatment for COD Facilities	0.43	0.23
氨氮排放量(万吨)	Ammonia Nitrogen Discharged (10 000 tons)	4.59	4.56
#工业氨氮排放量	Industrial Ammonia Nitrogen Discharged	1.14	1.09
城镇生活氨氮排放量	Urban Living Ammonia Nitrogen Discharged	2.18	2.23
农业氨氮排放量	Agricultural Ammonia Nitrogen Discharged	1.25	1.21
集中式治理设施氨氮排放量	Amount of Centralized Treatment for Ammonia Nitrogen Facilities	0.02	0.02
大气环境	**Atmosphere Environment**		
工业废气排放量(亿标立方米)	Industrial Waste Gas Emission (100 million cu.m)	22846.46	21037.66
二氧化硫排放量(万吨)	Sulphur Dioxide Emission (10 000 tons)	85.30	77.82
#工业二氧化硫排放量	Industrial Sulphur Dioxide Emission	71.81	62.21
城镇生活二氧化硫排放量	Urban Living Sulphur Dioxide Emission	13.49	15.62
氮氧化物排放量(万吨)	Nitrogen Oxides Emission (10 000 tons)	86.17	73.65

注：自然保护区只包含自治区及国家级自然保护区。
Note: The nature reserves contain the municipality and state level nature protection area.

6-5 续表 1 Continued

项　　目	Item	2014	2015
#工业氮氧化物排放量	Industrial Nitrogen Oxides Emission	53.90	41.48
城镇生活氮氧化物排放量	Urban Living Nitrogen Oxides Emission	2.18	2.86
机动车氮氧化物排放量	Nitrogen Oxides Emission	30.09	29.30
烟(粉)尘排放量(万吨)	Volume of Sulphur Dioxide Emission (10 000 tons)	81.38	59.75
#工业烟(粉)尘排放量	Volume of Industrial Soot Emission	67.60	46.42
城镇生活烟(粉)尘排放量	Urban Living Soot Emission	11.54	11.03
机动车烟(粉)尘排放量(总颗粒物排放量)	Soot Emission by Motor Vehicle	2.23	2.30
固体废物	**Solid Wastes**		
一般工业固体废物产生量(万吨)	Common Industrial Solid Wastes Produced (10 000 tons)	7789.67	7263.83
一般工业固体废物综合利用量(万吨)	Common Industrial Solid Wastes Comprehensively Utilized (10 000 tons)	4333.62	4133.69
一般工业固体废物处置量(万吨)	Common Industrial Solid Wastes Disposed (10 000 tons)	806.79	755.52
一般工业固体废物储存量(万吨)	Stock of Common Industrial Solid Wastes (10 000 tons)	2627.91	2368.41
一般工业固体废物倾倒丢弃量(万吨)	Common Industrial Solid Wastes Discharged (10 000 tons)	26.84	15.39
危险废物产生量（万吨）	Hazardous Waste Produced (10 000 tons)	319.33	328.16
生态环境	**Eco-Environment**		
当年造林面积(万公顷)	Area of Afforestation of the Year (10 000 hectares)	14.91	18.69
自然保护区数(个)	Number of Nature Reserves (unit)	29	29
#国家级	Nation Level	11	11
自然保护区面积(万公顷)	Area of Nature Reserves (10 000 hectares)	1968.93	2136.00
#国家级	Nation Level	1222.59	1222.59

6-5 续表 2 Continued

项　目	Item	2014	2015
自然保护区面积占辖区面积比重(%)	Proportion of Area of Nature Reserves in Total Area of Territory Regions (%)	11.82	12.87
农村生态示范建设个数(个)	Number of Demonstration Zones of Ecology (unit)	48	42
国家级生态乡镇数	Number of Nation Level Eco-towns	41	35
国家级生态村数	Number of Nation Level Eco-village	7	7
自然灾害	**Natural Disaster**		
发生地质灾害起数(次)	Geological Disaster(case)	15	13
发生地震灾害次数(次)	Seismic Disaster(case)	6	4
#5.0 级以上	Magnitude above 5 Richter Scale	5	4
森林火灾次数(次)	Forest Fire (case)	28	19
森林火灾受灾面积 (公顷)	Fire-Affected Forest Area (hectare)	90.71	117.28
森林病虫害发生面积(万公顷)	Forest Area Affected by Disease and Pests (10 000 hectares)	138.30	146.42
森林病虫害防治面积(万公顷)	Forest Area of Prevention from Disease and Pests (10 000 hectares)	62.58	118.94
森林病虫害防治率(%)	Prevention Rate (%)	45.3	81.2
环境污染治理投资	**Investment in the Treatment of Environmental Pollution**		
环境污染治理投资总额(亿元)	Total Investment in Pollution Treatment (100 million yuan)	363.32	211.87
城镇环境基础设施建设投资额	Investment in Urban Environment Infrastructure Construcion	127.56	0.88
工业污染治理项目年完成投资总额	Investment Completed in Treatment Projects of Industrial Pollution	36.77	15.26
当年完成环保验收项目环保投资总额	Investment Completed in Projects of Environmental Protection Acceptance Pollution	198.99	133.67
环境污染治理投资总额相当于新疆生产总值比例(%)	Investment in Pollution Treatment Out of XJ GDP (%)	3.9	2.3
当年施工工业污染治理项目数(个)	Number of Projects in Industrial Pollution Treatment under Construction of The Year (unit)	70	79
当年竣工工业污染治理项目数(个)	Number of Projects Completed in Industrial Pollution Treatment of the Year Projects (unit)	76	52

6-6 水资源情况
Water Resource

年份 Year	地区 Region	水资源总量(亿立方米) Total Amount Of Water Resources (100 million cu.m)	地表水资源量 Surface Water Resources	地下水资源量 Ground Water Resources	地表水与地下水资源重复量 Duplicated Measurement Between surface Water and Groundwater	人均水资源量(立方米/人) Per Capita Water Resources (cu.m/person)
	2000	952.40	897.10	636.29	580.99	5255
	2001	1024.40	966.90	692.31	634.81	5500
	2002	1068.60	1006.00	724.85	662.25	5652
	2003	920.10	863.20	604.30	547.40	4793
	2004	855.40	809.20	502.60	456.40	4390
	2005	962.82	910.66	562.57	510.41	4789
	2006	953.12	903.84	554.13	504.85	4695
	2007	863.80	816.60	514.10	466.90	4168
	2008	802.60	759.50	518.50	475.36	3798
	2009	754.29	713.64	470.47	429.82	3517
	2010	1124.00	1063.00	624.30	563.20	5120
	2011	885.70	841.00	539.80	495.10	4035
	2012	903.20	854.20	557.00	508.00	4141
	2013	956.07	905.58	561.27	510.89	4223
	2014	726.93	686.55	443.93	403.55	3130
	2015	930.40	880.10	545.00	494.70	3943
乌鲁木齐市	Urumqi City	13.29	12.91	5.74	5.36	498
克拉玛依市	Karamay City	0.65	0.05	1.03	0.42	218
石河子市	Shihezi City	0.15	0.07	0.62	0.54	24
吐鲁番市	Turpan City	10.20	8.92	5.20	3.92	1565
哈密地区	Hami [Kumul] Administrative Offices	14.76	13.11	9.72	8.06	2393
昌吉回族自治州	Changji Hui Autonomous Prefecture	40.11	36.08	24.04	20.01	2880
伊犁州直属县(市)	Counties (Cities) Direct Under Ili Prefecture	160.70	157.70	75.36	72.40	5349
塔城地区	Tacheng [Tarbagatai] Administrative Offices	63.71	59.23	31.67	27.19	6220
阿勒泰地区	Altay Administrative Offices	112.90	108.60	45.65	41.31	16901
博尔塔拉蒙古自治州	Bortala Mongol Autonomous Prefecture	26.62	24.36	15.59	13.33	5549
巴音郭楞蒙古自治州	Bayangol Mongol Autonomous Prefecture	141.70	134.80	75.57	68.68	10172
阿克苏地区	Aksu Administrative Offices	79.23	72.37	68.73	61.87	3131
克孜勒苏柯尔克孜自治州	Kizilsu Kirgiz Autonomous Prefecture	69.41	67.63	43.87	42.09	11644
喀什地区	Kashgar [Kaxgar] Administrative Offices	78.72	72.64	80.18	74.10	1750
和田地区	Hotan Administrative Offices	118.20	111.60	61.99	55.43	5085

6-7 供水和用水情况
Water Supply and Water Use

单位：亿立方米 (2015 年) (100 million cu.m)

地 区	Region	供水总量 Water Supply	地表水 Surface Water	地下水 Ground Water	中水利用量 Use of Intermediate Water	用水总量 Water Use	生产 for Production
总 计	**Total**	**577.17**	**456.88**	**119.40**	**0.89**	**577.17**	**561.38**
乌鲁木齐市	Urumqi City	10.91	5.68	4.87	0.36	10.91	8.08
克拉玛依市	Karamay City	6.06	5.13	0.88	0.05	6.06	3.87
石河子市	Shihezi City	5.84	3.32	2.52		5.84	4.77
吐鲁番市	Turpan City	13.46	5.59	7.87		13.46	12.80
哈密地区	Hami [Kumul] Administrative Offices	10.74	5.39	5.14	0.21	10.74	9.87
昌吉回族自治州	Changji Hui Autonomous Prefecture	45.03	23.31	21.66	0.06	45.03	42.67
伊犁州直属县(市)	Counties (Cities) Direct Under Ili Prefecture	52.76	48.44	4.29	0.03	52.76	50.99
塔城地区	Tacheng [Tarbagatai] Administrative Offices	43.13	25.59	17.43	0.11	43.13	42.57
阿勒泰地区	Altay Administrative Offices	32.79	32.43	0.34	0.02	32.79	32.23
博尔塔拉蒙古自治州	Bortala Mongol Autonomous Prefecture	16.08	9.88	6.20		16.08	15.72
巴音郭楞蒙古自治州	Bayangol Mongol Autonomous Prefecture	55.26	38.55	16.70	0.01	55.26	52.93
阿克苏地区	Aksu Administrative Offices	107.63	100.23	7.40		107.63	106.44
克孜勒苏柯尔克孜自治州	Kizilsu Kirgiz Autonomous Prefecture	12.23	11.52	0.67	0.04	12.23	12.03
喀什地区	Kashgar [Kaxgar] Administrative Offices	118.96	97.47	21.49		118.96	117.94
和田地区	Hotan Administrative Offices	46.29	44.35	1.94		46.29	45.65

地 区	Region	第一产业 Primary Industry	第二产业 Secondary Industry	第三产业 Tertiary Industry	居民生活 for Residents' life	生态环境 for Ecological Protection	人均用水量(立方米/人) Per Capita Water Use (cu.m/person)
总 计	**Total**	**546.43**	**12.81**	**2.14**	**10.02**	**5.80**	**2446**
乌鲁木齐市	Urumqi City	6.25	1.50	0.32	1.50	0.97	409
克拉玛依市	Karamay City	3.61	0.18	0.09	0.18	1.23	2022
石河子市	Shihezi City	4.51	0.23	0.03	0.23	0.27	923
吐鲁番市	Turpan City	12.48	0.29	0.03	0.29	0.19	2065
哈密地区	Hami [Kumul] Administrative Offices	9.22	0.53	0.12	0.53	0.22	1741
昌吉回族自治州	Changji Hui Autonomous Prefecture	41.61	0.82	0.24	0.82	0.47	3233
伊犁州直属县(市)	Counties (Cities) Direct Under Ili Prefecture	49.33	1.47	0.19	1.47	0.51	1697
塔城地区	Tacheng [Tarbagatai] Administrative Offices	41.83	0.73	0.02	0.73	0.11	4211
阿勒泰地区	Altay Administrative Offices	31.86	0.26	0.11	0.26	0.13	4909
博尔塔拉蒙古自治州	Bortala Mongol Autonomous Prefecture	15.41	0.24	0.07	0.24	0.17	3276
巴音郭楞蒙古自治州	Bayangol Mongol Autonomous Prefecture	51.83	0.57	0.53	0.59	0.56	3965
阿克苏地区	Aksu Administrative Offices	105.77	0.67		0.67	0.03	4253
克孜勒苏柯尔克孜自治州	Kizilsu Kirgiz Autonomous Prefecture	11.70	0.31	0.02	0.31	0.09	2052
喀什地区	Kashgar [Kaxgar] Administrative Offices	116.25	1.52	0.17	1.52	0.39	2644
和田地区	Hotan Administrative Offices	44.77	0.68	0.21	0.68	0.46	1992

注：石河子市用水量中包含莫索湾灌区用水量。The water use of Shihezi city included irrgated distict of Mosuowan.

6-8 主要年份环保系统机构、人员数

Number of Environmental Protection Agencies and Persons Engaged in Main Years

年 份 Year	机构数 (个) Number of Agencies (unit)	人员数 (人) Total Number of Staff & Workers (person)	#科技人员 Scientific and Technical Personnel	#监测人员 Monitoring Personnel	#监察人员 Supervising and Administrative Personnel
2000	208	1965	110	654	416
2001	208	2096	109	636	420
2002	238	2386	99	692	523
2003	275	2588	107	766	671
2004	288	2694	107	763	701
2005	304	2796	120	758	790
2006	326	2968	125	777	923
2007	326	2962	77	786	955
2008	296	2962	100	812	993
2009	319	3197	103	857	998
2010	324	3237	109	936	1126
2011	335	3372	121	967	1194
2012	324	3459	111	995	1112
2013	335	3438	104	985	1042
2014	440	3854	113	1193	1210
2015	392	3857	61	1068	1150

注：本表数据从 2009 年开始不包含兵团数据（6-12、6-13、6-14 同）。
Note: The date of this table don't cover the date of XJPCC from 2009 (the same as the table of 6-12,6-13,6-14).

6-9 工业按行业重点调查工业企业废气及污染物排放情况

Emission and Treatment of Waste Water and Pollutant in Industrial Enterprises by Sector

单位：吨　　(2015 年)　　(ton)

行 业	Sector	工业废气排放量 (亿立方米) Total Volume of Industrial Waste Gas Emission (100 million cu.m)	工业二氧化硫排放量 Volume of Sulphur Dioxide Emission by Industry	工业氮氧化物排放量 Volume of Nitrogen Oxide Emission by Industry	工业烟(粉)尘排放量 Volume of Industrial Soot Emission
合 计	**Total**	**21037.66**	**622123.10**	**414822.29**	**464213.35**
黑色金属矿采选业	Mining and Processing of Ferrous Metal Ores	18.41	68.11	22.61	3670.85
有色金属矿采选业	Mining and Processing of Non-Ferrous Metal Ores	148.51	713.19	590.82	6989.70
农副产品加工业	Processing of Food from Agricultural Products	155.52	7476.35	3986.21	4402.43
造纸及纸制品业	Manufacture of Paper and Paper Products	12.60	2125.50	433.28	4694.87
石油加工、炼焦及核燃料加工业	Oil Processing, Coking and Nuclear Fuel Processing	1436.60	33668.83	35643.10	15581.04
化学原料及化学制品制造业	Raw Chemical Material and Chemical Products	1605.46	52935.21	41353.13	18905.17
非金属矿物制品业	Nonmetal Mineral Products Manufacturing	2332.18	43640.66	63018.08	79711.59
黑色金属冶炼及压延加工业	Smelting and Pressing of Ferrous Metals	2098.75	45049.29	25331.9	38514.18
有色金属冶炼及压延加工业	Smelting and Pressing of Non-ferrous Metals	3908.02	208365.92	40515.94	33971.30
电力、热力的生产和供应业	Electricity and Thermal Production and Supply	8145.70	193929.28	172164.54	108886.32
其他行业	Ohters	1175.91	34150.77	29019.01	141332.11

6-10 工业按行业重点调查工业企业废水及污染物排放情况

Emission and Treatment of Waste Water and Pollutant in Industrial Enterprises by Sector

(2015 年)

行业	Sector	工业废水排放量(万吨) Volume Of Waste Water Discharged (10 000 tons)	工业废水中化学需氧量排放量(吨) COD Discharge From Industral WasteWater (ton)	工业废水中氨氮排放量(吨) Ammonia Nitrogen Discharge form Industrial Waste Water (ton)
合　计	**Total**	**28410.04**	**183374.85**	**10963.31**
农副食品加工业	Processing of Food from Agricultural Products	2508.65	7686.81	257.32
食品制造业	Food Manufacturing	3015.40	9332.00	309.34
酒、饮料和精制茶制造业	Processing of Food from Agricultural Products	521.39	6438.80	76.04
纺织业	Textile Industry	1104.64	4753.62	138.68
造纸及纸制品业	Paper and Paper Products Manufacturing	1355.54	5722.16	138.49
石油加工、炼焦及核燃料加工业	Oil Processing, Coking and Nuclear Fuel Processing	1922.65	6237.36	2727.97
化学原料及化学制品制造业	Raw Chemical Material and Chemical Products	3774.59	12370.16	3767.96
化学纤维制造业	Chemical Fiber Manufacturing	5747.03	107640.50	2857.83
黑色金属冶炼及压延加工业	Smelting and Pressing of Ferrous Metals	1624.77	11404.83	241.46
电力、热力的生产和供应业	Electricity and Thermal Production and Supply	2151.07	1665.50	149.77
其他行业	Ohters	3792.70	4961.30	221.44

6-11 工业按行业重点调查工业企业固体废物产生量及处理利用情况

Production and Treatment of Waste Solid in Industrial Enterprises by Region

单位：万吔　　(2015 年)　　(10 000 ton)

行业 Sector	一般工业固体废物产生量 Common Industrial Solid Wastes Produced	一般工业固体废物综合利用量 Common Industrial Solid Wastes Comprehensively Utilized	一般工业固体废物贮存量 Stock of Common Industrial Solid Wastes	一般工业固体废物处置量 Common Industrial Solid Wastes Disposed	一般工业固体废物倾倒丢弃量 Common Industrial Solid Wastes Discarded (10 000 tons)
合　计 Total	**7196.03**	**4077.60**	**2363.03**	**750.20**	**14.39**
煤炭开采和洗选业 Mining and Washing of Coal	769.14	599.43	5.68	164.13	0.07
黑色金属矿采选业 Processing of Ferrous Metals Ores	1645.27	422.70	920.89	296.19	5.49
有色金属矿采选业 Processing of Nonferrous Metals Ores	1067.71	87.61	935.48	44.62	
农副产品加工业 Processing of Food from Agricultural Products	34.56	32.56	1.22	0.79	0.45
食品制造业 Food Manufacturing	33.73	31.46		2.11	0.16
纺织业 Textile Industry	1.60	1.43		0.16	0.01
化学原料及化学制品制造业 Raw Chemical Material and Chemical Products	711.82	518.58	179.40	13.81	0.04
非金属矿物制品业 Nonmetal Mineral Products Manufacturing	153.71	142.52	7.97	3.90	0.31
黑色金属冶炼及压延加工业 Smelting and Pressing of Ferrous Metals	349.24	268.68	72.39	8.23	
电力、热力的生产和供应业 Electricity and Thermal Production and Supply	918.30	746.62	109.69	60.80	6.51
其他行业 Ohters	1510.95	1226.01	130.31	155.46	1.35

6-12 环境污染治理投资

Investment in the Treatment of Environment Pollution

项 目	Item	2014	2015
环境污染治理投资总额(万元)	**Total Investment in the Treatment of Environment Pollution (10 000 yuan)**	**3633195**	**5239564**
城镇环境基础设施建设投资	Investment in Urban Environmental Infrastructure Construction	1275620	3750220
#污水处理	Waste Water Dispose	83309	367957
垃圾处理	Volume of Garbage Dispose	120378	
燃 气	Gas Supply	301488	
集中供热	Centralized Heating	352056	
园林绿化	Gardening and Greening	418389	
工业污染源治理投资	Investment in the Treatment of Industrial Pollution	367661	152646
#工业废水治理项目	Number of Project in Industrial Waste Water Treatment	38974	28969
工业废气脱硫治理项目	Number of Project in Desulfuration of Industrial Waste Gas	167574	31162
工业废气脱硝治理项目	Number of Project in Denitration of Industrial Waste Gas	143985	53465
污染物自动在线监测仪器安装项目	Number of Project of Installation of Pollution Automatic on-Line Monltoring Instrument	544	64
当年完成环保验收项目环保投资	Investment Completed in Projects of Environmental Protection Acceptance Pollution	1989914	1336698
#废水治理环保投资	Investment of Pollution in Waste Water Treatment	848369	265851
废气治理环保投资	Investment of Pollution in Waste Gas Treatment	409980	701075
固体废物治理环保投资	Investment of Pollution in Solid Wastes Treatment	24298	40096
噪声治理环保投资	Investment of Pollution in Noise Treatment	25824	30396
绿化及生态环保投资	Investment of Pollution in Landscape and Greening	49106	28501
环境污染治理投资总额相当于新疆生产总值比例(%)	**Investment in the Treatment of Environmental Pollution as Percent of GDP (%)**	**3.9**	**2.3**

6-13 主要年份工业污染治理投资完成情况

Investment Completed in the Treatment of Industrial Pollution in Main Years

年 份 Year	汇总工业企业数(个) Number of Industrial Enterprises (unit)	污染治理项目本年完成投资(万元) Investment In the Treatment of Industrial Pollution (10 000 yuan)	治理废水 Treatment of Waste Water	治理废气 Treatment of Waste Gas	治理固体废物 Treatment of Solid Waste	治理噪声 Treatment of Noise Pollution	治理其他 Treatment of Other Pollution	本年施工项目数(个) Projects Under Construction (unit)	本年竣工项目数(个) Projects Completed (unit)
2000	154	22311	8528	9116	349	4109	209	203	198
2001	113	32009	25917	4886	723	66	416	113	106
2002	89	16952	5015	8241	2206	261	1229	129	85
2003	83	26509	9298	9514	4865	21	2811	104	94
2004	94	29622	12334	13114	2756	92	1327	146	110
2005	97	44008	23549	9656	371	321	10111	162	153
2006	92	45229	26876	12036	2582	32	3703	143	132
2007	90	60138	29958	23891	1676	219	4394	117	103
2008	72	68004	33123	31999	1964	270	648	120	120
2009	99	125435	22242	99849	600	170	2574	109	100
2010	66	66813	19687	46276	800		50	56	48
2011	81	231693	36028	195202			317	154	92
2012	79	79106	37905	40483			718	72	54
2013	83	223866	38658	167383	8187	38	9599	83	79
2014	70	367661	38974	326871	42	38	1736	70	76
2015	80	152646	28969	121003	328		2346	79	52

6-14 工业污染治理投资来源
Source of Investment in the Treatment of Industrial Pollution

单位：万元 (10 000 yuan)

项　　目	Item	2014	2015
施工项目本年投资来源	Source of Funds for Investment of Projects Under Construcion	367661	152646
排污费补助	Pollution Charges Subsidies	2101	110
政府其他补助	Other Government Subsidies	3883	2432
企业自筹	Self-raising Funds	313844	150104
#银行贷款	Bank Loans	41477	10830

6-15 主要城市空气质量指标
Ambient Air Quality in Main Cities

单位:微克/立方米 (2015 年) (microgram/cu.m)

城　　市	City	可吸入颗粒物 Paticulate Matters (PM10)	二氧化硫 (SO_2)	二氧化氮 (NO_2)	一氧化氮均值第 95 百分位数(毫克/立方米) 95th Percentile Daily Average Concentration of No (mg/m^3)	臭氧日最大 8 小时滑动均值第 90 百分位数 90th Percentile Daily Maximum 8 Hours Average Concentration of O_3	细颗粒物 PM2.5	空气质量好于二级天数比例(%) Percentage of Days of Air Quality Egual to or Above Grade Ⅱ（%）
乌鲁木齐市	Urumqi City	133	15	52	3.5	120	66	65.2
克拉玛依市	Karamay City	64	8	19	2.0	120	31	91.2
石河子市	Shihezi City	92	14	33	3.1	133	49	77.5
吐鲁番市	Turpan City	143	20	35	4.0	116	67	62.2
哈 密 市	Hami [Kumul] City	122	8	14	2.0	62	39	82.1
昌 吉 市	Changji City	106	12	40	2.6	114	45	81.5
阜 康 市	Fukang City	87	16	39	3.6	94	40	75.8
奎 屯 市	Kuytun City	91	7	27	3.4	137	53	76.0
伊 宁 市	Yining [Gulja] City	76	18	32	4.6	119	41	83.4
塔 城 市	Tacheng [Qoqek] City	39	10	16	2.4	116	22	100.0
乌 苏 市	Usu City	84	5	21	2.8	122	42	77.8
阿勒泰市	Altay City	25	20	19	2.2	110	13	99.7
博 乐 市	Bole [Bortala] City	66	20	18	1.7	61	30	92.3
库尔勒市	Korla City	144	8	28	2.2	113	49	65.8
阿克苏市	Aksu City	211	18	31	2.5	146	79	41.3
阿图什市	Artux City	211	8	13	2.0	131	55	47.4
喀 什 市	Kashgar [Kaxgar] City	307	19	33	3.6	120	124	22.0
和 田 市	Hotan City	359	72	27	2.2	116	98	19.0
五家渠市	Wujiaqu City	105	16	33	3.2	114	59	76.5

6-16 主要城市道路交通噪声监测情况
Monitoring of Urban Road Traffic Noise in Major Cities

(2015 年)

城　市	City	等效声级 dB(A) Average Noise Value dB(A)
乌鲁木齐市	Urumqi City	66.2
克拉玛依市	Karamay City	64.9
石河子市	Shihezi City	61.3
高 昌 区	Gaochang District	68.9
哈 密 市	Hami [Kumul] City	64.9
昌 吉 市	Changji City	62.5
阜 康 市	Fukang City	63.0
奎 屯 市	Kuytun City	65.5
伊 宁 市	Yining [Gulja] City	65.0
塔 城 市	Tacheng [Qoqek] City	64.5
阿勒泰市	Altay City	67.4
博 乐 市	Bole [Bortala] City	62.7
库尔勒市	Korla City	64.5
阿克苏市	Aksu City	62.3
阿图什市	Artux City	63.8
喀 什 市	Kashgar [Kaxgar] City	67.6
和 田 市	Hotan City	72.7

6-17 主要城市区域环境噪声监测情况
Monitoring of Urban Environment Noise in Major Cities under National Control Programme

(2015 年)

城　市	City	等效声级 dB(A) Average Noise Value dB(A)
乌鲁木齐市	Urumqi City	53.7
克拉玛依市	Karamay City	53.3
石河子市	Shihezi City	52.1
高 昌 区	Gaochang District	49.2
哈 密 市	Hami [Kumul] City	53.9
昌 吉 市	Changji City	51.5
阜 康 市	Fukang City	54.2
奎 屯 市	Kuytun City	51.1
伊 宁 市	Yining [Gulja] City	52.1
塔 城 市	Tacheng [Qoqek] City	48.7
阿勒泰市	Altay City	54.5
博 乐 市	Bole [Bortala] City	50.9
库尔勒市	Korla City	53.4
阿克苏市	Aksu City	56.3
阿图什市	Artux City	65.8
喀 什 市	Kashgar [Kaxgar] City	52.8
和 田 市	Hotan City	57.2

6-18 主要年份自然保护区基本情况
Basic Situation of Natural Protection in Main Years

年 份 Year	自然保护区个数（个） Number of Nature Reserves (unit)	#国家级 Nation level	自然保护区面积（万公顷） Area of Nature Reserves (10 000 hectares)	#国家级 Nation Level	自然保护区占辖区面积比重（%） Percentage of Nature Reserves in the Region (%)
2000	23	5	1594.05	869.08	9.6
2001	26	7	2042.40	1105.50	12.3
2005	28	8	2183.49	1275.86	13.1
2006	28	8	2162.49	1275.86	13.0
2007	34	8	2257.60	1275.86	13.6
2008	34	8	2257.60	1275.86	13.6
2009	34	8	2257.60	1275.86	13.6
2010	34	8	2257.60	1275.86	13.6
2011	28	9	2096.00	1365.53	12.6
2012	28	9	2140.56	1365.53	12.9
2013	28	9	1972.56	1196.30	11.9
2014	29	11	1968.93	1222.59	11.8
2015	29	11	2136.00	1222.59	12.9

注：自然保护区自 2011 年起只包含自治区及国家级自然保护区。
Note: Since 2011,The nature reserves contain the municipality and state leuel nature protection area.

6-19 各地区城市生活垃圾清运和处理情况
Collection, Transport and Disposal of Consumption Wastes in Cities by Region

(2015 年)

城 市	City	生活垃圾清运量（万吨） Consumption Wastes Collected and Transported (10 000 tons)	生活垃圾处理量（万吨） Disposal of Consumption Wastes Treatment (10 000 tons)	无害化处理厂数（座） Number of Factories for Wastes Treatment (unit)	无害化处理能力（吨/日） Treatment Capacity (ton/day)	无害化处理量（万吨） Volume of Wastes Disposed (10 000 tons)	生活垃圾处理率（%） Treatment Rate of Consumption Wastes (%)
总 计	**Total**	**380.04**	**364.55**	**23**	**9205**	**307.40**	**95.92**
乌鲁木齐市	Urumqi City	138.55	133.59	2	3636	132.73	96.42
克拉玛依市	Karamay City	16.57	16.57	3	700	16.40	100.00
高 昌 区	Gaochang District	7.20	6.85	1	300	6.85	95.14
哈 密 市	Hami [Kumul] City	10.50	9.60	1	350	9.60	91.43
昌 吉 市	Changji City	16.06	15.30	1	440	15.30	95.27
阜 康 市	Fukang City	4.08	3.84	1	150	3.84	94.12
伊 宁 市	Yining [Gulja] City	29.21	29.21	1	600	29.21	100.00
奎 屯 市	Kuytun City	7.90	7.90	1	600	7.90	100.00
霍尔果斯市	Huoerguosi City	2.04	2.00				98.04
塔 城 市	Tacheng [Qoqek] City	6.72	6.52	1	207	6.52	97.02
乌 苏 市	Usu City	2.97	2.88	1	165	2.88	96.97
阿勒泰市	Altay City	3.06	3.03	1	140	3.03	99.02
博 乐 市	Bole [Bortala] City	5.80	5.22	1	150	5.22	90.00
阿拉山口市	Alashankou City	1.78	1.52				85.39
库尔勒市	Korla City	30.18	28.83	1	500	28.83	95.53
阿克苏市	Aksu City	13.82	12.70				91.90
阿图什市	Artux City	5.00	4.91	1	189	4.91	98.20
喀 什 市	Kashgar [Kaxgar] City	25.66	25.16	1	500	25.16	98.05
和 田 市	Hotan City	22.00	20.19				91.77
石河子市	Shihezi City	19.71	19.71				100.00
阿拉尔市	Aral City	3.17	2.74	2	135	2.74	86.44
图木舒克市	Tumxuk City	1.32	1.14	1	110	1.14	86.36
五家渠市	Wujiaqu City	3.00	2.88	1	250	2.88	96.00
北 屯 市	Beitur City	2.35	2.26	1	83	2.26	96.17
铁门关市	Tiemenguan City	0.73					
双河市	Shuanghe City	0.66					

注：表中无害化处理数据均为二级以上无害化处理厂数据。
Note: Data on wastes disposed are provided by secondary and above factories for wastes treatment.

6-20 造林面积
Area of Afforestation

单位:公顷 (hectare)

年份 地区 Year Region	造林总面积 Total Area of Afforestation	按造林方式分 By Approach 人工造林 Manual Planting	飞机播种 Airplane Planting	无林地和疏林地新封 Area without Forest or of Sparse Forest	按林种用途分 By Function 用材林 Timber Forests	经济林 By-product Forests	防护林 Protection Forests	薪炭林 Fuel Forests	特种用途林 Forests for Special Purpose
2000	64173	63793	200		1605	44564	16512	1012	480
2001	106771	106771			2149	78203	24536	1424	459
2002	216924	216924			3034	78302	134723	706	159
2003	263781	253781	10000		10152	59777	191380	2390	82
2004	176540	176540			3897	73103	96897	2638	5
2005	136990	130323	6667		3226	40523	92449	738	54
2006	97424	97424			1780	38495	56548	588	13
2007	146632	124642		21990	2991	71667	71325	589	60
2008	239951	217429		22522	8744	136046	94820	341	
2009	301438	266301		35137	9387	155503	135584	954	10
2010	199629	156964		42665	1996	104527	90546	2298	262
2011	186197	140262		45935	823	92656	89942	2356	420
2012	187321	114287		73034	3702	51435	128692	3309	183
2013	147357	99659		47698	3675	42170	98541	2948	23
2014	135986	97413	1954	36619	3633	35204	96593	511	45
2015	186699	123577	333	62789	2214	48341	134265	444	1435
乌鲁木齐市 Urumqi City	1853	1853					1853		
克拉玛依市 Karamay City	2747	1413		1334			2747		
石河子市 Shihezi City	113	113					113		
吐鲁番市 Turpan City	4866	2200		2666	1	1279	2158		1428
哈密地区 Hami [Kumul] Administrative Offices	4037	370		3667			4037		
昌吉回族自治州 Changji Hui Autonomous Prefecture	24292	14292		10000	46	1845	22401		
伊犁州直属县(市) Counties (Cities) Direct Under Ili Prefecture	8566	6900		1666	1517	4557	2492		
塔城地区 Tacheng [Tarbagatai] Administrative Offices	15682	9314		6368	317	1045	14213	100	7
阿勒泰地区 Altay Administrative Offices	20493	13093		7400	333	2869	17291		
博尔塔拉蒙古自治州 Bortala Mongol Autonomous Prefecture	5949	2329		3620		31	5918		
巴音郭楞蒙古自治州 Bayangol Mongol Autonomous Prefecture	20286	10552		9734		7446	12840		
阿克苏地区 Aksu Administrative Offices	18819	15152		3667			18819		
克孜勒苏柯尔克孜自治州 Kizilsu Kirgiz Autonomous Prefecture	6454	4054		2400		1386	5022	46	
喀什地区 Kashgar [Kaxgar] Administrative Offices	29875	25608		4267		18230	11645		
和田地区 Hotan Administrative Offices	22334	16334		6000		9653	12383	298	
自治区直属单位 Directly under Unit Autonomous Regions	333		333				333		

6-21 林业重点工程造林面积
Area of Key Afforestation Projects

单位:公顷 (hectare)

年份 Year	地区 Region	造林总面积 Total Area of Afforestation	#天然林保护工程 Protection for Natural Forests Projects	#退耕还林工程 Grain for Green Projects	#三北及长江流域等防护林工程 Project on Protection Forests in North China andYangtze River Basin
	2001	102317		13173	
	2002	199324		113010	
	2003	235924		175314	
	2004	152967		82838	70129
	2005	133778		62457	71321
	2006	88744		38160	50584
	2007	138700		32926	105774
	2008	187318		50977	136341
	2009	270997		48120	222877
	2010	177674		38034	139640
	2011	186197		31066	107390
	2012	187321		47091	113213
	2013	116713		33460	83253
	2014	113756	2248	15588	95920
	2015	169773	999	33316	135458
乌鲁木齐市	Urumqi City	1853			1853
克拉玛依市	Karamay City	2001			2001
石河子市	Shihezi City				
吐鲁番市	Turpan City	4866		201	4665
哈密地区	Hami [Kumul] Administrative Offices	4037			4037
昌吉回族自治州	Changji Hui Autonomous Prefecture	24292		4627	19665
伊犁州直属县(市)	Counties (Cities) Direct Under Ili Prefecture	8559		120	8439
塔城地区	Tacheng [Tarbagatai] Administrative Offices	15368			15368
阿勒泰地区	Altay Administrative Offices	20193		4834	15359
博尔塔拉蒙古自治州	Bortala Mongol Autonomous Prefecture	3886			3886
巴音郭楞蒙古自治州	Bayangol Mongol Autonomous Prefecture	19687		600	19087
阿克苏地区	Aksu Administrative Offices	18819		9200	9619
克孜勒苏柯尔克孜自治州	Kizilsu Kirgiz Autonomous Prefecture	2940		400	2540
喀什地区	Kashgar [Kaxgar] Administrative Offices	28739		9534	19205
和田地区	Hotan Administrative Offices	13534		3800	9734
自治区直属单位	Directly under Unit Autonomous Regions	999	999		

6-22 森林火灾情况
Forest Fires

年份 Year	地区 Region	森林火灾次数(次) Forest Fires (case)	一般火灾 Ordinary Fires	较大火灾 Large Fires	火场总面积(公顷) Total Area of Fires (hectare)
	2005	28	1		42.33
	2006	35	5		258.27
	2007	47	13		137.09
	2008	67	19		191.38
	2009	51	35	16	83.58
	2010	34	27	7	65.95
	2011	59	46	13	713.72
	2012	41	40	1	19.16
	2013	31	29	2	64.61
	2014	28	19	9	118.08
	2015	19	15	4	143.69
乌鲁木齐市	Urumqi City				
克拉玛依市	Karamay City				
石河子市	Shihezi City				
吐鲁番市	Turpan City				
哈密地区	Hami [Kumul] Administrative Offices	2	2		0.58
昌吉回族自治州	Changji Hui Autonomous Prefecture				
伊犁州直属县(市)	Counties (Cities) Direct Under Ili Prefecture	3	3		7.50
塔城地区	Tacheng [Tarbagatai] Administrative Offices	1		1	53.00
阿勒泰地区	Altay Administrative Offices	7	6	1	40.15
博尔塔拉蒙古自治州	Bortala Mongol Autonomous Prefecture				
巴音郭楞蒙古自治州	Bayangol Mongol Autonomous Prefecture	5	4	1	40.46
阿克苏地区	Aksu Administrative Offices	1		1	2.00
克孜勒苏柯尔克孜自治州	Kizilsu Kirgiz Autonomous Prefecture				
喀什地区	Kashgar [Kaxgar] Administrative Offices				
和田地区	Hotan Administrative Offices				
五家渠市	Wujiaqu City				

6-22 续表 Continued

年 份 Year	地 区 Region	受灾森林总面积(公顷) Destructed Forest Area (hectare)	#天然林 Natural Forest	#人工林 Man-made Forest	经济损失(万元) Economic Loss (10 000 yuan)
	2005	11.62	10.63	0.99	12.52
	2006	94.10	78.28	1.39	9.26
	2007	75.34	31.44	39.37	19.47
	2008	122.74	58.39	65.64	145.53
	2009	72.66	8.24	49.86	52.29
	2010	43.82	17.56	15.70	5.48
	2011	150.16	114.36	35.80	1426.91
	2012	17.35	4.66	12.70	45.88
	2013	12.79	3.48	9.31	14.65
	2014	90.71	34.97	55.74	6.94
	2015	117.28	117.28		12.47
乌鲁木齐市	Urumqi City				
克拉玛依市	Karamay City				
石河子市	Shihezi City				
吐鲁番市	Turpan City				
哈密地区	Hami [Kumul] Administrative Offices	0.19	0.19		0.12
昌吉回族自治州	Changji Hui Autonomous Prefecture				
伊犁州直属县(市)	Counties (Cities) Direct Under Ili Prefecture				
塔城地区	Tacheng [Tarbagatai] Administrative Offices	43.00	43.00		
阿勒泰地区	Altay Administrative Offices	31.63	31.63		10.55
博尔塔拉蒙古自治州	Bortala Mongol Autonomous Prefecture				
巴音郭楞蒙古自治州	Bayangol Mongol Autonomous Prefecture	40.46	40.46		
阿克苏地区	Aksu Administrative Offices	2.00	2.00		1.80
克孜勒苏柯尔克孜自治州	Kizilsu Kirgiz Autonomous Prefecture				
喀什地区	Kashgar [Kaxgar] Administrative Offices				
和田地区	Hotan Administrative Offices				
五家渠市	Wujiaqu City				

6-23 森林病虫害防治情况
Prevention of Forest Diseases and Pests

单位：公顷 (hectare)

年份 Year	地区 Region	合计 Total 发生面积 Area of Occurrence	防治面积 Area of Prevention	防治率(%) Prevention Rate (%)	森林病害 Forest Diseases 发生面积 Area of Occurrence	防治面积 Area of Prevention	防治率(%) Prevention Rate (%)
	2005	241713	221720	91.7	4467	3440	77.0
	2006	400127	344146	86.0	21993	19273	87.6
	2007	787087	441533	56.1	30194	23393	77.5
	2008	1066659	609457	57.1	147035	92811	63.1
	2009	990580	572735	57.8	82273	68525	83.3
	2010	1051060	570973	54.3	80820	73573	91.0
	2011	1223633	547200	45.0	73747	61240	83.0
	2012	1261386	539040	42.7	68426	57025	83.3
	2013	1403008	537534	38.3	77270	64638	83.7
	2014	1382628	625803	45.3	71029	59530	83.8
	2015	1464242	1189353	81.2	82776	66307	80.1
乌鲁木齐市	Urumqi City	7261	6926	95.4			
吐鲁番市	Turpan City	10687	10687	100.0			
哈密地区	Hami [Kumul] Administrative Offices	21249	19056	89.7	1547	1353	87.5
昌吉回族自治州	Changji Hui Autonomous Prefecture	394569	378136	95.8	911	818	89.8
伊犁州直属县(市)	Counties (Cities) Direct Under Ili Prefecture	21089	21080	100.0	3199	3199	100.0
塔城地区	Tacheng [Tarbagatai] Administrative Offices	9843	8744	88.8	644	443	68.7
阿勒泰地区	Altay Administrative Offices	27527	507	1.8	2117		
博尔塔拉蒙古自治州	Bortala Mongol Autonomous Prefecture	183948	104417	56.8	5333		
巴音郭楞蒙古自治州	Bayangol Mongol Autonomous Prefecture	42109	40593	96.4	286	280	98.1
阿克苏地区	Aksu Administrative Offices	195886	163903	83.7	11967	11256	94.1
克孜勒苏柯尔克孜自治州	Kizilsu Kirgiz Autonomous Prefecture	33200	26351	79.4	94	47	49.7
喀什地区	Kashgar [Kaxgar] Administrative Offices	359145	280465	78.1	31570	27634	87.5
和田地区	Hotan Administrative Offices	149438	125955	84.3	21045	20809	98.9
自治区林业厅	Xinjiang Forestry Bureau	8289	2533	30.6	4063	470	11.6

注：自治区林业厅数据中包括石河子市和克拉玛依市的数据。
Note: The data on Bureau of Forestry include the data of Shihezi City and Karamay City.

6-23 续表 Continued

单位：公顷 (hectare)

年份 Year	地区 Region	森林虫害 Forest Damage by Insects 发生面积 Area of Occurrence	防治面积 Area of Prevention	防治率(%) Prevention Rate (%)	森林鼠害 Forest Rat Plague 发生面积 Area of Occurrence	防治面积 Area of Prevention	防治率(%) Prevention Rate (%)
	2005	221500	199700	89.9	21747	18580	85.4
	2006	340320	290693	85.4	37813	34180	90.4
	2007	350592	331735	94.6	406301	86405	21.3
	2008	527465	446766	84.7	392159	69880	17.8
	2009	474213	431197	90.9	434093	73013	16.8
	2010	470961	432316	91.8	499279	65084	13.0
	2011	582653	457627	79.0	567233	28333	5.0
	2012	518263	455652	87.9	674697	26363	3.9
	2013	517802	443262	85.6	807936	29634	3.7
	2014	589471	479782	81.4	722127	86492	12.0
	2015	656448	570110	86.8	725018	552936	71.1
乌鲁木齐市	Urumqi City	5261	4926	93.6	2000	2000	100.0
吐鲁番市	Turpan City	8887	8887	100.0	1800	1800	100.0
哈密地区	Hami [Kumul] Administrative Offices	12876	11703	90.6	6827	6000	87.0
昌吉回族自治州	Changji Hui Autonomous Prefecture	8945	8945	100.0	384713	368373	90.1
伊犁州直属县(市)	Counties (Cities) Direct Under Ili Prefecture	15036	15033	100.0	2854	2849	95.8
塔城地区	Tacheng [Tarbagatai] Administrative Offices	2368	1716	72.5	6832	6585	96.4
阿勒泰地区	Altay Administrative Offices	3613	507	14.0	21797		
博尔塔拉蒙古自治州	Bortala Mongol Autonomous Prefecture	18677	17965	96.2	159938	86452	48.8
巴音郭楞蒙古自治州	Bayangol Mongol Autonomous Prefecture	37075	36149	97.5	4749	4164	97.5
阿克苏地区	Aksu Administrative Offices	183920	152648	83.0			
克孜勒苏柯尔克孜自治州	Kizilsu Kirgiz Autonomous Prefecture	28294	21503	76.0	4812	4802	99.8
喀什地区	Kashgar [Kaxgar] Administrative Offices	200692	184491	91.9	126883	68340	53.3
和田地区	Hotan Administrative Offices	126860	103613	81.7	1533	1533	100.0
自治区林业厅	Xinjiang Forestry Bureau	3946	2027	51.4	281	37	13.1

6-24 林业系统营林固定资产投资完成情况
Investment in Fixed Assets for Afforestation in Forest System

单位：万元 (10 000 yuan)

年份 Year	地区 Region	本年完成投资 Investment Completed During the Year	#国家投资 State Investment	本年新增固定资产 Newly Increased Fixed Assets
	2000	23582	11686	4542
	2001	45890	23725	12492
	2002	68861	35835	
	2003	71277	40821	27223
	2004	60631	43475	23047
	2005	80150	57680	24988
	2006	96062	82235	31047
	2007	115523	94094	33091
	2008	158416	129294	55295
	2009	193818	153538	52765
	2010	168930	142678	28725
	2011	85365	39304	41378
	2012	97849	39318	35863
	2013	130356	41129	119451
	2014	115666	73849	20066
	2015	133414	117347	9997
乌鲁木齐市	Urumqi City	57042	53070	
克拉玛依市	Karamay City			
石河子市	Shihezi City			
吐鲁番市	Turpan City			
哈密地区	Hami [Kumul] Administrative Offices	725		725
昌吉回族自治州	Changji Hui Autonomous Prefecture	5237	5237	5237
伊犁州直属县(市)	Counties (Cities) Direct Under Ili Prefecture	3295	1510	
塔城地区	Tacheng [Tarbagatai] Administrative Offices			
阿勒泰地区	Altay Administrative Offices	12384	9094	1258
博尔塔拉蒙古自治州	Bortala Mongol Autonomous Prefecture	7093	5614	1951
巴音郭楞蒙古自治州	Bayangol Mongol Autonomous Prefecture			
阿克苏地区	Aksu Administrative Offices	28677	28677	
克孜勒苏柯尔克孜自治州	Kizilsu Kirgiz Autonomous Prefecture			
喀什地区	Kashgar [Kaxgar] Administrative Offices			
和田地区	Hotan Administrative Offices	10501	9306	
林业厅直属	Xinjiang Forestry Bureau	8460	4839	826

注：自 2011 年起固定资产投资统计范围为单项投资 500 万元以上项目，2010 年及以前年份统计范围是只要形成固定资产的投资均需统计。
Note: In 2011,Statistical range of investment in fixed assets is above of 5million yuan single investment project.Before 2010,Statistical range is the formation of the investment fixed direct under Foresary Bureau.

6-25 地震灾害情况
Earthquake Disasters

年 份 Year	地 区 Region	地震次数(次) Number of Earthquakes (case)	5.0-5.9 级 5.0-5.9 Richterscale	6.0-6.9 级 6.0-6.9 Richterscale	7.0 级以上 Over 7.0 Richterscale
	2005	4	3	1	
	2006	2	2		
	2007	1	1		
	2008	4	2	1	1
	2009	6	6		
	2010	2	2		
	2011	8	7	1	
	2012	11	8	3	
	2013	5	5		
阿图什市	Artux City	1	1		
昌吉、乌鲁木齐交界	Changji City border on Urumqi City	1	1		
乌鲁木齐市	Urumqi City	1	1		
且末县	Qiemo [Qargan] County	1	1		
柯坪县	Kalpin County	1	1		
	2014	6	5		
于田县	Yutian [Keriya] County	1	1		
于田县	Yutian [Keriya] County	1			
于田县	Yutian [Keriya] County	1	1		
于田县	Yutian [Keriya] County	1	1		
哈密市	Hami [Kumul] City	1	1		
麦盖提县	Makit County	1	1		
	2015	4	3	1	
阿图什市	Artux City	1	1		
沙湾县	Shawan County	1	1		
托克逊县	Toxsun County	1	1		
皮山县	Pishan [Guma] County	1		1	

注：本表数据由自治区地震局提供。
Note: The data in this table is Provided by the Bureau of Earthquake.

6-25 续表 Continued

年 份 Year	地 区 Region	人员伤亡（人） Casualties (person)	#死亡人数 Deaths	经济损失（万元） Economic Losses (10 000 yuan)	失去住所（户） Homeless (household)
	2005			16316	5823
	2006			126	
	2007			11060	5074
	2008			38437	5702
	2009			20498	4393
	2010			2408	675
	2011			105059	15964
	2012			272095	25713
	2013			6696	1755
阿图什市	Artux City			2397	792
昌吉、乌鲁木齐交界	Changji City border on Urumqi City			792	193
乌鲁木齐市	Urumqi City				
且末县	Qiemo [Qargan] County				
柯坪县	Kalpin County			3507	770
	2014			110553	14120
于田县	Yutian [Keriya] County				
于田县	Yutian [Keriya] County			108061	13662
于田县	Yutian [Keriya] County				
于田县	Yutian [Keriya] County				
哈密市	Hami [Kumul] City				
麦盖提县	Makit County			2492	458
	2015	264	3	549595	39560
阿图什市	Artux City			1422	333
沙湾县	Shawan County	1		5173	311
托克逊县	Toksun County				
皮山县	Pishan [Guma] County	263	3	543000	38916

主要统计指标解释

自然资源 指人类可以直接从自然界获得，并用于生产和生活的物质资源。自然资源一般可以分成可再生资源和非再生资源两大类。可再生资源指在较短时间内可以再生、可以循环利用的资源，包括土地资源、水资源、气候资源、生物资源和海洋资源等。非再生资源指在使用后不能再生的资源，包括矿产资源和地热能源。

土地资源 土地指陆地的表层部分，它主要由岩石、岩石的风化物和土壤构成。土地资源按利用类型可以分为农用地、建筑用地和未利用地。农用地包括耕地、园地、林地、牧草地和水面。建筑用地包括居民点及工矿用地、交通用地和水利设施用地。未利用地指农用地和建筑用地以外的土地，包括滩涂、荒漠、戈壁、冰川和石山等。

耕地 指种植农作物的土地，包括熟地，新开发、复垦、整理地，休闲地（含轮歇地、轮作地）；以种植农作物（含蔬菜）为主，间有零星果树、桑树或其他树木的土地；平均每年能保证收获一季的已垦滩地和海涂。耕地中包括南方宽度<1.0米，北方宽度<2.0米固定的沟、渠、路和地坎（埂）；临时种植药材、草皮、花卉、苗木等的耕地，以及其他临时改变用途的耕地。

园地 指种植以采集果、叶、根、茎、汁等为主的集约经营的多年生木本和草本作物，覆盖度大于50%和每亩株数大于合理株数70%的土地。包括用于育苗的土地。

林地 指生长乔木、竹类、灌木的土地，及沿海生长红树林的土地。包括迹地，不包括居民点内部的绿化林木用地，铁路、公路征地范围内的林木，以及河流、沟渠的护堤林。

草地 指生长草本植物为主的土地。

矿产资源 矿产资源指由地质作用形成的，具有利用价值的，呈固态、液态、气态的自然资源，是社会生产发展的重要物质基础。目前我国已发现矿种有170多种，按其特点和用途，可分为能源矿产(如煤炭、石油、天然气、地热)、金属矿产(如铁矿、锰矿、铜矿、铅矿、铝土矿)、非金属矿产(如金刚石、石灰岩、粘土)和水气矿产(如地下水、矿泉水、二氧化碳气)四大类。其中：金属矿产按其物质成份和性质又可分为：黑色金属矿产、有色金属矿产、贵金属矿产、稀有金属矿产、稀土金属矿产、分散元素金属矿产六类。

矿产基础储量 基础储量是查明矿产资源的一部分。它能满足现行采矿和生产所需的指标要求，是控制的、探明的并通过可行性或预可行性研究认为属于经济的、边界经济的部分，用未扣除设计、采矿损失的数量表示。

平均气温 气温指空气的温度，我国一般以摄氏度为单位表示。气象观测的温度表是放在离地面约1.5米处通风良好的百叶箱里测量的，因此，通常说的气温指的是离地面1.5米处百叶箱中的温度。计算方法：月平均气温是将全月各日的平均气温相加，除以该月的天数而得。年平均气温是将12个月的月平均气温累加后除以12而得。

降水量 指从天空降落到地面的液态或固态(经融化后)水，未经蒸发、渗透、流失而在地面上积聚的深度。计算方法为：月降水量是将全月各日的降水量累加而得。年降水量是将12个月的月降水量累加而得。

全年日照时数 指太阳实际照射地面的时数，通常以小时为单位表示。其统计方法与降水量相同。

水资源总量 指当地降水形成的地表和地下产水总量，即地表径流量与降水入渗补给量之和。

地表水资源量 指河流、湖泊以及冰川等地表水体中可以逐年更新的动态水量，即天然河川径流量。

地下水资源量 指地下饱和含水层逐年更新的动态水量，即降水和地表水入渗对地下水的补给量。

地表水与地下水重复计算量 指地表水和地下水相互转化的部分，即天然河川径流量中的地下水排泄量和地下水补给量中来源于地表水的入渗补给量。

供水总量 指各种水源为用水户提供的包括输水损失在内的毛水量。

地表水源供水量 指地表水体工程的取水量，按蓄、引、提、调四种形式统计。从水库、塘坝中引水或提水，均属蓄水工程供水量；从河道或湖泊中自流引水的，无论有闸或无闸，均属引水工程供水量；利用扬水站从河道或湖泊中直接取水的，属提水工程供水量；跨流域调水指水资源一级区或独立流域之间的跨流域调配水量，不包括在蓄、引、提水量中。

地下水源供水量 指水井工程的开采量，按浅层谈水、深层承压水和微咸水分别统计。城市地下水源供水量包括自来水厂的开采量和工矿企业自备井的开采量。

其他水源供水量 包括污水处理再利用、集雨工程、海水淡化等水源工程的供水量。

用水总量 指各类用水户取用的包括输水损失在内的毛用水量。

农业用水 包括农田灌溉用水、林果地灌溉用水、草地灌溉用水和鱼塘补水和畜禽用水。

工业用水 指工矿企业在生产过程中用于制造、加工、冷却、空调、净化、洗涤等方面的用水，按新水取用量计，不包括企业内部的重复利用水量。

生活用水 包括城镇生活用水和农村生活用水。城镇生活用水由居民用水和公共用水(含第三产业及建筑业等用水)组成；农村生活用水指居民生活用水。

生态环境补水 仅包括人为措施供给的城镇环境用水和部分河湖、湿地补水，而不包括降水、径流自然满足的水量。

一般工业固体废物产生量 指未被列入《国家危险废物名录》或者根据国家规定的危险废物鉴别标准（GB5085）、固体废物浸出毒性浸出方法（GB5086）及固体废物浸出毒性测定方法（GB／T 15555）鉴别方法判定不具有危险特性的工业固体废物。计算公式是：

一般工业固体废物产生量=（一般工业固体废物综合利用量－其中：综合利用往年贮存量）+一般工业固体废物贮存量+（一般工业固体废物处置量－其中：处置往年贮存量）+一般工业固体废物倾倒丢弃量

一般工业固体废物综合利用量 指报告期内企业通过回收、加工、循环、交换等方式，从固体废物中提取或者使其转化为可以利用的资源、能源和其他原材料的固体废物量（包括当年利用的往年工业固体废物累计贮存量）。如用作农业肥料、生产建筑材料、筑路等。综合利用量由原产生固体废物的单位统计。

一般工业固体废物处置量 指报告期内企业将工业固体废物焚烧和用其他改变工业固体废物的物理、化学、生物特性的方法，达到减少或者消除其危险成分的活动，或者将工业固体废物最终置于符合环境保护规定要求的填埋场的活动中，所消纳固体废物的量。

一般工业固体废物贮存量 指报告期内企业以综合利用或处置为目的，将固体废物暂时贮存或堆存在专设的贮存设施或专设的集中堆存场所内的量。专设的固体废物贮存场所或贮存设施必须有防扩散、防流失、防渗漏、防止污染大气、水体的措施。

一般工业固体废物倾倒丢弃量 指报告期内企业将所产生的固体废物倾倒或者丢弃到固体废物污染防治设施、场所以外的量。

生活垃圾清运量 指报告期收集和运送到各生活垃圾处理厂(场)和生活垃圾最终消纳点的生活垃圾数量。生活垃圾指城市日常生活或为城市日常生活提供服务的活动中产生的固体废物以及法律行政规定的视为城市生活垃圾的固体废物。包括：居民生活垃圾、商业垃圾、集市贸易市场垃圾、街道清扫垃圾、公共场所垃圾和机关、学校、厂矿等单位的生活垃圾。

生活垃圾无害化处理率 指报告期生活垃圾无害化处理量与生活垃圾产生量比率。在统计上，由于生活垃圾产生量不易取得，可用清运量代替。计算公式为：

生活垃圾无害化处理率=生活垃圾无害化处理量/生活垃圾产生量×100%

森林面积 包括郁闭度 0.2 以上的乔木林地面积和竹林面积，国家特别规定的灌木林地面积，农田林网以及村旁、路旁、水旁、宅旁林木的覆盖面积。

人工林面积 指由人工播种、植苗或扦插造林形成的生长稳定，(一般造林 3-5 年后或飞机播种 5-7 年后)每公顷保存株数大于或等于造林设计植树株数 80%或郁闭度 0.20 以上(含 0.20)的林分面积。

森林覆盖率 以行政区域为单位的森林面积占区域土地总面积的百分比。计算公式为：

森林覆盖率(%)=森林面积／土地总面积×100%

活立木总蓄积量 指一定范围内土地上全部树木蓄积的总量，包括森林蓄积、疏林蓄积、散生木蓄积和四旁树蓄积。

森林蓄积量 指一定森林面积上存在着的林木树干部分的总材积。

造林面积 指在宜林荒山荒地、宜林沙荒地、无立木林地、疏林地和退耕地等其它宜林地上通过人工措施形成或恢复森林、林木、灌木林的过程。

人工造林 指在宜林荒山荒地、宜林沙荒地、无立木林地、疏林地和退耕地等其他宜林地上通过播种、植苗和分植来提高森林植被覆被率的技术措施。

无林地和疏林地本年新封山育林 指本年开始对具有天然下种或萌蘖能力的疏林地、灌丛地、采伐迹地、火烧迹地以及荒山荒地、沙荒地等有条件的地方采取划界封禁和人工辅助措施，使其成为森林或灌草植被的面积。

用材林 指以生产木材为主要目的的森林和林木，包括以生产竹材为主要目的的竹林。

经济林 指以生产果品，食用油料、饮料、调料，工业原料和药材为主要目的的林木。经济林是人们为了取得林木的果实、叶片、皮层、胶液等产品作为工业原料或者供食用所营造的林木，如油茶、油桐、核桃、樟树、花椒、茶、桑、果等。

防护林 指以防护为主要目的的森林、林木和灌木丛。包括水源涵养林，水土保持林，防风固沙林，农田、牧场防护林，护岸林，护路林等。

薪炭林 指以生产燃料为主要目的的林木。

特种用途林 指以国防、环境保护、科学实验等为主要目的的森林和林木。包括国防林、实验林、母树林、环境保护林、风景林，名胜古迹和革命纪念地的林木，自然保护区的森林。

三北和长江流域等重点防护林体系建设工程 三北和长江中下游地区等重点防护林体系建设工程,是我国涵盖面最大、内容最丰富的防护林体系建设工程。具体包括三北防护林四期工程、长江中下游及淮河太湖流域防护林二期工程、沿海防护林二期工程、珠江防护林二期工程、太行山绿化二期工程和平原绿化二期工程。主要解决三北地区的防沙治沙问题和其他区域各不相同的生态问题。

湿地 指天然或人工、长久或暂时性的沼泽地、泥炭地或水域地带，包括静止或流动、淡水、半咸水、咸水体，低潮时水深不超过 6 米的水域以及海岸地带地区的珊瑚滩和海草床、滩涂、红树林、河口、河流、淡水沼泽、沼泽森林、湖泊、盐沼及盐湖。

自然保护区 指为了保护自然环境和自然资源，促进国民经济的持续发展，将一定面积的陆地和水体划分出来，并经各级人民政府批准而进行特殊保护和管理的区域个数。根据保护对象，自然保护区分为自然生态系统类、野生生物类、自然遗迹类。风景名胜区、文物保护区不计在内。

森林火灾次数 指发生在城市市区外的一切森林、林木和林地的火灾次数。按照受害森林面积和伤亡人数，森林火灾分为一般森林火灾、较大森林火灾、重大森林火灾和特别重大森林火灾：1.一般森林火灾：受害森林面积在 1 公顷以下或者其他林地起火的，或者死亡 1 人以上 3 人以下的，或者重伤 1 人以上 10 人以下的；2.较大森林火灾：受害森林面积在 1 公顷以上 100 公顷以下的，或者死亡 3 人以上 10 人以下的，或者重伤 10 人以上 50 人以下的；3.重大森林火灾：受害森林面积在 100 公顷以上 1000 公顷以下的，或者死亡 10 人以上 30 人以下的，或者重伤 50 人以上 100 人以下的；4.特别重大森林火灾：受害森林面积在 1000 公顷以上的，或者死亡 30 人以上的，或者重伤 100 人以上的。本条所称“以上”包括本数，“以下”不包括本数。

森林病虫鼠害 指对森林、林木、林木种苗及木材、竹材形成的病害、虫害和鼠害。森林病害是指林木机体遭受真菌、细菌、病毒、寄生性种子植物和线虫等的危害，而使林木在生理机能、细胞和组织结构以及外部形态等方面发生的病理性变化。森林虫害是指林木机体遭受松毛虫、金花虫、竹蝗、金龟子、蝼蛄等各种昆虫的危害，而造成一定面积森林的生长衰弱或死亡。森林鼠害是指森林、林木、林木种苗遭受各种鼠类的危害，而造成一定程度的损失或死亡。

发生地震灾害次数 指发生形成灾害(包括人员伤亡或经济损失)的所有震级的地震次数。

Explanatory Notes on Main Statistical Indicators

Natural Resources refer to material resources that could be obtained from the nature by human being and used for production and living. Natural resources in general can be classified as renewable resources and non-renewable resources. Renewable resources refer to resources that could be renewed and recycled during a relatively short period of time, including land resource, water resource, climate resource, biology resource and marine resource. Non-renewable resources include resources that could not be renewed, such as minerals and geothermal resource.

Land Resource Land refers to the surface of the earth, consisting of mainly rocks and its weathering and earth. Land resource can be classified, by its utilization, as land for agriculture, land for construction and unused land. Land for agriculture includes cultivated land, plantation land, forestland, grassland and waters. Land for construction includes land for residential purpose, for manufacturing and mining, for transportation and for water-conservancy projects. Unused land refers to land other than land for agriculture and construction, including beaches, deserts, Gobi, glaciers and rock mountains.

Cultivated Land refers to land mainly for the regular cultivation of farm crops (including vegetables), with some fruit trees, mulberry trees and others, covers cultivated land, newly-developed land, reclaimed land, consolidated land, fallow, beach land that can guarantee one harvest per year on average. It also covers fixed ditch, canal, road and sill (ridge) with width less than 1 meter in the South and 2 meters in the North, lands planted temporarily with herbs, grass, flowers and nursery stocks, and other cultivated land with temporary change of use.

Garden Land refers to land for intensive cultivation of perennial woody plants and herbs to collect fruits, leaves, roots, stems and juice, with a covering rate over 50% and plant number per mu over 70% of rational plant number. Land for nursery is included.

Forestland refers to land for planting arbor, bamboo, bush shrub and land in coastal zones for planting mangrove. It includes slash, but not the green belts in residential area, forests requested for railway and highway, and the dike protection forest around rivers and ditches.

Pastureland refers to land mainly for the growth of herbs.

Mineral Resources refer to useful minerals, with solid state, liquid state, gaseity, due to the geological process. Minerals are important natural resources, and important material base for social development. At present, there are more than 170 types of minerals discovered in China. They can be categorized into four groups: energy producing minerals (including coal, petroleum, natural gas and terrestrial heat), metallic minerals (including iron, manganese, copper, lead and bauxite), non metallic minerals (including diamond, limestone and clay), and water/gas related minerals (including ground water, mineral water and carbon dioxide). Metallic minerals can be further classified as ferrous, non-ferrous, noble metal, rare metal, rare earth metal and dispersed metals.

Ensured Mineral Reserves refer to the actual mineral reserves, which equal to the proven mineral reserves (including industrial reserves and prospective reserves) minus extracted parts and underground losses.

Average Temperature refers to the air temperature. China uses centigrade as the unit. The thermometry used for weather observation is put in a breezy shutter, which is 1.5 meters high from the ground. Therefore, the commonly used temperature refers to the temperature in the breezy shutter 1.5 meters away from the ground. The calculation method is as follows:

Monthly average temperature is the summation of average daily temperature of one month divided by the actual days of that particular month.

Annual average temperature is the summation of monthly average of a year divided by 12 months.

Volume of Precipitation refers to the deepness of liquid state or solid state (thawed) water falling from the sky to the ground that has not been evaporated, infiltrated or run off. The calculation method is as follows:

Monthly precipitation is the summation of daily precipitation of a month.

Annual precipitation is the summation of 12 months precipitation of a year.

Annual Sunshine Hours refer to the actual hours of sun irradiating the earth, usually expressed in hours. The calculation method is the same as that of the precipitation.

Total Water Resources refers to total volume of surface water and groundwater and is measured as run-off for surface water and replenishment of groundwater with rainfall in local area.

Surface Water Resources refers to total volume of year by year renewable dynamic resources which exist in rivers, lakes, glaciers and other surface water and are the natural run-off of rivers.

Groundwater Resources refers to total volume of year by year renewable dynamic resources which exist in saturation acquifers of groundwater and are measured as replenishment of groundwater with rainfall and surface water.

Duplicated Measurement between Surface Water and Groundwater refers to mutual exchange between surface water and groundwater, i.e. run-off of rivers includes some depletion into groundwater while groundwater includes some replenishment from surface water.

Water Supply refers to gross water of various sources supplied to consumers, including losses during distribution.

Surface Water Supply refers to withdrawals by surface water supply system, broken down with storage, flow, pumping and transfer. Supply from storage projects includes withdrawals from reservoirs; supply from flow includes withdrawals from rivers and lakes with natural flows no matter if there are locks or not; supply from pumping projects includes withdrawals from rivers or lakes with pumping stations; and supply from transfer refers to water supplies transferred from first-level regions of water resources or independent river drainage areas to others, and should not be covered under supplies of storage, flow and pumping.

Groundwater Supply refers to withdrawals from supplying wells, broken down with shallow layer freshwater, deep layer freshwater and slightly brackish water. Groundwater supply for urban areas includes water mining by both waterworks and own wells of enterprises.

Other Water Supply Sources include supplies by waste-water treatment, rain collection, seawater desalinization and other water projects.

Water Use refers to gross water used by various water users, including losses during distribution.

Water Use by Agriculture includes uses of water by irrigation of farming fields, forestry and orchards, irrigation of grassland, replenishment of fishing farms and water used by animal husbandry.

Water Use by Industry refers to new withdrawals of water, excluding reuse of water within enterprises.

Water Use by Living Consumption includes use of water for living consumption in both urban and rural areas. Urban water use by living consumption is composed of household use and public use (including tertiary industry and construction). Rural water use by living consumption includes water used by households.

Water Use by Ecological and Environmental Protection includes replenishment of rivers and lakes and use for urban environment.

Common Industrial Solid Wastes Produced refers to the industrial solid wastes that are not listed in the 《National Catalogue of Hazardous Wastes》, or not regarded as hazardous according to the national hazardous waste identification standards (GB5085), solid waste-Extraction procedure for leaching toxicity (GB5086) and solid waste-Extraction procedure for leaching toxicity (GB/T 15555). The calculation formula is as followed:

Common Industrial Solid Wastes Produced = (common industrial solid wastes utilized – the proportion of utilized stock of previous years) + common industrial solid waste stock + (common industrial solid wastes disposed – the proportion of disposed stock of previous years) + common industrial solid wastes discharged.

Common Industrial Solid Wastes Comprehensively Utilized refers to volume of solid wastes from which useful materials can be extracted or which can be converted into usable resources, energy or other materials by means of reclamation, processing, recycling and exchange (including utilizing in the year the stocks of industrial solid wastes of the previous year) during the report period, e.g. being used as agricultural fertilizers, building materials or as material for paving road. Examples of such utilizations include fertilizers, building materials and road materials. The information shall be collected by the producing units of the wastes.

Common Industrial Solid Wastes Disposed refers to the quantity of industrial solid wastes which are burnt or specially disposed using other methods to alter the physical, chemical and biological properties and thus to reduce or eliminate the hazard, or placed ultimately in the sites meeting the requirements for environmental protection during the report period.

Stock of Common Industrial Solid Wastes refers to the volume of solid wastes placed in special facilities or special sites by enterprises for purposes of utilization or disposal during the report period. The sites or facilities should take measures against dispersion, loss, seepage, and air and water contamination.

Common Industrial Solid Wastes Discharged refers to the volume of industrial solid wastes dumped or discharged by producing enterprises to disposal facilities or to other sites.

Consumption Wastes Transported refers to volume of consumption wastes collected and transported to disposal factories or sites during the reference period. Consumption wastes are solid wastes produced from urban households or from service activities for urban households, and solid wastes regarded by laws and regulations as urban consumption wastes, including those from households, commercial activities, markets, cleaning of streets, public sites, offices, schools, factories, mining units and other sources.

Ratio of Consumption Wastes Treated refers to consumption wastes treated over that produced. In practical statistics, as it is difficult to estimate, the volume of consumption wastes produced is replaced with that transported. It is calculated as:

$$\text{Ratio of consumption wastes treated} = \frac{\text{consumption wastes treated}}{\text{consumption wastes produced}} \times 100\%$$

Forest Area refers to the area of trees and bamboo grow with a canopy density above 0.2 degree, the area of shrubby tree according to regulations of the government, the area of forest land inside farm land and the area of trees planted by the side of villages, farm houses and along roads and rivers.

Area of Man-made Forests refer to the area of stable growing forests, planted manually or by airplanes, with a survival rate of 80% or higher of the designed number of trees per hectare, or with a canopy density of 0.20 degree or above after 3-5 years of manual planting or 5-7 years of airplane planting.

Forest Coverage Rate Taking the administrative jurisdiction as the unit, the percentage of area of afforested land to the area of total land. The formula for calculating forest coverage rate is as follows:

$$\text{Forestry coverage rate} = \frac{\text{Area of Afforested Land}}{\text{Area of Total Land}} \times 100\%$$

Total Standing Stock Volume refers to the total stock volume of trees growing in land, including trees in forest, trees in sparse forest, scattered trees and trees planted by the side of villages, farm houses and along roads and rivers.

Stock Volume of Forest refers to total stock volume of wood growing in forest area, which shows the total size and level of forest resources of a country or a region.

Area of Afforestation refers to the total area of land suitable for afforestation, including barren hills, idle land, sand dunes, non-timber forest land, woodland and "grain for green" land, on which acres of forests, trees and shrubs are planted through manual planting.

Manual Planting refers to technical measures of sowing, planting seedlings and divided transplanting on land suitable for afforestation, including barren hills, idle land, sand dunes, non-timber forest land, woodland and "grain for green" land to increase vegetation coverage rate of forests.

No-stocked Land and Sparse Forest Land Newly Closed for Afforestation This Year refers to the area of sparse forest land, brush shrub land, stump land, burned land, barren hills, barren land, sand dunes where trees can naturally grow or sprout, which are demarcated, closed down and returned to forest, shrubbery and grass land with the assistance of special measures by men.

Timber Forests refer to forests which are mainly for the production of timber, including bamboo groves planted to harvest bamboos.

By-product Forests refer to forests that mainly produce fruits, nuts, edible oil, beverages, indigents, raw materials and medicine materials. By-product forests are planted to harvest the fruits, leaves, bark or liquid of trees, and consume them as food or raw materials for the manufacturing industry, such as tea-oil trees, tung oil trees, walnut trees, camphor trees, tea bushes, mulberry trees, fruit trees, etc.

Protection Forests refer to forests, trees and bushes planted mainly for protection or preservation purpose, including water resource conservation forests, water and soil conservation forests, windbreak and dune-fixing forests, farmland and pasture protection forests, riverside protection forests, roadside protection forests, etc.

Fuel Forests refer to forests planted mainly for fuels.

Forests for Special Purpose refer to forests planted mainly for national defence, environment protection or scientific experiments, including national defence forests, experimental forests, mother-tree forests, environment protection forests, scenery forests, trees in historical or scenic spots, forests in natural reserves.

Projects on Protection Forests in North China and Yangtze River Basin covering the widest areas in China with a rich variety of contents, these projects aim at solving the problem of sand and dust in northeastern China, northern China and northwestern China and the ecological issues in other areas. More specifically, they include phase IV of Project on North China protection forests, phase II of Project on protection forests at the middle and lower streams of Yangtze River and at the Huihe River and Taihu Lake valley, phase II of Project on coastal protection forests, phase II of Project on Pearl River protection forests, phase II Project on greenery of Taihang Mountain and phase II Projects on greenery of plains.

Wetlands refer to marshland and peat bog, whether natural or man-made, permanent or temporary; water covered areas, whether stagnant or flowing, with fresh or semi-fresh or salty water that is less than 6 meters deep at low tide; as well as coral beach, weed beach, mud beach, mangrove, river outlet, rivers, fresh-water marshland, marshland forests, lakes, salty bog and salt lakes along the coastal areas.

Natural Reserves refer to number of certain areas of land, or waters that have been set aside and put under special protection and management in order to protect natural environment and natural resources, and promote the sustainable development of national economy. They are subject to formal approval from governments of various levels. According to the protected targets, natural reserves can be divided into three categories: reserves of natural ecological system, natural reserves of wildlife species, and natural heritage of historical significance.Scenic spots and cultural preservation zones are not included.

Number of Forest Fires refers to the number of fires in forests, woods and woodland outside of the downtown areas of cities. In light of the area plagued by fires and the number of casualties, forest fires can be categorized into usual forest fires, relatively larger fires, serious forest fires and extraordinary serous forest fires: 1). Usual forest fires: the destructed forest area is less than 1 hectare, or the fire erupts in other woodland, or the number of deaths is no less than 1 but less than 3, or the number of seriously injured persons is no less than 1 but less than 10 persons. 2). Relatively larger forest fires: the destructed forest area is no less than 1 hectare but less than 100 hectares, or the number of deaths is no less than 3 but less than 10, or the number of seriously injured persons is no less than 10 but less than 50 persons. 3). Serious forest fires: the destructed forest area is no less than 100 hectares but less than 1000 hectares, or the number of deaths is no less than 10 but less than 30, or the number of seriously injured persons is no less than 50 but u less than 100 persons. 4). Extraordinary serious forest fires: the destructed forest area is no less than 1000 hectares, or the number of deaths is no less than 30, or the number of seriously injured persons is no less than 100 persons.

Forest Diseases, Pest and Rat Plagues refers to the diseases, pests and rats that plague forests, woods, seedlings and timbers, and bamboos. Forest diseases refer to the plague of fungi, bacteria, virus, parasitic seed plants and nematode suffered by wood organism, which will cause pathologic changes in trees in terms of physiology function, cells, texture and shape. Forest pest plague means wood organism is plagued by pests such as pine moth, leaf beetle, bamboo locust, cockchafer, and mole cricket that damage a certain area of forest, and slow down the growth or cause them to die. Forest rat plague means the forest, trees, seedlings are damaged by rats, resulting in a certain amount of loss or death.

Number of Earthquakes the number of earthquakes of all magnitude that cause damages (including casualties or economic losses).

能 源

PRODUCTION AND CONSUMPTION OF ENERGY

第七篇 能源

本篇主要内容和资料来源

本篇包括的主要内容有能源生产、消费总量及品种构成，综合能源平衡表和主要能源品种单项平衡表，分行业、分主要能源品种的消费量，能源生产和消费弹性系数，能源加工转换效率及生活用能源消费量等。

本篇资料由新疆维吾尔自治区统计局能源与资源统计处依据能源年报整理提供。

Production and Consumption of Energy

Main Content and Source of Data

Data in this chapter cover mainly the energy production and consumption and their composition, the overall balance of energy and the balance by different types of energy, the consumption of energy by sector and by types of energy the elasticity ratio of energy production and consumption, efficiency of energy conversion and the consumption of energy for non-production uses.

Data in this chapter are provided and processed in accordance with the statistical reporting scheme on energy by the Department of Energy and Resources of Xinjiang Bureau of Statistics.

7-1 主要年份能源生产总量及构成
Total Production of Energy and Its Composition in Main Years

年 份 Year	能源生产总量 (万吨标准煤) Total Energy Production (10 000 tons of SCE)	占能源生产总量的比重(%) Percentage of Total Energy Production (%)			
		原 煤 Coal	原 油 Crude Oil	天然气 Natural Gas	水电、风电、太阳能及其它能源发电 Hydro- Power, Wind Power, Solar Power and others
1978	1410.75	60.0	35.8	2.4	1.8
1980	1518.70	58.8	36.7	3.1	1.4
1985	2077.10	60.5	34.3	3.5	1.7
1990	2775.10	59.4	36.1	2.4	2.1
1995	4239.00	50.4	43.8	3.6	2.2
2000	5419.77	40.6	48.7	7.9	2.8
2001	5720.04	38.7	48.6	9.7	3.0
2002	6156.05	39.5	47.3	10.5	2.7
2003	6657.43	41.1	46.0	10.2	2.7
2004	7112.95	41.4	45.3	10.7	2.6
2005	8175.74	37.9	42.1	17.3	2.7
2006	9528.72	37.3	37.1	22.9	2.7
2007	10735.84	36.7	34.7	26.0	2.6
2008	12669.13	41.9	30.6	24.8	2.7
2009	13542.33	46.5	26.5	24.1	2.9
2010	14696.76	49.2	24.9	22.6	3.3
2011	16117.37	54.1	23.2	19.4	3.3
2012	17744.42	55.7	21.5	19.0	3.8
2013	18943.23	53.4	21.1	19.9	5.6
2014	19473.20	53.0	21.1	20.3	5.6
2015	19779.97	53.3	20.2	19.7	6.8

注：电力折算标准煤的系数根据当年平均发电煤耗计算。
Note: The coefficient for conversion of electric power into SCE (standard coal equivalent) is calculated on the basic of the data on the average coal consumption in generating electric power in the same year.

7-2 主要年份能源消费总量及构成
Total Consumption of Energy and Its Composition in Main Years

年份 Year	能源消费总量 (万吨标准煤) Total Energy Consumption (10 000 tons of SCE)	占能源消费总量的比重(%) As percentage of Total Energy Consumption (%)			
		煤炭 Coal	石油 Crude Oil	天然气 Natural Gas	水电、风电、太阳能及其它能源发电 Hydro- Power, Wind Power,Solar Power and others
1978	979.27	72.5	21.5	3.4	2.6
1980	1017.30	72.0	21.3	4.6	2.1
1985	1395.50	72.7	19.6	5.2	2.5
1990	1898.00	70.6	22.8	3.5	3.1
1995	2707.90	66.8	24.1	5.6	3.5
2000	3316.03	63.6	23.3	8.6	4.5
2001	3496.44	60.4	21.6	13.2	4.8
2002	3622.40	62.2	20.5	12.7	4.6
2003	4064.43	60.3	21.7	13.1	4.9
2004	4784.83	61.0	20.1	15.0	3.9
2005	5506.49	56.1	26.2	13.7	4.0
2006	6047.27	56.7	24.7	14.3	4.3
2007	6575.92	57.8	23.9	14.1	4.2
2008	7069.39	61.7	20.3	13.1	4.9
2009	7525.56	65.9	16.9	12.0	5.2
2010	8290.20	66.3	15.8	12.4	5.5
2011	9926.50	67.9	14.7	12.3	5.1
2012	11831.62	68.4	14.4	11.5	5.7
2013	13631.79	66.1	13.6	12.5	7.8
2014	14926.08	65.1	12.4	15.2	7.3
2015	15651.20	65.8	13.2	12.4	8.6

7-3 主要年份分品种生活能源年消费总量
Annual Energy Consumption for Households by Type of Energy in Main Years

年份 Year	合计 (万吨标准煤) Total (10 000 tons of SEC)	煤炭 (万吨) Coal (10 000 tons)	煤油 (万吨) Kerosene (10 000 tons)	液化石油气 (万吨) Liquefied Petroleum Gas (10 000 tons)	天然气 (亿立方米) Natural Gas (100 million cu.m)	热力 (万百万千焦) Heating Power (10 000 million kj)	电力 (亿千瓦小时) Electric Power (100 000 kwh)
1980	330.44	404.10					1.70
1985	355.65	421.72	0.71	3.00			2.38
1990	428.04	479.37	0.58	5.35		160.02	4.22
1995	499.84	527.00	0.50	8.94		177.29	10.11
2000	650.91	590.00	0.75	10.89	0.13	1611.81	17.60
2001	703.97	600.00	0.67	12.31	0.46	2209.66	19.50
2002	752.10	610.00	0.10	14.22	0.32	3112.58	19.20
2003	782.21	625.04		16.62	0.60	3191.14	20.37
2004	901.88	605.00		17.00	1.00	3363.45	24.26
2005	978.54	500.79	0.55	12.96	1.92	6219.00	27.10
2006	612.66	211.00	0.55	14.10	2.60	5008.00	31.90
2007	652.36	213.00	0.42	14.53	2.70	5097.43	33.52
2008	752.73	232.20	0.35	11.60	2.89	7371.00	38.55
2009	855.56	255.00	0.35	13.50	3.90	9073.84	42.62
2010	831.13	252.00	0.34	12.30	4.60	10511.04	47.10
2011	925.38	256.00	0.34	11.42	5.71	12103.27	55.15
2012	992.04	255.00	0.35	11.25	5.79	12795.81	61.94
2013	1166.68	257.00	0.33	9.29	8.97	15511.63	67.65
2014	1203.81	257.00	0.32	9.26	9.97	15716.37	73.15
2015	1332.30	292.79	0.35	9.54	10.64	17917.52	80.19

注：表 7-3 和 7-4 中，2006 年以前数据未按新口径进行调整。
Note:Data of before 2006 did not adjusted by new caliber in table of 7-3and 7-4.

7-4 主要年份能源加工转换效率
Efficiency of Energy Conversion in Main Years

单位：%　　　　(%)

年 份 Year	总效率 Total Efficiency	发 电 Electricity Generation	供 热 Heating	炼 焦 Coking	炼 油 Petroleum Refining
1980	73.90	21.20		72.00	96.90
1985	74.90	21.10		75.50	98.10
1990	73.90	20.90	69.40	85.50	98.00
1995	72.70	23.60	71.20	78.60	96.60
2000	73.60	26.60	75.00	89.40	94.70
2001	73.70	26.10	74.60	78.20	97.40
2002	73.60	26.80	73.50	83.40	96.80
2003	73.80	26.00	78.00	92.00	97.90
2004	70.20	25.90	70.30	78.80	96.20
2005	72.30	27.00	77.70	75.70	97.10
2006	74.80	27.80	76.70	85.00	97.60
2007	73.30	28.60	73.50	86.30	96.40
2008	73.80	30.00	76.60	84.80	96.60
2009	73.50	30.40	77.40	82.20	96.30
2010	74.20	32.30	76.70	80.80	96.10
2011	74.00	33.50	76.00	81.20	97.00
2012	70.80	33.90	76.20	81.90	97.20
2013	69.60	35.90	78.00	79.90	98.00
2014	68.50	37.20	79.50	81.80	98.50
2015	65.70	38.40	81.20	81.10	97.80

7-5 主要年份能源生产弹性系数
Elasticity Ratio of Energy Production in Main Years

年 份 Year	能源生产比上年增长(%) Growth Rate of Energy Production Over Preceding Year(%)	电力生产比上年增长(%) Growth Rate of Electricity Production over Preceding Year(%)	新疆生产总值比上年增长(%) Growth Rate of Gross Domestic Product (GDP) Over Preceding Year(%)	能源生产弹性系数 Elasticity Ratio of Energy Production	电力生产弹性系数 Elasticity Ratio of Electricity Production
1980	7.80	3.60	7.30	1.07	0.49
1985	11.60	11.50	16.90	0.69	0.68
1990	5.70	10.80	11.70	0.49	0.92
1995	7.90	13.40	9.10	0.87	1.47
2000	3.30	8.10	8.70	0.38	0.93
2001	5.50	8.00	8.60	0.64	0.93
2002	7.60	7.40	8.20	0.93	0.90
2003	8.10	10.50	11.20	0.72	0.94
2004	6.80	13.30	11.40	0.60	1.17
2005	14.90	16.60	10.90	1.37	1.52
2006	16.60	15.20	11.00	1.51	1.38
2007	12.70	16.70	12.20	1.04	1.37
2008	18.00	16.00	11.00	1.64	1.45
2009	6.90	14.30	8.10	0.85	1.77
2010	8.50	21.40	10.60	0.80	2.02
2011	9.70	28.80	12.00	0.81	2.40
2012	10.10	35.80	12.00	0.84	2.98
2013	6.80	40.40	11.00	0.62	3.67
2014	2.80	25.40	10.00	0.28	2.54
2015	1.60	18.50	8.80	0.18	2.10

注：新疆生产总值增速按可比价格计算，下表同。
Note: The growth rate of GDP in Xinjiang is calculated at comparable prices and the same as in the 7-6 table.

7-6 主要年份能源消费弹性系数
Elasticity Ration of Energy Consumption in Main Years

年 份 Year	能源消费比上年增长(%) Growth Rate of Energy Consumption Over Preceding Year(%)	电力消费比上年增长(%) Growth Rate of Electricity Consumption over Preceding Year(%)	新疆生产总值比上年增长(%) Growth Rate of Gross Domestic Product (GDP) Over Preceding Year(%)	能源消费弹性系数 Elasticity Ratio of Energy Consumption	电力消费弹性系数 Elasticity Ratio of Electricity Consumption
1980	4.40	3.60	7.30	0.60	0.49
1985	13.70	11.50	16.90	0.81	0.68
1990	9.20	10.80	11.70	0.79	0.92
1995	4.40	13.40	9.10	0.48	1.47
2000	3.10	8.10	8.70	0.36	0.93
2001	5.40	8.00	8.60	0.63	0.93
2002	3.60	7.40	8.20	0.44	0.90
2003	12.20	10.50	11.20	1.09	0.94
2004	17.70	13.30	11.40	1.55	1.17
2005	15.10	16.60	10.90	1.39	1.52
2006	9.80	14.80	11.00	0.89	1.35
2007	8.70	16.00	12.20	0.71	1.31
2008	7.50	16.00	11.00	0.68	1.45
2009	6.50	14.30	8.10	0.80	1.77
2010	10.20	20.80	10.60	0.96	1.96
2011	19.70	26.80	12.00	1.64	2.23
2012	19.20	37.20	12.00	1.60	3.10
2013	20.70	39.20	11.00	1.88	3.56
2014	9.50	19.60	10.00	0.95	1.96
2015	4.90	15.90	8.80	0.56	1.81

7-7 主要年份平均每天各种能源消费量
Average Daily Energy Consumption by Type of Energy in Main Years

年 份 Year	总 计(万吨标准煤) Total (10 000 tons of SCE)	煤 炭(万吨) Coal (10 000 tons)	焦 炭(万吨) Coke (10 000 tons)	原 油(万吨) Crude Oil (10 000 tons)	燃料油(万吨) Fuel Oil (10 000 tons)	汽 油(万吨) Gasoline (10 000 tons)	煤 油(万吨) Kerosene (10 000 tons)	柴 油(万吨) Diesel Oil (10 000 tons)	天然气(万立方米) Natural Gas (10 000 cu.m)	电 力(亿千瓦时) Electricity (100 000 kwh)
1980	2.79	2.57	0.09	0.57	0.05	0.12	0.01	0.13	96.71	0.06
1985	3.82	3.54	0.12	0.82	0.07	0.15	0.01	0.16	149.59	0.10
1990	5.20	5.04	0.16	1.33	0.25	0.20	0.01	0.24	137.53	0.19
1995	7.42	6.67	0.20	1.99	0.32	0.28	0.04	0.33	314.52	0.33
2000	9.09	7.48	0.20	2.94	0.16	0.28	0.06	0.43	642.19	0.50
2001	9.58	7.49	0.20	2.95	0.14	0.24	0.07	0.46	949.04	0.54
2002	9.92	8.10	0.23	3.07	0.09	0.24	0.05	0.46	947.12	0.58
2003	11.09	8.92	0.24	3.26	0.13	0.29	0.04	0.50	1110.96	0.64
2004	13.11	9.95	0.43	3.60	0.06	0.30	0.05	0.54	1480.55	0.73
2005	15.09	10.58	0.50	4.46	0.05	0.29	0.07	0.83	1546.85	0.85
2006	16.57	12.15	0.63	4.97	0.05	0.32	0.08	0.93	1781.92	0.98
2007	18.02	13.54	0.78	5.13	0.06	0.34	0.09	1.04	1912.60	1.14
2008	19.37	15.64	1.25	5.32	0.07	0.34	0.10	0.92	1913.40	1.31
2009	20.62	20.32	1.45	5.47	0.06	0.33	0.09	0.91	1861.10	1.50
2010	22.71	22.21	1.78	6.32	0.04	0.36	0.09	1.00	2195.89	1.81
2011	27.20	26.70	2.41	7.12	0.01	0.38	0.10	1.07	2603.01	2.30
2012	32.42	32.51	2.77	7.13	0.02	0.45	0.12	1.30	2793.15	3.15
2013	37.35	38.92	3.04	7.02	0.04	0.57	0.06	1.50	3485.21	4.39
2014	40.89	44.08	2.94	7.38	0.02	0.59	0.06	1.54	4652.88	5.25
2015	42.88	47.56	2.05	6.82	0.01	0.70	0.08	1.75	3994.80	6.00

7-8 主要年份每人年平均生活用能源

Annual Per Capita Energy Consumption of Households in Main Years

年 份 Year	平均每人生活消费能源(公斤标准煤/人) Annual Per Capita Consumption for Households (kg of SCE/person)	煤 炭(公斤) Coal (kg)	电 力(千瓦小时) Electricity (kwh)	煤 油(公斤) Kerosene (kg)	液化石油气(公斤) Liquefied Petroleum Gas (kg)	天然气(立方米) Natural Gas (cu.m)
1980	258	315	13.25			
1985	261	310	17.49	0.52	2.20	
1990	268	313	27.60	0.38	3.50	
1995	301	317	65.60	0.30	5.33	
2000	353	320	95.33	0.41	5.90	0.70
2001	375	320	103.93	0.36	6.56	2.45
2002	395	320	100.78	0.08	7.46	1.68
2003	404	323	105.33	0.16	8.59	3.10
2004	459	308	123.58	0.15	8.66	5.09
2005	487	249	134.80	0.27	6.45	9.55
2006	302	104	157.13	0.27	6.95	12.81
2007	311	102	159.99	0.20	6.93	12.89
2008	352	109	180.92	0.16	5.44	13.56
2009	396	118	197.44	0.16	6.25	18.07
2010	381	115	215.90	0.16	5.64	21.09
2011	419	116	249.69	0.15	5.17	25.85
2012	426	114	277.41	0.16	5.04	25.93
2013	515	114	298.77	0.15	4.10	39.61
2014	524	112	318.26	0.14	4.03	43.38
2015	565	124	339.79	0.15	4.04	45.08

7-9 主要年份综合能源平衡表
Overall Energy Balance Sheet in Main Years

单位:万吨标准煤 (10 000 tons of SCE)

项　目	Item	1990	2000	2010	2013	2014	2015
可供消费的能源总量	**Total Energy Available for Consumption**	**2045.32**	**3430.05**	**8272.30**	**11924.92**	**12465.34**	**13035.43**
一次能源生产量	Primary Energy Output	2801.57	5419.77	14989.75	18943.23	19473.20	19779.97
进口量	Imports		107.39	1419.75	5423.74	5576.25	4560.98
外省调入量	Inflow from Other Provinces (Autonomons Regions and Municipalities)	2.26	25.59	175.17	432.66	422.00	182.34
出口量(-)	Exports (-)	4.84	31.90	19.89	31.85	7.78	7.67
本区调出量(-)	Outflow (-)	694.89	2144.79	8121.48	12444.19	12953.56	11653.29
年初年末库存差额	Stock Changes in the Year	-58.78	53.99	-171.00	-398.67	-44.78	173.10
能源消费总量	**Total Energy Consumption**	**1898.00**	**3316.03**	**8290.20**	**13631.79**	**14926.08**	**15651.20**
在总量中：	Consumption by Sector						
农、林、牧、渔、水利业	Agriculture, Forestry, Animal Husbandry, Fishery and Water Conservancy	134.91	274.97	408.45	644.85	689.30	705.79
工　业	Industry	1068.77	1860.26	5958.10	10329.22	11467.90	11772.25
建筑业	Construction	41.16	81.73	74.07	157.76	150.15	155.57
交通运输和邮电通讯业	Transport, Post and Telecommunication Services	99.72	189.76	632.52	791.70	851.34	1016.41
商业、饮食、物资供销和仓储业	Commerce, Catering Services, Material Supply, Marketing and Storage	26.28	93.83	175.97	249.44	251.00	298.26
其　他	Others	99.12	164.57	214.67	292.14	312.58	370.62
生活消费	Household Consumption	428.04	650.91	826.42	1166.68	1203.81	1332.30
在总量中：	Consumption by Usage						
终端消费	End-use Consumption	1825.44	3148.77	7300.37	12369.42	13607.47	14157.71
#工　业	Industry	996.27	1692.96	4913.17	9066.84	10149.29	10278.76
加工转换损失量	Losses During the Process of Energy Conversion	27.90	91.25	679.78	858.87	853.58	1039.07
#炼　焦	Coking	13.00	72.05	303.82	581.25	547.11	438.18
炼　油	Petroleum Refining	13.16	75.99	70.58	73.29	59.50	79.18
损失量	Energy Losses	71.11	76.01	310.06	403.50	465.03	454.42
平衡差额	**Balance**	**120.87**	**114.02**	**27.18**	**-1706.88**	**-2460.75**	**-2615.77**

注：1.村办工业包括在工业中(下同)。
2.电力按等价热值折算，因此加工转换损失量中不包括发电损失量。
3.进口量包括新疆飞机在国外加油量，出口量包括外国飞机在新疆的加油量。

Note: a) Data on industry includes the data of village-run industry. (The same is as in the following tables).
b) Electric power and heat are converted on the basic of equal caloric value. Therefore, losses in processing and transformation exclude losses in power generation and heating.
c) Data on imports include the petroleum consumed by the Xinjiang airplanes in refueling abroad. Data on exports include the petroleum consumed by the foreign airplanes in refueling in Xinjiang.

7-10 主要年份煤炭平衡表
Coal Balance Sheet in Main Years

单位:万吨 (10 000 tons)

项 目	Item	1990	2000	2010	2013	2014	2015
可供量	**Total Energy Available for Consumption**	**1816.32**	**2702.81**	**8106.35**	**11815.31**	**12631.24**	**13866.33**
生产量	Output	2100.20	2798.90	9926.73	14203.87	14519.53	15221.48
进口量	Imports		10.70	213.43	488.30	485.47	213.58
外省调入量	Inflow from other Provinces (Autonomons Regions and Municipalities)			0.52	25.45	6.79	37.33
出口量(-)	Exports (-)	0.01	0.22		0.10	0.08	0.04
本区调出量(-)	Outflow (-)	232.76	203.12	1916.20	2841.34	1943.76	1816.41
年初年末库存差额	Stock Changes in the Year	-51.11	96.55	-118.13	-60.87	-436.71	210.39
消费量	**Total Energy Consumption**	**1716.11**	**2702.40**	**8106.35**	**14205.50**	**16088.03**	**17359.29**
在消费量中:	Consumption by Sector						
农、林、牧、渔、水利业	Agriculture, Forestry, Animal Husbandry, Fishery and Water Conservancy	23.96	100.00	101.00	104.99	105.10	112.94
工 业	Industry	1080.07	1801.40	7593.35	13672.01	15554.59	16743.62
建筑业	Construction	11.67	26.00	19.00	27.50	27.52	28.89
交通运输和邮电通讯业	Transportation, Post and Telecommunication Services	25.42	55.00	50.00	51.00	50.90	61.16
商业、饮食、物资供销和仓储业	Commerce, Catering Services, Material Supply, Marketing and Storage	20.50	40.00	47.00	50.99	50.01	62.00
其 他	Others	79.48	90.00	44.00	42.01	43.11	57.89
生活消费	Household Consumption	479.37	590.00	252.00	257.00	256.80	292.79
在消费量中:	Consumption by Usage						
终端消费	End-use Consumption	1163.46	1502.63	2350.51	2476.94	2360.57	2712.51
#工 业	Industry	523.06	601.63	1837.51	1943.45	1827.13	2096.84
中间消费(用于加工转换)	Intermediate Consumption	525.51	1199.77	5755.84	11728.56	13727.46	14646.77
#发 电	Power Generation	372.01	849.20	2501.72	6453.63	8198.85	9493.73
供 热	Heating	32.32	204.46	1096.50	1420.87	1374.60	1580.70
此外:当年炼油投入量	Petroleum Refining Input	111.39	137.77	1988.54	3622.25	3688.22	2780.64
平衡差额	**Balance**	**100.21**	**0.41**		**-2390.19**	**-3456.79**	**-3492.95**

注:生产量为原煤产量。 Note: Data on output refer to the output of raw coal.

7-11 主要年份原油平衡表
Crude Oil Balance Sheet in Main Years

单位:万吨 (10 000 tons)

项目	Item	1990	2000	2010	2013	2014	2015
可供量	**Total Energy Available for Consumption**	**480.75**	**1071.88**	**2308.44**	**2560.76**	**2693.05**	**2489.49**
生产量	Output	701.26	1848.43	2558.16	2792.50	2875.28	2795.09
进口量	Imports		74.60	991.93	1184.08	1180.03	1136.32
外省调入量	Inflow from other Provinces (Autonomons Regions and Municipalities)						
出口量(-)	Exports (-)						
本区调出量(-)	Outflow (-)	218.85	838.69	1241.20	1258.09	1609.88	1453.51
年初年末库存差额	Stock Changes in the Year	-1.66	-12.46	-0.45	-157.73	247.60	11.59
消费量	**Total Energy Consumption**	**480.73**	**1071.29**	**2308.44**	**2560.76**	**2693.05**	**2489.49**
在消费量中:	Consumption by Sector						
农、林、牧、渔、水利业	Agriculture, Forestry, Animal Husbandry, Fishery and Water Conservancy						
工　业	Industry	480.73	1071.29	2228.18	2560.76	2693.05	2489.49
建筑业	Construction						
交通运输和邮电通讯业	Transportation, Post and Telecommunications Services			80.26			
商业、饮食、物资供销和仓储业	Commerce, Catering Services, Materials Supply, Marketing and Storage						
其　他	Others						
生活消费	Household Consumption						
在消费量中:	Consumption by Usage						
终端消费	End-use Consumption	16.44	69.92	45.22	51.36	48.65	64.94
#工　业	Industry	16.44	69.92	45.22	51.36	48.65	64.94
中间消费(用于加工转换)	Intermediate Consumption	464.29	1001.37	2182.96	2509.40	2644.40	2424.55
#发　电	Power Generation		0.05				
供　热	Heating						
此外：当年炼油投入量	Petroleum Refining Input	464.29	1001.32	2182.96	2509.40	2644.40	2424.55
平衡差额	**Balance**	**0.02**	**0.59**				

注：1.生产量为原油产量。2.进口量包括新疆飞机在国外加油量，出口量包括外国飞机在新疆的加油量。
Note: a) Data on output refer to the aotput of crude oil. b) The Refueling by Xinjiang airplanes aboard is included in imports.The refueling by foreign airplanes in Xinjiang is in included in Exports.

7-12 主要年份石油平衡表
Petroleum Balance Sheet in Main Years

单位:万吨 (10 000 tons)

项目	Item	1990	2000	2010	2013	2014	2015
可供量	**Total Energy Available for Consumption**	**333.19**	**616.14**	**869.02**	**1270.84**	**1269.79**	**1422.81**
生产量	Output	701.26	1848.43	2558.16	2792.50	2875.30	2795.09
进口量	Imports		75.16	993.43	1221.41	1221.35	1140.84
外省调入量	Inflow from other Provinces (Autonomons Regions and Municipalities)	1.44	10.85		26.09	25.75	22.82
出口量(-)	Exports (-)	3.29	11.17	1.08	15.49	0.86	0.82
本区调出量(-)	Outflow (-)	353.59	1285.38	2682.12	2593.82	3097.22	2541.46
年初年末库存差额	Stock Changes in the Year	-12.63	-21.75	0.63	-159.85	245.47	6.34
消费量	**Total Energy Consumption**	**300.16**	**527.71**	**869.02**	**1270.84**	**1269.79**	**1422.81**
在消费量中:	Consumption by Sector						
农、林、牧、渔、水利业	Agriculture, Forestry, Animal Husbandry, Fishery and Water Conservancy	42.46	63.65	71.27	90.45	100.23	106.20
工　业	Industry	171.96	273.95	298.42	512.76	486.12	514.45
建筑业	Construction	16.87	32.10	23.81	62.07	57.25	60.24
交通运输和邮电通讯业	Transportation, Post and Telecommunications Services	48.30	86.89	360.79	414.88	430.49	509.73
商业、饮食、物资供销和仓储业	Commerce, Catering Services, Material Supply, Marketing and Storage	3.66	18.78	40.15	57.87	54.40	66.18
其　他	Others	8.48	32.70	44.91	63.19	67.43	88.84
生活消费	Household Consumption	8.43	19.64	29.67	69.62	73.87	77.18
在消费量中:	Consumption by Usage						
终端消费	End-use Consumption	257.06	457.99	687.45	1233.04	1238.30	1382.68
#工　业	Industry	128.86	204.23	197.11	474.96	454.63	474.31
中间消费(用于加工转换)	Intermediate Consumption	15.69	17.34	101.31	37.80	31.49	40.13
#发　电	Power Generation	15.69	2.10	13.31	0.70	0.77	0.95
供　热	Heating		1.24	27.43	6.28	6.22	6.62
此外：当年炼油投入量	Petroleum Refining Input	464.29	1001.32	2182.96	2509.40	2644.40	2424.55
平衡差额	**Balance**	**33.03**	**88.43**				

注：1.生产量为石油产量。2.进口量包括新疆飞机在国外加油量，出口量包括外国飞机在新疆的加油量。
Note: a) Data on output refer to the output of crude oil. b) The Refueling by Xinjiang airplanes aboard is included in imports.The refueling by foreign airplanes in Xinjiang is in included in Exports.

7-13 主要年份电力平衡表
Electricity Balance Sheet in Main Years

单位:亿千瓦小时 (100 million kwh)

项　目	Item	1990	2000	2010	2013	2014	2015
可供量	**Total Energy Available for Consumption**	**69.79**	**182.98**	**675.56**	**1602.50**	**1915.73**	**2190.68**
生产量	Output	69.79	182.98	679.32	1667.80	2090.94	2478.51
火　电	Thermal Power	55.46	150.71	550.91	1357.30	1759.55	2059.96
水　电	Hydropower	14.25	30.54	97.07	207.00	161.41	209.05
风　电	Wind Power	0.08	1.73	31.34	96.00	126.61	147.83
太阳能发电	Solar Power				6.27	41.66	59.38
其他能源发电	Other Energy Generation				1.23	1.71	2.29
本区调出量(-)	Callout Volume			-3.76	-65.30	-175.21	-287.83
消费量	**Total Energy Consumption**	**69.79**	**182.98**	**675.56**	**1602.50**	**1915.73**	**2190.68**
在消费量中:	Consumption by Sector						
农、林、牧、渔、水利业	Agriculture, Forestry, Animal Husbandry, Fishery and Water Conservancy	9.16	22.30	61.12	128.12	141.90	147.50
工　业	Industry	48.86	118.85	508.54	1310.17	1588.52	1837.71
建筑业	Construction	1.18	3.50	6.86	14.93	15.04	15.68
交通运输和邮电通讯业	Transportation, Post and Telecommunications Services	1.48	4.00	6.68	16.99	24.08	29.39
商业、饮食、物资供销和仓储业	Commerce, Catering Services, Material Supply, Marketing and Storage	0.81	6.90	16.74	22.78	25.79	28.89
其　他	Others	4.08	9.83	28.52	41.86	47.25	51.32
生活消费	Household Consumption	4.22	17.60	47.10	67.65	73.15	80.19
在消费量中:	Consumption by Usage						
终端消费	End-use Consumption	65.74	170.86	622.31	1484.68	1775.01	2048.69
#工　业	Industry	44.81	106.73	455.29	1192.35	1447.80	1695.72
输配电损失量	Losses in Transmission	4.05	12.12	53.25	117.82	140.72	141.99

7-14 分行业能源消费总量和主要能源消费量

(2015 年)

行　业	Sector	能源消费总量(万吨标准煤) Total Energy Consumption (10 000 tons of SCE)	煤炭消费量(万吨) Coal Consumption (10 000 tons)	焦炭消费量(万吨) Coke Consumption (10 000 tons)
消费总量	**Total Consumption**	**15651.20**	**17359.29**	**748.59**
农、林、牧、渔业	**Agriculture, Forestry, Animal Husbandry, and Fishery**	**705.79**	**112.94**	
工　业	**Industry**	**11772.25**	**16743.62**	**748.59**
采 掘 业	**Mining and Quarrying**	**1401.97**	**464.72**	**2.67**
煤炭开采和洗选业	Mining and Washing of Coal	184.41	362.07	
石油和天然气开采业	Extraction of Petroleum and Natural Gas	1077.46	59.82	
黑色金属矿采选业	Mining and Processing of Ferrous Metals Ores	43.85	18.88	
有色金属矿采选业	Mining and Processing of Nonferrous Metals Ores	32.99	5.55	2.67
非金属矿采选业	Mining and Processing of Non-metal Ores	9.35	5.14	
开采辅助活动	Support Activities for Mining	49.62	7.31	
其他采矿业	Mining of Other Ores	4.29	5.95	
制 造 业	**Manufacturing**	**8974.89**	**10183.23**	**743.92**
农副食品加工业	Processing of Food from Agricultural Products	130.42	108.37	2.23
食品制造业	Manufacture of Food	172.72	177.53	
酒、饮料和精制茶制造业	Manufacture of Liguor,Beverage and Refined Tea	21.23	15.96	
烟草制品业	Manufacture of Tobacco	1.12		
纺织业	Manufacture of Textile	64.59	9.24	
纺织服装、鞋、帽制造业	Manufacture of Textile, Wearing Apparel,Footware and Caps	1.78	2.74	
皮革、毛皮、羽绒及其制品业	Manufacture of Leather, Fur, Feather and Related Products	0.44	0.31	
木材加工及木、竹、藤、棕、草制品业	Processing of Timber Manufacture of Wood, Bamboo, Rattan,Palm and straw Products	8.98	6.83	
家具制造业	Manufacture of Furniture	0.41	0.25	
造纸及纸制品业	Manufacture of Paper and Paper Products	13.36	6.71	
印刷和记录媒介复制业	Printing and Repruduction of Recording Media	1.21	0.15	
文教、工美、体育和娱乐用品制造业	Manufacture of Articles for Culture,Education Art,Sport and Entertainment Activities	0.80	0.52	
石油加工、炼焦及核燃料加工业	Processing of Petroleum, Coking and Nuclear Fuel	1392.53	2898.93	3.61

Total Consumption of Energy and Its Main Varieties by Sector

原油消费量 (万吨) Crude Oil Consumption (10 000 tons)	汽油消费量 (万吨) Gasoline Consumption (10 000 tons)	煤油消费量 (万吨) Kerosene Consumption (10 000 tons)	柴油消费量 (万吨) Diesel Oil Consumption (10 000 tons)	燃料油消费量 (万吨) Fuel Oil Consumption (10 000 tons)	天然气消费量 (亿立方米) Natural Gas Consumption (100 million cu.m)	电力消费量 (亿千瓦小时) Electricity Consumption (100 million kwh)
2489.49	**254.50**	**27.98**	**637.13**	**1.76**	**145.81**	**2190.68**
	15.00		**90.01**			**147.50**
2489.49	**9.65**	**0.13**	**64.75**	**1.76**	**119.19**	**1837.71**
60.72	**4.65**	**0.01**	**39.73**	**0.24**	**67.85**	**68.74**
	3.34		9.99		0.02	12.06
60.72	0.63		1.03		67.42	38.45
	0.04		5.13		0.04	7.07
	0.07		1.36			7.65
	0.09	0.01	1.99			0.85
	0.46		20.17	0.24	0.37	2.65
	0.02		0.05			0.01
2428.78	**3.41**	**0.12**	**24.23**	**1.52**	**37.26**	**1460.03**
	0.84	0.01	0.55		0.14	22.27
	0.13		0.47		0.15	12.64
	0.05		0.04		0.15	2.22
					0.04	0.20
	0.06		0.05		0.06	16.90
	0.04		0.02		0.01	0.09
	0.01		0.01			0.06
	0.01		0.08			1.40
	0.02		0.01			0.04
	0.03		0.11		0.07	1.89
	0.04		0.02		0.01	0.09
	0.01					0.07
2415.67	0.09	0.01	1.04	1.52	10.95	53.49

7-14 续表

行　　业	Sector	能源消费总量(万吨标准煤) Total Energy Consumption (10 000 tons of SCE)	煤炭消费量(万吨) Coal Consumption (10 000 tons)	焦炭消费量(万吨) Coke Consumption (10 000 tons)
化学原料及化学制品制造业	Manufacture of Raw Chemical Materials and Chemical Products	2697.91	2913.76	280.67
医药制造业	Manufacture of Medicines	22.83	36.70	
化学纤维制造业	Manufacture of Chemical Fibers	90.83	120.70	
橡胶和塑料制品业	Manufacture of Rubber and Plastics Products	22.88	8.62	
非金属矿物制品业	Manufacture of Non-metallic Mineral Products	743.70	587.13	6.30
黑色金属冶炼及压延加工业	Smelting and Pressing of Ferrous Metals	824.17	507.06	445.69
有色金属冶炼及压延加工业	Smelting and Pressing of Non-ferrous Metals	2732.37	2770.41	5.20
金属制品业	Manufacture of Metal Products	7.75	2.02	0.22
通用设备制造业	Manufacture of General Purpose Machinery	1.44	0.41	
专用设备制造业	Manufacture of Special Purpose Machinery	3.91	0.99	
汽车制造业	Manufacture of Automobile	3.48	0.06	
铁路、船舶、航空航天和其他运输设备制造业	Manufacture of Railway,Ships,Aerospace and Other Transportation Equipments	0.07	0.03	
电气机械和器材制造业	Manufacture of Electrical Machinery and Apparatus	9.24	6.35	
通信设备、计算机及其他电子设备制造业	Manufacture of Communication Equipment, Computer and Other Electronic Equipment	1.63	0.03	
仪器仪表制造业	Manufacture of Measuring Instruments	0.09		
其他制造业	Other Manufacture	0.04	0.03	
废弃资源综合利用业	Utiligation of Waste Resources	2.63	1.29	
金属制品、机械和设备修理业	Repair Service of Metal Products,Machinery and Equipment	0.30	0.11	
电力、燃气及水的生产和供应业	**Electric Power, Gas and Water Production and Supply**	**1395.39**	**6095.66**	**2.00**
电力、热力的生产和供应业	Production and Supply of Electric Power, and Heatpower	1157.14	5738.10	2.00
燃气生产和供应业	Production and Supply of Gas	227.06	344.03	
水的生产和供应业	Production and Supply of Water	11.18	13.53	
建筑业	**Construction**	**155.57**	**28.89**	
交通运输、仓储和邮政业	**Transport, Storage and Post**	**1016.41**	**61.16**	
批发、零售业和住宿、餐饮业	**Wholesale, Retail Trades,and Hotel,Restaurants**	**298.26**	**62.00**	
其他行业	**Others**	**370.62**	**57.89**	
生活消费	**Household Consumption**	**1332.30**	**292.79**	

Continued

原油消费量 (万吨) Crude Oil Consumption (10 000 tons)	汽油消费量 (万吨) Gasoline Consumption (10 000 tons)	煤油消费量 (万吨) Kerosene Consumption (10 000 tons)	柴油消费量 (万吨) Diesel Oil Consumption (10 000 tons)	燃料油消费量 (万吨) Fuel Oil Consumption (10 000 tons)	天然气消费量 (亿立方米) Natural Gas Consumption (100 million cu.m)	电力消费量 (亿千瓦小时) Electricity Consumption (100 million kwh)
13.11	0.31	0.05	3.67		23.83	366.24
	0.03		0.03		0.06	3.75
	0.03		0.05			7.85
	0.15		0.13		0.05	4.83
	0.83	0.05	15.68		1.25	61.17
	0.11		1.21		0.16	71.34
	0.07	0.01	0.72		0.14	828.42
	0.22		0.17		0.06	1.32
	0.05		0.03			0.21
	0.05		0.06		0.03	0.68
	0.03		0.01		0.07	0.30
	0.01					0.01
	0.14		0.04		0.02	1.61
						0.48
	0.02					0.01
			0.01		0.01	0.44
	0.02		0.03			0.01
	1.60		**0.79**		**14.07**	**308.94**
	0.99		0.64		13.49	299.55
	0.07		0.08		0.55	7.48
	0.55		0.07		0.03	1.91
	5.77		**21.76**		**0.04**	**15.68**
	110.68	**27.50**	**363.69**		**9.97**	**29.39**
	16.30		**40.53**		**3.76**	**28.89**
	48.50		**38.08**		**2.21**	**51.32**
	48.60	**0.35**	**18.31**		**10.64**	**80.19**

7-15 各地、州、市规模以上工业企业能源消费量

Energy Consumption of Industry above Designated Size by Prefecture, Autonomous Prefecture and City

(2015 年)

能源品种	Item	合 计 Total	乌鲁木齐市 Urumqi City	克拉玛依市 Karamay City	吐鲁番市 Turpan City
原煤(吨)	Coal (ton)	163856178	16763985	4465544	4347545
洗精煤(吨)	Washed Coal(ton)	9439248	3777230		
其他洗煤(吨)	Other Washed Coal (ton)	193984	39548		
焦炭(吨)	Coke (ton)	7433409	2233716		712926
焦炉煤气(万立方米)	Coke Oven Gas (10 000 cu.m)	160330	99083		11378
高炉煤气(万立方米)	High Oven Gas (10 000 cu.m)	942334	619157		
天然气(万立方米)	Natural Gas (10 000 cu.m)	1104806	216476	421898	19862
原油(吨)	Crude Oil (ton)	24694879	7478179	12298604	477860
汽油(吨)	Gasoline (ton)	42694	13463	7225	934
煤油(吨)	Kerosene (ton)	197	55		
柴油(吨)	Diesel Oil (ton)	527648	32699	196718	30902
燃料油(吨)	Fuel Oil (ton)	17572	13258	2944	
液化石油气(吨)	Liquefied Petroleum Gas (ton)	161927	195	149316	1756
炼厂干气(吨)	Refinary Dry Gas (ton)	1183605	179187	816026	
其他石油制品(吨)	Other Oil Product (ton)	1293855	511773	574767	27457
热力(百万千焦)	Heat (million KJ)	129433222	19940944	29917157	1291350
电力(万千瓦时)	Electricity (10 000 kwh)	18235328	2224479	540468	528129
其他燃料(吨标准煤)	Other (ton of SCE)	104212	4940		
能源合计(吨标准煤)	Energy Total (ton of SCE)	114145693	16102501	11889702	3574447

能源品种	Item	塔城地区 Tacheng [Tarbagatai] Administrative Office	阿勒泰地区 Altay Administrative Offices	巴音郭楞蒙古自治州 Bayangol Mongol Autonomous Prefecture	阿克苏地区 Aksu Administrative Offices
原煤(吨)	Coal (ton)	3456334	414166	3982431	8956764
洗精煤(吨)	Washed Coal (ton)			5279	1300995
其他洗煤(吨)	Other Washed Coal (ton)			16538	
焦炭(吨)	Coke (ton)	4914	156311	484941	231252
焦炉煤气(万立方米)	Coke Oven Gas (10 000 cu.m)	30			9186
高炉煤气(万立方米)	High Oven Gas (10 000 cu.m)			161275	55159
天然气(万立方米)	Natural Gas (10 000 cu.m)	193	38071	282137	89243
原油(吨)	Crude Oil (ton)	1		63293	4301115
汽油(吨)	Gasoline (ton)	651	603	2787	1631
煤油(吨)	Kerosene (ton)		1	3	
柴油(吨)	Diesel Oil (ton)	6892	14910	23701	13191
燃料油(吨)	Fuel Oil (ton)				
液化石油气(吨)	Liquefied Petroleum Gas (ton)			6015	
炼厂干气(吨)	Refinary Dry Gas (ton)				188392
其他石油制品(吨)	Other Oil Product (ton)			45	49715
热力(百万千焦)	Heat (million KJ)	2969658		21092209	2702796
电力(万千瓦时)	Electricity (10 000 kwh)	175167	88672	414256	291554
其他燃料(吨标准煤)	Other (ton of SCE)	125	11321		26566
能源合计(吨标准煤)	Energy Total (ton of SCE)	1359623	600695	6328733	4535311

注：各地区数含兵团工业在内。
Note:Figures in different prefectures include data of XPCG enterprises.

7-15 续表 Continued

能源品种	Item	哈密地区 Hami [kumul] Administrative Offices	昌吉回族自治州 Changji Hui Autonomous Prefecture	博尔塔拉蒙古自治州 Bortala Mongol Autonomous Prefecture	伊犁州直属县(市) Counties (Cities) Direct Under Ili Prefecture
原煤(吨)	Coal (ton)	21226227	42907324	914627	7549263
洗精煤(吨)	Washed Coal (ton)	5657	2171984		738391
其他洗煤(吨)	Other Washed Coal (ton)		21544		
焦炭(吨)	Coke (ton)	21421	1014992	20111	866246
焦炉煤气(万立方米)	Coke Oven Gas (10 000 cu.m)				21998
高炉煤气(万立方米)	High Oven Gas (10 000 cu.m)				105416
天然气(万立方米)	Natural Gas (10 000 cu.m)		14210		282
原油(吨)	Crude Oil (ton)		52677		14196
汽油(吨)	Gasoline (ton)	1279	3182	120	1847
煤油(吨)	Kerosene (ton)	5	29		3
柴油(吨)	Diesel Oil (ton)	44669	63436	2746	16593
燃料油(吨)	Fuel Oil (ton)		1370		
液化石油气(吨)	Liquefied Petroleum Gas (ton)				22
炼厂干气(吨)	Refinary Dry Gas (ton)				
其他石油制品(吨)	Other Oil Product (ton)		119066		8209
热力(百万千焦)	Heat (million KJ)	19832	1244427		106698
电力(万千瓦时)	Electricity (10 000 kwh)	323454	6140928	46337	501328
其他燃料(吨标准煤)	Other (ton of SCE)			52	3857
能源合计(吨标准煤)	Energy Total (ton of SCE)	7339097	25815200	656948	5438167

能源品种	Item	克孜勒苏柯尔克孜自治州 Kizilsu Kirgiz Autonomous Prefecture	喀什地区 Kashgar [kaxgar] Administrative Offices	和田地区 Hotan Administrative Offices	生产建设兵团 Xinjiang Production and Construction Group
原煤(吨)	Coal (ton)	160662	2063610	197063	46450633
洗精煤(吨)	Washed Coal (ton)				1439711
其他洗煤(吨)	Other Washed Coal (ton)				116354
焦炭(吨)	Coke (ton)	35235	42216		1609129
焦炉煤气(万立方米)	Coke Oven Gas (10 000 cu.m)				18655
高炉煤气(万立方米)	High Oven Gas (10 000 cu.m)		1327		
天然气(万立方米)	Natural Gas (10 000 cu.m)	2368	2239		17827
原油(吨)	Crude Oil (ton)		2		8953
汽油(吨)	Gasoline (ton)	154	103	4746	3968
煤油(吨)	Kerosene (ton)		34		67
柴油(吨)	Diesel Oil (ton)	7895	2888	1190	69218
燃料油(吨)	Fuel Oil (ton)				
液化石油气(吨)	Liquefied Petroleum Gas (ton)		4060		563
炼厂干气(吨)	Refinary Dry Gas (ton)				
其他石油制品(吨)	Other Oil Product (ton)				2824
热力(百万千焦)	Heat (million KJ)		52		50148099
电力(万千瓦时)	Electricity (10 000 kwh)	59078	95636	148296	6657547
其他燃料(吨标准煤)	Other (ton of SCE)				57351
能源合计(吨标准煤)	Energy Total (ton of SCE)	238614	1126392	335305	28804957

主要统计指标解释

能源生产总量 指一定时期内，一个地区一次能源生产量的总和。该指标是观察一个地区能源生产水平、规模、构成和发展速度的总量指标。一次能源生产量包括原煤、原油、天然气、水电、核能及其他动力能(如风能、地热能等)发电量，不包括低热值燃料生产量、生物质能、太阳能等的利用和由一次能源加工转换而成的二次能源产量。

能源消费总量 指一定地域内，国民经济各行业和居民家庭在一定时间消费的各种能源的总和。包括：原煤、原油、天然气、水能、核能、风能、太阳能、地热能、生物质能等一次能源；一次能源通过加工转换产生的洗煤、焦炭、煤气、电力、热力、成品油等二次能源和同时产生的其他产品；其他化石能源、可再生能源和新能源，是指人们通过一定技术手段获得的，并作为商品能源使用的部分。在核算过程中，一次能源、二次能源消费不能重复计算。能源消费总量分为终端能源消费量、能源加工转换损失量和能源损失量三部分。

(1)终端能源消费量：指一定时期内，一个地区生产和生活消费的各种能源在扣除了用于加工转换二次能源消费量和损失量以后的数量。

(2)能源加工转换损失量：指一定时期内，一个地区投入加工转换的各种能源数量之和与产出各种能源产品之和的差额，该指标是观察能源在加工转换过程中损失量变化的指标。

(3)能源损失量：指一定时期内，能源在输送、分配、储存过程中发生的损失和由客观原因造成的各种损失量，不包括各种气体能源放空、放散量。

能源生产弹性系数 是研究能源生产增长速度与国民经济增长速度之间关系的指标。计算公式为：

能源生产弹性系数 = 能源生产总量年平均增长速度 / 国民经济年平均增长速度

国民经济年平均增长速度，可根据不同的目的或需要，用国民生产总值、国内生产总值等指标来计算，本年鉴是采用国内生产总值指标计算的。

电力生产弹性系数 是研究电力生产增长速度与国民经济增长速度之间关系的指标。一般来说，电力的发展应当快于国民经济的发展，也就是说电力应超前发展。计算公式为：

电力生产弹性系数 = 电力生产量年平均增长速度 / 国民经济年平均增长速度

能源消费弹性系数 是反映能源消费增长速度与国民经济增长速度之间比例关系的指标。计算公式为：

能源消费弹性系数 = 能源消费量年平均增长速度 / 国民经济年平均增长速度

电力消费弹性系数 反映电力消费增长速度与国民经济增长速度之间比例关系的指标。计算公式为：

电力消费弹性系数 = 电力消费量年平均增长速度 / 国民经济年平均增长速度

能源加工转换效率 指一定时期内，能源经过加工、转换后，产出的各种能源产品的数量与同期内投入加工转换的各种能源数量的比率。该指标是观察能源加工转换装置和生产工艺先进与落后、管理水平高低等的重要指标。计算公式为：

能源加工转换效率 = 能源加工转换产出量 / 能源加工转换投入量 × 100%

单位国内生产总值能耗 指一定时期内，一个国家或地区每生产一个单位的国内生产总值所消耗的能源。计算公式为：

单位国内生产总值能耗=能源消费总量/国内生产总值

单位国内生产总值电耗 指一定时期内，一个国家或地区每生产一个单位的国内生产总值所消耗的电力。计算公式为：

单位国内生产总值电耗=全社会用电量/国内生产总值

单位工业增加值能耗 指一定时期内，一个国家或地区每生产一个单位的工业增加值所消耗的能源。计算公式为：

单位工业增加值能耗=工业能源消费量/工业增加值

Explanatory Notes on Main Statistical Indicators

Total Energy Production refers to the total production of primary energy by all energy producing enterprises in the country in a given period of time. It is a comprehensive indicator to show the level, scale, composition and pace of development of energy production of the country. The production of primary energy includes that of coal, crude oil, natural gas, hydro-power and electricity generated by nuclear energy and other means such as wind power and geothermal power. However, it does not include the production of fuels of low calorific value, bio-energy, solar energy and secondary energy converted from primary energy.

Total Energy Consumption refers to the total consumption of energy of various kinds by the production sectors of the economy and the households in a given period of time. It includes the primary kinds of energy such as coal, crude oil, natural gas, hydro-power, nuclear power, wind power, solar power, geothermal power and bio-energy; the secondary kinds of energy and their products which are transformed from the primary energy such as washed coal, coke, coal gas, electricity, heating, and petroleum products; and other kinds of fossil energy, renewable energy and new energy. The renewable energy, including hydro-power, wind power, solar power, geothermal power and bio-energy, refers to the part attained with some given technical means and used for commercial purposes. Total energy consumption can be divided into three parts: end-use energy consumption; loss during the process of energy conversion; and energy loss.

(1)End-use Energy Consumption: It refers to the total energy consumption by the production sectors and the households in the country (region) in a given period of time. It does not include the consumption during the conversion of primary energy into secondary energy and the loss in the process of energy conversion.

(2)Loss During the Process of Energy Conversion: It refers to the total input of various kinds of energy for conversion, minus the total output of various kinds of energy in the country in a given period of time. It is an indicator to show the loss that occurs during the process of energy conversion.

(3)Energy Loss: It refers to the total of the loss of energy during the course of energy transport, distribution and storage and the loss caused by any objective reason in a given period of time. The loss of various kinds of gas due to gas discharges and stocktaking is not included.

Elasticity Ratio of Energy Production is an indicator to show the relationship between the growth rate of energy production and the growth rate of the national economy. The formula is:

$$\text{Elasticity Ratio of Energy Production} = \frac{\text{Average Annual Growth Rate of Energy Production}}{\text{Average Annual Growth Rate of National Economy}}$$

The average annual growth rate of the national economy can be measured by indicators such as the Gross National Product and the Gross Domestic Product, depending on the purposes or needs. The Gross Domestic Product has been used in the calculation of the ratio in this Yearbook.

Elasticity Ratio of Electricity Production is an indicator to show the relationship between the growth rate of electricity production and the growth rate of the national economy. Generally speaking, the growth rate of electricity production should be higher than that of the national economy.

Its formula is:

$$\text{Elasticity Ratio of Electricity Production} = \frac{\text{Average Annual Growth Rate of Electricity Production}}{\text{Average Annual Growth Rate of National Economy}}$$

Elasticity Ratio of Energy Consumption is an indicator to show the relationship between the growth rate of energy consumption and the growth rate of the national economy. The formula is:

$$\text{Elasticity Ratio of Energy Consumption} = \frac{\text{Average Annual Growth Rate of Energy Consumption}}{\text{Average Annual Growth Rate of National Economy}}$$

Elasticity Ratio of Electricity Consumption is an indicator to show the relationship between the growth rate of electricity consumption and the growth rate of the national economy. The formula is:

$$\text{Elasticity Ratio of Electricity Consumption} = \frac{\text{Average Annual Growth Rate of Electricity Consumption}}{\text{Average Annual Growth Rate of National Economy}}$$

Efficiency of Energy Processing and Conversion refers to the ratio of the total output of energy products of various kinds after processing and conversion to the total input of energy of various kinds for processing and conversion in the same reference period. It is an important indicator to show the current conditions of energy processing and conversion equipment, production technique and management. The formula is:

$$\text{Efficiency of Energy Processing \& Conversion} = \frac{\text{Output of Energy After Processing \& Conversion}}{\text{Input of Energy for Processing \& Conversion}} \times 100\%$$

Energy Consumption per Unit of GDP refers to the energy consumption per unit of Gross Domestic Product in a country or the Gross Regional Product in a region in the same reference period. The formula is:

$$\text{Energy Consumption per Unit of GDP} = \frac{\text{Total Energy Consumption}}{\text{Gross Domestic Product}}$$

Electricity Consumption per Unit of GDP refers to the electricity consumption per unit of Gross Domestic Product in a country or the Gross Regional Product in a region in the same reference period. The formula is:

$$\text{Electricity Consumption per Unit of GDP} = \frac{\text{Total Electricity Consumption}}{\text{Gross Domestic Product}}$$

Energy Consumption per Unit of Industrial Value-added refers to the energy consumption per unit of industrial value-added in a country or region in the same reference period. The formula is:

$$\text{Energy Consumption per Unit of Industrial Value-added} = \frac{\text{Total Energy Consumption}}{\text{Industrial Value-added}}.$$

财 政

GOVERNMENT FINANCE

第八篇　财政

Government Finance

本篇主要内容和资料来源

本篇包括自治区地方财政收支及各地州、县（市）公共财政收支资料。

本篇资料来源于新疆维吾尔自治区财政厅年度决算，由新疆维吾尔自治区统计局国民经济综合统计处编辑整理。

Main Content and Source of Data

The data in this chapter show the government revenue and expenditure of Xinjiang Uygur Autonomous region,and the data of public budgetary revenue and expenditure by prefecture,autonomous prefecture and city.

Data on the government revenue and expenditure come from the final state financial accounts.Data in this chapter are compiled and collected by the Division of comprehensive of the Xinjing Bureau of Statistics on the basis of data from the relative departments.

8-1 主要年份一般公共预算收支及增长速度
General Public Budget Revenue and Expenditure and Their Increase Rates

单位：亿元 (100 million yuan)

年 份 Year	一般公共预算收入 General public Budget Revenue	一般公共预算支出 General public Budget Expenditure	收支差额 Balance	指数(上年=100) Indices (precding year=100) 一般公共预算收入 General public Budget Revenue	一般公共预算支出 General public Budget Expenditure
1978	7.14	17.02	-9.88	196.5	153.3
1980	4.03	16.22	-12.19	73.4	95.4
1985	8.47	28.60	-20.14	117.2	122.6
1990	21.78	47.62	-25.84	118.9	114.2
1995	38.28	96.40	-58.12	133.4	135.6
2000	79.07	190.95	-111.88	110.9	114.8
2001	95.09	263.32	-168.23	120.3	137.9
2002	116.47	361.17	-244.70	122.5	137.2
2003	128.22	368.47	-240.25	110.1	102.0
2004	155.70	421.04	-265.34	121.4	114.3
2005	180.32	519.02	-338.70	115.8	123.3
2006	219.46	678.47	-459.01	121.7	130.7
2007	285.86	795.15	-509.29	130.3	117.2
2008	361.06	1059.36	-698.30	126.3	133.2
2009	388.78	1346.91	-958.13	107.7	127.1
2010	500.58	1698.91	-1198.34	128.8	126.1
2011	720.43	2284.49	-1564.05	143.9	134.5
2012	908.97	2720.07	-1811.10	126.2	119.1
2013	1128.49	3067.12	-1938.64	124.2	112.8
2014	1282.34	3317.79	-2035.45	113.6	108.2
2015	1330.85	3804.87	-2474.02	103.8	114.7

8-2 主要年份一般公共预算收入占新疆生产总值的比重
Proportion of General Public Budgetary Revenue to GDP of Xinjiang in Main Years

单位：亿元 (100 million yuan)

年 份 Year	一般公共预算收入 General public Budget Revenue	新疆生产总值 Gross Domestic Product of Xinjiang	一般公共预算收入相当于新疆生产总值的比例(%) Proportion of General Public Revenue to GDP of Xinjiang (%)
1978	7.14	39.07	18.27
1980	4.03	53.24	7.57
1985	8.47	112.24	7.56
1990	21.78	261.44	8.34
1995	38.28	814.85	4.70
2000	79.07	1363.56	5.80
2001	95.09	1491.60	6.37
2002	116.47	1612.65	7.22
2003	128.22	1886.35	6.79
2004	155.70	2209.09	7.05
2005	180.32	2604.14	6.92
2006	219.46	3045.26	7.21
2007	285.86	3523.16	8.11
2008	361.06	4183.21	8.63
2009	388.78	4277.05	9.09
2010	500.58	5437.47	9.21
2011	720.43	6610.05	10.90
2012	908.97	7505.31	12.11
2013	1128.49	8360.24	13.50
2014	1282.34	9273.46	13.83
2015	1330.85	9324.80	14.27

8-3 地方财政收支情况

Statistics on Total Government Revenue and Expenditures in Local Finance

单位：亿元 (100 million yuan)

项　目	Item	2014	2015
收入合计	**Total Revenue**	**1710.25**	**1666.07**
一般公共预算收入	General Public Budgetary Revenue	1282.34	1330.85
税收收入	Tax Revenue	887.79	861.73
增值税	Value-added Tax	156.39	140.72
营业税	Business Tax	282.23	265.12
企业所得税（含退税）	Corporate Income Tax	90.29	92.34
个人所得税	Individual Income Tax	48.13	55.55
资源税	Resources Tax	78.17	66.36
城市维护建设税	City Maintenance and Construction Tax	51.92	51.76
房产税	House Property Tax	24.57	26.62
契　税	Deed Tax	37.04	41.93
其他税收收入	Other Tax Revenue	119.04	121.33
非税收入	Non-tax Revenue	394.55	469.12
专项收入	Special Program Receipts	205.71	245.31
行政性收费收入	Charge of Administrative and Institutional Units	58.65	63.56
罚没收入	Penalty Receipts	24.77	26.86
其他收入	Other Non-tax Receipts	105.42	133.39
国有资本经营预算收入	Operation Budget Revenue of Stateowned Assets	1.78	2.18
基金预算收入	Fund Budget Revenue	426.13	333.04
支出合计	**Total Expenditures**	**3778.03**	**4169.19**
一般公共预算支出	General Public Budget Expenditure	3317.79	3804.87
一般公共服务	Expenditure for General Public Services	324.88	366.41
教　育	Expenditure for Education	567.20	647.93
科学技术	Expenditure for Science and Technology	40.34	41.64
文化体育与传媒	Expenditure for Culture ,Sport and Media	74.32	78.96
社会保障和就业	Expenditure for Social Safety Net and Employment Effort	300.85	371.90
医疗卫生	Expenditure for Medical and Health Care	202.32	244.01
节能环保	Expenditure for Environment Protection	70.86	71.51
城乡社区事务	Expenditure for Urban and Rural Community Affairs	286.76	323.04
农林水事务	Expenditure for Agriculture, Forestry and Water Conservancy	477.27	605.34
交通运输	Expenditure for Transportation	215.53	270.75
资源勘探电力信息等事务	Expenditure for Miming and Quarrying,Electriaty and Information Technology	56.75	72.11
其他各项支出	Other Expenditure	700.71	711.27
国有资本经营预算支出	Operation Budgetary Expenditure of Stateowned Assets	1.47	1.33
基金预算支出	Fund Budgetary Expenditure	458.77	362.99

8-4 各地、州、市、县(市)一般公共预算收支

General Public Budget Revenue and Expenditure by Prefecture, Autonomous Prefecture, City and County

单位：万元 (2015 年) (10 000 yuan)

地 区	Region	收 入 Revenue	支 出 Expenditure
总 计	**Total**	**13308464**	**38048687**
自治区本级	Autonomous regional Level	2417340	10302472
乌鲁木齐市	**Urumqi City**	**3686663**	**4466709**
乌鲁木齐市本级	Urumqi City Level	1099943	1911268
经济技术开发区（头屯河区）	Economic and Technological DeveloPment Zone（Tou Tunhe District）	655020	378687
高新技术开发区	New and High-tech Industrial DeveloPment Zone	544813	585163
乌鲁木齐县	Urumqi County	58524	170588
天山区	Tianshan District	250100	251126
沙依巴克区	Shayibak District	201923	228494
新市区	Xinshi District	300118	239228
水磨沟区	Shui Mogou District	237734	252643
米东区	Midong District	302660	369134
达坂城区	Da Bancheng District	35828	80378
昌吉回族自治州	**Changji Hui Autonomous Prefecture**	**1104442**	**2163946**
昌吉州本级	Changji Prefecture Level	108280	337588
昌吉市	Changji City	352991	495190
阜康市	Fukang City	199200	269291
呼图壁县	Hutubi County	97821	240701
玛纳斯县	Manas County	98961	213776
奇台县	Qitai County	90424	250981
吉木萨尔县	Jimsar County	123504	206686
木垒哈萨克自治县	Mori Kazak Autonomous County	33261	149733
克拉玛依市	**Karamay City**	**749926**	**896640**
市本级	City Level	438627	464361
克拉玛依区	Karamay District	190584	211002
独山子区	Dushanzi District	81619	138265
白碱滩区	Bai Jiantan District	30076	59809
乌尔河区	Urhe District	9020	23203
吐鲁番市	**Turpan City**	**302628**	**716703**
市本级	City Level	35247	100553
高昌区	Gaochang District	74809	231939
鄯善县	Shanshan [Piqan] County	110006	221448
托克逊县	Toksun County	82566	162763
哈密地区	**Hami [Kumul] Administrative Offices**	**545273**	**1007135**
地区本级	Prefecture Level	49335	232590

8-4 续表 1 Continued

单位：万元 (10 000 yuan)

地　　区	Region	收 入 Revenue	支 出 Expenditure
哈密市	Hami [Kumul] City	418729	523170
巴里坤哈萨克自治县	Barkol Kazak Autonomous County	38096	156104
伊吾县	Yiwu [Araturuk] County	39113	95271
伊犁哈萨克自治州	**Ili Kazak Autonomous Prefecture**	**1380889**	**5111968**
伊犁州直属县(市)	**Counties (Cities) Direct Under Ili Prefecture**	**672568**	**2536964**
伊犁州直属县(市)本级	Counties (Cities) Direct Under Ili Prefecture Level	28332	276858
伊宁市	Yining [Gulja] City	246891	454948
奎屯市	Kuytun City	113659	210364
霍尔果斯市	Huoerguosi City	34759	77272
伊宁县	Yining [Gulja] County	46447	245763
察布查尔锡伯自治县	Qapqal Xibe Autonomous County	26700	177671
霍城县	Huocheng [Korgas] County	43117	232738
巩留县	Gongliu [Tokkuztara] County	19600	166356
新源县	Xinyuan [Kunes] County	50441	205420
昭苏县	Zhaosu [Mongolkure] County	14696	170407
特克斯县	Tekes County	20610	157297
尼勒克县	Nilka County	27316	161870
塔城地区	**Tacheng [Tarbagatai] Administrative Office**	**404123**	**1370425**
地区本级	Prefecture Level	18837	123661
塔城市	Tacheng [Qoqek] City	50530	188734
乌苏市	Usu City	133377	290137
额敏县	Emin [Dorbiljin] County	38480	198016
沙湾县	Shawan County	82824	240604
托里县	Toli County	20010	115426
裕民县	Yumin [Qagantokay] County	7722	89688
和布克赛尔蒙古自治县	Hoboksar Mongol Autonomous County	52343	124159
阿勒泰地区	**Altay Administrative Offices**	**304198**	**1204579**
阿勒泰地区本级	Altay Administrative Offices Level	29914	131645
阿勒泰市	Altay City	62000	238169
布尔津县	Burqin County	29602	134980
富蕴县	Fuyun [Koktokay] County	77007	193653
福海县	Fuhai [Burultokay] County	25601	131740
哈巴河县	Habahe [Kaba] County	50007	151860

8-4 续表 2 Continued

单位：万元 (10 000 yuan)

地　区	Region	收 入 Revenue	支 出 Expenditure
青河县	Qinghe [Qinggil] County	20017	129690
吉木乃县	Jeminay County	10050	92842
博尔塔拉蒙古自治州	**Bortala Mongol Autonomous Prefecture**	**171261**	**758226**
博尔塔拉州本级	Bortala Mongol Autonomous Prefecture Level	13507	164592
博乐市	Bole [Bortala] City	90632	266912
阿拉山口市	AlashanKon City	22531	65105
精河县	Jinghe [Jing] County	33433	150309
温泉县	Wenquan [Araxang] County	11158	111308
巴音郭楞蒙古自治州	**Bayangol Mongol Autonomous Prefecture**	**700081**	**1797775**
巴音郭楞州本级	Bayangol Mongol Autonomous Prefecture Level	115539	281834
库尔勒市	Korla City	311000	446322
轮台县	Luntai [Bugur] County	69010	146615
尉犁县	Yuli [Lopnur] County	21298	130086
若羌县	Ruoqiang [Qarkilik] County	66075	136973
且末县	Qiemo [Qarqan] County	20615	133181
焉耆回族自治县	Yanqi Hui Autonomous County	30551	136576
和静县	Hejing County	35500	182745
和硕县	Hoxud County	15730	107623
博湖县	Bohu [Bagrax] County	14763	95820
阿克苏地区	**Aksu Administrative Offices**	**769712**	**2527768**
地区本级	Prefecture Level	33414	339634
阿克苏市	Aksu City	165032	358281
温宿县	Wensu [Onsu] County	43467	222537
库车县	Kuqa County	260292	455366
沙雅县	Xayar County	76498	215482
新和县	Xinhe [Toksu] County	39000	171660
拜城县	Baicheng [Bay] County	117010	257888
乌什县	Wushi [Uxturpan] County	10925	203646
阿瓦提县	Awat County	19039	216274
柯坪县	Kalpin County	5035	87000
克孜勒苏柯尔克孜自治州	**Kizilsu Kirgiz Autonomous Prefecture**	**109721**	**1008315**
州本级	Autonomous Prefecture Level	25469	181265

8-4 续表 3 Continued

单位：万元 (10 000 yuan)

地　　区	Region	收 入 Revenue	支 出 Expenditure
阿图什市	Artux City	30725	268570
阿克陶县	Akto County	24374	294168
阿合奇县	Akqi County	7751	116011
乌恰县	Wuqia [Ulugqat] County	21402	148301
喀什地区	**Kashgar [Kaxgar] Administrative Offices**	**573702**	**4201329**
地区本级	Prefecture Level	30555	247362
喀什市	Kashgar [Kaxgar] City	181115	545027
疏附县	Shufu County	31387	277925
疏勒县	Shule County	43745	302187
英吉沙县	Yengisar County	20026	270140
泽普县	Zepu [Poskam] County	24267	204393
莎车县	Shache [Yarkant] County	48669	609891
叶城县	Yecheng [Kagilik] County	51237	438248
麦盖提县	Makit County	26000	245510
岳普湖县	Yopurga County	19806	198494
伽师县	Jiashi [Payzawat] County	42178	353053
巴楚县	Bachu [Maralbexi] County	38501	378156
塔什库尔干塔吉克自治县	Taxkorgan Tajik Autonomous County	16216	130943
和田地区	**Hotan Administrative Offices**	**186119**	**2331481**
地区本级	Prefecture Level	10553	277996
和田市	Hotan City	69586	288914
和田县	Hotan County	16022	246035
墨玉县	Moyu [Karakax] County	23477	424480
皮山县	Pishan [Guma] County	13792	333733
洛浦县	Lop County	17316	258798
策勒县	Qira County	8550	167824
于田县	Yutian [Keriya] County	18295	245820
民丰县	Minfeng [Niya] County	8528	87881
自治区直辖县级市	**County level City directly under the Autonomous Region**	**610707**	**758220**
石河子市	Shihezi City	368259	445888
阿拉尔市	Aral City	66882	83578
图木舒克市	Tumxuk City	31040	53854
五家渠市	Wujiaqu City	117059	139434
北屯市	Beitun City	22634	30456
铁门关市	Tiemenuan City	4833	5010

主要统计指标解释

地方财政收入 包括一般公共预算收入、国有资本经营预算收入和基金预算收入。

一般公共预算收入 指国家财政参与社会产品分配所取得的收入，是实现国家职能的财力保证。主要包括：（1）各项税收：包括国内增值税、国内消费税、进口货物增值税和消费税、出口货物退增值税和消费税、营业税、企业所得税、个人所得税、资源税、城市维护建设税、房产税、印花税、城镇土地使用税、土地增值税、车船税、船舶吨税、车辆购置税、关税、耕地占用税、契税、烟叶税等。（2）**非税收收入**：包括专项收入、行政事业性收费、罚没收入和其他收入。

基金预算收入 是按规定收取，转入或通过当年财政安排，由财政管理并具有指定用途的政府性基金预算收入等。

地方财政支出 是以国家为主体，以财政的事权为依据进行的一种财政资金分配活动，集中反映了国家的职能活动范围及其所发生的耗费，包括一般公共预算支出、国有资本经营预算支出和基金预算支出。

一般公共预算支出 指国家财政将筹集起来的资金进行分配使用，以满足经济建设和各项事业的需要。主要包括：一般公共服务、外交、国防、公共安全、教育、科学技术、文化体育与传媒、社会保障和就业、医疗卫生和计划生育、节能环保、城乡社区、农林水、交通运输、资源勘探信息等、商业服务业等、金融、援助其他地区、国土海洋气象等、住房保障、粮油物资储备等、债务付息等方面的支出。

基金预算支出 是各级财政部门用基金预算收入安排的支出。

Explanatory Notes on Main Statistical Indicators

Local Government Revenue includes local public budgetary financial revenue state-owned capital operating budget revenue and fund budget revenue.

General Public Budget Revenue refers to income for the government finance through participating in the distribution of social products. It is the financial guarantee to ensure government functioning. The government revenue includes the following main items: (1) Various tax revenues including domestic value added tax (VAT), domestic consumption tax, VAT and consumption tax from imports, VAT and consumption tax rebate for exports, business tax, corporate income tax, individual income tax, resource tax, city maintenance and construction tax, house property tax, stamp tax, urban land use tax, land appreciation tax, tax on vehicles and boat operation, ship tonnage tax, vehicle purchase tax, tariffs, farm land occupation tax, deed tax, and tobacco tax, etc. (2) Non-tax revenue, including special program receipts, charge of administrative and institutional units, penalty receipts and others non-tax receipts.

Fund Budget Revenue refers to governmental fund budget revenues collected, transferred in or arranged by government finance the same year in accordance with regulations, governed by government finance and for specific use of purpose.

Local Financial Expenditure refers to a sort of allocation activity of financial funds by the state based on the position of finance.It is a concentrated reflection of the functional activity scope of the state and the expenditure incurred by it. It includes local public budgetary financial expenditure. state-owned capital operating budget exependiture and fund budget expenditure.

General Public Budget Expenditure refers to the distribution and use of the funds which the government finance has raised, so as to meet the needs of economic construction and various undertakings. It includes the following main items: expenditure for general public services, expenditure for foreign affairs, expenditure for national defence expenditure for public security, expenditure for education, expenditure for science and technology, expenditure for culture, sport and media, expenditure for social safety net and employment effort, expenditure for medical and health care and family planning, expenditure for energy conservation and environment protection, expenditure for urban and rural community affairs, expenditure for agriculture, forestry and water conservancy, expenditure for transportation, expenditure for resource exploration and information, expenditure for affairs of commerce and services, expenditure for finance, aid to other regions, expenditure for land, ocean and weather, expenditure for housing security, expenditure for grain & oil reserves, interest payment for public debts. General public budget expenditure is divided into general public budget expenditure of central government and general public budget expenditure of local government according to the different functions of the governments played in economic and social activities,

Fund Budget Expenditure refers to the expenditure arranged by finance authorities at all level with the fund budget revenue.

物价
PRICE

第九篇　物价

本篇主要内容和资料来源

本篇价格指数资料，反映生产、流通、消费与投资环节的价格变动趋势和变动幅度，主要包括居民消费价格指数、商品零售价格指数、农业生产资料价格指数、工业生产者出厂价格指数、工业生产者购进价格指数、固定资产投资价格指数。

居民消费价格指数、商品零售价格指数和农业生产资料价格指数出自国家统计局新疆调查总队消费价格调查处；工业生产者出厂价格指数、工业生产者购进价格指数、固定资产投资价格指数出自国家统计局新疆调查总队生产投资价格调查处。

Price

Main Content and Source of Data

Data on the price indices in this chapter show the changing trend and the change rates in production, circulation, consumption and investment, including mainly consumer price indices of residents, retail price indices, price indices of agricultural means of production, purchasing price indices of farm products, producers' price indices of industrial products, purchasing price indices of raw materials, fuels and power, price indices of investment in fixed assets, and real estate price indices.

Data on the consumer price index, retail price index and price indices of agriculture production come from Division of Consumer Price of NBS Survey Office in Xinjiang.Data on the price indices of industrial products, indices of purchasing price of raw materials, fuels and power, price indices of investment in fixed assets, price indices for real estate come from Division of Consumer Price of NBS Survey Office in Xinjiang.

9-1 主要年份各种物价指数
Price Indices in Main Years

年 份 Year	居民消费价格指数 Consumer Price Indiex	城市居民消费价格指数 Urban Household	农村居民消费价格指数 Rural Household	商品零售价格指数 Retail Price Indiex
上年=100 Preceding year=100				
1978	101.2	101.4	100.3	101.4
1980	102.8	104.1	102.0	104.2
1985	107.8	109.5	106.4	108.1
1990	105.0	104.5	105.9	104.1
1995	119.7	118.4	122.5	116.7
2000	99.4	100.1	97.6	98.3
2001	104.0	104.0	103.8	102.5
2002	99.4	98.9	100.9	97.9
2003	100.4	100.5	100.2	99.2
2004	102.7	102.1	104.5	100.7
2005	100.7	100.6	101.2	99.4
2006	101.3	101.0	102.0	101.8
2007	105.5	104.6	107.2	105.1
2008	108.1	107.3	109.5	108.5
2009	100.7	100.2	102.0	100.4
2010	104.3	103.6	105.8	104.6
2011	105.9	105.5	106.8	105.1
2012	103.8	103.4	104.7	103.3
2013	103.9	103.8	104.1	103.3
2014	102.1	102.3	101.7	101.7
2015	100.6	100.5	100.6	99.6
1978 年=100 Year 1978 =100				
1978	100.0	100.0	100.0	100.0
1980	105.1	106.6	103.8	107.8
1985	120.9	125.6	117.9	124.2
1990	194.3	206.0	184.0	197.6
1995	392.7	422.7	364.2	381.0
2000	436.5	471.9	398.6	397.9
2001	454.0	490.8	413.8	407.8
2002	451.3	485.4	417.5	399.3
2003	453.1	487.8	418.3	396.1
2004	465.3	498.1	437.1	398.9
2005	468.6	501.1	442.3	396.5
2006	474.7	506.1	451.1	403.6
2007	500.8	529.4	483.6	424.2
2008	541.4	568.0	529.5	460.3
2009	545.2	569.1	540.1	462.1
2010	568.6	589.6	571.4	483.4
2011	602.1	622.0	610.3	508.1
2012	625.0	643.1	639.0	524.9
2013	649.7	667.7	665.6	541.9
2014	663.4	683.0	677.2	551.1
2015	667.4	686.4	681.3	548.9

9-2 居民消费价格分类指数
Consumer Price Indices by Category

(上年=100) (2015 年) (preceding year=100)

项目	Item	全区 Autonomous Region	城市 Urban Indices	农村 Rural Indices
居民消费价格总指数	**Consumer Price Indiex**	**100.6**	**100.5**	**100.6**
食品	**Food**	**99.2**	**99.0**	**99.5**
粮食	Grain	101.7	101.4	102.1
大米	Rice	102.0	101.9	102.2
面粉	Flour	101.7	101.8	101.6
粮食制品	Grain Products	100.5	100.6	100.3
其它	Others	107.1	103.8	109.7
淀粉及制品	Starches and Tubers	102.5	105.1	99.1
干豆类及豆制品	Beans and Bean Products	103.8	105.8	100.5
油脂	Oil or Fat	97.7	98.8	96.2
肉禽及其制品	Meat, Poultry and Processed Products	93.5	93.5	93.4
蛋	Eggs	92.8	92.5	93.3
水产品	Aquatic Products	98.3	98.3	98.3
菜	Vegetables	101.3	101.4	101.0
鲜菜	Fresh Vegetables	101.4	101.5	101.1
干菜及菜制品	Dried Vegetables and Vegetable Products	102.4	102.1	103.1
薯类	Tubers	96.3	97.2	94.2
调味品	Flavoring	102.2	102.0	102.5
糖	Carbohydrate	101.3	102.5	100.0
食糖	Sugar	101.6	102.2	101.1
糖果	Candy	101.3	103.0	99.4
巧克力制品	Chocolate Goods	101.8	104.0	99.0
糖类小食品	Carbohydrate Products	100.5	100.9	99.9
茶及饮料	Tea and Beverages	102.6	103.5	101.2
干鲜瓜果	Dried and Fresh Melons and Fruits	101.5	96.9	110.3
鲜瓜果	Fresh melons and Fruits	101.6	94.7	113.4
干(坚)果	Drie (nut) Fruits	101.1	101.9	98.9
糕点饼干面包	Cake and Biscuit	101.6	101.4	102.2
液体乳及乳制品	Milk and Its Products	99.0	98.8	99.5
在外用膳食品	Dining Out	103.8	104.1	102.7
主食	Staple Food	104.3	104.1	104.8
炒菜	Fried Dishes	102.9	103.5	101.1
地方小吃	Local Snack	104.1	104.5	102.3
其他	Others	103.8	104.9	102.4
其他食品	Other Foods	100.8	100.6	101.2
烟酒	**Tobacco, Liquor**	**102.0**	**101.7**	**102.6**
烟草	Tobacco	105.5	105.4	105.7
酒	Liquor	98.8	98.0	99.9
衣着	**Clothing**	**103.4**	**103.3**	**103.5**
服装	Garments	103.7	103.5	104.2
衣着材料	Clothing Material	101.3	101.4	101.2
棉布	Cotton Cloth	101.4	103.0	100.1

9-2 续表 Continued

(上年=100) (preceding year=100)

项　目	Item	全　区 Autonomous Region	城　市 Urban Areas	农　村 Rural Areas
化纤布	Chemical Fiber Cloth	100.0	100.1	100.0
毛　线	Wool	100.5	100.1	100.9
其　他	Others	103.7	102.3	104.8
鞋袜帽	Footwear and Hats	102.6	102.7	102.4
鞋	Shoes	102.9	103.0	102.8
袜　子	Socks and Stockings	100.8	101.0	100.6
帽　子	Hats	103.1	102.8	103.9
衣着加工服务费	Clothing Manufacturing Services	106.9	109.6	104.1
家庭设备用品及维修服务	**Household Facilities,Articles and Services**	**100.6**	**100.6**	**100.5**
耐用消费品	Durable Consumer Goods	99.7	99.5	100.0
家　具	Furniture	100.7	100.7	100.7
家庭设备	Household Facilities	99.0	98.6	99.5
室内装饰品	Interior Decorations	101.0	100.8	101.4
床上用品	Bed Articles	99.6	99.1	100.4
家庭日用杂品	Daily Use Household Articles	100.1	100.2	99.9
家庭服务及加工维修服务	Household Service and Mainteance and Renovation	104.9	106.1	102.8
医疗保健和个人用品	**Health Care and Personal Articles**	**101.5**	**101.6**	**101.3**
医疗保健	Health Cares	102.0	102.2	101.5
医疗器具及用品	Medical Instruments and Articles	99.8	99.4	100.3
中药材及中成药	Traditional Chinese Medicine	100.8	100.3	102.2
西　药	Western Medicine	104.5	105.1	102.2
保健器具及用品	Health Care Appliances and Articles	100.9	101.1	100.4
医疗保健服务	Health Care Services	100.0	100.0	100.0
个人用品及服务	Personal Articles and Services	100.8	100.5	101.1
交通和通信	**Transportation and Communication**	**99.3**	**99.1**	**99.5**
交　通	Transportation	99.1	98.8	99.5
通　信	Communication	99.4	99.4	99.5
娱乐教育文化用品及服务	**Recreation, Education, Culture Articles**	**100.9**	**100.8**	**101.1**
文娱用耐用消费品及服务	Durable Consumer Goods for Cultural and Recreationl Use and Services	99.2	99.4	98.8
教　育	Education	101.2	101.1	101.4
文化娱乐	Culture and Recreation Articles	101.3	101.7	100.4
文化娱乐用品	Cultural and Recreational Articles	99.0	98.5	100.0
书报杂志	Newspapers and Magazines	102.0	102.7	100.6
文娱费	Expenditure on Culture and Recreation	102.8	103.5	100.7
旅　游	Touring and Outing	101.6	100.4	103.7
居　住	**Residence**	**102.0**	**102.4**	**101.3**
建房及装修材料	Building and Building Decoration Materials	100.7	101.1	99.8
住房租金	Renting	101.7	102.2	99.6
自有住房	Private Housing	102.6	102.9	102.2
水、电、燃料	Water, Electricity and Fuels	100.6	101.8	99.4
服务项目价格指数	**Services**	**101.8**	**101.8**	**101.9**

9-3 各调查市县居民消费价格分类指数

(上年=100) (2015 年)

项 目	Item	乌鲁木齐市 Urumqi City	喀什市 Kashgar [Kaxgar] City	伊宁市 Yining [Gulja] City	和田市 Hotan City	克拉玛依市 Karamay City	哈密市 Hami [Kumul] City
居民消费价格总指数	**Consumer Price Indiex**	**100.7**	**100.4**	**101.2**	**100.6**	**100.4**	**100.9**
食 品	**Food**	**102.2**	**105.8**	**101.7**	**103.6**	**101.1**	**102.5**
粮 食	Grain	99.2	96.6	101.1	98.6	98.0	99.8
大 米	Rice	102.1	101.0	101.8	101.1	102.9	100.0
面 粉	Flour	103.1	100.8	103.4	102.4	105.3	97.9
粮食制品	Grain Products	101.8	101.2	100.6	100.3	100.4	102.1
其 它	Others	101.4	100.0	100.4	99.4	101.8	97.9
淀粉及制品	Starches and Tubers	102.2	102.0	128.7	105.0	107.9	103.7
干豆类及豆制品	Beans and Bean Products	109.1	100.0	99.1	102.0	100.0	102.8
油 脂	Oil or Fat	106.5	102.8	114.6	98.5	111.3	101.7
肉禽及其制品	Meat, Poultry and Processed Products	98.4	89.9	105.6	96.9	100.7	105.4
蛋	Eggs	95.0	91.8	95.4	92.9	94.4	93.8
水产品	Aquatic Products	92.7	92.2	96.9	96.0	95.5	94.4
菜	Vegetables	98.0	94.8	106.6	96.3	98.2	98.4
鲜 菜	Fresh Vegetables	101.8	99.6	101.4	100.2	96.0	105.0
干菜及菜制品	Dried Vegetables and Vegetable Products	102.2	99.5	100.8	100.1	95.4	105.7
薯 类	Tubers	101.1	102.5	111.0	103.4	100.0	100.0
调味品	Flavoring	92.6	99.1	99.6	95.0	105.4	96.9
糖	Carbohydrate	103.5	99.6	100.2	102.4	102.5	103.3
食 糖	Sugar	106.1	101.7	100.7	100.3	100.8	101.0
糖 果	Candy	102.2	107.5	100.0	100.4	100.3	102.8
巧克力制品	Chocolate Goods	107.2	100.0	101.0	100.0	100.0	100.0
糖类小食品	Carbohydrate Products	108.3	100.0	101.8	101.2	104.1	100.0
茶及饮料	Tea and Beverages	105.0	100.0	100.0	100.2	100.0	100.0
干鲜瓜果	Dried and Fresh Melons and Fruits	103.3	100.0	105.7	99.4	105.0	102.7
鲜瓜果	Fresh melons and Fruits	95.2	90.3	95.0	95.0	91.8	108.3
干(坚)果	Drie (nut) Fruits	91.5	86.1	92.0	94.9	88.0	113.9
糕点饼干面包	Cake and Biscuit	104.2	100.4	104.1	95.2	107.7	96.6
液体乳及乳制品	Milk and Its Products	101.2	99.9	104.7	101.9	101.1	100.4
在外用膳食品	Dining Out	100.2	101.8	101.8	93.8	100.3	91.6
主 食	Staple Food	104.1	102.9	112.6	107.6	102.5	102.0
炒 菜	Fried Dishes	102.3	102.2	121.9	112.7	101.0	101.5
地方小吃	Local Snack	104.2	106.3	105.8	109.0	101.8	102.4
其他	Others	106.7	101.5	105.2	100.0	104.1	102.1
其他食品	Other Foods	106.8	100.0	100.0	102.0	100.0	102.9
烟 酒	**Tobacco, Liquor**	**101.0**	**100.3**	**100.9**	**100.5**	**101.2**	**98.7**
烟 草	Tobacco	101.7	103.0	102.6	101.2	100.8	103.4
酒	Liquor	106.5	106.9	106.2	106.0	105.7	105.2
衣 着	**Clothing**	**96.8**	**99.3**	**100.2**	**97.7**	**96.9**	**101.9**
服 装	Garments	102.7	102.7	101.3	103.2	107.1	103.0
衣着材料	Clothing Material	102.6	103.8	101.0	103.9	108.2	102.9
棉 布	Cotton Cloth	100.0	98.9	100.0	100.0	106.1	98.1

Consumer Price Indices by Category in Surveyed Cities and Counties

(preceding year=100)

昌吉市 Changji City	库尔勒市 Korla City	阿克苏市 Aksu City	焉耆回族自治县 Yanqi Hui Autonomous County	塔城市 Tacheng [Qoqek] City	阿勒泰市 Altay City	沙湾县 Shawan County	博乐市 Bole [Bortala] City	高昌区 Gaochang District	库车县 Kuqa County	阿图什市 Artux City	莎车县 Shache [Yarkant] County	奎屯市 Kuytun City	石河子市 Shihezi City
101.4	**99.7**	**99.9**	**100.1**	**99.7**	**101.0**	**100.0**	**100.5**	**101.4**	**101.0**	**100.0**	**99.7**	**101.1**	**100.5**
101.3	**102.5**	**103.2**	**102.8**	**101.3**	**102.3**	**101.5**	**101.3**	**105.6**	**100.9**	**101.5**	**100.3**	**103.9**	**100.0**
100.9	96.7	97.8	98.5	98.2	100.2	99.3	99.0	98.8	101.0	98.7	98.3	99.3	100.5
99.8	99.8	105.0	103.3	103.2	101.4	99.9	103.6	101.5	105.3	101.0	101.3	99.8	100.4
100.0	99.5	99.4	107.4	110.4	102.0	100.0	104.4	101.4	108.6	102.2	98.1	100.8	99.7
100.5	100.1	111.0	97.4	100.3	99.7	99.4	101.5	100.2	104.0	100.2	103.8	98.3	100.8
96.6	100.0	101.1	99.1	100.0	102.7	100.0	104.0	100.0	103.1	101.0	95.5	100.0	100.0
100.0	99.8	100.7	122.0	106.9	107.9	106.5	109.9	111.7	103.4	101.9	108.0	100.2	102.2
105.3	100.0	100.0	100.5	100.8	103.1	100.0	103.4	100.0	97.0	81.8	100.4	100.0	100.9
106.0	102.0	93.5	103.1	102.0	101.1	103.3	98.8	102.0	99.7	99.9	101.1	109.9	104.8
84.6	98.9	101.0	93.9	99.6	96.2	101.1	95.1	92.3	93.1	91.8	98.8	100.0	99.1
91.0	92.5	93.7	93.4	93.5	95.7	95.7	93.7	93.6	93.7	93.0	92.6	95.4	98.7
93.3	83.9	95.9	89.8	95.7	100.1	95.1	89.4	90.8	91.1	96.5	95.8	94.5	87.9
96.7	94.8	89.5	100.3	100.8	102.8	105.3	104.2	94.5	98.7	87.1	93.5	106.8	99.7
110.9	99.9	100.2	97.4	98.4	99.8	105.1	102.8	100.4	103.6	102.4	99.6	99.4	99.5
111.7	99.7	100.2	96.5	99.7	100.5	106.1	103.1	101.6	104.2	102.2	99.6	99.3	99.6
100.0	102.3	101.9	104.9	100.0	107.1	99.3	106.0	107.0	100.1	99.9	100.8	100.0	102.4
104.3	97.6	87.9	92.7	85.0	90.9	105.1	94.3	92.1	100.0	116.1	94.4	107.7	92.8
101.4	97.7	99.9	104.2	100.0	103.7	100.3	100.5	108.4	99.8	103.2	100.0	101.2	101.2
100.2	100.0	103.5	92.6	100.0	97.5	100.0	103.5	102.7	102.1	98.5	99.3	102.1	99.8
100.0	100.0	109.8	94.0	100.0	93.8	100.0	101.9	110.0	105.9	96.8	99.1	102.9	96.1
100.0	100.0	102.8	87.7	100.0	99.0	100.0	104.0	100.0	100.3	99.3	99.6	102.4	100.0
101.7	100.0	100.0	99.6	100.0	100.0	100.0	102.0	100.3	98.8	100.0	95.2	100.0	100.6
100.0	100.0	100.0	100.0	100.0	100.0	100.0	108.6	98.6	95.9	98.8	100.0	100.0	102.4
100.6	102.2	100.9	101.2	100.0	103.2	100.7	103.9	100.0	100.4	103.7	100.0	100.0	100.3
120.0	94.5	89.4	109.5	98.7	109.0	95.1	101.0	98.2	110.4	103.9	100.2	100.1	101.7
129.2	96.5	90.4	110.7	98.1	113.5	93.2	100.5	97.4	114.1	106.8	101.8	95.9	100.8
106.8	85.7	85.3	107.2	100.0	94.5	101.5	102.7	100.2	97.8	95.5	96.1	107.8	105.1
100.0	104.6	97.4	99.1	101.2	103.2	103.8	100.0	115.7	99.2	103.6	100.0	101.3	100.6
92.0	100.1	96.9	99.0	96.9	98.6	100.0	99.9	103.5	99.9	104.3	100.5	100.0	103.3
101.5	101.8	104.9	100.6	100.0	102.8	100.6	100.5	106.2	105.2	104.2	103.5	103.6	103.4
101.9	103.7	100.0	100.0	100.0	103.0	100.9	100.0	109.3	105.1	107.4	108.0	102.2	100.0
100.1	101.0	100.1	100.0	100.0	100.0	101.2	100.0	104.1	104.0	100.4	100.0	104.2	101.5
102.6	100.0	109.3	102.0	100.0	106.1	100.0	102.9	105.0	106.8	102.1	100.0	100.0	111.8
100.0	100.0	125.0	101.8	100.0	100.5	100.0	100.0	102.0	108.9	118.0	101.4	116.4	100.0
100.0	**100.0**	**100.2**	**97.3**	**100.0**	**100.0**	**100.8**	**101.9**	**100.0**	**100.6**	**115.8**	**100.0**	**101.3**	**104.2**
103.4	102.7	104.6	99.8	101.9	102.4	102.6	102.7	102.7	103.5	102.0	102.5	99.0	104.0
105.6	105.3	105.7	105.9	106.1	104.7	105.4	105.8	106.0	106.0	105.5	104.8	100.0	106.0
100.9	**100.0**	**103.5**	**92.9**	**99.3**	**100.5**	**100.3**	**99.9**	**100.0**	**101.4**	**99.3**	**100.0**	**98.2**	**101.8**
107.6	103.5	100.3	102.3	99.2	105.2	102.5	106.9	103.4	102.7	103.5	104.0	102.5	101.9
106.7	103.4	96.8	102.4	97.6	105.8	100.0	109.8	103.7	102.4	102.3	106.1	102.3	102.2
108.7	101.2	102.8	100.9	101.6	100.0	100.0	104.7	99.2	101.7	100.0	100.0	100.0	102.3

9-3 续表

(上年=100)

项 目	Item	乌鲁木齐市 Urumqi City	喀什市 Kashgar [Kaxgar] City	伊宁市 Yining [Gulja] City	和田市 Hotan City	克拉玛依市 Karamay City	哈密市 Hami [Kumul] City
化纤布	Chemical Fiber Cloth	100.0	95.7	100.0	100.0	110.4	100.0
毛 线	Wool	100.0	100.0	100.0	100.0	99.5	93.1
其 他	Others	100.0	100.0	100.1	100.0	104.2	100.0
鞋袜帽	Footwear and Hats	100.0	100.0	100.0	100.0	100.0	100.0
鞋	Shoes	100.7	100.0	101.9	103.4	106.0	102.4
袜 子	Socks and Stockings	100.7	100.0	102.2	104.4	106.5	103.1
帽 子	Hats	100.0	100.0	100.0	100.0	102.1	100.0
衣着加工服务费	Clothing Manufacturing Services	102.1	100.0	100.0	105.6	104.0	100.1
家庭设备用品及维修服务	**Household Facilities,Articles and Services**	**119.2**	**104.0**	**103.5**	**99.4**	**101.0**	**111.7**
耐用消费品	Durable Consumer Goods	100.9	100.5	99.5	98.4	101.8	101.5
家 具	Furniture	100.5	99.1	98.8	96.9	101.7	97.8
家庭设备	Household Facilities	102.0	98.1	98.4	94.7	103.8	98.3
室内装饰品	Interior Decorations	99.5	99.8	98.9	98.7	99.9	97.6
床上用品	Bed Articles	101.9	100.0	101.4	100.0	100.2	100.0
家庭日用杂品	Daily Use Household Articles	98.0	100.0	99.4	100.0	99.8	97.1
家庭服务及加工维修服务	Household Service and Mainteance and Renovation	100.3	100.0	99.7	99.9	100.4	100.0
医疗保健和个人用品	**Health Care and Personal Articles**	**106.1**	**108.2**	**100.0**	**100.0**	**107.1**	**115.2**
医疗保健	Health Cares	102.2	101.0	103.2	100.7	100.5	103.3
医疗器具及用品	Medical Instruments and Articles	102.3	101.9	104.6	100.8	101.4	103.3
中药材及中成药	Traditional Chinese Medicine	98.0	100.0	101.6	100.0	100.0	100.0
西 药	Western Medicine	99.5	102.2	104.0	102.7	100.3	101.9
保健器具及用品	Health Care Appliances and Articles	104.8	102.7	106.0	100.3	102.7	106.1
医疗保健服务	Health Care Services	101.1	100.4	105.9	100.0	100.4	101.8
个人用品及服务	Personal Articles and Services	100.0	100.1	100.4	100.0	100.0	100.0
交通和通信	**Transportation and Communication**	**101.8**	**99.5**	**100.7**	**100.5**	**99.5**	**103.4**
交 通	Transportation	99.6	98.9	99.4	98.9	97.9	98.0
通 信	Communication	99.6	98.2	99.4	98.2	96.6	97.6
娱乐教育文化用品及服务	**Recreation, Education, Culture Articles**	**99.6**	**99.8**	**99.5**	**99.6**	**99.5**	**98.7**
文娱用耐用消费品及服务	Durable Consumer Goods for Cultural and Recreationl Use and Services	101.0	104.1	103.4	107.2	101.4	101.4
教 育	Education	99.0	100.6	100.0	101.1	100.8	97.4
文化娱乐	Culture and Recreation Articles	102.1	105.0	104.0	112.8	102.0	104.0
文化娱乐用品	Cultural and Recreational Articles	102.2	99.6	99.8	100.6	101.1	104.4
书报杂志	Newspapers and Magazines	96.7	98.1	99.5	99.8	99.2	101.3
文娱费	Expenditure on Culture and Recreation	107.1	100.1	100.0	104.0	100.0	113.5
旅 游	Touring and Outing	103.2	100.7	100.0	100.0	106.3	98.3
居 住	**Residence**	**98.9**	**113.3**	**107.1**	**100.5**	**101.9**	**97.1**
建房及装修材料	Building and Building Decoration Materials	102.7	107.8	99.8	101.6	101.2	101.1
住房租金	Renting	101.0	102.4	99.7	98.9	103.6	100.4
自有住房	Private Housing	104.3	102.5	100.0	101.4	100.0	104.6
水、电、燃料	Water, Electricity and Fuels	104.8	112.1	100.5	102.3	101.1	100.0
服务项目价格指数	**Services**	**102.8**	**102.0**	**95.5**	**101.1**	**100.0**	**99.5**

Continued

(preceding year=100)

昌吉市 Changji City	库尔勒市 Korla City	阿克苏市 Aksu City	焉耆回族自治县 Yanqi Hui Autonomous County	塔城市 Tacheng [Qoqek] City	阿勒泰市 Altay City	沙湾县 Shawan County	博乐市 Bole [Bortala] City	高昌区 Gaochang District	库车县 Kuqa County	阿图什市 Artux City	莎车县 Shache [Yarkant] County	奎屯市 Kuytun City	石河子市 Shihezi City
107.6	102.9	102.8	100.0	100.0	100.0	100.0	100.0	100.0	101.0	100.0	100.0	100.0	105.4
111.3	101.5	103.8	100.0	110.8	100.0	100.0	100.0	100.0	99.5	100.0	100.0	100.0	100.3
107.6	100.2	95.3	104.7	100.0	100.0	100.0	100.0	96.7	106.0	100.0	100.0	100.0	100.8
110.1	101.1	108.7	100.0	104.4	100.0	100.0	120.0	100.0	100.4	100.0	100.0	100.0	100.0
108.7	104.0	101.1	101.3	100.0	101.0	99.6	102.5	104.4	105.1	108.1	100.3	103.5	101.5
109.1	104.4	101.3	101.4	100.0	101.2	98.7	103.2	105.5	105.8	109.2	100.3	104.3	101.4
105.4	100.0	103.0	100.0	100.0	100.0	101.5	100.0	101.8	100.4	102.5	100.0	100.0	101.5
115.0	104.1	89.1	102.8	100.0	100.0	100.0	115.9	101.3	109.7	100.7	100.0	103.1	102.6
113.7	**105.6**	**109.9**	**107.0**	**142.4**	**121.7**	**158.5**	**100.6**	**100.0**	**100.0**	**100.8**	**102.2**	**103.6**	**99.9**
100.3	98.6	101.0	99.2	101.1	100.1	100.2	99.7	101.9	101.0	102.1	99.9	102.1	101.2
99.3	94.9	100.6	99.5	100.0	100.1	100.2	98.7	101.4	100.0	99.6	99.8	101.1	101.3
102.0	97.9	100.4	102.8	100.0	100.6	100.0	99.4	107.4	99.7	99.7	99.6	102.6	101.8
98.8	93.3	100.7	97.3	100.0	99.8	100.3	98.1	98.9	100.4	99.6	99.8	100.3	101.1
102.1	99.5	101.1	100.3	100.0	100.0	100.0	102.3	102.7	100.5	96.0	99.8	103.4	101.7
97.9	100.0	107.1	100.5	100.0	100.0	100.0	100.0	101.1	104.0	101.3	100.0	103.4	102.5
101.0	100.0	100.1	97.5	100.4	100.1	100.0	100.2	98.8	101.1	98.9	100.0	101.2	100.0
104.0	**108.5**	**100.0**	**100.0**	**109.1**	**100.7**	**101.0**	**100.0**	**106.8**	**102.6**	**111.2**	**100.0**	**105.1**	**102.4**
100.8	102.9	100.4	101.0	101.9	100.9	100.3	101.2	102.8	102.5	100.5	101.1	103.6	101.0
100.2	104.4	100.9	101.7	101.3	100.9	100.3	101.3	102.9	102.5	100.6	101.5	100.3	101.4
100.0	98.1	100.0	101.3	102.8	100.0	102.8	100.0	100.0	98.8	102.8	100.0	104.0	105.9
100.2	100.1	100.4	102.2	102.4	99.8	100.2	100.8	107.5	107.6	100.4	101.4	100.9	101.5
100.3	109.7	101.7	101.6	103.4	103.5	100.3	102.7	102.8	101.3	101.1	102.5	100.0	103.3
100.0	98.0	102.5	103.9	100.0	100.0	100.0	100.0	97.8	101.5	101.1	100.0	99.9	99.1
100.0	100.0	100.0	100.0	100.0	100.0	100.0	100.0	100.0	100.0	100.0	100.0	100.0	100.0
101.8	**100.5**	**99.6**	**99.9**	**103.4**	**100.9**	**100.1**	**100.9**	**102.6**	**102.6**	**100.4**	**100.5**	**108.2**	**100.1**
99.1	99.1	99.2	98.5	100.9	99.1	98.8	97.1	99.7	99.0	98.4	100.0	99.4	98.4
99.0	99.2	98.7	96.8	101.1	98.5	97.8	95.5	99.8	98.7	98.4	100.6	99.7	97.2
99.2	**98.9**	**100.0**	**100.0**	**100.5**	**100.0**	**100.0**	**98.9**	**99.5**	**99.7**	**98.4**	**99.3**	**99.0**	**99.9**
100.1	99.8	103.3	98.8	100.1	102.4	100.8	99.4	101.7	101.4	103.2	100.1	100.1	99.6
99.4	96.6	100.0	95.9	100.0	100.4	100.0	98.4	97.2	98.9	98.9	99.3	99.8	98.5
100.1	100.7	101.6	99.4	100.0	100.2	100.0	100.9	103.2	101.7	104.9	99.9	100.4	100.0
101.0	100.3	101.8	100.7	100.2	102.3	100.1	98.9	103.4	100.9	100.3	100.0	100.9	99.8
102.6	100.3	102.2	100.2	100.5	102.2	100.2	100.3	96.3	100.4	99.8	100.0	100.2	99.4
100.0	100.0	100.0	100.0	100.0	100.0	100.0	100.0	113.3	98.1	100.0	100.0	101.5	100.0
100.8	100.6	103.3	101.9	100.0	105.5	100.0	96.5	109.5	103.4	101.3	100.0	101.1	100.5
99.9	**101.7**	**112.2**	**100.0**	**100.0**	**108.7**	**104.7**	**96.9**	**102.2**	**104.4**	**108.6**	**103.4**	**99.0**	**99.8**
101.1	102.7	101.5	104.3	100.1	100.8	100.0	102.3	107.2	99.7	98.7	98.9	104.2	99.9
101.4	99.7	98.3	96.2	99.9	100.0	100.2	100.1	98.7	99.4	100.0	101.1	102.2	100.1
103.4	103.4	104.0	100.0	100.2	101.2	100.0	100.0	101.9	98.3	102.9	95.9	103.6	100.0
100.0	104.0	102.5	108.2	100.3	101.1	100.0	103.6	111.1	100.4	98.1	98.4	105.5	100.0
100.0	**100.0**	**91.1**	**100.8**	**98.7**	**100.0**	**100.2**	**100.0**	**99.9**	**98.5**	**98.2**	**99.4**	**100.2**	**98.8**

9-4 商品零售价格分类指数
Retail Price Indices by Category

(上年=100) (2015 年) (preceding year=100)

项目	Item	全区 Autonomous Region	城市 Urban Indices	农村 Rural Indices
商品零售价格总指数	**Retail Price Indice**	**99.6**	**99.5**	**99.8**
食品	**Food**	**99.3**	**99.3**	**99.4**
粮食	Grain	101.7	101.8	101.6
油脂	Oil or Fat	97.7	98.7	96.2
肉禽及其制品	Meat, Poultry and Processed Products	95.1	95.5	94.2
猪肉	Pork	103.7	104.8	101.4
牛肉	Beef	91.6	91.1	92.7
羊肉	Mutton	83.7	84.0	83.1
鸡	Chicken	100.9	101.8	98.7
鲜蛋	Fresh Eggs	91.6	91.6	91.4
水产品	Aquatic Products	98.2	98.1	98.3
鲜瓜果	Fresh Melons and Fruits	99.1	93.9	111.2
糕点、饼干、面包	Cake, Biscuit and Bread	101.6	101.2	102.8
饮料、烟酒	**Beverages, Tobacco and Liquor**	**102.2**	**102.2**	**102.2**
茶及饮料	Tea and Beverages	102.7	103.3	101.4
#饮料	Beverages	103.4	103.9	102.3
烟草	Tobacco	106.1	106.2	105.7
酒	Liquor	98.2	97.7	99.6
服装鞋帽	**Garments, Shoes and Hats**	**102.9**	**102.4**	**103.9**
服装	Garments	103.4	102.9	104.6
鞋袜帽	Footgear and Hats	102.0	101.7	102.5
#鞋	Shoes	102.0	101.9	102.4
纺织品	**Textiles**	**99.5**	**98.9**	**101.0**
棉布	Cotton Cloth	100.9	101.6	100.1
化纤布	Chemical Fiber Cloth	100.3	100.3	100.4
毛线	Wool	100.4	100.3	100.9
其他	Others	101.5	100.7	103.4
家用电器及音响器材	**Household Appliances,Music andVideo Equipment**	**99.3**	**99.2**	**99.7**
家庭设备	Household Facilities	99.2	99.2	99.3
文娱用耐用消费品	Durable Consuming Goods for Entertainment	99.5	99.0	100.3
专业音像器材	Sound Apparatus	99.8	100.1	99.3

9-4 续表 Continued

(上年=100) (preceding year=100)

项　目	Item	全　区 Autonomous Region	城　市 Urban Indices	农　村 Rural Indices
文化办公用品	**Cultural and Office Appliances**	**98.0**	**96.8**	**100.3**
日用品	**Articles for Daily Use**	**100.3**	**100.5**	**100.1**
日用百货	General Merchandise for Daily Use	100.2	100.2	100.2
日用杂品	Miscellaneous for Daily Use	99.9	100.1	99.5
洗涤用品	Washing and Cleaning Goods	100.6	100.6	100.9
其他日用品	Other Daily-use Goods	100.5	100.9	99.6
体育娱乐用品	**Sports and Recreation Articles**	**100.0**	**99.8**	**100.5**
体育用品	Sports Articles	100.4	100.3	100.6
娱乐用品	Recreational Articles	99.6	99.4	100.4
交通、通信用品	**Transportation communication Appliances**	**99.7**	**99.6**	**99.8**
交通运输机械	Traffic and Transport Machinery	100.2	100.4	99.6
通信器材	Telecommunication Apparatus	98.9	98.3	100.0
家　具	**Furniture**	**101.5**	**101.5**	**101.5**
化妆品	**Cosmetics**	**100.4**	**100.3**	**100.6**
金银珠宝	**Gold , Silver and Jewelry**	**95.6**	**95.8**	**95.1**
中西药品及医疗保健用品	**Traditional Chinese and Western Medicines, Health Care Articles**	**102.4**	**102.5**	**102.1**
医疗器具及用品	Medical Apparatus and Article	99.2	98.6	100.4
中药材及中成药	Traditional Chinese Medicinal Materials and Medicines	100.9	100.0	102.3
西　药	Western Medicines	104.0	104.5	102.4
保健器具及用品	Health Care Devices and Articles	101.0	101.2	100.3
书报杂志及电子出版物	**Books,Newspapers,Magazines and Electronic Publications**	**102.3**	**102.9**	**100.6**
教材及参考书	Texts and Reference Books	100.3	100.4	100.3
书报杂志	Newspapers and Magazines	104.5	105.4	101.2
电子音像制品	Electronic Audio and Video Products	101.0	101.3	100.4
燃　料	**Fuels**	**91.8**	**91.6**	**92.2**
煤炭及制品	Coal and Its Products	98.0	98.6	97.3
石油及制品	Oil and Its Products	89.4	89.8	88.1
建筑材料及五金电料	**Building Materials and, Hardwares**	**100.1**	**100.3**	**99.9**
建筑装璜材料	Building Decoration Materials	99.9	100.2	99.5
五金电料	Hardware	100.5	100.4	100.8

9-5 各调查市县商品零售价格分类指数

(上年=100) (2015 年)

项 目	Item	乌鲁木齐市 Urumqi City	喀什市 Kashgar [Kaxgar] City	伊宁市 Yining [Gulja] City	和田市 Hotan City	克拉玛依市 Karamay City	哈密市 Hami [Kumul] City
商品零售价格总指数	**General Retail Price Index**	**99.4**	**99.8**	**99.6**	**99.0**	**99.7**	**99.6**
食 品	**Food**	**99.1**	**97.1**	**101.1**	**98.7**	**97.8**	**99.9**
粮 食	Grain	102.1	100.9	101.8	101.2	102.9	100.2
油 脂	Oil or Fat	98.6	89.8	105.7	96.9	100.7	105.8
肉禽及其制品	Meat, Poultry and Their Products	95.3	93.9	95.4	93.0	94.9	93.1
猪 肉	Pork	105.6	98.7	99.9	96.3	104.1	104.8
牛 肉	Beef	91.2	86.5	94.1	92.9	91.2	93.8
羊 肉	Mutton	84.8	84.2	83.6	83.0	82.6	81.0
鸡	Chicken	101.1	104.7	105.5	96.9	100.9	101.5
鲜 蛋	Fresh Egg	91.1	91.5	95.9	95.6	94.8	92.5
水产品	Aquatic Products	98.1	97.0	106.6	96.0	98.2	97.9
鲜瓜果	Fresh Fruits	91.5	86.1	92.0	94.9	88.0	113.9
糕点、饼干、面包	Cake, Biscuit and Bread	101.3	99.9	104.6	101.9	101.1	100.2
饮料、烟酒	**Beverages, Tobacco and Liquor**	**101.8**	**103.5**	**103.1**	**99.5**	**102.2**	**103.4**
茶及饮料	Tea and Beverages	103.1	100.0	104.9	99.7	104.7	102.5
#饮 料	Beverages	103.1	99.9	106.6	99.2	107.0	98.6
烟 草	Tobacco	106.5	106.9	106.2	102.9	105.5	105.2
酒	Liquor	96.6	99.4	100.3	97.7	96.9	102.3
服装鞋帽	**Garments, Shoes and Hats**	**102.0**	**102.7**	**101.3**	**103.8**	**107.2**	**102.2**
服 装	Garments	102.6	103.8	101.0	103.9	108.2	102.8
鞋袜帽	Footgear and Hats	100.7	100.0	101.9	103.8	105.9	102.9
#鞋	Shoes	100.7	100.0	102.1	104.9	106.5	104.0
纺织品	**Textiles**	**97.7**	**99.3**	**99.6**	**100.0**	**101.7**	**97.4**
棉 布	Cotton Cloth	100.0	95.7	100.0	100.0	110.4	100.0
化纤布	Chemical Fiber Cloth	100.0	100.0	100.0	100.0	99.5	93.1
毛 线	Wool	100.0	100.0	100.1	100.0	104.2	100.0
其 他	Others	100.0	100.0	100.0	100.0	100.0	100.0
家用电器及音响器材	**Household Appliances, Music and Sound Apparatus**	**99.5**	**99.8**	**99.3**	**99.3**	**99.9**	**97.9**
家庭设备	Household Facilities	99.6	99.8	99.0	98.6	99.9	97.8
文娱用耐用消费品	Durable Consuming Goods for Entertainment	99.2	99.7	99.8	100.7	100.7	97.6
专业音像器材	Sound Apparatus	**102.5**	**100.0**	**100.0**	**100.0**	**95.4**	**100.0**

Retail Price Indices by Category in Surveyed Cities and Counties

(preceding year=100)

昌吉市 Changji City	库尔勒市 Korla City	阿克苏市 Aksu City	焉耆回族自治县 Yanqi Hui Autonomous County	塔城市 Tacheng [Qoqek] City	阿勒泰市 Altay City	沙湾县 Shawan County	博乐市 Bole [Bortala] City	高昌区 Gaochang District	库车县 Kuqa County	阿图什市 Artux City	莎车县 Shache [Yarkant] County	奎屯市 Kuytun City	石河子市 Shihezi City
100.5	**99.1**	**97.9**	**99.0**	**98.4**	**99.8**	**99.4**	**100.3**	**100.3**	**100.6**	**99.1**	**99.0**	**100.3**	**100.2**
100.9	**98.7**	**97.7**	**98.8**	**98.4**	**99.7**	**99.1**	**99.7**	**98.3**	**100.9**	**98.2**	**98.7**	**99.9**	**100.8**
100.2	99.8	105.2	104.0	103.2	101.3	99.9	104.6	101.5	105.2	101.0	100.5	99.6	100.4
88.2	98.4	100.8	93.4	99.6	95.8	101.1	95.9	92.2	93.1	91.4	98.7	100.0	99.0
91.4	98.8	93.7	94.9	93.5	95.7	96.9	96.3	93.6	98.1	93.3	93.9	98.0	99.0
106.3	101.1	104.7	104.9	95.3	100.0	105.1	104.3	107.9	100.9	104.3	100.0	96.8	101.2
89.5	88.9	86.9	89.9	95.1	90.8	92.7	98.6	93.7	89.8	92.6	91.4	93.7	94.2
81.0	81.3	76.8	83.3	80.5	84.3	88.7	75.7	83.9	81.0	83.3	84.8	84.0	89.9
98.7	102.7	113.1	96.8	102.5	100.0	97.7	98.4	98.8	99.8	104.5	95.2	106.8	106.5
92.4	82.5	95.7	89.4	95.1	98.4	85.9	86.9	89.5	89.7	96.6	95.4	94.1	85.2
97.0	99.1	89.2	99.3	100.8	102.0	104.8	103.9	94.5	100.3	86.7	94.5	106.4	99.5
129.2	96.5	90.4	110.7	98.1	113.5	93.2	100.5	97.4	114.1	106.8	101.8	95.9	100.8
100.0	104.9	97.3	99.0	101.2	103.6	104.5	100.0	115.7	99.1	103.4	100.0	100.9	100.4
103.2	**102.6**	**104.2**	**100.0**	**102.2**	**102.6**	**102.2**	**103.5**	**102.4**	**102.0**	**102.8**	**102.0**	**99.5**	**102.8**
100.8	102.0	100.9	101.4	100.0	103.9	101.0	104.6	100.0	100.4	103.3	100.0	100.0	100.1
101.2	103.3	101.1	100.8	100.0	106.6	101.3	105.6	100.1	100.1	109.9	100.0	100.0	100.2
105.7	105.6	105.7	105.9	106.1	104.7	105.3	105.8	105.8	106.0	105.5	105.0	100.0	105.2
100.7	100.0	103.5	92.5	99.3	100.5	100.3	99.7	100.0	101.3	99.3	100.0	98.8	102.3
107.4	**103.3**	**98.8**	**101.8**	**98.3**	**103.7**	**99.9**	**109.5**	**104.5**	**103.1**	**103.7**	**104.4**	**103.2**	**102.1**
107.0	103.2	97.6	102.2	97.6	105.9	100.2	112.2	103.7	102.3	102.3	105.7	102.9	102.2
108.6	103.6	100.8	101.3	100.0	100.4	99.5	105.9	104.4	104.0	105.9	100.4	103.8	101.9
109.1	104.2	101.3	101.4	100.0	100.8	98.8	104.9	105.5	105.8	108.8	100.6	104.6	101.7
101.7	**100.6**	**103.9**	**100.6**	**100.6**	**100.0**	**100.0**	**102.0**	**100.5**	**104.1**	**101.5**	**100.0**	**103.0**	**102.6**
107.6	102.9	102.8	100.0	100.0	100.0	100.0	100.0	100.0	101.0	100.0	100.0	100.0	105.4
111.3	101.5	103.8	100.0	110.8	100.0	100.0	100.0	100.0	99.5	100.0	100.0	100.0	100.3
107.6	100.2	95.3	104.7	100.0	100.0	100.0	100.0	96.7	106.0	100.0	100.0	100.0	100.8
110.1	101.1	108.7	100.0	104.4	100.0	100.0	120.0	100.0	100.4	100.0	100.0	100.0	100.0
98.2	**94.6**	**100.3**	**96.9**	**100.0**	**100.1**	**100.2**	**98.2**	**101.7**	**99.0**	**99.0**	**99.6**	**99.3**	**100.0**
98.4	94.0	100.7	97.4	100.0	99.8	100.3	98.4	99.1	99.4	99.7	100.0	100.5	101.1
97.9	94.5	100.0	95.2	100.0	100.3	100.0	97.7	109.1	98.6	97.8	98.9	98.0	98.2
100.0	**101.3**	**100.0**	**99.7**	**100.0**	**102.1**	**100.0**	**100.0**	**98.2**	**98.6**	**100.0**	**100.0**	**98.7**	**100.0**

9-5 续表

(上年=100)

项　　目	Item	乌鲁木齐　市 Urumqi City	喀什市 Kashgar [Kaxgar] City	伊宁市 Yining [Gulja] City	和田市 Hotan City	克拉玛依　市 Karamay City	哈密市 Hami [Kumul] City
文化办公用品	**Cultural and Office Appliances**	**95.5**	**99.1**	**99.6**	**99.7**	**99.7**	**100.3**
日用品	**Articles for Daily Use**	**100.5**	**100.0**	**100.4**	**99.7**	**100.4**	**101.6**
日用百货	General Merchandise for Daily Use	100.3	99.9	100.0	99.2	101.0	98.6
日用杂品	Miscellaneous for Daily Use	100.0	100.0	98.5	100.3	100.0	100.0
洗涤用品	Washing and Cleaning Goods	100.6	100.0	101.1	99.5	99.6	103.8
其他日用品	Other Daily-use Goods	100.7	100.0	100.8	100.0	101.3	102.1
体育娱乐用品	**Sports and Recreation Articles**	**99.3**	**100.0**	**100.2**	**100.0**	**100.0**	**99.5**
体育用品	Sports Articles	100.0	100.0	100.5	99.9	100.0	100.0
娱乐用品	Recreational Articles	98.6	100.0	100.0	100.0	99.9	98.6
交通、通信用品	**Transportation communication Appliances**	**99.2**	**109.3**	**98.1**	**97.4**	**99.9**	**95.4**
交通运输机械	Traffic and Transport Machinery	100.0	114.8	100.0	98.1	100.0	95.3
通信器材	Telecommunication Apparatus	98.2	97.6	96.2	96.2	99.8	95.5
家　具	**Furniture**	**102.6**	**98.2**	**98.4**	**95.0**	**103.8**	**98.6**
化妆品	**Cosmetics**	**100.4**	**100.1**	**100.2**	**100.6**	**100.6**	**99.4**
金银珠宝	**Gold , Silver and Jewelry**	**95.0**	**95.5**	**89.4**	**93.7**	**101.0**	**98.4**
中西药品及医疗保健用品	**Traditional Chinese and Western Medicines, Health Care Articles**	**102.5**	**102.8**	**105.1**	**100.9**	**101.2**	**103.3**
医疗器具及用品	Medical Apparatus and Article	98.0	100.0	101.6	100.0	100.0	100.0
中药材及中成药	Traditional Chinese Medicinal Materials and Medicines	99.0	102.2	104.0	102.7	100.3	101.9
西　药	Western Medicines	105.0	103.8	106.0	100.3	102.3	105.5
保健器具及用品	Health Care Devices and Articles	101.1	100.3	105.9	100.0	100.4	101.9
书报杂志及电子出版物	**Books,Newspapers,Magazines and Electronic Publications**	**104.1**	**98.9**	**102.5**	**101.3**	**100.0**	**106.3**
教材及参考书	Texts and Reference Books	100.0	97.4	105.6	100.0	100.0	102.4
书报杂志	Newspapers and Magazines	107.1	100.1	100.0	103.7	100.0	113.7
电子音像制品	Electronic Audio and Video Products	101.3	100.0	100.0	100.0	100.0	100.0
燃　料	**Fuels**	**91.7**	**97.7**	**84.9**	**94.2**	**91.9**	**92.0**
煤炭及制品	Coal and Its Products	100.0	102.2	101.3	95.0	100.0	96.2
石油及制品	Oil and Its Products	91.2	96.0	82.6	94.0	87.6	89.8
建筑材料及五金电料	**Building Materials and, Hardwares**	**100.5**	**100.6**	**98.1**	**98.8**	**103.5**	**97.9**
建筑装璜材料	Building Decoration Materials	100.6	101.0	96.9	98.5	103.4	98.4
五金电料	Hardware	100.4	99.1	101.6	99.4	103.7	96.9

Continued

(preceding year=100)

昌吉市 Changji City	库尔勒市 Korla City	阿克苏市 Aksu City	焉耆回族自治县 Yanqi Hui Autonomous County	塔城市 Tacheng [Qoqek] City	阿勒泰市 Altay City	沙湾县 Shawan County	博乐市 Bole [Bortala] City	高昌区 Gaochang District	库车县 Kuqa County	阿图什市 Artux City	莎车县 Shache [Yarkant] County	奎屯市 Kuytun City	石河子市 Shihezi City
99.9	**100.4**	**100.3**	**100.2**	**100.1**	**101.3**	**100.1**	**101.0**	**101.0**	**99.3**	**100.0**	**100.0**	**99.1**	**99.3**
101.0	**100.2**	**100.7**	**99.8**	**100.1**	**100.3**	**100.0**	**100.0**	**101.1**	**101.5**	**99.1**	**99.9**	**101.5**	**100.3**
100.2	100.5	100.2	101.4	100.2	100.2	100.0	100.3	102.0	100.8	97.2	100.0	99.6	100.0
102.9	100.0	100.0	96.0	100.1	100.0	100.0	100.2	96.0	101.9	98.6	100.0	104.2	99.9
100.0	100.0	100.9	100.0	100.0	101.0	100.0	100.3	103.2	102.0	101.5	100.0	100.5	99.9
102.9	100.2	101.4	100.0	100.0	100.0	100.0	98.8	100.2	101.5	97.2	99.5	103.8	102.9
101.6	**99.4**	**102.9**	**99.2**	**100.0**	**105.3**	**100.0**	**100.4**	**97.1**	**101.6**	**100.6**	**100.0**	**101.1**	**100.3**
102.5	99.1	106.2	98.4	100.0	108.9	100.0	100.0	96.5	102.9	101.1	100.0	103.3	100.0
100.8	99.9	101.7	100.2	100.0	103.2	100.0	100.7	98.3	100.3	100.0	100.0	99.4	100.7
99.3	**98.9**	**100.2**	**100.0**	**101.2**	**100.5**	**100.0**	**98.9**	**105.8**	**99.7**	**97.7**	**98.4**	**98.2**	**99.5**
100.0	100.1	100.2	100.0	99.7	100.9	100.0	100.0	96.3	99.2	100.1	99.8	100.0	99.3
98.4	95.7	100.1	100.0	103.9	100.1	100.0	97.3	114.9	100.4	94.8	97.1	96.8	99.7
101.9	**98.2**	**100.3**	**102.8**	**100.0**	**100.5**	**100.0**	**99.1**	**107.3**	**100.2**	**99.3**	**99.4**	**103.5**	**101.5**
100.3	**100.7**	**99.2**	**100.3**	**100.0**	**100.2**	**100.0**	**99.8**	**101.8**	**102.8**	**100.0**	**99.6**	**103.0**	**100.3**
98.8	**97.1**	**92.4**	**94.4**	**95.3**	**95.1**	**97.2**	**95.2**	**98.8**	**101.4**	**93.1**	**88.1**	**100.0**	**98.4**
100.3	**105.1**	**101.2**	**102.3**	**102.4**	**101.1**	**100.1**	**101.6**	**104.0**	**103.2**	**101.0**	**101.8**	**100.5**	**102.1**
100.0	98.1	100.0	101.3	102.8	100.0	102.8	100.0	100.0	98.8	102.8	100.0	104.0	105.9
100.2	100.2	100.4	102.7	102.4	99.8	100.2	101.0	107.5	107.2	100.3	101.2	100.8	101.5
100.4	109.8	101.7	101.5	103.4	103.5	99.7	103.0	103.1	101.3	101.1	102.4	100.0	103.1
100.0	98.3	102.5	103.7	100.0	100.0	100.0	100.0	97.8	102.0	101.3	100.0	99.4	99.5
100.0	**100.6**	**100.0**	**100.3**	**100.0**	**100.0**	**100.0**	**100.3**	**105.4**	**100.0**	**100.4**	**100.0**	**101.1**	**99.9**
100.2	100.5	100.0	100.5	100.0	100.0	100.0	100.1	100.3	101.1	102.0	100.0	100.7	100.0
100.0	100.0	100.0	100.0	100.0	100.0	100.0	100.0	113.3	98.1	100.0	100.0	102.6	100.0
99.7	101.9	100.0	100.0	100.0	100.0	100.0	101.2	100.0	100.6	100.0	100.0	100.0	99.7
91.4	**88.9**	**78.8**	**91.2**	**83.2**	**91.0**	**95.3**	**90.5**	**94.2**	**90.6**	**93.5**	**91.3**	**96.0**	**90.0**
100.0	100.0	88.4	92.7	89.0	100.0	104.6	102.2	98.0	90.7	110.1	95.8	100.0	95.0
90.9	85.9	75.4	90.4	81.7	86.5	88.7	86.1	91.1	90.5	88.2	88.7	94.1	88.6
101.4	**97.9**	**98.9**	**96.9**	**99.6**	**99.9**	**99.8**	**101.4**	**99.1**	**100.7**	**99.7**	**100.6**	**101.5**	**100.5**
101.2	97.6	98.6	96.0	99.5	99.9	99.7	99.9	98.7	99.3	99.5	100.9	101.7	100.2
102.3	98.4	100.0	99.5	101.0	100.0	100.0	104.7	99.8	101.8	100.0	99.9	100.4	101.1

9-6 主要年份农业生产资料价格分类指数

Price Indices for Means of Agricultural Production by Category in Main Years

(上年=100) (preceding year=100)

项 目	Item	2010	2014	2015
农业生产资料价格指数	**Price Indices for Means of Agricultural Production**	**103.1**	**97.7**	**98.6**
农用手工工具	Farm Handtools	101.0	102.5	102.2
饲料类	Forage	114.0	101.6	99.3
产品畜	Commodity Animals	127.1	96.9	95.5
半机械化农具	Semi-mechanized Farm Tools	101.7	100.3	99.8
机械化农具	Mechanized Farm Machinery	100.1	100.2	99.9
化学肥料	Chemical Fertilizer	95.3	88.4	96.4
农药及农药械	Pesticide and Its Appliances	101.7	100.4	100.0
农用机油	Oil for Farm Machinery	110.1	99.2	92.2
其他农业生产资料	Other Means of Agricultural Production	100.7	104.1	100.0
农业生产服务	Service for Agriculture Production	102.0	106.2	103.8

9-7 各市县农业生产资料价格指数

Price Indices for Means of Agricultural Production in Cities and Counties

(上年=100) (2015 年) (preceding year=100)

项 目	Item	喀什市 Kashgar [Kaxgar] City	阿勒泰市 Altay City	沙湾县 Shawan County	博乐市 Bole [Bortala] City	高昌区 Gaochang District	库车县 Kuqa County	阿图什市 Artux City	莎车县 Shache [Yarkant] County	焉耆回族自治县 Yanqi Hui Autonomous County
农业生产资料价格指数	**Price Indices for Means of Agricultural Production**	**98.9**	**98.9**	**97.3**	**98.5**	**101.9**	**99.0**	**97.9**	**97.1**	**100.0**
农用手工工具	Farm Handtools	108.4	113.2	100.0	100.0	97.6	102.0	105.2	100.0	102.5
饲料类	Forage	100.1	92.4	102.0	102.1	111.1	101.2	93.3	97.4	97.6
产品畜	Commodity Animals	81.8	89.9	93.7	93.8	96.3	98.9	82.0	98.3	100.7
半机械化农具	Semi-mechanized Farm Tools	100.0	100.0	100.0	100.0	92.9	100.9	108.6	100.0	100.0
机械化农具	Mechanized Farm Machinery	100.9	100.0	100.0	99.0	100.6	99.1	100.2	100.0	100.0
化学肥料	Chemical Fertilizer	98.1	97.7	96.4	98.4	97.1	99.6	98.7	92.0	102.9
农药及农药械	Pesticide and Its Appliances	100.1	99.6	100.1	100.9	98.0	102.0	100.0	99.5	101.2
农用机油	Oil for Farm Machinery	99.0	91.1	80.3	89.4	89.4	85.3	91.0	100.0	89.3
其他农业生产资料	Other Means of Agricultural Production	100.9	101.2	100.8	103.0	99.0	100.9	99.3	98.8	97.9
农业生产服务	Service for Agriculture Production	103.1	111.7	100.4	99.1	117.4	100.3	111.9	100.3	104.2

9-8 主要年份工业生产者出厂价格分类指数
Producer Price Indices for Industrial Products by Category in Main Years

(上年=100) (preceding year=100)

项目	Item	2010	2014	2015
全部工业品	**Total Industrial Products**	**125.3**	**96.2**	**82.4**
按轻、重工业分	**By Light and Heavy Industry**			
轻工业	**Light Industry**	**108.9**	**98.3**	**98.7**
以农产品为原料	Using Farm Produces as Raw Materials	111.2	99.4	98.0
以非农产品为原料	Using Non-farm Produces as Raw Materials	104.6	92.7	102.1
重工业	**Heavy Industry**	**128.7**	**95.9**	**79.7**
采　掘	Mining and Quarrying	153.1	95.9	65.2
原　料	Raw Materials	114.0	96.1	83.2
加　工	Processing	105.6	95.2	93.0
按部类分	**By Sector**			
生产资料	**Means of Production**	**127.1**	**95.8**	**80.9**
采　掘	Mining and Quarrying	151.9	95.9	65.2
原　料	Raw Materials	115.1	95.9	83.9
加　工	Processing	107.3	95.6	93.8
生活资料	**Consumer Goods**	**104.1**	**100.3**	**98.6**
食　品	Food	104.4	100.2	98.4
衣　着	Clothing	101.5	100.1	99.5
一般日用品	Articles for Daily Use	101.4	101.0	99.3
耐用消费品	Durable Consumer Goods	102.3	100.2	100.0
按工业部门分	**Division of Industrial Setors**			
冶金工业	Metallurgical Industry	114.4	93.3	84.5
电力工业	Power Industry	100.7	100.2	99.9
煤炭及炼焦工业	Coal and Coking Industry	104.0	94.3	94.2
石油工业	Petroleum Industry	141.6	95.9	67.3
化学工业	Chemical Industry	112.1	94.4	93.1
机械工业	Machine Manufacturing Industry	97.4	99.3	99.3
建筑材料工业	Building Materials Industry	101.1	95.7	97.2
森林工业	Timber Industry	101.7	99.8	97.1
食品工业	Food Industry	104.9	100.3	97.8
纺织工业	Textile Industry	122.8	97.7	97.4
缝纫工业	Tailoring Industry	101.5	100.4	99.4
皮革工业	Leather Industry	101.1	101.1	98.9
造纸工业	Paper Industry	127.8	99.9	100.2
文教艺术用品工业	Cultural, Educational and Handicrafts Articles	101.1	100.2	100.2
其他工业	Other Industry	107.7	100.5	101.2

9-9 主要年份工业生产者购进价格分类指数

Purchasing Price Indices for Industrial Producers by Category in Main Years

(上年=100) (preceding year=100)

项　目	Iterm	2010	2014	2015
全部原材料价格指数	**Total of Raw Material**	**123.9**	**97.5**	**84.3**
燃料、动力类	Fuel and Power	137.6	97.0	69.9
黑色金属材料类	Ferrous Metals	105.0	95.2	88.7
#钢　材	Rolled Steel	102.5	95.6	93.2
其　他	Others	112.3	94.4	80.4
有色金属材料及电线类	Nonferrous Metals and Wire Type	139.6	96.9	91.5
化工原料类	Raw Chemistry Materiasls	106.8	98.5	96.4
木材及纸浆类	Timber and Paper Pulp	104.0	98.8	99.7
建筑材料及非金属类	Building Material and Non-metal Ore	103.0	98.7	98.1
其他工业原材料及半成品类	Other Industrial Raw Material and Semi-finished Category	101.1	98.7	97.1
农副产品类	Agricultural Products	118.7	99.2	94.1
纺织原料类	Textile Raw Materials	144.2	99.1	95.3

9-10 主要年份固定资产投资价格指数

Price Indices for Investment in Fixed Assets in Main Years

(上年=100) (preceding year=100)

项　目	Item	2010	2014	2015
固定资产投资价格指数	**Investment in Fixed Assets**	**104.6**	**100.3**	**98.3**
建筑安装工程	**Construction and Installtion**	**105.9**	**100.2**	**97.6**
人工费	Manpower Expenses	110.6	106.1	102.7
材料费	Material Expenses	104.8	97.5	95.0
#钢　材	Rolled Steel	104.4	93.5	90.8
木　材	Timber	104.8	101.6	100.1
水　泥	Cement	104.7	97.0	96.1
地方材料	Local Material	104.6	98.9	98.6
化工材料	Chemical Material	104.9	101.5	96.0
电　料	Electrical Wire	105.1	101.8	97.4
其他材料	Other Material	101.7	100.5	100.0
机械使用费	Expenses of Machine Use	103.3	102.9	100.8
设备工器具	**Purchase of Equipment,Tools and Instruments**	**100.4**	**99.3**	**99.1**
其他费用	**Others**	**105.2**	**103.7**	**102.6**

主要统计指标解释

居民消费价格指数 简称 CPI，是反映一定时期内城乡居民所购买的生活消费品和服务项目价格变动趋势和程度的相对数，是对城市居民消费价格指数和农村居民消费价格指数进行综合汇总计算的结果。通过该指数可以观察和分析消费品的零售价格和服务项目价格变动对城乡居民实际生活费支出的影响程度。

城市居民消费价格指数 是反映一定时期内城市居民家庭所购买的生活消费品价格和服务项目价格变动趋势和程度的相对数。通过该指数可以观察和分析消费品的零售价格和服务项目价格变动对城镇居民收入和消费支出的影响。

农村居民消费价格指数 是反映一定时期内农村居民家庭所购买的生活消费品价格和服务项目价格变动趋势和程度的相对数。该指数可以观察农村消费品的零售价格和服务项目价格变动对农村居民收入和生活消费支出的影响。

商品零售价格指数 是反映一定时期内城乡商品零售价格变动趋势和程度的相对数。商品零售价格的变动与国家的财政收入、市场供需的平衡、消费与积累的比例关系有关。因此，该指数可以从一个侧面对上述经济活动进行观察和分析。

农业生产资料价格指数 指反映一定时期内，农业生产资料价格变动趋势和程度的相对数。其编制目的是了解农业生产中物质资料投入价格的变动状况，服务于国民经济核算。1994年以前，农业生产资料价格指数仅仅是商品零售价格指数的一个类别，此后，从商品零售价格指数中分离出来，单独编制。

工业生产者出厂价格指数 简称PPI，是反映一定时期内全部工业产品出厂价格（工业企业产品第一次出售时的价格）总水平的变动趋势和程度的相对数，包括工业企业售给本企业以外所有单位的各种产品和直接售给居民用于生活消费的产品。该指数可以观察出厂价格变动对工业总产值及增加值的影响。

工业生产者购进价格指数 是反映工业企业作为生产投入，而从物资交易市场和能源、原材料生产企业购买原材料、燃料和动力产品时，所支付的价格水平变动趋势和程度的统计指标。是扣除工业企业物质消耗成本中的价格变动影响的重要依据。

目前，我国编制的工业生产者购进价格指数所调查的产品包括燃料动力、黑色金属、有色金属、化工、建材等九大类。

固定资产投资价格指数 是反映一定时期内固定资产投资品及取费项目的价格变动趋势和程度的相对数。固定资产投资额是由建筑安装工程投资完成额、设备工器具购置投资完成额和其他费用投资完成额三部分组成的。编制固定资产投资价格指数应首先分别编制上述三部分投资的价格指数，然后采用加权算术平均法求出固定资产投资价格总指数。

该指数可以准确地反映固定资产投资中涉及的各类投资品和取费项目价格变动趋势和变动幅度，消除按现价计算的固定资产投资指标中的价格变动因素，真实地反映固定资产投资的规模、速度、结构和效益，为国家科学地制定、检查固定资产投资计划并提高宏观调控水平，为完善国民经济核算体系提供科学的、可靠的依据。

Explanatory Notes on Main Statistical Indicators

Consumer Price Indices reflect the trend and degree of changes in prices of consumer goods and services purchased by urban and rural households during a given period.They are obtained by combining Consumer Price Indices of Urban Household and Consumer Price Indices of Rural Household. The Indices enable the observation and analysis of the degree of impact of the changes in the prices of retailed goods and services on the actual living expenses of urban and rural residents

Consumer Price Indices of Urban Household reflect the trend and degree of changes in prices of consumer goods and services purchased by urban households during a given period. It can be used to observe and analyze the impact of price changes in consumer goods and services on urban household income and consumption expenditure.

Consumer Price Indices of Rural Household reflect the trend and degree of changes in prices of consumer goods and services purchased by rural households during a given period. It can be used to observe the impact of change in retail prices of consumer goods and service prices on rural household income and consumption expenditure on living.

Retail Price Indices reflect the trend and degree of change in retail prices of commodities during a given period. The change in retail prices of commodities is related to government revenue, the equilibrium of market supply and demand, and the ratio of consumption to accumulation. Therefore, the retail price indices are useful from an oblique perspective for observing and analyzing the changes of the above economic activities.

Price Indices for Means of Agricultural Production reflect the trend and degree of changes in the prices of the means of agricultural production during a given period. Compilation of these indices helps to understand the price changes of material input in agricultural production and facilitate the compilation of national accounts. Before 1994, price indices for means of agricultural production were a sub-category in the retail price indices for commodities, and it has been compiled separately since 1994.

Producer Price Indices for Industrial Products reflect the trend and degree of changes in general ex-factory prices of all manufactured goods during a given period, including sales of manufactured goods by an industrial enterprise to all units outside the enterprise, as well as sales of consumer goods to residents. It can be used to analyze the impact of ex-factory prices on gross output value and value-added of the industrial sector.

Purchasing Price Indices for Industrial Producers reflect changes in the level and degree of prices paid by industrial enterprises when they purchase production input such as raw materials, fuels and power from the market or from other energy or raw materials producing enterprises. These indices provide an important basis for measuring the material consumption of industrial enterprises after removing the influence of price changes.

At present, products in 9 categories, including fuels and power, ferrous metals, non-ferrous metals, chemicals, building materials, are covered in China for the survey to produce indices for purchasing' prices for industrial producers.

Price Indices for Investment in Fixed Assets reflect the trend and degree of changes in prices of investment goods and projects in fixed assets during a given period. The investment in fixed assets consists of three components, namely the investment in construction and installation, the investment in purchases of equipment and instrument, and the investment in other items. Price indices for investment in fixed assets are calculated as the weighted arithmetic mean of the price indices for the three components of investment in fixed assets.

Removing the factor of price change in the aggregates of investment at current prices, this indicator shows the changes in the prices of commodities and fees involved in the investment of fixed assets, and can be used to observe the actual size, growth, structure, and efficiency of investment in fixed assets and provides reliable and scientific data for government planning, management, decision-making, and further improving the current national accounting system..

10 人民生活

PEOPLE'S LIVELIHOOD AND SOCIAL WELFARE

第十篇　人民生活

本篇主要内容和资料来源

本篇资料反映新疆居民生活现状及城镇居民社会保障情况，主要包括居民家庭基本情况、家庭收入、支出情况、主要食品消费量、耐用消费品的拥有量及居民社会保险情况等。

从2013年起，国家统计局开展了城乡一体化住户收支与生活状况调查。2014年，国家统计局新疆调查总队按照国家方法制度要求进行了城乡一体化住户收支与生活状况调查，由于与2013年前的分城镇和农村住户调查范围、调查方法、指标口径有所不同，历史数据无法延续，本章只反映2015年新疆居民生活基本情况。

居民生活状况的数据来源于国家统计局新疆调查总队居民收支调查处。

居民社会保险情况数据来源于新疆维吾尔自治区人力资源和社会保障厅。

People’s Livelihood and Social Welfare

Main Content and Source of Data

Data in this chapter show the condition of people’s livelihood in Xinjiang and social security in urban, including mainly basic condition of people’s household, income of households, income and expenditure of the household, the quantity and the expenditure on major commodities purchased, the housing condition and the possession of the durable consumer goods and people’s social securiyt, etc.

Since 2013, the National Bureau of statistics carried out the urban and rural household income and expenditure survey. 2014 the National Bureau of Statistics Investigation Corps in Xinjiang, in accordance with national system requirements conducted a survey of the integration of urban and rural household budget and living conditions, because the 2013 before the urban and rural households scope of investigation, survey methods, standards and different, historical data can not be extended, this chapter reflect only the 2015 Xinjiang residents basic living conditions.

Data on the livelihood of residents are from the Department of Households Survey , NBS Survey Office in Xinjiang.

Data on social security in urban and rural are from Bureau of Human Resources and Social Security of Xinjiang Uygur Autonomous Region.

10-1 居民家庭基本情况
Basic Living Conditions of Households

(2015 年) (抽样调查 Sampled Survey)

项 目	Item	全体居民 Total Resident	城镇居民 Urban Permanet Residents	农村居民 Rural Permanet Residents
基本情况	**Basic Condition**			
调查户数 (户)	Number of Households Surveyed (household)	3180	1355	1825
户均常住人口(人/户)	Average Number of Permanent Residents Per Household (person/household)	3.41	2.85	4.03
户均常住从业人口(人/户)	Average Number Permanent Employee per Household (person/househdd)	1.82	1.33	2.37
平均每户家庭从业人口比重	Proportion of Employed Population Per Household	0.54	0.47	0.59
户主文化程度(%)	**Housemaster's Degree of Education(%)**			
未上过学	No Schooling	3.28	1.91	4.82
小 学	Primary Schools	24.76	11.08	40.04
初 中	Junior Secondary Schools	37.42	30.08	45.62
高 中	Senior Secondary Schools	16.17	24.05	7.37
大学专科	Junior College	11.90	20.86	1.88
大学本科以上	Bachelor's Degree or Above	6.47	12.02	0.27
常住从业人员就业类型(%)	**Employment Type of Permanent Employee(%)**			
雇 主	Employer	0.46	0.84	0.23
公职人员	Public Employee	3.51	8.74	0.22
事业单位人员	Business Unit Personel	5.11	12.15	0.69
国有企业雇员	State Owned Enterprise Employee	5.01	12.92	0.03
其他雇员	Other Employee	22.03	46.73	6.50
农业自营	Agricultural Self	53.86	3.77	85.34
非农自营	Non-agricultural Self	10.02	14.85	6.99
常住从业人员按产业类型分(%)	**Industry Type of Permanent Employees(%)**			
第一产业	Primary Industry	54.60	6.19	85.05
第二产业	Secondary Industry	8.97	17.66	3.50
第三产业	Tertiary Industry	36.43	76.15	11.45

10-1 续表 Continued

项　　目	Item	全体居民 Total Resident	城镇居民 Urban Permanet Residents	农村居民 Rural Permanet Residents
居民可支配收入(元)	**Disposable Income(yuan)**	**16859**	**26275**	**9425**
工资性收入	Income from Wages and Salaries	9108	17943	2131
经营净收入	Net Business Income	4204	2693	5397
财产净收入	Income from Porperty	676	1268	209
转移净收入	Income from Transfer	2871	4370	1687
平均每人消费性支出(元)	**Average Expenditure per Capita(yuan)**	**12867**	**19415**	**7698**
食品烟酒	Food, Tobacco and Liquor	4093	5955	2623
衣　着	Clothing	1274	2013	691
居　住	Residence	2228	3167	1487
生活用品及服务	Household Facilities ,Articles and Services	789	1286	396
交通通信	Transport and Communications	1842	2869	1032
教育文化和娱乐	Education , Cultural and Recreation	1282	2105	632
医疗保健	Health Care and Medical Services	1078	1517	732
其他商品和服务	Miscellaneous Goods and Services	281	502	106
平均每人消费性支出构成(%)	**Constitue of Consumption Expenditure per Capita(%)**	**100**	**100**	**100**
(人均消费支出=100)	**(Consumption Expenditure per Capita=100)**			
食品烟酒	Food, Tobacco and Liquor	31.8	30.7	34.1
衣　着	Clothing	9.9	10.4	9.0
居　住	Residence	17.3	16.3	19.3
生活用品及服务	Household Facilities , Articles and Services	6.1	6.6	5.1
交通通信	Transport and Communications	14.3	14.8	13.4
教育文化和娱乐	Education , Cultural and Recreation	10.0	10.8	8.2
医疗保健	Health Care and Medical Services	8.4	7.8	9.5
其他商品和服务	Miscellaneous Goods and Services	2.2	2.6	1.4

10-2 分地区城乡居民人均可支配收入
Per Capita Disposable Income of Urban and Rural Households by Region

单位：元　　(2015 年) (抽样调查　Sampled Survey)　　(yuan)

地　区	Region	城镇居民 Urban Households	农村居民 Rural Households
乌鲁木齐市	Urumqi City	31604	15007
克拉玛依市	Karamay City	33430	
吐鲁番市	Turpan City	25869	10322
哈密地区	Hami [Kumul] Administrative Offices	27975	12951
昌吉回族自治州	Changji Hui Autonomous Prefecture	25856	15633
伊犁哈萨克自治州直属县市	Counties (Cities) Direct Under Ili Prefecture	24207	10591
塔城地区	Tacheng [Tarbagatai] Administrative Offices	25097	13583
阿勒泰地区	Altay Administrative Offices	23478	9377
博尔塔拉蒙古自治州	Bortala Mongol Autonomous Prefecture	24775	13127
巴音郭楞蒙古自治州	Bayangol Mongol Autonomous Prefecture	26523	14154
阿克苏地区	Aksu Administrative Offices	23987	9831
克孜勒苏柯尔克孜自治州	Kizilsu Kirgiz Autonomous Prefecture	22465	5434
喀什地区	Kashgar [Kaxgar] Administrative Offices	20662	7201
和田地区	Hotan Administrative Offices	22549	6346

10-3 居民人均可支配收入
Per Capita Disposable Income of Households

单位：元　　(2015 年) (抽样调查　Sampled Survey)　　(yuan)

项　目	Item	2014	2015
一、全疆居民可支配收入	**Per Capita Disposable Income of Whoie Xinjiang**	**15097**	**16859**
工资性收入	Income from Wages and Salaries	7810	9108
经营净收入	Net Business Income	3997	4204
财产净收入	Net Income from Porperties	674	676
转移净收入	Net Income from Transfer	2616	2871
二、城镇居民可支配收入	**Per Capita Disposable Income of urban Households**	**23214**	**26275**
工资性收入	Income from Wages and Salaries	15404	17943
经营净收入	Net Business Income	2491	2693
财产净收入	Net Income from Porperties	1240	1268
转移净收入	Net Income from Transfer	4078	4370
三、农村居民可支配收入	**Per Capita Disposable Income of Rural Households**	**8724**	**9425**
工资性收入	Income from Wages and Salaries	1848	2131
经营净收入	Net Business Income	5179	5397
财产净收入	Net Income from Porperties	229	209
转移净收入	Net Income from Transfer	1468	1687

10-4 城镇居民人均可支配收入（按收入分组）
Per Capita Disposable Income of Urban Households by Income

单位：元　　(2015 年)(抽样调查 Sampled Survey)　　(yuan)

项目	Item	全区 Whole Region	最低收入户 Lowest Income Households	#困难户 Poor Households	低收入户 Low Income Households	中等偏下户 Lower Middle Income Households
可支配收入	**Disposable Income**	**26275**	**6144**	**4339**	**12672**	**19498**
工资性收入	Income from Wages and Salaries	17943	2815	1726	8570	13808
工　资	Salary	16700	2014	975	7553	13073
其他收入	Other Income	1243	801	751	1017	735
经营净收入	Net Business Income	2693	1189	777	2353	3386
财产净收入	Net Income from Porperties	1268	543	495	630	1034
转移净收入	Net Income from Transfer	4371	1597	1341	1119	1270
转移性收入	Income from Transfer	6366	1950	1607	2357	3183
#养老金或离退休金收入	Income of pension	5723	706	187	1505	2840
转移性支出	Transfer Expenditure	1996	353	266	1238	1912
#社会保障支出	Security Expenditure	1686	324	265	1082	1648

项目	Item	中等收入户 Middle Income Households	中等偏上户 Upper Middle Income Households	高收入户 High Income Households	最高收入户 Highest Income Households	#更高 More Highest
可支配收入	**Disposable Income**	**27637**	**35621**	**43932**	**56709**	**63082**
工资性收入	Income from Wages and Salaries	19187	23522	30929	39955	41957
工　资	Salary	18146	22250	28671	36860	38873
其他收入	Other Income	1041	1272	2258	3095	3084
经营净收入	Net Business Income	3627	1908	2494	3602	5719
财产净收入	Income from Porperties	1079	1586	2202	2870	4033
转移净收入	Income from Transfer	3744	8605	8307	10282	11373
转移性收入	Income from Transfer	5879	10992	11274	14227	15124
#养老金或离退休金收入	Income of pension	5441	10516	10549	13309	14304
转移性支出	Transfer Expenditure	2135	2387	2967	3946	3750
#社会保障支出	Security Expenditure	1874	2052	2519	2874	2354

10-5 农村居民人均可支配收入(按收入分组)
Per Capita Disposable Income of Rural Households by Income

单位：元　　(2015 年) (抽样调查　Sampled Survey)　　(yuan)

项　目	Item	全　区 Whole Region	低收入户 Low Income Households	中低收入户 Lower Middle Income Households	中等收入户 Middle Income Households	中高收入户 Upper Middle Income Households	高收入户 High Income Households
人均可支配收入	**Per Capita Disposable Income**	**9425**	**2362**	**5056**	**7385**	**11407**	**25393**
工资性收入	Income from Wages and Salaries	2131	1147	1419	2194	2608	3835
工　资	Salary	1448	428	863	1483	1903	3089
其他收入	Other Income	683	719	556	711	705	746
经营净收入	Net Business Income	5397	750	2788	3780	6547	16063
第一产业	Primary Industry	3903	383	1990	2750	5254	11246
第二产业	Secondary Industry	194	24	114	138	60	765
第三产业	Tertiary Industry	1300	343	684	892	1233	4052
财产净收入	Net Income from Porperties	209	-11	43	105	236	842
转移净收入	Net Income from Transfer	1687	476	806	1306	2016	4653
转移性收入	Income from Transfer	1934	754	939	1447	2296	5107
#养老金或离退休金收入	Income of pension	287	68	127	149	365	890
政策性生活补贴	Living Aullowance by Policy	335	51	88	266	511	943
政策性惠农补贴	Benefits of Agricltur Subsidier by Policy	815	361	340	491	834	2470
转移性支出	Transfe Expenditurer	247	277	133	141	280	454
#社会保障支出	Security Expenditure	191	243	115	119	194	312

10-6 居民人均现金可支配收入(按收入分组)

Per Capita Disposable Cash Income of Households by Income

单位：元 (2015 年) (抽样调查 Sampled Survey) (yuan)

项　目	Item	全　区 Whole Region	低收入户 Low Income Households	中低收入户 Lower Middle Income Households
人均可支配收入	**Per Capita Disposable Income**	**15914**	**3080**	**7507**
工资性收入	Income from Wages and Salaries	9094	1293	2841
工　资	Salary	8177	638	2044
其他收入	Other Income	917	655	797
经营净收入	Net Business Income	3940	1141	3318
第一产业	Primary Industry	1806	511	2038
第二产业	Secondary Industry	230	71	132
第三产业	Tertiary Industry	1904	559	1148
财产净收入	Net Income from Porperties	198	33	123
转移净收入	Net Income from Transfer	2682	613	1225
转移性收入	Income from Transfer	3700	828	1494
#养老金或离退休金收入	Income of pension	2685	96	361
政策性生活补贴	Living Aullowance by Policy	221	62	256
政策性惠农补贴	Benefits of Agriclture Subsidier by Policy	468	332	455
转移性支出	Transfe Expenditurer	1018	215	269
#社会保障支出	Security Expenditure	851	191	209

项　目	Item	中等收入户 Middle Income Households	中高收入户 Upper Middle Income Households	高收入户 High Income Households
人均可支配收入	**Per Capita Disposable Income**	**14962**	**25464**	**43443**
工资性收入	Income from Wages and Salaries	7446	16380	27443
工　资	Salary	6771	15421	25561
其他收入	Other Income	675	959	1882
经营净收入	Net Business Income	5409	5335	6455
第一产业	Primary Industry	2841	2029	2131
第二产业	Secondary Industry	181	104	896
第三产业	Tertiary Industry	2387	3202	3428
财产净收入	Net Income from Porperties	225	127	666
转移净收入	Net Income from Transfer	1882	3622	8879
转移性收入	Income from Transfer	2865	5501	11640
#养老金或离退休金收入	Income of pension	1445	4539	10797
政策性生活补贴	Living Aullowance by Policy	437	270	102
政策性惠农补贴	Benefits of Agriclture Subsidier by Policy	574	523	532
转移性支出	Transfe Expenditurer	983	1879	2761
#社会保障支出	Security Expenditure	845	1620	2223

10-7 城镇居民人均现金可支配收入(按收入分组)
Per Capita Disposable Cash Income by Urban Households by Income

单位：元　　(2015 年) (抽样调查 Sampled Survey)　　(yuan)

项　目	Item	全　区 Whole Region	最低收入户 Lowest Income Households	#困难户 Poor Households	低收入户 Low Income Households	中　等 偏下户 Lower Middle Income Households
人均现金可支配收入	**Per Captia Disposable cash Income**	**25057**	**5750**	**3724**	**11871**	**18759**
工资性收入	Income from Wages and Salaries	17915	2814	1726	8554	13785
工　资	Salary	16700	2014	975	7552	13073
其他收入	Other Income	1215	800	751	1002	712
经营净收入	Net Business Income	2826	1328	748	2356	3666
财产净收入	Net Income from Porperties	183	168	171	61	131
转移净收入	Net Income from Transfer	4133	1440	1078	900	1177
转移性收入	Income from Transfer	6128	1793	1344	2139	3089
#养老金或离退休金收入	Income of pension	5723	706	187	1505	2840
转移性支出	Transfer Expenditure	1995	353	266	1239	1912
#社会保障支出	Security Expenditure	1686	324	265	1082	1648

项　目	Item	中　等 收入户 Middle Income Households	中　等 偏上户 Upper Middle Income Households	高　收 入　户 High Income Households	最　高 收入户 Highest Income Households	#更高 More Highest
人均现金可支配收入	**Per Captia Disposable cash Income**	**26443**	**33860**	**41751**	**54325**	**60870**
工资性收入	Income from Wages and Salaries	19166	23492	30889	39847	41871
工　资	Salary	18146	22250	28671	36860	38873
其他收入	Other Income	1020	1242	2218	2987	2998
经营净收入	Net Business Income	3750	2035	2524	3664	5812
财产净收入	Net Income from Porperties	-33	11	440	1185	2420
转移净收入	Net Income from Transfer	3560	8322	7898	9629	10767
转移性收入	Income from Transfer	5696	10710	10851	13575	14517
#养老金或离退休金收入	Income of pension	5441	10516	10549	13309	14304
转移性支出	Transfer Expenditure	2136	2388	2953	3946	3750
#社会保障支出	Security Expenditure	1874	2052	2519	2874	2354

10-8 农村居民人均现金可支配收入(按收入分组)
Per Capita Disposable Cash Income of Rural Households by Income

单位：元　　(2015 年) (抽样调查 Sampled Survey)　　(yuan)

项　目	Item	全　区 Whole Region	低收入户 Low Income Households	中低收入户 Lower Middle Income Households
人均现金可支配收入	**Per Captia Disposable cash Income**	**8695**	**1998**	**4306**
工资性收入	Income from Wages and Salaries	2130	1147	1417
工　资	Salary	1449	428	863
其他收入	Other Income	681	719	554
经营净收入	Net Business Income	4819	452	2134
第一产业	Primary Industry	3196	46	1301
第二产业	Secondary Industry	224	25	115
第三产业	Tertiary Industry	1399	381	718
财产净收入	Net Income from Porperties	209	-11	43
转移净收入	Net Income from Transfer	1537	410	712
转移性收入	Income from Transfer	1783	687	845
#养老金或离退休金收入	Income of pension	287	68	127
政策性生活补贴	Living Aullowance by Policy.	335	51	88
政策性惠农补贴	Benefits of Agriclture Subsidier by Policy	815	361	340
转移性支出	Transfer Expenditure	247	277	133
#社会保障支出	Security Expenditure	191	243	115

项　目	Item	中等收入户 Middle Income Households	中高收入户 Upper Middle Income Households	高收入户 High Income Households
人均现金可支配收入	**Per Captia Disposable cash Income**	**6567**	**10484**	**24519**
工资性收入	Income from Wages and Salaries	2190	2607	3831
工　资	Salary	1484	1903	3089
其他收入	Other Income	708	704	742
经营净收入	Net Business Income	3133	5820	15460
第一产业	Primary Industry	2042	4416	10160
第二产业	Secondary Industry	139	61	943
第三产业	Tertiary Industry	952	1343	4357
财产净收入	Net Income from Porperties	105	236	842
转移净收入	Net Income from Transfer	1139	1821	4386
转移性收入	Income from Transfer	1280	2101	4840
#养老金或离退休金收入	Income of pension	149	365	890
政策性生活补贴	Living Aullowance by Policy.	266	511	943
政策性惠农补贴	Benefits of Agriclture Subsidier by Policy	491	834	2470
转移性支出	Transfer Expenditure	141	280	454
#社会保障支出	Security Expenditure	119	194	312

10-9 主要年份城乡居民人均收入
Per Capita Annual Income of Urban and Rural Households in Main Years

(抽样调查 Sampled Survey)

年 份 Year	农村居民家庭人均纯收入 Per Capita Annual Net Income of Rural Households		城镇居民家庭人均可支配收入 Per Capita Annual Disposable Income of Urban Households	
	绝对数（元） Value (yuan)	指数(1978=100) Index	绝对数（元） Value (yuan)	指数(1978=100) Index
1978	119	100	319	100
1980	201	168.9	427	133.9
1985	394	331.1	735	230.4
1990	684	574.8	1314	411.8
1995	1137	955.5	4163	1172.3
2000	1618	1359.3	5645	1589.4
2001	1710	1437.0	6215	1749.9
2002	1863	1564.9	6554	1979.1
2003	2106	1768.3	7006	2115.7
2004	2245	1885.0	7503	2265.9
2005	2482	2084.0	7990	2412.9
2006	2737	2300.0	8871	2679.0
2007	3183	2674.8	10313	3114.5
2008	3503	2943.7	11432	3452.4
2009	3883	3263.0	12258	3701.8
2010	4643	3901.7	13644	4120.0
2011	5442	4573.1	15514	4684.4
2012	6394	5373.4	17921	5410.5
2013	7296	6131.5	19874	6230.1
2014	8113	6817.8	21881	6859.3
2015	8765	7365.9	24767	7764.1

注: 1992 年以前城镇居民人均年可支配收入为人均年生活费收入。
Note: Per capita disposal income of urban households before the year 1992 is Per capita annual income as life expense.

10-10 居民家庭平均每人全年消费性支出

Per Capita Annual Consumption Expenditure of Resident Households

单位：元 (2015 年) (抽样调查 Sampled Survey) (yuan)

项 目	Item	全 区 Whole Region	低收入户 Low Income Households	中低收入户 Lower Middle Income Households
消费性支出	**Consumption Expenditures**	**12867.40**	**5533.49**	**7524.39**
食品烟酒	Food, Tobacco, Liquor	4092.75	2120.83	2666.52
#谷 物	Cereal	585.71	510.58	543.82
肉禽类	Meat, Poultry	1054.89	674.53	876.56
水产品	Aquatic Products	71.87	10.35	15.77
蛋 类	Eggs	70.13	52.09	56.36
奶 类	Milk	159.59	42.39	74.81
衣 着	Clothing	1274.47	548.11	683.05
居 住	Residence	2227.93	1116.47	1582.83
生活用品及服务	Household Facilities, Articles and Services	788.82	270.91	360.51
交通通信	Transport and Communications	1842.43	509.68	757.47
教育文化娱乐	Education , Cultural and Recreation	1282.08	387.37	584.51
#文化娱乐用品	Recreation Articles	180.45	42.23	60.74
医疗保健	Health Care and Medical Services	1078.31	533.21	781.85
其他商品和服务	Miscellaneous Goods and Services	280.62	46.90	107.65

项 目	Item	中等收入户 Middle Income Households	中高收入户 Upper Middle Income Households	高收入户 High Income Households
消费性支出	**Consumption Expenditures**	**12416.38**	**19238.19**	**28277.83**
食品烟酒	Food, Tobacco, Liquor	3903.20	6080.12	7997.92
#谷 物	Cereal	587.71	646.44	718.95
肉禽类	Meat, Poultry	1073.36	1405.55	1614.02
水产品	Aquatic Products	65.86	131.12	215.64
蛋 类	Eggs	68.17	86.81	109.05
奶 类	Milk	153.83	311.36	345.17
衣 着	Clothing	1171.11	2023.03	2846.58
居 住	Residence	2144.88	3090.25	4439.23
生活用品及服务	Household Facilities, Articles and Services	670.08	1303.46	2005.34
交通通信	Transport and Communications	1700.51	2734.55	5216.21
教育文化娱乐	Education , Cultural and Recreation	1489.27	2086.34	2838.03
#文化娱乐用品	Recreation Articles	173.66	273.14	530.61
医疗保健	Health Care and Medical Services	1080.52	1427.47	2156.12
其他商品和服务	Miscellaneous Goods and Services	256.82	492.97	778.40

10-11 农村居民家庭平均每人全年消费性支出
Per Capita Annual Expenditure of Rural Households

单位：元 (2015 年) (抽样调查 Sampled Survey) (yuan)

项 目	Item	全 区 Whole Region	低收入户 Low Income Households	中低收入户 Lower Middle Income Households
消费性支出	**Consumption Expenditures**	**7697.95**	**5374.82**	**5214.60**
食品烟酒	Food, Tobacco, Liquor	2622.52	2064.23	2072.13
#谷 物	Cereal	538.27	499.63	513.07
肉禽类	Meat, Poultry	900.65	661.30	682.22
水产品	Aquatic Products	15.63	12.43	4.52
蛋 类	Eggs	55.00	53.36	51.48
奶 类	Milk	55.42	46.11	27.50
衣 着	Clothing	691.27	540.95	534.95
居 住	Residence	1486.55	1028.22	1048.38
生活用品及服务	Household Facilities, Articles and Services	396.00	271.74	214.56
交通通信	Transport and Communications	1031.63	507.92	526.42
教育文化娱乐	Education , Cultural and Recreation	632.02	392.42	346.73
#文化娱乐用品	Recreation Articles	69.70	45.65	29.52
医疗保健	Health Care and Medical Services	731.85	512.58	427.32
其他商品和服务	Miscellaneous Goods and Services	106.11	56.76	44.11

项 目	Item	中等收入户 Middle Income Households	中高收入户 Upper Middle Income Households	高收入户 High Income Households
消费性支出	**Consumption Expenditures**	**6696.80**	**8879.52**	**14176.93**
食品烟酒	Food, Tobacco, Liquor	2497.30	2883.53	3999.00
#谷 物	Cereal	533.87	556.59	610.35
肉禽类	Meat, Poultry	892.90	992.77	1432.53
水产品	Aquatic Products	7.84	19.26	40.72
蛋 类	Eggs	50.89	56.25	65.74
奶 类	Milk	59.96	74.74	78.38
衣 着	Clothing	613.22	787.09	1098.66
居 住	Residence	1381.73	1647.96	2661.59
生活用品及服务	Household Facilities, Articles and Services	303.86	487.52	824.25
交通通信	Transport and Communications	690.36	1104.83	2785.10
教育文化娱乐	Education , Cultural and Recreation	482.05	847.43	1289.98
#文化娱乐用品	Recreation Articles	50.91	83.09	165.71
医疗保健	Health Care and Medical Services	651.31	972.68	1272.12
其他商品和服务	Miscellaneous Goods and Services	76.97	148.48	246.22

10-12 居民家庭平均每人全年现金消费性支出
Per Capita Cash Consumption Expenditure of Resident Households

单位：元 (2015 年) (抽样调查 Sampled Survey) (yuan)

项　目	Item	全　区 Whole Region	低收入户 Low Income Households	中低收入户 Lower Middle Income Households
消费性支出	**Consumption Expenditures**	**11164.92**	**4486.84**	**6180.18**
食品烟酒	Food, Tobacco, Liquor	3737.69	1635.02	2172.94
#谷 物	Cereal	466.76	292.01	373.63
肉禽类	Meat, Poultry	901.49	503.51	663.81
水产品	Aquatic Products	71.56	10.35	15.77
蛋 类	Eggs	58.86	34.50	40.08
奶 类	Milk	148.17	25.89	55.09
衣 着	Clothing	1272.76	545.64	680.92
居 住	Residence	1063.16	649.22	878.27
生活用品及服务	Household Facilities, Articles and Services	787.38	270.54	359.73
交通通信	Transport and Communications	1842.30	509.68	757.47
教育文化娱乐	Education , Cultural and Recreation	1282.00	387.07	584.51
#文化娱乐用品	Recreation Articles	180.37	41.93	60.74
医疗保健	Health Care and Medical Services	899.55	442.99	639.35
其他商品和服务	Miscellaneous Goods and Services	280.09	46.67	106.99

项　目	Item	中等收入户 Middle Income Households	中高收入户 Upper Middle Income Households	高收入户 High Income Households
消费性支出	**Consumption Expenditures**	**10837.62**	**17010.49**	**25221.02**
食品烟酒	Food, Tobacco, Liquor	3544.92	5922.43	7883.36
#谷 物	Cereal	509.02	619.83	703.72
肉禽类	Meat, Poultry	878.77	1320.04	1567.41
水产品	Aquatic Products	65.86	131.12	213.45
蛋 类	Eggs	58.44	83.35	106.36
奶 类	Milk	143.15	309.42	344.47
衣 着	Clothing	1169.12	2022.83	2845.62
居 住	Residence	1088.09	1228.85	1899.61
生活用品及服务	Household Facilities, Articles and Services	667.11	1302.82	2002.03
交通通信	Transport and Communications	1700.51	2734.55	5215.25
教育文化娱乐	Education , Cultural and Recreation	1489.27	2086.34	2838.03
#文化娱乐用品	Recreation Articles	173.66	273.14	530.61
医疗保健	Health Care and Medical Services	923.05	1219.93	1758.90
其他商品和服务	Miscellaneous Goods and Services	255.56	492.75	778.21

10-13 农村居民家庭平均每人全年现金消费性支出
Per Capita Cash Consumption Expenditure of Rural Households

单位：元 (2015 年)(抽样调查 Sampled Survey) (yuan)

项目	Item	全区 Whole Region	低收入户 Low Income Households	中低收入户 Lower Middle Income Households
消费性支出	**Consumption Expenditures**	**6332.36**	**4371.90**	**4089.08**
食品烟酒	Food, Tobacco, Liquor	2029.08	1558.13	1518.60
#谷 物	Cereal	333.67	283.78	241.41
肉禽类	Meat, Poultry	635.51	473.82	502.21
水产品	Aquatic Products	15.63	12.43	4.52
蛋 类	Eggs	35.43	34.04	32.23
奶 类	Milk	34.97	21.94	16.25
衣 着	Clothing	688.42	538.18	532.49
居 住	Residence	856.99	599.14	563.20
生活用品及服务	Household Facilities, Articles and Services	394.50	271.04	214.48
交通通信	Transport and Communications	1031.63	507.92	526.42
教育文化娱乐	Education , Cultural and Recreation	632.02	392.42	346.73
#文化娱乐用品	Recreation Articles	69.70	45.65	29.52
医疗保健	Health Care and Medical Services	594.40	448.74	343.49
其他商品和服务	Miscellaneous Goods and Services	105.33	56.34	43.67

项目	Item	中等收入户 Middle Income Households	中高收入户 Upper Middle Income Households	高收入户 High Income Households
消费性支出	**Consumption Expenditures**	**5376.28**	**7328.40**	**12141.26**
食品烟酒	Food, Tobacco, Liquor	1910.63	2236.42	3284.13
#谷 物	Cereal	323.60	387.51	478.79
肉禽类	Meat, Poultry	641.28	664.58	1000.02
水产品	Aquatic Products	7.84	19.26	40.72
蛋 类	Eggs	31.89	36.07	45.37
奶 类	Milk	32.64	48.90	65.34
衣 着	Clothing	610.27	783.74	1095.87
居 住	Residence	796.94	920.71	1615.35
生活用品及服务	Household Facilities, Articles and Services	303.73	484.93	819.25
交通通信	Transport and Communications	690.36	1104.83	2785.10
教育文化娱乐	Education , Cultural and Recreation	482.05	847.43	1289.98
#文化娱乐用品	Recreation Articles	50.91	83.09	165.71
医疗保健	Health Care and Medical Services	506.24	801.90	1007.85
其他商品和服务	Miscellaneous Goods and Services	76.06	148.45	243.73

10-14 居民平均每人全年主要食品消费量

Per Capita Consumption of Major Foods of Households

单位：公斤 (2015 年) (抽样调查 Sampled Survey) (kg)

项　目	Item	全　区 Whole Region	城　镇 Urban Households	农　村 Rural Households
粮食	Grain	181.87	153.71	204.11
#谷物	Cereal	178.26	146.97	202.97
薯类	Tuber	0.70	0.96	0.50
豆类	Beans and the Products	2.91	5.78	0.64
油脂类	Oil and Fats	13.89	13.85	13.91
#食用植物油	Edible Vegetable Oil	13.80	13.79	13.81
蔬菜及菜制品	Vegetable and Vegetable Products	103.55	120.75	89.96
#鲜菜	Fresh Vegetables	101.90	117.63	89.49
肉禽及其制品	Meats,Poultry and Processed Products	23.15	26.22	20.73
#猪　肉	Pork	4.16	7.40	1.59
牛　肉	Beef	4.63	5.39	4.03
羊　肉	Mutton	13.23	11.23	14.81
家　禽	Poultry	5.17	7.47	3.36
水产品	Aquatic Products	3.16	6.03	0.90
蛋类	Eggs	6.82	8.66	5.36
奶类	Milk and Dairy Products	19.53	27.95	12.89
干鲜瓜果类	Dried and Fresh Melons and Fruits	58.18	70.43	48.51
#鲜瓜果	Fresh Fruits	52.95	63.07	44.95
坚果类	Nuts	4.09	5.64	2.86
糖果糕点类	Cake and Biscuit	4.60	7.39	2.40

10-15 居民家庭平均每百户年底耐用品拥有量
Number of Durable Consume Goods Owned of Resident Household

(2015 年) (抽样调查 Sampled Survey)

项 目	Item	全 区 Whole Region	城 镇 Urban Households	农 村 Rural Households
家用汽车(辆)	Automobile (unit)	19.93	26.45	12.64
摩托车(辆)	Motorcycle (unit)	48.86	13.91	87.91
助力车(辆)	Mope (unit)	33.37	24.78	42.96
洗衣机(台)	Washing Machine (unit)	92.81	97.28	87.82
电冰箱(台)	Refrigerator (unit)	91.07	95.99	85.56
微波炉(台)	Microwave Oven (unit)	23.57	39.40	5.88
彩色电视机(台)	Color Tv (set)	100.06	100.16	99.94
#接入有线电视	Cable Tv Insert	53.62	83.22	20.55
空调(台)	Air Conditioner (unit)	9.23	16.51	1.10
热水器 (台)	Water Heater (unit)	53.23	81.62	21.52
#太阳能热水器	Solar Water Heater	14.53	20.68	7.67
消毒碗柜(台)	Disinfectant Tank (unit)	1.39	2.22	0.46
洗碗机(台)	Dishwasher (unit)	0.86	1.61	0.03
抽油烟机(台)	Exhaust Fan(unit)	44.84	76.93	8.97
固定电话(部)	Telephone(set)	43.97	60.93	25.02
移动电话(部)	Mobile Phone (set)	192.69	209.08	174.38
#接入互联网	Access the Internet	77.71	103.90	48.45
计算机(台)	Computer (unit)	39.76	62.55	14.30
#接入互联网	Access the Internet	32.57	52.93	9.82
摄像机(架)	Video Camera (set)	3.99	7.15	0.46
照像机(架)	Camera (set)	17.01	29.93	2.57
中高档乐器	Middle grade Musical Instruments	3.67	6.42	0.61
健身器材	Body Building Apparstus	2.81	5.21	0.13
组合音响	Music Center	3.47	4.46	2.36

10-16 社会保险基本情况
Basic Statistics of Social Insurance

指　　标	Item	2014	2015
基本养老保险	**Basic Pension Insurance**		
职工基本养老保险年末参保人数(万人)	Employee Basic Pension Insurance Contributors at Year-end (10 000 persons)	338.50	345.35
参保职工	Number of Employees	247.84	250.20
离退休人员	Number of Retirees	90.66	95.15
城乡居民社会养老保险年末参保人数(万人)	Urban and Rural Basic Penion Insurance Contributors at Year-end (10 000 persons)	530.61	530.83
享受待遇人数（万人）	Beneficiaries at Year-end (10000 persons)	102.82	105.79
基本医疗保险	**Basic Medical Care Insurance**		
职工基本医疗保险年末参保人数（万人）	Employee Basic Medical Care Insurance Contributors at Year-end (10 000 persons)	368.84	376.48
城镇居民基本医疗保险年末参保人数（万人）	Urban Residents Basic Medical care Insurance Contributors at Year-end (10 000 persons)	285.04	280.41
工伤保险年末参保人数(万人)	**Work Injury Insurance Contributors at Year-end (10 000 persons)**	**247.54**	**253.55**
年末享受待遇人次数（万人次）	Beneficiaries at Year-end (10000 persons)	2.26	2.30
失业保险年末参保人数(万人)	**Unemployment Insurance Contributors at Year-end (10 000 persons)**	**225.09**	**229.45**
年末享受待遇人次数（万人次）	Beneficiaries at Year-end (10 000 persons)	6.49	7.44
生育保险年末参保人数(万人)	**Maternity Insurance Contributors at Year-end (10 000 persons)**	**236.23**	**241.10**
年末享受待遇人数（万人）	Beneficiaries at Year-end (10 000 persons)	10.78	10.54

注：基本医疗保险数据不含新型农村合作医疗。
Note: Data of basic medical care insurance did not include new cooperative health care in agricultural and pastoral areas.

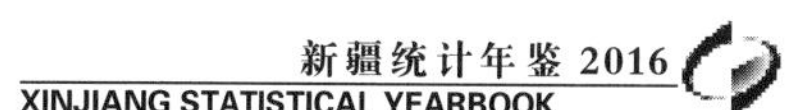

10-17 各地、州、市社会保险年末参保人数

Number of Social Insured Persons at the Year-end by Prefecture, Autonomous Prefecture and City

单位：万人 (10 000 persons)

年 份 Year	地 区 Region	基本养老保险 Basic Endowment Insurance		基本医疗保险 Basic Medical Care Insurance
		职工基本养老保险 Employee Basic Pension Insurance	城乡居民社会养老保险 Urban Non-employment Social Pension Insurance	职工基本医疗保险 Employee Basic Medical Care Insurance
	2001	148.08		116.17
	2002	152.06		148.12
	2003	160.04		176.37
	2004	173.76		195.97
	2005	181.88		211.85
	2006	191.97		227.15
	2007	205.00		244.78
	2008	222.17		263.54
	2009	232.08		279.09
	2010	259.67		296.72
	2011	291.99	518.07	322.73
	2012	312.16	528.71	342.56
	2013	326.04	530.35	358.93
	2014	338.50	530.61	368.84
	2015	345.35	530.83	376.48
乌鲁木齐市	Urumqi City	112.40	11.61	118.58
克拉玛依市	Karamay City	5.64	0.19	20.76
吐鲁番市	Turpan City	6.10	21.56	8.47
哈密地区	Hami [Kumul] Administrative Offices	12.51	8.24	12.78
昌吉回族自治州	Changji Hui Autonomous Prefecture	25.36	30.36	26.44
伊犁州直属县(市)	Counties (Cities) Direct Under Ili Prefecture	28.45	58.16	29.81
塔城地区	Tacheng [Tarbagatai] Administrative Offices	13.30	21.52	13.12
阿勒泰地区	Altay Administrative Offices	8.80	14.09	11.90
博尔塔拉蒙古自治州	Bortala Mongol Autonomous Prefecture	5.81	7.89	6.72
巴音郭楞蒙古自治州	Bayangol Mongol Autonomous Prefecture	25.21	21.65	28.42
阿克苏地区	Aksu Administrative Offices	13.65	7.39	19.57
克孜勒苏柯尔克孜自治州	Kizilsu Kirgiz Autonomous Prefecture	3.87	18.10	8.31
喀什地区	Kashgar [Kaxgar] Administrative Offices	16.63	149.55	26.85
和田地区	Hotan Administrative Offices	6.31	94.52	12.24

注：基本医疗保险数据不含新型农村合作医疗。
Note: Data of basic medical care insurance did not include new cooperative health care in agricultural and pastoral areas.

10-17 续表 Continued

单位：万人 (10 000 persons)

年 份 Year	地 区 Region	基本医疗保险 Basic Medical Care Insurance：城镇居民基本医疗保险 Urban Non-employment Basic Medical Insurance	工伤保险 Work Injury Insurance	失业保险 Unemployment Insurance	生育保险 Maternity Insurance
	2001		30.53	126.47	30.52
	2002		29.45	131.29	29.72
	2003		41.08	135.12	32.16
	2004		60.93	138.58	59.23
	2005		79.51	140.82	103.48
	2006		102.40	145.04	135.90
	2007		132.55	151.55	151.60
	2008	175.07	151.08	162.76	165.02
	2009	256.90	167.70	169.60	176.07
	2010	274.60	184.13	180.29	188.23
	2011	282.68	208.18	196.72	206.14
	2012	286.59	225.95	208.95	217.96
	2013	291.41	239.87	218.52	230.22
	2014	285.04	247.54	225.09	236.23
	2015	280.41	253.55	229.45	241.10
乌鲁木齐市	Urumqi City	60.08	76.56	78.05	67.04
克拉玛依市	Karamay City	7.30	18.89	8.08	17.49
吐鲁番地区	Turpan Administrative Offices	3.06	6.59	4.83	5.45
哈密地区	Hami [Kumul] Administrative Offices	9.31	10.57	7.84	7.49
昌吉回族自治州	Changji Hui Autonomous Prefecture	21.63	26.06	16.96	20.19
伊犁州直属县(市)	Counties (Cities) Direct Under Ili Prefecture	31.72	17.20	16.74	19.01
塔城地区	Tacheng [Tarbagatai] Administrative Offices	12.27	7.19	6.77	8.05
阿勒泰地区	Altay Administrative Offices	11.37	7.72	5.60	6.75
博尔塔拉蒙古自治州	Bortala Mongol Autonomous Prefecture	6.12	4.99	4.01	4.67
巴音郭楞蒙古自治州	Bayangol Mongol Autonomous Prefecture	25.92	19.31	17.60	18.85
阿克苏地区	Aksu Administrative Offices	27.14	11.46	11.01	12.64
克孜勒苏柯尔克孜自治州	Kizilsu Kirgiz Autonomous Prefecture	4.59	4.74	4.80	4.57
喀什地区	Kashgar [Kaxgar] Administrative Offices	45.20	21.69	16.67	18.86
和田地区	Hotan Administrative Offices	14.79	7.28	7.21	8.58

主要统计指标解释

住户调查

一、城乡一体化住户收支与生活状况调查指标解释

从2012年四季度起，国家统计局对分别进行的城乡住户调查实施了一体化改革，规范了城乡划分范围，统一了城乡居民收入指标名称、分类和统计标准，建立了城乡统一的一体化住户调查，并据此采集全国居民有关数据。

（一）居民可支配收入

居民可支配收入指居民可用于最终消费支出和储蓄的总和，即居民可用于自由支配的收入。既包括现金收入，也包括实物收入。按照收入的来源，可支配收入包含四项，分别为：工资性收入、经营性净收入、财产性净收入和转移性净收入。

工资性收入 指就业人员通过各种途径得到的全部劳动报酬和各种福利，包括受雇于单位或个人、从事各种自由职业、兼职和零星劳动得到的全部劳动报酬和福利。

经营净收入 指住户或住户成员从事生产经营活动所获得的净收入，是全部经营收入中扣除经营费用、生产性固定资产折旧和生产税之后得到的净收入。计算公式为：

经营净收入=经营收入-经营费用-生产性固定资产折旧-生产税

财产净收入 指住户或住户成员将其所拥有的金融资产、住房等非金融资产和自然资源交由其他机构单位、住户或个人支配而获得的回报并扣除相关的费用之后得到的净收入。财产净收入包括利息净收入、红利收入、储蓄性保险净收益、转让承包土地经营权租金净收入、出租房屋净收入、出租其他资产净收入和自有住房折算净租金等。财产净收入不包括转让资产所有权的溢价所得。

转移净收入 计算公式为：转移净收入=转移性收入—转移性支出

转移性收入 指国家、单位、社会团体对住户的各种经常性转移支付和住户之间的经常性收入转移。包括养老金或退休金、社会救济和补助、政策性生产补贴、政策性生活补贴、救灾款、经常性捐赠和赔偿、报销医疗费、住户之间的赡养收入，本住户非常住成员寄回带回的收入等。转移性收入不包括住户之间的实物馈赠。

转移性支出 指调查户对国家、单位、社会团体或个人的经常性或义务性转移支付。包括缴纳的税款、各项社会保障支出、赡养支出、经常性捐赠和赔偿支出以及其他经常性转移支出等。

（二）居民消费支出

居民消费支出是指居民用于满足家庭日常生活消费需要的全部支出，既包括现金消费支出，也包括实物消费支出。消费支出可划分为食品烟酒、衣着、居住、生活用品及服务、交通通信、教育文化娱乐、医疗保健以及其他用品及服务八大类。

食品烟酒 指用于各种食品和烟草、就类的支出。

衣着 指与居民穿着有关的支出，包括服装、服装材料、鞋类、其他衣类及配件、衣着相关加工服务的支出。

居住 指与居住有关的支出，包括房租、水、电、燃料、物业管理等方面的支出，也包括自有住房折算租金。

生活用品及服务 指家庭及个人的各类生活用品及家庭服务。包括家具及室内装饰品、家用器具、家用纺织品、家庭日用杂品、个人用品和家庭服务。

交通通信 指用于交通和通信工具及相关的各种服务费、维修费和车辆保险等支出。

教育文化娱乐 指用于教育、文化和娱乐方面的支出。

医疗保健 指用于医疗和保健的药品、用品和服务的总费用。包括医疗器具及药品，以及医疗服务。

其他用品及服务 指无法直接归入上述各类支出的其他用品与服务支出。

二、城镇住户调查和农村住户调查指标解释

2012年及以前年份，中国的住户调查一直分城乡分别开展。城镇与农村居民收入、支出等指标的统计口径有所不同，数据不完全可比，城镇调查城镇居民可支配收入，农村调查农村居民纯收入。为了保持历史数据的可比，本年鉴中2012年及以前年份的数据和指标解释仍保持了原城镇住户调查和农村住户调查方案的原貌。

（一）城镇住户调查

城镇家庭人口 指居住在一起，经济上合在一起共同生活的家庭成员。凡计算为家庭人口的成员其全部收支都包括在本家庭中。

城镇就业面 指就业人口占家庭人口的百分比。

城镇就业者负担人数 指家庭人口与就业人口之比。

城镇家庭总收入 指家庭成员得到的工资性收入、经营净收入、财产性收入和转移性收入之和，不包括出售财物收入和借贷收入。

城镇居民家庭可支配收入 指家庭成员得到可用于最

终消费支出和其它非义务性支出以及储蓄的总和，即居民家庭可以用来自由支配的收入。它是家庭总收入扣除交纳的个人所得税、个人交纳的社会保障支出以及记账补贴后的收入。计算公式为：

城镇居民家庭可支配收入=家庭总收入-交纳的个人所得税-个人交纳的社会保障支出-记账补贴

城镇家庭总支出 指家庭除借贷支出以外的全部实际支出。包括现金消费支出、财产性支出、转移性支出、社会保障支出、购房与建房支出。

城镇家庭现金消费支出 指家庭用于日常生活的全部现金支出，包括食品、衣着、居住、家庭设备及用品、交通通信、文教娱乐、医疗保健、其他等八大类支出。

城镇家庭服务性消费支出 指家庭用于支付社会提供的各种文化和生活方面的非商品性服务费用。

城镇家庭收入分组方法 是将所有调查户按户人均可支配收入由低到高排队，按20%，20%，20%，20%，20%的比例依次分成：低收入户、中等偏下收入户、中等收入户、中等偏上收入户、高收入户五组。

（二）农村住户调查

农村住户 指农村常住户。农村常住户指长期（一年以上）居住在乡镇（不包括城关镇）行政管理区域内的住户，以及长期居住在城关镇所辖行政村范围内的农村住户。户口不在本地而在本地居住一年以上的住户也包括在本地农村常住户范围内；有本地户口，但举家外出谋生一年以上的住户，无论是否保留承包耕地都不包括在本地农村住户范围内。

常住人口 指全年经常在家或在家居住6个月以上，而且经济和生活与本户连成一体的人口。外出从业人员在外居住时间虽然在6个月以上，但收入主要带回家中，经济与本户连为一体，仍视为家庭常住人口；在家居住，生活和本户连成一体的国家职工、退休人员也为家庭常住人口。但是现役军人、中专及以上(走读生除外)的在校学生、以及常年在外(不包括探亲、看病等)且已有稳定的职业与居住场所的外出从业人员，不算家庭常住人口。家庭常住人口主要作为计算农村住户平均每人收入、消费和积累水平及分析家庭人口状况的依据。

总收入 指调查期内农村住户和住户成员从各种来源渠道得到的收入总和。按收入的性质划分为工资性收入、家庭经营收入、财产性收入和转移性收入。

工资性收入 指农村住户成员受雇于单位或个人，靠出卖劳动而获得的收入。

家庭经营收入 指农村住户以家庭为生产经营单位进行生产筹划和管理而获得的收入。农村住户家庭经营活动按行业划分为农业、林业、牧业、渔业、工业、建筑业、交通运输业邮电业、批发和零售贸易餐饮业、社会服务业、文教卫生业和其他家庭经营。

财产性收入 指金融资产或有形非生产性资产的所有者向其他机构单位提供资金或将有形非生产性资产供其支配，作为回报而从中获得的收入。

转移性收入 指农村住户和住户成员无须付出任何对应物而获得的货物、服务、资金或资产所有权等，不包括无偿提供的用于固定资本形成的资金。一般情况下，是指农村住户在二次分配中的所有收入。

现金收入 指农村住户和住户成员在调查期内得到以现金形态表现的收入。按来源分成工资性收入、家庭经营现金收入、财产性收入、转移性收入。

农村居民家庭纯收入 指农村住户当年从各种来源得到的总收入相应扣除所发生的费用后的收入总和。计算公式为：

农村居民家庭纯收入=总收入-家庭经营费用支出-税费支出-生产性固定资产折旧-赠送农村内部亲友

纯收入主要用于再生产投入和当年生活消费支出，也可用于储蓄和各种非义务性支出。“农民人均纯收入”是按人口平均的纯收入水平，反映的是一个地区农村居民的平均收入水平。

总支出 指农村住户用于生产、生活和再分配的全部支出。包括家庭经营费用支出、购置生产性固定资产支出、税费支出、消费支出、财产性支出和转移性支出。

社会保险

城镇职工基本养老保险

1.参保职工人数：指报告期末按照国家法律、法规和有关政策规定参加基本养老保险并在社保经办机构已建立缴费记录档案的职工人数。包括中断缴费但未终止养老关系的职工人数，不包括只登记未建立缴费记录档案的人数。

2. 参保离退休人员人数:指报告期末参加基本养老保险的离休、退休和退职人员的人数。

3.基金收入：指根据国家有关规定，由纳入基本养老保险范围的缴费单位和个人按照国家规定的缴费基数和缴费比例缴纳的养老保险基金，以及通过其他方式取得的形成基金来源的收入。包括单位和职工个人缴纳的基本养老保险费、基本养老保险基金利息收入、上级补助收入、下级上解收入、转移收入、财政补贴和其他收入。

4.基金支出：指按照国家政策规定的开支范围和开支标准从养老保险基金中支付给参加基本养老保险的个人的养老金、丧葬抚恤补助，以及由于保险关系转移、上下级之间调剂资金等原因而发生的支出。包括:离休金、退休金、退职金、各种补贴、医疗费、死亡丧葬补助费、抚恤救济费、社会保险经办机构管理费、补助下级支出、上解上级支出、转移支出、其他支出等。

5.基金累计结余：指截止报告期末基本养老保险基金收支相抵后的累计余额。

城乡居民基本养老保险

1.参保人数　指报告期末，参加城乡居民养老保险（在经办机构参保登记并已建立缴费记录以及制度实施当年已经年满 60 周岁并在经办机构参保登记）的总人数（不包括已经办理注销登记手续的人数）。

2. 基金收入　指根据国家有关规定，由参加城乡居民基本养老保险的个人按规定缴费的城乡居民基本养老保险基金，以及通过集体补助、财政补助等其他方式取得的形成基金来源的收入。包括个人缴费收入、集体补助收入、政府补贴收入、利息收入、转移收入、上级补助收入、下级上解收入和其他收入。

3.基金支出　指按照国家政策规定的开支范围和开支标准从城乡居民基本养老保险基金中支付给参加城乡居民基本养老保险的个人养老金待遇支出，以及由于参保人员跨统筹地区流动而发生的支出等。包括养老金待遇支出、转移支出、补助下级支出、上解上级支出、其他支出。

4.基金累计结余　指截止报告期末城乡居民基本养老保险基金收支相抵后的累计余额。

基本医疗保险

1.参保人数：指报告期末按国家有关规定参加相应基本医疗保险的人数。

2.基金收入：指由用人单位和个人按照国家规定的缴费基数、缴费比例或缴费标准缴纳的基本医疗保险基金，财政补助资金以及通过其他方式取得的形成基金来源的款项，包括：单位缴纳收入、个人缴纳收入、财政补助收入（含医疗救助补助个人收入）、财政补贴收入、利息收入和其他收入。

3.基金支出：指按照国家政策规定的开支范围和开支标准，从基本医疗保险基金中支付给参保人员的医疗保险待遇支出，以及其他支出。包括住院医疗费用支出、门急诊医疗费用支出、个人账户基金支出、其他支出。

4.基金累计结余：指截止报告期末基本医疗保险基金累计结余金额。

失业保险

1.参保人数: 指报告期末按照国家法律、法规和有关政策规定参加了失业保险的城镇企业、事业单位的职工及地方政府规定参加失业保险的其他人员的人数。

2.基金收入: 指报告期内筹集的失业保险基金的总额，包括失业保险费收入、利息收入、财政补贴收入、其他收入、转移收入、上级补助收入、下级上解收入。

3.基金支出：指报告期内为保障失业人员基本生活、促进其再就业等支出的基金总额，包括失业保险金支出、医疗补助金支出、丧葬补助金和抚恤金支出、职业培训和职业介绍补贴支出、农民合同制工人一次性生活补助支出、其他支出、转移支出、上级补助支出、下级上解支出。

4.基金累计结余：指截止报告期末失业保险基金收支相抵后的累计余额。

工伤保险

1.参加保险人数: 指报告期末依据国家有关规定参加工伤保险的职工人数和有雇工的个体工商户的雇工数。

2.享受保险待遇人数: 指年初至报告期末因工伤或职业病而享受工伤保险待遇的人数。为享受工伤医疗待遇中未评定等级的人数、享受伤残待遇人数以及享受因工死亡待遇人数之和。

3.基金收入: 指根据国家有关规定，由参加工伤保险的单位按国家规定的缴费基数和缴费比例缴纳的工伤保险基金，以及通过其他形式取得的形成基金来源的款项。包括：单位缴纳的社会统筹基金收入、财政补贴收入、利息收入、其他收入。

4.基金支出: 指按照国家政策规定的开支范围和开支标准从工伤保险基金中支付给参加工伤保险的人员及供养直系亲属工伤保险待遇支出及其他支出。包括工伤医疗费、伤残补助金、工亡补助金、护理费、丧葬补助费、工伤预防费用、职业康复费用和其他支出。

5.基金累计结余: 指截止报告期末工伤保险基金累计结余金额。

生育保险

1.参保人数: 指报告期末依据有关规定参加生育保险的人数。

2.基金收入: 指根据国家有关规定，由参加生育保险的单位按照国家规定的缴费基数和缴费比例缴纳的生育保险基金，以及通过其他方式取得的形成基金来源的款项，包括：单位缴纳的基金收入、利息收入和其他收入。

3.基金支出: 指按照国家政策规定的开支范围和开支标准，从生育保险基金中支付给参加生育保险的职工，因妊娠、分娩和计划生育手术而享受的待遇及其他支出。包括：生育津贴、医疗费用支出及其他支出。

4.基金累计结余: 指截止报告期末生育保险基金累计结余金额。

Explanatory Notes on Main Statistical Indicators

Ⅰ. Integrated Urban and Rural Households Survey on Income and Expenditures and Living Conditions

Since the fourth quarter of 2012, the NBS has launched its reform on the household survey programme, to form an integrated survey, instead of the two separate urban and rural household surveys. The reform regulates the division of urban and rural areas, integrates the concepts, classifications and standards, conducts the integrated household survey, and collects household data in the whole country thereafter.

1. Disposable Income of Households

Disposable Income of Households refers to the income of households for purpose of final expenditure and savings. It includes income both in cash and in kind. By sources of income, disposable income includes four categories: income from wages and salaries, net business income, net income from properties and net income from transfer.

Income from Wages and Salaries refers to remuneration of labour and salaries from all kinds of sources, including those employed by other units or individuals, freelance work, part-time jobs, and sporadic labour.

Net Business Income refers to net income earned by households and their members engaged in production and business activities. It refers to the net income of operating revenue minus operating costs, depreciation of productive fixed assets, and production tax. The formula is:

Net Business Income=Operating Revenue-Operating Costs-Depreciation of Productive Fixed Assets-Production Tax

Net Income from Properties refers to the net income received as returns by households or members of financial assets, non-financial assets such as housing, to other institutions, households or individuals, and minus relevant costs. Net income from properties includes net income of interest, bonus income, net income of saving insurance, net income of rents of transferring management right of contract land, income of renting housing, income of renting other assets, net converted rents of self-owned housing. Net income from properties do not include premium of transferring ownership of assets.

Net Income from Transfer The formula is:

Net Income from Transfer=Income from Transfers-Expenditure from Transfer

Income from Transfer refers to the regular transfer from country, institutions, social communities to households and between households. It includes old-age and retirement pension, disaster relief funds, regular donation and compensation, applying for medical fees, supporting income between households, income from non-usual-residing members of households, etc. Income from transfer do not include presents in kinds between households.

Expenditure from Transfer refers to regular or deontic transfer from households to country, institutions, households or individuals. It includes taxes paid, expenditure of all kinds of social security, supporting expenditure, regular donation and compensation and other regular transfer expenditure, etc.

2. Consumption Expenditure of Households

Consumption Expenditure of Households refers to all expenditure of households for living expenditure to satisfy family daily living. It includes expenditure in cash and in kind. It includes eight categories: food, tobacco and liquor; clothing; residence; household facilities, articles and services; transport and communications; education, cultural and recreational activities; health care and medical services, and miscellaneous goods and services.

Food, Tobacco and Liquor refers to expenditure for food, tobacco and liquor of all kinds.

Clothing refers to expenditure related to clothing, including clothes, clothing materials, footwear, other clothing and accessories, processing services related to clothing.

Residence refers to expenditure related to residence, including housing rents, water, electricity, fuel, property management, and including converted self-owned housing rents.

Household Facilities, Articles and Services refers to expenditure for family and individual articles for living purpose and family services. It includes furniture and interior decoration, home appliances, home textiles, household miscellaneous daily articles, personal articles, and family services.

Transport and Communications refers to expenditure for transport and communication and related services, maintenance and repairs, and vehicle insurance.

Education, Cultural and Recreational Activities refers to expenditure on education, cultural and recreational activities.

Health Care and Medical Services refers to expenditure on drugs, supplies and services of medical and health care. It includes medical appliances and drugs, and medical services.

Miscellaneous Goods and Services refers to expenditure of all kinds of expenditure of other articles and services that can not divided into the category above.

II. Urban and Rural Households Survey

Prior to 2012, household surveys in China were conducted separately in urban and rural areas. Statistical coverage of indicators of household income and expenditure of urban and rural households were different, data were not comparable completely. Disposable income was surveyed in urban households, and net income was surveyed in rural households. For comparable reason, data prior to 2012 in this yearbook were still original urban households and rural households survey.

1. Urban Household Survey

Population of Urban Households refer to members of households living and sharing economically together in the urban areas. All the income and expenditure of all the members of such households are included in the income and expenditure of the household.

Proportion of Urban Employment refers to the proportion of employed population to the population of urban households.

Number of Dependents per Urban Employee refers to the ratio between number of persons in an urban household and the number of employed persons.

Total Income of Urban Households refers to the sum of wage income; net business income; income from properties; and income from transfers of members of the households. Income from selling of properties and income from borrowing are not included.

Disposable Income of Urban Households refers to the actual income at the disposal of members of the households which can be used for final consumption, other non-compulsory expenditure and savings. This equals to total income minus income tax, personal contribution to social security and subsidy for keeping diaries in being a sample household. The following formula is used:

Disposable Income of Urban Households= total household income - income tax - personal contribution to social security - subsidy for keeping diaries for a sampled household.

Total Expenditure of Urban Households refers to all actual expenditure of households except expenditure on lending. It includes cash expenditure; property expenditure, transfer expenditure, social insurance expenditure and expenditure on house purchasing or house building.

Consumption Expenditure of Urban Households in Cash refers to total cash expenditure of households for consumption in daily life, including expenditure on the eight categories of food; clothing; housing; household appliances; transport and communications; education, cultural and recreational activities and medical care.

Consumption Expenditure of Urban Households on Services refers to non-commodity service expenditure of households on various kinds of cultural and living activities provided by society.

Urban Households by Income Group All households in the sample are grouped, by per capita disposable income of the household, into groups of low income, lower middle income, middle income, upper middle income, high income, each group consisting of 20%, 20%, 20%, 20%, and 20% of all households respectively.

2. Rural Households

Rural Households refer to usual resident households in rural areas. Usual resident households in rural areas are households residing on a long term basis(for more than one year) in the areas under the administration of township governments (not including county towns), and in the areas under the administration of villages in county towns. Households residing in the current addresses for over one year with their household registration in other places are still considered as resident households of the locality. For households with their household registration in one place but all members of the households having moved away to make a living in another place for over one year, they will not be included in the rural households of the area where they are registered, irrespective of whether they still keep their contracted land.

Usual Resident Population refers to persons staying at home regularly or for over 6 months during a year and integrated with the household economically and in terms of living. Members of the household staying away from the household for over 6 months but keeping a close economic relation with the household by sending the majority of income to the household are regarded as usual resident of the household. Government staff and workers or retirees living as close members of the household are also considered as usual resident. However, servicemen, students of secondary technical schools or schools of higher education and persons with stable jobs and residence outside the household (excluding those visiting relatives or seeking medical service) are not included as resident population of the household. Resident population is used in calculating income, consumption, accumulation on per capita basis of rural households and in analyzing composition of rural households.

Total Income refers to the sum of income earned from various sources by the rural households and their members during the reference period, and is classified as income from wages and salaries, income from household operations, income from properties and income from transfers.

Income from Wages and Salaries refers to income from labour earned by the members of rural households employed by other units or individuals.

Income from Household Operations refers to income by the rural households as units of production and operation. Operations by rural households are classified according to their economic activities namely agriculture, forestry, animal husbandry, fishery, manufacturing, construction, transportation, post and telecommunications, wholesale, retail and catering, social service, culture, education, health, and other household operations.

Income from Properties refers to the income received as returns by owners of financial assets or tangible non-productive assets by providing capitals or tangible non-productive assets to other institutional units.

Income from Transfers refers to the receipt by rural households and their members of goods, services, capital or rights of assets without giving or repaying accordingly, excluding capital provided to them for the formation of fixed assets. In general, it refers to all income received by rural households through redistribution.

Cash Income refers to income received by rural households and their members in the form of cash during the reference period. It is classified, by source of income, into income from wages and salaries, cash income from household operations, income from properties and income from transfers.

Net Income of Rural Households refers to the total income of rural households from all sources minus all corresponding expenses. The formula for calculation is as follows:

Net income of rural households = total income - household operation expenses - taxes and fees-depreciation of fixed assets for production - gifts to rural relatives.

Net income is mainly used as input for reinvestment in production and as consumption expenditure of the year, and also used for savings and non-compulsory expenses of various forms. "Per capita net income of farmers" is the level of net income averaged by population, reflecting the average income level of rural population in a given area.

Total Expenditure refers to total expenses of rural households on production, consumption and redistribution, including expenditure on household operations; purchase of productive fixed assets; taxes and fees; consumption expenditure; expenses on properties; and expenses on transfers.

Ⅲ Social Insurance

Basic Pension Insurance for Urban Staff and Workers

1. Number of staff and workers covered refers to staff and workers participating in the basic pension insurance for urban staff and workers programme according to national laws, regulations and related policies at the end of the reference period, who have already had payment records in social security management agencies, including those who have interrupt payment without terminating the insurance programme. Those who have registered in the programme but with no payment records are not included.

2. Number of retirees refers to the number of retirees participating in the basic pension insurance for urban staff and workers programmes by the end of the reference period.

3. Revenue of the basic pension insurance programme refers to payments made by employers and individuals participating in the pension insurance programme in accordance with the basis and proportion stipulated in State regulations, and income from other sources that become the source of pension insurance fund, including the premium paid by employers and staff and workers, interest income, subsidies from higher level agencies, income as transfer from subordinate agencies, transferred income, government financial subsidies and other income.

4. Expenditure of basic pension insurance programme refer to payment made on pensions and funeral subsidies to those covered in pension insurance programmes according to related national policies on scope and standard of expenditure. Also included are expenditure which arises due to shift of the insurance relationship or adjustment of funds among agencies. More specifically, included are pensions for resigned people, pensions for retired people, pension for people quitting jobs, various subsidies, medical fees, funeral subsidies, compensation payments, management fees for social security agencies, expenses on subsidies to lower subordinates, expenses as transfer to agencies at higher level, transferred expenditure and other expenditure.

5. Balance of basic pension insurance programme refers to the balance of basic pension insurance funds at the end of the reference period after deducting expenses from revenue.

Basic Pension Insurance for Urban and Rural Residents

1. Number of participants refers to people participating in the basic pension insurance for urban and rural residents programme who registered with the participation and established payment records, and who were 60 years old or above when the system was established and registered with the participation.. Those who cancelled their registration are not included.

2. Revenue of the insurance programme refers to the revenue from the payments made, in accordance with related regulations of the government, by individuals participating in the basic pension insurance for urban and rural residents programme and from the subsidies contributed by collective subsidies, public finance and other sources. It includes the payment by individual participants, collective subsidies, government subsidies, interest income, transferred income, subsidies from higher levels, contributions from lower levels, and income from other sources.

3. Expenditure of the insurance programme refers to payment made to those covered in the basic pension insurance for urban and rural residents according to related national policies on scope and standard of expenditure. Also included are expenditures which arise due to movement of participants among different locations. It includes the payment to the individual participants, transferred expenditures, expenses on subsidies to lower subordinates, expenses as transfer to agencies at higher level, and other expenditures.

4. Balance of insurance programme refers to the balance of basic pension insurance funds for urban and rural residents at the end of the reference period after deducting expenses from revenue.

Basic Medical Care Insurance

1. Number of people participating in the insurance programme refers to people participating in the basic medical care insurance programme according to related regulations at the end of the reference period.

2. Revenue of the insurance programme refers to payments made by employers and individuals participating in the medical care insurance programme in accordance with the basis and proportion stipulated in State regulations, government subsidies and income from other sources that become the source of medical insurance fund, including payment by employers and individuals, financial assistance (including medical assistance subsidiaries to individuals), financial subsidies, interest income and other incomes.

3. Expenditure of the insurance programme refers to medical care payment made to people covered in basic medical care insurance programme within the scope and standards of expenditure according to related national policies, and other expenses, including medical expenses of hospital inpatients, medical expenses for outpatients and emergency patients, payment to individual accounts and other expenditure.

4. Balance of the basic medical care insurance programme refers to the balance of medical care insurance funds at the end of the reference period after deducting expenses from revenue.

Unemployment Insurance

1. Number of people covered refers to staff and workers in urban enterprises or institutions who have participated in the unemployment insurance programme according to relevant policies and regulations, and other people who have participated according to local government regulations at the end of the reference period.

2. Revenue of the unemployment insurance programme refers to the total unemployment insurance funds raised in the reference period, including unemployment insurance premium, interest income, financial subsidies, other incomes, transferred income, subsidies from higher level agencies and income as transfer from subordinate agencies.

3. Expenditure of the unemployment insurance programme refers to total expenses during the reference period to guarantee the basic livelihood of unemployed people, and to encourage their re-employment. Included are unemployment relief, medical fees, funeral subsidies, compensation payments, training expenses, job placement expenses, one-time subsistence allowance for contracted migrant workers, other expenditures, transferred expenditure, expenses as transfer to higher level agencies and subsidies to lower level agencies.

4. Balance of the unemployment insurance programme refers to the balance of revenue of the programme after deducting expenses at the end of the reference period.

Work Injury Insurance

1. Number of people covered refers to staff and workers who have participated in the work injury insurance programme and employees who work for the self employed and have participated in the work injury insurance programme according to relevant national regulations at the end of the reference period.

2. Number of beneficiaries refers to number of people benefited from work injury insurance, as a result of work injury or occupational disease. It is the sum of beneficiaries of medical treatment of unrated work injuries, disability benefits for work injuries and compensation for deaths at work places.

3. Revenue of the work injury insurance programme refers to payments made by employers participating in the work injury insurance programme in accordance with the basis and proportion stipulated in State regulations, and income from other sources that become source of work injury insurance fund, including income of social comprehensive funds paid by employers, government financial subsidies, interest income and other incomes.

4. Expenditure of the work injury insurance programme refers to payments made from work injury insurance funds to those who participated in the work injury insurance programme and their direct dependents within the scope and standards of expenditure according to related national policies, and other expenditure, including medical fees for work injury, injury and disability subsidies, death subsidies, nursing fees, funeral subsidies, injury prevention fees, occupational rehabilitation fees and other expenditure.

5. Balance of the work injury insurance programme refers to the balance of the work injury funds at the end of the reference period.

Maternity Insurance

1. Number of people covered refers to people who have participated in the maternity insurance programme according to relevant regulation at the end of the reference period.

2. Revenue of maternity insurance programme refers to payments made by employers participating in the maternity insurance programme in accordance with the basis and proportion stipulated in State regulations, and income from other sources that become source of maternity insurance fund, including income of funds paid by employers, interest income and other income.

3. Expenditure of the maternity insurance programme refers to payments made from maternity insurance funds to staff and workers who participate in the maternity insurance programme within the scope and standards of expenditure in accordance with related national policies, expenses paid for pregnancy, child delivery or surgeries related to family planning, and other expenditure, including allowance for child bearing, medical fees and other expenditure.

4. Balance of the maternity programme refers to the balance of the maternity insurance funds at the end of the reference period.

11 城市概况

GENERAL SURVEY OF CITIES

第十一篇　城市概况

本篇主要内容和资料来源

本篇资料反映新疆城市社会、经济发展和城市建设的基本情况。

城市概况资料主要包括城市公用事业基本情况、主要经济指标、市政设施、园林绿化、环境卫生、供水供气等。

本篇资料由新疆维吾尔自治区统计局国民经济综合统计处根据新疆维吾尔自治区住建厅和新疆维吾尔自治区统计局相关处室提供的年度数据整理。

General Survey of Cities

Main Content and Source of Data

Data in this chapter show the social and economic development and the urban construction of Xinjiang.

Data on the general survey cities include the basic condition of urban public facilities, main economic indicators, civil facilities, urban greenery, environment and sanitation, supply of gas and heating, public transportation, etc.

Data on this chapter are compiled by the Department of Comprehensive of the Xinjiang Bureau of Statistics according to the data of yearly statistics, which are provided by the Construction Bureau of Xinjiang Uygur Autonomous Region and related departments of Statistics Bureau of Xinjiang Uygur Autonomous Region.

11-1 城市公用事业基本情况
Basic Statistics on City Public Utilities

项　目	Item	2014	2015
城市及建筑物面积	**City Areas and Floor Space of Buildings**		
建成区面积(平方公里)	Area of Built Districts(sq.km)	986	1041
征用土地面积(平方公里)	Land Put in Requisition for State Construction Projects (sq. km)	19.9	20.4
城市人口密度(人/平方公里)	Population Density of City Districts(persons/sq.km)	5083	2764
供水、供气及供热	**Water Supply, Gas Supply and Heating**		
自来水年供水量(万立方米)	Annual Volume of Tap Water Supply (10 000 cu.m)	79884	79007
#生活用水量	Water Consumption for Residential use	29522	30206
平均每人日生活用水量(升)	Per -Capita Water Consumption for Residential Use (litre)	170	168
用水普及率(%)	Coverage Rate of Urban Population with Access to Tap Water (%)	98.2	99.1
人工煤气供气量(万立方米)	Gaswork Gas Supply (10 000 cu.m)	1752	1752
#家庭用量	Consumption of Gaswork Gas for Residential Use	1752	1752
天然气供气量(万立方米)	Natural Gas Supply (10 000 cu.m)	422189	416973
#家庭用量	Consumption of Natural Gas for Residential Use	87911	86490
液化石油气供气量(吨)	Liquefied Petroleum Gas (ton)	56790	57924
#家庭用量	Consumption of Liquefied Gas for Residential Use	47014	44650
天然气、煤气管道长度(公里)	Length of Gas Pipelines (km)	10887	11587
燃气普及率(%)	Coverage Rate of Urban Population with Access to Gas (%)	97.3	98.0
集中供热面积(万平方米)	Area of Centralized Heating (10 000 sq.m)	22782	27499
#住　宅	Residential Buildings	16376	19418
市政工程	**Municipal Engineering**		
道路长度(公里)	Length of Paved Roads (km)	5686	6139
平均每万人拥有 (公里)	Length of Paved Roads per 10 000 Persons (km)	7.1	7.7
道路面积(万平方米)	Area of Paved Roads (10 000 sq.m)	10173	10957
平均每人拥有(平方米)	Per Capita Area of Paved Roads (sq.m)	12.7	16.5
下水道长度(公里)	Length of Sewer Pipelines (km)	5140	5655
平均每万人拥有 (公里)	Length of Sewer Pipelines 10 000 Persons (km)	6.4	5.4
城市绿化	**City Greening**		
建成区绿化覆盖面积(公顷)	Green Areas of Completed Area (hectare)	33855	39395
每万人建成区绿地面积(公顷)	Green Areas of Completed Area per 10 000 Persons (hectare)	42.2	37.9
公园数(个)	Number of Parks and Zoos(unit)	134	148
公园面积(公顷)	Area of Parks (hectare)	3747	4106
环境卫生	**Environmental Sanitation**		
清运生活垃圾(万吨)	Volume of Garbage Disposal (10 000 tons)	339	349
清运粪便(万吨)	Volume of Disposal of Excrement and Urine (10 000 tons)	0.3	0.1
每万人拥有公共厕所(座)	Number of Public Toilets per 10 000 Persons (unit)	2.8	2.9

11-2 各城市主要经济指标
Major Economic Indicators by Cities

单位：万元　　(2015 年)　　(10 000 yuan)

城市名称	City	地区生产总值（当年价格）Gross Region Production (current-year price)	第一产业 Primary Industry	第二产业 Secondary Industry	第三产业 Tertiary Industry
乌鲁木齐市	Urumqi City	26316398	316439	7873749	18126210
克拉玛依市	Karamay City	6294299	51436	4105309	2137554
高 昌 区	Gaochang District	760387	197376	170613	392398
哈 密 市	Hami [Kumul] City	3307375	243603	1725646	1338126
昌 吉 市	Changji City	3909619	399071	2002446	1508102
阜 康 市	Fukang City	1404974	274511	765410	365053
伊 宁 市	Yining [Gulja] City	2053177	68879	440159	1544139
奎 屯 市	Kuytun City	1203643	71148	479365	653130
霍尔果斯市	Huoerguosi City				
塔 城 市	Tacheng [Qoqek] City	825951	216086	146278	463587
乌 苏 市	Usu City	1677908	638062	589235	450611
阿勒泰市	Altay City	607916	88424	110053	409439
博 乐 市	Bole [Bortala] City	1448654	302012	458342	688300
阿拉山口市	Alashankou City	490377		111047	379330
库尔勒市	Korla City	6637443	400500	4939658	1297285
阿克苏市	Aksu City	1672126	208866	367146	1096114
阿图什市	Artux City	451236	64303	114904	272029
喀 什 市	Kashgar [Kaxgar] City	2161929	78307	674499	1409123
和 田 市	Hotan City	655113	38760	123223	493130
石河子市	Shi Hezi City	3157843	107540	1854032	1196271
阿拉尔市	Aral City				
图木舒克市	Tumxuk City				
五家渠市	Wujiaqu City				
北 屯 市	Beitun City				
铁门关市	Tiemenguan City				

城市名称	City	#工 业 Industry	#交通运输、仓储和邮政业 Transport, Storage and Post	人均地区生产总值（元）Per Capita GDP (yuan)
乌鲁木齐市	Urumqi City	6321387	3359386	74340
克拉玛依市	Karamay City	4658887	126526	131014
高 昌 区	Gaochang District	108114	74290	26741
哈 密 市	Hami [Kumul] City	1160491	351864	68252
昌 吉 市	Changji City	1605633	264679	78982
阜 康 市	Fukang City	606880	46076	84030
伊 宁 市	Yining [Gulja] City	174421	86688	37957
奎 屯 市	Kuytun City	320395	83110	77256
霍尔果斯市	Huoerguosi City			
塔 城 市	Tacheng [Qoqek] City	44108	49796	49491
乌 苏 市	Usu City	444235	50503	54635
阿勒泰市	Altay City	41253	34494	31255
博 乐 市	Bole [Bortala] City	288678	51997	55841
阿拉山口市	Alashankou City	91549	116290	206259
库尔勒市	Korla City	4410784	127572	112222
阿克苏市	Aksu City	180729	101692	32514
阿图什市	Artux City	71981	24830	16732
喀 什 市	Kashgar [Kaxgar] City	503999	127050	32316
和 田 市	Hotan City	6389	28736	18718
石河子市	Shi Hezi City	1345620	137506	83701
阿拉尔市	Aral City			
图木舒克市	Tumxuk City			
五家渠市	Wujiaqu City			
北 屯 市	Beitun City			
铁门关市	Tiemenguan City			

11-2 续表 Continued

单位: 万元 (10 000 yuan)

城市名称	City	固定资产投资总额 Investment in Fixed Assets	规模以上工业总产值（当年价格） Gross Industrial Output Value above Designated Size (At Current Prices)	一般公共预算收入 General Public Budget Revenue in Local Finance	一般公共预算支出 General Public Budget Expenditure in Local Finance
乌鲁木齐市	Urumqi City	12260603	20632531	3686663	4466709
克拉玛依市	Karamay City	3965392	10743381	749926	896640
高 昌 区	Gaochang District	2043884	345247	74809	231939
哈 密 市	Hami [Kumul] City	6260865	3597404	418729	523170
昌 吉 市	Changji City	2785588	3540619	352991	495190
阜 康 市	Fukang City	2273813	2317819	199200	269291
伊 宁 市	Yining [Gulja] City	986405	349455	246891	454948
奎 屯 市	Kuytun City	1198133	902165	113659	210364
霍尔果斯市	Huoerguosi City		75936	34759	77272
塔 城 市	Tacheng [Qoqek] City	553152	37035	50530	188734
乌 苏 市	Usu City	977815	604588	133377	290137
阿勒泰市	Altay City	791658	115064	62000	238169
博 乐 市	Bole [Bortala] City	1808258	518457	90632	266912
阿拉山口市	Alashankou City		158950	22531	65105
库尔勒市	Korla City	4378999	5997726	311000	446322
阿克苏市	Aksu City	1122874	891721	165032	358281
阿图什市	Artux City	400561	140076	30725	268570
喀 什 市	Kashgar [Kaxgar] City	2088595	375773	181115	545027
和 田 市	Hotan City	811471	26419	69586	288914
石河子市	Shi Hezi City	2108337	4775122	368259	445888
阿拉尔市	Aral City	1211213	1336337	66882	83578
图木舒克市	Tumxuk City	634630	520027	31040	53854
五家渠市	Wujiaqu City	654562	2883368	117059	139434
北 屯 市	Beitun City			22634	30456
铁门关市	Tiemenguan City			4833	5010

城市名称	City	居民消费价格指数(上年=100) Consumer Price Index (preceding year=100)	社会消费品零售总额 Total Retail Sales of Consumer Goods	在岗职工平均工资(元) Average Wage of Staff and Workers (yuan)
乌鲁木齐市	Urumqi City	100.7	9405087	68603
克拉玛依市	Karamay City	100.4	588146	83194
高 昌 区	Gaochang District	101.4	258814	63189
哈 密 市	Hami [Kumul] City	100.9	756221	60414
昌 吉 市	Changji City	101.4	995708	63574
阜 康 市	Fukang City		322382	62277
伊 宁 市	Yining [Gulja] City	101.2	760927	58640
奎 屯 市	Kuytun City	101.1	248510	54271
霍尔果斯市	Huoerguosi City			59813
塔 城 市	Tacheng [Qoqek] City	99.7	186501	51801
乌 苏 市	Usu City		157189	43326
阿勒泰市	Altay City	101.0	248834	48323
博 乐 市	Bole [Bortala] City	100.5	293110	50823
阿拉山口市	Alashankou City			60250
库尔勒市	Korla City	99.7	679391	66035
阿克苏市	Aksu City	99.9	638367	58292
阿图什市	Artux City	100.0	113383	54740
喀 什 市	Kashgar [Kaxgar] City	100.4	717768	55204
和 田 市	Hotan City	100.6	178007	55707
石河子市	Shi Hezi City	100.5		60819
阿拉尔市	Aral City			55941
图木舒克市	Tumxuk City			57739
五家渠市	Wujiaqu City			59000
北 屯 市	Beitun City			
铁门关市	Tiemenguan City			

11-3 各城市市区设施水平
Level of Urban Public Facilities in Cities

(2015 年)

城市名称	City	城市用水普及率 (%) Coverage Rate of Urban Population with Access to Tap Water (%)	城市燃气普及率 (%) Coverage Rate of Population with Access to Gas (%)	人均城市道路面积 (平方米) Per Capita Area of Paved Roads (sq.m)	人均公园绿地面积 (平方米) Per Capita Area of Parks and Green Land (sq.m)	排水管道密度 (公里/平方公里) Density of Sewage Pipes (km/sq.km)
总　计	**Total**	98.81	94.63	14.37	9.34	5.52
乌鲁木齐市	Urumqi City	99.98	99.85	10.34	10.93	4.05
克拉玛依市	Karamay City	100.00	100.00	29.24	11.62	6.29
高 昌 区	Gaochang District	99.24	95.84	27.78	17.96	8.41
哈 密 市	Hami [Kumul] City	99.90	93.95	21.16	13.34	9.02
昌 吉 市	Changji City	99.20	98.37	17.13	11.29	4.70
阜 康 市	Fukang City	99.89	98.72	28.39	19.75	8.63
伊 宁 市	Yining [Gulja] City	99.92	96.74	21.31	9.72	14.40
奎 屯 市	Kuytun City	93.99	99.40	19.27	9.19	10.15
霍尔果斯市	Huoerguosi City	66.67	54.00	41.35	9.00	1.25
塔 城 市	Tacheng [Qoqek] City	97.95	83.52	15.17	13.41	10.72
乌 苏 市	Usu City	95.07	93.36	20.79	8.05	7.12
阿勒泰市	Altay City	98.87	93.62	16.43	27.23	7.53
博 乐 市	Bole [Bortala] City	98.74	89.23	14.60	12.53	12.02
阿拉山口市	Alashankou City	61.58		76.50	7.59	3.61
库尔勒市	Korla City	99.95	99.52	25.81	14.54	4.45
阿克苏市	Aksu City	96.17	99.97	14.96	11.34	5.16
阿图什市	Artux City	100.00	100.00	25.91	9.87	4.25
喀 什 市	Kashgar [Kaxgar] City	100.00	96.70	24.59	13.84	2.70
和 田 市	Hotan City	97.62	99.94	18.74	6.96	3.84
石河子市	Shihezi City	100.00	98.24	31.80	10.36	9.26
阿拉尔市	Alar City	97.41	87.16	21.04	10.64	3.56
图木舒克市	Tumxuk City	66.67	58.33	51.20	8.89	9.96
五家渠市	Wujiaqu City	100.00	100.00	20.58	11.32	2.85
北 屯 市	Beitun City	82.70	98.89	39.43	7.77	4.75
铁门关市	Tiemenguan City	100.00	100.00	19.91	10.00	3.11
双河市	Shuanghe City	100.00	71.43	24.62	8.67	3.82

11-4 主要年份城市自来水情况
Basic Statistics on Tap Water Supply in Cities in Main Years

指　　标	Item	2010	2014	2015
年末水厂生产能力(万吨/日)	Production Capacity of TapWater Supply (10 000 tons/day)	292	373	463
年末供水管道总长度(公里)	Length of Water Supply Piplines (km)	4448	6507	8047
全年供水总量(亿立方米)	Total Annual Volume of Water Supply (100 millon cu.m)	5.0	7.7	7.9
#生活用水	For Residential Use	2.5	2.6	3.0
生产用水	For Productive Use	2.0	2.1	2.1
平均每人日生活用水量(升)	Per-Capita Daily Consumption of Tap Water for Residential Use (litre)	165.1	150.8	167.7
用水人口(万人)	Number of Residents with Access to Tap Water (10 000 persons)	418	626	659

11-5 主要年份城市市政建设情况
Statistics on City Construction in Cities in Main Years

指　　标	Item	2010	2014	2015
实有道路长度(公里)	Length of Paved Roads (km)	2809	5178	6139
实有道路面积(万平方米)	Area of Paved Roads (10 000 sq.m)	3654	8323	10957
城市桥梁(座)	Number of City Bridges (unit)	253	384	457
城市下水道总长度(公里)	Length of City Sewer Pipes (km)	2008	4372	5655
城市污水日处理能力(万立方米)	Daily Disposal Capacity of City Sewage (10 000 cu.m)	46	157	200
城市路灯盏数(千盏)	Number of Street Light (1 000 units)	72.9	400.1	490.1

注：城市污水日处理能力指污水处理厂处理能力，不包括其他污水处理设施处理量。
Note: The daily treatment capacity in urban area refers to the treatment capacity of a waste- water treatment plant, excluding the volume handled by other polluted-water treatment facility.

11-6 主要年份城市园林绿化情况
Basic Statistics on Parks and Green Areas in Cities in Main Years

指　　标	Item	2010	2014	2015
城市园林绿地面积(公顷)	Area of Park and Green Land (hectare)	19124	37686	60074
#建成区绿地面积	Green Land of Completed Area		27773	39395
每万人建成区绿地面积(公顷)	Green Areas of Completed Area Per 10 000 Persons (hectare)	53.4	35.7	65.6
建成区绿化覆盖率(%)	Green Covrage Rate of Completed Area (%)	29.1	36.4	37.9
平均每人公园绿地面积(平方米)	Per Capita Parks Green Areas (sq.m)	6.4	8.6	9.6
公园数(个)	Number of Parks and Zoos (unit)	84	131	148
公园面积(公顷)	Area of Parks (hectare)	1568	3156	4106

11-7 主要年份城市环境卫生情况
Basic Statistics on Urban Environment in Cities in Main Years

指　　标	Item	2000	2010	2015
环卫专用车辆设备数量(辆)	Number of Special Vehicles for Environmental Sanitation (unit)	767	1690	5034
公共厕所(座)	Number of Public Lavatories (unit)	1684	2119	2308
每万人拥有公共厕所(座)	Number of Public Lavatories Per 10 000 Population (unit)	4.7	2.5	2.9
道路清扫面积(万平方米)	Area under Cleaning Program (10 000 sq.m)	3224	8080	12708
#机械化	Mechanization		3163	5428
清运生活垃圾(万吨)	Volum of Garbage Disposal (10 000 tons)	259	317	336
清运粪便 (万吨)	Volum of Excrement and Urine Disposal (10 000 tons)	16.0	4.0	0.1

11-8 主要年份城市煤气、液化石油气、天然气情况

Basic Statistics on Supply of Gas, Liquefied Petroleum Gas and Natural Gas in Cities in Main Years

指　标	Item	2000	2010	2015
人工煤气生产能力(万立方米/日)	Production Capacity of Gaswork Gas (10 000 cu.m/day)		49	46
管道长度(公里)	Length of Gas Pipelines (km)	385	7298	11662
人工煤气	Coal Gas		71	61
液化石油气	Liquefied Petroleum Gas		82	75
天然气	Natural Gas	385	7145	11526
全年供气总量(万立方米)	Volume of Gas Supply (10 000 cu.m)		216080	476869
人工煤气	Coal Gas		1752	1752
液化石油气(吨)	Liquefied Petroleum Gas (ton)	244018	79617	58144
天然气	Natural Gas	5385	134711	416973
用气人口(万人)	Population with Access to Gas (10 000 persons)		604.37	651.45
人工煤气	Coal Gas		8.75	5.00
液化石油气	Liquefied Petroleum Gas	305.70	150.64	49.00
天然气	Natural Gas	27.00	444.98	597.45

11-9 主要年份城市集中供热情况

Basic Statistics on Heating in Cities in Main Years

指　标	Item	2000	2010	2015
供应能力	**Heating Capacity**			
蒸汽(吨/小时)	Steam (ton/hour)	1638	1376	660
热水(兆瓦)	Hot Water (1 billion kw)	6145	18897	28944
供热总量(万吉焦)	**Quantity of Heat Supplied (10 000 gigajoules)**			
蒸 汽	Steam		1242	255
热 水	Hot Water		16866	14134
管道长度(公里)	**Length of Heating Pipelines (km)**			
蒸 汽	Steam	250	207	22
热 水	Hot Water	2064	5912	8609
供热面积(万平方米)	**Area of Centralized Heating (10 000 sq.m)**	**5170**	**19162**	**27499**
#住 宅	Residential Buildings		13298	19418

主要统计指标解释

供水综合生产能力 指按供水设施取水、净化、送水、出厂输水干管等环节设计能力计算的综合生产能力。包括在原设计能力的基础上，经挖、革、改增加的生产能力。计算时，以四个环节中最薄弱的环节为主确定能力。

供水管道长度 指从送水泵至用户水表之间所有管道的长度。不包括新安装尚未使用、水厂内以及用户建筑物内的管道。

城市供水总量 指报告期供水企业(单位)供出的全部水量。包括有效供水量和漏损水量。

生产运营用水 指在城区范围内生产、运营的农、林、牧、渔业、工业、建筑业、交通运输业等单位在生产、运营过程中的用水。

公共服务用水 指为城区社会公共生活服务的用水。包括行政事业单位、部队营区和公共设施服务、批发零售业、住宿餐饮业以及社会服务业等单位的用水。

居民家庭用水 指城市范围内所有居民家庭的日常生活用水。包括城市居民、农民家庭、公共供水站用水。

用水普及率 指报告期末城区用水人口数与城市人口总数的比率。计算公式为：

用水普及率＝城区用水人口数（含暂住人口）／(城区人口+城区暂住人口)×100%

人工煤气生产能力 指报告期末人工煤气生产厂制气、净化、输送等环节的综合生产能力，不包括备用设备能力。一般按设计能力计算，当实际生产能力大于设计能力时，应按实际测定的生产能力计算。测定时应以制气、净化、输送三个环节中最薄弱的环节为主。

供气管道长度 指报告期末从气源厂压缩机的出口或门站出口至各类用户引入管之间的全部已经通气、投入使用的管道长度。不包括煤气生产厂、输配站、液化气储存站、灌瓶站、储配站、气化站、混气站、供应站等厂(站)内的管道。

城市供气总量 指报告期燃气企业(单位)向用户供应的燃气数量。包括销售量和损失量。

燃气普及率 指报告期末城区使用燃气的城市人口数与城市人口总数的比率。其中燃气包括人工燃气、天然气、液化石油气三种。计算公式为：

燃气普及率＝城区用气人口（含暂住人口）／(城区人口+城区暂住人口)×100%

城市供热能力 指供热企业（单位）向城市热用户输送热源的设计能力。

城市供热总量 指在报告期供热企业（单位）向城市热用户输送全部蒸汽和热水的总热量。

城市供热管道长度 指从各类热源到热用户建筑物接入口之间的全部蒸汽和热水的管道长度。不包括各类热源厂内部的管道长度。

道路长度 指道路长度和与道路相通的桥梁、隧道的长度，按车行道中心线计算。

城市桥梁 指为跨越天然或人工障碍物而修建的构筑物。包括跨河桥、立交桥、人行天桥以及人行地下通道等。

城市排水管道长度 指所有排水总管、干管、支管、检查井及连接井进出口等长度之和。

城市污水日处理能力 指污水处理厂（污水处理装置）每昼夜处理污水量的设计能力。

城市绿地面积 指报告期末用作园林和绿化的各种绿地面积。包括公园绿地、生产绿地、防护绿地、附属绿地和其他绿地面积。

公园绿地 城市中向公众开放的、以游憩为主要功能，有一定的游憩设施和服务设施，同时兼有健全生态、美化景观，防灾减灾等综合作用的绿化用地。包括综合公园、社区公园、专类公园、带状公园和街旁绿地。其中综合公园、专类公园和带状公园面积之和为公园面积。

道路清扫保洁面积 指报告期末对城市道路和公共场所（主要包括城市行车道、人行道、车行隧道、人行过街地下通道、道路附属绿地、地铁站、高架路、人行过街天桥、立交桥、广场、停车场及其他设施等）进行清扫保洁的面积。一天清扫多次的，按清扫保洁面积最大的一次计算。

市容环卫专用车辆设备 指用于环境卫生作业、监察的专用车辆和设备，包括用于道路清扫、冲洗、洒水、除雪、垃圾粪便清运、市容监察以及与其配套使用的车辆和设备。

Explanatory Notes on Main Statistical Indicators

Production Capacity of Water Supply refers to the designed overall production capacity of water facilities, covering the four segments of water collection, purification, conveyance, and outflow through trunk pipelines. Increased capacity through transformation and innovation projects is included as well. The capacity is determined mainly on the weakest of the above-mentioned four segments.

Length of Water Supply Pipelines refers to the total length of all the pipelines between the water pumps and the user water meters, excluding pipelines newly installed but not used yet, pipeline in the water factory, and pipeline in the user's buildings.

Total Volume of Urban Water Supply refers to the total volume of water supplied by water-works (units) during the reference period, including both the effective water supply and loss during the water supply.

Consumption of Water for Production and Operation Use refers to water consumption in the process of production and operation by production and operation units of agriculture, forestry, animal husbandry, fisheries, industry, construction industry, and transportation industry, etc. in urban areas.

Consumption of Water for Public Service Use refers to water consumption for public service in the urban areas. It includes water consumption of administrative institutions, army camps, public facilities, wholesale and retail, accommodation and catering industry and social service industry, etc.

Consumption of Water for Households Use refers to consumption of water for daily life of all households in cities, including households of urban residents and farmers, and public water supply stations.

Coverage Rate of Urban Population with Access to Tap Water refers to the ratio of the urban population with access to tap water to the total urban population at the end of reference period. The formula is:

$$\text{Coverage of urban population with access to tap water} = \frac{\text{Urban population with access to tap water}}{\text{Urban population}} \times 100\%$$

Production Capacity of Gaswork Gas refers to the overall production capacity of the urban gasworks in gas generation, purification and delivery at the end of the reference period, excluding capacity of the reserved facilities. In general, it is determined by the designed capacity, and when actual production capacity is larger than the designed capacity, the capacity is determined by the actual measurement on the weakest segment in the production, purification and delivery.

Length of Gas Pipelines refers to the total length of pipelines in use between the outlet of the compressor of gas-work or outlet of gas stations and the leading pipe of users, excluding pipelines within gasworks, delivery stations, LPG storage stations, refilling stations, gas-mixing stations and supply stations.

Volume of Gas Supply refers to the total volume of gas provided to users by gas-producing enterprises (units) during the reporting period,, including the volume sold and the volume lost.

Coverage Rate of Urban Population with Access to Gas refers to the ratio of the urban population with access to gas to the total urban population at the end of the reference period. Gas here includes artificial coal gas, natural gas and liquefied petroleum gas. The formula is:

$$\text{Coverage rate of urban population with access to gas} = \frac{\text{Urban population with access to gas}}{\text{Urban population}} \times 100\%$$

Heating Capacity in Urban Areas refers to the designed capacity of heating enterprises (units) in supplying heating energy to urban users during the reference period.

Quantity of Heat Supplied in Urban Areas refers to the total quantity of heat from steam and hot water supplied to urban users by heating enterprises (units) during the reference period.

Length of Urban Heating Pipelines refers to the total length of steam or hot water pipelines for sources of heat to the leading pipelines of the buildings of the users, excluding internal pipelines in heat generating enterprises.

Length of Paved Roads refers to the length of roads with paved surface including bridges and tunnels connected with roads. Length of the roads is measured by the central lines.

Urban Bridges refer to bridges built to cross over natural or man-made barriers, including bridges over rivers, overpasses for traffic and for pedestrians, underpasses for pedestrians, etc.

Length of Urban Sewage Pipes refers to the total length of general drainage, trunks, branch and inspection wells, connection wells, inlets and outlets, etc.

Daily Disposal Capacity of Urban Sewage refers to the designed 24-hour capacity of sewage disposal by the sewage treatment works or facilities.

Area of Urban Green Land refers to the total area occupied for green projects at the end of the reference period, including park green land, production green land, protection green land, green land attached to institutions, and other green areas.

Park Green Area refers to green areas open to the public for amusement and rest with the facilities of amusement, rest and services. Its function includes perfecting ecology, beautifying landscape, and preventing and reducing disaster. Park green areas include comprehensive park, community park, theme park, linear park and roadside green space. Total areas of comprehensive park, topic park and belt-shaped is the area of park.

Road Area Cleaned refers to the area which are regularly cleaned, as at the end of the reference period, at urban roads and public places (mainly including urban roadways, pedestrian walkways, vehicular tunnels, pedestrian underpasses, underground railway stations, lifted roads, pedestrians walk bridges, overpasses, plazas, parking lots and other facilities). If there are several times of cleaning in a day at a location, the area of that time of cleaning with the largest area cleaned will be taken.

Vehicles and Facilities Dedicated to Urban Cleanliness and Environmental Sanitation refer to vehicles and facilities dedicated for use in the operation, management and monitoring of environmental hygiene work. They include vehicles for road cleaning, washing, showering, ice removal, disposal of garbage and human wastes, cleanliness monitoring and related activities.

12 农业 AGRICULTURE

第十二篇　农业

本篇主要内容和资料来源

本篇资料反映新疆维吾尔自治区农业生产和农村经济基本情况，主要内容包括农村基层组织情况、乡村从业人员、国有农、林、牧、渔场情况、主要农业生产条件、农林牧渔业产值、主要农产品生产情况、特色农作物生产情况、乡镇企业情况等。

本篇资料除表12-4来自新疆维吾尔自治区国土资源厅，12-10、12-11、12-12来自新疆维吾尔自治区水利厅，乡镇企业主要指标来自新疆维吾尔自治区乡镇企业局外，其余资料均由新疆维吾尔自治区统计局农村统计处提供。

Agriculture

Main Content and Source of Data

The data in this chapter show the basic conditions of agricultural production and rural economy in Xinjiang Uygur Autonomous Region, mainly including Statistics on rural grassroots units, rural employed labor force, basic conditions of township enterprises, statistic on forest products, cultivated land, gross output value farming, forest, animal husbandry and fishery, output of major farm products and condition on the township enterprises, etc.

Data on table12-4 are provided by Xinjiang Bureau of State Land and Resources.Data on table 12-10,12-11,12-12 are provided by the Xinjiang Bureau of Water Resources.Data on the township enterprises are from the Xinjiang Bureau of Township Enterprises. Others are provided by the Department of Rural statistics, Xinjiang Bureau of Statistics.

12-1 主要年份农村基本情况
Basic Statistics of Rural Grass-roots Unit in Main Years

指　标	Item	2014	2015
乡村户数(户)	**Number of Rural Households (household)**	**2878213**	**2948327**
#牧业户数	Stock-Breeding Households	415888	433400
乡村人口数（人）	**Rural Population (person)**	**11737472**	**11929400**
#牧业人口数	Population Engaged in Live-stocks	1602943	1679377
男	Male	6083245	6192081
女	Female	5654227	5737319
乡村劳动力合计（人）	**Total Population of Rural Labourers (Person)**	**6231531**	**6463589**
男	Male	3419807	3541399
女	Female	2811724	2922190
乡村从业人员数（人）	**Number of Engaged Persons in Rural Area (person)**	**5692206**	**5835441**
#从事农业人员数	Engaged in Agriculture	4558659	4759422
男	Male	3149508	3233498
女	Female	2542698	2601943
自来水受益村数（个）	**Number of Tap Water benefit Villages（unit）**	**7929**	**8009**
通有线电视村数（个）	**Number of Cable TV Villages（unit）**	**4466**	**4485**
通宽带村数（个）	**Number of Through Broadband Villages（unit）**	**5009**	**6374**

12-2 国有农林牧渔场基本情况
Basic statistics of State Agriculture, Forestry, Animal Husbandry and Fishery

指　标	Item	2014	2015
场数合计(个)	**Total (unit)**	**470**	**465**
农 场	Number of Agriculture Farms	285	282
林 场	Number of Forest Farms	48	48
牧 场	Number of Livestock Farms	127	125
渔 场	Number of Fishing Ground	10	10
场内户数(户)	**Number of Households in Farms (household)**	**856918**	**851323**
#牧业户数	Number of Stock-breeding Households	82330	84776
场内人口(人)	**Farm Populations (person)**	**2537497**	**2533889**
#牧业人口	Stock-breeding Population	270703	279787
男	Male	1324548	1319826
女	Female	1212949	1214063
场内劳动力（人）	**Number of Labourers (Person)**	**1383668**	**1393443**
男	Male	756037	757774
女	Female	627631	635669
场内实有从业人员(人)	**Persons Actually Engaged in Farms (person)**	**1208942**	**1248897**
#从事农业人员数	Engaged in Agriculture	687475	699139
男	Male	668958	690826
女	Female	539984	558071

12-3 各地、州、市、县(市)农村基本情况

(2015 年)

地　区	Region	乡村户数(户) Number of Rural Households (household)	#牧业户数 Stock-Breeding Households	乡村人口数(人) Rural Population (person)	#牧业人口数 Population Engaged in Live-stocks
总　计	**Total**	**2948327**	**433400**	**11929400**	**1679377**
乌鲁木齐市	**Urumqi City**	**71676**	**9818**	**218869**	**30104**
#乌鲁木齐县	Urumqi County	13396	5004	43042	15678
克拉玛依市	**Karamay City**	**673**	**57**	**2128**	**182**
吐鲁番市	**Turpan City**	**116867**	**3987**	**466166**	**15756**
高昌区	Gaochang District	47179	2330	198762	10129
鄯善县	Shanshan [piqan]County	41758	352	168912	1308
托克逊县	Toksun County	27930	1305	98492	4319
哈密地区	**Hami [Kumul]Administrative Offices**	**57803**	**15353**	**187316**	**53734**
哈密市	Hami [Kumul]City	36058	7760	118800	23614
巴里坤哈萨克自治县	Barkol KazakAutonomous County	18834	6354	60534	25552
伊吾县	Yiwu [Araturuk]County	2911	1239	7982	4568
昌吉回族自治州	**Changji Hui Autonomous Prefecture**	**199739**	**34275**	**694130**	**122059**
昌吉市	Changji City	37069	6185	123021	19957
阜康市	Fukang City	21874	3588	72052	13435
呼图壁县	Hutubi County	22251	4680	85674	17253
玛纳斯县	Manas County	27394	4339	93617	15315
奇台县	Qitai County	38240	5102	153917	20784
吉木萨尔县	Jimsar County	29845	3098	94989	10705
木垒哈萨克自治县	Mori Kazak Autonomous County	23066	7283	70860	24610
伊犁哈萨克自治州	**Ili Kazak Autonomous Prefecture**	**646222**	**107022**	**2485091**	**435608**
伊犁州直属县(市)	**Counties (Cities) Direct Under Ili Prefecture**	**393846**	**52274**	**1616281**	**240127**
伊宁市	Yining [Gulja]City	49460	684	197430	3702
奎屯市	Kuytun City	453	436	1444	1378
伊宁县	Yining [Gulja]County	80228	4718	363608	25112
察布查尔锡伯自治县	Qapqal Xibe Autonomous County	35379	2150	132592	9261
霍城县	Huocheng [korgas]County	53614	3454	193460	12561
巩留县	Gongliu [Tokkuzlara]County	29825	4652	131170	23182
新源县	Xinyuan [kunes]County	41734	7965	211990	39753
昭苏县	Zhaosu [mongolkure]County	38207	8944	122063	38927
特克斯县	Tekes County	30214	9785	126132	45781
尼勒克县	Nilka County	34732	9486	136392	40470
塔城地区	**Tacheng [Tarbagatai] Administrative Offices**	**156277**	**20223**	**539343**	**69190**
塔城市	Tacheng [Qoqek] City	20787	1572	67167	5014
乌苏市	Usu City	34775	1060	117800	3868
额敏县	Emin [Dorbiljin] County	19629	1290	83990	5131
沙湾县	Shawan County	44231	1574	153769	5521
托里县	Toli County	18548	10079	61513	34818
裕民县	Yumin [Qagantokay] County	10445	2682	35392	9003
和布克赛尔蒙古自治县	Hoboksar Mongol Autonomous County	7862	1966	19712	5835
阿勒泰地区	**Altay Administrative Offices**	**96099**	**34525**	**329467**	**126291**
阿勒泰市	Altay City	16616	3733	64810	16468
布尔津县	Burqin County	16995	6386	50978	19338
富蕴县	Fuyun [Koktokay] County	12142	4423	47533	17691
福海县	Fuhai [Burultokay] County	11793	4722	40113	20132
哈巴河县	Habahe [Kaba] County	20416	7702	66971	26595
青河县	Qinghe [Qinggil] County	10891	5931	41695	21639
吉木乃县	Jeminay County	7246	1628	17367	4428

Basic statistics of Rural Grass-roots Units by Prefecture, Autonomous Prefecture, City and County

乡村劳动力（人） Rural Labourers (person)	#男 Male	乡村从业人员（人） Engaged Persons in Rural Area (person)	#男 Male	#从事农业人员 Engaged in Agriculture	自来水受益村数（个） Number of Tap Water benefit village (unit)	通有线电视村数（个） Number of Cable TV Village (unit)	通宽带村数（个） Number of Through Broadband Village (unit)
6463589	**3541399**	**5835441**	**3233498**	**4759422**	**8009**	**4485**	**6374**
146481	**78366**	**131541**	**70882**	**76765**	**171**	**160**	**168**
27840	14487	24355	12729	15972	41	35	40
1137	**681**	**967**	**512**	**770**	**6**	**6**	**6**
286331	**154181**	**266644**	**147792**	**214192**	**174**	**133**	**175**
116264	62883	106084	60918	79965	60	60	60
105860	56163	104560	55868	89237	66	66	65
64207	35135	56000	31006	44990	48	7	50
116097	**61686**	**110681**	**59120**	**82800**	**155**	**119**	**154**
74703	39706	71288	38261	56249	81	87	78
36304	19195	34365	18077	21749	48		44
5090	2785	5028	2782	4802	26	32	32
430112	**232281**	**379143**	**209450**	**296172**	**457**	**452**	**436**
75217	40419	65380	35532	55387	84	79	79
46942	25789	42094	24183	26460	60	60	57
52219	27502	45754	24594	38482	52	52	51
55866	30702	48417	26444	38417	85	85	77
91072	49342	79643	45470	59196	60	60	60
62987	33601	57231	30584	45756	56	56	52
45809	24926	40624	22643	32474	60	60	60
1412804	**803988**	**1259967**	**717895**	**947286**	**1597**	**1353**	**1662**
900117	**513835**	**790471**	**453173**	**566056**	**614**	**314**	**585**
113653	61559	96969	53349	36950	46	15	46
1008	521	920	495	839	4	4	4
195211	115611	181235	108919	135568	125	14	122
72889	42852	67317	39149	52910	65	49	60
120167	64949	117289	63268	102520	64	64	64
72571	42791	57822	31731	43366	49	3	45
101646	58878	91180	52694	65061	72	53	72
63886	37544	49677	30733	35553	68	66	71
79248	43423	66089	37344	48785	54		36
79838	45707	61973	35491	44504	67	46	65
337194	**191097**	**308901**	**173260**	**256991**	**675**	**610**	**689**
45300	28076	40716	24671	35921	110	114	112
77734	41324	68909	37215	63355	141	141	141
50394	30236	49572	30116	39716	64	7	98
89960	46112	87516	45251	71448	237	220	221
40187	26700	35395	22118	22000	46	38	44
20609	10938	19792	10244	18912	41	45	45
13010	7711	7001	3645	5639	36	45	28
175493	**99056**	**160595**	**91462**	**124239**	**308**	**429**	**388**
37053	21929	36012	21812	31980	42	82	64
27642	16093	24045	13609	16234	37	61	49
26378	14820	22080	12414	11793	69	53	67
21226	11723	20372	11207	15271	53	62	60
33102	17765	30037	16569	26751	76	88	70
20242	10323	18399	9578	13046	7	42	37
9850	6403	9650	6273	9164	24	41	41

12-3 续表

地　区	Region	乡村户数（户） Number of Rural Households (household)	#牧业户数 Stock-Breeding Households	乡村人口数（人） Rural Population (person)	#牧业人口数 Population Engaged in Livestocks
博尔塔拉蒙古自治州	**Bortala Mongol Autonomous Prefecture**	**60677**	**6675**	**191778**	**22631**
博乐市	Bole [Bortala] City	24479	2832	90714	11047
精河县	Jinghe [Jing] County	22597	1880	63674	6151
温泉县	Wenquan [Araxang] County	13601	1963	37390	5433
巴音郭楞蒙古自治州	**Bayangol Mongol Autonomous Prefecture**	**136339**	**14904**	**514265**	**49996**
库尔勒市	Korla City	21806	718	84290	2510
轮台县	Luntai [Bugur] County	20180	1067	78949	3349
尉犁县	Yuli [Lopnur] County	13662	2278	49521	9132
若羌县	Ruoqiang [Qarkilik] County	6499	243	25351	717
且末县	Qiemo [Qarqan] County	11430	1803	42268	6151
焉耆回族自治县	Yanqi Hui Autonomous County	21804	1340	82919	5163
和静县	Hejing County	21919	4835	79861	14911
和硕县	Hoxud County	10411	2045	36311	6125
博湖县	Bohu [Bagrax] County	8628	575	34795	1938
阿克苏地区	**Aksu Administrative Offices**	**362405**	**34039**	**1592765**	**133629**
阿克苏市	Aksu City	36556	9762	175254	36225
温宿县	Wensu [Onsu] County	35614	4020	152725	19328
库车县	Kuqa County	71053	5377	316132	23605
沙雅县	Xayar County	48994	1776	207898	7372
新和县	Xinhe [Toksu] County	37616	5294	162011	16361
拜城县	Baicheng [Bay] County	42781	4149	173276	14765
乌什县	Wushi [Uxturpan] County	44528	1815	183842	7141
阿瓦提县	Awat County	37247	1055	183215	5277
柯坪县	Kalpin County	8016	791	38412	3555
克孜勒苏柯尔克孜自治州	**Kizilsu Kirgiz Autonomous Prefecture**	**105446**	**33731**	**457798**	**134167**
阿图什市	Artux City	42047	9438	201023	36537
阿克陶县	Akto County	44022	10313	182467	38699
阿合奇县	Akqi County	9133	5571	35358	26519
乌恰县	Wuqia [Ulugqat] County	10244	8409	38950	32412
喀什地区	**Kashgar [Kaxgar] Administrative Offices**	**725479**	**134994**	**3181864**	**552869**
喀什市	Kashgar [Kaxgar] City	61677	15908	261300	40718
疏附县	Shufu County	48975	5387	199980	21549
疏勒县	Shule County	60430	2890	296720	6970
英吉沙县	Yengisar County	56861	7537	259010	33916
泽普县	Zepu [Poskam] County	29116	1846	122595	6889
莎车县	Shache [Yarkant] County	166773	40981	704765	170175
叶城县	Yecheng [Kagilik] County	76243	12319	330748	60617
麦盖提县	Makit County	33826	1041	133430	4685
岳普湖县	Yopurga County	30554	12983	129499	67512
伽师县	Jiashi [Payzawat] County	85301	8988	395983	41704
巴楚县	Bachu [Maralbexi] County	68713	18814	318734	71984
塔什库尔干塔吉克自治县	Taxkorgan Tajik Autonomous County	7010	6300	29100	26150
和田地区	**Hotan Administrative Offices**	**461313**	**38034**	**1923774**	**126614**
和田市	Hotan City	50147	2870	233997	10811
和田县	Hotan County	65745	5403	311103	15528
墨玉县	Moyu [Karakax] County	119113	9944	504093	32636
皮山县	Pishan [Guma] County	54459	2771	218010	8918
洛浦县	Lop County	58943	4819	251487	15169
策勒县	Qira County	43406	6928	141102	23695
于田县	Yutian [Keriya] County	61149	3756	238614	14461
民丰县	Minfeng [Niya] County	8351	1543	25368	5396
生产建设兵团	**Xinjiang Production and Construction Group**	**3688**	**511**	**13456**	**2028**

Continued

乡村劳动力（人） Rural Labourers (person)	#男 Male	乡村从业人员（人） Engaged Persons in Rural Area (person)	#男 Male	#从事农业人员 Engaged in Agriculture	自来水受益村数（个） Number of Tap Water benefit village（unit）	通有线电视村数（个） Number of Cable TV Village（unit）	通宽带村数（个） Number of Through Broadband Village（unit）
121236	**67083**	**99816**	**56401**	**73623**	**220**	**220**	**213**
53744	29090	45612	25963	35151	107	107	106
42315	23277	31792	17615	20483	52	52	52
25177	14716	22412	12823	17989	61	61	55
305135	**175411**	**265191**	**154098**	**208061**	**355**	**263**	**357**
43505	24671	40330	23252	30741	59	15	59
40421	22670	35135	18903	32060	64	11	64
27127	15473	21898	12388	18997	48	48	48
19338	12490	18316	11817	9899	18	18	18
23972	13682	19260	11043	16137	46	36	46
52944	32192	47575	29168	33225	40	44	44
52393	28654	45636	26356	34610	30	37	28
23307	13413	18920	10950	16454	28	28	25
22128	12166	18121	10221	15938	22	26	25
872092	**466769**	**834641**	**449033**	**746373**	**1051**	**1062**	**766**
82236	43929	77476	42128	61542	122	122	78
85388	47160	82194	44906	70965	98	60	13
167550	87126	157497	81898	146536	208	210	135
119233	66138	115570	64098	108558	146	150	138
83514	45545	77887	44863	65873	110	110	92
91488	49965	87800	47957	80832	143	151	90
129434	66011	129385	66000	124733	93	107	68
95277	50751	89120	47147	70021	99	119	119
17972	10144	17712	10036	17313	32	33	33
206483	**116120**	**185327**	**106664**	**146536**	**226**	**227**	**167**
99665	58953	83786	52897	62776	75	75	43
77532	42004	75140	40190	64925	95	96	91
10634	5423	10315	5261	6292	22	22	22
18652	9740	16086	8316	12543	34	34	11
1681917	**921459**	**1498681**	**839232**	**1269301.4**	**2270**	**234**	**1263**
128990	77753	112254	76353	82833	149	80	149
123475	67411	111200	61160	93964	121	6	116
239376	142232	227695	135581	194459	218		218
140963	78940	112770	57513	104256	163	6	163
51409	25762	41061	20778	33393	129		62
335203	186528	289298	174931	218935	486		257
190852	101413	172575	91514	139222	271		101
65028	34367	65014	34360	55424	129	129	13
66694	33690	59800	30776	52097	87		31
175464	89452	156167	79614	142589	297	13	53
152245	77645	140065	71153	136982	186		95
12218	6266	10782	5499	15147	34		5
876783	**459903**	**795861**	**418948**	**693275**	**1311**	**239**	**993**
92832	51049	76280	42998	66045	112	28	68
160881	82748	155263	81670	137356	166		97
216379	112828	188019	96640	160058	353	25	186
81263	43227	77327	41066	63830	163	4	166
128448	66488	117111	60619	101345	200	12	207
72290	38988	62020	33943	49979	117		114
110894	56735	109783	56167	107281	166	166	121
13796	7840	10058	5845	7381	34	4	34
6981	**3471**	**6981**	**3471**	**4268**	**16**	**17**	**14**

12-4 各地、州、市、县(市)耕地面积

Area of Cultivated land by Prefecture, Autonomous Prefecture, City and County

单位：公顷　　(2008 年)　　(hectare)

地　区	Region	年末耕地面积 Cultivated Land at Year-end	#水浇地 #Irrigable Land	#旱　地 Driy Land
总　计	**Total**	**4124563.70**	**3812247.55**	**204501.81**
乌鲁木齐市	**Urumqi City**	**96950.66**	**78328.45**	**4035.06**
#乌鲁木齐县	Urumqi County	55412.44	48787.55	2206.13
克拉玛依市	**Karamay City**	**41926.31**	**41150.26**	**34.34**
石河子市	**Shihezi City**	**21886.21**	**21444.27**	
吐鲁番市	**Turpan City**	**48182.08**	**47560.93**	
高昌区	Gaochang District	17365.34	16883.43	
鄯善县	Shanshan [piqan]County	13707.94	13577.23	
托克逊县	Toksun County	17108.80	17100.27	
哈密地区	**Hami [Kumul]Administrative Offices**	**87087.69**	**83783.52**	**2617.09**
哈密市	Hami [Kumul]City	48101.16	47484.37	0.91
巴里坤哈萨克自治县	Barkol KazakAutonomous County	33793.67	31248.76	2494.56
伊吾县	Yiwu [Araturuk]County	5192.86	5050.39	121.62
昌吉回族自治州	**Changji Hui Autonomous Prefecture**	**629255.41**	**575551.19**	**48255.72**
昌吉市	Changji City	81216.70	79559.30	
阜康市	Fukang City	45008.84	43705.99	438.04
呼图壁县	Hutubi County	108240.93	107083.42	
玛纳斯县	Manas County	142651.23	140149.81	1646.14
奇台县	Qitai County	141463.80	125593.52	15405.67
吉木萨尔县	Jimsar County	59196.71	54743.95	4118.61
木垒哈萨克自治县	Mori Kazak Autonomous County	51477.20	24715.20	26647.26
伊犁哈萨克自治州	**Ili Kazak Autonomous Prefecture**	**1370619.63**	**1206934.23**	**147541.35**
伊犁州直属县(市)	**Counties (Cities) Direct Under Ili Prefecture**	**565724.94**	**462766.85**	**93380.19**
伊宁市	Yining [Gulja]City	13143.75	12397.65	157.73
奎屯市	Kuytun City	13830.81	13416.21	
伊宁县	Yining [Gulja]County	91060.36	87325.21	3074.98
察布查尔锡伯自治县	Qapqal Xibe Autonomous County	78010.92	67482.83	8691.95
霍城县	Huocheng [korgas]County	90103.57	86672.14	2627.72
巩留县	Gongliu [Tokkuzlara]County	42300.77	34067.58	5769.73
新源县	Xinyuan [kunes]County	69968.00	64130.84	3631.87
昭苏县	Zhaosu [mongolkure]County	89646.90	46655.06	42897.45
特克斯县	Tekes County	29857.44	23166.80	6399.81
尼勒克县	Nilka County	47802.42	27452.53	20128.95
塔城地区	**Tacheng [Tarbagatai] Administrative Offices**	**623638.56**	**574819.09**	**44346.27**
塔城市	Tacheng [Qoqek] City	116362.76	111668.61	4375.15
乌苏市	Usu City	90090.34	88675.34	
额敏县	Emin [Dorbiljin] County	147338.60	125362.73	21758.60
沙湾县	Shawan County	189499.02	186954.94	254.66
托里县	Toli County	24924.02	24791.30	70.37
裕民县	Yumin [Qagantokay] County	44247.45	26309.92	17887.49
和布克赛尔蒙古自治县	Hoboksar Mongol Autonomous County	11176.37	11056.25	
阿勒泰地区	**Altay Administrative Offices**	**181256.13**	**169348.29**	**9814.89**
阿勒泰市	Altay City	40931.04	40585.26	24.04
布尔津县	Burqin County	20584.37	16887.53	3469.38
富蕴县	Fuyun [Koktokay] County	14892.11	11654.88	2860.36
福海县	Fuhai [Burultokay] County	48402.20	47386.39	105.63
哈巴河县	Habahe [Kaba] County	31714.03	29103.31	2462.77
青河县	Qinghe [Qinggil] County	9825.27	8902.88	892.71
吉木乃县	Jeminay County	14907.11	14828.04	

12-4 续表 Continued

单位：公顷 (hectare)

地区	Region	年末耕地面积 Cultivated Land at Year-end	#水浇地 #Irrigable Land	#旱地 Ariy Land
博尔塔拉蒙古自治州	**Bortala Mongol Autonomous Prefecture**	**135223.32**	**133774.95**	**23.79**
博乐市	Bole [Bortala] City	65574.44	64586.74	
精河县	Jinghe [Jing] County	36147.89	35728.97	23.79
温泉县	Wenquan [Araxang] County	33500.99	33459.24	
巴音郭楞蒙古自治州	**Bayangol Mongol Autonomous Prefecture**	**322556.95**	**312340.71**	
库尔勒市	Korla City	63399.62	55645.29	
轮台县	Luntai [Bugur] County	32947.41	32914.37	
尉犁县	Yuli [Lopnur] County	68263.86	67857.08	
若羌县	Ruoqiang [Qarkilik] County	7132.15	7070.05	
且末县	Qiemo [Qarqan] County	15088.73	15059.49	
焉耆回族自治县	Yanqi Hui Autonomous County	36128.76	35999.77	
和静县	Hejing County	45540.81	45088.93	
和硕县	Hoxud County	36168.43	35167.26	
博湖县	Bohu [Bagrax] County	17887.18	17538.47	
阿克苏地区	**Aksu Administrative Offices**	**614943.17**	**585562.62**	**1674.65**
阿克苏市	Aksu City	168847.83	161536.10	394.20
温宿县	Wensu [Onsu] County	78711.69	67549.42	831.61
库车县	Kuqa County	65204.00	63182.13	6.41
沙雅县	Xayar County	56653.34	56359.21	
新和县	Xinhe [Toksu] County	37933.16	34910.01	
拜城县	Baicheng [Bay] County	72601.88	71028.51	
乌什县	Wushi [Uxturpan] County	46465.29	43538.75	
阿瓦提县	Awat County	79372.13	78323.46	442.43
柯坪县	Kalpin County	9153.85	9135.03	
克孜勒苏柯尔克孜自治州	**Kizilsu Kirgiz Autonomous Prefecture**	**52859.60**	**50149.91**	**252.68**
阿图什市	Artux City	15715.38	15293.50	223.54
阿克陶县	Akto County	29250.53	27006.77	11.71
阿合奇县	Akqi County	6164.41	6140.43	
乌恰县	Wuqia [Ulugqat] County	1729.28	1709.21	17.43
喀什地区	**Kashgar [Kaxgar] Administrative Offices**	**530457.07**	**516515.12**	**66.56**
喀什市	Kashgar [Kaxgar] City	7165.97	6271.21	
疏附县	Shufu County	51747.77	48541.95	
疏勒县	Shule County	49364.21	47766.47	
英吉沙县	Yengisar County	5718.17	5537.15	60.69
泽普县	Zepu [Poskam] County	37625.15	36203.14	
莎车县	Shache [Yarkant] County	98935.41	95867.11	
叶城县	Yecheng [Kagilik] County	53928.82	52503.91	4.67
麦盖提县	Makit County	50533.09	50138.07	
岳普湖县	Yopurga County	22224.51	22149.50	
伽师县	Jiashi [Payzawat] County	52288.15	51455.31	0.54
巴楚县	Bachu [Maralbexi] County	96950.39	96108.71	0.66
塔什库尔干塔吉克自治县	Taxkorgan Tajik Autonomous County	3975.44	3972.59	
和田地区	**Hotan Administrative Offices**	**172615.60**	**159151.39**	**0.57**
和田市	Hotan City	5996.45	5300.40	
和田县	Hotan County	30130.79	27035.19	
墨玉县	Moyu [Karakax] County	34013.32	28767.52	
皮山县	Pishan [Guma] County	27499.96	27193.71	
洛浦县	Lop County	26977.43	26784.99	
策勒县	Qira County	16489.41	16046.82	0.57
于田县	Yutian [Keriya] County	27445.86	24235.45	
民丰县	Minfeng [Niya] County	4062.38	3787.31	

12-5 农、林、牧、渔业总产值

Gross Output Value of Agriculture, Forestry, Animal Husbandry and Fishery

单位：万元 (10 000 yuan)

年份 Year	地区 Region	农林牧渔业总产值 Total	农业产值 Farming	林业产值 Forestry	牧业产值 Animal Husbandry	渔业产值 Fishery	农林牧渔服务业产值 Output Value of Services for Farming, Forestry, Animal Husbandry and Fishery
1978		191184	142460	3397	44990	337	
1980		220135	164187	5394	50148	406	
1985		565699	429519	25906	108598	1676	
1990		1446535	1104742	38152	294963	8678	
1995		4057332	3150055	56381	823351	27545	
1996		4309617	3340735	61940	875560	31382	
1997		4764743	3738602	64913	925923	35305	
1998		4992355	3873616	74394	1008783	35562	
1999		4611503	3409380	75565	1092279	34279	
2000		4872005	3605405	83451	1145142	38007	
2001		4968125	3488409	100847	1340236	38633	
2002		5250446	3627669	110897	1480382	31498	
2003		6883187	4827597	136936	1619823	32065	266766
2004		7506792	5150018	138204	1874660	42985	300925
2005		8310614	5958464	152851	1835206	43405	320688
2006		8835409	6385954	171994	1890700	46945	339816
2007		10634648	7669468	208623	2315097	70149	371311
2008		11766907	7841922	231830	3182256	99097	411802
2009		12976109	8986167	266451	3183730	111403	428358
2010		18461828	13768852	352701	3757905	126663	455707
2011		19553884	14378900	380808	4150000	141653	502523
2012		22756726	16750000	430407	4853719	152600	570000
2013		25388809	18061099	481323	6041994	171741	632652
2014		27440062	19551099	493949	6511994	196023	686997
2015		28044163	20053799	531503	6495094	217706	746061
乌鲁木齐市	Urumqi City	402296	170123	10987	207657	7219	6310
克拉玛依市	Karamay City	125771	45629	29501	41622	990	8029
吐鲁番市	Turpan City	779627	645575	6341	117426	703	9582
哈密地区	Hami [Kumul] Administrative Offices	524009	284059	14997	215929	2463	6561
昌吉回族自治州	Changji Hui Autonomous Prefecture	3492034	1493599	26798	1917315	20770	33552
伊犁哈萨克自治州	Ili Kazak Autonomous Prefecture	6094421	3337500	97672	2525366	37074	96809
伊犁州直属县(市)	Counties (Cities) Direct Under Ili Prefecture	2652667	1158994	63175	1369985	16884	43629
塔城地区	Tacheng [Tarbagatai] Administrative Offices	2683334	1778175	17711	842304	5120	40024
阿勒泰地区	Altay Administrative Offices	758420	400331	16786	313077	15070	13156
博尔塔拉蒙古自治州	Bortala Mongol Autonomous Prefecture	855894	666986	5256	131041	4363	48248
巴音郭楞蒙古自治州	Bayangol Mongol Autonomous Prefecture	2735505	2107967	41633	493411	10756	81738
阿克苏地区	Aksu Administrative Offices	3086945	2452367	31320	492519	21788	88951
克孜勒苏柯尔克孜自治州	Kizilsu Kirgiz Autonomous Prefecture	307020	177337	7075	106675	301	15632
喀什地区	Kashgar [Kaxgar] Administrative Offices	4790888	3371722	109689	1201521	14655	93301
和田地区	Hotan Administrative Offices	1291237	858843	26506	384767	3896	17225
生产建设兵团	Xinjiang Production and Construction Group	9712236	7413143	155861	1448661	74028	620543

注：本表按当年价格计算。
Note: The data in this form is caculated by current price.

12-6 主要年份农、林、牧、渔业总产值指数

Indices of Gross Output Value of Agriculture, Forestry, Animal Husbandry and Fishery in Main Years

年份 Year	农林牧渔业总产值 Total	#农业产值 Farming	#林业产值 Forestry	#牧业产值 Animal Husbandry	#渔业产值 Fishery
(上年=100) (preceding year=100)					
1978	113.0	118.6	108.8	105.4	106.7
1980	108.9	108.4	151.2	104.4	112.7
1985	110.9	111.5	131.3	104.6	135.1
1990	115.1	119.2	95.2	102.0	111.3
1995	107.1	107.0	88.5	109.0	127.0
1996	104.2	103.3	101.0	107.7	112.3
1997	109.5	109.6	100.5	110.2	108.6
1998	110.8	111.5	105.5	109.0	102.0
1999	104.8	103.9	100.9	108.1	106.3
2000	105.3	104.2	110.3	108.0	116.4
2001	104.5	103.9	116.1	105.8	104.2
2002	105.2	103.9	111.5	108.9	102.1
2003	106.3	105.2	120.7	108.7	101.7
2004	106.4	104.5	100.7	112.0	108.2
2005	107.4	107.0	105.8	109.0	105.3
2006	107.5	107.7	106.5	107.8	105.3
2007	108.2	108.9	108.6	106.0	115.2
2008	106.7	106.1	107.5	109.4	107.5
2009	105.1	107.8	106.5	98.5	106.9
2010	104.9	104.7	106.4	105.1	105.5
2011	106.9	108.3	105.9	102.0	107.1
2012	107.4	106.8	107.6	109.8	104.1
2013	107.2	107.1	108.1	107.8	107.8
2014	106.8	107.2	105.8	105.7	105.7
2015	106.3	106.9	107.9	104.1	109.5
(1978 年=100) (1978=100)					
1978	100	100	100	100	100
1980	115.9	115.5	158.8	111.1	120.5
1985	188.4	194.3	245.4	160.0	140.9
1990	303.7	322.6	244.4	243.7	442.4
1995	420.7	453.3	247.4	325.5	863.7
1996	438.4	468.1	249.8	350.6	970.0
1997	480.2	512.8	251.1	386.4	1053.2
1998	531.8	571.7	265.1	421.1	1073.9
1999	557.1	593.8	267.5	455.3	1141.6
2000	586.3	618.8	295.0	491.9	1328.4
2001	612.9	642.8	342.5	520.6	1384.1
2002	644.8	668.1	381.9	566.9	1413.2
2003	685.4	702.6	460.9	616.0	1437.2
2004	729.3	734.2	464.1	689.9	1555.1
2005	783.3	785.6	491.0	752.0	1637.5
2006	842.0	846.1	522.9	810.7	1724.3
2007	911.0	921.4	567.9	859.3	1986.4
2008	972.0	977.6	610.5	940.1	2135.4
2009	1021.6	1053.9	650.2	926.0	2282.7
2010	1071.7	1103.4	691.8	973.2	2408.2
2011	1145.6	1195.0	732.6	992.7	2579.2
2012	1230.4	1276.3	788.3	1090.0	2684.9
2013	1319.0	1366.9	852.2	1175.0	2894.3
2014	1409.0	1465.0	902.0	1242.0	3059.0
2015	1497.8	1566.1	973.3	1292.9	3349.6

12-7 各地、州、市、县(市)农林牧渔业总产值

Gross Output Value of Agriculture, Forestry, Animal Husbandry and Fishery by Prefecture, Autonomous Prefecture, City and County

单位：万元 (2015 年) (10 000 yuan)

地　区	Region	农林牧渔业总产值 Total	农业产值 Farming	林业产值 Forestry	牧业产值 Animal Husbandry	渔业产值 Fishery	农林牧渔服务业产值 Services for Farming, Forestry, Animal Husbandary and Fishery
总　计	**Total**	**28044163**	**20053799**	**531503**	**6495094**	**217706**	**746061**
乌鲁木齐市	**Urumqi City**	**402296**	**170123**	**10987**	**207657**	**7219**	**6310**
#乌鲁木齐县	Urumqi County	119085	43072	3696	70161	256	1900
克拉玛依市	**Karamay City**	**125771**	**45629**	**29501**	**41622**	**990**	**8029**
吐鲁番市	**Turpan City**	**779627**	**645575**	**6341**	**117426**	**703**	**9582**
高昌区	Gaochang District	336677	283713	3099	44130	560	5175
鄯善县	Shanshan [piqan]County	275690	235773	1382	36708	100	1727
托克逊县	Toksun County	167260	126089	1860	36588	43	2680
哈密地区	**Hami [Kumul]Administrative Offices**	**524009**	**284059**	**14997**	**215929**	**2463**	**6561**
哈密市	Hami [Kumul]City	267003	189297	3502	69475	1966	2763
巴里坤哈萨克自治县	Barkol KazakAutonomous County	174723	64574	455	107027	449	2218
伊吾县	Yiwu [Araturuk]County	82283	30188	11040	39427	48	1580
昌吉回族自治州	**Changji Hui Autonomous Prefecture**	**3492034**	**1493599**	**26798**	**1917315**	**20770**	**33552**
昌吉市	Changji City	511936	179716	4374	312972	10672	4202
阜康市	Fukang City	444140	198753	2441	240429	505	2012
呼图壁县	Hutubi County	578667	212135	4647	342959	4653	14273
玛纳斯县	Manas County	665079	358902	3075	289194	2795	11113
奇台县	Qitai County	754901	284542	3900	466182		277
吉木萨尔县	Jimsar County	307635	143035	6183	154952	2145	1320
木垒哈萨克自治县	Mori Kazak Autonomous County	229676	116516	2178	110627		355
伊犁哈萨克自治州	**Ili Kazak Autonomous Prefecture**	**6094421**	**3337500**	**97672**	**2525366**	**37074**	**96809**
伊犁州直属县(市)	**Counties (Cities) Direct Under Ili Prefecture**	**2652667**	**1158994**	**63175**	**1369985**	**16884**	**43629**
伊宁市	Yining [Gulja]City	128348	68936	433	53417	2262	3300
奎屯市	Kuytun City	41716	28453	96	11598		1569
霍尔果斯市	Huoerguosi City	37057	33651	334	1767	22	1283
伊宁县	Yining [Gulja]County	524661	233340	2577	269074	9833	9837
察布查尔锡伯自治县	Qapqal Xibe Autonomous County	305822	188795	10844	100141	1523	4519
霍城县	Huocheng [korgas]County	308938	167263	4293	130063	1063	6256
巩留县	Gongliu [Tokkuzlara]County	232926	106457	2413	122719	904	433
新源县	Xinyuan [kunes]County	418272	135616	38307	238269	822	5258
昭苏县	Zhaosu [mongolkure]County	207403	66489	274	138147	9	2484
特克斯县	Tekes County	177551	58057	964	117349	56	1125
尼勒克县	Nilka County	269973	71937	2640	187441	390	7565

注：本表按当年价格计算。
Note: The number in this form is caculated by current price.

12-7 续表 1 Continued

单位：万元 (10 000 yuan)

地区	Region	农林牧渔业总产值 Total	农业产值 Farming	林业产值 Forestry	牧业产值 Animal Husbandry	渔业产值 Fishery	农林牧渔服务业产值 Services for Farming, Forestry, Animal Husbandary and Fishery
塔城地区	**Tacheng [Tarbagatai] Administrative Offices**	**2683334**	**1778175**	**17711**	**842304**	**5120**	**40024**
塔城市	Tacheng [Qoqek] City	383133	230988	3466	140939	990	6750
乌苏市	Usu City	719896	551201	5396	154673	1092	7534
额敏县	Emin [Dorbiljin] County	408905	278498	2110	120606	179	7512
沙湾县	Shawan County	852431	590501	2950	241554	2766	14660
托里县	Toli County	127344	37717	1819	86497		1311
裕民县	Yumin [Qagantokay] County	94421	55353	1419	36696	76	877
和布克赛尔蒙古自治县	Hoboksar Mongol Autonomous County	97204	33917	551	61339	17	1380
阿勒泰地区	**Altay Administrative Offices**	**758420**	**400331**	**16786**	**313077**	**15070**	**13156**
阿勒泰市	Altay City	141151	71653	852	65205	1238	2203
布尔津县	Burqin County	76680	35462	1976	36610	677	1955
富蕴县	Fuyun [Koktokay] County	109869	46509	2702	58454	684	1520
福海县	Fuhai [Burultokay] County	188203	123736	1433	47803	11310	3921
哈巴河县	Habahe [Kaba] County	130100	71902	4727	51435	980	1056
青河县	Qinghe [Qinggil] County	81397	39137	4766	36180	121	1193
吉木乃县	Jeminay County	31020	11932	330	17390	60	1308
博尔塔拉蒙古自治州	**Bortala Mongol Autonomous Prefecture**	**855894**	**666986**	**5256**	**131041**	**4363**	**48248**
博乐市	Bole [Bortala] City	320386	236080	975	66149	2860	14322
精河县	Jinghe [Jing] County	411500	352896	2292	30858	688	24766
温泉县	Wenquan [Araxang] County	124008	78010	1989	34034	815	9160
巴音郭楞蒙古自治州	**Bayangol Mongol Autonomous Prefecture**	**2735505**	**2107967**	**41633**	**493411**	**10756**	**81738**
库尔勒市	Korla City	593145	490345	791	88654	769	12586
轮台县	Luntai [Bugur] County	297748	235201	414	52391	627	9115
尉犁县	Yuli [Lopnur] County	336954	280027	2992	34704		19231
若羌县	Ruoqiang [Qarkilik] County	287592	273190	430	11282	8	2682
且末县	Qiemo [Qarqan] County	212495	148420	3528	51550	647	8350
焉耆回族自治县	Yanqi Hui Autonomous County	240070	122588	24157	80668	456	12201
和静县	Hejing County	282053	159257	5941	109630	474	6751
和硕县	Hoxud County	317262	268260	1071	40755	80	7096
博湖县	Bohu [Bagrax] County	168186	130679	2309	23777	7695	3726
阿克苏地区	**Aksu Administrative Offices**	**3086945**	**2452367**	**31320**	**492519**	**21788**	**88951**
阿克苏市	Aksu City	491398	371032	1245	99166	3218	16737
温宿县	Wensu [Onsu] County	592357	480360	4226	75361	7735	24675
库车县	Kuqa County	518526	392306	5921	115646	642	4011

12-7 续表 2 Continued

单位：万元 (10 000 yuan)

地 区	Region	农林牧渔业总产值 Total	农业产值 Farming	林业产值 Forestry	牧业产值 Animal Husbandry	渔业产值 Fishery	农林牧渔服务业产值 Services for Farming, Forestry, Animal Husbandary and Fishery
沙雅县	Xayar County	317891	264580	5887	36868	562	9994
新和县	Xinhe [Toksu] County	296341	243688	4345	32898	554	14856
拜城县	Baicheng [Bay] County	261380	175018	5434	70571	7800	2557
乌什县	Wushi [Uxturpan] County	172136	139783	1861	25742	1180	3570
阿瓦提县	Awat County	375989	342546	1673	21845	97	9828
柯坪县	Kalpin County	60927	43054	728	14422		2723
克孜勒苏柯尔克孜自治州	**Kizilsu Kirgiz Autonomous Prefecture**	**307020**	**177337**	**7075**	**106675**	**301**	**15632**
阿图什市	Artux City	138062	82798	2200	46598	256	6210
阿克陶县	Akto County	128862	84369	3388	34210	45	6850
阿合奇县	Akqi County	20219	5192	1245	12675		1107
乌恰县	Wuqia [Ulugqat] County	19877	4978	242	13192		1465
喀什地区	**Kashgar [Kaxgar] Administrative Offices**	**4790888**	**3371722**	**109689**	**1201521**	**14655**	**93301**
喀什市	Kashgar [Kaxgar] City	210695	102375	6462	94942	1261	5655
疏附县	Shufu County	344146	228947	3371	103548	1400	6880
疏勒县	Shule County	448909	275530	15519	156386	830	644
英吉沙县	Yengisar County	270794	187797	4880	70964	143	7010
泽普县	Zepu [Poskam] County	338726	257349	4079	72214	3984	1100
莎车县	Shache [Yarkant] County	860894	641178	39968	152981	4068	22699
叶城县	Yecheng [Kagilik] County	661336	468884	13297	169512	1219	8424
麦盖提县	Makit County	424537	338281	5099	71797	360	9000
岳普湖县	Yopurga County	219018	159660	7704	47560	231	3863
伽师县	Jiashi [Payzawat] County	504336	345402	6941	140538	700	10755
巴楚县	Bachu [Maralbexi] County	482615	358547	2369	105179	459	16061
塔什库尔干塔吉克自治县	Taxkorgan Tajik Autonomous County	24882	7772		15900		1210
和田地区	**Hotan Administrative Offices**	**1291237**	**858843**	**26506**	**384767**	**3896**	**17225**
和田市	Hotan City	99090	52183	1910	41804	776	2417
和田县	Hotan County	226531	169050	4488	50273	1197	1523
墨玉县	Moyu [Karakax] County	332856	224471	4681	98992	1230	3482
皮山县	Pishan [Guma] County	141839	93945	4541	39709	39	3605
洛浦县	Lop County	152126	106645	3827	39388	291	1975
策勒县	Qira County	112963	72405	2108	37292	42	1116
于田县	Yutian [Keriya] County	187872	125125	3485	56714	258	2290
民丰县	Minfeng [Niya] County	37960	15019	1466	20595	63	817
生产建设兵团	**Xinjiang Production and ConstructionGroup**	**9712236**	**7413143**	**155861**	**1448661**	**74028**	**620543**

12-8 各地、州、市、县(市)农业机械拥有量

Agricultural Machinery by Prefecture, Autonomous Prefecture, City and County

(2015 年)

地 区	Region	农业机械总动力(千瓦) Total Power of Agricultural Machinery (kw)	农用大中型拖拉机 Large and Medium-siged Agricultural Tractors		小型拖拉机 Small Tractors	
			数量(台) Number (unit)	动力(千瓦) Capacity (kw)	数量(台) Number (unit)	动力(千瓦) Capacity (kw)
总 计	**Total**	**24834890**	**470591**	**14896674**	**280914**	**3529686**
乌鲁木齐市	**Urumqi City**	**302223**	**3014**	**85291**	**2086**	**26610**
#乌鲁木齐县	Urumqi County	57735	1266	28600	591	8168
克拉玛依市	**Karamay City**	**36857**	**559**	**19859**	**82**	**1052**
吐鲁番市	**Turpan City**	**552112**	**3269**	**104012**	**8157**	**95004**
高昌区	Gaochang District	221609	1128	31032	2973	32792
鄯善县	Shanshan [piqan]County	221722	1038	37427	3211	40767
托克逊县	Toksun County	108781	1103	35553	1973	21445
哈密地区	**Hami [Kumul]Administrative Offices**	**376901**	**5424**	**171745**	**8309**	**98548**
哈密市	Hami [Kumul]City	203180	3534	103365	3294	39242
巴里坤哈萨克自治县	Barkol KazakAutonomous County	139476	1480	53313	4219	48773
伊吾县	Yiwu [Araturuk]County	34245	410	15067	796	10533
昌吉回族自治州	**Changji Hui Autonomous Prefecture**	**2283821**	**25583**	**1034072**	**37900**	**452016**
昌吉市	Changji City	425002	3684	178896	7370	91440
阜康市	Fukang City	200180	1797	82286	3141	33746
呼图壁县	Hutubi County	374188	4847	191157	4436	62974
玛纳斯县	Manas County	362446	5989	209785	6021	69469
奇台县	Qitai County	545588	4770	205658	9042	99647
吉木萨尔县	Jimsar County	207256	2049	84538	3625	42967
木垒哈萨克自治县	Mori Kazak Autonomous County	169161	2447	81752	4265	51773
伊犁哈萨克自治州	**Ili Kazak Autonomous Prefecture**	**5026679**	**91675**	**3055792**	**55078**	**704605**
伊犁州直属县(市)	**Counties (Cities) Direct Under Ili Prefecture**	**1914456**	**32699**	**1179738**	**21077**	**268371**
伊宁市	Yining [Gulja]City	92800	1286	55836	1175	15256
奎屯市	Kuytun City	20356	317	6386	47	518
伊宁县	Yining [Gulja]County	340264	5720	213709	5536	69033
察布查尔锡伯自治县	Qapqal Xibe Autonomous County	234670	4189	152943	1040	11466
霍城县	Huocheng [korgas]County	193200	4110	133334	780	9936
巩留县	Gongliu [Tokkuzlara]County	231162	3395	122760	4992	64896
新源县	Xinyuan [kunes]County	302241	5921	210776	869	11023
昭苏县	Zhaosu [mongolkure]County	170601	2261	95995	2743	36415
特克斯县	Tekes County	125051	2328	69626	1287	16741
尼勒克县	Nilka County	165471	2370	90122	2324	29957
霍尔果斯市	Huoerguosi City	38640	802	28250	284	3130
塔城地区	**Tacheng [Tarbagatai] Administrative Offices**	**2283109**	**41628**	**1371273**	**19755**	**261125**
塔城市	Tacheng [Qoqek] City	304500	5492	177772	2684	34438
乌苏市	Usu City	680743	13709	445102	5344	76954
额敏县	Emin [Dorbiljin] County	307822	4119	141459	2487	34365
沙湾县	Shawan County	671269	13079	434009	6824	84511
托里县	Toli County	119195	1713	56212	858	10885
裕民县	Yumin [Qagantokay] County	148179	2530	85385	1083	14019
和布克赛尔蒙古自治县	Hoboksar Mongol Autonomous County	51401	986	31334	475	5954
阿勒泰地区	**Altay Administrative Offices**	**829114**	**17348**	**504781**	**14246**	**175109**
阿勒泰市	Altay City	178045	4761	148932	2600	33717
布尔津县	Burqin County	96120	1940	47145	2446	30575
富蕴县	Fuyun [Koktokay] County	140041	3109	87245	1720	20548
福海县	Fuhai [Burultokay] County	176271	3810	108783	1517	19517
哈巴河县	Habahe [Kaba] County	152391	1900	62603	4300	49265
青河县	Qinghe [Qinggil] County	57708	1181	29595	1273	16730
吉木乃县	Jeminay County	28538	647	20480	390	4757

12-8 续表 1 Continued

地　　区	Region	农业机械总动力(千瓦) Total Power of Agricultural Machinery (kw)	农用大中型拖拉机 Large and Medium-siged Agricultural Tractors		小型拖拉机 Small Tractors	
			数量(台) Number (unit)	动力(千瓦) Capacity (kw)	数量(台) Number (unit)	动力(千瓦) Capacity (kw)
博尔塔拉蒙古自治州	**Bortala Mongol Autonomous Prefecture**	**745683**	**11563**	**435358**	**13008**	**159582**
博乐市	Bole [Bortala] City	280787	4724	148650	5060	61534
精河县	Jinghe [Jing] County	325770	5025	224035	5641	69999
温泉县	Wenquan [Araxang] County	139126	1814	62673	2307	28049
巴音郭楞蒙古自治州	**Bayangol Mongol Autonomous Prefecture**	**2233021**	**49810**	**1619730**	**23259**	**296622**
库尔勒市	Korla City	539122	12861	358729	8704	113152
轮台县	Luntai [Bugur] County	216961	4675	134488	4021	49356
尉犁县	Yuli [Lopnur] County	431630	10322	409246	1441	20174
若羌县	Ruoqiang [Qarkilik] County	63148	2338	63874	274	3480
且末县	Qiemo [Qarqan] County	136882	3696	99850	1887	23614
焉耆回族自治县	Yanqi Hui Autonomous County	278923	4357	170797	3093	38999
和静县	Hejing County	218739	5050	154082	1005	13966
和硕县	Hoxud County	186044	3316	127144	1332	16633
博湖县	Bohu [Bagrax] County	161572	3195	101520	1502	17248
阿克苏地区	**Aksu Administrative Offices**	**2753812**	**61946**	**1755865**	**59520**	**762439**
阿克苏市	Aksu City	259733	6133	164167	4650	58974
温宿县	Wensu [Onsu] County	459601	12345	383642	5508	63345
库车县	Kuqa County	366108	8450	225625	8970	112117
沙雅县	Xayar County	315937	7294	222836	7250	80566
新和县	Xinhe [Toksu] County	211329	4410	131534	4779	57306
拜城县	Baicheng [Bay] County	416650	8052	238580	8250	115500
乌什县	Wushi [Uxturpan] County	288632	8268	189276	5954	74396
阿瓦提县	Awat County	390392	6028	173492	13557	192396
柯坪县	Kalpin County	45430	966	26714	602	7839
克孜勒苏柯尔克孜自治州	**Kizilsu Kirgiz Autonomous Prefecture**	**439547**	**13523**	**333620**	**5197**	**64252**
阿图什市	Artux City	137097	3401	94428	1149	12608
阿克陶县	Akto County	247130	7815	191792	3671	46607
阿合奇县	Akqi County	31555	1251	26904	156	2078
乌恰县	Wuqia [Ulugqat] County	23765	1056	20495	221	2959
喀什地区	**Kashgar [Kaxgar] Administrative Offices**	**4173254**	**127674**	**3118997**	**33284**	**415134**
喀什市	Kashgar [Kaxgar] City	164401	5568	132782	1807	22527
疏附县	Shufu County	412270	11163	229866	5019	62122
疏勒县	Shule County	537777	15780	432658	3559	47121
英吉沙县	Yengisar County	216464	6769	158541	3048	36753
泽普县	Zepu [Poskam] County	274167	9912	214907	2056	25309
莎车县	Shache [Yarkant] County	777443	22898	561564	8345	102514
叶城县	Yecheng [Kagilik] County	394000	12739	291429	2000	26371
麦盖提县	Makit County	274632	9014	229580	1827	22491
岳普湖县	Yopurga County	184421	6388	162583	1216	14539
伽师县	Jiashi [Payzawat] County	407879	11892	280833	2473	30819
巴楚县	Bachu [Maralbexi] County	499903	14155	398418	1654	20508
塔什库尔干塔吉克自治县	Taxkorgan Tajik Autonomous County	29896	1396	25836	280	4060
和田地区	**Hotan Administrative Offices**	**914504**	**25753**	**660669**	**5288**	**62393**
和田市	Hotan City	84449	2375	75103	195	2478
和田县	Hotan County	116347	3154	70841	929	9663
墨玉县	Moyu [Karakax] County	232117	6495	169330	653	6334
皮山县	Pishan [Guma] County	95685	3206	70323	310	4108
洛浦县	Lop County	125047	3679	89382	582	7020
策勒县	Qira County	82729	2011	55687	1129	14903
于田县	Yutian [Keriya] County	143721	4032	106949	1083	12996
民丰县	Minfeng [Niya] County	34409	801	23054	407	4892
生产建设兵团	**Xinjiang Production and Construction Group**	**4996477**	**50798**	**2501663**	**29746**	**391431**

12-8 续表 2 Continued

地　　区	Region	大中型拖拉机配套农具（部）Number of Large and Medium Tractor Towing Farm Machinery (unit)	小型拖拉机配套农具（部）Number of Small Tractor Towing Farm Machinery (unit)	农用排灌柴油机 Diesel Engines	
				数　量（台）Number (unit)	动　力（千瓦）Capacity (kw)
总　计	**Total**	**794245**	**628044**	**12066**	**185401**
乌鲁木齐市	**Urumqi City**	**4205**	**3062**	**5**	**33**
#乌鲁木齐县	Urumqi County	1321	2080	5	33
克拉玛依市	**Karamay City**	**1140**	**231**	**4**	**80**
吐鲁番市	**Turpan City**	**5370**	**17395**	**13**	**158**
高昌区	Gaochang District	1109	4428		
鄯善县	Shanshan [piqan]County	2009	5734		
托克逊县	Toksun County	2252	7233	13	158
哈密地区	**Hami [Kumul]Administrative Offices**	**12258**	**18132**		
哈密市	Hami [Kumul]City	8008	4896		
巴里坤哈萨克自治县	Barkol KazakAutonomous County	3422	11449		
伊吾县	Yiwu [Araturuk]County	828	1787		
昌吉回族自治州	**Changji Hui Autonomous Prefecture**	**52670**	**65614**	**136**	**2483**
昌吉市	Changji City	8369	12595		
阜康市	Fukang City	4938	4105		
呼图壁县	Hutubi County	14520	17931		
玛纳斯县	Manas County	7867	16791	17	207
奇台县	Qitai County	9788	6900		
吉木萨尔县	Jimsar County	4054	3812		
木垒哈萨克自治县	Mori Kazak Autonomous County	3134	3480	119	2276
伊犁哈萨克自治州	**Ili Kazak Autonomous Prefecture**	**198092**	**108285**	**4296**	**55185**
伊犁州直属县(市)	**Counties (Cities) Direct Under Ili Prefecture**	**63925**	**18068**	**844**	**9490**
伊宁市	Yining [Gulja]City	2895	870	33	702
奎屯市	Kuytun City	608	51		
伊宁县	Yining [Gulja]County	7382	5556	223	2156
察布查尔锡伯自治县	Qapqal Xibe Autonomous County	10651	1358	45	793
霍城县	Huocheng [korgas]County	10450	1125	146	1091
巩留县	Gongliu [Tokkuzlara]County	4061	2317	33	1450
新源县	Xinyuan [kunes]County	10578	3097	103	1334
昭苏县	Zhaosu [mongolkure]County	3560	370	110	
特克斯县	Tekes County	7646	1658	8	382
尼勒克县	Nilka County	5370	1390	122	1330
霍尔果斯市	Huoerguosi City	724	276	21	252
塔城地区	**Tacheng [Tarbagatai] Administrative Offices**	**113375**	**76322**	**1344**	**16435**
塔城市	Tacheng [Qoqek] City	13454	11696	16	320
乌苏市	Usu City	46611	18170	978	11255
额敏县	Emin [Dorbiljin] County	12813	10899	254	3736
沙湾县	Shawan County	31486	31113	68	863
托里县	Toli County	2401	853		
裕民县	Yumin [Qagantokay] County	5137	3234		
和布克赛尔蒙古自治县	Hoboksar Mongol Autonomous County	1473	357	28	261
阿勒泰地区	**Altay Administrative Offices**	**20792**	**13895**	**2108**	**29260**
阿勒泰市	Altay City	4200	2040	51	601
布尔津县	Burqin County	1800	2450	190	2675
富蕴县	Fuyun [Koktokay] County	4116	1495	632	10254
福海县	Fuhai [Burultokay] County	6648	2612	400	6000
哈巴河县	Habahe [Kaba] County	2245	2647	600	6000
青河县	Qinghe [Qinggil] County	1192	1632	217	3417
吉木乃县	Jeminay County	591	1019	18	313

12-8 续表 3 Continued

地　　区	Region	大中型拖拉机配套农具(部) Number of Large and Medium Tractor Towing Farm Machinery (unit)	小型拖拉机配套农具(部) Number of Small Tractor Towing Farm Machinery (unit)	农用排灌柴油机 Diesel Engines	
				数　量(台) Number (unit)	动　力(千瓦) Capacity (kw)
博尔塔拉蒙古自治州	**Bortala Mongol Autonomous Prefecture**	**16787**	**10354**	**8**	**187**
博乐市	Bole [Bortala] City	7795	3501	3	33
精河县	Jinghe [Jing] County	6825	5841		
温泉县	Wenquan [Araxang] County	2167	1012	5	154
巴音郭楞蒙古自治州	**Bayangol Mongol Autonomous Prefecture**	**75596**	**74376**	**2385**	**34064**
库尔勒市	Korla City	18841	29037	1278	13414
轮台县	Luntai [Bugur] County	5511	8429		
尉犁县	Yuli [Lopnur] County	9050	5505	766	13328
若羌县	Ruoqiang [Qarkilik] County	2949	2032	231	6202
且末县	Qiemo [Qarqan] County	4774	6967		
焉耆回族自治县	Yanqi Hui Autonomous County	15703	8482		
和静县	Hejing County	10340	5526	50	760
和硕县	Hoxud County	4848	3426	60	360
博湖县	Bohu [Bagrax] County	3580	4972		
阿克苏地区	**Aksu Administrative Offices**	**125493**	**137718**	**1139**	**12727**
阿克苏市	Aksu City	19820	14268	138	1758
温宿县	Wensu [Onsu] County	16748	10742	51	630
库车县	Kuqa County	22798	19562	55	681
沙雅县	Xayar County	16979	18080	593	5978
新和县	Xinhe [Toksu] County	8561	11120	17	186
拜城县	Baicheng [Bay] County	14132	20156	9	120
乌什县	Wushi [Uxturpan] County	12592	10386	210	2625
阿瓦提县	Awat County	12310	32416	66	748
柯坪县	Kalpin County	1553	988		
克孜勒苏柯尔克孜自治州	**Kizilsu Kirgiz Autonomous Prefecture**	**20065**	**8264**	**1**	**4**
阿图什市	Artux City	6128	2466		
阿克陶县	Akto County	10279	5184		
阿合奇县	Akqi County	2298	302		
乌恰县	Wuqia [Ulugqat] County	1360	312	1	4
喀什地区	**Kashgar [Kaxgar] Administrative Offices**	**174270**	**144948**	**949**	**14874**
喀什市	Kashgar [Kaxgar] City	1730	5806		
疏附县	Shufu County	9597	30905		
疏勒县	Shule County	22619	21359		
英吉沙县	Yengisar County	10115	6405		
泽普县	Zepu [Poskam] County	8853	20701	15	144
莎车县	Shache [Yarkant] County	27803	19265	393	7018
叶城县	Yecheng [Kagilik] County	25302	16535		
麦盖提县	Makit County	14885	8828	136	1999
岳普湖县	Yopurga County	10988	4362	30	264
伽师县	Jiashi [Payzawat] County	17940	7466	225	3094
巴楚县	Bachu [Maralbexi] County	21648	2754	150	2355
塔什库尔干塔吉克自治县	Taxkorgan Tajik Autonomous County	2790	562		
和田地区	**Hotan Administrative Offices**	**26272**	**13308**	**70**	**1574**
和田市	Hotan City	1918	235		
和田县	Hotan County	2443	1843	19	244
墨玉县	Moyu [Karakax] County	6110	1227		
皮山县	Pishan [Guma] County	3546	2403	30	441
洛浦县	Lop County	4460	1268		
策勒县	Qira County	1450	2741	17	742
于田县	Yutian [Keriya] County	5742	3100		
民丰县	Minfeng [Niya] County	603	491	4	147
生产建设兵团	**Xinjiang Production and Construction Group**	**82027**	**26357**	**3060**	**64031**

12-9 各地、州、市、县(市)农村物质消耗情况

Statistics on Material Consumption in Rural Areas by Prefecture, Autonomous Prefecture, City and County

(2015 年)

地　区	Region	化 肥 施用量 (吨)(折纯) Consumption of Chemical Fertilizer (ton) (100% Purity)	氮 肥 Nitrogenous Fertilizer	磷 肥 Phosphate Fertilizer	钾 肥 Potash Fertilizer
总　计	**Total**	**2480930**	**1097961**	**662020**	**205729**
乌鲁木齐市	**Urumqi City**	**8034**	**4852**	**1653**	**707**
#乌鲁木齐县	Urumqi County	1757	759	488	341
克拉玛依市	**Karamay City**	**7138**	**4019**	**1151**	**880**
吐鲁番市	**Turpan City**	**28710**	**14088**	**4293**	**3118**
高昌区	Gaochang District	13662	6665	713	1358
鄯善县	Shanshan [piqan]County	10059	5835	1222	911
托克逊县	Toksun County	4989	1588	2358	849
哈密地区	**Hami [Kumul]Administrative Offices**	**28264**	**16290**	**7184**	**2547**
哈密市	Hami [Kumul]City	17897	12229	2855	1847
巴里坤哈萨克自治县	Barkol KazakAutonomous County	6317	2941	3009	20
伊吾县	Yiwu [Araturuk]County	4050	1120	1320	680
昌吉回族自治州	**Changji Hui Autonomous Prefecture**	**167529**	**82573**	**44833**	**10625**
昌吉市	Changji City	28168	11010	6719	1887
阜康市	Fukang City	9958	5021	2873	76
呼图壁县	Hutubi County	46184	24751	14149	2838
玛纳斯县	Manas County	34086	16688	11058	1741
奇台县	Qitai County	25907	12979	6381	1175
吉木萨尔县	Jimsar County	12856	6740	1598	1951
木垒哈萨克自治县	Mori Kazak Autonomous County	10370	5384	2054	957
伊犁哈萨克自治州	**Ili Kazak Autonomous Prefecture**	**435720**	**165222**	**124995**	**37187**
伊犁州直属县(市)	**Counties (Cities) Direct Under Ili Prefecture**	**122265**	**37779**	**22280**	**6299**
伊宁市	Yining [Gulja]City	3904	1651	399	239
奎屯市	Kuytun City	7692	3052	3064	220
伊宁县	Yining [Gulja]County	34575	9500	4658	1531
察布查尔锡伯自治县	Qapqal Xibe Autonomous County	18146	6259	5904	1671
霍城县	Huocheng [korgas]County	9868	2040	1490	957
巩留县	Gongliu [Tokkuzlara]County	10873	4449		
新源县	Xinyuan [kunes]County	13195	3699	1589	649
昭苏县	Zhaosu [mongolkure]County	8422	3231	2702	596
特克斯县	Tekes County	3356	788	935	
尼勒克县	Nilka County	12234	3110	1539	436
塔城地区	**Tacheng [Tarbagatai] Administrative Offices**	**267067**	**103023**	**88037**	**26660**
塔城市	Tacheng [Qoqek] City	44680	20225	16733	4761
乌苏市	Usu City	61731	19023	34094	3883
额敏县	Emin [Dorbiljin] County	51333	20820	9801	8121
沙湾县	Shawan County	91158	35143	23661	9767
托里县	Toli County	6383	3711	2610	31
裕民县	Yumin [Qagantokay] County	8006	2651	863	7
和布克赛尔蒙古自治县	Hoboksar Mongol Autonomous County	3776	1450	275	90
阿勒泰地区	**Altay Administrative Offices**	**46388**	**24420**	**14678**	**4228**
阿勒泰市	Altay City	7701	4322	3030	255
布尔津县	Burqin County	2794	1504	1072	101
富蕴县	Fuyun [Koktokay] County	3927	2370	1121	322
福海县	Fuhai [Burultokay] County	23505	11273	6959	2676
哈巴河县	Habahe [Kaba] County	2640	1890	567	143
青河县	Qinghe [Qinggil] County	3759	2176	943	540
吉木乃县	Jeminay County	2062	885	986	191

12-9 续表 1 Continued

地区	Region	化肥施用量(吨)(折纯) Consumption of Chemical Fertilizer (ton) (100% Purity)	氮肥 Nitrogenous Fertilizer	磷肥 Phosphate Fertilizer	钾肥 Potash Fertilizer
博尔塔拉蒙古自治州	**Bortala Mongol Autonomous Prefecture**	**71751**	**34380**	**21869**	**3907**
博乐市	Bole [Bortala] City	24771	10218	7557	1504
精河县	Jinghe [Jing] County	32163	16819	8597	1388
温泉县	Wenquan [Araxang] County	14817	7343	5715	1015
巴音郭楞蒙古自治州	**Bayangol Mongol Autonomous Prefecture**	**199231**	**98454**	**55364**	**14480**
库尔勒市	Korla City	44725	24527	13328	3550
轮台县	Luntai [Bugur] County	25438	13816	5015	554
尉犁县	Yuli [Lopnur] County	58172	23007	17381	5764
若羌县	Ruoqiang [Qarkilik] County	7573	3914	1685	357
且末县	Qiemo [Qarqan] County	10706	6850	1731	282
焉耆回族自治县	Yanqi Hui Autonomous County	13656	7119	2494	1262
和静县	Hejing County	11482	4971	4466	1301
和硕县	Hoxud County	16777	9034	6232	336
博湖县	Bohu [Bagrax] County	10702	5216	3032	1074
阿克苏地区	**Aksu Administrative Offices**	**333205**	**128406**	**125648**	**23749**
阿克苏市	Aksu City	73096	28803	33280	7799
温宿县	Wensu [Onsu] County	33401	3999	6336	5520
库车县	Kuqa County	45995	17785	13237	1544
沙雅县	Xayar County	53277	24356	22497	2082
新和县	Xinhe [Toksu] County	35778	16458	15027	3220
拜城县	Baicheng [Bay] County	20359	7737	8305	2260
乌什县	Wushi [Uxturpan] County	13441	8580	820	
阿瓦提县	Awat County	54554	18952	24578	1324
柯坪县	Kalpin County	3304	1736	1568	
克孜勒苏柯尔克孜自治州	**Kizilsu Kirgiz Autonomous Prefecture**	**21804**	**11195**	**7441**	**1292**
阿图什市	Artux City	10195	5256	4784	
阿克陶县	Akto County	11414	5816	2588	1289
阿合奇县	Akqi County	80	50	30	
乌恰县	Wuqia [Ulugqat] County	115	73	39	3
喀什地区	**Kashgar [Kaxgar] Administrative Offices**	**337767**	**168339**	**111164**	**30612**
喀什市	Kashgar [Kaxgar] City	6102	2295	2276	
疏附县	Shufu County	24800	12155	10972	1215
疏勒县	Shule County	29357	14367	10695	2397
英吉沙县	Yengisar County	24077	12737	9304	291
泽普县	Zepu [Poskam] County	33014	14875	10080	2900
莎车县	Shache [Yarkant] County	44076	22655	7425	12271
叶城县	Yecheng [Kagilik] County	35949	18828	8296	4268
麦盖提县	Makit County	18896	12877	5335	69
岳普湖县	Yopurga County	36980	15120	12075	5887
伽师县	Jiashi [Payzawat] County	40625	24089	12044	851
巴楚县	Bachu [Maralbexi] County	42506	18188	21430	463
塔什库尔干塔吉克自治县	Taxkorgan Tajik Autonomous County	1385	153	1232	
和田地区	**Hotan Administrative Offices**	**76413**	**39111**	**23008**	**5416**
和田市	Hotan City	6123	3972	1579	369
和田县	Hotan County	11294	6301	2478	1551
墨玉县	Moyu [Karakax] County	19277	8262	3672	1836
皮山县	Pishan [Guma] County	11036	7358	2627	526
洛浦县	Lop County	9268	4482	4786	
策勒县	Qira County	6694	3068	2914	161
于田县	Yutian [Keriya] County	10176	4590	3622	891
民丰县	Minfeng [Niya] County	2545	1079	1331	83
生产建设兵团	**Xinjiang Production and Construction Group**	**765365**	**331031**	**133417**	**71209**

12-9 续表 2 Continued

地　　区	Region	复合肥 Compound Fertilizer	地膜覆盖面积(公顷) Area of Covering (hectare)	农用柴油使用量(吨) Consumption of Agricultural Diesel Oil (ton)	农村用电量(万千瓦小时) Electricity Consumed in Rural Areas (10 000 kwh)
总　计	**Total**	**515220**	**3463530**	**862968**	**1040684**
乌鲁木齐市	**Urumqi City**	**822**	**6451**	**8758**	**19028**
#乌鲁木齐县	Urumqi County	169	693	2947	940
克拉玛依市	**Karamay City**	**1088**	**5533**	**3282**	**350**
吐鲁番市	**Turpan City**	**7211**	**20587**	**16541**	**43808**
高昌区	Gaocang Offices	4926	5255	7103	17604
鄯善县	Shanshan [piqan]County	2091	10007	7024	20015
托克逊县	Toksun County	194	5325	2414	6189
哈密地区	**Hami [Kumul]Administrative Offices**	**2243**	**36442**	**26462**	**26594**
哈密市	Hami [Kumul]City	966	33028	14380	21082
巴里坤哈萨克自治县	Barkol KazakAutonomous County	347	868	10160	3674
伊吾县	Yiwu [Araturuk]County	930	2547	1922	1838
昌吉回族自治州	**Changji Hui Autonomous Prefecture**	**29498**	**280252**	**85400**	**92638**
昌吉市	Changji City	8551	57140	9976	16972
阜康市	Fukang City	1988	35061	6338	7646
呼图壁县	Hutubi County	4446	60478	12404	21931
玛纳斯县	Manas County	4599	63553	13721	9591
奇台县	Qitai County	5372	40891	22388	25589
吉木萨尔县	Jimsar County	2567	16644	15497	3885
木垒哈萨克自治县	Mori Kazak Autonomous County	1975	6486	5076	7025
伊犁哈萨克自治州	**Ili Kazak Autonomous Prefecture**	**108316**	**534207**	**150687**	**95748**
伊犁州直属县(市)	**Counties (Cities) Direct Under Ili Prefecture**	**55907**	**43080**	**54816**	**38035**
伊宁市	Yining [Gulja]City	1615	2542	3679	2113
奎屯市	Kuytun City	1356	6400	793	5610
伊宁县	Yining [Gulja]County	18886	1338	5947	4451
察布查尔锡伯自治县	Qapqal Xibe Autonomous County	4312	11477	6790	3182
霍城县	Huocheng [korgas]County	5381	16667	10455	12410
巩留县	Gongliu [Tokkuzlara]County	6424	2432	3745	1360
新源县	Xinyuan [kunes]County	7258	74	4249	4193
昭苏县	Zhaosu [mongolkure]County	1893	207	5250	1396
特克斯县	Tekes County	1633	533	4130	1032
尼勒克县	Nilka County	7149	1411	9778	2288
塔城地区	**Tacheng [Tarbagatai] Administrative Offices**	**49347**	**408291**	**60484**	**37326**
塔城市	Tacheng [Qoqek] City	2961	62288	5897	1950
乌苏市	Usu City	4731	125597	16348	3722
额敏县	Emin [Dorbiljin] County	12591	58960	3498	2601
沙湾县	Shawan County	22587	143922	20791	10728
托里县	Toli County	31	791	6685	7850
裕民县	Yumin [Qagantokay] County	4485	16433	4255	8431
和布克赛尔蒙古自治县	Hoboksar Mongol Autonomous County	1961	300	3010	2044
阿勒泰地区	**Altay Administrative Offices**	**3062**	**82836**	**35387**	**20387**
阿勒泰市	Altay City	94	7000	4050	3510
布尔津县	Burqin County	117	4180	4141	2936
富蕴县	Fuyun [Koktokay] County	114	11672	6420	4949
福海县	Fuhai [Burultokay] County	2597	49480	12426	3662
哈巴河县	Habahe [Kaba] County	40	3170	5100	2339
青河县	Qinghe [Qinggil] County	100	6667	1580	1759
吉木乃县	Jeminay County		10000	1670	1232

12-9 续表 3 Continued

地　区	Region	复合肥 Compound Fertilizer	地膜覆盖面积(公顷) Area of Covering (hectare)	农用柴油使用量(吨) Consumption of Agricultural Diesel Oil (ton)	农村用电量(万千瓦小时) Electricity Consumed in Rural Areas (10 000 kwh)
博尔塔拉蒙古自治州	**Bortala Mongol Autonomous Prefecture**	**11595**	**151260**	**23011**	**34510**
博乐市	Bole [Bortala] City	5492	59417	6381	17165
精河县	Jinghe [Jing] County	5359	66405	14717	15353
温泉县	Wenquan [Araxang] County	744	25438	1913	1992
巴音郭楞蒙古自治州	**Bayangol Mongol Autonomous Prefecture**	**30933**	**334305**	**67493**	**92756**
库尔勒市	Korla City	3320	83489	23758	27868
轮台县	Luntai [Bugur] County	6053	54050	9138	14176
尉犁县	Yuli [Lopnur] County	12020	81198	6449	13466
若羌县	Ruoqiang [Qarkilik] County	1617	3252	1786	7794
且末县	Qiemo [Qarqan] County	1843	16297	7512	2290
焉耆回族自治县	Yanqi Hui Autonomous County	2781	14737	3880	4095
和静县	Hejing County	744	26259	4290	1848
和硕县	Hoxud County	1175	37415	7330	17846
博湖县	Bohu [Bagrax] County	1380	17608	3350	3373
阿克苏地区	**Aksu Administrative Offices**	**55402**	**605578**	**108215**	**63594**
阿克苏市	Aksu City	3214	76953	6896	4733
温宿县	Wensu [Onsu] County	17546	60136	7714	3385
库车县	Kuqa County	13429	124870	18706	13642
沙雅县	Xayar County	4342	126127	16033	12266
新和县	Xinhe [Toksu] County	1073	65675	18523	12428
拜城县	Baicheng [Bay] County	2057	27481	6427	5564
乌什县	Wushi [Uxturpan] County	4041	15884	5320	2560
阿瓦提县	Awat County	9700	101133	26193	5653
柯坪县	Kalpin County		7320	2403	3362
克孜勒苏柯尔克孜自治州	**Kizilsu Kirgiz Autonomous Prefecture**	**1876**	**17202**	**6772**	**6582**
阿图什市	Artux City	155	7265	1184	1904
阿克陶县	Akto County	1721	9263	5247	3999
阿合奇县	Akqi County			210	411
乌恰县	Wuqia [Ulugqat] County		674	131	268
喀什地区	**Kashgar [Kaxgar] Administrative Offices**	**27652**	**501970**	**80054**	**155035**
喀什市	Kashgar [Kaxgar] City	1531	11819	3352	765
疏附县	Shufu County	458	30000	10050	4025
疏勒县	Shule County	1898	28000	5300	1548
英吉沙县	Yengisar County	1745	22040	5538	3650
泽普县	Zepu [Poskam] County	5159	27380	5473	7209
莎车县	Shache [Yarkant] County	1725	86793	16015	13513
叶城县	Yecheng [Kagilik] County	4557	28981	2996	1515
麦盖提县	Makit County	615	50431	5918	17673
岳普湖县	Yopurga County	3898	59868	5036	3423
伽师县	Jiashi [Payzawat] County	3641	69547	9715	24389
巴楚县	Bachu [Maralbexi] County	2425	86600	10199	77116
塔什库尔干塔吉克自治县	Taxkorgan Tajik Autonomous County		512	462	209
和田地区	**Hotan Administrative Offices**	**8878**	**47397**	**29846**	**78846**
和田市	Hotan City	203	1973	3751	11041
和田县	Hotan County	964	9673	2764	13418
墨玉县	Moyu [Karakax] County	5508	12763	3958	13802
皮山县	Pishan [Guma] County	525	7963	2837	9542
洛浦县	Lop County		2733	4800	12331
策勒县	Qira County	551	6080	6338	7038
于田县	Yutian [Keriya] County	1073	5912	5025	9383
民丰县	Minfeng [Niya] County	53	300	372	2291
生产建设兵团	**Xinjiang Production and Construction Group**	**229708**	**922345**	**256447**	**331195**

12-10 灌溉、水库和除涝、治水情况
Irrigation, Reservoirs, Flood Prevention, Water and Soil Conservation

项　目	Item	2015
灌溉面积(千公顷)	Irrigated Areas (1000 hectares)	4910.23
耕地灌溉面积	Irrigated Cultivated-land Areas	3799.62
林地灌溉面积	Irrigated Wooded-land Areas	593.21
园地灌溉面积	Irrigated Orchard Areas	248.07
牧草灌溉面积	Irrigated Pasture-land Areas	268.22
其他灌溉面积	Other Irrigated Areas	1.11
水库(座)	Number of Reservoirs (unit)	530
大型水库	Large Reservoir	20
中型水库	Medium-sized Reservoir	106
小型水库	Small Reservoir	404
塘坝(座)	Dam (unit)	376
泵站(处)	Pumping Station (unit)	435
节水灌溉面积(千公顷)	Water-saving Irrigated Areas (1000 hectares)	2418.95
#微灌面积	Micro Irrigated Area	1939.71
除涝面积(千公顷)	Areas wish Flood Prevention Measures (1000 hectares)	20.75
水土流失治理面积(千公顷)	Area of Soil Erosion under Control (1000 hectares)	926.15
#小流域综合治理面积	Area of Comprehensive Management of Small Watershed	190.36
堤防长度(公里)	Total Length of Dikes (km)	5390.434
#河堤长度	Length of River Bank	5101.774
堤防保护人口数(万人)	Dikes Protected Population (10000 people)	952.14
堤防保护耕地面积(千公顷)	Area of Land Protected by Dikes (1000 hectares)	1922.95

注:大型水库库容: 1 亿立方米以上; 中型水库库容: 1 千万至 1 亿立方米;小型水库库容: 10 万至 1 千万立方米。
Note: The capacity of the large reservoirs is over 100 million cubic meters, while that of the medium ones is from 10 million to 100 million cubic meters, and that of the small ones is from 100 000 to 10 million cubic meters.

12-11 各地、州、市水利设施和节水灌溉面积

Water Conservancy Facilities and Water-saving Irrigated Area by Prefecture, Autonomous Prefecture and City

(2015 年)

地区	Region	水库数 (座) Number of Reservoirs (unit)	泵站 (座) Pumping Station (unit)	节水灌溉面积 (千公顷) Water-saving Irrigated Area (1 000 hectares)	水土流失治理面积 (千公顷) Area of Soil Erosion under Control (1 000 hectares)
总　计	**Total**	**530**	**435**	**2418.95**	**926.15**
乌鲁木齐市	Urumqi City	25	10	6.40	27.11
克拉玛依市	Karamay City	7	20	19.65	7.36
吐鲁番市	Turpan City	17		59.12	20.36
哈密地区	Hami [Kumul]Administrative Offices	52	3	70.68	24.95
昌吉回族自治州	Changji HuiAutonomous Prefecture	92	34	384.40	61.44
伊犁州直属县(市)	Counties (Cities) Direct Under Ili Prefecture	22	16	258.39	214.35
塔城地区	Tacheng [Tarbagatai] Administrative Offices	66	9	433.86	70.57
阿勒泰地区	Altay Administrative Offices	81	190	183.53	80.73
博尔塔拉蒙古自治州	Bortala Mongol Autonomous Prefecture	8		111.34	43.52
巴音郭楞蒙古自治州	Bayangol Mongol Autonomous Prefecture	18	77	315.27	98.32
阿克苏地区	Aksu Administrative Offices	22	8	263.29	83.56
克孜勒苏柯尔克孜自治州	Kizilsu Kirgiz Autonomous Prefecture	14	1	15.92	22.49
喀什地区	Kashgar [Kaxgar] Administrative Offices	58	59	161.49	97.84
和田地区	Hotan Administrative Offices	48	8	135.61	73.55

12-12 各地、州、市农村集中式供水工程情况

Projects of Centralized Water Supply in Rural by Prefecture,Autonomous Prefecture and City

单位:处　　(2015 年)　　(unit)

地区	Region	合计 Total	城镇管网延伸工程 Project of Urban Pipe Network Extension	联村供水工程 Joint Village Water-supply Project	单村供水工程 Village Water-supply Project
总　计	**Total**	**2319**	**110**	**960**	**1249**
乌鲁木齐市	Urumqi City	90	1	35	54
克拉玛依市	Karamay City	2		2	
吐鲁番市	Turpan City	40	1	31	8
哈密地区	Hami [Kumul]Administrative Offices	148	13	29	106
昌吉回族自治州	Changji HuiAutonomous Prefecture	521	10	69	442
伊犁州直属县(市)	Counties (Cities) Direct Under Ili Prefecture	239	18	136	85
塔城地区	Tacheng [Tarbagatai] Administrative Offices	270	6	92	172
阿勒泰地区	Altay Administrative Offices	193	14	65	114
博尔塔拉蒙古自治州	Bortala Mongol Autonomous Prefecture	171		114	57
巴音郭楞蒙古自治州	Bayangol Mongol Autonomous Prefecture	184	38	47	99
阿克苏地区	Aksu Administrative Offices	155	1	142	12
克孜勒苏柯尔克孜自治州	Kizilsu Kirgiz Autonomous Prefecture	116	3	29	84
喀什地区	Kashgar [Kaxgar] Administrative Offices	126	3	112	11
和田地区	Hotan Administrative Offices	64	2	57	5

12-13 主要年份农作物播种面积
Total Sown Areas of Farm Crops in Main Years

单位：千公顷 (1 000 hectares)

年份 Year	农作物播种面积 Total Sown Area	粮食作物播种面积 Sown Area of Grain Crops	谷物 Cereal	#水稻 Rice	#小麦 Wheat	#玉米 Corn	#大麦 Barley	豆类 Soybeans	薯类 Tubers	棉花 Cotton
1978	3021.67	2310.71	2297.44	105.59	1348.82	621.39	50.01	13.27	23.09	150.42
1980	2993.71	2162.37	2147.60	98.39	1354.83	555.79	23.24	14.77	17.55	181.22
1985	2846.63	1853.04	1844.47	74.50	1278.43	418.43	13.63	8.57	10.56	253.52
1990	2979.51	1826.61	1813.16	84.13	1180.11	442.40	42.92	13.45	10.67	435.22
1995	3051.44	1593.29	1528.62	73.38	952.58	439.16	41.58	64.67	10.34	742.90
2000	3388.76	1445.77	1353.99	78.15	838.99	382.45	33.50	91.78	22.59	1012.39
2001	3404.12	1394.96	1281.38	73.28	744.27	410.29	34.11	113.58	20.77	1129.72
2002	3478.37	1493.96	1386.81	74.96	749.74	501.93	36.45	107.15	20.65	943.97
2003	3470.28	1307.02	1202.61	67.16	626.09	454.14	38.25	104.41	23.89	1037.05
2004	3571.89	1378.61	1273.03	66.77	658.08	505.69	24.53	105.58	24.23	1127.55
2005	3728.11	1471.76	1371.89	69.07	761.84	497.64	27.42	99.87	20.51	1157.99
2006	4206.28	1465.82	1369.68	68.00	740.11	496.43	50.96	96.14	22.79	1664.43
2007	4394.25	1379.00	1300.58	70.95	634.02	528.91	55.86	78.42	33.15	1782.60
2008	4536.87	1649.97	1554.43	70.12	877.97	545.39	54.68	95.54	36.02	1668.01
2009	4710.26	1993.50	1867.77	73.49	1153.32	598.38	31.73	125.73	37.68	1409.31
2010	4758.64	1991.61	1879.36	66.93	1120.01	653.82	28.94	112.25	36.99	1460.60
2011	4983.48	2000.36	1916.10	70.59	1077.98	728.00	24.81	84.26	47.12	1638.06
2012	5136.74	2103.20	2034.45	69.23	1081.04	855.72	14.13	68.75	27.97	1720.80
2013	5212.26	2204.22	2130.28	67.29	1120.98	920.80	10.07	73.94	30.58	1718.26
2014	5994.47	2220.20	2147.84	75.06	1142.35	910.80	10.13	72.36	35.65	2421.33
2015	6126.06	2365.55	2293.89	66.17	1239.33	961.87	12.09	71.66	29.47	2273.11

年份 Year	#长绒棉 Long-Staple Cotton	油料 Oil Bearing Crops	#油菜 Rapeseeds	#胡麻 Flax	#葵花 Helianthus	甜菜 Beetroots	蔬菜 Vegetables	果用瓜 Melon	#甜瓜 Musk-melon	苜蓿 Lucerne
1978	29.05	202.13	90.90	65.49	23.68	17.67	55.12	41.95		174.9
1980	38.50	269.39	107.47	81.85	50.08	24.27	46.99	39.54		191.65
1985	26.28	294.78	89.82	81.12	111.39	15.51	54.91	53.69	27.95	132.07
1990	62.69	269.27	117.35	46.04	96.11	66.87	58.07	28.84	15.09	159.34
1995	8.35	306.70	130.11	26.75	140.10	71.10	71.54	25.15	9.72	120.25
2000	49.29	310.07	96.23	24.57	157.05	55.75	127.75	55.99	26.01	120.49
2001	67.69	217.64	72.85	17.10	99.76	85.54	125.96	58.19	26.55	165.06
2002	46.30	215.05	70.00	23.84	96.60	85.32	164.21	82.47	48.47	235.11
2003	70.13	226.38	74.48	22.30	100.07	67.31	163.84	62.45	32.82	294.13
2004	70.63	215.47	67.52	13.74	85.55	59.88	185.60	61.29	36.07	301.10
2005	73.38	185.49	59.92	17.37	84.62	69.90	176.66	70.57	36.02	275.91
2006	106.94	151.73	49.25	14.28	64.29	94.42	186.82	74.02	41.27	242.38
2007	142.53	176.47	59.48	12.32	96.41	94.02	234.88	103.40	62.81	231.36
2008	132.18	286.68	83.67	9.51	172.44	71.14	258.04	110.60	68.22	171.42
2009	82.60	270.05	76.95	12.43	155.74	63.74	262.17	143.47	86.70	165.34
2010	96.79	273.37	70.15	8.75	164.87	75.27	303.59	122.78	69.44	150.14
2011	83.87	264.28	64.47	7.83	163.65	75.43	322.61	118.85	57.78	145.29
2012	53.33	242.34	59.64	8.68	148.19	82.63	306.94	130.08	63.12	149.69
2013	38.28	221.74	43.71	8.08	145.77	65.90	296.68	136.45	66.13	184.70
2014	63.33	220.53	48.52	8.13	143.29	62.89	310.16	144.38	66.69	206.01
2015	243.79	218.33	43.68	6.57	147.33	61.23	323.67	162.97	81.79	214.16

注：粮食、棉花播种面积为国家审定数。
Note: Total sown areas of grain,cotton refer to the statistical data of state approved.

12-14 各地、州、市、县(市)农作物播种面积

单位：千公顷 (2015 年)

地区	Region	农作物播种面积 Total Sown Area	粮食 Grain Crops	谷物 Cereal	#水稻 Rice	#小麦 Wheat	#玉米 Corn	豆类 Soy-beans
总　计	**Total**	**6126.06**	**2365.55**	**2293.89**	**66.17**	**1239.33**	**961.87**	**71.66**
乌鲁木齐市	**Urumqi City**	**44.43**	**13.43**	**13.15**	**4.90**	**4.21**	**3.05**	**0.28**
#乌鲁木齐县	Urumqi County	11.82	1.52	1.43		0.46	0.02	0.08
克拉玛依市	**Karamay City**	**16.06**	**3.80**	**3.80**	**0.01**	**0.28**	**3.48**	
吐鲁番市	**Turpan City**	**61.32**	**3.02**	**2.98**		**0.01**	**0.31**	**0.04**
高昌区	Gaochang Offices	18.51						
鄯善县	Shanshan [piqan]County	14.53	0.53	0.51		0.01	0.28	0.01
托克逊县	Toksun County	28.28	2.49	2.47			0.03	0.03
哈密地区	**Hami [Kumul]Administrative Offices**	**74.28**	**28.44**	**28.27**		**21.47**	**2.51**	**0.17**
哈密市	Hami [Kumul]City	41.86	6.52	6.51		2.90	2.50	0.01
巴里坤哈萨克自治县	Barkol KazakAutonomous County	26.16	19.10	19.09		18.12	0.01	0.01
伊吾县	Yiwu [Araturuk]County	6.25	2.82	2.68		0.45		0.14
昌吉回族自治州	**Changji Hui Autonomous Prefecture**	**547.36**	**307.53**	**299.43**	**0.64**	**185.72**	**108.24**	**8.10**
昌吉市	Changji City	84.40	31.52	31.25	0.51	13.33	17.41	0.27
阜康市	Fukang City	54.47	20.65	20.58		14.31	5.94	0.07
呼图壁县	Hutubi County	97.61	40.05	40.01	0.08	16.49	23.07	0.04
玛纳斯县	Manas County	74.09	27.96	27.92	0.06	4.64	20.25	0.04
奇台县	Qitai County	130.29	103.69	102.68		78.75	23.44	1.01
吉木萨尔县	Jimsar County	53.88	36.10	34.81		22.60	11.65	1.29
木垒哈萨克自治县	Mori Kazak Autonomous County	52.62	47.56	42.17		35.60	6.49	5.39
伊犁哈萨克自治州	**Ili Kazak Autonomous Prefecture**	**1357.40**	**831.56**	**793.45**	**15.97**	**367.44**	**404.59**	**38.11**
伊犁州直属县(市)	**Counties (Cities) Direct Under Ili Prefecture**	**505.39**	**395.71**	**363.83**	**15.97**	**197.26**	**146.70**	**31.88**
伊宁市	Yining [Gulja]City	17.96	12.05	10.96	0.90	4.00	6.06	1.09
奎屯市	Kuytun City	11.31	4.80	4.80		4.00	0.80	
伊宁县	Yining [Gulja]County	91.80	80.68	68.81	0.02	18.60	50.19	11.87
察布查尔锡伯自治县	Qapqal Xibe Autonomous County	84.98	61.95	59.47	12.63	23.28	23.50	2.49
霍城县	Huocheng [korgas]County	42.91	26.75	25.74		12.33	13.41	1.01
巩留县	Gongliu [Tokkuzlara]County	61.49	52.25	39.38	0.11	22.13	17.05	12.87
新源县	Xinyuan [kunes]County	68.01	58.62	56.26	2.29	31.26	22.50	2.37
昭苏县	Zhaosu [mongolkure]County	55.25	42.35	42.35		41.77	0.23	
特克斯县	Tekes County	33.33	24.27	24.18		17.35	5.23	0.09
尼勒克县	Nilka County	38.35	31.98	31.88	0.02	22.54	7.71	0.10
塔城地区	**Tacheng [Tarbagatai] Administrative Offices**	**620.74**	**344.30**	**343.66**		**130.09**	**212.18**	**0.64**
塔城市	Tacheng [Qoqek] City	106.85	94.09	94.09		35.45	58.63	
乌苏市	Usu City	154.39	43.18	43.08		16.34	26.02	0.10
额敏县	Emin [Dorbiljin] County	116.48	107.80	107.80		41.91	65.75	
沙湾县	Shawan County	159.44	37.62	37.09		15.89	21.18	0.53
托里县	Toli County	32.37	31.25	31.25		9.15	21.60	
裕民县	Yumin [Qagantokay] County	38.79	26.49	26.49		9.17	17.31	
和布克赛尔蒙古自治县	Hoboksar Mongol Autonomous County	12.42	3.88	3.87		2.18	1.69	0.01
阿勒泰地区	**Altay Administrative Offices**	**231.27**	**91.55**	**85.96**		**40.08**	**45.71**	**5.59**
阿勒泰市	Altay City	37.03	13.05	11.36		3.81	7.55	1.69
布尔津县	Burqin County	29.40	9.09	8.37		1.18	7.15	0.72
富蕴县	Fuyun [Koktokay] County	29.33	17.68	16.61		10.10	6.51	1.07
福海县	Fuhai [Burultokay] County	65.55	24.10	24.04		9.35	14.69	0.06
哈巴河县	Habahe [Kaba] County	43.71	14.67	12.80		3.99	8.69	1.87
青河县	Qinghe [Qinggil] County	18.23	9.30	9.13		8.88	0.24	0.17
吉木乃县	Jeminay County	8.02	3.66	3.66		2.77	0.89	

注:全区农作物播种面积及棉花面积合计不等于地方和生产建设兵团汇总数。

Sown Areas of Farm Crops by Prefecture, Autonomous Prefecture, City and County

(1 000 hectares)

薯 类 Tubers	棉 花 Cotton	#长绒棉 Longstaple Cotton	油 料 Oil Bearing Crops	#油 菜 Rapeseeds	#胡 麻 Flax	#葵 花 Helianthus	甜 菜 Beetroots	蔬 菜 Vegetables	果用瓜 Melon	#甜 瓜 Muskmelon	苜 蓿 Lucerne
29.47	**2273.11**	**243.79**	**218.33**	**43.68**	**6.57**	**147.33**	**61.23**	**323.67**	**162.97**	**81.79**	**214.16**
3.98	**0.44**		**2.56**	**0.31**	**0.01**	**1.88**	**0.01**	**13.57**	**0.31**		**3.14**
2.60			0.24	0.23		0.01		3.52			1.91
0.01	**5.53**		**2.09**			**2.03**	**0.44**	**1.00**	**0.19**	**0.03**	**0.69**
0.08	**23.25**		**0.38**					**6.31**	**14.87**	**11.40**	**0.23**
	6.13							3.97	5.60	2.81	
	4.69							1.06	7.47	7.06	0.03
0.08	12.43		0.38					1.28	1.80	1.53	0.20
1.05	**28.19**		**1.42**	**1.01**	**0.04**	**0.37**		**2.66**	**5.07**	**4.80**	**5.49**
0.02	28.05		1.24	0.83	0.04	0.37		1.41	2.34	2.08	1.27
1.01	0.13		0.11	0.11				1.21	0.17	0.17	4.16
0.02	0.01		0.07	0.07				0.04	2.56	2.56	0.06
6.34	**80.28**		**39.31**	**0.06**	**0.34**	**36.75**	**5.73**	**34.39**	**7.55**	**1.64**	**6.67**
0.08	16.65		15.60			15.54	1.34	6.21	5.10	0.65	0.97
1.12	0.40		10.44			10.41	1.60	9.65	0.42	0.09	0.65
0.27	25.98		4.97	0.03		4.88	1.27	8.79	1.07	0.59	3.43
0.48	37.26		1.40	0.01		1.29	0.10	1.11	0.23		0.78
1.25			2.74	0.01		1.79	1.27	4.74	0.23	0.07	0.18
2.16			2.44			1.47	0.15	3.76	0.14	0.07	0.48
0.98			1.73	0.01	0.34	1.37		0.14	0.36	0.18	0.17
5.74	**199.03**	**95.83**	**88.43**	**11.35**	**1.79**	**63.31**	**16.31**	**34.86**	**4.71**	**1.53**	**63.40**
1.96	**8.60**	**8.60**	**26.19**	**10.21**	**1.47**	**13.94**	**13.93**	**15.19**	**1.84**	**0.10**	**16.02**
0.09			0.34			0.33	0.11	3.03	0.69		0.21
0.03	6.40	6.40						0.03	0.01		0.04
0.41			3.12	0.09	0.07	2.97	0.48	3.67	0.35		1.42
0.05	0.48	0.48	1.61		0.28	1.26	1.86	1.78	0.43	0.03	5.25
0.33	1.71	1.71	2.87			2.87	4.50	3.01	0.20	0.07	
0.06			1.95			1.95	1.59	0.55	0.09		3.13
0.39			3.01	0.41		2.11	1.53	0.41	0.03		2.85
0.34			9.43	8.93	0.21	0.30	1.52	0.13			0.07
0.04			2.53	0.25	0.20	2.07	1.09	1.74	0.03		1.04
0.23			1.32	0.53	0.72	0.07	1.26	0.84	0.01		2.01
0.67	**190.44**	**87.24**	**24.76**	**1.15**	**0.30**	**11.91**	**2.07**	**18.49**	**0.31**	**0.12**	**12.91**
0.02			0.41	0.40		0.01	0.35	2.36	0.03		6.77
0.23	86.82	86.82	5.03		0.17	4.24	0.46	6.08	0.24	0.11	2.01
			0.43	0.02	0.14	0.27	0.90	1.02			2.34
0.27	101.70		4.15	0.07		3.63	0.27	7.92	0.05		0.66
0.03	0.41	0.41	0.65	0.65				0.03			
0.09			10.33				0.09	0.05			1.14
0.04	1.50		3.76			3.76		1.03			
3.10			**37.48**		**0.01**	**37.47**	**0.32**	**1.18**	**2.55**	**1.31**	**34.46**
0.05			7.28		0.01	7.26	0.29	0.21	1.17	1.16	5.33
0.09			9.01			9.01		0.12	0.02	0.02	2.85
0.28			2.86			2.86		0.15	0.02		4.91
0.93			5.34			5.34	0.02	0.15	1.08	0.13	8.30
0.20			10.11			10.11		0.42	0.26		5.85
1.45			1.68			1.68		0.08			4.79
0.11			1.21			1.21		0.04			2.43

Note:Total of sown areas of farm crops and cotton areas by region do not mean that summary number of local and Production&Construction Corps.

12-14 续表

单位：千公顷

地区	Region	农作物播种面积 Total Sown Area	粮食 Grain Crops	谷物 Cereal	#水稻 Rice	#小麦 Wheat	#玉米 Corn	豆类 Soybeans
博尔塔拉蒙古自治州	**Bortala Mongol Autonomous Prefecture**	**184.16**	**78.62**	**78.61**	**0.05**	**22.06**	**56.50**	**0.01**
博乐市	Bole [Bortala] City	62.72	31.97	31.96	0.05	5.24	26.67	0.01
精河县	Jinghe [Jing] County	82.09	11.46	11.46		6.75	4.71	
温泉县	Wenquan [Araxang] County	39.35	35.19	35.18		10.07	25.11	0.01
巴音郭楞蒙古自治州	**Bayangol Mongol Autonomous Prefecture**	**417.65**	**108.11**	**107.86**	**0.23**	**60.95**	**46.30**	**0.25**
库尔勒市	Korla City	96.99	6.46	6.39	0.03	1.22	5.14	0.06
轮台县	Luntai [Bugur] County	63.59	23.67	23.67		13.84	9.83	
尉犁县	Yuli [Lopnur] County	82.64	1.05	1.05		0.26	0.79	
若羌县	Ruoqiang [Qarkilik] County	7.88	2.41	2.41		1.90	0.51	
且末县	Qiemo [Qarqan] County	29.32	14.59	14.50		8.73	5.48	0.09
焉耆回族自治县	Yanqi Hui Autonomous County	32.60	17.51	17.51	0.01	13.03	4.47	
和静县	Hejing County	35.70	18.33	18.24		7.98	10.16	0.09
和硕县	Hoxud County	42.53	15.79	15.79		10.42	5.37	
博湖县	Bohu [Bagrax] County	26.41	8.30	8.30	0.18	3.58	4.54	
阿克苏地区	**Aksu Administrative Offices**	**844.23**	**271.68**	**270.91**	**15.32**	**146.51**	**107.47**	**0.77**
阿克苏市	Aksu City	88.94	15.29	15.29	2.10	8.78	4.41	
温宿县	Wensu [Onsu] County	96.44	37.91	37.63	8.83	18.98	9.73	0.27
库车县	Kuqa County	164.77	52.16	52.12		29.71	22.40	0.04
沙雅县	Xayar County	160.86	38.95	38.95		21.76	17.19	0.01
新和县	Xinhe [Toksu] County	91.41	24.40	24.40		16.33	8.07	
拜城县	Baicheng [Bay] County	66.77	47.31	47.07	0.59	19.34	25.96	0.24
乌什县	Wushi [Uxturpan] County	35.10	27.55	27.34	3.80	16.20	7.01	0.21
阿瓦提县	Awat County	126.53	23.15	23.15		12.44	10.71	
柯坪县	Kalpin County	13.42	4.95	4.95		2.97	1.98	
克孜勒苏柯尔克孜自治州	**Kizilsu Kirgiz Autonomous Prefecture**	**73.41**	**55.42**	**55.32**	**0.61**	**29.29**	**24.64**	**0.10**
阿图什市	Artux City	25.63	17.65	17.65	0.10	10.60	6.92	
阿克陶县	Akto County	39.86	31.76	31.76	0.52	14.79	16.34	
阿合奇县	Akqi County	4.69	3.82	3.78		2.60	0.60	0.04
乌恰县	Wuqia [Ulugqat] County	3.24	2.19	2.13		1.29	0.78	0.06
喀什地区	**Kashgar [Kaxgar] Administrative Offices**	**1177.96**	**456.19**	**435.85**	**3.78**	**235.36**	**194.89**	**20.35**
喀什市	Kashgar [Kaxgar] City	44.73	21.27	21.27	0.58	10.97	9.71	
疏附县	Shufu County	65.11	37.95	37.95	0.53	20.29	17.13	
疏勒县	Shule County	115.13	40.14	40.14	0.29	22.14	17.72	
英吉沙县	Yengisar County	61.06	32.07	31.57		17.35	14.23	0.49
泽普县	Zepu [Poskam] County	50.38	28.32	21.99	0.35	12.73	8.90	6.33
莎车县	Shache [Yarkant] County	200.10	88.27	84.37	1.43	45.21	37.73	3.90
叶城县	Yecheng [Kagilik] County	113.11	72.49	62.87	0.59	30.64	31.63	9.62
麦盖提县	Makit County	108.21	28.49	28.49		17.08	11.41	
岳普湖县	Yopurga County	83.99	19.09	19.09		10.65	8.44	
伽师县	Jiashi [Payzawat] County	168.26	48.05	48.05		26.87	21.18	
巴楚县	Bachu [Maralbexi] County	162.26	35.40	35.40		19.03	16.37	
塔什库尔干塔吉克自治县	Taxkorgan Tajik Autonomous County	5.61	4.65	4.65		2.40	0.43	
和田地区	**Hotan Administrative Offices**	**266.39**	**177.90**	**177.60**	**7.95**	**93.44**	**76.05**	**0.30**
和田市	Hotan City	20.14	15.09	15.09	0.46	8.70	5.93	
和田县	Hotan County	41.25	26.75	26.75	2.42	15.98	8.35	
墨玉县	Moyu [Karakax] County	69.84	48.12	48.12	2.25	25.87	20.00	
皮山县	Pishan [Guma] County	35.53	19.39	19.25		9.40	9.85	0.13
洛浦县	Lop County	32.26	26.78	26.77	0.01	13.33	13.42	
策勒县	Qira County	25.19	15.18	15.02		7.38	7.54	0.16
于田县	Yutian [Keriya] County	37.64	24.17	24.17	2.80	11.43	9.90	
民丰县	Minfeng [Niya] County	4.54	2.42	2.42		1.35	1.06	
生产建设兵团	**Xinjiang Production and Construction Group**	**1353.99**	**316.85**	**308.99**	**17.24**	**174.53**	**112.60**	**7.85**

Continued

(1 000 hectares)

薯类 Tubers	棉花 Cotton	#长绒棉 Longstaple Cotton	油料 Oil Bearing Crops	#油菜 Rapeseeds	#胡麻 Flax	#葵花 Helianthus	甜菜 Beetroots	蔬菜 Vegetables	果用瓜 Melon	#甜瓜 Muskmelon	苜蓿 Lucerne
0.06	**80.47**		**3.62**			**2.90**	**2.31**	**1.12**	**0.39**	**0.15**	**2.52**
0.03	28.89		0.03			0.03	0.30	0.83	0.09	0.02	0.12
	51.58		1.23			0.90	1.07	0.26	0.28	0.13	1.94
0.03			2.35			1.97	0.94	0.02	0.02		0.45
0.46	**220.59**	**2.64**	**3.26**	**0.49**	**0.01**	**2.00**	**5.08**	**49.28**	**5.04**	**4.19**	**4.31**
0.07	81.51		0.33	0.02	0.01	0.12	0.23	1.18	0.35	0.13	2.01
	36.70						0.69	0.46	1.02	0.92	0.28
	77.96		0.40				0.38	0.22	0.41	0.24	
	1.87							0.17	2.67	2.65	0.05
	10.12		0.36	0.01		0.25	0.03	1.00	0.23	0.18	1.26
	0.86		0.47	0.02		0.44	1.44	7.65	0.03	0.01	0.33
0.26	0.10		0.72	0.36		0.34	0.98	12.58	0.08	0.01	0.11
0.12	8.83		0.33	0.08		0.19	0.43	13.64	0.12	0.02	0.23
	2.64	2.64	0.66			0.66	0.91	12.39	0.15	0.03	0.04
2.47	**479.56**	**127.50**	**8.61**	**6.49**	**1.53**	**0.59**	**10.35**	**25.80**	**15.94**	**4.84**	**10.80**
	64.61	35.88					2.70	3.26	1.97	0.23	0.74
0.84	43.78	3.96	0.71	0.68	0.03		0.85	5.61	1.67	0.18	1.75
0.12	102.56	0.51	0.37	0.29		0.09	0.73	3.64	2.66	1.18	1.03
0.15	107.60	12.63	1.28	1.21		0.07	1.03	2.53	3.34	1.61	0.85
0.04	62.16	0.02	0.07	0.07			1.05	1.65	1.01	0.31	1.00
1.32			4.14	3.29	0.81	0.04	2.31	3.28	1.36	0.15	4.26
	0.49		1.38	0.78	0.59		0.63	3.81	0.73	0.11	0.51
	91.04	73.96	0.41	0.16	0.09	0.16	1.05	1.36	3.14	1.04	0.48
	7.32	0.53	0.24			0.24		0.66	0.07	0.03	0.19
0.06	**11.09**	**5.25**	**0.44**	**0.11**	**0.30**	**0.02**		**1.67**	**1.19**	**0.61**	**2.03**
0.01	5.25	5.25	0.03		0.01	0.01		0.52	0.35	0.32	0.65
	5.83		0.01			0.01		0.94	0.78	0.29	0.19
0.03			0.32	0.03	0.29			0.07			0.44
0.01			0.08	0.08				0.15	0.06		0.75
4.67	**481.01**		**6.49**	**4.99**	**0.22**	**1.10**		**53.68**	**74.63**	**33.89**	**36.74**
	15.61							5.73	1.69	0.95	0.34
0.53	9.69		0.07		0.07			8.11	8.29	2.40	
0.11	50.84							8.35	11.80	3.73	2.33
	18.06		0.07	0.07				3.66	4.99	2.00	2.20
2.00	14.30		0.08		0.02	0.01		2.39	1.79	0.15	1.07
0.56	83.87		4.93	4.92	0.01			8.83	9.73	2.87	3.04
1.47	16.57		1.15		0.12	0.89		7.48	1.85	0.43	7.42
	47.28							2.80	4.35	1.27	4.51
	45.45		0.20			0.20		0.95	5.03	3.43	4.60
	96.08							3.30	16.18	12.91	4.55
	82.93							1.98	8.92	3.73	6.43
	0.32							0.10			0.25
0.58	**38.24**		**4.25**	**1.77**	**1.52**	**0.56**		**11.67**	**5.13**	**2.64**	**24.06**
	1.48		0.11					1.29	0.30	0.19	0.76
0.26	9.67		0.41	0.41				1.70	1.12	0.67	0.97
0.01	12.36		0.19	0.15	0.04			2.14	1.10	0.35	5.74
0.13	5.93		0.56	0.32		0.23		1.50	0.26	0.11	7.15
0.01	1.38		1.04	0.11	0.81			0.91	0.56	0.21	1.24
0.03	2.05		1.00	0.02	0.67	0.22		1.62	0.68	0.33	3.26
0.13	5.36		0.93	0.75		0.11		2.12	0.57	0.23	3.83
	0.01							0.38	0.54	0.54	1.11
5.63	**629.35**	**12.57**	**57.46**	**17.10**	**0.83**	**35.81**	**20.99**	**87.65**	**27.96**	**16.08**	**54.09**

12-15 主要年份农作物种植结构
Planting Structure of Major Farm Crops in Main Years

单位：%　　(%)

项　目	Item	1995	2000	2010	2015
农作物总播种面积	**Total Sown Areas of Farm Crops**	**100**	**100**	**100**	**100**
粮食作物	**Grain Crops**	**52.21**	**42.66**	**41.85**	**38.61**
谷　物	Cereal	50.10	39.95	39.49	37.44
稻　谷	Rice	2.40	2.31	1.41	1.08
小　麦	Wheat	31.22	24.75	23.54	20.23
玉　米	Corn	14.39	11.29	13.74	15.70
谷　子	Millet	0.02	0.04	0.02	0.09
高　粱	Jowar	0.47	0.39	0.12	0.07
其它谷物	Other Cereal	1.59	1.18	0.67	0.27
豆　类	Soybeans	2.12	2.71	2.36	1.17
#大 豆	Soja	0.94	1.85	1.56	0.94
杂 豆	Miscellaneous Beans	1.18	0.20	0.80	0.15
薯　类	**Tubers**	**0.34**	**0.66**	**0.78**	**0.48**
油　料	**Oil-bearing Crops**	**10.05**	**9.15**	**5.74**	**3.56**
#花　生	Peanuts		0.14	0.08	0.05
油菜籽	Rapeseeds	4.26	2.84	1.47	0.71
芝　麻	Sesame		0.02	0.03	0.19
胡麻籽	Benne	0.88	0.72	0.18	0.11
向日葵	Helianthus	4.59	4.63	3.46	2.40
棉　花	**Cotton**	**24.35**	**29.87**	**30.69**	**37.11**
麻　类	**Fiber Crops**	**0.14**	**0.21**	**0.05**	**0.06**
甜　菜	**Beetroots**	**2.33**	**1.65**	**1.58**	**1.00**
烟　叶	**Tobacco**	**0.03**	**0.08**	**0.02**	
药　材	**Medicinal Materials**	**0.22**	**0.38**	**0.42**	**1.10**
蔬菜、瓜类	**Vegetables and Melon**	**3.17**	**5.42**	**8.96**	**7.94**
#蔬 菜	Vegetables	2.34	3.77	6.38	5.28
其他农作物	**Other Farm Crops**	**7.16**	**9.92**	**9.91**	**10.14**
#青饲料	Succulence	3.94	3.56	1.26	1.93

12-16 主要年份农作物产品产量

Output of Major Farm Crops in Main Years

单位：万吨 (10 000 tons)

年 份 Year	粮 食 Grain	谷 物 Cereal	#水 稻 Rice	#小 麦 Wheat	#玉 米 Corn	#大 麦 Barley	豆 类 Soybeans	薯 类 Tubers	棉 花 Cotton	#长绒棉 Long-staple Cotton
1978	370.01	367.71	27.39	180.02	134.45	5.01	2.30	22.91	5.50	1.19
1980	386.13	384.16	25.62	213.19	126.43	3.50	1.97	16.03	7.92	1.74
1985	496.65	495.16	30.63	314.52	139.38	1.93	1.49	15.14	18.78	1.40
1990	676.89	673.18	47.27	390.80	209.42	10.51	3.71	22.57	46.88	3.48
1995	730.16	716.83	48.25	381.21	266.74	12.82	13.33	26.43	93.50	1.13
1996	818.20	808.67	51.49	420.32	312.54	17.39	9.53	32.50	94.04	1.72
1997	825.34	813.07	55.27	437.60	294.31	17.92	12.27	26.73	115.00	3.10
1998	830.00	814.54	49.56	444.00	302.25	11.00	15.46	33.12	140.00	1.39
1999	838.78	821.70	54.14	423.29	323.06	8.00	17.08	46.06	140.75	1.67
2000	808.60	782.93	60.35	405.80	298.22	11.75	25.67	64.01	150.00	6.16
2001	796.00	767.53	56.79	374.14	318.41	11.86	28.47	60.02	157.00	9.71
2002	875.87	849.48	60.62	386.44	379.05	13.78	26.39	62.41	150.00	6.67
2003	801.64	774.62	50.73	335.67	366.25	14.33	27.02	71.80	160.00	10.10
2004	828.53	800.04	51.31	345.94	388.12	8.06	28.49	70.79	175.25	11.22
2005	877.21	852.00	54.18	400.71	380.36	10.23	25.22	65.86	195.70	11.87
2006	895.22	870.21	59.27	400.31	386.80	17.85	25.01	76.50	267.53	18.59
2007	867.04	846.35	62.52	359.22	396.00	24.26	20.69	101.36	290.00	25.02
2008	909.00	885.99	56.50	395.69	416.41	14.75	23.01	107.62	301.55	19.73
2009	1152.00	1119.77	58.30	630.70	439.38	14.30	32.23	126.06	252.40	11.04
2010	1150.20	1121.88	58.98	623.49	421.61	12.54	28.32	102.50	247.90	13.03
2011	1200.75	1171.64	60.64	576.64	517.67	11.06	29.11	119.75	289.77	12.16
2012	1259.83	1234.81	59.36	576.54	592.11	3.46	25.02	65.85	353.95	5.95
2013	1360.83	1339.71	59.82	622.08	649.02	4.92	21.12	80.85	351.80	5.35
2014	1390.81	1369.14	76.17	642.27	641.09	4.95	21.67	118.30	451.00	8.24
2015	1501.30	1480.47	65.08	698.25	705.05	6.04	20.83	99.82	429.80	40.45

年 份 Year	油 料 Oil bearing Crops	#油 菜 Rapeseeds	#胡 麻 Flax	#葵 花 Helianthus	甜 菜 Beetroots	蔬 菜 Vegetables	果用瓜 Melons	#甜 瓜 Muskmelon	苜 蓿 Lucerne
1978	10.33	3.30	3.14	2.29	16.37	91.26	44.05		
1980	17.59	5.59	5.17	4.59	38.52	73.44	55.68		
1985	34.25	7.29	8.10	16.90	40.69	111.08	103.18	47.02	49.69
1990	38.96	12.17	6.32	18.17	224.37	187.42	93.38	37.75	89.29
1995	49.41	15.12	3.79	29.06	288.14	269.56	68.75	18.31	82.62
1996	30.95	10.15	3.12	16.91	354.52	301.94	67.16	17.33	75.42
1997	29.95	8.92	2.53	17.69	388.71	295.59	86.78	25.90	70.05
1998	37.52	12.32	2.53	20.82	513.12	321.79	88.32	29.45	67.56
1999	60.46	16.37	2.75	35.69	354.24	406.18	143.49	46.38	69.98
2000	60.14	14.75	3.60	35.47	292.65	527.84	151.03	51.22	76.32
2001	42.64	12.19	2.47	23.31	455.12	486.74	156.87	56.86	103.12
2002	44.37	12.90	3.69	23.26	466.81	674.96	233.40	107.49	149.93
2003	50.13	15.43	3.49	25.80	381.65	761.00	189.32	77.61	249.60
2004	44.54	12.16	2.10	21.90	344.21	919.13	186.06	92.54	273.04
2005	38.94	9.22	2.39	21.69	419.12	862.23	220.65	95.58	295.74
2006	32.82	9.73	2.52	16.17	555.53	958.04	237.28	109.98	240.15
2007	40.30	9.60	1.58	25.39	586.93	1173.99	338.67	192.63	205.47
2008	56.85	10.67	1.23	42.87	438.88	970.67	404.17	248.81	150.83
2009	63.91	15.72	1.89	41.40	418.41	1383.21	491.20	286.30	154.90
2010	66.62	15.14	1.32	44.11	486.97	1734.40	435.00	222.58	132.93
2011	66.76	15.18	1.23	45.36	518.95	1866.15	434.31	193.06	139.94
2012	59.04	11.20	1.40	41.44	577.19	1656.02	485.35	213.35	149.62
2013	60.63	11.29	1.37	41.90	476.47	1669.92	544.24	239.46	212.39
2014	59.33	10.31	1.49	43.51	471.94	1819.79	608.26	234.95	225.10
2015	62.88	10.79	1.34	46.33	448.32	1933.92	673.58	288.88	225.45

注：粮食、棉花总产量为国家审定数。

Note:Total grain and cotton output refer to approvable dafa by NBS

12-17 各地、州、市、县(市)主要农产品产量

单位：吨 (2015 年)

地区	Region	粮食作物 Grain Crops	谷物 Cereal	#水稻 Rice	#小麦 Wheat	#玉米 Corn	豆类 Soy-beans
总　计	**Total**	**15013000**	**14804700**	**650800**	**6982500**	**7050500**	**208300**
乌鲁木齐市	**Urumqi City**	**102912**	**101758**	**45576**	**24006**	**28636**	**1154**
#乌鲁木齐县	Urumqi County	5797	5468		2076	82	329
克拉玛依市	**Karamay City**	**35187**	**35187**	**44**	**830**	**34197**	
吐鲁番市	**Turpan City**	**14952**	**14874**		**16**	**1700**	**78**
高昌区	Gaochang District						
鄯善县	Shanshan [piqan]County	2298	2256		16	1442	42
托克逊县	Toksun County	12654	12618			258	36
哈密地区	**Hami [Kumul]Administrative Offices**	**151579**	**150936**		**112642**	**22993**	**643**
哈密市	Hami [Kumul]City	41574	41458		14631	22844	116
巴里坤哈萨克自治县	Barkol KazakAutonomous County	100540	100498		95726	149	42
伊吾县	Yiwu [Araturuk]County	9465	8980		2285		485
昌吉回族自治州	**Changji Hui Autonomous Prefecture**	**2273832**	**2253650**	**5699**	**1102575**	**1114472**	**20182**
昌吉市	Changji City	261570	260890	4553	81398	174921	680
阜康市	Fukang City	144103	143933		92539	49494	170
呼图壁县	Hutubi County	353488	353399	774	100241	250469	89
玛纳斯县	Manas County	226943	226860	372	26493	178812	83
奇台县	Qitai County	744563	741652		493608	247467	2911
吉木萨尔县	Jimsar County	281770	277605		135730	138021	4165
木垒哈萨克自治县	Mori Kazak Autonomous County	261395	249311		172566	75288	12084
伊犁哈萨克自治州	**Ili Kazak Autonomous Prefecture**	**7188467**	**7085338**	**148421**	**1997104**	**4915674**	**103129**
伊犁州直属县(市)	**Counties (Cities) Direct Under Ili Prefecture**	**3093864**	**3004647**	**148421**	**1047720**	**1793094**	**89217**
伊宁市	Yining [Gulja]City	104234	101229	10408	21912	68907	3005
奎屯市	Kuytun City	26640	26640		18000	8640	
伊宁县	Yining [Gulja]County	784173	751244	75	111204	639965	32929
察布查尔锡伯自治县	Qapqal Xibe Autonomous County	507548	501283	124085	130911	246032	6265
霍城县	Huocheng [korgas]County	272614	268787		82507	186280	3827
巩留县	Gongliu [Tokkuzlara]County	326624	288004	1190	79076	207198	38620
新源县	Xinyuan [kunes]County	479892	475976	12483	177683	284724	3916
昭苏县	Zhaosu [mongolkure]County	209808	209808		205836	2625	
特克斯县	Tekes County	150020	149720		88820	56200	300
尼勒克县	Nilka County	232311	231956	180	131771	92523	355
塔城地区	**Tacheng [Tarbagatai] Administrative Offices**	**3427222**	**3425201**		**750328**	**2666439**	**2021**
塔城市	Tacheng [Qoqek] City	961768	961768		200143	761625	
乌苏市	Usu City	467188	467067		99700	360304	121
额敏县	Emin [Dorbiljin] County	1053952	1053952		254796	798822	
沙湾县	Shawan County	383798	381928		101285	280560	1870
托里县	Toli County	270513	270513		40491	229068	
裕民县	Yumin [Qagantokay] County	263288	263288		46388	216900	
和布克赛尔蒙古自治县	Hoboksar Mongol Autonomous County	26715	26685		7525	19160	30
阿勒泰地区	**Altay Administrative Offices**	**667381**	**655490**		**199056**	**456141**	**11891**
阿勒泰市	Altay City	91137	88088		17868	70212	3049
布尔津县	Burqin County	74291	72094		5493	66501	2197
富蕴县	Fuyun [Koktokay] County	120542	118948		49934	69014	1594
福海县	Fuhai [Burultokay] County	219806	219657		47259	172398	149
哈巴河县	Habahe [Kaba] County	91692	87218		17945	69099	4474
青河县	Qinghe [Qinggil] County	49186	48758		46623	2124	428
吉木乃县	Jeminay County	20727	20727		13934	6793	

注: 1.地方与生产建设兵团合计不等于全区总计数。2.全区总计数为国家统计局审定数。

Output of Major Farm Crops by Prefecture, Autonomous Prefecture, City and County

(ton)

薯 类 Tubers	棉 花 Cotton	#长绒棉 Longstaple Cotton	油 料 Oil Bearing Crops	#油 菜 Rapeseeds	#胡 麻 Flax	#葵 花 Helianthus	甜 菜 Beetroots	蔬 菜 Vegetables	果用瓜 Melon	#甜 瓜 Muskmelon	苜 蓿 Lucerne
998200	4298000	404491	628830	107934	13407	463275	4483153	19339200	6735761	2888796	2254500
105467	1166	1	8032	426	13	7422	507	583572	4960	88	28891
61699			330	298		32		110045	95		14581
145	10375		4824			4261	26400	37330	7552	500	9425
3728	32321		1694					252280	428186	310028	1440
	6892							159300	155400	71802	
	7159							36480	220455	195759	1440
3728	18270		1694					56500	52331	42467	
41507	52123		1461	709	74	666		131262	167961	154167	40334
487	51879		1119	374	74	659		67741	76661	62867	13307
40312	229		222	215		7		60241	3054	3054	26649
708	15		120	120				3280	88246	88246	378
255931	149907		133187	84	833	128841	441932	2122515	487708	68754	105732
3078	29886		55694			55534	104027	535720	397119	30537	13080
44946	1909		34405			34398	132923	366448	11668	3630	8755
7894	42741		18149	25		17917	97496	597388	49899	24581	40695
16373	75371		4529	10		4173	8312	75694	7262	8	26021
63191			8078	30		6577	89114	268965	5599	1566	3028
89255			6789			5551	10060	275576	4179	2192	5581
31194			5543	19	833	4691		2724	11982	6240	8572
219377	420817	200202	222026	23159	2857	175845	1099885	2297947	161906	48048	643149
73903	13258	13258	71041	20314	2133	39530	933747	756647	71202	4105	262858
3493			801	1		772	8214	192330	20756		3126
1500	10560	10560						460	600		446
14739	1	1	8322	261	50	8011	30472	123993	11909		12736
1914	592	592	11008		342	3114	135954	95851	21796	1505	82753
12954	2105	2105	10317			10317	317860	156054	8600	2600	
1800			6270			6270	119500	28700	4651		15477
17445			6741	937		4320	91806	25720	1474		33443
10552			18034	17004	310	720	85602	2498			367
1110			6507	513	240	5754	72535	87000	1250		85800
8396			3041	1598	1191	252	71804	44041	166		28710
25929	407559	186944	53658	2845	682	39030	151347	1541300	14763	4241	118057
900			754	732		22	24206	150561	1325	125	49742
10888	186251	186251	15091		496	14028	34777	714637	11218	4116	24084
			820	45	186	589	68244	75428			28841
9987	218139		14912	200		11991	17670	588591	2220		5926
312	693	693	1865	1865				1350			
3532			7816	3			6450	1457			9464
310	2476		12400			12400		9276			
119545			97327		42	97285	14791		75941	39702	262234
1945			20050		42	20008	13532		35022	34712	48769
4041			24302			24302			990	990	21356
8855			6452			6452			680		39680
35050			11883			11883	1259		33400	4000	56215
6567			25594			25594			5849		52655
60697			5043			5043					32365
2390			4003			4003					11194

Note:a) The region total output of grain is not equal to the sum of local and Production and Construction Groups.b) The region total data of grain refer to approvable data by NBS.

12-17 续表

单位：吨

地　区	Region	粮食作物 Grain Crops	谷物 Cereal	#水稻 Rice	#小麦 Wheat	#玉米 Corn	豆类 Soy-beans
博尔塔拉蒙古自治州	**Bortala Mongol Autonomous Prefecture**	**902565**	**902526**	**402**	**116346**	**785776**	**39**
博乐市	Bole [Bortala] City	413624	413607	402	31987	381216	17
精河县	Jinghe [Jing] County	89096	89096		33074	56022	
温泉县	Wenquan [Araxang] County	399845	399823		51285	348538	22
巴音郭楞蒙古自治州	**Bayangol Mongol Autonomous Prefecture**	**788621**	**788066**	**1468**	**379332**	**405832**	**555**
库尔勒市	Korla City	26315	26188	200	5098	20890	127
轮台县	Luntai [Bugur] County	133096	133096		77743	55353	
尉犁县	Yuli [Lopnur] County	6475	6475		1089	5386	
若羌县	Ruoqiang [Qarkilik] County	9803	9803		8182	1621	
且末县	Qiemo [Qarqan] County	88957	88716	12	54408	33449	241
焉耆回族自治县	Yanqi Hui Autonomous County	139900	139900	55	85864	53981	
和静县	Hejing County	170528	170341	15	54204	115556	187
和硕县	Hoxud County	136458	136458		67459	68978	
博湖县	Bohu [Bagrax] County	77089	77089	1186	25285	50618	
阿克苏地区	**Aksu Administrative Offices**	**2056790**	**2054328**	**162047**	**951423**	**936381**	**2462**
阿克苏市	Aksu City	115118	115118	19362	60029	35727	
温宿县	Wensu [Onsu] County	308169	307964	97418	119588	90699	205
库车县	Kuqa County	345357	344757		190969	153767	600
沙雅县	Xayar County	270792	270768		141380	129388	24
新和县	Xinhe [Toksu] County	148168	148168		102793	45375	
拜城县	Baicheng [Bay] County	458923	458045	5460	130101	318997	878
乌什县	Wushi [Uxturpan] County	219009	218258	39807	103962	73779	751
阿瓦提县	Awat County	157509	157505		84030	73475	4
柯坪县	Kalpin County	33745	33745		18571	15174	
克孜勒苏柯尔克孜自治州	**Kizilsu Kirgiz Autonomous Prefecture**	**351865**	**351490**	**5415**	**176031**	**168113**	**375**
阿图什市	Artux City	108399	108399	666	63816	43854	
阿克陶县	Akto County	218753	218753	4749	95706	118015	
阿合奇县	Akqi County	14771	14595		10765	2430	176
乌恰县	Wuqia [Ulugqat] County	9942	9743		5744	3814	199
喀什地区	**Kashgar [Kaxgar] Administrative Offices**	**2962980**	**2917148**	**35987**	**1448633**	**1425835**	**45832**
喀什市	Kashgar [Kaxgar] City	128650	128650	9524	65004	54122	
疏附县	Shufu County	266647	266647	2320	128050	136277	
疏勒县	Shule County	277810	277810	2527	140803	134480	
英吉沙县	Yengisar County	210314	209204		109687	99517	1110
泽普县	Zepu [Poskam] County	159243	142001	2199	79380	60422	17242
莎车县	Shache [Yarkant] County	571496	567694	13588	300873	253233	3802
叶城县	Yecheng [Kagilik] County	477923	454245	5829	179958	268458	23678
麦盖提县	Makit County	168431	168431		96075	72356	
岳普湖县	Yopurga County	127112	127112		63920	63192	
伽师县	Jiashi [Payzawat] County	322795	322795		163723	159072	
巴楚县	Bachu [Maralbexi] County	233626	233626		112201	121426	
塔什库尔干塔吉克自治县	Taxkorgan Tajik Autonomous County	18933	18933		8959	3280	
和田地区	**Hotan Administrative Offices**	**1122718**	**1122011**	**58362**	**533647**	**529516**	**707**
和田市	Hotan City	90579	90579	3888	46103	40588	
和田县	Hotan County	154181	154181	16491	89921	47769	
墨玉县	Moyu [Karakax] County	294830	294830	17830	148840	128160	
皮山县	Pishan [Guma] County	138401	138141		53540	84575	260
洛浦县	Lop County	160530	160516	60	76116	84317	14
策勒县	Qira County	107061	106628		44062	62298	433
于田县	Yutian [Keriya] County	161352	161352	20093	67242	73849	
民丰县	Minfeng [Niya] County	15784	15784		7823	7960	
生产建设兵团	**Xinjiang Production and Construction Group**	**2586631**	**2558708**	**192565**	**1205268**	**1128241**	**27923**

Continued

(ton)

薯类 Tubers	棉花 Cotton	#长绒棉 Longstaple Cotton	油料 Oil Bearing Crops	#油菜 Rapeseeds	#胡麻 Flax	#葵花 Helianthus	甜菜 Beetroots	蔬菜 Vegetables	果用瓜 Melon	#甜瓜 Muskmelon	苜蓿 Lucerne
1586	**164765**		**10011**			**8384**	**108968**	**77597**	**19059**	**6483**	**18098**
900	57675		116			116	20295	68449	4560	690	450
	107090		3465			2820	44900	8415	13692	5793	15281
686			6430			5448	43773	733	807		2367
19017	**438105**	**3890**	**10445**	**802**	**20**	**4384**	**443948**	**3327544**	**116301**	**73124**	**51694**
3240	171912		701	77	20	92	18900		11489	3050	30168
	75805						70000	27200	17452	15715	1696
	152027		4184				25520	7654	19486	8936	
	2649							5185	39597	38900	300
52	16691		769	8		548	1031	36627	5318	4358	12257
	956		1166	53		1113	135921	616771	1018	246	3000
12003	140		1349	484		850	86043	668175	5728	363	1001
3722	14035		885	180		390	26976	1139904	6467	928	2571
	3890	3890	1391			1391	79557	826028	9746	628	701
86575	**841753**	**168000**	**17338**	**12090**	**3419**	**1829**	**517420**	**985028**	**389096**	**105621**	**128134**
	120438	51400					154457	219948	75376	10095	12462
23942	80239	5400	1065	1019	46		27982	174252	44238	4103	22000
4468	186783	700	477	368	2	107	34458	90008	66900	29804	34510
4830	197738	18700	1884	1784		100	15226	34580	55082	26534	
1250	119728		140	140			18840	62890	36300	13500	24000
52085			8035	6176	1754	105	221907	110110	60114	4849	35162
	542		3300	1883	1417		38570	234213	18762	4752	
	123344	91200	1372	720	200	452	5980	49077	30847	11392	
	12941	600	1065			1065		9950	1477	592	
461	**18485**	**9253**	**606**	**227**	**308**	**58**		**45855**	**39713**	**22719**	
322	9253	9253	48	5	16	14		18618	11939	10994	
	9232		44			44		23014	27486	11725	
100			337	45	292			1105			
39			177	177				3118	288		
199902	**799841**		**14949**	**10574**	**389**	**3124**		**2475017**	**3132275**	**1362739**	**341374**
	10536							310935	72259	40499	2550
24000	14584		160		160			431766	447840	129600	
3792	64800							385991	512370	173290	28000
	27572		201	201				177540	225975	91275	16500
76500	23595		394		104	44		107623	91278	6900	14490
22680	144178		10377	10373	4			225780	437700	129300	27360
72930	26278		3577		121	2840		455088	89857	21524	121753
	88295							146547	195900	57300	33800
	78399		240			240		32800	168698	119400	34500
	176120							139240	577037	464337	12321
	144952							60667	313361	129314	48250
	532							1040			1850
14550	**55828**		**11027**	**5669**	**2857**	**1771**		**350808**	**160995**	**71438**	**247343**
	2092		362	14				49907	11129	6184	9112
9375	13441		621	621				35731	23358	12936	7055
177	15763		229	174	55			69500	38612	10580	55400
2597	10451		1215	664	3	533		29923	5465	2211	49968
225	1796		1556	158	1190	3		31480	22095	7050	38980
1276	3679		2265	24	1609	470		52561	26522	12016	28375
891	8594		4775	4010		765		77262	22788	9528	45840
9	12		4	4				4444	11026	10933	12613
285115	**1465007**	**23145**	**193230**	**54194**	**2637**	**126690**	**1844093**	**6820671**	**1620048**	**665087**	**705734**

12-18 各地、州、市、县(市)农作物单位面积产量

Output of Major Farm Products Per Hectare by Prefecture, Autonomous Prefecture, City and County

单位：公斤/公顷　　(2015 年)　　(kg / hectare)

地　区	Region	粮 食 Grain	#谷 物 Cereal	#小 麦 Wheat	#玉 米 Corn	棉 花 Cotton	油 料 Oil-Bearing Crops	甜 菜 Beetroots
总　计	**Total**	**6347**	**6454**	**5634**	**7330**	**1891**	**2880**	**73221**
乌鲁木齐市	**Urumqi City**	**7661**	**7737**	**5702**	**9394**	**2672**	**3133**	**64449**
#乌鲁木齐县	Urumqi County	3826	3822	4483	4046		1378	
克拉玛依市	**Karamay City**	**9250**	**9250**	**3000**	**9825**	**1875**	**2307**	**60000**
吐鲁番市	**Turpan City**	**4950**	**4991**	**3200**	**5457**	**1390**	**4442**	
高昌区	Gaochang District					1125		
鄯善县	Shanshan [piqan]County	4350	4388	3200	5098	1525		
托克逊县	Toksun County	5077	5117		9000	1470	4442	
哈密地区	**Hami [Kumul]Administrative Offices**	**5330**	**5339**	**5247**	**9153**	**1849**	**1027**	
哈密市	Hami [Kumul]City	6376	6373	5044	9143	1849	900	
巴里坤哈萨克自治县	Barkol KazakAutonomous County	5264	5265	5283	10956	1801	1960	
伊吾县	Yiwu [Araturuk]County	3356	3351	5100		1271	1800	
昌吉回族自治州	**Changji Hui Autonomous Prefecture**	**7394**	**7527**	**5937**	**10296**	**1867**	**3388**	**77149**
昌吉市	Changji City	8299	8348	6107	10045	1795	3569	77849
阜康市	Fukang City	6979	6993	6467	8334	4829	3295	83077
呼图壁县	Hutubi County	8826	8833	6077	10858	1645	3655	76732
玛纳斯县	Manas County	8118	8125	5714	8831	2023	3239	84759
奇台县	Qitai County	7181	7223	6268	10558		2952	70058
吉木萨尔县	Jimsar County	7804	7974	6006	11850		2786	66476
木垒哈萨克自治县	Mori Kazak Autonomous County	5496	5912	4847	11604		3210	
伊犁哈萨克自治州	**Ili Kazak Autonomous Prefecture**	**8645**	**8930**	**5435**	**12150**	**2114**	**2511**	**67422**
伊犁州直属县(市)	**Counties (Cities) Direct Under Ili Prefecture**	**7819**	**8258**	**5311**	**12223**	**1542**	**2712**	**67025**
伊宁市	Yining [Gulja]City	8651	9239	5481	11367		2328	72905
奎屯市	Kuytun City	5550	5550	4500	10800	1650		
伊宁县	Yining [Gulja]County	9720	10918	5979	12750	1500	2665	63749
察布查尔锡伯自治县	Qapqal Xibe Autonomous County	8193	8430	5624	10470	1230	6857	73275
霍城县	Huocheng [korgas]County	10190	10441	6690	13890	1228	3594	70658
巩留县	Gongliu [Tokkuzlara]County	6251	7313	3573	12150		3210	75000
新源县	Xinyuan [kunes]County	8186	8461	5684	12654		2238	60166
昭苏县	Zhaosu [mongolkure]County	4954	4954	4928	11250		1912	56275
特克斯县	Tekes County	6182	6192	5118	10739		2575	66750
尼勒克县	Nilka County	7265	7276	5846	12000		2299	56999
塔城地区	**Tacheng [Tarbagatai] Administrative Offices**	**9954**	**9967**	**5768**	**12567**	**2140**	**2168**	**73230**
塔城市	Tacheng [Qoqek] City	10222	10222	5646	12990		1844	70095
乌苏市	Usu City	10821	10842	6102	13849	2145	3003	75004
额敏县	Emin [Dorbiljin] County	9777	9777	6080	12149		1898	76109
沙湾县	Shawan County	10202	10298	6375	13245	2145	3597	65999
托里县	Toli County	8656	8656	4424	10605	1685	2849	
裕民县	Yumin [Qagantokay] County	9940	9940	5057	12528		757	69107
和布克赛尔蒙古自治县	Hoboksar Mongol Autonomous County	6882	6898	3450	11355	1650	3300	
阿勒泰地区	**Altay Administrative Offices**	**7290**	**7626**	**4966**	**9978**		**2597**	**46906**
阿勒泰市	Altay City	6983	7754	4695	9300		2755	46502
布尔津县	Burqin County	8173	8618	4650	9300		2698	
富蕴县	Fuyun [Koktokay] County	6818	7161	4942	10607		2259	
福海县	Fuhai [Burultokay] County	9120	9138	5054	11738		2226	51740
哈巴河县	Habahe [Kaba] County	6249	6814	4500	7950		2532	
青河县	Qinghe [Qinggil] County	5289	5343	5250	8777		2993	
吉木乃县	Jeminay County	5667	5667	5026	7673		3313	

注：个别县(市)油料等作物种植在边角地头，未计面积，故单产偏高。
Note: The oil-bearing crop planted at the edge or margin of fields in small number of counties (cities), whose area is not calculated, thus per-unit output is relatively higher.

12-18 续表 Continued

单位：公斤/公顷 (kg/ hectare)

地　区	Region	粮 食 Grain	#谷 物 Cereal	#小 麦 Wheat	#玉 米 Corn	棉 花 Cotton	油 料 Oil-Bearing Crops	甜 菜 Beet-roots
博尔塔拉蒙古自治州	**Bortala Mongol Autonomous Prefecture**	**11480**	**11482**	**5274**	**13908**	**2047**	**2766**	**47080**
博乐市	Bole [Bortala] City	12939	12941	6106	14292	1996	3480	67755
精河县	Jinghe [Jing] County	7775	7775	4899	11897	2076	2806	41832
温泉县	Wenquan [Araxang] County	11362	11364	5093	13878		2734	46485
巴音郭楞蒙古自治州	**Bayangol Mongol Autonomous Prefecture**	**7295**	**7306**	**6224**	**8766**	**1986**	**3200**	**87343**
库尔勒市	Korla City	4076	4097	4179	4066	2109	2122	82485
轮台县	Luntai [Bugur] County	5623	5623	5618	5628	2065		102080
尉犁县	Yuli [Lopnur] County	6193	6193	4246	6826	1950	10502	67501
若羌县	Ruoqiang [Qarkilik] County	4067	4067	4311	3162	1420		
且末县	Qiemo [Qarqan] County	6096	6118	6230	6108	1649	2111	30992
焉耆回族自治县	Yanqi Hui Autonomous County	7990	7990	6592	12063	1108	2495	94215
和静县	Hejing County	9302	9339	6795	11369	1443	1884	87823
和硕县	Hoxud County	8643	8643	6476	12852	1590	2667	63166
博湖县	Bohu [Bagrax] County	9284	9284	7059	11150	1473	2123	87702
阿克苏地区	**Aksu Administrative Offices**	**7571**	**7583**	**6494**	**8713**	**1755**	**2013**	**49976**
阿克苏市	Aksu City	7527	7527	6837	8096	1864		57150
温宿县	Wensu [Onsu] County	8130	8184	6301	9319	1833	1491	33000
库车县	Kuqa County	6621	6615	6427	6865	1821	1275	46988
沙雅县	Xayar County	6951	6952	6498	7525	1838	1472	14850
新和县	Xinhe [Toksu] County	6072	6072	6293	5625	1926	1875	18000
拜城县	Baicheng [Bay] County	9699	9731	6727	12288		1940	96000
乌什县	Wushi [Uxturpan] County	7950	7984	6418	10523	1098	2394	60900
阿瓦提县	Awat County	6803	6803	6755	6858	1355	3324	5682
柯坪县	Kalpin County	6815	6815	6246	7671	1768	4500	
克孜勒苏柯尔克孜自治州	**Kizilsu Kirgiz Autonomous Prefecture**	**6349**	**6354**	**6011**	**6823**	**1667**	**1388**	
阿图什市	Artux City	6141	6141	6018	6340	1761	1787	
阿克陶县	Akto County	6887	6887	6471	7223	1583	3300	
阿合奇县	Akqi County	3863	3861	4140	4050		1053	
乌恰县	Wuqia [Ulugqat] County	4549	4580	4444	4874		2313	
喀什地区	**Kashgar [Kaxgar] Administrative Offices**	**6495**	**6693**	**6155**	**7316**	**1663**	**2303**	
喀什市	Kashgar [Kaxgar] City	6049	6049	5925	5572	675		
疏附县	Shufu County	7026	7026	6312	7954	1505	2400	
疏勒县	Shule County	6921	6921	6360	7590	1275		
英吉沙县	Yengisar County	6558	6626	6323	6994	1526	3015	
泽普县	Zepu [Poskam] County	5623	6459	6234	6789	1650	4728	
莎车县	Shache [Yarkant] County	6475	6729	6656	6712	1719	2106	
叶城县	Yecheng [Kagilik] County	6593	7226	5873	8487	1585	3119	
麦盖提县	Makit County	5911	5911	5625	6340	1867		
岳普湖县	Yopurga County	6658	6658	6000	7488	1725	1200	
伽师县	Jiashi [Payzawat] County	6717	6717	6092	7510	1833		
巴楚县	Bachu [Maralbexi] County	6600	6600	5895	7419	1748		
塔什库尔干塔吉克自治县	Taxkorgan Tajik Autonomous County	4075	4075	3733	7569	1663		
和田地区	**Hotan Administrative Offices**	**6311**	**6318**	**5711**	**6963**	**1460**	**2596**	
和田市	Hotan City	6003	6003	5301	6843	1417	3327	
和田县	Hotan County	5764	5764	5627	5721	1390	1505	
墨玉县	Moyu [Karakax] County	6127	6127	5754	6408	1275	1227	
皮山县	Pishan [Guma] County	7138	7175	5696	8589	1763	2157	
洛浦县	Lop County	5995	5996	5709	6284	1305	1491	
策勒县	Qira County	7052	7099	5970	8260	1798	2271	
于田县	Yutian [Keriya] County	6675	6675	5881	7459	1602	5116	
民丰县	Minfeng [Niya] County	6516	6516	5809	7492	1125	2400	
生产建设兵团	**Xinjiang Production and Construction Group**	**8164**	**8281**	**6906**	**10020**	**2328**	**3363**	**87867**

12-19 各地、州、市、县(市)特色农作物播种面积

Sown Areas of Characteristic Farm Crops by Prefecture,Autonomous Prefecture , City and County

单位：千公顷 (2015 年) (1000 hectares)

地 区	Region	番 茄 Tomato	#工业用番 茄 Tomato in Industr	辣 椒 Peppers	#工业用辣 椒 Capsicum	打瓜籽 Melon Seeds	啤酒花 Hop
总 计	**Total**	**92.01**	**69.41**	**65.17**	**48.90**	**100.96**	**1.67**
乌鲁木齐市	**Urumqi City**	**0.60**	**0.03**	**1.01**		**0.02**	
乌鲁木齐县	Urumqi County	0.02		0.41			
克拉玛依市	**Karamay City**	**0.15**	**0.12**	**0.42**	**0.39**	**1.50**	
吐鲁番市	**Turpan City**	**0.77**		**0.42**		**0.07**	
高昌区	Gaochang District	0.35		0.28			
鄯善县	Shanshan [piqan]County	0.21		0.11			
托克逊县	Toksun County	0.21		0.03		0.07	
哈密地区	**Hami [Kumul]Administrative Offices**	**0.19**		**0.16**		**0.14**	
哈密市	Hami [Kumul]City	0.16		0.12		0.14	
巴里坤哈萨克自治县	Barkol KazakAutonomous County	0.03		0.04			
伊吾县	Yiwu [Araturuk]County						
昌吉回族自治州	**Changji Hui Autonomous Prefecture**	**12.96**	**11.51**	**2.42**	**1.11**	**22.60**	**0.15**
昌吉市	Changji City	4.42	4.35	0.19		2.19	0.11
阜康市	Fukang City	1.60	0.85	0.89	0.19	8.14	
呼图壁县	Hutubi County	3.72	3.72	0.54	0.45	3.47	
玛纳斯县	Manas County	0.70	0.67	0.05		1.85	
奇台县	Qitai County	0.85	0.36	0.60	0.47	3.11	
吉木萨尔县	Jimsar County	1.67	1.56	0.15		2.61	0.04
木垒哈萨克自治县	Mori Kazak Autonomous County					1.24	
伊犁哈萨克自治州	**Ili Kazak Autonomous Prefecture**	**10.54**	**8.45**	**6.89**	**5.41**	**50.28**	**0.12**
伊犁州直属县(市)	**Counties (Cities) Direct Under Ili Prefecture**	**1.36**	**0.18**	**1.29**	**0.21**	**0.41**	
伊宁市	Yining [Gulja]City	0.37		0.37		0.04	
奎屯市	Kuytun City	0.01		0.01			
伊宁县	Yining [Gulja]County	0.12		0.08			
察布查尔锡伯自治县	Qapqal Xibe Autonomous County	0.17	0.05	0.28	0.07	0.16	
霍城县	Huocheng [korgas]County	0.25	0.13	0.21	0.13	0.11	
巩留县	Gongliu [Tokkuzlara]County	0.13		0.15			
新源县	Xinyuan [kunes]County	0.04		0.05		0.09	
昭苏县	Zhaosu [mongolkure]County						
特克斯县	Tekes County	0.25		0.11			
尼勒克县	Nilka County	0.02		0.01			

12-19 续表 1 Continued

单位：千公顷 (1000 hectares)

地　区	Region	番　茄 Tomato	#工业用番　茄 Tomato in Industr	辣　椒 Peppers	#工业用辣　椒 Capsicum	打瓜籽 Melon Seeds	啤酒花 Hop
塔城地区	**Tacheng[Tarbagatai] Administrative Officess**	**9.05**	**8.27**	**5.48**	**5.20**	**14.73**	
塔城市	Tacheng [Qoqek] City	0.62		0.06		2.83	
乌苏市	Usu City	4.33	4.28	0.16	0.09	4.55	
额敏县	Emin [Dorbiljin] County	0.94	0.93	0.01		1.52	
沙湾县	Shawan County	3.16	3.06	4.25	4.11	3.27	
托里县	Toli County						
裕民县	Yumin [Qagantokay] County					0.58	
和布克赛尔蒙古自治县	Hoboksar Mongol Autonomous County			1.00	1.00	1.97	
阿勒泰地区	**Altay Administrative Offices**	**0.12**		**0.11**		**35.14**	**0.12**
阿勒泰市	Altay City	0.02		0.03		4.83	
布尔津县	Burqin County	0.01		0.01		5.08	0.12
富蕴县	Fuyun [Koktokay] County	0.01		0.01		2.00	
福海县	Fuhai [Burultokay] County	0.02		0.02		13.77	
哈巴河县	Habahe [Kaba] County	0.05		0.04		8.42	
青河县	Qinghe [Qinggil] County	0.01		0.01		0.58	
吉木乃县	Jeminay County					0.48	
博尔塔拉蒙古自治州	**Bortala Mongol Autonomous Prefecture**	**0.47**	**0.39**	**0.13**	**0.04**	**0.90**	
博乐市	Bole [Bortala] City	0.41	0.39	0.06	0.04	0.02	
精河县	Jinghe [Jing] County	0.06		0.06		0.88	
温泉县	Wenquan [Araxang] County						
巴音郭楞蒙古自治州	**Bayangol Mongol Autonomous Prefecture**	**15.71**	**14.92**	**24.10**	**23.05**	**2.50**	**0.04**
库尔勒市	Korla City	0.08		0.06		0.39	
轮台县	Luntai [Bugur] County	0.04		0.02			
尉犁县	Yuli [Lopnur] County	0.02		0.08	0.03	0.20	
若羌县	Ruoqiang [Qarkilik] County	0.02		0.02			
且末县	Qiemo [Qarqan] County	0.02		0.77	0.75	0.12	
焉耆回族自治县	Yanqi Hui Autonomous County	3.44	3.43	3.62	3.61	0.51	
和静县	Hejing County	2.87	2.83	8.26	8.07	0.52	
和硕县	Hoxud County	5.07	4.66	6.44	6.07	0.36	
博湖县	Bohu [Bagrax] County	4.15	4.00	4.84	4.52	0.40	0.04
阿克苏地区	**Aksu Administrative Offices**	**4.88**	**0.39**	**2.48**	**0.26**	**0.33**	**0.06**
阿克苏市	Aksu City	0.17		0.03			
温宿县	Wensu [Onsu] County	0.31		0.33	0.11	0.33	0.02
库车县	Kuqa County	0.67	0.01	0.34			

12-19 续表 2 Continued

单位：千公顷 (1000 hectares)

地　区	Region	番　茄 Tomato	#工业用番　茄 Tomato in Industr	辣　椒 Peppers	#工业用辣　椒 Capsicum	打瓜籽 Melon Seeds	啤酒花 Hop
沙雅县	Xayar County	0.22		0.97			
新和县	Xinhe [Toksu] County	0.24		0.18			
拜城县	Baicheng [Bay] County	0.66	0.38	0.43	0.15		
乌什县	Wushi [Uxturpan] County	2.44		0.07			
阿瓦提县	Awat County	0.16		0.13			
柯坪县	Kalpin County	0.01					
克孜勒苏柯尔克孜自治州	**Kizilsu Kirgiz Autonomous Prefecture**	**0.22**	**0.00**	**0.18**			
阿图什市	Artux City	0.05		0.02			
阿克陶县	Akto County	0.11		0.11			
阿合奇县	Akqi County	0.02		0.01			
乌恰县	Wuqia [Ulugqat] County	0.04		0.04			
喀什地区	**Kashgar [Kaxgar] Administrative Offices**	**6.37**	**0.07**	**4.04**	**0.41**		
喀什市	Kashgar [Kaxgar] City	0.47		0.14			
疏附县	Shufu County	1.29		1.15			
疏勒县	Shule County	0.61		0.41			
英吉沙县	Yengisar County	1.01		0.69			
泽普县	Zepu [Poskam] County	0.25		0.20			
莎车县	Shache [Yarkant] County	0.42	0.07	0.40	0.21		
叶城县	Yecheng [Kagilik] County	0.26		0.30			
麦盖提县	Makit County	0.25		0.13			
岳普湖县	Yopurga County	0.26		0.04			
伽师县	Jiashi [Payzawat] County	1.23		0.30			
巴楚县	Bachu [Maralbexi] County	0.31		0.29	0.20		
塔什库尔干塔吉克自治县	Taxkorgan Tajik Autonomous County						
和田地区	**Hotan Administrative Offices**	**0.85**		**0.38**			
和田市	Hotan City	0.09		0.05			
和田县	Hotan County	0.28		0.19			
墨玉县	Moyu [Karakax] County	0.11		0.04			
皮山县	Pishan [Guma] County	0.03		0.02			
洛浦县	Lop County	0.06		0.02			
策勒县	Qira County	0.03		0.03			
于田县	Yutian [Keriya] County	0.24		0.03			
民丰县	Minfeng [Niya] County	0.01					
生产建设兵团	**Xinjiang Production and Construction Group**	**38.31**	**33.54**	**22.55**	**18.24**	**22.61**	**1.29**

12-20 各地、州、市、县(市)特色农作物产量
Output of Characteristic Farm Crops by Prefecture,Autonomous Prefectura,City and County

单位：吨 (2015 年) (ton)

地区	Region	番茄 Tomato	#工业用番茄 Tomato for Industrial use	辣椒 Pepper	#工业用辣椒 Pepper For Industrial use	枸杞 Medlar	打瓜籽 Melon Seeds	啤酒花 Hop
总计	**Total**	**9108897**	**7613028**	**2645133**	**1980025**	**52022**	**212990**	**5933**
乌鲁木齐市	**Urumqi City**	**34795**	**2130**	**45393**			**27**	
#乌鲁木齐县	Urumqi County	1938		17323				
克拉玛依市	**Karamay City**	**9162**	**7805**	**9438**	**9407**	**50**	**4508**	
吐鲁番市	**Turpan City**	**32989**		**8635**				
高昌区	Gaochang District	17733		6144				
鄯善县	Shanshan [piqan]County	6600		1531				
托克逊县	Toksun County	8656		960				
哈密地区	**Hami [Kumul]Administrative Offices**	**10650**		**6819**		**67**	**424**	
哈密市	Hami [Kumul]City	9603		5594		58	424	
巴里坤哈萨克自治县	Barkol KazakAutonomous County	961		1176		9		
伊吾县	Yiwu [Araturuk]County	86		50				
昌吉回族自治州	**Changji Hui Autonomous Prefecture**	**1300232**	**1176300**	**83238**	**30866**	**3668**	**51163**	**1027**
昌吉市	Changji City	459943	452164	4505		113	5091	901
阜康市	Fukang City	165758	84634	32182	1872		16371	
呼图壁县	Hutubi County	365056	364714	20582	15994	250	9143	
玛纳斯县	Manas County	62337	61416	1185		885	3652	
奇台县	Qitai County	65651	42680	17622	13000	2400	6259	
吉木萨尔县	Jimsar County	181387	170692	7134			8067	126
木垒哈萨克自治县	Mori Kazak Autonomous County	100		28		20	2580	
伊犁哈萨克自治州	**Ili Kazak Autonomous Prefecture**	**1080974**	**930735**	**272114**	**183493**	**711**	**86785**	**264**
伊犁州直属县(市)	**Counties (Cities) Direct Under Ili Prefecture**	**100464**	**13760**	**76983**	**7725**	**58**	**965**	
伊宁市	Yining [Gulja]City	30970		28888			70	
奎屯市	Kuytun City	400		60				
伊宁县	Yining [Gulja]County	4526		2625		58		
察布查尔锡伯自治县	Qapqal Xibe Autonomous County	14900	4760	17876	3225		214	
霍城县	Huocheng [korgas]County	17760	9000	8800	4500		421	
巩留县	Gongliu [Tokkuzlara]County	9287		8103				
新源县	Xinyuan [kunes]County	3466		2140			254	
昭苏县	Zhaosu [mongolkure]County	241		90				
特克斯县	Tekes County	17850		7883				
尼勒克县	Nilka County	1064		518			6	

12-20 续表 1 Continued

单位：吨 (ton)

地　区	Region	番　茄 Tomato	#工业用番　茄 Tomato for Industrial use	辣　椒 Peppers	#工业用辣　椒 Pepper For Industrial use	枸　杞 Medlar	打瓜籽 Melon Seeds	啤酒花 Hop
塔城地区	**Tacheng[Tarbagatai] Administrative Officess**	**976796**	**916975**	**191297**	**175768**	**191**	**29433**	
塔城市	Tacheng [Qoqek] City	50881		1846			5093	
乌苏市	Usu City	505083	503893	10620	2620		10247	
额敏县	Emin [Dorbiljin] County	70485	69035	262			2307	
沙湾县	Shawan County	350047	344047	169782	164453	191	7358	
托里县	Toli County	100		20	20			
裕民县	Yumin [Qagantokay] County	105		93			585	
和布克赛尔蒙古自治县	Hoboksar Mongol Autonomous County	95		8675	8675		3843	
阿勒泰地区	**Altay Administrative Offices**	**3714**		**3834**		**462**	**56387**	**264**
阿勒泰市	Altay City	773		739			7244	
布尔津县	Burqin County	400		720			7613	264
富蕴县	Fuyun [Koktokay] County	548		150			4462	
福海县	Fuhai [Burultokay] County	417		476		462	23937	
哈巴河县	Habahe [Kaba] County	1130		1695			11360	
青河县	Qinghe [Qinggil] County	378		48			951	
吉木乃县	Jeminay County	68		6			820	
博尔塔拉蒙古自治州	**Bortala Mongol Autonomous Prefecture**	**48405**	**45348**	**5231**	**2133**	**20968**	**2275**	
博乐市	Bole [Bortala] City	46354	45228	3068	1958	7	67	
精河县	Jinghe [Jing] County	1908	120	2141	175	20940	2208	
温泉县	Wenquan [Araxang] County	143		22		21		
巴音郭楞蒙古自治州	**Bayangol Mongol Autonomous Prefecture**	**1656529**	**1578868**	**1043088**	**998211**	**1754**	**5501**	**554**
库尔勒市	Korla City	6080		3480		1330	708	
轮台县	Luntai [Bugur] County	2212		1052		170		
尉犁县	Yuli [Lopnur] County	1057		2144	960		301	
若羌县	Ruoqiang [Qarkilik] County	670.59		450				
且末县	Qiemo [Qarqan] County	784		27957	27704	165	188	
焉耆回族自治县	Yanqi Hui Autonomous County	363896	362769	204954	204298		1437	
和静县	Hejing County	321421	316930	249056	242234		941	
和硕县	Hoxud County	578366	530275	326901	307792	49	641	
博湖县	Bohu [Bagrax] County	382042	368894	227095	215223	40	1285	554
阿克苏地区	**Aksu Administrative Offices**	**289019**	**30379**	**43862**	**1914**	**2491**	**900**	**154**
阿克苏市	Aksu City	10905		845				
温宿县	Wensu [Onsu] County	10799		10370	964	813	900	54
库车县	Kuqa County	18216	270	8266				

12-20 续表 2 Continued

单位：吨 (ton)

地　区	Region	番　茄 Tomato	#工业用番　茄 Tomato for Industrial use	辣　椒 Peppers	#工业用辣　椒 Pepper For Industrial use	枸　杞 Medlar	打瓜籽 Melon Seeds	啤酒花 Hop
沙雅县	Xayar County	4279		6861				
新和县	Xinhe [Toksu] County	14604		6600				
拜城县	Baicheng [Bay] County	38980	30109	5750	950			100
乌什县	Wushi [Uxturpan] County	182970		1200				
阿瓦提县	Awat County	8176		3916		1678		
柯坪县	Kalpin County	90		54				
克孜勒苏柯尔克孜自治州	**Kizilsu Kirgiz Autonomous Prefecture**	**7698.8**		**4363.2**				
阿图什市	Artux City	3000		1043				
阿克陶县	Akto County	3168		2519				
阿合奇县	Akqi County	405		243				
乌恰县	Wuqia [Ulugqat] County	1126		558				
喀什地区	**Kashgar [Kaxgar] Administrative Offices**	**346045**	**1689**	**138932**	**12220**			
喀什市	Kashgar [Kaxgar] City	53045		6674				
疏附县	Shufu County	81666		25950				
疏勒县	Shule County	16961		12200				
英吉沙县	Yengisar County	53095		33990				
泽普县	Zepu [Poskam] County	10800		4467				
莎车县	Shache [Yarkant] County	9421	1689	12632	6820			
叶城县	Yecheng [Kagilik] County	24681		18930				
麦盖提县	Makit County	12801		6487				
岳普湖县	Yopurga County	9804		842				
伽师县	Jiashi [Payzawat] County	55315		9000				
巴楚县	Bachu [Maralbexi] County	18456		7760	5400			
塔什库尔干塔吉克自治县	Taxkorgan Tajik Autonomous County							
和田地区	**Hotan Administrative Offices**	**32237**		**8401**				
和田市	Hotan City	4564		1982				
和田县	Hotan County	6542		3615				
墨玉县	Moyu [Karakax] County	3690		560				
皮山县	Pishan [Guma] County	1037		255				
洛浦县	Lop County	2305		645				
策勒县	Qira County	1478		755				
于田县	Yutian [Keriya] County	12104		429				
民丰县	Minfeng [Niya] County	517		160				
生产建设兵团	**Xinjiang Production and Construction Group**	**4260161**	**3839774**	**975619**	**741781**	**22313**	**61407**	**3934**

12-21 各地、州、市水果及坚果种植面积

Planted Area of Fruits and Nutd by Prefecture, Autonomous Prefecture, City

单位:公顷 (2015 年) (hectare)

地　区	Region	水 果 Fruits	苹 果 Apples	梨 Pears	葡 萄 Grapes
总　计	**Total**	**971783**	**63572**	**70265**	**150249**
乌鲁木齐市	Urumqi City	944	308		191
克拉玛依市	Karamay City	57	18		24
吐鲁番市	Turpan City	46696		9	32943
哈密地区	Hami [Kumul] Administrative Offices	29744	90	44	3773
昌吉回族自治州	Changji Hui Autonomous Prefecture	19550	2579	17	10668
伊犁哈萨克自治州	Ili Kazak Autonomous Prefecture	63143	19063	43	9144
伊犁州直属县(市)	Counties (Cities) Direct Under Ili Prefecture	36781	15761	16	8219
塔城地区	Tacheng [Tarbagatai] Administrative Offices	8867	3295	27	925
阿勒泰地区	Altay Administrative Offices	17495	7		
博尔塔拉蒙古自治州	Bortala MongolAutonomous Prefecture	1623	138		273
巴音郭楞蒙古自治州	Bayangol Mongol Autonomous Prefecture	104884	322	38873	16995
阿克苏地区	Aksu Administrative Offices	168985	17887	11635	5114
克孜勒苏柯尔克孜自治州	Kizilsu Kirgiz Autonomous Prefecture	24480	293	18	6931
喀什地区	Kashgar [Kaxgar] Administrative Offices	217843	4483	1318	4537
和田地区	Hotan Administrative Offices	88819	899		10998
生产建设兵团	Xinjiang Production and Construction Group	205015	17492	18308	48658

地　区	Region	桃 Peaches	杏 Apricots	红 枣 Jujubes	坚 果 Nuts	核 桃 Walnut
总　计	**Total**	**12687**	**125033**	**495548**	**462654**	**351677**
乌鲁木齐市	Urumqi City	9	342	17	13	
克拉玛依市	Karamay City	4				
吐鲁番市	Turpan City	12	4219	9250	793	793
哈密地区	Hami [Kumul] Administrative Offices	17	2327	21906	202	202
昌吉回族自治州	Changji Hui Autonomous Prefecture	535	1329	541	5321	1
伊犁哈萨克自治州	Ili Kazak Autonomous Prefecture	2193	8061	711	15993	3835
伊犁州直属县(市)	Counties (Cities) Direct Under Ili Prefecture	1951	8011	444	9369	3835
塔城地区	Tacheng [Tarbagatai] Administrative Offices	242	50	267	6362	
阿勒泰地区	Altay Administrative Offices				262	
博尔塔拉蒙古自治州	Bortala Mongol Autonomous Prefecture				9121	
巴音郭楞蒙古自治州	Bayangol Mongol Autonomous Prefecture	330	4958	41708	4250	1572
阿克苏地区	Aksu Administrative Offices	85	21086	111256	110060	109704
克孜勒苏柯尔克孜自治州	Kizilsu Kirgiz Autonomous Prefecture	502	12382	2054	8240	7955
喀什地区	Kashgar [Kaxgar] Administrative Offices	4562	51368	143617	187281	106531
和田地区	Hotan Administrative Offices	1077	13541	54241	108985	108826
生产建设兵团	Xinjiang Production and Construction Group	3361	5420	110247	12395	12258

12-22 各地、州、市水果及坚果产量

Output of Fruits and Nutd by Prefecture, Autonomous Prefecture, City

单位：吨 (2015 年) (ton)

地区	Region	水果 Total	苹果 Apples	梨 Pears	葡萄 Grapes
总计	**Total**	**9614479**	**1151301**	**1139823**	**2755981**
乌鲁木齐市	Urumqi City	7100	888		3744
克拉玛依市	Karamay City	541	155		288
吐鲁番市	Turpan City	956851		99	923848
哈密地区	Hami [Kumul] Administrative Offices	123712	85		89629
昌吉回族自治州	Changji Hui Autonomous Prefecture	172218	9971	187	145995
伊犁哈萨克自治州	Ili Kazak Autonomous Prefecture	347865	130025	100	125564
伊犁州直属县(市)	Counties (Cities) Direct Under Ili Prefecture	285747	100028	100	116844
塔城地区	Tacheng [Tarbagatai] Administrative Offices	50163	29986		8720
阿勒泰地区	Altay Administrative Offices	11955	11		
博尔塔拉蒙古自治州	Bortala MongolAutonomous Prefecture	3904	559		3345
巴音郭楞蒙古自治州	Bayangol Mongol Autonomous Prefecture	619695	1798	374831	47690
阿克苏地区	Aksu Administrative Offices	1745249	416479	328639	138048
克孜勒苏柯尔克孜自治州	Kizilsu Kirgiz Autonomous Prefecture	184880	204	4	87242
喀什地区	Kashgar [Kaxgar] Administrative Offices	1464122	119546	15388	98103
和田地区	Hotan Administrative Offices	499235	5149		225279
生产建设兵团	Xinjiang Production and Construction Group	3489107	466442	420575	867206

地区	Region	桃 Peachs	杏 Apricots	红枣 Jujubes	坚果 Nuts	核桃 Walnut
总计	**Total**	**175789**	**1197823**	**3054270**	**731200**	**600844**
乌鲁木齐市	Urumqi City	270	368	306	10	
克拉玛依市	Karamay City	28				
吐鲁番市	Turpan City	299	15840	15733	370	370
哈密地区	Hami [Kumul] Administrative Offices		903	33095		
昌吉回族自治州	Changji Hui Autonomous Prefecture	3093	1739	1341	2049	
伊犁哈萨克自治州	Ili Kazak Autonomous Prefecture	31772	36341	1549	14031	489
伊犁州直属县(市)	Counties (Cities) Direct Under Ili Prefecture	28503	36030	614	3894	489
塔城地区	Tacheng [Tarbagatai] Administrative Offices	3269	311	935	10089	
阿勒泰地区	Altay Administrative Offices				48	
博尔塔拉蒙古自治州	Bortala MongolAutonomous Prefecture				20000	
巴音郭楞蒙古自治州	Bayangol Mongol Autonomous Prefecture	2351	32396	156215	904	144
阿克苏地区	Aksu Administrative Offices	806	253264	591915	206812	205871
克孜勒苏柯尔克孜自治州	Kizilsu Kirgiz Autonomous Prefecture	930	90174	2675	2662	2337
喀什地区	Kashgar [Kaxgar] Administrative Offices	60650	590822	536317	309494	216912
和田地区	Hotan Administrative Offices	7789	133518	96535	154420	154420
生产建设兵团	Xinjiang Production and Construction Group	67801	42458	1618589	20448	20301

12-23 主要年份牲畜饲养情况
Number of Livestock in Main Years

单位：万头(只) (10 000 heads)

年 份 Year	大牲畜年底头数 Large Animals (year-end)	牛 Cattle and Buffaloes	马 Horses	驴 Donkeys	骡 Mules	骆驼 Camels
1978	446.19	222.39	112.39	96.61	1.61	13.19
1980	482.55	250.65	106.89	108.88	1.72	14.41
1985	517.55	293.26	99.54	106.57	2.17	16.05
1990	575.88	338.22	104.58	112.96	2.69	17.43
1995	580.04	343.54	100.47	117.04	2.77	16.22
1996	589.41	349.78	101.16	119.36	2.76	16.34
1997	600.12	359.81	100.32	120.74	2.87	16.38
1998	606.79	364.29	100.26	123.45	2.80	15.99
1999	615.91	370.52	101.47	124.99	2.78	16.15
2000	632.93	384.98	102.57	125.94	2.74	16.70
2001	630.67	386.40	99.38	126.06	2.84	15.99
2002	654.46	414.13	99.71	122.22	2.59	15.81
2003	694.53	453.06	99.39	124.02	2.48	15.58
2004	716.56	482.30	95.78	120.82	2.36	15.30
2005	739.72	504.16	94.19	123.90	2.38	15.09
2006	736.33	502.86	92.09	124.94	2.14	14.30
2007	702.03	486.98	86.09	113.92	1.83	13.20
2008	543.41	336.00	83.85	109.25	1.45	12.86
2009	536.83	330.76	84.60	107.17	1.35	12.95
2010	536.82	330.47	85.29	106.96	1.19	12.91
2011	523.00	318.20	85.66	104.73	1.08	13.33
2012	565.77	365.93	86.84	97.97	1.06	13.97
2013	564.92	371.14	87.52	90.31	0.91	15.04
2014	575.88	383.85	89.42	85.71	0.92	15.98
2015	584.89	396.90	89.91	80.30	0.82	16.96

年 份 Year	猪年底头数 Hogs (year-end)	羊年底只数 Sheep and Goats (year-end)	山羊 Goats	绵羊 Sheep	牲畜出栏头数 Slanghtered Fattened Animals with in ayear	#猪 Hogs	#牛 Cattle and Buffaloes	#羊 Sheep and Goats
1978	103.25	1927.34	349.63	1577.91	460.41	50.75	18.75	382.76
1980	84.62	2105.43	388.89	1716.54	584.09	67.32	24.22	477.81
1985	66.58	2431.91	394.79	2037.12	836.39	49.07	42.33	723.51
1990	89.71	2830.81	449.43	2381.38	1242.89	78.93	70.10	1070.43
1995	135.26	3009.02	471.38	2537.64	1709.93	122.32	101.20	1448.72
1996	138.18	3136.21	498.10	2638.11	1859.28	153.75	116.25	1550.65
1997	145.73	3261.81	514.60	2747.21	2096.67	173.06	125.72	1753.88
1998	169.82	3447.38	528.05	2919.33	2222.27	197.39	140.82	1837.57
1999	188.34	3592.29	555.21	3037.08	2223.89	203.87	145.95	1820.71
2000	201.53	3690.21	586.70	3103.51	2455.99	224.46	154.53	2017.36
2001	208.23	3764.88	601.14	3163.74	2633.83	246.00	179.32	2147.31
2002	219.08	3908.23	626.42	3281.81	2878.39	259.05	188.65	2363.02
2003	227.71	4104.30	657.15	3447.15	3201.99	307.74	202.23	2626.94
2004	223.08	4266.73	669.47	3597.26	3437.59	352.83	220.80	2790.53
2005	238.38	4355.50	659.75	3695.75	3756.92	358.71	249.41	3081.88
2006	243.88	4359.50	654.26	3705.24	4063.52	390.82	278.69	3317.99
2007	237.90	4083.44	608.10	3475.34	4108.28	393.70	271.76	3361.99
2008	177.00	3025.70	453.85	2571.85	3388.09	265.50	207.30	2842.30
2009	180.42	3127.50	469.13	2658.37	3135.72	254.23	210.89	2604.48
2010	171.96	3013.37	528.73	2484.64	3498.52	262.72	216.69	2947.22
2011	254.00	3016.40	489.70	2526.70	3606.61	411.94	203.90	2913.83
2012	265.43	3502.05	525.31	2976.74	3737.30	427.60	222.26	3001.24
2013	274.72	3663.22	505.54	3157.68	3862.06	439.57	230.26	3107.49
2014	303.60	3883.98	506.38	3377.60	4129.92	475.50	239.39	3327.60
2015	294.49	3995.65	523.64	3472.01	4340.05	463.13	247.29	3444.06

注：牲畜出栏数 1999 年以后计算口径与 1998 年以前不同。

Note: The calculating norm of cattles out of stock after 1999 was different from that prior to that in 1998.

12-24 各地、州、市、县(市)牲畜年底头数

Number of Livestock at the Year-end by Prefecture, Autonomous Prefecture, City and County

单位：万头(只)　　(2015 年)　　(10 000 heads)

地　区	Region	合 计 Total	#牛 Cattle and Buffaloes	#马 Horses	#驴 Donkeys	#猪 Hogs	#山羊 Goats	#绵羊 Sheep
总　计	**Total**	**4875.05**	**396.90**	**89.91**	**80.30**	**294.49**	**523.64**	**3472.01**
乌鲁木齐市	**Urumqi City**	**77.73**	**8.94**	**1.83**	**0.19**	**8.70**	**15.81**	**41.81**
#乌鲁木齐县	Urumqi County	30.63	3.37	1.45	0.09	0.03	3.78	21.81
克拉玛依市	**Karamay City**	**15.34**	**0.82**	**0.07**		**8.67**	**0.98**	**4.70**
吐鲁番市	**Turpan City**	**95.80**	**4.31**	**0.40**	**1.84**	**2.42**	**12.31**	**74.11**
高昌区	Gaochang District	31.79	1.45	0.03	0.57	1.25	6.25	22.21
鄯善县	Shanshan [piqan]County	31.30	0.47	0.10	0.45	1.08	2.96	26.09
托克逊县	Toksun County	32.71	2.39	0.27	0.82	0.09	3.10	25.81
哈密地区	**Hami [Kumul]Administrative Offices**	**121.32**	**7.44**	**1.53**	**0.78**	**11.48**	**16.00**	**83.14**
哈密市	Hami [Kumul]City	46.03	2.51	0.41	0.31	2.89	7.14	32.49
巴里坤哈萨克自治县	Barkol KazakAutonomous County	56.83	2.86	0.95	0.42	4.24	5.69	42.15
伊吾县	Yiwu [Araturuk]County	18.46	2.07	0.17	0.05	4.35	3.17	8.50
昌吉回族自治州	**Changji Hui Autonomous Prefecture**	**443.22**	**50.83**	**4.78**	**0.70**	**58.45**	**44.09**	**282.19**
昌吉市	Changji City	91.79	12.79	0.76	0.05	21.87	9.28	46.65
阜康市	Fukang City	29.30	4.50	0.42	0.04	3.80	7.03	13.33
呼图壁县	Hutubi County	56.34	9.44	1.22	0.05	4.35	7.88	33.09
玛纳斯县	Manas County	54.38	4.92	0.24	0.05	8.98	1.77	38.20
奇台县	Qitai County	101.18	10.15	0.73		8.94	7.02	73.99
吉木萨尔县	Jimsar County	58.28	7.04	0.65	0.30	8.72	5.11	36.35
木垒哈萨克自治县	Mori Kazak Autonomous County	51.95	2.01	0.76	0.22	1.78	6.00	40.58
伊犁哈萨克自治州	**Ili Kazak Autonomous Prefecture**	**1480.25**	**234.07**	**62.25**	**2.48**	**60.13**	**118.99**	**993.26**
伊犁州直属县(市)	**Counties (Cities) Direct Under Ili Prefecture**	**668.88**	**133.83**	**40.28**	**2.11**	**34.75**	**23.05**	**434.17**
伊宁市	Yining [Gulja]City	23.46	4.26	0.41	0.19	2.40	1.13	15.04
奎屯市	Kuytun City	4.98	0.24	0.01		2.76	0.13	1.84
伊宁县	Yining [Gulja]County	98.22	20.07	3.01	0.37	12.26	6.43	55.96
察布查尔锡伯自治县	Qapqal Xibe Autonomous County	44.98	7.00	1.63	0.49	2.64	2.16	31.06
霍城县	Huocheng [korgas]County	73.75	13.94	1.94	0.56	6.03	2.05	49.08
巩留县	Gongliu [Tokkuzlara]County	61.20	13.05	3.80	0.37	2.95	2.61	38.38
新源县	Xinyuan [kunes]County	100.36	24.23	8.26	0.05	2.31	2.58	62.91
昭苏县	Zhaosu [mongolkure]County	95.78	16.82	9.65	0.01	1.26	1.20	66.81
特克斯县	Tekes County	73.70	14.58	5.30	0.03	0.74	2.46	50.56
尼勒克县	Nilka County	92.44	19.64	6.27	0.03	1.40	2.30	62.52
塔城地区	**Tacheng [Tarbagatai] Administrative Offices**	**501.33**	**45.88**	**11.09**	**0.32**	**23.88**	**61.76**	**354.89**
塔城市	Tacheng [Qoqek] City	94.36	8.63	2.34	0.05	2.75	3.02	76.98
乌苏市	Usu City	82.20	4.91	0.79	0.07	4.20	9.34	62.46
额敏县	Emin [Dorbiljin] County	73.39	6.44	1.31		1.96	10.70	52.78
沙湾县	Shawan County	72.26	9.08	1.36	0.02	14.28	7.73	39.42
托里县	Toli County	63.74	7.08	1.74	0.05	0.23	8.66	45.11
裕民县	Yumin [Qagantokay] County	63.48	6.24	2.21		0.37	8.96	45.06
和布克赛尔蒙古自治县	Hoboksar Mongol Autonomous County	51.90	3.50	1.34	0.13	0.09	13.35	33.08
阿勒泰地区	**Altay Administrative Offices**	**310.04**	**54.36**	**10.88**	**0.06**	**1.50**	**34.18**	**204.20**
阿勒泰市	Altay City	59.14	12.55	2.10		0.38	3.42	40.17
布尔津县	Burqin County	36.05	8.27	1.80		0.10	3.58	22.00
富蕴县	Fuyun [Koktokay] County	66.04	7.75	2.87	0.01	0.08	9.73	44.32
福海县	Fuhai [Burultokay] County	46.60	6.77	0.80		0.74	3.83	32.57
哈巴河县	Habahe [Kaba] County	41.22	11.43	1.40		0.11	5.11	22.83
青河县	Qinghe [Qinggil] County	37.47	5.17	1.10	0.05	0.04	6.50	24.28
吉木乃县	Jeminay County	23.52	2.42	0.81		0.05	2.01	18.03

注：1.全区总计不等于地方与生产建设兵团汇总数。2.全区总计和兵团数为国家统计局审定数，各地州数据来自畜牧部门。
Note:a)The region total data is not equal to the sum of local and Production and Construction Groups.b)The region total data refer to approvable data of NBS.

12-24 续表 Continued

单位：万头(只) (10 000 heads)

地　区	Region	合 计 Total	#牛 Cattle and Buffaloes	#马 Horses	#驴 Donkeys	#猪 Hogs	#山羊 Goats	#绵羊 Sheep
博尔塔拉蒙古自治州	**Bortala Mongol Autonomous Prefecture**	**125.80**	**8.41**	**1.54**	**0.20**	**5.84**	**12.98**	**96.50**
博乐市	Bole [Bortala] City	39.97	3.41	0.37	0.10	2.62	3.35	29.93
阿拉山口市	Alashankou City	0.06				0.02		0.03
精河县	Jinghe [Jing] County	41.16	2.00	0.40	0.05	1.74	6.78	30.16
温泉县	Wenquan [Araxang] County	44.61	3.01	0.77	0.05	1.45	2.86	36.38
巴音郭楞蒙古自治州	**Bayangol Mongol Autonomous Prefecture**	**405.69**	**17.24**	**3.58**	**1.70**	**40.59**	**74.45**	**267.38**
库尔勒市	Korla City	50.55	0.84	0.08	0.07	12.62	7.39	29.55
轮台县	Luntai [Bugur] County	41.36	1.14	0.03	0.45	1.88	10.11	27.73
尉犁县	Yuli [Lopnur] County	46.19	0.78	0.04	0.13	0.54	23.88	20.81
若羌县	Ruoqiang [Qarkilik] County	11.74	0.31	0.03	0.04	0.69	0.74	9.89
且末县	Qiemo [Qarqan] County	64.87	1.77	0.11	0.85	1.20	17.24	43.41
焉耆回族自治县	Yanqi Hui Autonomous County	32.25	1.96	0.15	0.11	2.75	0.57	26.71
和静县	Hejing County	107.23	8.41	2.41	0.02	5.43	8.32	82.55
和硕县	Hoxud County	29.39	1.27	0.45		5.09	5.67	16.63
博湖县	Bohu [Bagrax] County	22.11	0.76	0.28	0.03	10.39	0.53	10.09
阿克苏地区	**Aksu Administrative Offices**	**585.09**	**34.36**	**5.44**	**9.45**	**23.42**	**135.36**	**376.08**
阿克苏市	Aksu City	65.59	3.03	0.12	0.31	11.55	6.77	43.81
温宿县	Wensu [Onsu] County	75.25	3.92	1.64	1.92	2.94	14.30	50.44
库车县	Kuqa County	96.37	5.74	0.62	1.33	2.94	25.84	59.75
沙雅县	Xayar County	56.86	3.20	0.39	1.06	1.72	24.89	25.55
新和县	Xinhe [Toksu] County	29.45	2.82	0.47	0.91	0.22	1.48	23.54
拜城县	Baicheng [Bay] County	119.33	8.32	0.72	1.56	3.21	26.99	78.49
乌什县	Wushi [Uxturpan] County	71.44	5.62	1.23	1.87	0.20	20.22	42.10
阿瓦提县	Awat County	45.78	1.49	0.22	0.29	0.64	4.50	38.64
柯坪县	Kalpin County	25.02	0.22	0.04	0.20		10.37	13.76
克孜勒苏柯尔克孜自治州	**Kizilsu Kirgiz Autonomous Prefecture**	**170.40**	**16.40**	**1.60**	**2.15**	**0.36**	**32.30**	**116.90**
阿图什市	Artux City	49.72	3.82	0.35	0.80	0.20	12.30	32.00
阿克陶县	Akto County	54.34	10.40	0.16	1.01	0.16	7.27	35.14
阿合奇县	Akqi County	33.93	0.58	0.58	0.04		8.53	24.15
乌恰县	Wuqia [Ulugqat] County	32.41	1.60	0.51	0.30		4.20	25.61
喀什地区	**Kashgar [Kaxgar] Administrative Offices**	**881.33**	**89.79**	**1.72**	**46.23**	**18.26**	**47.31**	**677.42**
喀什市	Kashgar [Kaxgar] City	53.86	1.92	0.05	0.85	1.92	0.91	48.13
疏附县	Shufu County	81.60	9.20	0.05	2.85	1.77	3.15	64.52
疏勒县	Shule County	90.79	9.83	0.04	4.27	8.18	0.73	67.70
英吉沙县	Yengisar County	39.75	6.05	0.04	2.26	0.80	1.50	29.08
泽普县	Zepu [Poskam] County	41.01	5.90		2.35	1.28	1.39	30.09
莎车县	Shache [Yarkant] County	129.64	11.20	0.25	7.50	1.15	5.50	104.04
叶城县	Yecheng [Kagilik] County	125.57	16.80	0.30	6.90	0.79	6.67	93.98
麦盖提县	Makit County	67.28	7.20	0.19	2.41	0.79	5.82	50.86
岳普湖县	Yopurga County	40.60	5.30	0.15	8.12	0.21	3.60	23.20
伽师县	Jiashi [Payzawat] County	110.55	6.40	0.28	6.70	0.25	6.70	90.21
巴楚县	Bachu [Maralbexi] County	78.51	5.78	0.12	1.49	1.11	5.60	64.41
塔什库尔干塔吉克自治县	Taxkorgan Tajik Autonomous County	22.18	4.22	0.26	0.53	0.00	5.75	11.20
和田地区	**Hotan Administrative Offices**	**521.20**	**24.76**	**1.14**	**15.86**	**2.54**	**29.29**	**446.87**
和田市	Hotan City	33.71	1.54	0.03	0.32	1.53	0.74	29.52
和田县	Hotan County	82.92	5.76	0.13	3.49	0.31	2.99	70.16
墨玉县	Moyu [Karakax] County	124.67	8.96	0.19	3.87	0.19	2.39	109.00
皮山县	Pishan [Guma] County	53.48	1.02	0.15	2.27	0.15	3.32	46.50
洛浦县	Lop County	53.45	3.20	0.05	0.77	0.05	1.24	48.10
策勒县	Qira County	53.85	1.17	0.25	1.45	0.09	2.52	48.29
于田县	Yutian [Keriya] County	78.43	2.70	0.28	2.60	0.18	6.51	65.99
民丰县	Minfeng [Niya] County	40.69	0.41	0.07	1.09	0.04	9.59	29.30
生产建设兵团	**Xinjiang Production and Construction Group**	**766.90**	**46.80**	**3.00**	**1.03**	**147.40**	**53.40**	**519.30**

12-25 主要年份畜产品产量
Output of Livestock Products in Main Years

年 份 Year	肉类产量 (万吨) Output of Meat (10 000 tons)	#牛 Beef	#马 Horse Meat	#骆驼 Camels	#猪 Pork	#羊 Mutton	#禽兔肉 Poultry and Rabbit Meat
1978	9.65	1.85			2.48	5.32	
1980	12.70	2.20	0.60	0.05	3.29	6.48	
1985	18.37	4.23	0.86	0.15	3.09	9.97	
1990	30.46	7.08	1.18	0.18	4.93	15.75	1.22
1995	52.38	13.14	2.05	0.40	8.37	24.48	3.61
1996	60.31	15.18	2.24	0.38	10.43	26.93	4.82
1997	64.40	16.40	2.55	0.38	11.52	27.72	5.38
1998	75.19	19.19	2.82	0.47	13.60	32.49	6.16
1999	81.36	20.61	2.93	0.62	16.02	33.57	6.94
2000	90.00	22.24	3.57	0.63	17.18	37.50	7.76
2001	97.00	23.99	3.55	0.72	18.36	40.48	8.66
2002	105.44	25.90	3.65	0.68	19.70	43.06	10.38
2003	115.00	28.77	3.88	0.69	22.41	45.54	11.46
2004	128.13	30.42	4.34	0.70	24.58	52.65	13.27
2005	141.46	34.22	4.67	0.77	26.18	59.89	13.46
2006	158.21	39.25	4.80	0.90	28.78	66.99	14.92
2007	160.58	42.25	5.09	0.94	31.73	65.02	13.74
2008	114.74	32.40	4.29	0.95	22.30	45.40	7.89
2009	115.31	33.88	4.33	0.73	22.03	43.77	8.52
2010	121.74	35.47	4.67	0.78	23.05	46.95	8.71
2011	127.28	33.80	4.86	0.73	29.80	46.40	9.50
2012	134.23	36.16	4.96	0.80	30.15	48.01	10.54
2013	139.26	37.82	5.04	0.79	31.33	49.71	11.86
2014	149.10	39.16	5.58	0.87	33.86	53.61	13.33
2015	155.84	40.45	5.87	0.89	33.08	55.43	14.66

12-25 续表 Continued

年份 Year	羊毛 (万吨) Wool (10 000 tons)	#绵羊毛 Sheep Wool	山羊绒 (吨) Cashmere (ton)	牛奶 (万吨) Cow Milk (10 000 tons)	羊奶 (万吨) Sheep Milk (10 000 tons)	禽蛋 (万吨) Poultry Eggs (10 000 tons)
1978	3.08	3.00	324	4.50	0.75	
1980	3.31	3.21	263	5.84	1.44	
1985	7.07	3.91	325	16.43	3.27	4.29
1990	5.09	4.93	607	30.81	4.83	6.30
1995	5.66	5.45	716	45.21	4.60	9.51
1996	5.99	5.77	780	48.76	5.46	10.33
1997	6.25	6.01	813	54.18	4.60	12.16
1998	6.48	6.22	811	59.96	5.06	13.34
1999	6.76	6.50	849	64.81	5.62	16.68
2000	6.98	6.67	893	72.54	5.69	18.53
2001	7.30	6.99	973	81.09	6.76	20.37
2002	7.78	7.44	1034	94.87	5.84	22.64
2003	8.21	7.84	1143	113.00	6.21	23.62
2004	8.91	8.49	1228	133.32	6.41	24.99
2005	9.38	8.98	1258	152.22	5.62	24.99
2006	9.62	8.96	1263	179.81	5.60	25.80
2007	9.34	8.92	1265	196.23	5.54	28.37
2008	9.03	8.40	1157	137.40	4.96	28.92
2009	7.60	7.16	1261	120.88	4.27	23.20
2010	8.69	8.40	1324	128.60	4.22	24.35
2011	9.01	8.69	1261	130.50	3.41	25.60
2012	9.20	8.85	1225	132.21	4.11	25.89
2013	9.68	9.16	1227	134.99	4.20	28.17
2014	9.68	9.29	1200	147.53	3.17	30.52
2015	10.11	9.69	1218	155.77	2.79	32.64

12-26 各地、州、市、县(市)总产肉量
Total Output of Meat by Prefecture, Autonomous Prefecture, City and County

单位：吨 (2015 年) (ton)

地 区	Region	合 计 Total	#牛 Beef	#马 Horse	#骆 驼 Camels	#猪 Pork	#山 羊 Goats	#绵 羊 Sheep	#禽 肉 Poultry Meat	#兔肉 Rabbit Meat
总 计	**Total**	**1558360**	**404500**	**58700**	**8900**	**330800**	**55000**	**499300**	**142900**	**3633**
乌鲁木齐市	**Urumqi City**	**65336**	**19639**	**1387**	**185**	**19337**	**2549**	**15965**	**6166**	**98**
#乌鲁木齐县	Urumqi County	14368	4467	1256	166	32	910	6925	531	71
克拉玛依市	**Karamay City**	**11449**	**445**			**9619**	**103**	**969**	**313**	
吐鲁番市	**Turpan City**	**43372**	**9245**	**130**	**90**	**3295**	**2590**	**26655**	**1274**	**11**
高昌区	Gaochang District	22116	3490	20		1710	1150	15500	224	
鄯善县	Shanshan [piqan]County	12242	1850	72	40	1470	990	7020	740	
托克逊县	Toksun County	9014	3905	38	50	115	450	4135	310	11
哈密地区	**Hami [Kumul]Administrative Offices**	**65144**	**9420**	**765**	**543**	**20378**	**3817**	**26778**	**3231**	
哈密市	Hami [Kumul]City	32827	5800	100	100	6027	2200	15900	2600	
巴里坤哈萨克自治县	Barkol KazakAutonomous County	22432	2757	522	317	9535	536	8136	550	
伊吾县	Yiwu [Araturuk]County	9885	863	143	126	4816	1081	2742	81	
昌吉回族自治州	**Changji Hui Autonomous Prefecture**	**492934**	**81767**	**4150**	**2000**	**183129**	**10452**	**93989**	**116832**	**306**
昌吉市	Changji City	108588	20797	948	741	44692	3708	15791	21634	262
阜康市	Fukang City	57743	5376	669	238	17018	2148	10164	22115	1
呼图壁县	Hutubi County	79286	18812	1118	303	23660	897	12872	21544	26
玛纳斯县	Manas County	55650	7350	448	119	12825	408	15692	18797	3
奇台县	Qitai County	129952	15840	180	111	74696	1380	19795	17936	14
吉木萨尔县	Jimsar County	45266	10382	307	68	7828	1042	11855	13676	
木垒哈萨克自治县	Mori Kazak Autonomous County	16449	3210	480	420	2410	869	7820	1130	
伊犁哈萨克自治州	**Ili Kazak Autonomous Prefecture**	**593443**	**212250**	**43688**	**3394**	**111128**	**17580**	**157383**	**46668**	**195**
伊犁州直属县(市)	**Counties (Cities) Direct Under Ili Prefecture**	**321286**	**125726**	**31470**	**332**	**56284**	**3456**	**71758**	**31161**	**119**
伊宁市	Yining [Gulja]City	14834	5600	652	33	3580	174	2828	1889	
奎屯市	Kuytun City	5105	230			4095	6	374	399	
伊宁县	Yining [Gulja]County	62586	27986	1943	96	15492	758	9556	6525	
察布查尔锡伯自治县	Qapqal Xibe Autonomous County	18250	6846	930		3780	387	4080	1764	50
霍城县	Huocheng [korgas]County	46104	11610	3075		12402	397	8563	9960	13
巩留县	Gongliu [Tokkuzlara]County	36835	13740	3674	34	6432	427	6600	5760	40
新源县	Xinyuan [kunes]County	46661	20890	7205	6	3532	450	12415	2141	15
昭苏县	Zhaosu [mongolkure]County	31399	13498	5622	19	2285	173	9679	119	
特克斯县	Tekes County	20331	9058	1848	16	1288	319	7057	736	1
尼勒克县	Nilka County	39181	16268	6521	128	3398	365	10606	1868	

注：同 12-24 表。
Note:The same applies to 12-24 table following.

12-26 续表 1 Continued

单位：吨 (ton)

地　区	Region	合计 Total	#牛 Beef	#马 Horse	#骆驼 Camels	#猪 Pork	#山羊 Goats	#绵羊 Sheep	#禽肉 Poultry Meat	#兔肉 Rabbit Meat
塔城地区	**Tacheng [Tarbagatai] Administrative Officess**	**191032**	**50673**	**8776**	**1209**	**50041**	**9699**	**57732**	**12669**	**65**
塔城市	Tacheng [Qoqek] City	21052	5715	1242	40	3913	464	8416	1207	19
乌苏市	Usu City	39572	9000	1935	342	13408	3088	9947	1727	26
额敏县	Emin [Dorbiljin] County	27526	6690	1136	250	6477	1836	10531	605	
沙湾县	Shawan County	58415	14846	1190	196	24608	751	8298	8498	20
托里县	Toli County	18214	6599	1518	165	757	1529	7488	134	
裕民县	Yumin [Qagantokay] County	12639	3653	915	18	648	411	6554	440	
和布克赛尔蒙古自治县	Hoboksar Mongol Autonomous County	13614	4170	840	198	230	1620	6498	58	
阿勒泰地区	**Altay Administrative Offices**	**81125**	**35851**	**3442**	**1853**	**4803**	**4425**	**27893**	**2838**	**11**
阿勒泰市	Altay City	20050	10398	1136	1008	1322	458	5454	262	4
布尔津县	Burqin County	10832	4907	269	89	735	522	3410	900	
富蕴县	Fuyun [Koktokay] County	13668	4890	687	440	175	1085	6228	160	
福海县	Fuhai [Burultokay] County	13220	5150	144	77	2295	784	4367	402	1
哈巴河县	Habahe [Kaba] County	12449	7370	592	77	179	600	3156	470	6
青河县	Qinghe [Qinggil] County	5767	1629	320	90	43	668	2487	531	
吉木乃县	Jeminay County	5139	1507	293	72	54	308	2791	113	
博尔塔拉蒙古自治州	**Bortala Mongol Autonomous Prefecture**	**25200**	**4172**	**387**	**63**	**7399**	**1177**	**9931**	**2013**	**27**
博乐市	Bole [Bortala] City	11613	2064	125	40	4477	271	3373	1254	1
阿拉山口市	Alashankou City	178	27			60		61	30	
精河县	Jinghe [Jing] County	6377	553	63	1	1492	669	3046	536	7
温泉县	Wenquan [Araxang] County	7032	1528	199	22	1370	237	3451	193	19
巴音郭楞蒙古自治州	**Bayangol Mongol Autonomous Prefecture**	**111298**	**13791**	**1266**	**706**	**35799**	**7773**	**35194**	**15381**	**175**
库尔勒市	Korla City	25210	1145	4		9484	702	6103	7627	40
轮台县	Luntai [Bugur] County	10386	793	21	2	2943	1895	3222	1150	3
尉犁县	Yuli [Lopnur] County	6733	802	8		660	2036	2080	1110	12
若羌县	Ruoqiang [Qarkilik] County	2312	132	11		834	73	962	225	13
且末县	Qiemo [Qarqan] County	12585	2158	119	251	2002	2100	5140	185	65
焉耆回族自治县	Yanqi Hui Autonomous County	12006	2612	116		2815	70	4821	1458	28
和静县	Hejing County	25811	5039	629	103	8634	746	10127	511	11
和硕县	Hoxud County	7850	633	333	346	2737	71	1888	1842	
博湖县	Bohu [Bagrax] County	8405	477	25	4	5690	80	851	1272	3
阿克苏地区	**Aksu Administrative Offices**	**242262**	**49940**	**3162**	**708**	**32874**	**19088**	**60688**	**71910**	**103**
阿克苏市	Aksu City	59316	11435	50		17217	1806	9869	18515	90
温宿县	Wensu [Onsu] County	26187	3610	744	72	1743	1910	7180	10584	
库车县	Kuqa County	55407	15658	961	18	5008	5480	18004	8829	

12-26 续表 2 Continued

单位：吨 (ton)

地　区	Region	合 计 Total	#牛 Beef	#马 Horse	#骆 驼 Camels	#猪 Pork	#山 羊 Goats	#绵 羊 Sheep	#禽 肉 Poultry Meat	#兔 肉 Rabbit Meat
沙雅县	Xayar County	15929	2890	174		2508	2603	2897	4483	12
新和县	Xinhe [Toksu] County	9369	2604	196		251	185	2390	3466	
拜城县	Baicheng [Bay] County	29149	5655	310	15	4945	2254	8821	6845	
乌什县	Wushi [Uxturpan] County	22484	5460	660	252	486	2988	5352	6790	
阿瓦提县	Awat County	21036	2413	39		715	1084	4838	11876	
柯坪县	Kalpin County	3384	215	29	351		778	1337	522	
克孜勒苏柯尔克孜自治州	**Kizilsu Kirgiz Autonomous Prefecture**	**40611**	**11708**	**1041**	**584**	**1254**	**3301**	**17771**	**4177**	**48**
阿图什市	Artux City	15293	2537	85	72	1058	1561	7354	2417	48
阿克陶县	Akto County	15110	6831	75	75	196	844	5247	1541	
阿合奇县	Akqi County	4353	672	300	98		526	2595	120	
乌恰县	Wuqia [Ulugqat] County	5855	1668	581	339		370	2575	99	
喀什地区	**Kashgar [Kaxgar] Administrative Offices**	**427100**	**91640**	**547**	**55**	**34649**	**4600**	**183425**	**105365**	
喀什市	Kashgar [Kaxgar] City	39270	10200			6400	155	19745	2770	
疏附县	Shufu County	37958	10728	25	10	5814	333	15865	4758	
疏勒县	Shule County	44409	11140			6937	77	16969	8026	
英吉沙县	Yengisar County	14174	6825	20	10	328	100	4160	2231	
泽普县	Zepu [Poskam] County	29403	3378			6775	130	8349	10773	
莎车县	Shache [Yarkant] County	64630	8580	60		2050	490	31950	20840	
叶城县	Yecheng [Kagilik] County	59717	12408	120	30	2125	587	22584	20129	
麦盖提县	Makit County	27755	5378	96		1972	550	13154	6256	
岳普湖县	Yopurga County	17684	4000			298	250	6612	5499	
伽师县	Jiashi [Payzawat] County	49505	6475	140		352	590	26663	15035	
巴楚县	Bachu [Maralbexi] County	36355	8862	80		1598	527	15635	9048	
塔什库尔干塔吉克自治县	Taxkorgan Tajik Autonomous County	6238	3668	6	5		811	1739		
和田地区	**Hotan Administrative Offices**	**144995**	**22344**	**563**	**477**	**2179**	**3096**	**62384**	**47442**	**82**
和田市	Hotan City	13928	2013	17	23	1477	67	5675	4590	
和田县	Hotan County	18469	4222	110	113	157	215	6435	5879	3
墨玉县	Moyu [Karakax] County	38638	8241	82	44	294	264	14222	12942	15
皮山县	Pishan [Guma] County	16118	832	42	40	29	295	7230	7153	23
洛浦县	Lop County	15479	3726	29	54	14	168	6277	4614	3
策勒县	Qira County	15204	1058	62	53	113	375	8818	4128	2
于田县	Yutian [Keriya] County	20225	2040	165	17	90	929	10260	6009	35
民丰县	Minfeng [Niya] County	6935	212	56	133	5	783	3467	2126	1
生产建设兵团	**Xinjiang Production and Construction Group**	**386044**	**53000**	**1806**	**99**	**180000**	**8000**	**89000**	**51400**	**2275**

12-27 水产品产量和养殖面积
Output of Aquatic Products and Cultured Area

年份 Year	地区 Region	水产品产量 (吨) Total Output of Aquatic Products (ton)	#养殖产量 Cultured Output	养殖面积 (公顷) Culture Area (hectare)
1985		8958	3403	32775
1990		23217	15401	68838
1995		44432	35341	72538
1996		47890	38876	79006
1997		52366	42656	75895
1998		53391	44557	67473
1999		55840	48068	70524
2000		60065	50974	69806
2001		60876	50902	63340
2002		63906	55159	62629
2003		67278	57244	67374
2004		73296	60405	74996
2005		79320	65571	76037
2006		84539	71440	76606
2007		88879	78639	77590
2008		92587	82040	73909
2009		97037	87863	73433
2010		101063	90913	73289
2011		116916	103315	74000
2012		125283	112590	71108
2013		131704	118551	70707
2014		144007	130881	72407
2015		151361	140567	72690
乌鲁木齐市	Urumqi City	6850	6850	955
克拉玛依市	Karamay City	660	408	330
吐鲁番市	Turpan City	426	426	44
哈密地区	Hami [Kumul] Administrative Offices	1153	1151	855
昌吉回族自治州	Changji Hui Autonomous Prefecture	19640	19640	3333
伊犁哈萨克自治州	Ili Kazak Autonomous Prefecture	30588	26602	16764
伊犁州直属县(市)	Counties (Cities) Direct Under Ili Prefecture	16598	16422	1458
塔城地区	Tacheng [Tarbagatai] Administrative Offices	3975	3182	2183
阿勒泰地区	Altay Administrative Offices	10015	6988	13123
博尔塔拉蒙古自治州	Bortala Mongol Autonomous Prefecture	1113	796	1030
巴音郭楞蒙古自治州	Bayangol Mongol Autonomous Prefecture	9416	4576	2355
阿克苏地区	Aksu Administrative Offices	18908	18362	1456
克孜勒苏柯尔克孜自治州	Kizilsu Kirgiz Autonomous Prefecture	645	645	120
喀什地区	Kashgar [Kaxgar] Administrative Offices	13248	12961	12039
和田地区	Hotan Administrative Offices	2597	2465	498
生产建设兵团	Xinjiang Production and Construction Group	46117	45694	32911

12-28 乡镇企业主要指标
Main Indicators of Township Enterprises

单位：万元 (10 000 yuan)

年 份 Year	地 区 Region	企业个数 (个) Number of Enterprises (unit)	从业人数 (人) Employees of Enterprises (person)	总产值 Total Output Value
	1985	98826	367753	75179
	1990	144281	464027	222218
	1991	145762	472332	314765
	1992	155711	498132	402139
	1993	202274	600687	553616
	1994	250037	686425	924082
	1995	281130	745291	1319217
	1996	282733	781784	1622442
	1997	43548	355585	1219032
	1998	269048	712490	2457410
	1999	297147	749205	2736766
	2000	316524	806368	3022076
	2001	334694	824499	3316049
	2002	307963	866661	3629499
	2003	354640	880874	4119555
	2004	368553	933473	4562898
	2005	366883	954411	4994156
	2006	368724	990365	5574730
	2007	377385	1037023	4265895
	2008	378343	1063023	8629234
	2009	378983	1115703	8486719
	2010	383653	1167548	9574341
	2011	391680	1219552	12067084
	2012	398340	1271549	14102422
	2013	402951	1328364	16589649
	2014	407579	1356460	19006874
	2015	414418	1376471	21632012
乌鲁木齐市	Urumqi City	18618	49742	1773156
克拉玛依市	Karamay City	4	38	36
石河子市	Shihezi City	3492	23396	294032
吐鲁番市	Turpan City	21933	52667	508847
哈密地区	Hami [Kumul] Administrative Offices	10625	18230	362066
昌吉回族自治州	Changji Hui Autonomous Prefecture	42168	164734	5827377
伊犁州直属县(市)	Counties (Cities) Direct Under Ili Prefecture	53544	180046	2846545
塔城地区	Tacheng [Tarbagatai] Administrative Offices	32125	132189	2505412
阿勒泰地区	Altay Administrative Offices	23848	62108	585696
博尔塔拉蒙古自治州	Bortala Mongol Autonomous Prefecture	9549	38411	607227
巴音郭楞蒙古自治州	Bayangol Mongol Autonomous Prefecture	26349	147082	3637764
阿克苏地区	Aksu Administrative Offices	51407	156114	910399
克孜勒苏柯尔克孜自治州	Kizilsu Kirgiz Autonomous Prefecture	9609	24720	141021
喀什地区	Kashgar [Kaxgar] Administrative Offices	66910	180944	1164647
和田地区	Hotan Administrative Offices	44237	146050	467787

12-28 续表 Continued

单位：万元 (10 000 yuan)

年 份 Year	地 区 Region	营业收入 Business Income	利润总额 Total Profits	上缴税金 Total Taxes
	1985	105072	9357	3136
	1990	249906	8614	5206
	1991	299890	25974	13747
	1992	374810	34644	16976
	1993	584089	51880	27354
	1994	957701	75439	69494
	1995	1493924	110656	76479
	1996	1927425	136410	76479
	1997	1128271	43337	48945
	1998	2455629	156578	82365
	1999	2742029	164949	93490
	2000	3071497	191764	100444
	2001	3377589	211439	108864
	2002	3739524	225723	126732
	2003	4276322	264661	137880
	2004	4757808	304998	152243
	2005	5164593	294021	164604
	2006	5806803	332070	190833
	2007	6776709	318943	228386
	2008	7548573	563293	249122
	2009	8547580	671806	271759
	2010	9596967	756277	306105
	2011	12287481	937847	374096
	2012	14250102	1083776	420174
	2013	16522535	1215432	474829
	2014	18960834	1317944	552596
	2015	21000117	1608243	776980
乌鲁木齐市	Urumqi City	1698137	76884	39618
克拉玛依市	Karamay City	271	20	27
石河子市	Shihezi City	292055	8054	3315
吐鲁番市	Turpan City	510415	51176	21801
哈密地区	Hami [Kumul] Administrative Offices	329708	23121	13511
昌吉回族自治州	Changji Hui Autonomous Prefecture	5284063	339403	118242
伊犁州直属县(市)	Counties (Cities) Direct Under Ili Prefecture	2958979	214850	52920
塔城地区	Tacheng [Tarbagatai] Administrative Offices	2266469	238545	60151
阿勒泰地区	Altay Administrative Offices	656436	55312	19817
博尔塔拉蒙古自治州	Bortala Mongol Autonomous Prefecture	603222	14084	10306
巴音郭楞蒙古自治州	Bayangol Mongol Autonomous Prefecture	3798447	368757	365193
阿克苏地区	Aksu Administrative Offices	983144	66919	30160
克孜勒苏柯尔克孜自治州	Kizilsu Kirgiz Autonomous Prefecture	135423	9343	4776
喀什地区	Kashgar [Kaxgar] Administrative Offices	1038628	90591	20932
和田地区	Hotan Administrative Offices	444720	51184	16211

主要统计指标解释

农林牧渔业总产值 指以货币表现的农、林、牧、渔业全部产品和对农林牧渔业生产活动进行的各种支持性服务活动的价值总量，它反映一定时期内农林牧渔业生产总规模和总成果。1957年以前的农林牧渔业总产值中包括了厩肥和农民自给性手工业(如农民自制衣服、鞋、袜，自己从事粮食初步加工等)。1958年及以后，林业中增加了村及村以下竹木采伐产值；牧业中取消了厩肥产值；副业中取消了农民自给性手工业产值，增加了村及村以下办的工业产值；渔业中增加了海洋捕捞水产品产值。1980年及以后，在副业中增加了农民家庭兼营工业商品部分的产值。从1984年起村及村以下工业产值划归工业。从1993年起取消副业，将野生动物的捕猎划入牧业，野生植物采集和农民家庭兼营商品性工业划归农业。从2003年起，执行新的国民经济行业分类标准，农林牧渔业总产值中包括了农林牧渔服务业产值。林业中增加了森林采运业产值。农业中取消了家庭兼营商品性工业产值，将野生林产品的采集划归林业。

农林牧渔业总产值的计算方法通常是按农、林、牧、渔业产品及其副产品的产量分别乘以各自单位产品价格求得；少数生产周期较长，当年没有产品或产品产量不易统计的，则采用间接方法匡算其产值；然后将四业产品产值及农林牧渔服务业产值相加即为农林牧渔业总产值。

粮食产量 指农业生产经营者日历年度内生产的全部粮食数量。按收获季节包括夏收粮食、早稻和秋收粮食，按作物品种包括谷物、薯类和豆类。其产量计算方法：谷物按脱粒后的原粮计算，豆类按去豆荚后的干豆计算；薯类(包括甘薯和马铃薯，不包括芋头和木薯)1963年以前按每4公斤鲜薯折1公斤粮食计算，从1964年开始改为按5公斤鲜薯折1公斤粮食计算。城市郊区作为蔬菜的薯类(如马铃薯等)按鲜品计算，并且不作粮食统计。1989年以前全国粮食产量数据主要靠全面报表取得，1989年开始使用抽样调查数据。

棉花产量 指全社会的产量。包括春播棉和夏播棉。产量按皮棉计算。不包括木棉。

油料产量 指全部油料作物的生产量。包括花生、油菜籽、芝麻、向日葵籽、胡麻籽(亚麻籽)和其他油料。不包括大豆、木本油料和野生油料。花生以带壳干花生计算。

水产品产量 指渔业（捕捞和养殖）生产活动的最终有效成果，包括全部海水和淡水鱼类、甲壳类（虾、蟹）、贝类、头足类、藻类和其他类渔业产品的最终产量。水产品产量是通过各级水产和统计部门逐级上报取得数据。1995 年及以前，贝类中牡蛎按鲜肉计算；蚶、蛤、蛙按 5 斤鲜品折 1 斤计算。1996 年以后则统一按鲜品计算。

猪、牛、羊肉产量 指当年出栏并已屠宰、除去头蹄下水后带骨肉(即胴体重)的重量。包括全社会范围内的产量。1996年以前为全面统计并逐级上报数据。1999年以后，国家统计局在部分地区开展了猪、牛、羊、禽等主要畜禽品种的抽样调查，并用抽样数据作为国家定案数据使用。2008年，建立了主要畜禽监测调查制度，猪、牛、羊、禽等主要畜禽数据均以抽样调查数为法定数据。

期初(末)畜禽存栏头(只)数 指报告期初(末)农村各种合作经济组织和国营农场、农民个人、机关、团体、学校、工矿企业、部队等单位以及城镇居民饲养的大牲畜、猪、羊、家禽等畜禽的存栏数。数据上报方式及数据调整情况同猪、牛、羊肉产量。

农作物播种面积 指农业生产经营者应在日历年度内收获农作物在全部土地（耕地或非耕地）上的播种或移植面积。凡是本年内收获的农作物，无论是本年还是上年播种，都算为播种面积，但不包括本年播种，下年收获的农作物面积。

有效灌溉面积 指具有一定的水源，地块比较平整，灌溉工程或设备已经配套，在一般年景下能够进行正常灌溉的耕地面积。在一般情况下，有效灌溉面积应等于灌溉工程或设备已经配套，能够进行正常灌溉的水田和水浇地面积之和。它是反映我国农田水利建设的重要指标。

农用化肥施用量 指本年内实际用于农业生产的化肥数量，包括氮肥、磷肥、钾肥和复合肥。化肥施用量要求按折纯量计算数量。折纯量是指把氮肥、磷肥、钾肥分别按含氮、含五氧化二磷、含氧化钾的百分之百成份进行折算后的数量。复合肥按其所含主要成分折算。公式为:

折纯量= 实物量×某种化肥有效成份含量的百分比

农业机械总动力 指全部农业机械动力的额定功率之和。农业机械是指用于种植业、畜牧业、渔业、农产品初加工、农用运输和农田基本建设等活动的机械及设备。农机总动力按使用能源不同分为以下四部分：

柴油发动机动力：指全部柴油发动机额定功率之和；

汽油发动机动力：指全部汽油发动机额定功率之和；

电动机动力：指全部电动机（含潜水电泵的电动机）额定功率之和；

其他机械动力：指采用柴油、汽油、电力之外的其他能源，如水力、风力、煤炭、太阳能等动力机械功率之和。

这个指标的统计数据主要来源于农机部门。

Explanatory Notes on Main Statistical Indicators

Gross Output Value of Agriculture, Forestry, Animal Husbandry and Fishery refers to the total value of products of agriculture, forestry, animal husbandry and fishery, and total value of services in support of agriculture, forestry, animal husbandry and fishery activities. It reflects the total scale and results of agricultural production during a given period. Prior to 1957, China's gross agricultural output value included barnyard manure and handicraft products for self-consumption (clothes, shoes, stockings, and initial grain processing undertaken by peasants). Since 1958, cutting and felling of bamboo and trees by villages and other cooperative organizations under villages have been included in forestry; value of barnyard manure has been excluded from animal husbandry; self consumed handicrafts have not been included from sideline occupations, while the output value of industries run by villages and cooperative organizations under village has been included in sideline occupations; and the output value of fish catches by motor fishing boats has been added to fishery. Since 1980, the value of handicraft products made for sale by individuals in households has been added to sideline occupations. Since 1984, industries run by villages and under villages have been included in the sector of industry. Since 1993, the subdivision of sideline occupations has been cancelled, and the hunting of wild animals has been classified into animal husbandry, and the gathering of wild plants and commodity industry run by rural household have been included in farming. A new industrial classification of economic activities was introduced in 2003. Under the new classification, value of services to agriculture, forestry, animal husbandry and fishery is included in the gross output value of agriculture, value of wood felling and transport is included in forestry, value of industrial output by rural households is not included in agriculture.

Gross output value of agriculture is obtained by multiplying the output of each product or by-product by its price, resulting in the output value of each single item. For a small number of products, annual output of which is not available or difficult to get due to the long production (growing) process involved, the output value is estimated through an indirect approach. The sum of output values of all products of agriculture, forestry, animal husbandry and fishery and services in support to those industries is then equal to the gross output value of agriculture.

Grain Output refers to the total output of grains produced by agricultural producers within a calendar year. It includes summer grain, early rice and autumn grain if classified by harvest seasons; it covers cereal, tubers and beans if classified by type of crops. Output of cereal should be limited to husked grain only. Output of beans refers to dry beans without pods. The output of tubers (sweet potatoes and potatoes, not including taros and cassava) are converted into that of grain at the ratio 4:1, i.e. 4 kilograms of fresh tubers were equivalent to 1 kilogram of grain up to 1963. Since 1964 the ratio for conversion has been 5:1. Tubers supplied as vegetables (such as potatoes) in cities and suburbs are calculated as fresh vegetables and their output is not included in the output of grain. Data on grain production before 1989 were obtained through the Comprehensive Statistical Reporting System. Since 1989, data from sample surveys are used.

Cotton Output refers to cotton production in the whole country including cotton planted in spring and in autumn. Output is measured as the weight of ginned cotton. Ceiba is not included.

Output of Oil-bearing Crops refers to the total production of oil-bearing crops of various kinds, including peanuts (dry, in shell), rapeseeds, sesame, sunflower seeds, flax seeds, and other oil-bearing crops. Soybeans, oil-bearing woody plants, and wild oil-bearing crops are not included.

Output of Aquatic Products refers to final output actually yielded from fishing production (fishery and breeding), including all output of marine and freshwater fish, crustaceans (shrimps, crabs), shellfish, cephalopod, seaweed and other fishery products. Data on output of aquatic products are reported by aquatic product and statistical agencies level by level. Before 1995, among the shellfish, oyster was counted as fresh meat; 5 kilograms of ark shell, clams and frogs are equivalent to 1 kilogram of fresh aquatic products; they have all been counted as fresh aquatic products since 1996.

Output of Pork, Beef, and Mutton refers to the meat of slaughtered hogs, cattle, sheep and goats with head, feet, and offal taken away. Data refers to the production of the whole country. Before 1996, it was a comprehensive reporting from the lower level to the upper one. The First Agricultural Census of China in 1996 revealed some discrepancy between the production of animal products from the annual reports and that from the census. Efforts were made to adjust the output value of animal husbandry to make the figures from the annual reports consistent with the census data. Since 1999, the NBS conducted sample surveys for the major animal husbandry products, such as hogs, cattle, sheep and goats and fowls, and the data from sample surveys are used as national finalized data. In 2008, A Monitoring and Survey Program was set up on main livestock, the data on the main livestock such as hog, cattle, sheep and poultry became the official data based on the sampling survey.

Number of Livestock or Poultry in Stock at Beginning (or End) of Period refers to the total number of large animals, pigs, sheep, fowls, etc. raised by rural cooperative organizations, State farms, rural individuals, government agencies, schools, industrial and mining enterprises, army, and urban residents at the beginning (or end) of the reference period. Data reporting system and data adjustment are the same as that in the output of pork, beef and mutton.

Sown Area of Crops refers to area of all land (cultivated or non-cultivated area) sown or transplanted with crops that are harvested within the calendar year by agricultural producers. All crops harvested within the year are counted as sown area, regardless of being sown in this year or the previous year. Crops sown this year but will be harvested in the coming year are excluded.

Effective Irrigated Area refers to area of land that are effectively irrigated, i.e. relatively level land, where there are water sources or complete sets of irrigation facilities to lift and move adequate water for irrigation purpose under normal conditions. Under normal situations, irrigated area is the sum of watered fields and irrigated fields where irrigation systems or equipment have been installed for regular irrigation purpose. It is an important indicator to reflect the farmland water conservancy construction in China.

Consumption of Chemical Fertilizers in Agriculture refers to the quantity of chemical fertilizers applied in agriculture in the year, including nitrogenous fertilizer, phosphate fertilizer, potash fertilizer, and compound fertilizer. The consumption of chemical fertilizers is calculated in terms of volume of effective components by means of converting the gross weight of the respective fertilizers into weight containing effective component (e.g. nitrogen content in nitrogenous fertilizer, phosphorous pentoxide contents in phosphate fertilizer, and potassium oxide contents in potash fertilizer). Compound fertilizer is converted in regard to its major components. The formula is:

Volume of effective component= physical quantity× effective component of certain chemical fertilizer (%)

Total Power of Agricultural Machinery refers to the total rated capacity of all agricultural machinery. Agricultural machinery refers to the machineries and equipments which are used for activities of planting, animal husbandry, fishery, primary processing of agricultural products, agricultural transport and infrastructure construction of farmland. Total power of agricultural machinery is grouped into four parts according to the energy used:

Diesel engine power refers to the total rated capacity of all diesel engines.

Gasoline engine power refers to the total rated capacity of all gasoline engines.

Motor power refers to the total rated capacity of all motors (include submersible pump motors).

Other mechanical powers refer to the total mechanical capacity of the sources of energy besides diesel, gasoline and motor power, such as hydro power, wind power, coal and solar energy.

Data are mainly from agricultural machinery agencies.

13 工业

INDUSTRY

第十三篇　工业

本篇主要内容和资料来源

本篇资料反映了新疆工业的基本情况，主要包括：按登记注册类型、轻重工业、企业规模、工业行业大类等分组的主要经济指标，指标包括：单位数、工业总产值、工业增加值、资产总计、负债合计、主营业务收入、主营业务成本、主营业务税金及附加、利润总额、应交增值税、总资产贡献率、资产负债率、成本费用利润率、全员劳动生产率、主要工业产品产量等。

本章还包括国有控股工业企业、大中型工业企业的主要经济指标，按工业行业大类、轻重工业、企业规模等主要分组的数据。

规模以上工业企业的统计范围。1998年至2006年为全部国有和年主营业务收入500万元及以上的非国有工业企业；2007至2010年为年主营业务收入500万元及以上的工业企业（即规模以上工业企业）；从2011年开始，为年主营业务收入2000万元及以上的工业企业（即规模以上工业企业）。

本篇资料从2011年年报起，工业行业分类按2011年《国民经济行业分类标准》划分；企业规模划分按2011年《统计上大中小微型企业划分办法》标准执行，增加了微型企业分组。

本篇资料由新疆维吾尔自治区统计局工业交通统计处根据工业统计年度报表中有关资料整理提供。

Industry

Main Content and Source of Data

Data in this chapter reflect the basic condition of industrial sector including the gross industrial output and indices of industrial enterprises; Main indicator on economic and economic benefit of industrial enterprises above designated size by status of registration, light & heavy industries, size of enterprises, industrial sector. Main indicators including number of enterprises, gross industrial output value, value added of industry, total assets, total liabilities, revenue from principal business, cost of principle business, taxes and other charges on principal business, total profits, value added tax payable, ratio of total assets to industrial output value, assets liability ration, ratio of profits to cost, output of major industrial products, main economic indicator of state-owned and non-state-owned industrial enterprises.

This chapter covers main indicators on economic and economic benefit of all state-owned and non-state-owned industrial enterprises, cooperative enterprises, industrial enterprises with funds from Hong Kong, Macao and Taiwan, foreign funded industrial enterprises, and large & medium-sized enterprises.

Industrial enterprises above designated size refers to all State-owned industrial enterprises and non-State-owned industrial enterprises with revenue from principal business over 5 million yuan from 1998 to 2006. For 2007 to 2010, the scopes of industrial statistics were all industrial enterprises with revenue from principal business over 5 million yuan, (or the industrial enterprises above designated size). Since 2011, the scope is adjusted to all industrial enterprises with revenue from principal business above 20 million yuan (i.e. industrial enterprises above designated size).

Industrial sectors since 2011 in this chapter has been categorized in accordance with the 2011 Industrial Classification of the National Economy and the sizes of industrial enterprises have been categorized in accordance with the 2011 Interim Regulations on Statistical Categorization of Large, Medium , Small and Micro Industrial Enterprises. Micro industrial enterprises are added.

Data in this chapter are collected and compiled by the Department of Industry and transport, XBS in accordance with the annual report of industrial statistics.

13-1 主要年份工业总产值
Gross Industrial Output Value in Main Years

单位:亿元 (100 million yuan)

年　份 Year	工业总产值 Gross Industrial Output Value	国有工业 State-owned Enterprises	集体工业 Collective-owned Enterprises	其它经济类型工业 Enterprises of Other Types of Ownership
1978	33.91	30.22	3.69	
1980	40.71	36.20	4.50	0.01
1985	86.78	73.18	11.93	1.67
1990	219.92	176.52	36.72	6.68
1995	593.43	461.31	89.24	42.88
2000	1061.29	258.93	72.78	729.58
2005	2358.83	236.18	17.29	2105.36
2006	2894.88	272.06	16.14	2606.68
2007	3471.51	358.28	17.29	3095.94
2008	4639.02	387.53	15.70	4235.79
2009	4184.50	404.01	15.61	3764.88
2010	5766.51	382.00	25.54	5358.97
2011	7105.31	654.79	29.44	6421.08
2012	7886.25	713.43	20.41	7152.41
2013	9121.22	589.70	13.62	8517.89
2014	9877.27	593.66	9.73	9273.88
2015	8668.64	604.63	7.40	8056.61

13-2 主要年份工业总产值指数
Indices of Gross Industrial Output Value in Main Years

(1978 年=100)

年　份 Year	工业总产值 Gross Industrial Output Value	国有工业 State-owned Enterprises	集体工业 Collective-owned Enterprises	其它经济类型工业 Enterprises of Other Types of Ownership
1978	100.0	100.0	100.0	
1980	117.7	118.0	113.2	(1981 年=100)
1985	220.6	199.5	428.2	851.7
1990	380.3	326.0	915.9	2096.1
1995	670.8	506.1	2104.5	7441.5
2000	1000.4	227.3	1763.6	66265.2
2005	1821.8	218.2	388.9	160072.4
2006	2057.1	246.3	344.8	180922.4
2007	2322.8	319.9	339.3	201240.8
2008	2707.5	336.5	272.4	237624.5
2009	2942.2	353.4	289.2	259031.4
2010	3331.8	325.7	431.9	298801.3
2011	3721.3	527.1	451.7	323156.5
2012	4271.9	576.4	328.3	373388.6
2013	5152.3	479.2	234.6	464817.2
2014	5798.9	501.4	174.1	525989.1
2015	6183.9	620.5	160.9	555223.4

13-3 规模以上工业企业分行业工业增加值

Value-added of Industrial Enterprises above Designated Size by Sector

单位: 万元 (10000 yuan)

行　业	Sector	2014	2015
总　计	**Total**	**31512920.7**	**26626977.7**
煤炭开采和洗选业	Mining and Washing of Coal	1462461.4	1315528.7
石油和天然气开采业	Extraction of Petroleum and Natural Gas	11652310.5	6101049.1
黑色金属矿采选业	Mining and Processing of Ferrous Metals Ores	526373.6	273963.9
有色金属矿采选业	Mining and Processing of Nonferrous Metals Ores	387650.6	323622.9
非金属矿采选业	Mining and Processing of Nonmetal Ores	89206.9	97264.2
开采辅助活动	Support Activities for Mining	1000534.3	899124.2
农副食品加工业	Processing of Food from Agricultural Products	828999.8	956824.4
食品制造业	Manufacture of Foods	575651.1	606051.0
酒、饮料和精制茶制造业	Manufacture of Liquor,Beverages and Refined Tea	419875.0	476574.5
烟草制品业	Manufacture of Tobacco	325723.8	363547.2
纺织业	Manufacture of Textile	266473.7	323973.9
纺织服装、服饰业	Manufacture of Textile, Wearing Apparel and Accessories	15776.2	59538.1
皮革、毛皮、羽毛(绒)及其制品业	Manufacturie of Leather, Fur, Feather and Related Products	22038.7	8692.9
木材加工及木、竹、藤、棕、草制品业	Processing of Timber, Manufachure of Wood, Bamboo, Cane, Grass Products	21571.0	28433.6
家具制造业	Manufacture of Furniture	3891.2	8619.6
造纸及纸制品业	Manufacture of Paper and Paper Products	80218.8	93101.0
印刷业和记录媒介的复制	Printing and Reproduction of Recording Media	21858.4	21117.8
文教、工美、体育和娱乐用品制造业	Manufacture of Articles for Culture,Education,Arts and Crafts, Sports and Entertainment	10747.8	12967.5
石油加工、炼焦及核燃料加工业	Oil Processing of Petroleum, Coking and Processing of Nuclear Fuel	3776084.1	5014482.9

13-3 续表 Continued

单位: 万元 (10000 yuan)

行　业	Sector	2014	2015
化学原料及化学制品制造业	Manufacture of Raw Chemical Materials and Chemical Products	1968075.1	1807557.0
医药制造业	Manufacture of Medicines	83748.0	80787.2
化学纤维制造业	Manufacture of Chemical Fibers	184988.7	140327.2
橡胶和塑料制品业	Manufacture of Rubber and Plastics Products	251813.8	257547.7
非金属矿物制品业	Manufacture of Non-metallic Mineral Products	1120701.6	1052275.0
黑色金属冶炼及压延加工业	Smelting and Pressing of Ferrous Metals	498421.8	-143056.1
有色金属冶炼及压延加工业	Smelting and Pressing of Non-ferrous Metals	1524944.3	1508559.4
金属制品业	Manufacture of Metal Products	135628.2	177245.6
通用设备制造业	Manufacture of General Purpose Machinery	44302.2	42049.8
专用设备制造业	Manufacture of Special Purpose Machinery	118411.2	99779.4
汽车制造业	Manufacture of Automobile	-13486.7	-11177.4
铁路、船舶、航空航天和其他运输设备制造业	Manufacture of Rail Way,Ship,Aerospace and Other Transport Equipments	1259.1	2633.9
电气机械及器材制造业	Manufacture of Electrical Machinery and Apparatus	665487.1	953450.4
计算机、通信和其他电子设备制造业	Manufalture of Computers, Communication and Other Electronic Equipment	3717.0	1042.7
仪器仪表制造业	Manufacture of Measuring Instruments and Machinery	2878.6	2472.3
废弃资源综合利用业	Utilization of Waste Resources	24135.2	16725.7
金属制品、机械和设备修理业	Repair Service of Metal Products, Machinery and Eguipment	13384.3	14654.8
电力、热力生产和供应业	Production and Supply of Electric Power and Heat Power	3186374.7	3369367.6
燃气生产和供应业	Production and Supply of Gas	154824.5	180980.3
水的生产和供应业	Production and Supply of Water	55865.1	89277.6

13-4 规模以上工业企业主要经济指标

单位：万元 (2015 年)

项　　目	Item	企业单位数(个) Number of Enterprises (unit)	#亏损企业 Loss- Suffering Enterprises	工业总产值(当年价格) Gross Industrial Output Value (At Current Prices)
总　　计	**Total**	**2707**	**818**	**81325512.3**
按登记注册类型分	**By Status of Registration**			
内资企业	Domestic Funded Enterprises	2626	794	79446116.4
国有企业	State-owned Enterprises	61	20	5517056.3
#中央企业	Central Enterprises	20	4	4755374.2
地方企业	Local Enterprises	41	16	761682.1
#自治区属企业	Autonomous	11	5	326009.2
地区(州、市)属企业	Prefecture or City	7	4	107697.9
县(市)属企业	County or City	21	7	163939.4
集体企业	Collective-owned Enterprises	8	3	56489.9
#自治区属企业	Autonomous	3	1	33147.1
地区(州、市)属企业	Prefecture or City			
县(市)属企业	County or City	3		15994.6
镇属企业	Town	1	1	4546.6
乡属企业	Village			
股份合作企业	Cooperative Enterprises	1	1	17044.2
联营企业	Joint Ownership Enterprises	1		2844.6
#国有联营企业	State Joint Ownership Enterprises			
集体联营企业	Collective Joint Ownership Enterprises			
国有与集体联营企业	Joint State-collective Enterprises			
其他联营企业	Other Joint Ownership Enterprises	1		2844.6
有限责任公司	Limited Liability Corporations	1343	462	33145371.9
#国有独资公司	State Sole funded Corporations	138	46	4681758.0
其他有限责任公司	Other Limited Liability Corporations	1205	416	28463613.9
股份有限公司	Share-holding Corporations Ltd.	122	37	24460316.7
私营企业	Private Enterprises	1069	271	16105716.9
#私营独资企业	Private-funded Enterprises	14	2	132312.0
私营合伙企业	Private Partnership Enterprises	5	1	51431.3
私营有限责任公司	Private Limited Liability Corporations	998	254	13516048.1
私营股份有限公司	Private Share-holding Corporations Ltd.	52	14	2405925.5
港、澳、台商投资企业	Enterprises with Funds from Hong Kong, Macao and Taiwan	32	10	546817.9
外商投资企业	Foreign Funded Enterprises	49	14	1332578.0
在总计中：国有控股企业	Of the Total : State-owned and State-holding Enterprises	746	251	44006335.9
在总计中：农村工业	Of the Total : Rural Industry	4	2	27811.5
按轻、重工业分	**Grouped by Light & Heavy Industry**			
轻工业	Light Industry	864	196	13118375.1
以农产品为原料	Using Farm Produces as Raw Materials	797	182	12485459.8
以非农产品为原料	Using Non-Farm Produces as Raw Materials	67	14	632915.3
重工业	Heavy Industry	1843	622	68207137.2
采掘工业	Mining and Quarrying	300	131	15078465.3
原料工业	Raw Material Industry	770	303	38785350.3
加工工业	Manufacturing Industry	773	188	14343321.6
按企业规模分	**Grouped by Size of Enterprises (New Standard)**			
大型企业	Large Enterprises	88	39	45918432.3
中型企业	Medium-sized Enterprises	315	101	11495022.1
小型企业	Small Enterprises	1964	553	22190429.4
微型企业	Min Enterprises	340	125	1721628.5

Main Economic Indicators of Industrial Enterprises above Designated Size

(10 000 yuan)

工业增加值 Value-added of Industry	工业销售产值(当年价格) Sales Value of Industry Products (At Current Prices)	出口交货值 Delivery Value of Industry Export	实收资本 Total Capital Hold	资产合计 Total Assets	流动资产合计 Total Current Assets	#产成品 Finished Product	固定资产原价 Net Value of Fixed Assets
26626977.7	**79446617.0**	**629658.0**	**49672884.1**	**181641554.7**	**53470170.3**	**4795336.3**	**143877186.1**
26154234.5	77597080.3	592813.0	48740805.7	178861528.5	52498051.3	4692760.4	141943000.2
1496565.0	5505230.4	528.2	1116317.1	9400142.4	1507565.5	71188.6	10190832.3
1195901.5	4761119.5		476985.0	6215178.8	516924.8	21370.8	7641284.6
300663.4	744110.9	528.2	639332.1	3184963.6	990640.7	49817.8	2549547.7
178267.9	313912.5		336107.4	1055075.0	210758.9	16135.2	1061012.0
19798.7	137705.7	528.2	61421.7	1092310.8	542248.4	4435.7	648209.6
74394.1	159960.8		217072.1	724644.9	150298.5	4705.5	634586.9
17169.6	55953.8		8241.7	59990.9	42314.3	5301.9	23292.6
5917.0	33739.9		2367.2	31584.0	23283.8	3552.7	9018.3
7914.1	14761.5		5654.5	20538.6	15926.1	1458.7	7795.1
2985.4	4546.6		195.0	7039.0	2384.8		6320.1
6627.7	13969.1		20000.0	139647.8	54855.6	4237.0	91571.0
1171.7	2493.8		136.6	1809.8	826.3	265.1	1762.5
1171.7	2493.8		136.6	1809.8	826.3	265.1	1762.5
9525320.1	32065782.6	330372.8	20451259.5	88007240.0	25139798.7	2505557.4	56091623.8
2005246.2	4613660.1	5981.2	4339873.8	14419845.3	4386984.1	221100.6	9320429.2
7520073.9	27452122.5	324391.6	16111385.7	73587394.7	20752814.6	2284456.8	46771194.6
11288831.1	24105639.5	124517.2	22430313.8	55240595.4	13853617.4	915351.1	63817158.5
3773216.3	15708349.5	137394.8	4698536.8	25890075.1	11831572.8	1189302.1	11683019.5
80796.2	130763.9		20748.0	153442.1	87939.8	16543.4	89958.5
31005.6	49698.0		3713.2	15195.7	8819.4	3867.8	9235.5
3174004.7	12959696.9	91904.1	4154781.7	20622825.1	8871050.5	1110306.7	10930812.5
487409.8	2568190.7	45490.7	519293.9	5098612.2	2863763.1	58584.2	653013.0
152859.6	542849.3	17082.5	364454.1	999926.2	351307.7	56101.9	589898.9
319883.6	1306687.4	19762.5	567624.3	1780100.0	620811.3	46474.0	1344287.0
18040796.6	43276341.0	191886.8	36267532.9	109457461.5	23929635.0	2133728.0	108764124.8
1772.5	25770.1		4500.0	25130.3	17632.2	1782.9	4967.4
3289930.1	12569510.0	463483.9	5072799.7	18037500.6	8177662.2	1419674.0	9267688.3
3102549.4	11949313.7	451841.0	4078167.1	14881265.5	7279449.2	1372198.9	7713867.9
187380.7	620196.3	11642.9	994632.6	3156235.1	898213.0	47475.1	1553820.4
23337047.6	66877107.0	166174.1	44600084.4	163604054.1	45292508.1	3375662.3	134609497.8
9010553.1	14643408.4	4491.6	20214475.4	45098980.3	9527126.4	714947.9	56086384.5
11056018.6	38133539.5	85435.7	18797621.3	88682235.3	21440314.1	1921989.6	67663576.5
3270475.9	14100159.1	76246.8	5587987.7	29822838.5	14325067.6	738724.8	10859536.8
16919708.2	45499261.3	322549.8	30823717.5	98359550.0	25692483.6	1370456.8	94297376.6
3559819.1	10975866.6	76017.2	6973990.7	32457279.4	10284160.2	1287675.1	19094954.3
5668057.8	21297563.3	218269.4	10251013.1	42467805.5	15213366.5	1957721.6	25441212.1
479392.6	1673925.8	12821.6	1624162.8	8356919.8	2280160.0	179482.8	5043643.1

13-4 续表

单位：万元

项　目	Item	负债合计 Total Liabilities	#流动负债 Total Liquid Liabilities	#非流动负债 Total Non-liquid Liabilities	所有者权益合计 Total Owners' Equities
总　计	**Total**	**116448837.9**	**75023899.7**	**40743498.8**	**65185301.9**
按登记注册类型分	**By Status of Registration**				
内资企业	Domestic Funded Enterprises	114776039.4	73731248.8	40365176.1	64083016.6
国有企业	State-owned Enterprises	6429815.2	3390916.4	3038894.8	2970326.7
#中央企业	Central Enterprises	3921917.1	2508385.1	1413528.2	2293261.4
地方企业	Local Enterprises	2507898.1	882531.3	1625366.6	677065.3
#自治区属企业	Autonomous	709577.3	122290.8	587286.4	345497.6
地区(州、市)属企业	Prefecture or City	1069482.6	337194.4	732288.2	22828.3
县(市)属企业	County or City	503237.3	330636.9	172600.3	221407.4
集体企业	Collective-owned Enterprises	32705.1	31686.1	1018.9	27285.8
#自治区属企业	Autonomous	19146.6	18497.3	649.3	12437.4
地区(州、市)属企业	Prefecture or City				
县(市)属企业	County or City	9177.8	8811.6	366.1	11360.8
镇属企业	Town	4105.7	4105.7		2933.3
乡属企业	Village				
股份合作企业	Cooperative Enterprises	124162.9	100153.8	24009.1	15484.9
联营企业	Joint Ownership Enterprises	825.9	825.9		983.9
#国有联营企业	State Joint Ownership Enterprises				
集体联营企业	Collective Joint Ownership Enterprises				
国有与集体联营企业	Joint State-collective Enterprises				
其他联营企业	Other Joint Ownership Enterprises	825.9	825.9		983.9
有限责任公司	Limited Liability Corporations	63400483.5	41970114.2	21021960.9	24629900.0
#国有独资公司	State Sole funded Corporations	9944134.1	5843726.7	4077209.1	4499618.4
其他有限责任公司	Other Limited Liability Corporations	53456349.4	36126387.5	16944751.8	20130281.6
股份有限公司	Share-holding Corporations Ltd.	27410957.7	15339075.2	12067981.6	27826670.5
私营企业	Private Enterprises	17298574.7	12826017.5	4205259.8	8568852.1
#私营独资企业	Private-funded Enterprises	104496.6	100939.7	3556.9	48945.4
私营合伙企业	Private Partnership Enterprises	9194.3	8967.6	226.7	6001.4
私营有限责任公司	Private Limited Liability Corporations	13998026.4	10031344.6	3711523.0	6609187.4
私营股份有限公司	Private Share-holding Corporations Ltd.	3186857.4	2684765.6	489953.2	1904717.9
港、澳、台商投资企业	Enterprises with Funds from Hong Kong, Macao and Taiwan	593446.7	486425.4	105659.4	406478.9
外商投资企业	Foreign Funded Enterprises	1079351.8	806225.5	272663.3	695806.4
在总计中：国有控股企业	Of the Total : State-owned and State-holding Enterprises	67348310.7	37922472.2	29188137.2	42148695.0
在总计中：农村工业	Of the Total : Rural Industry	14945.1	12730.4	0.8	7219.1
按轻、重工业分	**Grouped by Light & Heavy Industry**				
轻工业	Light Industry	10876116.8	8479834.8	2253849.9	7154486.6
以农产品为原料	Using Farm Produces as Raw Materials	8928496.8	7422302.7	1364712.2	5945872.2
以非农产品为原料	Using Non-Farm Produces as Raw Materials	1947620.0	1057532.1	889137.7	1208614.4
重工业	Heavy Industry	105572721.1	66544064.9	38489648.9	58030815.3
采掘工业	Mining and Quarrying	24792953.7	14737132.8	10015255.8	20303799.0
原料工业	Raw Material Industry	61769588.9	37438577.9	23964691.5	26933854.9
加工工业	Manufacturing Industry	19010178.5	14368354.2	4509701.6	10793161.4
按企业规模分	**Grouped by Size of Enterprises (New Standard)**				
大型企业	Large Enterprises	60304617.3	37343297.9	22958689.7	38054931.8
中型企业	Medium-sized Enterprises	21585114.3	14309423.0	7225684.4	10872163.2
小型企业	Small Enterprises	28145539.3	19793946.0	8044439.6	14331809.1
微型企业	Min Enterprises	6413567.0	3577232.8	2514685.1	1926397.8

Continued

(10 000 yuan)

主营业务收入 Revenue from Principal Business	主营业务成本 Cost of Principal Business	主营业务税金及附加 Taxes and Other Charges on Principal Business	营业利润 Business Profit	利润总额 Total Profit	亏损企业亏损总额 Losses Value of Loss-Suffering Enterprises	利税总额 Total Profits and Taxes	本年应交增值税 Value-added Taxes Payable	全部从业人员年平均人数(人) Annual Average Employed Persons (person)
82037341.9	**65910732.9**	**3777572.7**	**2541058.3**	**3409656.9**	**3570382.2**	**10524057.2**	**3336827.6**	**720073**
80266443.8	64497698.1	3755659.0	2483041.7	3326575.1	3493208.7	10365210.6	3282976.5	701660
5512888.1	5159954.3	11980.5	171470.8	222293.5	37587.2	254520.0	20246.0	36643
4777725.3	4591323.8	8182.5	124827.3	134658.1	4240.5	141463.6	-1377.0	27503
735162.8	568630.5	3798.0	46643.5	87635.4	33346.7	113056.4	21623.0	9140
277764.6	147026.2	1631.2	80003.5	82840.6	9061.5	95817.4	11345.6	2902
138206.9	158584.4	277.6	-47647.9	-17396.0	19681.0	-20050.8	-2932.4	2806
158015.1	105314.7	1633.8	18965.5	20865.8	4604.2	34262.8	11763.2	2029
54929.7	49080.3	917.6	913.5	1254.5	1658.8	5204.9	3032.8	1496
31802.3	29822.0	210.3	158.2	226.6	142.6	1561.0	1124.1	777
15919.1	11817.9	370.7	2284.5	2544.1		4216.3	1301.5	499
4546.6	4961.0	329.4	-1319.9	-1330.6	1330.6	-476.0	525.2	150
13969.1	11724.4		-3489.3	-3434.5	3434.5	-1995.0	1439.5	598
2493.8	2053.1	20.0	157.1	157.1		377.1	200.0	120
2493.8	2053.1	20.0	157.1	157.1		377.1	200.0	120
32483843.5	27105604.4	947720.8	201225.9	601577.5	1606524.8	2963810.0	1414511.7	358059
4602356.3	3676703.7	259627.7	78358.7	167730.1	100998.3	716539.7	289181.9	72204
27881487.2	23428900.7	688093.1	122867.2	433847.4	1505526.5	2247270.3	1125329.8	285855
25753776.0	18563009.0	2721736.5	728194.8	1011566.1	1604484.9	5201999.7	1468697.1	163905
16315631.3	13512247.9	72994.8	1354647.6	1463090.6	239518.5	1910066.2	373980.8	139436
133374.1	96578.3	2668.0	13682.3	11674.8	4109.8	30541.3	16198.5	1699
50133.7	34205.2	158.1	7250.4	6340.1	7.8	14111.5	7613.3	551
13474032.7	11266062.1	59493.7	1012740.7	1114580.8	210525.0	1463836.8	289762.3	126959
2658090.8	2115402.3	10675.0	320974.2	330494.9	24875.9	401576.6	60406.7	10227
539744.1	424489.0	2450.9	28723.3	40751.2	17016.4	64616.3	21414.2	8960
1231154.0	988545.8	19462.8	29293.3	42330.6	60157.1	94230.3	32436.9	9453
44496409.4	34122793.3	3586473.2	780620.3	1321929.8	2470690.5	7143308.9	2234905.9	384230
26714.2	23070.4	27.6	659.9	884.7	134.4	1099.0	186.7	154
12678834.9	10182704.6	315301.0	965128.0	1161094.6	180075.9	1837344.5	360948.9	153823
12048722.3	9670366.6	312168.0	993293.4	1177652.3	116236.1	1829612.9	339792.6	139177
630112.6	512338.0	3133.0	-28165.4	-16557.7	63839.8	7731.6	21156.3	14646
69358507.0	55728028.3	3462271.7	1575930.3	2248562.3	3390306.3	8686712.7	2975878.7	566250
15729146.5	11451474.8	685977.5	391586.7	629673.8	1485501.5	2466558.2	1150906.9	185656
39059427.7	32438995.3	2658880.6	145425.3	430894.5	1598659.5	4602908.5	1513133.4	262222
14569932.8	11837558.2	117413.6	1038918.3	1187994.0	306145.3	1617246.0	311838.4	118372
47656054.4	37921256.6	3290110.6	882757.6	1359318.4	2281771.4	6825070.8	2175641.8	320387
11138179.6	9089245.8	314726.1	199239.8	378476.8	542651.0	1231543.3	538340.4	171427
21515933.8	17568306.6	162332.2	1352452.2	1552225.7	655233.1	2306263.8	591705.9	213750
1727174.1	1331923.9	10403.8	106608.7	119636.0	90726.7	161179.3	31139.5	14509

13-5 按行业分规模以上工业企业主要经济指标

单位：万元 (2015 年)

行业	Sector	企业单位数(个) Number of Enterprises (unit)	#亏损企业 Loss- Suffering Enterprises	工业总产值(当年价格) Gross Industrial Output Value (At Current Prices)
总　计	**Total**	**2707**	**818**	**81325512.3**
煤炭开采和洗选业	Mining and Washing of Coal	133	59	2426611.3
石油和天然气开采业	Extraction of Petroleum and Natural Gas	7	4	8966347.9
黑色金属矿采选业	Mining and Processing of Ferrous Metals Ores	54	33	957549.3
有色金属矿采选业	Mining and Processing of Nonferrous Metals Ores	43	22	634733.5
非金属矿采选业	Mining and Processing of Nonmetal Ores	25	6	190715.0
#采　盐	Extraction of Salt	5		46497.3
开采辅助活动	Support for Minning	38	7	1902508.3
农副食品加工业	Activities Processing of Food from Agricultural Products	401	90	5126781.3
#谷物磨制	Grain Grinding	64	19	617605.7
饲料加工	Fodder Processing	46	6	898094.8
制　糖	Sugar Making	13	7	235535.4
食品制造业	Manufacture of Foods	125	34	2326804.1
#罐头制造	Manufacture of can	49	12	406888.0
饮料制造业	Manufacture of Liguor,Beverages and Refined Tea	74	12	1328592.7
#酒的制造	Manufacture of Liguor	50	10	799044.9
烟草制品业	Manufacture of Tobacco	1		472468.0
纺织业	Manufacture of Textile	91	24	1481467.2
#棉、化纤纺织及印染精加工	Cotton, Chemical Fiber, Dyeing, Printing and Processing	79	19	1328371.9
毛纺织和染整精加工	Wool Textile, Dyeing and Printing	4	2	86746.4
纺织服装、鞋、帽制造业	Manufacture of Textile, Wearing Apparel and Accessories	18	1	216200.0
皮革、毛皮、羽毛(绒)及其制品业	Manufacturie of Leather, Fur, Feather and Related Products	5	4	87431.5
#皮革鞣制加工	Leather Tanning and Processing	4	3	83903.5
木材加工及木、竹、藤、棕、草制品业	Processing of Timber, Manufacture of Wood, Bamboo, Cane, Grass Products	16	4	118644.6
家具制造业	Manufacture of Furniture	7		30734.5
造纸及纸制品业	Manufacture of Paper and Paper Products	30	6	382140.8
印刷业和记录媒介的复制	Printing and Reproduction of Recording Media	13	3	47105.5
文教、工美、体育和娱乐用品制造业	Manufacture of Articles for Cultural, Educational,Sports and Entertainment	6	1	92276.4
石油加工、炼焦及核燃料加工业	Processing, Processing of Petroleeum,Coking and Nuclear Fuel	100	36	12181358.3
#炼　焦	Coking	50	21	1013073.3
化学原料及化学制品制造业	Manufacture of Raw Chemical Materials and Chemical Products	198	52	6785665.7
#基础化学原料制造	Basic Chemical Material	54	19	1491606.0
肥料制造	Manufacture of Fertilizer	59	12	1701113.9
合成材料制造	Manufacture of Synthetic Materials	20	8	2543875.2
医药制造业	Manufacture of Medicine	31	5	315113.1
化学纤维制造业	Manufacture of Chemical Fibers	15	6	743761.6
橡胶和塑料制品业	Manufacture of Rubber and Plastics Products	120	21	1244347.6
非金属矿物制品业	Manufacture of Non-metallic Mineral Products	419	146	4084433.1
#水泥制造	Manufacture of Cement	80	52	1004359.8
黑色金属冶炼及压延加工业	Smelting and Pressing of Ferrous Metals	86	63	3299614.7
有色金属冶炼及压延加工业	Smelting and Pressing of Non ferrous Metals	54	24	8382410.8
金属制品业	Manufacture of Metal Products	87	31	807217.0
通用设备制造业	Manufacture of General Purpose Machinery	26	6	208385.1
专用设备制造业	Manufacture of Special Purpose Machinery	27	7	428147.5
汽车制造业	Manufacture of Automobile	10	8	189178.7
铁路、船舶、航空航天和其他运输设备制造业	Manufacture of Railway ,Ship,Aeronautics and Other Transport Equipment	2		9405.9
电气机械及器材制造业	Manufacture of Electrical Machinery and Apparatus	57	10	5221711.0
计算机、通信和其他电子设备制造业	Manufacture of, Computer Communication and Other Electronic Equipment	4	1	20143.8
仪器仪表制造业	Measuring Instruments and Machinery	2		12314.6
废弃资源综合利用业	Comprehensive Utilization of Waste Resources	4	1	34993.5
金属制品、机械和设备修理业	Repair Service of Metal Prodults,Mouhinery and Equipment	3		28044.5
电力、热力的生产和供应业	Production and Supply of Electrici Power and Heat Power	312	84	9396557.5
#电力生产和电力供应	Production and Supply of Electric	254	64	8989067.2
燃气生产和供应业	Production and Supply of Gas	45	3	962919.8
水的生产和供应业	Production and Supply of Water	18	4	180676.6

Main Economic Indicators of Industrial Enterprises above Designated Size by Sectors

(10 000 yuan)

工业增加值 Value-added of Industry	工业销售产值(当年价格) Sales Value of Industry Products (At Current Prices)	出口交货值 Delivery Value of Industry Export	实收资本 Total Capital Hold	资产合计 Total Assets	流动资产合计 Total Current Assets	#产成品 Finished Product	固定资产原价 Original Value of Fixed Assets
26626977.7	**79446617.0**	**629658.0**	**49672884.1**	**181641554.7**	**53470170.3**	**4795336.3**	**143877186.1**
1315528.7	2317149.6	12.2	1838270.0	8736778.0	2240891.3	203628.8	4033347.6
6101049.1	8844445.0		15674602.3	28352694.9	3794423.5	138688.4	47752202.0
273963.9	834016.0		427448.2	2542869.8	1220658.5	227116.0	1016583.6
323622.9	558652.3	6.0	535357.9	2261331.6	574634.6	95321.8	1292775.9
97264.2	179546.7	2159.6	71332.5	273230.6	139950.5	35755.4	147156.6
30798.2	46477.0		22581.1	68516.8	38195.5	9701.9	22617.2
899124.2	1909598.8	2313.8	1667464.5	2932075.4	1556568.0	14437.5	1844318.8
956824.4	4959714.9	31296.0	961062.2	4399978.0	2574398.2	604077.0	1732584.7
71003.2	615649.9		86807.9	437900.0	241835.9	20995.0	145536.8
141806.6	905096.2		146122.3	694111.3	337568.5	25900.3	221983.1
52334.9	207593.7		69626.2	426651.2	293736.5	193381.3	274066.9
606051.0	2189161.2	331455.6	868520.9	3234311.1	1270715.1	290342.1	2179695.4
80203.6	380764.2	149058.0	249881.3	750201.6	428684.2	167126.8	483661.0
476574.5	1290800.3	2531.0	417237.1	1555533.0	713641.8	101844.8	785011.8
353583.6	782613.4		317770.6	1108493.3	585616.0	81595.5	458343.1
363547.2	476905.0		369850.0	505672.0	286298.0	3899.0	227535.5
323973.9	1391441.1	35789.8	840556.9	2676548.9	1242368.9	184816.6	1376257.3
279929.7	1243836.0	21881.8	701830.5	2143928.9	1072769.8	158471.2	1179208.0
29867.8	84696.9	10882.4	63748.0	227430.0	56885.3	16295.9	122295.8
59538.1	176059.6	30128.6	184215.6	368226.2	104169.6	15044.6	250645.9
8692.9	79384.6		10300.0	87177.7	69693.7	7823.8	15388.7
6951.8	75856.6		10000.0	85549.7	69144.2	7674.3	14198.7
28433.6	115520.3	325.0	36517.6	180865.9	86423.5	22473.5	74404.8
8619.6	32457.8	5648.3	9930.0	47009.7	33904.5	3466.1	11262.0
93101.0	347596.4	670.1	41533.4	278156.0	134239.0	40649.1	123052.3
21117.8	47096.9		25237.1	100384.1	55234.8	8686.8	80580.4
12967.5	88217.5	8764.4	12988.0	43071.4	23680.9	6351.5	20572.8
5014482.9	12005163.2		4887760.0	10253374.7	3060427.8	513920.5	10408487.7
205990.5	930092.8		659562.3	2771114.0	938284.0	212626.8	1474488.9
1807557.0	6671227.5	32685.7	4351518.3	19928151.1	4519887.4	399298.1	13847297.0
383655.4	1479139.3	5734.9	1044840.7	4920584.2	1058209.9	110888.2	3478933.6
606582.9	1636476.0	398.2	1044107.1	4848099.9	1296813.8	81365.6	3525040.7
515757.6	2533807.3	26102.3	1864154.5	7356322.5	1343060.2	162531.2	4997196.3
80787.2	296553.1	9583.7	516858.7	1261241.9	400213.3	64406.1	363376.1
140327.2	739129.4	7616.4	280123.9	1352742.8	628328.2	61754.1	832682.5
257547.7	1221045.0	5057.9	373343.8	1238360.8	706357.0	151567.4	505679.1
1052275.0	3966542.4		2846267.6	10947458.3	4556102.5	294407.9	5382337.5
262509.3	939743.8		1392023.5	5796060.5	1796289.7	72716.2	3242558.9
-143056.1	3262924.7	20749.9	2222223.6	10140647.0	2707377.8	495102.2	5973499.0
1508559.4	8042517.8	32520.4	1390270.3	13879177.8	5712511.9	525248.9	7776962.0
177245.6	771143.7	5893.0	298695.3	1178450.6	592406.5	66107.6	342607.9
42049.8	232736.2	6.3	59120.2	396311.5	288775.7	30810.5	101488.7
99779.4	367397.2	14358.7	226361.9	1132511.6	339876.0	56628.1	290637.9
-11177.4	185496.8	50.6	159658.2	360755.2	171614.9	14509.8	235769.2
2633.9	9635.1		8923.9	10861.2	7604.0	409.5	3397.5
953450.4	5221453.6	48444.5	972671.6	10414915.5	6599768.3	97843.0	714434.2
1042.7	15049.1	1587.3	21600.0	47203.4	10115.5	3040.5	38033.5
2472.3	12161.5		10000.0	76142.8	27299.1	1349.9	948.5
16725.7	33684.4		60598.3	124465.1	15165.3	4038.1	103780.5
14654.8	26946.7		4745.4	26151.3	22879.9	32.1	5878.1
3369367.6	9396223.3	3.2	5850787.0	35514611.8	5380592.2	6589.7	31360086.0
3282546.2	8954360.9	3.2	5542523.5	33142673.2	4397741.2	3856.7	29703413.1
180980.3	956737.5		700614.8	3099681.8	1101741.6	3849.5	1713938.9
89277.6	175084.8		438317.1	1682424.2	499231.0		912488.2

13-5 续表

单位：万元

行　业	Sector	负债合计 Total Liabilities	#流动负债 Total Liquid Liabilities	#非流动负债 Total Non-liquid Liabilities	所有者权益合计 Total Owners' Equities
总　计	**Total**	**116448837.9**	**75023899.7**	**40743498.8**	**65185301.9**
煤炭开采和洗选业	Mining and Washing of Coal	6313843.1	4859132.9	1425480.6	2420708.6
石油和天然气开采业	Extraction of Petroleum and Natural Gas	13210606.7	5501207.2	7709399.5	15142087.9
黑色金属矿采选业	Mining and Processing of Ferrous Metals Ores	1894755.8	1749353.8	145399.8	648113.7
有色金属矿采选业	Mining and Processing of Nonferrous Metals Ores	1359655.5	931762.3	427893.1	901675.8
非金属矿采选业	Mining and Processing of Nonmetal Ores	201217.4	188149.1	4139.0	72013.1
#采　盐	Extraction of Salt	22920.3	13491.0	500.0	45596.4
开采辅助活动	Support for Minning	1812875.2	1507527.5	302943.8	1119199.9
农副食品加工业	Activities Processing of Food from Agricultural Products	2745522.1	2473112.8	189687.6	1659384.8
#谷物磨制	Grain Grinding	251189.4	226251.4	20147.0	185472.3
饲料加工	Fodder Processing	283938.2	253073.2	21881.2	412246.3
制　糖	Sugar Making	327332.0	320888.4	6095.0	99319.0
食品制造业	Manufacture of Foods	2072341.7	1585704.1	473294.7	1155567.3
#罐头制造	Manufacture of can	588674.8	580741.0	7869.4	161526.5
饮料制造业	Manufacture of Liguor,Beverages and Refined Tea	842893.7	618643.4	222951.5	707697.5
#酒的制造	Manufacture of Liguor	603155.1	384942.4	216914.0	500396.5
烟草制品业	Manufacture of Tobacco	135822.0	127822.0	8000.0	369850.0
纺织业	Manufacture of Textile	1600037.2	1332704.9	256461.2	1076510.9
#棉、化纤纺织及印染精加工	Cotton, Chemical Fiber, Dyeing, Printing and Processing	1300529.0	1168068.9	124384.3	843399.2
毛纺织和染整精加工	Wool Textile, Dyeing and Printing	70328.3	51127.4	19200.9	157101.7
纺织服装、鞋、帽制造业	Manufacture of Textile, Wearing Apparel and Accessories	128138.2	61566.1	63046.6	240088.0
皮革、毛皮、羽毛(绒)及其制品业	Manufacturie of Leather, Fur, Feather and Related Products	68038.5	64801.8		18779.1
#皮革鞣制加工	Leather Tanning and Processing	67034.5	63797.8		18155.1
木材加工及木、竹、藤、棕、草制品业	Processing of Timber, Manufacture of Wood, Bamboo, Cane, Grass Products	110952.6	80059.4	30293.2	69913.2
家具制造业	Manufacture of Furniture	30919.3	30919.3		16090.4
造纸及纸制品业	Manufacture of Paper and Paper Products	147626.4	128107.4	18590.6	130529.5
印刷业和记录媒介的复制	Printing and Reproduction of Recording Media	42568.3	36116.0	6452.3	57815.7
文教、工美、体育和娱乐用品制造业	Manufacture of Articles for Cultural, Educational,Sports and Entertainment	25885.0	25309.9	575.1	17186.4
石油加工、炼焦及核燃料加工业	Processing, Processing of Petroleeum,Coking and Nuclear Fuel	4753402.2	3772636.9	899429.3	5477468.7
#炼　焦	Coking	1934012.4	1673440.6	179469.5	823708.4
化学原料及化学制品制造业	Manufacture of Raw Chemical Materials and Chemical Products	13565577.9	7469048.6	6056890.3	6358930.1
#基础化学原料制造	Basic Chemical Material	3413330.3	2002283.4	1404921.4	1503309.6
肥料制造	Manufacture of Fertilizer	3496907.4	2221557.4	1261399.9	1351192.2
合成材料制造	Manufacture of Synthetic Materials	5114889.4	2263967.7	2831358.4	2241735.2
医药制造业	Manufacture of Medicine	688787.7	617555.1	71232.6	572453.6
化学纤维制造业	Manufacture of Chemical Fibers	940194.3	798693.6	115943.8	412428.2
橡胶和塑料制品业	Manufacture of Rubber and Plastics Products	629700.1	575603.3	50930.7	608659.8
非金属矿物制品业	Manufacture of Non-metallic Mineral Products	7032640.8	5680232.1	1233292.7	3918102.7
#水泥制造	Manufacture of Cement	3580889.2	2599639.5	903294.5	2221425.0
黑色金属冶炼及压延加工业	Smelting and Pressing of Ferrous Metals	8734756.2	7569222.5	1144644.4	1416684.7
有色金属冶炼及压延加工业	Smelting and Pressing of Non ferrous Metals	10125355.7	7811880.2	2307373.9	3753822.0
金属制品业	Manufacture of Metal Products	744991.3	632709.7	100622.2	431386.5
通用设备制造业	Manufacture of General Purpose Machinery	301276.5	287590.6	13646.5	95034.8
专用设备制造业	Manufacture of Special Purpose Machinery	398135.4	339054.9	39150.8	726338.3
汽车制造业	Manufacture of Automobile	317646.9	246362.4	71284.5	43108.3
铁路、船舶、航空航天和其他运输设备制造业	Manufacture of Railway ,Ship,Aeronautics and Other Transport Equipment	4198.0	4135.3	62.7	6663.2
电气机械及器材制造业	Manufacture of Electrical Machinery and Apparatus	6456356.2	5262600.4	1153565.0	3952559.1
计算机、通信和其他电子设备制造业	Manufacture of, Computer Communication and Other Electronic Equipment	25930.5	18153.7	7776.8	21272.9
仪器仪表制造业	Measuring Instruments and Machinery	55255.1	51330.2	3924.9	20887.7
废弃资源综合利用业	Comprehensive Utilization of Waste Resources	35435.7	27531.7	7904.0	89029.5
金属制品、机械和设备修理业	Repair Service of Metal Prodults,Mouhinery and Equipment	19940.1	19940.1		6211.2
电力、热力的生产和供应业	Production and Supply of Electrici Power and Heat Power	25480679.9	10967357.5	14359573.9	10064239.5
#电力生产和电力供应	Production and Supply of Electric	23613037.5	10267968.9	13206885.6	9559943.5
燃气生产和供应业	Production and Supply of Gas	2315793.0	1273860.7	1039905.9	783471.0
水的生产和供应业	Production and Supply of Water	1079085.7	296400.3	781735.3	603338.3

Continued

(10 000 yuan)

主营业务收入 Revenue from Principal Business	主营业务成本 Cost of Principal Business	主营业务税金及附加 Taxes and Other Charges on Principal Business	营业利润 Business Profit	利润总额 Total Profit	亏损企业亏损总额 Losses Value of Loss-Suffering Enterprises	利税总额 Total Profits and Taxes	本年应交增值税 Value-added Taxes Payable	全部从业人员年平均人数（人） Annual Average Employed Persons (person)
82037341.9	**65910732.9**	**3777572.7**	**2541058.3**	**3409656.9**	**3570382.2**	**10524057.2**	**3336827.6**	**720073**
2366385.5	1820109.8	98797.6	-37883.0	-24581.9	172034.6	340523.2	266307.5	56244
9856712.7	6733484.7	522320.4	305988.4	507435.8	1188272.1	1654466.2	624710.0	70740
845979.3	636679.7	25432.3	31438.2	32486.3	51670.5	119150.6	61232.0	9893
558348.7	364150.7	13114.3	61613.9	60905.1	41611.2	126191.8	52172.4	9454
185228.9	112775.9	5928.3	14225.2	14261.1	6306.5	37718.1	17528.7	3124
46578.4	12622.6	4762.7	9929.0	10163.8		20088.1	5161.6	952
1916491.4	1784274.0	20384.6	16204.0	39167.4	25606.6	188508.3	128956.3	36201
5075262.2	4263373.3	9375.0	455042.5	484281.9	43314.1	551158.1	57501.2	41033
626679.0	570592.4	770.6	29881.4	36008.2	2419.0	40871.8	4093.0	3423
912833.1	757786.7	529.3	70344.6	73161.6	1905.1	78021.9	4331.0	6284
206230.2	186034.8	780.1	-9910.3	-3733.5	7217.3	5792.4	8745.8	5804
2184104.9	1749674.1	9032.7	169468.1	192942.9	33940.7	278003.7	76028.1	25901
379906.0	307242.8	1426.9	7432.8	18215.9	11858.7	27438.0	7795.2	5966
1226550.2	821762.8	63320.6	207843.5	212549.9	6062.3	334351.3	58480.8	12595
764672.2	467285.6	61714.3	151437.2	156619.0	3962.0	263999.1	45665.8	9017
476905.0	179636.0	219745.0	53774.4	52767.4		328980.4	56468.0	761
1479280.2	1336405.2	4517.3	24143.3	120945.9	18318.6	171941.8	46478.6	32501
1335856.9	1224986.5	3537.6	16000.7	109616.9	13743.8	156537.0	43382.5	27889
80085.0	59252.0	833.7	7154.8	8840.6	268.4	14944.6	5270.3	1907
210735.4	162451.2	1050.9	15776.3	21038.4	176.6	24241.3	2152.0	8511
67891.2	64788.4	118.2	-474.3	-234.7	234.9	936.4	1052.9	450
64363.2	61859.1	48.2	-462.0	-222.4	222.6	875.9	1050.1	445
119411.2	97766.2	223.8	11042.4	13051.4	3894.3	14733.4	1458.2	1445
33047.5	27106.6	141.5	2550.6	3927.8		4963.6	894.3	816
335116.9	270638.7	1298.4	48091.6	46793.1	592.6	53824.6	5733.1	4133
47561.6	37306.3	381.8	1158.0	3448.3	262.0	6213.4	2383.3	1717
79969.5	63722.7	209.7	5967.4	6345.3	35.3	7917.2	1362.2	992
12259234.6	8224720.5	2602594.1	572992.3	577289.7	133881.2	4005289.5	825405.7	45969
900475.6	804795.3	1351.6	917.0	1082.3	71240.8	20213.5	17779.6	11556
6556941.9	5407953.6	86787.9	44317.7	131049.0	346255.7	368027.0	150190.1	72770
1497981.8	1310286.2	8178.5	-45423.5	-33194.5	103295.7	17738.1	42754.1	19875
1672863.5	1148719.8	65336.5	112429.7	154948.1	54689.8	242558.6	22274.0	15438
2307817.2	2097560.2	8482.8	-69460.8	-61597.8	139789.2	11113.1	64228.1	24751
283181.4	207037.9	1583.1	-573.0	4395.1	15267.5	20087.9	14109.7	7137
709579.8	610392.9	2415.6	8073.4	28030.3	12693.9	55530.5	25084.6	8342
1265061.8	1075311.8	4285.2	88551.5	96581.3	14220.6	124940.2	24073.7	13776
4002744.3	3441074.1	15968.6	65429.7	99945.5	208776.2	278042.8	162128.7	58810
938518.8	844811.5	4984.7	-87789.9	-65797.1	140990.0	3922.6	64735.0	18772
3407894.2	3645339.2	6853.2	-760331.9	-727631.7	742342.2	-687440.2	33338.3	40492
8797852.3	8113352.1	3652.6	28597.8	63648.2	192262.4	321043.8	253743.0	42878
804783.2	701469.0	3124.5	53763.3	61615.1	14990.6	74270.8	9531.2	10697
203321.1	171303.8	717.1	10995.1	13719.4	1867.6	16427.1	1990.6	2847
376500.2	288680.0	829.5	37977.2	44299.8	6444.7	49649.0	4519.7	4911
210917.9	201665.1	5882.1	-59807.5	-52942.2	53687.5	-44694.2	2365.9	2488
9375.9	7181.3	62.2	870.3	1507.6		2097.4	527.6	150
5556063.5	4564054.3	19525.2	589954.1	610649.0	7502.2	756052.5	125878.3	14796
31272.4	29726.0	69.9	-3285.7	-695.2	1563.0	-1153.6	-528.3	753
14704.9	11868.9	72.9	770.0	1218.4		1606.7	315.4	178
33737.3	25471.7	206.4	2163.2	2137.9	724.9	4532.6	2188.3	268
28038.2	25738.5	488.0	123.7	187.5		2590.3	1914.8	1163
9283848.2	7739583.6	21472.1	487889.8	655484.7	126427.1	887606.1	210649.3	63059
8806832.6	7233171.4	20573.8	588878.5	647826.4	99117.4	875283.9	206883.7	53622
977454.2	784043.5	4610.7	-18479.5	-1535.0	93197.7	24617.8	21542.1	8492
159852.3	108658.8	979.4	5096.3	13171.1	5944.3	21109.8	6959.3	3586

13-6 各地、州、市、县(市)规模以上工业企业主要经济指标

单位: 万元 (2015 年)

地区	Region	企业单位数(个) Number of Enterprises (unit)	#亏损企业 Loss- Suffering Enterprises	工业总产值(当年价格) Gross Industrial Output Value (At Current Prices)
总 计	**Total**	**2707**	**818**	**81325512.3**
乌鲁木齐市	**Urumqi City**	**396**	**133**	**20632531.3**
天山区	Tianshan District	16	5	360775.5
沙依巴克区	Shayibak District	25	8	671111.9
新市区	Xinshi District	90	21	3720084.0
水磨沟区	Shui Mogou District	12	4	4546497.7
头屯河区	Tou Tunhe District	130	40	6405200.6
达坂城区	Da Bancheng District	21	5	216723.2
米东区	Midong District	97	49	4668627.7
乌鲁木齐县	Urumqi County	5	1	43510.7
克拉玛依市	**Karamay City**	**94**	**20**	**10743380.6**
独山子区	Dushanzi District	10	4	3769153.9
克拉玛依区	Karamay District	67	13	6779719.4
白碱滩区	Bai Jiantan District	15	2	190698.5
乌尔河区	Urhe District	2	1	3808.8
吐鲁番市	**Turpan City**	**118**	**53**	**2099787.5**
高昌区	Gaochang District	37	16	345247.1
鄯善县	Shanshan [Piqan] County	42	18	1148161.2
托克逊县	Toksun County	39	19	606379.2
哈密地区	**Hami [Kumul] Administrative Offices**	**180**	**54**	**4255918.3**
哈密市	Hami [Kumul] City	136	36	3597404.2
巴里坤哈萨克自治县	Barkol Kazak Autonomous County	28	10	248214.4
伊吾县	Yiwu [Araturuk] County	16	8	410299.7
昌吉回族自治州	**Changji Hui Autonomous Prefecture**	**426**	**105**	**12841383.2**
昌吉市	Changji City	141	24	3540618.5
阜康市	Fukang City	76	29	2317818.6
呼图壁县	Hutubi County	70	10	964240.5
玛纳斯县	Manas County	63	16	1942675.5
奇台县	Qitai County	40	11	783283.2
吉木萨尔县	Jimsar County	31	15	3253756.5
木垒哈萨克自治县	Mori Kazak Autonomous County	5		38990.4
伊犁哈萨克自治州	**Ili Kazak Autonomous Prefecture**	**466**	**180**	**6633144.3**
伊犁州直属县(市)	**Counties (Cities) Direct Under Ili Prefecture**	**247**	**94**	**3816400.9**
伊宁市	Yining [Gulja] City	37	16	349455.4
奎屯市	Kuytun City	53	20	902164.5
霍尔果斯市	Huoerguosi City	3		75935.5
伊宁县	Yining [Gulja] County	39	17	556807.1
察布查尔锡伯自治县	Qapqal Xibe Autonomous County	17	5	138694.7
霍城县	Huocheng [Korgas] County	35	9	483308.2
巩留县	Gongliu [Tokkuztara] County	21	5	375036.5
新源县	Xinyuan [Kunes] County	19	13	572160.1
昭苏县	Zhaosu [Mongolkure] County	7	1	147785.9
特克斯县	Tekes County	4	4	42304.1
尼勒克县	Nilka County	12	4	172748.9
塔城地区	**Tacheng [Tarbagatai] Administrative Offices**	**126**	**42**	**1835095.0**
塔城市	Tacheng [Qoqek] City	5	3	37034.5
乌苏市	Usu City	25	9	604587.5
额敏县	Emin [Dorbiljin] County	13	6	125468.2

Main Economic Indicators of Industrial Enterprises above Designated Size by Prefecture, Autonomous Prefecture, City and County

(10 000 yuan)

工业增加值 Value-added of Industry	工业销售产值(当年价格) Sales Value of Industry Products (At Current Prices)	出口交货值 Delivery Value of Industry Export	实收资本 Total Capital Hold	资产合计 Total Assets	流动资产合计 Total Current Assets	#产成品 Finished Product	固定资产原价 Original Value of Fixed Assets
26626977.7	**79446617.0**	**629658.0**	**49672884.1**	**181641554.7**	**53470170.3**	**4795336.3**	**143877186.1**
5392571.0	**20554641.4**	**283583.5**	**9118159.5**	**42468682.7**	**12953334.6**	**698576.6**	**32090625.5**
126433.8	380021.1	39045.2	284046.5	1785568.7	838627.5	54375.6	1435855.3
76053.2	669585.3		512910.2	3036852.8	1345058.0	8715.6	1006769.2
1327324.3	3511993.4	46900.9	2660758.0	10957852.4	3028777.6	224320.9	11991662.1
1077377.3	4544545.3		422792.8	6038987.9	349909.7	6239.0	7576074.3
1019528.0	6551039.0	191756.7	2418054.6	13089160.0	5361136.0	211046.7	4331359.8
97231.8	220160.8		292553.7	1536949.5	201716.6	18733.4	1077054.1
1636309.0	4633785.8	5880.7	2422844.6	5617895.0	1757654.3	174771.4	4357221.5
32313.7	43510.7		104199.1	405416.4	70454.9	374.0	314629.2
4630564.0	**10678928.2**	**5283.0**	**13706861.2**	**20678535.8**	**5290733.8**	**188377.0**	**26742029.0**
1499210.2	3744248.1		2510319.2	3400802.4	709600.7	79457.8	5038397.0
3053256.8	6742788.1	3488.2	11144433.0	16959404.9	4400923.5	105803.1	21549245.0
75731.2	188209.9	1794.8	50849.0	295384.9	171123.4	2913.4	147093.5
2365.7	3682.1		1260.0	22943.6	9086.2	202.7	7293.5
544840.4	**2053445.5**	**14880.3**	**1832355.5**	**7694821.9**	**2155022.7**	**234087.3**	**8082906.9**
93866.1	367893.3	11315.1	275869.7	1168819.6	421341.0	22435.3	725085.5
321377.7	1086593.7	199.1	280479.1	3483999.5	923181.7	171108.7	5411179.8
129596.6	598958.5	3366.1	1276006.7	3042002.8	810500.0	40543.3	1946641.6
1257155.2	**4147973.2**	**1273.8**	**2944233.2**	**13524421.5**	**3395104.1**	**201316.5**	**8760071.0**
963516.1	3488686.8	1273.8	2126196.8	10076622.7	2829891.5	139703.8	6245612.1
106626.3	247838.2		401861.4	1591706.9	289122.6	31276.7	1045653.5
187012.8	411448.2		416175.0	1856091.9	276090.0	30336.0	1468805.4
2923327.8	**12315250.0**	**76733.4**	**3893943.3**	**25134411.7**	**8941715.6**	**775082.4**	**12743416.6**
889130.0	3475272.9	51956.1	825426.9	6219662.2	3000797.1	161397.7	1933063.9
448597.6	2177707.6	1978.2	1147608.2	5201330.2	1361902.7	274478.9	3361212.0
271344.6	945685.3	8851.5	308183.9	1112168.0	326222.9	67585.9	755539.0
390576.5	1810299.6	6023.9	440785.5	2915665.6	1083944.4	105341.1	1602991.5
274057.3	698956.7		139057.1	1061602.4	401496.4	60400.8	385615.5
635595.1	3174832.0	7923.7	1027156.7	8528325.2	2716664.9	99625.0	4662322.0
14026.7	32495.9		5725.0	95658.1	50687.2	6253.0	42672.7
1990426.6	**6398787.9**	**34373.3**	**4806235.9**	**19282833.6**	**5461647.1**	**758365.0**	**12733107.0**
1176551.4	**3720042.0**	**18133.3**	**3003047.3**	**11582783.5**	**3334259.4**	**451845.1**	**7636269.6**
118628.8	337928.0	2684.0	570081.1	1611657.7	370108.0	29912.1	872671.3
263515.3	907073.3		590506.0	2498663.2	767003.9	83167.2	1901231.2
52770.9	75935.5	1904.8	20865.0	168311.6	24754.8	749.0	119717.5
112494.7	540226.7	3363.1	703281.7	2697244.5	840303.9	65100.3	1559395.8
31969.7	139326.1		88927.0	373070.2	185339.4	27408.8	192428.2
162750.0	466695.0	10181.4	138263.9	514765.5	183332.8	62420.3	395375.2
106460.1	374603.5		357007.2	1102976.8	268873.4	9451.0	787318.6
166367.7	533342.6		220814.7	1242715.0	520040.8	152234.7	582910.4
55567.6	144802.8		10213.7	173468.4	31120.8	5472.6	135649.8
12109.4	32042.4		70738.8	236748.5	43508.0	7408.4	172099.2
93917.3	168066.1		232348.2	963162.1	99873.6	8520.7	917472.4
448480.8	**1750299.9**	**7728.5**	**1029521.1**	**3856188.6**	**1149810.2**	**190365.8**	**2630467.6**
3379.3	37245.2	2990.0	7109.2	71666.7	35914.4	2614.8	34913.3
136566.1	581315.3	461.2	489522.4	1105379.6	275953.8	40752.9	874547.5
36283.0	123370.3	4205.9	93111.2	346929.2	141039.5	49074.7	224829.3

13-6 续表 1

单位：万元

地　区	Region	企业单位数（个）Number of Enterprises (unit)	#亏损企业 Loss- Suffering Enterprises	工业总产值（当年价格）Gross Industrial Output Value (At Current Prices)
沙湾县	Shawan County	51	10	696379.5
托里县	Toli County	17	7	175003.0
裕民县	Yumin [Qagantokay] County	1	1	4180.2
和布克赛尔蒙古自治县	Hoboksar Mongol Autonomous County	14	6	192442.1
阿勒泰地区	**Altay Administrative Offices**	**93**	**44**	**981648.4**
阿勒泰市	Altay City	17	8	115063.9
布尔津县	Burqin County	15	6	81423.6
富蕴县	Fuyun [Koktokay] County	19	13	353591.9
福海县	Fuhai [Burultokay] County	17	7	93520.4
哈巴河县	Habahe [Kaba] County	10	3	189712.7
青河县	Qinghe [Qinggil] County	11	7	65125.2
吉木乃县	Jeminay County	4		83210.7
博尔塔拉蒙古自治州	**Bortala Mongol Autonomous Prefecture**	**96**	**31**	**848832.8**
博乐市	Bole [Bortala] City	61	19	518457.1
阿拉山口市	Alashankou City	11	3	158950.2
精河县	Jinghe [Jing] County	18	9	156239.0
温泉县	Wenquan [Araxang] County	6		15186.5
巴音郭楞蒙古自治州	**Bayangol Mongol Autonomous Prefecture**	**203**	**57**	**7782797.8**
库尔勒市	Korla City	83	20	5997726.4
轮台县	Luntai [Bugur] County	15	6	209714.1
尉犁县	Yuli [Lopnur] County	13	1	141695.0
若羌县	Ruoqiang [Qarkilik] County	11	5	521113.7
且末县	Qiemo [Qarqan] County	1	1	8224.9
焉耆回族自治县	Yanqi Hui Autonomous County	16	6	103229.1
和静县	Hejing County	40	10	689502.1
和硕县	Hoxud County	17	6	76999.4
博湖县	Bohu [Bagrax] County	7	2	34593.1
阿克苏地区	**Aksu Administrative Offices**	**221**	**65**	**4046894.6**
阿克苏市	Aksu City	64	12	891721.3
温宿县	Wensu [Onsu] County	42	9	251613.3
库车县	Kuqa County	49	23	1971810.1
沙雅县	Xayar County	16	2	215521.7
新和县	Xinhe [Toksu] County	8		129739.8
拜城县	Baicheng [Bay] County	24	13	453914.2
乌什县	Wushi [Uxturpan] County	8		43184.3

Continued

(10 000 yuan)

工业增加值 Value-added of Industry	工业销售产值(当年价格) Sales Value of Industry Products (At Current Prices)	出口交货值 Delivery Value of Industry Export	实收资本 Total Capital Hold	资产合计 Total Assets	流动资产合计 Total Current Assets	#产成品 Finished Product	固定资产原价 Original Value of Fixed Assets
128433.3	664612.6	71.4	156142.6	738753.6	381682.6	59663.1	415343.5
56197.5	158914.3		92453.2	726509.6	210221.1	20333.4	444095.6
-331.9	3846.0		3500.0	5646.3	2948.2	996.9	2410.2
87953.5	180996.2		187682.5	861303.6	102050.6	16930.0	634328.2
365394.3	**928446.0**	**8511.5**	**773667.5**	**3843861.5**	**977577.5**	**116154.1**	**2466369.8**
32025.9	98664.4	8505.5	53268.3	275540.2	123880.8	15671.6	154466.9
36814.8	74381.7	6.0	59694.1	557788.7	105911.2	1103.8	468555.4
78861.8	337002.3		357538.2	1498008.7	346883.8	68688.5	944219.0
29236.5	87659.1		93273.6	199000.4	69796.9	13087.8	83173.7
134793.4	191883.9		66526.0	660625.4	154934.0	2304.8	381814.9
11150.9	56148.8		87381.3	355518.6	86165.9	14699.4	224889.6
42511.0	82705.8		55986.0	297379.5	90004.9	598.2	209250.3
283884.7	**732841.3**	**927.7**	**400883.8**	**1890663.9**	**680812.8**	**100648.6**	**1176785.4**
144778.1	445797.9	885.1	217440.9	1026435.6	443309.6	55114.1	579823.5
78530.8	143667.0	40.0	95831.0	486084.2	106417.0	27493.8	394922.4
54633.2	125923.9	2.6	75397.9	344380.3	121667.0	15546.0	173570.8
5942.5	17452.5		12214.0	33763.8	9419.2	2494.7	28468.7
4969920.6	**7684207.5**	**87376.1**	**6034059.0**	**16349239.9**	**3483101.6**	**434526.7**	**20357553.1**
4330415.2	5960408.3	11468.2	5188238.2	11877278.4	1989955.4	131055.0	17115300.1
35373.6	210483.4	2837.5	150659.7	530317.8	200773.3	29103.8	351945.9
33373.1	141001.5	2159.6	60177.0	161327.8	74963.2	3482.1	88705.2
333123.1	467843.3		90809.9	1024816.9	325177.9	42932.4	778537.2
-1281.9	7449.0		50000.0	81820.4	4417.0	1869.5	52973.0
28652.1	92251.1	13947.1	34958.1	210754.8	112450.1	25792.7	130809.2
187599.9	694205.3	19305.9	397427.6	2160771.1	654998.4	169212.3	1614045.8
10251.6	77541.4	19898.3	42924.6	220796.6	88172.5	16182.4	149017.7
12414.1	33024.2	17759.5	18863.9	81356.1	32193.8	14896.5	76219.0
1478978.8	**3868714.0**	**6275.3**	**2186916.7**	**8909402.1**	**2552953.6**	**401566.5**	**5739309.0**
201939.1	861803.1		597298.7	2052526.8	661744.1	68103.1	1099011.0
88273.2	230677.7	5132.5	127713.6	576017.5	176516.9	47143.6	390826.3
981867.0	1988124.2	462.5	785343.5	2776679.2	816692.3	103698.8	2049101.9
57715.8	180557.1	680.3	105228.4	385138.0	143954.2	35863.7	269378.0
37963.0	100771.2		12950.0	165085.6	82800.0	10366.7	69904.7
73172.5	391588.4		481533.6	2659566.0	595853.0	111585.9	1657029.2
15968.0	38780.8		36138.0	98078.4	27604.9	7158.1	71974.6

13-6 续表 2

单位：万元

地　区	Region	企业单位数（个） Number of Enterprises (unit)	#亏损企业 Loss- Suffering Enterprises	工业总产值（当年价格） Gross Industrial Output Value (At Current Prices)
阿瓦提县	Awat County	7	4	55079.2
柯坪县	Kalpin County	3	2	34310.7
克孜勒苏柯尔克孜自治州	**Kizilsu Kirgiz Autonomous Prefecture**	**37**	**23**	**387809.9**
阿图什市	Artux City	15	6	140076.0
阿克陶县	Akto County	10	10	127128.2
阿合奇县	Akqi County	1		19633.6
乌恰县	Wuqia [Ulugqat] County	11	7	100972.1
喀什地区	**Kashgar [Kaxgar] Administrative Offices**	**146**	**30**	**1326818.6**
喀什市	Kashgar [Kaxgar] City	28	8	375773.4
疏附县	Shufu County	2		4896.0
疏勒县	Shule County	20	2	185233.4
英吉沙县	Yengisar County	10	3	48801.7
泽普县	Zepu [Poskam] County	6	3	17289.7
莎车县	Shache [Yarkant] County	7	1	125422.6
叶城县	Yecheng [Kagilik] County	24	2	158178.7
麦盖提县	Makit County	11	2	91026.2
岳普湖县	Yopurga County	12	3	121083.2
伽师县	Jiashi [Payzawat] County	11		113094.1
巴楚县	Bachu [Maralbexi] County	12	3	68968.3
塔什库尔干塔吉克自治县	Taxkorgan Tajik Autonomous County	3	3	17051.3
和田地区	**Hotan Administrative Offices**	**29**	**10**	**211359.7**
和田市	Hotan City	5	3	26419.3
和田县	Hotan County	6	2	53197.9
墨玉县	Moyu [Karakax] County	8	2	62510.9
皮山县	Pishan [Guma] County	3		17724.5
洛浦县	Lop County	4	2	34148.1
策勒县	Qira County			
于田县	Yutian [Keriya] County	3	1	17359.0
民丰县	Minfeng [Niya] County			
自治区直辖县级市	**County level City directly under the Autonomous Region**	**295**	**57**	**9514853.7**
石河子市	Shihezi City	100	33	4775122.1
阿拉尔市	Aral City	109	8	1336337.0
图木舒克市	Tumxuk City	38	1	520026.8
五家渠市	Wujiaqu City	48	15	2883367.8

Continued

(10 000 yuan)

工业增加值 Value-added of Industry	工业销售产值（当年价格） Sales Value of Industry Products (At Current Prices)	出口交货值 Delivery Value of Industry Export	实收资本 Total Capital Hold	资产合计 Total Assets	流动资产合计 Total Current Assets	#产成品 Finished Product	固定资产原价 Original Value of Fixed Assets
16439.6	44348.1		23112.5	109103.4	32959.2	15455.2	109953.4
5640.6	32063.4		17598.4	87207.2	14829.0	2191.4	22129.9
139976.5	**326695.7**		**422444.1**	**1820358.7**	**554980.4**	**93224.7**	**1063735.8**
61733.4	141040.7		196359.8	632088.9	295012.5	33705.1	334193.0
24657.9	87340.5		130788.0	637362.5	197818.4	43762.6	347536.2
13745.2	19533.6			160533.7	4197.0		171087.6
39840.0	78780.9		95296.3	390373.6	57952.5	15757.0	210919.0
355174.1	**1240847.6**	**18318.2**	**486342.4**	**2380809.6**	**966650.5**	**172762.5**	**1504368.8**
109426.8	390576.1	6355.5	178851.4	801772.2	196710.6	5109.5	695755.3
1114.3	4676.6		960.0	9136.2	3982.5	441.2	2258.2
41142.8	176629.6		53135.8	276120.2	149792.0	16186.7	133614.5
15891.4	45001.9	2420.0	46080.0	118309.3	32734.9	4934.7	97217.4
4935.5	15662.0		9740.0	48495.2	25508.9	2639.1	32980.9
29327.9	116832.8	4038.2	31633.0	171939.0	96442.9	9806.2	77068.8
43315.7	105398.5	2231.4	72510.0	261798.1	137048.4	69409.0	143738.7
24769.3	91961.8		16233.7	134256.1	92175.4	5140.3	39554.0
24324.6	106324.0		35887.8	148809.1	78449.3	33896.7	43662.6
45537.7	114533.9	3273.1	12684.6	130102.8	57184.8	9682.5	85495.8
9520.7	61914.2		20306.1	90092.6	52051.8	9820.7	43386.5
5867.3	11336.2		8320.0	189978.8	44569.0	5695.9	109636.1
87962.1	**205252.5**		**325460.6**	**930171.2**	**281951.8**	**14882.9**	**770590.0**
6115.6	26344.4		6696.9	50135.3	26247.3	997.5	29625.0
25649.7	54358.9		192094.2	473881.3	134258.2	1704.9	416334.1
25976.8	56008.7		34864.5	133044.0	68983.8	1703.2	83816.9
8391.8	17724.5		13098.0	70201.6	15891.1	391.2	52539.3
15246.1	33336.4		48107.0	101617.0	17729.9	6498.1	93416.6
6582.1	17479.6		30600.0	101292.0	18841.5	3588.0	94858.1
2572196.1	**9239032.2**	**100633.4**	**3514988.9**	**20577202.1**	**6752161.7**	**721919.6**	**12112688.0**
1253223.9	4599708.5	13548.5	1887938.0	11305128.4	3105459.0	384480.9	7551088.8
425809.7	1304779.4		498060.8	2532893.2	905096.5	74256.6	1097911.8
143809.0	482480.1		159341.8	733964.9	319741.1	79028.8	509447.9
749353.5	2852064.2	87084.9	969648.3	6005215.6	2421865.1	184153.3	2954239.5

13-6 续表 3

单位：万元

地 区	Region	负债合计 Total Liabilities	#流动负债 Total Liquid Liabilities	#非流动负债 Total Non-liquid Liabilities	所有者权益合计 Total Owners' Equities
总 计	**Total**	**116448837.9**	**75023899.7**	**40743498.8**	**65185301.9**
乌鲁木齐市	**Urumqi City**	**26982959.0**	**19086049.1**	**7863760.5**	**15480423.9**
天山区	Tianshan District	1444215.5	552180.6	892034.9	341353.1
沙依巴克区	Shayibak District	2032314.7	1380179.7	650421.4	1004538.0
新市区	Xinshi District	6499474.5	4665386.7	1828983.3	4458377.6
水磨沟区	Shui Mogou District	3699101.1	2306529.9	1392535.2	2339886.8
头屯河区	Tou Tunhe District	8891499.3	7746516.7	1135606.1	4195588.2
达坂城区	Da Bancheng District	1113861.6	569470.1	544391.5	423087.9
米东区	Midong District	3007126.8	1670931.4	1327194.3	2609767.1
乌鲁木齐县	Urumqi County	295365.5	194854.0	92593.8	107825.2
克拉玛依市	**Karamay City**	**8827637.0**	**4512153.5**	**4312099.8**	**11841787.4**
独山子区	Dushanzi District	996842.6	728385.5	268457.0	2403959.7
克拉玛依区	Karamay District	7643326.3	3624276.7	4015666.0	9306968.1
白碱滩区	Bai Jiantan District	180826.8	152850.0	27976.8	114557.5
乌尔河区	Urhe District	6641.3	6641.3		16302.1
吐鲁番市	**Turpan City**	**5250456.8**	**3139448.1**	**2108844.8**	**2443945.5**
高昌区	Gaochang District	763140.2	534597.5	228089.7	405678.8
鄯善县	Shanshan [Piqan] County	2220606.4	1255876.0	963019.7	1262974.6
托克逊县	Toksun County	2266710.2	1348974.6	917735.4	775292.1
哈密地区	**Hami [Kumul] Administrative Offices**	**9775066.4**	**5395987.2**	**4272219.6**	**3727947.0**
哈密市	Hami [Kumul] City	7352043.1	3724199.0	3520984.8	2703171.6
巴里坤哈萨克自治县	Barkol Kazak Autonomous County	1092095.3	579987.5	512107.6	499611.5
伊吾县	Yiwu [Araturuk] County	1330928.0	1091800.7	239127.2	525163.9
昌吉回族自治州	**Changji Hui Autonomous Prefecture**	**17286053.7**	**12500677.1**	**4599415.2**	**7872077.0**
昌吉市	Changji City	3260634.3	2632414.9	603968.0	2952502.0
阜康市	Fukang City	3565539.4	2244521.9	1321017.3	1635790.5
呼图壁县	Hutubi County	791111.4	393633.6	397477.8	350866.9
玛纳斯县	Manas County	2347721.9	1646613.0	650830.5	566052.2
奇台县	Qitai County	714020.0	534626.9	126336.3	341043.0
吉木萨尔县	Jimsar County	6535935.6	4993450.7	1484110.3	2001255.4
木垒哈萨克自治县	Mori Kazak Autonomous County	71091.1	55416.1	15675.0	24567.0
伊犁哈萨克自治州	**Ili Kazak Autonomous Prefecture**	**13497047.5**	**8521759.4**	**4823749.0**	**5781659.6**
伊犁州直属县(市)	**Counties (Cities) Direct Under Ili Prefecture**	**8184567.7**	**5063363.2**	**3052643.1**	**3394211.8**
伊宁市	Yining [Gulja] City	966058.2	698239.1	265605.2	642632.7
奎屯市	Kuytun City	1930770.8	1257811.7	609762.9	567892.1
霍尔果斯市	Huoerguosi City	104364.2	25736.8	78627.3	63947.4
伊宁县	Yining [Gulja] County	2053916.2	1009802.4	1044113.2	643327.7
察布查尔锡伯自治县	Qapqal Xibe Autonomous County	256141.9	216706.6	39435.3	116928.1
霍城县	Huocheng [Korgas] County	343932.2	294044.8	49887.3	170833.1
巩留县	Gongliu [Tokkuztara] County	662577.2	322607.6	339848.7	439364.5
新源县	Xinyuan [Kunes] County	824680.2	682266.0	142414.2	418034.0
昭苏县	Zhaosu [Mongolkure] County	138621.8	72836.4	64949.6	34846.6
特克斯县	Tekes County	192666.1	103378.1	87094.2	44082.4
尼勒克县	Nilka County	710838.9	379933.7	330905.2	252323.2
塔城地区	**Tacheng [Tarbagatai] Administrative Offices**	**2610674.9**	**1924855.7**	**625325.6**	**1245391.5**
塔城市	Tacheng [Qoqek] City	57284.4	50584.7	6699.7	14382.3
乌苏市	Usu City	525584.3	453752.7	71831.2	579794.8
额敏县	Emin [Dorbiljin] County	246028.6	149533.6	96494.8	100900.4

Continued

(10 000 yuan)

主营业务收入 Revenue from Principal Business	主营业务成本 Cost of Principal Business	主营业务税金及附加 Taxes and Other Charges on Principal Business	营业利润 Business Profit	利润总额 Total Profit	亏损企业亏损总额 Losses Value of Loss-Suffering Enterprises	利税总额 Total Profits and Taxes	本年应交增值税 Value-added Taxes Payable	全部从业人员年平均人数(人) Annual Average Employed Persons (person)
82037341.9	**65910732.9**	**3777572.7**	**2541058.3**	**3409656.9**	**3570382.2**	**10524057.2**	**3336827.6**	**720073**
21115550.1	**17982747.2**	**1279400.3**	**-97090.1**	**160660.5**	**775843.5**	**2005454.3**	**565393.5**	**152962**
367548.8	336625.2	2037.6	-34532.7	16550.0	21933.2	30299.2	11711.6	7311
670069.6	624970.1	3981.7	-35386.7	1728.8	40200.7	12714.5	7004.0	10001
3790088.1	3211001.0	62239.0	-150547.7	-62753.8	218280.0	136881.7	137396.5	32565
4544150.5	4387133.3	5184.8	109785.2	128857.8	339.4	112657.3	-21385.3	23651
6637868.8	5656324.4	248360.0	39415.8	88025.7	419262.7	497986.8	161601.1	41911
225726.9	161911.7	4143.6	14466.3	15538.4	7201.8	-3601.7	-23283.7	6188
4839794.7	3586226.1	953148.0	-50845.6	-40303.8	68579.4	1202792.0	289947.8	31186
40302.7	18555.4	305.6	10555.3	13017.4	46.3	15724.5	2401.5	149
11833048.7	**9288391.6**	**1404462.0**	**-476162.1**	**-224651.8**	**714152.5**	**1931020.4**	**751210.2**	**107062**
3905971.1	2794773.5	636345.3	87123.8	108277.5	55200.9	1020305.0	275682.2	18477
7724361.7	6330838.8	766042.0	-577191.1	-349545.8	657337.9	879416.7	462920.5	84766
196912.7	157461.5	1999.0	14186.3	16465.5	1504.8	30677.1	12212.6	3668
5803.2	5317.8	75.7	-281.1	151.0	108.9	621.6	394.9	151
2193290.8	**1945037.8**	**50429.0**	**-424334.4**	**-423953.6**	**523986.4**	**-301952.0**	**71572.6**	**25659**
357638.0	303106.0	2767.0	-2199.2	398.6	18341.3	24292.9	21127.3	5013
1236517.4	1108323.3	37145.4	-355005.8	-360232.8	402070.5	-286538.6	36548.8	12138
599135.4	533608.5	10516.6	-67129.4	-64119.4	103574.6	-39706.3	13896.5	8508
4099530.1	**3237206.3**	**31845.7**	**285562.8**	**308128.3**	**114769.3**	**515205.2**	**175231.2**	**36118**
3467705.9	2764395.0	23632.7	259394.1	277963.1	72318.1	407936.7	106340.9	29193
224024.1	168697.4	2893.6	2483.6	4967.1	15147.5	19651.7	11791.0	2956
407800.1	304113.9	5319.4	23685.1	25198.1	27303.7	87616.8	57099.3	3969
13069855.0	**11355600.3**	**52060.4**	**388710.1**	**442742.2**	**329991.1**	**765513.1**	**270710.5**	**95065**
3620689.8	3004891.1	10037.7	345835.4	367932.2	22810.5	484933.3	106963.4	23671
2186903.6	2056652.0	7175.1	-112526.4	-106553.5	166905.2	-1035.5	98342.9	25238
948587.9	779194.5	6766.0	93975.7	97493.1	1576.8	148593.1	44334.0	8876
1823249.7	1573300.2	7801.5	42457.5	52186.1	26674.2	24579.1	-35408.5	12961
624809.1	509641.4	9571.3	30124.7	31595.1	15899.0	66830.5	25664.1	4570
3837227.4	3410176.7	10110.5	-13826.3	-2241.3	96125.4	36760.8	28891.6	18771
28387.5	21744.4	598.3	2669.5	2330.5		4851.8	1923.0	978
6486589.7	**5149349.2**	**94894.7**	**177636.9**	**239246.3**	**454708.2**	**563322.9**	**229181.9**	**89103**
3849684.2	**3093683.7**	**54139.2**	**114630.7**	**149930.8**	**299186.6**	**357468.1**	**153398.1**	**53813**
346863.0	295755.7	2615.0	-4994.2	504.6	32336.2	18166.6	15047.0	8038
996917.1	817431.2	3842.6	67364.8	81551.0	36179.4	107384.6	21991.0	12184
75227.4	60876.9	121.2	2369.4	2867.6		10752.9	7764.1	1349
546860.4	461708.8	5212.6	-81873.9	-72174.5	102901.7	-44263.9	22698.0	9214
142000.8	116808.2	201.2	7024.5	8969.3	9515.6	11023.6	1853.1	1795
465849.5	312083.0	8858.9	79872.5	78706.7	9575.8	100440.9	12875.3	4039
385464.4	300146.5	950.1	37430.4	38751.6	6073.8	50907.0	11205.3	3511
548894.0	481179.4	28866.3	-27819.7	-24497.3	81111.1	37132.7	32763.7	9123
144212.8	96484.0	894.1	33921.9	33748.6	1356.0	43860.5	9217.8	733
30392.2	26673.5	349.3	-6630.5	-6443.6	6443.6	-4279.5	1814.8	883
167002.6	124536.5	2227.9	7965.5	7946.8	13693.4	26342.7	16168.0	2944
1708584.3	**1427795.3**	**23911.5**	**29712.7**	**50188.1**	**73756.4**	**106965.8**	**32866.2**	**22492**
38636.5	33249.4	106.7	-2038.3	-1566.1	1758.0	-1512.2	-52.8	457
574172.6	489440.7	13895.5	-3938.4	4107.6	24301.9	18248.5	245.4	5683
122337.7	104194.9	277.8	5349.4	10609.8	5574.8	17505.6	6618.0	1828

13-6 续表 4

单位：万元

地　区	Region	负债合计 Total Liabilities	#流动负债 Total Liquid Liabilities	#非流动负债 Total Non-liquid Liabilities	所有者权益合计 Total Owners' Equities
沙湾县	Shawan County	512340.6	479629.4	24385.1	226292.2
托里县	Toli County	598019.1	395137.5	159647.8	128489.9
裕民县	Yumin [Qagantokay] County	4129.2	3688.3	440.9	1517.1
和布克赛尔蒙古自治县	Hoboksar Mongol Autonomous County	667288.7	392529.5	265826.1	194014.8
阿勒泰地区	**Altay Administrative Offices**	**2701804.9**	**1533540.5**	**1145780.3**	**1142056.3**
阿勒泰市	Altay City	211608.9	129553.7	82055.2	63931.4
布尔津县	Burqin County	453655.1	209236.6	227793.2	104133.5
富蕴县	Fuyun [Koktokay] County	1045766.5	635357.0	410409.4	452242.1
福海县	Fuhai [Burultokay] County	96660.6	74742.6	21918.0	102339.8
哈巴河县	Habahe [Kaba] County	437063.3	176356.6	260706.6	223562.1
青河县	Qinghe [Qinggil] County	284866.2	207784.7	71222.9	70652.3
吉木乃县	Jeminay County	172184.3	100509.3	71675.0	125195.1
博尔塔拉蒙古自治州	**Bortala Mongol Autonomous Prefecture**	**1434111.4**	**910309.7**	**501564.7**	**456552.3**
博乐市	Bole [Bortala] City	801245.0	564774.5	216628.2	225190.5
阿拉山口市	Alashankou City	359872.9	143020.1	216852.8	126211.3
精河县	Jinghe [Jing] County	254538.5	184060.1	68083.7	89841.8
温泉县	Wenquan [Araxang] County	18455.0	18455.0		15308.7
巴音郭楞蒙古自治州	**Bayangol Mongol Autonomous Prefecture**	**9200651.5**	**4523894.8**	**4673146.4**	**7148586.8**
库尔勒市	Korla City	6246666.0	2487719.7	3758946.1	5630611.9
轮台县	Luntai [Bugur] County	308253.6	265539.9	41592.4	222063.7
尉犁县	Yuli [Lopnur] County	67127.2	50824.7	16041.5	94200.5
若羌县	Ruoqiang [Qarkilik] County	688037.2	477416.3	210620.7	336779.8
且末县	Qiemo [Qarqan] County	41815.5	41815.5		40004.9
焉耆回族自治县	Yanqi Hui Autonomous County	149090.9	120844.6	27694.5	61663.9
和静县	Hejing County	1483076.6	933715.3	548285.5	677694.1
和硕县	Hoxud County	167707.3	121416.9	45690.4	53089.2
博湖县	Bohu [Bagrax] County	48877.2	24601.9	24275.3	32478.8
阿克苏地区	**Aksu Administrative Offices**	**6124232.6**	**4333931.3**	**1751682.6**	**2778765.0**
阿克苏市	Aksu City	1254390.4	685167.8	568216.4	798136.0
温宿县	Wensu [Onsu] County	431580.0	279776.0	138686.3	138035.7
库车县	Kuqa County	1565061.5	1089152.0	474220.3	1211615.8
沙雅县	Xayar County	247161.7	163410.5	83751.2	137976.2
新和县	Xinhe [Toksu] County	136980.2	90209.4	44970.8	28105.1
拜城县	Baicheng [Bay] County	2286111.3	1902791.7	362316.3	373454.7
乌什县	Wushi [Uxturpan] County	49483.1	32137.6	17345.4	48595.3

Continued

(10 000 yuan)

主营业务收入 Revenue from Principal Business	主营业务成本 Cost of Principal Business	主营业务税金及附加 Taxes and Other Charges on Principal Business	营业利润 Business Profit	利润总额 Total Profit	亏损企业亏损总额 Losses Value of Loss-Suffering Enterprises	利税总额 Total Profits and Taxes	本年应交增值税 Value-added Taxes Payable	全部从业人员年平均人数(人) Annual Average Employed Persons (person)
624071.3	542652.5	2631.9	26896.4	30306.0	6660.2	47760.0	14822.1	6671
166641.2	125670.0	965.2	5912.7	7600.2	13424.3	7345.2	-1220.2	3276
3765.0	3754.0		-927.8	-833.4	833.4	-891.4	-58.0	100
178960.0	128833.8	6034.4	-1541.3	-36.0	21203.8	18510.1	12511.7	4477
928321.2	**627870.2**	**16844.0**	**33293.5**	**39127.4**	**81765.2**	**98889.0**	**42917.6**	**12798**
93848.6	81961.6	460.1	-1992.1	618.2	3497.0	3666.1	2587.8	2171
77387.4	51306.9	298.8	1468.3	4320.7	2820.0	8819.5	4200.0	712
335773.7	232410.8	10588.3	-39243.4	-38520.1	55128.9	-14584.2	13347.6	4496
89951.9	67525.6	1532.1	7592.6	8831.7	6273.9	11531.2	1167.4	1235
191793.3	92056.0	3418.5	53602.4	51031.3	2080.8	71012.5	16562.7	2212
56857.9	52467.8	85.1	-12615.9	-11673.1	11964.6	-11842.9	-254.9	1762
82708.4	50141.5	461.1	24481.6	24518.7		30286.8	5307.0	210
716301.9	**579704.7**	**2057.4**	**33799.2**	**43434.6**	**24194.1**	**67203.0**	**21711.0**	**9212**
440146.7	372765.5	1401.0	8736.0	15800.1	17893.1	27409.4	10208.3	6265
134462.6	92254.9	102.2	26340.4	26570.9	612.5	33324.8	6651.7	849
124021.3	100109.4	488.3	-3406.1	-1173.4	5688.5	3930.6	4615.7	1930
17671.3	14574.9	65.9	2128.9	2237.0		2538.2	235.3	168
7897266.3	**4572384.3**	**360551.5**	**1801216.1**	**1866072.2**	**188856.2**	**2711430.1**	**484806.4**	**53032**
6033438.0	3196916.1	288875.5	1704859.8	1731534.3	76622.9	2426561.8	406152.0	33483
208385.3	183621.3	1252.7	-23166.5	-23025.5	28997.9	-17938.5	3834.3	2147
154557.8	130306.6	313.7	15048.5	16491.1	392.7	20790.0	3985.2	1193
466654.7	208294.4	63885.0	83766.7	116123.7	5331.9	214600.8	34592.1	4482
7553.3	7961.3	312.0	-4463.5	-4419.7	4419.7	-4109.0	-1.3	127
103184.0	81587.6	937.9	1160.0	1470.7	5994.6	5135.3	2726.7	1432
809120.0	671677.3	4279.5	30503.9	33751.0	51774.7	64778.7	26748.2	8199
81470.1	67030.1	585.9	-8026.7	-7691.3	15024.0	-4785.3	2320.1	1449
32903.1	24989.6	109.3	1533.9	1837.9	297.8	6396.3	4449.1	520
3909194.2	**2863103.1**	**460393.5**	**143672.1**	**175512.0**	**238229.2**	**830284.6**	**194379.1**	**35096**
871532.8	734172.2	2664.2	49734.2	66200.9	7514.1	82995.3	14130.2	9293
234258.2	163486.4	1750.5	34841.2	38262.0	11766.7	46061.9	6049.4	3652
2009246.9	1260690.6	447260.8	153414.0	154231.2	60942.8	754045.2	152553.2	9984
188144.7	142602.7	438.3	20080.2	24461.5	747.6	26282.9	1383.1	2076
96848.6	61270.4	43.2	29636.7	32245.1		32679.2	390.9	1247
404590.2	410471.7	5824.2	-145926.4	-145644.8	153934.7	-126175.6	13645.0	7062
33093.9	23289.0	1579.6	4295.5	4832.5		9177.8	2765.7	496

13-6 续表 5

单位：万元

地　区	Region	负债合计 Total Liabilities	#流动负债 Total Liquid Liabilities	#非流动负债 Total Non-liquid Liabilities	所有者权益合计 Total Owners' Equities
阿瓦提县	Awat County	87852.1	60474.0	27375.9	21251.3
柯坪县	Kalpin County	65612.3	30812.3	34800.0	21594.9
克孜勒苏柯尔克孜自治州	**Kizilsu Kirgiz Autonomous Prefecture**	**1343580.8**	**985648.4**	**357932.3**	**476777.8**
阿图什市	Artux City	377366.2	348669.2	28696.9	254722.6
阿克陶县	Akto County	516941.7	269005.3	247936.4	120420.9
阿合奇县	Akqi County	160533.7	160533.7		
乌恰县	Wuqia [Ulugqat] County	288739.2	207440.2	81299.0	101634.3
喀什地区	**Kashgar [Kaxgar] Administrative Offices**	**1614596.7**	**1052107.0**	**513148.7**	**766211.7**
喀什市	Kashgar [Kaxgar] City	556197.7	248508.1	304980.1	245574.1
疏附县	Shufu County	6403.2	3993.1	2410.0	2733.0
疏勒县	Shule County	176642.4	149761.9	26880.5	99477.5
英吉沙县	Yengisar County	62910.3	30408.1	21794.0	55398.9
泽普县	Zepu [Poskam] County	28359.1	12090.5	5100.0	20136.0
莎车县	Shache [Yarkant] County	103900.5	71882.1	31123.3	68038.5
叶城县	Yecheng [Kagilik] County	190820.0	164445.1	24182.5	70978.0
麦盖提县	Makit County	85440.0	85440.0		48816.0
岳普湖县	Yopurga County	89654.6	81638.7	8015.9	59154.4
伽师县	Jiashi [Payzawat] County	54806.5	54025.5	-2744.4	75296.2
巴楚县	Bachu [Maralbexi] County	63173.9	43236.8	1795.5	26918.8
塔什库尔干塔吉克自治县	Taxkorgan Tajik Autonomous County	196288.5	106677.1	89611.3	-6309.7
和田地区	**Hotan Administrative Offices**	**484172.1**	**273352.5**	**210685.5**	**445998.7**
和田市	Hotan City	36057.8	22034.8	14023.0	14077.4
和田县	Hotan County	253679.7	100064.6	153615.1	220201.5
墨玉县	Moyu [Karakax] County	60421.0	56279.3	4104.9	72623.0
皮山县	Pishan [Guma] County	27837.6	7495.1	20342.5	42363.9
洛浦县	Lop County	36270.4	35573.1	600.0	65346.6
策勒县	Qira County				
于田县	Yutian [Keriya] County	69905.6	51905.6	18000.0	31386.3
民丰县	Minfeng [Niya] County				
自治区直辖县级市	**County level City directly under the Autonomous Region**	**14628272.4**	**9788581.6**	**4755249.7**	**5964569.2**
石河子市	Shihezi City	7791913.7	4501108.0	3244198.2	3519770.5
阿拉尔市	Aral City	1594595.5	1099583.9	490483.8	938297.3
图木舒克市	Tumxuk City	454262.0	289126.5	149641.8	288787.4
五家渠市	Wujiaqu City	4787501.2	3898763.2	870925.9	1217714.0

Continued

(10 000 yuan)

主营业务收入 Revenue from Principal Business	主营业务成本 Cost of Principal Business	主营业务税金及附加 Taxes and Other Charges on Principal Business	营业利润 Business Profit	利润总额 Total Profit	亏损企业亏损总额 Losses Value of Loss-Suffering Enterprises	利税总额 Total Profits and Taxes	本年应交增值税 Value-added Taxes Payable	全部从业人员年平均人数(人) Annual Average Employed Persons (person)
40837.2	39916.3	140.3	-4413.7	-1153.1	3153.3	1581.6	2594.4	1118
30641.7	27203.8	692.4	2010.4	2076.7	170.0	3636.3	867.2	168
324543.2	**250841.2**	**7196.8**	**24342.9**	**24625.6**	**22754.4**	**56455.1**	**24632.7**	**4411**
134519.0	107758.7	968.5	22514.8	25294.9	8501.2	38154.4	11891.0	1495
88702.8	76482.0	1389.0	-7981.8	-8076.9	8076.9	-2892.3	3795.6	1669
19533.6	8844.1	310.9	2626.3	2617.4		5969.5	3041.2	49
81787.8	57756.4	4528.4	7183.6	4790.2	6176.3	15223.5	5904.9	1198
1263390.4	**1023024.0**	**4117.7**	**92711.2**	**116808.2**	**18530.8**	**171163.8**	**50237.9**	**19193**
402406.1	319724.2	2109.7	27886.5	35484.7	2578.0	50296.2	12701.8	5444
4361.8	3865.5	4.1	209.6	204.6		239.8	31.1	135
192025.9	161967.1	138.4	13385.6	16919.0	2415.2	22856.7	5799.3	1646
44798.0	34679.7	333.2	2618.4	4649.6	96.7	7654.1	2671.3	893
15658.2	13826.0	67.0	-1423.5	-407.0	2006.8	151.3	491.3	413
117039.2	102070.3	118.7	6624.0	8974.2	39.0	11052.1	1959.2	1198
107512.2	79892.1	269.9	11476.9	13649.3	3032.9	20205.2	6286.0	2831
98712.0	80734.7	105.8	11746.8	12273.5	738.6	16434.8	4055.5	876
83046.6	71731.5	38.4	3730.5	5467.1	763.9	6808.5	1303.0	1956
117497.1	85961.9	733.8	20401.8	22497.5		35332.4	12101.1	2528
68906.9	60969.9	97.3	1675.3	3010.9	944.5	4659.7	1551.5	927
11426.4	7601.1	101.4	-5620.7	-5915.2	5915.2	-4527.0	1286.8	346
199649.2	**158930.9**	**1291.3**	**5196.9**	**13908.6**	**5416.1**	**27841.6**	**12641.7**	**5087**
26170.8	25308.7	111.7	-1070.9	447.5	448.6	1090.4	531.2	773
54143.9	38285.4	698.5	-1058.6	982.9	3294.3	5053.6	3372.2	701
52717.6	45576.9	171.2	1251.0	4221.6	187.6	11425.5	7032.7	1178
15395.2	10833.9	228.8	2414.8	2762.4		3629.0	637.8	1141
34004.8	23911.6	59.8	4586.9	5834.1	420.2	6921.7	1027.8	934
17216.9	15014.4	21.3	-926.3	-339.9	1065.4	-278.6	40.0	360
8929132.3	**7504412.3**	**28872.4**	**585796.7**	**667123.8**	**158950.4**	**1181115.1**	**485118.9**	**88073**
4267477.8	3556921.1	15793.3	229356.8	280095.0	71437.1	435725.0	139836.7	50234
1290246.6	951159.1	8893.5	225176.4	231222.4	27138.1	266541.0	26425.1	15068
482853.6	389071.8	1029.8	55831.4	58819.8	843.7	85268.2	25418.6	5683
2888554.3	2607260.3	3155.8	75432.1	96986.6	59531.5	393580.9	293438.5	17088

13-7 规模以上工业企业主要经济效益指标

单位: % (2015 年)

项 目	Item	产值利税率 Ratio of Profits and Taxes to Industrial Output Value
总 计	**Total**	**12.9**
按登记注册类型分	**Grouped by Registry Type**	
内资企业	Domestic Funded Enterprises	13.0
国有企业	State-owned Enterprises	4.6
#中央企业	Central Enterprises	3.0
地方企业	Local Enterprises	14.8
#自治区属企业	Autonomous	29.4
地区(州、市)属企业	Prefecture or City	-18.6
县(市)属企业	County or City	20.9
集体企业	Collective-owned Enterprises	9.2
#自治区属企业	Autonomous	4.7
地区(州、市)属企业	Prefecture or City	
县(市)属企业	County or City	26.4
镇属企业	Town	-10.5
乡属企业	Village	
股份合作企业	Share-holding Cooperative Enterprises	-11.7
联营企业	Joint Ownership Enterprises	13.3
#国有联营企业	State Joint Ownership Enterprises	
集体联营企业	Collective Joint Ownership Enterprises	
国有与集体联营企业	Joint State-collective Enterprises	
其他联营企业	Other Joint Ownership Enterprises	13.3
有限责任公司	Limited Liability Corporations	8.9
#国有独资公司	State Sole funded Corporations	15.3
其他有限责任公司	Other Limited Liability Corporations	7.9
股份有限公司	Share-holding Corporations Ltd.	21.3
私营企业	Private Enterprises	11.9
#私营独资企业	Private-funded Enterprises	23.1
私营合伙企业	Private Partnership Enterprises	27.4
私营有限责任公司	Private Limited Liability Corporations	10.8
私营股份有限公司	Private Share-holding Corporations Ltd.	16.7
港、澳、台商投资企业	Enterprises with Funds from Hong Kong, Macao and Taiwan	11.8
外商投资企业	Foreign Funded Enterprises	7.1
在总计中: 国有控股企业	Of the Total: State-owned and State-holding Enterprises	16.2
在总计中: 农村工业	Of the Total: Rural Industry	4.0
按轻、重工业分	**Grouped by Light & Heavy Industry**	
轻工业	Light Industry	14.0
以农产品为原料	Using Farm Produces as Raw Materials	14.7
以非农产品为原料	Using Non-Farm Produces as Raw Materials	1.2
重工业	Heavy Industry	12.7
采掘工业	Mining and Quarrying	16.4
原料工业	Raw Materials Industry	11.9
加工工业	Manufacturing Industry	11.3
按企业规模分	**Grouped by Size of Enterprises (Old Standard)**	
大型企业	Large Enterprises	14.9
中型企业	Medium-sized Enterprises	10.7
小型企业	Small Enterprises	10.4
微型企业	Mini Enterprises	9.4

Main Indicators on Economic Efficiency of Industrial Enterprises above Designated Size

(%)

总资产贡献率 Ratio of Profits, Taxes and Interests to Average Value	资本保值增值率 Ratio of Capital-hold and Rise	资产负债率 Ratio of debts to Assets	流动资产周转次数(次/年) Turnover of Currents Assets (times/year)	成本费用利润率 Ratio of Profits to Industrial Costs	全员劳动生产率(万元/人) Overall Labour Productivity (10 000yuan/person)
7.4	**105.1**	**64.1**	**1.5**	**4.5**	**36.98**
7.5	105.4	64.2	1.5	4.5	37.27
4.1	95.1	68.4	3.7	4.1	40.84
3.4	94.9	63.1	9.2	2.9	43.48
5.4	95.6	78.7	0.7	12.5	32.90
10.5	101.4	67.3	1.3	41.2	61.43
-0.7	27.5	97.9	0.3	-9.4	7.06
7.6	115.0	69.4	1.1	15.1	36.67
9.2	88.8	54.5	1.3	2.4	11.48
5.6	102.1	60.6	1.4	0.7	7.62
21.0	82.3	44.7	1.0	18.8	15.86
-6.8	65.5	58.3	1.9	-24.0	19.90
1.2		88.9	0.3	-20.7	11.08
20.8	118.5	45.6	3.0	6.8	9.76
20.8	118.5	45.6	3.0	6.8	9.76
5.4	108.8	72.0	1.3	1.9	26.60
6.6	99.1	69.0	1.0	3.9	27.77
5.1	111.2	72.6	1.3	1.6	26.31
10.8	104.2	49.6	1.9	4.6	68.87
8.5	103.7	66.8	1.4	9.8	27.06
21.1	124.8	68.1	1.5	10.0	47.56
93.0	119.5	60.5	5.7	14.8	56.27
8.4	109.9	67.9	1.5	9.0	25.00
8.4	86.3	62.5	0.9	13.9	47.66
6.7	116.6	59.3	1.5	8.0	17.06
6.5	78.9	60.6	2.0	3.7	33.84
8.2	101.0	61.5	1.9	3.3	46.95
6.6	75.2	59.5	1.5	3.4	11.51
11.3	116.1	60.3	1.6	10.1	21.39
13.4	109.4	60.0	1.7	10.9	22.29
1.4	166.8	61.7	0.7	-2.5	12.79
7.0	103.9	64.5	1.5	3.5	41.21
6.7	98.9	55.0	1.7	4.5	48.53
7.2	104.9	69.7	1.8	1.2	42.16
6.8	111.8	63.7	1.0	8.8	27.63
8.5	100.0	61.3	1.9	3.2	52.81
5.4	109.1	66.5	1.1	3.5	20.77
7.1	113.3	66.3	1.4	7.7	26.52
4.0	140.9	76.7	0.8	7.4	33.04

13-8 分行业规模以上工业企业主要经济效益指标

单位: % (2015 年)

行　业	Sector	产　值 利税率 Ratio of Profits and Taxes to Industrial Output Value
总　计	**Total**	**12.9**
煤炭开采和洗选业	Mining and Washing of Coal	14.0
石油和天然气开采业	Extraction of Petroleum and Natural Gas	18.5
黑色金属矿采选业	Mining and Processing of Ferrous Metals Ores	12.4
有色金属矿采选业	Mining and Processing of Nonferrous Metals Ores	19.9
非金属矿采选业	Mining and Processing of Nonmetal Ores	19.8
#采　盐	Extraction of Salt	43.2
开采辅助活动	Support for Minning	9.9
农副食品加工业	Activities Processing of Food from Agricultural Products	10.8
#谷物磨制	Grain Grinding	6.6
饲料加工	Fodder Processing	8.7
制　糖	Sugar Making	2.5
食品制造业	Manufacture of Foods	11.9
#罐头制造	Manufacture of can	6.7
饮料制造业	Manufacture of Liguor,Beverages and Refined Tea	25.2
#酒的制造	Manufacture of Liguor	33.0
烟草制品业	Manufacture of Tobacco	69.6
纺织业	Manufacture of Textile	11.6
#棉、化纤纺织及印染精加工	Cotton, Chemical Fiber, Dyeing, Printing and Processing	11.8
毛纺织和染整精加工	Wool Textile, Dyeing and Printing	17.2
纺织服装、鞋、帽制造业	Manufacture of Textile, Wearing Apparel and Accessories	11.2
皮革、毛皮、羽毛(绒)及其制品业	Manufacturie of Leather, Fur, Feather and Related Products	1.1
#皮革鞣制加工	Leather Tanning and Processing	1.0
木材加工及木、竹、藤、棕、草制品业	Processing of Timber, Manufacture of Wood, Bamboo, Cane, Grass Products	12.4
家具制造业	Manufacture of Furniture	16.1
造纸及纸制品业	Manufacture of Paper and Paper Products	14.1
印刷业和记录媒介的复制	Printing and Reproduction of Recording Media	13.2
文教、工美、体育和娱乐用品制造业	Manufacture of Articles for Cultural, Educational,Sports and Entertainment	8.6
石油加工、炼焦及核燃料加工业	Processing, Processing of Petroleeum,Coking and Nuclear Fuel	32.9
#炼　焦	Coking	2.0
化学原料及化学制品制造业	Manufacture of Raw Chemical Materials and Chemical Products	5.4
#基础化学原料制造	Basic Chemical Material	1.2
肥料制造	Manufacture of Fertilizer	14.3
合成材料制造	Manufacture of Synthetic Materials	0.4
医药制造业	Manufacture of Medicine	6.4
化学纤维制造业	Manufacture of Chemical Fibers	7.5
橡胶制品业	Manufacture of Rubber and Plastics Products	10.0
非金属矿物制品业	Manufacture of Non-metallic Mineral Products	6.8
#水泥制造	Manufacture of Cement	0.4
黑色金属冶炼及压延加工业	Smelting and Pressing of Ferrous Metals	-20.8
有色金属冶炼及压延加工业	Smelting and Pressing of Non ferrous Metals	3.8
金属制品业	Manufacture of Metal Products	9.2
通用设备制造业	Manufacture of General Purpose Machinery	7.9
专用设备制造业	Manufacture of Special Purpose Machinery	11.6
汽车制造业	Manufacture of Automobile	-23.6
铁路、船舶、航空航天和其他运输设备制造业	Manufacture of Railway ,Ship,Aeronautics and Other Transport Equipment	22.3
电气机械及器材制造业	Manufacture of Electrical Machinery and Apparatus	14.5
计算机、通信和其他电子设备制造业	Manufacture of, Computer Communication and Other Electronic Equipment	-5.7
仪器仪表制造业	Measuring Instruments and Machinery	13.0
废弃资源综合利用业	Comprehensive Utilization of Waste Resources	13.0
金属制品、机械和设备修理业	Repair Service of Metal Prodults,Mouhinery and Equipment	9.2
电力、热力的生产和供应业	Production and Supply of Electrici Power and Heat Power	9.4
#电力生产和电力供应	Production and Supply of Electric	9.7
燃气生产和供应业	Production and Supply of Gas	2.6
水的生产和供应业	Production and Supply of Water	11.7

Main Indicators on Economic Efficiency of Industrial Enterprises above Designated Size by Sectors

(%)

总资产贡献率 Ratio of Profits, Taxes and Interests to Average Value	资本保值增值率 Ratio of Capital-hold and Rise	资产负债率 Ratio of debts to Assets	流动资产周转次数(次/年) Turnover of Currents Assets (times/year)	成本费用利润率 Ratio of Profits to Industrial Costs	全员劳动生产率（万元/人） Overall Labour Productivity (10 000yuan/person)
7.4	**105.1**	**64.1**	**1.5**	**4.5**	**36.98**
5.1	88.4	72.3	1.1	-1.1	23.39
7.1	102.7	46.6	2.6	6.0	86.25
6.1	83.3	74.5	0.7	4.1	27.69
6.8	101.1	60.1	1.0	12.9	34.23
15.4	103.5	73.6	1.3	8.6	31.13
29.5	119.1	33.5	1.2	31.7	32.35
7.2	85.6	61.8	1.2	2.1	24.84
13.8	103.4	62.4	2.0	10.5	23.32
10.4	116.9	57.4	2.6	6.0	20.74
12.3	118.0	40.9	2.7	8.7	22.57
2.3	87.6	76.7	0.7	-1.7	9.02
10.1	128.6	64.1	1.7	9.5	23.40
5.0		78.5	0.9	5.0	13.44
22.1	110.4	54.2	1.7	21.7	37.84
24.5	108.8	54.4	1.3	27.4	39.21
65.1	101.9	26.9	1.7	25.9	477.72
7.3	107.2	59.8	1.2	8.3	9.97
8.2	106.8	60.7	1.2	8.3	10.04
7.2	101.6	30.9	1.4	12.4	15.66
7.1	1353.0	34.8	2.0	10.8	7.00
1.6	97.0	78.0	1.0	-0.3	19.32
1.6	97.1	78.4	0.9	-0.3	15.62
10.8	127.2	61.3	1.4	12.1	19.68
10.8	5.4	65.8	1.0	12.6	10.56
20.3	89.2	53.1	2.5	16.4	22.53
6.9	105.7	42.4	0.9	7.2	12.30
19.3	156.4	60.1	3.4	8.6	13.07
39.8	102.3	46.4	4.0	6.4	109.08
1.6	100.0	69.8	1.0	0.1	17.83
4.0	112.0	68.1	1.5	2.0	24.84
2.9	108.3	69.4	1.4	-2.1	19.30
6.8	100.2	72.1	1.3	10.3	39.29
2.2	117.0	69.5	1.7	-2.6	20.84
2.1	319.0	54.6	0.7	1.5	11.32
5.8	137.5	69.5	1.1	4.0	16.82
10.9	96.9	50.8	1.8	8.2	18.70
4.2	96.3	64.2	0.9	2.5	17.89
2.0	91.0	61.8	0.5	-6.1	13.98
-4.5	62.1	86.1	1.3	-17.4	-3.53
4.1	127.1	73.0	1.5	0.7	35.18
7.4	104.2	63.2	1.4	8.1	16.57
5.1	109.3	76.0	0.7	7.2	14.77
4.7	245.9	35.2	1.1	13.0	20.32
-11.5	46.7	88.1	1.2	-22.2	-4.49
19.6	129.1	38.7	1.2	17.9	17.56
8.5	114.6	62.0	0.8	12.2	64.44
0.1	112.5	54.9	3.1	-2.0	1.38
2.6	115.0	72.6	0.5	8.5	13.89
4.3	97.5	28.5	2.2	6.8	62.41
10.2	122.1	76.2	1.2	0.7	12.60
4.9	110.2	71.7		7.4	53.43
5.1	110.2	71.2		7.8	61.22
3.1	89.3	74.7		-0.2	21.31
2.5	136.8	64.1		8.0	24.90

13-9 各地、州、市、县(市)规模以上工业企业主要经济效益指标

单位: % (2015 年)

地区	Region	产值利税率 Ratio of Profits and Taxes to Industrial Output Value
总计	**Total**	**12.9**
乌鲁木齐市	**Urumqi City**	**9.7**
天山区	Tianshan District	8.4
沙依巴克区	Shayibak District	1.9
新市区	Xinshi District	3.7
水磨沟区	Shui Mogou District	2.5
头屯河区	Tou Tunhe District	7.8
达坂城区	Da Bancheng District	-1.7
米东区	Midong District	25.8
乌鲁木齐县	Urumqi County	36.1
克拉玛依市	**Karamay City**	**18.0**
独山子区	Dushanzi District	27.1
克拉玛依区	Karamay District	13.0
白碱滩区	Bai Jiantan District	16.1
乌尔河区	Urhe District	16.3
吐鲁番市	**Turpan City**	**-14.4**
高昌区	Gaochang District	7.0
鄯善县	Shanshan [Piqan] County	-25.0
托克逊县	Toksun County	-6.5
哈密地区	**Hami [Kumul] Administrative Offices**	**12.1**
哈密市	Hami [Kumul] City	11.3
巴里坤哈萨克自治县	Barkol Kazak Autonomous County	7.9
伊吾县	Yiwu [Araturuk] County	21.4
昌吉回族自治州	**Changji Hui Autonomous Prefecture**	**6.0**
昌吉市	Changji City	13.7
阜康市	Fukang City	
呼图壁县	Hutubi County	15.4
玛纳斯县	Manas County	1.3
奇台县	Qitai County	8.5
吉木萨尔县	Jimsar County	1.1
木垒哈萨克自治县	Mori Kazak Autonomous County	12.4
伊犁哈萨克自治州	**Ili Kazak Autonomous Prefecture**	**8.5**
伊犁州直属县(市)	**Counties (Cities) Direct Under Ili Prefecture**	**9.4**
伊宁市	Yining [Gulja] City	5.2
奎屯市	Kuytun City	11.9
霍尔果斯市	Huoerguosi City	14.2
伊宁县	Yining [Gulja] County	-7.9
察布查尔锡伯自治县	Qapqal Xibe Autonomous County	7.9
霍城县	Huocheng [Korgas] County	20.8
巩留县	Gongliu [Tokkuztara] County	13.6

Main Indicators on Economic Efficiency of Industrial Enterprises above Designated Size by Prefecture, Autonomous Prefecture, City and County

(%)

总资产贡献率 Ratio of Profits, Taxes and Interests to Average Value	资本保值增值率 Ratio of Capital-hold and Rise	资产负债率 Ratio of debts to Assets	流动资产周转次数(次/年) Turnover of Currents Assets (times/year)	成本费用利润率 Ratio of Profits to Industrial Costs	全员劳动生产率(万元/人) Overall Labour Productivity (10 000yuan/person)
7.4	**105.1**	**64.1**	**1.5**	**4.5**	**36.98**
6.1	**99.7**	**63.5**	**1.6**	**0.8**	**35.25**
3.2	204.7	80.9	0.4	4.1	17.29
1.6	92.8	66.9	0.5	0.2	7.60
3.0	99.8	59.3	1.3	-1.6	40.76
3.1	97.1	61.3	13.0	2.9	45.55
5.2	97.7	67.9	1.2	1.4	24.33
1.6	108.1	72.5	1.1	7.5	15.71
22.4	98.1	53.5	2.8	-1.0	52.47
6.0	195.0	72.9	0.6	44.4	216.87
10.3	**96.4**	**42.7**	**2.2**	**-2.1**	**43.25**
30.9	88.5	29.3	5.5	3.4	81.14
6.1	98.3	45.1	1.8	-4.8	36.02
11.1	130.9	61.2	1.2	9.0	20.65
2.8	118.0	28.9	0.6	2.5	15.67
-2.0	**105.4**	**68.2**	**1.0**	**-17.9**	**21.23**
3.7	112.0	65.3	0.8	0.1	18.72
-6.5	98.2	63.7	1.3	-26.6	26.48
1.0	115.7	74.5	0.7	-9.8	15.23
6.0	**120.1**	**72.3**	**1.2**	**8.1**	**34.81**
6.1	125.6	73.0	1.2	8.7	33.01
3.3	113.2	68.6	0.8	2.3	36.07
8.0	102.6	71.7	1.5	6.6	47.12
5.1	**111.3**	**68.8**	**1.5**	**3.5**	**30.75**
9.5	103.5	52.4	1.2	11.2	37.56
2.3	87.4	68.6	1.6	-4.6	17.77
15.4	105.2	71.1	2.9	11.5	30.57
3.0	109.4	80.5	1.7	2.9	30.13
7.3	94.9	67.3	1.6	5.5	59.97
2.7	180.7	76.6	1.4	-0.1	33.86
5.9	83.5	74.3	0.6	9.1	14.34
4.9	**113.7**	**70.0**	**1.2**	**3.9**	**22.34**
5.0	**110.3**	**70.7**	**1.2**	**4.1**	**21.86**
2.3	222.1	59.9	0.9	0.1	14.76
5.6	95.0	77.3	1.3	8.7	21.63
9.9	107.9	62.0	3.0	4.0	39.12
1.4	108.8	76.1	0.7	-11.6	12.21
5.6	95.4	68.7	0.8	6.7	17.81
21.2	85.1	66.8	2.5	21.0	40.29
6.4	112.5	60.1	1.4	11.1	30.32

13-9 续表 1

单位: %

地　　区	Region	产　值 利税率 Ratio of Profits and Taxes to Industrial Output Value
新源县	Xinyuan [Kunes] County	6.5
昭苏县	Zhaosu [Mongolkure] County	29.7
特克斯县	Tekes County	-10.1
尼勒克县	Nilka County	15.2
塔城地区	**Tacheng [Tarbagatai] Administrative Offices**	**5.8**
塔城市	Tacheng [Qoqek] City	-4.1
乌苏市	Usu City	3.0
额敏县	Emin [Dorbiljin] County	14.0
沙湾县	Shawan County	6.9
托里县	Toli County	4.2
裕民县	Yumin [Qagantokay] County	-21.3
和布克赛尔蒙古自治县	Hoboksar Mongol Autonomous County	9.6
阿勒泰地区	**Altay Administrative Offices**	**10.1**
阿勒泰市	Altay City	3.2
布尔津县	Burqin County	10.8
富蕴县	Fuyun [Koktokay] County	-4.1
福海县	Fuhai [Burultokay] County	12.3
哈巴河县	Habahe [Kaba] County	37.4
青河县	Qinghe [Qinggil] County	-18.2
吉木乃县	Jeminay County	36.4
博尔塔拉蒙古自治州	**Bortala Mongol Autonomous Prefecture**	**7.9**
博乐市	Bole [Bortala] City	5.3
阿拉山口市	Alashankou City	21.0
精河县	Jinghe [Jing] County	2.5
温泉县	Wenquan [Araxang] County	16.7
巴音郭楞蒙古自治州	**Bayangol Mongol Autonomous Prefecture**	**34.8**
库尔勒市	Korla City	40.5
轮台县	Luntai [Bugur] County	-8.6
尉犁县	Yuli [Lopnur] County	14.7
若羌县	Ruoqiang [Qarkilik] County	41.2
且末县	Qiemo [Qarqan] County	-50.0
焉耆回族自治县	Yanqi Hui Autonomous County	5.0
和静县	Hejing County	9.4
和硕县	Hoxud County	-6.2
博湖县	Bohu [Bagrax] County	18.5
阿克苏地区	**Aksu Administrative Offices**	**20.5**
阿克苏市	Aksu City	9.3
温宿县	Wensu [Onsu] County	18.3
库车县	Kuqa County	38.2

Continued

(%)

总资产贡献率 Ratio of Profits, Taxes and Interests to Average Value	资本保值增值率 Ratio of Capital-hold and Rise	资产负债率 Ratio of debts to Assets	流动资产周转次数(次/年) Turnover of Currents Assets (times/year)	成本费用利润率 Ratio of Profits to Industrial Costs	全员劳动生产率(万元/人) Overall Labour Productivity (10 000yuan/person)
3.9	86.2	66.4	1.1	-4.5	18.24
28.6	145.4	79.9	4.6	30.8	75.81
0.7	94.4	81.4	0.7	-17.2	13.71
5.0	93.9	73.8	1.7	5.0	31.90
4.5	**143.5**	**67.7**	**1.5**	**3.0**	**19.94**
2.0	174.3	79.9	1.1	-3.8	7.39
2.7	254.2	47.5	2.1	0.7	24.03
6.5	91.2	70.9	0.9	9.1	19.85
7.9	119.7	69.4	1.6	5.1	19.25
2.9	108.2	82.3	0.8	4.7	17.15
-15.4		73.1	1.3	-18.5	-3.32
4.6	91.1	77.5	1.8		19.65
4.9	**100.1**	**70.3**	**0.9**	**4.5**	**28.55**
2.9	117.5	76.8	0.8	0.6	14.75
5.4	105.7	81.3	0.7	5.6	51.71
1.5	95.1	69.8	1.0	-10.6	17.54
8.5	103.2	48.6	1.3	10.9	23.67
12.1	85.7	66.2	1.2	42.1	60.94
-1.7	135.5	80.1	0.7	-16.8	6.33
12.4	125.0	57.9	0.9	42.4	202.43
5.3	**155.8**	**75.9**	**1.1**	**6.3**	**30.82**
4.1	154.3	78.1	1.0	3.7	23.11
9.0	178.2	74.0	1.3	24.0	92.50
3.2	121.7	73.9	1.0	-0.9	28.31
8.0	638.0	54.7	1.9	14.4	35.37
18.2	**106.8**	**56.3**	**2.3**	**32.6**	**93.72**
21.9	109.4	52.6	3.0	43.0	129.33
-2.5	88.5	58.1	1.0	-10.0	16.48
14.1	123.7	41.6	2.1	11.9	27.97
22.0	104.4	67.1	1.4	36.3	74.32
-2.2	90.0	51.1	1.7	-37.6	-10.09
3.6	111.5	70.7	0.9	1.4	20.01
5.2	95.4	68.6	1.2	4.4	22.88
2.1	79.9	76.0	0.9	-8.6	7.07
10.1	155.6	60.1	1.0	5.8	23.87
11.0	**84.1**	**68.7**	**1.5**	**5.3**	**42.14**
5.8	55.3	61.1	1.3	8.0	21.73
9.8	125.4	74.9	1.3	20.2	24.17
28.6	111.3	56.4	2.5	10.9	98.34

13-9 续表 2

单位: %

地　区	Region	产　值利税率 Ratio of Profits and Taxes to Industrial Output Value
沙雅县	Xayar County	12.2
新和县	Xinhe [Toksu] County	25.2
拜城县	Baicheng [Bay] County	-27.8
乌什县	Wushi [Uxturpan] County	21.3
阿瓦提县	Awat County	2.9
柯坪县	Kalpin County	10.6
克孜勒苏柯尔克孜自治州	**Kizilsu Kirgiz Autonomous Prefecture**	**14.6**
阿图什市	Artux City	27.2
阿克陶县	Akto County	-2.3
阿合奇县	Akqi County	30.4
乌恰县	Wuqia [Ulugqat] County	15.1
喀什地区	**Kashgar [Kaxgar] Administrative Offices**	**12.9**
喀什市	Kashgar [Kaxgar] City	13.4
疏附县	Shufu County	4.9
疏勒县	Shule County	12.3
英吉沙县	Yengisar County	15.7
泽普县	Zepu [Poskam] County	0.9
莎车县	Shache [Yarkant] County	8.8
叶城县	Yecheng [Kagilik] County	12.8
麦盖提县	Makit County	18.1
岳普湖县	Yopurga County	5.6
伽师县	Jiashi [Payzawat] County	31.2
巴楚县	Bachu [Maralbexi] County	6.8
塔什库尔干塔吉克自治县	Taxkorgan Tajik Autonomous County	-26.5
和田地区	**Hotan Administrative Offices**	**13.2**
和田市	Hotan City	4.1
和田县	Hotan County	9.5
墨玉县	Moyu [Karakax] County	18.3
皮山县	Pishan [Guma] County	20.5
洛浦县	Lop County	20.3
策勒县	Qira County	
于田县	Yutian [Keriya] County	-1.6
民丰县	Minfeng [Niya] County	
自治区直辖县级市	**Municpality Country-LevelCity directly under the Central Government**	**12.4**
石河子市	Shihezi City	9.1
阿拉尔市	Aral City	19.9
图木舒克市	Tumxuk City	16.4
五家渠市	Wujiaqu City	13.7

Continued

(%)

总资产贡献率 Ratio of Profits, Taxes and Interests to Average Value	资本保值增值率 Ratio of Capital-hold and Rise	资产负债率 Ratio of debts to Assets	流动资产周转次数(次/年) Turnover of Currents Assets (times/year)	成本费用利润率 Ratio of Profits to Industrial Costs	全员劳动生产率(万元/人) Overall Labour Productivity (10 000yuan/person)
9.7	95.5	64.2	1.3	14.5	27.80
20.6	70.0	83.0	1.2	47.7	30.44
-3.1	88.1	86.0	0.7	-27.4	10.36
9.9	268.9	50.5	1.2	17.8	32.19
3.4	78.5	80.5	1.2	-2.5	14.70
5.0	222.6	75.2	2.1	7.4	33.58
4.4	**140.9**	**73.8**	**0.6**	**7.9**	**31.73**
6.7	151.7	59.7	0.5	19.7	41.29
0.6	101.1	81.1	0.4	-8.5	14.77
8.5		100.0	4.7	15.8	280.51
5.3	197.7	74.0	1.4	6.7	33.26
9.1	**113.5**	**67.8**	**1.3**	**10.0**	18.51
9.0	100.1	69.4	2.0	9.5	20.10
3.1	75.3	70.1	1.1	4.9	8.25
10.1	111.2	64.0	1.3	9.5	25.00
8.9	105.6	53.2	1.4	11.1	17.80
1.7	105.5	58.5	0.6	-2.4	11.95
7.9	115.6	60.4	1.2	8.2	24.48
9.5	132.4	72.9	0.8	14.1	15.30
12.5	120.5	63.6	1.1	14.2	28.28
5.1	199.3	60.2	1.1	6.9	12.44
28.1	116.8	42.1	2.1	23.2	18.01
6.5	160.1	70.1	1.3	4.5	10.27
0.2		103.3	0.3	-34.2	16.96
4.4	**114.2**	**52.1**	**0.7**	**7.2**	**17.29**
3.4	78.4	71.9	1.0	1.6	7.91
3.4	105.3	53.5	0.4	1.8	36.59
9.0	123.4	45.4	0.8	8.3	22.05
6.8	197.4	39.7	1.0	21.6	7.35
6.9	108.7	35.7	1.9	19.8	16.32
-0.2	135.0	69.0	0.9	-1.9	18.28
7.3	**121.0**	**71.1**	**1.3**	**8.0**	**29.21**
5.4	108.7	68.9	1.4	6.9	24.95
12.6	395.0	63.0	1.4	21.9	28.26
13.0	85.3	61.9		13.8	25.31
8.1	109.4	79.7		3.4	43.85

13-10 国有控股工业企业主要经济指标

单位: 万元 (2015 年)

项　目	Item	企业单位数(个) Number of Enterprises (unit)	#亏损企业 Loss- Suffering Enterprises	工业总产值(当年价格) Gross Industrial Output Value (At Current Prices)
总　计	**Total**	**746**	**251**	**44006335.9**
按登记注册类型分	**Grouped by Registration**			
内资企业	Domestic Funded Enterprises	740	248	43820720.8
国有企业	State-owned Enterprises	61	20	5517056.3
#中央企业	Central Enterprises	20	4	4755374.2
地方企业	Local Enterprises	41	16	761682.1
#自治区属企业	Autonomous	11	5	326009.2
地区(州、市)属企业	Prefecture or City	7	4	107697.9
县(市)属企业	County or City	21	7	163939.4
股份合作企业	Cooperative Enterprises	1	1	17044.2
有限责任公司	Limited Liability Corporations	605	203	17265435.1
#国有独资公司	StateSole Funded Corporations	138	46	4681758.0
其他有限责任公司	Other Limited Liability Corporations	467	157	12583677.1
股份有限公司	Share-holding Corporations Ltd.	73	24	21021185.2
港、澳、台商投资企业	Enterprises with Funds from Hongkong,Macao and Taiwan	1		4159.4
外商投资企业	Foreign Funded Enterprises	5	3	181455.7
按轻、重工业分	**Grouped by Light & Heavy Industry**			
轻工业	Light Industry	191	43	3598548.3
以农产品为原料	Using Farm Products as Raw Materials	171	40	3310494.8
以非农产品为原料	Using Non-Farm Products as Raw Materials	20	3	288053.5
重工业	Heavy Industry	555	208	40407787.6
采掘工业	Mining and Quarrying	92	37	12522824.2
原料工业	Raw Material Industry	319	130	24812542.1
加工工业	Manufacturing Industry	144	41	3072421.3
按企业规模分	**Grouped by Size of Enterprises**			
大型企业	Large Enterprises	52	24	32125285.0
中型企业	Medium-sized Enterprises	142	55	5772977.0
小型企业	Small Enterprises	468	146	5720428.4
微型企业	Mini Enterprises	84	26	387645.5

Main Economic Indicators Efficiency of State-holding Industrial Enterprises

(10 000 yuan)

工业增加值 Value-added of Industry	工业销售产值(当年价格) Sales Value of Industry Products (At Current Prices)	出口交货值 Delivery Value of Industry Export	实收资本 Total Capital Hold	资产合计 Total Assets	流动资产合计 Total Current Assets	#产成品 Finished Product	固定资产原价 Original Value of Fixed Assets
18040796.6	**43276341.0**	**191886.8**	**36267532.9**	**109457461.5**	**23929635.0**	**2133728.0**	**108764124.8**
18009182.7	43094917.1	191886.8	36085896.8	109109217.3	23822254.9	2128059.4	108416720.3
1496565.0	5505230.4	528.2	1116317.1	9400142.4	1507565.5	71188.6	10190832.3
1195901.5	4761119.5		476985.0	6215178.8	516924.8	21370.8	7641284.6
300663.4	744110.9	528.2	639332.1	3184963.6	990640.7	49817.8	2549547.7
178267.9	313912.5		336107.4	1055075.0	210758.9	16135.2	1061012.0
19798.7	137705.7	528.2	61421.7	1092310.8	542248.4	4435.7	648209.6
74394.1	159960.8		217072.1	724644.9	150298.5	4705.5	634586.9
6627.7	13969.1		20000.0	139647.8	54855.6	4237.0	91571.0
5937398.3	16765731.4	104391.7	14211377.5	55189516.5	13034742.1	1310247.5	38267937.3
2005246.2	4613660.1	5981.2	4339873.8	14419845.3	4386984.1	221100.6	9320429.2
3932152.0	12152071.3	98410.5	9871503.7	40769671.2	8647758.0	1089146.9	28947508.1
10568591.8	20809986.2	86966.9	20738202.2	44379910.6	9225091.7	742386.3	59866379.7
3532.5	4159.4		13000.0	36193.7	2094.1		35938.8
28081.4	177264.5		168636.1	312050.5	105286.0	5668.6	311465.7
1213605.7	3453973.0	140296.1	2056774.6	6146660.1	2875616.4	592091.5	3324876.0
1119717.7	3171540.8	140082.2	1612597.5	4548400.6	2360186.0	582691.5	2325618.1
93888.0	282432.2	213.9	444177.1	1598259.5	515430.4	9400.0	999257.9
16827190.9	39822368.0	51590.7	34210758.3	103310801.4	21054018.6	1541636.5	105439248.8
7904354.8	12302135.9		19166019.7	38601291.2	7100416.1	415673.3	53275961.0
8144635.6	24625940.6	48337.0	13679838.0	58177681.8	11041692.0	875101.5	48609792.8
778200.5	2894291.5	3253.7	1364900.6	6531828.4	2911910.5	250861.7	3553495.0
14024507.7	31896937.8	72506.6	26237900.3	65949818.3	12686596.2	852064.5	78682719.3
2032141.8	5547254.5	39328.4	4261975.2	19091855.8	5463927.1	734250.7	12459026.9
1803158.1	5439616.6	80051.2	5001943.5	20526610.2	4926301.2	504551.0	15142682.0
180989.0	392532.1	0.6	765713.9	3889177.2	852810.5	42861.8	2479696.6

13-10 续表

单位：万元

项目	Item	负债合计 Total Liabilities	#流动负债 Total Liquid Liabilities	#非流动负债 Total Non-liquid Liabilities	所有者权益合计 Total Owners' Equities
总计	**Total**	**67348310.7**	**37922472.2**	**29188137.2**	**42148695.0**
按登记注册类型分	**Grouped by Registration**				
内资企业	Domestic Funded Enterprises	67141209.6	37766532.7	29136975.6	42007552.0
国有企业	State-owned Enterprises	6429815.2	3390916.4	3038894.8	2970326.7
#中央企业	Central Enterprises	3921917.1	2508385.1	1413528.2	2293261.4
地方企业	Local Enterprises	2507898.1	882531.3	1625366.6	677065.3
#自治区属企业	Autonomous	709577.3	122290.8	587286.4	345497.6
地区(州、市)属企业	Prefecture or City	1069482.6	337194.4	732288.2	22828.3
县(市)属企业	County or City	503237.3	330636.9	172600.3	221407.4
股份合作企业	Cooperative Enterprises	124162.9	100153.8	24009.1	15484.9
有限责任公司	Limited Liability Corporations	39216017.4	23110292.2	15869445.6	16013044.5
#国有独资公司	StateSole Funded Corporations	9944134.1	5843726.7	4077209.1	4499618.4
其他有限责任公司	Other Limited Liability Corporations	29271883.3	17266565.5	11792236.5	11513426.1
股份有限公司	Share-holding Corporations Ltd.	21371214.1	11165170.3	10204626.1	23008695.9
港、澳、台商投资企业	Enterprises with Funds from Hongkong,Macao and Taiwan	21294.9	15994.9	5300.0	14898.7
外商投资企业	Foreign Funded Enterprises	185806.2	139944.6	45861.6	126244.3
按轻、重工业分	**Grouped by Light & Heavy Industry**				
轻工业	Light Industry	3411921.6	2664032.3	719835.0	2737420.6
以农产品为原料	Using Farm Products as Raw Materials	2451637.4	2258705.4	165827.9	2099445.4
以非农产品为原料	Using Non-Farm Products as Raw Materials	960284.2	405326.9	554007.1	637975.2
重工业	Heavy Industry	63936389.1	35258439.9	28468302.2	39411274.4
采掘工业	Mining and Quarrying	20281729.9	10739800.6	9532995.8	18319560.4
原料工业	Raw Material Industry	39205854.5	21051585.7	17972800.4	19008691.0
加工工业	Manufacturing Industry	4448804.7	3467053.6	962506.0	2083023.0
按企业规模分	**Grouped by Size of Enterprises**				
大型企业	Large Enterprises	37798083.0	21150666.6	16647269.8	28151734.6
中型企业	Medium-sized Enterprises	12579884.0	7240751.5	5326793.8	6511970.9
小型企业	Small Enterprises	13853702.7	7937076.9	5818827.7	6672904.4
微型企业	Mini Enterprises	3116641.0	1593977.2	1395245.9	812085.1

Continued

(10 000 yuan)

主营业务收入 Revenue from Principal Business	主营业务成本 Cost of Principal Business	主营业务税金及附加 Taxes and Other Charges on Principal Business	营业利润 Business Profit	利润总额 Total Profit	亏损企业亏损总额 Losses Value of Loss-Suffering Enterprises	利税总额 Total Profits and Taxes	本年应交增值税 Value-added Taxes Payable	全部从业人员年平均人数(人) Annual Average Employed Persons (person)
44496409.4	**34122793.3**	**3586473.2**	**780620.3**	**1321929.8**	**2470690.5**	**7143308.9**	**2234905.9**	**384230**
44312315.4	33968726.4	3579933.6	798690.0	1333531.8	2443312.7	7138971.3	2225505.9	383089
5512888.1	5159954.3	11980.5	171470.8	222293.5	37587.2	254520.0	20246.0	36643
4777725.3	4591323.8	8182.5	124827.3	134658.1	4240.5	141463.6	-1377.0	27503
735162.8	568630.5	3798.0	46643.5	87635.4	33346.7	113056.4	21623.0	9140
277764.6	147026.2	1631.2	80003.5	82840.6	9061.5	95817.4	11345.6	2902
138206.9	158584.4	277.6	-47647.9	-17396.0	19681.0	-20050.8	-2932.4	2806
158015.1	105314.7	1633.8	18965.5	20865.8	4604.2	34262.8	11763.2	2029
13969.1	11724.4		-3489.3	-3434.5	3434.5	-1995.0	1439.5	598
16802289.1	13475318.6	861004.3	-18549.7	233566.0	952594.6	1886784.0	792213.7	212953
4602356.3	3676703.7	259627.7	78358.7	167730.1	100998.3	716539.7	289181.9	72204
12199932.8	9798614.9	601376.6	-96908.4	65835.9	851596.3	1170244.3	503031.8	140749
21983169.1	15321729.1	2706948.8	649258.2	881106.8	1449696.4	4999662.3	1411606.7	132895
4159.4	2439.9	40.9	560.5	890.5		1569.9	638.5	25
179934.6	151627.0	6498.7	-18630.2	-12492.5	27377.8	2767.7	8761.5	1116
3549410.7	2620196.2	262370.5	235073.0	301284.0	84625.1	720834.8	157180.3	47796
3244945.9	2362259.7	260877.8	269462.3	327204.1	40607.4	735802.9	147721.0	41406
304464.8	257936.5	1492.7	-34389.3	-25920.1	44017.7	-14968.1	9459.3	6390
40946998.7	31502597.1	3324102.7	545547.3	1020645.8	2386065.4	6422474.1	2077725.6	336434
13375971.1	9636741.8	618581.8	340297.1	577593.0	1311123.6	2147075.0	950900.2	146073
24606796.9	19442236.8	2628158.8	197169.6	363968.0	914195.3	4027535.6	1035408.8	154800
2964230.7	2423618.5	77362.1	8080.6	79084.8	160746.5	247863.5	91416.6	35561
32913749.5	25072710.9	3260693.8	450391.7	815604.3	1914572.5	5812884.1	1736586.0	238001
5680034.0	4384645.8	274257.4	128585.1	210501.3	271563.8	789488.2	304729.5	80216
5519342.3	4415812.5	49615.3	172268.7	258700.8	256480.1	489948.3	181632.2	61492
383283.6	249624.1	1906.7	29374.8	37123.4	28074.1	50988.3	11958.2	4521

13-11 分行业国有控股工业企业主要经济指标

单位：万元 (2015 年)

行业	Sector	企业单位数(个) Number of Enterprises (unit)	#亏损企业 Loss- Suffering Enterprises	工业总产值(当年价格) Gross Industrial Output Value (At Current Prices)
总计	**Total**	**746**	**251**	**44006335.9**
煤炭开采和洗选业	Mining and Washing of Coal	40	18	1289769.4
石油和天然气开采业	Extraction of Petroleum and Natural Gas	6	4	8897661.9
黑色金属矿采选业	Mining and Processing of Ferrous Metals Ores	14	5	500769.9
有色金属矿采选业	Mining and Processing of Nonferrous Metals Ores	17	8	376603.0
非金属矿采选业	Mining and Processing of Nonmetal Ores	12	1	103358.0
#采盐	Extraction of Salt	4		44200.1
开采辅助活动	Support for Minning	3	1	1354662.0
农副食品加工业	Activities Processing of Food from Agricultural Products	79	15	1391923.7
#谷物磨制	Grain Grinding	18	3	156601.5
饲料加工	Fodder Processing	8		261371.8
制糖	Sugar Making	11	6	219036.5
食品制造业	Manufacture of Foods	38	8	668076.5
#罐头制造	Manufacture of can	17	5	219765.6
饮料制造业	Manufacture of Liguor,Beverages and Refined Tea	15	6	261611.3
#酒的制造	Manufacture of Liguor	12	6	253419.8
烟草制品业	Manufacture of Tobacco	1		472468.0
纺织业	Manufacture of Textile	14	5	305960.8
#棉、化纤纺织及印染精加工	Cotton, Chemical Fiber, Dyeing, Printing and Processing	12	4	250844.1
毛纺织和染整精加工	Wool Textile, Dyeing and Printing	2	1	55116.7
纺织服装、鞋、帽制造业	Manufacture of Textile, Wearing Apparel and Accessories	5	1	38532.1
皮革、毛皮、羽毛(绒)及其制品业	Manufacturie of Leather, Fur, Feather and Related Products			
#皮革鞣制加工	Leather Tanning and Processing			
木材加工及木、竹、藤、棕、草制品业	Processing of Timber, Manufacture of Wood, Bamboo, Cane, Grass Products	1		3660.0
家具制造业	Manufacture of Furniture			
造纸及纸制品业	Manufacture of Paper and Paper Products	2		33022.7
印刷业和记录媒介的复制	Printing and Reproduction of Recording Media	10	2	39253.2
文教、工美、体育和娱乐用品制造业	Manufacture of Articles for Cultural, Educational,Sports and Entertainment			
石油加工、炼焦及核燃料加工业	Processing, Processing of Petroleeum,Coking and Nuclear Fuel	13	6	10357754.8
#炼焦	Coking	5	3	189538.4
化学原料及化学制品制造业	Manufacture of Raw Chemical Materials and Chemical Products	48	20	3905135.7
#基础化学原料制造	Basic Chemical Material	12	5	645693.7
肥料制造	Manufacture of Fertilizer	13	3	802754.5
合成材料制造	Manufacture of Synthetic Materials	13	7	2299590.7
医药制造业	Manufacture of Medicine	7	1	60242.2
化学纤维制造业	Manufacture of Chemical Fibers	3	1	61927.7
橡胶制品业	Manufacture of Rubber and Plastics Products	21	6	367645.2
非金属矿物制品业	Manufacture of Non-metallic Mineral Products	101	47	1160742.6
#水泥制造	Manufacture of Cement	39	27	502879.9
黑色金属冶炼及压延加工业	Smelting and Pressing of Ferrous Metals	17	14	2160467.3
有色金属冶炼及压延加工业	Smelting and Pressing of Non ferrous Metals	12	8	477096.5
金属制品业	Manufacture of Metal Products	9	3	155331.5
通用设备制造业	Manufacture of General Purpose Machinery	3		12965.3
专用设备制造业	Manufacture of Special Purpose Machinery	8	2	105533.0
汽车制造业	Manufacture of Automobile	5	4	162251.1
铁路、船舶、航空航天和其他运输设备制造业	Manufacture of Railway ,Ship,Aeronautics and Other Transport Equipment	1		6046.0
电气机械及器材制造业	Manufacture of Electrical Machinery and Apparatus	6	1	320981.1
计算机、通信和其他电子设备制造业	Manufacture of, Computer Communication and Other Electronic Equipment			
仪器仪表制造业	Measuring Instruments and Machinery	1		7581.6
废弃资源综合利用业	Comprehensive Utilization of Waste Resources	1		6510.0
金属制品、机械和设备修理业	Repair Service of Metal Prodults,Mouhinery and Equipment	1		10917.7
电力、热力的生产和供应业	Production and Supply of Electrici Power and Heat Power	207	59	8308987.0
#电力生产和电力供应	Production and Supply of Electric	177	50	8064718.3
燃气生产和供应业	Production and Supply of Gas	10	2	472991.9
水的生产和供应业	Production and Supply of Water	15	3	147895.2

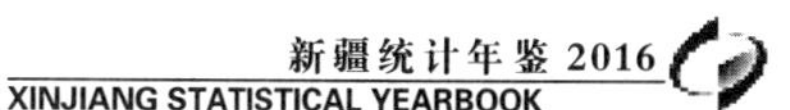

Main Economic Indicators of state-holding Industrial Enterprises by Sectors

(10 000 yuan)

工业增加值 Value-added of Industry	工业销售产值(当年价格) Sales Value of Industry Products (At Current Prices)	出口交货值 Delivery Value of Industry Export	实收资本 Total Capital Hold	资产合计 Total Assets	流动资产合计 Total Current Assets	#产成品 Finished Product	固定资产原价 Net Value of Fixed Assets
18040796.6	**43276341.0**	**191886.8**	**36267532.9**	**109457461.5**	**23929635.0**	**2133728.0**	**108764124.8**
748281.3	1240994.7		1380646.5	5425917.6	1305640.5	113719.0	2755808.8
6068818.3	8776263.9		15651302.3	28210412.6	3725188.7	138090.2	47670468.7
163626.2	483807.2		258745.9	1469519.9	671991.9	79021.2	604423.0
210947.5	341577.2		349967.1	1428302.2	343100.6	50889.2	834544.5
48433.7	97903.9		42701.0	159329.8	74505.0	21442.6	90727.3
28944.3	43879.8		22381.1	66193.0	36159.5	9701.9	22542.0
664247.9	1361589.0		1482656.9	1907809.1	979989.4	12511.1	1319988.7
275146.5	1328064.8	8505.5	334967.4	1584282.8	899062.6	298624.1	686734.3
19553.3	155340.9		32584.3	150795.3	78699.7	6122.6	50034.5
57495.6	271707.8		102328.3	411969.3	164187.3	11451.3	108772.1
50695.8	190846.1		63366.2	382979.3	270571.6	182071.0	248684.9
166750.9	638987.6	117082.1	269149.1	950276.1	472043.3	160703.7	615190.4
44166.9	210862.3	113370.2	155656.4	417614.7	238003.9	123590.2	324982.2
168776.6	259591.8		185053.2	413737.9	197534.6	13631.7	146134.9
165768.9	250771.0		179530.5	405343.4	193819.9	12789.8	140364.7
363547.2	476905.0		369850.0	505672.0	286298.0	3899.0	227535.5
82693.5	270524.8	10072.9	313521.5	679265.6	252967.6	48918.4	455800.5
59213.1	220267.8		260073.5	473606.7	210282.9	34917.1	339367.3
23480.4	50257.0	10072.9	53448.0	205658.9	42684.7	14001.3	116433.2
11765.8	37328.3	3978.5	19570.8	45392.3	25925.7	6396.6	18906.6
1552.5	3642.0		3000.0	4282.2	18.0	18.0	5042.5
11285.4	30774.8		2092.8	21806.1	10529.5	3765.5	13646.7
19417.8	39476.5		22737.1	88783.5	50377.6	8597.9	72942.7
4704594.4	10310691.6		4128787.3	6539686.5	1737011.2	229575.0	8556980.4
25722.5	147055.3		158941.2	602222.8	150994.6	70390.9	384663.9
1085955.8	3812834.0	27596.9	2398301.7	11241541.6	2199303.5	231685.5	8167593.0
182062.5	612307.2	1494.6	439745.7	2373636.4	521922.5	39953.9	1643638.7
381896.8	758985.3		394441.8	2017576.3	386704.4	35925.9	1878851.8
494501.2	2284716.8	26102.3	1434256.4	6218740.6	1070100.6	145819.9	4249656.1
16285.6	45284.3	657.1	48093.4	174282.5	105401.4	36390.5	47633.7
16450.5	68126.2		60198.6	146576.4	87584.5	4426.7	66562.4
66659.1	364294.5	2668.4	214848.3	488022.5	281142.5	86724.1	217376.4
322468.9	1139368.2		1355864.6	6215034.0	2342934.8	83858.7	2858343.9
119323.6	481830.2		1074304.2	4352332.1	1340903.2	36980.5	2163076.7
-184863.5	2167890.2	20739.5	1583169.6	7376135.8	1685037.1	239569.5	4416314.1
71696.6	390979.9		154736.0	1318930.1	538634.6	176939.0	403213.5
29175.7	128429.1		84071.0	280983.0	143084.7	25935.4	83172.8
3739.9	13674.6		13991.0	27229.6	14714.7	495.7	1735.4
23130.3	84227.7	534.7	45300.0	243461.9	102323.2	23019.2	93156.3
-9608.2	161611.6	50.6	133448.2	238062.8	108594.5	4156.7	180508.2
1519.9	6046.0		7423.9	8039.7	6173.3	30.0	2596.9
49167.3	240337.9		21460.0	303694.4	264660.7	22222.9	41290.7
1811.5	7428.5		5000.0	28748.9	18327.2	991.9	673.8
2200.0	6886.0		7798.3	41735.1	3172.4	663.8	24940.5
9543.1	10917.7		2400.0	3845.8	3551.8		366.4
2740355.6	8318172.4	0.6	4838479.5	29847768.9	4125988.5	5880.6	27050605.0
2682979.9	8039499.7	0.6	4636616.4	28196501.3	3409466.2	3856.7	25906151.0
12224.0	468886.6		105249.8	755419.1	419231.8	934.6	343014.2
72999.2	142822.5		372950.1	1283473.2	447589.6		690152.1

13-11 续表

单位：万元

行　业	Sector	负债合计 Total Liabilities	#流动负债 Total Liquid Liabilities	#非流动负债 Total Non-liquid Liabilities	所有者权益合计 Total Owners' Equities
总　计	**Total**	**67348310.7**	**37922472.2**	**29188137.2**	**42148695.0**
煤炭开采和洗选业	Mining and Washing of Coal	3942242.7	2750458.1	1191780.5	1483674.8
石油和天然气开采业	Extraction of Petroleum and Natural Gas	13153587.3	5446462.8	7707124.5	15056825.1
黑色金属矿采选业	Mining and Processing of Ferrous Metals Ores	1081954.5	1014139.5	67814.9	387565.3
有色金属矿采选业	Mining and Processing of Nonferrous Metals Ores	816218.2	484694.8	331523.4	612083.8
非金属矿采选业	Mining and Processing of Nonmetal Ores	106557.3	93875.6	3752.4	52772.3
#采　盐	Extraction of Salt	21806.3	12377.0	500.0	44386.6
开采辅助活动	Support for Minning	1181169.9	950169.8	231000.1	726639.1
农副食品加工业	Activities Processing of Food from Agricultural Products	998494.2	917915.4	66817.6	594872.8
#谷物磨制	Grain Grinding	102349.3	87365.1	14984.2	48446.0
饲料加工	Fodder Processing	129066.0	115174.4	13891.6	282903.1
制　糖	Sugar Making	293237.6	288906.0	3983.0	89741.5
食品制造业	Manufacture of Foods	607031.8	552715.5	40973.4	336842.7
#罐头制造	Manufacture of can	343130.9	338064.4	5002.1	74483.6
饮料制造业	Manufacture of Liguor,Beverages and Refined Tea	128463.8	123204.9	5258.9	285274.1
#酒的制造	Manufacture of Liguor	126559.3	121642.7	4916.6	278784.1
烟草制品业	Manufacture of Tobacco	135822.0	127822.0	8000.0	369850.0
纺织业	Manufacture of Textile	302691.4	271068.8	31622.5	376574.0
#棉、化纤纺织及印染精加工	Cotton, Chemical Fiber, Dyeing, Printing and Processing	240014.9	226670.2	13344.6	233591.6
毛纺织和染整精加工	Wool Textile, Dyeing and Printing	62676.5	44398.6	18277.9	142982.4
纺织服装、鞋、帽制造业	Manufacture of Textile, Wearing Apparel and Accessories	34015.8	28764.7	5251.1	11376.5
皮革、毛皮、羽毛(绒)及其制品业	Manufacturie of Leather, Fur, Feather and Related Products				
#皮革鞣制加工	Leather Tanning and Processing				
木材加工及木、竹、藤、棕、草制品业	Processing of Timber, Manufacture of Wood, Bamboo, Cane, Grass Products	10.7	10.7		4271.5
家具制造业	Manufacture of Furniture				
造纸及纸制品业	Manufacture of Paper and Paper Products	4466.6	4026.6	440.0	17339.4
印刷业和记录媒介的复制	Printing and Reproduction of Recording Media	35037.1	29976.9	5060.2	53746.3
文教、工美、体育和娱乐用品制造业	Manufacture of Articles for Cultural, Educational,Sports and Entertainment				
石油加工、炼焦及核燃料加工业	Processing, Processing of Petroleeum,Coking and Nuclear Fuel	2237198.2	1693241.5	543440.9	4302488.1
#炼　焦	Coking	480970.8	459920.9	20680.5	121251.9
化学原料及化学制品制造业	Manufacture of Raw Chemical Materials and Chemical Products	7837058.3	3811710.4	4005784.4	3404785.2
#基础化学原料制造	Basic Chemical Material	1684537.0	816471.1	868065.7	689099.3
肥料制造	Manufacture of Fertilizer	1442589.6	876894.6	565695.0	574986.7
合成材料制造	Manufacture of Synthetic Materials	4295544.0	1794803.1	2481177.6	1923498.7
医药制造业	Manufacture of Medicine	90906.2	85914.1	4992.1	83376.3
化学纤维制造业	Manufacture of Chemical Fibers	127349.9	126106.6	1243.3	19226.5
橡胶制品业	Manufacture of Rubber and Plastics Products	241976.1	228203.0	12800.2	246046.3
非金属矿物制品业	Manufacture of Non-metallic Mineral Products	3622221.0	2747135.4	815820.8	2599066.4
#水泥制造	Manufacture of Cement	2450923.9	1783370.3	624847.3	1907662.2
黑色金属冶炼及压延加工业	Smelting and Pressing of Ferrous Metals	6239848.7	5398481.2	841367.4	1136287.0
有色金属冶炼及压延加工业	Smelting and Pressing of Non ferrous Metals	567622.8	422620.9	145001.9	751307.2
金属制品业	Manufacture of Metal Products	186797.2	159249.1	25834.5	94185.7
通用设备制造业	Manufacture of General Purpose Machinery	17571.1	16808.1	763.0	9658.6
专用设备制造业	Manufacture of Special Purpose Machinery	149294.9	126097.3	23197.6	94167.0
汽车制造业	Manufacture of Automobile	199750.6	155337.5	44413.1	38312.2
铁路、船舶、航空航天和其他运输设备制造业	Manufacture of Railway ,Ship,Aeronautics and Other Transport Equipment	2594.3	2531.6	62.7	5445.4
电气机械及器材制造业	Manufacture of Electrical Machinery and Apparatus	275135.6	272578.7	2556.9	28558.8
计算机、通信和其他电子设备制造业	Manufacture of, Computer Communication and Other Electronic Equipment				
仪器仪表制造业	Measuring Instruments and Machinery	21503.1	18876.3	2626.8	7245.8
废弃资源综合利用业	Comprehensive Utilization of Waste Resources	18380.4	13842.6	4537.8	23354.7
金属制品、机械和设备修理业	Repair Service of Metal Prodults,Mouhinery and Equipment	1445.4	1445.4		2400.4
电力、热力的生产和供应业	Production and Supply of Electrici Power and Heat Power	21587026.3	9035484.0	12432859.6	8291050.8
#电力生产和电力供应	Production and Supply of Electric	20215532.0	8610002.8	11486846.6	8011277.6
燃气生产和供应业	Production and Supply of Gas	645455.3	594475.8	50979.4	109963.8
水的生产和供应业	Production and Supply of Water	751412.0	217026.6	533435.3	532061.1

Continued

(10 000 yuan)

主营业务收入 Revenue from Principal Business	主营业务成本 Cost of Principal Business	主营业务税金及附加 Taxes and Other Charges on Principal Business	营业利润 Business Profit	利润总额 Total Profit	亏损企业亏损总额 Losses Value of Loss-Suffering Enterprises	利税总额 Total Profits and Taxes	本年应交增值税 Value-added Taxes Payable	全部从业人员年平均人数(人) Annual Average Employed Persons (person)
44496409.4	**34122793.3**	**3586473.2**	**780620.3**	**1321929.8**	**2470690.5**	**7143308.9**	**2234905.9**	**384230**
1301641.5	1013054.2	61755.8	-21428.3	-7680.5	75932.8	196571.7	142496.4	39146
9788530.8	6690603.7	521859.3	283673.0	485088.4	1188272.1	1627677.8	620730.1	70578
489431.9	352333.6	12692.1	34206.5	39055.2	13499.5	96029.5	44282.2	5087
336228.6	209118.3	5264.7	42117.2	40626.6	29526.2	79019.2	33127.9	5211
97807.4	54264.8	4654.7	11537.8	11775.3	1832.9	24010.2	7580.2	2287
43981.2	11963.0	4152.1	9067.7	9302.5		18296.3	4841.7	944
1362330.9	1317367.2	12355.2	-9809.1	8728.0	2060.1	123766.6	102683.4	23764
1372088.3	1131729.4	2609.4	106454.6	122675.3	8936.6	147955.1	22670.4	14438
163115.2	146871.2	220.2	8361.4	12262.1	455.8	13929.5	1447.2	986
278751.2	204862.5	290.2	30635.8	31111.7		33604.0	2202.1	2174
188447.3	168543.7	721.1	-7606.1	-1876.9	4580.6	7508.6	8664.4	5097
645763.9	496269.0	3470.7	42310.8	54076.8	21243.0	79433.3	21885.8	9023
209652.7	165924.9	808.5	-2635.5	6019.7	9080.4	12430.7	5602.5	3462
259447.4	130285.3	32687.4	61262.8	62778.9	2507.6	118640.8	23174.5	4107
250736.3	123664.0	32620.0	60494.2	61986.7	2507.6	117543.5	22936.8	3827
476905.0	179636.0	219745.0	53774.4	52767.4		328980.4	56468.0	761
295163.0	260449.6	1312.8	7574.7	26911.0	3168.6	42425.0	14201.2	7513
244188.5	225742.3	649.6	2091.8	20184.0	2992.6	30718.4	9884.8	6156
50974.5	34707.3	663.2	5482.9	6727.0	176.0	11706.6	4316.4	1357
35314.3	28833.7	124.3	-1112.6	495.5	176.6	1314.1	694.3	1477
3642.0	2658.7	18.2	857.4	857.4		948.4	72.8	80
30633.2	25538.4	611.4	3260.0	3257.4		5709.5	1840.7	1018
40256.0	32068.9	326.2	1163.2	3037.7	232.1	5435.9	2072.0	1568
10532740.6	6702285.9	2593822.2	544609.2	546643.3	35294.1	3936712.6	796247.1	31807
154263.5	148652.5	280.9	-24183.1	-24279.6	25933.8	-20182.5	3816.2	3347
3684222.9	3092754.4	75942.4	-8135.4	49607.2	186188.6	249314.1	123764.5	41651
633228.0	560445.5	3275.6	-10807.4	-1239.1	23480.8	20870.3	18833.8	9914
763528.4	475486.8	64248.2	51107.4	82553.6	42600.3	182772.6	35970.8	7322
2094625.6	1873118.6	7538.9	-9337.4	-2467.2	73582.7	67535.2	62463.5	20634
45636.0	34136.8	264.0	1261.1	2145.3	786.7	4677.0	2267.7	1320
67150.3	56888.5	102.8	-3053.5	2443.7	3552.2	7059.6	4513.1	1020
387757.8	357671.8	814.4	-2220.3	960.7	11596.2	13522.0	11746.9	6016
1168428.0	1018156.2	4913.9	-46380.1	-29329.5	128705.1	40529.2	64944.8	23184
476513.5	442632.2	2537.1	-63376.1	-49645.0	99092.9	-7849.3	39258.6	11701
2231734.0	2433029.8	3300.7	-554828.6	-533551.5	535249.0	-522835.0	7415.8	20920
392789.8	355917.7	262.9	-5112.7	-4532.1	22873.1	4793.3	9062.5	4662
123528.1	114203.8	843.1	-49.9	2620.8	4118.6	5871.7	2407.8	1638
14661.0	11482.7	112.5	366.8	408.8		483.9	-37.4	499
92864.4	68167.9	289.1	5984.2	8227.0	1888.3	10142.8	1626.7	1507
162708.9	153424.6	5741.5	-42937.2	-36870.1	36944.6	-29553.7	1574.9	1549
6046.0	4906.9	57.9	185.0	305.3		715.5	352.3	114
239709.3	217399.6	654.2	5850.9	6889.6	2017.7	14560.1	7016.3	826
11551.8	9566.3	61.8	57.6	505.9		779.2	211.5	140
5726.0	4761.1	45.3	1.0	3.0		406.4	358.1	133
10917.2	10192.2	292.3	69.1	34.4		1330.7	1004.0	632
8183280.3	7025860.8	17195.3	305355.5	418425.6	113932.3	536487.1	100866.2	54406
7892334.2	6703254.1	16771.2	378298.7	421665.6	91900.1	535729.2	97292.4	48943
472182.8	437841.6	1646.5	-41141.2	-29786.8	39078.7	-26492.0	1648.3	2849
127590.0	89933.9	623.2	4896.4	12328.8	1077.2	16886.9	3934.9	3299

13-12 各地、州、市、县(市)国有控股工业企业主要经济指标

单位: 万元 (2015 年)

地　区	Region	企业单位数(个) Number of Enterprises (unit)	#亏损企业 Loss- Suffering Enterprises	工业总产值(当年价格) Gross Industrial Output Value (At Current Prices)
总　计	**Total**	**746**	**251**	**44006335.9**
乌鲁木齐市	**Urumqi City**	**141**	**46**	**14423219.5**
天山区	Tianshan District	11	4	320407.2
沙依巴克区	Shayibak District	16	5	613191.2
新市区	Xinshi District	32	8	1751122.2
水磨沟区	Shui Mogou District	5	1	4495322.1
头屯河区	Tou Tunhe District	39	15	2890061.1
达坂城区	Da Bancheng District	15	3	188292.6
米东区	Midong District	20	10	4126032.2
乌鲁木齐县	Urumqi County	3		38790.9
克拉玛依市	**Karamay City**	**24**	**10**	**9944434.1**
独山子区	Dushanzi District	8	4	3759085.5
克拉玛依区	Karamay District	13	5	6147046.1
白碱滩区	Bai Jiantan District	3	1	38302.5
乌尔河区	Urhe District			
吐鲁番市	**Turpan City**	**40**	**14**	**1197478.9**
高昌区	Gaochang District	11	5	81826.3
鄯善县	Shanshan [Piqan] County	13	3	848179.3
托克逊县	Toksun County	16	6	267473.3
哈密地区	**Hami [Kumul] Administrative Offices**	**67**	**24**	**1708988.5**
哈密市	Hami [Kumul] City	51	15	1574015.9
巴里坤哈萨克自治县	Barkol Kazak Autonomous County	13	7	111510.8
伊吾县	Yiwu [Araturuk] County	3	2	23461.8
昌吉回族自治州	**Changji Hui Autonomous Prefecture**	**61**	**18**	**2117818.2**
昌吉市	Changji City	14	4	445392.4
阜康市	Fukang City	15	7	1111160.4
呼图壁县	Hutubi County	11	1	239663.1
玛纳斯县	Manas County	9	2	52175.3
奇台县	Qitai County	6	3	164059.4
吉木萨尔县	Jimsar County	4	1	90359.4
木垒哈萨克自治县	Mori Kazak Autonomous County	2		15008.2
伊犁哈萨克自治州	**Ili Kazak Autonomous Prefecture**	**160**	**62**	**2997538.4**
伊犁州直属县(市)	**Counties (Cities) Direct Under Ili Prefecture**	**76**	**26**	**1721958.3**
伊宁市	Yining [Gulja] City	11	5	166661.9
奎屯市	Kuytun City	21	4	573509.8
霍尔果斯市	Huoerguosi City	2		74030.7
伊宁县	Yining [Gulja] County	10	2	169617.3
察布查尔锡伯自治县	Qapqal Xibe Autonomous County	6	1	54593.4
霍城县	Huocheng [Korgas] County	7	4	73517.5
巩留县	Gongliu [Tokkuztara] County	5	2	131571.5
新源县	Xinyuan [Kunes] County	7	4	360273.4
昭苏县	Zhaosu [Mongolkure] County	2	1	30437.5
特克斯县	Tekes County	1	1	7295.0
尼勒克县	Nilka County	4	2	80450.3
塔城地区	**Tacheng [Tarbagatai] Administrative Offices**	**40**	**16**	**692850.8**
塔城市	Tacheng [Qoqek] City	1		17520.1
乌苏市	Usu City	6	3	203431.0
额敏县	Emin [Dorbiljin] County	9	4	84048.0

Main Economic Indicators of State-holding Industrial Enterprises by Prefecture, Autonomous Prefecture, City and County

(10 000 yuan)

工业增加值 Value-added of Industry	工业销售产值(当年价格) Sales Value of Industry Products (At Current Prices)	出口交货值 Delivery Value of Industry Export	实收资本 Total Capital Hold	资产合计 Total Assets	流动资产合计 Total Current Assets	#产成品 Finished Product	固定资产原价 Net Value of Fixed Assets
18040796.6	**43276341.0**	**191886.8**	**36267532.9**	**109457461.5**	**23929635.0**	**2133728.0**	**108764124.8**
4245409.1	**14367724.1**	**74030.3**	**7396284.9**	**30152427.9**	**6710243.5**	**402216.9**	**28598460.6**
118985.0	340111.8	39045.2	274254.9	1724095.7	799075.6	54245.0	1401271.2
67226.1	612281.8		498960.2	2933413.7	1280449.1	7779.6	953969.6
965058.6	1654138.9	10651.7	2049687.1	6044929.7	778321.0	131427.2	9937337.3
1072461.7	4493702.8		403392.8	5949076.0	297775.6	4693.2	7523634.0
325680.8	2930461.4	22838.8	1641134.1	7091040.4	2206539.6	95721.1	3486746.4
84587.3	191246.6		237222.7	1398566.9	163706.5	13427.9	975731.8
1582180.6	4106989.9	1494.6	2200434.0	4652039.4	1129563.0	94922.9	4032748.1
29229.1	38790.9		91199.1	359266.1	54813.1		287022.2
4344605.7	**9895010.8**		**13413948.8**	**19200315.9**	**4511213.6**	**151823.7**	**26077482.8**
1495149.7	3734558.0		2503670.1	3384812.9	696690.0	78678.3	5032124.1
2832599.7	6123398.4		10888188.9	15738537.0	3785040.0	70831.9	20996413.9
16856.3	37054.4		22089.8	76966.0	29483.6	2313.5	48944.8
393144.3	**1188578.1**		**588793.3**	**4784066.9**	**1014260.4**	**76382.3**	**6601496.9**
43661.4	81318.0		147598.7	577921.0	121727.2	1107.8	462076.0
262723.8	844864.5		183643.8	2967122.1	670924.4	67521.5	5124862.1
86759.0	262395.6		257550.8	1239023.8	221608.8	7753.0	1014558.8
606456.8	**1628352.6**		**1864926.5**	**8613314.0**	**1933809.0**	**86242.0**	**5749870.5**
533894.6	1494045.6		1682688.8	7419546.4	1687293.8	61207.4	4993292.3
61151.5	110767.0		151737.7	1035201.5	208302.5	24356.7	644068.2
11410.7	23540.0		30500.0	158566.1	38212.7	677.9	112510.0
611528.0	**1963409.6**	**47575.5**	**910668.7**	**5289446.2**	**987451.0**	**255662.6**	**4035809.9**
146414.0	432894.1	34298.0	150512.8	924509.9	198568.6	35512.2	784152.3
251745.1	1017820.2		531959.7	3066835.0	587673.0	172228.1	2241461.1
80950.7	230899.8		148930.6	575563.8	78706.3	13012.7	472575.9
15640.6	47007.1	5353.8	5228.1	41802.2	23745.2	8540.7	32813.6
70509.2	131584.8		27280.9	275201.5	49276.6	16129.6	115542.1
40802.8	92257.5	7923.7	45486.6	367410.5	37537.0	7187.2	362714.9
5465.5	10946.1		1270.0	38123.3	11944.3	3052.1	26550.0
1204711.9	**2867841.7**	**16093.9**	**2619699.4**	**10710414.3**	**2492456.2**	**390025.9**	**7913551.2**
683742.5	**1663440.1**	**3382.5**	**1417206.9**	**5758860.5**	**1487789.5**	**238091.9**	**4308924.3**
80040.7	166614.1	19.4	110554.5	570414.7	124483.4	3043.7	503276.3
223843.9	570686.9		390843.0	1632483.5	474130.6	30369.7	1284242.6
52363.5	74030.7		20665.0	161841.4	18856.6		118533.4
30809.2	160247.3	3363.1	111619.4	483044.1	159406.7	42742.7	346971.0
11766.5	54229.5		32330.0	131596.2	26934.4	1704.1	106858.8
16666.1	64950.2		29007.4	119241.3	66428.6	41828.0	89748.2
45751.2	131676.8		333925.6	875361.5	205345.5	488.9	654818.2
151986.9	323230.1		154609.0	783637.0	358795.5	111632.9	214602.3
12272.0	30437.5		1976.0	130193.2	11828.5		113668.3
4683.1	7295.0		27838.8	108711.0	4394.0		108093.0
53559.3	80042.0		203838.2	762336.6	37185.7	6281.9	768112.2
229731.6	**654708.9**	**4205.9**	**762814.7**	**2399355.5**	**452726.7**	**101560.9**	**1857484.5**
884.1	17509.6		4529.2	8909.4	5470.2	117.4	4895.5
71334.4	197279.2		418762.2	659663.7	43768.1	10916.4	662949.3
29056.9	81148.8	4205.9	75389.0	311246.0	124873.3	47707.8	215429.4

13-12 续表 1

单位：万元

地　区	Region	企业单位数（个） Number of Enterprises (unit)	#亏损企业 Loss- Suffering Enterprises	工业总产值（当年价格） Gross Industrial Output Value (At Current Prices)
沙湾县	Shawan County	6	1	98532.7
托里县	Toli County	9	3	153857.4
裕民县	Yumin [Qagantokay] County			
和布克赛尔蒙古自治县	Hoboksar Mongol Autonomous County	9	5	135461.6
阿勒泰地区	**Altay Administrative Offices**	**44**	**20**	**582729.3**
阿勒泰市	Altay City	8	4	72619.5
布尔津县	Burqin County	12	5	63627.1
富蕴县	Fuyun [Koktokay] County	9	7	232840.1
福海县	Fuhai [Burultokay] County	3	1	27209.2
哈巴河县	Habahe [Kaba] County	6	1	163080.3
青河县	Qinghe [Qinggil] County	3	2	8828.4
吉木乃县	Jeminay County	3		14524.7
博尔塔拉蒙古自治州	**Bortala Mongol Autonomous Prefecture**	**16**	**6**	**200463.9**
博乐市	Bole [Bortala] City	9	5	144621.5
阿拉山口市	Alashankou City	3		31580.2
精河县	Jinghe [Jing] County	2	1	19275.5
温泉县	Wenquan [Araxang] County	2		4986.7
巴音郭楞蒙古自治州	**Bayangol Mongol Autonomous Prefecture**	**57**	**15**	**5640514.1**
库尔勒市	Korla City	22	7	4639268.4
轮台县	Luntai [Bugur] County			
尉犁县	Yuli [Lopnur] County	2		38999.1
若羌县	Ruoqiang [Qarkilik] County	4	1	472992.7
且末县	Qiemo [Qarqan] County	1	1	8224.9
焉耆回族自治县	Yanqi Hui Autonomous County	5	1	41088.7
和静县	Hejing County	14	4	391540.0
和硕县	Hoxud County	5	1	22049.4
博湖县	Bohu [Bagrax] County	4		26350.9
阿克苏地区	**Aksu Administrative Offices**	**49**	**21**	**2342274.8**
阿克苏市	Aksu City	16	6	345586.1
温宿县	Wensu [Onsu] County	9	6	64413.3
库车县	Kuqa County	13	5	1685006.2
沙雅县	Xayar County			
新和县	Xinhe [Toksu] County			
拜城县	Baicheng [Bay] County	7	3	229822.0
乌什县	Wushi [Uxturpan] County	3		15794.2

Continued

(10 000 yuan)

工业增加值 Value-added of Industry	工业销售产值(当年价格) Sales Value of Industry Products (At Current Prices)	出口交货值 Delivery Value of Industry Export	实收资本 Total Capital Hold	资产合计 Total Assets	流动资产合计 Total Current Assets	#产成品 Finished Product	固定资产原价 Net Value of Fixed Assets
16639.4	92427.8		27632.2	106955.8	69524.6	16219.7	72533.1
50013.5	139067.2		74278.2	555448.8	132923.1	14290.5	350334.9
61803.4	127276.3		162223.9	757131.8	76167.4	12309.1	551342.3
291237.9	**549692.7**	**8505.5**	**439677.8**	**2552198.3**	**551940.0**	**50373.1**	**1747142.4**
19481.3	60804.2	8505.5	21999.0	165180.2	66700.5	6843.0	114809.4
33206.9	58188.8		52945.9	502334.5	92544.9	826.1	431292.5
85292.3	216533.5		204092.6	889638.9	204391.3	40700.1	607338.3
13020.4	26900.6		68818.5	78008.0	11217.4	1235.0	12689.1
126885.2	164071.5		49396.0	609521.1	136967.4	768.9	340493.3
3071.6	8669.4		9739.8	152418.4	19348.4		113002.8
10280.1	14524.7		32686.0	155097.2	20770.1		127517.0
68639.2	**162872.0**		**126164.9**	**610413.0**	**129618.6**	**27859.7**	**513905.5**
31533.4	106278.2		60877.9	249881.9	79463.7	26051.6	184473.2
25977.8	30957.6		61081.0	325082.2	40347.8		300687.4
9126.7	18628.4		2900.0	31669.4	7356.1	1191.0	23581.6
2001.2	7007.8		1306.0	3779.5	2451.0	617.1	5163.3
4527355.4	**5573343.2**	**49227.7**	**5386811.2**	**12522030.3**	**1915443.8**	**283694.3**	**18077273.6**
4075906.5	4606194.0	3092.2	4865737.4	9637163.2	1127108.8	68325.2	15753435.0
4654.3	38826.1		1600.0	7679.2	5518.8	173.0	2467.5
321918.5	420543.1		63899.9	760830.0	163597.2	29403.6	721577.5
-1281.9	7449.0		50000.0	81820.4	4417.0	1869.5	52973.0
11564.1	38423.8	13947.1	9269.1	95233.1	59773.5	19943.5	49696.8
95379.3	414556.8	12650.5	366349.5	1815373.2	511637.5	147711.7	1382978.7
7992.5	22556.9	4029.4	16675.3	58888.9	19675.8	3360.4	45727.3
11222.2	24793.5	15508.5	13280.0	65042.3	23715.2	12907.4	68417.8
1048978.0	**2273945.5**		**1499681.5**	**5136760.1**	**1053054.4**	**141367.7**	**3907229.4**
88627.6	343357.3		372751.8	1288643.7	336315.3	16585.3	697166.9
22562.5	53331.5		79315.6	348958.8	67753.6	20267.7	292054.6
933770.0	1666281.9		649321.4	2054847.3	473585.5	62943.9	1784239.3
-5348.7	195554.6		373486.7	1332511.3	161967.9	38283.1	1084164.9
8492.3	13767.2		11800.0	40235.0	9571.1	3287.7	33577.7

13-12 续表 2

单位：万元

地　区	Region	企业单位数(个) Number of Enterprises (unit)	#亏损企业 Loss- Suffering Enterprises	工业总产值(当年价格) Gross Industrial Output Value (At Current Prices)
阿瓦提县	Awat County			
柯坪县	Kalpin County	1	1	1653.0
克孜勒苏柯尔克孜自治州	**Kizilsu Kirgiz Autonomous Prefecture**	**8**	**3**	**75912.2**
阿图什市	Artux City	4	1	41419.0
阿克陶县	Akto County	1	1	6823.0
阿合奇县	Akqi County	1		19633.6
乌恰县	Wuqia [Ulugqat] County	2	1	8036.6
喀什地区	**Kashgar [Kaxgar] Administrative Offices**	**17**	**6**	**231264.3**
喀什市	Kashgar [Kaxgar] City	6	2	120980.5
疏附县	Shufu County			
疏勒县	Shule County	1	1	4415.4
英吉沙县	Yengisar County	1	1	2102.1
泽普县	Zepu [Poskam] County			
莎车县	Shache [Yarkant] County	1		14502.4
叶城县	Yecheng [Kagilik] County	1		3124.5
麦盖提县	Makit County	1		5658.2
岳普湖县	Yopurga County			
伽师县	Jiashi [Payzawat] County	1		47191.4
巴楚县	Bachu [Maralbexi] County	3		16537.5
塔什库尔干塔吉克自治县	Taxkorgan Tajik Autonomous County	2	2	16752.3
和田地区	**Hotan Administrative Offices**	**11**	**3**	**106451.7**
和田市	Hotan City	2	1	7248.9
和田县	Hotan County	4	2	32508.9
墨玉县	Moyu [Karakax] County	3		42235.1
皮山县	Pishan [Guma] County	1		4027.9
洛浦县	Lop County	1		20430.9
策勒县	Qira County			
于田县	Yutian [Keriya] County			
民丰县	Minfeng [Niya] County			
自治区直辖县级市	**County level City directly under the Autonomous Region**	**95**	**23**	**3019977.3**
石河子市	Shihezi City	38	13	2192681.1
阿拉尔市	Aral City	31	7	434337.9
图木舒克市	Tumxuk City	17	1	328662.2
五家渠市	Wujiaqu City	9	2	64296.1

Continued

(10 000 yuan)

工业增加值 Value-added of Industry	工业销售产值(当年价格) Sales Value of Industry Products (At Current Prices)	出口交货值 Delivery Value of Industry Export	实收资本 Total Capital Hold	资产合计 Total Assets	流动资产合计 Total Current Assets	#产成品 Finished Product	固定资产原价 Net Value of Fixed Assets
874.1	1653.0		13006.0	71564.0	3861.0		16026.0
47999.1	**76987.0**		**214272.0**	**796255.0**	**123856.8**	**2822.6**	**636709.4**
29040.6	42594.6		144872.0	232704.0	60005.9	2603.3	198311.8
2905.0	6823.0		38000.0	311041.1	49414.7		195063.9
13745.2	19533.6			160533.7	4197.0		171087.6
2308.3	8035.8		31400.0	91976.2	10239.2	219.3	72246.1
72735.4	**230050.0**		**149423.5**	**733913.3**	**161202.0**	**20023.2**	**680008.7**
43165.2	122343.1		101091.4	430188.9	51169.8	1579.8	477167.8
739.7	3826.7		7000.0	27622.7	12784.5	2664.0	16145.1
1346.3	2102.1		13800.0	26176.7	3927.1		26367.7
3667.6	12395.3		15000.0	28579.4	10761.5	1768.5	19543.2
1298.5	3124.5		3000.0	9228.6	3798.4	156.2	5360.1
1582.5	5555.7		350.0	9669.4	5218.9	250.8	4450.5
11346.4	53024.2		3000.0	38210.8	31762.0	4416.1	10530.6
3391.8	16641.2		5862.1	25511.4	7649.5	3491.9	20563.9
6197.6	11037.2		320.0	138725.4	34130.3	5695.9	99879.8
52865.1	**99395.5**		**254302.0**	**575243.0**	**185942.0**	**3531.2**	**478139.3**
3471.4	6814.0		2621.7	30194.9	11982.1	934.2	21869.5
16653.9	33253.3		169094.2	345392.5	117905.8	1437.6	286747.0
20367.9	34820.1		28486.1	93414.3	47339.5	910.1	63816.5
1699.1	4027.9		11100.0	30890.2	5473.2	14.0	27950.4
10672.8	20480.2		43000.0	75351.1	3241.4	235.3	77755.9
816368.6	**2948830.9**	**4959.4**	**1842556.2**	**10332861.6**	**2711083.7**	**292075.9**	**5494187.0**
604559.1	2165589.7	4959.4	1105691.9	7091939.3	1535446.0	180393.5	4343145.2
105822.2	426126.3		397010.2	1728437.0	573009.8	36952.3	661022.5
93058.3	298184.3		120749.7	530768.2	245435.3	70468.0	367668.6
12929.1	58930.6		219104.4	981717.1	357192.6	4262.1	122350.7

13-12 续表 3

单位: 万元

地　区	Region	负债合计 Total Liabilities	#流动负债 Total Liquid Liabilities	#非流动负债 Total Non-liquid Liabilities	所有者权益合计 Total Owners' Equities
总　计	**Total**	**67348310.7**	**37922472.2**	**29188137.2**	**42148695.0**
乌鲁木齐市	**Urumqi City**	**19440612.2**	**13405993.1**	**6027784.9**	**10711815.2**
天山区	Tianshan District	1416974.1	524968.8	892005.3	307121.5
沙依巴克区	Shayibak District	1948070.4	1297809.8	648547.0	985343.2
新市区	Xinshi District	3417450.5	2734981.0	677385.0	2627479.0
水磨沟区	Shui Mogou District	3641186.6	2261304.7	1379845.9	2307889.4
头屯河区	Tou Tunhe District	5394422.3	4771986.6	622435.7	1696618.1
达坂城区	Da Bancheng District	1043708.5	553978.5	489730.0	354858.4
米东区	Midong District	2312448.2	1065866.4	1246581.7	2339591.1
乌鲁木齐县	Urumqi County	266351.6	195097.3	71254.3	92914.5
克拉玛依市	**Karamay City**	**8042780.8**	**3832635.2**	**4209253.3**	**11157534.6**
独山子区	Dushanzi District	989561.4	721753.5	267807.9	2395251.4
克拉玛依区	Karamay District	6999682.9	3084109.4	3914681.2	8738854.0
白碱滩区	Bai Jiantan District	53536.5	26772.3	26764.2	23429.2
乌尔河区	Urhe District				
吐鲁番市	**Turpan City**	**3211694.0**	**1546500.3**	**1665193.1**	**1572371.5**
高昌区	Gaochang District	412447.1	201104.0	211342.8	165473.8
鄯善县	Shanshan [Piqan] County	1824611.5	900744.7	923866.6	1142509.5
托克逊县	Toksun County	974635.4	444651.6	529983.7	264388.2
哈密地区	**Hami [Kumul] Administrative Offices**	**6501345.4**	**3061473.8**	**3439871.2**	**2111968.4**
哈密市	Hami [Kumul] City	5559136.6	2580324.2	2978812.2	1860409.7
巴里坤哈萨克自治县	Barkol Kazak Autonomous County	813507.6	456353.6	357153.8	221693.8
伊吾县	Yiwu [Araturuk] County	128701.2	24796.0	103905.2	29864.9
昌吉回族自治州	**Changji Hui Autonomous Prefecture**	**3608379.8**	**2010601.9**	**1552404.0**	**1711376.9**
昌吉市	Changji City	559270.1	424620.1	134650.0	365239.8
阜康市	Fukang City	2065672.6	1021501.6	1044171.0	1001162.3
呼图壁县	Hutubi County	484480.9	121615.4	362865.5	121393.6
玛纳斯县	Manas County	33974.0	33931.7	42.3	7828.1
奇台县	Qitai County	245987.5	200524.6	89.0	29214.1
吉木萨尔县	Jimsar County	187004.6	186468.4	536.2	180405.8
木垒哈萨克自治县	Mori Kazak Autonomous County	31990.1	21940.1	10050.0	6133.2
伊犁哈萨克自治州	**Ili Kazak Autonomous Prefecture**	**7352772.0**	**4042495.3**	**3221521.7**	**3357640.9**
伊犁州直属县(市)	**Counties (Cities) Direct Under Ili Prefecture**	**4040541.7**	**2137932.5**	**1839413.0**	**1718318.3**
伊宁市	Yining [Gulja] City	371650.6	127342.2	244308.4	198764.1
奎屯市	Kuytun City	1185316.6	585983.1	536137.4	447166.9
霍尔果斯市	Huoerguosi City	101558.4	22981.0	78577.3	60283.0
伊宁县	Yining [Gulja] County	324938.5	251254.3	73684.2	158105.4
察布查尔锡伯自治县	Qapqal Xibe Autonomous County	88967.3	59394.6	29572.7	42628.9
霍城县	Huocheng [Korgas] County	94845.6	94466.7	378.9	24395.6
巩留县	Gongliu [Tokkuztara] County	597351.0	260296.1	337054.9	278010.3
新源县	Xinyuan [Kunes] County	497691.2	407721.7	89969.5	285945.8
昭苏县	Zhaosu [Mongolkure] County	110232.6	45768.1	64464.5	19960.6
特克斯县	Tekes County	88980.0	19580.0	69400.0	19731.0
尼勒克县	Nilka County	579009.9	263144.7	315865.2	183326.7
塔城地区	**Tacheng [Tarbagatai] Administrative Offices**	**1520855.3**	**1031757.3**	**480164.6**	**878499.5**
塔城市	Tacheng [Qoqek] City	3753.8	3753.8		5155.6
乌苏市	Usu City	200872.6	180539.2	20333.3	458791.0
额敏县	Emin [Dorbiljin] County	228492.5	132764.1	95728.3	82753.3

Continued

(10 000 yuan)

主营业务收入 Revenue from Principal Business	主营业务成本 Cost of Principal Business	主营业务税金及附加 Taxes and Other Charges on Principal Business	营业利润 Business Profits	利润总额 Total Profits	亏损企业亏损总额 Losses Value of Loss-Suffering Enterprises	利税总额 Total Profits and Taxes	本年应交增值税 Value-added Taxes Payable	全部从业人员年平均人数(人) Annual Average Employed Persons (person)
44496409.4	**34122793.3**	**3586473.2**	**780620.3**	**1321929.8**	**2470690.5**	**7143308.9**	**2234905.9**	**384230**
14504525.5	**12509477.0**	**1251907.1**	**-509724.1**	**-344043.2**	**716173.0**	**1356168.7**	**448304.8**	**105012**
325948.1	302302.5	1826.3	-36419.8	14844.3	21789.7	27852.1	11181.5	6178
610448.1	572527.3	3826.4	-32854.2	-798.2	39208.8	9195.8	6167.6	9020
1675370.8	1404602.4	56200.2	-185901.9	-156338.5	206997.6	15781.9	115920.2	15098
4492695.3	4335690.8	5006.6	117205.7	128117.0	291.8	110499.9	-22623.7	22451
2900978.1	2679354.6	230401.4	-355093.8	-321562.2	395505.6	-14248.9	76911.9	23086
197026.1	145116.7	4090.0	8953.8	9880.3	6621.9	-9194.9	-23165.2	5934
4266918.4	3051655.3	950280.9	-34677.5	-29711.3	45757.6	1202134.4	281564.8	23174
35140.6	18227.4	275.3	9063.6	11525.4		14148.4	2347.7	71
10955445.0	**8574398.2**	**1390389.6**	**-527674.1**	**-285925.3**	**698489.2**	**1823018.8**	**718554.5**	**90910**
3894814.1	2785922.7	636257.4	86061.6	106977.0	55200.9	1018198.9	274964.5	18160
7023602.6	5760145.9	754082.6	-617127.1	-397375.7	641827.9	797455.9	440749.0	72197
37028.3	28329.6	49.6	3391.4	4473.4	1460.4	7364.0	2841.0	553
1279185.9	**1098474.2**	**44210.9**	**-347714.1**	**-350594.2**	**403721.9**	**-250011.4**	**56371.9**	**12287**
79958.8	54664.8	1047.6	-5626.0	-4472.4	8176.4	8589.6	12014.4	1177
932730.9	836161.7	35620.8	-341566.2	-347628.8	378753.8	-280632.0	31376.0	8854
266496.2	207647.7	7542.5	-521.9	1507.0	16791.7	22031.0	12981.5	2256
1621642.4	**1230901.1**	**12253.8**	**66450.0**	**86419.7**	**46492.5**	**151761.2**	**53087.7**	**20874**
1490818.4	1149968.0	9728.1	63186.8	81278.7	37688.5	134966.5	43959.7	19010
107284.0	66680.6	2389.5	4131.9	5406.4	6763.2	14791.5	6995.6	1719
23540.0	14252.5	136.2	-868.7	-265.4	2040.8	2003.2	2132.4	145
1973585.9	**1707008.2**	**9390.7**	**20953.7**	**28712.7**	**70204.1**	**121519.3**	**83415.9**	**21745**
438831.3	384605.8	1754.7	8036.0	11297.5	14746.4	39349.8	26297.6	4637
1024951.4	912407.4	2748.4	-20503.0	-19313.1	47018.4	18281.3	34846.0	11648
228983.8	189995.6	2243.6	12580.5	15544.9	399.0	28442.6	10654.1	2556
47247.5	40175.9	181.3	1683.7	2051.4	1485.7	2193.4	-39.3	1011
130415.7	104408.9	2030.8	12064.9	11994.5	4394.7	19879.1	5853.8	678
92509.2	67413.8	342.9	5345.3	5538.7	2159.9	10759.2	4877.6	964
10647.0	8000.8	89.0	1746.3	1598.8		2613.9	926.1	251
2931688.6	**2185121.7**	**59833.4**	**160838.9**	**190378.0**	**165016.9**	**390772.8**	**140561.4**	**41839**
1696623.0	**1290543.1**	**32512.4**	**119763.0**	**136530.2**	**86124.3**	**252993.3**	**83950.7**	**23819**
160535.5	124152.1	911.7	11923.3	15313.7	10057.3	26729.1	10503.7	2828
601861.5	447737.2	2588.8	90042.1	96102.2	4392.5	111910.2	13219.2	7034
73322.6	59187.6	121.2	2266.3	2764.6		10649.9	7764.1	1280
160318.3	150271.3	1551.6	-28594.0	-26391.5	31190.2	-21360.9	3479.0	4092
56088.2	47653.5	111.7	95.5	464.6	6371.6	1924.2	1347.9	642
64448.0	55366.9	245.4	213.6	552.9	2025.5	3594.4	2796.1	1348
138519.8	101607.4	821.4	-964.2	-183.3	2820.2	10336.7	9698.6	895
324213.1	228646.3	25123.8	37356.0	40367.4	14403.1	87958.1	22466.9	4484
29847.5	17521.2	356.8	4910.7	4910.7	1356.0	7786.6	2519.1	200
7288.1	5134.1	117.5	-1581.0	-1579.0	1579.0	-266.0	1195.5	69
80180.4	53265.5	562.5	4094.7	4207.9	11928.9	13731.0	8960.6	947
692096.8	**558507.0**	**17100.6**	**-11841.0**	**-2621.5**	**55100.7**	**27382.4**	**12903.3**	**10997**
15627.5	14899.5	15.1	132.9	97.1		112.2		86
210763.1	178469.5	10719.0	-17510.5	-14139.0	17892.7	-8171.4	-4751.4	2550
79929.6	68550.9	230.0	1833.3	6859.1	4568.4	12811.0	5721.9	1531

13-12 续表 4

单位：万元

地区	Region	负债合计 Total Liabilities	#流动负债 Total Liquid Liabilities	#非流动负债 Total Non-liquid Liabilities	所有者权益合计 Total Owners' Equities
沙湾县	Shawan County	50644.7	49845.2	799.4	56311.1
托里县	Toli County	443103.6	311240.2	131863.4	112344.9
裕民县	Yumin [Qagantokay] County				
和布克赛尔蒙古自治县	Hoboksar Mongol Autonomous County	593988.1	353614.8	231440.2	163143.6
阿勒泰地区	**Altay Administrative Offices**	**1791375.0**	**872805.5**	**901944.1**	**760823.1**
阿勒泰市	Altay City	141984.3	64797.1	77187.2	23196.0
布尔津县	Burqin County	406835.0	186741.4	203468.3	95499.4
富蕴县	Fuyun [Koktokay] County	572755.5	294995.2	277760.2	316883.3
福海县	Fuhai [Burultokay] County	7717.9	7717.9		70290.1
哈巴河县	Habahe [Kaba] County	412126.8	157203.9	254922.9	197394.3
青河县	Qinghe [Qinggil] County	134790.6	115585.1	19205.5	17627.7
吉木乃县	Jeminay County	115164.9	45764.9	69400.0	39932.3
博尔塔拉蒙古自治州	**Bortala Mongol Autonomous Prefecture**	**536769.6**	**292649.9**	**244007.5**	**73643.3**
博乐市	Bole [Bortala] City	241968.3	177530.8	64325.4	7913.5
阿拉山口市	Alashankou City	258210.4	80596.5	177613.9	66871.8
精河县	Jinghe [Jing] County	34368.8	32300.5	2068.2	-2699.4
温泉县	Wenquan [Araxang] County	2222.1	2222.1		1557.4
巴音郭楞蒙古自治州	**Bayangol Mongol Autonomous Prefecture**	**6533271.4**	**2530586.1**	**4002111.5**	**5988758.2**
库尔勒市	Korla City	4643049.3	1317692.1	3325357.1	4994113.7
轮台县	Luntai [Bugur] County				
尉犁县	Yuli [Lopnur] County	4502.3	4502.3		3176.9
若羌县	Ruoqiang [Qarkilik] County	448847.5	279487.0	169360.5	311982.4
且末县	Qiemo [Qarqan] County	41815.5	41815.5		40004.9
焉耆回族自治县	Yanqi Hui Autonomous County	57923.4	44889.0	12621.4	37309.7
和静县	Hejing County	1256633.9	806447.4	450025.8	558739.0
和硕县	Hoxud County	39733.4	19091.0	20642.4	19155.5
博湖县	Bohu [Bagrax] County	40766.1	16661.8	24104.3	24276.1
阿克苏地区	**Aksu Administrative Offices**	**3436369.7**	**2217700.6**	**1205003.8**	**1693988.6**
阿克苏市	Aksu City	822560.9	326684.3	495876.6	466082.7
温宿县	Wensu [Onsu] County	280280.1	149977.8	117184.7	62277.3
库车县	Kuqa County	1047130.4	722569.8	324044.6	1007716.6
沙雅县	Xayar County				
新和县	Xinhe [Toksu] County				
拜城县	Baicheng [Bay] County	1203125.3	983735.9	219357.8	129386.0
乌什县	Wushi [Uxturpan] County	25518.0	11777.8	13740.1	14717.0

Continued

(10 000 yuan)

主营业务收入 Revenue from Principal Business	主营业务成本 Cost of Principal Business	主营业务税金及附加 Taxes and Other Charges on Principal Business	营业利润 Business Profits	利润总额 Total Profits	亏损企业亏损总额 Losses Value of Loss-Suffering Enterprises	利税总额 Total Profits and Taxes	本年应交增值税 Value-added Taxes Payable	全部从业人员年平均人数(人) Annual Average Employed Persons (person)
119307.2	104100.5	150.3	3240.8	3552.4	2481.1	6342.5	2639.8	1152
138864.2	102548.3	797.6	8869.1	9188.4	9031.5	8618.0	-1368.0	2733
127605.2	89938.3	5188.6	-8406.6	-8179.5	21127.0	7670.1	10661.0	2945
542968.8	**336071.6**	**10220.4**	**52916.9**	**56469.3**	**23791.9**	**110397.1**	**43707.4**	**7023**
57167.4	52259.0	104.1	-2155.1	-252.8	2773.9	766.3	915.0	1145
59590.9	37161.6	238.8	719.7	3542.4	2189.7	7651.2	3870.0	658
213506.2	146051.7	5830.2	631.1	1442.2	13397.0	27418.6	20146.2	3021
25585.9	17182.9	1201.0	1964.7	2483.9	823.5	6308.2	2623.3	249
163907.5	69531.0	2829.6	53082.2	50015.6	1674.4	67671.0	14825.8	1728
8684.4	6624.9	16.7	-3491.9	-2933.3	2933.4	-2916.6		174
14526.5	7260.5	0.0	2166.2	2171.3		3498.4	1327.1	48
165763.4	**129639.4**	**573.4**	**-3694.4**	**-1422.5**	**10784.6**	**7195.1**	**8044.2**	**2970**
107756.4	91090.8	226.7	-6070.7	-3803.8	8779.7	-1425.8	2151.3	2492
31156.8	19134.6	9.9	2847.3	2849.8		7249.2	4389.5	88
19123.7	12915.2	271.8	-1333.2	-1397.8	2004.9	142.1	1268.1	306
7726.5	6498.8	65.0	862.2	929.3		1229.6	235.3	84
5745032.1	**2729291.4**	**351171.3**	**1736228.5**	**1770595.0**	**76071.7**	**2552136.5**	**430370.2**	**30456**
4679976.9	1998164.3	284201.4	1673014.3	1671761.8	20962.0	2327507.9	371544.7	18846
38826.1	35035.2	21.2	1730.6	1730.6		2105.1	353.3	418
420853.7	172461.8	63663.8	84002.2	116300.5	139.1	212789.0	32824.7	3659
7553.3	7961.3	312.0	-4463.5	-4419.7	4419.7	-4109.0	-1.3	127
37671.4	28102.0	178.0	3304.3	3343.0	124.3	4497.7	976.7	607
514084.8	455813.0	2557.0	-26969.6	-23810.8	50378.6	-1508.2	19745.6	6138
21947.6	14579.1	141.2	3554.3	3604.7	48.0	4225.8	479.9	314
24118.3	17174.7	96.7	2055.9	2084.9		6628.2	4446.6	347
2294253.1	**1524866.6**	**450812.5**	**44115.2**	**48178.9**	**186323.0**	**666218.7**	**167227.3**	**14799**
349465.4	292218.5	1104.2	9929.3	12953.1	6345.1	19959.4	5902.1	3103
48542.0	32794.2	349.4	-6890.3	-5857.4	10883.6	-1451.9	4056.1	1160
1671194.0	967329.9	444560.2	160958.4	160513.7	40893.5	750511.9	145438.0	6602
210033.8	223914.7	3436.0	-121892.5	-121435.4	128153.8	-108320.9	9678.5	3727
13364.9	7578.3	1362.7	2057.3	2051.9		5567.2	2152.6	154

13-12 续表 5

单位: 万元

地　　区	Region	负债合计 Total Liabilities	#流动负债 Total Liquid Liabilities	#非流动负债 Total Non-liquid Liabilities	所有者权益合计 Total Owners' Equities
阿瓦提县	Awat County				
柯坪县	Kalpin County	57755.0	22955.0	34800.0	13809.0
克孜勒苏柯尔克孜自治州	**Kizilsu Kirgiz Autonomous Prefecture**	**553330.0**	**277243.1**	**276086.9**	**242925.1**
阿图什市	Artux City	83484.8	65692.3	17792.5	149219.2
阿克陶县	Akto County	249238.7	21418.7	227820.0	61802.4
阿合奇县	Akqi County	160533.7	160533.7		
乌恰县	Wuqia [Ulugqat] County	60072.8	29598.4	30474.4	31903.5
喀什地区	**Kashgar [Kaxgar] Administrative Offices**	**586770.5**	**286687.0**	**289052.3**	**147142.7**
喀什市	Kashgar [Kaxgar] City	341340.9	121174.4	219215.4	88848.0
疏附县	Shufu County				
疏勒县	Shule County	20367.0	20367.0		7255.6
英吉沙县	Yengisar County	12278.1	2198.1		13898.5
泽普县	Zepu [Poskam] County				
莎车县	Shache [Yarkant] County	11580.4	11580.3		16999.0
叶城县	Yecheng [Kagilik] County	3215.6	665.6	2550.0	6013.0
麦盖提县	Makit County	8346.0	8346.0		1323.4
岳普湖县	Yopurga County				
伽师县	Jiashi [Payzawat] County	22230.8	21830.8	400.0	15979.9
巴楚县	Bachu [Maralbexi] County	17298.7	17282.2	16.5	8212.8
塔什库尔干塔吉克自治县	Taxkorgan Tajik Autonomous County	150113.0	83242.6	66870.4	-11387.5
和田地区	**Hotan Administrative Offices**	**261036.3**	**139541.2**	**121397.8**	**314206.5**
和田市	Hotan City	19681.7	6793.9	12887.8	10513.1
和田县	Hotan County	162738.4	76673.3	86065.1	182654.1
墨玉县	Moyu [Karakax] County	31023.9	26944.0	4079.9	62390.4
皮山县	Pishan [Guma] County	19296.2	931.2	18365.0	11593.9
洛浦县	Lop County	28296.1	28198.8		47055.0
策勒县	Qira County				
于田县	Yutian [Keriya] County				
民丰县	Minfeng [Niya] County				
自治区直辖县级市	**County level City directly under the Autonomous Region**	**7283179.0**	**4278364.7**	**2934449.2**	**3065323.1**
石河子市	Shihezi City	5130737.7	2834457.4	2249761.6	1967757.7
阿拉尔市	Aral City	1024671.1	772757.5	251913.4	703765.8
图木舒克市	Tumxuk City	358988.5	196828.9	148859.2	180864.2
五家渠市	Wujiaqu City	768781.7	474320.9	283915.0	212935.4

Continued

(10 000 yuan)

主营业务收入 Revenue from Principal Business	主营业务成本 Cost of Principal Business	主营业务税金及附加 Taxes and Other Charges on Principal Business	营业利润 Business Profits	利润总额 Total Profits	亏损企业亏损总额 Losses Value of Loss-Suffering Enterprises	利税总额 Total Profits and Taxes	本年应交增值税 Value-added Taxes Payable	全部从业人员年平均人数（人） Annual Average Employed Persons (person)
1653.0	1031.0		-47.0	-47.0	47.0	-47.0		53
76427.5	**51787.7**	**643.3**	**3842.2**	**5568.1**	**1292.0**	**17959.1**	**11747.7**	**896**
41937.6	34472.7	309.9	1832.3	3572.2	394.1	12462.9	8580.8	639
6830.0	2808.7		-26.6	-26.6	26.6	-125.0	-98.4	67
19533.6	8844.1	310.9	2626.3	2617.4		5969.5	3041.2	49
8126.3	5662.2	22.5	-589.8	-594.9	871.3	-348.3	224.1	141
229815.6	**182498.6**	**707.4**	**2690.7**	**6590.6**	**7864.3**	**20940.3**	**13642.3**	**3151**
119595.5	89081.1	420.8	5965.5	7411.7	1295.3	11074.3	3241.8	1689
4191.2	4164.8	0.2	-2590.6	-2157.3	2157.3	-1865.8	291.3	139
2102.1	1573.1		-57.7	-57.7	57.7	-57.7		9
12395.3	10473.1	81.7	-835.0	550.4		1977.7	1345.6	298
3822.1	3318.5	1.9	-153.2	29.3		37.6	6.4	176
5555.7	4498.9	1.6	822.3	822.3		992.1	168.2	61
54385.1	48490.1	38.3	2669.6	2696.9		9603.7	6868.5	232
16641.2	13739.8	61.5	1229.3	1649.0		2144.2	433.7	231
11127.4	7159.2	101.4	-4359.5	-4354.0	4354.0	-2965.8	1286.8	316
97183.3	**73118.6**	**698.1**	**3847.3**	**8161.1**	**3397.6**	**17310.1**	**8450.9**	**1610**
7190.0	5603.0	16.4	592.5	592.7	103.3	1102.8	493.7	127
33902.3	25683.2	624.6	-3328.2	-2006.1	3294.3	339.1	1720.6	513
32108.8	27501.3	57.1	566.6	3537.2		10009.8	6415.5	683
3442.6	1872.3		314.3	314.3		314.3		60
20539.6	12458.8		5702.1	5723.0		5544.1	-178.9	227
2621861.1	**2126210.6**	**13881.7**	**130460.5**	**159310.9**	**84859.7**	**268319.7**	**95127.1**	**37681**
1855819.2	1507613.8	9903.8	81489.7	90649.5	52604.9	167656.8	67103.5	26803
420421.3	339556.7	3170.0	21839.2	37695.3	26340.8	50836.3	9971.0	6117
297423.6	235629.1	759.8	31723.5	33997.4	843.7	51667.3	16910.1	3430
48197.0	43411.0	48.1	-4591.9	-3031.3	5070.3	-1840.7	1142.5	1331

13-13 国有控股工业企业主要经济效益指标

单位: % (2015 年)

项　目	Item	产　值 利税率 Ratio of Profits and Taxes to Industrial Output Value
总　计	**Total**	**16.2**
按登记注册类型分	**Grouped by Registry Type**	
内资企业	Domestic Funded Enterprises	16.3
国有企业	State-owned Enterprises	4.6
#中央企业	Central Enterprises	3.0
地方企业	Local Enterprises	14.8
#自治区属企业	Autonomous	29.4
地区(州、市)属企业	Prefecture or City	-18.6
县(市)属企业	County or City	20.9
股份合作企业	Cooperative Enterprises	-11.7
有限责任公司	Limited Liability Corporations	10.9
#国有独资公司	Sole State-funded Corporations	15.3
其他有限责任公司	Other Limited Liability Corporations	9.3
股份有限公司	Share-holding Corporations Ltd.	23.8
港、澳、台商投资企业	Enterprises with Funds from Hongkong,Macao and Taiwan	37.7
外商投资企业	Foreign Funded Enterprises	1.5
在总计中: 国有控股企业	Of the Total: State-owned and State-holding Enterprises	16.2
按轻、重工业分	**Grouped by Light & Heavy Industry**	
轻工业	Light Industry	20.0
以农产品为原料	Using Farm Products as Raw Materials	22.2
以非农产品为原料	Using Non-Farm Products as Raw Materials	-5.2
重工业	Heavy Industry	15.9
采掘工业	Mining and Quarrying	17.1
原料工业	Raw Material Industry	16.2
加工工业	Manufacturing Industry	8.1
按企业规模分	**Grouped by Size of Enterprises**	
大型企业	Large Enterprises	18.1
中型企业	Medium-sized Enterprises	13.7
小型企业	Small Enterprises	8.6
微型企业	Mini Enterprises	13.2

Main Indicators on Economic Efficiency of State-holding Industrial Enterprises

(%)

总资产贡献率 Ratio of Profits, Taxes and Interests to Average Value	资本保值增值率 Ratio of Capital-hold and Rise	资产负债率 Ratio of debts to Assets	流动资产周转次数(次/年) Turnover of Currents Assets (times/year)	成本费用利润率 Ratio of Profits to Industrial Costs	全员劳动生产率（万元/人） Overall Labour Productivity (10 000yuan/person)
8.2	**101.0**	**61.5**	**1.9**	**3.3**	**46.95**
8.2	101.1	61.5	1.9	3.4	47.01
4.1	95.1	68.4	3.7	4.1	40.84
3.4	94.9	63.1	9.2	2.9	43.48
5.4	95.6	78.7	0.7	12.5	32.90
10.5	101.4	67.3	1.3	41.2	61.43
-0.7	27.5	97.9	0.3	-9.4	7.06
7.6	115.0	69.4	1.1	15.1	36.67
1.2		88.9	0.3	-20.7	11.08
5.5	107.0	71.1	1.3	1.5	27.88
6.6	99.1	69.0	1.0	3.9	27.77
5.1	110.4	71.8	1.4	0.6	27.94
12.5	98.1	48.2	2.4	4.9	79.53
4.3	98.3	58.8	2.0	23.5	141.30
1.6	85.8	59.5	1.7	-7.2	25.16
8.2	101.0	61.5	1.9	3.3	46.95
12.7	117.5	55.5	1.2	9.9	25.39
17.0	118.3	53.9	1.4	12.1	27.04
0.3	115.2	60.1	0.6	-7.7	14.69
7.9	100.1	61.9	1.9	2.8	50.02
6.8	100.4	52.5	1.9	4.9	54.11
9.0	100.0	67.4	2.2	1.7	52.61
5.3	97.6	68.1	1.0	2.8	21.88
10.3	95.1	57.3	2.6	2.8	58.93
6.0	103.0	65.9	1.0	3.9	25.33
4.5	124.9	67.5	1.1	4.9	29.32
3.6	180.9	80.1	0.4	10.5	40.03

13-14 分行业国有控股工业企业主要经济效益指标

单位: %　　　　(2015 年)

行　业	Sector	产　值 利税率 Ratio of Profits and Taxes to Industrial Output Value
总　计	**Total**	**16.2**
煤炭开采和洗选业	Mining and Washing of Coal	15.2
石油和天然气开采业	Extraction of Petroleum and Natural Gas	18.3
黑色金属矿采选业	Mining and Processing of Ferrous Metals Ores	19.2
有色金属矿采选业	Mining and Processing of Nonferrous Metals Ores	21.0
非金属矿采选业	Mining and Processing of Nonmetal Ores	23.2
#采　盐	Extraction of Salt	41.4
开采辅助活动	Support for Minning	9.1
农副食品加工业	Activities Processing of Food from Agricultural Products	10.6
#谷物磨制	Grain Grinding	8.9
饲料加工	Fodder Processing	12.9
制　糖	Sugar Making	3.4
食品制造业	Manufacture of Foods	11.9
#罐头制造	Manufacture of can	5.7
饮料制造业	Manufacture of Liguor,Beverages and Refined Tea	45.4
#酒的制造	Manufacture of Liguor	46.4
烟草制品业	Manufacture of Tobacco	69.6
纺织业	Manufacture of Textile	13.9
#棉、化纤纺织及印染精加工	Cotton, Chemical Fiber, Dyeing, Printing and Processing	12.2
毛纺织和染整精加工	Wool Textile, Dyeing and Printing	21.2
纺织服装、鞋、帽制造业	Manufacture of Textile, Wearing Apparel and Accessories	3.4
皮革、毛皮、羽毛(绒)及其制品业	Manufacturie of Leather, Fur, Feather and Related Products	
#皮革鞣制加工	Leather Tanning and Processing	
木材加工及木、竹、藤、棕、草制品业	Processing of Timber, Manufacture of Wood, Bamboo, Cane, Grass Products	25.9
家具制造业	Manufacture of Furniture	
造纸及纸制品业	Manufacture of Paper and Paper Products	17.3
印刷业和记录媒介的复制	Printing and Reproduction of Recording Media	13.8
文教、工美、体育和娱乐用品制造业	Manufacture of Articles for Cultural, Educational,Sports and Entertainment	
石油加工、炼焦及核燃料加工业	Processing, Processing of Petroleeum,Coking and Nuclear Fuel	38.0
#炼　焦	Coking	-10.6
化学原料及化学制品制造业	Manufacture of Raw Chemical Materials and Chemical Products	6.4
#基础化学原料制造	Basic Chemical Material	3.2
肥料制造	Manufacture of Fertilizer	22.8
合成材料制造	Manufacture of Synthetic Materials	2.9
医药制造业	Manufacture of Medicine	7.8
化学纤维制造业	Manufacture of Chemical Fibers	11.4
橡胶制品业	Manufacture of Rubber and Plastics Products	3.7
非金属矿物制品业	Manufacture of Non-metallic Mineral Products	3.5
#水泥制造	Manufacture of Cement	-1.6
黑色金属冶炼及压延加工业	Smelting and Pressing of Ferrous Metals	-24.2
有色金属冶炼及压延加工业	Smelting and Pressing of Non ferrous Metals	1.0
金属制品业	Manufacture of Metal Products	3.8
通用设备制造业	Manufacture of General Purpose Machinery	3.7
专用设备制造业	Manufacture of Special Purpose Machinery	9.6
汽车制造业	Manufacture of Automobile	-18.2
铁路、船舶、航空航天和其他运输设备制造业	Manufacture of Railway ,Ship,Aeronautics and Other Transport Equipment	11.8
电气机械及器材制造业	Manufacture of Electrical and Machinery and Apparatus	4.5
计算机、通信和其他电子设备制造业	Manufacture of, Computer Communicationand Other Electronic Equipment	
仪器仪表制造业	Measuring Instruments and Machinery	10.3
废弃资源综合利用业	Comprehensive Utilization of Waste Resources	6.2
金属制品、机械和设备修理业	Repair Service of Metal Prodults,Mouhinery and Equipment	12.2
电力、热力的生产和供应业	Production and Supply of Electrici Power and Heat Power	6.5
#电力生产和电力供应	Production and Supply of Electric	6.6
燃气生产和供应业	Production and Supply of Gas	-5.6
水的生产和供应业	Production and Supply of Water	11.4

Main Indicators on Economic Efficiency of State-holding Industrial Enterprises by Sectors

(%)

总资产贡献率 Ratio of Profits, Taxes and Interests to Average Value	资本保值增值率 Ratio of Capital-hold and Rise	资产负债率 Ratio of debts to Assets	流动资产周转次数(次/年) Turnover of Currents Assets (times/year)	成本费用利润率 Ratio of Profits to Industrial Costs	全员劳动生产率(万元/人) Overall Labour Productivity (10 000yuan/person)
8.2	**101.0**	**61.5**	**1.9**	**3.3**	**46.95**
5.0	97.3	72.7	1.0	-0.6	19.12
7.0	102.1	46.6	2.6	5.7	85.99
8.0	92.6	73.6	0.7	8.7	32.17
6.8	104.9	57.1	1.0	14.7	40.48
16.8	104.0	66.9	1.3	14.4	21.18
27.8	115.9	32.9	1.2	30.1	30.66
7.1	78.3	61.9	1.4	0.6	27.95
10.6	97.8	63.0	1.5	9.7	19.06
10.1	125.2	67.9	2.1	7.8	19.83
8.7	119.1	31.3	1.7	12.5	26.45
2.8	88.1	76.6	0.7	-0.9	9.95
9.4	259.8	63.9	1.4	9.2	18.48
4.6		82.2	0.9	2.9	12.76
28.8	105.1	31.0	1.3	37.7	41.09
29.2	105.5	31.2	1.3	39.1	43.32
65.1	101.9	26.9	1.7	25.9	477.72
6.7	143.5	44.6	1.2	9.3	11.01
6.9	190.6	50.7	1.2	8.3	9.62
6.3	102.2	30.5	1.2	15.3	17.30
3.1	105.6	74.9	1.4	1.3	7.97
22.2		0.2	202.3	31.0	19.41
27.2	38.9	20.5	2.9	12.0	11.09
6.8	113.9	39.5	0.8	7.5	12.38
60.7	99.8	34.2	6.1	7.5	147.91
-1.4	82.7	79.9	1.0	-13.5	7.69
4.3	106.7	69.7	1.7	1.4	26.07
3.5	142.9	71.0	1.2	-0.2	18.36
11.3	94.9	71.5	2.0	12.6	52.16
3.0	102.6	69.1	2.0	-0.1	23.97
3.4	96.4	52.2	0.4	4.8	12.34
7.3		86.9	0.8	3.5	16.13
3.1	94.4	49.6	1.4	0.2	11.08
2.6	94.8	58.3	0.5	-2.3	13.91
1.8	93.5	56.3	0.4	-8.3	10.20
-4.5	65.7	84.6	1.3	-19.1	-8.84
1.0	105.0	43.0	0.7	-1.1	15.38
3.4	121.7	66.5	0.9	2.1	17.81
4.0	124.8	64.5	1.0	2.9	7.49
4.9	98.3	61.3	0.9	9.4	15.35
-11.5	62.7	83.9	1.5	-20.6	-6.20
8.9		32.3	1.0	5.3	13.33
6.5	89.8	90.6	0.9	3.0	59.52
4.0	108.2	74.8	0.6	4.4	12.94
1.8	91.6	44.0	1.8	0.1	16.54
34.6	100.4	37.6		0.3	15.10
4.1	105.7	72.3		5.3	50.37
4.3	106.0	71.7		5.6	54.82
-3.1	76.7	85.4		-5.8	4.29
2.1	132.2	58.5		9.2	22.13

13-15 各地、州、市、县(市)国有控股工业企业主要经济效益指标

单位: % (2015 年)

地 区	Region	产 值 利税率 Ratio of Profits and Taxes to Industrial Output Value
总 计	**Total**	**16.2**
乌鲁木齐市	**Urumqi City**	**9.4**
天山区	Tianshan District	8.7
沙依巴克区	Shayibak District	1.5
新市区	Xinshi District	0.9
水磨沟区	Shui Mogou District	2.5
头屯河区	Tou Tunhe District	-0.5
达坂城区	Da Bancheng District	-4.9
米东区	Midong District	29.1
乌鲁木齐县	Urumqi County	36.5
克拉玛依市	**Karamay City**	**18.3**
独山子区	Dushanzi District	27.1
克拉玛依区	Karamay District	13.0
白碱滩区	Bai Jiantan District	19.2
乌尔河区	Urhe District	
吐鲁番市	**Turpan City**	**-20.9**
高昌区	Gaochang District	10.5
鄯善县	Shanshan [Piqan] County	-33.1
托克逊县	Toksun County	8.2
哈密地区	**Hami [Kumul] Administrative Offices**	**8.9**
哈密市	Hami [Kumul] City	8.6
巴里坤哈萨克自治县	Barkol Kazak Autonomous County	13.3
伊吾县	Yiwu [Araturuk] County	8.5
昌吉回族自治州	**Changji Hui Autonomous Prefecture**	**5.7**
昌吉市	Changji City	8.8
阜康市	Fukang City	1.6
呼图壁县	Hutubi County	11.9
玛纳斯县	Manas County	4.2
奇台县	Qitai County	12.1
吉木萨尔县	Jimsar County	11.9
木垒哈萨克自治县	Mori Kazak Autonomous County	17.4
伊犁哈萨克自治州	**Ili Kazak Autonomous Prefecture**	**13.0**
伊犁州直属县(市)	**Counties (Cities) Direct Under Ili Prefecture**	**14.7**
伊宁市	Yining [Gulja] City	16.0
奎屯市	Kuytun City	19.5
霍尔果斯市	Huoerguosi City	14.4
伊宁县	Yining [Gulja] County	-12.6
察布查尔锡伯自治县	Qapqal Xibe Autonomous County	3.5
霍城县	Huocheng [Korgas] County	4.9
巩留县	Gongliu [Tokkuztara] County	7.9
新源县	Xinyuan [Kunes] County	24.4
昭苏县	Zhaosu [Mongolkure] County	25.6
特克斯县	Tekes County	-3.6
尼勒克县	Nilka County	17.1
塔城地区	**Tacheng [Tarbagatai] Administrative Offices**	**4.0**
塔城市	Tacheng [Qoqek] City	0.6
乌苏市	Usu City	-4.0
额敏县	Emin [Dorbiljin] County	15.2

Main Indicators on Economic Efficiency of State-holding Industrial Enterprises by Prefecture, Autonomous Prefecture, City and County

(%)

总资产贡献率 Ratio of Profits, Taxes and Interests to Average Value	资本保值增值率 Ratio of Capital-hold and Rise	资产负债率 Ratio of debts to Assets	流动资产周转次数(次/年) Turnover of Currents Assets (times/year)	成本费用利润率 Ratio of Profits to Industrial Costs	全员劳动生产率(万元/人) Overall Labour Productivity (10 000yuan/person)
8.2	**101.0**	**61.5**	**1.9**	**3.3**	47.0
6.1	**93.9**	**64.5**	**2.2**	**-2.5**	40.4
3.2	196.7	82.2	0.4	4.1	19.3
1.5	92.5	66.4	0.5	-0.1	7.5
2.0	86.4	56.5	2.2	-8.6	63.9
3.1	97.1	61.2	15.1	2.9	47.8
2.0	83.7	76.1	1.3	-10.6	14.1
1.1	108.1	74.6	1.2	5.3	14.3
26.7	99.2	49.7	3.8	-0.9	68.3
5.9	174.7	74.1	0.6	44.9	411.7
10.4	**96.0**	**41.9**	**2.4**	**-2.9**	47.8
31.0	88.6	29.2	5.6	3.4	82.3
6.0	98.0	44.5	1.9	-6.0	39.2
9.9	309.8	69.6	1.3	13.5	30.5
					0.0
-3.3	**114.5**	**67.1**	**1.3**	**-25.4**	**32.0**
3.7	122.4	71.4	0.7	-5.3	37.1
-7.8	107.1	61.5	1.4	-33.5	29.7
4.2	154.7	78.7	1.2	0.6	38.5
4.1	**120.2**	**75.5**	**0.8**	**5.6**	29.1
4.1	121.2	74.9	0.9	5.7	28.1
4.0	109.7	78.6	0.5	5.3	35.6
5.3	151.3	81.2	0.6	-1.1	78.7
4.7	**94.6**	**68.2**	**2.0**	**1.5**	28.1
6.3	83.0	60.5	2.2	2.6	31.6
3.4	93.6	67.4	1.7	-1.8	21.6
7.3	100.1	84.2	2.9	7.2	31.7
6.2	424.3	81.3	2.0	4.5	15.5
8.4	3107.6	89.4	2.6	10.4	104.0
4.6	109.5	50.9	2.5	6.4	42.3
7.6	55.2	83.9	0.9	18.3	21.8
5.6	**112.8**	**68.7**	**1.2**	**7.0**	28.8
6.4	**101.1**	**70.2**	**1.1**	**8.8**	28.7
6.9	89.2	65.2	1.3	10.1	28.3
8.3	105.7	72.6	1.3	18.6	31.8
10.2	108.2	62.8	3.9	3.9	40.9
-1.6	98.9	67.3	1.0	-14.3	7.5
4.3	108.2	67.6	2.1	0.8	18.3
4.8	106.4	79.5	1.0	0.9	12.4
3.3	100.4	68.2	0.7	-0.1	51.1
11.8	102.4	63.5	0.9	15.4	33.9
10.3	1240.7	84.7	2.5	20.0	61.4
3.7	125.9	81.9	1.7	-16.7	67.9
4.3	90.4	76.0	2.2	5.5	56.6
2.9	**158.8**	**63.4**	**1.5**	**-0.4**	20.9
2.7	111.0	42.1	2.9	0.6	10.3
-0.6	461.2	30.5	4.8	-6.6	28.0
5.7	92.7	73.4	0.6	8.8	19.0

13-15 续表 1

单位: %

地区	Region	产值利税率 Ratio of Profits and Taxes to Industrial Output Value
沙湾县	Shawan County	6.4
托里县	Toli County	5.6
裕民县	Yumin [Qagantokay] County	
和布克赛尔蒙古自治县	Hoboksar Mongol Autonomous County	5.7
阿勒泰地区	**Altay Administrative Offices**	**18.9**
阿勒泰市	Altay City	1.1
布尔津县	Burqin County	12.0
富蕴县	Fuyun [Koktokay] County	11.8
福海县	Fuhai [Burultokay] County	23.2
哈巴河县	Habahe [Kaba] County	41.5
青河县	Qinghe [Qinggil] County	-33.0
吉木乃县	Jeminay County	24.1
博尔塔拉蒙古自治州	**Bortala Mongol Autonomous Prefecture**	**3.6**
博乐市	Bole [Bortala] City	-1.0
阿拉山口市	Alashankou City	23.0
精河县	Jinghe [Jing] County	0.7
温泉县	Wenquan [Araxang] County	24.7
巴音郭楞蒙古自治州	**Bayangol Mongol Autonomous Prefecture**	**45.2**
库尔勒市	Korla City	50.2
轮台县	Luntai [Bugur] County	
尉犁县	Yuli [Lopnur] County	5.4
若羌县	Ruoqiang [Qarkilik] County	45.0
且末县	Qiemo [Qarqan] County	-50.0
焉耆回族自治县	Yanqi Hui Autonomous County	10.9
和静县	Hejing County	-0.4
和硕县	Hoxud County	19.2
博湖县	Bohu [Bagrax] County	25.2
阿克苏地区	**Aksu Administrative Offices**	**28.4**
阿克苏市	Aksu City	5.8
温宿县	Wensu [Onsu] County	-2.3
库车县	Kuqa County	44.5
沙雅县	Xayar County	
新和县	Xinhe [Toksu] County	
拜城县	Baicheng [Bay] County	-47.1
乌什县	Wushi [Uxturpan] County	35.2

Continued

(%)

总资产贡献率 Ratio of Profits, Taxes and Interests to Average Value	资本保值增值率 Ratio of Capital-hold and Rise	资产负债率 Ratio of debts to Assets	流动资产周转次数(次/年) Turnover of Currents Assets (times/year)	成本费用利润率 Ratio of Profits to Industrial Costs	全员劳动生产率（万元/人） Overall Labour Productivity (10 000yuan/person)
6.8	98.3	47.4	1.7	3.1	14.4
3.7	114.0	79.8	1.0	7.0	18.3
					0.0
3.6	80.0	78.5	1.7	-6.3	21.0
6.6	**105.2**	**70.2**	**1.0**	**12.0**	41.5
2.1	89.3	86.0	0.9	-0.4	17.0
5.4	102.9	81.0	0.6	5.9	50.5
5.3	127.5	64.4	1.0	0.7	28.2
12.3	91.5	9.9	2.3	11.1	52.3
12.3	83.8	67.6	1.2	53.0	73.4
-1.1	188.4	88.4	0.4	-24.1	17.7
5.4	116.8	74.3	0.7	17.6	214.2
3.9	**97.9**	**87.9**	**1.3**	**-0.8**	23.1
1.6	66.2	96.8	1.4	-3.4	12.7
5.1	133.0	79.4	0.8	9.7	295.2
5.3		108.5	2.6	-6.9	29.8
35.0		58.8	3.2	13.6	23.8
21.9	**110.2**	**52.2**	**3.0**	**48.9**	148.7
25.6	111.7	48.2	4.2	62.2	216.3
					0.0
27.5		58.6	7.0	4.7	11.1
29.1	102.4	59.0	2.6	42.5	88.0
-2.2		51.1	1.7	-37.6	-10.1
5.9	105.9	60.8	0.6	9.7	19.1
2.1	95.4	69.2	1.0	-4.4	15.5
9.4	97.0	67.5	1.1	19.5	25.5
12.8	122.6	62.7	1.0	9.4	32.3
15.1	**75.2**	**66.9**	**2.2**	**2.7**	70.9
3.8	43.3	63.8	1.0	3.7	28.6
2.0	86.5	80.3	0.7	-12.6	19.5
38.1	121.1	51.0	3.5	15.0	141.4
					0.0
					0.0
-5.0	50.6	90.3	1.3	-38.8	-1.4
14.2	144.9	63.4	1.4	20.7	55.2

13-15 续表 2

单位: %

地　　区	Region	产值利税率 Ratio of Profits and Taxes to Industrial Output Value
阿瓦提县	Awat County	
柯坪县	Kalpin County	-2.8
克孜勒苏柯尔克孜自治州	**Kizilsu Kirgiz Autonomous Prefecture**	**23.7**
阿图什市	Artux City	30.1
阿克陶县	Akto County	-1.8
阿合奇县	Akqi County	30.4
乌恰县	Wuqia [Ulugqat] County	-4.3
喀什地区	**Kashgar [Kaxgar] Administrative Offices**	**9.1**
喀什市	Kashgar [Kaxgar] City	9.2
疏附县	Shufu County	
疏勒县	Shule County	-42.3
英吉沙县	Yengisar County	-2.7
泽普县	Zepu [Poskam] County	
莎车县	Shache [Yarkant] County	13.6
叶城县	Yecheng [Kagilik] County	1.2
麦盖提县	Makit County	17.5
岳普湖县	Yopurga County	
伽师县	Jiashi [Payzawat] County	20.4
巴楚县	Bachu [Maralbexi] County	13.0
塔什库尔干塔吉克自治县	Taxkorgan Tajik Autonomous County	-17.7
和田地区	**Hotan Administrative Offices**	**16.3**
和田市	Hotan City	15.2
和田县	Hotan County	1.0
墨玉县	Moyu [Karakax] County	23.7
皮山县	Pishan [Guma] County	7.8
洛浦县	Lop County	27.1
策勒县	Qira County	
于田县	Yutian [Keriya] County	
民丰县	Minfeng [Niya] County	
自治区直辖县级市	**County level City directly under the Autonomous Region**	**8.9**
石河子市	Shihezi City	7.6
阿拉尔市	Aral City	11.7
图木舒克市	Tumxuk City	15.7
五家渠市	Wujiaqu City	-2.9

Continued

(%)

总资产贡献率 Ratio of Profits, Taxes and Interests to Average Value	资本保值增值率 Ratio of Capital-hold and Rise	资产负债率 Ratio of debts to Assets	流动资产周转次数(次/年) Turnover of Currents Assets (times/year)	成本费用利润率 Ratio of Profits to Industrial Costs	全员劳动生产率(万元/人) Overall Labour Productivity (10 000yuan/person)
0.9	242.0	80.7	0.4	-2.8	16.5
4.0	**137.7**	**69.5**	**0.6**	**7.8**	53.6
5.4	130.2	35.9	0.7	9.0	45.5
1.2	103.9	80.1	0.1	-0.4	43.4
8.5		100.0	4.7	15.8	280.5
2.2	1335.4	65.3	0.8	-6.8	16.4
6.0	**88.5**	**80.0**	**1.4**	**2.9**	23.1
6.0	82.8	79.3	2.3	6.5	25.6
-4.3	74.2	73.7	0.3	-31.6	5.3
2.1	90.0	46.9	0.5	-2.7	149.6
10.3	103.3	40.5	1.2	4.2	12.3
4.0	128.9	34.8	1.0	0.7	7.4
10.3	74.5	86.3	1.1	17.4	25.9
25.1	100.8	58.2	1.7	5.2	48.9
11.9	982.4	67.8	2.2	10.7	14.7
1.3		108.2	0.3	-27.7	19.6
4.5	**101.8**	**45.4**	**0.5**	**8.8**	32.8
5.6	59.7	65.2	0.6	8.9	27.3
2.0	104.4	47.1	0.3	-5.4	32.5
11.1	106.0	33.2	0.7	11.3	29.8
4.6	89.9	62.5	0.6	10.0	28.3
7.4	106.2	37.6	6.3	38.5	47.0
4.4	**130.3**	**70.5**	**1.0**	**6.4**	21.7
4.2	109.4	72.3	1.2	5.1	22.6
5.1	474.9	59.3	0.7	9.5	17.3
11.5	84.3	67.6		12.8	27.1
0.3	111.5	78.3		-5.8	9.7

13-16 分行业大中型工业企业主要经济指标

单位：万元 (2015 年)

行 业	Sector	企业单位数(个) Number of Enterp-rises (unit)	#亏损企业 Loss- Suffering Enterprises	工业总产值(当年价格) Gross Industrial Output Value (At Current Prices)
总 计	**Total**	**403**	**140**	**57413454.4**
煤炭开采和洗选业	Mining and Washing of Coal	35	14	1401756.8
石油和天然气开采业	Extraction of Petroleum and Natural Gas	5	3	8747092.8
黑色金属矿采选业	Mining and Processing of Ferrous Metals Ores	8	1	456389.6
有色金属矿采选业	Mining and Processing of Nonferrous Metals Ores	6	3	241211.4
非金属矿采选业	Mining and Processing of Nonmetal Ores	2		25215.3
#采 盐	Extraction of Salt	2		25215.3
开采辅助活动	Support for Minning	16	4	1750216.2
农副食品加工业	Activities Processing of Food from Agricultural Products	28	8	1055436.2
#谷物磨制	Grain Grinding			
饲料加工	Fodder Processing	4		394899.9
制 糖	Sugar Making	13	7	235535.4
食品制造业	Manufacture of Foods	17	3	1486557.9
#罐头制造	Manufacture of can	1		69688.9
饮料制造业	Manufacture of Liguor,Beverages and Refined Tea	9	1	445742.8
#酒的制造	Manufacture of Liguor	7	1	343069.2
烟草制品业	Manufacture of Tobacco	1		472468.0
纺织业	Manufacture of Textile	38	9	1013914.6
#棉、化纤纺织及印染精加工	Cotton, Chemical Fiber, Dyeing, Printing and Processing	32	7	895302.8
毛纺织和染整精加工	Wool Textile, Dyeing and Printing	2		80716.7
纺织服装、鞋、帽制造业	Manufacture of Textile, Wearing Apparel and Accessories	7	1	177901.5
皮革、毛皮、羽毛(绒)及其制品业	Manufacturie of Leather, Fur, Feather and Related Products			
#皮革鞣制加工	Leather Tanning and Processing			
木材加工及木、竹、藤、棕、草制品业	Processing of Timber, Manufacture of Wood, Bamboo, Cane, Grass Products			
家具制造业	Manufacture of Furniture			
造纸及纸制品业	Manufacture of Paper and Paper Products	1		7776.4
印刷业和记录媒介的复制	Printing and Reproduction of Recording Media	1		7169.5
文教、工美、体育和娱乐用品制造业	Manufacture of Articles for Cultural, Educational,Sports and Entertainment	2		16258.4
石油加工、炼焦及核燃料加工业	Processing, Processing of Petroleeum,Coking and Nuclear Fuel	23	10	10776428.3
#炼 焦	Coking	13	7	525523.9
化学原料及化学制品制造业	Manufacture of Raw Chemical Materials and Chemical Products	48	18	5399669.5
#基础化学原料制造	Basic Chemical Material	15	6	1082953.5
肥料制造	Manufacture of Fertilizer	13	4	1306162.4
合成材料制造	Manufacture of Synthetic Materials	12	7	2411249.4
医药制造业	Manufacture of Medicine	5	1	96967.3
化学纤维制造业	Manufacture of Chemical Fibers	9	5	655679.7
橡胶制品业	Manufacture of Rubber and Plastics Products	5	3	234696.2
非金属矿物制品业	Manufacture of Non-metallic Mineral Products	34	15	1260698.4
#水泥制造	Manufacture of Cement	14	8	379032.3
黑色金属冶炼及压延加工业	Smelting and Pressing of Ferrous Metals	18	15	2588560.2
有色金属冶炼及压延加工业	Smelting and Pressing of Non ferrous Metals	21	11	7574082.5
金属制品业	Manufacture of Metal Products	4	1	82463.7
通用设备制造业	Manufacture of General Purpose Machinery			
专用设备制造业	Manufacture of Special Purpose Machinery	3		142941.7
汽车制造业	Manufacture of Automobile	3	3	149237.1
铁路、船舶、航空航天和其他运输设备制造业	Manufacture of Railway ,Ship,Aeronautics and Other Transport Equipment			
电气机械及器材制造业	Manufacture of Electrical Machinery and Apparatus	8		3343286.5
计算机、通信和其他电子设备制造业	Manufacture of, Computer Communication and Other Electronic Equipment	1		7108.7
仪器仪表制造业	Measuring Instruments and Machinery			
废弃资源综合利用业	Comprehensive Utilization of Waste Resources			
金属制品、机械和设备修理业	Repair Service of Metal Prodults,Mouhinery and Equipment	1		10917.7
电力、热力的生产和供应业	Production and Supply of Electrici Power and Heat Power	38	9	7123049.2
#电力生产和电力供应	Production and Supply of Electric	29	8	6935293.4
燃气生产和供应业	Production and Supply of Gas	5	2	598999.0
水的生产和供应业	Production and Supply of Water	1		63561.3

Main Indicators of Large-scale and Medium-scale Industrial Enterprises by Sectors

(10 000 yuan)

工业增加值 Value-added of Industry	工业销售产值(当年价格) Sales Value of Industry Products (At Current Prices)	出口交货值 Delivery Value of Industry Export	实收资本 Total Capital Hold	资产合计 Total Assets	流动资产合计 Total Current Assets	#产成品 Finished Product	固定资产原价 Original Value of Fixed Assets
20479527.3	**56475127.9**	**398567.0**	**37797708.2**	**130816829.4**	**35976643.8**	**2658131.9**	**113392330.9**
834916.2	1329905.9		1421639.0	6058526.9	1598220.0	114830.3	3048964.7
6016260.8	8625694.8		15270234.1	27742605.9	3723095.5	138090.2	47168242.2
138581.1	454551.6		167314.8	879063.8	366798.1	45415.5	381513.2
161825.8	240453.7		223760.0	931382.8	234310.6	19703.7	494992.9
20966.8	24151.5		20500.0	54073.3	25913.0	8702.0	21105.8
20966.8	24151.5		20500.0	54073.3	25913.0	8702.0	21105.8
823198.3	1757306.7	1794.8	1588185.5	2598812.4	1354310.6	13897.8	1697239.3
212099.0	1002219.4	10450.3	235935.4	1189722.7	675346.7	257110.1	534700.2
72450.8	409713.4		106763.5	433748.7	177587.0	14630.2	118806.7
52334.9	207593.7		69626.2	426651.2	293736.5	193381.3	274066.9
413245.2	1386891.0	201326.3	555508.5	2066403.6	643463.4	97340.4	1512198.6
9152.7	53695.5	39045.2	97451.2	185141.3	107728.8	49108.6	116216.0
214919.7	438217.1		212612.3	709138.4	368612.8	9116.7	296575.3
187940.3	335052.2		198738.5	623469.8	351257.1	5815.4	206425.1
363547.2	476905.0		369850.0	505672.0	286298.0	3899.0	227535.5
221625.0	968994.3	28596.2	660308.9	1972544.3	822667.5	111377.0	1056652.5
187455.1	854419.0	14688.2	537381.0	1484099.0	681316.0	87939.0	882631.2
29337.4	78596.1	10882.4	56049.5	216606.1	49080.3	15298.4	112347.6
45589.0	139693.6	7251.6	171509.1	326376.9	75746.5	10147.4	238755.2
2376.4	7311.3	670.1	200.0	6345.8	2369.6	820.8	3139.9
4573.2	7543.0		5727.4	26367.7	11343.6	2995.5	29738.1
4901.6	11576.3	8764.4	6000.0	17650.9	8879.4	4778.4	6715.2
4789554.8	10678274.2		4185376.4	7710174.3	2162214.3	333073.9	9518940.9
84840.7	447953.2		323103.1	1904516.8	663297.3	157439.6	993674.9
1476452.2	5302383.3	27702.9	3799988.8	17826198.4	3638551.4	305166.1	12591996.9
282546.3	1075809.6	752.1	754706.3	4012473.2	762964.6	72526.4	2818718.3
516558.7	1245011.6	398.2	935745.3	4361467.8	1079707.7	59937.5	3257882.5
501914.3	2399985.3	26102.3	1832863.9	7225460.4	1273124.3	151444.3	4937101.8
34478.8	99602.0	2878.5	420960.6	869586.0	183659.2	15004.6	250989.1
116153.1	653473.6	7616.4	258528.5	1227086.9	555707.6	55092.4	787542.1
40943.4	240645.9	2649.0	179430.1	329678.6	169469.5	65483.1	166324.0
299656.8	1220229.1		905229.2	5718836.1	2309692.0	119178.0	2008612.1
82903.8	348189.1		525948.8	3287479.8	1142712.2	31291.8	1190805.8
-142688.5	2516121.8	20739.5	1833096.9	8777930.1	2124728.4	400741.6	5225520.0
1370404.1	7261516.8	32520.4	1244417.9	13125225.3	5321652.3	464556.0	7429060.4
25094.3	82246.0		18775.8	151455.5	72301.6	950.7	21939.6
35322.3	128051.3	528.2	161436.0	657953.3	143090.2	19037.0	85184.0
-12959.5	151829.0		126970.0	238354.2	97338.6	2378.9	191465.1
637649.3	3452024.8	45078.4	824315.6	8940758.2	5401057.2	35444.9	536735.6
451.9	6905.4		1000.0	8853.8	1893.6	328.7	7066.3
9543.1	10917.7		2400.0	3845.8	3551.8		366.4
2236901.9	7137941.3		2091118.8	16865701.0	2438545.0	2097.3	16155946.3
2177033.4	6918722.0		1970009.1	15466678.6	1764065.0	1512.8	15149153.9
52869.3	597989.2		585187.6	2603459.4	954262.9	1373.9	1386327.2
31074.8	63561.3		250191.0	677045.1	201552.9		310246.3

13-16 续表

单位：万元

行　业	Sector	负债合计 Total Liabilities	#流动负债 Total Liquid Liabilities	#非流动负债 Total Non-liquid Liabilities
总　计	**Total**	**81889731.6**	**51652720.9**	**30184374.1**
煤炭开采和洗选业	Mining and Washing of Coal	4455543.8	3220476.4	1235063.3
石油和天然气开采业	Extraction of Petroleum and Natural Gas	13060377.4	5372800.1	7687577.3
黑色金属矿采选业	Mining and Processing of Ferrous Metals Ores	610986.8	560411.9	50574.8
有色金属矿采选业	Mining and Processing of Nonferrous Metals Ores	539724.8	293143.5	246581.3
非金属矿采选业	Mining and Processing of Nonmetal Ores	17674.9	8245.6	500.0
#采　盐	Extraction of Salt	17674.9	8245.6	500.0
开采辅助活动	Support for Minning	1619374.3	1321225.6	298144.0
农副食品加工业	Activities Processing of Food from Agricultural Products	688063.4	643910.4	43804.1
#谷物磨制	Grain Grinding			
饲料加工	Fodder Processing	127753.5	115034.6	12718.9
制　糖	Sugar Making	327332.0	320888.4	6095.0
食品制造业	Manufacture of Foods	1309119.2	894414.9	414704.2
#罐头制造	Manufacture of can	160798.3	157732.8	3065.5
饮料制造业	Manufacture of Liguor,Beverages and Refined Tea	382088.6	191536.9	190551.7
#酒的制造	Manufacture of Liguor	312320.6	121768.9	190551.7
烟草制品业	Manufacture of Tobacco	135822.0	127822.0	8000.0
纺织业	Manufacture of Textile	1099310.3	867349.6	226441.4
#棉、化纤纺织及印染精加工	Cotton, Chemical Fiber, Dyeing, Printing and Processing	824829.8	726669.5	95436.3
毛纺织和染整精加工	Wool Textile, Dyeing and Printing	65644.5	46443.6	19200.9
纺织服装、鞋、帽制造业	Manufacture of Textile, Wearing Apparel and Accessories	98609.0	34167.2	60916.4
皮革、毛皮、羽毛(绒)及其制品业	Manufacturie of Leather, Fur, Feather and Related Products			
#皮革鞣制加工	Leather Tanning and Processing			
木材加工及木、竹、藤、棕、草制品业	Processing of Timber, Manufacture of Wood, Bamboo, Cane, Grass Products			
家具制造业	Manufacture of Furniture			
造纸及纸制品业	Manufacture of Paper and Paper Products	4960.4	4960.4	
印刷业和记录媒介的复制	Printing and Reproduction of Recording Media	13691.6	9139.6	4552.0
文教、工美、体育和娱乐用品制造业	Manufacture of Articles for Cultural, Educational,Sports and Entertainment	9112.5	9112.5	
石油加工、炼焦及核燃料加工业	Processing, Processing of Petroleeum,Coking and Nuclear Fuel	3108438.4	2514880.5	572218.2
#炼　焦	Coking	1498873.3	1331420.1	146259.9
化学原料及化学制品制造业	Manufacture of Raw Chemical Materials and Chemical Products	12314447.3	6501791.5	5812655.5
#基础化学原料制造	Basic Chemical Material	2856686.0	1596661.7	1260024.2
肥料制造	Manufacture of Fertilizer	3197779.9	2003542.3	1194237.6
合成材料制造	Manufacture of Synthetic Materials	5043870.7	2216207.2	2827663.4
医药制造业	Manufacture of Medicine	418050.2	400914.2	17136.0
化学纤维制造业	Manufacture of Chemical Fibers	868110.3	756840.5	102943.8
橡胶制品业	Manufacture of Rubber and Plastics Products	148759.4	135178.3	12608.2
非金属矿物制品业	Manufacture of Non-metallic Mineral Products	3619923.4	2757564.8	862158.1
#水泥制造	Manufacture of Cement	1982506.9	1318832.2	663474.3
黑色金属冶炼及压延加工业	Smelting and Pressing of Ferrous Metals	7472159.2	6471195.3	999404.6
有色金属冶炼及压延加工业	Smelting and Pressing of Non ferrous Metals	9653387.2	7383801.2	2269586.0
金属制品业	Manufacture of Metal Products	101594.0	74548.2	25140.0
通用设备制造业	Manufacture of General Purpose Machinery			
专用设备制造业	Manufacture of Special Purpose Machinery	91590.0	84670.8	6919.2
汽车制造业	Manufacture of Automobile	229903.7	164651.0	65252.7
铁路、船舶、航空航天和其他运输设备制造业	Manufacture of Railway ,Ship,Aeronautics and Other Transport Equipment			
电气机械及器材制造业	Manufacture of Electrical Machinery and Apparatus	5440158.5	4354358.4	1085800.1
计算机、通信和其他电子设备制造业	Manufacture of, Computer Communication and Other Electronic Equipment	7503.2	7503.2	
仪器仪表制造业	Measuring Instruments and Machinery			
废弃资源综合利用业	Comprehensive Utilization of Waste Resources			
金属制品、机械和设备修理业	Repair Service of Metal Prodults,Mouhinery and Equipment	1445.4	1445.4	
电力、热力的生产和供应业	Production and Supply of Electrici Power and Heat Power	11933627.2	5326997.7	6606629.4
#电力生产和电力供应	Production and Supply of Electric	10731470.9	4971623.8	5759847.0
燃气生产和供应业	Production and Supply of Gas	2050620.9	1090996.6	959624.2
水的生产和供应业	Production and Supply of Water	385554.3	66666.7	318887.6

Continued

(10 000 yuan)

所有者权益合计 Total Owners' Equities	主营业务收入 Revenue from Principal Business	主营业务成本 Cost of Principal Business	主营业务税金及附加 Taxes and Other Charges on Principal Business	营业利润 Business Profits	利润总额 Total Profits	亏损企业亏损总额 Losses Value of Loss-Suffering Enterprises	利税总额 Total Profits and Taxes	本年应交增值税 Value-added Taxes Payable	全部从业人员年平均人数(人) Annual Average Employed Persons (person)
48927095.0	**58794234.0**	**47010502.4**	**3604836.7**	**1081997.4**	**1737795.2**	**2824422.4**	**8056614.1**	**2713982.2**	**491814**
1602982.9	1392091.5	1103476.6	65807.6	-66359.1	-49284.3	93224.2	195338.2	178814.9	44062
14682228.4	9637961.7	6568352.7	512658.5	291763.4	493178.8	1180181.7	1635669.4	629832.1	70329
268077.0	455361.7	339561.0	11061.5	23665.6	27792.8	2122.3	76518.8	37664.5	5165
391657.9	240588.6	138704.8	3954.9	43258.8	42300.1	14475.2	72368.4	26113.4	4146
36398.3	24328.3	8550.1	1873.3	6743.0	6977.8		11917.2	3066.1	897
36398.3	24328.3	8550.1	1873.3	6743.0	6977.8		11917.2	3066.1	897
979437.9	1754950.3	1656768.4	18084.8	-5285.6	15956.9	25502.7	154284.9	120243.2	33054
501659.1	995054.8	820787.6	1491.0	62080.1	73578.5	9708.2	95038.7	19969.2	13137
305995.2	410115.3	318380.6	371.0	40815.9	41394.0		44293.9	2528.9	3053
99319.0	206230.2	186034.8	780.1	-9910.3	-3733.5	7217.3	5792.4	8745.8	5804
757284.3	1394940.1	1110603.9	5112.9	122870.1	138050.5	13512.3	200349.8	57186.4	14446
24343.0	54704.3	43680.3	14.2	-2937.6	5154.8		4499.1	-669.9	1273
327049.8	427349.5	252432.7	34387.1	88702.9	91469.8	932.7	151947.8	26090.9	6127
311149.2	333820.0	186729.1	34265.1	81882.9	84111.2	932.7	142693.4	24317.1	5096
369850.0	476905.0	179636.0	219745.0	53774.4	52767.4		328980.4	56468.0	761
873233.8	1017699.4	921640.1	3332.4	8810.7	84341.6	12442.5	122707.8	35033.8	24223
659269.0	906196.3	835306.8	2419.9	5614.4	78215.1	8194.1	114101.5	33466.5	20001
150961.6	75399.6	54709.0	830.9	7574.0	9109.0		15142.3	5202.4	1754
227767.9	174448.5	135021.9	918.0	13869.6	15454.5	176.6	17705.5	1333.0	7128
1385.4	7311.3	6920.1		38.6	14.1		-226.7	-240.8	265
12676.1	8308.7	7161.8	97.8	-634.1	144.6		483.6	241.2	488
8538.4	13647.0	10350.4	15.8	2628.3	2710.3		2726.1		638
4601735.5	10917478.5	7069609.9	2595401.1	504405.5	506047.3	85458.8	3908939.2	807490.8	37250
405643.3	449077.4	437823.8	1038.6	-50745.6	-51106.1	58159.7	-38344.2	11723.3	7710
5511750.7	5098664.9	4230926.9	79417.8	-42524.2	37981.4	292821.5	227658.1	110258.9	57810
1155787.1	1089720.5	970029.2	5764.5	-42854.3	-32297.9	69367.3	2149.4	28682.8	13830
1163687.7	1278925.4	854453.4	64415.5	65115.3	105851.8	44665.0	186162.7	15895.4	12421
2181589.7	2170487.3	1971936.2	7977.1	-71498.3	-64879.6	135280.8	4007.9	60910.4	23962
451535.7	99598.0	70705.2	701.6	-4112.9	-2560.6	8616.2	4939.8	6798.8	3817
358976.6	624712.3	544900.1	2183.5	-2204.0	17475.5	11333.4	41403.9	21744.9	7589
180919.1	247838.7	234834.8	575.7	-7003.5	-5242.6	6478.8	4832.7	9499.6	3938
2098912.4	1262362.5	1134665.9	3484.3	13113.1	23379.3	61869.7	86233.3	59369.7	17531
1304972.9	353881.9	322319.6	1617.5	-15384.8	-7942.6	43546.6	18535.6	24860.7	7300
1305770.9	2639096.3	2892727.8	5695.6	-664424.0	-641520.4	645012.6	-600023.4	35801.4	31710
3471838.1	8020354.8	7400368.0	2824.2	5138.0	38069.2	172095.8	274993.5	234100.1	37650
49861.5	90735.6	81294.0	371.8	7571.1	8278.8	95.0	8748.7	98.1	1375
566363.3	124795.8	91773.4	234.4	13695.7	15734.4		16518.2	549.4	2193
8450.5	151997.5	143009.4	5750.7	-53600.2	-46785.0	46785.0	-39164.8	1869.5	1833
3500599.7	3777513.7	3055276.0	13156.3	399606.1	421405.6		512823.4	78261.5	10259
1350.6	22030.1	20365.7	66.1	-630.3	156.5		222.6		530
2400.4	10917.2	10192.2	292.3	69.1	34.4		1330.7	1004.0	632
4932073.6	7033718.4	6216991.0	13687.4	350911.7	432111.8	48778.5	585279.8	139480.6	46360
4735207.5	6806574.6	5974511.5	13404.4	400463.8	436021.7	30678.1	587498.2	138072.1	42025
552838.4	600286.2	519359.6	2308.6	-83649.7	-68286.2	92798.7	-51674.2	14303.4	5210
291490.8	51187.1	33534.4	144.7	-290.8	6062.4		7742.7	1535.6	1261

13-17 分行业大中型工业企业主要经济效益指标

单位: %　　　　(2015 年)

行　业	Sector	产值利税率 Ratio of Profits and Taxes to Industrial Output Value
总　计	**Total**	**14.0**
煤炭开采和洗选业	Mining and Washing of Coal	13.9
石油和天然气开采业	Extraction of Petroleum and Natural Gas	18.7
黑色金属矿采选业	Mining and Processing of Ferrous Metals Ores	16.8
有色金属矿采选业	Mining and Processing of Nonferrous Metals Ores	30.0
非金属矿采选业	Mining and Processing of Nonmetal Ores	47.3
#采　盐	Extraction of Salt	47.3
开采辅助活动	Support for Minning	8.8
农副食品加工业	Activities Processing of Food from Agricultural Products	9.0
#谷物磨制	Grain Grinding	
饲料加工	Fodder Processing	11.2
制　糖	Sugar Making	2.5
食品制造业	Manufacture of Foods	13.5
#罐头制造	Manufacture of can	6.5
饮料制造业	Manufacture of Liguor,Beverages and Refined Tea	34.1
#酒的制造	Manufacture of Liguor	41.6
烟草制品业	Manufacture of Tobacco	69.6
纺织业	Manufacture of Textile	12.1
#棉、化纤纺织及印染精加工	Cotton, Chemical Fiber, Dyeing, Printing and Processing	12.7
毛纺织和染整精加工	Wool Textile, Dyeing and Printing	18.8
纺织服装、鞋、帽制造业	Manufacture of Textile, Wearing Apparel and Accessories	10.0
皮革、毛皮、羽毛(绒)及其制品业	Manufacturie of Leather, Fur, Feather and Related Products	
#皮革鞣制加工	Leather Tanning and Processing	
木材加工及木、竹、藤、棕、草制品业	Processing of Timber, Manufacture of Wood, Bamboo, Cane, Grass Products	
家具制造业	Manufacture of Furniture	
造纸及纸制品业	Manufacture of Paper and Paper Products	-2.9
印刷业和记录媒介的复制	Printing and Reproduction of Recording Media	6.7
文教、工美、体育和娱乐用品制造业	Manufacture of Articles for Cultural, Educational,Sports and Entertainment	16.8
石油加工、炼焦及核燃料加工业	Processing, Processing of Petroleeum,Coking and Nuclear Fuel	36.3
#炼 焦	Coking	-7.3
化学原料及化学制品制造业	Manufacture of Raw Chemical Materials and Chemical Products	4.2
#基础化学原料制造	Basic Chemical Material	0.2
肥料制造	Manufacture of Fertilizer	14.3
合成材料制造	Manufacture of Synthetic Materials	0.2
医药制造业	Manufacture of Medicine	5.1
化学纤维制造业	Manufacture of Chemical Fibers	6.3
橡胶制品业	Manufacture of Rubber and Plastics Products	2.1
非金属矿物制品业	Manufacture of Non-metallic Mineral Products	6.8
#水泥制造	Manufacture of Cement	4.9
黑色金属冶炼及压延加工业	Smelting and Pressing of Ferrous Metals	-23.2
有色金属冶炼及压延加工业	Smelting and Pressing of Non ferrous Metals	3.6
金属制品业	Manufacture of Metal Products	10.6
通用设备制造业	Manufacture of General Purpose Machinery	
专用设备制造业	Manufacture of Special Purpose Machinery	11.6
汽车制造业	Manufacture of Automobile	-26.2
铁路、船舶、航空航天和其他运输设备制造业	Manufacture of Railway ,Ship,Aeronautics and Other Transport Equipment	
电气机械及器材制造业	Manufacture of Electrical Machinery and Apparatus	15.3
计算机、通信和其他电子设备制造业	Manufacture of, Computer Communication and Other Electronic Equipment	3.1
仪器仪表制造业	Measuring Instruments and Machinery	
废弃资源综合利用业	Comprehensive Utilization of Waste Resources	
金属制品、机械和设备修理业	Repair Service of Metal Prodults,Mouhinery and Equipment	12.2
电力、热力的生产和供应业	Production and Supply of Electrici Power and Heat Power	8.2
#电力生产和电力供应	Production and Supply of Electric	8.5
燃气生产和供应业	Production and Supply of Gas	-8.6
水的生产和供应业	Production and Supply of Water	12.2

Main Indicators on Economic Efficiency of Large-scale and Medium-scale Industrial Enterprises by Sectors

(%)

总资产贡献率 Ratio of Profits, Taxes and Interests to Average Value	资本保值增值率 Ratio of Capital-hold and Rise	资产负债率 Ratio of debts to Assets	流动资产周转次数(次/年) Turnover of Currents Assets (times/year)	成本费用利润率 Ratio of Profits to Industrial Costs	全员劳动生产率(万元/人) Overall Labour Productivity (10 000yuan/person)
7.8	**101.9**	**62.6**	**1.6**	**3.2**	**41.64**
4.6	81.6	73.5	0.9	-3.6	18.95
7.1	99.6	47.1	2.6	5.9	85.54
10.5	55.3	69.5	1.2	6.6	26.83
8.8	80.6	57.9	1.0	23.3	39.03
22.2	85.3	32.7	0.9	44.1	23.37
22.2	113.7	32.7	0.9	44.1	23.37
6.7	81.6	62.3	1.3	0.9	24.90
9.2	106.0	57.8	1.5	7.9	16.15
10.7	124.5	29.5	2.3	11.2	23.73
2.3	87.6	76.7	0.7	-1.7	9.02
11.6	154.9	63.4	2.2	10.6	28.61
4.1		86.9	0.5	9.2	7.19
22.1	104.8	53.9	1.2	27.7	35.08
23.6	104.6	50.1	1.0	35.2	36.88
65.1	101.9	26.9	1.7	25.9	477.72
7.1	113.1	55.7	1.2	8.3	9.15
8.6	115.7	55.6	1.3	8.7	9.37
7.6	101.3	30.3	1.5	13.8	16.73
5.9	1691.6	30.2	2.3	9.7	6.40
-3.6	3.4	78.2	3.1	0.2	8.97
2.9	100.9	51.9	0.7	1.5	9.37
16.8	791.9	51.6	1.5	24.6	7.68
51.4	99.0	40.3	5.0	6.5	128.58
-1.0	106.7	78.7	0.7	-10.2	11.00
3.5	111.9	69.1	1.4	0.7	25.54
2.7	102.3	71.2	1.4	-2.8	20.43
6.2	104.0	73.3	1.2	9.2	41.59
2.1	117.6	69.8	1.7	-2.9	20.95
0.8	941.8	48.1	0.5	-2.5	9.03
5.0	135.8	70.7	1.1	2.8	15.31
1.6	93.1	45.1	1.5	-2.1	10.40
3.3	89.4	63.3	0.5	1.8	17.09
2.7	82.4	60.3	0.3	-1.9	11.36
-4.5	63.3	85.1	1.2	-19.3	-4.50
3.9	126.0	73.5	1.5	0.5	36.40
6.9	60.7	67.1	1.3	9.4	18.25
2.8	465.8	13.9	0.9	14.2	16.11
-15.5	14.8	96.5	1.6	-26.8	-7.07
7.0	110.3	60.8	0.7	12.3	62.16
5.0	113.1	84.7	11.6	0.7	0.85
34.6	47.2	37.6	3.1	0.3	15.10
5.4	96.4	70.8	2.9	6.4	48.25
5.8	97.2	69.4	3.9	6.8	51.80
0.4	102.4	78.8	0.6	-10.0	10.15
2.1	117.5	56.9	0.3	10.2	24.64

13-18 主要工业产品产量
Output of Major Industrial Products

产品名称	Item	2014	2015
原煤(万吨)	Coal (10 000 tons)	14519.53	15221.48
天然原油(万吨)	Crude Oil (10 000 tons)	2875.28	2795.09
天然气(亿立方米)	Natural Gas (100 million cu.m)	296.70	293.02
铁矿石原矿量(吨)	Crudeiron Ore (ton)	43281166	26130693
铜选矿含铜量(吨)	Cuproaurite (ton)	261816	112108
硫铁矿(折含 S 35%)(吨)	Pyritel with Content of (S35%)(ton)	374295	193571
原盐(吨)	Salt (ton)	3830499	4157403
发电量(亿千瓦小时)	Electricity (100 million kwh)	2090.94	2478.51
#火 电	Thermalpower	1759.56	2059.97
水 电	Hydropower	161.41	209.05
风 电	Windpower	126.61	147.83
太阳能发电	Solarpwer	41.66	59.38
供热量(万吉焦)	Heat Supply (10 000 gigajoules)	32469	51209
大米(吨)	Rice (ton)	469959	433247
小麦粉(万吨)	Wheate Flour (10 000 tons)	304	327
精制食用植物油(吨)	Refined Edible Vegetable Oil (ton)	1862776	1879246
成品糖(吨)	Refined Sugar (ton)	445308	440194
饲料(吨)	Forage (ton)	3835659	4207647
糖果(吨)	Candy (ton)	8658	5479
乳制品(吨)	Dairy Products (ton)	438233	486403
罐头(吨)	Canned Food (ton)	831291	876480
#番茄酱	Tomato Jam	784189	825233
味精(吨)	Monosodium Glutamate (ton)	93	103
酱油(吨)	Soy (ton)	22543	20903
方便面(吨)	Instant Noodles(ton)	52277	50177
发酵酒精(千升)	Zymolytic Alcohol (kilo-liter)	85359	71957
饮料酒(千升)	Alcohol Beverage(kilo-liter)	621570	665587
#白 酒	Liquor	77881	85951
啤 酒	Beer	461813	467756
葡萄酒	Grape Wine	80826	87456
软饮料(吨)	Soft Drink (ton)	2163194	2603244
#碳酸饮料	Carbonic Drink	191067	146064
果汁和蔬菜汁饮料	Fruit Juice and Vegetable Juice Drink	715481	971690
包装饮用水	Bottled Water	1032799	1252200
冷冻饮品(吨)	Ice Beverage (ton)	54707	47395

注：钢材里包括钢材生产中消耗的外购国内钢。
Note: Rolled steel contain that manufacture of steel consumed outsourcing of internal steel.

13-18 续表 1 Continued

产品名称	Item	2014	2015
卷烟(万支)	Cigarettes (10 000 pieces)	1900000	2015000
纱(吨)	Yarn (ton)	439926	602259
布(万米)	Cloth (10 000 m)	6541	6859
#棉 布	Pure Cotton Cloth	5477	5914
绒线(毛线)(吨)	Knitting Wool (ton)	230	225
呢绒(万米)	Woolen Cloth Goods (10 000 m)	272	391
服装(万件)	Garments (10 000 units)	2149	4111
轻革(平方米)	Light Leather (sq.m)	8057119	6269300
人造板(立方米)	Artificial Board (cu.m)	1534276	1647333
#胶合板	Plywood	309114	272611
纤维板	Fiberboard	653078	368101
刨花板	Chip Board	429418	715275
家具(件)	Furniture (unit)	2097759	2239129
#木制家具	Wooden Furniture	1629596	1799732
金属家具	Steal Furniture	306799	366572
纸浆(吨)	Paper Pulp (ton)	173769	118493
纸制品(吨)	Paper Products (ton)	660129	679238
#瓦楞纸箱(纸箱)	Corrugaled Case(unit)	562023	548009
机制纸及纸板(吨)	Machine-made Paper and Paperboard (ton)	488132	376230
原油加工量(吨)	Processed Crude Oil (ton)	26443984	24245451
汽油(吨)	Gasoline (ton)	3208819	3236319
溶剂油(吨)	Megilp (ton)	47619	26206
煤油(吨)	Kerosene (ton)	652697	722485
柴油(吨)	Diesel Oil (ton)	12133764	10495786
润滑油(吨)	Lubricating Oil (ton)	425046	418019
燃料油(吨)	Fuel Oil (ton)	467673	454355
石油沥青(吨)	Petroleum Bitumen (ton)	1356222	1750931
液化石油气(吨)	Liquefied Petroleum Gas (ton)	741087	633456
焦炭(万吨)	Coke (10 000ton)	2235.24	1643.53
#机械化焦炉生产的焦炭	Coke Turned out by Mechanized Coke Oven	2188.45	1643.53
煤气(万立方米)	Coal Gas (10 000 cu.m)	1361705	948458
硫酸(折 100%)(吨)	Sulfuric Acid (ton)	673347	664425
盐酸(含量 31%以上)(吨)	Hydrochloric Acid (With Content of 31%) (ton)	402394	358016

13-18 续表 2 Continued

产品名称	Item	2014	2015
氢氧化钠(烧碱)(折 100%)(吨)	Caustic Soda (ton)	2398303	2448908
碳化钙(电石)(折 300 升/千克)(吨)	Calcium Carbide (ton)	5189690	5372599
合成氨(吨)	Synthetic Ammonia (ton)	1999069	2182393
农用氮、磷、钾化学肥料(折纯)(吨)	Chemical Fertilizers (ton)	3122729	3224019
#氮肥(折含 N 100%)	Nitrogen Fertilizers	2231056	2316495
#尿 素	Carbamide	2168294	2236508
磷肥(折合 P_2O_5 100%)	Phosphate Fertilizers	14752	23031
乙烯(吨)	Ethylene(ton)	1284704	1091130
涂料(吨)	Paint (ton)	221861	171197
合成洗涤剂(吨)	Synthetic Detergents (ton)	47281	60112
化学原料药(吨)	Chemical Medicines(ton)	3292	2695
中成药(吨)	Traditional Chinese Medicine (ton)	5159	7594
轮胎外胎(条)	Outer Tires (unit)	1582756	1487505
塑料制品(吨)	Plastic Products (ton)	2121554	2280656
#塑料薄膜	Plastic Film	282741	301432
#农用薄膜	Farm Plastic Sheet	251575	271653
塑料型材(含板片材)	Plastic Moulding Material	208162	73912
塑料制管子及其附件(吨)	Plastic Pipe and Accessory (ton)	886323	944227
塑料编织袋(吨)	Woven Plastic Bag (ton)	180059	155339
泡沫塑料(吨)	Foamed Plastics (ton)	77850	75139
塑料包装箱及容器(吨)	Plastic Packing Case and Container (ton)	66926	82892
日用塑料制品(吨)	Household Plastic Products (ton)	56757	96547
水泥熟料(万吨)	Cement Chamotte (10 000 tons)	3389	2911
窑外分解窑熟料(预分解窑熟料)(万吨)	Clinker Cement (10 000 tons)	3249	2827
水泥(万吨)	Cement (10 000 tons)	5082	4279
水泥电杆(根)	Cement Electric Pole Piece (unit)	478181	540431
商品混凝土(立方米)	Commercial Concrete (cu.m)	53990412	47963016
预应力混凝土桩 (米)	Prestressed Concrete Piles (m)	1110699	769928
砖(折标准砖)(万块)	Brick (Standard Brick) (10 000 pieces)	2405233	2461965
瓦(万片)	Tile (10 000 pieces)	790	1037
大理石板材(平方米)	Marble Slab (sq.m)	1010452	1130819
花岗石板材(平方米)	Granite Sheet (sq.m)	41880866	36017820

13-18 续表 3 Continued

产品名称	Item	2014	2015
石膏板(万平方米)	Plasterboard (10 000sq.m)	7000	1598
平板玻璃(重量箱)	Plate Glass (weight case)	7961706	11083969
沥青和改性沥青防水卷材(平方米)	Bitumen and Rolled Waterproof Material (sq.m)	5573910	15829904
中空玻璃(平方米)	Insulating Glass (sq.m)	358599	288685
钢化玻璃(平方米)	Toughened Glass (sq.m)	1020307	1175992
夹层玻璃(平方米)	Laminated Glass (sq.m)	90664	36996
日用玻璃制品(吨)	Household Glass Products (ton)	73395	76717
玻璃保温容器(万个)	Glass Attemperator (10 000 units)	1094	897
陶质砖(平方米)	Carbonic Bricks (sq.m)	16902779	13612464
耐火材料制品(吨)	Fire Proof Material (ton)	606932	581037
石墨及碳素制品(吨)	Graphite and Carbon Products (ton)	1605714	1857543
玻璃纤维增强塑料制品(吨)	Glass Fibre Reinforced Plastices Products (ton)	58125	37753
生铁(吨)	Pig Iron (ton)	13387168	7595172
粗钢(吨)	Crude Steel (ton)	12703179	7857790
钢材(吨)	Rolled Steel (ton)	15669486	11240120
中小型型钢	Medium and Small Rolled Steel	193563	273927
钢　筋	Corrugated Steel Bar	4115969	2183566
盘　条(线材)	Wire Rod	3146117	2426721
铁合金(吨)	Ferroalloy (ton)	255045	197834
铜(吨)	Copper (ton)	75677	78885
镍(吨)	Nickel (ton)	11167	11618
铝(吨)	Aluminium (ton)	4268180	5864454
铝材(吨)	Aluminium Material (ton)	611678	746667
工业锅炉(蒸发量吨)	Industrial Boiler (evaporating quantity ton)	1893	1916
泵(台)	Pump (unit)	12306	672
风机(台)	Fan (unit)	7504	7575
农作物收获机械(台)	Grop Harvesting Machinery (unit)	6389	9467
汽车(辆)	Motor Vehicles(unit)	10829	16186
#载货汽车	Trucks	2511	270
改装汽车(辆)	Modified Truck (unit)	5617	5030
发电设备(千瓦)	Power Generating Equipment (kw)	4512301	5988021
变压器(千伏安)	Transformer (kva)	70618993	73112199
电力电缆(公里)	Electric Cable (km)	233395	201874

13-19 各地、州、市主要工业产品产量

年份 Year	地区 Region	纱(吨) Yarn (ton)	布(万米) Cloth (10 000 m)	绒线(吨) Knitting Wool (ton)	呢绒(万米) Woolen Piece Goods (10 000 m)
	1978	28008	15616	1239	189
	1980	31272	16931	1614	240
	1985	39130	21150	2396	680
	1990	101941	30017	2179	1230
	1995	244689	30460	2286	1262
	1996	208526	27186	2202	1361
	1997	247143	29862	2393	1227
	1998	220332	26719	1361	979
	1999	294378	27450	1349	798
	2000	334307	28060	1184	754
	2001	302654	25380	843	399
	2002	316095	20679	811	265
	2003	292713	15239	744	206
	2004	291386	13989	980	206
	2005	340864	14047	1118	284
	2006	357324	15415	799	327
	2007	408870	16000	637	368
	2008	397417	15302	578	412
	2009	386085	15148	533	376
	2010	415783	15069	741	326
	2011	399094	7303	444	383
	2012	402151	6676	545	332
	2013	434569	7451	323	259
	2014	439926	6541	230	272
	2015	602259	6859	225	391
乌鲁木齐市	Urumqi City	11064	70	98	
克拉玛依市	Karamay City		1		
吐鲁番市	Turpan City	3501			
哈密地区	Hami [Kumul] Administrative Offices	6956			
昌吉回族自治州	Changji Hui Autonomous Prefecture	29751			
伊犁哈萨克自治州	Ili Kazak Autonomous Prefecture	20123	39	127	
伊犁州直属县(市)	Counties (Cities) Direct Under Ili Prefecture	10614			
塔城地区	Tacheng [Tarbagatai] Administrative Offices	9509	39	127	
阿勒泰地区	Altay Administrative Offices				
博尔塔拉蒙古自治州	Bortala Mongol Autonomous Prefecture	34684	57		
巴音郭楞蒙古自治州	Bayangol Mongol Autonomous Prefecture	77399	144		
阿克苏地区	Aksu Administrative Offices	96876			
克孜勒苏柯尔克孜自治州	Kizilsu Kirgiz Autonomous Prefecture				
喀什地区	Kashgar [Kaxgar] Administrative Offices	42874	150		
和田地区	Hotan Administrative Offices	6595			
新疆生产建设兵团	XinJiang Prodiction and Construction Group	272438	6398		391

Output of Major Industrial Products by Prefecture, Autonomous Prefecture and City

机制纸及纸板(吨) Machine-made Paper and Paperboard (ton)	原盐(万吨) Salt (10 000 tons)	成品糖(万吨) Sugar (10 000 tons)	饮料酒(千升) Alcohol Beverage (kilo-liter)	卷烟(亿支) Cigarettes (100 million pieces)	原煤(万吨) Coal (10 000 tons)	原油(万吨) Crude Oil (10 000 tons)	天然气(万立方米) Natural gas (10 000 cu.m)	发电量(亿千瓦时) Electricity (100 million kwh)	#水电 Hydropower
19851	51.71	2.08	9336	15.05	1079.01	353.05	25100	21.17	4.64
23838	38.18	4.43	17082	15.55	1136.84	390.58	35298	23.58	5.25
41521	35.09	7.18	74809	40.20	1600.22	499.00	54556	38.11	8.64
90857	159.00	16.84	118585	61.70	2100.00	695.00	50161	69.79	14.25
180440	25.98	30.18	249481	68.05	2720.74	1267.83	114821	120.43	22.82
169789	36.54	36.34	219961	67.80	2986.00	1457.10	140609	136.03	24.49
161659	39.85	42.28	259015	66.05	3021.37	1629.25	213006	150.58	26.97
168799	27.53	47.59	271056	60.20	2926.91	1628.38	237826	157.76	28.23
180138	36.14	46.36	269453	55.00	2778.16	1739.65	310600	169.3	30.06
176477	31.78	30.76	269761	52.50	2798.90	1848.43	353930	182.98	30.53
193389	46.02	41.98	296187	55.20	2819.61	1946.95	417429	197.62	34.10
226950	50.75	51.84	307167	60.00	3098.67	2036.19	485237	212.24	34.67
233365	52.71	45.43	317260	62.50	3482.86	2141.39	502942	234.62	36.2
263066	87.32	37.26	345770	70.00	3749.40	2253.02	574805	266.3	37.08
289318	85.35	42.92	355275	70.00	3898.81	2408.32	1066437	306.92	43.27
295338	153.21	53.79	401771	85.00	4518.52	2474.74	1642099	357.15	53.43
252329	111.53	64.94	438502	100.00	5018.64	2604.31	2103348	416.87	58.78
301606	153.06	53.78	486007	120.00	6763.41	2715.13	2358941	489.17	73.84
355762	129.36	40.77	484936	135.00	8812.55	2512.86	2453887	571.31	79.84
371032	174.67	45.10	565041	150.00	9926.72	2558.16	2499096	679.33	97.07
422924	258.05	46.11	645919	160.00	11991.71	2615.63	2353798	875.19	114.57
410547	301.40	53.64	657637	170.00	13646.99	2670.68	2530101	1187.48	158.62
457449	318.63	46.72	662124	180.00	14203.90	2792.47	2839777	1667.82	172.91
488132	383.05	44.53	621570	190.00	14519.53	2875.28	2966988	2090.94	161.41
376230	415.74	44.02	665587	201.50	15221.48	2795.09	2930196	2478.51	209.05
83656	8.60		139121	201.50	1239.03	703.00	160069	320.12	9.29
	0.03		9			1180.01	313901	63.44	
	265.04		6148		756.07	210.02	93526	61.76	1.10
	0.63		5451		2305.56			266.12	0.17
173232		7.24	52554		6563.23	10.05		692.48	3.00
338	127.45	13.61	133217		1789.91	102.00		185.28	92.40
338		12.58	39825		1000.23			112.69	67.41
	127.45		92897		789.68	102.00		32.92	1.58
		1.03	495					39.67	23.41
	9.04	3.66	919					14.09	3.86
3328	2.69	2.85	20912		108.49	590.01	2362700	75.29	36.18
	2.26	2.52	29267		1502.42			66.03	16.13
								14.71	13.80
1186		0.03	47147		4.31			44.52	8.35
542		0.03	1095		65.76			14.02	10.69
113948		14.08	229747		886.70			660.65	14.08

13-19 续表

年 份 Year	地 区 Region	生铁(万吨) Pig Iron (10 000 tons)	粗钢(万吨) Crude Steel (10 000 tons)	大理石板材(平方米) Marble Plate (sq.m)	钢材(万吨) Steel Rolled (10 000 tons)
	1978	17.52	8.46		6.83
	1980	15.81	10.74		8.59
	1985	22.87	19.79		16.73
	1990	40.57	36.49	9589	28.48
	1995	69.53	70.59	34169	66.55
	1996	85.64	87.47	6420	86.70
	1997	93.82	97.21	53588	99.89
	1998	100.40	107.67	9197	116.19
	1999	101.30	105.60	7807	117.30
	2000	106.42	109.70	6294	131.26
	2001	111.73	131.83	22786	134.42
	2002	122.78	175.45	34185	173.07
	2003	144.86	204.12	117306	203.10
	2004	193.89	249.13	109663	238.52
	2005	258.66	306.54	78577	326.96
	2006	324.08	394.19	176025	411.45
	2007	394.97	447.24	119926	470.94
	2008	505.70	536.60	160011	576.62
	2009	764.62	653.32	190480	690.81
	2010	941.12	825.54	328249	891.70
	2011	1088.45	892.98	1240465	985.14
	2012	1328.32	1138.23	1364368	1289.84
	2013	1431.13	1276.77	400912	1512.90
	2014	1338.72	1270.32	1010452	1566.95
	2015	759.52	785.78	1130819	1124.01
乌鲁木齐市	Urumqi City	409.52	417.17	27296	585.91
克拉玛依市	Karamay City			2571	6.14
吐鲁番市	Turpan City	21.44	0.07	69294	
哈密地区	Hami [Kumul] Administrative Offices				
昌吉回族自治州	Changji Hui Autonomous Prefecture	3.42	18.56		44.99
伊犁哈萨克自治州	Ili Kazak Autonomous Prefecture	187.14	179.91	351261	219.13
伊犁州直属县(市)	Counties (Cities) Direct Under Ili Prefecture	182.63	177.74		202.89
塔城地区	Tacheng [Tarbagatai] Administrative Offices		2.17		1.25
阿勒泰地区	Altay Administrative Offices	4.51		351261	14.99
博尔塔拉蒙古自治州	Bortala Mongol Autonomous Prefecture				
巴音郭楞蒙古自治州	Bayangol Mongol Autonomous Prefecture	98.37	100.74	5000	100.89
阿克苏地区	Aksu Administrative Offices				46.17
克孜勒苏柯尔克孜自治州	Kizilsu Kirgiz Autonomous Prefecture	3.78		499561	
喀什地区	Kashgar [Kaxgar] Administrative Offices	6.08	45.94		49.31
和田地区	Hotan Administrative Offices			1274	
新疆生产建设兵团	XinJiang Prodiction and Construction Group	29.77	23.39	174561	71.47

Continued

水 泥 (万吨) Cement (10 000 tons)	硫 酸 (吨) Sulfuric Acid (ton)	烧 碱 (吨) Caustic Soda (ton)	合成氨 (吨)(折纯) Synthetic Ammonia (ton)	农用氮、磷、钾化肥(吨) Farm Nitrogen Phophate and Potassium (ton)	碳化钙 (电石)(吨) Calcium Crbide (ton)	塑料制品 (吨) Plastic Products (ton)
78.15	20262	4164	33155	20276	4895	3194
90.89	19153	3542	13762	9207	4486	2051
201.05	23921	5045	85728	58080	5989	17974
285.00	47732	15063	397062	287640	15976	40958
489.88	88491	24732	492754	383279	12344	100739
562.87	76413	28008	488337	372056	15901	129059
628.00	77187	35544	581449	428711	28350	143916
728.94	64836	39614	688069	520681	28999	168372
805.83	68169	42161	896632	685587	40216	139497
895.67	71458	51831	947511	754668	51749	197756
981.29	72511	68589	884340	729034	65763	262873
1029.71	70407	93362	956732	766291	73680	230729
1128.98	85322	114110	1082601	854530	82057	314891
1212.99	114046	174445	1015630	869795	115991	388270
1241.74	126901	295917	1192001	1285346	290591	349151
1334.50	160073	423901	1303586	1290802	501283	412032
1536.77	183484	485880	1325017	1385279	711277	517069
1672.76	201993	630314	1471312	1609409	910659	653230
2049.60	300423	814393	1407674	1591027	1560762	697269
2400.96	326112	916205	1484103	1591043	1845104	830651
3171.71	361779	1315745	1775660	2335610	2784380	1041107
4315.93	389819	1464433	1889044	3041687	3125805	1399683
5410.34	531812	2133953	1335922	3747746	4421861	1866580
5081.66	673347	2398303	1999069	3122729	5189690	2121554
4279.00	664425	2448908	2182393	3224019	5372599	2280656
226.60	18282	545910	610348	442700	171458	551107
						19626
168.26	95223	126799			828126	
121.37				3671		826
540.78	228751	831635	401946	280964	1865409	607217
527.71	297491			33305	279929	125226
279.07	170354					55571
117.09	26692			33305	279929	67936
131.55	100445					1720
87.89						72417
150.52			626937	1452012		43760
392.76			44656	472984		37160
146.61						1360
516.15	23133					23523
196.51						4656
1203.40	1545	944564	498507	538383	2227677	793777

13-20 国有控股企业主要指标占全区规模以上工业比重

Percentage of Main Indicators in State-holding Enterprises to Enterprises above Designated Size

单位：万元 (2015 年) (10 000 yuan)

指　标	Item	全区规模以上工业企业 Enterprises Above Designated Size	国　有控股企业 State-Holding Enterprises	占全区比重(%) Percentage (%)
企业单位数(个)	Number of Enterprises(unit)	2707	746	27.56
从业人员(人)	Employed Person (person)	720073	384230	53.36
工业总产值	Gross Industrial Output Value	81325512.3	44006335.9	54.11
工业销售产值	Sales Value of Industry Products	79446617.0	43276341.0	54.47
出口交货值	Delivery Value of Industry Export	629658.0	191886.8	30.47
资产总计	Total Assets	181641554.7	109457461.5	60.26
负债合计	Total Liabilities	116448837.9	67348310.7	57.84
所有者权益	Owners'Equities	65185301.9	42148695.0	64.66
实收资本	Substantial Capital	49672884.1	36267532.9	73.01
主营业务收入	Revenue from Principal Business	82037341.9	44496409.4	54.24
主营业务税金及附加	Taxes and Other Charges on Principal Business	3777572.7	3586473.2	94.94
利润总额	Total Profits	3409656.9	1321929.8	38.77
利税总额	Total Profits and Taxes	10524057.2	7143308.9	67.88
亏损单位数(个)	Number of Loss-suffering Enterprises (unit)	818	251	30.68
亏损企业亏损额	Losses Value of Loss-suffering	3570382.2	2470690.5	69.20

13-21 重点行业主要指标占全区规模以上工业比重
Percentage of Main Indicators in Key Industrial Sectors to Xinjiang's Industry above Designated Size

(2015 年)

指 标	Item	合 计 Total	占全区比重 (%) Percentage (%)
从业人员(人)	**Employed Persons (person)**	**720073**	**100.0**
石油和天然气开采业	Extraction of Petroleum and Natural Gas	70740	9.8
石油加工、炼焦及核燃料加工业	Processing of Petroleum, Coking and of Nuclear Fuel Processing	45969	6.4
黑色金属冶炼及压延加工业	Smelting and Pressing of Ferrous Metal	40492	5.6
电力、热力的生产和供应业	Production and Supply of Electric Power and Heat Power	63059	8.8
化学原料及化学制品制造业	Manufactue of Raw Chemical Materials and Chemical Products	72770	10.1
纺织业	Manufactue of Textile	32501	4.5
农副食品加工业	Processing of Food from Agricultural Products	41033	5.7
工业总产值(万元)	**Gross Industrial Output Value (10 000 yuan)**	**81325512.3**	**100.0**
石油和天然气开采业	Extraction of Petroleum and Natural Gas	8966347.9	11.0
石油加工、炼焦及核燃料加工业	Processing of Petroleum, Processing Coking and of Nuclear Fuel	12181358.3	15.0
黑色金属冶炼及压延加工业	Smelting and Pressing of Ferrous Metal	3299614.7	4.1
电力、热力的生产和供应业	Production and Supply of Electric Power and Heat Power	9396557.5	11.6
化学原料及化学制品制造业	Manufactue of Raw Chemical Materials and Chemical Products	6785665.7	8.3
纺织业	Manufactue of Textile	1481467.2	1.8
农副食品加工业	Processing of Food from Agricultural Products	5126781.3	6.3
工业销售产值(万元)	**Sales Value of Industry Products (10 000 yuan)**	**79446617.0**	**100.0**
石油和天然气开采业	Extraction of Petroleum and Natural Gas	8844445.0	11.1
石油加工、炼焦及核燃料加工业	Processing of Petroleum, Processing Coking and of Nuclear Fuel	12005163.2	15.1
黑色金属冶炼及压延加工业	Smelting and Pressing of Ferrous Metal	3262924.7	4.1
电力、热力的生产和供应业	Production and Supply of Electric Power and Heat Power	9396223.3	11.8
化学原料及化学制品制造业	Manufactue of Raw Chemical Materials and Chemical Products	6671227.5	8.4
纺织业	Manufactue of Textile	1391441.1	1.8
农副食品加工业	Processing of Food from Agricultural Products	4959714.9	6.2

注：所列行业为工业总产值百亿元以上行业。
Note: Listed sector of gross industrial output value were above ten billion sector.

13-21 续表 Continued

指　标	Item	合　计 Total	占全区比重 (%) Percentage (%)
资产总计(万元)	**Total of Assets (10 000 yuan)**	**181641554.7**	**100.0**
石油和天然气开采业	Extraction of Petroleum and Natural Gas	28352694.9	15.6
石油加工、炼焦及核燃料加工业	Processing of Petroleum, Processing Coking and of Nuclear Fuel	10253374.7	5.6
黑色金属冶炼及压延加工业	Smelting and Pressing of Ferrous Metal	10140647.0	5.6
电力、热力的生产和供应业	Production and Supply of Electric Power and Heat Power	35514611.8	19.6
化学原料及化学制品制造业	Manufactue of Raw Chemical Materials and Chemical Products	19928151.1	11.0
纺织业	Manufactue of Textile	2676548.9	1.5
农副食品加工业	Processing of Food from Agricultural Products	4399978.0	2.4
利润总额(万元)	**Total Profits (10 000 yuan)**	**3409656.9**	**100.0**
石油和天然气开采业	Extraction of Petroleum and Natural Gas	507435.8	14.9
石油加工、炼焦及核燃料加工业	Processing of Petroleum, Processing Coking and of Nuclear Fuel	577289.7	16.9
黑色金属冶炼及压延加工业	Smelting and Pressing of Ferrous Metal	-727631.7	-21.3
电力、热力的生产和供应业	Production and Supply of Electric Power and Heat Power	655484.7	19.2
化学原料及化学制品制造业	Manufactue of Raw Chemical Materials and Chemical Products	131049.0	3.8
纺织业	Manufactue of Textile	120945.9	3.5
农副食品加工业	Processing of Food from Agricultural Products	484281.9	14.2
利税总额(万元)	**Total Profits and Tax (10 000 yuan)**	**10524057.2**	**100.0**
石油和天然气开采业	Extraction of Petroleum and Natural Gas	1654466.2	15.7
石油加工、炼焦及核燃料加工业	Processing of Petroleum, Processing Coking and of Nuclear Fuel	4005289.5	38.1
黑色金属冶炼及压延加工业	Smelting and Pressing of Ferrous Metal	-687440.2	-6.5
电力、热力的生产和供应业	Production and Supply of Electric Power and Heat Power	887606.1	8.4
化学原料及化学制品制造业	Manufactue of Raw Chemical Materials and Chemical Products	368027.0	3.5
纺织业	Manufactue of Textile	171941.8	1.6
农副食品加工业	Processing of Food from Agricultural Products	551158.1	5.2
主营业务收入(万元)	**Revenue from Principal Business (10 000 yuan)**	**82037341.9**	**100.0**
石油和天然气开采业	Extraction of Petroleum and Natural Gas	9856712.7	12.0
石油加工、炼焦及核燃料加工业	Processing of Petroleum, Processing Coking and of Nuclear Fuel	12259234.6	14.9
黑色金属冶炼及压延加工业	Smelting and Pressing of Ferrous Metal	3407894.2	4.2
化学原料及化学制品制造业	Production and Supply of Electric Power and Heat Power	9283848.2	11.3
电力、热力的生产和供应业	Manufactue of Raw Chemical Materials and Chemical Products	6556941.9	8.0
纺织业	Manufactue of Textile	1479280.2	1.8
农副食品加工业	Processing of Food from Agricultural Products	5075262.2	6.2

13-22 规模以上工业主要产品生产能力
Production Capacity of Major Industrial Products above Designated Size

产品名称	Item	2014	2015
原煤(吨)	Raw Coal (ton)	205079466	229133862
天然原油(吨)	Crude Oil (ton)	26964300	28071400
发电设备容量(万千瓦)	Installed Capcity of Power Generation (10 000 kw)	4783	5741
卷烟(万支)	Cigarettes (10 000 pieces)	2376000	3132000
化学纤维(吨)	Chemical Fiber (ton)	643000	580000
棉纺锭(环锭纺)(锭)	Cotton Hasp (unit)	4352890	4675616
气流纺锭(转杯纺)(头)	Airflow Hasp (unit)	148168	249700
棉布织机(台)	Calico Spinning Machine (set)	2190	2690
原油加工能力(吨)	Crude Oil Processing Capacity (ton)	33700000	33660000
焦炭(吨)	Coke (ton)	40840585	43685000
烧碱(折 100%)(吨)	Caustic Soda (ton)	2845000	2835000
炭化钙(电石)(折 300 升/千克)(吨)	Calcium Carbide (ton)	5453000	6830000
农用氮、磷、钾化学肥料(折纯)(吨)	Chemical Fertilizers (ton)	4776160	5368160
初级形态塑料(吨)	Primary Plastic (ton)	6288600	6184000
水泥熟料(吨)	Cement Chamotte (ton)	66375439	70169250
水泥(吨)	Cement (ton)	91423717	97608200
平板玻璃(重量箱)	Plate Glass (weight case)	9025000	12020000
生铁(吨)	Pig Iron (ton)	17836454	17946454
粗钢(吨)	Crude Steel (ton)	18953052	17858000
钢材(吨)	Rolled Steel (ton)	25331023	25864900
铁合金(吨)	Ferroalloy (ton)	450200	434200
原铝(电解铝)(吨)	Electrolyzed Aluminium (ton)	5766700	6954700
汽车(辆)	Motor Vehicles(unit)	30000	30000

主要统计指标解释

工业 指从事自然资源的开采，对采掘品和农产品进行加工和再加工的物质生产部门。具体包括：(1)对自然资源的开采，如采矿、晒盐等(但不包括禽兽捕猎和水产捕捞)；(2)对农副产品的加工、再加工，如粮油加工、食品加工、缫丝、纺织、制革等；(3)对采掘品的加工、再加工，如炼铁、炼钢、化工生产、石油加工、机器制造、木材加工等，以及电力、自来水、煤气的生产和供应等；(4)对工业品的修理、翻新，如机器设备的修理等。

工业统计调查单位为工业法人单位。

工业法人单位指从事工业生产经营活动的法人单位。工业法人单位应同时具备以下条件：①依法成立，有自己的名称、组织机构和场所，能够独立承担民事责任；②独立拥有（或授权）使用资产，承担负债，有权与其他单位签订合同；③具有包括资产负债表在内的账户，或者能够根据需要编制账户。

国有控股企业 既原来的国有及国有控股企业。根据企业实收资本中国有经济成分的出资人的实际投资情况，或国有经济成分的出资人对企业资产的实际控制、支配程度进行分类。以下情况为国有控股：（1）在企业的全部实收资本中，国有经济成分的出资人拥有的实收资本（股本）所占企业全部实收资本（股本）的比例大于50%的国有绝对控股。（2）在企业的全部实收资本中，国有经济成分的出资人拥有的实收资本（股本）所占比例虽不大于50%，但相对大于其他任何一方经济成分的出资人所占比例的国有相对控股；或者虽不大于其他经济成分，但根据协议规定拥有企业实际控制权的国有协议控股。（3）投资双方各占50%，且未明确由谁绝对控股的企业，若其中一方为国有经济成分的，一律按国有控股处理。

本篇涉及的企业登记注册类型的解释详见综合篇。

轻工业 指主要提供生活消费品和制作手工工具的工业。按其所使用的原料不同，可分为两大类：(1)以农产品为原料的轻工业，是指直接或间接以农产品为基本原料的轻工业。主要包括食品制造、饮料制造、烟草加工、纺织、缝纫、皮革和毛皮制作、造纸以及印刷等工业；(2)以非农产品为原料的轻工业，是指以工业品为原料的轻工业。主要包括文教体育用品、化学药品制造、合成纤维制造、日用化学制品、日用玻璃制品、日用金属制品、手工工具制造、医疗器械制造、文化和办公用机械制造等工业。

重工业 指为国民经济各部门提供物质技术基础的主要生产资料的工业。按其生产性质和产品用途，可以分为下列三类：(1)采掘(伐)工业，是指对自然资源的开采，包括石油开采、煤炭开采、金属矿开采、非金属矿开采等工业；(2)原材料工业，指向国民经济各部门提供基本材料、动力和燃料的工业。包括金属冶炼及加工、炼焦及焦炭、化学、化工原料、水泥、人造板以及电力、石油和煤炭加工等工业；(3)加工工业，是指对工业原材料进行再加工制造的工业。包括装备国民经济各部门的机械设备制造工业、金属结构、水泥制品等工业，以及为农业提供的生产资料如化肥、农药等工业。

根据上述划分原则，修理业中以重工业产品为修理作业对象的划为重工业，反之划为轻工业。

工业总产值

(1)定义：

工业总产值是工业企业在一定时期内生产的以货币形式表现的工业最终产品和提供工业性劳务活动的总价值量。它反映一定时间内工业生产的总规模和总水平。

(2)计算原则：

工业生产的原则，即凡是企业在报告期内生产的最终产品和提供的劳务，均应包括在内。其中的最终产品，不管是否在报告期内销售，只要是报告期内生产的，就应包括在内。凡不是工业生产的产品，均不得计入工业总产值。

最终产品的原则，即企业生产的成品价值必须是本企业生产的，经检验合格不需再进行任何加工的最终产品。企业对外销售的半成品也应视为最终产品计入工业总产值。而在本企业内各车间转移的半成品和在制品只能计算其期末期初差额价值。

工厂法原则，即以法人工业企业作为一个整体计算工业总产值，是其报告期内生产的最终产品和提供劳务的总价值量。

(3)内容及计算方法：

1995年全国工业普查对工业总产值(原规定)的内容及计算原则和方法做了某些修订，修订后的工业总产值(新规定)包括三项内容：即本期生产成品价值、对外加工费收入、在制品半成品期末期初差额价值三部分。

本期生产成品价值：指企业本期生产，并在报告期内不再进行加工，经检验、包装入库的全部工业成品(半成品)价值合计，包括企业生产的自制设备及提供给本企业在建工程、其他非工业部门和福利部门等单位使用的成品价值。本期生产成品价值为按自备原材料生产的产品的数量乘以本期不含增值税(销项税额)的产品实际销售平均单价计算；会计核算中按成本价格转帐的自制设备和自产自用的成品，按成本价格计算生产成品价值。生产成品价值中不包括用定货者来料加工的成品(半成品)价值。

对外加工费收入：指企业在报告期内完成的对外承接的工业品加工(包括用定货者来料加工产品)的加工费收入和对外工业修理作业所取得的加工费收入。对外加工费收入按不含增值税(销项税额)的价格计算，可根据会计“产品销售收入”科目的有关资料取得。

对于本企业对内非工业部门提供的加工修理、设备安装的劳务收入，如果企业会计核算基础较好，能取得这部分资料，而且这部分价值所占比重较大，应包括在对外加工费收入中。

自制半成品在制品期末期初差额价值: 指企业报告期在制品期末减期初的差额价值，本指标一般可以从会计核算资料中取得。如果会计产品成本核算中不计算半成品、在制品的成本，则总产值中也不包括这部分价值，反之则包括。

资产总计 指企业过去的交易或者事项形成的、由企业拥有或者控制的、预期会给企业带来经济利益的资源。资产一般按流动性分为流动资产和非流动资产。其中流动资产可分为货币资金、交易性金融资产、应收票据、应收账款、预付款项、其他应收款、存货等；非流动资产可分为长期股权投资、固定资产、无形资产及其他非流动资产等。来源于会计“资产负债表”中“资产总计”项目的期末余额数。

流动资产合计 资产满足以下条件之一应归为流动资产：（1）预计在一个正常营业周期中变现、出售或耗用，主要包括存货、应收账款等；（2）主要为交易目的而持有；（3）预计在资产负债表日起一年内（含一年）变现；（4）自资产负债日起一年内，交换其他资产或清偿负债的能力不受限制的现金或现金等价物。包括货币资金、应收票据、应收账款、存货等项目。来源于会计“资产负债表”中“流动资产合计”项目的期末余额数。

固定资产原价 指固定资产的成本，包括企业在购置、自行建造、安装、改建、扩建、技术改造某项固定资产时所发生的全部支出总额。根据会计“固定资产”科目的期末借方余额填报。

负债合计 指企业过去的交易或者事项形成的，预期会导致经济利益流出企业的现时义务。负债一般按偿还期长短分为流动负债和非流动负债。来源于会计“资产负债表”中“负债合计”项目的期末余额数。

流动负债合计 负债满足下列条件之一的应归为流动负债：（1）预计在一个正常营业周期中清偿；（2）主要为交易目的而持有；（3）自资产负债表日起一年内到期应予清偿；（4）企业无权自主地将清偿推迟至资产负债表日后一年以上。包括短期借款、应付票据、应付账款、应付职工薪酬、应交税费等项目。根据会计“资产负债表”中“流动负债合计”项目的期末余额数填报。

所有者权益合计 指企业资产扣除负债后由所有者享有的剩余权益。公司的所有者权益又称股东权益。包括实收资本、资本公积、盈余公积、未分配利润等。来源于会计“资产负债表”中“所有者权益合计”项目的期末余额数。

主营业务收入 指企业确认的销售商品、提供劳务等主营业务的收入。来源于会计“主营业务收入”科目的期末贷方余额（结转前）。

主营业务成本 指企业经营主要业务所发生的成本总额。来源于会计“主营业务成本”科目的期末借方余额（结转前）。

主营业务税金及附加 指企业经营主要业务应负担的营业税、消费税、城市维护建设税、教育费附加等。来源于会计“主营业务税金及附加”科目的期末借方余额(结转前)。

利润总额 指企业在一定会计期间的经营成果，是生产经营过程中各种收入扣除各种耗费后的盈余，反映企业在报告期内实现的亏盈总额。来源于会计“利润表”中“利润总额”项目的本期金额数。

应交增值税 指企业按税法规定，从事货物销售或提供加工、修理修配劳务等增加货物价值的活动本期应交纳的税金。计算公式为：

应交增值税=销项税额-（进项税额-进项税额转出）-出口抵减内销产品应纳税额-减免税款+出口退税

进项税额指企业在报告期内购入货物或接受应税劳务而支付的、准予从销项税额中抵扣的增值税额。

销项税额指工业企业在报告期内销售货物或提供应税劳务应收取的增值税额。

总资产贡献率 反映企业全部资产的获利能力，是企业经营业绩和管理水平的集中体现，是评价和考核企业盈利能力的核心指标。计算公式为：

总资产贡献率(%)=(利润总额+税金总额+利息支出)/ 平均资产总额*100%

公式中：税金总额为主营业务税金及附加与应交增值税之和；平均资产总额为期初期末资产之和的算术平均值。

资产负债率 该指标既反映企业经营风险的大小，也反映企业利用债权人提供的资金从事经营活动的能力。计算公式为：

资产负债率（%）=负债总额 / 资产总额 *100%

资产与负债均为报告期期末数。

流动资产周转次数 指一定时期内流动资产完成的周转次数，反映投入工业企业流动资金的周转速度。计算公式为：

流动资产周转次数=主营业务收入 / 全部流动资产平均余额

公式中：全部流动资产平均余额为期初和期末的流动资产之和的算术平均值。

成本费用利润率 反映企业投入的生产成本及费用的经济效益，同时也反映企业降低成本所取得的经济效益。计算公式为：

成本费用利润率（%）=利润总额 / 成本费用总额*100%

公式中：成本费用总额为主营业务成本、销售费用、管理费用、财务费用之和。

产品销售率 该指标反映工业产品已实现销售的程度，是分析工业产销衔接情况，研究工业产品满足社会需求的指标。计算公式为：

产品销售率(%)=工业销售产值 / 工业总产值*100%

Explanatory Notes on Main Statistical Indicators

Industry refers to the material production sector which is engaged in the extraction of natural resources and processing and reprocessing of minerals and agricultural products, including (1) extraction of natural resources, such as mining, salt production (but not including hunting and fishing); (2) processing and reprocessing of farm and sideline produces, such as grain and oil processing, food processing, silk reeling, spinning and weaving and leather making; (3) processing and reprocessing of mineral products, such as steel making, iron smelting, chemicals manufacturing, petroleum processing, machine building, timber processing, and production and supply of electricity, gas and water; (4) repairing and renovating of industrial products such as the machinery.

In industrial surveys, the units of enquiry are industrial corporate units.

Industrial corporate units refer to corporate units engaging in industrial production and operation activities, which meet the following requirements: (1) They are established legally, having their own names, organizations, location, and are able to take civil liability independently; (2) They possess (or are authorized to use) assets independently, assume liabilities and are entitled to sign contracts with other units; (3) They have accounts including the balance sheets or can compile the accounts according to the need.

State-holding Enterprises cover the original state-owned enterprises and state-holding enterprises. They are classified according to the actual investment made by the contribor of state-owned part in the paid-in capital of the enterprises, or the degree of control or dominance of the contributor on the assets of the enterprises. The following cases are regarded as state-holding: (1) Absolute state-holding in which the contribors of state-owned parts possess more than 50% of all the paid-in capital (stocks) of the enterprises; (2) Relative state-holding in which the contribors of state-owned parts possess no more than 50% of the paid-in capital (stocks) of the enterprises, but more than that of any other contributors; or Agreed state-holding in which the contribors of state-owned parts possess no more than other contributors but have actual control over the enterprises according to agreements; (3) In the case both contributors possess 50% and it is not clear which one is in absolute holding position, the enterprise is regarded as state-holding enterprise if one of the contributor has state-owned elements.

For explanation of types of registration covered in this chapter, please refer to General Survey.

Light Industry refers to the industry that produces consumer goods and hand tools. It consists of two categories, depending on the materials used:

(1) Industries using farm products as raw materials. These are the branches of light industry which directly or indirectly use farm products as basic raw materials, including the manufacture of food and beverages, tobacco processing, textile, clothing, fur and leather manufacturing, paper making, printing, etc.

(2) Industries using non-farm products as raw materials. These are the branches of light industry which use manufactured goods as raw materials, including the manufacture of cultural, educational articles and sports goods, chemicals, synthetic fibre, chemical products for daily use, glass products for daily use, metal products for daily use, hand tools, medical apparatus and instruments, and the manufacture of cultural and office machinery.

Heavy Industry refers to the industry which produces capital goods, and provides various sectors of the national economy with necessary material and technical basis for production. It consists of the following three branches according to the purpose of production or the use of products:

(1) Mining, quarrying and logging industry, which refers to the industry that extracts natural resources, including extraction of petroleum, coal, metal and non-metal ores.

(2) Raw materials industry refers to the industry that provides various sectors of the national economy with raw materials, fuels and power. It includes smelting and processing of metals, coking and coke chemistry, chemical materials and building materials such as cement, plywood, and power, petroleum refining and coal dressing.

(3) Manufacturing industry which refers to the industry that processes raw materials. It includes machine-building industries which equip sectors of the national economy; industries producing metal structure and cement products; and industries producing means of agricultural production, such as chemical fertilizers and pesticides.

In accordance with the above principles of classification, the repairing trades, which are engaged primarily in repairing products of heavy industry, are classified as heavy industry while those which are engaged in repairing products of light industry are classified as light industry.

Gross Industrial Output Value

(1) Definition: Gross industrial output value is the total volume of final industrial products produced and industrial services provided during a given period in monetary terms. It reflects the total achievements and overall scale of industrial production during a given period.

(2) Principles for calculation:

Statistics on industrial production follow the principle that all final industrial products produced and industrial services provided during the reference period are to be included. The final industrial products are included as long as being produced during the reference period, no matter whether they are sold or not during the reference period. The gross industrial output value will not cover those products that are not from industrial production.

Determination of final products follows the principle that all products that are included in the calculation of gross industrial output value are the final products of the enterprise. which have been accepted through quality check and require no further processing. The intermediate products sold by enterprises are considered as the final products of the enterprise and counted into the gross industrial output value. However, for the intermediate products being transferred among workshops and the work-in-progress products, only the balance value from the beginning to the end of the period is calculated.

Gross industrial output value is calculated following the principle of factory approach, i.e. industrial enterprise with legal entity is used as a whole in calculating the gross industrial output value, which will cover the total value of final industrial products produced and industrial services provided by these enterprises during the reference period.

(3) Content and method of calculation: The old definition of gross industrial output value was modified during the 1995 National Industrial Census. The revised (new) definition of gross industrial output value consists of 3 components: value of the finished products during the reference period, income from processing for external parties, and value of change in semi-finished products between the end and the beginning of the reference period.

Value of finished products during the reference period: refers to the value of all finished (semi-finished) industrial products that are produced during the reference period without the need for further processing, checked for acceptance, packed and put into the warehouse of the enterprise, including the value of own-produced equipment and the value of products provided to the projects under construction of the enterprise, and to other non-industrial or welfare units. Value of finished products during the reference period is calculated by the quantity of products produced using own materials multiplied by the average unit prices at which products are sold (excluding value-added tax). Own-produced equipment and products produced for own use are valued at cost prices as in the case of enterprise accounting. Value of finished products does not include the value of finished products (semi-finished products) that are produced using the materials from the clients who place the orders.

Income from external processing: refers to income from contracted external processing of industrial products (including processing of industrial products using materials from the clients), and the income from industrial repairing work provided to other parties. Income from external processing is calculated using information from the item "products sales income" in the enterprise accounting at the prices with value-added tax excluded.

For income from services such as processing, repairing and installation of equipment provided to non-industrial units within the enterprise, if the accounting work of the enterprise is good enough to separate it from other records, and the share of such services is significant, it should also be included in the income from external processing.

Value of change in semi-finished products between the end and the beginning of the reference period: refers to the value of change in semi-finished products between the end and the beginning of the reference period, which generally can be obtained from accounting records of enterprises. If the enterprise accounting excludes the cost of semi-finished products, then it should not be included in the gross industrial output value, and the reverse if otherwise.

Total Assets refer to all resources that are owned or controlled by enterprises through previous trades or transactions with expectation of making economic profits. Classified by the degree of liquidity, total assets include current assets, and non-current assets. Current assets can be classified into monetary assets, trading financial assets, notes receivable, accounts receivable, advanced payments, other prepaid money and inventories. Non-current assets can be divided into long-term equity investment, fixed assets, intangible assets and other non-current assets. Data on this indicator can be obtained from the year-end figures of total assets in the *Balance Sheet* of accounting records.

Total Current Assets refer to the assets that meet one of the following requirements: (1) expected to be cashed, sold or used in a normal operation cycle, mainly including inventory and accounts receivable; (2) be owned for trading purpose mainly; (3) expected to be cashed in one year (including one year) from the day of the *Balance Sheet*; (4) unlimited cash or cash equivalents that can be exchanged with other assets or being capable of settling debts during one year since the day of *the Balance Sheet*. Included are monetarycapital, notes receivable, accounts receivable and inventories. Data on this indicator can be obtained by the year-end figures of total current assets in the Balance Sheet of accounting records.

Original Value of Fixed Assets refers to the cost of fixed assets, or the total expenditure of an enterprise spent on certain fixed assets, through purchase, construction, installation, transformation, expansion or technical upgrading. It is reported according to the year-end debit balance of fixed assets of accounting records.

Total Liabilities refer to payable liabilities of enterprises that accumulated from previous trades or transactions with expectation of economic profits leaking out. In terms of payment, it can be divided into liquid liabilities and long-term liabilities. Data on this indicator can be obtained from the year-end figures of total liabilities in the *Balance Sheet* of accounting records.

Total Liquid Liabilities refer to the liabilities that meet one of the following requirements: (1) expected to be repaid in a normal operation cycle; (2) be owned for trading purpose mainly; (3) expected to be repaid in one year from the day of the *Assets and Liability Table*; (4) enterprise has no right to postpone the settlement of which over a year from the day of the *Assets and Liability Table*. Included are short-term loans, notes payable, accounts payable, employee compensations, taxes and expenses due. Data on this indicator can be obtained by the year-end figures of total liquid liabilities in the *Balance Sheet* of accounting records.

Total Equity refers to the residual ownership of enterprise investors by deducting total liabilities from the total assets, including the paid-in capital, accumulation of capital, operating surplus and non-distributed profits. Data are obtained from the year-end figures of total equity in the *Balance Sheet* of accounting records.

Revenue from Principal Business refers to the income confirmed of an enterprise from the principal business of selling products and providing labor services. Data on this indicator can be obtained from the year-end credit balance of "revenue from principal business" in the accounting record of enterprise(before carryover).

Cost of Principal Business refers to the total cost occurred from the principal business of the enterprise. Data can be obtained from the year-end debit balance of "cost of principal business" in the accounting record of enterprise(before carryover).

Tax and Extra Charges from Principal Business refer to the sales tax, consumption tax, urban maintenance and construction tax and education expenses shouldered by the enterprise from its principal business. Data are obtained from the year-end debit balance of "tax and extra charges from principal business" in the accounting record of enterprise(before carryover).

Total Profits refers to the operation results in a certain accounting period, and it is the balance of various incomes minus various spendings in the course of operation, reflecting the total profits and losses of enterprises in reference period. Data are obtained from the amount of total profits in the profit statement of the accounting record of enterprise.

Value-added Tax Payable refers to the payable tax according to Tax Law of enterprises which engaged in selling goods or providing services that bring added value to the goods, such as processing, repairing, fitting and other activities. The formula is as follows:

Value-added Tax Payable = tax on sales-(tax on purchase-transferred tax on purchase)-exports deduct tax payable on domestic sales-tax relief+the export tax rebate.

Tax on Purchase refers to the value-added tax payable by enterprises that purchase goods or receiving taxable services during the reference period and this part of the tax is allowed to be deducted from the tax on sales.

Tax on Sales refers to the value-added tax chargeable by enterprises that sell goods or provide taxable services during the reference period.

Ratio of Profits, Taxes and Interests to Average Assets reflects the profit-making capability of all assets, manifests the performance and management of the enterprise, and is a key indicator for evaluating the profit-making potential of the enterprise. It is calculated as follows:

$$\text{Ratio of Profits, Taxes and Interests to Average Assets (\%)} = \frac{\text{total profits + total taxes + interest payment}}{\text{average assets}} \times 100\%$$

In the above formula, total taxes is the sum of tax and extra charges on the principal business and value-added tax payable; and average assets is the arithmetic mean of the sum of beginning assets and ending assets.

Ratio of Debts to Assets reflects both the operation risk and the capability of the enterprise in making use of the capital from the creditors. It is calculated as follows:

$$\text{Ratio of Debts to Assets (\%)} = \frac{\text{total debts}}{\text{total assets}} \times 100\%$$

Both assets and debts are figures at the end of the reference period.

Turnover of Current Assets refers to the number of times of turnover of current assets in a given period of time, which reflects the speed of the turnover of current assets of industrial enterprises, and is calculated as follows:

$$\text{Turnover of Current Assets} = \frac{\text{revenue from principal business}}{\text{average balance of total current assets}}$$

In the above formula, average balance of total current assets refers to the arithmetic mean of the sum of current assets at the beginning and at the end of the reference period.

Ratio of Profits to Total Industrial Costs reflects the economic efficiency of input cost and cost reduction. It is calculated as follows:

$$\text{Ratio of Profits to Total Industrial Cost (\%)} = \frac{\text{total profits}}{\text{total costs}} \times 100\%$$

Total costs in the above formula are the sum of cost of principal business, marketing cost, management cost and financial cost.

Sales Ratio of Products is an indicator reflecting the actual sale of industrial products, analyzing the production-selling and supply-demand relations. It is calculated as:

$$\text{Sales Ratio of Products (\%)} = \frac{\text{value of industrial sales}}{\text{gross industrial output value (current prices)}} \times 100\%$$

新疆统计年鉴
XINJIANG STATISTICAL YEARBOOK

14 建筑业

CONSTRUCTION

第十四篇　建筑业

本篇主要内容和资料来源

本篇资料反映在新疆维吾尔自治区注册的建筑法人企业概况及发展情况，包括建筑业企业基本情况和生产经营情况。主要指标有企业个数、从业人员和建筑企业签定合同情况、承包工程完成情况及总产值、企业技术装备情况、房屋建筑面积、利润、税金、劳动生产率等。

根据建筑业发展的实际情况，建筑业统计范围从2002年起，由原具有建筑业资质等级四级及四级以上的独立核算的建筑业企业调整为具有施工总承包、专业承包和劳务分包的法人建筑业企业。

本篇建筑业企业统计数据是根据国家统计局制定的《建筑业统计报表制度》整理汇总的。建筑业统计数据采取全面调查的方法。资料由新疆维吾尔自治区统计局固定资产投资统计处提供。

Construction

Main Content and Source of Data

Data in this chapter show the general situation and the development of the construction in Xinjiang Uygur Autonomous Region. They cover the situation of production and management of the enterprises on construction, including the number of enterprises, number of employed persons, complete and gross output value of construction industry, value added floor space of the buildings, profits and taxes of enterprises and labor productivity, etc.

According to the development of construction industry, starting from 2002,the coverage of construction statistics has been adjusted to include all the construction enterprises of various types of ownership with qualification certificates and with independent accounting system ,instead of the original criteria that required construction enterprises of various types of ownership to have qualification certificates at or above Class 4 with independent accounting system.

Data on construction enterprises are collected in accordance with the Reporting System of Construction Statistics stipulated by the National Bureau of Statistics. Data on the construction industry are collected through comprehensive reporting system and provided by the Department of Investment in Fixed Assets Statistics, Xinjiang Bureau of Statistics.

14-1 建筑企业概况
Main Indicators on Construction Enterprises

年份 地区	Year Region	企业个数(个) Number of Enterprises (unit)				从业人员(万人) Number of Persons Employed (10 000 persons)			
		合计 Total	国有 State-owned	集体 Collec-tive-owned	其他 Others	合计 Total	国有 State-owned	集体 Collec-tive-owned	其他 Others
	1985	275	117	158		25.85	19.21	6.64	
	1990	353	183	170		22.86	18.36	4.50	
	1995	928	481	432	15	35.33	26.33	8.72	0.28
	1996	886	478	386	22	24.97	18.53	6.09	0.35
	1997	650	313	312	25	30.75	20.39	8.56	1.80
	1998	682	269	348	65	22.14	14.83	6.42	0.89
	1999	711	272	344	95	19.35	13.00	4.94	1.41
	2000	690	226	293	171	26.16	17.69	4.25	4.22
	2001	594	175	152	267	25.27	14.77	2.68	7.82
	2002	730	146	109	475	23.57	8.64	1.89	13.04
	2003	776	112	77	587	20.81	6.16	1.12	13.53
	2004	932	105	51	776	33.22	7.21	0.84	25.17
	2005	881	107	43	731	34.37	8.70	0.90	24.77
	2006	914	102	39	773	33.84	8.81	0.84	24.19
	2007	967	103	35	829	37.02	9.63	0.92	26.47
	2008	998	99	32	867	42.37	11.28	0.48	30.61
	2009	993	90	28	875	48.18	12.01	0.52	35.65
	2010	1004	81	28	895	56.48	12.66	0.52	43.30
	2011	1025	89	22	914	52.73	9.89	0.40	42.44
	2012	1045	89	20	936	63.81	12.86	0.48	50.47
	2013	1123	76	19	1028	79.11	13.68	0.61	64.82
	2014	1146	76	15	1055	75.84	11.05	0.26	64.53
	2015	1256	74	15	1167	72.19	9.51	0.29	62.39
乌鲁木齐市	Urumqi City	479	33	6	440	24.02	3.96	0.13	19.93
克拉玛依市	Karamay City	65	2	2	61	2.25	0.20	0.03	2.02
吐鲁番市	Turpan City	19	2		17	0.58	0.01		0.57
哈密地区	Hami [Kumul] Administrative Offices	57	3	1	53	0.62	0.06	0.01	0.55
昌吉回族自治州	Changji Hui Autonomous Prefecture	113	2		111	4.37	0.12		4.25
伊犁哈萨克自治州	Ili Kazak Autonomous Prefecture	154	17	4	133	10.60	1.65	0.03	8.92
伊犁州直属县(市)	Counties (Cities) Direct Under Ili Prefecture	80	9	1	70	6.18	1.25		4.93
塔城地区	Tacheng [Tarbagatai] Administrative Offices	38	4	3	31	3.50	0.22	0.03	3.25
阿勒泰地区	Altay Administrative Offices	36	4		32	0.92	0.18		0.74
博尔塔拉蒙古自治州	Bortala Mongol Autonomous Prefecture	42	1	1	40	1.28		0.09	1.19
巴音郭楞蒙古自治州	Bayangol Mongol Autonomous Prefecture	75	5	1	69	5.33	0.12		5.21
阿克苏地区	Aksu Administrative Offices	67	2		65	3.16	0.08		3.08
克孜勒苏柯尔克孜自治州	Kizilsu Kirgiz Autonomous Prefecture	22	1		21	0.66	0.05		0.61
喀什地区	Kashgar [Kaxgar] Administrative Offices	62	1		61	2.75			2.75
和田地区	Hotan Administrative Offices	24	1		23	1.53	0.32		1.21
石河子市	Shihezi City	33	3		30	8.53	2.43		6.10
阿拉尔市	Aral City	13	1		12	2.01	0.51		1.50
图木舒克市	Tumxuk City	10			10	2.01			2.01
五家渠市	Wujiaqu City	21			21	2.49			2.49

注：1.2000 年至 2002 年建筑业所有指标数据均包括克拉玛依石油管理局工业部分，2003 年起将此部分扣除(以下同)。
2.2004 年建筑业所有数据为经济普查数，企业个数及其他指标包括没有工作量或者停业企业，往年未包括(以下同)。
3.根据我区建筑特点，建筑业从业人员为年平均人数。

Note: a) All the quota indices in building sector from 2000 to 2002 include the industrial part of Karamay Oil Administration. From 2003, this part was omitted. (the same as in the following) . b) All the data in architectural sector are the statistics of economic census, enterprise numbers and other quota exclude work volume or closed enterprises except for previous years. (the same as in the following) . c)In view of the features of the construction, the number of employed persons refers to the annual average.

14-2 按登记注册类型分建筑企业总产值

Total Output Value of Construction Enterprises by Registration Status

单位：万元 (10 000 yuan)

年份 Year	地区 Region	合计 Total	国有经济 State-owned Units	集体经济 Collective -owned Units	其他经济 Others Units
	1985	175165	138138	37027	
	1990	273893	220574	53319	
	1995	1070085	816396	238387	15302
	1996	1284669	977358	283776	23535
	1997	1141318	828482	288081	24755
	1998	1434787	1002235	378956	53596
	1999	1569486	1085080	365588	118818
	2000	2349506	1436653	362649	550204
	2001	2742800	1394099	252076	1096625
	2002	3136257	1270601	170319	1695337
	2003	3221502	739953	147256	2334293
	2004	3439968	910264	89189	2440515
	2005	3615674	1138005	102580	2375089
	2006	3856223	1269722	88474	2498027
	2007	4541026	1548285	97418	2895323
	2008	6292562	1879497	86431	4326634
	2009	7913768	2245048	119717	5549003
	2010	9694741	2486878	119917	7087946
	2011	13278310	3302487	104738	9871085
	2012	16331061	3670127	161626	12499308
	2013	20988887	3532297	222053	17234537
	2014	23321204	3792924	140514	19387766
	2015	23040672	3710417	113887	19216368
乌鲁木齐市	Urumqi City	6396013	1385893	49281	4960839
克拉玛依市	Karamay City	880604	18300	18629	843675
吐鲁番市	Turpan City	285130	10114		275016
哈密地区	Hami [Kumul] Administrative Offices	649083	305796	17612	325675
昌吉回族自治州	Changji Hui Autonomous Prefecture	1383289	36164		1347125
伊犁哈萨克自治州	Ili Kazak Autonomous Prefecture	3762087	849962	6812	2905313
伊犁州直属县(市)	Counties (Cities) Direct Under Ili Prefecture	2396337	612504	1034	1782799
塔城地区	Tacheng [Tarbagatai] Administrative Offices	954537	151292	5778	797467
阿勒泰地区	Altay Administrative Offices	411213	86166		325047
博尔塔拉蒙古自治州	Bortala Mongol Autonomous Prefecture	832016	477	21500	810039
巴音郭楞蒙古自治州	Bayangol Mongol Autonomous Prefecture	1722512	45583	53	1676876
阿克苏地区	Aksu Administrative Offices	1169908	19385		1150523
克孜勒苏柯尔克孜自治州	Kizilsu Kirgiz Autonomous Prefecture	197639	5585		192054
喀什地区	Kashgar [Kaxgar] Administrative Offices	742459	5517		736942
和田地区	Hotan Administrative Offices	482401	152809		329592
石河子市	Shihezi City	2061973	593215		1468758
阿拉尔市	Aral City	948184	281617		666567
图木舒克市	Tumxuk City	610196			610196
五家渠市	Wujiaqu City	917178			917178

14-3 按构成分建筑企业总产值

Total Output Value of Construction Enterprises by Composition

单位：万元 (10 000 yuan)

年份 Year	地区 Region	总产值 Total Output Value	建筑工程 Output Value of Construction Projects	安装工程 Output Value of Installation Projects	其他 Others
	1985	175165	154496	18042	2627
	1990	273893	241574	28211	4108
	1995	1070085	942158	106744	21183
	1996	1284669	1124271	132079	28319
	1997	1141318	1009082	105891	26345
	1998	1434787	1270483	139104	25200
	1999	1569486	1398179	146154	25153
	2000	2349506	2073166	214425	61915
	2001	2742800	2403688	279909	59203
	2002	3136257	2637362	405115	93780
	2003	3221502	2708269	336535	176698
	2004	3439968	2836668	396509	206791
	2005	3615674	2981373	487239	147062
	2006	3856223	3209192	510770	136261
	2007	4541026	3822922	564228	153876
	2008	6292562	5359129	804719	128714
	2009	7913768	6924156	867812	121800
	2010	9694741	8450628	1107006	137107
	2011	13278310	11850908	1223095	204307
	2012	16331061	14545263	1420629	365169
	2013	20988887	18887487	1691824	409576
	2014	23321204	21147170	1747407	426637
	2015	23040672	20876242	1790308	374122
乌鲁木齐市	Urumqi City	6396013	5502208	814699	79106
克拉玛依市	Karamay City	880604	518468	322744	39392
吐鲁番市	Turpan City	285130	200878	83249	1003
哈密地区	Hami [Kumul] Administrative Offices	649083	614027	29666	5390
昌吉回族自治州	Changji Hui Autonomous Prefecture	1383289	1209155	117588	56546
伊犁哈萨克自治州	Ili Kazak Autonomous Prefecture	3762087	3622208	91031	48848
伊犁州直属县(市)	Counties (Cities) Direct Under Ili Prefecture	2396337	2338091	49869	8377
塔城地区	Tacheng [Tarbagatai] Administrative Offices	954537	889228	27008	38301
阿勒泰地区	Altay Administrative Offices	411213	394889	14154	2170
博尔塔拉蒙古自治州	Bortala Mongol Autonomous Prefecture	832016	768223	34508	29285
巴音郭楞蒙古自治州	Bayangol Mongol Autonomous Prefecture	1722512	1628166	76617	17729
阿克苏地区	Aksu Administrative Offices	1169908	1147564	22344	
克孜勒苏柯尔克孜自治州	Kizilsu Kirgiz Autonomous Prefecture	197639	171899	4792	20948
喀什地区	Kashgar [Kaxgar] Administrative Offices	742459	687579	47514	7366
和田地区	Hotan Administrative Offices	482401	436948	9226	36227
石河子市	Shihezi City	2061973	1962239	73560	26174
阿拉尔市	Aral City	948184	933258	8818	6108
图木舒克市	Tumxuk City	610196	604084	6112	
五家渠市	Wujiaqu City	917178	869338	47840	

14-4 按行业和登记注册类型分建筑企业总产值

Total Output Value of Construction Enterprises by Registration Status and Sectors

单位：万元 (10 000 yuan)

项 目	Item	2014	2015
总 计	**Total**	**23321204**	**23040672**
#一、二级企业	First Grade and Second Grade Enterprises	18846157	18706810
#国有及国有控股	State-owned and State-holding	11997822	12130754
按登记注册类型分组	**Grouped by Registration Status**		
内资企业	Domestic Funded	23321053	23040508
#国有企业	State-owned Enterprises	1383114	1481402
集体企业	Collective-owned Enterprises	140514	113887
有限责任公司	Limited Liability Corporations	15319225	14899323
国有独资公司	Sole State -funded Corporations	2409810	2229015
其他有限责任公司	Other Limited Liability Corporations	12909415	12670308
股份有限公司	Share-holding Corporations Ltd	1181723	1064848
私营企业	Private Enterprises	5296477	5470548
#私营独资企业	Private funded Enterprises		3976
私营有限责任公司	Private Limited Liability Corporations	5199619	5343323
私营股份有限公司	Private share-holding Corporations Ltd	96578	123249
其他企业	Other Enterprises		10500
港、澳、台商投资企业	Enterprises With Funds from Hong Kong, Macao , and Taiwan	27	30
#合资经营企业(港或澳、台资)	Joint-Venture Enterprises	27	30
外商投资企业	Foreign Funded Enterprises	124	134
按国民经济行业分组	**Grouped by National Economic Sectors**		
房屋工程建筑业	Building Construction	16968203	16491471
土木工程建筑业	Civil Engineering Construction	5277539	5301684
铁路、道路、隧道和桥梁	Railways, Roads, Tunnels and Bridges	2297246	2136985
水利和内河港口工程建筑	Water Conservancy and Seaport Construction	1877271	2053397
工矿工程建筑	Mine Project	280312	380507
架线和管道工程建筑	Cabling and Piping Project	793907	680992
其他土木工程建筑	Other Civil Engineering	28803	49803
建筑安装业	Construction and Installation	757049	730982
电气安装	Electrical Installation		388108
管道和设备安装	Piping and Eguipment Installatiou		92479
其他建筑安装业	Other Construction and Installation		250395
建筑装饰和其他建筑业	Building Decoration and Other Construction	318413	516535
建筑装饰业	Architectural Decoration Industry		180241
工程准备活动	Poject Preparation Activities		168602
提供施工设备服务	Provide Construction Equipment Service		84227
其他未列明建筑业	Not Listed Other Construction		83465
按隶属关系分组	**Grouped by Subordination**		
中 央	Central Government	8764148	9157736
地 方	Local	14557056	13882936
按企业资质等级分组	**Grouped by Enterprise's Qualification**		
施工总承包	Undertaking Porjects	21292659	21302977
特 级	Special Grade	440418	702999
一 级	First Grade	8306709	8215450
二 级	Second Grade	8666396	8627073
三级及以下	Third Grade and Below	3879136	3757455
专业承包	Specialized Undertaking	1331744	1254426
一 级	First Grade	343699	400670
二 级	Second Grade	505441	392130
三级及以下	Third Grade and Below	482604	461626
劳务分包	Work Subcontractors	696801	483269
一 级	First Grade	43496	141931
二 级	Second Grade	102321	226557
三级及以下	Third Grade and Below	550984	114781

14-5 建筑企业利税总额

Total Pre-tax Profits of Construction Enterprises

单位：万元 (10 000 yuan)

年份 Year	地区 Region	利税总额合计 Total Pre-tax Profits	利润总额 Total Profits	工程结算税金及附加 Taxes and Extra Charges on Project Settlement Accounts	管理费用中的税金 Taxes in Management Expenses	产值利税率(%) Ratio of Pre-tax Profits to Output Value (%)	资金利税率(%) Ratio of Pre-tax Profits to Assets (%)
	1994	28199	5535	20195	2469	3.81	4.11
	1995	30156	2974	24916	2266	3.44	3.46
	1996	20752	-8625	26816	2561	1.97	-0.93
	1997	31970	-4347	33360	2957	2.80	2.51
	1998	37596	-5875	41162	2309	2.62	2.41
	1999	64777	13359	48995	2423	4.13	3.72
	2000	19274	-48005	64614	2665	0.82	0.63
	2001	28688	-47485	74206	1967	1.05	0.84
	2002	84833	-11089	92484	3438	2.70	2.18
	2003	169594	67146	96888	5560	5.26	5.51
	2004	174255	65037	102990	6228	5.07	5.65
	2005	165236	46909	112565	5762	4.57	4.91
	2006	177102	54570	116426	6106	4.59	4.83
	2007	221117	67796	145119	8202	4.87	5.40
	2008	328484	120146	198718	9620	5.22	6.67
	2009	422062	156541	252547	12974	5.33	7.08
	2010	536197	208372	317056	10769	5.53	7.54
	2011	725740	274797	438927	12016	5.47	7.68
	2012	928871	356595	555058	17218	5.69	8.06
	2013	1126029	421152	678809	26068	5.36	7.94
	2014	1236134	519651	697592	18935	5.30	7.66
	2015	1229471	491944	717703	19848	5.34	6.66
乌鲁木齐市	Urumqi City	327250	138705	183271	5285	5.12	4.09
克拉玛依市	Karamay City	63475	25948	35854	1678	7.21	3.76
吐鲁番市	Turpan City	23015	13899	8375	742	8.07	7.84
哈密地区	Hami [Kumul] Administrative Offices	39567	19944	19120	500	6.10	8.19
昌吉回族自治州	Changji Hui Autonomous Prefecture	112322	44170	65528	2631	8.12	10.47
伊犁哈萨克自治州	Ili Kazak Autonomous Prefecture	175926	67134	107422	1388	4.68	10.63
伊犁州直属县(市)	Counties (Cities) Direct Under Ili Prefecture	92276	29345	62069	869	3.85	8.48
塔城地区	Tacheng [Tarbagatai] Administrative Offices	51976	23274	28300	407	5.45	14.02
阿勒泰地区	Altay Administrative Offices	31674	14515	17053	112	7.70	16.14
博尔塔拉蒙古自治州	Bortala Mongol Autonomous Prefecture	56205	24501	31290	411	6.75	22.61
巴音郭楞蒙古自治州	Bayangol Mongol Autonomous Prefecture	116579	51272	64429	877	6.77	12.76
阿克苏地区	Aksu Administrative Offices	49177	12775	34592	1804	4.20	6.48
克孜勒苏柯尔克孜自治州	Kizilsu Kirgiz Autonomous Prefecture	11247	3656	7377	208	5.69	5.53
喀什地区	Kashgar [Kaxgar] Administrative Offices	55786	19294	35176	1316	7.51	8.01
和田地区	Hotan Administrative Offices	21929	8752	12878	299	4.55	11.19
石河子市	Shihezi City	59648	19024	39734	892	2.89	4.89
阿拉尔市	Aral City	49578	23570	25298	712	5.23	17.58
图木舒克市	Tumxuk City	20617	3992	15841	783	3.38	7.86
五家渠市	Wujiaqu City	47150	15308	31518	322	5.14	9.54

14-6 建筑企业劳动生产率
Labor Productivity of Construction Enterprises

单位：元/人 (yuan/person)

年 份 Year	地 区 Region	按总产值计算的劳动生产率 Overall Labor Productivity in Terms of Total Output Value	#国有经济 State-owned Enterprises	#集体经济 Collective-owned Enterprises
	1994	29871	32616	23023
	1995	34668	38483	26617
	1996	32606	36557	25291
	1997	38808	40629	33658
	1998	47698	51465	40819
	1999	55593	61196	44235
	2000	74994	87999	48767
	2001	84666	94344	62458
	2002	86302	108857	66231
	2003	94165	98095	86190
	2004	107150	112145	107185
	2005	112214	137966	127587
	2006	121506	149550	118932
	2007	126303	134275	139988
	2008	152795	182536	168023
	2009	173714	204170	233869
	2010	176404	200435	231859
	2011	226848	284263	176207
	2012	249202	245195	286875
	2013	265325	257911	369964
	2014	285958	317490	387942
	2015	290120	317627	277907
乌鲁木齐市	Urumqi City	254012	271744	233557
克拉玛依市	Karamay City	262797	213036	240379
吐鲁番市	Turpan City	477043	871862	
哈密地区	Hami [Kumul] Administrative Offices	402806	427566	1558584
昌吉回族自治州	Changji Hui Autonomous Prefecture	278036	302373	
伊犁哈萨克自治州	Ili Kazak Autonomous Prefecture	344788	492418	296130
伊犁州直属县(市)	Counties (Cities) Direct Under Ili Prefecture	407312	487352	287194
塔城地区	Tacheng [Tarbagatai] Administrative Offices	236687	389126	297789
阿勒泰地区	Altay Administrative Offices	413237	1070385	
博尔塔拉蒙古自治州	Bortala Mongol Autonomous Prefecture	264584	170214	249710
巴音郭楞蒙古自治州	Bayangol Mongol Autonomous Prefecture	309921	401970	59111
阿克苏地区	Aksu Administrative Offices	308528	241713	
克孜勒苏柯尔克孜自治州	Kizilsu Kirgiz Autonomous Prefecture	251735	107410	
喀什地区	Kashgar [Kaxgar] Administrative Offices	253062	1282930	
和田地区	Hotan Administrative Offices	335512	475594	
石河子市	Shihezi City	256091	208695	
阿拉尔市	Aral City	449674	555677	
图木舒克市	Tumxuk City	376316		
五家渠市	Wujiaqu City	273108		

14-7 建筑企业签订合同情况
Contracts Signed by Construction Enterprises

单位：万元 (10 000 yuan)

年 份 Year	地 区 Region	合同总额 Total Value Of Contracts	上年结转合同 Value from Contracts Signed In Last Year	本年新签合同 Value from New Contracts Signed In This Year
	2002	3962086	988485	2973601
	2003	4312515	1236887	3075628
	2004	4725501	1351086	3374415
	2005	4857604	1557300	3300304
	2006	5692120	1483664	4208455
	2007	7220300	1986086	5234214
	2008	9907859	2906991	7000868
	2009	12473691	3859836	8613855
	2010	15883584	5459941	10423643
	2011	21956637	6083819	15872818
	2012	27266741	9965704	17301037
	2013	34204813	11167870	23036943
	2014	36223617	13189051	23034566
	2015	36362040	13175677	23186363
乌鲁木齐市	Urumqi City	12423270	5764121	6659149
克拉玛依市	Karamay City	1791321	893233	898088
吐鲁番市	Turpan City	563506	202624	360882
哈密地区	Hami [Kumul] Administrative Offices	934778	377445	557333
昌吉回族自治州	Changji Hui Autonomous Prefecture	2183012	716809	1466203
伊犁哈萨克自治州	Ili Kazak Autonomous Prefecture	5045044	1258400	3786644
伊犁州直属县(市)	Counties (Cities) Direct Under Ili Prefecture	3181157	731832	2449325
塔城地区	Tacheng [Tarbagatai] Administrative Offices	1315680	398708	916972
阿勒泰地区	Altay Administrative Offices	548207	127860	420347
博尔塔拉蒙古自治州	Bortala Mongol Autonomous Prefecture	1136561	302824	833737
巴音郭楞蒙古自治州	Bayangol Mongol Autonomous Prefecture	2171362	694764	1476598
阿克苏地区	Aksu Administrative Offices	1889428	952912	936516
克孜勒苏柯尔克孜自治州	Kizilsu Kirgiz Autonomous Prefecture	225132	52616	172516
喀什地区	Kashgar [Kaxgar] Administrative Offices	1158598	421833	736765
和田地区	Hotan Administrative Offices	786471	236130	550341
石河子市	Shihezi City	3187861	881847	2306014
阿拉尔市	Aral City	1029185	118588	910597
图木舒克市	Tumxuk City	789738	200582	589156
五家渠市	Wujiaqu City	1046773	100949	945824

14-8 建筑企业承包工程完成情况
Completion of Contracted Projects by Construction Enterprises

单位：万元 (10 000 yuan)

年 份 Year	地 区 Region	直接从建设单位承揽工程完成产值 Completed Output Value of Projects Contracted Directly from Investors	自行完成施工产值 Own-Completed Output Value	分包出去工程产值 Output Value Of Out-Sourced Projects	从建设单位以外承揽工程产值 Completed Output Value of Projects Contracted From Non-investors
	2002	3141928	3048086	93842	88171
	2003	3238170	3135725	102445	85777
	2004	3443802	3377532	66270	62436
	2005	3634746	3563947	70799	51727
	2006	3856300	3775975	80325	80248
	2007	4534324	4420958	113366	120068
	2008	6309803	6128312	181492	164251
	2009	7993048	7805261	187787	108507
	2010	9723428	9503630	219798	191111
	2011	13382657	13026735	355922	251577
	2012	16409068	16042803	366265	288258
	2013	21128364	20726750	401614	262137
	2014	23448958	23204836	244122	116371
	2015	23044581	22903385	141195	137289
乌鲁木齐市	Urumqi City	6364605	6313853	50752	82162
克拉玛依市	Karamay City	946107	867829	78278	12775
吐鲁番市	Turpan City	282713	281663	1050	3467
哈密地区	Hami [Kumul] Administrative Offices	648923	648923		160
昌吉回族自治州	Changji Hui Autonomous Prefecture	1374212	1373612	600	9677
伊犁哈萨克自治州	Ili Kazak Autonomous Prefecture	3762023	3761390	633	697
伊犁州直属县(市)	Counties (Cities) Direct Under Ili Prefecture	2396337	2396337		
塔城地区	Tacheng [Tarbagatai] Administrative Offices	954473	953840	633	697
阿勒泰地区	Altay Administrative Offices	411213	411213		
博尔塔拉蒙古自治州	Bortala Mongol Autonomous Prefecture	830649	830649		1367
巴音郭楞蒙古自治州	Bayangol Mongol Autonomous Prefecture	1719669	1718870	799	3643
阿克苏地区	Aksu Administrative Offices	1169175	1169175		733
克孜勒苏柯尔克孜自治州	Kizilsu Kirgiz Autonomous Prefecture	196784	196784		855
喀什地区	Kashgar [Kaxgar] Administrative Offices	742351	739507	2843	2951
和田地区	Hotan Administrative Offices	482401	482401		
石河子市	Shihezi City	2049411	2049411		12562
阿拉尔市	Aral City	948184	941944	6240	6240
图木舒克市	Tumxuk City	610196	610196		
五家渠市	Wujiaqu City	917178	917178		

14-9 建筑企业资产及资本金
Assets and Capital Principal of Construction Enterprises

单位：万元 (10 000 yuan)

年份 Year	地区 Region	资产合计 Total Assets	流动资产合计 Total of Circulating Funds	固定资产合计 Total of Fixed Assets	固定资产净值 Net Value of Fixed Assets	本年折旧 Depreciation in the Year	资本金合计 Total of Principal Value	#国家资本金 National Principal
1995		939205	647608	240076	225084	18463	221212	110987
2000		3256421	1855185	1215525	1106384	65383	892851	208214
2001		3740312	2187385	1243161	1048023	82884	1055531	227457
2002		4244587	2527414	1364782	1179599	95565	1327186	227601
2003		3375330	2292828	787690	675947	61335	835618	219826
2004		3810825	2632242	825567	722019	62725	929293	225884
2005		3818087	2665404	826376	700835	72103	936389	184447
2006		4115800	2952267	796558	712740	69191	985436	202670
2007		4611598	3387459	804007	706591	76979	1095997	222967
2008		5527993	4040796	958379	862286	91915	1408249	429579
2009		6565349	4966204	1080129	960338	103188	1528701	396188
2010		7906943	6141713	1078910	939519	99050	1585475	412634
2011		10577644	8275111	1395723	1176365	119913	1960348	1948237
2012		13091083	10327841	1462446	1200685	152195	2149972	2138479
2013		16337241	12804962	1656199	1373052	193299	3569213	3553059
2014		18158723	14735677	1643777	1406323	193047	3026862	3007719
2015		20719991	17085448	1745699	1374189	194348	3349629	3327636
乌鲁木齐市 Urumqi City		9352981	7435350	680262	561718	81440	1410639	1393368
克拉玛依市 Karamay City		1898506	1581855	118006	101824	15882	227351	224834
吐鲁番市 Turpan City		307137	261029	38888	32386	3598	63307	63307
哈密地区 Hami [Kumul] Administrative Offices		509559	449411	38575	33365	3276	89655	88295
昌吉回族自治州 Changji Hui Autonomous Prefecture		1206020	1015363	82614	57646	7659	283412	282637
伊犁哈萨克自治州 Ili Kazak Autonomous Prefecture		1777654	1464897	220623	190886	26133	337114	337085
伊犁州直属县(市) Counties (Cities) Direct Under Ili Prefecture		1149872	947598	156200	141187	19288	178960	178960
塔城地区 Tacheng [Tarbagatai] Administrative Offices		393297	345916	38266	24760	3213	92584	92584
阿勒泰地区 Altay Administrative Offices		234485	171383	26157	24939	3632	65570	65541
博尔塔拉蒙古自治州 Bortala Mongol Autonomous Prefecture		269697	210749	53268	37855	2340	79369	79369
巴音郭楞蒙古自治州 Bayangol Mongol Autonomous Prefecture		1004076	831207	112757	82152	8873	240659	240659
阿克苏地区 Aksu Administrative Offices		840754	697346	105811	60921	13021	157086	157086
克孜勒苏柯尔克孜自治州 Kizilsu Kirgiz Autonomous Prefecture		214964	185596	20176	17538	989	46840	46799
喀什地区 Kashgar [Kaxgar] Administrative Offices		728673	630330	72067	66299	6283	138323	138323
和田地区 Hotan Administrative Offices		215685	174752	24010	21250	3010	46731	46731
石河子市 Shihezi City		1278643	1151894	101317	67619	3966	143092	143092
阿拉尔市 Aral City		299835	251922	36138	30099	16244	30152	30152
图木舒克市 Tumxuk City		298093	254280	30641	7938	765	27465	27465
五家渠市 Wujiaqu City		517714	489467	10546	4693	869	28434	28434

14-10 建筑企业负债及所有者权益
Liabilities and Owner's Equity of Construction Enterprises

单位：万元 (10 000 yuan)

年份 Year	地区 Region	负债合计 Total Liabilities	所有者权益 Owners' Equity
1994		540403	192618
1995		699997	239208
1996		815330	324051
1997		1018007	350659
1998		1175839	385913
1999		1325825	415026
2000		2068439	1187982
2001		2300621	1439690
2002		2717728	1526859
2003		2327382	1047948
2004		2631252	1174864
2005		2651255	1159206
2006		2886203	1220298
2007		3240248	1359137
2008		3806899	1707855
2009		4553885	1996439
2010		5798936	2089888
2011		7857731	2707722
2012		9797466	3167556
2013		12275613	4018977
2014		13804129	4326661
2015		15646174	5039745
乌鲁木齐市	Urumqi City	7194627	2140144
克拉玛依市	Karamay City	1555291	329732
吐鲁番市	Turpan City	223124	84016
哈密地区	Hami [Kumul] Administrative Offices	381421	126815
昌吉回族自治州	Changji Hui Autonomous Prefecture	796173	408827
伊犁哈萨克自治州	Ili Kazak Autonomous Prefecture	1320407	457225
伊犁州直属县(市)	Counties (Cities) Direct Under Ili Prefecture	881778	268099
塔城地区	Tacheng [Tarbagatai] Administrative Offices	268334	124962
阿勒泰地区	Altay Administrative Offices	170295	64164
博尔塔拉蒙古自治州	Bortala Mongol Autonomous Prefecture	152787	116914
巴音郭楞蒙古自治州	Bayangol Mongol Autonomous Prefecture	625657	378421
阿克苏地区	Aksu Administrative Offices	551095	289662
克孜勒苏柯尔克孜自治州	Kizilsu Kirgiz Autonomous Prefecture	154911	60010
喀什地区	Kashgar [Kaxgar] Administrative Offices	505827	222852
和田地区	Hotan Administrative Offices	153190	62498
石河子市	Shihezi City	1079584	199064
阿拉尔市	Aral City	239418	60418
图木舒克市	Tumxuk City	259436	38659
五家渠市	Wujiaqu City	453226	64488

14-11 建筑企业总收入
Total Income of Construction Enterprises

单位：万元 (10 000 yuan)

年 份 Year	地 区 Region	企业总收入 Total Income of Enterprises	工程结算收入 Revenue of Project Settlement Accounts	#工程结算成本 Costs of Project Settlement Accounts	其他业务收入 Revenue from Other Business	#其他业务利润 Profits from Other Business
	1994	813369	714469	627830	98900	9332
	1995	898810	821713	713940	77097	9445
	1996	983170	904800	799183	78370	8765
	1997	1210813	1081666	950091	129147	17368
	1998	1454758	1346748	1193276	108010	19146
	1999	1595986	1500818	1320898	95167	14882
	2000	2659696	2514011	2252154	145686	30012
	2001	2961754	2807549	2521902	154205	34532
	2002	3360613	3199880	2854350	160733	30853
	2003	3221521	3090768	2716009	130753	21692
	2004	3395793	3276421	2900842	119372	21601
	2005	3685197	3566042	3202712	119155	23629
	2006	3766819	3643783	3255171	123036	20730
	2007	4584374	4431221	3983622	153154	22186
	2008	6382510	6225083	5635311	157427	33187
	2009	7958865	7788105	7074708	170760	39289
	2010	9849630	9610000	8752747	239630	46564
	2011	13467486	13201119	12045042	266367	39679
	2012	17359472	17075648	15598630	283824	64353
	2013	21758625	21427070	19539511	331555	25951
	2014	23526289	23230811	21130769	295478	22406
	2015	23127209	22796846	20782394	330359	14928
乌鲁木齐市	Urumqi City	7153539	7004486	6351574	149052	5044
克拉玛依市	Karamay City	1330573	1298713	1182151	31860	1273
吐鲁番市	Turpan City	328478	324327	291472	4151	692
哈密地区	Hami [Kumul] Administrative Offices	594178	592252	537112	1926	1735
昌吉回族自治州	Changji Hui Autonomous Prefecture	1294619	1265391	1121822	29227	239
伊犁哈萨克自治州	Ili Kazak Autonomous Prefecture	3697489	3668471	3412109	29017	2404
伊犁州直属县(市)	Counties (Cities) Direct Under Ili Prefecture	2415969	2393724	2249049	22244	2296
塔城地区	Tacheng [Tarbagatai] Administrative Offices	833037	827971	758293	5066	224
阿勒泰地区	Altay Administrative Offices	448483	446776	404767	1707	-115
博尔塔拉蒙古自治州	Bortala Mongol Autonomous Prefecture	799870	789680	719617	10189	30
巴音郭楞蒙古自治州	Bayangol Mongol Autonomous Prefecture	1781463	1772969	1614977	8493	1459
阿克苏地区	Aksu Administrative Offices	853887	853750	751670	137	119
克孜勒苏柯尔克孜自治州	Kizilsu Kirgiz Autonomous Prefecture	202693	194299	177898	8394	13
喀什地区	Kashgar [Kaxgar] Administrative Offices	908404	886104	789270	22299	895
和田地区	Hotan Administrative Offices	500845	470460	441425	30385	208
石河子市	Shihezi City	1357641	1353724	1252448	3916	383
阿拉尔市	Aral City	913102	913043	843031	59	49
图木舒克市	Tumxuk City	448801	447674	411033	1127	268
五家渠市	Wujiaqu City	961627	961502	884787	125	118

14-12 建筑企业亏损额及从业人数
Losses and Employed Persons of Construction Enterprises

(2015 年)

项 目	Item	企业数(个) Number of Enterprises (unit)	#亏损企业个数 Number of Losssuffering Enterprises	亏损企业亏损额(万元) Amount of Total Loss (10000 yuan)	计算劳动生产率的平均人数(人) Average Number of Staff for Calculation of Labour Productivity (person)	期末从业人数(人) Employees atYear- end (person)
总计	**Total**	**1256**	**371**	**72572**	**722777**	**353691**
#一、二级企业	First, Second Enterprises	556	134	44942	584153	253303
#国有及国有控股	State-owned and State-holding	189	23	9226	372262	139446
按登记注册类型分组	**Grouped by Registration Status**					
内资企业	Domestic Funede	1253	370	72569	722768	353682
国有企业	State-owned Enterprises	38	6	511	46528	29808
集体企业	Collective-owned Enterprises	15	4	1319	2843	1947
有限责任公司	Limited Liability Corporations	514	126	26556	468406	198509
国有独资公司	Sole State -funded Corporations	36	3	1667	48612	27290
其他有限责任公司	Other Limited Liability Corporations	478	123	24889	419794	171219
股份有限公司	Share-holding Corporations Ltd	13	3	1984	29773	11927
私营企业	Private Enterprises	672	230	41948	174965	111191
#私营独资企业	Private-funded Enterprises	2			55	35
私营有限责任公司	Private Limited Liability Corporations	664	228	41893	169513	109132
私营股份有限公司	Private share-holding Corporations Ltd	6	2	55	5397	2024
其他企业	Other Enterprises	1	1	251	253	300
港、澳、台商投资企业	Enterprises With Funds from Hong Kong, Macao , Taiwan and Foreign	2	1	3	4	4
#合资经营企业(港或澳、台资)	Joint-Venture	1			2	2
港、澳、台商独资经济企业	Enterprises With Funds from Hong Kong,Macao and Taiwan	1	1	3	2	2
外商投资企业	Foreign Funded Enterprises	1			5	5
中外合资经营企业	Joint-venture Enterprises	1			5	5
按国民经济行业分组	**Grouped by National Economic Sectors**					
房屋建筑业	Building	625	166	48989	527022	238435
土木工程建筑业	Civil Engineering	276	71	11465	141973	81664
铁路、道路、隧道和桥梁工程建筑业	Railways, Roads, Tunnels and Bridges	115	28	6895	56005	38806
水利和内河港口工程建筑业	Water Conservancy and Seaport	51	11	1197	58246	17261
工矿工程建筑业	Mining Project	26	11	666	8517	8368
架线和管道工程建筑业	Cabling and Piping Project	66	16	2550	17634	16264
其他土木工程建筑业	Other Civil Engineering	18	5	157	1571	965
建筑安装业	Construction and Installation	172	56	8069	22183	20578
建筑装饰和其他建筑业	Building Decoration and other Construction	183	78	4049	31599	13014
按隶属关系分组	**Grouped by Subordination**					
中 央	Central Government	87	9	4747	309477	96120
地 方	Local	1169	362	67825	413300	257571
按企业资质等级分组	**Grouped by Enterprise's Qualification**					
施工总承包	Undertaking Porjects	831	217	62196	646173	299054
特 级	Special Grade	4	1	625	15490	4722
一 级	First Grade	71	11	12312	266465	106598
二 级	Second Grade	319	62	27400	251199	118870
三级及以下	Third Grade	437	143	21859	113019	68864
专业承包	Specialized Undertaking	334	118	9298	38293	29640
一 级	First Grade	31	10	1711	11570	8511
二 级	Second Grade	84	34	2581	10964	7132
三级及以下	Third Grade	219	74	5006	15759	13997
劳务分包	Work Subcontractors	91	36	1078	38311	24997
一 级	First Grade	8	2	56	18892	3221
二 级	Second Grade	39	14	257	9573	4249
三级及以下	Third Grade	44	20	765	9846	17527

14-13 建筑企业工程施工情况

Condition of Building Works by Construction Enterprise

单位：万平方米 (10 000 sq.m)

年份 Year	地区 Region	房屋建筑施工面积 Floor Space of Buildings Under Construction	#本年新开工面积 New-opened Works for This Year	施工面积中实行投标承包面积 Space of Building and Contracting	房屋建筑竣工面积 Floor Space of Buildings Completed
	1995	1212.45	657.34	214.65	609.84
	1996	1207.45	673.17	397.83	645.89
	1997	1400.28	778.14	653.90	747.24
	1998	1662.36	1032.15	1023.88	879.67
	1999	1943.05	1068.05	1210.90	1042.51
	2000	2241.48	1448.34	1666.87	1261.42
	2001	2659.69	1679.41	2056.30	1467.54
	2002	2572.62	1489.38	2133.56	1469.59
	2003	2719.22	1735.19	2411.27	1450.80
	2004	2812.30	1791.50	2426.79	1483.35
	2005	2767.64	1639.80	2512.79	1429.36
	2006	2889.64	1854.91	2687.63	1645.02
	2007	3552.36	2421.17	3299.73	1849.64
	2008	4234.71	2862.31	3982.24	2155.98
	2009	5151.60	3560.54	4812.84	2517.79
	2010	6620.14	4449.78	6119.70	2891.45
	2011	8947.71	5796.89	8318.62	3465.49
	2012	11026.49	6247.32	9563.64	4553.97
	2013	13096.18	7550.88	11318.17	5775.28
	2014	14340.27	7647.42	13156.85	6115.37
	2015	12233.29	5583.87	10675.23	5247.30
乌鲁木齐市	Urumqi City	3684.68	984.10	3398.82	990.81
克拉玛依市	Karamay City	367.06	74.68	319.47	117.82
吐鲁番市	Turpan City	79.90	53.65	72.49	44.06
哈密地区	Hami [Kumul] Administrative Offices	475.14	253.98	439.12	206.09
昌吉回族自治州	Changji Hui Autonomous Prefecture	654.82	426.14	424.35	366.62
伊犁哈萨克自治州	Ili Kazak Autonomous Prefecture	1852.52	1032.94	1631.89	861.65
伊犁州直属县(市)	Counties (Cities) Direct Under Ili Prefecture	1076.67	573.52	949.37	448.78
塔城地区	Tacheng [Tarbagatai] Administrative Offices	503.15	265.69	454.06	282.64
阿勒泰地区	Altay Administrative Offices	272.70	193.73	228.46	130.23
博尔塔拉蒙古自治州	Bortala Mongol Autonomous Prefecture	398.20	178.33	343.28	194.08
巴音郭楞蒙古自治州	Bayangol Mongol Autonomous Prefecture	976.40	402.39	748.75	484.36
阿克苏地区	Aksu Administrative Offices	712.33	329.28	618.46	360.17
克孜勒苏柯尔克孜自治州	Kizilsu Kirgiz Autonomous Prefecture	135.72	80.10	96.72	58.54
喀什地区	Kashgar [Kaxgar] Administrative Offices	594.30	344.09	494.81	285.03
和田地区	Hotan Administrative Offices	289.10	179.50	252.49	195.40
石河子市	Shihezi City	1157.28	564.00	1021.71	472.77
阿拉尔市	Aral City	333.98	269.51	321.62	270.58
图木舒克市	Tumxuk City	211.63	137.57	207.69	177.25
五家渠市	Wujiaqu City	310.23	273.61	283.56	162.07

注：该表口径为总承包和专业承包企业，以下同。
Note: The data of the table refer to all general construction contractors and professional contractors (the same as in the following).

14-14 按登记注册类型分建筑企业工程施工情况

Condition of Building Works by Construction Enterprise by Registration Status

单位：万平方米 (2015 年) (10 000 sq.m)

项目	Item	房屋建筑施工面积 Floor Space of Buildings Under Construction	#本年新开工面积 New-opened Works for This Year	施工面积中实行投标承包面积 Space of Buildings and Contracting	房屋建筑竣工面积 Floor Space of Buildings Completed
总　计	**Total**	**12233.29**	**5583.87**	**10675.23**	**5247.18**
#一、二级企业	First, Second Enterprises	9890.00	4115.67	8988.37	4033.60
#国有及国有控股	State-owned and State-holding	6241.58	2384.54	5831.41	2380.23
按登记注册类型分组	**Grouped by Registration Status**				
内资企业	Domestic Funede	12233.29	5583.87	10675.23	5247.18
国有企业	State-owned Enterprises	739.24	351.27	735.10	283.45
集体企业	Collective-owned Enterprises	30.58	11.00	29.92	12.10
有限责任公司	Limited Liability Corporations	7942.93	3461.65	7063.26	3514.02
国有独资公司	Sole State -funded Corporations	966.16	478.71	944.21	423.73
其他有限责任公司	Other Limited Liability Corporations	6976.77	2982.94	6119.05	3090.29
股份有限公司	Share-holding Corporations Ltd	576.91	165.03	556.90	136.07
私营企业	Private Enterprises	2943.63	1594.92	2290.05	1301.54
私营有限责任公司	Private Limited Liability Corporations	2868.44	1579.96	2214.86	1276.13
私营股份有限公司	Private Share-holcling Corporations Ltd	75.19	14.96	75.19	25.41
按国民经济行业分组	**Grouped by National Economic Sectors**				
房屋工程建筑业	Building Construction	11530.87	5234.64	10072.08	4910.65
土木工程建筑业	Civil Engineering Construction	649.75	332.70	558.45	318.86
铁路、道路、隧道和桥梁工程建筑业	Railways, Roads, Tunnels and Bridges	225.80	148.03	199.71	110.58
水利和内河港口工程建筑业	Water Conservancy and Seaport	400.42	180.66	341.47	200.22
工矿工程建筑业	Mine Project	6.33	2.65	1.87	2.15
架线和管道工程建筑业	Cabling and Piping Project	15.30	1.26	15.30	4.09
其他土木工程建筑	Other Civil Engineering	1.90	0.10	0.10	1.82
建筑安装业	Construction and Installation	52.12	15.98	44.15	17.12
建筑装饰和其他建筑业	Others Construction	0.55	0.55	0.55	0.55
按隶属关系分组	**Grouped by Subordination**				
中　央	Central Government	4737.94	1679.92	4536.99	1824.32
地　方	Local	7495.35	3903.95	6138.24	3422.86
按企业资质等级分组	**Grouped by Enterprise's Qualification**				
施工总承包	Undertaking Porjects	11926.27	5539.93	10398.37	5165.54
特　级	Special Grade	490.49	105.67	487.37	143.00
一　级	First Grade	4905.88	1684.89	4567.97	1566.97
二　级	Second Grade	4233.24	2324.50	3675.30	2257.46
三级及以下	Third Grade	2296.66	1424.87	1667.73	1198.11
专业承包	Specialized Undertaking	307.02	43.94	276.86	81.64
一　级	First Grade	7.82	0.06	5.16	5.16
二　级	Second Grade	252.57	0.55	252.57	61.01
三级及以下	Third Grade	46.63	43.33	19.13	15.47

14-15 按登记注册类型分建筑企业竣工房屋建筑面积
Floor Space of Buildings Constructed of Construction Enterprises by Registration Status

单位：平方米　　(2015 年)　　(sq.m)

项　目	Item	合　计 Total	住宅用房 Residential Building	商业、居民服务业用房 Houses for Commercial and Residential Service	办公用房 Office Occupancy
总　计	**Total**	**52471821**	**33696358**	**5607999**	**3401958**
#一、二级企业	First, Second Enterprises	40336048	26848804	4059786	2274160
#国有及国有控股	State-owned and State-holding	23802289	16403054	2512319	986468
按登记注册类型分组	**Grouped by Registration Status**				
内资企业	Domestic Funede	52471821	33696358	5607999	3401958
#国有企业	State-owned Enterprises	2834483	2047720	180836	314842
集体企业	Collective-owned Enterprises	120974	64699	34019	5808
有限责任公司	Limited Liability Corporations	35140200	22523970	3844017	1839098
国有独资公司	Sole State -funded Corporations	4237324	2814666	656068	93840
其他有限责任公司	Other Limited Liability Corporations	30902876	19709304	3187949	1745258
股份有限公司	Share-holding Corporations Ltd	1360739	1125014	23063	59577
私营企业	Private Enterprises	13015425	7934955	1526064	1182633
#私营有限责任公司	Private Limited Liability Corporations	12761265	7774416	1526064	1182633
私营股份有限公司	Private Share-holcling Corporations Ltd	254160	160539		
按国民经济行业分组	**Grouped by National Economic Sectors**				
房屋工程建筑业	Building Construction	49106543	31816147	5314089	3210381
土木工程建筑业	Civil Engineering Construction	3188599	1810521	292898	185358
铁路、道路、隧道和桥梁工程建筑业	Railways, Roads, Tunnels and Bridges	1105790	554085	86827	57650
水利和内河港口工程建筑业	Water Conservancy and Seaport	2002178	1254033	206071	127308
工矿工程建筑业	Mine Project	21475	2403		400
架线和管道工程建筑业	Stringing and Pipeline Constrnction Project	40906			
其他土木工程建筑	Other Civil Engineering Construction	18250			
建筑安装业	Construction and Installation	171199	69690	1012	6219
建筑装饰和其他建筑业	Building Decoration and Other Construction	5480			
按隶属关系分组	**Grouped by Subordination**				
中　央	Central Government	18243217	12721129	2321217	475627
地　方	Local	34228604	20975229	3286782	2926331
按企业资质等级分组	**Grouped by Enterprise's Qualification**				
施工总承包	Undertaking Porjects	51655454	32918551	5607999	3401958
特　级	Special Grade	1430032	1006248	244886	25056
一　级	First Grade	15669725	11016964	1219799	1080929
二　级	Second Grade	22574553	14186182	2595101	1168175
三级及以下	Third Grade	11981144	6709157	1548213	1127798
专业承包	Specialized Undertaking	816367	777807		
一　级	First Grade	51617	51617		
二　级	Second Grade	610121	587793		
三级及以下	Third Grade	154629	138397		

14-15 续表 Continued

单位：平方米 (sq.m)

项目	Item	科研、教育、医疗用房 House for Science Medical and Education	文化、体育、娱乐用房 House for Culture and Sports and Entertainment	厂房及建筑物用房 House for Plant and Buildings	仓库 Warehouses	其他 Others
总计	**Total**	**3315887**	**658569**	**2360866**	**577993**	**2852191**
#一、二级企业	First, Second Enterprises	2683305	451964	1336270	436854	2244905
#国有及国有控股	State-owned and State-holding	918039	328137	997817	322497	1333958
按登记注册类型分组	**Grouped by Registration Status**					
内资企业	Domestic Funede	3315887	658569	2360866	577993	2852191
#国有企业	State-owned Enterprises	132731	20688	113638	2855	21173
集体企业	Collective-owned Enterprises	14903			1545	
有限责任公司	Limited Liability Corporations	2304011	511805	1519165	457650	2140484
国有独资公司	Sole State -funded Company	153569	48815	117208	96895	256263
其他有限责任公司	Other Limited Liability Companies	2150442	462990	1401957	360755	1884221
股份有限公司	Share-holding Corporations Ltd	3668	62104	73333		13980
私营企业	Private Enterprises	860574	63972	654730	115943	676554
#私营有限责任公司	Private Limited Liability Companies	831237	63972	628146	115943	638854
私营股份有限公司	Private Stock Limited Companies	29337		26584		37700
按国民经济行业分组	**Grouped by National Economic Sectors**					
房屋工程建筑业	Building	3091981	645897	1843009	473806	2711233
土木工程建筑业	Civil Engineering	171906	6444	476327	104187	140958
铁路、道路、隧道和桥梁工程建筑业	Railways, Roads, Tunnels and Bridges	91190	700	307528	700	7110
水利和内河港口工程建筑业	Water Conservancy and Seaport	51261	5494	120676	103487	133848
工矿工程建筑业	Mine Project	10775		7897		
架线和管道工程建筑业	Stringing and Pipeline Constrnction Project	18680		22226		
其他土木工程建筑	Other Civil Engineering Construction		250	18000		
建筑安装业	Construction and Installation	52000	6228	36050		
建筑装饰和其他建筑业	Building Decoration and Other Construction			5480		
按隶属关系分组	**Grouped by Subordination**					
中央	Central Government	711177	215156	723165	258480	817266
地方	Local	2604710	443413	1637701	319513	2034925
按企业资质等级分组	**Grouped by Enterprise's Qualification**					
施工总承包	Undertaking Porjects	3295057	658319	2343386	577993	2852191
特级	Special Grade	46960		89382	6800	10700
一级	First Grade	1085790	222889	478599	93708	471047
二级	Second Grade	1533707	229075	762809	336346	1763158
三级及以下	Third Grade	628600	206355	1012596	141139	607286
专业承包	Specialized Undertaking	20830	250	17480		
一级	First Grade					
二级	Second Grade	16848		5480		
三级及以下	Third Grade	3982	250	12000		

主要统计指标解释

建筑业统计单位 指从事房屋、构筑物建造和设备安装活动的法人企业。建筑业法人企业应具有建筑业资质并能够独立核算，同时还应具备以下条件：①依法成立，有自己的名称、组织机构和场所，能够承担民事责任；②独立拥有和使用资产，承担负债，有权与其他单位签订合同；③独立核算盈亏，能够编制资产负债表。

建筑业总产值 是以货币形式表现的建筑业企业在一定时期内生产的建筑业产品和提供服务的总和。建筑业总产值包括：

(1)建筑工程产值：指列入建筑工程预算内的各种工程价值。

(2)安装工程产值：指设备安装工程价值，不包括被安装设备本身价值。

(3)其他产值：建筑业总产值中除建筑工程、安装工程以外的产值。包括房屋构筑物修理产值、非标准设备制造产值、总包企业向分包企业收取的管理费以及不能明确划分的施工活动所完成的产值。

a.房屋构筑物修理产值：指房屋和构筑物修理所完成的产值，但不包括被修理房屋、构筑物本身价值和生产设备的修理价值。

b.非标准设备制造产值：指加工制造没有定型的非标准生产设备的加工费和原材料价值(如化工厂、炼油厂用的各种罐、槽，矿井生产统一使用的各种漏斗、三角槽、阀门等)以及附属加工厂为本企业承建工程制作的非标准设备的价值。

建筑业增加值 指建筑业企业在报告期内以货币形式表现的建筑业生产经营活动的最终成果。

从2004年第一次全国经济普查开始，建筑业现价增加值按生产法和分配法(收入法)两种方法计算，以收入法的计算结果为准，即从收入的角度出发，根据生产要素在生产过程中应得的收入份额计算。具体计算方法：经济普查年度建筑业增加值按照《经济普查年度GDP核算方案》计算，非经济普查年度建筑业增加值按照《非经济普查年度GDP核算方案》计算

房屋施工面积 指在报告期内施工的全部房屋建筑面积，包括本期新开工的房屋建筑面积、上期跨入本期继续施工的房屋建筑面积、上期停缓建在本期恢复施工的房屋建筑面积、本期竣工的房屋建筑面积及本期施工后又停缓建的房屋建筑面积。

房屋竣工面积 指在报告期内房屋建筑按照设计要求已全部完工，达到住人和使用条件，经验收鉴定合格或达到竣工验收标准，可正式移交使用单位的各栋房屋建筑面积的总和。

工程结算收入 指企业承包工程实现的工程价款结算收入，以及向发包单位收取的除工程价款以外的按规定列作营业收入的各种款项，如临时设施费、劳动保险费、施工机械调迁费等以及向发包单位收取的各种索赔款。

企业总收入 指与企业生产经营直接有关的各项收入，包括工程结算收入和其他业务收入。计算公式为：

企业总收入 = 工程结算收入 + 其他业务收入

Explanatory Notes on Main Statistical Indicators

Statistical Unit in the Construction Industry refers to a corporate enterprise engaged in the construction of buildings and structures and in the installation of equipment. A corporate construction enterprise should have qualification certificates with independent accounting system, and should meet the following 3 requirements: a) being set up in line with relevant legal basis, having its full name, organization and location, and capable of taking civil liabilities; b) independently possessing and using its assets and assuming its liabilities, and entitled to sign contracts with other institutions; and c) making independent accounts of its profits and losses, and capable of compiling its own balance sheet.

Gross Output Value of Construction refers to total of construction products and services, expressed in money terms, produced or rendered by construction and installation enterprises during a given period of time. It includes:

(1) Output value of construction projects: the value of projects covered by the project budgets;

(2) Output value of installation projects: the value of the installation of equipment, (excluding the value of the equipment to be installed);

(3) Other output values: the output value of construction industry apart from that of construction projects and installation projects. It includes: output value of repair of buildings and structures; output value of non-standard equipment manufacture-ing; overhead expenses received by contracted enterprises from the sub-contracted enterprises and the completed output value of construction activities for which there is no clear definition.

a. Output value of repair of buildings and structures: the value created through the repairs of buildings or structures. It does not include the value of buildings or structures being repaired and the value of the repair of production equipment;

b. Output value of manufactured non-standard equipment: the value of non-standard production equipment, including raw materials and manufacturing cost, made for the construction project (i.e., chemical plant; kettles or tanks used by refineries; various fillers, triangle tanks, valves used by mines). It also includes the output value of equipment manufactured by subsidiary workshops.

Value-added of Construction refers to the final result of the activities of production and operation of enterprises of the construction industry in monetary terms during the reference period.

Starting from the 2004 economic census, value-added of construction is calculated by both production approach and income approach, with the figures from the income approach as the final figures., Under the income approach,, calculation starts from the perspective of income and is based on the share of income derived from the production process by the relevant factors of production. Specifically, value-added of construction for the Census years is calculated in accordance with the *Programme of Compilation of GDP and National Accounts for the Year of Economic Census*, and value-added of construction for other years is calculated in accordance with the *Programme of Compilation of GDP and National Accounts for the Non Economic Census Years.*

Floor Space of Buildings refers to floor space of buildings under construction in the reference period, including the space of buildings for which construction has newly started; buildings for which construction has started earlier and is continuing during the reference period; and buildings for which construction has been suspended earlier but has restarted during the reference period; buildings completed during the reference period; and buildings under construction but construction has subsequently been during the reference period.

Floor Space of Buildings Completed refers to the total floor space of each building that has been completed in the reference period in accordance with the requirements of the design, up to the standard for being resided in and put into use, or has been checked and accepted by departments concerned as qualified ones or up to the standard of buildings completed and can be handed over for putting into use.

Income from Settlement of Projects refers to the income received by the construction enterprise from the contracted project through settlement procedures, and other charges to the contractoree as operational costs in addition to the value of the project, such as temporary facility fee,labour insurance premium, moving cost of construction equipment,as well as various types of claims to the contractee.

Total Revenue of Enterprises refers to the sum of income from production and operation of enterprises, including income from settlement of projects and other operational income, namely:

Total Revenue of Enterprises=Income from Settlement of Projects+Other Operational Incom

交通运输和邮政业

TRANSPORT, POSTAL AND TELECOMMUNICATION SERVICES

第十五篇　交通运输和邮政业

本篇主要内容和资料来源

本篇资料反映新疆维吾尔自治区交通运输业和邮政、电信业发展的基本状况。

运输业资料主要包括：铁路、公路、民航、管道四种运输方式的线路条数、里程、总运量及周转量、货物运输平均运距、铁路运输主要技术经济指标；民用机动车辆情况。

邮政、电信业资料主要包括：邮政、电信业务完成情况，邮政、电信业务发展水平等资料。

铁路资料来自乌鲁木齐铁路局；公路资料来自新疆维吾尔自治区公路局；民航运输数据资料来自中国南方航空股份有限公司新疆分公司；电信资料来自新疆维吾尔自治区通信管理局；邮政数据来自新疆维吾尔自治区邮政公司。

本篇资料由新疆维吾尔自治区统计局工业交通统计处收集整理。

Transport, Postal and Telecommunication Services

Main Content and Source of Data

Data in this chapter cover mainly the basic condition of the development of transportation, post and telecommunications in Xinjiang Uygur Autonomous Region.

Data on transport cover mainly the length of the routes of four means of railway, highways, civil aviation and pipeline. total fright traffic, total freight ton-kilometers, average transport distance of fright, principal economic and technical indicators of railway transport, possession of civil vehicles.

Data on post and telecommunication cover mainly the complete business volume of post and telecommunication services, and the development of the post and telecommunication service, etc.

Data on railways transportation come from the Urumqi Bureau of the Railway. Data on the highways come from the Bureau of Transportation. Data on the civil aviation transport come from the China Southwest Airlines, Xinjiang Branch. Data on telecommunication services come from telecommunication Bureau. Data on post are provided by the Post Bureau.

Data in this chapter are collected and compiled by the Division of Industry and Transport Statistics, Xinjiang Bureau of Statistics.

15-1 主要年份运输业基本情况
Basic Conditions of Transport in Main Years

指 标	Item	2000	2010	2015
运输线路长度(公里)	**Length of Transport Routes (km)**			
铁路营业里程	Railways in Operation	3010	4393	6165
公路里程	Highways	80875	152843	178263
民用航线里程	Total Civil Aviation Routes	152941	176992	209300
管道输油(气)里程	Petroleum and Gas Pipelines	2696	11464	13050
客运量(万人)	**Total Passenger Traffic (10 000 persons)**	**23191**	**46346**	**35824**
铁 路	Railways	1147	1523	2751
公 路	Highways	21877	44333	32310
民用航空	Civil Aviation	167	490	763
旅客周转量(亿人公里)	**Total Passenger-Kilometers (100 million passenger-km)**	**292.80**	**670.75**	**645.52**
铁 路	Railways	97.40	170.10	252.46
公 路	Highways	158.20	404.00	241.57
民用航空	Civil Aviation	37.20	96.65	151.49
货运量(万吨)	**Total Freight Traffic (10 000 tons)**	**33090.50**	**64596.70**	**80190.60**
铁 路	Railways	4199.00	6853.00	6234.00
公 路	Highways	27048.00	50448.00	64505.00
民用航空	Civil Aviation	3.50	3.70	6.60
输油(气)管道	Petroleum and Gas Pipelines	1840.00	7292.00	9445.00
货物周转量(亿吨公里)	**Total Freight Ton-kilometers (100 million ton-km)**	**660.88**	**2053.82**	**2605.46**
铁 路	Railways	355.00	814.03	819.04
公 路	Highways	272.90	767.14	1060.46
民用航空	Civil Aviation	0.98	0.98	1.66
输油(气)管道	Petroleum and Gas Pipelines	32.00	471.67	724.30
民用汽车拥有量(万辆)	**Possession of Civil Motor Vehicles (10 000 units)**	**37.00**	**135.90**	**298.26**
#载客汽车辆数	Buses and Cars	18.00	87.60	232.10
载货汽车辆数	Trucks	17.50	37.00	58.64
#私人汽车拥有量	Privat Vehicles	13.90	85.80	234.52

注：1.2000 年以后公路里程包括兵团数据。2.2006 年起新疆公路通车里程包含村道里程(以下同)。
Note: a) Since 2000 the highway mileage cover the data of XJPCC. b) Length of highways include the village road since 2006 (the same as in the following table).

15-2 主要年份运输线路长度
Length of Transport Routes in Main Years

单位:公里 (km)

年 份 Year	铁路营业里程 Length of Railways in Operation	#新疆境内 Inside Xinjiang	公 路 Length of Highways	#有铺装和简易铺装路(高级次高级路面) Simple Pavement and Pavement Roads	民用航空 Length of the Civil Aviation	#新疆境内 Inside Xinjiang	管道输油(气)里程 Petroleurn and Gas Pipelines
1978	1031	796	23818	5810	4783	4783	443
1980	1103	868	21148	6390	4412	4412	443
1985	1579	1344	22232	8369	4527	4527	473
1990	1578	1343	25425	12566	36465	5159	740
1995	2038	1803	30298	19013	69789	6693	875
1996	2038	1803	31609	20461	122089	9183	928
1997	2038	1803	32053	21495	123664	9717	1373
1998	2038	1803	32762	22485	150473	9717	1955
1999	3008	2780	33484	23214	141872	9719	2496
2000	3010	2775	80875	31059	152941	9719	2696
2001	3010	2774	80947	31635	161814	9719	2965
2002	3010	2775	82929	32541	132483	9898	3153
2003	3009	2775	83633	33891	141456	9898	3008
2004	2999	2763	86824	40679	111768	8664	3003
2005	2925	2761	89531	43803	119481	8664	3003
2006	2925	2761	143736	50119	138564	9064	4631
2007	2925	2761	145219	55080	160354	11363	6793
2008	2925	2925	146652	60233	147753	10560	9455
2009	3837	3673	150683	67684	152392	10754	11235
2010	4393	4228	152843	72887	176992	9939	11464
2011	4480	4316	155150	80974	175797	9939	11077
2012	4914	4315	165909	92456	179054	11727	12843
2013	4911	4741	170154	99887	226089	11721	11666
2014	5760	5463	175468	106378	211827	7782	12367
2015	6165	5868	178263	113455	209300	10329	13050

15-3 主要年份运输线路质量
Quality of Transport Routes in Main Years

单位：公里 (km)

指 标	Item	1995	2000	2010	2015
铁路营业里程	Length of Railways in Operation	2038	3010	4393	5868
#复线里程	Double-Tracking Length		986	1324	2759
#自动闭塞里程	Automatic Blocking Length	273	685	1408	3246
公路线路里程	Length of Highways	30298	80875	152843	178263
#水泥沥青路面	Lenth of bituminous Pavement	27982	33035	72887	113455

15-4 主要年份客运量及周转量
Passenger Traffic and Passenger kilometers in Main Years

年 份 Year	客运量(万人) Passenger Traffic (10 000 persons)				旅客周转量(亿人公里) Passenger-Kilometers (100 million passenger-km)			
	总 计 Total	铁 路 Railways	公 路 Highways	民用航空 Civil Aviation	总 计 Total	铁 路 Railways	公 路 Highways	民用航空 Civil Aviation
1978	941	148	786	7	25.23	13.72	10.96	0.55
1980	1356	193	1152	10	30.49	18.83	10.83	0.83
1985	3728	320	3399	9	63.16	33.16	29.13	0.87
1986	4058	362	3674	22	73.87	36.40	34.00	3.74
1987	4439	377	4327	34	83.67	37.14	39.44	7.09
1988	5205	459	4698	48	99.17	42.86	46.35	9.96
1989	8740	453	8240	47	120.69	44.52	66.37	9.80
1990	9602	388	9161	53	103.80	37.96	55.11	10.73
1991	14582	383	14142	56	122.08	41.94	68.05	12.09
1992	14997	425	14490	82	138.24	44.48	75.38	18.38
1993	16352	513	15749	90	174.23	50.04	103.51	20.73
1994	17181	670	16405	106	195.58	58.08	112.50	25.00
1995	17533	672	16739	122	204.89	58.00	117.17	29.68
1996	18858	610	18110	138	218.79	57.80	128.58	32.20
1997	20237	748	19360	129	233.39	64.70	139.00	29.69
1998	21747	878	20735	134	256.90	76.90	149.60	30.40
1999	22763	1000	21618	145	270.74	81.90	157.05	31.79
2000	23191	1147	21877	167	292.80	97.40	158.20	37.20
2001	24344	932	23255	157	309.70	104.10	170.30	35.30
2002	26016	950	24883	183	330.80	106.00	185.60	39.20
2003	26972	879	25878	215	342.00	106.10	195.00	40.90
2004	29782	1023	28473	286	423.80	121.90	249.00	52.90
2005	33220	1134	31747	339	457.42	125.20	271.20	61.02
2006	34471	1272	32835	364	498.30	138.90	292.10	67.30
2007	38434	1873	36159	402	548.10	144.46	326.70	76.94
2008	42111	1311	40392	408	594.60	149.89	363.60	81.11
2009	43410	1371	41604	435	614.66	152.90	376.30	85.46
2010	46346	1523	44333	490	670.75	170.10	404.00	96.65
2011	50461	2002	47927	532	758.26	216.16	437.90	104.16
2012	55298	2162	52473	663	849.25	236.72	478.50	134.03
2013	59024	2318	56000	706	895.50	250.83	499.40	145.27
2014	55880	2355	52798	727	849.80	245.60	458.70	145.50
2015	35824	2751	32310	763	645.52	252.46	241.57	151.49

注：2015 年民航旅客吞吐量为 2536 万人。
Note: Air passenger handling capacity was25.36million persons in 2015.

15-5 主要年份货运量及货物周转量
Freight Traffic and Ton-kilometers in Main Years

年份 Year	货运量(万吨) Freight Traffic (10 000 tons)				
	总计 Total	铁路 Railways	公路 Highways	民用航空 Civil Aviation	输油(气)管道 Petroleum and Gas Pipelines
1978	6064.12	923	4843	0.12	298
1980	8422.16	884	7209	0.16	329
1990	13919.87	1691	11551	0.87	677
1995	25406.00	2733	21754	2.00	917
2000	33090.50	4199	27048	3.50	1840
2001	33589.00	3904	27751	2.00	1932
2002	34966.70	4121	28861	2.70	1982
2003	37485.20	4602	30881	2.20	2000
2004	38885.50	5083	31700	2.50	2100
2005	40600.20	5397	33000	3.20	2200
2006	43096.40	6001	34835	3.40	2256
2007	49009.62	7430	38427	3.62	3149
2008	57187.80	6120	44987	3.80	6077
2009	60162.80	6413	46787	3.80	6959
2010	64596.70	6853	50448	3.70	7292
2011	70361.90	6904	55965	3.90	7489
2012	78248.80	6933	61850	5.80	9460
2013	83716.66	7399	68528	6.66	7783
2014	90249.16	7529	74432	7.16	8281
2015	80190.60	6234	64505	6.60	9445

年份 Year	货物周转量(亿吨公里) Freight Ton-kilometers (100 million ton-km)				
	总计 Total	铁路 Railways	公路 Highways	民用航空(万吨公里) Civil Aviation (10 000 ton-km)	输油(气)管道 Petroleum and Gas Pipelines
1978	106.96	67.76	32.06	98.10	7.13
1980	121.14	67.27	45.89	137.80	7.97
1990	262.29	141.16	108.09	2048.00	12.84
1995	474.39	240.88	219.72	5744.00	13.22
2000	660.88	355.00	272.90	9776.00	32.00
2001	714.43	403.90	275.90	6300.00	34.00
2002	759.62	425.30	298.00	8238.00	35.50
2003	837.04	475.00	325.00	6400.00	36.40
2004	947.24	548.50	361.00	7400.00	37.00
2005	1032.75	586.90	405.00	8500.00	40.00
2006	1143.31	647.10	425.68	8921.00	69.64
2007	1264.31	678.53	468.80	9085.78	116.07
2008	1656.88	758.74	672.30	9285.43	224.91
2009	1815.81	751.09	705.90	9700.00	357.85
2010	2053.82	814.03	767.14	9837.00	471.67
2011	2199.52	857.01	852.17	9700.00	488.38
2012	2558.68	910.58	946.90	14400.00	699.76
2013	2490.29	996.71	1055.20	15999.00	436.78
2014	2777.28	970.46	1156.40	17284.60	648.69
2015	2605.46	819.04	1060.46	16598.62	724.30

15-6 主要年份货物运输平均运距
Average Transport Distance of Freight in Main Years

单位：公里 (km)

年 份 Year	合 计 Total	铁 路 Railways	公 路 Highways	民用航空 Civil Aviation	输油(气)管道 Petroleum and Gas Pipelines
1978	168	565	66	818	239
1980	139	566	64	861	242
1985	158	624	69	945	206
1990	188	835	94	2354	190
1995	187	881	101	2872	144
2000	200	845	101	2857	174
2001	211	1023	99	3150	176
2002	217	1032	103	3051	179
2003	224	865	105	2909	182
2004	244	904	114	2960	176
2005	254	901	122	2656	182
2006	265	894	122	2598	308
2007	257	913	122	2528	368
2008	289	926	149	2456	370
2009	301	873	151	2552	518
2010	317	934	152	2637	514
2011	312	935	152	2480	652
2012	327	945	153	2486	646
2013	297	958	154	2616	561
2014	308	943	152	2530	783
2015	325	933	164	2518	767

15-7 主要年份铁路运输主要财务指标
Main Financial Indicators of Railway Transport in Main Years

单位：万元 (10 000 yuan)

指 标	Item	1990	1995	2000	2010	2015
运输总收入	**Total Transport Revenue**	**86686**	**192555**	**509480**	**1926749**	**2630143**
旅客票价收入	Passenger Fares	18763	33560	82121	234979	473431
货物运费收入	Freight Revenue	62516	142168	318485	1197619	1581890
运输清算收入	**Transportation Claring Revenue**	**59765**		**467142**	**1311275**	**2293527**
运输总支出	**Toatl Transport Expenditure**	**51875**	**193693**	**418497**	**1552877**	**21974394**
#工 资	Wages and Salaries	11163	38429	98293	238570	4754017
材 料	Materials	6702	23183	36210	79181	914953
燃 料	Fuel	9308	32996	74487	340960	649742
电 力	Electricity	666	2433	4701	8022	1286972
折 旧	Depreciation	17174	13137	60859	127368	3522811
营业外收支净额	**Non-operating Net Revenue or Expenditure**	**6886**	**14503**	**23236**	**-21947**	**10413**
实现利润	**Profits**	**6291**	**-12591**	**34130**	**-273121**	**-286929**
#运输利润	Transport Profits	5501	-11649	33195	-266910	-52516

注：运输总收入、旅客票价收入、货物运费收入是运送到全国范围的客、货运输收入。
Note: Revenue from transport,passenger traffic and freight traffic refer to revenue from transport to allover China.

15-8 铁路运输技术经济主要指标
Main Technical and Economic Indicators of Railway Transport

指　　标	Item	2014	2015
货运机车日产量(万吨公里)	Average Daily Ton-kilometers of Freight Locomotives (10 000 ton-km)	146.1	154.5
#内燃机车	Diesel Locomotives	65.2	68.4
货运列车平均总重(吨)	Average Total Tonnage of Freight Locomotives (ton)	2933	2897
#内燃机车	Diesel Locomotives	2219	2133
货运机车日车公里(公里)	Daily Distance per Freight Locomotive (km)	603	613
客运机车日车公里(公里)	Daily Distance per Passenger Locomotive (km)	910	1043
内燃机车每万吨公里耗油(公斤)	Oil Consumption of Diesel Locomotives (kg/10 000 ton-km)	41.4	33.0
货物列车出发正点率(%)	Punctuality Rate of Freight Trains at Departure (%)	98.5	98.7
货物列车运行正点率(%)	Punctuality Rate of Freight Trains in Running (%)	98.4	98.6
旅客列车出发正点率(%)	Punctuality Rate of Passenger Trains at Departure (%)	99.5	99.7
旅客列车运行正点率(%)	Punctuality Rate of Passenger Trains in Running (%)	98.0	99.3
旅客列车技术速度(公里/小时)	Technical Speed of Passenger Trains (km/hr)	79.4	86.3
旅客列车旅行速度(公里/小时)	Travelling Speed of Passenger Trains (km/hr)	69.6	75.3
客运密度(万人公里/公里)	Density of Passenger Transport (10 000 passenger-km/km)	493.9	518.5
货物列车技术速度(公里/小时)	Technical Speed of Freight Trains (km/hr)	54.0	56.2
货物列车旅行速度(公里/小时)	Running Speed of Freight Trains (km/hr)	42.5	44.8
货运密度(万吨公里/公里)	Density of Freight Transport (10 000 ton-km/km)	2014.7	1280.2
货车周转时间(天)	Turning Around Time of Freight Cars (day)	4.2	4.2
一次货物作业时间(小时)	Handling Time of Freight (hour)	15.5	15.1
货车中转停留时间(小时)	Transfer Waiting Time per Car (hour)	2.9	3.0
货车静载重(准轨) (吨)	Static Load of Freight Cars (Standard Gauge) (ton)	58.6	57.5

15-9 民用车辆拥有量
Number of Civil Vehicles

单位：辆 (unit)

指　　标	Item	2014		2015	
		总　计 Total	#私　人 Private	总　计 Total	#私　人 Private
民用汽车	**Civil Vehicles**	**2772748**	**2086209**	**2982553**	**2345241**
载客汽车	Passenger Vehicles	2078924	1769976	2320981	2031122
大　型	Large	32042	1539	29695	1056
中　型	Medium	32545	10982	28400	8517
小　型	Small	1982633	1728093	2234542	1995047
微　型	Minicar	31704	29362	28344	26502
载货汽车	Trucks	605535	276246	586351	282192
重　型	Large	167503	15623	154612	14394
中　型	Medium	48701	12634	42202	11466
轻　型	Light	387105	246256	387659	254865
微　型	Mini	2226	1733	1878	1467
其它汽车	Others	88289	39987	75221	31927

15-10 主要年份邮电事业情况
Basic Conditions of Postal and Telecommunication Services in Main Years

指 标	Item	2000	2010	2015
邮政局营业网点(处)	**Number of Post Offices (unit)**		**1276**	**1525**
邮路长度(单程)(公里)	**Length of Postal Routes (km)**	**134109**	**75571**	**71432**
#农 村	Rural	55852	18238	19305
邮政业务总量(万元)	**Business Volume of Postal Services(10 000 yuan)**	**59370**	**165794**	**222501**
电信业务总量(万元)	**Business Volume of Telecommunication Services (10 000 yuan)**	**413630**	**5654665**	**3797773**
函件(万件)	Number of Letters (10 000 pieces)	7148	2926	2049
包件(万件)	Number of Parcels (10 000 pieces)	163	174	164
快递(万件)	Pieces of Express Mail Services (10 000 pieces)	124	487	7051
报刊期发数(万份)	Issue of Newspapers and Magazines Circulation (10 000 copies)	535	307	350
长途电话(万分钟)	Length of Long-distance Calls (10 000 minutes)	34712	105001	1111967
固定电话年末用户(万户)	Number of Fixed Telephone Subscribers at Year-end (10 000 subscribers)	191.0	547.5	523.6
城市电话年末数	Number Urban Telephone Subscribers at Year-end	136.3	395.8	396.2
乡村电话年末数	Number of Rural Telephones Subscribers at Year-end	54.7	132.1	105.4
移动电话年末用户(万户)	Number of Mobile Telephones Subscribers at Year-end (10 000 subscribers)	78.0	1359.8	2067.2
长途电信线路	**Telecommunication Lines**			
光缆线路长度(公里)	Length of Long Distance Optical Cable Lines (km)	10828	259307	611570
邮电通信设备	**Telecommunication Facilities**			
固定长途交换机容量(路端)	Capacity of long-distance Telephone Exchanges (circuit)	102540	315982	27930
本地电话局用交换机容量(万门)	Capacity of Local Office Telephone Exchange (10 000 line)	241.7	928.2	453.9
邮电通信水平	**Level of Postal and Telecommunication Services**			
平均每百人每年发函件数(件)	Annual Arerage Number of Letters Mailed Per 100 persons (piece)	387	122	88
平均每百人每年订报刊数(份)	Annual Arerage Number of Newspaper Subscribed Per 100 Persons (piece)	28.9	12.6	14.9
平均每百人拥有电话机数(固定) (部)	Number of Fixed Telephone Sets Owned per 100 Persons(stable) (set)	15.0	25.4	22.8
平均每百人拥有电话机数(移动) (部)	Number of Mobile Telephone Sets Owned per 100 Persons (mobile) (set)		63.0	89.9
农村邮电通信水平	**Rural Level**			
通电话的乡(镇)比重(%)	Percentage of Townships with Telephone Communication (%)	100	100	100

15-11 主要年份邮电业务情况
Conditions of Postal and Telecommunication Services in Main Years

年份 Year	邮政业务总量(万元) Business Volume of Postal Services (10000 yuan)	电信业务总量(万元) Business Volume of Telecommunication Services (10000 yuan)	函件(万件) Number of Letters (10 000 pieces)	快递(万件) Pieces of Express Mail Services (10 000 pieces)	报刊期发数(万份) Issue of Newspapers and Magazines (10 000 copies)	集邮业务(万枚) Stamps for Collection (10 000 pieces)
1978			4842.7		223.8	
1980			5890.8		329.6	
1985			7032.6		578.9	
1990	8203	8312	7380.5	…	805.7	1034.5
1995	17322	71220	9041.8	93.6	478.1	3086.6
2000	59370	413630	7148.0	124.0	534.5	5766.0
2001	62265	572073	5601.0	147.0	358.0	5491.0
2002	68032	878968	6814.0	163.0	399.0	4620.0
2003	72007	1072831	5987.0	199.0	587.3	3112.8
2004	74835	1457000	4756.7	238.1	283.0	3141.3
2005	80500	1643259	4450.0	266.0	293.0	2072.0
2006	94188	2195000	4129.8	291.0	341.7	2205.1
2007	100498	2936000	3177.0	324.0	305.0	2134.0
2008	113802	3673709	2900.0	362.0	296.0	2335.0
2009	133535	4663000	2800.0	412.0	296.0	2520.0
2010	165794	5654665	2926.0	487.0	307.0	2672.0
2011	138398	2126602	3202.4	579.0	296.4	2306.8
2012	181720	2466653	2529.0	583.0	310.0	2253.5
2013	187804	2681682	2041.0	5092.0	353.0	2795.4
2014	202280	3290297	1907.8	5940.5	357.6	2531.0
2015	222501	3797773	2049.0	7050.7	349.6	2856.7

年份 Year	长途电话(万分钟) Length of Long-distance Calls (10 000 minutes)	移动电话用户(万户) Number of Mobile Telephone Subscribers (10 000 subscribers)	国际互联网络用户(万户) Number of Subscribers of Internet Services (10 000 subscribers)	固定电话年末用户(万户) Number of Subscribers of Fnixed Telephone at Year-end (10 000 subscribers)	城市电话用户 Urban Fixed Telephone Subscribers	乡村电话用户 Rural Fixed Telephone Subscribers
1978	258.8			2.9	1.9	1.1
1980	276.5			3.2	2.1	1.0
1985	425.1			4.7	3.7	1.0
1990	762.5			8.9	7.9	1.1
1995	11705.9	2.7		44.6	42.0	2.6
2000	34712.0	78.0		191.0	136.3	54.7
2001	89844.0	180.9	12.8	262.6	196.1	66.5
2002	45769.0	297.0	17.3	337.5	238.3	79.5
2003	35554.2	421.2	60.8	431.0	293.9	93.5
2004	62526.0	489.7	78.0	516.7	387.0	108.2
2005	52482.0	531.3	105.8	612.2	457.5	135.2
2006	46478.0	671.1	123.7	706.9	533.6	154.5
2007	67660.0	808.3	157.8	678.1	520.6	157.5
2008	42550.0	1051.3	142.8	634.9	462.2	150.0
2009	48816.0	1119.6	133.7	573.1	409.6	140.8
2010	105001.0	1359.8	161.1	547.5	395.8	132.1
2011	91298.0	1670.9	208.8	540.5	390.8	127.5
2012	14024.8	2008.5	255.0	540.1	391.0	126.9
2013	1246123.0	2133.9	293.0	544.8	393.6	125.1
2014	1259238.0	2077.7	305.7	535.4	391.8	121.4
2015	1111967.0	2067.2	322.6	523.6	396.2	105.4

注：从 1997 年起，市内电话户数统计口径有了较大调整，故农村电话户数增幅较大。

Note: Since 1997, greater adjustment has been made on the Statistic Method about the number of telephone subscribers and the number of rural subscribers has gone up by a bigger margin.

主要统计指标解释

铁路营业里程 又称营业长度，指投入客货运输营业或临时营业的线路长度。

铁路自动、半自动闭塞里程 为保证列车安全运行，在一个区间、同一时间内，一般只允许一列列车运行，这种保证列车在这个区间安全间隔运行的技术方法称为“闭塞”。自动闭塞是根据列车运行及有关闭塞分区状态，自动变换通过信号机显示而司机凭信号显示行车的闭塞方法，采用此方式的闭塞公里为自动闭塞里程。半自动闭塞是由人工办理闭塞手续，列车凭信号显示发车后，出站信号机自动关机闭塞，靠车站值班员确认列车整列到达，办理区间闭塞复原的一种闭塞方式，采用此方式的闭塞公里为半自动闭塞里程。

公路里程 指报告期末公路的实际长度。统计范围：包括城间、城乡间、乡（村）间能行驶汽车的公共道路，公路通过城镇街道的里程，公路桥梁长度、隧道长度、渡口宽度。不包括城市街道里程，断头路里程，农（林）业生产用道路里程，工（矿）企业等内部道路里程。统计原则：按已竣工验收或交付使用的实际里程计算；两条或多条公路共同经由同一路段的重复里程，只计算一次。

定期航班航线里程 指定期航班营运里程的总长度，以万公里为计算单位。航线里程的统计分为按重复距离计算和按不重复距离计算两种形式。“按重复距离计算”是指不同航线的相同航段距离可以重复累加；“按不重复距离计算”则不同航线相同航段只统计一次。

管道输油(气)里程 指油、气、成品油等各类介质实际输送距离，是反映运输管线长度的指标，也是计算周转量的依据。对于有复线和备用线的地段，原则上按单线计算管输里程。双线同时输送又不能分开计量的情况下，管输里程为双线长度之和除以 2。

货(客)运量 指在一定时期内，各种运输工具实际运送的货物重量(旅客数量)。该指标是反映运输业为国民经济和人民生活服务的数量指标，也是制定和检查运输生产计划、研究运输发展规模和速度的重要指标。货运按吨计算，客运按人计算。货物不论运输距离长短、货物类别，均按实际重量统计。旅客不论行程远近或票价多少，均按一人一次客运量统计；半价票、小孩票也按一人统计。

货物(旅客)周转量 指在一定时期内，由各种运输工具运送的货物(旅客)数量与其相应运输距离的乘积之总和。该指标可以反映运输业生产的总成果，也是编制和检查运输生产计划，计算运输效率、劳动生产率以及核算运输单位成本的主要基础资料。计算货物周转量通常按发出站与到达站之间的最短距离，也就是计费距离计算。计算公式为：

货物(旅客)周转量=∑（货物（旅客）运输量×运输距离）

铁路货车平均静载重 **指货物在装车时的静止装载重量。**计算公式为：

货车平均静载重=货物发送吨数/装车数

铁路货运机车日产量 指在一定时期内，平均每台货运机车在一昼夜内所完成的总重吨公里数，包括载运货物的重量和车辆本身的自重。该指标从时间和牵引能力两方面反映了机车运用效率。计算公式为：

货运机车平均日产量=货运总重吨公里数/货运机车台日数

民用汽车拥有量 指报告期末，在公安交通管理部门按照《机动车注册登记工作规范》，已注册登记领有民用车辆牌照的全部汽车数量。汽车拥有量统计的主要分类：根据汽车结构分为载客汽车、载货汽车及其他汽车；根据汽车所有者不同分为个人(私人)汽车、单位汽车；根据汽车的使用性质分为营运汽车、非营运汽车；根据汽车大小规格不同，载客汽车分为大型、中型、小型和微型，载货汽车分为重型、中型、轻型和微型。

邮电业务总量 邮电业务总量 指以货币形式表现的邮电企业为社会提供各类邮电通信服务的总数量。该指标是用于观察邮电业务发展变化总趋势的综合性总量指标，分别按邮政业务总量和电信业务总量统计。邮电业务总量是以各类业务的实物量分别乘以相应的不变单价，求出各类业务的货币量加总求得。不变单价是一定时期内计算业务总量的同度量因素，是根据基年各类邮电业务量与相对应的邮电业务收入测算的平均单价。

移动电话用户 指在电信运营企业营业网点办理开户登记手续，通过移动电话交换机进入移动电话网，占用移动电话号码的各类电话用户。包括各类签约用户、智能网预付费用户、无线上网卡用户。

互联网上网人数　指过去半年内使用过互联网的6周岁及以上中国居民人数。

固定电话用户　指在电信企业营业网点办理开户登记手续并已接入固定电话网上的全部电话用户。包括普通电话用户、无线市话用户、公用电话用户、窄带综合业务数字网（N—ISDN）用户、智能网专用接入终端用户等。

城市电话用户　指按行政区划属于中央直辖市、省辖市、地级市、县级市的市区、市郊区及县城区范围内的电话用户数。包括分布在农村地区但以县团级以上建制的独立工矿区、林区、驻军的电话用户。

农村电话用户　指按行政区划属于城市范围以外的乡（镇）、村电话用户。

住宅电话用户　指私人付费或安装在居民住宅并按照私人或住宅电话用户登记注册和收费的各类电话用户。

长途电话交换机容量　指电信企业用于接入长途电话网的电话交换机的设备额定容量。

局用交换机容量　指安装在电信运营企业内用于接续本地固定电话的电话交换机容量，包括接入网设备容量（安装在电信运营企业用于连接语音用户的远端节点的设备容量）。

移动电话交换机容量　指移动电话交换机根据一定话务模型和交换机处理能力计算出来的最大同时服务用户的数量。按报告期末已割接入网正式投入使用的设备实际容量统计。

互联网宽带接入端口　指用于接入互联网用户的各类实际安装运行的接入端口的数量，包括xDSL用户接入端口、LAN 接入端口、其他类型接入端口等，不包括窄带拨号接入端口。

Explanatory Notes on Main Statistical Indicators

Length of Railways in Operation refers to the total length of the trunk line for passenger and freight transportation in full operation or temporary operation.

Length of Automatic-blocking and Semi- automatic-blocking Railways Blocking is a spacing technique by which a section of the railway only allows one train to pass at a time with the aim of ensuring traffic safety. Automatic-blocking is the blocking method that signal display transforms automatically based on the state of train operation and related block partition, while the driver operates according to the signal display. The section which is blocked using the above method is called as length of automatic-blocking railways. Semi-blocking is realized manually. After the train departs based on signal display, the departure signal machine will perform automatic shutdown blocking, while the station attendant will conduct restoration of section blocking with arrival confirmation of the entire train. The section which is blocked using the above method is called as length of semi-automatic-blocking railways.

Length of Highways refers to the actual length of highways at the end of reference period. It covers public roads running vehicles among cities, city and rural areas, township (villages), highways passing through streets at small cities and towns, length of bridges and tunnels, width of ferry piers. It does not include the length of streets in cities, dead end highways, the length of streets built for agricultural (forest) production and inside factories (mines). It can only be calculated with the actual mileage having been completed, checked and accepted or put into operation. If two or more highways go the same section of the way, the length of the section is only calculated for once.

Length of Routes with Scheduled Flights refers to the total length of all routes for scheduled flights, which is calculated using million kilometres as the unit. There are usually two ways to calculate the route length: duplicated calculation and non-duplicated calculation. Duplicated calculation means that the same segment of different routes can be added duplicately, while the non-duplicated calculation allows the same segment of different routes be counted once only.

Length of Oil (Gas) Pipelines refers to the actual transport distance of oil, gas and oil products, an indicator reflecting the length of transportation routes and a reference to calculate the freight-kilometers. For those sections with double pipelines and alternate pipeline, the length will be calculated according to the length of single pipeline in principle. If the double pipelines perform the transportation at the same time and unable to be counted separately, the length of pipelines will be the length of double pipelines divided by 2.

Freight (Passenger) Traffic refers to the weight of freight (number of passenger) transported with various means within a specific period of time. This indicator reflects the service of the transport industry towards the national economy and people's living conditions, as well as an important indicator used in formulating and monitoring transport production plans and research into the scale and pace of transport development. Freight transport is calculated in tons and passenger traffic is calculated in terms of number of persons. Freight transport is calculated in terms of the actual weight of the goods and takes no account of the type of freight and distance of travel. Passenger traffic is calculated by the principle that one person can be counted only once in one trip and takes no account of the travelling distance and ticket price. The passengers who travel with a half price ticket or a child's ticket is also calculated as one person.

Freight Ton-kilometres (Passenger-kilometres) refers to the sum of the product of the volume of transported cargo (passengers) multiplied by the transport distance. It is an important indicator to reflect the achievement of the transportation industry. This is an important indicator to show the total results of the transport industry; to prepare and examine the transport plan; and to serve as the main basic data for calculating the efficiency, labour productivity and unit cost of transport. Normally, the shortest distance between the departure station and the destination station (i.e., the payable distance) is the basis in calculating the freight ton-kilometres. The formula is as follows:

$$\text{Freight ton kilometres (passenger kilometres)} = \sum \text{freight (passenger) traffic} \times \text{distance of transportation}$$

Average Static Load of Freight Cars refers to the average cargo weight when loaded onto each freight car under the static condition. For its calculation the following formula is applied:

$$\text{Average static load of freight cars (tons)} = \frac{\text{Tonnage of goods dispatched}}{\text{Number of freight cars loaded}}$$

Average Daily Haul of Freight Locomotives refers to the average total ton-kilometres accomplished by each freight transport locomotive over one day and night during a given period of time. It includes both the weight of the goods carried and the dead weight of the train itself. It is a comprehensive indicator reflecting the locomotive efficiency in terms of both time and the pulling force.

$$\text{Average daily haul of freight transport locomotive (ton kilometre)} = \frac{\text{Total ton kilometres of freight}}{\text{Daily number of freight transport locomotive}}$$

Possession of Civil Motor Vehicles refer to the total numbers of vehicles that are registered and received vehicles license tags according to the *Work Standard for Motor Vehicles Registration* formulated by the Transport Management Office under the department of public security at the end of the reference period. They are divided into categories. According to the structure of motor vehicles, they are divided into passenger vehicles, trucks and others; according to ownership into private vehicles and vehicles for the unit's use; according to kind of usage into working vehicles and non-working vehicles; and according to size of vehicles into large passenger vehicles, medium-sized passenger vehicles, small passenger vehicles and mini passenger vehicles, heavy trucks, light-heavy trucks, light trucks and mini-trucks.

Business Volume of Post and Telecommunications refers to the total amount of postal and telecommunication services, expressed in value terms, provided by the post and telecommunications departments for society. This indicator reflects the overall results of development of postal and telecommunication services. It can be classificated as postal services and telecommunication services. Business volume of post and telecommunications is the sum of each service in kind multiplying with its correspondent unit price (constant price).

Mobile Telephone Subscribers refers to persons who have gone through registration procedures in the operation points of enterprises engaged in telecommunications and are hence connected with the mobile telephone communication network through the mobile telephone switchboards and occupy mobile phone numbers. Included are various types of subscriber, prepaid users for intelligent network and wireless network card users.

Internet Users refer to the number of Chinese citizens aged 6 and over who use the Internet in the past six months.

Local Telephone Subscribers refer to all subscribers who have gone through registration procedures in the operation points of enterprises engaged in telecommunications and are hence connected to the local telecommunications service provider through fixed line network. Included are general subscribers, wireless local telephone subscribers, public telephones subscribers, N-ISDN subscribers and intelligent network terminal subscribers.

Urban Telephone Subscribers refer to the number of telephone subscribers, located at the municipalities directly under the Central Government, cities under the jurisdiction of province, cities at prefecture level, downtown and suburb of city at county level town and county towns according to the administrative division, including subscribers in rural mineral area, forest area, military area that are at or above county level.

Rural Telephone Subscribers refer to telephone subscribers, located at the towns and villages outside the coverage of urban areas according to the administrative division.

Household Telephone Subscribers refers to all kinds of subscribers with telephone sets paid privately or installed in the dwelling units of residents, and registered as private subscribers or residence subscribers for payment.

Capacity of Long Distance Telephone Exchanges refers to the rated capacity of telephone exchanges to connect long distance telephone network by enterprises engaged in telecommunications.

Capacity of Office Telephone Exchanges refers to the capacity (measured in gate) of telephone exchanges installed in the offices of telecommunication service providers for communication between fixed telephones.It includes the capacity of access network equipment(capacity of equipment installed in the offices of telecommunication service providers for connecting distant nodes of voice users).

Capacity of Mobile Telephone Exchanges refers to the capacity of the maximum services provided to subscribers at any one time as computed based on a certain model of calls distribution and transacting capacity of the mobile telephone exchanges. It is calculated based on the actual capacity of equipments connected to network through cutover and put into operation officially at the end of the reference period.

Broadband Connection Terminals refer to the connection terminals to internet users actually installed and put into operation, including connection terminals for XDSL, connection terminals for LAN, and other types of connection terminals. N-ISDN connection terminals are not included.

批发和零售业、住宿和餐饮业

WHOLESALE AND RETAIL TRADES, HOTELS AND CATERING SERVICES

第十六篇　批发和零售业、住宿和餐饮业

本篇主要内容和资料来源

本篇资料反映新疆维吾尔自治区商品流通市场发展及批发和零售业、住宿和餐饮业经营情况。主要内容有社会消费品零售额，限额以上批发和零售业、住宿和餐饮业情况，限额以上批发和零售业商品销售及商品分类销售情况，限额以上批发和零售贸易企业及住宿和餐饮企业主要财务情况，亿元商品交易市场成交情况，连锁经营情况等。

限额以上批发和零售业、住宿和餐饮业统计限额标准：批发业年销售额2000万元及以上，零售业年销售额500万元及以上，餐饮业年营业额200万元及以上，住宿业为年主营业务收入200万元以上企业。

本篇资料由新疆维吾尔自治区统计局贸易外经统计处提供。

Wholesale and Retail Trades, Hotels and Catering Services

Main Content and Source of Data

Data in this chapter reflect the development of Xinjiang' s circulation of domestic market and the management situation of wholesale and retail & hotels and catering services, etc. Main contents include the total retail sales, condition of wholesales & retail trades and hotels and catering services above designated size,condition of sale value of enterprises above designated size of wholesales and retail trade and sale value of trade by category of main commodities,financial status of enterprises above designated size of wholesales & retail trade and catering service,turn over of large commodity transaction markets with transaction over 100 million yuan,development of chain stores .

Criteria for wholesale and retail sale trades, hotels and catering services above designated size is defined as follows: wholesale trade has annual sales over 20 million yuan; retail sale trade have annual sale over 5 million yuan; catering services have annual income over 2 million yuan. Enterprise above designated size in accommodation refers to star-rated unit.

Data in this chapter are provided by the Division of Trade Statistics, the Xinjiang Bureau of Statistics.

16-1 主要年份国内贸易基本情况
Basic Conditions of Domestic Trade in Main Years

指　　标	Item	2000	2005	2010	2015
法人企业(个)	**Number of Corporation Enterprises (unit)**	**394**	**1097**	**1449**	**2529**
批发和零售业	Wholesale and Retail Trades	370	800	1175	2181
住宿和餐饮业	Hotels and Catering Servicess	24	297	274	348
#餐饮业	Catering Services	24	65	53	93
产业活动单位(个)	**Number of Establishments (unit)**	**431**	**2396**	**4563**	**4305**
批发和零售业	Wholesale and Retail Trades	382	1998	4137	4026
住宿和餐饮业	Hotels and Catering Services	49	398	426	279
#餐饮业	Catering Services	49	96	122	152
批发和零售业	**Wholesale and Retail Trades**				
商品销售总额（亿元)	Total Sales (100 million yuan)	478.3	1182.0	4230.9	8627.0
社会消费品零售总额(亿元)	**Total Retail Sales of Consumer Goods (100 million yuan)**	**374.5**	**640.2**	**1386.1**	**2606.0**
按销售单位所在地分	By Location of Establishments				
城　镇	Urban	233.7	443.9	1236.2	2373.8
#城　区	Urban Area	65.2	95.6	989.0	1949.8
乡　村	Rural	75.6	100.7	149.9	232.2
按行业分	By Sector				
商品零售	Retail Trades	242.3	509.3	1210.4	2276.2
餐费收入	Catering Services	38.2	92.8	175.7	329.8
其他	Others	94.0	38.1		

注：1.法人企业、产业活动单位统计范围为限额以上企业(单位)。2.商品销售总额、社会消费品零售总额为全口径数据。3.2008 年限额以上住宿业数据为年主营业务收入 200 万元以上企业。4.从 2010 年开始,按销售单位所在地分组由市、县、县以下调整为城镇、城区、乡村。5.从 2010 年开始,按行业分组取消其他行业。6.2010-2014 年数据依据第三次经济普查数据调整。7.2010 年以前为按行业(批发和零售业、住宿和餐饮业、其他行业)分组，2010 年开始调整为按经营形式（商品零售、餐费收入）分组。

Note: a) Scope of corporation enterprises,industrial activity units covers enterprises(units)above designated size. b) Data of total sales and total retail sales of consumer goods are those of full coverage. c) Data of hotels and catering services above designated size in 2008 are figures from enterprises of annual income over 2 million yuan. d) Since 2010 By the sales units of the group was adjusted,from city,county and under county level to town,city and country.e) Since 2010 data of other sector was canceled .f)Data of 2010-2014 was adjusted by the Third Economic Census. g)before 2010 data was grouped by sector,since 2010 data was adjusted by operate situation.

16-2 主要年份社会消费品零售总额
Total Retail Sales of Consumer Goods in Main Years

单位：亿元 (100 million yuan)

年 份 Year	社会消费品零售总额 Total Retail Sales of Consumer Goods	按销售单位所在地分 By Location			按行业分 By Sector		
		城 镇 Urban	#城 区 Urban Area	乡 村 Rural	商品零售 Retail Trades	餐费收入 Catering Services	其他行业 Others
1978	21.89	7.44	4.80	9.65	17.34	0.57	3.98
1980	29.36	11.06	6.05	12.25	22.95	0.94	5.47
1985	57.38	24.55	10.70	22.13	40.83	2.51	14.04
1990	104.30	57.17	24.27	22.86	72.68	6.06	25.56
1995	253.65	145.74	50.03	57.88	169.16	17.27	67.22
1996	295.36	171.51	55.38	68.47	191.14	19.44	84.78
1997	310.42	186.37	57.54	66.51	198.73	22.22	89.47
1998	327.52	197.89	59.89	69.74	206.92	27.84	92.76
1999	347.40	213.96	61.51	71.93	222.57	32.76	92.07
2000	374.50	233.66	65.15	75.69	242.29	38.21	94.00
2001	406.35	256.58	69.73	80.04	266.38	44.57	95.40
2002	442.88	284.74	74.32	83.82	296.13	53.04	93.71
2003	421.16	311.33	49.20	60.63	341.90	60.64	18.62
2004	563.41	385.81	85.79	91.81	450.65	76.22	36.54
2005	640.20	443.95	95.60	100.65	509.25	92.82	38.13
2006	733.20	513.12	107.68	112.40	582.28	111.55	39.37
2007	857.50	606.74	123.64	127.12	685.94	130.51	41.05
2008	1041.50	740.85	150.78	149.87	841.65	156.49	43.36
2009	1180.06	836.95	171.76	171.35	959.17	177.21	43.68
2010	1386.06	1236.19	988.97	149.87	1210.40	175.66	
2011	1662.35	1512.11	1244.06	150.24	1455.78	206.57	
2012	1916.06	1754.47	1498.21	161.59	1677.14	238.92	
2013	2179.45	1995.66	1645.59	183.79	1910.51	268.94	
2014	2436.50	2220.82	1825.94	215.68	2139.88	296.62	
2015	2605.96	2373.80	1949.79	232.16	2276.12	329.84	

注:1.2010-2014 年数据依据第三次经济普查数据调整。 2.2010 年以前为按行业(批发和零售业、住宿和餐饮业、其他行业)分组，2010 年开始调整为按经营形式（商品零售、餐费收入）分组。 3.从 2010 年开始,按销售单位所在地分组由市、县、县以下调整为城镇、城区、乡村。

Note:1.Data of 2010 -2014 adjusted by the Third Economic Census.2.Data of this table grouped by sector before 2010 , Since 2010,data of this table grouped by status of operation.3. Since 2010 data of location grouped by urban,urban area and rural.

16-3 分类型、分地区限额以上批发和零售业、住宿和餐饮业基本情况

Basic Conditions of Enterprises above Designated Size in Wholesale and Retail Trades, Hotels and Catering Services by Category and Region

(2015 年)

指　标	Item	法人企业数(个) Number of Corporation Enterprises (unit)	产业活动单位数(个) Number of Establishments (unit)	从业人员数(人) Engaged Persons (person)
总　计	**Total**	**2529**	**4305**	**166362**
批发业	**Wholesale Trades**	**1311**	**2067**	**65984**
内资企业	Domestic Funded Enterprises	1304	2049	64806
国有企业	State-owned Enterprises	73	394	8180
集体企业	Collective-owned Enterprises	18	63	1373
联营企业	Joint Ownership Enterprises	1	13	22
集体联营企业	Collective Joint Ownership Enterprises	1	13	22
有限责任公司	Limited Liability Corporations	419	835	25249
国有独资公司	State Sole Funded Corporations	73	199	6165
其他有限责任公司	Other Limited Liability Corporations	346	636	19084
股份有限公司	Share-holding Corporations Ltd.	45	589	9643
私营企业	Private Enterprises	726	155	19201
私营独资企业	Private-funded Enterprises	3		25
私营合伙企业	Private Partnership Enterprises	2		23
私营有限责任公司	Private Limited Liability Corporations	713	142	17907
私营股份有限公司	Private Share-holding Corporation Ltd.	8	13	1246
其他企业	Other Enterprises	22		1138
港、澳、台商投资企业	Enterprises With Funds from Hong Kong, Macao and Taiwan	2	3	658
港、澳、台商独资经营企业	Enterprises With Sole Fund from Hong Kong, Macao and Taiwan	2	2	243
其他港、澳、台投资企业	Other Enterprises With Funds from Hong Kong, Macao and Tai wan		1	415
外商投资企业	Foreign Funded Enterprises	5	15	520
中外合资经营企业	Joint-venfure Enterprises	3	6	230
外资企业	Enterprises with Sole Fund	2	9	290
零售业	**Retail Trades**	**870**	**1959**	**57181**
内资企业	Domestic Funded Enterprises	858	1950	54680
国有企业	State-owned Enterprises	26	152	2336
集体企业	Collective-owned Enterprises	2	10	83
股份合作企业	Cooperative Enterprises	1		64
有限责任公司	Limited Liability Corporations	286	484	16839
国有独资公司	State Sole Funded Corporation	7	12	225
其他有限责任公司	Other Limited Liability Corporations	279	472	16614
股份有限公司	Share-holding Corporations Ltd.	9	131	7408
私营企业	Private Enterprises	533	1172	27932
私营独资企业	Private-funded Enterprises	5	12	82
私营合伙企业	Private Partnership Enterprises	2		36
私营有限责任公司	Private Limited Liability Corporations	523	1160	27750
私营股份有限公司	Private Share-holding Corporation Ltd.	3		64
其他企业	Other Enterprises	1	1	18
港、澳、台商投资企业	Enterprises With Funds from Hong Kong, Macao and Taiwan	6	3	783
港、澳、台商独资经营企业	Enterprises With Sole Fund from Hong Kong, Macaoand Taiwan	5		585
港、澳、台商投资股份有限公司	Share-holding Corporatons Ltd With Investment from Hong Kong, Macao and Taiwan	1	3	198
外商投资企业	Other Enterprises With funds From Hong Kong,Macao anf Tai Wan	6	6	1718
中外合资经营企业	Joint-venfure Enterprises	4		629
外资企业	Enterprises with Sole Fund	1	6	1066
外商投资股份有限公司	Share-holding Corpotions Ltd.With Foreign Investment	1		23
住宿业	**Hotels**	**255**	**127**	**30612**
内资企业	Domestic-funded Enterprises	253	126	30219
国有企业	State-owned Enterprises	66	37	9883
集体企业	Collective-owned Enterprises	4	2	454
联营企业	Joint Ownership Enterprises	1		40
国有联营企业	State Joint Ownership Enterprises	1		40

16-3 续表 Continued

指　　标	Item	法人企业数(个) Number of Corporation Enterprises (unit)	产业活动单位数(个) Number of Establishments (unit)	从业人员数(人) Engaged Persons (person)
有限责任公司	Limited Liability Corporations	86	43	10942
国有独资公司	State Sole Funded Corporations	12		734
其他有限责任公司	Other Limited Liability Corporations	74	43	10208
股份有限公司	Share-holding Corporations Ltd.	6	7	1112
私营企业	Private Enterprises	89	37	7734
私营独资企业	Private-funded Enterprises	10	12	462
私营合伙企业	Private Partnership Enterprises	1	3	71
私营有限责任公司	Private Limited Liability Corporations	76	21	7003
私营股份有限公司	Private Share-holding Corporation Ltd.	2	1	198
其他企业	Other Enterprises	1		54
港、澳、台商投资企业	Enterprises With Funds from Hong Kong, Macao and Taiwan	1		25
合资经营企业（港或澳、台资）	Joint-venture Enterprises (Funds from HongKong, Macao and Taiwan)	1		25
外商投资企业	Foreign Funded Enterprises	1	1	368
中外合资经营企业	Joint-venfure Enterprises		1	347
外资企业	Enterprises with Sole Fund	1		21
餐饮业	**Catering Services**	**93**	**152**	**12585**
内资企业	Domestic Funded Enterprises	91	123	11897
国有企业	State-owned Enterprises	7	9	1406
有限责任公司	Limited Liability Corporations	22	17	1796
国有独资公司	State Sole Funded Corporations	2		53
其他有限责任公司	Other Limited Liability Corporations	20	17	1743
股份有限公司	Share-holding Corporations Ltd.	1		114
私营企业	Private Enterprises	60	96	8305
私营独资企业	Private-funded Enterprises	8		639
私营合伙企业	Private Partnership Enterprises	2		272
私营有限责任公司	Private Llimited Liability Corporations	48	88	7112
私营股份有限公司	Private Share-holding Corporations Ltd.	2	8	282
其他企业	Other Enterprises	1	1	276
港、澳、台商投资企业	Enterprises With Funds from Hong Kong, Macao and Taiwan	1		55
与港澳台商合资经营企业	Joint-venture Enterprises (Funds from HongKong, Macao and Taiwan)	1		55
外商投资企业	Foreign Funded Enterprises	1	29	633
外资企业	Enterprises With Sole Fund	1	29	633
按地区分	**By Region**			
乌鲁木齐市	Urumqi City	865	1312	71910
克拉玛依市	Karamay City	94	101	6591
吐鲁番市	Turpan City	39	70	2049
哈密地区	Hami [Kumul] Administrative Offices	92	169	5043
昌吉回族自治州	Changji Hui Autonomous Prefecture	100	211	6408
伊犁哈萨克自治州	Ili Kazak Autonomous Prefecture	340	385	15460
伊犁州直属县(市)	Counties (Cities) Direct Under Ili Prefecture	238	186	10354
塔城地区	Tacheng [Tarbagatai] Administrative Offices	58	124	2574
阿勒泰地区	Altay Administrative Offices	44	75	2532
博尔塔拉蒙古自治州	Bortala Mongol Autonomous Prefecture	50	45	2290
巴音郭楞蒙古自治州	Bayangol Mongol Autonomous Prefecture	163	436	10979
阿克苏地区	Aksu Administrative Offices	231	487	11067
克孜勒苏柯尔克孜自治州	Kizilsu Kirgiz Autonomous Prefecture	33	2	1284
喀什地区	Kashgar [Kaxgar] Administrative Offices	126	256	8612
和田地区	Hotan Administrative Offices	38	35	2225
生产建设兵团	Production and Construction Corps	358	796	22444

16-4 分行业、分地区限额以上批发和零售业商品销售额

Total Sales Values of Enterprises above Designated Size of Wholesale and Retail Trades by Sector and Region

单位：万元　　　　(2015 年)　　　　(10 000 yuan)

指　标	Item	销售总额 Total Sales Value	批　发 Wholesale Value	零　售 Retail Value
总　计	**Total**	**69107934**	**58166039**	**10941895**
批发业	**Wholesale Trade**	**59587363**	**57401689**	**2185674**
农、林、牧产品批发	Wholesale of Agricultunal,Forestry	8289044	8249046	39998
谷物、豆及薯类批发	Wholesale of Grain,Bean and Potato	620301	613130	7171
种子批发	Wholesale of Seed	319404	310509	8895
饲料批发	Wholesale of Secdstuff	36843	36794	49
棉、麻批发	Wholesale of Cotton and Liner	7184339	7170087	14252
林业产品批发	Wholesale of Forestry Produccts	17628	7997	9631
牲畜批发	Wholesale of Livestock	52809	52809	
其他农牧产品批发	Wholesale of Other Agricultural Products and Livestock Products	57720	57720	
食品、饮料及烟草制品批发	Wholesale of Food,Beverages and Tobaccos	4939112	4921843	17269
米、面制品及食用油批发	Wholesale of Rice, Flour and Edible Oil	361664	361664	
糕点、糖果及糖批发	Wholesale of Pastry,Candy and Sugar	45318	44848	470
果品、蔬菜批发	Wholesale of Fruit and Vegetable	828339	820957	7382
肉、禽、蛋及水产品批发	Wholesale of Meat,Birds and Equatic Products	50584	50584	
盐及调味品批发	Wholesale of Salt and Condiment Flavoring Material	84354	83719	635
营养及保健品批发	Wholesale of Nutritious and Healeh Food	13944	13944	
酒、饮料及茶叶批发	Wholesale of Soft Drink and Tea Leaf	146741	143997	2744
烟草制品批发	Wholesale of Tobaccos	3379699	3373971	5728
其他食品批发	Wholesale of Other Food	28469	28159	310
纺织、服装及家庭用品批发	Wholesale of Textitles, Wearing Apparel and Household Articles	620964	590857	30107
纺织品、针织品及原料批发	Wholesale of Textiles,Hosiery and Raw Material	143555	143555	
服装批发	Wholesale of Wearing Apparel	129517	124257	5260
化妆品及卫生用品批发	Wholesale of Cosmetics and Health Aids	43808	43265	543
家用电器批发	Wholesale of Household Electrcal Appliances	285326	261023	24303
其他家庭用品批发	Wholesale of Other Household Articles	18758	18757	1
文化、体育用品及器材批发	Wholesale of Culture, Sports Appliances and Equipments	266066	241780	24286
文具用品批发	Wholesale of Stationery	2452	2452	
图书批发	Wholesale of Books	199481	187557	11924
首饰、工艺品及收藏品批发	Wholesale of Jewellery、Handicraft、Collection	6558	6534	24
其他文化用品批发	Wholesale of Other Culture Products	57575	45237	12338
医药及医疗器材批发	Wholesale of Medicines and Medical Appliances	1233399	1218659	14740
西药批发	Wholesale of Western Medicine	1061946	1048185	13761
中药批发	Wholesale of Chinese Medicinal Plant	53106	52322	784
医疗用品及器材批发	Wholesale of Medical Supplies and Appliances	118347	118152	195
矿产品、建材及化工产品批发	Wholesale of Mineral Products, Building Materials and Chemical Products	40605023	38831705	1773318
煤炭及制品批发	Wholesale of Coal and Related Products	475509	472509	3000
石油及制品批发	Wholesale of Petroleum and Related Products	28974028	27413928	1560100
非金属矿及制品批发	Wholesale of Non-Metal Materials	5944	5944	
金属及金属矿批发	Wholesale of Metal and Metal Materials	6131567	5938067	193500
建材批发	Wholesale of Building Materials	675064	670391	4673

16-4 续表 1 Continued

单位：万元 (10 000 yuan)

指　标	Item	销售总额 Total Sales Value	批 发 Wholesale Value	零 售 Retail Value
化肥批发	Wholesale of Chemical Fertilizer	2110384	2100832	9552
农药批发	Wholesale of Pesticides	46741	46531	210
其他化工产品批发	Wholesale of Other Chemical Products	2185786	2183503	2283
机械设备、五金交电及电子产品批发	Wholesale of Machinery, Hardware and Electronic Products	3423029	3137143	285886
农业机械批发	Wholesale of Agriculture Machinery	248013	211358	36655
汽车批发	Wholesale of Motor Vehicles	144795	135026	9769
汽车零配件批发	Wholesale of Motor Vehicle Parts	852060	837498	14562
摩托车及零配件批发	Wholesale of Motorcycles and Parts	10831	10831	
五金产品批发	Wholesale of Hardware	132546	128696	3850
电气设备批发	Wholesale of Electric Machinery	223395	19040	204355
计算机、软件及辅助设备批发	Wholesale of Computer, Software and Assistant Appliances	124107	113107	11000
通讯及广播电视设备批发	Wholesale of Communicating and Broadcasting Television Device	63758	62076	1682
其他机械设备及电子产品批发	Wholesale of Other Mechanical Equipment and Electronic Products	1623524	1619511	4013
贸易经纪与代理	Trade Broker and Agency	90094	90094	
贸易代理	Trade Agency	90094	90094	
其他批发业	Other Wholesale not Classified Elsewhere	120632	120562	70
再生物资回收与批发	Recovery and Wholesale of Regeneration Material	71598	71528	70
其他未列明的批发	Wholesale of Un-listed	49034	49034	
零售业	**Retail Trades**	**9520571**	**764350**	**8756221**
综合零售	Integrated Retail	1945657	27914	1917743
百货零售	Retail of General Merchandise	1432388	25118	1407270
超级市场零售	Retail of Supermarkets	509458	2796	506662
其他综合零售	Retail of Other Integrate	3811		3811
食品、饮料及烟草制品专门零售	Special Retail of Food, Beverages and Tobaccos	25757	6838	18919
粮油零售	Retail of Grain and Oil	2507	46	2461
果品、蔬菜零售	Retail of Fruite and Vegetables	4331	500	3831
肉、禽、蛋及水产品零售	Retail of Meat,Poultry ,Eggs and Aquatic Products	903	305	598
营养和保健品零售	Retail of Health Products	2912	1718	1194
酒、饮料及茶叶零售	Retail of Soft Drink and Tea Leaf	11355	4269	7086
烟草制品零售	Retail of Tobaccos	3749		3749
纺织、服装及日用品专门零售	Special Retail of Textile, Garments and Daily Consumer Articles	458570	19819	438751
纺织品及针织品零售	Retail of Textile Fabric and Hosiery	42382	7368	35014
服装零售	Retail of Garment	306508	6812	299696
鞋帽零售	Retail of Shoes and Hats	17630	1489	16141
化妆品及卫生用品零售	Retail of Cosmetics and Health Aids	5604	1470	4134
钟表、眼镜零售	Retail of Timelkeeper and Spectacle	14196	1359	12837
厨房用具及日用杂品零售	Retail of Kitchenware and Household goods	1321	1321	
其他日用品零售	Retail of Other Covenience Goods	70929		70929
文化、体育用品及器材专门零售	Speciad Retail of Cultural, Sports Goods and Appliances	239650	720	238930
文具用品零售	Retail of Stationery and Office Supplies	6043		6043

16-4 续表 2 Continued

单位：万元 (10 000 yuan)

指标	Item	销售总额 Total Sales Value	批发 Wholesale Value	零售 Retail Value
体育用品及器材零售	Retail of Sports Appliances and Eguipments	720	720	
图书、报刊零售	Retail of Books,Newspapers and Magazines	200154		200154
珠宝首饰零售	Retail of Jewelry	32733		32733
医药及医疗器材专门零售	Special Retail of Medicines and Medical Appliances	1196014	212247	983767
药品零售	Retail of Medcine	1133174	207207	925967
医疗用品及器材零售	Retaul of Medical Treatment and Equipment	62840	5040	57800
汽车、摩托车、燃料及零配件专门零售	Special Retail of Car, Motor, Fuel and Parts	5073862	443887	4629975
汽车零售	Retail of Motor Vehicles	3657590	130029	3527561
汽车零配件零售	Retail of Automobiles' Parts	178047		178047
摩托车及零配件零售	Retail of Motorcycle and Fittings	8419	505	7914
机动车燃料零售	Retail of Auto Fuel	1229806	313353	916453
家用电器及电子产品专门零售	Special Retail of House hold Electric Appliancesaund Electronic Products	486386	31686	454700
家用视听设备零售	Retail of Home audio-visual Equipments	231118	812	230306
日用家电设备零售	Retail of Household Electric Appliances	112881	6831	106050
计算机、软件及辅助设备零售	Retail of Cumputer,Software and Assistant Appliances	79464	10533	68931
通信设备零售	Retail of Communication Equipments	51808	9912	41896
其他电子产品零售	Retail of other Electronic Products	11115	3598	7517
五金、家具及室内装修材料专门零售	Special Retail of Hardware, Furniture and Interor Decorating Material	15394	280	15114
五金零售	Retail of Hardware	11986	280	11706
陶瓷、石材装饰材料零售	Retaul of Ceramics and Stone Decorating Material	1567		1567
其他室内装饰材料零售	Retaul of other Interior Decorating Material	1841		1841
货摊、无店铺及其他零售业	Stalls,Non-shop and Other Retail	79281	20959	58322
邮购及电视、电话零售	Retoul of Post and E-commerce	865		865
生活用燃料零售	Retail of Life Fuels	78416	20959	57457
按地区分	**By Region**			
乌鲁木齐市	Urumqi City	44015029	37998533	6016496
克拉玛依市	Karamay City	1103342	759660	343682
吐鲁番市	Turpan Cit	461482	302025	159457
哈密地区	Hami [Kumul] Administrative Offices	1181437	816540	364897
昌吉回族自治州	Changji Hui Autonomous Prefecture	1299081	836628	462453
伊犁哈萨克自治州	Ili Kazak Autonomous Prefecture	3107092	2446464	660628
伊犁州直属县(市)	Counties (Cities) Direct Under Ili Prefecture	2135192	1620828	514364
塔城地区	Tacheng [Tarbagatai] Administrative Offices	687866	596915	90951
阿勒泰地区	Altay Administrative Offices	284034	228721	55313
博尔塔拉蒙古自治州	Bortala Mongol Autonomous Prefecture	768886	641654	127232
巴音郭楞蒙古自治州	Bayangol Mongol Autonomous Prefecture	2189693	1600059	589634
阿克苏地区	Aksu Administrative Offices	2128184	1518311	609873
克孜勒苏柯尔克孜自治州	Kizilsu Kirgiz Autonomous Prefecture	154616	139444	15172
喀什地区	Kashgar [Kaxgar] Administrative Offices	1472755	1118531	354224
和田地区	Hotan Administrative Offices	322752	236060	86692
生产建设兵团	Production and Construction Group	10903585	9752130	1151455

16-5 限额以上餐饮企业经营情况
Operations of Enterprises above Designated Size of Catering Services

单位：万元 (2015 年) (10 000 yuan)

项 目	Item	法人企业数(个) Number of Corporation Enterprises (unit)	产业活动单位数(个) Number of Establishments (unit)	营业额 Business Revenue	#商品零售额 Retail Sales of Commodities
总 计	**Total**	**93**	**152**	**196096**	**171505**
正餐服务	Dinner	86	42	142643	119046
快餐服务	Snack	7	110	53453	52459
按地区分	**By Region**				
乌鲁木齐市	Urumqi City	29	116	129347	123236
克拉玛依市	Karamay City	2	10	3594	3289
吐鲁番市	Turpan City	1		397	397
哈密地区	Hami [Kumul] Administrative Offices	2		935	926
昌吉回族自治州	Changji Hui Autonomous Prefecture	4	5	5559	3881
伊犁哈萨克自治州	Ili Kazak Autonomous Prefecture	22	7	21185	13127
伊犁州直属县(市)	Counties (Cities) Direct Under Ili Prefecture	20	5	19639	11918
塔城地区	Tacheng [Tarbagatai] Administrative Offices	2	2	1546	1209
巴音郭楞蒙古自治州	Bayangol Mongol Autonomous Prefecture	14	6	11518	8898
阿克苏地区	Aksu Administrative Offices	8		6659	5470
喀什地区	Kashgar [Kaxgar] Administrative Offices	2	1	1550	1268
生产建设兵团	Production and Construction Group	9	7	15352	11013

16-6 限额以上住宿企业经营情况
Operation of Enterprises above Designated Size in Hotels Services

单位：万元 (2015 年) (10 000 yuan)

项 目	Item	营业额 Business Revenue	客房收入 From Hotel Rooms	餐费收入 From Meals
总 计	**Total**	**438987**	**211962**	**176016**
五 星	Five-Star	87743	36490	38843
四 星	Four-Star	112612	50366	43403
三 星	Three-Star	140879	68576	60127
二 星	Two-Star	16152	11446	2633
其 他	Others	81601	45084	31010
按行业分	**By Sector**			
旅游饭店	Tourist Hotel	376390	175273	155029
一般旅馆	Fonda	61924	36200	20804
其他住宿服务	Others	672	489	183
按地区分	**By Region**			
乌鲁木齐市	Urumqi City	228448	101789	90673
克拉玛依市	Karamay City	15613	6743	8034
吐鲁番市	Turpan City	5328	3843	1337
哈密地区	Hami [Kumul] Administrative Offices	15754	6117	9138
昌吉回族自治州	Changji Hui Autonomous Prefecture	10757	3780	5599
伊犁哈萨克自治州	Ili Kazak Autonomous Prefecture	40301	21634	16311
伊犁州直属县(市)	Counties (Cities) Direct Under Ili Prefecture	17848	9651	6697
塔城地区	Tacheng [Tarbagatai] Administrative Offices	4943	2488	2398
阿勒泰地区	Altay Administrative Offices	17510	9495	7216
博尔塔拉蒙古自治州	Bortala Mongol Autonomous Prefecture	5704	2508	2435
巴音郭楞蒙古自治州	Bayangol Mongol Autonomous Prefecture	24705	12167	10688
阿克苏地区	Aksu Administrative Offices	12415	9020	3097
克孜勒苏柯尔克孜自治州	Kizilsu Kirgiz Autonomous Prefecture	4058	1933	1937
喀什地区	Kashgar [Kaxgar] Administrative Offices	17240	9865	5485
和田地区	Hotan Administrative Offices	9002	5524	3248
生产建设兵团	Xinjiang Production and Construction Group	49662	27039	18034

16-6 续表 Continued

单位：万元 (10 000 yuan)

项目	Item	商品销售收入 From Commodities	其他收入 Others	床位数（张） Number of Beds (unit)
总计	**Total**	**4327**	**46682**	**88045**
五星	Five-Star	1674	10736	11252
四星	Four-Star	871	17972	22316
三星	Three-Star	1090	11086	31740
二星	Two-Star	75	1998	4951
其他	Others	617	4890	17786
按行业分	**By Sector**			
旅游饭店	Tourist Hotel	3086	43003	72874
一般旅馆	Fonda	1241	3679	14824
其他住宿服务	Others			347
按地区分	**By Region**			
乌鲁木齐市	Urumqi City	2430	33556	30150
克拉玛依市	Karamay City	32	804	2808
吐鲁番市	Turpan City		148	2271
哈密地区	Hami [Kumul] Administrative Offices	118	381	2617
昌吉回族自治州	Changji Hui Autonomous Prefecture	70	1308	2229
伊犁哈萨克自治州	Ili Kazak Autonomous Prefecture	314	2042	14324
伊犁州直属县(市)	Counties (Cities) Direct Under Ili Prefecture	110	1390	6338
塔城地区	Tacheng [Tarbagatai] Administrative Offices	25	32	1381
阿勒泰地区	Altay Administrative Offices	179	620	6605
博尔塔拉蒙古自治州	Bortala Mongol Autonomous Prefecture	384	377	1120
巴音郭楞蒙古自治州	Bayangol Mongol Autonomous Prefecture	482	1368	5614
阿克苏地区	Aksu Administrative Offices	127	171	4708
克孜勒苏柯尔克孜自治州	Kizilsu Kirgiz Autonomous Prefecture		188	918
喀什地区	Kashgar [Kaxgar] Administrative Offices	121	1769	7074
和田地区	Hotan Administrative Offices	104	126	2277
生产建设兵团	Xinjiang Production and Construction Group	145	4444	11935

16-7 各地、州、市、县(市)社会消费品零售总额

Total Retail Sales of Consumer Goods by Prefecture, Autonomous Prefecture, City and County

单位：万元 (2015 年) (10 000 yuan)

地 区	Region	社会消费品零售总额 Total Retail Sales of Consumer Goods	城 镇 Urban	城 区 Urban Area	乡 村 Rural
总 计	**Total**	**26059563**	**23738024**	**19497950**	**2321539**
乌鲁木齐市	**Urumqi City**	**9405087**	**9375810**	**7365195**	**29277**
#乌鲁木齐县	Urumqi County	81096	7378	7378	73718
克拉玛依市	**Karamay City**	**588146**	**588146**	**588146**	
吐鲁番市	Turpan City	**443524**	**323656**	**184068**	**119868**
高昌区	Gaochang District	258814	214471	184068	44343
鄯善县	Shanshan [piqan]County	135045	83331		51714
托克逊县	Toksun County	49665	25854		23811
哈密地区	**Hami [kumul]Administrative Offices**	**847259**	**804262**	**720791**	**42997**
哈密市	Hami [kumul]City	756221	733155	720791	23066
巴里坤哈萨克自治县	Barkol KazakAutonomous County	68040	48724		19316
伊吾县	Yiwu [Araturuk]County	22998	22383		615
昌吉回族自治州	**Changji Hui Autonomous Prefecture**	**2364260**	**2071601**	**1861855**	**292659**
昌吉市	Changji City	995708	846352	731528	149356
阜康市	Fukang City	322382	283696	254682	38686
呼图壁县	Hutubi County	274068	246661	229395	27407
玛纳斯县	Manas County	301963	271767	252744	30196
奇台县	Qitai County	266270	239643	222868	26627
吉木萨尔县	Jimsar County	126712	114041	106058	12671
木垒哈萨克自治县	Mori Kazak Autonomous County	77157	69441	64580	7716
伊犁哈萨克自治州	**Ili Kazak Autonomous Prefecture**	**3303244**	**2670868**	**1567362**	**632376**
伊犁州直属县(市)	**Counties (Cities) Direct Under Ili Prefecture**	**1913419**	**1561952**	**1239270**	**351467**
伊宁市	Yining [Gulja]City	760927	743751	722879	17176
奎屯市	Kuytun City	248510	248510	248510	
伊宁县	Yining [Gulja]County	149709	107298	56980	42411
察布查尔锡伯自治县	Qapqal Xibe Autonomous County	32887	23713	11998	9174
霍城县	Huocheng [korgas]County	174095	102161	46699	71934
巩留县	Gongliu [Tokkuzlara]County	64165	39755	15189	24410
新源县	Xinyuan [kunes]County	250983	136278	64415	114705
昭苏县	Zhaosu [mongolkure]County	57100	40138	14674	16962
特克斯县	Tekes County	95303	58228	30479	37075
尼勒克县	Nilka County	79740	62120	27447	17620
塔城地区	**Tacheng [Tarbagatai] Administrative Offices**	**782752**	**564862**	**152482**	**217890**
塔城市	Tacheng [Qoqek] City	186501	129160	80767	57341
乌苏市	Usu City	157189	130379	71715	26810
额敏县	Emin [Dorbiljin] County	155816	91971		63845
沙湾县	Shawan County	176473	136188		40285
托里县	Toli County	42123	30929		11194
裕民县	Yumin [Qagantokay] County	30690	19850		10840
和布克赛尔蒙古自治县	Hoboksar Mongol Autonomous County	33960	26385		7575
阿勒泰地区	**Altay Administrative Offices**	**607073**	**544054**	**175610**	**63019**
阿勒泰市	Altay City	248834	231711	175610	17123
布尔津县	Burqin County	131086	115698		15388
富蕴县	Fuyun [Koktokay] County	68310	57918		10392
福海县	Fuhai [Burultokay] County	63626	57128		6498
哈巴河县	Habahe [Kaba] County	51452	45884		5568
青河县	Qinghe [Qinggil] County	31313	26265		5048
吉木乃县	Jeminay County	12452	9450		3002

16-7 续表 Continued

单位：万元 (10 000 yuan)

地　区	Region	社会消费品零售总额 Total Retail Sales of Consumer Goods	城　镇 Urban	#城　区 Urban Area	乡　村 Rural
博尔塔拉蒙古自治州	**Bortala Mongol Autonomous Prefecture**	**389778**	**341590**	**242272**	**48188**
博乐市	Bole [Bortala] City	293110	263460	242272	29650
精河县	Jinghe [Jing] County	67880	54459		13421
温泉县	Wenquan [Araxang] County	28788	23671		5117
巴音郭楞蒙古自治州	**Bayangol Mongol Autonomous Prefecture**	**982763**	**916038**	**639825**	**66725**
库尔勒市	Korla City	679391	661361	639825	18030
轮台县	Luntai [Bugur] County	50116	40907		9209
尉犁县	Yuli [Lopnur] County	25055	18745		6310
若羌县	Ruoqiang [Qarkilik] County	10367	8526		1841
且末县	Qiemo [Qarqan] County	12796	10903		1893
焉耆回族自治县	Yanqi Hui Autonomous County	88951	82416		6535
和静县	Hejing County	58105	46714		11391
和硕县	Hoxud County	22800	18561		4239
博湖县	Bohu [Bagrax] County	35182	27905		7277
阿克苏地区	**Aksu Administrative Offices**	**1247776**	**1009897**	**531865**	**237879**
阿克苏市	Aksu City	638367	579530	531865	58837
温宿县	Wensu [Onsu] County	112999	65829		47170
库车县	Kuqa County	193124	140957		52167
沙雅县	Xayar County	104809	81078		23731
新和县	Xinhe [Toksu] County	43431	32360		11071
拜城县	Baicheng [Bay] County	77700	60891		16809
乌什县	Wushi [Uxturpan] County	18900	7749		11151
阿瓦提县	Awat County	52234	38951		13283
柯坪县	Kalpin County	6212	2552		3660
克孜勒苏柯尔克孜自治州	**Kizilsu Kirgiz Autonomous Prefecture**	**187832**	**163969**	**158838**	**23863**
阿图什市	Artux City	113383	101506	101505	11877
阿克陶县	Akto County	42825	34467	29857	8358
阿合奇县	Akqi County	12224	11725	11725	499
乌恰县	Wuqia [Ulugqat] County	19400	16271	15751	3129
喀什地区	**Kashgar [Kaxgar] Administrative Offices**	**1681248**	**1223104**	**549585**	**458144**
喀什市	Kashgar [Kaxgar] City	717768	549585	549585	168183
疏附县	Shufu County	35934	28557		7377
疏勒县	Shule County	78896	56723		22173
英吉沙县	Yengisar County	56900	35600		21300
泽普县	Zepu [Poskam] County	62960	42609		20351
莎车县	Shache [Yarkant] County	151400	99657		51743
叶城县	Yecheng [Kagilik] County	145101	103046		42055
麦盖提县	Makit County	123075	80866		42209
岳普湖县	Yopurga County	39500	29773		9727
伽师县	Jiashi [Payzawat] County	113244	85643		27601
巴楚县	Bachu [Maralbexi] County	138625	97489		41136
塔什库尔干塔吉克自治县	Taxkorgan Tajik Autonomous County	17845	13556		4289
和田地区	**Hotan Administrative Offices**	**360601**	**276658**	**219409**	**83943**
和田市	Hotan City	178007	167818	158658	10189
和田县	Hotan County	22617	559		22058
墨玉县	Moyu [Karakax] County	44273	31301	21318	12972
皮山县	Pishan [Guma] County	22315	8312	5939	14003
洛浦县	Lop County	23641	17453	7538	6188
策勒县	Qira County	26102	16864		9238
于田县	Yutian [Keriya] County	32038	24928	19748	7110
民丰县	Minfeng [Niya] County	11608	9423	6208	2185
生产建设兵团	**Xinjiang Production and Construction Group**	**5523395**	**4932108**	**3380290**	**591287**

16-8 各地、州、市、县(市)社会消费品零售总额(按行业分)

Total Retail Sales of Consumer Goods by Sector and Prefecture, Autonomous Prefecture, City and County

单位：万元　　(2015 年)　　(10 000 yuan)

地　区	Region	社会消费品零售总额 Total Retail Sales of Consumer Goods	批发和零售业 Wholesale And Retail Sale Trades	住宿和餐饮业 Hotels and Catering Services
总　计	**Total**	**26059563**	**22744543**	**3315020**
乌鲁木齐市	**Urumqi City**	**9405087**	**8423147**	**981940**
#乌鲁木齐县	Urumqi County	81096	76023	5073
克拉玛依市	**Karamay City**	**588146**	**517875**	**70271**
吐鲁番市	**Turpan City**	**443524**	**393113**	**50411**
高昌区	Gaochang District	258814	236613	22201
鄯善县	Shanshan [piqan]County	135045	116278	18767
托克逊县	Toksun County	49665	40222	9443
哈密地区	**Hami [kumul]Administrative Offices**	**847259**	**686296**	**160963**
哈密市	Hami [kumul]City	756221	620271	135950
巴里坤哈萨克自治县	Barkol KazakAutonomous County	68040	50932	17108
伊吾县	Yiwu [Araturuk]County	22998	15093	7905
昌吉回族自治州	**Changji Hui Autonomous Prefecture**	**2364260**	**1940377**	**423883**
昌吉市	Changji City	995708	843225	152483
阜康市	Fukang City	322382	250610	71772
呼图壁县	Hutubi County	274068	218274	55794
玛纳斯县	Manas County	301963	248087	53876
奇台县	Qitai County	266270	212482	53788
吉木萨尔县	Jimsar County	126712	103382	23330
木垒哈萨克自治县	Mori Kazak Autonomous County	77157	64317	12840
伊犁哈萨克自治州	**Ili Kazak Autonomous Prefecture**	**3303244**	**2733755**	**569489**
伊犁州直属县(市)	**Counties (Cities) Direct Under Ili Prefecture**	**1913419**	**1592288**	**321131**
伊宁市	Yining [Gulja]City	760927	632629	128298
奎屯市	Kuytun City	248510	227319	21191
伊宁县	Yining [Gulja]County	149709	130552	19157
察布查尔锡伯自治县	Qapqal Xibe Autonomous County	32887	23858	9029
霍城县	Huocheng [korgas]County	174095	149574	24521
巩留县	Gongliu [Tokkuzlara]County	64165	51356	12809
新源县	Xinyuan [kunes]County	250983	195501	55482
昭苏县	Zhaosu [mongolkure]County	57100	49405	7695
特克斯县	Tekes County	95303	80567	14736
尼勒克县	Nilka County	79740	51527	28213
塔城地区	**Tacheng [Tarbagatai] Administrative Offices**	**782752**	**655000**	**127752**
塔城市	Tacheng [Qoqek] City	186501	153192	33309
乌苏市	Usu City	157189	126658	30531
额敏县	Emin [Dorbiljin] County	155816	142985	12831
沙湾县	Shawan County	176473	147474	28999
托里县	Toli County	42123	36028	6095
裕民县	Yumin [Qagantokay] County	30690	24961	5729
和布克赛尔蒙古自治县	Hoboksar Mongol Autonomous County	33960	23702	10258
阿勒泰地区	**Altay Administrative Offices**	**607073**	**486467**	**120606**
阿勒泰市	Altay City	248834	202456	46378
布尔津县	Burqin County	131086	87239	43847
富蕴县	Fuyun [Koktokay] County	68310	57603	10707
福海县	Fuhai [Burultokay] County	63626	55794	7832
哈巴河县	Habahe [Kaba] County	51452	45396	6056
青河县	Qinghe [Qinggil] County	31313	27648	3665
吉木乃县	Jeminay County	12452	10331	2121

16-8 续表 Continued

单位：万元 (10 000 yuan)

地　区	Region	社会消费品零售总额 Total Retail Sales of Consumer Goods	批发和零售业 Wholesale And Retail Sale Trades	住宿和餐饮业 Hotels and Catering Services
博尔塔拉蒙古自治州	**Bortala Mongol Autonomous Prefecture**	**389778**	**332876**	**56902**
博乐市	Bole [Bortala] City	293110	262809	30301
精河县	Jinghe [Jing] County	67880	46789	21091
温泉县	Wenquan [Araxang] County	28788	23278	5510
巴音郭楞蒙古自治州	**Bayangol Mongol Autonomous Prefecture**	**982763**	**877080**	**105683**
库尔勒市	Korla City	679391	630529	48862
轮台县	Luntai [Bugur] County	50116	39843	10273
尉犁县	Yuli [Lopnur] County	25055	19786	5269
若羌县	Ruoqiang [Qarkilik] County	10367	7764	2603
且末县	Qiemo [Qarqan] County	12796	9091	3705
焉耆回族自治县	Yanqi Hui Autonomous County	88951	84787	4164
和静县	Hejing County	58105	44649	13456
和硕县	Hoxud County	22800	11309	11491
博湖县	Bohu [Bagrax] County	35182	29322	5860
阿克苏地区	**Aksu Administrative Offices**	**1247776**	**1106050**	**141726**
阿克苏市	Aksu City	638367	600268	38099
温宿县	Wensu [Onsu] County	112999	109418	3581
库车县	Kuqa County	193124	147256	45868
沙雅县	Xayar County	104809	83838	20971
新和县	Xinhe [Toksu] County	43431	34009	9422
拜城县	Baicheng [Bay] County	77700	70687	7013
乌什县	Wushi [Uxturpan] County	18900	17094	1806
阿瓦提县	Awat County	52234	38084	14150
柯坪县	Kalpin County	6212	5396	816
克孜勒苏柯尔克孜自治州	**Kizilsu Kirgiz Autonomous Prefecture**	**187832**	**164459**	**23373**
阿图什市	Artux City	113383	104077	9306
阿克陶县	Akto County	42825	35639	7186
阿合奇县	Akqi County	12224	10443	1781
乌恰县	Wuqia [Ulugqat] County	19400	14300	5100
喀什地区	**Kashgar [Kaxgar] Administrative Offices**	**1681248**	**1434797**	**246451**
喀什市	Kashgar [Kaxgar] City	717768	676348	41420
疏附县	Shufu County	35934	32806	3128
疏勒县	Shule County	78896	63380	15516
英吉沙县	Yengisar County	56900	44710	12190
泽普县	Zepu [Poskam] County	62960	49691	13269
莎车县	Shache [Yarkant] County	151400	123159	28241
叶城县	Yecheng [Kagilik] County	145101	115241	29860
麦盖提县	Makit County	123075	97695	25380
岳普湖县	Yopurga County	39500	27980	11520
伽师县	Jiashi [Payzawat] County	113244	80723	32521
巴楚县	Bachu [Maralbexi] County	138625	106110	32515
塔什库尔干塔吉克自治县	Taxkorgan Tajik Autonomous County	17845	16954	891
和田地区	**Hotan Administrative Offices**	**360601**	**312271**	**48330**
和田市	Hotan City	178007	164293	13714
和田县	Hotan County	22617	16967	5650
墨玉县	Moyu [Karakax] County	44273	40299	3974
皮山县	Pishan [Guma] County	22315	20292	2023
洛浦县	Lop County	23641	15703	7938
策勒县	Qira County	26102	20484	5618
于田县	Yutian [Keriya] County	32038	25273	6765
民丰县	Minfeng [Niya] County	11608	8960	2648
生产建设兵团	**Xinjiang Production and Construction Group**	**5523395**	**4595430**	**927965**

16-9 限额以上批发企业资产及负债情况

Assets and Liabilities of Enterprises above Designated Size of Wholesale Trades

单位：万元 (2015 年) (10 000 yuan)

指标	Item	资产合计 Total Assets	#流动资产 Current Working Capitals	#固定资产 Fixed Assets	负债合计 Total Liabilities
总计	**Total**	**28887153**	**20622645**	**1919127**	**23100979**
按登记注册类型分	**By Type of Registration**				
内资企业	Domestic Funded Enterprises	28582461	20340848	1905952	22858190
国有企业	State-owned Enterprises	3413491	2787667	239395	2599949
集体企业	Collective-owned Enterprises	231350	181953	33423	165288
联营企业	Joint Ownership Enterprises	1540	1250	278	438
集体联营企业	Collective Joint Ownership Enterprises	1540	1250	278	438
有限责任公司	Limited Liability Corporations	11142021	8273298	797128	8662290
国有独资公司	State Sole Funded Corporations	2329574	1034181	191343	1945182
其他有限责任公司	Other Limited Liability Corporations	8812447	7239117	605785	6717108
股份有限公司	Share-holding Corporations Ltd.	7946487	4306818	431295	6973698
私营企业	Private Enterprises	5779691	4739125	388243	4421218
私营独资企业	Private-funded Enterprises	13220	13094	96	12447
私营合伙企业	Private Partnership Enterprises	864	791	53	809
私营有限责任公司	Private Limited Liability Corporations	5583218	4632979	338165	4311812
私营股份有限公司	Private Share-holding Corporations Ltd.	182389	92261	49929	96150
其他企业	Other Enterprises	67881	50737	16190	35309
港、澳、台商投资企业	Enterprises With Funds from Hong Kong, Macao and Taiwan	238544	236742	769	181598
港、澳、台商独资经营企业	Enterprises with Sole Funds from Hong Kong, Macao and Taiwan	238544	236742	769	181598
外商投资企业	Foreign Funded Enterprises	66148	45055	12406	61191
中外合资经营企业	Joint-venture Enterprise	18184	13442	3636	4805
外资企业	Enterprises with Sole Funds	47964	31613	8770	56386
按批发行业小类分组	**By Sector of Wholesale**				
农、林、牧产品批发	Wholesale of Agriculturel,Forestry and Livestock Products	6318332	5116464	539246	5074009
谷物、豆及薯类批发	Wholesale of Grain,Bean and Potato	755172	578415	109161	604654
种子批发	Wholesale of Feed	532371	359692	84718	294659
饲料批发	Wholesale of Secdstuffe	745	632	113	245
棉、麻批发	Wholesale of Cotton and Liner	4940532	4104675	339606	4111903
林业产品批发	Wholesale of Forestry Producets	4207	3550	2	6874
牲畜批发	Wholesale of Livestock	28330	25888	2381	11380
其他农牧产品批发	Wholesale of Other Agicultural Product and Livestock Products	56975	43612	3265	44294
食品、饮料及烟草制品批发	Wholesale of Food,Beverages and Tobaccos	2669067	1822043	299922	1246644
米、面制品及食用油批发	Wholesale of Rice, Flour and Edible Oil	316801	245370	40730	257203
糕点、糖果及糖批发	Wholesale of Pastry,Candy and Sugar	21092	11795	188	11269
果品、蔬菜批发业	Wholesale of Fruit and Vegetable	795018	367591	170655	523767
肉、禽、蛋及水产品批发	Wholesale of Meat,Poultry,Eggs and Aquatic Products	37322	19855	5915	38752
盐及调味品批发	Wholesale of Salt and Condiment Flavoring Material	81318	29632	5955	31879
营养及保健品批发	Wholesale of Nutritious and Healeh Food	5396	5385	8	5226
酒、饮料及茶叶批发	Wholesale of Soft Drink and Tea Leaf	501019	386204	14033	174678
烟草制品批发	Wholesale of Tobaccos	877196	731902	54658	180807
其他食品批发	Wholesale of Other Food	33905	24309	7780	23063
纺织、服装及日用品批发	Wholesale of Textitle, Wearing Apparel and Household Articles	349230	271393	15630	290405
纺织品、针织品及原料批发	Wholesale of Textile,Hosiery and Raw Material	172281	125824	7013	128423
服装批发	Wholesale of Garment	60808	55689	286	59520
化妆品及卫生用品批发	Wholesale of Cosmetics and Health Aids	19390	17929	1244	18002
家用电器批发	Wholesale of Household Electric Appliances	86233	63439	6105	78916
其他家庭用品批发	Wholesale of Household Goods	10518	8512	982	5544
文化、体育用品及器材批发	Wholesale of Culture, Sports Goods and Apparatus	240594	162596	19244	172874
文具用品批发	Whoiesale of Stationery	1242	1105	137	1096
图书批发	Wholesale of Books	179073	105821	16213	116909

16-9 续表 Continued

单位：万元 (10 000 yuan)

指标	Item	资产合计 Total Assets	#流动资产 Working Capitals	#固定资产 Fixed Assets	负债合计 Total Liabilities
首饰、工艺品及收藏品批发	Wholesale of Jewellery、Handicraft、Collectim	19535	18645	870	18665
其他文化用品批发	Wholesale of Other Culture Products	40744	37025	2024	36204
医药及医疗器械批发	Wholesale of Medicines and Medical Appliances	746420	654700	61300	583121
西药批发	Wholesale of Western Medicine	632465	555705	53776	508099
中药批发	Wholesale of Chinese Medicinal Plant and Chinese Patent Medicine	39597	32342	3810	28699
医疗用品及器材批发	Wholesale of Medical Supplies and Appliances	74358	66653	3714	46323
矿产品、建材及化工产品批发	Wholesale of Mineral Products, Building Material and Chemical Products	16050642	10468857	890545	13759468
煤炭及制品批发	Wholesale of Coal and Related Products	2679164	1674435	30421	1683595
石油及制品批发	Wholesale of Petroleum and Related Products	6166295	3982358	675783	6687717
非金属矿及制品批发	Wholesale of Non-Metal Materials	5159	4359	628	4636
金属及金属矿批发	Wholesale of Metal and Metal Materials	2904315	2588385	38950	2421311
建材批发	Wholesale of Building Materials	466958	414422	13323	388729
化肥批发	Wholesale of Fertilizer	1173221	974048	56433	978155
农药批发	Wholesale of Pesticides	28822	24121	1415	20671
其他化工产品批发	Wholesale of Other Chemical Product	2626708	806729	73592	1574654
机械设备、五金交电及电子产品批发	Wholesale of Machinery, Hardware and Electronic Products	2340966	2021160	74591	1837530
农业机械批发	Wholesale of Agriculture Machinery	150039	118977	18258	106363
汽车批发	Wholesale of Motor Vehicles, Motorcycles and Parts	215946	203560	7044	168140
汽车零配件批发	Wholesales of Motor Vehicle Parts	1079706	960090	14960	817067
摩托车及零配件批发	Wholesales of Motorcycle and Parts	6005	5909	83	5573
五金产品批发	Wholesale of Hardware	101660	94303	2376	82818
电气设备批发	Wholesale of Electric Appliances	62372	61968	25	56795
计算机、软件及辅助设备批发	Wholesale of Computer, Software and Assistant Equipment	32727	29062	376	22302
通讯及广播电视设备批发	Wholesale of Communicating and Broadcasting Television Device	26914	25021	314	20586
其他机械设备及电子产品批发	Wholesale of Other Mechanical Equipment and Electromic Products	665597	522270	31155	557886
贸易经纪与代理	Trade Broker and Agency	48701	37889	5730	42138
贸易代理	Trades Broker and Agency	48701	37889	5730	42138
其他批发业	Others Wholesale not classified Elsewhere	123201	67543	12919	94790
再生物资回收与批发业	Recovery and Wholesale of Regeneration Material	93322	51011	4092	83181
其他未列明的批发业	Wholesale of Un-listed	29879	16532	8827	11609
按地区分	**By Region**				
乌鲁木齐市	Urumqi City	15051766	10941316	413121	10742097
克拉玛依市	Karamay City	426269	191735	114796	505212
吐鲁番市	Turpan City	162600	97068	38220	107092
哈密地区	Hami [Kumul] Administrative Offices	449242	361670	43832	604981
昌吉回族自治州	Changji Hui Autonomous Prefecture	720526	456468	116154	738623
伊犁哈萨克自治州	Ili Kazak Autonomous Prefecture	2136346	1058769	184013	1569019
伊犁州直属县(市)	Counties (Cities) Direct Under Ili Prefecture	1563002	675157	122755	937458
塔城地区	Tacheng [Tarbagatai] Administrative Offices	483829	338767	33665	386336
阿勒泰地区	Altay Administrative Offices	89515	44845	27593	245225
博尔塔拉蒙古自治州	Bortala Mongol Autonomous Prefecture	319772	207346	54751	251987
巴音郭楞蒙古自治州	Bayangol Mongol Autonomous Prefecture	1015077	714563	174468	797021
阿克苏地区	Aksu Administrative Offices	1269959	955568	169017	1300108
克孜勒苏柯尔克孜自治州	Kizilsu Kirgiz Autonomous Prefecture	183212	147515	14218	120951
喀什地区	Kashgar [Kaxgar] Administrative Offices	863370	554457	132086	974258
和田地区	Hotan Administrative Offices	107058	63996	23932	96905
生产建设兵团	Xinjiang Production and Construction Group	6181956	4872174	440519	5292725

16-10 限额以上零售企业资产及负债情况
Assets and Liabilities of Enterprises above Designated Size of Retail Trades

单位：万元 (2015 年) (10 000 yuan)

指标	Item	资产合计 Total Asset	#流动资产 Working Capitals	#固定资产 Fixed Asset	负债合计 Total Liabilities
总计	**Total**	**6240890**	**4134479**	**952097**	**4934779**
按登记注册类型分	**By Status of Registration**				
内资企业	Domestic Funded Enterprises	5294986	3545093	899324	4497937
国有企业	State-owned Enterprises	264232	122069	81514	120538
集体企业	Collective-owned Enterprises	12331	7591	2598	9997
股份合作企业	Cooperative Enterprises	1490	825	465	950
有限责任公司	Limited Liability Corporations	2002252	1504298	292412	1399958
国有独资公司	State Sole Funded Corporations	79124	70353	3593	71934
其他有限责任公司	Other Limited Liability Corporations	1923128	1433945	288819	1328024
股份有限公司	Share-holding Corporations Ltd.	730602	213191	239847	1124887
私营企业	Private Enterprises	2283228	1696293	282463	1841116
私营独资企业	Private-funded Enterprises	2134	2049	48	1516
私营合伙企业	Private Partnership Enterises	1801	1197	274	948
私营有限责任公司	Private Limited Liability Corporations	2244787	1685854	281803	1807163
私营股份有限公司	Private Share-holding Corporation Ltd.	34506	7193	338	31489
其他企业	Other Enterprises	851	826	25	491
港、澳、台投资企业	Enterprises With Funds from Hong Kong, Macao and Taiwan	859394	521531	35570	381657
港、澳、台商独资经营企业	Enterprises with Sole Funds from Hong Kong, Macao and Taiwan	58259	43904	7196	29029
港、澳、台商投资股份有限公司	Share-holcling Corporatin Ltd with Funds From Aongkong Macao and Faiwan	801135	477627	28374	352628
外商投资企业	Foreign Funded Enterprises	86510	67855	17203	55185
中外合资经营企业	Joint Venture Enterprises	54554	41977	11291	36920
外资企业	Enterprises with Sole Fund	28142	22627	5353	12968
外商投资股份有限公司	Share-holcling Corporatin Ltd with Foreign Investhment	3814	3251	559	5297
按零售行业小类分组	**By Sector of Retail**				
综合零售	Integrated Retail	1439063	695415	363978	1181527
百货零售	Retail of Merchandise	1182923	525181	319275	961435
超级市场零售	Retail of Supermarkets	253954	168229	44658	219432
其他综合零售	Retail of other integrate	2186	2005	45	660
食品、饮料及烟草制品专门零售	Special Retail of Food, Beverages and Tobaccos	52670	39582	3685	49727
粮油零售	Retail of Grain and Oil	17813	17218	575	18907
果品、蔬菜零售	Retail of Fruit and Vegetables	10820	5351	1272	7823
肉、禽、蛋及水产品零售	Retail of Meat,Poultry ,Eggs and Aquatic Products	2106	928	775	695
营养和保健品零售	Retail of Nutritious and Healeh Food	1213	1174	37	1032
酒、饮料及茶叶零售	Retail of Soft Drink and Tea Leaf	14306	12359	742	17666
烟草制品零售	Retail of Tobaccos	6412	2552	284	3604
纺织、服装及日用品专门零售	Special Retail of Textile, Garments and Daily Consumer Articles	286666	201453	51425	267505
纺织品及针织品零售	Retail of Textile Fabric and Hosiery	52658	51492	1021	51304
服装零售	Retail of Garment	192015	130357	32765	189879
鞋帽零售	Retail of Shoes and Hats	11085	10412	656	8640
化妆品及卫生用品零售	Retail of Cosmetics and Health Aids	1202	1187	15	1197
钟表、眼镜零售	Retail of Timekeeper and Spectacle	6024	5007	22	5013
厨房用具及日用杂品零售	Retail of kitchenware and Household goods	1234	717	43	675
其他日用品零售	Retail of Other Covenience Goods	22448	2281	16903	10797
文化、体育用品及器材专门零售业	Special Retail of Cultural, Sports goods and Appliances	313661	156222	76120	154870

16-10 续表 Continued

单位：万元 (10 000 yuan)

指 标	Item	资产合计 Total Assets	#流动资产 Working Capitals	#固定资产 Fixed Assets	负债合计 Total Liabilities
文具用品零售	Retail of Stationery and Office Supplies	4029	4020	9	2373
体育用品及器材零售	Retail of Sports Appliances and Eqwipments	2322	2316	6	1838
图书、报刊零售	Retail of Books,Newspapers and Magazines	210851	89203	68517	90800
珠宝首饰零售	Retail of Jewelry	96459	60683	7588	59859
医药及医疗器材专门零售	Special Retail of Medicines and Medical- Appliances	711912	637044	44974	489769
药品零售	Retail of Medcine	679228	611790	44229	470651
医疗用品及器材零售	Retocil of Medical Treatment and Equipment	32684	25254	745	19118
汽车、摩托车、燃料及零配件专门零售	Special Retail of Car, Motor, Fuel and Parts	3125370	2176754	362197	2591222
汽车零售	Retail of Motor Vehicles	1871035	1487156	216997	1413984
汽车零配件零售	Retail of Automobiles' Parts	70167	44797	10864	22264
摩托车及零配件零售	Retail of Motorcycle and Fittings	12003	11151	464	9819
机动车燃料零售	Retail of Auto Fuel	1172165	633650	133872	1145155
家用电器及电子产品专门零售	Special Retail of House hold Electric Appliances and Electronic Products	207484	189365	4221	142960
家用视听设备零售	Retail of Home audio-Visual Appliances	83780	76614	1058	61393
日用家电设备零售	Retail of Household Electric Appliances	42738	40376	1573	28397
计算机、软件及辅助设备零售	Retail of Cumputers,Software and Assistant Appliances	49524	41674	1192	30452
通讯设备零售	Retail of Communication Equipments	22393	21774	321	16566
其他电子产品零售	Retail of other Electronic Products	9049	8927	77	6152
五金、家具及室内装修材料专门零售	Special Retail of Hardware, Furniture and Interior Decorating Material	7517	7045	462	5516
五金零售	Retail of Hardware	5608	5384	224	4533
陶瓷、石材装饰材料零售	Retaul of Ceramics and Stone Decorating Material	539	301	237	42
其他室内装饰材料零售	Retaul of other Interior Decorating Material	1370	1360	1	941
货摊、无店铺及其他零售业	Stalls,Non-shop and Other Retail	96547	31599	45035	51683
邮购及电视、电话零售	Retoul of Post and E-commerce	3181	1643	51	3142
生活用燃料零售业	Retail of Life Fuels	93366	29956	44984	48541
按地区分	**By Region**				
乌鲁木齐市	Urumqi City	4004379	2679952	536249	3278986
克拉玛依市	Karamay City	190983	147053	22718	167387
吐鲁番市	Turpan City	27452	13914	5769	14772
哈密地区	Hami [Kumul] Administrative Offices	156092	91374	28454	111814
昌吉回族自治州	Changji Hui Autonomous Prefecture	222034	152513	26876	166357
伊犁哈萨克自治州	Ili Kazak Autonomous Prefecture	389312	243135	78278	278594
伊犁州直属县(市)	Counties (Cities) Direct Under Ili Prefecture	314344	207987	56631	233444
塔城地区	Tacheng [Tarbagatai] Administrative Offices	61764	27070	19404	35445
阿勒泰地区	Altay Administrative Offices	13204	8078	2243	9705
博尔塔拉蒙古自治州	Bortala Mongol Autonomous Prefecture	16696	10528	2051	14691
巴音郭楞蒙古自治州	Bayangol Mongol Autonomous Prefecture	317425	190783	72387	272255
阿克苏地区	Aksu Administrative Offices	318657	206119	77463	263031
克孜勒苏柯尔克孜自治州	Kizilsu Kirgiz Autonomous Prefecture	13419	5949	4309	8364
喀什地区	Kashgar [Kaxgar] Administrative Offices	149148	97538	34539	100442
和田地区	Hotan Administrative Offices	23626	13715	5073	12745
生产建设兵团	Xinjiang Production and Construction Group	411667	281906	57931	245341

16-11 限额以上餐饮企业资产及负债情况
Assets and Liabilities of Enterprises above Designated Size of Catering Services

单位：万元 (2015 年) (10 000 yuan)

指 标	Item	资产合计 Total Assets	#流动资产 Current Capitals	#固定资产 Fixed Assets	负债合计 Total Liabilities
总 计	**Total**	**359557**	**102931**	**112696**	**176948**
按登记注册类型分	**By Status of Registration**				
内资企业	Domestic-funded Enterprises	351187	100553	111521	170241
国有企业	State – owned Enterprises	127636	10547	35253	9178
有限责任公司	Limited Liability Corporations	63028	23176	24928	36023
国有独资公司	Stata Sole Funded Corporations	3085	654	2419	528
其他有限责任公司	Other Limited Liability Corporations	59943	22522	22509	35495
股份有限公司	Share-holding Corporations Ltd.	31564	14826	2314	22900
私营企业	Private Enterprises	128855	51914	49012	102078
私营独资企业	Private-funded Enterprises	13611	3519	7556	16137
私营合伙企业	Private Partnership Enterprises	3868	2914	433	689
私营有限责任公司	Private Limited Liability Corporations	108163	43266	40793	83802
私营股份有限公司	Private Share-holding Corporation Ltd.	3213	2215	230	1450
其他企业	Other Enterprises	104	90	14	62
港、澳、台商投资企业	Enterprises With Funds from Hong Kong, Macao and Taiwan	307	301	6	1836
与港澳台商合资经营企业	Joint-venture Enterprises	307	301	6	1836
外商投资企业	Foreign Funded Enterprises	8063	2077	1169	4871
外资企业	Enterprises with Sole Fund	8063	2077	1169	4871
按餐饮行业小类分组	**By Sector of Catering**				
正餐服务	Dinner	330217	94241	102357	164891
快餐服务	Snack	29340	8690	10339	12057
按地区分	**By Region**				
乌鲁木齐市	Urumqi City	180121	32603	49172	51708
克拉玛依市	Karamay City	2145	1838	76	2808
吐鲁番市	Turpan City	47	44	3	7
哈密地区	Hami [Kumul] Administrative Offices	1195	717	125	890
昌吉回族自治州	Changji Hui Autonomous Prefecture	3775	1685	1812	3534
伊犁哈萨克自治州	Ili Kazak Autonomous Prefecture	76757	30161	28964	52605
伊犁州直属县(市)	Counties (Cities) Direct Under Ili Prefecture	72651	28965	28387	47938
塔城地区	Tacheng [Tarbagatai] Administrative Offices	4106	1196	577	4667
巴音郭楞蒙古自治州	Bayangol Mongol Autonomous Prefecture	17995	9904	4005	15553
阿克苏地区	Aksu Administrative Offices	18917	5629	9738	15046
喀什地区	Kashgar [Kaxgar] Administrative Offices	618	186	431	281
生产建设兵团	Xinjiang Production and Construction Group	57987	20164	18370	34516

16-12 限额以上住宿企业资产及负债情况

Assets and Liabilities of Enterprises above Designated Size of Accommodation Services

单位：万元 (2015 年) (10 000 yuan)

指 标	Item	资产合计 Total Assets	#流动资产 Current Capitals	#固定资产 Fixed Assets	负债合计 Total Liabilities
总 计	**Total**	**1185463**	**341867**	**537645**	**846308**
按登记注册类型分	**By Status of Registration**				
内资企业	Domestic-funded Enterprises	1184810	341574	537285	846366
国有企业	State-owned Enterprises	241883	79448	137408	125849
集体企业	Collective-owned Enterprises	45077	1558	2418	50015
联营企业	Joint Ownership Enterprises	2237	1428	809	1287
国有联营企业	State Joint Ownership Enterprises	2237	1428	809	1287
有限责任公司	Limited Liability Corporations	566012	162608	250986	393935
国有独资公司	State Sole Funded Corporations	49070	9131	36470	38558
其他有限责任公司	Other Limited Liability Corporations	516942	153477	214516	355377
股份有限公司	Share-holding Corporations Ltd.	37081	4571	15447	11895
私营企业	Private Enterprises	292144	91881	129921	263123
私营独资企业	Private-funded Enterprises	15382	3490	10701	12959
私营合伙企业	Private Partnership Enterprises	2953	221	2459	4330
私营有限责任公司	Private Limited Liability Corporations	271785	88154	116176	244602
私营股份有限公司	Private Share-holding Corporations Ltd	2024	16	585	1232
其他企业	Others Enterprises	376	80	296	262
港、澳、台商投资企业	Enterprises With Funds from Hong Kong, Macao and Taiwan	544	186	358	74
合资经营企业（港或澳、台资）	Joint-venture Enterprises (Funds from Hong Kong, Macao and Taiwan)	544	186	358	74
外商投资企业	With Foreign Investment Enterprises	109	107	2	-132
外资企业	Enterprises with Sole Foreign Fund	109	107	2	-132
按住宿行业分组	**By Sector of**				
旅游饭店	Tourist Hotels	1079816	308868	479409	766532
一般旅馆	Ordinary Hotels	105491	32953	58182	78825
其他住宿业	Other Hotels	156	46	54	951
按星级等级分	**Classified by Stars**				
五 星	Five-Star	287649	64897	132970	214677
四 星	Four-Star	309468	121658	135235	219140
三 星	Three-Star	453971	99256	204618	310312
二 星	Two-Star	31631	12937	16167	23076
其 他	Other	102744	43119	48655	79103
按地区分	**By Region**				
乌鲁木齐市	Urumqi City	427683	154376	167322	262068
克拉玛依市	Karamay City	40657	2164	37639	56236
吐鲁番市	Turpan City	35991	14147	12239	31136
哈密地区	Hami [Kumul] Administrative Offices	36868	8999	17072	15884
昌吉回族自治州	Changji Hui Autonomous Prefecture	9155	2401	3933	9855
伊犁哈萨克自治州	Ili Kazak Autonomous Prefecture	147631	37243	71406	97084
伊犁州直属县(市)	Counties (Cities) Direct Under Ili Prefecture	57908	15159	26657	40727
塔城地区	Tacheng [Tarbagatai] Administrative Offices	22141	8327	12779	18465
阿勒泰地区	Altay Administrative Offices	67582	13757	31970	37892
博尔塔拉蒙古自治州	Bortala Mongol Autonomous Prefecture	14513	5051	7850	10158
巴音郭楞蒙古自治州	Bayangol Mongol Autonomous Prefecture	78181	22264	45871	73857
阿克苏地区	Aksu Administrative Offices	88494	21092	59401	76725
克孜勒苏柯尔克孜自治州	Kizilsu Kirgiz Autonomous Prefecture	6758	880	5693	3938
喀什地区	Kashgar [Kaxgar] Administrative Offices	168540	37575	42117	154665
和田地区	Hotan Administrative Offices	23019	5156	15109	11060
生产建设兵团	Xinjiang Production and Construction Group	107973	30519	51993	43642

16-13 限额以上批发企业主要财务指标
Main Financial Indicators of Wholesale Enterprises above Designated Size

单位：万元　　(2015 年)　　(10 000 yuan)

指 标	Item	商品销售收入 Revenue of Product Sales	商品销售成本 Cost of Product Sales	商品销售税金及附加 Sales Tax and Extra Changes	商品销售利润 Profits of Product Sales
总 计	**Total**	**51826050**	**50003616**	**223984**	**1598450**
按登记注册类型分	**By Status of Registration**				
内资企业	Domestic Funded Enterprises	51499336	49683818	223838	1591680
国有企业	State-owned Enterprises	5711252	5250012	90716	370524
集体企业	Collective-owned Enterprises	260458	238580	250	21628
联营企业	Joint Ownership Enterprises	4550	4269	1	280
集体联营企业	Collective Joint Ownership Enterprises	4550	4269	1	280
有限责任公司	Limited Liability Corporations	22256477	21401038	116241	739198
国有独资公司	State Sole Funded Corporations	3566835	3307651	95204	163980
其他有限责任公司	Other Limited Liability Corporations	18689642	18093387	21037	575218
股份有限公司	Share-holding Corporations Ltd.	15276262	15218330	7972	49960
私营企业	Private Enterprises	7824800	7436121	8477	380202
私营独资企业	Private-funded Enterprises	22059	20817	21	1221
私营合伙企业	Private Partnership Enterprises	1464	1334	2	128
私营有限责任公司	Private Limited Liability Corporations	7734899	7361424	8356	365119
私营股份有限公司	Private Share-holding Corporation Ltd.	66378	52546	98	13734
其他企业	Other Enterprises	165537	135468	181	29888
港、澳、台商投资企业	Enterprises With Funds from Hong Kong, Macao and Taiwan	292908	290291	20	2597
港、澳、台商独资经营企业	Enterprises with Sole Funds from Hong Kong, Macao and Taiwan	292908	290291	20	2597
外商投资企业	Foreign funded Enterprises	33806	29507	126	4173
中外合资经营企业	Joint Venture Enterprises	8903	7057	46	1800
外资企业	Enterprises with Sole Fund	24903	22450	80	2373
按批发行业小类分组	**By Sector of Wholesale**				
农、林、牧产品批发	Wholesale of Agricultunal,Forestry	7826123	7457183	1956	366984
谷物、豆及薯类批发	Wholesale of Grain,Bean and Potato	622028	582619	130	39279
种子批发	Wholesale of Seed	273722	219562	43	54117
饲料批发	Wholesale of feedstuff	3549	3017		532
棉、麻批发	Wholesale of Cotton and Liner	6799269	6530848	1713	266708
林业产品批发	Wholesale of Foresry Produccts	16787	18979	8	-2200
牲畜批发	Wholesale of Livestoch	53129	46455	26	6648
其他农牧产品批发	Wholesale of Other Agricudtural Produce and Livestoclc Products	57639	55703	36	1900
食品、饮料及烟草制品批发	Wholesale of Food,Beverages and Tobaccos	4323864	3697848	200409	425607
米、面制品及食用油批发	Wholesale of Rice, Flour and Edible Oil	291139	282631	147	8361
糕点、糖果及糖批发	Wholesale of Pastry,Candy and Sugar	25769	22838	50	2881
果品、蔬菜批发	Wholesale of Fruit and Vegetable	784826	665411	14753	104662
肉、禽、蛋及水产品批发	Wholesale of Meat,Poultry,Eggs and Aquatic Products	53562	43889	315	9358
盐及调味品批发	Wholesale of Salt and Condiment Flavoring Material	76226	62431	220	13575
营养及保健品批发	Wholesale of Nutritious and Healeh Food	11918	10443	25	1450
酒、饮料及茶叶批发	Wholesale of Soft Drink and Tea Leaf	142472	117651	1759	23062
烟草制品批发	Wholesale of Tobaccos	2910979	2469291	183036	258652
其他食品批发	Wholesale of Other Food	26973	23263	104	3606
纺织、服装及家庭用品批发	Wholesale of Textitles, Wearing Apparel and Household Articles	482979	451527	580	30872
纺织品、针织品及原料批发	Wholesale of Textiles,Hosiery and Raw Material	148458	140871	50	7537
服装批发	Wholesale of Wearing Appardl	90261	83920	157	6184
化妆品及卫生用品批发	Wholesale of Cosmetics and Health Aids	39238	35117	59	4062
家用电器批发	Wholesale of Household Electrcal Appliances	187223	176178	271	10774
其他家庭用品批发	Wholesale of Other Household Articles	17799	15441	43	2315
文化、体育用品及器材批发	Wholesale of Culture, Sports Goods and Apparatus	204750	184552	232	19966

16-13 续表 Continued

单位：万元 (10 000 yuan)

指　标	Item	商品销售收入 Revenue of Product Sales	商品销售成本 Cost of Product Sales	商品销售税金及附加 Sales Tax and Extra Changes	商品销售利润 Product Sales Profits
文具用品批发	Wholesale of Stationery	2452	901	2	1549
图书批发	Wholesale of Books	146772	132183	123	14466
首饰、工艺品及收藏品批发	Wholesale of Jewellery、Handicraft、Collection	6316	5236	66	1014
其他文化用品批发	Wholesale of Other Culture Products	49210	46232	41	2937
医药及医疗器械批发	Wholesale of Medicines and Medical Appliances	1146938	1043996	1747	101195
西药批发	Wholesale of Western Medicine	999738	922727	1270	75741
中药批发	Wholesale of Chinese Medicinal Plant	49603	45042	96	4465
医疗用品及器材批发	Wholesale of Medical Supplies and Appliances	97597	76227	381	20989
矿产品、建材及化工产品批发	Wholesale of Mineral Products, Building Materials and Chemical Products	34718563	34181292	15706	521565
煤炭及制品批发	Wholesale of Coal and Related Products	438256	410495	862	26899
石油及制品批发	Wholesale of Petroleum and Related Products	24751258	24648606	8235	94417
非金属矿及制品批发	Wholesale of Non-Metal Materials	4807	3996	30	781
金属及金属矿批发	Wholesale of Metal and Metal Materials	5250455	5131075	2310	117070
建材批发	Wholesale of Building Materials	590647	569793	666	20188
化肥批发	Wholesale of chemical Fertilizer	1738490	1672149	327	66014
农药批发	Wholesale of Pesticides	36488	32362	25	4101
其他化工产品批发	Wholesale of Other Chemical Products	1908162	1712816	3251	192095
机械设备、五金交电及电子产品批发	Wholesale of Machinery, Hardware and Electronic Products	2935676	2817686	2937	115053
农业机械批发	Wholesale of Agriculture Machinery	246927	231803	83	15041
汽车批发	Wholesale of Motor Vehicles	134246	125987	335	7924
汽车零配件批发	Wholesale of Motor Vehicles Parts	724467	699113	384	24970
摩托车及零配件批发	Wholesale of Motorcycles and Parts	10028	8963	20	1045
五金产品批发	Wholesale of Hardware	146740	131076	1078	14586
电气设备批发	Wholesale of Electric Equipments	191312	186271	98	4943
计算机、软件及辅助设备批发	Wholesale of Computer, Software and Accessory Equipment	67113	65203	61	1849
通讯及广播电视设备批发	Wholesale of Communicating and Broadcasting Television Device	58121	55033	79	3009
其他机械设备及电子产品批发	Wholesale of Other Mechanical Equipment and Electromic Products	1356722	1314237	799	41686
贸易经纪与代理	Trade Broker and Agency	87322	84702	31	2589
贸易代理	Trades Agency	87322	84702	31	2589
其他批发业	Others Wholesale	99835	84830	386	14619
再生物资回收与批发业	Recovery and Wholesale of Regeneration Material	61859	57609	204	4046
其他未列明的批发业	Wholesale of Un-listed	37976	27221	182	10573
按地区分	**By Region**				
乌鲁木齐市	Urumqi City	32550334	31956320	60092	533922
克拉玛依市	Karamay City	737967	673225	6549	58193
吐鲁番市	Turpan City	377187	345168	6006	26013
哈密地区	Hami [Kumul] Administrative Offices	838344	780839	9139	48366
昌吉回族自治州	Changji Hui Autonomous Prefecture	885289	792996	18332	73961
伊犁哈萨克自治州	Ili Kazak Autonomous Prefecture	2389713	2240814	35249	113650
伊犁州直属县(市)	Counties (Cities) Direct Under Ili Prefecture	1561224	1474153	15992	71079
塔城地区	Tacheng [Tarbagatai] Administrative Offices	590986	557443	12797	20746
阿勒泰地区	Altay Administrative Offices	237503	209218	6460	21825
博尔塔拉蒙古自治州	Bortala Mongol Autonomous Prefecture	549301	522102	5007	22192
巴音郭楞蒙古自治州	Bayangol Mongol Autonomous Prefecture	1667544	1566755	16099	84690
阿克苏地区	Aksu Administrative Offices	1533905	1427781	17161	88963
克孜勒苏柯尔克孜自治州	Kizilsu Kirgiz Autonomous Prefecture	148418	141180	78	7160
喀什地区	Kashgar [Kaxgar] Administrative Offices	1190892	1098582	17467	74843
和田地区	Hotan Administrative Offices	287919	260582	5458	21879
生产建设兵团	Xinjiang Production and Construction Group	8669237	8197272	27347	444618

16-14 限额以上零售企业主要财务指标
Main Financial Indicators of Retail Enterprises above Designated Size

单位：万元 (2015 年) (10 000 yuan)

指 标	Item	商品销售收入 Revenue of Product Sales	商品销售成本 Cost of Product Sales	商品销售税金及附加 Sales Tax and Extra Changes	商品销售利润 Product Sales Profits
总 计	**Total**	**8356626**	**7424137**	**32621**	**899868**
按登记注册类型分	**By Status of Registration**				
内资企业	Domestic Funded Enterprises	7924638	7045704	30772	848162
国有企业	State-owned Enterprises	229290	173697	660	54933
集体企业	Collective-owned Enterprises	8983	8084	18	881
股份合作企业	Cooperative Enterprises	896	780	1	115
有限责任公司	Limited Liability Corporations	3219475	2889111	8512	321852
国有独资公司	State Sole Funded Corporations	61282	53465	51	7766
其他有限责任公司	Other Limited Liability Corporations	3158193	2835646	8461	314086
股份有限公司	Corporations Ltd.	1092741	964532	9638	118571
私营企业	Private Enterprises	3371883	3008786	11931	351166
私营独资企业	Private-funded Enterprises	3249	2686	25	538
私营合伙企业	Private Partnership Enterprises	2029	1913	10	106
私营有限责任公司	Private Limited Liability Corporations	3363906	3002035	11890	349981
私营股份有限公司	Private Share-holding Corporation Ltd.	2699	2152	6	541
其他企业	Other Enterprises	1370	714	12	644
港、澳、台投资企业	Enterprises With Funds from Hong Kong, Macao and Taiwan	230839	206376	575	23888
港、澳、台商独资经营企业	Enterprises with Sole Funds from Hong Kong, Macao and Taiwan	184735	167867	520	16348
港、澳、台商投资股份有限公司	Share-holding Corporatin Ltd with Funds FromAongkong Macao and Faiwan	46104	38509	55	7540
外商投资企业	Foreign funded Enterprises	201149	172057	1274	27818
中外合资经营企业	Joint Venture Enterprises	143762	123536	874	19352
外资企业	Enterprises with Sole Fund	49787	41456	399	7932
外商投资股份有限公司	Share-holcling Corporations Ltd with Foreign Investhment	7600	7065	1	534
按零售行业小类分组	**By Sector of Retail**				
综合零售	Integrated Retail	1588577	1355631	16236	216710
百货零售	Retail of General Merchandise	1123400	945049	14618	163733
超级市场零售	Retail of Supermarket	461366	408049	1617	51700
其他综合零售	Retail of Other Integrate	3811	2533	1	1277
食品、饮料及烟草制品专门零售	Special Retail of Foods, Beverages and Tobaccos	24101	20885	73	3143
粮油零售	Retail of Grain and Oil	2506	2578		-72
果品、蔬菜零售	Retail of Fruite and Vegetables	4331	4135	10	186
肉、禽、蛋及水产品零售	Retail of Meat,Poultry, Eggs and Aquatic products	903	662	2	239
营养和保健品零售	Retail of Nutritious and Healeh Food	2645	2348	4	293
酒、饮料及茶叶零售	Retail of Soft Drink and Tea Leaf	10512	8441	52	2019
烟草制品零售	Retail of Tobaccos	3204	2721	5	478
纺织、服装及日用品专门零售	Special Retail of Textile, Garments and Daily Consumer Articles	387333	324267	3026	60040
纺织品及针织品零售	Retail of Textile Fabric and Hosiery	42383	39946		2437
服装零售	Retail of Garment	272820	226984	2440	43396
鞋帽零售	Retail of Shoes and Hats	21345	14815	123	6407
化妆品及卫生用品零售	Retail of Cosmetics and Health Aids	1470	1360	2	108
钟表、眼镜零售	Retail of Timekeeper and Spectacle	13954	11955	56	1943
厨房用具及日用杂品零售	Retail of kitchenware and Househald goods	1315	1128	2	185
其他日用品零售	Retail of other Covenience Goods	34046	28079	403	5564
文化、体育用品及器材专门零售	Special Retail of Cultural, Sports Goods And Apparatus	225424	168511	672	56241

16-14 续表 Continued

单位：万元 (10 000 yuan)

指标	Item	商品销售收入 Revenue of Product Sales	商品销售成本 Cost of Product Sales	商品销售税金及附加 Sales Taxes and Extra Changes	商品销售利润 Product Sales Profits
文具用品零售	Retail of Sports Stationery and office Supplies	5278	4799	7	472
体育用品及器材零售	Retail of Sports Appliances and Eguipments	820	720	4	96
图书、报刊零售	Retail of Books,Newspapers and Magazines	190732	144327	114	46291
珠宝首饰零售	Retail of Jewelry	28594	18665	547	9382
医药及医疗器材专门零售	Special Retail of Medicines and Medical Appliances	1032079	919450	2360	110269
药品零售	Retail of Medcine	973377	877986	2063	93328
医疗用品及器材零售	Retaul of Medical Treatment and Equipment	58702	41464	297	16941
汽车、摩托车、燃料及零配件专门零售	Special Retail of Car, Motor, Fuel and Parts	4564011	4170598	9031	384382
汽车零售	Retail of Motor Vehicles	3324871	3081623	5891	237357
汽车零配件零售	Retail of Automobiles' Parts	175044	116507	1491	57046
摩托车及零配件零售	Retail of Motorcycle and Fittings	7759	7199	15	545
机动车燃料零售	Retail of Auto Fuel	1056337	965269	1634	89434
家用电器及电子产品专门零售	Special Retail of House hold Electric Appliancesaund Electronic Products	446255	395577	910	49768
家用视听设备零售	Retail of Home audio-visual Equipments	214590	187702	490	26398
日用家电设备零售	Retail of Household Electric Appliances	101579	91859	177	9543
计算机、软件及辅助设备零售	Retail of Cumputer,Software and Assistant Appliances	72929	66519	124	6286
通讯设备零售	Retail of Communication Equipments	45607	39779	102	5726
其他电子产品零售	Retail of other Electronic Products	11550	9718	17	1815
五金、家具及室内装修材料专门零售	Special Retail of Hardware, Furniture and Interor Decorating Material	16642	15163	14	1465
五金零售	Retail of Hardware	11667	11060	9	598
陶瓷、石材装饰材料零售	Retaul of Ceramics and Stone Decorating Material	3134	2354	5	775
其他室内装饰材料零售	Retaul of other Interior Decorating Material	1841	1749		92
货摊、无店铺及其他零售	Stalls,Non-shop and Other Retail	72204	54055	299	17850
邮购及电视、电话零售	Retoul of Post and E-commerce	612	538		74
生活用燃料零售	Retail of Life Fuels	71592	53517	299	17776
按地区分	**By Region**				
乌鲁木齐市	Urumqi City	5072634	4538134	22633	511867
克拉玛依市	Karamay City	225935	203398	745	21792
吐鲁番市	Turpan City	23931	19309	61	4561
哈密地区	Hami [Kumul] Administrative Offices	192555	170355	319	21881
昌吉回族自治州	Changji Hui Autonomous Prefecture	316440	283246	776	32418
伊犁哈萨克自治州	Ili Kazak Autonomous Prefecture	475076	416317	1305	57454
伊犁州直属县(市)	Counties (Cities) Direct Under Ili Prefecture	400087	352191	1210	46686
塔城地区	Tacheng [Tarbagatai] Administrative Offices	61777	53535	75	8167
阿勒泰地区	Altay Administrative Offices	13212	10591	20	2601
博尔塔拉蒙古自治州	Bortala Mongol Autonomous Prefecture	29752	26988	31	2733
巴音郭楞蒙古自治州	Bayangol Mongol Autonomous Prefecture	394949	359689	1908	33352
阿克苏地区	Aksu Administrative Offices	368309	329871	958	37480
克孜勒苏柯尔克孜自治州	Kizilsu Kirgiz Autonomous Prefecture	9553	7066	35	2452
喀什地区	Kashgar [Kaxgar] Administrative Offices	208135	186416	364	21355
和田地区	Hotan Administrative Offices	26402	21836	34	4532
生产建设兵团	Production and Construction Group	1012955	861512	3452	147991

16-15 限额以上餐饮企业主要财务指标
Main Financial Indicators of Catering Enterprises above Designated Size

单位：万元　　(2015 年)　　(10 000 yuan)

指　　标	Item	主营业务收　入 Revenue from Principal Business	主营业务成　本 Cost of Principal Business	主营业务税金及附加 Tax and Addition of Major Business	主营业务利　润 Profit From Principal Business
总　计	**Total**	**144181**	**66849**	**7621**	**69711**
按登记注册类型分	**By Status of Registration**				
内资企业	Domestic-funded Enterprises	121105	55385	6328	59392
国有企业	State – owned Enterprises	7343	3331	418	3594
有限责任公司	Limited Liability Corporations	27190	11461	1415	14314
国有独资公司	State Sole Funded Corporations	1998	1014	95	889
其他有限责任公司	Other Limited Liability Corporations	25192	10447	1320	13425
股份有限公司	Share-holding Corporations Ltd	990	217	43	730
私营企业	Private Enterprises	83518	39476	4336	39706
私营独资企业	Private-funded Enterprises	5549	3415	260	1874
私营合伙企业	Private Partnership Enterprises	2745	1304	140	1301
私营有限责任公司	Private Limited Liability Corporations	70394	32615	3689	34090
私营股份有限公司	Private Share-holding Corporation Ltd.	4830	2142	247	2441
其他企业	Other Enterprises	2064	900	116	1048
港、澳、台商投资企业	Enterprises With Funds from Hong Kong, Macao and Taiwan	765	518	43	204
与港澳台商合资经营企业	Joint-venture Enterprises	765	518	43	204
外商投资企业	Foreign Funded Enterprises	22311	10946	1250	10115
外资企业	Enterprises with Sole Fund	22311	10946	1250	10115
按餐饮行业小类分组	**By Sector of Catering**				
正餐服务	Dinner	98469	46713	5164	46592
快餐服务	Snack	45712	20136	2457	23119
按地区分	**By Region**				
乌鲁木齐市	Urumqi City	89505	40236	4981	44288
克拉玛依市	Karamay City	2960	1311	100	1549
吐鲁番市	Turpan City	397	344	22	31
哈密地区	Hami [Kumul] Administrative Offices	931	549	53	329
昌吉回族自治州	Changji Hui Autonomous Prefecture	4204	1691	175	2338
伊犁哈萨克自治州	Ili Kazak Autonomous Prefecture	21605	9157	1085	11363
伊犁州直属县(市)	Counties (Cities) Direct Under Ili Prefecture	20074	8231	1025	10818
塔城地区	Tacheng [Tarbagatai] Administrative Offices	1531	926	60	545
巴音郭楞蒙古自治州	Bayangol Mongol Autonomous Prefecture	10332	5302	563	4467
阿克苏地区	Aksu Administrative Offices	6378	3284	346	2748
喀什地区	Kashgar [Kaxgan] Administratine Offices	1194	700	49	445
生产建设兵团	Xinjiang Production and Construction Group	6675	4275	247	2153

16-16 限额以上住宿企业主要财务指标

Main Financial Indicators of Hotels Enterprises above Designated

单位：万元 (2015 年) (10 000 yuan)

指 标	Item	主营业务收入 Revenue from Principal Business	主营业务成本 Cost of Principal Business	主营业务税金及附加 Tax and Addition of Principal Business	主营业务利润 Profit From Principal Business
总 计	**Total**	**321787**	**148163**	**18415**	**155209**
按登记注册类型分	**By Status of Registration**				
内资企业	Domestic-funded Enterprises	321331	148160	18389	154782
国有企业	State-owned Enterprises	103884	47343	5870	50671
集体企业	Collective-owned Enterprises	5381	1637	257	3487
联营企业	Joint Ownership Enterprises	217	16	31	170
国有联营企业	State Joint Ownership Enterprises	217	16	31	170
有限责任公司	Limited Liability Corporations	121071	61838	6989	52244
国有独资公司	State Sole Funded Corporations	12388	4295	728	7365
其他有限责任公司	Other Limited Liability Corporations	108683	57543	6261	44879
股份有限公司	Share-holding Corporations Ltd.	6869	4856	387	1626
私营企业	Private Enterprises	83486	32314	4831	46341
私营独资企业	Private-funded Enterprises	9355	1625	570	7160
私营合伙企业	Private Partnership Enterprises	436	500	24	-88
私营有限责任公司	Private Limited Liability Corporation	72161	29889	4155	38117
私营股份有限公司	Private Share-holding Corporation Ltd.	1534	300	82	1152
其他企业	Others	423	156	24	243
港、澳、台商投资企业	Enterprises With Funds from Hong Kong, Macao and Taiwan	280	3	16	261
合资经营企业（港或澳、台资）	Joint-venture Enterprises (Funds from Hong Kong, Macao and Taiwan)	280	3	16	261
外商投资企业	Foreign Funded Enterprises	176		10	166
外资企业	Enterprises with Sole Fund	176		10	166
按住宿行业小类分组	**By Sector of National Economic**				
旅游饭店	Tourist Hotels	269945	116884	15373	137688
一般旅馆	Ordinary Hotels	51480	31155	3010	17315
其他住宿业	Other Hotels	362	124	32	206
按星级等级分	**Classified by Stars**				
五 星	Five-Star	66766	39462	3763	23541
四 星	Four-Star	77844	30477	4425	42942
三 星	Three-Star	112862	52738	6478	53646
二 星	Two-Star	14290	4473	788	9029
其 他	Other	50025	21013	2961	26051
按地区分	**By Region**				
乌鲁木齐市	Urumqi City	151133	64581	8713	77839
克拉玛依市	Karamay City	7367	8375	402	-1410
吐鲁番地区	Turpan Administrative Offices	5142	2217	310	2615
哈密地区	Hami [Kumul] Administrative Offices	15779	5869	799	9111
昌吉回族自治州	Changji Hui Autonomous Prefecture	5672	2766	309	2597
伊犁哈萨克自治州	Ili Kazak Autonomous Prefecture	35513	20046	2071	13396
伊犁州直属县(市)	Counties (Cities) Direct Under Ili Prefecture	16940	9165	1015	6760
塔城地区	Tacheng [Tarbagatai] Administrative Offices	5138	3412	331	1395
阿勒泰地区	Altay Administrative Offices	13435	7469	725	5241
博尔塔拉蒙古自治州	Bortala Mongol Autonomous Prefecture	5574	3108	320	2146
巴音郭楞蒙古自治州	Bayangol Mongol Autonomous Prefecture	23752	8852	1364	13536
阿克苏地区	Aksu Administrative Offices	10238	3892	605	5741
克孜勒苏柯尔克孜自治州	Kizilsu Kirgiz Autonomous Prefecture	2184	1225	127	832
喀什地区	Kashgar [Kaxgar] Administrative Offices	18281	7449	1004	9828
和田地区	Hotan Administrative Offices	9710	5187	499	4024
生产建设兵团	Xinjiang Production and Construction Group	31442	14596	1892	14954

16-17 限额以上批发和零售业商品销售类值

Total Sales of Enterprises above Designated Size in Wholesale and Retail Trades by Category of Commodities

单位：万元 (10 000 yuan)

项　目	Item	销售总额 Total Sales Value		批　发 Wholesale Trades		零　售 Retail Trades	
		2014	2015	2014	2015	2014	2015
总　计	**Total**	**70065126**	**66791706**	**60404962**	**56549460**	**9660164**	**10242246**
粮油、食品类	Girain, oil and Foods	2211474	2539663	1638151	1893778	573323	645885
饮料类	Beverages	108385	124702	40243	50494	68142	74208
烟酒类	Tobacco and Liquor	3505074	3616545	3379350	3470465	125724	146080
服装、鞋帽类、针纺织品类	Garments, Shoes and Hats, Knitted Goods and Textiles	1310324	1283727	352702	250113	957622	1033614
化妆品类	Cosmetics	184674	197044	36383	43829	148291	153215
金银珠宝类	Gold and Silver Jewelry	253909	272503	13146	12593	240763	259910
日用品类	Commodity Categories	303835	242289	90883	21264	212952	221025
五金、电料类	Hardwares, Electrical Materials	48400	73201	29795	44231	18605	28970
体育、娱乐用品类	Sports, Recreational Articles and Magayines	22337	19709	3141	961	19196	18748
书报杂志类	Books, Newspapers and Magazines	367517	400476	167983	187241	199534	213235
电子出版物及音像制品类	E-journal and Video Products	3346	3688	49		3297	3688
家用电器及音像器材类	Household Appliances and Video Equipments	579831	655237	220120	275808	359711	379429
中西药品类	Chinese Traditional Medicine and Western Medicines	1836456	2144105	961453	1175651	875003	968454
文化办公用品类	Office Articles	233194	284966	127031	164673	106163	120293
家具类	Furnitures	212603	41290	7659	160	204944	41130
通讯器材类	Communication Appliances	78669	155902	22757	43113	55912	112789
煤炭及制品类	Coal and Related Products	712052	895728	700860	889029	11192	6699
木材及制品类	Wood and Wooden Products	145	8095	145	8095		
石油及制品类	Petroleum and Related Products	36843144	30148525	34380753	27860307	2462391	2288218
化工材料及制品类	Raw Chemical Materials and Related Products	3314438	4621753	3314438	4621753		
金属材料类	Metal Materials	5484696	5747712	5484696	5747712		
建筑装潢材料类	Building and Decoration Materials	191418	257033	179209	218323	12209	38710
机电产品及设备类	Mechanical and Electrical Products and Accessories	859626	925570	847250	904895	12376	20675
汽车类	Automobile	4031530	4417963	1099707	1070714	2931823	3347249
种子饲料类	Seed and Feedstuff	295696	381786	295696	381786		
棉麻类	Cotton and Hemp	6483809	6638158	6483258	6637525	551	633
其他类	Others	588544	694336	528104	574947	60440	119389

16-18 亿元以上商品交易市场总体情况
Statistics on Commodity Exchange Markets of Transaction Value over 100 Million Yuan

项　目	Item	市场数(个) Number of Markets (unit)		总摊位数(个) Number of Booths (unit)		年末出租摊位数(个) Number of Rental Booths at Year-end (unit)	
		2014	2015	2014	2015	2014	2015
总　计	**Total**	**89**	**98**	**87150**	**96948**	**76782**	**86061**
按市场类别分组	**By Market Categories**						
综合市场	**Integrated Markets**	**35**	**38**	**48373**	**53151**	**44386**	**47845**
生产资料综合市场	Production Comprehensive Market	3	3	4256	4256	4209	3920
工业消费品综合市场	Industrial Consumable Comprehensive Markets	12	13	11492	15701	10900	14091
农产品综合市场	Farm Produce Comprehensive Markets	10	10	6293	6829	5733	6138
其他综合市场	Other Comprehensive Markets	10	12	26332	26365	23544	23696
专业市场	**Special Markets**	**54**	**60**	**38777**	**43797**	**32396**	**38216**
生产资料市场	Production Markets	12	10	14593	13859	11205	11194
农业生产用具市场	Agricultural Production Equiment Markets	1	1	548	548	350	350
农用生产资料	Agricultural Production Markets	2	2	238	238	157	152
煤炭市场	Coal and Charcoal Markets	1		60		30	
建材市场	Building Material Markets	2	2	7386	7386	5406	5407
金属材料市场	Metal Materials Markets	3	2	1256	443	1105	443
机械设备市场	Mechanical Equipments Markets	1	1	1200	1200	1200	1100
其他生产资料市场	Others	2	2	3905	4044	2957	3742
农产品市场	Farm Produce Markets	15	17	6680	9960	5439	8698
粮油市场	Grain and Oil Markets	1	1	208	180	173	152
肉禽蛋市场	Meat, Poultry and Eggs Markets	4	5	508	3522	498	3472
蔬菜市场	Vegetables Markets	5	5	3140	3115	2663	2660
干鲜果市场	Dried and Fresh Melons and Fruits Markets	3	4	2412	2730	1693	2001
其他农产品市场	Others	2	2	412	413	412	413
食品、饮料及烟酒市场	Food, Beverages, Tobacco and Liquor Markets	1	1	200	200	146	146
食品饮料市场	Food and Beverages Markets	1	1	200	200	146	146
纺织、服装、鞋帽市场	Textiles, Clothing, Shoes and Hats Markets	13	14	12218	12501	10736	11285
服装市场	Clothing Markets	9	10	10393	10673	8911	9467
其他纺织服装鞋帽市场	Others	4	4	1825	1828	1825	1818
日用品及文化用品市场	Daily Use Articles and Cultural Goods Markets	1	1	360	360	265	292
小商品市场	Merchandise Markets	1	1	360	360	265	292
黄金、珠宝、玉器等首饰市场	Gold, Jeweller, Jade Markets	1	1	724	724	724	724
电器、通讯器材、电子设备市场	Electrical Appliances, Communication Appliances and Electronical Appliances Markets	3	4	1058	1768	1016	1702
通讯器材市场	Communication Appliances Markets		1		710		698
计算机及辅助设备市场	Computer and Auxillary Equipments Markets	3	3	1058	1058	1016	1004
家具、五金及装饰材料市场	Furniture, Hardware and Decoration Materials Markets	3	5	1647	2400	1647	2306
家具市场	Furniture Markets	1	1	510	510	510	459
装饰材料市场	Decoration Materials Markets	1	1	325	523	325	480
厨具、盥洗设备市场	Kitchen Utensils,Washing Equipments Markets		1		32		32
五金材料市场	Hardware Materials markets		1		890		890
其他装饰市场	Others	1	1	812	445	812	445
汽车、摩托车及零配件市场	Cars, Motorcycles and Spare Parts Markets	4	6	997	1725	918	1569
汽车市场	Cars Markets	4	5	997	1136	918	980
机动车零配件市场	Vehicle Spare Parts Markets		1		589		589
花、鸟、鱼、虫市场	Flower, Bird, Fish and Insects Markets	1	1	300	300	300	300
花卉市场	Flower Markets	1	1	300	300	300	300
按营业状态分组	**By Operating State**						
常年营业	Business Year	87	97	86779	96632	76441	85745
季节性营业	Seasonal Business	1		60		30	
其他	Others	1	1	311	316	311	316
按经营方式分组	**By Mode of Operating**						
以批发为主	Mainly in the Wholesale	56	62	67930	72530	59038	64011
以零售为主	Mainly in the Retail	33	36	19220	24418	17744	22050
按经营环境分组	**By Operating Environment**						
露天式	Open Type	19	17	10017	9374	8957	9089
封闭式	Closed Type	60	70	64185	74272	57538	66242
其　他	Others	10	11	12948	13302	10287	10730

16-18 续表 Continued

项　目	Item	营业面积(平方米) Operating Area (sq.m)		成交额(万元) Turnouer (10 000 yuan)	
		2014	2015	2014	2015
总　计	**Total**	**12657859**	**13435444**	**15398868**	**17936073**
按市场类别分组	**By Market Categories**				
综合市场	**Integrated Markets**	**5576142**	**5922332**	**4233505**	**4305242**
生产资料综合市场	Production Comprehensive Market	615120	615120	326180	320402
工业消费品综合市场	Industrial Consumable Comprehensive Markets	1004829	1249209	870592	903610
农产品综合市场	Farm Produce Comprehensive Markets	2077542	2139903	1338970	1278938
其他综合市场	Other Comprehensive Markets	1878651	1918100	1697763	1802292
专业市场	**Special Markets**	**7081717**	**7513112**	**11165363**	**13630831**
生产资料市场	Production Markets	4676152	4442735	6058760	6663523
农业生产用具市场	Agricultural Production Equiment Markets	49506	49506	18622	17579
农用生产资料	Agricultural Production Markets	56168	56168	63787	57261
煤炭市场	Coal and Charcoal Markets	2550		14239	
建材市场	Building Materials Markets	3876536	3877625	651735	674650
金属材料市场	Metal Materials Markets	342744	110788	4961053	5325684
机械设备市场	Mechanical Equipments Markets	49000	49000	40000	300000
其他生产资料市场	Others	299648	299648	309324	288349
农产品市场	Farm Produce Markets	1195627	1438697	3147668	3812929
粮油市场	Grain and Oil Markets	25000	25000	35600	30400
肉禽蛋市场	Meat, Poultry and Eggs Markets	722229	928623	342505	697395
蔬菜市场	Vegetables Markets	235998	235998	1087252	1346110
干鲜果市场	Dried and Fresh Melons and Fruits Markets	145000	181676	1579457	1652868
其他农产品市场	Others	67400	67400	102854	86156
食品、饮料及烟酒市场	Food, Beverages, Tobacco and Liquor Markets	7013	7013	28075	27948
食品饮料市场	Food and Beverages Markets	7013	7013	28075	27948
纺织、服装、鞋帽市场	Textiles, Clothing, Shoes and Hats Markets	394963	506014	913611	845780
服装市场	Clothing Markets	311963	423004	799778	740814
其他纺织服装鞋帽市场	Others	83000	83010	113833	104966
日用品及文化用品市场	Daily Use Articles and Cultural Goods Markets	6000	6000	11050	11250
小商品市场	Merchandise Markets	6000	6000	11050	11250
黄金、珠宝、玉器等首饰市场	Gold, Jeweller, Jade Markets	57420	57420	34917	34327
电器、通讯器材、电子设备市场	Electrical Appliances, Communication Appliances and Electronical Appliances Markets	26048	46798	139621	305008
通讯器材市场	Communication Appliances Markets		18000		153660
计算机及辅助设备市场	Computer and Auxillary Equipments Markets	26048	28798	139621	151348
家具、五金及装饰材料市场	Furniture, Hardware and Decoration Materials Markets	212656	336513	124670	500575
家具市场	Furniture Markets	44056	44056	30550	20350
装饰材料市场	Decoration Materials Markets	70000	107526	22992	21992
厨具、盥洗设备市场	Kitchen Utensils,Washing Equipments Markets		53300		12929
五金材料市场	Hardware Materials markets		24000		375000
其他装饰市场	Others	98600	107631	71128	70304
汽车、摩托车及零配件市场	Cars, Motorcycles and Spare Parts Markets	475838	641922	691991	1414491
汽车市场	Cars Markets	475838	527628	691991	1241327
机动车零配件市场	Vehicle Spare Parts Markets		114294		173164
花、鸟、鱼、虫市场	Flower, Bird, Fish and Insects Markets	30000	30000	15000	15000
花卉市场	Flower Markets	30000	30000	15000	15000
按营业状态分组	**By Operating State**				
常年营业	Business Year	12650109	13430234	15374594	17925963
季节性营业	Seasonal Business	2550		14239	
其他	Others	5200	5210	10035	10110
按经营方式分组	**By Mode of Operating**				
以批发为主	Mainly in the Wholesale	11403335	11566282	13697243	15731629
以零售为主	Mainly in the Retail	1254524	1869162	1701625	2204444
按经营环境分组	**By Operating Environment**				
露天式	Open Type	3314721	3497505	1636960	1623878
封闭式	Closed Type	5181128	5670539	6586279	7906956
其　他	Others	4162010	4267400	7175629	8405239

16-19 亿元以上商品交易市场成交情况(按摊位分)

Basic Statistics on Commodity Exchange Markets of Transaction Value over 100 Million Yuan (by Booths)

项目	Item	年末出租摊位数(个) Number of Booths at Year-end (unit)		成交额(万元) Turnover (10 000 yuan)	
		2014	2015	2014	2015
总计	**Total**	**76782**	**86061**	**15398868**	**17936073**
粮油、食品类	Grain and Oil, Food	15045	19217	4551283	5197729
粮油类	Grain and Oil	1009	1806	144229	202111
肉禽蛋类	Meat, Poultry and Eggs	1669	4687	524589	852428
水产品类	Aquatic Products	746	813	354110	430929
蔬菜类	Vegetables	5754	6244	1365803	1523989
干鲜果品类	Dried and Fresh Melons and Fruits	5264	4752	2119060	2147511
饮料类	Beverages	732	680	65882	62498
烟酒类	Tobacco and Liquor	955	732	68866	77850
服装、鞋帽、针纺织品类	Clothing, Shoes, Hats and Textiles	14383	17658	1086777	1068574
服装类	Clothing	10387	12355	849906	825012
鞋帽类	Footwear and Hats	2170	2606	159533	142435
针纺织品类	Knitwear and Textiles	1826	2697	77338	101127
化妆品类	Cosmetics	688	804	40474	47589
金银珠宝类	Gold, Silver and Jewellery	990	1108	130010	143540
日用品类	Articles for Daily Use	2903	4337	149930	230698
儿童玩具类	Children Toys	471	557	14510	23225
五金、电料类	Hardware & Electrical Materials	3061	4883	197054	608743
体育、娱乐用品类	Sports & Recreational Articles	353	424	23318	12693
照相器材类	Photographic Equipments	39	73	3246	3794
书报杂志类	Newspapers and Magazines	165	303	2924	17762
电子出版物及音像制品类	E-journal and Video Products	173	132	7685	6486
家用电器和音像器材类	Household Appliances and Video Equipments	1256	1605	157976	140081
中西药品类	Traditional Chinese and Western Medicine	295	301	19019	16539
西药类	Western Medicine	75	61	11509	11366
中草药及中成药类	Traditional Chinese	33	147	1682	4360
文化办公用品类	Cultural and Official Goods	1728	1732	204720	206448
计算机及其配套产品	Computer and Corollary Eguipment	884	874	126552	135722
家具类	Furniture	3318	3573	310038	286286
通讯器材类	Communication Appliances	874	1590	35337	192401
煤炭及制品类	Coal and Related Products	157	127	16387	2156
木材及制品类	Wood and Wooden Products	765	1069	22496	44514
石油及制品类	Petroleum and Related Products	26	31	15785	17178
化工材料及制品类	Raw Chemical Materials and Related Products	1096	1206	301367	324832
化肥类	Fertilizer	769	768	281853	301119
金属材料类	Metal Materials	1220	2810	4891641	5540478
建筑及装潢材料类	Building and Decoration Materials	15790	10596	1075474	868181
机电产品及设备类	Mechanical & Electrical Products	3075	4782	368639	708970
农机类	Agricultural Machinery	230	227	53970	51128
汽车类	Automobile	1137	2342	932652	1724090
种子饲料类	Seed and Feedstuff	413	456	73240	79047
棉麻类	Cotton and Hemp	19	265	498	1576
其他类	Others	6165	3298	649396	309134

16-20 各地区亿元以上商品交易市场总体情况
Basic Statistics on Commodity Exchange Markets of Transaction Value over 100 Million Yuan by Region

项　目	Item	市场数(个) Number of Markets (unit)		总摊位数(个) Number of Booths (unit)		年末出租摊位数(个) Number of Rental booths at Year-end (unit)	
		2014	2015	2014	2015	2014	2015
总　计	**Total**	**89**	**98**	**87150**	**96948**	**76782**	**86061**
乌鲁木齐市	Urumqi City	25	25	44060	42356	39951	38725
克拉玛依市	Karamay City	1	1	510	510	461	457
吐鲁番市	Turpan City	1	1	650	650	650	650
哈密地区	Hami [Kumul] Administrative Offices	2	2	1285	1285	1285	1283
昌吉回族自治州	Changji Hui Autonomous Prefecture	2	2	3631	3541	3242	3028
伊犁哈萨克自治州	Ili Kazak Autonomous Prefecture	19	21	9511	16992	8748	16043
伊犁州直属县(市)	Counties (Cities) Direct Under Ili Prefecture	19	20	9511	13992	8748	13043
塔城地区	Tacheng [Tarbagatai] Administrative Offices		1		3000		3000
巴音郭楞蒙古自治州	Bayangol Mongol Autonomous Prefecture	9	9	8120	8797	4835	5450
阿克苏地区	Aksu Administrative Offices	5	4	2798	2738	2571	2555
喀什地区	Kashgar [Kaxgar] Administrative Offices	8	8	6519	6570	6376	5629
和田地区	Hotan Administrative Offices	2	2	1575	1575	1495	1427
生产建设兵团	Xinjiang Production and Construction Group	15	23	8491	11934	7168	10814

项　目	Item	营业面积(平方米) Operating Area (sq.m)		成交额(万元) Turnover (10 000 yuan)	
		2014	2015	2014	2015
总　计	**Total**	**12657859**	**13435444**	**15398868**	**17936073**
乌鲁木齐市	Urumqi City	7142700	7204173	5115508	5427529
克拉玛依市	Karamay City	30000	30000	71100	71000
吐鲁番市	Turpan City	15000	15000	130000	110500
哈密地区	Hami [Kumul] Administrative Offices	1764520	1764520	128257	138299
昌吉回族自治州	Changji Hui Autonomous Prefecture	305103	326948	141546	134963
伊犁哈萨克自治州	Ili Kazak Autonomous Prefecture	1075907	1434472	843722	1110959
伊犁州直属县(市)	Counties (Cities) Direct Under Ili Prefecture	1075907	1419472	843722	830959
塔城地区	Tacheng [Tarbagatai] Administrative Offices		15000		280000
巴音郭楞蒙古自治州	Bayangol Mongol Autonomous Prefecture	683894	683894	447535	405844
阿克苏地区	Aksu Administrative Offices	408550	406000	408938	394451
喀什地区	Kashgar [Kaxgar] Administrative Offices	585170	309020	836774	619782
和田地区	Hotan Administrative Offices	99859	99859	128668	120982
生产建设兵团	Production and Construction Group	547156	1161558	7146820	9401764

16-21 连锁批发和零售企业总体情况
Total Conditions of Chain Wholesale and Retail Enterprises

项目 Item	合计 Total		直营店 Straight Camp Shop		加盟店 Join in Store	
	2014	2015	2014	2015	2014	2015
连锁总店数(个) Number of Head Stores (unit)		95				
连锁门店总数(个) Number of Stores (unit)	4486	4446	3644	3462	842	984
年末从业人员数(人) Engaged Persons at Year-end (person)	30848	33365	28273	30603	2575	2762
年末零售营业面积(平方米) Operating Area of Retail Enterprises at Year-end (sq.m)	3316068	3390738	3178926	3256590	137142	134148
连锁门店商品购进总额(万元) Total Purchases Value of Chain Stores (10 000 yuan)	7204730	6180948	7030226	6028158	174504	152790
#统一配送商品购进额(万元) Centralized Purchase and Delivery (10 000 yuan)	6325151	5455351	6198548	5323794	126604	131557
#自有配送中心配送商品购进额(万元) Own Purchase and Delivery (10 000 yuan)	3822426	3235443	3715689	3134431	106736	101011
非自有配送中心配送商品购进额(万元) Public Puchase and Delivery(10 000 yuan)	2045602	2191474	2037017	2160948	8585	30526
商品销售额(万元) Total Sales of Commodities (10 000 yuan)	8001035	7095141	7814821	6931475	186214	163665
#零售额(万元) Of which:Retail of value(10 000 yuan)	3757593	3958486	3660326	3862043	97267	96443

16-22 连锁批发和零售企业基本情况
Basic Condition of Chain Wholesale and Retail Enterprises

项 目	Item	连锁总店数(个) Number of Chain Stores (unit)	门店数合计(个) Total Stores (unit)	
			2014	2015
总 计	**Total**	**95**	**4486**	**4446**
按登记注册类型分组	**by Status of Registration**			
内资企业	Domestic Funded Enterprises	94	4482	4442
国有企业	State-owned Enterprises	34	2494	2188
集体企业	Collective-owned Enterprises	1	8	8
有限责任公司	Limited Liability Corporations	18	405	600
其他有限责任公司	Other Limited Liability Corporations	18	405	600
股份有限公司	Share-holding Corporations Ltd.	9	390	390
私营企业	Private Enterprises	31	1152	1223
私营有限责任公司	Private-funded Enterprises	31	1152	1223
其他企业	Other Enterprises	1	33	33
外商投资企业	Foreign Funded Enterprises	1	4	4
外资企业	Enterprises with Sole Fund	1	4	4
按行业分组	**By Sector**			
批发业	**Wholesale**	**28**	**2681**	**2262**
食品、饮料及烟草制品批发	Special Wholesale of Food, Beverages and Tobaccos	4	9	10
医药及医疗器材批发	Wholesale of Medicines and Medical Appliances	2	7	7
矿产品、建材及化工产品批发	Wholesale of Minerals、Building Materials and Chemical Materials	22	2665	2245
零售业	**Retail Trades**	**67**	**1805**	**2184**
综合零售	Integrated Retail	15	400	501
食品、饮料及烟草制品专门零售	Special Retail of Foods, Beverages and Tobacco	1	6	6
纺织、服装及日用品专门零售	Special Retail of Textile, Garments and Daily Consumer Articles	1	3	3
文化、体育用品及器材专门零售	Special Retail of Cultural, Sports Goods and Apparatus	14	117	125
医药及医疗器材专门零售	Special Retail of Medicine and Medical- care Apparatus	23	992	1246
汽车、摩托车、燃料及零配件专门零售	Special Retail of Car, Motor, Fuel and Parts	3	125	124
家用电器及电子产品专门零售	Special Retail of House hold Electric Appliances and Electronic Products	9	93	94
五金、家具及室内装修材料专门零售	Special Retail of Hardware, Furniture and Interior Decorating Material	1	69	85
按业态分组	**By Business Categories**			
便利店	Convenience Store	1	138	169
超 市	Supermarket	6	67	83
大型超市	Hypermarket	3	23	10
百货店	Department Store	1	83	83
专业店	Specialty Store	75	4062	3963
# 加油站	Gas Station	19	885	908
专卖店	Franchised Store	6	82	99
厂家直销中心	Factory Outlets Center	1		7
其 他	Other Store	2	31	32

16-22 续表 1 Continued

项目	Item	年末从业人员数(人) Engaged Persons at Year-end (person)		年末零售营业面积(平方米) Operating Area of Retail Enterprises at Year-end (sq.m)	
		2014	2015	2014	2015
总计	**Total**	**30848**	**33365**	**3316068**	**3390738**
按登记注册类型分组	**by Status of Registration**				
内资企业	Domestic Funded Enterprises	29991	32538	3287326	3361996
国有企业	State-owned Enterprises	9281	9591	1142250	1359225
集体企业	Collective-owned Enterprises	56	56	200	200
有限责任公司	Limited Liability Corporations	4604	6754	284097	234664
其他有限责任公司	Other Limited Liability Corporations	4604	6754	284097	234664
股份有限公司	Share-holding Corporations Ltd.	6093	5669	1431979	1324146
私营企业	Private Enterprises	9819	10348	425905	441281
私营有限责任公司	Private-funded Enterprises	9819	10348	425905	441281
其他企业	Other Enterprises	138	120	2895	2480
外商投资企业	Foreign Funded Enterprises	857	827	28742	28742
外资企业	Enterprises with Sole Fund	857	827	28742	28742
按行业分组	**By Sector**				
批发业	**Wholesale**	**11113**	**11288**	**1778718**	**1692743**
食品、饮料及烟草制品批发	Wholesale of Food, Beverages and Tobaccos	500	500	401	401
医药及医疗器材批发	Wholesale of Medicines and Medical Appliances	137	133	961	961
矿产品、建材及化工产品批发	Wholesale of Minerals、Building Materials and Chemical Materiac	10476	10655	1777356	1691381
零售业	**Retail Trades**	**19735**	**22077**	**1537350**	**1697995**
综合零售	Integrated Retail	7108	6827	820691	963970
食品、饮料及烟草制品专门零售	Special Retail of Foods, Beverages and Tobacco	24	24	445	445
纺织、服装及日用品专门零售	Special Retail of Textile, Garments and Daily Consumer Articles	7	7	200	200
文化、体育用品及器材专门零售	Special Retail of Cultural, Sports Goods and Apparatus	1650	1554	87938	94919
医药及医疗器材专门零售	Special Retail of Medicine and Medical- care Apparatus	5031	6030	120276	142359
汽车、摩托车、燃料及零配件专门零售	Special Retail of Car, Motor, Fuel and Parts	1866	1677	269707	269707
家用电器及电子产品专门零售	Special Retail of House hold Electric Appliances and Electronic Products	1690	1853	128084	123646
五金、家具及室内装修材料专门零售	Special Retail of Hardware, Furniture and Interior Decorating Material	2359	4105	110009	102749
按业态分组	**By Business Categories**				
便利店	Convenience Store	514	574	31900	23741
超　市	Supermarket	2252	3494	608453	817118
大型超市	Hypermarket	3508	1943	168162	94320
百货店	Department Store	98	98	3561	3561
专业店	Specialty Store	21357	22340	2384159	2322395
# 加油站	Gas Station	9689	10217	1881358	1869883
专卖店	Franchised Store	2927	4673	116828	109698
厂家直销中心	Factory Outlets Center		19		
其　他	Other Store	192	224	3005	19905

16-22 续表 2 Continued

项　目	Item	直营店门店数(个) Straight Camp Shop (unit)		年末从业人员数(人) Engaged Persons at Year-end (person)	
		2014	2015	2014	2015
总　计	**Total**	**3644**	**3462**	**28273**	**30603**
按登记注册类型分组	**by Status of Registration**				
内资企业	Domestic Funded Enterprises	3640	3458	27416	29776
国有企业	State-owned Enterprises	2028	1772	8802	9162
集体企业	Collective-owned Enterprises	8	8	56	56
有限责任公司	Limited Liability Corporations	356	389	4531	6173
其他有限责任公司	Other Limited Liability Corporations	356	389	4531	6173
股份有限公司	Share-holding Corporations Ltd.	390	390	6093	5669
私营企业	Private Enterprises	827	868	7801	8600
私营有限责任公司	Private-funded Enterprises	827	868	7801	8600
其他企业	Other Enterprises	31	31	133	116
外商投资企业	Foreign Funded Enterprises	4	4	857	827
外资企业	Enterprises with Sole Fund	4	4	857	827
按行业分组	**By Sector**				
批发业	**Wholesale**	**2252**	**1892**	**10670**	**10895**
食品、饮料及烟草制品批发	Wholesale of Food, Beverages and Tobaccos	9	10	500	500
医药及医疗器材批发	Wholesale of Medicines and Medical Appliances	7	7	137	133
矿产品、建材及化工产品批发	Wholesale of Minerals、Building Materials and Chemical Materiac	2236	1875	10033	10262
零售业	**Retail Trades**	**1392**	**1570**	**17603**	**19708**
综合零售	Integrated Retail	192	262	5318	5312
食品、饮料及烟草制品专门零售	Special Retail of Foods, Beverages and Tobacco	6	6	24	24
纺织、服装及日用品专门零售	Special Retail of Textile, Garments and Daily Consumer Articles	3	3	7	7
文化、体育用品及器材专门零售	Special Retail of Cultural, Sports Goods and Apparatus	117	125	1650	1554
医药及医疗器材专门零售	Special Retail of Medicine and Medical- care Apparatus	787	871	4689	5176
汽车、摩托车、燃料及零配件专门零售	Special Retail of Car, Motor, Fuel and Parts	125	124	1866	1677
家用电器及电子产品专门零售	Special Retail of House hold Electric Appliances and Electronic Products	93	94	1690	1853
五金、家具及室内装修材料专门零售	Special Retail of Hardware, Furniture and Interior Decorating Material	69	85	2359	4105
按业态分组	**By Business Categories**				
便利店	Convenience Store	23	23	132	136
超　市	Supermarket	48	56	2060	2496
大型超市	Hypermarket	15	10	2371	1943
百货店	Department Store	17	17	19	19
专业店	Specialty Store	3428	3218	20572	21093
# 加油站	Gas Station	885	908	9689	10217
专卖店	Franchised Store	82	99	2927	4673
厂家直销中心	Factory Outlets Center		7		19
其　他	Other Store	31	32	192	224

16-22 续表 3 Continued

项目	Item	年末零售营业面积(平方米) Operating Area of Retail Enterprises at Year-end (sq.m)		加盟店门店数(个) Number of Join in Stores (unit)	
		2014	2015	2014	2015
总 计	**Total**	**3178926**	**3256590**	**842**	**984**
按登记注册类型分组	**by Status of Registration**				
内资企业	Domestic Funded Enterprises	3150184	3227848	842	984
国有企业	State-owned Enterprises	1116082	1336057	466	416
集体企业	Collective-owned Enterprises	200	200		
有限责任公司	Limited Liability Corporations	281497	223514	49	211
其他有限责任公司	Other Limited Liability Corporations	281497	223514	49	211
股份有限公司	Share-holding Corporations Ltd.	1431979	1324146		
私营企业	Private Enterprises	317711	341631	325	355
私营有限责任公司	Private-funded Enterprises	317711	341631	325	355
其他企业	Other Enterprises	2715	2300	2	2
外商投资企业	Foreign Funded Enterprises	28742	28742		
外资企业	Enterprises with Sole Fund	28742	28742		
按行业分组	**By Sector**				
批发业	**Wholesale**	**1754718**	**1671743**	**429**	**370**
食品、饮料及烟草制品批发	Wholesale of Food, Beverages and Tobaccos	401	401		
医药及医疗器材批发	Wholesale of Medicines and Medical Appliances	961	961		
矿产品、建材及化工产品批发	Wholesale of Minerals、Building Materials and Chemical Materiac	1753356	1670381	429	370
零售业	**Retail Trades**	**1424208**	**1584847**	**413**	**614**
综合零售	Integrated Retail	720382	871820	208	239
食品、饮料及烟草制品专门零售	Special Retail of Foods, Beverages and Tobacco	445	445		
纺织、服装及日用品专门零售	Special Retail of Textile, Garments and Daily Consumer Articles	200	200		
文化、体育用品及器材专门零售	Special Retail of Cultural, Sports Goods and Apparatus	87938	94919		
医药及医疗器材专门零售	Special Retail of Medicine and Medical- care Apparatus	107443	121361	205	375
汽车、摩托车、燃料及零配件专门零售	Special Retail of Car, Motor, Fuel and Parts	269707	269707		
家用电器及电子产品专门零售	Special Retail of House hold Electric Appliances and Electronic Products	128084	123646		
五金、家具及室内装修材料专门零售	Special Retail of Hardware, Furniture and Interior Decorating Material	110009	102749		
按业态分组	**By Business Categories**				
便利店	Convenience Store	7681	7681	115	146
超 市	Supermarket	573164	743196	19	27
大型超市	Hypermarket	129529	94320	8	
百货店	Department Store	1393	1393	66	66
专业店	Specialty Store	2347326	2280397	634	745
# 加油站	Gas Station	1881358	1869883		
专卖店	Franchised Store	116828	109698		
厂家直销中心	Factory Outlets Center				
其 他	Other Store	3005	19905		

16-22 续表 4 Continued

项　目	Item	年末从业人员数(人) Engaged Persons at Year-end (person)		年末零售营业面积(平方米) Operating Area of Retail Enterprises at Year-end (sq.m)	
		2014	2015	2014	2015
总　计	**Total**	**2575**	**2762**	**137142**	**134148**
按登记注册类型分组	**by Status of Registration**				
内资企业	Domestic Funded Enterprises	2575	2762	137142	134148
国有企业	State-owned Enterprises	479	429	26168	23168
集体企业	Collective-owned Enterprises				
有限责任公司	Limited Liability Corporations	73	581	2600	11150
其他有限责任公司	Other Limited Liability Corporations	73	581	2600	11150
股份有限公司	Share-holding Corporations Ltd.				
私营企业	Private Enterprises	2018	1748	108194	99650
私营有限责任公司	Private-funded Enterprises	2018	1748	108194	99650
其他企业	Other Enterprises	5	4	180	180
外商投资企业	Foreign Funded Enterprises				
外资企业	Enterprises with Sole Fund				
按行业分组	**By Sector**				
批发业	**Wholesale**	**443**	**393**	**24000**	**21000**
食品、饮料及烟草制品批发	Wholesale of Food, Beverages and Tobaccos				
医药及医疗器材批发	Wholesale of Medicines and Medical Appliances				
矿产品、建材及化工产品批发	Wholesale of Minerals、Building Materials and Chemical Materiac	443	393	24000	21000
零售业	**Retail Trades**	**2132**	**2369**	**113142**	**113148**
综合零售	Integrated Retail	1790	1515	100309	92150
食品、饮料及烟草制品专门零售	Special Retail of Foods, Beverages and Tobacco				
纺织、服装及日用品专门零售	Special Retail of Textile, Garments and Daily Consumer Articles				
文化、体育用品及器材专门零售	Special Retail of Cultural, Sports Goods and Apparatus				
医药及医疗器材专门零售	Special Retail of Medicine and Medical- care Apparatus	342	854	12833	20998
汽车、摩托车、燃料及零配件专门零售	Special Retail of Car, Motor, Fuel and Parts				
家用电器及电子产品专门零售	Special Retail of House hold Electric Appliances and Electronic Products				
五金、家具及室内装修材料专门零售	Special Retail of Hardware, Furniture and Interior Decorating Material				
按业态分组	**By Business Categories**				
便利店	Convenience Store	382	438	24219	16060
超　市	Supermarket	192	998	35289	73922
大型超市	Hypermarket	1137		38633	
百货店	Department Store	79	79	2168	2168
专业店	Specialty Store	785	1247	36833	41998
# 加油站	Gas Station				
专卖店	Franchised Store				
厂家直销中心	Factory Outlets Center				
其　他	Other Store				

16-23 连锁住宿和餐饮企业总体情况
Total Conditions of Chain Hotels and Catering Enterprises

项　目	Item	合 计 Total		直营店 Straight Camp Shop	
		2014	2015	2014	2015
连锁总店数(个)	Number of Head Stores (unit)		10		
门店总数(个)	Number of Stores (unit)	188	193	131	133
年末从业人员数(人)	Engaged Persons at Year-end (person)	3965	4147	3185	3290
年末餐饮营业面积(平方米)	Operating Area of Catering Enterprises at Year-end (sq.m)	56997	61275	49447	53525
客房数(间)	Number of Hotel Rooms (unit)	3455	3993	3395	3993
床位数(个)	Number of Beds (unit)	4510	5500	4430	5500
餐位数(位)	Number of Dining-seats (unit)	18567	18089	15624	14746
连锁门店商品购进（采购）额(万元)	Total Purchases Value of Chain Stores (10 000 yuan)	16128	16772	14184	14808
#统一配送商品购进（采购）额	Centralized Purchase and Delivery	14673	15142	12743	13192
#自有配送中心配送商品购进（采购）额	Purchases Value of Its Own Distribution Center	9760	9156	7830	7206
非自有配送中心配送商品购进（采购）额	Purchases Value of Non Its Own Distribution Cente		5986		5986
连锁门店营业额(万元)	Business Revenue of Chain Store (10 000 yuan)	72238	74480	63468	65552
#餐费收入	From Meals	57890	56748	49560	47820
商品销售额	Total Sales of Commodities	289	1033	268	1033

项　目	Item	加盟店 Join in Store	
		2014	2015
连锁总店数(个)	Number of Head Stores (unit)		
门店总数(个)	Number of Stores (unit)	57	60
年末从业人员数(人)	Engaged Persons at Year-end (person)	780	857
年末餐饮营业面积(平方米)	Operating Area of Catering Enterprises at Year-end (sq.m)	7550	7750
客房数(间)	Number of Hotel Rooms (unit)	60	
床位数(个)	Number of Beds (unit)	80	
餐位数(位)	Number of Dining-seats (unit)	2943	3343
连锁门店商品购进（采购）额(万元)	Total Purchases Value of Chain Stores (10 000 yuan)	1944	1964
#统一配送商品购进（采购）额	Centralized Purchase and Delivery	1930	1950
#自有配送中心配送商品购进（采购）额	Purchases Value of Its Own Distribution Center	1930	1950
非自有配送中心配送商品购进（采购）额	Purchases Value of Non Its Own Distribution Cente		
连锁门店营业额(万元)	Business Revenue of Chain Store (10 000 yuan)	8770	8928
#餐费收入	From Meals	8330	8928
商品销售额	Total Sales of Commodities	21	

16-24 连锁住宿和餐饮企业基本情况
Basic Condition of Chain Hotels and Catering Enterprises

项　目	Item	连锁总店数(个) Number of Head Stores (unit)	门店数合计(个) Total Stores (unit)		年末从业人员数(人) Engaged Persons at Year-end (person)	
			2014	2015	2014	2015
总　计	**Total**	**10**	**188**	**193**	**3965**	**4147**
住宿业	**Hotels**	**2**	**24**	**24**	**1140**	**1166**
按登记注册类型分组	**By Status of Registration**					
内资企业	Domestic Funded Enterprises	2	24	24	1140	1166
有限责任公司	Limited Liability Corporations	1	11	11	845	906
其他有限责任公司	Other Limited Liability Corporations	1	11	11	845	906
私营企业	Private Enterprises	1	13	13	295	260
私营有限责任公司	Private-Limited Liability Corporations	1	13	13	295	260
按行业分组	**By Sector**					
旅游饭店	Tourist Hotels	2	24	24	1140	1166
餐饮业	Catering Enterprises	8	164	169	2825	2981
按登记注册类型分组	**By Status of Registration**					
内资企业	Domestic Funded Enterprises	7	138	145	2155	2348
有限责任公司	Limited Liability Corporations	1	2	2	105	139
其他有限责任公司	Other Limited Liability Corporations	1	2	2	105	139
股份有限公司	Share-holding Corporations Ltd.	1	53	58	976	1039
私营企业	Private Enterprises	5	83	85	1074	1170
私营有限责任公司	Private-funded Enterprises	5	83	85	1074	1170
外商投资企业	Foreign Funded Enterprises	1	26	24	670	633
外资企业	Enterprises with Sole Fund	1	26	24	670	633
按行业分组	**By Sector**					
正餐服务	Restaurant Services	3	14	14	315	346
快餐服务	Fast Food Services	5	150	155	2510	2635

16-24 续表 1 Continued

项　目	Item	年末餐饮营业面积(平方米) Operating Area of Catering Enterprises at Year-end (sq.m)		#直营店门店数(个) Number of Straight Camp Shop (unit)	
		2014	2015	2014	2015
总　计	**Total**	**56997**	**61275**	**131**	**133**
住宿业	**Hotels**	**16418**	**15548**	**23**	**24**
按登记注册类型分组	**By Status of Registration**				
内资企业	Domestic Funded Enterprises	16418	15548	23	24
有限责任公司	Limited Liability Corporations	15768	14898	11	11
其他有限责任公司	Other Limited Liability Corporations	15768	14898	11	11
私营企业	Private Enterprises	650	650	12	13
私营有限责任公司	Private-funded Enterprises	650	650	12	13
按行业分组	**By Sector**				
旅游饭店	Tourist Hotels	16418	15548	23	24
餐饮业	Catering Enterprises	40579	45727	108	109
按登记注册类型分组	**By Status of Registration**				
内资企业	Domestic Funded Enterprises	30217	36167	82	85
有限责任公司	Limited Liability Corporations	3795	3795	2	2
其他有限责任公司	Other Limited Liability Corporations	3795	3795	2	2
股份有限公司	Share-holding Corporations Ltd.	13486	19436	53	58
私营企业	Private Enterprises	12936	12936	27	25
私营有限责任公司	Private-funded Enterprises	12936	12936	27	25
外商投资企业	Foreign Funded Enterprises	10362	9560	26	24
外资企业	Enterprises with Sole Fund	10362	9560	26	24
按行业分组	**By Sector**				
正餐服务	Restaurant Services	7057	7057	14	14
快餐服务	Fast Food Services	33522	38670	94	95

16-24 续表 2 Continued

项　目	Item	年末从业人员数(人) Engaged Persons at Year-end (person)		年末餐饮营业面积(平方米) Operating Area of Catering Enterprises at Year-end (sq.m)		#加盟店门店数(个) Number of Join in Store (unit)	
		2014	2015	2014	2015	2014	2015
总　计	**Total**	**3185**	**3290**	**49447**	**53525**	**57**	**60**
住宿业	**Hotels**	**1117**	**1166**	**16418**	**15548**	**1**	
按登记注册类型分组	**By Status of Registration**						
内资企业	Domestic Funded Enterprises	1117	1166	16418	15548	1	
有限责任公司	Limited Liability Corporations	845	906	15768	14898		
其他有限责任公司	Other Limited Liability Corporations	845	906	15768	14898		
私营企业	Private Enterprises	272	260	650	650	1	
私营有限责任公司	Private-funded Enterprises	272	260	650	650	1	
按行业分组	**By Sector**						
旅游饭店	Tourist Hotels	1117	1166	16418	15548	1	
餐饮业	Catering Enterprises	2068	2124	33029	37977	56	60
按登记注册类型分组	**By Status of Registration**						
内资企业	Domestic Funded Enterprises	1398	1491	22667	28417	56	60
有限责任公司	Limited Liability Corporations	105	139	3795	3795		
其他有限责任公司	Other Limited Liability Corporations	105	139	3795	3795		
股份有限公司	Share-holding Corporations Ltd.	976	1039	13486	19436		
私营企业	Private Enterprises	317	313	5386	5186	56	60
私营有限责任公司	Private-funded Enterprises	317	313	5386	5186	56	60
外商投资企业	Foreign Funded Enterprises	670	633	10362	9560		
外资企业	Enterprises with Sole Fund	670	633	10362	9560		
按行业分组	**By Sector**						
正餐服务	Restaurant Services	315	346	7057	7057		
快餐服务	Fast Food Services		1778		30920		60

16-24 续表 3 Continued

项目	Item	年末从业人员数(人) Engaged Persons at Year-end (person)		年末餐饮营业面积(平方米) Operating Area of Catering Enterprises at Year-end (sq.m)	
		2014	2015	2014	2015
总　计	**Total**	**780**	**857**	**7550**	**7750**
住宿业	**Hotels**	**23**			
按登记注册类型分组	**By Status of Registration**				
内资企业	Domestic Funded Enterprises	23			
有限责任公司	Limited Liability Corporations				
其他有限责任公司	Other Limited Liability Corporations				
私营企业	Private Enterprises	23			
私营有限责任公司	Private-funded Enterprises	23			
按行业分组	**By Sector**				
旅游饭店	Tourist Hotels	23			
餐饮业	Catering Enterprises	757	857	7550	7750
按登记注册类型 分组	**By Status of Registration**				
内资企业	Domestic Funded Enterprises	757	857	7550	7750
有限责任公司	Limited Liability Corporations				
其他有限责任公司	Other Limited Liability Corporations				
股份有限公司	Share-holding Corporations Ltd.				
私营企业	Private Enterprises	757	857	7550	7750
私营有限责任公司	Private-funded Enterprises	757	857	7550	7750
外商投资企业	Foreign Funded Enterprises				
外资企业	Enterprises with Sole Fund				
按行业分组	**By Sector**				
正餐服务	Restaurant Services				
快餐服务	Fast Fo od Services		857		7750

主要统计指标解释

批发业 指向其他批发或零售单位（含个体经营者）及其他企事业单位、机关团体等批量销售生活用品、生产资料的活动，以及从事进出口贸易和贸易经纪与代理的活动，包括拥有货物所有权，并以本单位(公司)的名义进行交易活动，也包括不拥有货物的所有权，收取佣金的商品代理、商品代售活动；还包括各类商品批发市场中固定摊位的批发活动，以及以销售为目的的收购活动。

零售业 指百货商店、超级市场、专门零售商店、品牌专卖店、售货摊等主要面向最终消费者（如居民等）的销售活动，以互联网、邮政、电话、售货机等方式的销售活动，还包括在同一地点，后面加工生产，前面销售的店铺（如面包房）；谷物、种子、饲料、牲畜、矿产品、生产用原料、化工原料、农用化工产品、机械设备（乘用车、计算机及通信设备除外）等生产资料的销售不作为零售活动；多数零售商对其销售的货物拥有所有权，但有些则是充当委托人的代理人，进行委托销售或以收取佣金的方式进行销售。

批发和零售业商品购进、销售、库存额 指各种登记注册类型的批发和零售业企业(单位)以本企业(单位)为总体的，从国内、国外市场购进的商品总量，销售和出口的商品总量、库存的商品总量等情况。该指标可以反映商品流转过程中商品的购进、销售、库存之间的比例关系和存在的问题。

商品购进额 指从本企业以外的单位和个人购进（包括从国外直接进口）作为转卖或加工后转卖的商品金额（含增值税）。商品购进包括：（1）从工农业生产者、批发和零售业企业、住宿和餐饮业企业、出版社或报社的出版发行部门和其他服务业企业购进的商品；（2）从机关团体、事业单位购进的商品；（3）从海关、市场管理部门购进的缉私和没收的商品；（4）从居民收购的废旧商品等。不包括：（1）企业为本单位自身经营用，不是作为转卖而购进的商品，如材料物资、包装物、低值易耗品、办公用品等；（2）未通过买卖行为而收入的商品，如接受其他部门移交的商品、借入的商品、收入代其他单位保管的商品、其他单位赠送的样品、加工回收的成品等；（3）经本单位介绍，由买卖双方直接结算，本单位只收取手续费的业务；（4）销售退回和买方拒付货款的商品；（5）商品溢余。

商品销售额 指对本单位以外的单位和个人出售的商品金额（包括售给本单位消费用的商品，含增值税）。商品销售包括（1）售给城乡居民和社会集团消费用的商品；（2）售给农业、工业、建筑业、服务业等国民经济各行业用于生产、经营用的商品，包括售予批发和零售业作为转卖或加工后转卖的商品；（3）对国（境）外直接出口的商品，不包括：（1）未通过买卖行为付出的商品，如随机构变动移交给其他企业单位的商品、借出的商品、归还受其他单位委托代保管的商品、付出的加工原料和赠送给其他单位的样品等；（2）经本单位介绍，由买卖双方直接结算，本单位只收取手续费的业务；（3）购货退回的商品；（4）商品损耗和损失；（5）出售本单位自用的废旧物资。

商品库存额 对于批发和零售业法人单位和个体经营户，是指报告期末取得所有权的全部商品金额（含增值税）；对于批发和零售业产业活动单位，是指报告期末实际在库且归属法人具有所有权的全部商品金额（含增值税）。库存商品包括：(1)存放在本单位(如门市部、批发站、采购站、经营处)的仓库、货场、货柜和货架中的商品；(2)挑选、整理、包装中的商品；(3)已记入购进而尚未运到本单位的商品，即发货单或银行承兑凭证已到而货未到的商品；(4)寄放他处的商品，如因购货方拒绝付款而暂时存在购货方的商品；(5)委托其他单位代销(未作销售或调出)尚未售出的商品；(6)代其他单位购进尚未交付的商品。不包括：所有权不属于本单位的商品；委托外单位加工的商品；外贸企业代理其他单位从国外进口，尚未付给订货单位的商品；代国家储备部门保管的商品。

连锁总店（总部） 指负责连锁企业资源（商号、商誉、经营模式、服务标准、管理模式等等）的开发、配置、控制或使用等功能的企业核心管理机构。连锁经营是指经营同类商品或服务，使用统一商号的若干店铺，在同一总店（总部）的管理下，采取统一采购或特许经营等方式，实现规模效益的组织形式，包括直营连锁、特许连锁和自愿连锁三种形式。其中，直营连锁是指连锁店铺由连锁公司全资或控股开设，在总部的直接控制下，开展统一经营的连锁经营形式；特许连锁是指拥有注册商标、企业标志、专利、专有技术等经营资源的企业（特许人），以合同形式将其拥有的经营资源许可其他经营者（被特许人）使用，被特许人按合同约定在统一的经营模式下开展经营，并向特许人支付特许经营费用的连锁经营形式；自愿连锁是指若干个店铺或企业自愿组合起来，在不改变各自资产所有权关系的情况下，以同一个品牌形象面对消费者，以共同进货为纽带开展的连锁经营形式。

亿元以上商品交易市场　指年成交额在亿元及以上的商品交易市场。商品交易市场是指经有关部门和组织批准设立，有固定场所、设施，有经营管理部门和监管人员，若干市场经营者入内，常年或实际开业三个月以上，集中、公开、独立地进行生活消费品、生产资料等现货商品交易以及提供相关服务的交易场所，包括各类消费品市场、生产资料市场等。

社会消费品零售总额　指企业（单位、个体户）通过交易直接售给个人、社会集团非生产、非经营用的实物商品金额，以及提供餐饮服务所取得的收入金额。个人包括城乡居民和入境人员，社会集团包括机关、社会团体、部队、学校、企事业单位、居委会或村委会等。

住宿业　指为旅行者提供短期留宿场所的活动，有些单位只提供住宿，也有些单位提供住宿、饮食、商务、娱乐一体的服务，不包括主要按月或按年长期出租房屋住所的活动。

餐饮业　指通过即时制作加工、商业销售和服务性劳动等，向消费者提供食品和消费场所及设施的服务。

营业额　指住宿和餐饮业单位在经营活动中因提供服务或销售商品等取得的收入。包括：客房收入、餐费收入、商品销售额（含增值税）和其他收入。其中，客房收入指住宿和餐饮业单位在经营活动中因提供住宿服务取得的收入。餐费收入指本单位为顾客提供就餐服务取得的收入，包括：经烹饪、调制加工后出售的各种食品，如主食、炒菜、凉拌菜等的收入。

Explanatory Notes on Main Statistical Indicators

Wholesale Trade refers to the activities of selling wholesale commodities for daily use and capital goods to enterprises of wholesale and retail trades (including self-employed individuals) and other enterprises, institutions and government organs and organizations, and the activities of engaging in import and export and acting as a trade agent. The wholesaler may have the ownership of the commodities for wholesale and trade in the name of its own (a company), and the wholesaler can act as commission agent or commodity broker without the ownership of commodities. Also included are the wholesale activities at the fixed stalls in wholesale market and the acquisition for sales purpose.

Retail Trade refers to the activities of department store, supermarket, franchised store, brand store, retail stall and on-the-spot-making-selling store selling commodities to the final consumers (residents) by any means including internet, post, telephone, sales machine. It also includes shops with sales and production localted in the same places (such as bakeries). Retail trade excludes the activities of sales of capital goods such as grain, seed, feed, livestock, mineral products, raw material for production, industrial chemicals, chemical products for agricultural use, machine and equipment (excluding vehicles, computers and communication equipment). Most retailers have the ownership of commodities to sell, but some are acting as agents or brokers to make transactions for a commission.

Purchase, Sales and Stock of Commodities by Wholesale and Retail Trades refer to the total volume of commodities purchased, total volume of sales and exports, and the stock of commodities by wholesale and retail enterprises (establishments) of different status of registration from domestic and overseas markets. This indicator reflects the relationship among purchase, sales and stock of commodities in the circulation of goods and reveals the existing problems.

Total Purchases of Commodities refer to the total value of purchases of commodities by enterprises (establishments) from other establishments or individuals (including direct import from abroad) for the purpose of re-selling, either with or without further processing of the commodities purchased. The commodities include: (1)commodities purchased from agricultural and industrial producer, wholesaler, retailer, publishing house and other service business, (2) commodities purchased from institutions and government departments, (3) confiscated goods purchased from the customs authorities or market management agencies, (4) second-hand goods and wastes purchased from residents. The commodities exclude (1)commodities purchased by enterprises (establishments) for use in their own business operation, commodities obtained without buying or selling procedures such as materials, consumable goods of low value, office appliance,etc. (2) received goods without trading, such as goods handed over from others, borrowed goods, preserved goods for others, donated goods from others, processed and retrieved goods, etc. (3) goods of direct settlement between buyer and seller with handling fees introduced by others, (4)goods returned or refused to pay by the buyer,(5) excessive goods.

Total Sales of Commodities refer to value of commodities sold by the establishments to other establishments and individuals (including goods sold for self consumption, including the value-added tax). The commodities include: (1) commodities sold to urban and rural residents and social groups for their consumption; (2) commodities sold to establishments in all industries for their production and operation, including agriculture, industry, construction, and catering services including commodities sold to wholesale and retail establishments for re-selling, with or without further processing; and (3) commodities for direct export to abroad. Excluded are (1) extended commodities without trading, such as goods handed over to other enterprises and institutions because of the change of organizations, lent goods, returned goods preserved for others, extended processing materials and samples donated to others, (2) goods of direct settlement between buyer and seller with handling fees introduced by others,(3) goods returned after purchase, (4) damaged and spoiled goods, (5) waste and used goods of self use.

Total Stock of Commodities For the legal entities and self-employed individuals engaged in wholesale and retail trade, it refers to total value (including VAT) of commodities possessed at the end of the reference period; and for wholesale and retail establishments, it refers to the value (including VAT) of all commodities actually in stock and owned by their legal persons at the end of reference period. The commodities in stock includes: (1) commodities located in storage, garages, counters, and shelves of operating places of wholesale and retail trades (such as sale stores, wholesale centres, procurement stations and operating offices); (2) commodities in the process of being selected, sorted, and packed; (3) commodities not arrived but recorded as purchase in the account, i.e. commodities not arrived but payment receipts for the commodities from the sellers or the banks arrived; (4) commodities deposited in other places rather than places mentioned above, for instance: commodities in the hold of purchasers temporarily due to the refusal of payment; (5)

commodities entrusted to other units to sell but not sold yet; (6) commodities purchased for other units but not delivered yet. Commodities not included as stock are those not owned by the enterprises (units), commodities on commission for processing, imported commodities of agency of foreign trade enterprise but not yet delivered to ordering units and finally those put in stock on behalf of the state reserves units.

Chain Head Stores (headquarter) refer to the core leading stores responsible for development, allocation, administration and utilization of resources (name of stores, brand of stores, operation model, service standard, management way, etc.) of chain stores. Chain stores refers to the stores engaged in providing homogeneous commodities or services, with the central leadership of head store(headquarters) and guided by common policies, conduct centralized purchase and distributed selling of commodities, in order to gain better efficiency through standardized operation. The chain stores include regular chain stores, franchise chain stores and voluntary chain stores.

Regular Chain store refers to chain stores that are invested or controlled by the headquarters. They operate under direct and unified management from the headquarters.

Franchise chain store refers to the chain stores (franchisees) which are franchised with operation resources such as trade marks, names, patent and operation know-how by the franchisors in form of contract and pay the operation fees to the franchisors.

Voluntary chain store refers to the stores operate jointly on the voluntary bases while maintaining their status of independent legal entities with full ownership of their assets. They sell goods of same brand from same channel of resource to the consumers.

Large Commodity Markets with Transaction Value over 100 Million Yuan refers to the commodity markets with an annual transaction at and above 100 million. The commodity market refers to the markets approved and managed by related departments, where there are fixed sites, facilities, managers and administration offices, where there are a certain number of traders to operate for three month and above or all the year, where the commodities including the articles for daily consumption and capital goods and services are traded in a centralized, independent and open way. Such market includes markets of daily goods and market of capital goods, etc.

Total Retail Sales of Consumer Goods refer to the amount obtained by enterprises (units, self-employed individuals) through direct sales of non-production and non-business physical commodity to individuals, social institutions, and revenue from providing catering services. Individuals include rural and urban households, population from abroad, social institutions include government agencies, social organizations, military units, schools, institutions, neighbourhood (village) committees.

Hotel Services refer to the accommodation services provided to visitors. Some units may provide only accommodation while others provide a combination of accommodation, meals, business services and/or recreational facilities. It excludes activities related to the provision of long-term primary residences in facilities such as apartments typically leased on a monthly or annual basis.

Catering Services refer to the activities of providing foods, serving locations and facilities to customers through instant processing, commercial sales and service-type labor.

Business Revenue refers to revenue of hotels and catering services received from providing services or selling commodities through business activities, including income from hotels, from catering services, from selling of commodities (including VAT) and from other services. Income from hotels refers to income of hotels and catering services by providing lodging services through business activities. Income from catering services refers to income from providing catering services, including selling of cooked or prepared foods, such as staple food, cooked dishes, or cold dishes.

金融业
FINANCIAL
INTERMEDIATION
17

第十七篇 金融业

本篇主要内容和资料来源

本篇反映新疆金融和保险业发展情况,有以下两个部分：一是金融机构存贷等活动情况；二是保险业务情况。

金融资料来自中国人民银行乌鲁木齐中心支行金融机构信贷统计月报及年报；保险业务资料取自中国保险监督管理委员会新疆监管局保险统计年报。

本篇金融部分数据由新疆维吾尔自治区统计局国民经济综合统计处根据中国人民银行乌鲁木齐中心支行所提供的资料整理；保险部分数据由中国保险监督管理委员会新疆监管局相关部门整理提供。

Financial Intermediation

Main Content and Source of Data

Data in this chapter show the development of Xinjiang’s financial and insruance industries in the following two aspects:(1)the financial activities of the deposit and loan interests;(2)the situation regarding the insurance business.

Data of finanicial come from statistics monthly and yearly sheet of crdeit funds by the Urumqi Central Sub-branch of the People’s Bank of China;Data of insruance compiled by he China Insruance Regulatory Commission Xinjiang Bureau.

Data of finanicial are compiled by the Department of Comprehensive of the Xinjiang Bureau of Statistics according to the data of yearly statistics, which are provided by the Urumqi Central Sub-branch of the People’s Bank of China;Data of insurance are compiled by the China Insruance Regulatory Commission. Xinjiang Bureau.

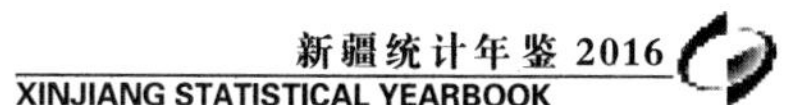

17-1 1978-2015 年历年金融机构人民币各项存款和贷款年底余额
Balance of Deposits and Loans of Financial Institutions (1978-2015)

单位：亿元 (100 million yuan)

年 份 Year	各项存款 Total Deposits	非金融企业及机关团体存款 Deposits by Non-financial Companies and Organizations	#储蓄存款 Savings Deposit	各项贷款 Total Loans
1978	32.07	6.86	6.42	18.26
1979	33.44	7.03	7.21	21.19
1980	38.56	9.60	9.52	24.74
1981	45.59	12.21	12.29	28.84
1982	53.47	15.23	15.30	32.86
1983	61.94	17.95	19.01	38.85
1984	73.63	23.35	24.31	52.02
1985	82.96	29.87	29.55	72.68
1986	102.75	38.15	40.37	93.18
1987	124.93	44.13	53.25	111.14
1988	141.10	47.41	66.25	139.43
1989	167.03	52.76	83.33	173.02
1990	221.80	71.23	114.13	233.72
1991	282.21	92.78	145.01	299.59
1992	336.58	119.51	175.62	380.26
1993	397.39	129.98	220.45	467.81
1994	634.44	214.13	347.71	632.32
1995	838.42	274.24	477.18	843.38
1996	1012.47	364.51	575.79	1016.20
1997	1180.78	442.76	676.13	1215.39
1998	1336.58	461.02	759.14	1318.41
1999	1548.72	544.22	824.68	1386.78
2000	1863.48	702.21	908.55	1403.13
2001	1972.55	691.74	994.00	1584.73
2002	2225.31	705.82	1137.87	1801.15
2003	2661.65	763.49	1371.59	2099.09
2004	2959.78	832.50	1534.67	2214.66
2005	3427.48	909.45	1816.38	2272.08
2006	4040.78	1106.42	2035.63	2412.69
2007	4614.62	1452.25	2054.91	2685.00
2008	5399.34	1473.24	2550.95	2826.53
2009	6845.07	2043.54	3049.91	3782.92
2010	8870.72	2791.72	3713.47	4973.16
2011	10387.00	5573.38	4421.93	6270.21
2012	12330.89	6588.72	5281.83	7914.00
2013	14088.83	7677.24	5884.50	9840.46
2014	15055.39	8156.28	6187.67	11671.39
2015	17123.95	9342.59	6791.62	13041.00

注：非金融企业及机关团体存款 2010 年及以前年份为企业存款，2011 年至 2014 年为单位存款。

Note: Before 2010 the deposits by Non-financial companies and organigations . refer to the deposits of enterprises,and in 2011-2014 reposits of units.

17-2　金融机构和人员数

Number of Financial Institutions and Staff

单位：个、人　　　　(2015 年)　　　　(unit, person)

项　目	Item	合　计 Total		法人机构 Legal Institution		一级分行 The Branch Level	
		机 构 Institutions	人 员 Employees	机 构 Institutions	人 员 Employees	机 构 Institutions	人 员 Employees
总　计	**Total**	**3785**	**69048**	**113**	**8739**	**27**	**6068**
人民银行	**The People's Bank of China**	**69**	**3539**			**1**	**417**
银监会新疆监管局	**China Banking Regulatory Commission Xingjiang Bureau**	**44**	**893**			**1**	**152**
全国性大型银行	**Large National Bank**	**1946**	**37614**			**8**	**3387**
工商银行	Industrial and Commercial Bank	259	8403			1	789
农业银行	Agricultural Bank	349	8542			1	299
兵团分行	XPCG Branch	243	3983			1	228
中国银行	Bank of China	173	4063			1	769
建设银行	Bank of Construction	216	5590			1	702
国家开发银行	State Development Bank	3	193			1	161
交通银行	Bank of Communication	47	996			1	310
邮政储蓄银行	Postal Savings Bank	656	5844			1	129
全国性中小型银行	**Small and Medium-sized National Bank**	**252**	**7320**	**1**	**634**	**11**	**1826**
中国进出口银行	Export and Import Bank of China	2	63			1	55
农业发展银行	Agricultural Development Bank	91	2249			1	121
中信银行	China Citic Bank	10	354			1	164
光大银行	Guang Da Bank	5	187			1	135
华夏银行	Hua Xia Bank	11	408			1	232
广发银行	GuangFa Bank	6	219			1	145
招商银行	Merchants Bank	17	658			1	353
浦发银行	Shanghai PuDong Development Bank	25	507			1	236
兴业银行	Xing Ye Bank	34	658			1	230
民生银行	Mingsheng Bank	1	85			1	85
北京银行	Beijing Bank	1	70			1	70
昆仑银行	KunLun Bank	49	1862	1	634		
区域性中小型银行	**Small and Medium-sized Regional Bank**	**561**	**8269**	**35**	**3251**	**1**	**50**
城市商业银行	City Commercial Bank	145	2794	4	1203		
农村商业银行	Rural Commercila Bank	274	3656	9	1192	1	50
农村合作银行	Rural Cooperation Bank	25	318	1	130		
村镇银行	County Bank	117	1501	21	726		
外资银行	**Foreign Bank**	**2**	**69**			**1**	**61**
农村信用社	**Rural Credit Cooperative**	**904**	**10710**	**74**	**4395**		
财务公司	**Finance Company**	**1**	**16**			**1**	**16**
信托投资公司	**Trust and Investment Company**	**2**	**362**	**2**	**362**		
金融租赁公司	**Financial Leasing Company**	**1**	**97**	**1**	**97**		
资产管理公司	**Assets Management Company**	**3**	**159**			**30**	**159**

17-2 续表 Continued

单位：个、人 (unit, person)

项 目	Item	二级分行 The Second Level Branch		支行及网点 Branches and Outlets		乡镇及农牧团场网点 and Outlets	
		机 构 Institutions	人 员 Employees	机 构 Institutions	人 员 Employees	机构 Institutions	人员 Employees
总 计	**Total**	**147**	**13832**	**3498**	**40409**	**1216**	**8425**
人民银行	**The People's Bank of China**	**14**	**1761**	**54**	**1361**		
银监会新疆监管局	**China Banking Regulatory Commission Xingjiang Bureau**	**14**	**630**	**29**	**111**		
全国性大型银行	**Large National Bank**	**86**	**9753**	**1852**	**24474**	**414**	**2367**
工商银行	Industrial and Commercial Bank	15	3005	243	4609	1	5
农业银行	Agricultural Bank	14	2058	334	6185	26	216
兵团分行	XPCG Branch	3	450	239	3305	118	1026
中国银行	Bank of China	14	1102	158	2192	4	23
建设银行	Bank of Construction	15	1877	200	3011	3	33
国家开发银行	State Development Bank	2	32				
交通银行	Bank of Communication	5	223	41	463		
邮政储蓄银行	Postal Savings Bank	18	1006	637	4709	262	1064
全国性中小型银行	**Small and Medium-sized National Bank**	**25**	**1402**	**215**	**3458**	**3**	**49**
中国进出口银行	Export and Import Bank of China	1	8				
农业发展银行	Agricultural Development Bank	16	663	74	1465	2	23
中信银行	China Citic Bank			9	190		
光大银行	Guang Da Bank			4	52		
华夏银行	Hua Xia Bank			10	176		
广发银行	GuangFa Bank	1	20	4	54		
招商银行	Merchants Bank			16	305		
浦发银行	Shanghai PuDong Development Bank	2	58	22	213		
兴业银行	Xing Ye Bank	1	37	32	391		
民生银行	Mingsheng Bank						
北京银行	Beijing Bank						
昆仑银行	KunLun Bank	4	616	44	612	1	26
区域性中小型银行	**Small and Medium-sized Regional Bank**	**8**	**286**	**517**	**4682**	**170**	**1277**
城市商业银行	City Commercial Bank	7	256	134	1335	8	42
农村商业银行	Rural Commercila Bank	1	30	263	2384	95	703
农村合作银行	Rural Cooperation Bank			24	188	12	108
村镇银行	County Bank			96	775	55	424
外资银行	**Foreign Bank**			**1**	**8**		
农村信用社	**Rural Credit Cooperative**			**830**	**6315**	**629**	**4732**
财务公司	**Finance Company**						
信托投资公司	**Trust and Investment Company**						
金融租赁公司	**Financial Leasing Company**						
资产管理公司	**Assets Management Company**						

17-3 金融机构人民币信贷资金平衡表

Balance Sheet of Credit Funds of Financial Institutions

单位：亿元 (100 million yuan)

项　　目	Item	2015
资金来源合计	**All Sources of Funds**	**17317.63**
各项存款	Total Deposits	17123.95
非金融企业及机关团体存款	Deposits by Non-finanial Companies and Organigations	9342.59
#活期存款	Current Deposits	3323.05
定期存款	Time Deposits	1945.35
个人存款	Personal Desposits	6791.62
#储蓄存款	Savings Desposits	6791.62
其他存款	Other Desposits	998.72
卖出回购资产	Financicd Assets Sold for Repurchase	37.45
借款及非存款类金融机构折入	Borrowing and Invagination from Non-deposit Financicd Instifutions	
联行往来（净）	Interbanrs Account	
应付及暂收款	Payable and Temporary Collection	328.60
各项准备金	Various Preparations	375.13
所有者权益	Owner's Right and Interest	825.00
其　他	Others	-1800.38
资金运用合计	**All Uses**	**16898.74**
各项贷款	Total Loans	12704.71
#境内贷款	Domestic Loans	13030.31
短期贷款	Short-term Loans	4063.04
个人贷款	Personal Loans	1132.12
#消费贷款	Personal Consumption Loans	181.01
经营贷款	Loans to Business	951.11
单位贷款	Unit Loans	2930.91
中长期贷款	Medium & Long-term Loans	7557.13
个人贷款	Personal Loans	1930.51
#消费贷款	Personal Consumption Loans	1378.45
经营贷款	Loans to Business	552.06
单位贷款	Unit Loans	5626.63
票据融资	Bills Financing	1000.69
融资租赁	Finance Leasing	394.04
各项垫付	The various Funds	13.44
境外贷款	Foreign Loans	70.41
债券投资	Bond Investment	844.88
股权及其他投资	Equity and other Investment	728.29
买入返购资产	Buying back the Sale of Financial Assetd	85.22
存放非存款类金融机构款项	Deposit in Non-deposit Financial Institution	28.46
联行往来（净）	Interbanks Account	2186.16
外汇占款	Funds Outstanding for Foreign Exchange	2.87
应收及预付款	Receivables and Advance Payment	88.46
投资性房地产	Investment Proberty	0.16
固定资产	Fixed Assets	218.39

17-4 大型银行信贷收支情况
Deposits and Loans of Stock-holding in Large Commercial Banks

单位：亿元 (2015 年) (100 million yuan)

项　目	Item	年末余额 Funds Sources		比年初增减数 The Beginning of Growth and Reduction
		绝对数 Absolute Value	比重(%) Proportion (%)	绝对数 Absolute Value
资金来源总计	**All Sources**	**11581.50**	**100.0**	**642.36**
各项存款	Total Deposits	9718.25	83.9	523.29
单位存款	Unit Deposit	5079.38	43.9	406.40
个人存款	Individual Deposits	4519.43	39.0	170.10
其他存款	Other Deposits	119.44	1.0	-53.21
代理财政性存款	Agency Financial Savings	13.20	0.1	6.86
金融债券	Financial Bonds			
向中央银行借款	Borrowing from the Central Bank	8.53	0.1	4.64
银行业存款类金融机构往来	Banking Deposit Financial Institutions Accounts	46.77	0.4	-11.68
借款及非存款类金融机构拆入	Borrowing and Invagination from Non-deposit Financial Institutions			-1.70
联行往来（净）	Interbanks Account	1428.79	12.3	127.78
应付及暂收款	Account Payable and Deposit Received	150.95	1.3	-28.65
所有者权益	Creditors' Equity	134.71	1.2	16.51
其他	Others	80.30	0.7	5.31
资金运用总计	**All Uses**	**11581.50**	**100.0**	**642.36**
各项贷款	Total Loans	7142.40	61.7	739.44
境内贷款	Domestic Loans	7131.78	61.6	736.00
短期贷款	Short-term Loans	1555.72	13.4	-25.53
中长期贷款	Medium-term & Long-term Loans	5236.15	45.2	612.86
其他贷款	Others	339.91	2.9	148.67
境外贷款	Overseas Loans	10.61	0.1	3.44
债券投资	Bond Investment	30.54	0.3	26.23
存放中央银行存款	Reserve Deposits Leaving in Central Bank	206.39	1.8	-22.97
联行往来（净）	Interbanks Account	3959.21	34.2	124.98
库存现金	Storage Cash	76.11	0.7	-1.39
其他	Others	166.85	1.4	-969.00

注：大型银行包括工商银行、建设银行、农业银行、兵团分行、中国银行、国家开发银行、交通银行和邮政储蓄银行。
Note:Large Banks include ICBC, CCB, ABC, BOC, CDB, BOC and PSBC.

17-5 中小型银行信贷收支情况

Deposits and Loans of Stock-holding in Medium and Small Commercial Banks

单位：亿元 (2015 年) (100 million yuan)

项　目	Item	年末余额 Funds Sources		比年初增减数 The Beginning of Growth and Reduction
		绝对数 Absolute Value	比重(%) Proportion (%)	绝对数 Absolute Value
资金来源总计	**All Sources**	**4834.97**	**100.0**	**208.54**
各项存款	Total Deposits	2986.10	61.8	591.24
单位存款	Unit Deposit	2242.49	46.4	542.44
个人存款	Individual Deposits	413.90	8.6	44.75
其他存款	Other Deposits	329.71	6.8	4.05
代理财政性存款	Agency Financial Savings	48.18	1.0	-21.47
金融债券	Financial Bonds			
向中央银行借款	Borrowing from the Central Bank	19.66	0.4	0.64
银行业存款类金融机构往来	Banking Deposit Financial Institutions Accounts	546.57	11.3	-216.15
联行往来（净）	Interbanks Account	799.21	16.5	-96.19
应付及暂收款	Account Payable and Deposit Received	61.80	1.3	-7.45
所有者权益	Creditors' Equity	248.16	5.1	12.93
其他	Others	125.29	2.6	-55.01
资金运用总计	**All Uses**	**4834.97**	**100.0**	**208.54**
各项贷款	Total Loans	2817.91	58.3	280.50
境内贷款	Domestic Loans	2817.83	58.3	280.53
短期贷款	Short-term Loans	1273.21	26.3	92.88
中长期贷款	Medium-term & Long-term Loans	1260.84	26.1	110.78
其他贷款	Others	283.78	5.9	76.87
境外贷款	Overseas Loans	0.08		-0.03
债券投资	Bond Investment	358.45	7.4	-59.87
存放中央银行存款	Reserve Deposits Leaving in Central Bank	309.69	6.4	48.80
联行往来（净）	Interbanks Account	352.04	7.3	181.61
库存现金	Storage Cash	5.91	0.1	-0.64
其他	Others	990.97	20.5	-241.86

注：中小型银行包括招商银行、农业发展银行、浦东发展银行、中信银行、兴业银行、民生银行、中国进出口银行、昆仑银行、光大银行和广东发展银行、北京银行、华夏银行。

Note:Small and Medium Banks included CMB, ADBC, SPDB, China Citic Bank,CIB,CMBC,EIBC,KLB,CEB and Guangdong Development Bank.

17-6 区域性中小型银行信贷收支情况
Deposits and Loans of Stock-holding in Regional Commercial Banks

单位：亿元 (2015 年) (100 million yuan)

项　目	Item	年末余额 Funds Sources		比年初增减数 The Beginning of Growth and Reduction
		绝对数 Absolute Value	比重(%) Proportion (%)	绝对数 Absolute Value
资金来源总计	**All Sources**	**2776.21**	**100.0**	**867.44**
各项存款	Total Deposits	2157.02	77.7	650.18
单位存款	Unit Deposit	1248.07	45.0	334.56
个人存款	Individual Deposits	908.82	32.7	316.54
其他存款	Other Deposits	0.13		-0.92
代理财政性存款	Agency Financial Savings	12.70	0.5	-8.17
金融债券	Financial Bonds			
向中央银行借款	Borrowing from the Central Bank	45.07	1.6	20.61
银行业存款类金融机构往来	Banking Deposit Financial Institutions Accounts	145.38	5.2	83.37
联行往来（净）	Interbanks Account	0.30		-0.19
应付及暂收款	Account Payable and Deposit Received	81.08	2.9	54.93
所有者权益	Creditors' Equity	255.33	9.2	75.82
其他	Others	79.33	2.9	-9.11
资金运用总计	**All Uses**	**2776.21**	**100.0**	**867.44**
各项贷款	Total Loans	1458.91	52.6	369.50
境内贷款	Domestic Loans	1458.91	52.6	369.50
短期贷款	Short-term Loans	678.50	24.4	193.69
中长期贷款	Medium-term & Long-term Loans	612.72	13.5	82.46
其他贷款	Others	167.69	14.6	93.35
境外贷款	Overseas Loans			
债券投资	Bond Investment	425.46	15.3	257.14
存放中央银行准备金存款	Reserve Deposits Leaving in Central Bank	402.99	14.5	49.55
联行往来（净）	Interbanks Account	37.25	1.3	22.72
库存现金	Storage Cash	17.08	0.6	3.41
其他	Others	434.52	15.7	165.12

注：区域性中小银行包括城市商业银行、农村商业银行、农村合作银行和村镇银行。
Note:Regional Small and Medium Banks included Urban commercial Banks, Rural Commercial Banks, Rural Cooperative Banks and Town Bank.

17-7 个人消费贷款情况

Basic Conditions of Personal Consumption Loans

单位：亿元 (100 million yuan)

项　目	Item	2014	2015
个人消费贷款	**Personal Consumption Loans**	**1364.10**	**1559.46**
短期个人消费贷款	Short-term Loans for Personal Consumption	139.47	181.01
住房贷款	Housing Loans	1.38	1.43
汽车贷款	Auto Loans	0.44	0.42
其他贷款	Other Loans	26.57	41.18
个人卡透支	Personalized Card is Overdrawn	111.08	137.99
长期个人消费贷款	Long-term Loans for Personal Consumption	1224.63	1378.45
住房贷款	Housing Loans	1080.66	1217.03
汽车贷款	Auto Loans	9.37	8.11
助学贷款	Student Loans	0.64	0.66
其他贷款	Other Loans	133.96	152.65

17-8 各地区金融机构存贷款年底余额

Deposits and Loans of Financial Institution by Region

单位：亿元 (2015 年) (100 million yuan)

项　目	Item	各项存款余额 Balance of Deposits	非金融企业及机关团体存款 Deposits by Non-financial Companies and Orgaigations	各项贷款余额 Banlance of Loans	#中长期贷款 Medium and Long-term
总　计	**Total**	**17123.95**	**9390.98**	**13041.00**	**7557.13**
乌鲁木齐市	Urumqi City	6984.60	4295.89	4957.43	2718.73
克拉玛依市	Karamay City	1286.78	765.10	509.73	162.14
吐鲁番市	Turpan City	228.61	97.99	171.35	99.60
哈密地区	Hami [Kumul] Administrative Offices	520.09	258.49	460.14	351.03
昌吉回族自治州	Changji Hui Autonomous Prefecture	1038.13	483.13	897.86	446.12
博尔塔拉蒙古自治州	Bortala Mongol Autonomous Prefecture	300.29	159.03	145.76	60.25
巴音郭楞蒙古自治州	Bayangol Mongol Autonomous Prefecture	978.17	415.75	593.80	267.68
阿克苏地区	Aksu Administrative Offices	1075.09	465.64	627.44	286.27
克孜勒苏柯尔克孜自治州	Kizilsu Kirgiz Autonomous Prefecture	164.34	93.69	72.75	43.52
喀什地区	Kashgar [Kaxgar] Administrative Offices	1206.26	668.65	564.78	312.50
和田地区	Hotan Administrative Offices	481.44	289.43	169.91	91.20
伊犁哈萨克自治州直属	Ili Kazak Autonomous Prefecture	1204.06	569.41	948.21	520.55
塔城地区	Tacheng [Tarbagatai] Administrative Offices	497.94	190.80	297.28	111.50
阿勒泰地区	Altay Administrative Offices	351.54	181.28	227.67	119.08
石河子市	Shihezi City	538.85	190.19	374.50	122.25

17-9 主要年份国内保险业务情况
Conditions of Domestic Insurance Service in Main Years

单位：亿元 (100 million yuan)

年份 Year	承保额 Amount Insured		保费 Premium		赔款及给付 Claim and Payment	
	财产险 Property Insurance	人身险 Life Insurance	财产险 Property Insurance	人身险 Life Insurance	财产险 Property Insurance	人身险 Life Insurance
1980	4.00		0.01			
1985	70.00	2.00	0.40	0.01	0.15	…
1990	241.00	41.00	1.04	0.53	0.47	0.08
1995	613.00	168.00	4.59	2.06	2.38	0.41
2000	1612.00	1711.00	12.49	15.72	5.99	3.72
2001	2112.00	1371.00	14.17	19.98	7.43	4.37
2002	2283.00	3524.00	16.48	35.25	7.84	5.02
2003	5588.00	1362.00	19.12	43.06	10.36	7.10
2004	3072.79	14089.56	20.04	48.09	10.65	7.70
2005	3839.10	14527.72	20.93	51.57	12.60	7.65
2006	4636.45	30724.13	24.61	60.79	12.92	10.34
2007	7554.92	17714.46	34.67	70.95	18.78	18.64
2008	7718.08	22143.88	44.25	108.26	23.61	20.79
2009	9673.90	24888.46	51.82	104.87	26.60	21.51
2010	11078.62	22816.35	63.00	127.92	29.21	20.12
2011	14293.63	25782.66	78.51	125.11	34.24	23.24
2012	16843.77	22272.27	93.68	141.88	50.34	29.77
2013	21000.73	34431.98	113.23	160.26	62.35	44.24
2014	26366.82	50433.68	131.63	185.78	76.60	44.57
2015	32385.67	63749.88	142.96	224.47	76.91	59.95

注：对 2004-2014 年承保额按新口径进行了调整。

17-10 保险业务经济技术指标
Economic and Technical Indicators of Insurance Service

单位：万元 (10 000 yuan)

项目	Item	保费 Premium 2014	保费 Premium 2015	赔款及给付 Claim and Payment 2014	赔款及给付 Claim and Payment 2015
财产保险业务	**Property Insurance**	**1316283**	**1429642**	**766028**	**769063**
企业财产险	Enterprise Property Insurance	69923	68548	34568	32781
家庭财产险	Family Property Insurance	9925	10639	913	1380
机动车辆险	Motor Vehicle Insurance	818963	878117	427919	452980
工程保险	Engineering Insurance	8288	8396	6760	6414
责任保险	Liability Insurance	54756	66007	20441	18991
信用保险	Credit Insurance	296	783	1	210
保证保险	Guarantee Insurance	25255	37126	1770	5816
船舶险	Ship Insurance	21	24	…	18
货物运输险	Freight Transpor Insurance	9315	8505	2076	2526
特殊风险保险	Special risks insurance	1251	778	641	141
农业保险	Agriculture Insurance	318245	350520	270901	247710
其他险	Other Insurance	47	199	39	94
人身保险业务	**Life Insurance**	**1857817**	**2244706**	**445711**	**599462**
寿　险	Life Insurance	1412275	1694327	283628	406994
健康险	Health Insurance	323184	418554	130186	154562
人身意外伤害险	Personal Insurance	122358	131825	31897	37906

17-11 新疆辖区保险机构

Number of Insurance Institutions in Xinjiang

单位：个 (2015 年) (unit)

项目	Item	机构数 Number of Institutions	总公司 Head Offices	自治区分公司 Xinjiang Branch Companies
总计	**Total**	**1782**	**1**	**29**
中国人民财产保险股份有限公司	The People's Insurance Corporation Ltd.of china	564		1
中国人寿保险股份有限公司	The Life Insurance Corporation Ltd.of China	289		1
中国大地财产保险股份有限公司	Da Di Property Insurance Corporation Ltd of China	16		1
中华联合财产保险股份有限公司	The Pacific Insurance Corporation Ltd.Property Insruance Company of China	314		1
中国太平洋财产保险股份有限公司	The Pacific Insurance Corporation Ltd., Property Insurance Company of China	27		1
中国太平洋人寿保险股份有限公司	The Pacific Insurance Corporation Ltd.,Life Insurance Company of China	33		1
中国平安财产保险股份有限公司	The Ping An Insurance Corporation Ltd., Property Insurance Company of China	57		1
中国平安人寿保险股份有限公司	The Ping An Insurance Corporation Ltd.,Life Insurance Company of China	74		1
新华人寿保险股份有限公司	Xin Hua Life Insurance Corporation Ltd.	48		1
泰康人寿保险股份有限公司	Tai Kang Life Insurance Corporation Ltd.	64		1
天安保险股份有限公司	Tian An Property Insurance Corporation Ltd.	14		1
永安财产保险股份有限公司	Yong An Property Insurance Corporation Ltd.	53		1
太平人寿保险有限公司	Taiping Life Insurance Corporation Ltd.	16		1
中银保险有限公司	Zhongyin Insurance Corporation Ltd.	1		1
生命人寿保险股份有限公司	The Life Insurance Corporation Ltd.	10		1
永诚财产保险股份有限公司	Yong chen Insurance Corporation Ltd.	4		1
平安养老保险股份有限公司	The Pingan Old-age Pension Insurance Company	2		1
合众人寿保险股份有限公司	Union Life Insurance Corporation Ltd.	12		1
中国人民健康保险股份有限公司	PICC Health Insurance Corporation Ltd.	8		1
阳光财产保险股份有限公司	Sunshine Property Insurance Corporation Ltd.	45		1
都邦财产保险股份有限公司	Du-bang Property Insurance Corporation Ltd.	1		1
渤海财产保险股份有限公司	Bohai Property Insurance Corporation Ltd.	5		1
中国人民人寿保险股份有限公司	PICC Life Insurance Corporation Ltd.of China	23		1
中国人寿财产保险股份有限公司	The Life Insurance Corporation Ltd.,Property Insurance Company	46		1
泰康养老保险股份有限公司	The Taikang Old-age Pension Insurance Company	1		1
阳光人寿保险股份有限公司	The Sun of Life Insurance Corporation Ltd.	13		1
信达财产保险股份有限公司	Xinda Property Insurance Corporation Ltd.	8		1
华泰财产保险有限公司	The Taikang Property Insurance Corporation Ltd.	1		1
安邦财产保险股份有限公司	An Bang Property Insurance Corporation Ltd.	32		1
中石油专属财产保险股份有限公司	The Oil in the Exclusive Property Insurance Limited by Share Ltd.	1	1	

17-11 续表 Continued

单位：个 (unit)

项 目	Item	地区级中心支公司 Branch Companies at Prefecture Level	县级支公司 Branch Companies at County Level	营业部 Business Departments	营销服务部 Marketing Departments
总 计	**Total**	**223**	**643**	**7**	**879**
中国人民财产保险股份有限公司	The People's Insurance Corporation Ltd.of china	15	105	5	438
中国人寿保险股份有限公司	The Life Insurance Corporation Ltd.of China	15	69		204
中国大地财产保险股份有限公司	Da Di Property Insurance Corporation Ltd of China	4	11		
中华联合财产保险股份有限公司	The Pacific Insurance Corporation Ltd.Property Insruance Company of China	19	216	1	77
中国太平洋财产保险股份有限公司	The Pacific Insurance Corporation Ltd., Property Insurance Company of China	9	17		
中国太平洋人寿保险股份有限公司	The Pacific Insurance Corporation Ltd.,Life Insurance Company of China	9	22		1
中国平安财产保险股份有限公司	The Ping An Insurance Corporation Ltd., Property Insurance Company of China	15	37		4
中国平安人寿保险股份有限公司	The Ping An Insurance Corporation Ltd.,Life Insurance Company of China	12	20		41
新华人寿保险股份有限公司	Xin Hua Life Insurance Corporation Ltd.	10	19		18
泰康人寿保险股份有限公司	Tai Kang Life Insurance Corporation Ltd.	11	18		34
天安保险股份有限公司	Tian An Property Insurance Corporation Ltd.	8	3		2
永安财产保险股份有限公司	Yong An Property Insurance Corporation Ltd.	14	6		32
太平人寿保险有限公司	Taiping Life Insurance Corporation Ltd.	7	7	1	
中银保险有限公司	Zhongyin Insurance Corporation Ltd.				
生命人寿保险股份有限公司	The Life Insurance Corporation Ltd.	5	1		3
永诚财产保险股份有限公司	Yong chen Insurance Corporation Ltd.	2			1
平安养老保险股份有限公司	The Pingan Old-age Pension Insurance Company	1			
合众人寿保险股份有限公司	Union Life Insurance Corporation Ltd.	7	4		
中国人民健康保险股份有限公司	PICC Health Insurance Corporation Ltd.	2	1		4
阳光财产保险股份有限公司	Sunshine Property Insurance Corporation Ltd.	11	27		6
都邦财产保险股份有限公司	Du-bang Property Insurance Corporation Ltd.				
渤海财产保险股份有限公司	Bohai Property Insurance Corporation Ltd.	4			
中国人民人寿保险股份有限公司	PICC Life Insurance Corporation Ltd.of China	10	12		
中国人寿财产保险股份有限公司	The Life Insurance Corporation Ltd.,Property Insurance Company	13	30		2
泰康养老保险股份有限公司	The Taikang Old-age Pension Insurance Company				
阳光人寿保险股份有限公司	The Sun of Life Insurance Corporation Ltd.	5	7		
信达财产保险股份有限公司	Xinda Property Insurance Corporation Ltd.	3	4		
华泰财产保险有限公司	The Taikang Property Insurance Corporation Ltd.				
安邦财产保险股份有限公司	An Bang Property Insurance Corporation Ltd.	12	7		12
中石油专属财产保险股份有限公司	The Oil in the Exclusive Property Insurance Limited by Share Ltd.				

17-12 新疆辖区保险事业发展情况

Statistics on Development of Insurance in Xinjiang

单位：万元 (2015 年) (10 000 yuan)

项　目	Item	承保额(亿元) Amount Insured (100 million yuan)	保 费 Premium	赔款及给付 Claim and Payment
总　计	**Total**	**96135.55**	**3674347.88**	**1368524.91**
财产险公司小计	**Sub-total of property Insurance Companies**	**75724.83**	**1586744.15**	**863680.17**
中国人民财产保险股份有限公司	The People's Insurance Corporation Ltd.of China	37574.31	792183.64	442852.40
中华联合财产保险股份有限公司	The Property Insurance Corporation Ltd.XPCG	14115.97	452529.09	263732.89
中国太平洋财产保险股份有限公司	The Pacific Insurance Corporation Ltd., Property Insurance Company of China	5207.34	41694.35	27193.30
中国平安财产保险股份有限公司	The Ping An Insurance Corporation Ltd., Property Insurance Company of China	11310.95	168783.25	62637.56
天安保险股份有限公司	Tian An Property Insurance Corporation Ltd.	1110.60	9203.31	5816.57
永安财产保险股份有限公司	Yong An Property Insurance Corporation Ltd.	761.85	15979.16	8619.34
中国大地财产保险股份有限公司	Da Di Property Insurance Corporation Ltd.	368.83	13877.18	6672.58
安邦财产保险股份有限公司	An Bang Property Insurance Corporation Ltd.	105.11	6236.51	3963.79
阳光财产保险股份有限公司	Sunshine Property Insurance Corporation Ltd.	960.18	31099.95	15379.89
都邦财产保险股份有限公司	Du-bang Property Insurance Corporation Ltd.	364.38	2648.33	1020.49
渤海财产保险股份有限公司	Bohai Property Insurance Corporation Ltd.	16.05	856.89	550.74
永诚财产保险股份有限公司	Yongcheng Property Insurance Corporation Ltd.	377.42	2822.39	1106.51
中银财产保险股份有限公司	Zhongyin Property Insurance Corporation Ltd.	187.25	3316.99	625.53
信达财产保险股份有限公司	Xinda Property Insurance Corporation Ltd.	320.94	7187.90	5942.44
中国人寿财产保险股份有限公司	The Life Insurance Corporation Ltd.,Property Insurance Company	1635.44	37816.85	17491.93
华泰财产保险股份有限公司	The Taikang Property Insurance Corporation Ltd.	1.57	10.53	1.21
人身险公司小计	**Sub-total of Life Insurance Companies**	**20410.72**	**2087603.74**	**504844.74**
中国人寿保险股份有限公司	The Life Insurance Corporation Ltd.of China	8312.63	624457.92	237144.06
中国太平洋人寿保险股份有限公司	The Pacific Insurance Corporation Ltd.,Life Insurance Company of China	1825.66	318772.02	35951.10
中国平安人寿保险股份有限公司	The Ping An Insurance Corporation Ltd.,Life Insurance Company of China	2179.48	299186.06	50418.02
平安养老保险股份有限公司	The Pingan Old-age Pension Insurance Company	1667.27	9052.75	4481.29
新华人寿保险股份有限公司	Xin Hua Life Insurance Corporation Ltd.	2096.38	246039.25	42367.25
泰康人寿保险股份有限公司	Tai Kang Life Insurance Corporation Ltd.	959.39	172247.11	59224.43
中国人民人寿保险股份有限公司	PICC Life Insurance Corporation Ltd.of China	1144.10	136008.54	28060.90
太平人寿保险有限公司	Taiping Life Insurance Corporation Ltd.	183.16	118034.23	11814.28
中国人民健康保险股份有限公司	PICC Health Insurance Corporation Ltd.	992.03	62184.47	23065.56
合众人寿保险股份有限公司	Union Life Insurance Corporation Ltd.	69.63	36321.25	8992.83
阳光人寿保险股份有限公司	The Sun of Life Insurance Corporation Ltd.	113.78	24546.87	1328.72
生命人寿保险股份有限公司	The Life Insurance Corporation Ltd.	99.34	38063.25	1612.74
泰康养老保险股份有限公司	The Taikang Old-age Pension Insurance Company	767.88	2690.01	383.55

注：众安财险（虚拟）主要经营互联网保险销售业务，在新疆没有实体机构，其经营数据直接汇入财产险公司总数，未单列在表格中。

Zhong An Insurance minly engaged in sales of internet insurance,There is no entity in Xir Qieng. The total number of business data directly imported in the property insuance company is not listed in the form.

17-13 各地区保险业务情况
Conditions of Insurance Service by Region

单位：万元 (2015 年) (10 000 yuan)

地区	Region	全部业务 All Insurance Business 保费收入 Premium Income	全部业务 比上年增长(%) Increase Rate Over Preceding year(%)	财产保险公司业务 Property Insurance Business 保费收入 Premium Income	财产保险公司业务 比上年增长(%) Increase Rate Over Preceding year(%)
总　计	**Total**	**3674347.88**	**15.76**	**1586744.15**	**8.85**
乌鲁木齐市	Urumqi City	1220057.03	16.62	392785.00	8.04
昌吉回族自治州	Changji Hui Autonomous Prefecture	330284.62	10.84	155505.14	2.91
伊犁州直属县(市)	Counties (Cities) Direct Under Ili Prefecture	266917.46	19.96	133817.19	13.62
克拉玛依市	Karamay City	159108.16	12.67	54818.55	3.62
博尔塔拉蒙古自治州	Bortala Mongol Autonomous Prefecture	94175.28	23.97	41807.16	14.67
石河子市	Shihezi City	206884.82	20.56	97581.09	13.82
奎屯市	Kuytun City	101546.39	15.27	54758.79	11.10
阿勒泰地区	Altay Administrative Offices	81386.69	8.86	47844.08	10.45
塔城地区	Tacheng [Tarbagatai] Administrative Offices	138385.29	19.84	63542.93	17.67
克孜勒苏柯尔克孜自治州	Kizilsu Kirgiz Autonomous Prefecture	21836.70	22.08	17272.80	25.94
和田地区	Hotan Administrative Offices	59335.83	4.10	44707.78	2.86
喀什地区	Kashgar [Kaxgar] Administrative Offices	201944.13	14.17	123034.49	11.44
巴音郭楞蒙古自治州	Bayangol Mongol Autonomous Prefecture	292535.69	11.27	119728.26	-4.70
阿克苏地区	Aksu Administrative Offices	286475.22	18.22	161615.16	16.48
吐鲁番市	Turpan City	75370.22	25.99	31041.82	17.27
哈密地区	Hami [Kumul] Administrative Offices	138104.36	11.82	46883.89	3.85

地区	Region	人寿保险公司业务 Life Insurance Business 保费收入 Premium Income	人寿保险公司业务 比上年增长(%) Increase Rate Over Preceding year(%)	保险密度(元/人) Insurance Density (yuan)	保险深度(%) Insurance Depth(%)
总　计	**Total**	**2087603.74**	**21.63**	**1557.11**	**3.9**
乌鲁木齐市	Urumqi City	827272.03	21.19	4572.41	4.6
昌吉回族自治州	Changji Hui Autonomous Prefecture	174779.47	19.01	2371.37	2.9
伊犁州直属县(市)	Counties (Cities) Direct Under Ili Prefecture	133100.26	27.09	983.19	3.9
克拉玛依市	Karamay City	104289.61	18.09	5308.91	2.5
博尔塔拉蒙古自治州	Bortala Mongol Autonomous Prefecture	52368.12	32.56	1963.21	3.3
石河子市	Shihezi City	109303.73	27.30	3270.39	6.6
奎屯市	Kuytun City	46787.60	20.56	3508.86	8.4
阿勒泰地区	Altay Administrative Offices	33542.61	6.67	1218.36	3.7
塔城地区	Tacheng [Tarbagatai] Administrative Offices	74842.36	21.74	1351.15	2.3
克孜勒苏柯尔克孜自治州	Kizilsu Kirgiz Autonomous Prefecture	4563.90	9.40	366.33	2.2
和田地区	Hotan Administrative Offices	14628.05	8.05	255.28	2.5
喀什地区	Kashgar [Kaxgar] Administrative Offices	78909.64	18.71	448.84	2.6
巴音郭楞蒙古自治州	Bayangol Mongol Autonomous Prefecture	172807.43	25.88	2098.84	2.8
阿克苏地区	Aksu Administrative Offices	124860.06	20.57	1132.09	3.5
吐鲁番市	Turpan City	44328.40	32.90	1156.16	3.6
哈密地区	Hami [Kumul] Administrative Offices	91220.46	16.42	2239.41	3.3

注：乌鲁木齐市区数据中包含自治区本级数据。
Note:Data of Urumqi city include data of Autonomous Level.

主要统计指标解释

信贷资金 指金融机构以信用方式积聚和分配的货币资金。金融机构信贷资金的来源有各项存款、金融债券、对国际金融机构负债、流通中现金、其他项目等；信贷资金的运用有各项贷款、有价证券及投资、金银占款、外汇占款、财政借款及在国际金融机构中的资产等。

存款 指企业、机关、团体或居民根据资金必须收回的原则，把货币资金存入银行或其他信贷机构保管并取得一定利息的一种信用活动形式。根据存款对象或性质的不同可划分为单位存款、个人存款、财政性存款、临时性存款、城委托存款、其他存款等科目。它是银行信贷资金的主要来源。

贷款 指银行或其他信用机构根据资金必须归还的原则，按一定利率，为企业、个人等提供资金的一种信用活动形式。我国银行贷款分为短期贷款、委托及信托类贷款、其他类贷款等

保险金额 指保险人承担赔偿或者给付保险金责任的最高限额。

保费 指投保人为取得保险人在约定范围内所承担赔偿责任而支付给保险人的费用。

赔款 指保险人根据保险合同的规定，向被保险人支付的赔偿保险责任损失的金额。

给付 包括死伤医疗给付和满期给付。死伤医疗给付是指保险人根据人寿保险及长期健康保险合同的规定，因被保险人在保险期内发生保险责任范围内的保险事故支付给被保险人(或受益人)的金额。满期给付是指被保险人生存期满，保险人按人寿保险合同规定支付给被保险人的满期保险金额。

Explanatory Notes on Main Statistical Indicators

Credit Funds refer to the monetary funds accumulated and distributed in the means of credit by the financial institutions. The sources of credit funds include various deposits, financial bonds, liabilities to international financial institutions, currency in circulation, other items. The uses of credit funds include loans, securities and investment, position for bullion and silver purchase, position for foreign exchange purchase, advances to treasury, and assets with international financial institutions.

Deposit is a form of credit by which enterprises, institutions, organizations or households can put money into banks and other credit institutions for safekeeping and interest earning under the principle of free withdrawal. According to different depositors, deposits are divided into enterprise deposits, treasury deposits, deposits of government agencies and organizations, capital construction deposits, urban savings deposits, rural deposits and other deposits. Deposits are major sources of the credit funds of banks.

Loan is a form of credit by which banks and other credit institutions provide funds at certain interest rate to enterprises and individuals in the light of the principle of unconditional repayment. Loans from Chinese banks include short-term loan, medium-term and long-term loans, financial lease, bill financing, various money advanced, foreign loans.

Amount Insured refers to the maximum that the insurant will get for the claim of the case insured.

Premium is the fee paid by the insurant to the insurer to obtain the obligation of compensation from the insurance within the agreed terms.

Settled Claim is the compensation paid by the insurer to the insurant in accordance with the insurance contract.

Payment includes payment for death, injury or medical treatment and payment at maturity. Payment for death, injury or medical treatment refers to the money paid to the insurant (or the beneficiary) in accordance with the life or health insurance contract when the insurant encounters accidents within the insured period covered in the contract. payment at maturity refers to the payment to the insurant in accordance with the life insurance contract at the end of the insured period.

18 教育、科技和文化

EDUCATION SCIENCE & TECHNOLOGY AND CULTURE

第十八篇　教育、科技和文化

本篇主要内容和资料来源

教育统计资料包括研究生教育（高等学校研究生教育、科研机构研究生教育）、普通高等学校本专科教育、普通中等教育(中等专业教育、技工学校、普通中学、职业高中、工读学校)、初等教育(小学)、学前教育、特殊教育(盲聋哑和弱智儿童学校等)以及教育经费来源及使用等资料。

教育部分资料由新疆维吾尔自治区教育厅依据年报资料整理提供。

科技统计资料包括科技活动基本情况、县级以上政府部门属研究与开发机构及科技信息与文献机构人员数、重大科学技术研究成果及奖励、专利申请和批准情况、高等学校科技活动情况、企事业单位专业技术人员情况、大中型工业企业科技活动情况、各类技术合同鉴定及执行情况、技术经济合同成交情况、技术流向地域情况等。

科技统计范围包括新疆地区有科技活动的企事业单位，具体涵盖规模以上工业企业（标准见工业篇）、各级各部门所属国有独立核算的科学研究与技术开发机构及科技情报与文献机构、普通高等学校等。

科技部分资料由新疆维吾尔自治区统计局社会科技统计处根据科技年报和新疆维吾尔自治区科技厅提供资料整理。

文化部分主要包括艺术表演团体、艺术表演场所、公共图书馆、博物馆、文化馆（站）、广播、电影、电视以及文物等文化单位的机构、人员、经费和业务活动情况。

文化部分资料是由新疆维吾尔自治区统计局社会科技统计处根据部门统计报表资料加工整理而成。艺术事业、图书馆事业、群众文化事业的资料主要来自新疆维吾尔自治区文化厅；文物资料来自新疆维吾尔自治区文物局；广播、电影、电视资料来自新疆维吾尔自治区新闻出版广电局。

Education Science & Technology and Culture

Main Content and Source of Data

The data on education cover the situation on postgraduate (regular institutions of higher education,research institutions), regular institution of higher education(universities and colleges), regular secondary education, (professional secondary schools, technical schools, regular secondary school,vocational senior secondary schools,schools for juvenile delinquents);primary education (primary schools), preschool education, special education(schools for the blind, deaf-mutes and the retarded) and expenditure on education.

Statistical data on education compiled by the Statistics Bureau of Xinjiang in accordance with the data from the Bureau of Education.

Data on science and technology mainly include: condition of scientific and technological activities, state-owned research and development institutions and information and literature institutions at and above county level and persons engaged; the situation of science and technological achievements & prizes and patent applications, basic statistics on scientific and technological activities of high education, condition of professional scientific and technological personnel of enterprises and institutions, statistics on signing and implementing technical contracts, statistics on transaction in technical and economic contract, statistics on location of technical contract.

Statistical scope on technology include scientific and technical activities in enterprises and institution, they are mainly: industrial enterprises above designated size, state-owned research and development institutions and information and literature institutions at and above county level and persons engaged, regular institutions of high education, etc.

Data on technology compiled by the Statistics Bureau of Xinjiang in accordance with the data from the Bureau of Science &Technology.

Data on culture cover mainly the situations on institutions, personal and business activities of arts (performing groups and venues), libraries, museums, cultural centers, archives, cultural stations, broadcasting, films, televisions, news and publication.

Data on culture are collected and tabulated in accordance with the statistical reporting schemes stipulated by the Statistical Bureau of Xinjiang. Data of arts, libraries, mass culture are provided by the Xinjiang Bureau of Culture; Data on archives are from Xinjiang Bureau of Archives; Data on broadcasting, film and television are mainly from Xinjiang Bureau of Press,Publication,Radio Film and Television.

18-1 主要年份各级各类学校数

Number of Schools by Level and Type in Main Years

单位：所 (unit)

年 份 Year	普通高等学校 Regular Institutions of Higher Education	中等学校 Secondary Schools	普通中等专业学校 Specialized Secondary Schools	普通中学 Regular Secondary Schools	#高 中 Senior Secondary Schools	职业高中 Vocational Secondary Schools	技工学校 Technical Schools	小 学 Primary Schools	特殊教育学校 Special Schools
1978	10	2078	78	1997	673		10	9891	1
1980	12	2197	96	2032	720	21	48	9006	2
1981	12	2201	99	2037	689	13	52	8753	2
1982	12	2243	101	2072	663	23	47	8533	2
1983	13	2333	104	2133	744	47	49	8261	2
1984	13	2374	100	2143	790	82	49	8253	3
1985	14	2360	97	2147	794	65	51	8104	3
1986	17	2284	99	2053	796	68	64	8178	3
1987	20	2284	100	2052	819	68	64	7813	5
1988	20	2335	108	2054	809	109	64	7597	5
1989	20	2301	112	2008	797	119	62	7494	5
1990	21	2274	112	1958	766	134	70	7247	6
1991	21	2229	112	1915	752	140	62	7132	6
1992	21	2239	112	1903	715	160	64	7122	6
1993	21	2206	113	1851	650	170	72	7088	6
1994	21	2168	114	1830	586	157	67	7117	6
1995	21	2121	115	1792	554	145	69	7086	6
1996	18	2092	115	1776	536	137	64	7047	7
1997	18	2090	115	1770	531	131	74	6962	8
1998	17	2066	115	1763	517	121	67	6837	7
1999	17	2022	113	1725	488	116	68	6796	7
2000	20	2000	112	1711	484	112	65	6718	7
2001	21	2179	99	1929	472	89	62	6221	7
2002	24	2173	87	1945	507	83	58	6043	7
2003	26	2154	78	1932	500	86	58	5832	8
2004	28	2186	78	1965	498	84	59	5451	8
2005	31	2185	79	1961	503	87	58	5209	10
2006	31	2101	67	1891	486	84	59	4815	9
2007	32	2040	74	1830	454	75	61	4589	9
2008	32	1973	75	1759	444	82	57	4159	10
2009	32	1832	80	1610	413	82	60	3651	10
2010	32	1772	81	1545	385	83	63	3598	13
2011	32	1766	96	1525	368	71	74	3536	15
2012	34	1744	95	1497	366	69	83	3535	19
2013	36	1738	93	1468	366	69	108	3533	26
2014	39	1729	95	1463	363	63	108	3551	29
2015	39	1690	94	1426	357	62	108	3501	28

注：从 2006 年起，职业初中并入普通中学统计。（以下同）

Note: Number of regular secondary schools included the number of junior vocational secondary schools from 2006.(The sameas follows)

18-2 主要年份各级各类学校教师数

Number of Teachers by Level and Type of School in Main Years

单位：人 (person)

年份 Year	普通高等学校 Regular Institutions of Higher Education	中等学校 Secondary Schools	普通中等专业学校 Specialized Secondary Schools	普通中学 Regular Secondary Schools	#高中 Senior Secondary Schools	职业高中 Vocational Secondary Schools	技工学校 Technical Schools	小学 Primary Schools	特殊教育学校 Special Schools
1978	2458	44417	2543	41661	8064		213	82616	28
1980	3149	50056	3459	45232	9292	77	1288	89027	54
1981	3377	55547	3808	50143	10341	62	1534	94966	58
1982	3994	61518	3869	55819	11441	167	1663	105556	69
1983	4724	65096	4140	58591	12567	663	1702	104536	64
1984	5109	65703	4183	58451	13128	1194	1875	101025	56
1985	5473	69185	4554	60942	15059	1567	2122	98294	67
1986	6052	72828	5114	63631	17058	1646	2437	95473	79
1987	6789	76680	5162	66395	18510	2215	2908	93910	104
1988	6822	78449	5664	67429	19010	2319	3037	94342	106
1989	6898	77756	5989	65833	19149	2680	3254	94397	111
1990	7002	78596	6158	65814	19318	3117	3507	95060	139
1991	7269	78339	6134	64923	19488	3580	3702	95565	145
1992	7280	78403	6210	64465	19000	3769	3959	96729	154
1993	7158	77200	6271	63448	17142	3853	3628	99297	129
1994	7554	75546	6383	62087	15011	3531	3545	101863	145
1995	7687	76584	6540	62934	14434	3494	3616	106001	162
1996	7835	79424	6791	65228	14781	3685	3720	112149	114
1997	7837	82459	7089	68115	15111	3568	3687	119184	156
1998	7587	83952	7194	69845	15734	3641	3272	123308	163
1999	7516	86667	7229	72195	15673	3598	3645	126401	171
2000	7924	89211	6786	75895	16069	3104	3426	131259	183
2001	9123	93126	6842	79419	17025	2546	4319	132137	187
2002	10369	96469	6031	84714	19031	2399	3325	132435	200
2003	11237	103156	5157	89332	20976	2440	6227	132284	237
2004	12239	106839	5494	94381	22809	3079	3885	134915	257
2005	12733	112941	4993	102168	25153	1696	4084	134768	262
2006	13783	120777	4339	106975	26815	2832	6631	134718	286
2007	15096	123246	5553	108232	27970	2295	7166	133626	298
2008	15755	121898	5381	108729	28735	2586	5202	132797	313
2009	16234	125152	6086	110842	29402	2464	5760	134263	319
2010	16506	128306	6232	113990	30231	2708	5706	133963	347
2011	17256	132748	7210	116501	31258	2255	6782	135182	316
2012	17570	134900	7173	118299	32375	2347	7081	136130	452
2013	18327	137901	6778	121129	35020	2478	7516	140561	547
2014	19081	141295	6775	124848	37780	2310	7362	145067	693
2015	19374	141627	6776	124626	38877	2453	7772	144767	790

18-3 主要年份各级各类学校在校学生数
Number of Students Enrollment by Level and Type of School in Main Years

单位：人 (person)

年 份 Year	普通高等学校 Regular Institutions of Higher Education	中等学校 Secondary Schools	普通中等专业学校 Specialized Secondary Schools	普通中学 Regular Secondary Schools	#高 中 Senior Secondary Schools	职业高中 Vocational Secondary Schools	技工学校 Technical Schools	小 学 Primary Schools	特殊教育学校 Special Schools
1978	10229	838560	23696	806386	128376		8478	2028771	270
1980	14308	886740	42362	823161	147446	1416	19801	2055513	371
1981	16546	871359	34399	813269	155816	2065	21626	2010494	414
1982	16235	894831	24881	842757	165619	6236	20957	1985976	464
1983	16493	932761	22493	873657	175157	17909	18702	1941009	527
1984	19689	994078	28150	906862	192914	38563	20503	1962981	688
1985	26500	1054293	33251	955356	223405	41825	23861	1966306	706
1986	29928	1134562	36231	1023533	261191	47149	27649	1948151	737
1987	30145	1170333	39842	1046403	270586	53425	30663	1884884	797
1988	30747	1128662	42524	993674	265301	57180	35284	1847160	745
1989	31964	1042028	44920	893198	255151	64979	38931	1842100	730
1990	31271	1015214	45985	863118	251067	65862	40249	1857246	610
1991	31374	963948	47129	806702	246950	68460	41657	1955216	652
1992	33857	941656	52102	783130	212942	65330	41094	1980686	624
1993	39422	884083	63314	718607	166203	58509	43653	2039409	549
1994	43687	892041	73922	723596	137870	50894	43629	2105911	590
1995	44918	912597	68586	749788	141330	54122	40101	2301274	643
1996	44928	967253	72782	803856	149937	51952	38663	2301764	407
1997	46342	1045980	77837	876720	168483	54038	37385	2419700	629
1998	47464	1121675	82262	958420	183230	51458	29535	2502691	613
1999	54959	1233288	93445	1062380	189037	49871	27592	2507406	681
2000	74063	1311845	105255	1132912	198639	51270	22408	2477413	674
2001	109815	1390360	97321	1228566	225411	47673	16800	2435667	922
2002	134831	1493580	83902	1338836	272381	50787	20055	2359788	3876
2003	151256	1584700	71499	1448531	315178	45330	19340	2289066	1863
2004	168247	1676971	71324	1517948	359147	61502	26197	2218109	2549
2005	188752	1717403	86744	1587850	387763	63158	26219	2143833	4961
2006	207672	1739422	108131	1572502	402321	23488	35301	2097975	4843
2007	226012	1742947	141162	1529092	413452	31741	40952	2058884	6396
2008	241288	1722667	150715	1483550	418701	41611	46791	2012004	5574
2009	253272	1695984	147439	1444836	417139	54777	48932	1973890	5991
2010	263835	1684027	152227	1422419	419141	59593	49788	1935798	5974
2011	272818	1675169	161657	1409293	432724	60734	43485	1919457	4733
2012	284172	1651618	159069	1383886	440717	57269	51394	1900844	4909
2013	295292	1632875	160368	1366013	447540	53971	52523	1894401	5229
2014	307664	1638621	154011	1374440	462963	51932	58238	1942947	5915
2015	322713	1682124	151913	1405335	497935	56339	68537	2048874	6459

注：1.18-3、18-4、18-5 表中高等学校含研究生数。2.特殊教育学校 2002 年新增随班就读。(以下同)
Note: a) Institutions of higher education included the number of postgraduates with table 18-3,18-4,18-5.
b) In Special Schools for the blind,deaf, mute, new comers may follow the classes accordingly since 2002 (The same as follows).

18-4 主要年份各级各类学校招生数

Number of New Students Enrollment by Level and Type of School in Main Years

单位：人 (person)

年份 Year	普通高等学校 Regular Institutions of Higher Education	中等学校 Secondary Schools	普通中等专业学校 Specialized Secondary Schools	普通中学 Regular Secondary Schools	#高中 Senior Secondary Schools	职业高中 Vocational Secondary Schools	技工学校 Technical Schools	小学 Primary Schools	特殊教育学校 Special Schools
1978	4118	343088	12540	323948	68261		6600	459802	40
1980	3767	336402	14688	310931	73959	792	10531	433089	90
1981	3070	332717	9751	314200	80957	1236	7530	427439	86
1982	3809	343286	7946	323580	81738	4401	7356	435334	181
1983	5158	364291	9342	334769	85514	12336	7844	409257	40
1984	6527	377785	13433	332093	91060	23020	9239	415792	235
1985	9298	386074	13919	341123	93692	20429	10603	374643	91
1986	7941	406625	14428	358590	96858	21454	12153	359007	105
1987	8347	388507	14986	336693	88115	24118	12710	328980	189
1988	8557	358913	15067	305074	87698	23849	14923	334031	117
1989	8118	326282	15123	264271	86812	31361	15527	333392	197
1990	8034	356615	15586	297641	84567	27968	15420	335552	103
1991	8179	302489	16902	239511	77525	29354	16722	344432	15
1992	10985	334705	20611	269859	61673	27041	17194	359302	119
1993	13359	331884	26572	263683	56180	24778	16851	385535	102
1994	12099	326160	29248	259237	44552	21350	16325	400700	102
1995	12307	356814	25260	286318	58203	25643	19593	419717	165
1996	12421	366772	26311	299348	59400	23003	18110	428651	67
1997	12673	392571	27302	326494	64377	21741	17034	443238	120
1998	12880	426400	27497	365234	71302	19862	13807	429247	130
1999	19821	463579	36014	399516	69801	18828	9221	391298	175
2000	30689	486763	38866	418790	76744	20027	9080	364193	177
2001	42253	510469	26763	459878	93519	16621	7207	352975	135
2002	42808	551353	22241	501824	113366	16746	10442	346386	874
2003	44733	583033	24016	532987	126163	15378	10652	347619	369
2004	53204	606666	27990	536405	138315	27585	14686	347364	390
2005	58653	602335	34882	539922	145044	12416	15115	338539	847
2006	62395	599748	45536	522425	142853	13017	18770	337994	780
2007	68999	619218	65290	510080	146449	19201	24647	340108	1158
2008	74670	603352	62098	497579	147914	21610	22065	328647	840
2009	73904	593290	53692	489838	148869	28243	21517	318488	869
2010	79216	597621	60418	489356	153238	28767	19080	311861	1055
2011	79337	581939	60669	482450	156497	21777	17043	322436	939
2012	83732	571006	56096	469674	155276	22229	23007	331734	1137
2013	89657	575331	57447	477175	163582	21943	18766	348643	1473
2014	91383	585700	59905	479548	173862	20103	26144	368584	1293
2015	96695	598174	60859	486933	187672	21016	29366	397691	1368

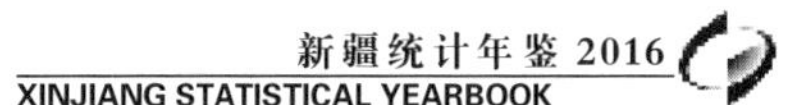

18-5 主要年份各级各类学校毕业生数
Number of Graduates by Level and Type of School in Main Years

单位：人 (person)

年 份 Year	普通高等学校 Regular Institutions of Higher Education	中等学校 Secondary Schools	普通中等专业学校 Specialized Secondary Schools	普通中学 Regular Secondary Schools	#高 中 Senior Secondary Schools	职业高中 Vocational Secondary Schools	技工学校 Technical Schools	小 学 Primary Schools	特殊教育学校 Special Schools
1978	1509	205862	8801	195542	53970		1519	388359	195
1980	814	264626	11946	246382	60370	341	5957	292515	37
1981	779	280171	17039	257478	67114	367	5287	397524	37
1982	4108	269927	17201	244853	69504	385	7488	310025	32
1983	4823	283120	11584	260906	77546	1144	9486	317227	27
1984	3426	275788	8130	257833	72191	2764	7061	295993	48
1985	3511	290077	8097	267302	68096	7424	7254	289045	73
1986	4797	296360	11551	268402	58585	8543	7864	307047	52
1987	8001	321981	10623	289556	73947	12280	9522	317820	101
1988	7792	346072	12026	311224	85718	12758	10064	288594	68
1989	6900	347719	12441	308467	86489	14650	12161	249888	57
1990	8603	343313	14260	297235	81062	17938	13880	259301	98
1991	7919	324031	15571	274913	79664	17505	16042	183350	159
1992	8402	310076	14950	260953	84518	18999	15174	268074	157
1993	7741	312284	16760	261502	78675	18558	15464	259468	104
1994	7734	250909	16206	198839	57090	18100	17764	262215	55
1995	10505	271992	18981	215756	44589	16490	20765	271227	57
1996	12272	271267	21701	215295	43478	15424	18847	279866	39
1997	10908	284580	21936	228287	37966	17181	17176	294420	71
1998	11401	313807	23090	259910	49702	18038	12769	321044	100
1999	11886	341434	25118	282486	52403	18826	15004	357801	84
2000	11220	363503	25879	308225	54985	17341	12058	371758	70
2001	16121	380946	26403	329801	59251	13881	10861	395010	104
2002	16380	410299	31598	356203	61932	15087	7411	411626	848
2003	25785	434523	31304	379269	70824	15685	8265	421443	264
2004	31013	468849	24758	420583	84418	15475	8033	417588	382
2005	37920	520798	19559	474621	103928	19492	7126	397592	714
2006	45810	541729	22515	501697	115422	5510	12007	373862	684
2007	48372	557512	25735	515494	127129	5943	10340	361921	716
2008	57076	557655	32537	507098	135240	6454	11566	349300	859
2009	60092	554905	41866	492259	137290	8883	11897	339836	935
2010	66903	547288	44478	473216	135706	14442	15152	334362	728
2011	67219	526007	47371	457944	129478	10256	10436	327704	652
2012	68664	529246	45833	454590	135089	16677	12146	321020	522
2013	74758	530205	50028	451275	139843	17257	11645	321294	680
2014	72395	519936	50983	441274	141332	13371	14308	309085	797
2015	75113	506055	44483	436574	139054	14514	10484	300407	706

18-6 主要年份研究生数
Number of Postgraduates in Main Years

单位: 人 (person)

年份 Year	招生数 Entrants	在校学生数 Total Enrollment	攻读博士学位 Working for Doctor's Degree	攻读硕士学位 Working for Master's Degree	毕业生数 Graduates	攻读博士学位 Working for Doctor's Degree	攻读硕士学位 Working for Master's Degree
1978	16	16		16			
1980	15	66		66			
1985	120	179		174	21		21
1990	73	256	3	253	112		112
1995	180	509	14	295	91		91
2000	544	1196	48	1148	235	5	230
2001	827	1749	80	1669	277	8	269
2002	1104	2495	112	2383	355	11	344
2003	1664	3629	186	3443	521	18	503
2004	2336	5120	283	4837	832	30	802
2005	2902	6938	415	6523	1066	35	1031
2006	3147	8421	489	7932	1628	90	1538
2007	3491	9623	549	9074	2244	110	2134
2008	3523	10317	595	9722	2786	132	2654
2009	4189	11635	653	10982	3021	121	2900
2010	4595	12675	713	11962	3360	158	3202
2011	4972	14099	840	13259	3421	133	3288
2012	5701	15456	844	14612	4073	159	3914
2013	6222	16867	1129	15738	4775	172	4603
2014	6097	17246	952	16294	4901	140	4761
2015	6481	18031	1050	16981	5453	150	5303

18-7 高等学校基本情况
Basic Statistics on Institutions of Higher Education

单位: 人 (2015 年) (person)

项目	Item	学校数(所) Schools (unit)	毕业生数 Graduates	招生数 Entrants	在校学生数 Total Enrollment	教职工数 Staff and Teachers	#专任教师 Full-time Teachers
普通高等学校	**Regular Institutions of Higher Education**	**39**	**69660**	**90214**	**304682**	**28893**	**19374**
本科院校	Universities with Full Undergraduate Courses	13	31080	40878	161878	18385	11848
专科院校	Universities with Specialized Courses	26	38580	49336	142804	10508	7526
高职学校	Colleges with Specialized Courses	22	27709	38296	105697	8989	6523
按类型分	**By Status**						
综合大学	Multiversity	8	15794	21794	76283	8530	5667
理工院校	Science Engineering	13	20785	29807	83454	6576	4697
农业院校	Agriculture	4	11792	12886	48351	3914	2623
医药院校	Medicine	4	4529	5047	20493	2276	1424
师范院校	Normal Institutions	5	11039	13539	48915	4726	3108
财经学院	Economics and Finance	1	3420	4190	16856	1608	1056
政法院校	Politics & Law	2	1442	1761	5991	692	438
体育院校	Sport	1	54	155	418	142	94
艺术院校	Art	1	805	1035	3921	429	267

注：在分类院校中含 5 所独立学院。
Note: Five independently established colleges are included in the number of classification of colleges and universities.

18-8 中等职业学校基本情况
Basic Statistics on Specialized Secondary Schools

单位：人 (2015 年) (person)

项 目	Item	毕业生数 Graduates	招生数 Entrants	在校学生数 Student Enrollment	专业课教师 Teachers of Various Subjects
总 计	**Total**	**65161**	**89493**	**221705**	**5398**
农林牧渔类	Agriculture,Foresty,Husbandry and Fishing	11503	10930	22389	617
资源环境类	Resource and Environment	899	339	1157	41
能源与新能源类	Energy and New Energy	1192	1212	3110	115
土木水利类	Civil and Hydraulic Engineering	5419	4405	14604	173
加工制造类	Processing and Manufacturing	5431	7301	17376	543
石油化工类	Petroleum and Chemical	1866	1016	3879	95
轻纺食品类	Textile and Food	2255	4193	11671	226
交通运输类	Transportation and Communication	6115	10351	27150	275
信息技术类	Information Technologies	3276	6992	14053	434
医药卫生类	Medcine and Health	8799	9211	28663	260
休闲保健类	Recreation and Health Care	641	1582	3577	149
财经商贸类	Economics and Finance	3097	5364	10422	303
旅游服务类	Trades and Tourism	2845	6930	15019	265
文化艺术类	Culture Arts and Physical Education	3697	8615	22385	501
体育与健身类	Sports and Fitness	807	1338	2958	213
教育类	Teacher Training	6017	8157	18736	760
司法服务类	Justice and Services	685	802	2385	88
公共管理与服务类	Scoial and Public Affairs	186	168	358	50
其 他	Others	431	587	1813	290

18-9 普通中学和其他学校基本情况
Basic Statistics on Regular Secondary Schools and Other Schools

单位：人 (2015 年) (person)

项 目	Item	学校数(所) Schools (unit)	毕业生数 Graduates	招生数 Enrollment	在校学生数 Total Enrollment	教职工数 Staff and Teachers	#专任教师 Full-time Teachers
普通中学	Regular Secondary Schools	1426	436574	486933	1405335	139064	124626
高 中	Senior Secondary Schools	357	139054	187672	497935	43564	38877
初 中	Junior Secondary Schools	1069	297520	299261	907400	95500	85749
职业高中	Vocational Secondary Schools	62	14514	21016	56339	3112	2453
技工学校	Technical Shools	108	10484	29366	68537	10530	7772
小 学	Primary Schools	3501	300407	397691	2048874	159024	144767
特殊教育学校	Special Schools	28	706	1368	6459	926	790

18-10 各类成人教育情况
Basic Statistics on Adult Education by Type

单位：人 (2015 年) (person)

项目	Item	学校数(所) Schools (unit)	毕业生数 Graduates	在校学生数 Total Enrollment	教职工数 Staff and Teachers	#专任教师 Full-time Teachers
成人高等教育	Institutions of Higher Education for Adults	7	30476	81565	4455	2830
职工高等学校	Istitutions of Higher Education for Employees	1	168	206	105	74
教育学院	Pedagogical Colleges	4	687	1308	867	679
广播电视大学	Radio and TV Universities	2	1450	3932	3483	2077
普通高校成人班	Regular Higher Education Institutions for Adults		28171	76119		
成人中等教育	Secondary Education for Adults	18	6164	13453	932	675
成人中学	Secondary Schools for Adults	10	28555	23777	14	11
成人技术培训学校	Technical adult college	1897	1093488	1220482	1886	1337
成人初等学校	Primary Schools for Adults	848	17866	28634	1028	455
#扫盲班	Literacy Courses		15146	24596	889	404

18-11 主要年份教育发展水平
Development Level of Education in Main Years

年份 Year	各类学校在校生占全区人口比重(%) Students as Percentage of Total Population (%)	平均每万人口中(人) Number of Students per 10 000 Population (person)			大中小学生各占普通学校学生总数的比重(%) Students of Different Level as Percentage of Total Students(%)		
		大学生 University and College Students	中学生 Secondary School students	小学生 Primary School Students	大学生 University and College Students	中学生 Secondary School Students	小学生 Primary School Students
1978	23.34	8.30	654.00	1645.38	0.36	28.02	70.50
1980	23.04	11.15	641.47	1601.82	0.48	27.80	69.52
1985	22.39	19.47	701.88	1444.60	0.87	31.35	64.52
1990	18.99	20.45	564.44	1208.01	1.08	29.72	63.94
1995	19.61	26.84	453.23	1330.61	1.38	23.00	70.60
2000	22.84	41.05	638.26	1395.72	1.82	27.93	61.09
2001	20.98	58.53	654.84	1298.22	2.79	31.21	61.87
2002	23.14	70.04	702.72	1238.61	3.21	31.87	56.18
2003	22.53	76.33	749.00	1183.62	3.39	33.25	52.54
2004	21.91	83.09	773.23	1129.89	4.18	38.92	56.90
2005	21.96	90.44	766.67	1066.40	4.70	39.86	55.44
2006	21.78	97.20	767.07	1023.40	5.10	40.64	54.26
2007	21.21	103.20	729.77	982.65	5.69	40.19	54.12
2008	20.68	108.44	696.24	911.60	6.20	39.81	54.00
2009	20.57	111.94	669.33	914.42	6.60	39.47	53.93
2010	20.62	115.13	652.09	887.34	6.96	39.41	53.63
2011	20.65	117.14	638.06	869.04	7.21	39.28	53.51
2012	20.48	120.35	619.80	851.34	7.56	38.94	53.49
2013	20.41	122.96	603.28	836.64	7.87	38.60	53.53
2014	20.60	126.35	597.98	845.32	8.05	38.10	53.85
2015	20.85	129.12	595.55	868.27	8.11	37.38	54.51

18-12 主要年份各级学校教师负担学生数
Student-teacher Ratio by Level of School in Main Years

单位：人 (person)

年 份 Year	高等学校 University and College		普通中学 Secondary Schools		小 学 Primary Schools	
	教师数 Number of Teachers	平均每个教师负担学生数 Student-Teacher Ratio	教师数 Number of Teachers	平均每个教师负担学生数 Student-Teacher Ratio	教师数 Number of Teachers	平均每个教师负担学生数 Student-Teacher Ratio
1978	2458	4.16	41661	19.36	82616	24.56
1980	3149	4.54	45232	18.20	89027	23.09
1985	5473	4.84	60942	15.68	98294	20.00
1990	7002	4.47	65814	13.12	95060	19.54
1995	7687	5.78	62934	11.91	106001	20.77
2000	7924	9.34	75895	14.92	131259	18.87
2005	12733	14.82	101701	15.16	134768	15.91
2006	13783	15.07	106975	14.70	134718	15.57
2007	15096	14.33	108232	14.13	133626	15.41
2008	15755	14.66	108729	13.64	132797	15.15
2009	16234	14.88	110842	13.04	134263	14.70
2010	16506	15.22	113990	12.48	133963	14.45
2011	17256	14.99	116501	12.10	135182	14.20
2012	17570	15.29	118299	11.70	136130	13.96
2013	18327	15.19	121129	11.28	140561	13.48
2014	19081	15.22	124848	11.01	145067	13.39
2015	19374	15.73	124626	11.28	144767	14.15

18-13 主要年份各级学校女学生和女教师数
Number of Female Students and Teachers by Level of School in Main Years

单位：人 (person)

项 目	Item	2000	2010	2014	2015
女学生	**Number of Female Students**	**1889552**	**1911185**	**1908792**	**1986789**
高等学校	Institutions of Higher Education	38419	136071	157462	166177
中等专业学校	Specialized Secondary Schools	49892	82554	75543	71551
普通中学	Regular Secondary Schools	568060	718438	696469	713270
职业高中	Vocational Secondary Schools	23670	26234	21184	23114
技工学校	Technical Shools	8740	13228	19413	20561
小 学	Primary Schools	1200513	932296	936317	989456
特殊教育学校	Special Schools for the Blind, Mute and Deaf	258	2364	2404	2660
女学生占学生总数的比重(%)	**Percentage of Female Students to Total Students (%)**	**48.9**	**49.3**	**49.2**	**49.8**
女教师	**Number of Female Teachers**	**134563**	**178259**	**202355**	**205449**
高等学校	Institutions of Higher Education	3192	8362	10130	11876
中等专业学校	Specialized Secondary Schools	3408	3421	3865	3890
普通中学	Regular Secondary Schools	40030	67901	77921	78498
职业高中	Vocational Secondary Schools	1601	1458	1264	1351
技工学校	Technical Schools	1264	3937	4417	4663
小 学	Primary Schools	84944	92917	104235	104569
特殊教育学校	Special Schools for the Blind, Mute and Deaf	124	263	523	602
女教师占教师总数的比重(%)	**Percentage of Female Teachers to Total Teachers (%)**	**58.9**	**63.1**	**66.1**	**65.9**

18-14 主要年份初中毕业生和小学生升学率及小学学龄儿童入学率
Promotion Rate of Graduates of Junior Secondary Schools and Primary Schools and Enrollment Rate of School-age Children in Main Years

单位：人、% (person,%)

年份 Year	初中毕业生升普通高中情况 Student of Graduates of Junior Secondary Schools Entering Senior Secondary Schools			小学毕业生升初中情况 Student of Graduates of Primary Schools Entering Junior Secondary Schools			小学学龄儿童入学情况 Student of School-Age Children Enrolled		
	初中毕业生数 Graduates of Junior Secondary Schools	高中招生数 Students Entering Senior Secondary Schools	升学率 Promotion Rate from Junior Secondary Schools to Senior Secondary Schools	小学毕业生数 Graduates of Primary Schools	初中招生数 Students Entering Junior Secondary Schools	升学率 Promotion Rate from Junior Secondary Schools to Senior Secondary Schools	学龄儿童数 School-Age Children	已入学学龄儿童数 School-Age Children Enrolled in Schools	入学率 Enrollment Rate
1978	141572	68261	48.22	788359	255687	88.67	1541148	1480400	96.00
1980	186012	73989	39.76	292515	236432	80.83	1637610	1548653	94.57
1985	199206	93692	47.03	289045	247431	85.60	1645055	1569328	95.40
1990	216173	84567	39.12	259301	213074	82.17	1502163	1465325	97.50
1995	171167	58203	34.00	271227	228115	84.10	2036541	1976120	97.03
2000	253240	76744	30.30	371758	342046	92.01	2313890	2245190	97.03
2005	370693	145044	39.13	397592	394878	99.33	2007742	1981569	98.70
2006	386275	142853	36.98	373862	379572	101.53	1957604	1941068	99.15
2007	388365	146449	37.71	361921	363631	100.47	1930074	1916265	99.28
2008	371858	147914	39.78	349300	349665	100.10	1865105	1856800	99.55
2009	354969	148869	41.94	339836	340969	100.33	1839775	1829016	99.41
2010	337510	153238	45.40	334362	336118	100.53	1801872	1797853	99.78
2011	328466	156497	47.64	327704	325953	99.47	1785583	1780729	99.73
2012	319501	155276	48.60	321020	314398	97.94	1767028	1763249	99.79
2013	311432	163582	52.53	321294	313593	97.60	1756979	1753563	99.81
2014	299942	173862	57.97	309085	305686	98.90	1799746	1796299	99.81
2015	297520	187672	63.08	300407	299261	99.62	1907150	1904282	99.85

18-15 主要年份各级各类学校少数民族在校学生数

Number of Students Enrollment of Minority Nationalities by Level and Type of School in Main Years

单位：人 (person)

年 份 Year	高等学校 Institutions of Higher Education	中等学校 Secondary Schools	中等专业学校 Specialized Secondary Schools	职业高中 Vocational Secondary Schools	技工学校 Technical Schools	普通中学 Regular Secondary Schools	#高 中 Senior Secondary Schools	#初 中 Junior Secondary Schools	小 学 (万人) Primary Schools (10 000 persons)
1978	7890	310987	10807			300180	38837	261343	106.58
1980	6455	311213	22263	592	4514	283844	50340	233504	101.73
1985	13996	346833	17888	4915	7649	316381	71199	245182	116.43
1990	17542	439140	23897	13577	13685	387981	94579	293402	126.78
1995	24125	477379	33264	20013	16040	408012	52570	355492	157.84
2000	31989	834390	62572	34992	12260	724566	91843	632723	171.44
2005	75744	993338	32698	54773	13371	892501	152244	740257	136.94
2006	77627	975346	36393	13216	18002	907735	149963	757772	132.94
2007	81978	958643	55224	19181	20476	863762	156478	707284	131.32
2008	85942	935350	62337	28387	23396	821230	160238	660992	130.44
2009	91243	927939	66502	41666	24466	795305	160720	634585	130.31
2010	94708	933338	75924	49388	24894	783132	162687	620445	129.37
2011	102358	940729	82524	54357	21743	782105	173913	608192	129.25
2012	106893	939713	85099	50841	25697	778076	185331	592745	130.10
2013	116256	956057	86810	53971	26261	789015	198588	590427	132.21
2014	129697	980149	88603	46587	29119	815840	218218	597622	138.15
2015	139443	1050936	94580	51369	34269	870718	257873	612845	149.45

18-16 各地、州、市各级各类学校数

Number of Schools by Level, Type and by Prefecture, Autonomous Prefecture and City

单位：所 (2015 年) (unit)

地　区	Region	普通高等学校 Regular Institutions of Higher Education	中等职业学校 Specialized Secondary Schools	#中等师范学校 Teacher Training Secondary Schools
总　计	**Total**	**39**	**172**	**11**
乌鲁木齐市	Urumqi City	21	30	
克拉玛依市	Karamay City	1	3	1
吐鲁番市	Turpan City		3	
哈密地区	Hami [Kumul] Administrative Offices	1	4	1
昌吉回族自治州	Changji Hui Autonomous Prefecture	3	6	
伊犁哈萨克自治州	Ili Kazak Autonomous Prefecture	3	39	3
伊犁州直属县(市)	Counties (Cities) Direct Under Ili Prefecture	3	20	1
塔城地区	Tacheng [Tarbagatai] Administrative Offices		11	1
阿勒泰地区	Altay Administrative Offices		8	1
博尔塔拉蒙古自治州	Bortala Mongol Autonomous Prefecture		1	
巴音郭楞蒙古自治州	Bayangol Mongol Autonomous Prefecture	1	7	1
阿克苏地区	Aksu Administrative Offices	1	8	
克孜勒苏柯尔克孜自治州	Kizilsu Kirgiz Autonomous Prefecture		9	1
喀什地区	Kashgar [Kaxgar] Administrative Offices	1	27	1
和田地区	Hotan Administrative Offices	2	12	1
生产建设兵团	Production and Construction Group	4	21	1
自治区直辖县级市	County level City directly under the Autonomous Region	1	2	1
石河子市	Shihezi City	1	2	1
阿拉尔市	Aral City			

地　区	Region	普通中学 Regular Secondary Schools	#高　中 Senior Secondary Schools	小　学 Primary Schools	特殊教育学校 Special Schools
总　计	**Total**	**1426**	**357**	**3501**	**28**
乌鲁木齐市	Urumqi City	136	53	129	4
克拉玛依市	Karamay City	19	13	29	1
吐鲁番市	Turpan City	55	13	87	1
哈密地区	Hami [Kumul] Administrative Offices	37	12	49	1
昌吉回族自治州	Changji Hui Autonomous Prefecture	45	17	102	1
伊犁哈萨克自治州	Ili Kazak Autonomous Prefecture	275	66	577	7
伊犁州直属县(市)	Counties (Cities) Direct Under Ili Prefecture	170	35	391	5
塔城地区	Tacheng [Tarbagatai] Administrative Offices	78	21	101	1
阿勒泰地区	Altay Administrative Offices	27	10	85	1
博尔塔拉蒙古自治州	Bortala Mongol Autonomous Prefecture	29	8	30	1
巴音郭楞蒙古自治州	Bayangol Mongol Autonomous Prefecture	58	20	98	1
阿克苏地区	Aksu Administrative Offices	139	38	595	2
克孜勒苏柯尔克孜自治州	Kizilsu Kirgiz Autonomous Prefecture	36	10	151	1
喀什地区	Kashgar [Kaxgar] Administrative Offices	180	37	929	5
和田地区	Hotan Administrative Offices	157	20	669	2
生产建设兵团	Production and Construction Group	247	47	50	
自治区直辖县级市	County level City directly under the Autonomous Region	13	3	6	1
石河子市	Shihezi City	13	3	6	1
阿拉尔市	Aral City				

18-17 各地、州、市各级各类学校教职工数

Number of Teachers and Staff by Level and Type of School and by Prefecture, Autonomous Prefecture and City

单位：人 (2015 年) (person)

地 区	Region	普通高等学校 Regular Institutions of Higher Education	中等职业学校 Specialized Secondary Schools
总 计	**Total**	**28893**	**13189**
乌鲁木齐市	Urumqi City	17256	3474
克拉玛依市	Karamay City	506	527
吐鲁番市	Turpan City		351
哈密地区	Hami [Kumul] Administrative Offices	320	272
昌吉回族自治州	Changji Hui Autonomous Prefecture	1782	450
伊犁哈萨克自治州	Ili Kazak Autonomous Prefecture	1671	2015
伊犁州直属县(市)	Counties (Cities) Direct Under Ili Prefecture	1671	992
塔城地区	Tacheng [Tarbagatai] Administrative Offices		537
阿勒泰地区	Altay Administrative Offices		486
博尔塔拉蒙古自治州	Bortala Mongol Autonomous Prefecture		203
巴音郭楞蒙古自治州	Bayangol Mongol Autonomous Prefecture	631	480
阿克苏地区	Aksu Administrative Offices	570	517
克孜勒苏柯尔克孜自治州	Kizilsu Kirgiz Autonomous Prefecture		366
喀什地区	Kashgar [Kaxgar] Administrative Offices	977	2130
和田地区	Hotan Administrative Offices	575	662
生产建设兵团	Production and Construction Group	4204	1638
自治区直辖县级市	County level City directly under the Autonomous Region	401	104
石河子市	Shihezi City	401	104
阿拉尔市	Aral City		

地 区	Region	普通中学 Regular Secondary Schools	小 学 Primary Schools	特殊教育学 校 Special Schools
总 计	**Total**	**139064**	**159024**	**926**
乌鲁木齐市	Urumqi City	12949	11437	183
克拉玛依市	Karamay City	2869	2072	12
吐鲁番市	Turpan City	3868	4849	17
哈密地区	Hami [Kumul] Administrative Offices	3150	3815	40
昌吉回族自治州	Changji Hui Autonomous Prefecture	7361	7291	51
伊犁哈萨克自治州	Ili Kazak Autonomous Prefecture	25449	34834	163
伊犁州直属县(市)	Counties (Cities) Direct Under Ili Prefecture	15304	21133	94
塔城地区	Tacheng [Tarbagatai] Administrative Offices	6230	7938	41
阿勒泰地区	Altay Administrative Offices	3915	5763	28
博尔塔拉蒙古自治州	Bortala Mongol Autonomous Prefecture	2666	3542	21
巴音郭楞蒙古自治州	Bayangol Mongol Autonomous Prefecture	7532	9752	72
阿克苏地区	Aksu Administrative Offices	13113	15698	63
克孜勒苏柯尔克孜自治州	Kizilsu Kirgiz Autonomous Prefecture	4856	7452	19
喀什地区	Kashgar [Kaxgar] Administrative Offices	25611	30996	175
和田地区	Hotan Administrative Offices	12056	13377	84
生产建设兵团	Production and Construction Group	16267	13187	
自治区直辖县级市	County level City directly under the Autonomous Region	1317	722	26
石河子市	Shihezi City	1317	722	26
阿拉尔市	Aral City			

18-18 各地、州、市各级各类学校教师数

Number of Teachers by Level and Type of School and by Prefecture, Autonomous Prefecture and City

单位：人 (2015 年) (person)

地 区	Region	普通高等学校 Regular Institutions of Higher Education	中等职业学校 Specialized Secondary Schools
总 计	**Total**	**19374**	**9904**
乌鲁木齐市	Urumqi City	11219	2302
克拉玛依市	Karamay City	284	283
吐鲁番市	Turpan City		274
哈密地区	Hami [Kumul] Administrative Offices	229	212
昌吉回族自治州	Changji Hui Autonomous Prefecture	1231	389
伊犁哈萨克自治州	Ili Kazak Autonomous Prefecture	1103	1540
伊犁州直属县(市)	Counties (Cities) Direct Under Ili Prefecture	1103	785
塔城地区	Tacheng [Tarbagatai] Administrative Offices		379
阿勒泰地区	Altay Administrative Offices		376
博尔塔拉蒙古自治州	Bortala Mongol Autonomous Prefecture		145
巴音郭楞蒙古自治州	Bayangol Mongol Autonomous Prefecture	518	396
阿克苏地区	Aksu Administrative Offices	445	451
克孜勒苏柯尔克孜自治州	Kizilsu Kirgiz Autonomous Prefecture		321
喀什地区	Kashgar [Kaxgar] Administrative Offices	764	1763
和田地区	Hotan Administrative Offices	376	570
生产建设兵团	Production and Construction Group	2843	1197
自治区直辖县级市	County level City directly under the Autonomous Region	362	61
石河子市	Shihezi City	362	61
阿拉尔市	Aral City		

地 区	Region	普通中学 Regular Secondary Schools	#高 中 Senior Secondary Schools	小 学 Primary Schools	特殊教育学 校 Special Schools
总 计	**Total**	**124626**	**38877**	**144767**	**790**
乌鲁木齐市	Urumqi City	11034	4312	10514	136
克拉玛依市	Karamay City	2454	945	1862	10
吐鲁番市	Turpan City	3548	1133	4634	16
哈密地区	Hami [Kumul] Administrative Offices	2732	1117	3380	29
昌吉回族自治州	Changji Hui Autonomous Prefecture	6452	2335	6804	47
伊犁哈萨克自治州	Ili Kazak Autonomous Prefecture	22546	7725	30695	142
伊犁州直属县(市)	Counties (Cities) Direct Under Ili Prefecture	13791	4528	19260	79
塔城地区	Tacheng [Tarbagatai] Administrative Offices	5374	1930	6699	38
阿勒泰地区	Altay Administrative Offices	3381	1267	4736	25
博尔塔拉蒙古自治州	Bortala Mongol Autonomous Prefecture	2303	745	3015	21
巴音郭楞蒙古自治州	Bayangol Mongol Autonomous Prefecture	6626	2428	8834	59
阿克苏地区	Aksu Administrative Offices	12050	3332	14792	52
克孜勒苏柯尔克孜自治州	Kizilsu Kirgiz Autonomous Prefecture	4618	1588	6835	19
喀什地区	Kashgar [Kaxgar] Administrative Offices	23651	5919	28627	159
和田地区	Hotan Administrative Offices	11572	2476	12522	76
生产建设兵团	Production and Construction Group	13833	4249	11576	
自治区直辖县级市	County level City directly under the Autonomous Region	1207	573	677	24
石河子市	Shihezi City	1207	573	677	24
阿拉尔市	Aral City				

18-19 各地、州、市各级各类学校在校学生数

Number of Students Enrollment by Level and Type of School and by Prefecture, Autonomous Prefecture and City

单位：人　　(2015 年)　　(person)

地　区	Region	普通高等学校 Regular Institutions of Higher Education	中等职业学校 Specialized Secondary Schools
总　计	**Total**	**304682**	**221705**
乌鲁木齐市	Urumqi City	179829	52121
克拉玛依市	Karamay City	5228	829
吐鲁番市	Turpan City		3373
哈密地区	Hami [Kumul] Administrative Offices	555	3001
昌吉回族自治州	Changji Hui Autonomous Prefecture	25318	12242
伊犁哈萨克自治州	Ili Kazak Autonomous Prefecture	17582	20806
伊犁州直属县(市)	Counties (Cities) Direct Under Ili Prefecture	17582	14116
塔城地区	Tacheng [Tarbagatai] Administrative Offices		3620
阿勒泰地区	Altay Administrative Offices		3070
博尔塔拉蒙古自治州	Bortala Mongol Autonomous Prefecture		1559
巴音郭楞蒙古自治州	Bayangol Mongol Autonomous Prefecture	4954	10581
阿克苏地区	Aksu Administrative Offices	4105	16944
克孜勒苏柯尔克孜自治州	Kizilsu Kirgiz Autonomous Prefecture		3173
喀什地区	Kashgar [Kaxgar] Administrative Offices	11527	40570
和田地区	Hotan Administrative Offices	7651	25203
生产建设兵团	Production and Construction Group	40505	29515
自治区直辖县级市	County level City directly under the Autonomous Region	7428	1788
石河子市	Shihezi City	7428	1788
阿拉尔市	Aral City		

地　区	Region	普通中学 Regular Secondary Schools	#高　中 Senior Secondary Schools	小　学 Primary Schools	特殊教育学校 Special Schools
总　计	**Total**	**1405335**	**497935**	**2048874**	**2846**
乌鲁木齐市	Urumqi City	154614	62105	198982	491
克拉玛依市	Karamay City	25546	9757	23773	33
吐鲁番市	Turpan City	34230	11931	56811	52
哈密地区	Hami [Kumul] Administrative Offices	32353	14930	33298	130
昌吉回族自治州	Changji Hui Autonomous Prefecture	73045	29663	80412	120
伊犁哈萨克自治州	Ili Kazak Autonomous Prefecture	238590	90510	351767	594
伊犁州直属县(市)	Counties (Cities) Direct Under Ili Prefecture	150398	54527	232547	453
塔城地区	Tacheng [Tarbagatai] Administrative Offices	55193	23188	69376	91
阿勒泰地区	Altay Administrative Offices	32999	12795	49844	50
博尔塔拉蒙古自治州	Bortala Mongol Autonomous Prefecture	20741	8421	28262	63
巴音郭楞蒙古自治州	Bayangol Mongol Autonomous Prefecture	70785	28532	109628	183
阿克苏地区	Aksu Administrative Offices	150344	50180	243186	202
克孜勒苏柯尔克孜自治州	Kizilsu Kirgiz Autonomous Prefecture	37180	13033	60855	109
喀什地区	Kashgar [Kaxgar] Administrative Offices	282479	83459	462458	560
和田地区	Hotan Administrative Offices	125096	31331	226960	242
生产建设兵团	Production and Construction Group	141730	55166	160032	
自治区直辖县级市	County level City directly under the Autonomous Region	18602	8917	12450	67
石河子市	Shihezi City	18602	8917	12450	67
阿拉尔市	Aral City				

18-20 各地、州、市各级各类学校招生数

Number of Entrants by Level and Type of School and by Prefecture, Autonomous Prefecture and City

单位：人 (2015 年) (person)

地 区	Region	普通高等学校 Regular Institutions of Higher Education	中等职业学校 Specialized Secondary Schools
总 计	**Total**	**90214**	**89493**
乌鲁木齐市	Urumqi City	51960	21281
克拉玛依市	Karamay City	1911	278
吐鲁番市	Turpan City		1393
哈密地区	Hami [Kumul] Administrative Offices	346	824
昌吉回族自治州	Changji Hui Autonomous Prefecture	8406	5160
伊犁哈萨克自治州	Ili Kazak Autonomous Prefecture	5302	8973
伊犁州直属县(市)	Counties (Cities) Direct Under Ili Prefecture	5302	6398
塔城地区	Tacheng [Tarbagatai] Administrative Offices		1475
阿勒泰地区	Altay Administrative Offices		1100
博尔塔拉蒙古自治州	Bortala Mongol Autonomous Prefecture		608
巴音郭楞蒙古自治州	Bayangol Mongol Autonomous Prefecture	1851	4172
阿克苏地区	Aksu Administrative Offices	1426	9079
克孜勒苏柯尔克孜自治州	Kizilsu Kirgiz Autonomous Prefecture		955
喀什地区	Kashgar [Kaxgar] Administrative Offices	2896	15200
和田地区	Hotan Administrative Offices	2589	9573
生产建设兵团	Production and Construction Group	10773	11312
自治区直辖县级市	County level City directly under the Autonomous Region	2754	685
石河子市	Shihezi City	2754	685
阿拉尔市	Aral City		

地 区	Region	普通中学 Regular Secondary Schools	#高 中 Senior Secondary Schools	小 学 Primary Schools	特殊教育学 校 Special Schools
总 计	**Total**	**486933**	**187672**	**397691**	**658**
乌鲁木齐市	Urumqi City	51704	21438	36923	97
克拉玛依市	Karamay City	8372	3216	4047	12
吐鲁番市	Turpan City	11637	4480	11345	16
哈密地区	Hami [Kumul] Administrative Offices	10684	5139	5664	12
昌吉回族自治州	Changji Hui Autonomous Prefecture	24046	10237	13909	21
伊犁哈萨克自治州	IliKazak Autonomous Prefecture	82174	31722	62887	175
伊犁州直属县(市)	Counties (Cities) Direct Under Ili Prefecture	52629	19283	42562	114
塔城地区	Tacheng [Tarbagatai] Administrative Offices	18295	7938	11435	11
阿勒泰地区	Altay Administrative Offices	11250	4501	8890	50
博尔塔拉蒙古自治州	Bortala Mongol Autonomous Prefecture	6865	2819	4914	
巴音郭楞蒙古自治州	Bayangol Mongol Autonomous Prefecture	24766	10514	20061	45
阿克苏地区	Aksu Administrative Offices	53611	20686	45687	73
克孜勒苏柯尔克孜自治州	Kizilsu Kirgiz Autonomous Prefecture	12863	4450	11298	35
喀什地区	Kashgar [Kaxgar] Administrative Offices	102259	36751	99556	86
和田地区	Hotan Administrative Offices	44511	14441	53583	76
生产建设兵团	Production and Construction Group	47296	18843	25647	
自治区直辖县级市	County level City directly under the Autonomous Region	6145	2936	2170	10
石河子市	Shihezi City	6145	2936	2170	10
阿拉尔市	Aral City				

18-21 各地、州、市各级各类学校毕业生数

Number of Graduates by Level and Type of School and by Prefecture, Autonomous Prefecture and City

单位：人 (2015 年) (person)

地区	Region	普通高等学校 Regular Institutions of Higher Education	中等职业学校 Specialized Secondary Schools
总计	**Total**	**69660**	**65161**
乌鲁木齐市	Urumqi City	39633	19132
克拉玛依市	Karamay City	1323	142
吐鲁番市	Turpan City		946
哈密地区	Hami [Kumul] Administrative Offices		1179
昌吉回族自治州	Changji Hui Autonomous Prefecture	6546	4750
伊犁哈萨克自治州	Ili Kazak Autonomous Prefecture	4151	6112
伊犁州直属县(市)	Counties (Cities) Direct Under Ili Prefecture	4151	3474
塔城地区	Tacheng [Tarbagatai] Administrative Offices		1040
阿勒泰地区	Altay Administrative Offices		1598
博尔塔拉蒙古自治州	Bortala Mongol Autonomous Prefecture		193
巴音郭楞蒙古自治州	Bayangol Mongol Autonomous Prefecture	1485	3676
阿克苏地区	Aksu Administrative Offices	917	2386
克孜勒苏柯尔克孜自治州	Kizilsu Kirgiz Autonomous Prefecture		668
喀什地区	Kashgar [Kaxgar] Administrative Offices	2743	6603
和田地区	Hotan Administrative Offices	1603	6971
生产建设兵团	Production and Construction Group	9148	11557
自治区直辖县级市	County level City directly under the Autonomous Region	2111	846
石河子市	Shihezi City	2111	846
阿拉尔市	Aral City		

地区	Region	普通中学 Regular Secondary Schools	#高中 Senior Secondary Schools	小学 Primary Schools	特殊教育学校 Special Schools
总计	**Total**	**436574**	**139054**	**300407**	**267**
乌鲁木齐市	Urumqi City	50432	19502	28387	102
克拉玛依市	Karamay City	8092	3210	3673	15
吐鲁番市	Turpan City	10463	3189	7862	
哈密地区	Hami [Kumul] Administrative Offices	10688	4591	5343	25
昌吉回族自治州	Changji Hui Autonomous Prefecture	25458	9905	12946	20
伊犁哈萨克自治州	Ili Kazak Autonomous Prefecture	77123	28770	52474	39
伊犁州直属县(市)	Counties (Cities) Direct Under Ili Prefecture	47037	16315	34103	25
塔城地区	Tacheng [Tarbagatai] Administrative Offices	19414	7989	11068	14
阿勒泰地区	Altay Administrative Offices	10672	4466	7303	
博尔塔拉蒙古自治州	Bortala Mongol Autonomous Prefecture	6900	2968	4317	
巴音郭楞蒙古自治州	Bayangol Mongol Autonomous Prefecture	22531	8547	14885	39
阿克苏地区	Aksu Administrative Offices	45291	12006	33438	8
克孜勒苏柯尔克孜自治州	Kizilsu Kirgiz Autonomous Prefecture	10443	3774	9270	
喀什地区	Kashgar [Kaxgar] Administrative Offices	77827	16884	67730	14
和田地区	Hotan Administrative Offices	35644	3961	30618	
生产建设兵团	Production and Construction Group	49629	18927	27596	
自治区直辖县级市	County level City directly under the Autonomous Region	6053	2820	1868	5
石河子市	Shihezi City	6053	2820	1868	5
阿拉尔市	Aral City				

18-22　各类学校教育经费情况
Educational Funds in Various Schools

单位：万元　　　　(2015 年)　　　　(10 000 yuan)

指　标	Item	合　计 Total	国家财政性教育经费 Government Appropriation for Education	#预算内教育经费 Budgetary Education Expense	民办学校中举办者投入 Investor Derotion	社会捐资 Donations	事业收入 Income from Under-takings	其　他 Others
总　计	**Total**	**7142500**	**6519221**	**6484239**	**2346**	**25895**	**327445**	**267593**
高等学校	**Institutions of Higher Education**	**897818**	**643273**	**630600**		**17671**	**162002**	**74872**
普通高等学校	Regular Institutions of Higher Education	866491	624410	611737		16871	150925	74285
普通高等本科学校	Universities with Full Undergraduate Course	547391	375628	363144		16675	100328	54761
普通高职高专学校	Regular Institutions of Specialized Course	319100	248783	248593		196	50597	19524
#高等职业学校	Universities With High Vocational Course	270402	207549	207360		66	44468	18319
成人高等学校	Institutions of Higher Education for Adults	31327	18863	18863		800	11077	587
中等职业学校	**Vocational Secondary Schools**	**381060**	**316687**	**312335**		**3394**	**18169**	**42810**
中等专业学校	Specialized Secondary Schools	242676	207630	205799		354	13262	21430
职业高中	Vocational Senior Secondary Schools	83469	71149	68629		3016	1991	7313
#农村	Rural Areas	50319	44454	44439		3008	556	2300
技工学校	Technical Schools	41046	25588	25588		24	2180	13254
成人中等专业学校	Specialized Secondary Schools for Adults	13869	12319	12319			737	813
中　学	**Secondary Schools**	**2337924**	**2234172**	**2228791**	**44**	**2798**	**61178**	**39732**
普通中学	Regular Secondary Schools	2337924	2234172	2228791	44	2798	61178	39732
普通高中	Regular Senior Secondary Schools	748532	679116	678400	25	2493	54774	12124
#农村	Rural Areas	358207	339824	339440		2399	10584	5400
普通初中	Regular Junior Secondary Schools	1589393	1555057	1550391	19	305	6404	27608
#农村	Rural Areas	1053630	1034144	1031878	1	257	362	18866
小　学	**Primary Schools**	**2524276**	**2473373**	**2468172**	**119**	**670**	**4957**	**45156**
#农村	Rural Areas	1894150	1869874	1866208	16	659	1041	22558
特殊教育	**Special Education**	**17529**	**17036**	**16793**		**8**	**137**	**347**
#特殊教育学校	Special Education Schools	17086	16611	16384		8	119	347
幼儿园	**Kindergartens**	**464026**	**378672**	**377470**	**2184**	**493**	**71004**	**11674**
#农村	Rural Areas	298899	274626	273469	407	433	17768	5666
教育行政单位	**Education Administrative Unit**	**190851**	**157624**	**156067**		**690**		**32537**
教育事业单位	**Education Institution**	**189415**	**171856**	**167924**		**169**	**7690**	**9699**
其　他	**Others**	**139600**	**126527**	**126086**			**2307**	**10766**

注：本表按隶属关系填列。 Note: Data in The table according to the membership listed.

18-23 科技活动基本情况
Basic Statistics on Scientific and Technological Activities

指 标	Item	2014	2015
研究与试验发展(R&D)投入情况	**Statistics on R&D Input**		
R&D 人员折合全时当量(人·年)	**Full-time Equivalent of Research and Development Personnel (person·year)**	**15662**	**16949**
#基础研究	Basic Research	2588	3034
应用研究	Applied Research	3888	4586
试验发展	Experimental Development	9184	9328
R&D 经费支出(万元)	**Expenditure on R&D (10000 yuan)**	**491587**	**520010**
#基础研究	Basic Research	33453	35778
应用研究	Applied Research	75308	106857
试验发展	Experimental Development	382826	377374
#日常性支出	Daily Expenditure	431476	425309
资产性支出	Capital Expenditure	60112	94701
#政府资金	Government Funds	122965	138234
企业资金	Self-raised Funds by Enterprises	360673	366498
研究与试验发展经费支出相当于新疆生产总值比例(%)	**Proportion of Expenditure on R&D to GDP of Xinjiang (%)**	**0.53**	**0.56**
科技产出及成果情况	**Statistics on S&T Outputs and Results**		
发表科技论文(篇)	Scientific Papers Issued (pieces)	21228	19197
出版科技著作(种)	Publication on Science and Technology (kind)	363	337
专利申请受理数(件)	Number of Patents Applications Accepted (piece)	3275	3601
#发明专利	Inventions	1277	1490
专利申请授权数(件)	Number of Patents Applications Granted (piece)	436	759
#发明专利	Inventions	183	277

18-24 县级以上政府部门属研究与开发机构及科技信息与文献机构数、人员数
State-owned Research and Development Institutions and Information and Literature Institutions at and above County Level and Persons Engaged

(2015 年)

指 标	Item	合 计 Total	理、工、农、医学领域机构 Field of Natural Sciences Technology Agncalture Medicines	社会、人文科学技术 领 域 Field of Social Sciences and Humanities	科技信息和文献机构 Scientific-technical Information and Document Institutions
机构数(个)	**Institutions (unit)**	**108**	**95**	**6**	**7**
科技活动人员(人)	**Personal Engaged in Scientific and Technological Activities (person)**	**6623**	**6064**	**379**	**180**
#大学本科及以上学历	University Graduate or above	5642	5189	314	139
研究与试验发展全时人员(人·年)	**Full-time Equivalent of Rearch and Development Personnel (person.year)**	**3560**	**3234**	**291**	**35**
科技活动收入(万元)	**Sources of Funds for S&T(10 000 yuan)**	**195012.8**	**180477.1**	**10181.9**	**4353.8**
#政府拨款	Government Funds	172751.2	159110.2	9581.9	4059.1
科技经费内部支出额(万元)	**Internal Expenditures on Scientific and Technological Activities (10 000 yuan)**	**175848.4**	**164323.8**	**7272.7**	**4251.9**
#劳务费	Service Fees	57381.5	51630.5	3704.9	2046.1
固定资产购建费	Purchases or Construction of Fixed Assets	32638.6	32336.7	110.9	191.0
研究与发展经费支出(万元)	**Expenditure on Research and Development(10 000 yuan)**	**86376.7**	**82567.1**	**2933.6**	**876.0**
#基础研究	Basic Research	15132.3	13101.0	2031.3	
应用研究	Applied Research	35216.8	33662.5	897.3	657.0
试验发展	Experimental Development	36027.6	35803.6	5.0	219.0

18-25 重大科学技术研究成果及奖励数

Number of Major Achievements in Scientific and Technological Research and Awarded Prizes

单位：项 (item)

年 份 Year	自治区级重大科技成果 Number of Major Achievements in Science and Technology of Autonomous Region	奖励情况 Awarded Prizes					
		国家级 National	自治区级 Autonomous Regional	一等奖 Frist Class Awards	二等奖 Second Class Awards	三等奖 Third Class Awards	四等奖 Fourth Class Awards
1978 年以前	1551	88	610				
1980-1985	1173	16	356	5	31	102	218
1990	444	3	129		18	56	55
1995	218	3	137	4	26	53	54
2000	250	2	90	5	18	67	
2001	285	6	92	4	23	65	
2002	207	5	99	5	30	64	
2003	232	3	111	8	34	69	
2004	218	4	108	4	33	71	
2005	225	3	101	6	27	68	
2006	212	3	107	8	37	62	
2007	220	8	118	10	42	66	
2008	69	8	108	9	40	59	
2009	166	12					
2010	228	9	130	15	47	68	
2011	205	6	121	14	46	61	
2012	236	6	126	15	45	66	
2013	257	5	150	21	62	67	
2014	246	9	134	17	60	57	
2015	220	6	146	21	48	77	

18-26 专利申请和批准数

Number of Patent Applications Examined and Approved

单位：件 (case)

年 份 Year	申 请 数 Number of Patent Applications Examined				批 准 数 Number of Patent Applications Granted				代理机构（个） Agency (unit)
	合 计 Total	发 明 Inventions	实用新型 Utility Models	外观设计 Designs	合 计 Total	发 明 Inventions	实用新型 Utility Models	外观设计 Designs	
1990	250	38	203	9	139	3	135	1	5
1995	609	92	467	50	312	11	285	16	6
2000	1088	179	699	210	717	66	475	176	7
2001	1088	189	683	216	755	90	522	143	5
2002	1239	216	779	244	627	61	407	159	4
2003	1472	253	940	279	751	75	520	156	5
2004	1492	272	870	350	792	75	530	187	5
2005	1851	320	1117	414	921	88	537	296	5
2006	2256	381	1166	709	1187	107	805	275	5
2007	2270	476	1255	539	1534	90	1035	409	5
2008	2412	482	1408	522	1493	82	1100	311	6
2009	2872	662	1865	345	1867	120	1261	486	6
2010	3560	914	2272	374	2562	189	2012	361	6
2011	4736	1273	2732	731	2642	302	1974	366	6
2012	7044	1679	3375	1990	3440	451	2383	606	6
2013	8224	2081	4620	1523	4998	540	3244	1214	6
2014	10210	2360	4935	2915	5238	605	3850	783	6
2015	12250	3024	6354	2872	8761	950	5049	2762	7

18-27 高等学校科技活动情况
Basic Statistics on Higher Education for Science and Technology Activities

指　标	Item	2014	2015
高等学校研发(R&D)情况	**Statistics on R&D of Higher Education**		
有 R&D 活动的单位数(个)	Number of Institntiens Having R&D Activities(unit)		
#理工农医	Natural Sciences & Technology	30	33
#人文社科	Social Sciences & Humanities	27	29
研究机构(个)	R&D Institutions(unit)	90	94
研究与试验发展(R&D)投入情况	**Statistics on R&D Input**		
R&D 人员折合全时当量(人·年)	Full-time Equivalent of R&D Personnel (man·years)	3503	3784
#基础研究	Basic Research	1892	2077
应用研究	Applied Research	1532	1625
试验发展	Experimental Development	78	82
R&D 经费支出(万元)	Expenditure on R&D(10 000 yuan)	32587	40103
#基础研究	Basic Research	17363	19795
应用研究	Applied Research	14300	19032
试验发展	Experimental Development	924	1277
#日常性支出	Daily Expenditure	29051	35005
资产性支出	Capital Expenditure	3535	5098
#政府资金	Government Funds	29580	34584
企业资金	Self-raised Funds by Enterprises	1605	4057
R&D 项目(课题)情况	**Statistics on R&D Topics**		
R&D 项目(课题)数(项)	R&D Projects (item)	7037	7932
R&D 项目(课题)人员全时当量(人·年)	Participants (person·years)	3499	3780
R&D 项目(课题)经费支出(万元)	Expenditure (10000 yuan)	27599	33744
科技产出及成果情况	**Statistics on S&T Outputs and Results**		
发表科技论文(篇)	Scientific Papers Issued (piece)	13613	14425
出版科技著作(种)	Publication on Science and Technology (kind)	217	251
专利申请受理数(件)	Number of Patents Applications Accepted (piece)	332	731
#发明专利	Inventions	185	415
专利申请授权数(件)	Number of Patents Applications Granted (piece)	191	385
#发明专利	Inventions	70	97

18-28 主要年份企事业单位主要专业技术人员数

Number of Main Scientific and Technical Personnel in Enterprises and Institutions in Main Years

单位：人 (person)

年份 Year	合计 Total	工程技术人员 Engineering Personnel	农业技术人员 Agriculture Personnel	卫生技术人员 Health Care Personnel	科学研究人员 Scientific Research Personnel	教学人员 Teaching Personnel
1978.6月末	85063	22198	13141	31741	3042	14941
1985	158709	51636	20730	57559	3416	25368
1990	241524	92383	25089	71906	4326	47820
2000	368262	58576	27764	62338	2409	217175
2001	385129	59913	30043	65585	2492	227096
2002	387726	58011	31867	65364	2337	230147
2003	385705	57506	30808	65622	2236	229533
2004	398318	55421	32831	68604	2928	238534
2005	402404	51915	32744	67945	2451	247349
2006	412977	52702	34131	68231	2460	255453
2007	411590	50680	33859	69101	2453	255497
2008	414277	49175	31799	71104	2261	259938
2009	411628	47525	30126	72827	2518	258632
2010	407651	47734	28433	77357	2071	252056
2011	421372	47357	27921	80290	6728	259076
2012	454975	47755	30422	85615	2224	288959
2013	446213	47967	30607	83161	2856	281622
2014	467724	50186	29805	90604	2849	294280
2015	478165	48674	28797	92317	2879	305498

注：1.1991 年起专业技术人员包括企事业单位(不含行政机关)人员数,教学人员包括社会和自然科技领域及小学教师人数。
2.1996 年后数据不包括中央单位的专业技术人员数，故人员减少较多。

Note: a) The Specialezed and technical personnel include those who work in enterprises and institutions (excluding administrative organs), teaching Staff, those work in social and nature scientific fields as well as elementary school teachers since 1991.

b) After 1996, the data exclude the figure of professionals with national establishments stationed to Xinjiang and thus the number of staff is reduced a lot.

18-29 主要年份企事业单位主要专业技术人员比重
Proportion of Scientific and Technical Personnel in Enterprises and Institutions in Main Years

单位：%　　(%)

年 份 Year	合 计 Total	工程技术人员 Engineering Personnel	农业技术人员 Agriculture Personnel	卫生技术人员 Health Care Personnel	科学研究人员 Scientific Researcn Personnel	教学人员 Teaching Personnel
1978. 6 月末	100	26.10	15.45	37.31	3.58	17.56
1985	100	32.54	13.06	36.27	2.15	15.98
1990	100	38.25	10.39	29.77	1.79	19.80
2000	100	15.91	7.54	16.93	0.65	58.97
2001	100	15.55	7.80	17.03	0.65	58.97
2002	100	14.96	8.22	16.86	0.60	59.36
2003	100	14.91	7.99	17.01	0.58	59.51
2004	100	13.91	8.24	17.22	0.74	59.89
2005	100	12.90	8.14	16.89	0.61	61.46
2006	100	12.76	8.26	16.52	0.60	61.86
2007	100	12.31	8.22	16.79	0.60	62.08
2008	100	11.87	7.68	17.16	0.55	62.74
2009	100	11.55	7.32	17.69	0.61	62.83
2010	100	11.71	6.97	18.98	0.51	61.83
2011	100	11.24	6.63	19.05	1.60	61.48
2012	100	10.50	6.68	18.82	0.49	63.51
2013	100	10.75	6.86	18.64	0.64	63.11
2014	100	10.73	6.37	19.37	0.61	62.92
2015	100	10.18	6.02	19.31	0.60	63.89

18-30 规模以上工业企业科技活动情况

(2015 年)

项目	Item	企业数(个) Nnmber of Industrial Enterprises (unit)	#有研究与试验发展活动的企业数 Number of Enterprises Having R&D Activities	企业办科技机构(个) R&D Institution
总　计	**Total**	**2707**	**265**	**208**
按企业规模分	**Grouped by Size of Enterprises**			
大型企业	Large Enterprises	88	37	39
中型企业	Medium-sized Enterprises	315	60	66
小型企业	Small Enterprises	1964	165	103
微型企业	Mini Enterprises	340	3	
按登记注册类型分	**Grouped by Ownership**			
内资企业	Domestic-funded Enterprises	2626	257	203
国有企业	State-owned Enterprises	61	6	5
有限责任公司	Limited Liability Corporations	1343	121	73
#国有独资公司	State Sole funded Corporations	138	6	10
其他有限责任公司	Other Limited Liability Corporations	1205	115	63
股份有限责任公司	Share-holding Corporations Ltd	122	36	68
私营企业	Private Enterprises	1069	92	56
私营有限责任公司	Private Limited Liability Corporations	998	79	50
私营股份有限公司	Private Stock Ltd. Co.	52	13	6
其他企业	Other Enterprises	21	2	1
港澳台商投资企业	Enterprises With Funds from Hong Kong, Macao and Taiwan	32	3	
#合资经营企业(港或澳、台资)	Joint-ventures Enterprises	16	1	
港、澳、台商独资经营企业	Enterprises With Sole Funds from Hong Kong, Macao and Taiwan	13	2	
外商投资企业	Foreign Funded Enterprises	49	5	5
外资企业	Enterprises with Sole Funds	29	4	2
外资投资股份有限公司	Share-holding Corporations Ltd	12	1	3
按工业行业大类分	**Grouped by Sector**			
采矿业	Mining and Quarrying	300	20	19
#煤炭开采和洗选业	Mining and Washing of Coal	133	6	4
石油和天然气开采业	Extraction of Petroleum and Natural Gas	7	3	7
黑色金属矿采选业	Mining and Processing of Ferrous Metals Ores	54	2	1
有色金属矿采选业	Mining and Processing of Nonferrous Metals Ores	43	2	
开采辅助活动	Support Activities for Mining	38	7	7
制造业	Manufacturing	2032	235	183
#农副食品加工业	Processing of Food from Agricultural Products	401	35	20
食品制造业	Manufacture of Food	125	20	11
酒、饮料和精制茶制造业	Manufacture of Liguor,Beverages and Refined Tea	74	10	4
纺织业	Manufacture of Textile	91	11	8

Basic Statistics on Science and Technology Activities of Industrial Enterprises above Designated Size

研究与试验发展人员数(人) Number of R&D Personnel (person)	研究人员 Research Personnel	研究与试验发展人员折合全时当量(人·年) Full-time Equivalent of R&D personnel (person·year)	研究人员 Research Personnel	研究与试验发展经费(万元) Expenditure on R&D (10 000 yuan)	其中 Of which 基础研究 Basic Research	应用研究 Applied Research	试验发展 Experimental Development
11075	**3955**	**7188**	**2585**	**366179.8**		**42103.7**	**324076.1**
5442	2178	3712	1451	198779.1		41132.0	157647.1
3126	1051	1949	707	108275.6		191.7	108083.9
2480	721	1519	425	58625.1		780.0	57845.1
27	5	9	2	500.0			500.0
10557	3748	6878	2458	359309.6		42103.7	317205.9
158	70	82	38	2507.9		181.5	2326.4
4398	1441	2579	820	136717.1		330.2	136386.9
689	247	594	202	9946.0			9946.0
3709	1194	1985	618	126771.1		330.2	126440.9
4452	1804	3191	1318	151607.4		40602.1	111005.3
1541	428	1023	280	68450.4		989.9	67460.5
1154	293	692	162	38436.3		989.9	37446.4
387	135	332	118	30014.1			30014.1
8	5	3	2	26.8			26.8
36	16	33	15	1014.4			1014.4
5	1	2		273.7			273.7
31	15	31	15	740.7			740.7
482	191	277	112	5855.8			5855.8
361	176	211	104	959.5			959.5
121	15	66	8	4896.3			4896.3
2847	1263	2137	941	72579.9		40470.6	32109.3
121	37	48	16	1961.4			1961.4
1763	882	1214	607	58385.5		40379.7	18005.8
26	12	19	10	1137.8			1137.8
38	12	11	3	254.5			254.5
899	320	844	305	10840.7		90.9	10749.8
7914	2560	4865	1571	281598.4		1116.3	280482.1
354	91	204	48	6652.2		100.0	6552.2
679	184	354	97	17177.5			17177.5
256	53	153	36	3071.5			3071.5
310	42	158	25	7977.9		100.8	7877.1

18-30 续表 1

项　目	Item	企业数(个) Number of Industrial Enterprises (unit)	#有研究与试验发展活动的企业数 Number of Enterprises Having R & D Activities	科技机构(个) Number of Scientific Technological Agencies (unit)
纺织服装、服饰业	Manufacture of Textile Wearing Apparel and Accessories	18	1	1
木材加工和木、竹、藤、棕、草制品业	Processing of Timber,Manufacture of Wood,Bamboo, Rattan Palm and Straw Products	16	1	
造纸及纸制品业	Manufacture of Paper and Paper Products	30	2	3
石油加工、炼焦及核燃料加工业	Processing of Petroleum,Coking and Processing of Nuclear Fuel	100	10	15
化学原料及化学制品制造业	Manufacture of Raw Chemical Material and Chemical Products	198	45	47
医药制造业	Manufacture of Medicine	31	14	10
化学纤维制造业	Manufacture of chemical Fibres	15	2	
橡胶和塑料制品业	Manufacture of Rubber and Plastic Products	120	17	16
非金属矿物制品业	Manufacture of Nonmetallic Mineral Products	419	20	26
黑色金属冶炼及压延加工业	Smelting and Pressing of Ferrous Metals	86	2	3
有色金属冶炼及压延加工业	Smelting and Pressing of Non-ferrous Metals	54	8	4
金属制品业	Manufacture of Metal Products	87	2	1
通用设备制造业	Manufacture of General Purpose Machinery	26	4	
专用设备制造业	Manufacture of Special Purpose Machinery	27	14	4
汽车制造业	Manufacture of Automobiles	10	4	3
电气机械及器材制造业	Manufacture of Electrical Machinery and Apparatus	57	9	3
计算机、通信和其他电子设备制造业	Manufacture of Computers Communication and other Electronic Equipment	4	1	3
仪器仪表制造业	Manufacture of Measuring Instruments and Machinery	2	2	3
金属制品、机械和设备修理业	Repair Service of Metal Products, Machinery and Equipment	3	1	1
电力、燃气及水的生产和供应业	Production and Suppoly of Electricity,Heot, Gas and Water	375	10	6
#电力、热力的生产和供应业	Production and Supply of Electric Power and Heat Power	312	10	6
按企业所在地区划分	**Grouped by Region**			
乌鲁木齐市	Urumqi City	396	69	70
克拉玛依市	Karamay City	94	16	21
吐鲁番市	Turpan City	118	3	2
哈密地区	Hami [Kumul] Administrative Offices	180	8	11
昌吉回族自治州	Changji Hui Autonomous Prefecture	426	19	22
伊犁州直属县(市)	Counties (Cities) Direct Under Ili Prefecture	247	31	21
塔城地区	Tacheng [Tarbagatai] Administrative Offices	126	8	3
阿勒泰地区	Altay Administrative Offices	93	4	2
博尔塔拉蒙古自治州	Bortala Mongol Autonomous Prefecture	96	6	3
巴音郭楞蒙古自治州	Bayangol Mongol Autonomous Prefecture	203	22	13
阿克苏地区	Aksu Administrative Offices	221	18	2
克孜勒苏柯尔克孜自治州	Kizilsu Kirgiz Autonomous Prefecture	37	3	1
喀什地区	Kashgar [Kaxgar] Administrative Offices	146	2	3
和田地区	Hotan Administrative Offices	29	1	3
自治区直辖县级市	County Level City Directly under the Autonomous Region	295	55	31

Continued

研究与试验发展人员数(人) Number of R&D Personnel (person)	研究人员 Research Personnel	研究与试验发展人员折合全时当量(人·年) Full-time Equivalent of R&D personnel (person·year)	研究人员 Research Personnel	研究与试验发展经费(万元) Expenditure on R&D (10 000 yuan)	其中 Of which		
					基础研究 Basic Research	应用研究 Applied Research	试验发展 Experimental Development
13	7	13	7	39.0			39.0
16	1	10	1	46.0			46.0
16	5	6	2	1124.0			1124.0
316	140	237	112	8670.9		29.9	8641.0
2213	699	1166	370	72215.8		390.6	71825.2
394	172	246	106	5687.3			5687.3
38	7	34	6	681.0			681.0
351	91	243	61	8373.1			8373.1
1089	326	953	282	68682.5			68682.5
353	157	94	41	6796.5			6796.5
419	110	302	76	33261.8		495.0	32766.8
34	10	10	2	1259.5			1259.5
34	13	23	8	356.6			356.6
307	112	155	50	5464.1			5464.1
372	171	225	104	1170.3			1170.3
296	144	231	115	32327.4			32327.4
30	15	28	14	187.2			187.2
13	6	13	6	165.0			165.0
11	4	7	2	211.3			211.3
314	132	187	73	12001.5		516.8	11484.7
314	132	187	73	12001.5		516.8	11484.7
3305	1333	2165	889	121976.4		181.5	121794.9
2141	929	1632	690	25434.5		677.1	24757.4
525	262	488	244	39119.1		37878.3	1240.8
74	26	25	9	1599.6		309.8	1289.8
683	262	201	69	21300.9			21300.9
770	192	381	79	29817.3		54.1	29763.2
109	21	62	9	1977.9			1977.9
53	16	24	8	556.0			556.0
87	17	48	10	82834.5		1037.4	81797.1
1008	367	648	228	1773.3			1773.3
297	86	233	70	24309.0		1965.5	22343.5
67	20	30	2	6551.3			6551.3
20	4	12	3	6392.1			6392.1
25	3	25	3	537.9			537.9
1911	417	1215	273	2000.0			2000.0

18-30 续表 2

项　目	Item	其中 Of which 政府资金 Government Appropriation Funds	企业资金 Self-raised Funds by Enterprises
总　计	**Total**	**11176.5**	**350689.6**
按企业规模分	**Grouped by Size of Enterprises**		
大型企业	Large Enterprises	3211.3	192299.3
中型企业	Medium-sized Enterprises	4482.5	103782.2
小型企业	Small Enterprises	3405.7	54185.1
微型企业	Mini Enterprises	77.0	423.0
按登记注册类型分	**Grouped by Ownership**		
内资企业	Domestic-funded Enterprises	10864.1	344131.8
国有企业	State-owned Enterprises	132.2	2375.7
有限责任公司	Limited Liability Corporations	3931.0	132190.8
#国有独资公司	State Sole funded Corporations	94.3	9851.7
其他有限责任公司	Other Limited Liability Corporations	3836.7	122339.1
股份有限责任公司	Share-holding Corporations Ltd	3958.8	147648.6
私营企业	Private Enterprises	2842.1	61889.9
私营有限责任公司	Private Limited Liability Corporations	1759.9	32958.0
私营股份有限公司	Private Stock Ltd. Co.	1082.2	28931.9
其他企业	Other Enterprises		26.8
港澳台商投资企业	Enterprises With Funds from Hong Kong, Macao and Taiwan	70.0	944.4
#合资经营企业(港或澳、台资)	Joint-ventures Enterprises		273.7
港、澳、台商独资经营企业	Enterprises With Sole Funds from Hong Kong, Macao and Taiwan	70.0	670.7
外商投资企业	Foreign Funded Enterprises	242.4	5613.4
外资企业	Enterprises with Sole Funds	100.0	859.5
外资投资股份有限公司	Share-holding Corporations Ltd	142.4	4753.9
按工业行业大类分	**Grouped by Sector**		
采矿业	Mining and Quarrying	2635.2	69923.7
#煤炭开采和洗选业	Mining and Washing of Coal	85.3	1876.1
石油和天然气开采业	Extraction of Petroleum and Natural Gas	1721.6	56663.9
黑色金属矿采选业	Mining and Processing of Ferrous Metals Ores	366.0	771.8
有色金属矿采选业	Mining and Processing of Nonferrous Metals Ores	43.0	190.5
开采辅助活动	Support Activities for Mining	419.3	10421.4
制造业	Manufacturing	8518.6	268787.1
#农副食品加工业	Processing of Food from Agricultural Products	373.9	6252.1
食品制造业	Manufacture of Food	511.6	16665.9
酒、饮料和精制茶制造业	Manufacture of Liguor,Beverages and Refined Tea	40.5	3031.0
纺织业	Manufacture of Textile	185.2	7792.7

Continued

研究与试验发展项目数(项) R&D Projects (unit)	新产品开发项目数(项) New Projects (unit)	专利申请数(件) Patent Applications (piece)	发明专利(件) Invention Patents (piece)	有效发明专利数(件) Number of Patents In Force (piece)	发表科技论文(篇) Pulish Scientific Papers (article)
972	**924**	**2340**	**788**	**1553**	**2246**
370	268	1521	445	643	1792
288	281	344	139	289	271
310	370	475	204	621	183
4	5				
953	905	2294	769	1522	2239
33	16	106	56	72	107
343	313	1078	267	573	619
61	44	221	75	133	252
282	269	857	192	440	367
359	310	811	307	575	1460
216	264	297	137	302	53
151	175	172	78	226	26
65	89	125	59	76	27
2	2	2	2		
8	10	21	10	26	5
1	1				1
7	9	21	10	26	4
11	9	25	9	5	2
4	2	4	1		2
7	7	21	8	5	
213	99	624	201	265	1153
13	5	26	9	1	26
112	49	310	98	109	880
3	1	6		6	
3	44	5	4		7
82	810	277	90	149	240
722	70	1611	540	1251	997
51	80	52	24	37	13
47	26	70	42	63	42
16	42	14	6	5	13
28	3	52	17	59	16

18-30 续表 3

项　目	Item	其中 Of which 政府资金 Government Appropriation Funds	企业资金 Self-raised Funds by Enterprises
纺织服装、服饰业	Manufacture of Textile Wearing Apparel, and Accessories	20.0	19.0
木材加工和木、竹、藤、棕、草制品业	Processing of Timber,Manufacture of Wood,Bamboo, Rattan.Palm and Straw Products		46.0
造纸及纸制品业	Manufacture of Paper and Paper Products		1124.0
石油加工、炼焦及核燃料加工业	Processing of Petroleum,Coking and Processing of Nuclear Fuel	524.6	8146.3
化学原料及化学制品制造业	Manufacture of Raw Chemical Material and Chemical Products	3004.1	69198.7
医药制造业	Manufacture of Medicine	853.4	4747.0
化学纤维制造业	Manufacture of chemical Fibres		565.5
橡胶和塑料制品业	Manufacture of Rubber and Plastic Products	535.4	7837.7
非金属矿物制品业	Manufacture of Nonmetallic Mineral Products	576.6	67823.0
黑色金属冶炼及压延加工业	Smelting and Pressing of Ferrous Metals		6796.5
有色金属冶炼及压延加工业	Smelting and Pressing of Non-ferrous Metals	384.6	29300.5
金属制品业	Manufacture of Metal Products	40.0	1219.5
通用设备制造业	Manufacture of General Purpose Machinery	48.6	237.0
专用设备制造业	Manufacture of Special Purpose Machinery	613.8	4729.8
汽车制造业	Manufacture of Automobiles		1170.3
电气机械及器材制造业	Manufacture of Electrical Machinery and Apparatus	677.9	31649.5
计算机、通信和其他电子设备制造业	Manufacture of Computers Communication and other Electronic Equipment	100.0	87.2
仪器仪表制造业	Manufacture of Measuring Instruments and Machinery	22.5	142.5
金属制品、机械和设备修理业	Repair Service of Metal Products, Machinery and Equipment	5.9	205.4
电力、燃气及水的生产和供应业	Production and Suppoly of Electricity,Heot, Gas and Water	22.7	11978.8
#电力、热力的生产和供应业	Production and Supply of Electric Power and Heat Power	22.7	11978.8
按企业所在地区划分	**Grouped by Region**		
乌鲁木齐市	Urumqi City	3881.0	117885.6
克拉玛依市	Karamay City	677.1	24507.4
吐鲁番市	Turpan City	361.0	38758.1
哈密地区	Hami [Kumul] Administrative Offices	33.0	1545.6
昌吉回族自治州	Changji Hui Autonomous Prefecture	2246.1	18984.1
伊犁州直属县(市)	Counties (Cities) Direct Under Ili Prefecture	487.4	28906.2
塔城地区	Tacheng [Tarbagatai] Administrative Offices	14.5	1963.4
阿勒泰地区	Altay Administrative Offices	30.0	526.0
博尔塔拉蒙古自治州	Bortala Mongol Autonomous Prefecture	1244.9	78425.7
巴音郭楞蒙古自治州	Bayangol Mongol Autonomous Prefecture	40.0	1733.3
阿克苏地区	Aksu Administrative Offices	2099.3	22094.2
克孜勒苏柯尔克孜自治州	Kizilsu Kirgiz Autonomous Prefecture	53.2	6439.0
喀什地区	Kashgar [Kaxgar] Administrative Offices	9.0	6383.1
和田地区	Hotan Administrative Offices		537.9
自治区直辖县级市	County Level City Directly under the Autonomous Region		2000.0

Continued

研究与试验发展项目数(项) R&D Projects (unit)	新产品开发项目数(项) New Projects (unit)	专利申请数(件) Patent Applications (piece)		有效发明专利数(件) Number of Patents In Force (piece)	发表科技论文(篇) Pulish Scientific Papers (article)
			发明专利(件) Invention Patents (piece)		
1	1	2	2		3
1	1	4		4	
2	3	11	11	1	2
58	68	54	44	186	155
142	127	358	156	395	307
58	62	42	35	75	11
2	1	1	1		
34	40	79	18	68	71
120	82	50	14	65	37
26	20	472	32	46	126
29	24	57	34	21	70
2	3	10	2	12	8
7	9	9	5	28	6
43	53	59	14	66	33
10	10	5		11	
39	76	176	68	81	78
2	2	15	11	16	
3	6	18	4	5	6
1	1	1		7	
37	15	105	47	37	96
37	15	105	47	37	96
347	339	1053	307	511	556
181	149	550	169	410	911
35	1	18	4	24	115
8	13	17	5	6	11
43	97	240	98	89	95
60	46	49	20	161	16
10	13	17	13	37	29
7	14				
156	174	2	2	2	
8	4	152	66	97	323
83	41	8	4	20	4
25	20	8	6	2	
3	1				
5	11				
1	1	226	94	194	186

18-31 各类技术合同签定及执行情况
Statistics on Signing and Implementing Technical Contracts by Type

单位：项、万元 (item,10 000 yuan)

项 目	Item	合同数 Number of Contracts		合同金额 Contract Amount		#技术交易额 Transaction Value in Technical Market	
		2014	2015	2014	2015	2014	2015
总 计	**Total**	**707**	**656**	**31628.31**	**35297.77**	**29834.62**	**34747.55**
技术开发合同	Technology Development	127	153	12137.64	16616.53	10672.38	16066.30
技术转让合同	Technology Transfer	49	34	6471.62	9649.28	6145.10	9649.28
技术咨询合同	Technology Consultation	223	100	6526.58	872.80	6526.58	872.80
技术服务合同	Technology Service	308	369	6492.47	8159.16	6490.57	8159.17

18-32 各级技术计划项目进入技术市场情况
Statistics on Projects for Technical Plan Entering Technical Market by Level

单位：项、万元 (2015 年) (item,10 000 yuan)

项 目	Item	合 计 Total		国家计划 National Plans		部门计划 Department Plans	
		项 数 Number of Items	金 额 Values	项 数 Number of Items	金 额 Values	项 数 Number of Items	金 额 Values
总 计	**Total**	**656**	**35297.77**	**1**	**30**	**4**	**332.30**
事业法人	Institntion Legal Person	311	4979.71	1	30	2	106.35
企业法人	Business Entity	345	30318.06			2	225.95
自然人	Natural Person						

项 目	Item	省、自治区计划 单列市计划 Provinces, Autonomous Plans		地、市、县计划 Perfecture, City and County Plans		计划外 Out of Plan	
		项 数 Number of Items	金 额 Values	项 数 Number of Items	金 额 Values	项 数 Number of Items	金 额 Values
总 计	**Total**	**3**	**890**	**1**	**65**	**647**	**33980.47**
事业法人	Institntion Legal Person	1	50			307	4793.36
企业法人	Business Entity	2	840	1	65	340	29187.11
自然人	Natural Person						

18-33 技术流向地域情况

Statistics on Location of Technical Contract

单位：项、万元 (2015 年) (item, 10 000 yuan)

地区 Region	合同类别合计 Contracts of Classification Total		技术开发 Technology Development		技术转让 Technology Transfer		技术咨询 Technology Consultation		技术服务 Technology Service	
	项数 Number of Items	金额 Values	项数 Number of Items	金额 Values	项数 Number of Items	金额 Values	项数 Number of Items	金额 Values	项数 Number of Items	金额 Values
总计 Total	**656**	**35297.77**	**153**	**16616.53**	**34**	**9649.28**	**100**	**872.80**	**369**	**8159.16**
北京 Beijing	22	1514.20	10	608.20	2	530.00			10	376.00
天津 Tianjing	1	3200.00	1	3200.00						
河北 Hebei	1	19.20							1	19.20
内蒙古 Inner Mongolia	1	1.80	1	1.80						
山西 Shanxi										
辽宁 Liaoning										
吉林 Jilin										
上海 Shanghai	6	221.00	6	221.00						
江苏 Jiangsu	3	39.56	2	39.00					1	0.56
浙江 Zhejiang	1	50.00			1	50.00				
安徽 Aanhui	1	9.60							1	9.60
福建 Fujian	1	18.00	1	18.00						
山东 Shandong	2	98.02	1	97.00					1	1.02
湖南 Hunan										
广东 Guangdong	1	69.36	1	69.36						
四川 Sichuan	2	27.59					1	26.00	1	1.59
云南 Yunnan										
西藏 Xizang	1	26.00	1	26.00						
陕西 Shanxi	1	1600.00			1	1600.00				
甘肃 Gansu										
青海 Qinghai										
新疆 Xinjiang	612	28403.00	129	12336.00	30	7469.00	99	847.00	354	7751.00

18-34 技术经济合同成交情况
Statistics on Transaction in Technical and Economic Contract

单位：项、万元　　(2015 年)　　(item, 10 000 yuan)

卖方类别 Classification of Sellers / 买方类别 Classification of Buyers		合 计 Total		事业法人 Institntion Legal Person		企业法人 Business Entity		自然人 Natural Person	
		项 数 Number of Items	金 额 Values	项 数 Number of Items	金 额 Values	项 数 Number of Items	金 额 Values	项 数 Number of Items	金 额 Values
总　计	**Total**	**656**	**35297.77**	**311**	**4979.71**	**345**	**30318.07**		
机关法人	Government Agency Legal Person	157	9020.68	47	904.32	110	8116.36		
事业法人	Institntion Legal Person	107	3166.69	49	726.09	58	2440.61		
社团法人	Corporation Aggregate	7	94.21			7	94.21		
企业法人	Business Entity	379	22425.89	215	3349.30	164	19076.59		
自然人	Natural Person	2	505.04			2	505.04		
其他组织	Others	4	85.26			4	85.26		

18-35 主要年份文化产业基本情况
Basic Statistics on Culture Institution in Main Years

项　目	Item	2005	2010	2015
文化产业机构数(个)	**Number of Culture Institutions (unit)**	**11777**	**9430**	**5600**
文化部门	Culture Departments	2404	1826	1886
其他部门	Other Departments	9373	7604	3714
文化产业人员数(人)	**Number of Person in Culture (person)**	**34001**	**37711**	**33599**
文化部门	Culture Departments	11515	13310	16321
其他部门	Other Departments	22486	24401	17278
各类文化艺术事业单位数(个)	**Number of Institutions on Various Culture and Art (unit)**			
文化馆	Cultural Centers	110	112	118
公共图书馆	Public Libraries	94	103	107
博物馆	Museums	28	71	86
艺术表演场所	Art Performance Places	47	15	12
艺术表演团体	Art Performance Troupes	89	108	109

18-36 文化艺术、文物事业机构和人员情况
Number of Institutions and Personnel in Culture, Art and Cultural Relics

(2015 年)

项 目	Item	机构数(个) Number of Institutions (unit)	从业人员数(人) Number of Persons Engaged (person)
艺术机构	**Art Institutions**	**171**	**5458**
艺术表演团体	Art Performance Troupes	109	5059
#话剧、儿童剧、滑稽剧团	Drama, Children Plays and Comedy Troupes	7	190
歌舞、音乐类	Song and Dance ,Musical	106	4402
京剧、昆曲类	Peking Opera and Kunqu Opera	2	73
地方戏曲类	Local Opera	4	138
杂技、魔术、马戏类	Acrobatics ,Magic and Circus	3	111
乌兰牧骑	Ulanmuchi	2	54
综合性艺术表演团体	Comprehensive Art Performance	7	367
艺术表演场所	Art Centers	12	231
#剧场、影剧院	Theaters and Music Halls	11	218
综合	Comprehensive	1	13
艺术展览创作机构(含美术馆)	Art Creation Institutions	50	168
图书馆机构	**Libraries**	**107**	**1083**
群众文化机构	**Mass Culture**	**1286**	**4801**
文化馆	Cultural Centers	118	1403
文化站	Cultural Stations	1168	3398
#乡镇文化站	Township Cultural Stations	1021	3084
艺术教育机构业	**Art Education**	**1**	**62**
艺术科研机构	**Art Research Institutions**	**2**	**49**
文化市场经营单位	**Entertainment Operators**	**3705**	**16972**
文化娱乐业	Entertainment Operators	1398	8191
文化市场其他经营单位	Cultural Market Operators	2307	8781
其他文化机构	**Other Cultural Units**	**9**	**123**
文物事业合计	**Cultural Relics**	**189**	**1849**
文物机构	Historical Relics Agency	189	1849
文物保护管理机构	Agency of Historical Relics Preservation	84	308
文物科研机构	Scientific and Research Historical Relics Agency	2	83
其他文物机构	Other Historical Relics Agency	16	334
博物馆	Museums	86	1098
#历史类	History Museum	35	453
文物商店	Cultural Relics Store	1	26

18-37 电影、电视、广播事业基本情况
Basic Statistics on Feature Film, Television and Broadcasting

项目	Item	2014	2015
电影制片厂(个)	**Number of Film Studios (unit)**	**1**	**1**
广播电台(座)	**Number of Broadcasting Stations (unit)**	**6**	**6**
中短波发射台及转播台(座)	Transmission and Relaying Stations of MW&SW (unit)	66	66
中短波广播发射功率(千瓦)	Power of MW & SW Transmitters (kw)	2910	2910
调频发射台及转播台(座)	FM Transmission and Relaying Stations (unit)	699	726
调频发射功率(千瓦)	Power of FM Transmitters (kw)	584.47	596.47
节目(套)	Program (set)	164	172
制作广播节目(小时)	Length of Radio Proqrams Produced (hour)	292469	310239
#新闻资讯类节目	News Programs	60066	67629
专题服务类节目	Feature Programs	90683	98623
综艺类节目	Variety Show	89672	93952
广播剧类节目	Radio Play	9254	8948
广告类节目	Advertisement Programs	24358	24632
其他类节目	Other Programs	18436	16455
广播人口覆盖率((%)	Radio Coverage Rate of the Population (%)	96.48	96.6
电视台(座)	**Number of Television Stations (unit)**	**8**	**8**
广播电视台(座)	**Radio and TV Stations (unit)**	**88**	**90**
#县级广播电视台(座)	Radio and TV Station at County-Level (unit)	80	82
电视发射机功率(千瓦)	Power of TV Transmitters (kw)	963.12	977.92
节目(套)	Program (set)	216	220
制作电视节目(小时)	length of TV Programs Produced (hour)	93188	93441
#新闻资讯类节目	News Programs	36083	38012
专题服务类节目	Feature Programs	22863	24022
综艺类节目	Variety Show	10457	9864
影视剧类节目	Film and TV Play Programs	3140	3644
广告类节目	Advertisement Programs	15919	12741
其他类节目	Other Programs	4726	5158
电视人口覆盖率(%)	TV Coverage Rate of Population (%)	96.94	97.04
有线电视用户(万户)	Numbe of Users of CATV (10 000 households)	219.92	217.73
#数字电视用户	Number of Users Digital TV	210.21	207.95
农村直播卫星用户(万户)	Numbe of Users of Rural Live Statellite(10 000 households)	301.72	325.84

主要统计指标解释

普通高等学校 指通过国家普通高等教育招生考试，招收高中毕业生为主要培养对象，实施高等学历教育的全日制大学、独立设置的学院、独立学院和高等专科学校、高等职业学校及其他机构。

大学、独立设置的学院主要实施本科及本科层次以上的教育。独立学院主要实施本科层次的教育。高等专科学校、高等职业学校实施专科层次的教育。其他机构是指承担国家普通招生计划任务不计校数的机构，包括普通高等学校分校、大专班等。

小学学龄儿童净入学率 指调查范围内已入小学学习的学龄儿童占校内外学龄儿童总数的比重。计算公式为：

小学学龄儿童净入学率=已入学的小学学龄儿童数/校内外小学学龄儿童总数*100%

国家财政性教育经费 包括公共财政预算教育经费，各级政府征收用于教育的税费，企业办学中的企业拨款，校办产业和社会服务收入用于教育的经费，其他属于国家财政性教育经费。

预算内教育经费 指中央、地方各级财政或上级主管部门在本年度内安排，并划拨到各级各类学校、教育行政单位、教育事业单位，列入国家预算支出科目的教育经费。包括教育事业费拨款、科研拨款、基本建设拨款和其他拨款。

研究与试验发展(R&D) 指在科学技术领域，为增加知识总量、以及运用这些知识去创造新的应用进行的系统的创造性的活动，包括基础研究、应用研究、试验发展三类活动。国际上通常采用R&D 活动的规模和强度指标反映一国的科技实力和核心竞争力。

基础研究 指为了获得关于现象和可观察事实的基本原理的新知识(揭示客观事物的本质、运动规律，获得新发现、新学说)而进行的实验性或理论性研究，它不以任何专门或特定的应用或使用为目的。其成果以科学论文和科学著作为主要形式。用来反映知识的原始创新能力。

应用研究 指为获得新知识而进行的创造性研究，主要针对某一特定的目的或目标。应用研究是为了确定基础研究成果可能的用途，或是为达到预定的目标探索应采取的新方法(原理性)或新途径。其成果形式以科学论文、专著、原理性模型或发明专利为主。用来反映对基础研究成果应用途径的探索。

试验发展 指利用从基础研究、应用研究和实际经验所获得的现有知识，为产生新的产品、材料和装置，建立新的工艺、系统和服务，以及对已产生和建立的上述各项作实质性的改进而进行的系统性工作。其成果形式主要是专利、专有技术、具有新产品基本特征的产品原型或具有新装置基本特征的原始样机等。在社会科学领域，试验发展是指把通过基础研究、应用研究获得的知识转变成可以实施的计划(包括为进行检验和评估实施示范项目)的过程。人文科学领域没有对应的试验发展活动。主要反映将科研成果转化为技术和产品的能力，是科技推动经济社会发展的物化成果。

R&D 人员 指参与研究与试验发展项目研究、管理和辅助工作的人员，包括项目(课题)组人员，企业科技行政管理人员和直接为项目(课题)活动提供服务的辅助人员。反映投入从事拥有自主知识产权的研究开发活动的人力规模。

R&D 人员全时当量 指全时人员数加非全时人员按工作量折算为全时人员数的总和。例如：有两个全时人员和三个非全时人员(工作时间分别为 20%、30%和 70%)，则全时当量为 2+0.2+0.3+0.7=3.2 人年。为国际上比较科技人力投入而制定的可比指标。

R&D 经费支出合计 指调查单位用于内部开展 R&D 活动（基础研究、应用研究和试验发展）的实际支出。包括用于 R&D 项目（课题）活动的直接支出，以及间接用于 R&D 活动的管理费、服务费、与 R&D 有关的基本建设支出以及外协加工费等。不包括生产性活动支出、归还贷款支出以及与外单位合作或委托外单位进行 R&D 活动而转拨给对方的经费支出。

R&D 经费支出中政府资金 指 R&D 经费内部支出中来自各级政府部门的各类资金，包括财政科学技术拨款、科学基金、教育等部门事业费以及政府部门预算外资金的实际支出。

R&D 经费支出中企业资金 指 R&D 经费内部支出中来自本企业的自有资金和接受其他企业委托而获得的经费，以及科研院所、高校等事业单位从企业获得的资金的实际支出。

R&D 项目（课题）数 指在当年立项并开展研究工作、以前年份立项仍继续进行研究的研发项目（课题）数，包括当年完成和年内研究工作已告失败的研发项目（课题），但不包括委托外单位进行的研发项目（课题）数。

R&D 项目（课题）人员全时当量 指实际参加研发项目（课题）活动人员折合的全时当量。

R&D 项目（课题）经费支出 指调查单位内部在报告年度进行研发项目（课题）研究和试制等的实际支出。包括劳务费、其他日常支出、固定资产购建费、外协加工费等，不包括委托或与外单位合作进行项目（课题）研究而拨付给对方使用的经费。

新产品销售收入 指报告期企业销售新产品实现的销售收入。新产品是指采用新技术原理、新设计构思研制、生产的全新产品，或在结构、材质、工艺等某一方面比原有产品有明显改进，从而显著提高了产品性能或扩大了使用功能的产品。既包括政府有关部门认定并在有效期内的新产品，也包括企业自行研制开发，未经政府有关部门认定，从投产之日起一年之内的新产品。

专利 是专利权的简称，是对发明人的发明创造经审查合格后，由专利局依据专利法授予发明人和设计人对该项发明创造享有的专有权。包括发明、实用新型和外观设计。反映拥有自主知识产权的科技和设计成果情况。

发明(专利) 指对产品、方法或者其改进所提出的新的技术方案。是国际通行的反映拥有自主知识产权技术的核心指标。

实用新型(专利) 指对产品的形状、构造或者其结合所提出的适于实用的新的技术方案。反映具有一定技术含量的技术成果情况。

外观设计(专利) 指对产品的形状、图案、色彩或者其结合所作出的富有美感并适于工业上应用的新设计。反映拥有自主知识产权的外观设计成果情况。

艺术表演团体 指由文化部门主办或实行行业管理（经文化行政部门审批或已申报登记并领取相关许可证），专门从事表演艺术等活动的各类专业艺术表演团体，含民间职业剧团。不包括群众业余文艺表演团体。

艺术表演场馆 指由文化部门主办或实行行业管理（经文化市场行政部门审批或已申报登记并领取相关许可证），有观众席、舞台、灯光设备，公开售票、专供文艺团体演出的文化活动场所。

文化市场经营机构 经文化市场行政部门审批或已申报登记并领取相关许可证的、从事文化经营和文化服务活动的机构。

广播/电视节目综合人口覆盖率 指根据原国家广电总局制定的《广播电视人口覆盖率统计技术标准和方法》进行统计调查的，在对象区内能接收到由中央、省、地市或县通过无线、有线或卫星等各种技术方式转播的各级广播/电视节目的人口数占全国总人口数的百分比。

Explanatory Notes on Main Statistical Indicators

Regular Institutions of Higher Education refer to educational establishments recruiting graduates from senior secondary schools as the main target through National Matriculation TEST. They include full-time universities, independently established colleges, colleges, and institutions of higher professional education, institutions of higher vocational education and others.

Universities and independently established colleges primarily provide undergraduate and above courses; colleges mainly impart undergraduate courses, institutions of higher professional education and institutions of higher vocational education primarily provide professional trainings; and others refer to educational establishments, which are responsible for enrolling higher education students under the State Plan but not enumerated in the total number of schools, including: branch schools of universities and colleges and junior colleges.

Net Enrolment Ratio of Primary Schools refers to the proportion of school age children enrolled at schools to the total number of school age children both in and outside schools (including retarded children, but excluding blind, deaf and mute children). The formula is:

$$\text{Net Enrolment Ratio of Primary Schools} = \frac{\text{Total Primary School - age Children at Schools}}{\text{Total Primary School - age Children Whether or Not Attending School}} \times 100\ \%$$

Government Appropriation for Education refers to the public budgetary fund for education, taxes and fees collected by governments at all levels that are used for education purpose, enterprise appropriation for enterprise-run schools, income from school-run enterprises and social services that are used for education purpose and other national appropriations for education.

Budget Education Fund refers to education funding from the central and local financial departments and supervision departments that is planned to be allocated to various schools, education administration institutions and education institutions within the reference year, which is within the State budgetary expenditure, including: appropriated funds for education, science and research, capital construction and others.

Research and Development (R&D) refers to systematic and creative activities in the field of science and technology aiming at increasing the knowledge and using the knowledge for new application. R&D includes 3 categories of activities: basic research, applied research and experiments and development. The scale and intensity of R&D are widely used internationally to reflect the strength of S&T and the core competitiveness of a country in the world.

Basic Research refers to empirical or theoretical research aiming at obtaining new knowledge on the fundamental principles regarding phenomena or observable facts to reveal the intrinsic nature and underlying laws and to acquire new discoveries or new theories. Basic research takes no specific or designated application as the aim of the research. Results of basic research are mainly released or disseminated in the form of scientific papers or monographs. This indicator reflects the innovation capacity for original knowledge.

Applied Research refers to creative research aiming at obtaining new knowledge on a specific objective or target. Purpose of the applied research is to identify the possible uses of results from basic research, or to explore new (fundamental) methods or new approaches. Results of applied research are expressed in the form of scientific papers, monographs, fundamental models or invention patents. This indicator reflects the exploration of ways to apply the results of basic research.

Experiments and Development refer to systematic activities aiming at using the knowledge from basic and applied researches or from practical experience to develop new products, materials and equipment, to establish new production process, systems and services, or to make substantial improvement on the existing products, process or services. Results of experiment and development activities are embodied in patents, exclusive technology, and monotype of new products or equipment. In social sciences, experiment and development activities refer to the process of converting the knowledge from basic or applied researches into feasible programmes (including conduct of demonstration projects for assessment and evaluation). There are no experiment and development activities in the science of humanities. This indicator reflects the capability of transferring the results of S&T into technique and products, and measures the realization of S&T in spearheading the economic and social development.

R&D Personnel refer to persons engaged in research, management and supporting activities of R&D, including persons in the project teams, persons engaged in the management of S&T activities of enterprises and supporting staff providing direct service to the research projects. This indicator reflects the size of personnel engaged in R&D activities with independent intellectual property.

Full-time Equivalent of R&D Personnel refers to the

sum of the full-time persons and the full-time equivalent of part-time persons converted by workload. For instance, if there are 2 full-time persons and 3 part-time workers (20%, 30% and 70% of working hours respectively on R&D activities), the full-time equivalent are 2+0.2+0.3+0.7=3.2 person-years. This is an internationally comparable indicator of S&T manpower input.

Total Expenditure of Funds on R&D refers to the real expenditure of surveyed units on their own R&D activities (basic research, applied research,experiments and development) including direct expenditure on R&D activities, indirect expenditure of management and services on R&D activities, expenditure on capital construction and material processing by others. Excluding the expenditure on production activities, return of loan, and fees transferred to cooperated or entrusted agencies on R&D activities.

Expenditure of Government Funds on R&D refers to the expenditure of funds on R&D activities from government agencies at different levels, including appropriate funds on science and technology from financial departments, scientific funds, operating expenses from education departments and the real expenditure of extra budgetary funds from government agencies.

Expenditure of Funds of Enterprises on R&D refers to the expenditure of funds on R&D activities from self-raised funds of enterprises and funds from other enterprises through entrustment, and the expenditure of funds of institutions, such as institution of scientific research and universities, from enterprises.

Number of R&D Projects (subjects) refers to the number of R&D projects (subjects) set up and implemented at the reference year, and the number of R&D projects (subjects) set up in former years and under implementation, including the projects (subjects) finished and failed at the reference year, excluding the projects (subjects) implemented by others through entrustment.

Full-time Equivalent of R&D Personnel refers to the full-time equivalent of persons actually engaged in R&D projects (subjects).

Expenditure of Funds on R&D Projects (subjects) refers to the real expenditure of internal funds of the surveyed units on research and test of R&D projects (subjects) at the reference year, including service fee, other daily expenditure, cost for fixed assets, cost of external process; excluding expenditure of funds transferred to other cooperated or entrusted units of the projects.

Sales Income of New Products refers to the sales income of new products of the enterprises at the reference period. New products refer to products developed and produced with new technologies and designs or improved in structure, material, process or other aspects so that their performance are improved or their functions expanded. New products include those affirmed by government authorities in their validity period and also those developed by enterprises without the affirmation of government authorities within one year after they are put into production.

Patent is an abbreviation for the patent right and refers to the exclusive right of ownership by the inventors or designers for the creation or inventions, given from the patent offices after due process of assessment and approval in accordance with the Patent Law. Patents are granted for inventions, utility models and designs. This indicator reflects the achievements of S&T and design with independent intellectual property.

Patented Inventions refer to new technical proposals to the products or methods or their modifications. This is universal core indicator reflecting the technologies with independent intellectual property.

Patented Utility Models refer to the practical and new technical proposals on the shape and structure of the product or the combination of both. This indicator reflects the condition of technological results with certain technical content.

Designs refer to the aesthetics and industrially applicable new designs for the shape, pattern and colour of the product, or their combinations. This indicator reflects the appearance design achievements with independent intellectual property.

Arts Performance Troupes refer to the various professional performing arts groups, which sponsored by the cultural sectors or guided by the cultural society (approved by the cultural administration authority, or registered and permitted with the relative certificate), including non-governmental troupes. The mass amateur arts performance troupes are not included.

Arts Performance Places refer to the various sites for cultural activities, which sponsored by the cultural sectors or guided by the cultural society (approved by the cultural market administration, or registered and permitted with the relative certificate), with the facility of auditorium, stage, and lighting, and selling tickets in public.

Cultural Market Operating Units refer to the units deal -ing in culture and cultural services, which registered and perm-itted with the relative certificate by cultural market administration.

The Population Coverage Rate of Radio/Television refers to the percentage of the whole country's population who can receive radio/television programmes transmitted by national, provincial, municipal or county stations through wireless, cable or satellite techniques, according to Statistical Standard and Method on Television and Radio Coverage of Population established by the former State Administration of Broadcasting, Film and Television.

卫生及其他

PUBLIC HEALTH AND OTHERS

第十九篇 卫生及其他

本篇主要内容和资料来源

本篇资料主要包括卫生事业、民政事业、公安机关案件受理处治情况、安全生产情况、道路交通事故和火灾事故等内容，除卫生事业外其他部门数据由新疆维吾尔自治区统计局社会科技处与综合处根据有关部门资料整理。

卫生部分资料是由新疆维吾尔自治区卫生和计划生育委员会依据年报资料整理提供。民政部分资料由新疆维吾尔自治区民政厅提供，治安、刑事案件资料由新疆维吾尔自治区公安厅提供，安全生产情况来自新疆维吾尔自治区安全生产监督管理局，道路交通事故和火灾事故分别由新疆维吾尔自治区公安交通管理局和新疆维吾尔自治区消防总队提供。

Public Health and Others

Main Content and Source of Data

Data in this chapter mainly include the development of public health, sports, civil affairs, labor and society protection, offense cases against public order handled by public Security organs, traffic accidents and fires. These statistics are provided by Department of Social Science &Technology in Statistics Bureau of Xinjiang according to the data from the related Department of Statistics Bureau.

Data on public health are from the Bureau of Public Health, these statistics are according to the data of yearly statistics; increased the data of condition of village clinic and basic condition of institution on new cooperative health care of agricultural and pastoral areas; Data on civil affairs and labor protection are provided respectively by the Bureau of Civil Affairs and the Bureau of Labor and Social Security. Data on public security, statistics on procuratorial, legal and judicial affairs are provided by the Bureau of Public Security. Data on production safety are come from Xinjiang Administration of Work Safety. Data on traffic accident and fire are respectively provided by the Xinjiang Traffic Management Bureau and the Xinjiang Fire Department.

19-1 卫生机构、床位、人员数

Number of Health Institutions, Beds and Persons Engaged by Type of Institutons

(2015 年)

项 目	Item	机构数(个) Number of Institutions (unit)	实有床位数(张) Beds (unit)	在岗职工合计(人) Total Number of Medical Personnel (person)	卫生技术人员小计 Medical Technical Personnel	执业(助理)医师 Licensed Assistant Doctor	执业医师 Licensed Doctors	注册护士 Registered Nurses	药剂人员 Pharmacist
总 计	**Total**	**18798**	**150263**	**208536**	**161841**	**57283**	**47226**	**63870**	**7543**
按经济类型分	**Grouped by Economic Type**								
公 立	State	12794	132213	178003	137380	46119	37570	55106	6391
国 有	State-owned	9765	129043	169428	133340	44498	36413	53534	6230
集 体	Collective-owned	3029	3170	8575	4040	1621	1157	1572	161
民 营	Non State	6004	18050	30533	24461	11164	9656	8764	1152
联 营	Joint Ownership	29	52	157	125	55	51	52	6
私 营	Private	5485	16104	26961	22038	10223	8830	7806	1022
其 他	Others	490	1894	3415	2298	886	775	906	124
按设置主办单位分	**Grouped by Sponsors**								
政府办	Run by Government	8498	125840	160595	126880	41580	33775	51081	5897
社会办	Run by Society	4895	7837	20094	12030	5136	4306	4655	588
个人办	Run by Private	5405	16586	27847	22931	10567	9145	8134	1058
按市县分	**Guouped by Ctiy and County**								
市	City	7269	86793	128031	103785	37972	34016	43140	4787
县	County	11529	63470	80505	58056	19311	13210	20730	2756
按城乡分	**Grouped by Rural and Urban**								
城 市	Urban	1797	31915	51991	41167	15337	14735	17737	1862
农 村	Rural	17001	118348	156545	120674	41946	32491	46133	5681
按营利性质分	**Grouped by Properties**								
非营利性	Non-profit	13255	133663	170980	131249	43951	35969	54711	6407
营利性	Profit	4838	16600	26711	22166	10036	8749	7999	1017
其 他	Others	705		10845	8426	3296	2508	1160	119
按机构分	**Grouped By Organizations**								
医 院	Total Number of Hospitals	914	118024	132110	108062	34905	30778	47753	5549
基层医疗卫生机构	Health Care Institution at Grass-root Level	17075	28987	61010	41615	17547	12734	13578	1712
专业公共卫生机构	Specalized Public Hedlth Institutions	802	3041	15234	12092	4799	3686	2515	277
其他卫生机机	Others	7	211	182	72	32	28	24	5

注：1.本表人员合计中包括乡村医生 13114 人和卫生员 1442 人；
2.不含乡镇卫生院在村卫生室工作的执业(助理)医师、注册护士数。

Note: a). Total data in this table included 13114 rural doctors and 1442medical personels.
b). Total data in this table didn't include licensed doctors and registered nurses in township and town health centers.

19-1 续表 1 Continued

项 目	Item	技师(士) Technician (artificer)	检验人员 Laboratory Technicians	其 他 Others	见习医师 Intern Doctor	其他技术人员 Other Technicians	管理人员 Administrative Personnel	工勤人员 Logistics Workers
总 计	**Total**	**9450**	**6456**	**23695**	**5649**	**9577**	**7592**	**14970**
按经济类型分	**Grouped by Economic Type**							
公 立	Public	8205	5688	21559	5187	8488	6216	12607
国 有	State-owned	8033	5565	21045	5040	8337	5984	12284
集 体	Collective-owned	172	123	514	147	151	232	323
民 营	Non-public	1245	768	2136	462	1089	1376	2363
联 营	Joint Ownership	6	4	6	4	6	4	8
私 营	Private	1092	673	1895	402	904	1186	2067
其 他	Others	147	91	235	56	179	186	288
按设置主办单位分	**Grouped by sponsors**							
政府办	Run by Government	7656	5304	20666	5015	8012	5617	11744
社会办	Run by Society	653	448	998	221	592	714	1113
个人办	Run by Private	1141	704	2031	413	973	1261	2113
按市县分	**Guouped by Ctiy and County**							
市	City	5806	4054	12080	3441	6130	5222	10067
县	County	3644	2402	11615	2208	3447	2370	4903
按城乡分	**Grouped by Rural and Urban**							
城 市	Urban	2031	1435	4200	1270	2663	2364	5797
农 村	Rural	7419	5021	19495	4379	6914	5228	9173
按营利性质分	**Grouped by Profit**							
非营利性	Non-profit	7103	4666	19077	5150	7837	5520	11954
营利性	Profit	1134	700	1980	428	947	1249	2213
其 他	Others	1213	1090	2638	71	793	823	803
按机构分	**Grouped By Organizations**							
医 院	Total Number of Hospitals	6304	3983	13551	4254	7127	5521	11400
基层医疗卫生机构	Health Care Institution at Grass-root Level	1603	1148	7175	1271	1463	923	2453
专业公共卫生机构	Specalized Public Hedlth Institutions	1537	1321	2964	123	967	1115	1060
其他卫生机机	Others	6	4	5	1	20	33	57

19-1 续表 2 Continued

项目	Item	机构数(个) Number of Institutions (unit)	实有床位数(张) Beds (unit)	在岗职工合计(人) Total Number of Medical Personnel (person)	卫生技术人员小计 Medical Technical Personnel	执业(助理)医师 Lecensed Assistant Doctor	执业医师 Lecensed Doctors	注册护士 Registered Nurses	药剂人员 Pharmacist
总计	**Total**	**18798**	**150263**	**208536**	**161841**	**57283**	**47226**	**63870**	**7543**
医院	Total Number of Hospitals	914	118024	132110	108062	34905	30778	47753	5549
综合医院	Comprehensive Hospitals	705	89394	107080	88543	28358	25085	39871	3994
中医医院	Hospitals of Traditional Chinese Medicine	57	9248	8304	6795	2451	2319	2726	532
中西医结合医院	TCM and Western Medicine Hospital	5	649	642	496	114	82	203	21
民族医院	Hospitals for Nationalities	46	7887	6583	5414	1809	1274	1707	710
专科医院	Specialist Hospitals	101	10846	9501	6814	2173	2018	3246	292
口腔医院	Nonnasality Hospitals	4	54	309	265	158	152	89	5
眼科医院	Ophthalmology Hospitals	10	250	361	236	79	69	105	14
耳鼻喉科医院	Otolaryngology Hospitals	2	173	250	191	66	59	69	13
肿瘤医院	Tumour Hospitals	1	1665	2243	1725	554	554	862	55
心血管病医院	Cardiovascular Hospitals	1	272	547	348	106	103	185	15
胸科医院	Chest Hospitals	1	527	580	456	134	134	228	19
妇产(科)医院	Hospitals for Gynaecology and Obsterics	20	757	1087	645	216	200	263	32
儿童医院	Children Hospitals	1	30	54	34	11	5	14	4
精神病医院	Mental Hospitals	13	4285	2097	1405	342	307	855	59
传染病医院	Infectous Diseases Hospitals	5	810	591	463	122	106	175	19
皮肤病医院	Skin Disease hospitals	3	124	127	96	28	23	56	6
结核病医院	Tubercuiosis Hospitals	1	474	199	171	75	64	70	6
职业病医院	Occupational Disease Hospitals	1							
骨科医院	Hospital of Orthopedics	4	137	117	94	26	19	29	7
康复医院	Recovery Hospitals	5	149	79	58	33	32	17	3
整形外科医院	Plastic Surgical Holpitals	2	52	63	33	15	12	12	3
美容医院	Hairdressing Hospitals	1	20	18	18	4	4	13	
其他专科医院	Other Specialist Hospitals	26	1067	779	576	204	175	204	32
基层医疗卫生机构	Health Care Institutions at Grass-root Level	17075	28987	61010	41615	17547	12734	13578	1712
社区卫生服务中心(站)	Health Service Center for Community (Stations)	800	3082	8958	7744	3158	2722	2986	486
社区卫生服务中心	Health Service Center for Community	185	2605	5602	4781	1756	1463	1792	345
社区卫生服务站	Health Service Station for Community	615	477	3356	2963	1402	1259	1194	141
卫生院	Public Health Center	927	25551	23466	20431	6401	3169	6126	898
乡镇卫生院	Public Health Center in Township and Towns	927	25551	23466	20431	6401	3169	6126	898
中心卫生院	Public Health Center	139	5724	4400	3859	1229	656	1131	184
乡卫生院	Public Health Center in Rural Area	788	19827	19066	16572	5172	2513	4995	714
村卫生室	Village Clinics	10439		15917	1361	1011	536	350	
门诊部	Outpatients Department	298	353	2371	2006	1011	886	643	87
综合门诊部	Comprehensive Department	225	308	1870	1584	741	664	541	74
中医门诊部	Department of Traditional Chinese Medicine	4	5	19	14	7	7	2	2
中西医结合门诊部	TCM and Western Medicine Department	8	5	21	20	13	11	5	
民族医门诊部	Department for Nationalities	4		42	35	22	13	6	4

19-1 续表 3 Continued

项　目	Item	技师(士) Technician (artificer)	检验人员 Laboratory Technicians	其　他 Others	见习医师 Intern Doctor	其他技术人员 Other Technicians	管理人员 Administrative Personnel	工勤人员 Logistics Workers
总　计	**Total**	**9450**	**6456**	**23695**	**5649**	**9577**	**7592**	**14970**
医　院	Total Number of Hospitals	6304	3983	13551	4254	7127	5521	11400
综合医院	Comprehensive Hospitals	5159	3274	11161	3567	5294	4478	8765
中医医院	Hospitals of Traditional Chinese Medicine	398	253	688	143	595	337	577
中西医结合医院	TCM and Western Medicine Hospital	24	13	134	55	14	48	84
民族医院	Hospitals for Nationalities	290	181	898	306	513	185	471
专科医院	Specialist Hospitals	433	262	670	183	711	473	1503
口腔医院	Nonnasality Hospitals	5	2	8	4	10	12	22
眼科医院	Ophthalmology Hospitals	15	11	23	3	18	27	80
耳鼻喉科医院	Otolaryngology Hospitals	11	6	32	2	11	23	25
肿瘤医院	Tumour Hospitals	80	34	174	44	131	29	358
心血管病医院	Cardiovascular Hospitals	15	11	27	14	48	20	131
胸科医院	Chest Hospitals	40	24	35		87	5	32
妇产(科)医院	Hospitals for Gynaecology and Obsterics	79	53	55	15	28	143	271
儿童医院	Children Hospitals	5	4			4	11	5
精神病医院	Mental Hospitals	66	42	83	46	290	77	325
传染病医院	Infectous Diseases Hospitals	39	18	108	12	28	23	77
皮肤病医院	Skin Disease hospitals	6	4				11	20
结核病医院	Tubercuiosis Hospitals	12	10	8	8	11	8	9
职业病医院	Occupational Disease Hospitals							
骨科医院	Hospital of Orthopedics	4	2	28	28	4	5	14
康复医院	Recovery Hospitals	4	3	1		7	7	7
整形外科医院	Plastic Surgical Holpitals	2	2	1			4	26
美容医院	Hairdressing Hospitals	1	1					
其他专科医院	Other Specialist Hospitals	49	35	87	7	34	68	101
基层医疗卫生机构	Health Care Institutions at Grass-root Level	1603	1148	7175	1271	1463	923	2453
社区卫生服务中心(站)	Health Service Center for Community (Stations)	403	281	711	117	437	360	417
社区卫生服务中心	Health Service Center for Community	327	220	561	86	304	213	304
社区卫生服务站	Health Service Station for Community	76	61	150	31	133	147	113
卫生院	Public Health Center	1026	736	5980	1048	986	515	1534
乡镇卫生院	Public Health Center in Township and Towns	1026	736	5980	1048	986	515	1534
中心卫生院	Public Health Center	232	153	1083	253	155	75	311
乡卫生院	Public Health Center in Rural Area	794	583	4897	795	831	440	1223
村卫生室	Village Clinics							
门诊部	Outpatients Department	117	87	148	32	40	48	277
综合门诊部	Comprehensive Department	105	78	123	26	34	40	212
中医门诊部	Department of Traditional Chinese Medicine			3				5
中西医结合门诊部	TCM and Western Medicine Department	1	1	1	1			1
民族医门诊部	Department for Nationalities	2	1	1			2	5

19-1 续表 4 Continued

项目	Item	机构数(个) Number of Institutions (unit)	实有床位数(张) Beds (unit)	在岗职工合计(人) Total Number of Medical Personnel (person)	卫生技术人员小计 Medical Technical Personnel	执业(助理)医师 Lecensed Assistant Doctor	执业医师 Lecensed Doctors	注册护士 Registered Nurses	药剂人员 Pharmacist
专科门诊部	Specialist Department	57	35	419	353	228	191	89	7
诊所、卫生所、医务室	Clinics, Health Centers,Health Rooms	4611	1	10298	10073	5966	5421	3473	241
诊所	Clinics	3973		8851	8707	5165	4811	3049	207
卫生所、医务室	Health Centers,Health Rooms	630		1437	1356	800	609	415	34
护理站	Nursing Department	8	1	10	10	1	1	9	
专业公共卫生机构	Specialized Public Health Institution	802	3041	15234	12092	4799	3686	2515	277
疾病预防控制中心	Center for Disease Control and Prevetion	223		6206	4966	2557	2010	573	72
自治区属	Autonoumous Run	1		422	291	166	163	4	
区辖市(地区)属	District Municipal Run	23		1294	1072	539	472	90	15
地辖市属	Run by Administer Under the Municipal l	27		1104	879	446	377	76	14
县属	County Run	77		2126	1640	774	536	213	31
其他	Others	95		1260	1084	632	462	190	12
专科疾病防治院(所、站)	Specialized Disease Prevention &Treatment Institution	4	85	93	47	24	15	9	1
专科疾病防治院	Specialized Disease Prevention &Treatment Centers	1	1	21	17	13	9	1	
其他	Others	1	1	21	17	13	9	1	
专科疾病防治所(站、中心)	Specialized Disease Prevention&Treatment Stations	3	84	72	30	11	6	8	1
药物戒毒所(中心)	The Drug Detoxificatio Center	2	84	72	30	11	6	8	1
其他	Others	1							
妇幼保健院(所、站)	Women and Children Care Agencies	92	2906	4226	3546	1449	1135	1305	155
区辖市(地区)属	District Municipal Run	5	492	830	685	199	187	350	27
地辖市属	Run by Administer Under the Municipal	19	755	1376	1180	517	439	442	56
县属	County Run	64	1619	1881	1556	670	456	468	68
其他	Others	4	40	139	125	63	53	45	4
妇幼保健院	Women and Children Care Hospitals	38	1719	2643	2246	883	750	928	106
妇幼保健所	Women and Children Care Center	5		128	107	50	35	31	2
妇幼保健站	Women and Children Care Stations	49	1187	1455	1193	516	350	346	47
急救中心(站)	Urgent Care Center	5	50	126	91	38	34	46	3
采供血机构	Blood Transfusion Services	21		565	406	66	55	142	3
卫生监督所(中心)	Health Inspection Institution (center)	158		1707	1442				
自治区属	Autonoumous Run	1		80	68				
区辖市(地区)属	District Municipal Run	14		276	231				
地辖市属	Run by Administer Under the Municipal	25		412	350				
县属	County Run	68		564	472				
其他	Others	50		375	321				
计划生育技术服务机构	The Family Planning Technical Service Institutions	299		2311	1594	665	437	440	43
其他卫生机构	Others	7	211	182	72	32	28	24	5
疗养院	Sanatoriums	3	211	126	54	24	22	19	4
卫生监督检验(监测、检测)所(站)	Health Inspection Institution (center)	1		4	4	2	2	1	
其他	Others	3		52	14	6	4	4	1

19-1 续表 5 Continued

项 目	Item	技师(士) Technician (artificer)	检验人员 Laboratory Technicians	其 他 Others	见习医师 Intern Doctor	其他技术人员 Other Technicians	管理人员 Administrative Personnel	工勤人员 Logistics Workers
专科门诊部	Specialist Department	9	7	20	5	6	6	54
诊所、卫生所、医务室	Clinics, Health Centers,Health Rooms	57	44	336	74			225
诊所	Clinics	39	28	247	66			144
卫生所、医务室	Health Centers,Health Rooms	18	16	89	8			81
护理站	Nursing Department							
专业公共卫生机构	Specialized Public Health Institution	1537	1321	2964	123	967	1115	1060
疾病预防控制中心	Center for Disease Control and Prevetion	887	801	877	50	324	407	509
自治区属	Autonoumous Run	21	21	100	0	58	14	59
区辖市(地区)属	District Municipal Run	272	262	156	3	47	75	100
地辖市属	Run by Administer Under the Municipal l	191	166	152	1	51	78	96
县属	County Run	314	266	308	12	108	161	217
其他	Others	89	86	161	34	60	79	37
专科疾病防治院(所、站)	Specialized Disease Prevention &Treatment Institution	7	4	6	3	1	44	1
专科疾病防治院	Specialized Disease Prevention &Treatment Centers	2		1		1	2	1
其他	Others	2		1		1	2	1
专科疾病防治所(站、中心)	Specialized Disease Prevention&Treatment Stations	5	4	5	3		42	
药物戒毒所(中心)	The Drug Detoxificatio Center	5	4	5	3		42	
其他	Others							
妇幼保健院(所、站)	Women and Children Care Agencies	314	225	323	49	179	254	247
区辖市(地区)属	District Municipal Run	69	46	40		27	77	41
地辖市属	Run by Administer Under the Municipal	110	72	55	10	62	64	70
县属	County Run	126	98	224	39	83	109	133
其他	Others	9	9	4		7	4	3
妇幼保健院	Women and Children Care Hospitals	201	139	128	10	108	165	124
妇幼保健所	Women and Children Care Center	12	10	12		3	8	10
妇幼保健站	Women and Children Care Stations	101	76	183	39	68	81	113
急救中心(站)	Urgent Care Center	4	2			11	8	16
采供血机构	Blood Transfusion Services	145	143	50	4	58	39	62
卫生监督所(中心)	Health Inspection Institution (center)			1442		5	155	105
自治区属	Autonoumous Run			68			3	9
区辖市(地区)属	District Municipal Run			231			26	19
地辖市属	Run by Administer Under the Municipal			350		2	30	30
县属	County Run			472		3	49	40
其他	Others			321			47	7
计划生育技术服务机构	The Family Planning Technical Service Institutions	180	146	266	17	389	208	120
其他卫生机构	Others	6	4	5	1	20	33	57
疗养院	Sanatoriums	5	4	2	1	3	19	50
卫生监督检验(监测、检测)所(站)	Health Inspection Institution (center)	1						
其他	Others			3		17	14	7

19-2 主要年份卫生机构数(不含村卫生室)

Number of Health Institutions in Main Years(Excluding Village Clinics)

单位：个 (unit)

年份 Year	合计 Total	医院、卫生院 Hospitals And Township Hospitals	#医院 Hospitals	疗养院 Sanitarium	门诊部 Clinics	专科防治所、站 Specialized Prevention & Treatment Centers or Stations	疾病防控中心 Sanitation and Antiepidemic Agencies	妇幼保健所、站 Maternity and Child Care Centers	社区卫生服务中心(站) Health Service Center for Community	卫生监督所(中心) Inspction Instietes of Medical Science	其他卫生机构 Other Institutions	诊所、医务保健室、医务室 Clinics Health Care Room Infirmary
1978	2581	806	204	2	1609	1	104	12			47	
1980	2818	884	270	4	1756	4	102	12			56	
1985	3320	947	389	5	2125	2	139	27			75	
1990	3945	1049	435	6	2536	13	191	59			91	
1995	3932	1292	507	8	2247	16	216	69			84	
2000	7314	1352	522	8	154	16	210	74			96	5404
2005	8087	1516	685	6	224	8	197	88	46	30	113	5859
2010	7650	1712	802	4	259	4	221	90	641	133	31	4555
2011	7587	1742	820	4	247	4	216	90	683	128	30	4443
2012	7820	1759	836	4	278	5	224	91	744	158	32	4525
2013	8096	1784	860	4	278	5	229	92	794	159	124	4627
2014	8285	1807	878	3	291	5	229	92	791	158	330	4579
2015	8359	1841	914	3	298	4	223	92	800	158	329	4611

注：1.2002 年起卫生部新制度规定持有"医疗执业许可证"所有卫生机构算为一个机构,兵团连队卫生室统计到卫生所中,所以卫生机构总数增加。2.从 2007 年开始卫生部门实行网络直报。

Note: a) From 2002, in line with new regulations of ministry of public health,all the health institutions that have medical service permit shall be counted as one and health care rooms shall be counted in health clinics,therefore the total number of health institutions increased.
b) Since 2007, health care institution carried out directly network report.

19-3 主要年份卫生人员数(不含村卫生室)

Number of Persons Engaged in Health Institutions in Main Years(Excluding Village Clinics)

单位：人 (person)

年份 Year	合计 Total	#卫生技术人员 Medical Technical Personnel	#医生 Doctors	执业医师 Licensed Doctors	执业助理医师 Licensed Assistant Doctor	#注册护士 Registered Nurses	平均每万人医生数 Number of Doctors per 10 000 Population
1978	66252	51050	16898	7368	9530	10765	13.70
1980	74627	57949	20614	10092	10522	12077	16.06
1985	88460	68961	25721	13330	12391	17136	18.90
1990	102053	79853	33683	24967	8716	23386	22.03
1995	116856	92028	39636	30038	9598	26350	23.86
2000	122064	98093	45402	34892	10510	30850	24.55
2005	117165	96266	41426	32563	8863	30657	20.61
2010	149069	122860	48166	39301	8865	44238	22.25
2011	155701	129354	48618	39763	8855	48422	22.49
2012	150083	135401	49558	40834	8724	52141	22.63
2013	159513	144462	51959	43006	8953	56250	23.39
2014	167598	152050	53789	44467	9322	59441	23.40
2015	178063	160480	56272	46690	9582	63520	23.85

注：2002 年以前执业医师为中医师、西医师、中西医结合医师，执业助理医师为中医士、西医士、中西医结合医士，注册护士为护师、护士。(以下同)

Note: Prior to 2002,doctors with license were doctors trained in western medicine,assistant doctors are practioners with secondary western medical education,and registered nurses are master nurses and nurses (The following is the same as below) .

19-4 主要年份卫生机构床位数
Number of Beds in Health Institutions in Main Years

单位：张 (unit)

年份 Year	合计 Total	医院卫生院 Hospitals And Health Centers	#医院 Hospitals	社区服务中心(站) Sanitarium	其他卫生机构 Other Health Institutions	每万人医院、卫生院床位数 Number of Hospital Beds per 10 000 Population
1978	57647	39179	25514		18468	31.78
1980	61075	47236	32944		13839	36.81
1985	60930	55298	42486		5632	40.63
1990	67414	60707	47924		6707	39.70
1995	72955	66696	53336		6259	40.15
2000	70542	65916	52438		4626	35.64
2005	79753	76002	63013	209	3542	37.81
2006	83722	80090	65589	445	3187	39.07
2007	90329	87131	71496	343	2855	41.59
2008	96852	93253	76321	843	2756	43.76
2009	107193	102620	83776	1851	2722	47.54
2010	116230	109851	89871	3588	2791	50.36
2011	125391	118781	97436	3691	2919	53.93
2012	131542	125064	103074	3084	3394	56.01
2013	137325	130889	107897	2951	3485	57.75
2014	142956	136722	112357	3087	3147	59.48
2015	150263	143575	118024	3082	3606	60.84

19-5 医疗卫生机构病床使用情况

(2015 年)

项目	Item	实有床位数(张) Number Of Beds (bed)	实际开放总床位(床日) Total Beds Opened (bed·day)	平均开放病床数(张) Average Beds Opended (bed)	实际占用总床日数(床日) Utilization Of Beds (bed·day)	出院者占用总床日数(床日) Total Stay Days in Hospital (bed·day)
总计	**Total**	**150263**	**51530371**	**141179**	**42956578**	**41803594**
医院	**Hospitals**	**118024**	**40743448**	**111626**	**35419947**	**34892674**
综合医院	Comprehensive Hospitals	89394	31234928	85575	26900791	26731463
中医医院	Hospitals of Traditional Chinese Medicine	9248	3224261	8834	3066250	2990246
中西医结合医院	TCM and Western Medicine Hospitals	649	192840	528	152426	150197
民族医院	Hospitals for Nationalities	7887	2581172	7072	2395695	2437000
专科医院	Specialized Hospitals	10846	3510247	9617	2904785	2583768
基层医疗卫生机构	**Basic Medical Institutions**	**28987**	**9812805**	**26884**	**6987480**	**6369293**
社区卫生服务中心(站)	Health Service Center for Community (Stations)	3082	1051943	2882	500929	415994
社区卫生服务中心	Health Service Center for Community	2605	917816	2515	447236	383327
社区卫生服务站	Health Service Station for Community	477	134127	367	53693	32667
卫生院	Total Number of Public Health Center	25551	8760497	24001	6486551	5953299
乡镇卫生院	Public Health Center in Township and Towns	25551	8760497	24001	6486551	5953299
中心卫生院	Public Health Center in Rural Area	5724	1960982	5373	1450523	1410560
乡卫生院	Public Health Center in Township	19827	6799515	18629	5036028	4542739
专业公共卫生机构	**Specialized Public Health Institution**	**3041**	**897103**	**2458**	**544700**	**538112**
专科疾病防治院(所、站)	Specialized Disease Prevention&Treatment Institutions	85	31025	85	12943	11875
妇幼保健院(所、站)	Women and Children Care Agencies	2906	866078	2373	531757	526237
#妇幼保健院	Women and Children Care Hospitals	1719	588431	1612	392929	390238
急救中心(站)	Urgent Care Center	50				
其他机构	**Others**	**211**	**77015**	**211**	**4451**	**3515**
疗养院	Sanatoriums	211	77015	211	4451	3515

Number of Beds in Health Care Instiutions

项　目	Item	观察床数（张）Obeserve Beds (bed)	全年开设家庭病床总数（张）Number Of Famlily Beds (bed)	病床周转次　数(次) Turnover Of Beds (time)	病床工作日（日）Working Days of Beds (bed)	病　床使用率(%) Utilization Rate of Beds(%)	出院者平均住院日（日）Average Stay Days in Hospital (day)
总计	**Total**	**28191**	**52469**	**36.1**	**304.3**	**83.36**	**8.2**
医院	**Hospitals**	**14292**	**13280**	**35.4**	**317.3**	**86.93**	**8.8**
综合医院	Comprehensive Hospitals	13298	13254	38.0	314.4	86.12	8.2
中医医院	Hospitals of TraditionalChinese Medicine	175		33.5	347.1	95.10	10.1
中西医结合医院	TCM and Western Medicine Hospital	4		25.2	288.5	79.04	11.3
民族医院	Hospitals for Nationalities	162	19	30.8	338.8	92.81	11.2
专科医院	Specialist Hospitals	653	7	17.9	302.0	82.75	15.0
基层医疗卫生机构	**Basic Medical Institutions**	**8780**	**39171**	**39.1**	**259.9**	**71.21**	**6.1**
社区卫生服务中心(站)	Health Service Center for Community (Stations)	1876	14709	16.9	173.8	47.62	8.6
社区卫生服务中心	Health Service Center for Community	1220	1129	17.5	177.9	48.73	8.7
社区卫生服务站	Health Service Station for Community	656	13580	12.4	146.1	40.03	7.2
卫生院	Health Center	6904	24462	41.5	270.3	74.04	6.0
乡镇卫生院	Public Health Center in Township and Towns	6904	24462	41.5	270.3	74.04	6.0
中心卫生院	Public Health Center in Rural Area	259	629	44.2	270.0	73.97	5.9
乡卫生院	Public Health Center in Township	6645	23833	40.7	270.3	74.06	6.0
专业公共卫生机构	**Specialized Public Health Institution**	**5119**	**18**	**38.9**	**221.6**	**60.72**	**5.6**
专科疾病防治院(所、站)	Specialized Disease Prevention& Treatment Institution			45.4	152.3	41.72	3.1
妇幼保健院(所、站)	Women and Children Care Agencies	5119	18	38.6	224.1	61.40	5.7
#妇幼保健院	Women and Children Care Hospitals	5081	4	38.3	243.7	66.78	6.3
急救中心(站)	Urgent Care Center						
其他机构	**Others**			**2.5**	**21.1**	**5.78**	**6.8**
疗养院	Sanatoriums			2.5	21.1	5.78	6.8

19-6 2000-2015 年医院床位和专业卫生技术人员数
Hospital Beds and Medical Technical Personnel (2000-2015)

年份 Year	医院床位(张) Number of Hospital Beds (unit)		专业卫生技术人员(人) Number of Medical Technical Personnel (person)		#执业医师、执业助理医师 Licensed Doctors & Assistant Doctors		#注册护士 Registered Nurses	
	市 City	县 County	市 City	县 County	市 City	县 County	市 City	县 County
2000	38398	27518	44115	31138	18408	13225	16805	9918
2001	38323	27685	44113	31055	18811	13271	16714	10105
2002	38700	26178	41850	27932	16689	10578	15965	8840
2003	42880	26915	44678	28228	17883	10916	17015	9087
2004	46300	27722	46956	28552	19207	10583	17185	9054
2005	50238	29515	54188	31132	23191	12323	18240	9289
2006	52275	31125	56701	32178	24033	13049	19365	9538
2007	54595	32536	68546	36125	28896	14655	24174	10488
2008	57242	36011	69292	37561	28215	15241	24976	11108
2009	58373	25403	54356	19490	20044	7242	22453	6979
2010	61157	28714	56706	21500	20953	7637	23777	8037
2011	65905	31531	61309	22893	21481	7881	26559	8964
2012	70217	32857	65326	24184	22081	8105	28960	9715
2013	71935	35962	69353	26708	23284	8425	30579	11177
2014	74767	37590	71957	29407	24199	8910	32189	12090
2015	78253	39771	76958	31104	25491	9414	34695	13058

19-7 2000-2015 年卫生院床位和专业卫生技术人员数
Hospital Beds and Medical Technical Personnel (2000-2015)

年份 Year	卫生院床位(张) Number of Hospital Beds (unit)		专业卫生技术人员(人) Number of Medical Technical Personnel (person)		#执业医师、执业助理医师 Licensed Doctors & Assistant Doctors		#注册护士 Registered Nurses	
	市 City	县 County	市 City	县 County	市 City	县 County	市 City	县 County
2000	2138	11119	3442	13131	1622	6299	1021	3756
2001	2141	11247	3602	13129	1782	6300	1095	3808
2002	2180	9991	4021	11215	1611	4370	970	2829
2003	2471	10147	3645	10901	1364	4227	946	2950
2004	2351	10479	3703	10936	1429	3963	992	2746
2005	5061	11679	10345	13646	5004	5704	2056	3024
2006	4732	13079	10930	14105	5370	6048	2207	3213
2007	2832	12803	18725	18220	9548	8000	4771	4182
2008	3037	13895	17745	19239	8888	8446	4710	4626
2009	3313	15531	3684	12578	1595	4435	1161	3527
2010	3383	16597	3641	13240	1536	4381	1180	3741
2011	3674	17671	3672	13653	1538	4334	1195	4097
2012	3768	18222	3694	14037	1466	4407	1241	4301
2013	3757	19235	3670	14642	1427	4502	1216	4448
2014	3974	20391	3912	15532	1464	4591	1252	4661
2015	3988	21563	4025	16406	1488	4913	1276	4850

19-8 各地、州、市卫生机构、床位和人员数

年 份 Year	地 区 Region	机构数 (个) Number of Institutions (unit)	床位数 (张) Beds (unit)	在岗职工合计 (人) Total Number of Medical Personnel (person)
	2005	8087	79753	117165
	2006	8175	83722	121400
	2007	7465	90329	127621
	2008	6739	96852	130174
	2009	7288	107193	138344
	2010	7650	116230	149069
	2011	17412	125391	167828
	2012	18320	131542	177085
	2013	18663	137325	189578
	2014	18873	142956	199649
	2015	18798	150263	208536
乌鲁木齐市	Urumqi City	1853	29301	47158
克拉玛依市	Karamay City	85	1780	3969
吐鲁番市	Turpan City	428	3394	5006
哈密地区	Hami [Kumul] Administrative Offices	522	4035	6466
昌吉回族自治州	Changji Hui Autonomous Prefecture	1442	9910	14879
伊犁哈萨克自治州	Ili Kazak Autonomous Prefecture	4191	28051	39002
伊犁州直属县(市)	Counties (Cities) Direct Under Ili Prefecture	2042	17938	23412
塔城地区	Tacheng [Tarbagatai] Administrative Offices	1330	5849	9097
阿勒泰地区	Altay Administrative Offices	819	4264	6493
博尔塔拉蒙古自治州	Bortala Mongol Autonomous Prefecture	677	2989	5473
巴音郭楞蒙古自治州	Bayangol Mongol Autonomous Prefecture	1259	9304	13003
阿克苏地区	Aksu Administrative Offices	1722	14048	15466
克孜勒苏柯尔克孜自治州	Kizilsu Kirgiz Autonomous Prefecture	360	3532	4730
喀什地区	Kashgar [Kaxgar] Administrative Offices	3423	23305	28629
和田地区	Hotan Administrative Offices	1809	13748	13859
自治区直辖县级市	County level City directly under the Autonomous Region	1027	6866	10896
石河子市	Shihezi City	739	5055	8099
阿拉尔市	Aral City	191	605	1039
图木舒克市	Tumxuk City	5	180	254
五家渠市	Wujiaqu City	92	1026	1504

注：1.本表人员合计中包括乡村医生 13907 人和卫生员 1435 人；
2.不含乡镇卫生院在村卫生室工作的执业(助理)医师、注册护士数。

Number of Health Institutions, Beds and Personnel by Prefecture, Autonomous Prefecture and City

卫生技术人员 Medical Technical Personnel	其他技术人员 Other Technicians	管理人员 Administrative Personnel	工勤人员 Logistics Workers	平均每万人床位数(张) Number of Beds per 10 000 Population (unit)
96266	4626	6330	9943	39.71
99839	5168	6258	10135	39.07
104671	5276	7143	10531	43.11
106853	5694	6419	11208	45.45
114521	6111	6453	11259	49.66
122860	6979	7089	12141	53.28
130604	6904	6837	12606	56.93
136691	6972	6631	13935	58.91
145851	7807	7179	14403	60.59
153417	8597	7471	14822	62.20
161841	9577	7592	14970	66.50
37100	2296	2141	5379	109.81
3199	271	158	339	59.39
3961	237	186	330	52.06
5519	262	201	300	65.43
12458	634	422	822	71.15
30964	1905	1341	2111	59.73
18835	1225	854	1286	59.71
7042	316	283	553	57.11
5087	364	204	272	63.83
4331	145	357	371	62.31
10961	594	388	556	66.75
11524	696	517	826	55.51
3673	220	120	198	59.25
19765	837	994	1771	51.80
9415	777	389	1508	59.15
8971	703	378	459	64.29
6616	605	302	367	79.91
809	35	33	41	33.76
233	10	8	3	11.04
1313	53	35	48	110.25

Note: a). Total data in this table included 13907 rural doctors and 1435 medical personels.
b). Total data in this table didn't include licensed doctors and registered nurses in township and town health centers.

19-9 各地、州、市卫生技术人员数

单位:人

年 份 Year	地 区 Region	卫生技术人员合计 Number of Medical Technical Personnel	执业医师 Doctors with License	执业助理医师 With Licence Assistant Doctors
	2005	96266	32563	8863
	2006	99839	33988	8787
	2007	104671	34838	8713
	2008	106853	35320	8136
	2009	114521	37223	8393
	2010	122860	39301	8865
	2011	130604	40265	9265
	2012	136691	41358	9182
	2013	145851	43582	9438
	2014	153417	44999	9806
	2015	161841	47226	10057
乌鲁木齐市	Urumqi City	37100	13269	595
克拉玛依市	Karamay City	3199	1221	33
吐鲁番市	Turpan City	3961	1152	326
哈密地区	Hami [Kumul] Administrative Offices	5519	1663	338
昌吉回族自治州	Changji Hui Autonomous Prefecture	12458	3717	650
伊犁哈萨克自治州	Ili Kazak Autonomous Prefecture	30964	8758	2465
伊犁州直属县(市)	Counties (Cities) Direct Under Ili Prefecture	18835	5318	1379
塔城地区	Tacheng [Tarbagatai] Administrative Offices	7042	1922	620
阿勒泰地区	Altay Administrative Offices	5087	1518	466
博尔塔拉蒙古自治州	Bortala Mongol Autonomous Prefecture	4331	1351	378
巴音郭楞蒙古自治州	Bayangol Mongol Autonomous Prefecture	10961	3297	723
阿克苏地区	Aksu Administrative Offices	11524	2877	841
克孜勒苏柯尔克孜自治州	Kizilsu Kirgiz Autonomous Prefecture	3673	870	394
喀什地区	Kashgar [Kaxgar] Administrative Offices	19765	4014	1760
和田地区	Hotan Administrative Offices	9415	2104	991
自治区直辖县级市	County level City directly under the Autonomous Region	8971	2933	563
石河子市	Shihezi City	6616	2357	378
阿拉尔市	Aral City	809	145	115
图木舒克市	Tumxuk City	233	43	15
五家渠市	Wujiaqu City	1313	388	55

注：1.本表人员合计中包括乡村医生 13114 人和卫生员 1442 人。
2.不含乡镇卫生院在村卫生室工作的执业(助理)医师、注册护士数。

Number of Medical Technical Personnel by Prefecture, Autonomous Prefecture and City

(person)

注册护士 Registered Nurses	药剂人员 Pharmacists	技师(士) Technicians (artificer)	检验人员 Laboratory Technicians	其他 Others	平均每万人医生数 Number of Doctors per 10 000 Population
30657	5848	4773		13562	20.61
32119	5948	4980		14017	20.87
34662	5647	6701	4746	14110	20.79
36084	5721	6876	4803	14716	20.39
40425	5989	7164	4977	15327	21.13
44238	6364	7742	5301	16350	22.25
48760	6483	7726	5391	18105	22.49
52449	6557	7984	5539	19161	22.63
56578	6923	8659	5903	20671	23.39
59792	7254	8966	6135	22600	23.84
63870	7543	9450	6456	23695	25.35
15853	1630	1760	1268	3993	51.96
1382	192	207	122	164	41.84
1598	203	239	170	443	22.67
2334	289	293	230	602	32.45
5079	642	799	513	1571	31.35
12022	1246	2077	1415	4396	22.59
7259	759	1300	901	2820	22.29
2769	289	468	296	974	24.82
1994	198	309	218	602	29.70
1720	218	243	181	421	36.04
4233	481	653	439	1574	28.84
4576	537	743	503	1950	14.69
1335	165	159	106	750	21.20
6802	984	1188	818	5017	12.83
3072	610	601	358	2037	13.32
3864	346	488	333	777	32.73
2867	261	352	241	401	43.23
351	26	53	35	119	14.51
98	7	9	7	61	3.56
548	52	74	50	196	47.60

Note: a). Total data in this table included 13114 rural doctors and 1442 medical personels.
b). Total data in this table didn't include licensed doctors and registered nurses in township and town health centers.

19-10 社区卫生服务中心(站)工作量
Medical Services in Health Service Centers for Community

年 份 Year	社区卫生服务中心 Health Service Centers for Community				社区卫生服务站诊疗人次(万人) Health Service Stations for Community (10 000 patients)
	诊疗人次 (万人次) Visits (10 000 patient-times)	入院人数(万人) Inpatients (10 000 patients)	病床使用率(%) Utilization Rate (%) of Beds	平均住院日(日) Average Duration of Hospitaliyation(day)	
2002	76.84	0.16	53.86	10.16	34.41
2003	88.10	0.60	89.51	16.13	33.75
2004	85.62	0.03	36.42	10.00	82.67
2005	67.04	0.03	16.71	11.08	152.68
2006	107.49	0.35	11.71	6.94	179.32
2007	105.73	0.24	59.77	11.70	109.22
2008	156.05	0.94	51.68	11.30	121.92
2009	232.95	2.36	49.93	9.90	207.23
2010	298.47	4.24	61.07	10.40	355.78
2011	323.93	4.37	53.51	9.80	351.28
2012	330.09	4.85	50.32	7.60	341.43
2013	410.08	4.32	50.85	8.80	359.09
2014	440.03	4.58	51.28	9.00	366.30
2015	476.51	4.42	48.73	8.70	350.02

19-11 乡村卫生室基本情况
Basic Conditions of Country Health Room

(2015 年)

项 目	Item	合 计 Total	中 医 Traditional Chinese Medicine	西 医 Western Medicine	中西医结合 Combination Traditional and Western Medicine
机构数(个)	Number of Institutions(unit)	10439	84	8952	1402
执业(助理)医师(人)	Licensed (Assistant) Doctors (person)	1011	26	887	98
注册护士(人)	Registered Nurses(person)	350	6	318	26
乡村医生和卫生员(人)	Country Doctor and Assistant Nurse(person)	14556	126	12256	2174
乡村医生	Country Doctor	13114	113	10997	2004
卫生员	Assistant Nurse	1442	13	1259	170
诊疗人次数(万人次)	Number of Patients Treated(10 000 patient-times)	926.52	10.41	792.71	123.41
#出 诊	Out-call	105.15	2.08	81.88	21.20

19-12 医疗卫生机构门诊服务情况
Basic Conditions of Outpatient Service Medical and Health Institutions

(2015 年)

项目	Item	总诊疗人次数(万人次) Number of Visits(10000 person times)	门、急诊 Outpatients with Emergency Treatment 小计 Total	门诊 Outpatients	急诊 Emergency Treatment	家庭卫生服务人次数 Vistits
总计	**Total**	**10333.27**	**9888.97**	**9477.02**	**411.95**	**41.18**
医院	Hospitals	4982.43	4826.90	4469.98	356.92	14.19
综合医院	General Hospital	4162.74	4034.36	3699.74	334.62	14.07
中医医院	Hospital Specialized in Traditional Chinese Medicine	457.60	453.88	439.69	14.19	0.05
中西医结合医院	Hospital Specialized in Combination Of Traditional Chinese and Western Medicine	22.25	22.05	21.94	0.11	
民族医院	National Hospital	146.23	126.66	122.02	4.64	0.01
专科医院	Specialized Hospital	193.61	189.94	186.58	3.36	0.05
基层医疗卫生机构	Health Care Instituions at Grass-root level	5030.93	4753.64	4708.40	45.24	23.43
社区卫生服务中心(站)	Health Service Center for Community (Stations)	826.52	790.72	781.56	9.17	14.33
社区卫生服务中心	Health Service Center for Community	476.51	450.72	445.33	5.38	8.51
社区卫生服务站	Health Service Station for Community	350.02	340.01	336.23	3.78	5.81
卫生院	Health Center	2010.40	1932.05	1895.97	36.08	9.11
乡镇卫生院	Public Health Center in Township and Towns	2010.40	1932.05	1895.97	36.08	9.11
中心卫生院	Public Health Center	440.49	423.58	414.58	9.01	3.20
乡卫生院	Public Health Center in Rural Area	1569.91	1508.47	1481.40	27.07	5.90
村卫生室	Village Clinics	926.52	821.37	821.37		
门诊部	Out-patients Department	143.39	131.81	131.81		
诊所、卫生所、医务室	Clinics, Health Centers,Health Rooms	1124.10	1077.70	1077.70		
诊所	Clinics	987.50	943.05	943.05		
卫生所、医务室	Health Centers, Health Rooms	135.23	133.28	133.28		
护理站	Nursing Department	1.36	1.36	1.36		
专业公共卫生机构	Specialized Public Health Institution	315.31	303.88	294.09	9.78	3.56
专科疾病防治院(所、站)	Specialized Disease Prevention & Treatment Institute	2.48	2.48	2.19	0.29	
妇幼保健院(所、站)	Hospitals for Maternity and Child Care	306.49	295.06	291.90	3.15	3.56
#妇幼保健院	Women and Children Care Agencies	187.71	184.85	183.20	1.64	1.81
急救中心(站)	Emergency center	6.34	6.34		6.34	
其他机构	Other Institutions	4.60	4.55	4.55		
疗养院	Sanatorium	4.60	4.55	4.55		

19-12 续表 Continued

项　　目	Item	观察室留观病例数(万人) Cases in Observation Room(10000 persons)	健康检查人数(万人) Number of Health Examinations (10000 persons)	急诊病死率(%) Fatality Rate among Emergency Admissions(%)	观察室病死率(%) Fatality Rate in Observation Room (%)
总　计	**Total**	**69.14**	**690.07**	**0.15**	**0.21**
医　院	Hospitals	48.30	382.59	0.17	0.30
综合医院	General Hospital	42.25	341.71	0.17	0.34
中医医院	Hospital Specialized in Traditional Chinese Medicine	3.73	20.00	0.21	0.01
中西医结合医院	Hospital Specialized in Combination Of Traditional Chinese and Western Medicine Medicine	0.02	0.03		
民族医院	National Hospital	1.47	6.01	0.04	0.03
专科医院	Specialized Hospital	0.84	14.84	0.04	0.18
基层医疗卫生机构	Health Care Institutions at Grass-root Level	20.03	253.47	0.02	0.01
社区卫生服务中心(站)	Health Service Center for Community (Stations)	13.23	69.80	0.07	0.01
社区卫生服务中心	Health Service Center for Community	8.12	36.64	0.11	0.02
社区卫生服务站	Health Service Station for Community	5.11	33.15	0.01	
卫生院	Health Center	6.79	166.62	0.01	0.01
乡镇卫生院	Public Health Center in Township and Towns	6.79	166.62	0.01	0.01
中心卫生院	Public Health Center	2.56	49.78	0.02	0.01
乡卫生院	Public Health Center in Rural Area	4.23	116.84	0.01	
村卫生室	Village Clinics				
门诊部	Out-patients Department		17.06		
诊所、卫生所、医务室	Clinics, Health Centers,Health Rooms				
诊所	Clinics				
卫生所、医务室	Health Centers,Health Rooms				
护理站	Nursing Department				
专业公共卫生机构	Specialized Public Health Institution	0.81	54.00		
专科疾病防治院(所、站)	Specialized Disease Prevention & Treatment Institute		0.05		
妇幼保健院(所、站)	Hospitals for Maternity and Child Care	0.81	53.95		
#妇幼保健院	Women and Children Care Agencies	0.65	24.03		
急救中心(站)	Emergency center				
其他机构	Other Institutions		0.02		
疗养院	Sanatorium		0.02		

19-13 医疗卫生机构住院服务情况
Basic Conditions of Service in Medical and Health Institutions

(2015 年)

项　目	Item	入院人数(人) Number of Inpatients (Person)	出院人数(人) Patients Discharged (Person)	死亡人数(人) Death toll (Person)
总　计	**Total**	**5121547**	**5100315**	**16860**
医　院	Hospitals	3971733	3953881	16684
综合医院	General Hospital	3266804	3255040	14742
中医医院	Hospital Specialized in Traditional Chinese Medicine	298157	296238	394
中西医结合医院	Hospital Specialized in Combination Of Traditional Chinese and Western Medicine	13327	13326	606
民族医院	National Hospital	219884	217515	53
专科医院	Specialized Hospital	173561	171762	889
基层医疗卫生机构	Health Care Institutions at Grass-root Level	1054137	1050420	164
社区卫生服务中心(站)	Health Service Center for Community (Stations)	48585	48595	136
社区卫生服务中心	Health Service Center for Community	44157	44041	131
社区卫生服务站	Health Service Station for Community	4428	4554	5
卫生院	Health Center	999838	996111	28
乡镇卫生院	Public Health Center in Township and Towns	999838	996111	28
中心卫生院	Public Health Center	238437	237390	9
乡卫生院	Public Health Center in Rural Area	761401	758721	19
门诊部	Village Clinics	5714	5714	
专业公共卫生机构	Specialized Public Health Institution	95160	95497	12
专科疾病防治院(所、站)	Specialized Disease Prevention & Treatment Institute	4355	3856	
妇幼保健院(所、站)	Hospitals for Maternity and Child Care	90805	91641	12
#妇幼保健院	Women and Children Care Agencies	61511	61689	12
其他机构	Other Institutions	517	517	
疗养院	Sanatorium	517	517	

项　目	Item	住院病人手术人次数(人次) Surgical Operation of Hospitalized (person-times)	每百门急诊的入院人数(人) Inpatients per 100 Outpatient and Emergency Visits (person)	入院病人死亡率(%) Inpatient mortality (%)
总　计	**Total**	**846306**	**6.52**	**0.33**
医　院	Hospitals	822326	8.23	0.42
综合医院	General Hospital	732912	8.10	0.45
中医医院	Hospital Specialized in Traditional Chinese Medicine	43722	6.57	0.13
中西医结合医院	Hospital Specialized in Combination Of Traditional Chinese and Western Medicine	50	6.04	4.55
民族医院	National Hospital	9097	17.36	0.02
专科医院	Specialized Hospital	36545	9.14	0.52
基层医疗卫生机构	Health Care Institutions at Grass-root Level		3.85	0.02
社区卫生服务中心(站)	Health Service Center for Community (Stations)		0.61	0.28
社区卫生服务中心	Health Service Center for Community		0.98	0.30
社区卫生服务站	Health Service Station for Community		0.13	0.11
卫生院	Health Center		5.18	
乡镇卫生院	Public Health Center in Township and Towns		5.18	
中心卫生院	Public Health Center		5.63	
乡卫生院	Public Health Center in Rural Area		5.05	
门诊部	Village Clinics			
专业公共卫生机构	Specialized Public Health Institution	23980	3.20	0.01
专科疾病防治院(所、站)	Specialized Disease Prevention & Treatment Institute		17.57	
妇幼保健院(所、站)	Hospitals for Maternity and Child Care	23980	3.08	0.01
#妇幼保健院	Women and Children Care Agencies	21446	3.33	0.02
其他机构	Other Institutions		1.14	
疗养院	Sanatorium		1.14	

19-14 医疗卫生机构门诊病人次均医疗费用

The Per Capita Medical Expenses of Patients Hospitalized in the Medical and Health Institutions

(2015 年)

项目	Item	门诊病人次均诊疗费用(元) The per Capita Medical Expenses of Outpatient (yuan)	挂号费 Registered Fee	诊察费 Diagnostic Fee	检查费 Inspection Fee	化验费 Laboratory Fee
总计	**Total**	**133.0**	**0.7**	**1.5**	**25.7**	**13.4**
医院	Hospitals	208.4	1.1	2.1	45.0	21.6
综合医院	General Hospital	201.1	1.1	2.1	46.9	21.6
中医医院	Hospital Specialized in Traditional Chinese Medicine	244.4	0.9	2.1	33.4	13.3
中西医结合医院	Hospital Specialized in Combination Of Traditional Chinese and Western Medicine	320.8	0.2	0.7	10.9	9.4
民族医院	National Hospital	128.0	1.2	1.6	21.6	7.3
专科医院	Specialized Hospital	328.5	1.5	2.8	51.7	52.5
基层医疗卫生机构	Health Care Institutions at Grass-root Level	40.7	0.1	0.3	2.3	1.7
社区卫生服务中心(站)	Health Service Center for Community	92.8	0.2	0.3	4.7	2.6
社区卫生服务中心	Health Service Center for Community	112.8	0.3	0.3	6.9	3.8
社区卫生服务站	Health Service Center for Community	65.6	0.1	0.2	1.6	1.1
卫生院	Total Number of Public Health Center	37.2	0.2	0.5	2.7	2.4
街道卫生院	Public Health Center in Neighbourhood	37.2	0.2	0.5	2.7	2.4
乡镇卫生院	Public Health Center in Township and Towns	36.0	0.1	0.6	3.2	2.4
中心卫生院	Public Health Center	37.5	0.2	0.5	2.6	2.3
乡卫生院	Public Health Center in Rural Area	108.5				
门诊部	Village Clinics	0.1				
护理站	Nursing Hospital	52.3				
专业公共卫生机构	Specialized Public Health Institution	140.8	1.0	7.9	27.0	38.0
专科疾病防治院(所、站)	Specialized Disease Prevention & Treatment Institute	116.7	0.5	0.4	0.2	0.6
妇幼保健院(所、站)	Hospitals for Maternity and Child Care	143.9	1.1	8.1	27.8	39.1
#妇幼保健院	Women and Children Care Agencies	176.5	1.3	11.7	31.3	47.5
其他机构	Other Institutions	139.9			9.8	2.4
疗养院	Sanatorium	139.9			9.8	2.4

项目	Item	治疗费 Treatment Costs	手术费 Operation Fee	卫生材料费 Sanitary Materials Fee	药费 Expenses for Medicine	药事服务费 Pharmaceutical Service Fee
总计	**Total**	**11.0**	**2.3**	**3.2**	**67.6**	**0.2**
医院	Hospitals	18.2	3.8	5.5	103.3	0.4
综合医院	General Hospital	15.5	3.3	5.8	97.1	0.4
中医医院	Hospital Specialized in Traditional Chinese Medicine	17.9	2.2	2.7	170.0	0.1
中西医结合医院	Hospital Specialized in Combination Of Traditional Chinese and Western Medicine	134.4	1.3	2.3	119.9	0.6
民族医院	National Hospital	10.8	0.8	1.8	78.7	0.4
专科医院	Specialized Hospital	69.4	21.4	7.6	94.2	2.0
基层医疗卫生机构	Health Care Institutions at Grass-root Level	2.4	0.2	0.4	26.5	
社区卫生服务中心(站)	Health Service Center for Community	5.9	0.5	1.0	74.0	
社区卫生服务中心	Health Service Center for Community	7.3	0.7	1.1	89.0	
社区卫生服务站	Health Service Center for Community	4.1	0.3	1.0	53.5	
卫生院	Total Number of Public Health Center	2.5	0.1	0.4	23.7	
街道卫生院	Public Health Center in Neighbourhood	2.5	0.1	0.4	23.7	
乡镇卫生院	Public Health Center in Township and Towns	2.6	0.3	0.5	22.0	
中心卫生院	Public Health Center	2.5	0.1	0.4	24.2	
乡卫生院	Public Health Center in Rural Area					
门诊部	Village Clinics					
护理站	Nursing Hospital	31.1			21.2	
专业公共卫生机构	Specialized Public Health Institution	8.7	4.6	4.7	36.8	0.4
专科疾病防治院(所、站)	Specialized Disease Prevention & Treatment Institute	107.5			7.5	
妇幼保健院(所、站)	Hospitals for Maternity and Child Care	8.1	4.7	4.8	37.8	0.4
#妇幼保健院	Women and Children Care Agencies	10.5	7.1	7.0	44.0	0.5
其他机构	Other Institutions	11.9			115.8	
疗养院	Sanatorium	11.9			115.8	

19-15 各地区医院门诊病人次均医疗费用

The Per Capita Medical Expenses of Patients Hospitalized in the Medical and Health Institutions

单位：元 （2015 年） (yuan)

地区	Region	门诊病人次均诊疗费用 The per Capita Medical Expenses of Outpatient	挂号费 Registered Fee	诊察费 Diagnostic Fee	检查费 Inspection Fee	化验费 Laboratory Fee
总计	**Total**	**208.4**	**1.1**	**2.1**	**45.0**	**21.6**
乌鲁木齐市	Urumqi City	264.0	0.9	2.2	46.4	26.6
克拉玛依市	Karamay City	279.5	0.7	2.2	34.8	28.6
吐鲁番市	Turpan City	188.4	1.3	1.6	47.3	23.7
哈密地区	Hami [Kumul] Administrative Offices	175.3	1.2	1.0	43.5	17.5
昌吉回族自治州	Changji Hui Autonomous Prefecture	158.5	1.0	1.0	31.5	15.4
伊犁哈萨克自治州	Counties (Cities) Direct Under Ili Prefecture	181.9	1.1	2.7	40.9	17.3
塔城地区	Tacheng [Tarbagatai] Administrative Offices	171.0	0.7	1.5	43.5	22.5
阿勒泰地区	Altay Administrative Offices	183.2	0.6	1.6	46.3	19.5
博尔塔拉蒙古自治州	Bortala Mongol Autonomous Prefecture	174.3	0.9	2.1	44.8	18.8
巴音郭楞蒙古自治州	Bayangol Mongol Autonomous Prefecture	194.6	1.3	2.0	42.4	17.7
阿克苏地区	Aksu Administrative Offices	194.1	0.9	1.3	60.4	29.5
克孜勒苏柯尔克孜自治州	Kizilsu Kirgiz Autonomous Prefecture	109.4	1.1	3.6	45.6	9.4
喀什地区	Kashgar [Kaxgar] Administrative Offices	160.0	1.6	3.2	56.0	16.6
和田地区	Hotan Administrative Offices	147.2	2.0	1.5	42.2	19.6
自治区直辖县级行政单位	County Level City Directly under the Autonomous Region	174.3	0.9	2.1	44.8	18.8

地区	Region	治疗费 Treatment Costs	手术费 Operation Fee	卫生材料费 Sanitary Materials Fee	药费 Expenses for Medicine	药事服务费 Pharmaceutical Service Fee
总计	**Total**	**18.2**	**3.8**	**5.5**	**103.3**	**0.4**
乌鲁木齐市	Urumqi City	28.1	6.0	5.7	140.3	0.3
克拉玛依市	Karamay City	23.2	3.0	7.6	146.1	
吐鲁番市	Turpan City	18.7	4.0	10.9	76.8	0.3
哈密地区	Hami [Kumul] Administrative Offices	13.3	1.8	4.6	89.8	0.2
昌吉回族自治州	Changji Hui Autonomous Prefecture	14.1	2.3	3.4	85.4	1.1
伊犁哈萨克自治州	Counties (Cities) Direct Under Ili Prefecture	11.7	2.5	6.9	94.3	0.2
塔城地区	Tacheng [Tarbagatai] Administrative Offices	14.7	3.0	7.0	69.5	0.7
阿勒泰地区	Altay Administrative Offices	8.7	1.7	4.3	96.8	0.9
博尔塔拉蒙古自治州	Bortala Mongol Autonomous Prefecture	11.6	3.8	5.5	83.6	0.1
巴音郭楞蒙古自治州	Bayangol Mongol Autonomous Prefecture	14.4	3.6	6.6	100.4	0.9
阿克苏地区	Aksu Administrative Offices	13.6	3.3	5.4	64.3	0.1
克孜勒苏柯尔克孜自治州	Kizilsu Kirgiz Autonomous Prefecture	9.3	1.1	3.3	29.7	0.7
喀什地区	Kashgar [Kaxgar] Administrative Offices	10.5	2.7	4.3	60.6	0.5
和田地区	Hotan Administrative Offices	8.3	3.3	3.5	64.1	0.5
自治区直辖县级行政单位	County Level City Directly under the Autonomous Region	11.6	3.8	5.5	83.6	0.1

19-16 医疗卫生机构住院病人次均医疗费用

The Per Capita Medical Expenses of Patients Hospitalized in the Medical and Health Institutions

单位：元　　　　(2015 年)　　　　(yuan)

项　目	Item	合 计 Total	床位费 Bed Fee	检查费 Inspection Fee	化验费 Laboratory Fee
总　计	**Total**	**5168.8**	**145.2**	**623.4**	**732.2**
医　院	Hospitals	6318.8	168.6	775.1	894.2
综合医院	General Hospital	6068.6	156.9	744.8	887.4
中医医院	Hospital Specialized in Traditional Chinese Medicine	7880.1	181.2	934.9	1018.9
中西医结合医院	Hospital Specialized in Combination Of Traditional Chinese and Western Medicine Medicine	7926.4	464.9	1835.8	1090.1
民族医院	National Hospital	3463.6	154.1	322.8	441.0
专科医院	Specialized Hospital	11858.7	364.6	1564.2	1366.3
基层医疗卫生机构	Health Care Institutions at Grass-root Level	1039.0	47.9	87.0	140.7
社区卫生服务中心(站)	Health Service Center for Community	2555.4	102.7	261.7	298.3
社区卫生服务中心	Health Service Center for Community	2618.5	106.5	259.7	307.4
社区卫生服务站	Health Service Center for Community	1945.1	66.3	280.9	210.8
卫生院	Total Number of Public Health Center	971.0	45.5	79.0	133.8
乡镇卫生院	Public Health Center in Township and Towns	971.0	45.5	79.0	133.8
中心卫生院	Public Health Center	1132.7	44.5	104.9	160.9
乡卫生院	Public Health Center in Rural Area	920.4	45.8	70.9	125.4
专业公共卫生机构	Specialized Public Health Institution	2991.2	231.3	246.2	537.1
专科疾病防治院(所、站)	Specialized Disease Prevention & Treatment Institute	103.7	13.0	23.3	13.0
妇幼保健院(所、站)	Hospitals for Maternity and Child Care	3112.7	240.4	255.6	559.1
#妇幼保健院	Women and Children Care Agencies	3884.0	320.0	341.2	708.4
其他机构	Other Institutions	3669.2	3518.4		1.9
疗养院	Sanatorium	3669.2	3518.4		1.9

项　目	Item	治疗费 Treatment Costs	手术费 Operation Fee	药　费 Expenses for Medicine	卫生材料费 Sanitoury Materials Fee
总　计	**Total**	**635.1**	**300.6**	**1875.9**	**655.7**
医　院	Hospitals	777.3	375.5	2262.5	833.3
综合医院	General Hospital	627.0	391.5	2181.0	858.4
中医医院	Hospital Specialized in Traditional Chinese Medicine	1822.2	327.7	2374.1	1040.4
中西医结合医院	Hospital Specialized in Combination Of Traditional Chinese and Western Medicine Medicine	1206.7	19.9	3028.7	11.9
民族医院	National Hospital	946.8	51.4	1222.5	75.6
专科医院	Specialized Hospital	1574.9	593.7	4872.1	1024.3
基层医疗卫生机构	Health Care Institutions at Grass-root Level	118.1	8.2	533.0	25.8
社区卫生服务中心(站)	Health Service Center for Community	363.5	82.0	1162.8	115.9
社区卫生服务中心	Health Service Center for Community	376.6	83.9	1191.4	123.7
社区卫生服务站	Health Service Center for Community	237.4	63.2	885.8	39.5
卫生院	Total Number of Public Health Center	106.8	4.6	505.4	21.6
乡镇卫生院	Public Health Center in Township and Towns	106.8	4.6	505.4	21.6
中心卫生院	Public Health Center	160.2	4.2	558.6	32.5
乡卫生院	Public Health Center in Rural Area	90.1	4.7	488.7	18.2
专业公共卫生机构	Specialized Public Health Institution	438.9	415.3	651.1	235.8
专科疾病防治院(所、站)	Specialized Disease Prevention & Treatment Institute	15.6		10.4	
妇幼保健院(所、站)	Hospitals for Maternity and Child Care	456.7	432.8	678.1	245.7
#妇幼保健院	Women and Children Care Agencies	582.0	567.8	774.0	333.7
其他机构	Other Institutions	135.4		9.7	
疗养院	Sanatorium	135.4		9.7	

19-17 各地区医院住院人次均医疗费用

The Per Capita Medical Expenses of Patients Hospitalized in the Medical and Health Institutions by Region

单位：元　　(2015 年)　　(yuan)

地　区	Region	门诊病人次均诊疗费用 The per Capita Medical Expenses of Outpatient	床位费 Bed Fee	诊察费 Diagnostic Fee	检查费 Inspection Fee	化验费 Laboratory Fee	治疗费 Treatment Costs
总　计	**Total**	**6318.8**	**168.6**	**41.0**	**775.1**	**894.2**	**777.3**
乌鲁木齐市	Urumqi City	12709.8	272.1	51.6	1598.3	1651.0	1527.7
克拉玛依市	Karamay City	10118.9	236.8	46.0	1064.1	1253.5	1002.1
吐鲁番市	Turpan City	3897.6	119.2	20.1	500.4	799.7	445.6
哈密地区	Hami [Kumul] Administrative Offices	6319.5	196.0	30.2	780.8	1193.8	790.1
昌吉回族自治州	Changji Hui Autonomous Prefecture	4519.3	137.9	21.9	552.8	672.0	657.1
伊犁哈萨克自治州	Counties (Cities) Direct Under Ili Prefecture	4774.4	155.3	42.5	531.7	644.0	581.5
塔城地区	Tacheng [Tarbagatai] Administrative Offices	4458.4	127.7	36.7	441.3	623.0	576.1
阿勒泰地区	Altay Administrative Offices	4239.9	127.1	26.1	564.1	682.3	404.0
博尔塔拉蒙古自治州	Bortala Mongol Autonomous Prefecture	4248.6	157.1	25.1	516.4	616.1	411.6
巴音郭楞蒙古自治州	Bayangol Mongol Autonomous Prefecture	5579.9	178.5	40.4	812.5	982.4	529.7
阿克苏地区	Aksu Administrative Offices	4332.5	151.7	29.1	469.8	702.5	525.0
克孜勒苏柯尔克孜自治州	Kizilsu Kirgiz Autonomous Prefecture	3577.1	117.0	29.5	400.6	614.9	322.6
喀什地区	Kashgar [Kaxgar] Administrative Offices	4229.8	120.3	48.8	466.7	600.0	547.1
和田地区	Hotan Administrative Offices	3432.7	112.7	33.4	353.0	499.2	391.8
自治区直辖县级行政单位	County Level City Directly under the Autonomous Region	7052.3	158.8	67.9	1133.3	874.5	1238.7

地　区	Region	手术费 Operation Fee	护理费 Nursing Fee	卫生材料费 Sanitoury Materials Fee	药费 Expenses for Medicine	药事服务费 Pharmaceutical Service Fee	出院者平均每日住院医疗费 Average Hcspital discharge per day	药费 Expenses for Medicine
总　计	**Total**	**375.5**	**91.6**	**833.3**	**2262.5**	**1.1**	**716.0**	**256.37**
乌鲁木齐市	Urumqi City	700.9	110.8	2194.2	4504.9	0.2	1235.0	437.73
克拉玛依市	Karamay City	504.1	179.3	2075.8	3680.5		984.1	357.93
吐鲁番市	Turpan City	290.7	88.2	353.2	1165.8	1.2	617.5	184.71
哈密地区	Hami [Kumul] Administrative Offices	266.7	109.3	797.0	2035.7	0.7	605.2	194.94
昌吉回族自治州	Changji Hui Autonomous Prefecture	265.1	62.2	465.9	1585.0		581.1	203.81
伊犁哈萨克自治州	Counties (Cities) Direct Under Ili Prefecture	290.0	89.2	536.3	1794.0	1.5	514.7	193.39
塔城地区	Tacheng [Tarbagatai] Administrative Offices	241.1	54.0	410.0	1791.7	1.9	501.4	201.50
阿勒泰地区	Altay Administrative Offices	245.6	51.7	398.4	1702.9		498.1	200.05
博尔塔拉蒙古自治州	Bortala Mongol Autonomous Prefecture	277.0	66.7	562.3	1586.6	1.7	517.2	193.16
巴音郭楞蒙古自治州	Bayangol Mongol Autonomous Prefecture	291.5	88.6	681.0	1849.9	2.2	644.7	213.74
阿克苏地区	Aksu Administrative Offices	444.1	97.2	282.7	1476.0	0.3	532.1	181.27
克孜勒苏柯尔克孜自治州	Kizilsu Kirgiz Autonomous Prefecture	189.6	60.4	344.6	1389.6	1.2	479.4	186.25
喀什地区	Kashgar [Kaxgar] Administrative Offices	247.0	94.9	512.6	1513.9	0.4	543.8	194.63
和田地区	Hotan Administrative Offices	219.0	83.2	272.4	1393.5	5.3	438.1	177.85
自治区直辖县级行政单位	County Level City Directly under the Autonomous Region	376.6	97.3	502.9	2539.1	1.3	654.3	235.57

19-18 法定报告传染病发病及死亡情况

Situations of Confirmed Incidence and Death from Infectious Diseases

项　目	Item	发病率（1/10万）Disease Incidence (1/100 000)		死亡率（1/10万）Death Rate (1/100 000)	
		2014	2015	2014	2015
总　计	**Total**	**611.78**	**635.11**	**3.52**	**4.30**
鼠　疫	The Plague				
霍　乱	Cholera				
传染性非典	SARS				
艾滋病	AIDS	7.11	8.13	1.42	2.96
肝　炎	Viral Hepatitis	249.29	233.58	0.06	0.0827
脊　灰	Epidemic Cerebrospinal Meningitis				
人禽流感	Highly Pathogenic Bird Flu				
甲型 H1N1 流感	A(H1N1) Flu				
麻　疹	Measles	5.57	12.10	0.01	0.05
出血热	Hemorrhage Fever	0.0044			
狂犬病	Hydrophobia				
乙　脑	Encephalitis B				
登革热	Dengue Fever	0.0044	0.0044		
炭　疽	Anthrax	0.15	0.06		0.0044
痢　疾	Dysentery	26.02	21.55		
肺结核	Plumonary Tuberculosis	175.99	184.53	0.94	1.17
伤寒+副伤寒	Typhoid and Paraty phoid Fever	0.764	0.875		
流　脑	Epidemic Encephalitis	0.37	0.12	0.01	0.01
百 日 咳	Pertussis	0.91	5.63		
白　喉	Diphtheria				
新生儿破伤风	Newborn Tetanus	0.21	0.14	0.0088	
猩 红 热	Scarlet Fever	9.32	13.54		
布鲁氏菌病	Brucellosis	33.02	38.37		
淋　病	Gonorrhea	9.36	8.91		0.0044
梅　毒	Syphilis	93.44	107.51	0.0088	0.0174
钩 体 病	Leptospirosis				
血吸虫病	Schistosomiasis				
疟　疾	Malaria	0.017	0.013		

注:新生儿破伤风死亡率单位为千分率。
Note: The unit of incidence disease rate and death rate of newborn baby tetanus is 1‰.

19-19 城市前十位疾病死亡原因及构成
Death Causes and Percentage of 10 Major Diseases in Urban Areas

(2015 年)

疾病死亡原因	Cause of Death	死亡总人数 (人) Total Deaths (person)	占死亡总人数的比重 (%) Percentage to Total Deaths (%)
总计	**Total**	**9032**	**100.00**
心脏病	Heart Disease	2160	23.91
恶性肿瘤	Malignant Tumour	2026	22.43
脑血管病	Cerebrovasculat Diseases	1391	15.40
呼吸系统疾病	Disease of the Respiratory System	1236	13.68
伤害	Infections and Parasitic Diseases	640	7.09
内分泌营养代谢疾病	Endocrine, Nutritional Metabolic Disease	320	3.54
传染病	Endocrine, Nutritional and Metabolic Diseases	250	2.77
消化系统疾病	Diseases of the Digestive System	212	2.35
其他疾病	Others	177	1.96
围生期疾病	Perinatal Disease	141	1.56

注：统计范围包括乌鲁木齐市及辖区资料。
Note: Statistics in data covers Urumqi and its Districts.

19-20 安全生产情况
Basic Statistics on Work Safety

单位：人 (person)

项　目	Item	2014	2015
亿元新疆生产总值生产安全事故死亡人数	Mortality Rate of Work Safety Accident Average 100 Billion Yuan GDP	0.11	0.10
工矿商贸企业就业人员生产安全事故十万人死亡人数	Mortality Rate of Work Safety Accident of Employment in Industrial & Mining and Commercial & Tradal Enterprises Average 100 000 Persons	4.5	3.3
煤矿百万吨死亡人数	Mortality Rate of Coal Procuction Average 1 Million Tons	0.29	6.26
道路交通万车死亡人数	Mortality Rate of Highway Traffic Accident Average 10 000 Vehicles	3.95	0.09

19-21 社会福利事业单位基本情况
Basic Statistics on Social Welfare Institutions

(2015 年)

指　标	Item	院　数(个) Number of Homes (unit)	工作人员数(人) Number of Persons Engaged (person)	床位数(张) Number of Beds (unit)	年末收养人数(人) Number of Persons Housed (person)	#女　性 Female
总　计	**Total**	**344**	**5317**	**36135**	**24729**	**4990**
社会福利院	Social Welfare Homes	40	714	5640	5237	962
儿童福利院	Children Welfare Homes	69	647	7212	3993	1082
光荣院	Homes for Disabled Veterans	11	64	499	163	5
社会福利医院	Psychopathy Welfare Homes	8	1177	2592	2379	676
城镇老年性福利机构	Urban Elderly Welfare Units	91	2091	11761	7456	1332
农村老年性福利机构	Rural Elderly Welfare Units	111	534	7388	5043	896
荣誉军人康复医院	Recuperative Hospital for Soldiers with Honour	1	32	100	8	
其他收养性机构	Other Residential Institutions	13	58	943	450	37

19-22 社会福利事业、企业单位数和工作人员数
Number of Social Welfare Institutions and Enterprises and Persons Engaged

(2015 年)

项　目	Item	机构数(个) Number of Institutions or Enterprises (unit)	工作人员数(人) Number of Persons Engaged (person)
收养性福利事业单位	Adopting Social Welfare Institutions	283	3699
工商部门登记	Administravie Office of Industry and Commerce	1	26
编制部门登记	Organization Department	140	1442
民政部门登记	Civil Administration Department	106	2071
未登记	Un-register	36	160
社会福利企业	Social Welfare Enterprises	157	16574
优抚安置事业单位	Administration Agencies for Martyrs	42	493
救助类单位	Salvaged Deparement	66	398
殡葬服务事业单位	Funeral and Interment Institutions	139	836
福利彩票发行单位	Welfare Lottery-Ticked Issuance Unit	18	197
社区服务机构	Community Service Institutions	2091	9869

19-23 社会救济情况
Basic Statistics on Social Relief

指 标	Item	2015
城镇居民最低生活保障人数(人)	**Number of Urban Residents Receiving Minimum Living Allowance (person)**	**778569**
按人员性质分类	**by Quality of Staff**	
#女性	Female	371814
#残疾人	Disabled Person	54323
#三无人员	Three Non Person	37370
按人员年龄分类	**by Aged of Staff**	
成年人	Adult	547244
老年人	Old Folks	111462
在职人员	Full Employed Staff and Workers	7086
灵活就业人员	Flexible Employed Persons	97086
登记失业人员	Registered Employed Persons	91702
未登记失业人员	Unregistered Employed Persons	239908
未成年人	Minors	231325
在校生	Enrollment	151617
其他未成年人	Others	79708
城镇居民最低生活保障家庭数(户)	**Number of Urban Family Receiving Minimum Living Allowance (household)**	**354631**
农村最低生活保障人数(人)	**Number of Rural Residents Receiving Minimum Living Allowance (person)**	**1317586**
#女性	Female	566733
#老年人	Old Folks	400671
#未成年人	Minors	217890
#残疾人	Disabled Person	91309
农村最低生活保障家庭数(户)	**Number of Rural Family Receiving Minimum Living Allowance (household)**	**631562**

19-24 主要年份工会组织情况
Basic Statistics on Trades Unions in Main Years

年 份 Year	工会基层组织个数(个) Number of Grassroots Unions (unit)	全区已建工会组织的基本单位职工与会员人数(万人) Membership and Number of Staff and Workers in Grassroots Unions (10 000 persons)				专职工会干部(万人) Number of Full-time Personnel of Unions (10 000 persons)
		职工人数 Number of Staff and Workers	#女 Female	会员人数 Number of Membership	#女 Female	
1980	3255	84.20	30.25	67.13	20.42	0.48
1990	10685	231.48	90.64	196.58	76.97	0.79
1995	14457	271.43	114.13	254.49	104.97	1.19
2000	13016	211.73	90.80	200.80	84.93	0.59
2005	11721	232.78	97.50	232.03	97.20	0.41
2006	13163	302.05	130.12	263.80	115.64	0.69
2007	15040	323.37	139.45	289.65	124.23	0.60
2008	16880	337.80	147.31	308.81	134.71	0.55
2009	17849	351.69	146.56	326.91	136.48	0.70
2010	19668	371.23	153.55	342.07	147.54	0.60
2011	21023	386.47	159.54	355.78	150.67	0.72
2012	22682	393.94	165.98	371.14	157.39	1.07
2013	24517	387.40	157.40	373.30	153.94	0.72
2014	26073	396.08	161.60	383.48	157.58	0.96
2015	27440	408.97	163.80	396.48	160.73	1.10

19-25 残疾人事业基本情况
Basic Statistics on the Work for Persons with Disabilities

项 目	Item	2014	2015
康 复	**Rehabilitation**		
白内障复明	Sight-restoring of Cataract Surgery		
白内障复明手术(万例)	Sight-restoring Surgeries for Cataract Patients (10 000 cases)	1.28	1.30
低视力配用助视器(人)	Vision-aids Provided for Individuds with Low-vision (person)	4446	6543
聋儿康复	Rehabilitation of Children With Hearing Disability		
年收训聋儿(人)	Hearing and Speech Training (person)	147	205
聋儿入普幼普小率(%)	Enrollment Rate to General Infant School or Elementary School (%)	33	21
培训家长(人)	Parents Trained (person)	408	434
精神病防治康复	Prevention and Treatment of Mental Diseases		
开展精神病防治康复工作市县数(个)	Number of Counties Carried on the Works (unit)	69	69
综合防治康复精神病人数(万人)	Number of Mental Sicks Synthetically Prevented, Cured and Rehabilitated (10 000 persons)	1.60	1.58
监护率(%)	Guardianship Rate (%)	68.72	67.39
显好率(%)	Rate of Getting Better (%)	47.54	48.43
社会参与率(%)	Social Participation Rate (%)	29.02	27.61
肇事率(%)	Violent Everds Rate (%)		
救济贫困患者数(人)	Number of Poor Sufferer Relieved (person)	5436	5990
用品用具供应件数(万件)	Number of Appliances Supplied (10 000 units)	3.28	3.47
康复训练与服务	Rehabilitation Training and Service		
肢体残疾康复训练数(人)	Rehabilitation Training of Body Disabilities (person)	6608	4746
智力残疾儿童康复训练数(人)	Rehabilitation Training of Mental Disabilities Children (person)	2087	3385
教 育	**Education**		
未入学适龄残疾儿童(万人)	Suhool-age Disabied Children Unable to Enter School (10 000 persons)	0.39	0.74
残疾人中等职业学校(班)	Secondary Vocational Schools for PWDS		
残联系统办	Run by Institution of Disabled Person's	1	1
教育部门办	Run by Education	1	1
在校学生(万人)	Number of Enrollments (10 000 persons)	0.044	0.049

19-25 续表 Continued

项　目	Item	2014	2015
就　业	**Employment**		
城镇残疾人就业状况(万人)	Employment of Urban Handicappeds (10 000 persons)	7.61	6.74
当年安排就业	Persons Employed in the Year	0.56	0.52
按比例就业	Employment by Quota Scheme	0.17	0.14
集中就业	Employed in Collective Form	0.10	0.10
个体就业	Individual Employment	0.29	0.22
未安排就业	Unemployed	1.25	2.15
农村残疾人就业状况(万人)	Employment of Rural Handicapped (10 000 persons)		
就　业	Employed	22.70	22.30
未就业	Unemployed	3.79	3.79
残疾人就业服务机构(个)	Number of Institutions Engaging in Handicappeds Employment (unit)		
省	Provinces	1	1
地	Prefectures	14	15
市(含县级市)	Cities (Cities at County Level)	46	24
县	County	68	68
市辖区	Districts under the Jurisdiction of Cities	11	11
实施分散按比例就业的地区数(个)	Number of Regions Implemented the Policy of the Disperse Employment by Proportion (unit)		
省	Provinces	1	1
地	Prefectures	14	15
市(含县级市)	Cities (Cities at County Level)	16	24
县	County	68	68
市辖区	Districts under the Jurisdiction of Cities	11	11
残联组织建设	**Organization of Association for the Handicapped**		
残疾人工作者(万人)	Number of Workers for the Handicappeds (10 000 persons)	0.29	0.29

19-26 历届全区人民代表大会代表人数

Number of Deputies to All the Previous People's Congresses of Xinjiang

项目 Item	第一届 (1954) First Congress	第二届 (1959) Second Congress	第三届 (1964) Third Congress	第四届 (1975) Fourth Congress	第五届 (1978) Fifth Congress	第六届 (1983) Sixth Congress	第七届 (1988) Seventh Congress	第八届 (1993) Eighth Congress	第九届 (1998) Ninth Congress	第十届 (2003) Tenth Congress	第十一届 (2008) Eleventh Congress	第十二届 (2013) Twelfth Congress
代表总数(人) Total Number of All Deputies (person)	**376**	**386**	**453**	**809**	**672**	**550**	**550**	**542**	**550**	**550**	**550**	**550**
#中国共产党党员 Deputies from the Communist Party of China	178		240			374	357	381	396	396	352	356
占总数比重(%) Percentage to Total (%)	47.3		53.0			68.0	64.9	70.3	72.0	72.0	64.0	64.8
#少数民族 Deputies from Ethnic Minorities	331		383	510	430	357	363	355	363	363	363	364
占总数比重(%) Percentage to Total(%)	88.0		84.5	63.8	64.0	64.9	66.0	65.5	66.0	66.0	66.0	66.2
#妇 女 Female Deputies	52	61	89	200	146	17	126	123	135	135	143	139
占总数比重(%) Percentage to Total(%)	13.8	15.8	19.6	24.7	21.7	21.3	22.9	22.7	24.5	24.5	26.0	25.3

19-27 历届全区政治协商会议委员人数

Number of Deputies to All the Previous People's Political Consultative Conferences of Xinjiang

项目 Item	第一届 (1954) First Congress	第二届 (1959) Second Congress	第三届 (1964) Third Congress	第四届 (1978) Fourth Congress	第五届 (1983) Fifth Congress	第六届 (1988) Sixth Congress	第七届 (1993) Seventh Congress	第八届 (1998) Eighth Congress	第九届 (2003) Ninth Congress	第十届 (2008) Tenth Congress	第十一届 (2013) Eleventh Congress
委员总数(人) Total Number of All Deputies (person)	**141**	**275**	**303**	**407**	**441**	**429**	**416**	**444**	**470**	**515**	**522**
#中国共产党党员 Deputies from the Communist Party of China	28	57	65	149	158	157	161	183	196	225	258
占总数比重(%) Percentage to Total(%)	19.9	20.7	21.5	36.6	35.8	36.6	38.7	41.2	41.7	43.7	49.4
#少数民族 Deputies from Ethnic Minorities	121	196	205	221	253	245	204	246	246	263	256
占总数比重(%) Percentage to Total(%)	85.8	71.3	67.7	54.3	57.4	57.0	49.0	55.4	52.3	51.1	9.5
#妇 女 Female Deputies	10	28	28	40	49	63	66	82	95	125	137
占总数比重(%) Percentage to Total(%)	7.1	10.2	9.2	9.8	11.1	14.7	15.9	18.5	20.2	24.3	26.2

19-28 主要年份律师、公证、调解工作基本情况
Basic Statistics on Lawyers, Notarization and Mediation in Main Years

项　目	Item	1995	2000	2005	2010	2015
律师工作	**Lawyers**					
律师事务所(个)	Number of Law Offices (unit)	169	227	243	318	430
律师(人)	Number of Lawyers (person)	1705	2414	2088	2900	4272
#专职律师	Full-time Lawyers	1209	1508	1987	2704	3857
兼职律师	Part-time Lawyers	336	418	101	114	128
聘请担任常年法律顾问的单位(处)	Number of Units with Permanent Legal Advisors (unit)	2560	2613	2663	3858	4951
民事诉讼代理(件)	Agent of Civil Cases (case)	6380	16165	23389	38822	42164
刑事辩护及代理(件)	Defender and Agent of Criminal Cases (case)	5850	5826	7716	8510	11049
非诉讼法律事务(件)	Agent of Non-Litigious Legal Affairs (case)	5357	4810	7066	2450	1836
解答法律咨询(万件)	Agent of Legal Advisory Services (10 000 cases)	4.21	7.45	8.14	10.13	11.52
代写法律事务文书(万件)	Agent of Legal Documents Written on Behalf of Clients (10 000 cases)	1.06	1.94	3.00	2.16	2.99
公证工作	**Notarization**					
公证处(个)	Number of Notary Offices (unit)	126	131	126	125	126
公证员(人)	Notaries (person)	266	332	457	416	464
办理公证文书(万件)	Number of Notarized Document (10 000 cases)	10.11	18.85	18.05	30.93	35.29
人民调解工作	**Number of People's Mediation**					
人民调解委员会(个)	Number of People's Mediation Committees (unit)	19045	22294	15852	14157	14061
调解人员(万人)	Number of Mediators (10 000 persons)	12.04	10.04	7.86	7.62	6.92
调解民间纠纷(万件)	Number of Civil Disputes Mediated (10 000 cases)	9.18	8.09	6.83	17.21	21.81

19-29 调解民间纠纷分类
Number of Civil Disputes Mediated by Type

(2015 年)

项　目	Item	调解纠纷(件) Civil Disputes (case)	各类纠纷所占比重(%) Percentage (%)
总　计	**Total**	**218098**	**100**
婚姻家庭	Marriage and Family	51906	23.80
合　同	Contract	14958	6.86
劳　动	Labor	11919	5.46
土　地	Land	11554	5.30
征地拆迁	Requisitioned Land Demolition	673	0.31
房屋宅基地	Housing and Housing Sites	4552	2.09
消费纠纷	Consume Dispute	1244	0.57
邻　里	Neighbour Dispute	51735	23.71
损害赔偿	Compensation for Damages	14690	6.74
环境保护	Environment Protection	556	0.25
道路交通事故	Road Traffic Accidents	13392	6.14
物　业	Property Management	6157	2.82
医　疗	Medical Treatment	448	0.21
生产经营	Production and Operation	6382	2.93
其　他	Others	27932	12.81

19-30 火灾事故发生情况
Basic Statistics on Fire Accidents

(2015 年)

指　标	Item	合　计 Total	按事故发生程度分 By Serious Dgree of Fires			
			特　大 Extraordinarily Serious	重　大 Serious	较　大 Comparatively Serious	一　般 Ordinary
发生起数(起)	Fires　(case)	11969			1	11968
死亡(人)	Death (person)	35			6	29
受伤(人)	Injuries (person)	39			2	37
损失折款(万元)	Losses Converted into Cash (10 000 yuan)	11774.90			184.40	11590.50
平均每起事故损失(元)	Average Loss per Fire (yuan)	9838			1843530	9685

19-31 2013-2015 年历年交通事故发生情况
Basic Statistics on Traffic Accidents (2013-2015)

指　标	Item	2013	2014	2015
发生起数(起)	Traffic Accidents (case)	4923	4919	4992
死亡(人)	Death (person)	1828	1765	1881
受伤(人)	Injuries (person)	5632	5628	5747
损失折款(万元)	Losses Converted into Cash (10 000 yuan)	1316	1228	1263
平均每起事故损失(元)	Average Loss per Fire (yuan)	2673	2496	2530

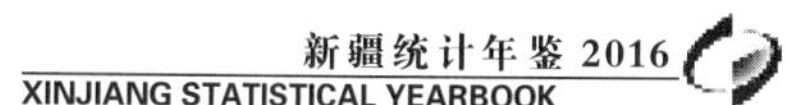

19-32 公安机关受理查处治安案件情况
Offense Cases Against Public Order Handled by Public Security Organs

单位：起 (2015 年) (case)

案件类别	Category of Cases	受理 Number of Cases Accepted to be Treated	查处 Number of Cases Investigated and Treated
总 计	**Total**	**121546**	**116132**
扰乱公共秩序	Disturbing Work or Public Order	3655	3581
扰乱单位秩序	Disturbing Business Orders	1152	1139
扰乱公共场所秩序	Disturbing the Orders in Public Places	723	720
寻衅滋事	Causing Quarrels and Making Troubles	856	821
其 他	Others	614	602
妨害公共安全	Disorderly Cordnct	710	696
非法携带枪支、弹药、管制刀具	Violation of Firearms Control Regulations	122	121
盗窃、损毁公共设施	Stealing and Damaging Public Facilities	162	149
其 他	Others	189	191
侵犯他人人身权利、财产权利	Offences Against, Citizens' Personal and Property Rights	78389	73252
侮辱、诽谤、诬告陷害	Insult, Slander and Circumvention	639	627
殴打他人	Beating Other Persons	54218	52372
故意伤害	Willfully Injuring Others	1860	1726
盗 窃	Stealing Property	13114	10846
诈 骗	Swindling, Seizing and Extorting Property	1284	987
抢 夺	Robbery and Snatch	82	71
敲诈勒索	Extertion and Blackmail	40	39
其 他	Others	1921	1869
妨害社会管理	Disorderly Social Management	38792	38603
阻碍执行职务	Obstructing Government Workers in Performing Their Duties	829	814
违反旅馆业管理	Violating the Hotel Management Regulations	2523	2517
违反房屋出租管理	Violating the Rent Control Regulations	10850	10849
卖淫、嫖娼	Prostitution or Soliciting Prostitutes	680	673
赌博或为赌博提供条件	Gambling	1749	1728
毒品违法活动	Illegal Drug Related Action	15417	15300
其 他	Others	5682	5666

19-33 2008-2015 年历年刑事案件中青少年犯罪情况
Juvenile Delinquency Among Criminal Cases(2008-2015)

单位：人 (person)

年 份 Year	刑事罪犯总数 Offenders	#青少年罪犯 Young Offenders	不满 18 岁 Less than 18	18 岁至 25 岁 Between 18 to 25	青少年罪犯占刑事罪犯 (%) Percentage to Total (%)
2008	37222	18317	5899	12418	49.20
2009	33121	15989	4538	11451	48.27
2010	29257	13299	4012	9287	45.45
2011	29690	12627	3697	8930	42.53
2012	30775	12738	3613	9125	41.39
2013	28981	11290	3215	8075	39.96
2014	34198	11846	2825	9021	34.64
2015	33176	10176	2491	7685	30.70

主要统计指标解释

医疗卫生机构 指从卫生行政部门取得《医疗机构执业许可证》、《计划生育技术服务许可证》，或从民政、工商行政、机构编制管理部门取得法人单位登记证书，为社会提供医疗保健、疾病控制、卫生监督服务或从事医学科研和医学在职培训等工作的单位。医疗卫生机构包括医院、基层医疗卫生机构、专业公共卫生机构、其他医疗卫生机构。

医院 包括综合医院、中医医院、中西医结合医院、民族医院、各类专科医院和护理院，不包括专科疾病防治院、妇幼保健院和疗养院。

基层医疗卫生机构 包括社区卫生服务中心、社区卫生服务站、街道卫生院、乡镇卫生院、村卫生室、门诊部、诊所(医务室)。

专业公共卫生机构 包括疾病预防控制中心、专科疾病防治机构、妇幼保健机构（含妇幼保健计划生育服务中心）、健康教育机构、急救中心（站）、采供血机构、卫生监督机构、取得《医疗机构执业许可证》或《计划生育技术服务许可证》的计划生育技术服务机构。

其他医疗卫生机构 包括疗养院、临床检验中心、医学科研机构、医学在职教育机构、医学考试中心、农村改水中心、人才交流中心、统计信息中心等卫生事业单位。

卫生人员 指在医院、基层医疗卫生机构、专业公共卫生机构及其他医疗卫生机构工作的职工，包括卫生技术人员、乡村医生和卫生员、其他技术人员、管理人员和工勤人员。一律按支付年底工资的在岗职工统计，包括各类聘任人员(含合同工)及返聘本单位半年以上人员，不包括临时工、离退休人员、退职人员、离开本单位仍保留劳动关系人员、本单位返聘和临聘不足半年人员。

卫生技术人员 包括执业医师、执业助理医师、注册护士、药师（士）、检验技师（士）、影像技师、卫生监督员和见习医（药、护、技）师（士）等卫生专业人员。不包括从事管理工作的卫生技术人员(如院长、副院长、党委书记等)。

执业医师 指《医师执业证》“级别”为“执业医师”且实际从事医疗、预防保健工作的人员，不包括实际从事管理工作的执业医师。执业医师类别分为临床、中医、口腔和公共卫生四类。

执业（助理）医师 指《医师执业证》“级别”为“执业助理医师”且实际从事医疗、预防保健工作的人员，不包括实际从事管理工作的执业助理医师。执业助理医师类别分为临床、中医、口腔和公共卫生四类。

每万人口执业(助理)医师 每万人口执业(助理)医师=（执业医师数+执业助理医师数)/人口数×10000。人口数系年末常住人口。

每万人口卫生技术人员 每万人口卫生技术人员=卫生技术人员数/人口数×10000。人口数系年末常住人口。

每万人口医疗卫生机构床位 每万人口医疗卫生机构床位=医疗卫生机构床位/人口数×10000。人口数系年末常住人口。

甲乙类法定报告传染病发病率 是指某年某地区每10万人口中甲、乙类法定报告传染病发病数。即甲乙类法定报告传染病发病率=甲、乙类法定报告传染病发病人数/人口数×100000。

甲乙类法定报告传染病死亡率 是指某年某地区每10万人口中甲、乙类法定报告传染病死亡数。即甲乙类法定报告传染病死亡率=甲、乙类法定报告传染病死亡人数/人口数×100000。

甲乙类法定报告传染病病死率 是指某年某地区甲、乙类法定报告传染病死亡人数与发病人数之比。即甲乙类法定报告传染病病死率=甲、乙类法定报告传染病死亡人数/发病人数×100%。

参加新农合人数 指根据本地新农合实施方案到年内新农合筹资截止时已缴纳新农合资金的人口数。

新农合当年基金支出 指本年度实际从新农合基金帐户中支出用于新农合补偿的资金。

新农合补偿受益人次 指年内新农合参合人员因病就医获得补偿的人次数，包括住院、家庭帐户形式、门诊、特殊病种大额门诊、住院正常分娩、体检和其他补偿人次之和。

新农合本年度筹资总额 指为本年度筹集的、实际进入新农合专用帐户的基金数额。包括本年度中央及地方财政配套资金、农民个人交纳资金（含民政部门及其他相关部门代缴的救助资金）、新农合基金本年度产生的全部利息收入及其他渠道实际筹集到的新农合基金额。筹资数额以进入新农合专用帐户的基金数额为准，不含上年结转额资金。

卫生总费用 指一个国家或地区在一定时期内，为开展卫生服务活动从全社会筹集的卫生资源的货币总额，按来源法核算。它反映一定经济条件下，政府、社会和居民个人对卫生保健的重视程度和费用负担水平，以及卫生筹资模式的主要特征和卫生筹资的公平性合理性。

政府卫生支出 指各级政府用于医疗卫生服务、医疗保障补助、卫生和医疗保险行政管理、人口与计划生育事务支出等各项事业的经费。

社会卫生支出 指政府支出外的社会各界对卫生事业的资金投入。包括社会医疗保障支出、商业健康保险费、社会办医支出、社会捐赠援助、行政事业性收费收入等。

个人现金卫生支出 指城乡居民在接受各类医疗卫生服务时的现金支付，包括享受多种医疗保险制度的居民就医时自付的费用。可分为城镇居民、农村居民个人现金卫生支出，反映城乡居民医疗卫生费用的负担程度。

人均卫生费用 即某年卫生总费用与同期平均人口数之比。

社会福利事业单位 指集中收养社会孤老、残、幼的机构，包括由民政部门管理的社会福利院、儿童福利院、精神病人福利院和城镇集体举办的福利院及农村集体举办的敬老院以及优抚医院和具有收养能力的社区服务中心等。该指标主要反映我国在社会福利性单位投入的水平。

社会福利事业单位收养人数 包括民政部门管理和城镇、农村集体举办的社会福利事业单位中收养的老人、少年儿童、缺乏生活自理能力的残疾人员和精神病人。该指标主要反映收养性社会福利单位的收养能力。

社会福利企业 指以集中安置有一定劳动能力的残疾人员就业为目的（残疾职工占生产人员 10%以上）、带有社会福利性质的企业总称。社会福利企业分类为：社会福利工厂、假肢厂和其他福利企业。性质分为：国有、集体和其他性质。

城市居民最低生活保障人数 指在报告期末家庭平均收入在当地规定的最低生活保障线以下的城镇居民数。包括“三无”对象，失业人员和在职、下岗、退休人员等。

农村居民最低生活保障人数 指报告期末在建立农村最低生活保障制度的地区，得到当地政府或集体给予最低生活保障的农业人口家庭人数。

综合防治康复精神病人数 指在开展精神病防治康复工作地区，采取不同形式，接受综合性防治康复措施、开放式管理的精神病人数。该指标主要反映精神病患者接受治疗康复情况。

监护率 指通过监护小组、家庭病床、工疗站、社会就业以及精神卫生机构，接受社会化、综合性、开放式治疗与康复的精神病人占经调查摸底、登记在册的精神病人数的百分比。该指标主要反映对精神病患者落实治疗康复措施的情况。

社会参与率 指生活能自理，并参加生产劳动和社会生活的精神病人数占监护精神病人数的百分比。该指标主要反映精神病人康复状况和参与社会的情况。

未入学学龄残疾儿童少年 指截止到本年度 12 月 31 日，《义务教育法》规定的入学年龄段（6-14 周岁或 7-15 周岁)内的，因各种原因未能入学的各类残疾儿童少年。

律师 指依法取得律师执业证书，担任法律顾问，民事(刑事、行政)案件代理人、刑事案件辩护人、办理非诉讼业务，解答法律询问，代写法律事务文书等，为社会提供法律服务的人员。

公证人员 指在公证处工作的人员总称，包括公证处主任、副主任、公证员、公证员助理(助理公证员)和其他从事辅助性工作的人员。

公证文书 指公证处根据当事人申请，依照事实和法律，按照法定程序制作的，具有法律效力的司法证明文书。

调解员 指在人民调解委员会担负调解民间纠纷工作的人员，包括调解委员会的委员和调解小组的调解员。该指标主要反映从事人民调解工作的人员数量。

调解民间纠纷 指调解委员会按照法律规定，根据自愿原则，用说服教育的方法调解民间发生的有关民事权利和义务争执的件数，包括调解成功数和调解未成功数。该指标主要反映人民调解委员会的工作量。

特大交通事故 指一次造成死亡 3 人以上，或者重伤 11 人以上，或者死亡 1 人，同时重伤 8 人以上，或者死亡 2 人，同时重伤 5 人以上，或者财产损失 6 万元以上的交通事故。

重大交通事故 指一次造成死亡 1 至 2 人，或者重伤 3 人以上 10 人以下，或者财产损失 3 万元以上不足 6 万元的交通事故。

特大火灾 指造成 30 人以上死亡，或者 100 人以上重伤，或者 1 亿元以上直接财产损失的火灾。

重大火灾 指造成 10 人以上 30 人以下死亡，或者 50 人以上 100 人以下重伤，或者 5000 万元以上 1 亿元以下直接财产损失的火灾。

较大火灾 指造成 3 人以上 10 人以下死亡，或者 10 人以上 50 人以下重伤，或者 1000 万元以上 5000 万元以下直接财产损失的火灾。

一般火灾 指造成3人以下死亡，或者10人以下重伤，或者1000万元以下直接财产损失的火灾。

Explanatory Notes on Main Statistical Indicators

Medical and Health Care Institutions refer to the units which have been qualified the Certification of Health Care Institution, certification of family planning technical service by the administration of public health, or qualified the Certification of Corporate Unit by the civil affairs, administration for industry and commerce, commission office for public sector reform, and engaging in medical care, disease prevention and control, health supervision and inspection, medicine research and on-job training, etc., including: hospitals, health care institutions at grass-root level, specialized public health institutions, and other medical and health care institutions.

Hospitals include general hospitals, hospitals specialized in traditional Chinese medicine, hospitals of integrated traditional Chinese and western medicine, ethnic hospitals, specialized hospitals and nursing hospitals, excluding specialized disease prevention and treatment institutes, maternal and child health care hospitals and convalescent hospitals.

Health Care Institutions at Grass-root Level include community health service centers,community health service stations, urban health centers, township health centers, village clinics, outpatient departments and clinics (health centers).

Specialized Public Health Institutions include centers for disease control and prevention, specialized disease prevention and treatment institutions, women and children care agencies(including women and children health care family planning service center), health education institutions, first aid centers, blood gathering and supplying institutions, health supervision and inspection agencies, and family planning technical service centers that obtained the Certification of Health Care Institution or certification of family planning technical service centers.

Other Medical and Health Care Institutions include sanatoriums, clinical laboratory centers, medicinal scientific research institutions, on-job training institutions, medical examination centers, rural water improvement centers, talent exchange centers, and statistical information centers, etc.

Health Care Employees refer to all employees engaged in the health care institutions, such as hospitals, health care institutions at grass-root level, specialized public health institutions, and other medical and health care institutions, including medical technical personnel, village doctors and assistants, other technical personnel, managerial and service staff. The data is based on the year end payroll, including personnel hired (including contract labor) and re-employed after retirement by the institution for over half a year and excluding temporary workers, retired personnel, resigned personnel, personnel who have left the institution but kept the contract relation and personnel who are re-employed after retirement or temporarily employed for less than half a year.

Medical Technical Personnel refer to the professional staff engaged in health care, including licensed doctors, licensed assistant doctors, registered nurses, pharmacists, laboratory technicians, imaging staff, health care supervisors and intern doctors, pharmacists, nurses, and technical personnel, excluding the medical technical personnel engaged in managerial job(e.g. president, vice president and secretary of the party committee etc).

Licensed Doctors refer to the medical workers who have obtained the licenses of qualified doctors and are employed in medical treatment, disease prevention or healthcare institutions, excluding the licensed doctors engaged in management job. The licensed doctors are divided into 4 categories: clinician, Chinese medicine physicians, dentist and public health physicians.

Licensed Assistant Doctors refer to the medical workers who have obtained the licenses of qualified assistant doctors and are employed in medical treatment, disease prevention or healthcare institutions, excluding the licensed assistant doctors engaged in management job. The classification of licensed assistant doctors is clinician, Chinese medicine, dentist and public health.

Number of Licensed (Assistant) Doctors per 10000 Population The formula is:

Number of Licensed Doctors per 10000 Population = (Number of Licensed Doctors + Number of Licensed Assistant Doctors) / Population *10000

The population is the figure of usual population at year-end.

Number of Medical Technical Personnel per 10000 Population The formula is:

Number of Medical Technical Personnel per 10000 Population = Number of Medical Technical Personnel / Population *10000

The population is the figure of usual population at year-end.

Number of Beds of Medical and Health Care Institutions per 10000 Population the formula is:

Number of Beds of Medical and Health Care Institutions per 10000 Population = Number of Beds of Medical and Health Care Institutions / Population *10000

The population is the figure of usual population at year-end.

Incidence Rate of A and B Type of Notifiable Infectious Diseases refer to the incidence cases notifiable class A and class B infectious diseases per 100 thousand population in the reference region in the reference year. The formula is:

Incidence Rate of A and B Type of Notifiable Infectious Diseases = Incidence Cases Notifiable Class A and Class B Infectious Diseases / Population *100000

Death Rate of A and B Type of Notifiable Infectious Diseases refer to the death cases notifiable class A and class B infectious diseases per 100 thousand population in the reference region in the reference year. The formula is:

Death Rate of A and B Type of Notifiable Infectious Diseases= Death Cases Notifiable Class A and Class B Infectious Diseases / Population *100000

Mortality Rate of A and B Type Notifiable Infectious Diseases refer to the ratio of death cases notifiable class A and class B infectious diseases to the incidence cases in the reference region in the reference year. The formula is:

Mortality Rate of A and B Type Notifiable Infectious Diseases = Death Cases Notifiable Class A and Class B Infectious Diseases / Incidence Cases *100%

Number of Persons Participated in the New Rural Cooperative Medical System refers to the number of persons who have given payment to the new cooperative medical system by the deadline of fundraising during the year according to the implementation plan of the new system.

Expenditure of Funds for the New Rural Cooperative Medical System This Year refers to expenditures on compensation funds for the new rural cooperative medical system from the fund account of new cooperative medical system this year.

Persons Benefited from the Compensation Expenditure of New Rural Cooperative Medical System refers to the number of person-times of those who participate in the new system and have been compensated for medical treatment in the year, including hospitalization, family account form, out-patient, large special diseases out-patient, normal childbirth in hospital, medical examination and other compensations.

Funds Raised for the New Rural Cooperative Medical System within the Reference Year refers to the amount of funds raised within the reference year and put into the special new rural cooperative medical account, including the matching funds of central and local governments, paid money by farmers (including relief funds paid by the civil affairs department and other relevant departments), all the interest income generated this year of the funds and funds actually raised from other channels this year. The amount of funding equals to the funds entering into the special new rural cooperative medical account, excluding the carry-over funds from the previous year.

Total Expenditure on Public Health refers to the total monetary value of health resources in a country or a region collected by the whole society for public health based on source approach. It reflects the attention and affordability of the government, society and individual for public health and the major characteristics, justice and rationality of the health fund-raising model under certain economic circumstance.

Government Expenditure on Public Health refers to the expenditure of the governments at all levels on medical and health care services, medical subsidies, health administration and health insurance management, and undertakings of family planning etc.

Social Expenditure on Public Health refers to all inputs of society except the government in public health including the expenditures on social medical security, commercial health insurance, private expenditure on operation of medical and health care, social donation and contribution, and income from administrative fees etc.

Individual Cash Expenditure on Health refers to expenditure in cash on various health services by rural and urban residents, including self payments of residents within the system of multi-medical insurance. It can be categorized as cash expenditure on health by urban and rural residents and reflects their affordability of public health.

Average Expenditure on Health refers to the ratio of total expenditure on health in a year to the average population.

Social Welfare Institutions refer to institutions taking care of old pople without children, handicapped people and orphans. They include social welfare institutions run by civil affairs departments, children welfare institutions, social welfare institutions for mental patients, collective-owned old peoples homes in rural areas, convalescent homes and community service centers with the capaCity of receiving those people. This indicator reflects the input in social welfare institutions.

Number of People Taken in by Social Welfare Institutions refers to the number of old people, children, totally dependent handicapped people and mental patients taken in by social welfare institutions run by civil affairs departments and those run by collective units in urban and rural areas. This indicator reflects the cap a City of social welfare institutions.

Social Welfare Enterprises refer to those welfare-oriented enterprises employing a significant number of handicapped people with certain labour ability (handicapped employees shall exceed 10% of the production staff). They can be categorized as welfare factories, artificial limb plants and other welfare enterprises. They can be in the form of state ownership, collective ownership or other kinds of ownership.

Number of Urban Residents Entitled to Minimum Living Allowances refers to the number of those whose average family income is below a minimum local standard by the end of the reporting period, including both the employed and unemployed, laid off and retired, and those jobless people without stable residence or valid IDs.

Number of Rural Residents Entitled to Minimum Living Allowances refers to the number of those receiving the minimum living allowances from the local government or community in the rural areas where this allowances system is in place as of the end of the reference period.

Number of Mental Patients under Integrated Prevention and Rehabilitation Program refers to mental disease patients receiving integrated prevention and rehabilitation treatment of various forms under open environment in areas with mental disease rehabilitation programs. This indicator reflects the condition of metal patients receiving rehabilitation treatment.

Supervision Rate refers to the percentage of patients among the total number of registered mental disease patients, who participate in social integrated and open treatment and rehabilitation programs through various forms such as supervision groups, family treatment, employment or guidance from psychiatric institutions. This indicator reflects the implementation of various measures aimed at rehabilitating those metal patients.

Social Participation Rate of Mental Patients refers to proportion of mental disease patients who are able to manage their daily life and participate in economic activities to the total number of mental disease patients under supervision. This indicator reflects the condition of recovery of those metal patient sand their participation in social activities.

Handicapped School-age Children without School Attendance refers to the number of handicapped children of the school age in accordance with the Law on Compulsory Education (6 to 14 years old or 7 to 15 years old) who fail to attend any schools for various reasons as of December 31 of the current year.

Lawyers are certified legal workers according to law, and who are employed by legal counseling firms to act as legal advisers, agents in criminal or civil lawsuits, or defenders in criminal lawsuits, or to handle non-litigious legal affairs, to advise on matters of law or t o write legal papers for others, and provide service to the public.

Notary Personnel refers to people working for notary offices including: directors, deputy directors, notaries, assistant notaries, and other people providing assistance.

Notary Documents refer to legally binding judicial notary documents developed at the request of the interested party based on facts and the law following certain legal proceedings.

Mediators refer to workers on peoples mediation committees responsible for mediating in civil disputes and cases of slight infraction of the law. They include members of the mediation committees and mediators of mediation groups. This indicator reflects the number of people engaged in meditation.

Mediation of Civil Disputes refers to number of cases made by mediation committees in mediating in civil disputes concerning civil rights and duties through persuasion and education in accordance witht he provisions of lawona voluntary basis, so as to solve disputes by helping the parties involved come to an agreement and understanding, including those unsuccessful ones. This indicator reflects the workload of the mediation committees.

Extraordinarily Serious Traffic Accident refers to an accident which has caused 3 or more deaths; or over 11 serious injuries; or 1 death and over 8 serious injuries; or 2 deaths and over 5 serious injuries; or a loss over 60 thousand yuan.

Serious Traffic Accident refers to an accident which has caused 1 or 2 deaths; or 3 to 10 serious injuries; or a loss over 30 thousand yuan to 60 thousand yuan.

Extraordinarily Serious Fire Case refers to a case which has caused over 30 deaths; or over 100 serious injuries; or a direct property loss over 100 million yuan.

Serious Fire Case refers to a case which has caused over 10 to 30 deaths; or over 50 to 100 serious injuries; or a direct property loss over 50 million to 100 million yuan.

Comparatively Serious Fire Case refers to a case which has caused over 3 to 10 deaths; or over 10 to 50 serious injuries; or a direct property loss over 10 million to 50 million yuan.

Ordinary Fire Case refers to a case which has caused less than 3 deaths; or less than 10 serious injuries; or a direct property loss less than 10 million yuan.

各地州市主要经济指标排序

RANKING OF MAIN ECONOMIC INDICATORS BY PREFECTURE, AUTONOMOUS PREFECTURE, CITY AND COUNTY OF XINJIANG

第二十篇　各地州市主要经济指标排序

本篇主要内容和资料来源

本篇反映2015年新疆各地州（市）主要经济指标排序情况。

本篇资料由新疆维吾尔自治区统计局国民经济综合统计处根据新疆维吾尔自治区统计局各相关专业处提供资料整理。

Ranking of Main Economic Indicators by prefecture, autonomous prefecture, city and county of Xinjiang

Main Content and Source of Data

Data in this chapter mainly include main social economic statistics by prefecture, autonomous prefecture, city and county in 2015.

Data on this chapter are compiled by the Department of Comprehensive Statistic, XBS according to the data provided by the related department of Statistics Bureau of Xinjiang Uygur Autonomous Region.

20-1 各地、州、市生产总值

Gross Regional Product by Prefecture, Autonomous Prefecture and City

单位：万元 (2015 年) (10 000 yuan)

地 区	Region	地区生产总值 Gross Regional Product	位次 Rank	第一产业增加值 Primary Industry	位次 Rank
乌鲁木齐市	Urumqi city	26316398	1	316439	12
克拉玛依市	Karamay city	6294299	7	51436	15
石河子市	Shihezi city	3157843	10	107540	14
吐鲁番市	Turpan City	2085846	14	457903	10
哈密地区	Hami [Kumul] Administrative Offices	4235687	9	394773	11
昌吉回族自治州	Changji Hui Autonomous Prefecture	11400132	2	2491462	1
伊犁哈萨克自治州	Ili Kazak Autonomous Prefecture	16243371		4486234	
伊犁州直属县(市)	Counties (Cities) Direct Under Ili Prefecture	8090572	5	1879565	5
塔城地区	Tacheng [Tarbagatai] Administrative Offices	5931633	8	2140806	4
阿勒泰地区	Altay Administrative Offices	2221166	13	465863	9
博尔塔拉蒙古自治州	Bortala Mongol Autonomous Prefecture	2872055	11	636151	7
巴音郭楞蒙古自治州	Bayangol Mongol Autonomous Prefecture	10390002	3	1814339	6
阿克苏地区	Aksu Administrative Offices	8101842	4	2362121	2
克孜勒苏柯尔克孜自治州	Kizilsu Kirgiz Autonomous Prefecture	1000297	15	141662	13
喀什地区	Kashgar [Kaxgar] Administrative Offices	7801202	6	2267496	3
和田地区	Hotan Administrative Offices	2340523	12	626682	8

地 区	Region	第二产业增加值 Secondary Industry	位次 Rank	第三产业增加值 Tertiary Industry	位次 Rank	人均地区生产总值(元) Per-capita GDP (yuan)	位次 Rank
乌鲁木齐市	Urumqi city	7873749	1	18126210	1	74340	3
克拉玛依市	Karamay city	4105309	4	2137554	7	131014	1
石河子市	Shihezi city	1854032	9	1196271	12	83701	2
吐鲁番市	Turpan City	785413	13	842530	14	32415	10
哈密地区	Hami [Kumul] Administrative Offices	2282926	8	1557988	9	68669	6
昌吉回族自治州	Changji Hui Autonomous Prefecture	5399622	3	3509048	3	71251	5
伊犁哈萨克自治州	Ili Kazak Autonomous Prefecture	4827709		6929428		34277	
伊犁州直属县(市)	Counties (Cities) Direct Under Ili Prefecture	2342445	7	3868562	2	28755	11
塔城地区	Tacheng [Tarbagatai] Administrative Offices	1682422	10	2108406	8	45964	8
阿勒泰地区	Altay Administrative Offices	802842	12	952461	13	34996	9
博尔塔拉蒙古自治州	Bortala Mongol Autonomous Prefecture	817767	11	1418137	10	59641	7
巴音郭楞蒙古自治州	Bayangol Mongol Autonomous Prefecture	5846537	2	2729126	6	73649	4
阿克苏地区	Aksu Administrative Offices	2561723	5	3177998	4	28477	12
克孜勒苏柯尔克孜自治州	Kizilsu Kirgiz Autonomous Prefecture	300533	15	558102	15	16777	14
喀什地区	Kashgar [Kaxgar] Administrative Offices	2407990	6	3125716	5	17431	13
和田地区	Hotan Administrative Offices	347220	14	1366621	11	10215	15

20-2 各地、州、市人口状况

Population Status by Prefecture, Autonomous Prefecture and City

单位：万人 (2015 年) (10 000 persons)

地区	Region	总人口 Total Population	位次 Rank	城镇人口 Urban Population	位次 Rank
乌鲁木齐市	Urumqi City	266.83	3	206.35	1
克拉玛依市	Karamay City	29.97	15	29.68	11
石河子市	Shihezi City	63.26	11	42.69	9
吐鲁番市	Turpan City	65.19	10	23.59	13
哈密地区	Hami [Kumul] Administrative Offices	61.67	12	33.71	10
昌吉回族自治州	Changji Hui Autonomous Prefecture	139.28	7	57.61	7
伊犁哈萨克自治州	Ili Kazak Autonomous Prefecture	469.63		203.58	
伊犁州直属县(市)	Counties (Cities) Direct Under Ili Prefecture	300.42	2	131.08	2
塔城地区	Tacheng [Tarbagatai] Administrative Offices	102.42	8	45.55	8
阿勒泰地区	Altay Administrative Offices	66.80	9	26.95	12
博尔塔拉蒙古自治州	Bortala Mongol Autonomous Prefecture	47.97	14	23.14	14
巴音郭楞蒙古自治州	Bayangol Mongol Autonomous Prefecture	139.38	6	63.75	5
阿克苏地区	Aksu Administrative Offices	253.05	4	83.04	4
克孜勒苏柯尔克孜自治州	Kizilsu Kirgiz Autonomous Prefecture	59.61	13	12.74	15
喀什地区	Kashgar [Kaxgar] Administrative Offices	449.92	1	109.01	3
和田地区	Hotan Administrative Offices	232.43	5	61.84	6

地区	Region	乡村人口 Rural Population	位次 Rank	人口自然增长率(‰) Natural Growth Rate (‰)	位次 Rank
乌鲁木齐市	Urumqi City	60.48	7	6.08	9
克拉玛依市	Karamay City	0.29	15	7.80	8
石河子市	Shihezi City	20.57	14	1.01	15
吐鲁番市	Turpan City	41.60	10	3.14	14
哈密地区	Hami [Kumul] Administrative Offices	27.96	12	3.48	13
昌吉回族自治州	Changji Hui Autonomous Prefecture	81.67	5	3.63	12
伊犁哈萨克自治州	Ili Kazak Autonomous Prefecture	266.05		9.10	
伊犁州直属县(市)	Counties (Cities) Direct Under Ili Prefecture	169.34	4	10.41	5
塔城地区	Tacheng [Tarbagatai] Administrative Offices	56.87	8	5.75	11
阿勒泰地区	Altay Administrative Offices	39.85	11	8.32	7
博尔塔拉蒙古自治州	Bortala Mongol Autonomous Prefecture	24.83	13	6.06	10
巴音郭楞蒙古自治州	Bayangol Mongol Autonomous Prefecture	75.63	6	8.33	6
阿克苏地区	Aksu Administrative Offices	170.01	3	18.41	2
克孜勒苏柯尔克孜自治州	Kizilsu Kirgiz Autonomous Prefecture	46.87	9	16.40	4
喀什地区	Kashgar [Kaxgar] Administrative Offices	340.91	1	26.06	1
和田地区	Hotan Administrative Offices	170.59	2	17.27	3

注：城镇、乡村人口按公安年报口径计算。
Note: The urban and rural population in Prefecture, Autonomous Prefecture and City are calculated on the annals of public security.

20-3 各地、州、市全社会固定资产投资
Total Investment in Fixed Assets by Prefecture, Autonomous Prefecture and City

单位：万元 (2015 年) (10 000 yuan)

地区	Region	合计 Total	位次 Rank	建筑工程 Construction Works	位次 Rank
乌鲁木齐市	Urumqi City	16074304	1	9099166	1
克拉玛依市	Karamay City	4199548	10	3231076	8
石河子市	Shihezi City	2347728	14	1001379	15
吐鲁番市	Turpan City	4587089	9	2818815	11
哈密地区	Hami [Kumul] Administrative Offices	9159381	3	3004080	9
昌吉回族自治州	Changji Hui Autonomous Prefecture	16026331	2	8985146	2
伊犁哈萨克自治州	Ili Kazak Autonomous Prefecture	14483694		10491600	
伊犁州直属县(市)	Counties (Cities) Direct Under Ili Prefecture	7017654	6	4703188	5
塔城地区	Tacheng [Tarbagatai] Administrative Offices	4875188	8	3653019	7
阿勒泰地区	Altay Administrative Offices	2590852	13	2135393	12
博尔塔拉蒙古自治州	Bortala Mongol Autonomous Prefecture	3010301	12	2080453	13
巴音郭楞蒙古自治州	Bayangol Mongol Autonomous Prefecture	7198562	5	4754290	4
阿克苏地区	Aksu Administrative Offices	6264621	7	4580829	6
克孜勒苏柯尔克孜自治州	Kizilsu Kirgiz Autonomous Prefecture	1354750	15	1116053	14
喀什地区	Kashgar [Kaxgar] Administrative Offices	9081682	4	7162484	3
和田地区	Hotan Administrative Offices	3284914	11	2849295	10

地区	Region	安装工程 Installation Works	位次 Rank	设备工具器具购置 Purchase of Equipment and Instruments	位次 Rank	其他费用 Others	位次 Rank
乌鲁木齐市	Urumqi City	1662126	1	2825212	3	2487800	1
克拉玛依市	Karamay City	407043	8	420037	12	141392	9
石河子市	Shi Hezi City	356194	9	839736	8	150419	8
吐鲁番市	Turpan City	429955	7	1218662	6	119657	10
哈密地区	Hami [Kumul] Administrative Offices	1035062	3	4387535	2	732704	2
昌吉回族自治州	Changji Hui Autonomous Prefecture	1414412	2	5292653	1	334120	6
伊犁哈萨克自治州	Ili Kazak Autonomous Prefecture	894850		2371118		726126	
伊犁州直属县(市)	Counties (Cities) Direct Under Ili Prefecture	527875	6	1271254	5	515337	3
塔城地区	Tacheng [Tarbagatai] Administrative Offices	256399	11	807637	9	158133	7
阿勒泰地区	Altay Administrative Offices	110576	12	292227	13	52656	14
博尔塔拉蒙古自治州	Bortala Mongol Autonomous Prefecture	128509	13	694027	11	107312	11
巴音郭楞蒙古自治州	Bayangol Mongol Autonomous Prefecture	318967	10	1610048	4	515257	4
阿克苏地区	Aksu Administrative Offices	836677	4	776763	10	70352	13
克孜勒苏柯尔克孜自治州	Kizilsu Kirgiz Autonomous Prefecture	44405	15	189023	14	5269	15
喀什地区	Kashgar [Kaxgar] Administrative Offices	593615	5	968380	7	357203	5
和田地区	Hotan Administrative Offices	229174	12	121605	15	84840	12

20-4 各地、州、市农林牧渔业总产值

Gross Output Value of Agriculture, Forestry, Animal Husbandry and Fishery by Prefecture, Autonomous Prefecture and City

单位：万元 (2015 年) (10 000 yuan)

地区	Region	农林牧渔业总产值 Total	位次 Rank	农业 Farming	位次 Rank	林业 Forestry	位次 Rank
乌鲁木齐市	Urumqi City	402296	12	170123	13	10987	11
克拉玛依市	Karamay City	125771	14	45629	14	29501	5
吐鲁番市	Turpan City	779627	9	645575	9	6341	13
哈密地区	Hami [Kumul] Administrative Offices	524009	11	284059	11	14997	10
昌吉回族自治州	Changji Hui Autonomous Prefecture	3492034	2	1493599	5	26798	6
伊犁哈萨克自治州	Ili Kazak Autonomous Prefecture	6094421		3337500		97672	
伊犁州直属县(市)	Counties (Cities) Direct Under Ili Prefecture	2652667	6	1158994	6	63175	2
塔城地区	Tacheng [Tarbagatai] Administrative Offices	2683334	5	1778175	4	17711	8
阿勒泰地区	Altay Administrative Offices	758420	10	400331	10	16786	9
博尔塔拉蒙古自治州	Bortala Mongol Autonomous Prefecture	855894	8	666986	8	5256	14
巴音郭楞蒙古自治州	Bayangol Mongol Autonomous Prefecture	2735505	4	2107967	3	41633	3
阿克苏地区	Aksu Administrative Offices	3086945	3	2452367	2	31320	4
克孜勒苏柯尔克孜自治州	Kizilsu Kirgiz Autonomous Prefecture	307020	13	177337	12	7075	12
喀什地区	Kashgar [Kaxgar] Administrative Offices	4790888	1	3371722	1	109689	1
和田地区	Hotan Administrative Offices	1291237	7	858843	7	26506	7

地区	Region	牧业 Animal Husbandry	位次 Rank	渔业 Fishery	位次 Rank	农林牧渔服务业 Serviceto Farming, Forestry, Animal Husbandary and Fishery	位次 Rank
乌鲁木齐市	Urumqi City	207657	10	7219	7	6310	14
克拉玛依市	Karamay City	41622	14	990	12	8029	12
吐鲁番市	Turpan City	117426	12	703	13	9582	11
哈密地区	Hami [Kumul] Administrative Offices	215929	9	2463	11	6561	13
昌吉回族自治州	Changji Hui Autonomous Prefecture	1917315	1	20770	2	33552	7
伊犁哈萨克自治州	Ili Kazak Autonomous Prefecture	2525366		37074		96809	
伊犁州直属县(市)	Counties (Cities) Direct Under Ili Prefecture	1369985	2	16884	3	43629	5
塔城地区	Tacheng [Tarbagatai] Administrative Offices	842304	4	5120	8	40024	6
阿勒泰地区	Altay Administrative Offices	313077	8	15070	4	13156	10
博尔塔拉蒙古自治州	Bortala Mongol Autonomous Prefecture	131041	11	4363	9	48248	4
巴音郭楞蒙古自治州	Bayangol Mongol Autonomous Prefecture	493411	5	10756	6	81738	3
阿克苏地区	Aksu Administrative Offices	492519	6	21788	1	88951	2
克孜勒苏柯尔克孜自治州	Kizilsu Kirgiz Autonomous Prefecture	106675	13	301	14	15632	9
喀什地区	Kashgar [Kaxgar] Administrative Offices	1201521	3	14655	5	93301	1
和田地区	Hotan Administrative Offices	384767	7	3896	10	17225	8

注：本表按当年价格计算。
Notes：Data in this table are calculated at current prices.

20-5 各地、州、市主要农产品产量

Yield of Major Farm Crops by Prefecture, Autonomous Prefecture and City

单位：吨 (2015 年) (ton)

地区	Region	粮食 Grain	位次 Rank	棉花 Cotton	位次 Rank
乌鲁木齐市	Urumqi City	102912	12	1166	13
克拉玛依市	Karamay City	35187	13	10375	12
吐鲁番市	Turpan City	14952	14	32321	9
哈密地区	Hami [Kumul] Administrative Offices	151579	11	52123	8
昌吉回族自治州	Changji Hui Autonomous Prefecture	2273832	4	149907	6
伊犁哈萨克自治州	Ili Kazak Autonomous Prefecture	7188467		420817	
伊犁州直属县(市)	Counties (Cities) Direct Under Ili Prefecture	3093864	2	13258	11
塔城地区	Tacheng [Tarbagatai] Administrative Offices	3427222	1	407559	4
阿勒泰地区	Altay Administrative Offices	667391	9		
博尔塔拉蒙古自治州	Bortala Mongol Autonomous Prefecture	902565	7	164765	5
巴音郭楞蒙古自治州	Bayangol Mongol Autonomous Prefecture	788621	8	438105	3
阿克苏地区	Aksu Administrative Offices	2056790	5	841753	1
克孜勒苏柯尔克孜自治州	Kizilsu Kirgiz Autonomous Prefecture	351865	10	18485	10
喀什地区	Kashgar [Kaxgar] Administrative Offices	2962980	3	799841	2
和田地区	Hotan Administrative Offices	1122718	6	55828	7

地区	Region	油料 Oil Bearing Crops	位次 Rank	甜菜 Beetroots	位次 Rank
乌鲁木齐市	Urumqi City	8032	10	507	9
克拉玛依市	Karamay City	4824	11	26400	7
吐鲁番市	Turpan City	1694	12		
哈密地区	Hami [Kumul] Administrative Offices	1461	13		
昌吉回族自治州	Changji Hui Autonomous Prefecture	133187	1	441932	4
伊犁哈萨克自治州	Ili Kazak Autonomous Prefecture	222026		1099885	
伊犁州直属县(市)	Counties (Cities) Direct Under Ili Prefecture	71041	3	933747	1
塔城地区	Tacheng [Tarbagatai] Administrative Offices	53658	4	151347	5
阿勒泰地区	Altay Administrative Offices	97327	2	14791	8
博尔塔拉蒙古自治州	Bortala Mongol Autonomous Prefecture	10011	9	108968	6
巴音郭楞蒙古自治州	Bayangol Mongol Autonomous Prefecture	10445	8	443948	3
阿克苏地区	Aksu Administrative Offices	17338	5	517420	2
克孜勒苏柯尔克孜自治州	Kizilsu Kirgiz Autonomous Prefecture	606	14		
喀什地区	Kashgar [Kaxgar] Administrative Offices	14949	6		
和田地区	Hotan Administrative Offices	11027	7		

20-6 各地、州、市规模以上工业企业主要经济指标

Main Indicators on Economic of Industrial Enterprises above Designated Sizeby Prefecture, Autonomous Prefecture and City

单位：% (2015 年) (%)

地 区	Region	工业总产值(万元) Gross Industrial Output Value (10 000 yuan)	位次 Rank	工业销售产值(万元) Sales Value of Industry Products (10 000 yuan)	位次 Rank
乌鲁木齐市	Urumqi City	20632531.3	1	20554641.4	1
克拉玛依市	Karamay City	10743380.6	3	10678928.2	3
石河子市	Shihezi City	4775122.1	5	4599708.5	5
吐鲁番市	Turpan City	2099787.5	9	2053445.5	9
哈密地区	Hami [Kumul] Administrative Offices	4255918.3	6	4147973.2	6
昌吉回族自治州	Changji Hui Autonomous Prefecture	12841383.2	2	12315250.0	2
伊犁哈萨克自治州	Ili Kazak Autonomous Prefecture	6633144.3		6398787.9	
伊犁州直属县(市)	Counties (Cities) Direct Under Ili Prefecture	3816400.9	8	3720042.0	8
塔城地区	Tacheng [Tarbagatai] Administrative Offices	1835095.0	10	1750299.9	10
阿勒泰地区	Altay Administrative Offices	981648.4	12	928446.0	12
博尔塔拉蒙古自治州	Bortala Mongol Autonomous Prefecture	848832.8	13	732841.3	13
巴音郭楞蒙古自治州	Bayangol Mongol Autonomous Prefecture	7782797.8	4	7684207.5	4
阿克苏地区	Aksu Administrative Offices	4046894.6	7	3868714.0	7
克孜勒苏柯尔克孜自治州	Kizilsu Kirgiz Autonomous Prefecture	387809.9	14	326695.7	14
喀什地区	Kashgar [Kaxgar] Administrative Offices	1326818.6	11	1240847.6	11
和田地区	Hotan Administrative Offices	211359.7	15	205252.5	15

地 区	Region	总资产贡献率 Ratio of Profits, Taxes and Interests to Average Assets	位次 Rank	资本保值增值率 Ratio of Capital Holding And Rise	位次 Rank
乌鲁木齐市	Urumqi City	6.1	5	99.7	13
克拉玛依市	Karamay City	10.3	3	96.4	14
石河子市	Shihezi City	5.4	7	108.7	9
吐鲁番市	Turpan City	-2.0	14	105.4	11
哈密地区	Hami [Kumul] Administrative Offices	6.0	6	120.1	4
昌吉回族自治州	Changji Hui Autonomous Prefecture	5.1	9	111.3	7
伊犁哈萨克自治州	Ili Kazak Autonomous Prefecture	4.9		113.7	
伊犁州直属县(市)	Counties (Cities) Direct Under Ili Prefecture	5.0	10	110.3	8
塔城地区	Tacheng [Tarbagatai] Administrative Offices	4.5	12	143.5	2
阿勒泰地区	Altay Administrative Offices	4.9	11	100.1	12
博尔塔拉蒙古自治州	Bortala Mongol Autonomous Prefecture	5.3	8	155.8	1
巴音郭楞蒙古自治州	Bayangol Mongol Autonomous Prefecture	18.2	1	106.8	10
阿克苏地区	Aksu Administrative Offices	11.0	2	84.1	15
克孜勒苏柯尔克孜自治州	Kizilsu Kirgiz Autonomous Prefecture	4.4	13	140.9	3
喀什地区	Kashgar [Kaxgar] Administrative Offices	9.1	4	113.5	6
和田地区	Hotan Administrative Offices	4.4	13	114.2	5

20-6 续表 Continued

单位：%　　　　(%)

地　区	Region	资产负债率 Ratio of Debts to Assets	位次 Rank	成本费用利润率 Ratio of Profits to Industrial Costs	位次 Rank
乌鲁木齐市	Urumqi City	63.5	12	0.8	13
克拉玛依市	Karamay City	42.7	15	-2.1	14
石河子市	Shihezi City	68.9	6	6.9	6
吐鲁番市	Turpan City	68.2	9	-17.9	15
哈密地区	Hami [Kumul] Administrative Offices	72.3	3	8.1	3
昌吉回族自治州	Changji Hui Autonomous Prefecture	68.8	7	3.5	11
伊犁哈萨克自治州	Ili Kazak Autonomous Prefecture	70.0		3.9	
伊犁州直属县(市)	Counties (Cities) Direct Under Ili Prefecture	70.7	4	4.1	10
塔城地区	Tacheng [Tarbagatai] Administrative Offices	67.7	11	3.0	12
阿勒泰地区	Altay Administrative Offices	70.3	5	4.5	9
博尔塔拉蒙古自治州	Bortala Mongol Autonomous Prefecture	75.9	1	6.3	7
巴音郭楞蒙古自治州	Bayangol Mongol Autonomous Prefecture	56.3	12	32.6	1
阿克苏地区	Aksu Administrative Offices	68.7	8	5.3	8
克孜勒苏柯尔克孜自治州	Kizilsu Kirgiz Autonomous Prefecture	73.8	2	7.9	4
喀什地区	Kashgar [Kaxgar] Administrative Offices	67.8	10	10.0	2
和田地区	Hotan Administrative Offices	52.1	13	7.2	5

地　区	Region	产值利税率 Ratio of Profits and Taxes to Industrial Output Value	位次 Rank	流动资产周转次数(次/年) Turnover of current Assets (times/year)	位次 Rank
乌鲁木齐市	Urumqi City	9.7	9	1.6	3
克拉玛依市	Karamay City	18.0	3	2.2	2
石河子市	Shihezi City	9.1	11	1.4	7
吐鲁番市	Turpan City	-14.4	15	1.0	12
哈密地区	Hami [Kumul] Administrative Offices	12.1	7	1.2	9
昌吉回族自治州	Changji Hui Autonomous Prefecture	6.0	13	1.5	4
伊犁哈萨克自治州	Ili Kazak Autonomous Prefecture	8.5		1.2	
伊犁州直属县(市)	Counties (Cities) Direct Under Ili Prefecture	9.4	10	1.2	9
塔城地区	Tacheng [Tarbagatai] Administrative Offices	5.8	14	1.5	4
阿勒泰地区	Altay Administrative Offices	10.1	8	0.9	13
博尔塔拉蒙古自治州	Bortala Mongol Autonomous Prefecture	7.9	12	1.1	11
巴音郭楞蒙古自治州	Bayangol Mongol Autonomous Prefecture	34.8	1	2.3	1
阿克苏地区	Aksu Administrative Offices	20.5	2	1.5	4
克孜勒苏柯尔克孜自治州	Kizilsu Kirgiz Autonomous Prefecture	14.6	4	0.6	15
喀什地区	Kashgar [Kaxgar] Administrative Offices	12.9	6	1.3	8
和田地区	Hotan Administrative Offices	13.2	5	0.7	14

20-7 各地、州、市主要工业产品产量

Output of Major Industrial Products by Prefecture, Autonomous Prefecture and City

(2015 年)

地区	Region	纱(吨) Yarn (ton)	位次 Rank	布(万米) Cloth (10 000 m)	位次 Rank	绒线(吨) Knitting Wool (ton)	位次 Rank
乌鲁木齐市	Urumqi City	11064	6	70	3	98	2
克拉玛依市	Karamay City			1	6		
吐鲁番市	Turpan City	3501	11				
哈密地区	Hami [Kumul] Administrative Offices	6956	9				
昌吉回族自治州	Changji Hui Autonomous Prefecture	29751	5				
伊犁哈萨克自治州	Ili Kazak Autonomous Prefecture	20123		39		127	
伊犁州直属县(市)	Counties (Cities) Direct Under Ili Prefecture	10614	7				
塔城地区	Tacheng [Tarbagatai] Administrative Offices	9509	8	39	5	127	1
阿勒泰地区	Altay Administrative Offices						
博尔塔拉蒙古自治州	Bortala Mongol Autonomous Prefecture	34684	4	57	4		
巴音郭楞蒙古自治州	Bayangol Mongol Autonomous Prefecture	77399	2	144	2		
阿克苏地区	Aksu Administrative Offices	96876	1				
克孜勒苏柯尔克孜自治州	Kizilsu Kirgiz Autonomous Prefecture						
喀什地区	Kashgar [Kaxgar] Administrative Offices	42874	3	150	1		
和田地区	Hotan Administrative Offices	6595	10				

地区	Region	成品糖(万吨) Refined Sugar (10 000 tons)	位次 Rank	饮料酒(千升) Alcohol Beverage (kilo-liter)	位次 Rank	塑料制品(吨) Plastic Products (ton)	位次 Rank
乌鲁木齐市	Urumqi City			139121	1	551107	2
克拉玛依市	Karamay City			9	13	19626	9
石河子市	Shihezi City						
吐鲁番市	Turpan City			6148	8		
哈密地区	Hami [Kumul] Administrative Offices			5451	9	826	13
昌吉回族自治州	Changji Hui Autonomous Prefecture	7.24	2	52554	3	607217	1
伊犁哈萨克自治州	Ili Kazak Autonomous Prefecture	13.61		133217		125226	
伊犁州直属县(市)	Counties (Cities) Direct Under Ili Prefecture	12.58	1	39825	5	55571	5
塔城地区	Tacheng [Tarbagatai] Administrative Offices			92897	2	67936	4
阿勒泰地区	Altay Administrative Offices	1.03	6	495	12	1720	11
博尔塔拉蒙古自治州	Bortala Mongol Autonomous Prefecture	3.66	3	919	11	72417	3
巴音郭楞蒙古自治州	Bayangol Mongol Autonomous Prefecture	2.85	4	20912	7	43760	6
阿克苏地区	Aksu Administrative Offices	2.52	5	29267	6	37160	7
克孜勒苏柯尔克孜自治州	Kizilsu Kirgiz Autonomous Prefecture					1360	12
喀什地区	Kashgar [Kaxgar] Administrative Offices	0.03		47147	4	23523	8
和田地区	Hotan Administrative Offices	0.03		1095	10	4656	10

20-7 续表 Continued

地区	Region	机制纸及纸板(吨) Machine-made Paper and Paper board (ton)	位次 Rank	粗钢(万吨) Crude Steel (10 000 tons)	位次 Rank	钢材(万吨) Steel Rolled (10 000 tons)	位次 Rank
乌鲁木齐市	Urumqi City	83656	2	417.17	1	585.91	1
克拉玛依市	Karamay City					6.14	8
吐鲁番市	Turpan City			0.07	7		
哈密地区	Hami [Kumul] Administrative Offices						
昌吉回族自治州	Changji Hui Autonomous Prefecture	173232	1	18.56	5	44.99	6
伊犁哈萨克自治州	Ili Kazak Autonomous Prefecture	338		179.91		219.13	
伊犁州直属县(市)	Counties (Cities) Direct Under Ili Prefecture	338	6	177.74	2	202.89	2
塔城地区	Tacheng [Tarbagatai] Administrative Offices			2.17	6	1.25	9
阿勒泰地区	Altay Administrative Offices					14.99	7
博尔塔拉蒙古自治州	Bortala Mongol Autonomous Prefecture						
巴音郭楞蒙古自治州	Bayangol Mongol Autonomous Prefecture	3328	3	100.74	3	100.89	3
阿克苏地区	Aksu Administrative Offices					46.17	5
克孜勒苏柯尔克孜自治州	Kizilsu Kirgiz Autonomous Prefecture						
喀什地区	Kashgar [Kaxgar] Administrative Offices	1186	4	45.94	4	49.31	4
和田地区	Hotan Administrative Offices	542	5				

地区	Region	水泥(万吨) Cement (10 000 tons)	位次 Rank	生铁(万吨) Pig Iron (10 000 tons)	位次 Rank	农用化肥(吨) Chemical Fertilizer (ton)	位次 Rank
乌鲁木齐市	Urumqi City	226.60	5	409.52	1	442700	3
克拉玛依市	Karamay City						
吐鲁番市	Turpan City	168.26	7	21.44	4		
哈密地区	Hami [Kumul] Administrative Offices	121.37	11			3671	6
昌吉回族自治州	Changji Hui Autonomous Prefecture	540.78	1	3.42	8	280964	4
伊犁哈萨克自治州	Ili Kazak Autonomous Prefecture	527.71		187.14		33305	
伊犁州直属县(市)	Counties (Cities) Direct Under Ili Prefecture	279.07	4	182.63	2		
塔城地区	Tacheng [Tarbagatai] Administrative Offices	117.09	12			33305	5
阿勒泰地区	Altay Administrative Offices	131.55	10	4.51	6		
博尔塔拉蒙古自治州	Bortala Mongol Autonomous Prefecture	87.89	13				
巴音郭楞蒙古自治州	Bayangol Mongol Autonomous Prefecture	150.52	8	98.37	3	1452012	1
阿克苏地区	Aksu Administrative Offices	392.76	3			472984	2
克孜勒苏柯尔克孜自治州	Kizilsu Kirgiz Autonomous Prefecture	146.61	9	3.78	7		
喀什地区	Kashgar [Kaxgar] Administrative Offices	516.15	2	6.08	5		
和田地区	Hotan Administrative Offices	196.51	6				

20-8 各地、州、市社会消费品零售总额

Total Retail Sales of Consumer Goods by Prefecture, Autonomous Prefecture and City

单位：万元 (2015 年) (10 000 yuan)

地　区	Region	社会消费品零售总额 Total Retail Sales of Consumer Goods	位次 Rank	城镇 Urban	位次 Rank
乌鲁木齐市	Urumqi City	9405087	1	9375810	1
克拉玛依市	Karamay City	588146	10	588146	8
吐鲁番市	Turpan City	443524	11	323656	12
哈密地区	Hami [Kumul] Administrative Offices	847259	7	804262	7
昌吉回族自治州	Changji Hui Autonomous Prefecture	2364260	2	2071601	2
伊犁哈萨克自治州	Ili Kazak Autonomous Prefecture	3303244		2670868	
伊犁州直属县(市)	Counties (Cities) Direct Under Ili Prefecture	1913419	3	1561952	3
塔城地区	Tacheng [Tarbagatai] Administrative Offices	782752	8	564862	9
阿勒泰地区	Altay Administrative Offices	607073	9	544054	10
博尔塔拉蒙古自治州	Bortala Mongol Autonomous Prefecture	389778	12	341590	11
巴音郭楞蒙古自治州	Bayangol Mongol Autonomous Prefecture	982763	6	916038	6
阿克苏地区	Aksu Administrative Offices	1247776	5	1009897	5
克孜勒苏柯尔克孜自治州	Kizilsu Kirgiz Autonomous Prefecture	187832	14	163969	14
喀什地区	Kashgar [Kaxgar] Administrative Offices	1681248	4	1223104	4
和田地区	Hotan Administrative Offices	360601	13	276658	13

地　区	Region	#城区 Urban Area	位次 Rank	乡村 Rural	位次 Rank
乌鲁木齐市	Urumqi City	7365195	1	29277	12
克拉玛依市	Karamay City	588146	6		
吐鲁番市	Turpan City	184068	11	119868	6
哈密地区	Hami [Kumul] Administrative Offices	720791	4	42997	11
昌吉回族自治州	Changji Hui Autonomous Prefecture	1861855	2	292659	3
伊犁哈萨克自治州	Ili Kazak Autonomous Prefecture	1567362		632376	
伊犁州直属县(市)	Counties (Cities) Direct Under Ili Prefecture	1239270	3	351467	2
塔城地区	Tacheng [Tarbagatai] Administrative Offices	152482	14	217890	5
阿勒泰地区	Altay Administrative Offices	175610	12	63019	9
博尔塔拉蒙古自治州	Bortala Mongol Autonomous Prefecture	242272	9	48188	10
巴音郭楞蒙古自治州	Bayangol Mongol Autonomous Prefecture	639825	5	66725	8
阿克苏地区	Aksu Administrative Offices	531865	8	237879	4
克孜勒苏柯尔克孜自治州	Kizilsu Kirgiz Autonomous Prefecture	158838	13	23863	13
喀什地区	Kashgar [Kaxgar] Administrative Offices	549585	7	458144	1
和田地区	Hotan Administrative Offices	219409	10	83943	7

20-9 各地、州、市海关进出口总额
Total Value of Imports and Exports by Prefecture, Autonomous Prefecture and City

单位：万美元　　(2015 年)　　(USD 10 000)

地　区	Region	进出口总额 Total Imports and Exports	位次 Rank	出口额 Exports	位次 Rank	进口额 Imports	位次 Rank
乌鲁木齐市	Urumqi City	584311	1	481117	1	103194	1
克拉玛依市	Karamay City	9522	13	5915	13	3607	9
石河子市	Shihezi City	120093	6	115835	6	4258	7
吐鲁番市	Turpan City	4200	14	1919	14	2281	13
哈密地区	Hami [Kumul] Administrative Offices	43345	8	40129	8	3216	10
昌吉回族自治州	Changji Hui Autonomous Prefecture	142422	5	124522	5	17900	4
伊犁哈萨克自治州	Ili Administrative Offices	594712		571322		23390	
伊犁州直属县(市)	Counties (Cities) Direct Under Ili Prefecture	469564	2	456656	2	12908	5
塔城地区	Tacheng [Tarbagatai] Administrative Offices	38506	9	35400	9	3106	11
阿勒泰地区	Altay Administrative Offices	86642	7	79266	7	7376	6
博尔塔拉蒙古自治州	Bortala Mongol Autonomous Prefecture	217505	3	188683	3	28822	2
巴音郭楞蒙古自治州	Bayangol Mongol Autonomous Prefecture	36930	10	13523	12	23407	3
阿克苏地区	Aksu Administrative Offices	28094	12	27836	10	258	14
克孜勒苏柯尔克孜自治州	Kizilsu Kirgiz Autonomous Prefecture	28196	11	25258	11	2938	12
喀什地区	Kashgar [Kaxgar] Administrative Offices	157480	4	153793	4	3687	8
和田地区	Hotan Administrative Offices	979	15	748	15	231	15

20-10 各地、州、市在岗职工工资总额和平均工资
Total Wages of Employed Staff and Workers and Average Wage by Prefecture, Autonomous Prefecture and City

(2015 年)

地　区	Region	在岗职工工资总额(万元) Total Wages of Staff and Workers (10 000 yuan)	位次 Rank	在岗职工平均货币工资(元) Average Wage of Staff and Workers (yuan)	位次 Rank
乌鲁木齐市	Urumqi City	5662789	1	68603	2
克拉玛依市	Karamay City	1442757	5	83194	1
石河子市	Shihezi City	960628	9	60819	6
吐鲁番市	Turpan City	528650	12	67829	3
哈密地区	Hami [Kumul] Administrative Offices	588571	11	59601	8
昌吉回族自治州	Changji Hui Autonomous Prefecture	1666109	3	62231	5
伊犁哈萨克自治州	Ili Kazak Autonomous Prefecture	3369645		49493	
伊犁州直属县(市)	Counties (Cities) Direct Under Ili Prefecture	1735115	2	53780	12
塔城地区	Tacheng [Tarbagatai] Administrative Offices	1119406	8	46288	14
阿勒泰地区	Altay Administrative Offices	515124	13	44266	15
博尔塔拉蒙古自治州	Bortala Mongol Autonomous Prefecture	465993	14	50431	13
巴音郭楞蒙古自治州	Bayangol Mongol Autonomous Prefecture	1395886	6	60118	7
阿克苏地区	Aksu Administrative Offices	1218043	7	54544	11
克孜勒苏柯尔克孜自治州	Kizilsu Kirgiz Autonomous Prefecture	296340	15	55551	10
喀什地区	Kashgar [Kaxgar] Administrative Offices	1588689	4	63804	4
和田地区	Hotan Administrative Offices	697898	10	55829	9

20-11 各地、州、市一般公共预算收支

General Public Budget Revenue and Expenditure of Local Finance by Prefecture, Autonomous Prefecture and City

单位：万元 (2015 年) (10 000 yuan)

地　区	Region	一般公共预算收入 Local Financial Revenue	位 次 Rank	一般公共预算支出 Local Financial Expenditure	位 次 Rank
乌鲁木齐市	Urumqi City	3686663	1	4466709	1
克拉玛依市	Karamay City	749926	4	896640	12
石河子市	Shihezi City	368259	10	445888	15
吐鲁番市	Turpan City	302628	12	716703	14
哈密地区	Hami [Kumul] Administrative Offices	545273	8	1007135	11
昌吉回族自治州	Changji Hui Autonomous Prefecture	1104442	2	2163946	6
伊犁哈萨克自治州	Ili Kazak Autonomous Prefecture	1380889		5111968	
伊犁州直属县(市)	Counties (Cities) Direct Under Ili Prefecture	672568	6	2536964	3
塔城地区	Tacheng [Tarbagatai] Administrative Offices	404123	9	1370425	8
阿勒泰地区	Altay Administrative Offices	304198	11	1204579	9
博尔塔拉蒙古自治州	Bortala Mongol Autonomous Prefecture	171261	14	758226	13
巴音郭楞蒙古自治州	Bayangol Mongol Autonomous Prefecture	700081	5	1797775	7
阿克苏地区	Aksu Administrative Offices	769712	3	2527768	4
克孜勒苏柯尔克孜自治州	Kizilsu Kirgiz Autonomous Prefecture	109721	15	1008315	10
喀什地区	Kashgar [Kaxgar] Administrative Offices	573702	7	4201329	2
和田地区	Hotan Administrative Offices	186119	13	2331481	5

20-12 分调查市县居民消费价格指数和商品零售价格指数

Consumer Price and Retail Price Index by Surveyed City/County

(上年=100) (2015 年)(抽样调查) (Sampled Survey) (preceding year=100)

地　区	Region	商品零售价格指数 Retail Price Index	位 次 Rank	居民消费价格指数 Consumer Price Index	位 次 Rank
乌鲁木齐市	Urumqi City	99.4	12	100.7	8
喀什市	Kashgar [Kaxgar] City	99.8	7	100.4	12
伊宁市	Yining [Gulja] City	99.6	10	101.2	3
和田市	Hotan City	99.0	16	100.6	9
克拉玛依市	Karamay City	99.7	9	100.4	12
哈密市	Hami [Kumul] City	99.6	10	100.9	7
昌吉市	Changji City	100.5	2	101.4	1
库尔勒市	Korla City	99.1	14	99.7	18
阿克苏市	Aksu City	97.9	20	99.9	17
焉耆回族自治县	Yanqi Hui Autonomous County	99.0	16	100.1	14
塔城市	Tacheng [Qoqek] City	98.4	19	99.7	18
阿勒泰市	Altay City	99.8	7	101.0	5
沙湾县	Shawan County	99.4	12	100.0	15
博乐市	Bole [Bortala] City	100.3	3	100.5	11
高昌区	Turpan City	100.3	3	101.4	1
库车县	Kuqa County	100.6	1	101.0	5
阿图什市	Artux City	99.1	14	100.0	15
莎车县	Shache [Yarkant] County	99.0	16	99.7	18
奎屯市	Kuytun City	100.3	3	101.1	4
石河子市	Shihezi City	100.2	6	100.5	9

20-13 各地、州、市各类学校在校学生数

Number of Enrollments of Formal Education by Type and Level and by Prefecture, Autonomous Prefecture and City

单位：人 (2015 年) (person)

地区	Region	普通高等学校 Regular Institutions of Higher Education	位次 Rank	中等职业学校 Specialized Secondary Schools	位次 Rank
乌鲁木齐市	Urumqi City	179829	1	52121	1
克拉玛依市	Karamay City	5228	7	829	15
石河子市	Shihezi City	7428	6	1788	13
吐鲁番市	Turpan City			3373	9
哈密地区	Hami [Kumul] Administrative Offices	555	10	3001	12
昌吉回族自治州	Changji Hui Autonomous Prefecture	25318	2	12242	6
伊犁哈萨克自治州	Ili Kazak Autonomous Prefecture	17582		20806	
伊犁州直属县(市)	Counties (Cities) Direct Under Ili Prefecture	17582	3	14116	5
塔城地区	Tacheng [Tarbagatai] Administrative Offices			3620	8
阿勒泰地区	Altay Administrative Offices			3070	11
博尔塔拉蒙古自治州	Bortala Mongol Autonomous Prefecture			1559	14
巴音郭楞蒙古自治州	Bayangol Mongol Autonomous Prefecture	4954	8	10581	7
阿克苏地区	Aksu Administrative Offices	4105	9	16944	4
克孜勒苏柯尔克孜自治州	Kizilsu Kirgiz Autonomous Prefecture			3173	10
喀什地区	Kashgar [Kaxgar] Administrative Offices	11527	4	40570	2
和田地区	Hotan Administrative Offices	7651	5	25203	3

地区	Region	普通中学 Regular Secondary Schools	位次 Rank	小学 Primary Schools	位次 Rank
乌鲁木齐市	Urumqi City	154614	2	198982	5
克拉玛依市	Karamay City	25546	13	23773	14
石河子市	Shihezi City	18602	15	12450	15
吐鲁番市	Turpan City	34230	10	56811	10
哈密地区	Hami [Kumul] Administrative Offices	32353	12	33298	12
昌吉回族自治州	Changji Hui Autonomous Prefecture	73045	6	80412	7
伊犁哈萨克自治州	Ili Kazak Autonomous Prefecture	238590		351767	
伊犁州直属县(市)	Counties (Cities) Direct Under Ili Prefecture	150398	3	232547	3
塔城地区	Tacheng [Tarbagatai] Administrative Offices	55193	8	69376	8
阿勒泰地区	Altay Administrative Offices	32999	11	49844	11
博尔塔拉蒙古自治州	Bortala Mongol Autonomous Prefecture	20741	14	28262	13
巴音郭楞蒙古自治州	Bayangol Mongol Autonomous Prefecture	70785	7	109628	6
阿克苏地区	Aksu Administrative Offices	150344	4	243186	2
克孜勒苏柯尔克孜自治州	Kizilsu Kirgiz Autonomous Prefecture	37180	9	60855	9
喀什地区	Kashgar [Kaxgar] Administrative Offices	282479	1	462458	1
和田地区	Hotan Administrative Offices	125096	5	226960	4

20-14 各地、州、市每万人口医院床位数和医生数

Number of Doctors and Hospital Beds Per 10 000 Population by Prefecture, Autonomous Prefecture and City

(2015 年)

地　区	Region	每万人床位数(张) Number of Beds per 10 000 Population (unit)	位次 Rank	平均每万人医生数(人) Number of Doctors Per 10 000 Population (person)	位次 Rank
乌鲁木齐市	Urumqi City	109.81	1	51.96	1
克拉玛依市	Karamay City	59.39	9	41.84	3
石河子市	Shihezi City	79.91	2	43.23	2
吐鲁番市	Turpan City	52.06	14	22.67	10
哈密地区	Hami [Kumul] Administrative Offices	65.43	5	32.45	5
昌吉回族自治州	Changji Hui Autonomous Prefecture	71.15	3	31.35	6
伊犁哈萨克自治州	Ili Kazak Autonomous Prefecture	59.73		22.59	
伊犁州直属县(市)	Counties (Cities) Direct Under Ili Prefecture	59.71	8	22.29	11
塔城地区	Tacheng [Tarbagatai] Administrative Offices	57.11	12	24.82	9
阿勒泰地区	Altay Administrative Offices	63.83	6	29.70	7
博尔塔拉蒙古自治州	Bortala Mongol Autonomous Prefecture	62.31	7	36.04	4
巴音郭楞蒙古自治州	Bayangol Mongol Autonomous Prefecture	66.75	4	28.84	8
阿克苏地区	Aksu Administrative Offices	55.51	13	14.69	13
克孜勒苏柯尔克孜自治州	Kizilsu Kirgiz Autonomous Prefecture	59.25	10	21.20	12
喀什地区	Kashgar [Kaxgar] Administrative Offices	51.80	15	12.83	15
和田地区	Hotan Administrative Offices	59.15	11	13.32	14

20-15 各地、州、市卫生技术人员和医生数

Medical Technical Personnel and Doctors by Prefecture, Autonomous Prefecture and City

单位：人　　(2015 年)　　(person)

地　区	Region	卫生技术人员 Medical Technical Personnel	位次 Rank	#执业医师 Doctors with Licence	位次 Rank	#执业助理医师 Assistant Doctors with Licence	位次 Rank
乌鲁木齐市	Urumqi City	37100	1	13269	1	595	8
克拉玛依市	Karamay City	3199	15	1221	13	33	15
石河子市	Shihezi City	6616	9	2357	7	378	11
吐鲁番市	Turpan City	3961	13	1152	14	326	14
哈密地区	Hami [Kumul] Administrative Offices	5519	10	1663	10	338	13
昌吉回族自治州	Changji Hui Autonomous Prefecture	12458	4	3717	4	650	6
伊犁哈萨克自治州	Ili Kazak Autonomous Prefecture	30964		8758		2465	
伊犁州直属县(市)	Counties (Cities) Direct Under Ili Prefecture	18835	3	5318	2	1379	2
塔城地区	Tacheng [Tarbagatai] Administrative Offices	7042	8	1922	9	620	7
阿勒泰地区	Altay Administrative Offices	5087	11	1518	11	466	9
博尔塔拉蒙古自治州	Bortala Mongol Autonomous Prefecture	4331	12	1351	12	378	11
巴音郭楞蒙古自治州	Bayangol Mongol Autonomous Prefecture	10961	6	3297	5	723	5
阿克苏地区	Aksu Administrative Offices	11524	5	2877	6	841	4
克孜勒苏柯尔克孜自治州	Kizilsu Kirgiz Autonomous Prefecture	3673	14	870	15	394	10
喀什地区	Kashgar [Kaxgar] Administrative Offices	19765	2	4014	3	1760	1
和田地区	Hotan Administrative Offices	9415	7	2104	8	991	3

附录

各省市区主要经济指标排序

RANKING OF MAIN ECONOMIC INDICATORS BY REGION

各省市区主要经济指标排序
Ranking of Main Economic Indicators by Region

(2015 年)

省市区	Region	地区生产总值 (亿元) Gross Regional Product (100 million yuan)	位次 Rank	地区生产总值比上年增长(%) Increase Rate of Gross Region Production over the Previous year(%)	位次 Rank
全 国	**China**	**676707.8**		**6.3**	
北 京	Beijing	22968.6	13	6.9	25
天 津	Tianjin	16538.2	19	9.3	4
河 北	Hebei	29806.1	7	6.8	27
山 西	Shanxi	12802.6	24	3.1	30
内蒙古	Inner Mongolia	18032.8	16	7.7	24
辽 宁	Liaoning	28743.4	10	3.0	31
吉 林	Jilin	14274.1	22	6.5	28
黑龙江	Heilongjiang	15083.7	21	5.7	29
上 海	Shanghai	24965.0	12	6.9	25
江 苏	Jiangsu	70116.4	2	8.5	12
浙 江	Zhejiang	42886.5	4	8.0	17
安 徽	Anhui	22005.6	14	8.7	9
福 建	Fujian	25979.8	11	9.0	6
江 西	Jiangxi	16723.8	18	9.1	5
山 东	Shandong	63002.3	3	8.0	17
河 南	Henan	37010.3	5	8.3	13
湖 北	Hubei	29550.2	8	8.9	7
湖 南	Hunan	29047.2	9	8.6	11
广 东	Guangdong	72812.6	1	8.0	17
广 西	Guangxi	16803.1	17	8.1	15
海 南	Hainan	3702.8	28	7.8	23
重 庆	Chongqing	15719.7	20	11.0	1
四 川	Sichuan	30103.1	6	7.9	22
贵 州	Guizhou	10502.6	25	10.7	3
云 南	Yunnan	13717.9	23	8.7	9
西 藏	Tibet	1026.4	31	11.0	1
陕 西	Shanxi	18171.9	15	8.0	17
甘 肃	Gansu	6790.3	27	8.1	15
青 海	Qinghai	2417.1	30	8.2	14
宁 夏	Ningxia	2911.8	29	8.0	17
新 疆	Xinjiang	9324.8	26	8.8	8

续表 1

省市区	Region	第一产业增加值(亿元) Value Added of the Primary Industry (100 million yuan)	位次 Rank	第二产业增加值(亿元) Value Added of the Secondary Industry (100 million yuan)	位次 Rank	第三产业增加值(亿元) Value Added of the Tertiary Industry (100 million yuan)	位次 Rank
全　国	**China**	**60863.0**		**274277.8**		**341566.9**	
北　京	Beijing	140.2	29	4526.4	24	18301.9	5
天　津	Tianjin	208.8	28	7688.7	18	8640.7	14
河　北	Hebei	3439.5	5	14388.0	6	11978.7	12
山　西	Shanxi	788.1	25	5224.3	22	6790.2	20
内蒙古	Inner Mongolia	1618.7	18	9200.6	14	7213.5	19
辽　宁	Liaoning	2384.0	12	13382.6	9	12976.8	8
吉　林	Jilin	1596.3	20	7337.1	19	5340.8	24
黑龙江	Heilongjiang	2633.5	9	4798.1	23	7652.1	16
上　海	Shanghai	109.8	30	7940.7	16	16914.5	6
江　苏	Jiangsu	3987.9	3	32043.6	2	34084.8	2
浙　江	Zhejiang	1832.8	15	19707.1	4	21346.6	4
安　徽	Anhui	2456.7	11	11342.3	12	8206.6	15
福　建	Fujian	2117.7	13	13218.7	10	10643.5	13
江　西	Jiangxi	1773.0	16	8487.3	15	6463.5	22
山　东	Shandong	4979.1	1	29485.9	3	28537.4	3
河　南	Henan	4209.6	2	18189.4	5	14611.3	7
湖　北	Hubei	3309.8	8	13503.6	8	12736.8	10
湖　南	Hunan	3331.6	7	12955.4	11	12760.2	9
广　东	Guangdong	3344.8	6	32511.5	1	36956.2	1
广　西	Guangxi	2566.0	10	7694.7	17	6542.4	21
海　南	Hainan	855.8	24	875.1	30	1971.8	28
重　庆	Chongqing	1150.2	22	7071.8	20	7497.8	17
四　川	Sichuan	3677.3	4	14293.2	7	12132.6	11
贵　州	Guizhou	1640.6	17	4146.9	25	4715.0	25
云　南	Yunnan	2055.7	14	5492.8	21	6169.4	23
西　藏	Tibet	96.9	31	376.2	31	553.3	31
陕　西	Shaanxi	1597.6	19	9360.3	13	7213.9	18
甘　肃	Gansu	954.5	23	2494.8	27	3341.0	27
青　海	Qinghai	208.9	27	1207.3	29	1000.8	30
宁　夏	Ningxia	238.5	26	1379.0	28	1294.3	29
新　疆	Xinjiang	1559.1	21	3596.4	26	4169.3	26

Continued

第一产业占GDP比重(%) Composition of Primary Industry Product to GDP(%)	位 次 Rank	第二产业占GDP比重(%) Composition of Secondary Industry Product to GDP(%)	位 次 Rank	第三产业占GDP比重(%) Composition of Tertiary Industrial Product to GDP(%)	位 次 Rank
9.0		**40.5**		**50.5**	
0.6	30	19.7	31	79.7	1
1.3	29	46.5	14	52.2	6
11.5	9	48.3	9	40.2	24
6.2	25	40.8	22	53.0	5
9.0	17	51.0	4	40.0	25
8.3	20	46.6	13	45.1	14
11.2	13	51.4	3	37.4	30
17.5	2	31.8	28	50.7	8
0.4	31	31.8	29	67.8	2
5.7	26	45.7	17	48.6	11
4.3	28	46.0	15	49.8	9
11.2	14	51.5	1	37.3	31
8.2	22	50.9	5	41.0	22
10.6	15	50.7	6	38.6	29
7.9	23	46.8	12	45.3	13
11.4	11	49.1	8	39.5	27
11.2	12	45.7	18	43.1	20
11.5	10	44.6	21	43.9	19
4.6	27	44.7	20	50.8	7
15.3	5	45.8	16	38.9	28
23.1	1	23.6	30	53.3	4
7.3	24	45.0	19	47.7	12
12.2	8	47.5	10	40.3	23
15.6	4	39.5	24	44.9	16
15.0	6	40.0	23	45.0	15
9.4	16	36.7	27	53.9	3
8.8	18	51.5	2	39.7	26
14.1	7	36.7	26	49.2	10
8.6	19	49.9	7	41.4	21
8.2	21	47.4	11	44.4	18
16.7	3	38.6	25	44.7	17

续表 2

省市区	Region	人均地区生产总值(元) Per Capita GDP (yuan)	位次 Rank	总人口(万人) Total Population (10 000 persons)	位次 Rank
全 国	**China**	**49351**		**137462**	
北 京	Beijing	106284	2	2171	26
天 津	Tianjin	107960	1	1547	27
河 北	Hebei	40255	19	7425	6
山 西	Shanxi	35017	27	3664	18
内蒙古	Inner Mongolia	71903	6	2511	23
辽 宁	Liaoning	65524	9	4382	14
吉 林	Jilin	51852	12	2753	21
黑龙江	Heilongjiang	39462	21	3812	16
上 海	Shanghai	103141	3	2415	24
江 苏	Jiangsu	87995	4	7976	5
浙 江	Zhejiang	77644	5	5539	10
安 徽	Anhui	35997	25	6144	8
福 建	Fujian	67966	7	3839	15
江 西	Jiangxi	36724	24	4566	13
山 东	Shandong	64168	10	9847	2
河 南	Henan	39131	22	9480	3
湖 北	Hubei	50654	13	5852	9
湖 南	Hunan	42968	16	6783	7
广 东	Guangdong	67503	8	10849	1
广 西	Guangxi	35190	26	4796	11
海 南	Hainan	40818	18	911	28
重 庆	Chongqing	52330	11	3017	20
四 川	Sichuan	36836	23	8204	4
贵 州	Guizhou	29847	29	3530	19
云 南	Yunnan	29015	30	4742	12
西 藏	Tibet	31999	28	324	31
陕 西	Shaanxi	48023	14	3793	17
甘 肃	Gansu	26165	31	2600	22
青 海	Qinghai	41252	17	588	30
宁 夏	Ningxia	43805	15	668	29
新 疆	Xinjiang	40036	20	2360	25

Continued

固定资产投资（亿元）Total Investment in Fixed Assets (100 million yuan)	位 次 Rank	居民消费价格指数 Consumer Price Index	位 次 Rank	城镇居民人均可支配收入(元) Per Capita Annual Disposable Income of Urban Households (yuan)	位 次 Rank	城镇居民人均消费性支出(元) Per Capita Annual Living Expenditures for Consumption (yuan)	位 次 Rank
546037.68		**101.4**		**31195**		**21392.4**	
7446.02	26	101.8	5	52859	2	36642.0	2
11814.57	21	101.7	9	34101	6	26229.5	4
28905.74	5	100.9	29	26152	22	17586.6	22
13744.59	17	100.6	30	25828	23	15818.6	31
13529.15	18	101.1	25	30594	10	21876.5	8
17640.37	13	101.4	19	31126	9	21556.7	9
12508.59	20	101.7	10	24901	27	17972.6	20
9884.28	24	101.1	26	24203	30	17152.1	26
6349.39	27	102.4	2	52962	1	36946.1	1
45905.17	2	101.7	8	37173	4	24966.0	6
26664.72	6	101.4	17	43714	3	28661.3	3
23803.93	10	101.3	21	26936	14	17233.5	24
20973.98	11	101.7	7	33275	7	23520.2	7
16993.90	14	101.5	15	26500	15	16731.8	29
47381.46	1	101.2	23	31545	8	19853.8	10
34951.28	3	101.3	20	25576	24	17154.3	25
26086.42	7	101.5	13	27051	13	18192.3	19
24324.17	9	101.4	18	28838	11	19501.4	12
29950.48	4	101.5	12	34757	5	25673.1	5
15654.95	15	101.5	14	26416	17	16321.2	30
3355.40	29	101.0	27	26356	19	18448.4	18
14208.15	16	101.3	22	27239	12	19742.3	11
24965.56	8	101.5	16	26205	21	19276.8	14
10676.70	23	101.8	6	24580	28	16914.2	28
13069.39	19	101.9	4	26373	18	17675.0	21
1295.68	31	102.0	3	25457	25	17022.0	27
18231.03	12	101.0	28	26420	16	18463.9	17
8626.60	25	101.6	11	23767	31	17450.9	23
3144.17	30	102.6	1	24542	29	19200.6	15
3426.42	28	101.1	24	25186	26	18983.9	16
10729.32	22	100.6	31	26275	20	19414.7	13

续表 3

省市区	Region	农村居民人均可支配收入(元) Annual Per Capita Disposable Income of Rural Households (yuan)	位次 Rank	农村居民人均生活消费支出(元) Annual Per Capita Living Expenditure of Rural Households (yuan)	位次 Rank
全　国	**China**	**11421.7**		**9222.6**	
北　京	Beijing	20568.7	3	15811.2	3
天　津	Tianjin	18481.6	4	14739.4	4
河　北	Hebei	11050.5	14	9022.8	12
山　西	Shanxi	9453.9	23	7421.2	27
内蒙古	Inner Mongolia	10775.9	19	10637.4	8
辽　宁	Liaoning	12056.9	9	8872.8	15
吉　林	Jilin	11326.2	11	8783.3	16
黑龙江	Heilongjiang	11095.2	13	8391.5	21
上　海	Shanghai	23205.2	1	16152.3	1
江　苏	Jiangsu	16256.7	5	12882.5	5
浙　江	Zhejiang	21125.0	2	16107.7	2
安　徽	Anhui	10820.7	18	8975.2	13
福　建	Fujian	13792.7	6	11960.8	6
江　西	Jiangxi	11139.1	12	8485.6	19
山　东	Shandong	12930.4	8	8747.6	17
河　南	Henan	10852.9	17	7887.4	24
湖　北	Hubei	11843.9	10	9803.1	9
湖　南	Hunan	10992.5	15	9690.6	10
广　东	Guangdong	13360.4	7	11103.0	7
广　西	Guangxi	9466.6	22	7582.0	26
海　南	Hainan	10857.6	16	8210.3	22
重　庆	Chongqing	10504.7	20	8937.7	14
四　川	Sichuan	10247.4	21	9250.6	11
贵　州	Guizhou	7386.9	30	6644.9	30
云　南	Yunnan	8242.1	28	6830.1	28
西　藏	Tibet	8243.7	27	5579.7	31
陕　西	Shaanxi	8688.9	26	7900.7	23
甘　肃	Gansu	6936.2	31	6829.8	29
青　海	Qinghai	7933.4	29	8566.5	18
宁　夏	Ningxia	9118.7	25	8414.9	20
新　疆	Xinjiang	9425.1	24	7697.9	25

Continued

农林牧渔业总产值(亿元) Gross Output Value of Agriculture, Forestry, Animal Husbandry and Fishery (100 million yuan)	位次 Rank	农林牧渔业总产值比上年增长(%) Output Value Increase Rate in 2015 over 2014 of Agriculture,Forestry, Animal Husbandry and Fishery(%)	位次 Rank	粮食产量 (万吨) Grain (10 000 tons)	位次 Rank	棉花产量 (万吨) Cotton (10 000 tons)	位次 Rank	油料产量 (万吨) Oil Bearing Crops (10 000 tons)	位次 Rank
107056.4		**3.9**		**62143.9**		**560.3**		**3537.0**	
368.2	28	-11.7	31	62.6	31			0.6	30
467.4	27	2.6	24	181.7	27	2.6	12	0.4	31
5978.9	5	2.7	23	3363.8	8	37.3	3	151.5	8
1522.6	24	1.1	29	1259.6	18	1.4	14	15.3	25
2751.6	20	2.4	26	2827.0	10			193.6	7
4686.7	10	3.8	18	2002.5	13			46.1	20
2880.6	16	4.3	13	3647.0	4			76.4	13
5044.9	9	5.2	7	6324.0	1			18.3	24
302.6	30	-6.7	30	112.1	28			1.2	29
7030.8	3	2.6	25	3561.3	5	11.7	8	143.1	9
2933.4	15	1.2	28	752.2	23	2.0	13	31.3	21
4390.8	11	4.2	15	3538.1	6	23.4	5	227.9	6
3717.9	13	3.9	17	661.1	24			30.7	22
2859.1	17	4.0	16	2148.7	12	11.5	9	124.0	10
9549.6	1	4.3	14	4712.7	3	53.7	2	324.1	3
7641.3	2	4.6	9	6067.1	2	12.6	7	599.7	1
5728.6	6	5.4	6	2703.3	11	29.8	4	339.6	2
5630.7	7	3.7	20	3002.9	9	14.5	6	242.9	5
5520.0	8	3.1	22	1358.1	17			110.3	11
4197.1	12	3.7	19	1524.8	15	0.3	16	64.7	16
1323.9	25	5.5	5	184.0	26			11.3	27
1738.1	22	4.6	10	1154.9	22			59.9	19
6377.8	4	3.6	21	3442.8	7	1.0	15	307.6	4
2738.7	21	6.8	1	1180.0	20	0.1	17	101.3	12
3383.1	14	6.0	3	1876.4	14			65.9	15
149.5	31	4.5	11	100.6	30			6.4	28
2813.5	18	5.0	8	1226.8	19	3.9	11	62.7	18
1722.1	23	5.7	4	1171.1	21	4.3	10	71.6	14
319.3	29	1.8	27	102.7	29			30.5	23
483.0	26	4.4	12	372.6	25			15.3	26
2804.4	19	6.3	2	1521.3	16	429.8	1	62.9	17

续表 4

省市区	Region	工业增加值(亿元) Value-added of Industry (100 million yuan)	位 次 Rank	天然气(亿立方米) Natural Gas (100 million cu. m)	位 次 Rank	原 油(万吨) Crude Oil (10 000 tons)	位 次 Rank
全 国	**China**	**228974.3**		**1346.1**		**21455.6**	
北 京	Beijing	3662.9	24	16.9	11		
天 津	Tianjin	6981.3	17	20.5	9	3496.8	3
河 北	Hebei	12626.2	6	10.4	12	580.1	9
山 西	Shanxi	4389.6	21	43.1	6		
内蒙古	Inner Mongolia	7939.2	13	9.2	13	45.8	16
辽 宁	Liaoning	11637.3	8	6.6	14	1037.1	7
吉 林	Jilin	6439.8	18	20.3	10	665.5	8
黑龙江	Heilongjiang	4053.8	22	35.8	7	3838.6	1
上 海	Shanghai	7109.9	15	1.9	17	6.8	20
江 苏	Jiangsu	27996.4	2	0.4	21	190.5	12
浙 江	Zhejiang	17209.4	4				
安 徽	Anhui	9659.8	12				
福 建	Fujian	10974.4	11				
江 西	Jiangxi	6987.0	16	0.4	22		
山 东	Shandong	25910.8	3	4.6	15	2608.0	5
河 南	Henan	16100.9	5	4.2	16	412.1	10
湖 北	Hubei	11532.6	9	1.4	19	71.0	13
湖 南	Hunan	11090.8	10				
广 东	Guangdong	30137.5	1	96.6	4	1572.6	6
广 西	Guangxi	6338.3	19	0.2	23	50.5	15
海 南	Hainan	485.9	30	1.9	18	30.0	17
重 庆	Chongqing	5557.5	20	33.3	8		
四 川	Sichuan	12084.9	7	267.2	3	15.4	18
贵 州	Guizhou	3315.6	25	0.9	20		
云 南	Yunnan	3925.2	23				
西 藏	Tibet	69.9	31				
陕 西	Shaanxi	7634.2	14	415.9	1	3736.7	2
甘 肃	Gansu	1778.1	27	0.1	24	66.6	14
青 海	Qinghai	893.9	29	61.4	5	223.0	11
宁 夏	Ningxia	979.7	28			13.4	19
新 疆	Xinjiang	2740.7	26	293.0	2	2795.1	4

Continued

建筑业总产值(亿元) Gross Output Value of Construction (100 million yuan)	位次 Rank	社会消费品零售总额(亿元) Total Retail Sales of Consumer Goods (100 million yuan)	位次 Rank	社会消费品零售总额比上年增长(%) Increase Rate in 2015 over 2014 of Total Retail Sales of Consumer Goods(%)	位次 Rank	进出口总额(亿美元) Total Value of Imports and Exports (USD 100 million)	位次 Rank
180757.5		**300930.8**		**10.7**		**39569.0**	
8436.7	7	10338.0	12	7.3	28	3196.2	5
4488.9	18	5257.3	23	10.7	13	1143.5	8
5252.6	15	12990.7	8	9.4	19	514.8	12
2931.3	21	6033.7	21	5.5	31	147.2	24
1123.5	27	6107.7	20	8.0	26	127.5	26
5413.8	14	12787.2	9	7.7	27	959.6	9
2216.3	23	6651.9	16	9.3	20	189.4	23
1680.4	26	7640.2	15	8.9	22	209.9	21
5652.5	13	10131.5	13	8.1	25	4492.4	3
24785.8	1	25876.8	3	10.3	15	5456.1	2
23980.6	2	19784.7	4	8.8	23	3473.4	4
5695.9	12	8908.0	14	12.0	6	479.7	15
7605.8	9	10505.9	11	12.4	2	1693.6	7
4602.5	17	5925.5	22	11.4	10	424.7	17
9381.7	4	27761.4	2	10.6	14	2417.5	6
8047.7	8	15740.4	5	12.4	2	738.4	11
10592.9	3	14003.2	6	12.3	4	456.0	16
6630.8	10	12024.0	10	12.1	5	293.3	19
8865.7	5	31517.6	1	10.1	17	10228.7	1
2953.4	20	6348.1	19	10.0	18	512.6	14
278.6	30	1325.1	28	8.2	24	139.6	25
6256.9	11	6424.0	18	12.5	1	744.8	10
8768.2	6	13877.7	7	12.0	6	514.7	13
1947.7	24	3283.0	25	11.8	9	122.2	27
3268.9	19	5103.2	24	10.2	16	245.2	20
106.9	31	408.5	31	12.0	6	9.1	31
4752.6	16	6578.1	17	10.8	12	305.0	18
1849.0	25	2907.2	26	9.0	21	80.0	28
409.5	29	691.0	30	11.3	11	19.3	30
524.5	28	789.6	29	7.1	29	37.9	29
2304.1	22	2606.0	27	7.0	30	196.8	22

续表 5 Continued

省市区	Region	#出口总额 (亿美元) Total Exports (USD 100 million)	位 次 Rank	一般公共预算收入 (亿元) General Public Budget Revenue in Local Finance (100 million yuan)	位 次 Rank	一般公共预算支出 (亿元) General Public Expenditure in Local Finance (100 million yuan)	位 次 Rank
全 国	**China**	**16819.5**		**82982.7**		**150218.8**	
北 京	Beijing	1017.8	5	4723.9	6	5751.4	9
天 津	Tianjin	706.8	7	2667.0	10	3233.0	25
河 北	Hebei	325.3	10	2648.5	11	5593.2	11
山 西	Shanxi	60.5	26	1642.2	21	3443.4	24
内蒙古	Inner Mongolia	77.8	25	1963.5	19	4293.4	17
辽 宁	Liaoning	560.0	8	2125.6	17	4461.8	14
吉 林	Jilin	146.4	19	1229.3	25	3217.1	26
黑龙江	Heilongjiang	100.0	23	1165.2	26	4022.1	19
上 海	Shanghai	2442.9	2	5519.5	4	6191.6	7
江 苏	Jiangsu	2321.7	3	8028.6	2	9681.5	2
浙 江	Zhejiang	763.4	6	4809.5	5	6645.6	6
安 徽	Anhui	149.6	18	2454.2	14	5233.2	12
福 建	Fujian	539.5	9	2544.1	12	3995.8	20
江 西	Jiangxi	105.7	21	2165.5	15	4419.9	15
山 东	Shandong	1310.1	4	5529.3	3	8249.9	3
河 南	Henan	312.3	12	3009.6	8	6806.5	5
湖 北	Hubei	175.1	15	3005.4	9	6094.2	8
湖 南	Hunan	102.5	22	2515.8	13	5657.3	10
广 东	Guangdong	4350.5	1	9364.8	1	12801.6	1
广 西	Guangxi	322.6	11	1515.1	22	4069.4	18
海 南	Hainan	112.4	20	627.7	28	1241.5	30
重 庆	Chongqing	187.8	13	2155.1	16	3793.8	23
四 川	Sichuan	187.0	14	3349.2	7	7506.7	4
贵 州	Guizhou	23.8	27	1503.3	23	3930.2	21
云 南	Yunnan	83.5	24	1808.1	20	4712.9	13
西 藏	Tibet	1.4	31	137.1	31	1383.9	29
陕 西	Shaanxi	152.6	17	2059.9	18	4375.5	16
甘 肃	Gansu	22.4	28	743.9	27	2964.6	27
青 海	Qinghai	2.2	30	267.1	30	1505.4	28
宁 夏	Ningxia	10.6	29	373.7	29	1138.2	31
新 疆	Xinjiang	175.1	16	1331.9	24	3804.9	22

中国统计出版社最新图书简目

(仅供参考,以实际出版为准)

统计资料

中国统计年鉴　中国统计摘要　中国发展报告
中国经济普查年鉴2013　国际统计年鉴　金砖国家联合统计手册
中国-东盟国家统计手册　中国农村统计年鉴　中国县域统计年鉴
中国城市统计年鉴　中国对外直接投资统计公报　中国地区经济监测报告
中国贸易外经统计年鉴　中国零售和餐饮连锁企业统计年鉴　中国商品交易市场统计年鉴
大中型批发零售和住宿餐饮企业统计年鉴　中国农产品价格调查年鉴　中国住户调查年鉴
中国价格统计年鉴　中国能源统计年鉴　全国农产品成本收益资料汇编
中国环境统计年鉴　中国建筑业统计年鉴　国外资源、能源和环境统计资料汇编
中国工业统计年鉴　中国城乡建设统计年鉴　中国房地产统计年鉴
中国城市建设统计年鉴　中国科技统计年鉴　中国第三产业统计年鉴
中国证券期货统计年鉴　中国劳动统计年鉴　中国高技术产业统计年鉴
工业企业科技活动资料　中国社会统计年鉴　中国人口和就业统计年鉴
中国人才资源统计报告　中国教育经费统计年鉴　中国文化及相关产业统计年鉴
文化及相关产业统计概览　中国民政统计年鉴　中国民族统计年鉴
中国残疾人事业统计年鉴　中国妇女儿童状况统计资料（英）　中国乡镇街道行政区域简册
中国基本单位统计年鉴

省级综合统计年鉴系列

北京 天津 河北 山西 内蒙古 辽宁 吉林 黑龙江 上海 江苏 浙江 安徽 福建 江西 山东 河南 湖北 湖南
广东 广西 海南 重庆 四川 贵州 云南 西藏 陕西 甘肃 青海 宁夏 新疆 新疆生产建设兵团

市(县)级综合统计年鉴系列

天津滨海新区 石家庄 唐山 邯郸 保定 沧州 邢台 廊坊 承德 衡水 秦皇岛 张家口 太原 大同 阳泉 长治 晋城
朔州 晋中 运城 忻州 临汾 呼和浩特 呼和浩特新城区 鄂尔多斯 包头 沈阳 大连 长春 延吉 四平 通化 哈尔滨
齐齐哈尔 黑龙江垦区 上海浦东新区 南京 无锡 徐州 常州 苏州 南通 连云港 淮安 盐城 扬州 镇江 泰州
宿迁 江阴 丹阳 杭州 宁波 温州 嘉兴 湖州 绍兴 金华 衢州 舟山 台州 丽水 合肥 安庆 马鞍山 福州 厦门
宁德 漳州 南昌 九江 上饶 新余 抚州 萍乡 赣州 吉安 景德镇 济南 青岛 潍坊 枣庄 日照 滕州 郑州 洛阳
平顶山 三门峡 商丘 信阳 济源 武汉 十堰 荆州 宜昌 荆门 咸宁 长沙 广州 深圳 惠州 东莞 南宁 柳州 桂林
来宾 海口 三亚 成都 贵阳 昆明 西安 安康 兰州 庆阳 银川 乌鲁木齐 兵团一师 兵团十师

调查年鉴系列

天津 山西 内蒙古 辽宁 吉林 上海　福建 江西 河南 湖北 湖南 广西　重庆 四川 云南 甘肃 宁夏 新疆

统计方法应用/实用手册

实用SAS统计分析教程　马克威统计分析与数据挖掘应用案例
乡镇统计人员岗位知识培训系列教材：辅助调查员岗位基础知识　乡镇统计人员岗位基础知识
县级统计人员岗位知识培训系列教材：Excel在统计工作中的应用　简明统计分析
EXCEL在基层统计工作中的应用　统计公文知识问答

统计通俗读物/统计科普图书

漫话诺贝尔经济学大师与数学情缘　魅力统计　漫话信息时代的统计学　统计使人更聪明
漫游数据王国　探访随机世界　新中国统计工作历史流变1949-1999　无处不在的统计

重点图书

新编英汉汉英统计大词典　中华医学统计百科全书
挑大学选专业2016—考研择校指南　挑大学选专业2016—高考志愿填报指南